THE

THEATRE GUILD

ANTHOLOGY

The THEATRE GUILD *Anthology*

With an Introduction by

THE BOARD OF DIRECTORS OF

THE THEATRE GUILD

RANDOM HOUSE · NEW YORK

FIRST EDITION

MANUFACTURED IN THE UNITED STATES OF AMERICA

CONTENTS

ACKNOWLEDGMENTS

For permission to reprint the plays in this volume, the editors gratefully make acknowledgment to the following playwrights and publishers:

John Ferguson—St. John G. Ervine and The Macmillan Co.

Mr. Pim Passes By—A. A. Milne and Alfred A. Knopf, Inc.

Liliom—Ferenc Molnar and Liveright Publishing Corp.

He Who Gets Slapped—Samuel French

The Adding Machine—Elmer Rice and Doubleday, Doran & Co.

Saint Joan—Bernard Shaw and Dodd, Mead & Co.

Goat Song—Franz Werfel and Doubleday, Doran & Co.

The Silver Cord—Sidney Howard and Samuel French

Porgy—Dorothy and DuBose Heyward and Doubleday, Doran & Co.

Strange Interlude—Eugene O'Neill and Random House, Inc.

Hotel Universe—Philip Barry and Samuel French

Reunion in Vienna—Robert E. Sherwood and Charles Scribner's Sons

Mary of Scotland—Maxwell Anderson and Doubleday, Doran & Co.

Rain from Heaven—S. N. Behrman and Random House, Inc.

INTRODUCTION

The Theatre Guild was founded on December 19, 1918, without a theatre, without a play, without an actor and without a scrap of scenery. Its sole artistic asset was an idea. If, in the years that have intervened, the Guild has achieved success, it is because the idea, revolutionary, has withstood the revolution it created and is still a driving force as potent as it was at the start.

The idea is simple. It is merely that the theatre itself is bigger than any of the workers in it and that it should be employed for the creation of the finest drama of the time, drama definitely and honestly reflecting the author's vision of life or sense of style and beauty.

The Guild is, then, primarily an "art theatre." It has from its inception produced only plays which it believed had something to say and which said it well. As to their content, it had no bias. It has not been in any sense of the word a propaganda theatre. It has been willing to produce a communistic play as quickly as an imperialistic play, so long as it was a good play with a definite idea to project.

It happened that the Guild dropped its idea into fertile soil in that year of 1918. It took root in an unusual state of unrest which had begun to take form in the American theatre shortly after the turn of the century and which with the end of the World War had grown to dangerous proportions. The organized drama was in the hands of commercially minded producers whose eyes were intent upon the box-office. They dominated the drama to the extent of imposing their own idea of what the public wanted upon helpless theatre-goers.

Play writing had been reduced to a formula. Producers refused to permit the violation of the formula in fear of failure. It was almost impossible to penetrate the stone wall with a new idea. If playwrights were unwilling to write the usual "happy-ending" drama, their chances of a hearing in the theatre were slight. There were exceptions, of course, but they were few.

However, signs of revolt against this "system" were beginning to appear. In communities throughout the country and in colleges a younger generation, realizing that the plays it saw reflected neither life nor beauty, sought to make a theatre of its own outside the pale of the commercial theatre. "Little Theatre" groups began to appear. For the most part they were voices crying in the wilderness. Their protest was sincere but ineffective. The economic cards were stacked against them. Their standing was strictly amateur. The professional theatre was strongly intrenched.

The founders of the Guild felt sure that there was a potential audience for the plays it hoped to produce. We felt that if we could get the co-operation of that audience it would be of tremendous help. Getting them interested was our problem until we hit upon the idea of taking them into partnership with us in the experiment we were about to launch.

The result of this decision was our subscription plan. By this plan we ask theatre-goers to pledge their confidence in us by buying, in advance, tickets to the six productions we promise to produce each year. In the beginning, in that first season of 1918, there were only one hundred and thirty-five theatre-goers who were brave enough to gamble with us. Today there are more than 25,000 in New York alone and an equal number in the five cities outside of New York to which we have extended our plan. We do not ask our subscribers to do all the gambling. In return for their confidence we offer them prices lower than box-office rates and preferred seat locations.

In this way we feel that we have brought an entirely new audience into the theatre and have organized that audience so that now it is available to all producers. It has not been an easy task, keeping 50,000 theatre-goers happy. Mr. X. must sit down front because he is slightly deaf. Mr. Y. must sit on an aisle because he is tall and his legs are long and can't be doubled up. Mr. and Mrs. Z. subscribe when they marry and hold hands in G 1-3. Five years later they are divorced and prefer to glare at each other from H 13 and C 8. Mrs. A. is infuriated by the play that Mrs. B. loves. It is a problem no other producing organization faces and we feel that we have met it successfully over a span of eighteen seasons.

The production history of the Guild is perhaps too well known to necessitate details in recounting. We have produced more than a hundred plays, more than half of which have been catalogued, under the Broadway definition, as hits. Many were failures from the box-office point of view, but also successes, we feel, because they were experimental—they opened new trails in which we, and often even other producers, later, were able to achieve better things in the theatre.

As a matter of fact, the Guild began with a failure. Seeking a meaningful manuscript which had been ignored by the commercial theatre, we selected *Bonds of Interest,* by Jacinto Benevente. It lingered for only a few weeks, undiscovered by its audience. But those who did see it were appreciative, and the dramatic critics were more than encouraging. The torch flickered, but the Guild held on.

For the second play, a neglected manuscript by an obscure author was chosen. It was *John Ferguson*, by St. John G. Ervine. Going on in the face of the dubious start was difficult, but through the co-operation of the group of actors and actresses that had been assembled and who believed, as whole-heartedly as we, in the experiment the play went forward. When the curtain went up on *John Ferguson* just $19.50 remained in the Guild's treasury. Failure then might have meant the end of a gesture. But the play did not fail. It achieved not only the artistic success which was the Guild's vindication, but financial success as well.

From that moment, the Guild's story is the story of the growth of the idea on which it was founded. The Guild continued to experiment, and theatre-goers, meeting an effort to approach them intelligently more than half way, continued to come into the fold.

Perhaps the most successful experiment of all was the one that brought George Bernard Shaw into the Guild's family. Mr. Shaw had written a play which could not find a producer on either side of the water, great as was his name as a dramatist. The play was *Heartbreak House*. The Guild finally prevailed upon the playwright, and the production not only gave us an artistic and financial success, but the prestige of a great name of the theatre.

Since then we have produced a number of Shaw plays, many of them in revival, but four of them in their world première, including *Back to Methuselah*, a play which he himself considered almost impossible of production, and *St. Joan*. Indeed, for a time the Irish playwright was known as the patron saint of the Guild.

The experiments went on through the years. Even in the lighter side of our program we sought to do what had not been done before. The Continental comedy, then at its height, has always been "Americanized" when produced here. We presented them in their own milieu and found that audiences were much more willing to accept an author in his own terms than otherwise. If he wrote of Budapest, he knew whereof he wrote. Transferring his story to New York for the sake of Americanization had merely diluted its native flavor.

The Guild was the first to produce a truly expressionistic play—*From Morn to Midnight*. It was the first to present a radical play—Elmer Rice's *The Adding Machine*. Among other experimental ventures were *Processional*, by John Howard Lawson, *Goat Song*, by Franz Werfel, *Man and the Masses*, by Ernst Toller, *The Failures* by H. R. Lenormand, and *Roar China*, by S. M. Tretyakov, to name only a few. Even *The Guardsman* might be included in this list, for it had been a complete failure when first presented in New York.

The Guild was accused, in its early days, of producing only foreign plays. There was, of course, some truth in the accusation. But once the American playwright, cowed by the refusal of commercial producers to permit him any range of ideas beyond the formula-play, realized that he had a platform from which to speak, he began turning out plays which fit perfectly into our program.

One by one these voices began to be heard—Elmer Rice, Sidney Howard, John Howard Lawson, S. N. Behrman, DuBose Heyward, Philip Barry, Robert E. Sherwood, Maxwell Anderson—until eventually the America drama surpassed that of Europe. Now the foreign play is a rarity in our programs.

It was natural that in this process of evolution Eugene O'Neill should become allied with the Guild. He came into our fold first with *Marco Millions* and followed this with what was perhaps the most unusual and successful experiment of the Guild's career, *Strange Interlude*. Here was a play in nine acts, a play which began at 5.30 in the afternoon, dismissed its audience for dinner, resumed at 8.30 and continued until 11 o'clock.

The Guild produced the play with a certain fear and trembling. It had no doubts of the play's artistic merits. But the question of its finding an audience was less certain of solution. The play found its audience in every state in the Union and in almost every foreign country as well. The Guild's most interesting experiment turned out to be its most successful.

The historical résumé of the Guild could go on at great length. It would not be complete without at least a brief word about the changing conditions in the theatre, which, in the years of its existence, the Guild has had to meet.

First came the rise of the actor as an important factor in the theatre. The Guild met this condition by the formation of an acting company. Then came the growth of the motion-picture industry, with its vast profits which permitted it to raid the theatre at will. The Guild through its acting company brought many an actor and actress to full flower, only to see the movies steal most of them away.

When the Guild was organized, the "road" was a vast field for production. The Guild, having achieved success with its experiment in New York, sought to do missionary work on the road as well. The advent of the motion picture meant the collapse of that factor too. When the Guild began, costs in the theatre were at a minimum. In the intervening years they have risen to a maximum.

However, the Guild's idea has come unscathed through the years. Its approach to the various problems of production may have changed in the years, but it still thrives on the belief that fine plays, honestly presented, represent the theatre at the height of its artistic achievement. That is still the aim of the Theatre Guild, and when it ceases to exist so will the Guild itself.

We submit the fourteen plays reprinted in this volume as a representative cross-section of the Guild's scope and activities. We purposely have chosen no two plays by any one author; the list includes commercial failures as well as our greatest successes; there are plays from our earliest season as well as our latest. In every case, however, we feel that there are those certain qualities that made us say "Here is a play that the Guild must produce!"

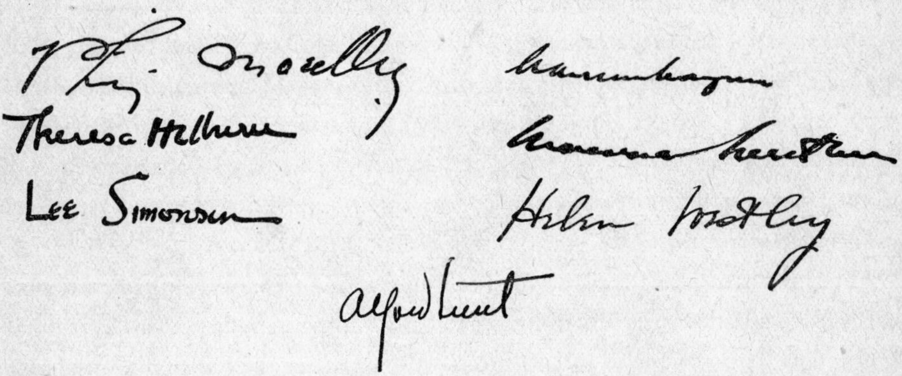

St. John G. Ervine

JOHN FERGUSON

To

the Memory of My Grandmother

Margaret Greer

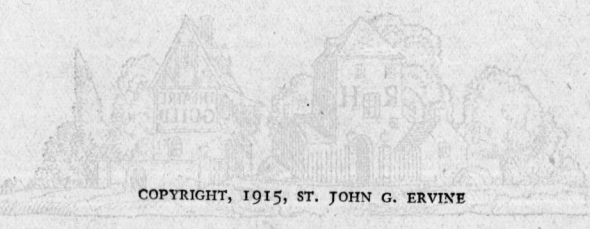

ST. JOHN G. ERVINE

It is to St. John G. Ervine's *John Ferguson* that the Theatre Guild owes its initial success. Faced at the beginning with the prospect of abandoning its experimental venture because of a depleted treasury, the play was an overnight hit and laid a firm foundation for the present organization. The Irish playwright who conferred this boon on the Theatre Guild was born in Belfast on December 28, 1883. His first play, *The Magnanimous Lover,* was produced in 1907. He achieved the distinction of having one of his works, *Mixed Marriage,* presented by the Abbey Theatre in Dublin in 1911. Subsequently Mr. Ervine became manager of this famous repertory company and helped produce several of his own plays. During the World War he served in France with the First Battalion of the Royal Dublin Fusiliers and was so seriously wounded that he suffered the loss of a leg. Mr. Ervine is quite as well known to American readers as a novelist and dramatic critic as he is a playwright. His critical articles in the old New York *World* stirred up violent controversy. His novels, of which *Changing Winds* is perhaps best known, indicate the wide range of his creative interests. His most successful plays are: *John Ferguson, Jane Clegg, The First Mrs. Fraser* and *The Wonderful Visit* (in collaboration with H. G. Wells).

CHARACTERS

JOHN FERGUSON, a farmer.
SARAH FERGUSON, his wife.
ANDREW FERGUSON, his son.
HANNAH FERGUSON, his daughter.
JAMES CAESAR, a grocer.
HENRY WITHEROW, a farmer and miller.
"CLUTIE" JOHN MAGRATH, a beggar.
SAM MAWHINNEY, a postman.
SERGEANT KERNAGHAN, R.I.C.
TWO CONSTABLES.
A CROWD OF MEN AND WOMEN, BOYS AND GIRLS.

The Scene is laid in the kitchen of a farm-house in County Down.
The Time is the late summer of the year 188-.
"CLUTIE" is a slang expression meaning "left-handed."
There is an interval of an hour between the First and Second Acts; of a night between the Second and Third; and of a fortnight between the Third and Fourth.

JOHN FERGUSON

ACT ONE

It is the afternoon of a warm day in the late summer of the year 188—, and soft sunlight enters the kitchen of JOHN FERGUSON'S *farm through the windows and the open door. The kitchen is comfortably furnished, although the* FERGUSONS *are no longer prosperous, for* MRS. FERGUSON, *who is now sitting by the door, mending socks, takes great pride in maintaining the appearance of fortune. She is a short, stout, healthy woman, pleasant and agreeable even when she is as harassed as she now is, and her mind is moulded in the kindliness of an Ulster woman. She is not a very intelligent woman, and so her sympathies are sometimes flattened by her lack of perception, but, within her limitations, she is an excellent wife and a very good mother.*

Her husband, JOHN FERGUSON, *is sitting in front of the turf fire, with a rug wrapped round his legs. He is reading a large Bible to himself, and his lips move as if he were silently pronouncing each word to himself. He is an elderly, tired, delicate-looking man, and his dark beard is turning gray. His eyes are set deeply in his head, and they are full of a dark, glowing color. His voice is slow but very firm, although his words are gentle. He looks like a portrait of Moses—not that Moses who led the Israelites out of Egypt and was a great captain of hosts, but the Moses who surveyed the Promised Land from Mount Nebo in the Plains of Moab.*

The furniture of the kitchen is good and substantial, and of the sort that one sees in a decent homestead. The door leading to the loaning ("loanie") or lane in front of the house is in the wall at the back of the scene. A person entering the kitchen from the "loanie" would have a large window on his right hand, in the same wall as the door, and a staircase on his left hand. Beyond the staircase, near the front of the scene, is a door leading to other rooms and also to the scullery and back of the farm. The fireplace is in the wall opposite that in which the staircase is set. Under the window is a large sofa. A dresser is set between the foot of the staircase and the door leading to the yard. A large table sits in the center of the room. JOHN FERGUSON'S *chair now stands against one end of this table, so that he can place his Bible on it easily when he is tired of holding it. The ornaments are those customary in such a house. Over the fireplace a gun is suspended.*

SARAH FERGUSON

I wonder where Hannah is. I haven't seen her for an hour past.

JOHN FERGUSON

(*Without looking up*). She's mebbe in the fields with Andrew. Listen to this, Sarah! (*He raises his voice as he reads from the thirtieth of the Psalms of David.*) "I will extol thee, O Lord; for thou hast lifted me up, and hast not made my foes to rejoice over me. O Lord, my God, I cried unto thee, and thou hast healed me. O Lord, thou hast brought up my soul from the grave: thou hast kept me alive, that I should not go down into the pit. Sing unto the Lord, O ye saints of his, and give thanks at the remembrance of his holiness. (*He emphasises what follows.*) For his anger endureth but a moment; in his favor, is life: weeping may endure for a night, but joy cometh in the morning." (*He turns to his wife.*) Do you hear that, Sarah? There's great comfort for you!

SARAH FERGUSON

Well, indeed, I hope it will, for we have need of joy in this house. We've bore enough trouble. Here's the farm mortgaged up to the hilt, and you sick and not able to do no work this long while, and Henry Witherow bothering you for the money you owe him! . . .

JOHN FERGUSON

(*Holding up the Bible so that she can see it*). "Weeping may endure for a night," Sarah, "but joy cometh in the morning." Them's grand words! Don't be complaining now, for sure God never deserts His own people. We have His word for that, Sarah. We're tried a while, and then we're given our reward.

SARAH FERGUSON

Well, we've earned ours anyway! It's a great pity Andrew's such a poor hand on the farm.

JOHN FERGUSON

The lad was never meant for the land, Sarah. You know rightly I dedicated him to the ministry the day he was born. It was a sore blow to the lad when I told him it couldn't be managed, but it was a sorer blow to me.

SARAH FERGUSON

Ay, indeed, it was, John. You were always quaren set on Andrew.

JOHN FERGUSON

(*Proudly*). He's my son! I have great hopes of Andrew.

SARAH FERGUSON

Well, well, you would have done better, mebbe, to let him go on with his learning, for he's no use at all on the farm. I hope to my goodness his uncle Andrew'll send the money to pay the mortgage. It's quare him not writing this long while.

JOHN FERGUSON

He's mebbe had bother. He'll write if he has the money by him. You may be sure of that.

SARAH FERGUSON

He never was much of a one for giving anything away, your brother Andrew, and mebbe he'll disappoint you the same as he's disappointed many another person.

JOHN FERGUSON

I know he's near with money, but all the same I think he'll be willing to lend me the price of the mortgage. Him and me was born in this house, and we played here together as wee lads. Our da was born here too, and his da before him. Andrew couldn't let the farm go out of the family after all them generations.

SARAH FERGUSON

I trust, indeed, he'll not, but it's a quare poor look-out when you think he's never answered your letters to him this long time, and him knowing well you were sick and helpless. Dear knows what'll become of us all if he doesn't send the money! Henry Witherow's a hard man, John, and he'll not be willing to wait long. (*She rises and looks out of the door.*) Here's Hannah now! I wonder is the mail in yet!

JOHN FERGUSON

We'll know in a wee while. (*He takes up the Bible again and resumes his reading.*) (HANNAH FERGUSON, *a beautiful girl of twenty, enters the kitchen from the "loanie." Her thick black hair is uncovered.*)

SARAH FERGUSON

Is the mail in yet?

HANNAH FERGUSON

(*Wearily*). The long-car only went by a minute or two ago. I met "Clutie" John at the end of the loanie, and he said the mail would be late the day. (*She goes to the window-seat and sits down.*) It's like Sam Mawhinney to be late the time we want him to be early.

JOHN FERGUSON

(*With gentle rebuke in his voice*). Hannah, child! You don't know what trouble the man may have had. It might not be his fault the mail's late. Sometimes there's a storm at sea, and that keeps the boats back. Mebbe the train was delayed. Many's a thing might have happened. You shouldn't be blaming Sam for what's mebbe not his fault.

HANNAH FERGUSON

(*Going to her father, and putting her arms round his neck*). Da, dear, aren't you the quare one for making excuses for people!

SARAH FERGUSON

Well, sure, a lot of them needs it.

(*She has resumed her seat by the door and is again busy with her work of mending socks.*)

HANNAH FERGUSON

How're you now, da? Are you better nor you were a while ago?

JOHN FERGUSON

(*Cheerfully*). Ah, boys-a-boys, Hannah, what did you mind me of it for? I was near forgetting I was sick at all. That shows I'm better in myself, doesn't it now?

HANNAH FERGUSON

(*Looking anxiously at him*). You're not letting on, are you, da?

SARAH FERGUSON

Letting on, indeed! Did you ever know your da to let on about anything?

JOHN FERGUSON

Indeed, now, and I let on many's a time! There's whiles, when I'm sitting here before the fire, or mebbe there in front of the door when the days is warm, I pretend to myself I'm better again and can go out and do a day's work in the fields with any man. (*His voice drops into complaint.*) I haven't been in the fields this long time.

SARAH FERGUSON

(*Sharply*). Now, don't be going and making yourself unhappy, John!

JOHN FERGUSON

No, woman, I won't. But it's hard for a man to be sitting here with a rug wrapped round his legs, and him not able to do a hand's turn for his wife and family.

HANNAH FERGUSON

(*Fondling him*). Ah, da, dear!

JOHN FERGUSON

(*Complaint now controlling his voice*). And me the man that was always active! There wasn't a one in the place could beat me at the reaping, not one.... (*He remembers the consolations of his faith, although his voice falters as he speaks the next sentence.*) But it's the will of God! (*He pauses for a moment, and then his mind wanders again to his illness.*) Sometimes, when I hear the men in the fields, cutting the corn and gathering the harvest, and them shouting to one another and laughing hearty together, I near cry. Me not able to go out and help them to bring in the harvest . . . tied here like a wee child! . . .

HANNAH FERGUSON

(*Tearfully*). Da, da, don't go on that way!

SARAH FERGUSON

(*Impatiently*). Ah, quit, the two of you! Hannah, I'm surprised at you coming in and upsetting your da, and him keeping his heart up all day!

HANNAH FERGUSON

I didn't mean to bother you, da.

JOHN FERGUSON

(*Patting her hair*). No, daughter, you didn't. I know that rightly. (*Stirring himself and speaking more briskly.*) Ah, well! "Weeping may endure for a night, but joy cometh in the morning." God always has a word to comfort you when your heart's down. Mebbe there's a letter in Sam Mawhinney's bag this minute that'll cheer us all up. I'm a poor, mealy man to be complaining like that, Hannah, when there's many is worse off nor me . . . only I can't help it sometimes. It's when the men are coming down the "loanie" in the evening with their scythes over their shoulders, and them tired and sweating and hungry for their suppers! . . . Well, God knows His own ways best, and there's many in the world has a harder time nor I have.

HANNAH FERGUSON

(*Trying to take his mind off his illness*). I was letting on too, da!

SARAH FERGUSON

Well, indeed, you might have employed your time to better advantage, Hannah. You can let on till you're tired, but you'll never alter anything that way.

JOHN FERGUSON

What were you letting on, daughter?

HANNAH FERGUSON

I was letting on that my Uncle Andrew had sent you all the money you need!

SARAH FERGUSON

Well, I hope your pretence will come true, for if he doesn't, we'll have to flit out of this. It'll break your da's heart to go, and it'll break my heart too. (*She rises and puts her work on the dresser.*) I come here as a young girl, no older nor yourself, Hannah, to be married on your da, and I've lived here ever since. I'll never be happy nowhere else.

JOHN FERGUSON

(*Ruminatingly*). Ay, it'll be hard to go.

SARAH FERGUSON

There's no sense or purpose in it, God forgive me for saying it!

JOHN FERGUSON

There's a meaning in it, whatever happens. I can't see God's purpose, but I know well there is one. His hand never makes a mistake.

HANNAH FERGUSON

(*Bitterly*). It's quare and hard to see what purpose there is in misfortune and trouble for people that never done nothing to deserve it!

SARAH FERGUSON

Ah, quit it, Hannah! If God was to hear you saying the like of that, He'd mebbe strike you dead.

JOHN FERGUSON

Daughter, dear, you're a young slip of a girl, or you'd never talk that way. (*Sternly.*) Do you think God doesn't know how to look after His own world? (*The severity of his voice relaxes.*) Everything that happens is made to happen, and everything in the world, the commonest wee fly in the bushes before the door there, has a purpose and a meaning. There's things hid from you and me because we're not fit to know them, but the more we fill ourselves with the glory of God, the better we get to understand the world. It's people that's full of sin, Hannah, that can't see or understand. That's sin—not knowing or understanding! Ignorance is sin. Keeping your mind shut is sin. Not letting the sun and the air and the warmth of God into your heart—that's sin, Hannah!
(*He sinks back in his chair, fatigued by his outburst.*)

SARAH FERGUSON

There, now, you've made yourself tired!

JOHN FERGUSON

(*Weakly*). I'm all right, woman!

HANNAH FERGUSON

(*Going towards the door*). I wish to my goodness that man Mawhinney would come with the letters!

JOHN FERGUSON

He'll soon be here now.

HANNAH FERGUSON

(*Looking out*). He's never in sight yet! (*She speaks the next sentence petulantly, returning to her seat on the sofa as she does so.*) Och, here's that man, Jimmy Caesar! I wonder what he wants!

SARAH FERGUSON

I wouldn't be surprised but it's you he's after! This isn't the first time he's been here lately, nor yet the second.

HANNAH FERGUSON

(*Crossly*). Och, ma, quit talking! I wouldn't marry him if he was the last man in the world.

SARAH FERGUSON

Well, dear bless us, if he was the last man in the world, and I wanted him for myself, I wouldn't like to run the risk of making you an offer of him! Sure, what's wrong with the man?

HANNAH FERGUSON

(*Contemptuously*). He's an old collie, that's what he is! He has no spirit in him at all! Look at the way he goes on about Henry Witherow and what he'll do to him when he gets the chance! He's had many a chance, but he's done nothing.

SARAH FERGUSON

Would you have him kill the man?

HANNAH FERGUSON

He shouldn't go about the place threatening to have Witherow's life when he doesn't mean to take it.

JOHN FERGUSON

Daughter, dear, I don't like to hear you speaking so bitterly. It's foolish of Jimmy Caesar to talk in the wild way he does, though, dear knows, he's had great provocation. But he doesn't mean the half he says!

HANNAH FERGUSON

Well, he shouldn't say it then!

SARAH FERGUSON

Ah, now, Hannah, if we were all to say just what we meant, more nor half of us would be struck dumb.

JOHN FERGUSON

Ay, you're right, woman! You are, indeed! Henry Witherow's a hard man, and he put many an indignity on Jimmy Caesar's family. If you knew all he's had to bear, Hannah, you'd pity him, and not be saying hard words against him.

SARAH FERGUSON

Ay, indeed, John! Witherow'll not be soft on us if we can't pay him what we owe him, and then, Hannah, you'll mebbe understand what Jimmy Caesar's feelings are.

HANNAH FERGUSON

I'll never understand the feelings of a collie. I like a man to have a spirit and do what he's said he'd do, or else keep his tongue quiet in his head.

SARAH FERGUSON

Now, it's brave and hard to be having a spirit in these times. Sure, the man must have some pluck in him to turn round and make a good business for himself after him losing near every halfpenny he had, and that man Witherow near bankrupting him, and killing his old da and ma with grief. That's not a poor, paltry spirit, is it?

JOHN FERGUSON

You'd better quit talking about him now. He'll step in the door any minute. Where was he when you saw him, Hannah?

HANNAH FERGUSON

He was at the foot of the "loanie."

SARAH FERGUSON

It's a credit to him the way he's slaved and saved. I daresay he has a big bit of money saved up in the Ulster Bank. (*She goes to the door and looks out.*) Ay, here he's coming! (*She calls out to* CAESAR.) Is that you, Jimmy? (CAESAR *is heard to shout in response.*) If Hannah was to marry him, the way he wants her. . . .

HANNAH FERGUSON

I wouldn't marry him if he was rolling in riches and had gallons of gold!

SARAH FERGUSON

(*Returning to the kitchen*). Och, wheesht with you! Sure, the man's right enough, and anyway one man's no worse nor another!

(JAMES CAESAR *comes to the door. He is a mean-looking man, about thirty-five years of age, and his look of meanness is not mitigated by his air of prosperity. His movements are awkward, and his speech is nervous. He is very eager to please* HANNAH, *whom he pretends not to see.*)

JAMES CAESAR

Good-day to you all!

JOHN FERGUSON

Good-day to you, Jimmy!

JAMES CAESAR

(*Hesitating at the door*). Can I come in?

SARAH FERGUSON

Sure, do! You know you're always welcome here, Jimmy!

JAMES CAESAR

(*Entering*). It's kind of you to say that! (*He puts his hat on the dresser.*) It's a brave day!

SARAH FERGUSON

It's not so bad.

JAMES CAESAR

It'll do good to harvest. (*Pretending to see* HANNAH *for the first time.*) Is that you, Hannah? I didn't see you when I come in first. I hope you're keeping your health?

HANNAH FERGUSON

(*Coldly*). I'm bravely, thank you!

JAMES CAESAR

I didn't see you this while back, and I was wondering to myself were you not well or something. I'm glad to see you looking so fine on it. (*To* JOHN FERGUSON.) Did you hear from your brother Andrew, John?

SARAH FERGUSON

Sam Mawhinney's not got this length yet. Did you see him as you were coming up?

JAMES CAESAR

I did not. Are you keeping well, John?

JOHN FERGUSON

I'm as well as can be expected, Jimmy.

JAMES CAESAR

That's good. I'm glad to hear it. It'll be a great blow to you if you have to leave the farm.

JOHN FERGUSON

It will.

JAMES CAESAR

(*Bitterness growing into his voice*). Ay, it's a quare blow to any man to have to leave the house he was born and reared in, the way I had to do. It's Witherow has your mortgage, isn't it?

JOHN FERGUSON

Ay.

JAMES CAESAR

God curse him!

JOHN FERGUSON

(*Reproachfully*). Jimmy, Jimmy!

JAMES CAESAR

Ah, you're a forgiving man, John Ferguson, but I'm not, and never will be. Look at the way he treated me and mine. I've never forgot that, and I never will if I live to be a hundred years old. (*Violently.*) I'll choke the life out of him one of these days!

HANNAH FERGUSON

(*Turning away scornfully*). Ah, quit, for dear sake. You're always talking, Jimmy Caesar!

JAMES CAESAR

(*Ashamedly*). Ay, I'm always talking, Hannah, and never doing! 'Deed and you're right! When I think of the things he done to me, I go near distracted with shame for taking it as quiet as I have done. I go out sometimes, demented mad, swearing to have his life—and I come home again, afeard to lay a finger on him. He's big and powerful, and he can take a holt of me and do what he likes with me. I'm heartsore at my weakness! That's the God's truth! You do well, Hannah, to be making little of me for a poor-natured man, but it's not for want of desire I don't do an injury to him. I haven't the strength—or the courage.

JOHN FERGUSON

What way is that to be talking, Jimmy Caesar? Would you sin your soul with a murder? Man, man, mind what you're saying and thinking! You're in God's grief already for the thoughts you have in your head. Them that has bad thoughts are no better in His eyes nor them that does bad deeds.

SARAH FERGUSON

Ah, sure, you can't help having thoughts, whatever kind of a mind you have!

JOHN FERGUSON

You can help brooding on them. What call has Jimmy to be wasting his mind on thinking bad about Henry Witherow? Your life isn't your own to do what you like with. It's God's life, and no one else's. And so is Henry Witherow's. If you take his life or any man's life, no matter why you do it, you're robbing God.

SARAH FERGUSON

Ah, for dear sake, quit talking about murders. You'll have me out of my mind with fear. Sure, nobody wants to kill anybody these times, what with civilization and all them things.

HANNAH FERGUSON

(*Sneeringly*). Och, ma, don't disturb yourself! Sure, you know it's only talk!

JAMES CAESAR

Hannah!

HANNAH FERGUSON

What?

JAMES CAESAR

I wanted to have a talk with you, and I was wondering would you be coming down the town the night?

HANNAH FERGUSON

(*Decisively*). I'm not.

SARAH FERGUSON

Ah, now, Hannah, you can just go down and get a few things from Jimmy's shop that I'm wanting. I was thinking of going myself, but sure you can just step that length and bring them back with you; and while you're on the way, Jimmy can say what he wants to say.

HANNAH FERGUSON

(*Sullenly*). You don't need the things till the morning, ma, and if you give Jimmy the order now, he can send them up the morrow.

JAMES CAESAR

Hannah, I want to speak to you particular. Will you not come out with me for a wee while?

HANNAH FERGUSON

I'm not in the way of going out again the night, thank you!

SARAH FERGUSON

Now, you've nothing to do, Hannah, and you can go along with him rightly.

HANNAH FERGUSON

I've plenty to do.

(HENRY WITHEROW *passes the window.*)

SARAH FERGUSON

Lord save us, there's Witherow.

(JAMES CAESAR *instinctively goes into the corner of the room farthest from the door.* HENRY WITHEROW, *a tall, heavy, coarse-looking man, with a thick, brutal jaw, comes into the kitchen. He has a look of great and ruthless strength, and all his movements are those of a man of decision and assurance. He does not ask if he may enter the kitchen and sit down; he assumes that he may do so.*)

HENRY WITHEROW

(*Sitting down*). Well, how're you all the day?

SARAH FERGUSON

(*Nervously*). We're rightly, thank God, Mr. Witherow!

HENRY WITHEROW

I'm glad to hear it. I was just passing, John, and I thought I'd drop in and hear how you were getting on.

JOHN FERGUSON

That was thoughtful of you, Henry.

HENRY WITHEROW

How're you, Hannah! (*He looks closely at her.*) Boys, but you're getting to be a fine-looking girl, Hannah! (*He turns to* MRS. FERGUSON.) You'll be having all the boys after her! Faith, I wouldn't mind going after her myself.

JAMES CAESAR

(*Pale with anger*). Keep your talk to yourself, Henry Witherow!

HENRY WITHEROW

(*Contemptuously*). Ah, you're there, are you? You haven't a notion of him, have you, Hannah?

HANNAH FERGUSON

Your manners could be better, Mr. Witherow.

HENRY WITHEROW

(*Laughing*). Could they, now? And who would improve them, eh? Mr. James Caesar, Esquire, mebbe?

JAMES CAESAR

We want no discourse with you, Henry Witherow. Your presence in this house is not welcome! . . .

HENRY WITHEROW

Oh, indeed! Have you bought the house? I've heard nothing about the sale, and I think I should have heard something about it. I hold the mortgage, you know. . . .

JOHN FERGUSON

There's no need for bitter talk, Henry. Jimmy forgot himself.

HENRY WITHEROW

Ah, well, as long as he admits it and says he's sorry!

JAMES CAESAR

I'm not sorry.

HENRY WITHEROW

God help you, your tongue's the strongest part of you. (*To* JOHN FERGUSON.) Now that I'm here, John, perhaps we could discuss a wee matter of business. I don't suppose you want to talk about your affairs before all the neighbours, and so if Mr. James Caesar will attend to his shop. . . .

SARAH FERGUSON

(*To* HANNAH). You can go down to the shop with him now, daughter, and leave your da and me to talk to Mr. Witherow. (*She speaks quietly to* HANNAH.) For God's sake, Hannah, have him if he asks you. Witherow'll not spare us, and mebbe Jimmy'll pay the mortgage.

HENRY WITHEROW

(*To* JOHN FERGUSON). I suppose you haven't had any word from Andrew yet?

JOHN FERGUSON

Not yet, Henry.

HENRY WITHEROW

H'm, that's bad!

(SAM MAWHINNEY, *the postman, goes past the window and then past the door.*)

SARAH FERGUSON

Lord bless us, there's Sam Mawhinney away past the door. (*She runs to the door.*) Hi, Sam, are you going past without giving us our letter?

SAM MAWHINNEY

(*Coming to the door*). What letter, Mrs. Ferguson?

SARAH FERGUSON

(*Anxiously*). Haven't you one for us? . . .

SAM MAWHINNEY

I have not.

HANNAH FERGUSON

You haven't! . . .

SARAH FERGUSON

Oh, God save us, he hasn't written after all!

HANNAH FERGUSON

Isn't the American mail in yet, Sam?

SAM MAWHINNEY

It's in, right enough. I left a letter at Braniel's from their daughter over in Boston. Were you expecting one?

JOHN FERGUSON

(*Desolation in his voice*). Ay, Sam, we were thinking there might be one, but it doesn't matter. We'll not keep you from your work.

SAM MAWHINNEY

I hope you're not put out by it. It's a quare disappointment not to get a letter and you expecting it.

JOHN FERGUSON

Ay, Sam, it is.

SAM MAWHINNEY

Well, good-evening to you!

JOHN FERGUSON

Good-evening to you, Sam!
(*The postman quits the door.* SARAH FERGUSON *sits down in a chair near the dresser and begins to cry.* HANNAH *stands at the window looking out with hard, set eyes.* JIMMY CAESAR *stands near her, twisting his cap awkwardly in his hands.* JOHN FERGUSON *lies back in his chair in silence. They are quiet for a few moments, during which* HENRY WITHEROW *glances about him, taking in the situation with satisfaction.*)

HENRY WITHEROW

I suppose that means you can't get the money to pay off the mortgage, John?

JOHN FERGUSON

I'm afeard so, Henry.

HENRY WITHEROW

(*Rising*). Well, I'm sorry for you. I have a great respect for you, John, and I'd do more for you nor for any one, but money's very close at present, and I need every penny I can put my hands on. I'll have to stand by my bargain. I'm sorry for you all!

JAMES CAESAR

That's a lie, Henry Witherow, and you know well it is! You're the fine man to come here letting on to be sorry for John Ferguson when you would do anything to get him out of this. If you were sorry for him, what did you call in your money for when you knew he couldn't pay it? You know rightly you've had your heart set on the farm these years past, and you're afeard of your life he'll mebbe pay the mortgage. . . .

HENRY WITHEROW

(*Going to him and shaking him roughly*). I've stood enough of your back-chat, Caesar, and I'll stand no more of it.

JAMES CAESAR

(*Feebly*). Let me go, will you?

HENRY WITHEROW

I'll let you go when I've done with you.

HANNAH FERGUSON

(*Going to* WITHEROW *and striking him in the face*). Go out of this house, Henry Witherow. It's not yours yet, and till it is, there's the door to you!

HENRY WITHEROW

(*Throwing* CAESAR *from him so that he falls on the floor, where he lies moaning and shivering*). Heth, Hannah, you're a fine woman! You are, in sang! It's a pity to waste you on a lad like that! (*He pushes* CAESAR *with his foot.*) You ought to marry a man, Hannah, and not an old Jenny-Jo! (*He turns to* JOHN FERGUSON.) John, I'll have to have a serious talk with you in a wee while, but it's no good stopping to have it now with all this disturbance. I'll go and see M'Conkey, the lawyer, first.

JOHN FERGUSON

Very well, Henry.

HENRY WITHEROW

I'm sorry for you, but I must look after myself.

JOHN FERGUSON

Ay, so you must. It's a hard thing to have to leave the home you're used to, but it can't be helped. I'm getting an old man, and I haven't much longer here. I'd like to end my days where they were begun, but . . .

HANNAH FERGUSON

(*Going to her father*). Don't take on, da! There'll mebbe be a way out of it all. (*To* WITHEROW.) Mr. Witherow, will you not let the mortgage go on for a while longer? We've had a great deal of trouble lately, and my brother Andrew's not accustomed to the farm yet. If you were to give us more time, mebbe my uncle'll send the money later on . . .

HENRY WITHEROW

Ay, and mebbe he'll not. Your Uncle Andrew's not over-anxious to part with anything as far as I can see. I'm sorry, Hannah, but I can't ruin myself to oblige other people.

JOHN FERGUSON

It was to be. You can foreclose, Henry.

SARAH FERGUSON

Andrew's a poor brother to you, John, to let you be brought to this bother and you sick and sore.

JOHN FERGUSON

Poor Andrew, he must be heart-scalded at not being able to send the money. He'd have sent it if he had had it by him. I know he would. I can picture him there, not writing because he hasn't the heart to tell us he can't send the money.
(CAESAR, *who has risen from the floor, comes to* JOHN FERGUSON *and speaks almost hysterically.*)

JAMES CAESAR

John, I know rightly that Witherow has set his heart on your farm. I know he has, and he's an old hypocrite if he says he's sorry for you! But I'll spite him yet, I will! I'm willing to pay off the mortgage for you if it costs me every penny I have . . .

SARAH FERGUSON

(*Rising and embracing him*). Oh, God reward you, Jimmy!

JAMES CAESAR

(*Putting her aside*). If Hannah'll listen to me . . .

HENRY WITHEROW

Ay, if Hannah'll listen to you! Huh! You'd make a bargain on your ma's coffin, Jimmy Caesar!

JAMES CAESAR

(*Weakly*). I don't want nothing more to say to you, Henry Witherow. Anything that passes between you and me now will come through a solicitor.

HENRY WITHEROW

Ay, you're mighty fond of the law. You'll get your fill of it one of these days. (*To* HANNAH.) Well, my bold girl, are you going to take the fine offer's been made for you here by Mr. James Caesar, Esquire? Because I'd like to know what the position is before I go. There's no good in me going to M'Conkey and incurring expense needlessly!

HANNAH FERGUSON

I bid you go before, Mr. Witherow. Will you have me bid you go again?

HENRY WITHEROW

Ah, now, quit talking!

HANNAH FERGUSON

It's well for you my da's sick and there's no man in the house to chastise you the way you deserve. I can't put you out myself, so you must stay if you won't go.

HENRY WITHEROW

(*Disconcerted, and beginning to bluster*). Oh, come now, Hannah, there's no need to go on like that.

HANNAH FERGUSON

(*Resuming her seat on the sofa*). I've said all I've got to say, Mr. Witherow. A decent man wouldn't be standing there after what I've said to you.
(*The sound of a tin whistle is heard outside.*)

JAMES CAESAR

Mebbe you'll go now, Witherow!

HENRY WITHEROW

If I go, it'll not be because you ask me! (*To* HANNAH.) You've a sharp tongue in your head, Hannah! I'd like to cut a bit of it off for you! (*To* JOHN FERGUSON.) Well, John, you'll mebbe let me know later on what course you'll take about the mortgage. I'll be up at the mill the rest of the day. Good-morning to you all!
(*He goes out.*)

JAMES CAESAR

Hell to him!
(*The whistling which has persisted all this time stops suddenly, and* HENRY WITHEROW *is heard outside shouting, "Get out of my road, damn you!" and then* "CLUTIE" JOHN MAGRATH, *the half-wit, is heard crying, "Ah, don't strike me,* MR. WITHEROW.")

SARAH FERGUSON

(*Going to the door*). Ah, dear save us, he's couped "Clutie" John into the hedge!

JAMES CAESAR

That's all he can do—strike weak lads like myself, and beat poor fellows that's away in the mind like "Clutie" John!

SARAH FERGUSON

(*Returning to the kitchen*). Ah, well, he's not much hurt anyway! (*Her eyes are still wet with tears, and she wipes them as she sits down.*)
(*The tin whistle is heard again, and continues to be heard until* "CLUTIE" JOHN *appears at the door.*)

JAMES CAESAR

(*To* JOHN FERGUSON). You heard what I said, John?

JOHN FERGUSON

(*Picking up his Bible and preparing to read it again*). Ay, Jimmy, I heard you. You have a heart of corn! (*He reads.*) "For his anger endureth not for a moment; in his favor is life: weeping may endure for a night, but joy cometh in the morning." (*To his wife, who still weeps silently.*) What are you crying for, Sarah? Do you not hear this from God's Word? "Weeping may endure for a night, but joy cometh in the morning." That's a promise, isn't it? Dry your eyes, woman! God's got everything planned, and He knows what's best to be done. Don't be affronting Him with tears! . . .

JAMES CAESAR

(*Touching him*). John, did you not hear me? I was saying I'd pay the mortgage if Hannah would only listen to me . . .

JOHN FERGUSON

Ay, Jimmy, I heard you right enough, and I'm thankful to you. It's kind and neighborly of you, but Hannah has to decide them things for herself with the help of God, not with mine. There's no good in a man and a woman marrying if they have no kindly feeling for each other. I would rather Henry Witherow foreclosed nor let Hannah do anything she didn't want to do.

HANNAH FERGUSON

Da! (*She kneels beside him.*)

JOHN FERGUSON

(*Drawing her close to him*). Ay, daughter?

HANNAH FERGUSON

(*Struggling to speak*). Da, I . . . I . . .

JAMES CAESAR

(*Eagerly*). I wouldn't make a hard bargain with you, John! Do you hear me, Hannah? Your da and ma could live on in the place where he was born . . .

SARAH FERGUSON

God'll reward you, Jimmy!
(HANNAH FERGUSON *gets up from her place by her father's side. She looks at the old man for a few moments. He takes her hand in his and presses it warmly, and then smiles at her.*)

JOHN FERGUSON

Whatever you think best'll be right, Hannah!

HANNAH FERGUSON

Ay, da. (*To* JAMES CAESAR.) I thank you for your offer, Jimmy! I'll . . . I'll have you!

JOHN FERGUSON

(*Hoarsely*). Hannah?

HANNAH FERGUSON

I'll have him, da!

SARAH FERGUSON

(*Embracing her*). Oh, thank God, Hannah, thank God!

JAMES CAESAR

(*Uncertainly*). I can't tell you all I feel, Hannah, but I'll be a good man to you.

JOHN FERGUSON

May God bless the two of you!
(*The sound of the tin whistle grows louder.* "CLUTIE" JOHN MAGRATH *appears at the door. He is a half-wit and his age is about thirty.*)

"CLUTIE" JOHN

I see you're all there!

SARAH FERGUSON

Och, away on with you, "Clutie"! We don't want you here with your whistle!

"CLUTIE" JOHN

(*Entering the kitchen*). Ah, now, Mrs. Ferguson, what harm does my whistle do to you? (*To* JAMES CAESAR.) Good-evening to you, Mr. Caesar!

JAMES CAESAR

(*Sharply*). I have nothing for you!

"CLUTIE" JOHN

That's a quare pity, Mr. Caesar! I was thinking to myself as I was coming along, "Clutie John, if you were to meet Mr. Caesar now, he'd mebbe give you the lend of a halfpenny!"

JAMES CAESAR

Well, you were thinking wrong then, and you can just march on out of this as quick as you like. There's no money here for you.

"CLUTIE" JOHN

Ah, well, the Lord will send relief, though you won't be the honored instrument. Sure, I'll just play a tune to you for the pleasure of the thing. (*He puts the whistle to his lips, and then takes it away again.*) You didn't kill Mr. Witherow yet, Mr. Caesar?

JAMES CAESAR

(*Furiously*). Go 'long to hell out of this, will you? (*He is about to strike* "CLUTIE" JOHN, *but* MRS. FERGUSON *prevents him from doing so.*)

SARAH FERGUSON

Ah, don't hurt the poor soul, Jimmy! Sure, you know rightly he's astray in the mind.

"CLUTIE" JOHN

Ay, that's true, Mrs. Ferguson! That's true enough. I'm away in the head and I ought to be locked up in the asylum! And I would be if I was worse nor I am! It's a quare pity of a man that's not distracted enough to be put in the madhouse and not wise enough to be let do what the rest of you do. It's a hard thing now that a man as harmless as myself can't be let play his whistle in peace.

JAMES CAESAR

Why don't you do some work?

"CLUTIE" JOHN

Sure, didn't I tell you I'm astray in the mind!

JAMES CAESAR

It's a nice thing when a big lump of a man like yourself goes tramping about the country playing tunes on an old whistle instead of turning your hand to something useful. You can work well enough if you like.

"CLUTIE" JOHN

(*Regarding his whistle affectionately*). I would rather be whistling. There's plenty can work, but few can whistle.

HANNAH FERGUSON

What do you want, "Clutie?"

"CLUTIE" JOHN

I want many's a thing that I'll never get. Did you ever hear me whistling, "Willie Reilly and his Colleen Bawn?" That's a grand tune, for all it's a Catholic tune!

JAMES CAESAR

We heard it many's a time, and we don't want to hear it again. Quit out of the place!

JOHN FERGUSON

Come here, "Clutie!" ("CLUTIE" JOHN *goes to him.*) Did you want anything to eat?

"CLUTIE" JOHN

I always want something to eat.

JOHN FERGUSON

Hannah, give him a sup of sweet milk and a piece of soda bread. Poor lad, his belly is empty many's a time.

(HANNAH *goes to get the bread and milk for* "CLUTIE.")

JAMES CAESAR

It's a nice thing for her to be attending on the like of him.

JOHN FERGUSON

Why shouldn't she serve him? We're all children of the one Father, and we're serving Him when we're serving each other.

"CLUTIE" JOHN

Will I whistle a tune to you, Mr. Ferguson? (*He does not wait for permission, but begins to play "Willie Reilly and his Colleen Bawn."*)

SARAH FERGUSON

Ah, quit it, will you? You'll have me deafened with your noise!

"CLUTIE" JOHN

Do you not like my whistle, Mrs. Ferguson? It's grand music. You should see the wee childher running after me when I play it. "Play us a tune, Clutie John!" they shout when I go by, and sure I just play one to them. They're quare and fond of my whistle. It's only people with bitter minds that doesn't like to hear it. (HANNAH *brings the bread and milk to him, and he puts down his whistle in order to take them from her.*) Ah, God love you, Hannah, for your kind heart!

HANNAH FERGUSON

Did Henry Witherow hurt you, "Clutie," when he couped you in the hedge?

"CLUTIE" JOHN

He did, in sang! He couped me head over heels, and me doing nothing at all to him. That's a bitter man, Hannah, that would take the bite out of your mouth if it would bring a happorth of profit to him. He never was known to give anything to anybody, that man! It's a poor and hungry house he has. I was there one day when he was at his dinner, and he never as much as asked me had I a mouth on me at all.

JAMES CAESAR

Ay, you're right there! You are, indeed! There's no charity or loving-kindness about him.

"CLUTIE" JOHN

Well, he's not the only one in the world that's like that!

JAMES CAESAR

There's people says he sold his soul to the devil.

"CLUTIE" JOHN

Ah, why would the devil be buying souls when he can get millions of them for nothing? (*To* JOHN FERGUSON.) Did your brother Andrew send the money to pay off the mortgage, Mr. Ferguson?

JAMES CAESAR

What do you know about his brother Andrew?

"CLUTIE" JOHN

I know many's a thing! I can tell you where a kingfisher has his nest this minute. I saw a golden eagle once! It was in the West I saw it when I was whistling in Connacht. It was a great big bird with a beak on it that would tear the life out of you if it was that way inclined. (*He finishes the milk.*) This is the grand sweet milk! And the fine new bread, too! Isn't it grand now to have plenty of that? Will you not let me play a tune to you to reward you? Sure, I'll not ask you to give me the lend of a halfpenny for it, though you can if you like! I'll do it just for the pleasure of it.

JOHN FERGUSON

No, "Clutie," we can't have you playing your whistle here the night. You must go home now. We have something important to talk about.

SARAH FERGUSON

Go on, "Clutie" John! Away home with you now! We've had enough of your chat for one night. You can finish your bread in the "loanie."

JAMES CAESAR

I'm going now, Hannah. Will you walk a piece of the road with me? I've not had you a minute to myself yet with all these interruptions!

HANNAH FERGUSON

(*Submissively*). Very well, Jimmy!

"CLUTIE" JOHN

(*Astonished*). Are you going to marry him, Hannah?

HANNAH FERGUSON

Ay, "Clutie."

"CLUTIE" JOHN

(*Incredulously*). Ah, you're codding!

JAMES CAESAR

Come on, Hannah, and not be wasting your time talking to him! (*He goes to the door.*) Here's Andrew coming across the fields. We'd better wait and tell him.

"CLUTIE" JOHN

It'll be a great surprise for him.

SARAH FERGUSON

Ay, and great joy to him when he knows we'll not have to quit the farm after all. (ANDREW FERGUSON *enters. He is a slight, delicate-looking lad of nineteen, nearer in looks to his father than his mother. He is very tired after his work in the fields, and he carelessly throws the bridle he is carrying into a corner of the kitchen as if he were too fatigued to put it in its proper place.*)

ANDREW FERGUSON

Good-evening to you, Jimmy!

JAMES CAESAR

Good-evening, Andrew! You're looking tired on it!

ANDREW FERGUSON

(*Sitting down heavily*). I am tired. How're you, da?

JOHN FERGUSON

I'm rightly, son!

ANDREW FERGUSON

Ma, can I have a drop of sweet milk to drink? I'm nearly dead with the drouth. (MRS. FERGUSON *goes to crock to get the milk for him.*)

JAMES CAESAR

Andrew, I've great news for you. Me and your sister's going to be married on it.

ANDREW FERGUSON

(*Starting up*). You're what? (*His mother puts a cup of milk into his hands.*) Thank you, ma!

JAMES CAESAR

Ay, we're going to be married, Andrew. Hannah's just settled it.

SARAH FERGUSON

And we'll not have to quit out of the farm after all, Andrew! Jimmy says he'll pay the mortgage off!

ANDREW FERGUSON

(*Vaguely*). But I thought! . . . (*He turns to* HANNAH.)

HANNAH FERGUSON

(*Quickly*). It's kind of Jimmy, isn't it, Andrew?

ANDREW FERGUSON

(*After a pause*). Ay . . . it's kind!

JAMES CAESAR

We just stopped to tell the news to you, Andrew, to hearten you up after your day's work, and now Hannah and me's going for a bit of a dandher together. We haven't had a chance of a word by ourselves yet, and you know the way a couple likes to be by their lone, don't you? Are you ready, Hannah?

HANNAH FERGUSON

Ay.

JAMES CAESAR

Well, come on! Good-night to you all!

OMNES

Good-night, Jimmy!

"CLUTIE" JOHN

God reward you, Mr. Caesar.

JAMES CAESAR

(*Contemptuously*). Och, you! (*He goes out.* HANNAH *follows him to the door.*)

HANNAH FERGUSON

I won't be long before I'm back. (*Exit.*)

ANDREW FERGUSON

Da, is it true about Hannah and Jimmy?

JOHN FERGUSON

Ay, son, it's true. You saw them going out together.

ANDREW FERGUSON

But . . . did she do it of her own free will?

JOHN FERGUSON

Would I force her to it, Andrew?

ANDREW FERGUSON

No . . . Only . . . I suppose my uncle Andrew didn't write, then?

JOHN FERGUSON

No.

ANDREW FERGUSON

I wonder what made her . . . It's a quare set-out, this!

"CLUTIE" JOHN

Did you never hear the story of the girl that killed herself over the head of love? It's a quare sad story.

SARAH FERGUSON

Ah, wheesht with you, "Clutie"! Didn't I tell you before to quit out of this?

"CLUTIE" JOHN

(*Coaxingly*). Let me stay a wee while longer here by the fire, Mrs. Ferguson. I'll not be disturbing you.

SARAH FERGUSON

Well, close the door, then, and don't be talking so much! ("CLUTIE" JOHN *does as she bids him.*) Go up there now by the fire, and content yourself.
("CLUTIE" *sits down in a corner of the fireplace.* MRS. FERGUSON *seats herself on the sofa.*)

ANDREW FERGUSON

I saw Witherow going down the "loanie." I suppose he was in here about the mortgage?

JOHN FERGUSON

Ay, he was. He knows about Hannah and Jimmy.

SARAH FERGUSON

There was a row between Witherow and Jimmy, and they had a bit of a scuffle. Witherow caught a holt of Jimmy and knocked him down, and then Hannah went forward and struck Witherow flat in the face. You could have knocked me down with a feather when she did it.

ANDREW FERGUSON

That was a queer thing for her to do. Mebbe she's changed her mind about him. She could hardly find a word hard enough for him one time. I suppose it's all right. It's a load off my mind anyway to hear that the farm's safe, though God knows I'm a poor hand at working it.

JOHN FERGUSON

You'll get into the way of it in a wee while, son, and mebbe I'll be able to give you more help now my mind's at ease. It's hard on you that was reared for the ministry to have to turn your hand to farming and you not used to it!

ANDREW FERGUSON

I daresay it'll do me some sort of good.

"CLUTIE" JOHN

Listen! The girl I was telling you about, the one that killed herself, it was because her boy fell out with her. That was the cause of it! She cried her eyes out to him, but it made no differs, and so she threw herself off a hill and was killed dead.

ANDREW FERGUSON

Wheesht, "Clutie"!

SARAH FERGUSON

Dear only knows where you get all them stories from that you're always telling, "Clutie"!

"CLUTIE" JOHN

I hear them in my travels.

SARAH FERGUSON

Do you never hear no comic ones?

"CLUTIE" JOHN

Ah, I can't mind the comic ones. I just mind the sad ones. Them's the easiest to mind. They say the man was sorry afterwards when he heard tell she'd killed herself, but sure it was no use being sorry then. He should have been sorry before. It was a great lep she took.

ANDREW FERGUSON

What's Jimmy going to do about the mortgage? Is he going to take it on himself or what?

JOHN FERGUSON

I suppose so. We haven't settled anything. He said I could stay on here, your ma and me, with you to manage the farm.

SARAH FERGUSON

It's brave and kind of him to do the like.

ANDREW FERGUSON

I don't see where the kindness comes in if he gets Hannah to marry him over it! I hope to God she's not doing it just to save the farm.

JOHN FERGUSON

It was her own choice, Andrew, son. I said to her I would rather go into the Poorhouse nor have her do anything against her will. I'm not saying I'm not glad she's consented to have Jimmy, for that would be a lie. I *am* glad . . .

ANDREW FERGUSON

Because the farm's safe, da?

JOHN FERGUSON

Ay, Andrew! (*They are silent for a few moments.*) What are you thinking, son? Are you thinking I'm letting her marry Jimmy against her will just to save the farm? Is that what you're thinking?

ANDREW FERGUSON

(*Evasively*). I don't know what to think, da.

JOHN FERGUSON

I left her to her own choice. Didn't I, Sarah?

SARAH FERGUSON

Ay, John, you did, and sure what does it matter anyway? She's a young slip of a girl with wayward fancies in her head, mebbe, but Jimmy's as good and substantial a man as she's likely to get, and he'll be a good husband to her. It's a great thing for a girl to get a comfortable home to go to when she leaves the one she was reared in. There's plenty of young women does be running after this and running after that, but sure there's nothing in the end to beat a kind man and a good home where the money is easy and regular.

ANDREW FERGUSON

It's easy to be saying that, ma, when you're past your desires.

SARAH FERGUSON

I got my desire, Andrew, when I got your da. I never desired no one else but him.

ANDREW FERGUSON

Would you like to have married Jimmy Caesar if he'd been your match when you were Hannah's age?

SARAH FERGUSON

There was never no question of me marrying any one but your da . . .

ANDREW FERGUSON

But if there had—if your da's farm had been mortgaged like this one? . . .

SARAH FERGUSON

Ah, what's the good of if-ing and supposing? There's a deal too much of that goes on in this house. And, anyway, we can't let your da be turned out of his home.

ANDREW FERGUSON

Then that *is* the reason! Hannah's marrying Jimmy Caesar for our sakes, not for her own!

JOHN FERGUSON

No, no, Andrew, son, that's not it. I tell you she took him of her own free will. I wouldn't put no compulsion on her . . .

ANDREW FERGUSON

No, da, I know you wouldn't; but are you sure you're not ready to believe she's taking him of her own free will just because she says she is?

SARAH FERGUSON

Sure, what else can he do?

JOHN FERGUSON

God knows, Andrew, it'd hurt me sore to leave this house, but I'd go gladly out of it sooner nor cause Hannah a moment's unhappiness. I'm trying hard to do what's right. I don't think I'm acting hypocritically, and I'm not deceiving myself . . .
(*The door opens suddenly, and* HANNAH *enters in a state of agitation. She closes the door behind her, and then stands with her face to it. She begins to sob without restraint.*)

JOHN FERGUSON

(*Rising from his chair*). What is it, daughter?

ANDREW FERGUSON

(*Going to her*). Hannah!

SARAH FERGUSON

Don't bother her! (*Going to her and drawing her into her arms.*) There, Hannah, dear, don't disturb yourself, daughter. (*To the others.*) She's overwrought with the excitement. That's what it is! (*To* HANNAH.) Come and sit down, dear!
(*She draws* HANNAH *towards the sofa, where they both sit down.* HANNAH *buries her face in her mother's shoulder and sobs bitterly.*)

SARAH FERGUSON

Control yourself, daughter! You're all right now! No one'll harm you here!

JOHN FERGUSON

Are you not well, Hannah?

ANDREW FERGUSON

(*Coming close to his mother and sister*). Hannah, do you not want to marry Jimmy Caesar?

SARAH FERGUSON

Ah, wheesht with you, Andrew, and not be putting notions into her head! It's just overwrought she is. You know well she's been as anxious about the farm as any of us, and about your da, too, and she bore the bother well, but now that it's all settled, she's had to give way. Sure, that's natural! There, daughter, dear, just cry away till you're better! (*She soothes* HANNAH *as she speaks to her.*)

JOHN FERGUSON

(*Kicking the rug from his legs and going unsteadily to his wife and daughter*). Hannah! (HANNAH, *still sobbing, does not reply.*) Hannah, daughter, do you hear me?

HANNAH FERGUSON

(*Without raising her head*). Ay, da!

JOHN FERGUSON

Listen to me a while! (*He tries to raise her face to his.*) Look up at me, daughter! (*She turns towards him.*) Don't cry, Hannah! I can't bear to see you crying, dear! (*He makes her stand up, and then he clasps her to him.*) Listen to me, Hannah! I've never deceived you nor been unjust to you, have I, daughter?

HANNAH FERGUSON

No, da.

JOHN FERGUSON

And you know I'd beg my bread from door to door sooner nor hurt you, don't you? Isn't that true?

HANNAH FERGUSON

Ay, da, it is.

JOHN FERGUSON

Well, don't be afeard to say what's in your mind, then! What is it that's upsetting you?

HANNAH FERGUSON

(*Putting her arms about his neck, and drawing herself closer to him*). Oh, da, I can't . . . I can't! . . .

SARAH FERGUSON

You can't what?

JOHN FERGUSON

Do you not want to marry Jimmy?

HANNAH FERGUSON

(*Sobbing anew*). I can't thole him, da! . . .

JOHN FERGUSON

Very well, daughter! That'll be all right! Don't annoy yourself no more about him, dear. It'll be all right.

HANNAH FERGUSON

I tried hard to want him, da, but I couldn't, and when he bid me good-night and tried to kiss me out in the "loanie," I near died! . . .

JOHN FERGUSON

I know, daughter.

SARAH FERGUSON

(*Starting up in fear and anger*). But you promised him, Hannah! John, you're never going to let her break her word to the man? . . .

JOHN FERGUSON

Wheesht, woman!

SARAH FERGUSON

(*To her son*). Andrew! . . . (*She sees that* ANDREW'S *sympathies are with* HANNAH.) Hannah, think shame of yourself!

HANNAH FERGUSON

I can't take him, ma, I can't!

SARAH FERGUSON

Do you want to see your da turned out of the home he was born in, and him old and sick and not able to help himself?

JOHN FERGUSON

(*Angrily*). Quit it, woman, when I tell you!

SARAH FERGUSON

What's wrong with the man that she won't take him? There isn't a decenter, quieter fellow in the place, and him never took drink nor played devil's cards in his life. There's plenty of girls would give the two eyes out of their head to have the chance of him. Martha M'Clurg and Ann Close and Maggie M'Conkey, the whole lot of them, would jump with joy if he was to give a word to them (*She turns on* HANNAH), and what call have you to be setting yourself up when a decent, quiet man offers for you, and you knowing all that depends on it?

ANDREW FERGUSON

Ma, that's no way to talk to her!

SARAH FERGUSON

I'll say what I want to say.

ANDREW FERGUSON

You'll say no more. If I hear you speaking another word to her like that, I'll walk out of the door and never come back again.

SARAH FERGUSON

(*Sitting down and weeping helplessly*). Oh, you're all again' me, your da and Hannah and you! I'll have to quit the house I was brought to when I was a young girl, and mebbe live in a wee house in the town or go into the Union!

JOHN FERGUSON

(*Putting* HANNAH *into his chair*). Sit down, daughter, and quieten yourself. (*To his wife.*) If we have to go into the Poorhouse, Sarah, we'll have to go. (*To his son.*) Put on your top-coat, Andrew, and go up to Witherow's and tell him he can take the farm . . .

HANNAH FERGUSON

(*Recovering herself slightly*). No, da, no. I'm all right again. I'll marry Jimmy! I'm ashamed of the way I went on just now. My ma was right. It was just the upset that made me like it.

SARAH FERGUSON

Ay, daughter, that was it.

JOHN FERGUSON

Wheesht, Sarah. Go on, Andrew.

ANDREW FERGUSON

All right, da.

SARAH FERGUSON

(*Angrily*). Let her go herself and finish her work! The lad's wore out with tiredness . . .

ANDREW FERGUSON

I'm not that tired, ma.

HANNAH FERGUSON

(*Firmly*). I'll go, Andrew. It'll quieten me down to have the walk. (*To her father.*) Jimmy doesn't know yet, da. I didn't tell him, and he's coming up here the night after he shuts his shop. Mebbe you'll tell him before I come back? . . .

JOHN FERGUSON

All right, daughter, I will (*To* ANDREW.) Hannah'll go, Andrew. She doesn't want to be here when Jimmy comes. (*To* HANNAH.) Put a shawl over your head, daughter, and wrap yourself well from the night-air.

HANNAH FERGUSON

Ay, da.
(*She goes upstairs to make herself ready to go out.* "CLUTIE" JOHN *makes a faint sound on his whistle.*)

JOHN FERGUSON

Ah, are you still there, "Clutie" John? I'd near forgot about you.

"CLUTIE" JOHN

Will I play "Willie Reilly and his Colleen Bawn" to you?

JOHN FERGUSON

No, boy, not the night. Just keep quiet there in the heat of the fire.

"CLUTIE" JOHN

It's a brave warm fire. It's well to be them that has a good fire whenever they want it.
(HANNAH, *wearing a shawl over her head, comes downstairs and goes across the kitchen to the door.*)

JOHN FERGUSON

You'll not be long, Hannah?

HANNAH FERGUSON

No, da.
(*She opens the door and goes out, closing it behind her.*)

JOHN FERGUSON

I wonder will Witherow let the farm to some one else or will he till it himself?

ANDREW FERGUSON

He'll mebbe till it himself.

SARAH FERGUSON

I'd better be laying the supper for you all. Is "Clutie" John to have his here?

JOHN FERGUSON

Ay, let him have a bite to eat. We'll mebbe not be able to . . . (*He breaks off suddenly and turns to his son.*) Light the lamp, Andrew, and draw the blinds. (*He seats himself again in his chair.*)

ANDREW FERGUSON

Draw the blinds, "Clutie."
(*He lights the lamp while* "CLUTIE" *draws the blinds and* MRS. FERGUSON *lays the table for supper.*)

ANDREW FERGUSON

I wonder what time Jimmy'll come.

JOHN FERGUSON

I hope he'll come soon so that he won't be here when Hannah comes back.

ANDREW FERGUSON

Ay. Will I set the lamp near your elbow, da?

JOHN FERGUSON

Ay, son, and reach the Bible to me, if you please. (ANDREW *hands the Bible to him.*) Thank you, son.

ACT TWO

IT *is more than an hour later, and it is quite dark outside.* JOHN FERGUSON *and his wife and son are sitting at the table, eating their supper.* "CLUTIE" JOHN MAGRATH *is still seated in the corner of the fireplace. He has laid his whistle aside and is engaged in eating the supper given to him by* MRS. FERGUSON.

SARAH FERGUSON

Hannah's gey and long in getting back from Witherow's.

JOHN FERGUSON

Ay.

SARAH FERGUSON

I wonder did she change her mind about Jimmy and go to the shop instead of going to Witherow's. It's quare him not coming before this!

ANDREW FERGUSON

Ah, I don't think she'd do that. Hannah's not the sort to change sudden.

SARAH FERGUSON

Well, she changed sudden enough the night!

ANDREW FERGUSON

Ah, that was because she was doing something she didn't want to do.

SARAH FERGUSON

Well, if she hasn't changed her mind, and Jimmy comes now, we'll have to give him his supper, and then Hannah'll mebbe be here before he goes away again. It'll be quare and awkward for us all.

ANDREW FERGUSON

Well, sure, you can tell him when he comes, and then he'll not be wanting to stop to his supper.

SARAH FERGUSON

Och, we'd have to offer the man something to eat anyway! It's only neighborly to do that much. (*She turns to* "CLUTIE" JOHN.) Will you have some more tea, "Clutie"?

"CLUTIE" JOHN

Ay, if you please, Mrs. Ferguson. It's quare nice tea. I don't often get the like of that any place I go.

ANDREW FERGUSON

It's a quare thing to me the way Jimmy runs after Hannah, and her showing him plain enough that she never had any regard for him.

"CLUTIE" JOHN

'Deed, Andrew, there's many a thing in the world is quarer nor that. It's a quare thing now for a man to be blowing wind into a bit of a pipe and it to be making up tunes for him. That's quare if you like!

SARAH FERGUSON

Ah, you're daft about that old whistle of yours! (*She hands a cup of tea to him.*) Here, drink up that, and don't talk so much! I suppose I'll have to let you sleep in the loft the night?

"CLUTIE" JOHN

Sure, that'll be a grand bed for me, lying on the hay.

SARAH FERGUSON

I do believe you're not such a fool as you make out, "Clutie"! You've the fine knack of getting into people's houses and making them give you your meals and a bed without them meaning to do it!

"CLUTIE" JOHN

I don't try to make them do it, Mrs. Ferguson. I just come in the house and sit down. That's all I do.

SARAH FERGUSON

Ay, that's all you do. If you did any more, they'd mebbe have to keep you for the rest of your life! Once you're settled down, it's hard to persuade you to get up again.

"CLUTIE" JOHN

You're letting on you're vexed with me, Mrs. Ferguson, but sure I know rightly you're not. A woman that has as kind a heart as you have . . .

SARAH FERGUSON

Ah, wheesht with your talk! Will I cut another piece for you?

"CLUTIE" JOHN

Ay, if you please!
(*She cuts a piece of bread and gives it to him.*)

ANDREW FERGUSON

I wonder, da, would you be willing to go up to Belfast to live? I think I could mebbe get a place in a linen office there, and I daresay Hannah might get work in a ware-room or a shop. Between the two of us, we could keep my ma and you rightly.

JOHN FERGUSON

I'd be as willing to go there as anywhere, son, if I have to quit out of this.

ANDREW FERGUSON

When I was thinking of going into the ministry, I got acquainted with a young fellow named M'Kinstry that was very well connected. His da kept a linen mill in Belfast, and I daresay he'd be willing to put a word in for me if I was to ask him.

JOHN FERGUSON

Ay.

ANDREW FERGUSON

I think I'll go up to Belfast on Saturday and see young M'Kinstry. I'll write a letter to him the night to tell him I'm coming, and I'll just let him know the position of things so that he can tell his da about me.

SARAH FERGUSON

(*To* ANDREW). Will I pour you out a wee drop more tea, son?

ANDREW FERGUSON

Thank you, ma!
(*She takes his cup and fills it, and then passes it back to him.*)

JOHN FERGUSON

Who knows but my health will be better in Belfast nor it has been here? I'm not sure, when I think of it, but the mists that lie on the hills at night are bad for me. They say there's a fine air in Belfast blowing up the Lough from the sea.
(*There is a knock at the door.*)

SARAH FERGUSON

There's someone at the door now. It'll either be Hannah or Jimmy. "Clutie" John, away and open it, will you?
("CLUTIE" JOHN *goes to the door and opens it.* JAMES CAESAR *steps in. The assured manner which he assumed when* HANNAH *accepted him has become more pronounced.*)

JAMES CAESAR

I'm later nor I expected to be. (*He turns to* "CLUTIE.") Here, "Clutie," help me off with my coat, will you? ("CLUTIE" JOHN *helps him to take off his overcoat.*) It's turned a bit cold the night! (*To* "CLUTIE.") Hang it up there on the rack, "Clutie." ("CLUTIE" *does as he is bid, and then goes to his seat by the fire.*) I thought it would be as well to wear my topcoat, for you get quare and damp coming up the loanie in the mist! (*He goes to the fire and rubs his hands in the warmth.*) Where's Hannah?

SARAH FERGUSON

She's out, Jimmy!

JAMES CAESAR

Out, is she? It's very late for her to be out! She'll have to keep better hours nor this when she's married, eh? (*His attempt to be jovial falls heavy.*) Has she not had her supper yet?

SARAH FERGUSON

No, not yet. We're expecting her in every while.

JAMES CAESAR

I hope she'll not be long. I want to discuss the wedding with her . . .

SARAH FERGUSON

The wedding!

JAMES CAESAR

Ay. Sure, there's no sense in our waiting long, is there? If people's able to get married, they ought to get the ceremony over quick. That's what I think, Mrs. Ferguson. Och, listen to me calling you Mrs. Ferguson, just like a stranger! I ought to start calling you "Ma" to get into the way of it, or would you rather I called you "Mother"?

SARAH FERGUSON

(*Nervously*). I'm not particular, Jimmy.

JAMES CAESAR

Some people's quare and particular about a thing like that. They think it's common to say "ma" and "da," and they never let their children call them anything but "father" and "mother." I knew a family once up in Belfast that always called their parents "papa" and "mamma." It was quare and conceited of them—just as if they were English or anything like that.

JOHN FERGUSON

Jimmy, I want to say something to you!

JAMES CAESAR

Ay, John! (*Jovially.*) I can't start calling you "da" or "papa" or anything else but John, can I? (*To* MRS. FERGUSON.) Do you know, I'm near dead of the drouth! If you could spare me a wee drop of tea! . . .

SARAH FERGUSON

(*Rising and speaking hurriedly*). Of course, Jimmy, I will. I don't know what I'm thinking about not to ask you to sit down to your supper. (*She goes to the dresser for a cup and saucer.*) Draw a chair up to the table, will you, and sit down!

JAMES CAESAR

Ah, now, I don't want to be putting you to any inconvenience.

SARAH FERGUSON

Sure, it's no bother at all. Just come and content yourself. I'm all throughother with the ups and downs we've had this day, and my manners is all shattered over the head of it. Sit down here.

JAMES CAESAR

(*Taking his place at the table.*) Thank you, ma.

SARAH FERGUSON

Will you have soda-bread or wheaten?

JAMES CAESAR

Wheaten, if you please!

(ANDREW FERGUSON *rises from the table and goes to the side of the fire opposite to that on which* "CLUTIE" JOHN *is seated.*)

SARAH FERGUSON

Help yourself to anything you want.

JAMES CAESAR

Thank you! (*He bows his head.*) Thank God for this meal, Amen! (*To* JOHN FERGUSON.) I've been making plans in my head, John, about the future of the farm.

JOHN FERGUSON

Jimmy, I want to say something to you! . . .

JAMES CAESAR

(*Slightly impatient.*) Ay, but wait till I tell you about my plans! Now, how would it be if you were to let the land by itself, and you and the rest of you stay on in the house? Me and Hannah'll be getting married in a wee while, and there'll only be the three of you left . . .

JOHN FERGUSON

Jimmy! . . .

JAMES CAESAR

Now, let me get it all out before I forget any of it. Andrew could mebbe resume his studies for the ministry. I might be able to advance him the money for it.

ANDREW FERGUSON

That's a kindly thought, Jimmy!

JAMES CAESAR

Ah, I've often thought I would like to be related to a minister. It looks well to be able to say the Reverend Mr. So-and-So is your brother-in-law, particular if he's a well-known man such as you might be yourself, Andrew. Or I was thinking if you didn't fancy the ministry any more, mebbe you'd come into the shop and learn the grocery! The fact is, betwixt ourselves, I'm thinking seriously of opening a branch establishment over at Ballymaclurg, and if I had you trained under me, Andrew, you'd do rightly as the manager of it.

JOHN FERGUSON

Jimmy, I'll never be able to thank you sufficient for your kindness . . .

JAMES CAESAR

Ah, don't mention it! Sure, it's a pleasure, and anyway it's in the family, you might say! I wonder what's keeping Hannah! Where is she at all?

JOHN FERGUSON

Jimmy . . . Hannah's changed her mind!

JAMES CAESAR

Changed her mind! What do you mean?

JOHN FERGUSON

She's changed her mind, Jimmy!

JAMES CAESAR

(*Getting up and going to him: the assured manner has dropped from him*). Do you mean she doesn't want to marry me no more?

JOHN FERGUSON

Ay, that's what I mean.

JAMES CAESAR

But! . . . Ah, quit your codding, for dear sake! (*He goes back to his seat and begins to eat again.*) You've been letting "Clutie" John put you up to this—trying to scare me. I wouldn't wonder but Hannah's upstairs all the while, splitting her sides . . . (*He gets up and goes to the foot of the staircase and calls up it.*) Hi, Hannah, are you there?

"CLUTIE" JOHN

I never put them up to anything, Mr. Caesar. It's not my nature to do a thing like that.

JAMES CAESAR

(*Calling up the stairs*). Come on down out of that, Hannah, and not be tormenting me!

JOHN FERGUSON

She's not there, Jimmy.

JAMES CAESAR

(*Coming back to the table*). Are you in earnest, John?

JOHN FERGUSON

I am, Jimmy. I'm quare and sorry for you . . .

JAMES CAESAR

But she gave her promise to me an hour ago! You heard her yourself!

JOHN FERGUSON

I know, but she's changed her mind since.

JAMES CAESAR

What's come over her?

JOHN FERGUSON

I can't tell you, Jimmy. She just didn't feel that she could go on with the match. It's a thing that you can't explain, Jimmy.

JAMES CAESAR

But . . . the farm . . . and the mortgage!

JOHN FERGUSON

When I saw the way her mind was set, I told her to go up to Witherow's and tell him to foreclose!

JAMES CAESAR

But, man alive! . . .

JOHN FERGUSON

That's the way of it, Jimmy. I'm heartsore about it, but it can't be helped, can it?

JAMES CAESAR

(*Angrily*). Do you mean to sit there and tell me you're going to let her treat me like dirt beneath her feet after the way I've offered to help you?

JOHN FERGUSON

I can't force her to do things against her will, Jimmy. No good would come of the like of that either to her or to you.

JAMES CAESAR

I suppose you never thought of my position, John Ferguson? I've told all my neighbors already that Hannah and me are to be married, and now I'll have to tell them that she won't have me!

ANDREW FERGUSON

My da can't help it, can he, if Hannah doesn't want to marry you?

JAMES CAESAR

What'll Witherow say when he hears about it? My God, he'll be the first to know! (*He becomes wild with rage as this idea expands in his mind.*) Had you no consideration at all, the whole pack of you? I was willing to cripple myself to get you out of your difficulty, and then you turn on me and affront me before the man I hate most in the world! That's kindness for you! That's the reward a man gets for being neighborly!

JOHN FERGUSON

Ay, you may well complain, Jimmy! I'm not denying your right to do so. I'd have spared you from this if I could.

JAMES CAESAR

Can't you make her keep her promise to me? A man has the right to be respected by his own child, and if she doesn't obey you and do what you tell her, you should make her.

ANDREW FERGUSON

Would you marry a woman that doesn't want you?

JAMES CAESAR

(*Fiercely*). I want her, don't I? What does it matter to me whether she wants me or not so long as I'm married to her? My heart's hungry for her! (*His ferocity passes into complaint.*) Don't I know rightly she doesn't want me? But what does that matter to me? I've loved her since she was a wee child, and I'd be happy with her if she was never to give me a kind look. Many and many a time, when the shop was closed, I went and sat out there in the fields and imagined her and me married together and living happy, us with two or three wee children, and them growing up fine and strong. I could see her them times walking about in a fine silk dress, and looking grand on it, and all the neighbors nudging each other and saying the fine woman she was and how well we must be getting on in the world for her to be able to dress herself that nice! I could hardly bear it when I used to meet her afterwards, and her hadn't hardly a civil word for me; but I couldn't keep out of her way for all that; and many's a time I run quick and dodged round corners so's I should meet her again and have the pleasure of looking at her. When she said she'd have me, I could feel big lumps rolling off me, and I was light-hearted and happy for all I knew she was only consenting to have me to save your farm, John. I had my heart's desire, and I never felt so like a man before! . . . And now! . . .

(*He rests his head on the table and begins to sob.*)

SARAH FERGUSON

(*In anguish*). I can't bear to see a man crying! (*She goes to* JIMMY.) Quit, Jimmy, son! It'll mebbe be all right in the end. Don't disturb yourself so much, man!

ANDREW FERGUSON

(*Contemptuously*). There's no sense in going on that way!

JOHN FERGUSON

Don't speak to him, Andrew! Leave the man to his grief!

JAMES CAESAR

(*Looking up, and addressing* ANDREW). I know rightly I'm making a poor show of myself, but I can't help it. Wouldn't anybody that's had the life that I've had do the same as me? You're right and fine, Andrew, and full of your talk, but wait till you've had to bear what I have, and you'll see then what you'll do when something good that you've longed for all your life comes to you and then is taken from you. (*He rises from the table, trying to recover himself and speak in an ordinary voice.*) I'm sorry I bothered you all! I'll not trouble you with my company any longer. It'll be better for me to be going nor to be here when she comes back. (*He moves towards the door.*) I said some harsh words to you, John! . . .

JOHN FERGUSON

I'm not minding them, Jimmy. I know well the state you're in.

JAMES CAESAR

I'm sorry I said them to you, all the same. It was in anger I said them . . .
("CLUTIE" JOHN *starts up from his seat in the corner, and holds up his hand for silence.*)

"CLUTIE" JOHN

Wheesht!

SARAH FERGUSON

What is it, "Clutie"?

"CLUTIE" JOHN

Wheesht, wheesht!
(*He goes to the door and opens, while the others stand staring at him. He listens for a moment or two, and then he darts swiftly into the darkness.*)

SARAH FERGUSON

In the name of God, what ails the fellow?

ANDREW FERGUSON

(*Going to the door*). He's heard something.

SARAH FERGUSON

(*Drawing a blind and peering out*). Oh, what is it?

ANDREW FERGUSON

(*Looking out*). I can't see anything . . . Wait! (*He pauses a moment.*) There's someone coming up the "loanie." I hear steps . . .

JAMES CAESAR

(*Coming to his side and listening*). It's someone running!

ANDREW FERGUSON

Ay! . . . It's Hannah! (*He shouts to his sister.*) What ails you, Hannah?

JAMES CAESAR

I hope nothing's happened to her.

SARAH FERGUSON

She must have been scared or something. (*She goes to the door and stands beside* CAESAR. ANDREW FERGUSON *is heard outside speaking inquiries to his sister. Then* CAESAR *and* MRS. FERGUSON *come away from the door into the kitchen, and* HANNAH, *in a state of terrible agitation, appears in the doorway. She pauses wildly for a moment, glancing round the room without seeing anything because of the sudden change from darkness to light.*)

SARAH FERGUSON

Hannah, what ails you, dear?
(HANNAH *goes quickly to her father and throws herself against his knees.*)

HANNAH FERGUSON

Da, da!

JOHN FERGUSON

What is it, daughter? What is it?
(ANDREW FERGUSON, *followed by* "CLUTIE" JOHN, *returns to the kitchen. He closes the door.*)

ANDREW FERGUSON

What ails her? Has she hurt herself?

JOHN FERGUSON

Hannah! (*He tries to lift her face to his, but she resists him.*) Hannah, what is it? Tell me, daughter!

HANNAH FERGUSON

(*Brokenly*). Da, da, I can't! . . .

JOHN FERGUSON

You can't what, Hannah?

HANNAH FERGUSON

It's . . . it's fearful, da!

JAMES CAESAR

Has anyone harmed her? Hannah, has anyone harmed you? (*To* JOHN FERGUSON.)

She was at Witherow's, wasn't she? (*Turning to the others.*) That's where she was—at Witherow's! (*To* HANNAH.) Hannah, do you hear me, girl? Has anyone harmed you? Was it Witherow?

HANNAH FERGUSON

I can't . . . can't . . .

JAMES CAESAR

You must tell us. (*Looking wildly about him.*) My God, I'll go mad if any harm's happened to her!

ANDREW FERGUSON

(*Taking hold of his arm and leading him away from* HANNAH). Quieten yourself, Jimmy. She'll tell us in a minute when she's herself again.

JOHN FERGUSON

Hannah, dear! Come closer to me, daughter! (*He lifts her head from his knees and draws her up so that her face rests against his.*) Just keep quiet, daughter! No one'll harm you here. Keep quite quiet! (*To* JAMES CAESAR.) She was always a wee bit afeard of the dark, for she has a great imagination, and she mebbe thought she saw something fearful in the night. Get her a wee sup of sweet milk, one of you! (MRS. FERGUSON *goes to get the milk for her.*) It's mebbe nothing but fright. I've seen her as startled as this once before when she was a child. (HANNAH *gives a great sob, and starts a little.*) There, daughter, you needn't be scared! You're safe here from any harm. (MRS. FERGUSON *brings a cup of milk to him.*) Thank you, Sarah! Here, Hannah, drink a wee sup of this! It'll do you good!

HANNAH FERGUSON

(*Clinging closer to him*). No, da, no!

JOHN FERGUSON

Ay, daughter, it'll help to steady you! (*He puts the cup to her lips, and she drinks some of the milk.*) That's right! That's right! You'll have a wee drop more, now! (*She averts her head.*) Ay, daughter, just have some more, and then you'll mebbe be quieter in yourself. (*He compels her to drink some more of the milk, and then he puts the cup away.*) That'll do you a power of good! (*He draws her head down to his breast.*) Just rest your head on me, daughter, and keep still!

"CLUTIE" JOHN

She was crying bitter out there. She was running up the "loanie" when I found her, and she let a screech out of her when I touched her arm, and then she run that hard I couldn't keep pace with her. It must have been a fearful thing that scared her that way!

SARAH FERGUSON

I hope to my goodness it's no more sorrow for us. We've had more nor our share already.

JOHN FERGUSON

Wheesht, wheesht, woman. Wheesht!

JAMES CAESAR

If Witherow's harmed her, I'll kill him. I will, so help me, God!

JOHN FERGUSON

Quit, quit! (*To* HANNAH.) Are you better now, Hannah? (*She still sobs a little, but her agitation has subsided, and she is now able to speak more or less coherently.*) Just tell me, daughter. What happened you?

HANNAH FERGUSON

Da, I'm ashamed! . . .

JOHN FERGUSON

Ashamed, daughter!

SARAH FERGUSON

She said she was ashamed! Oh, my God!

JOHN FERGUSON

What are you ashamed of, daughter?

HANNAH FERGUSON

I . . . (*She relapses.*) I can't tell you, da, I can't tell you!

JAMES CAESAR

Was it Witherow, Hannah?

JOHN FERGUSON

Don't bother her, Jimmy?

JAMES CAESAR

I know it was Witherow. I know it was him!

JOHN FERGUSON

Hannah! Look up, daughter!

HANNAH FERGUSON

Yes, da!

JOHN FERGUSON

Tell me about it!

HANNAH FERGUSON

(*Making an effort to control herself, now and then she speaks brokenly*). I went up to Witherow's farm, the way you told me, and there were two people waiting to talk to him.

JOHN FERGUSON

Ay.

HANNAH FERGUSON

He kept me waiting till after he had done with them. I told him we couldn't pay the money and he was to foreclose, and then he begun laughing at me and making a mock of . . . of Jimmy . . .
(*She looks up and sees* CAESAR *and hesitates to finish her sentence.*)

JAMES CAESAR

Was it me he made a mock of? (*To* JOHN FERGUSON.) Ah, didn't I tell you what he would do? Didn't I, now? (*He turns to the others.*) Didn't I, Mrs. Ferguson? . . .

JOHN FERGUSON

Go on, daughter!

HANNAH FERGUSON

He said he supposed it couldn't be helped, and I was just coming away when he said he would walk the length of the "loanie" with me, and I waited for him. (*Her voice grows feeble.*) We were walking along, talking about one thing and another . . .

JOHN FERGUSON

(*Nervously*). Ay, ay!

HANNAH FERGUSON

And he begun telling me what a fine girl I am, and wishing he could kiss me! . . .

JAMES CAESAR

God starve him!

HANNAH FERGUSON

And then he tried to kiss me, but I wouldn't let him. We were going over Musgrave's meadow together, and all of a sudden he put his arms round me and threw me down! . . . Oh, da, da!
(*Her grief overcomes her again, and she buries her head against his breast and is unable to speak further.*)

JAMES CAESAR

What did she say, John? What was it she said?

JOHN FERGUSON

(*Brokenly*). I can't speak, Jimmy—I can't speak. Hannah, dear! (*He tries to comfort her.*)

JAMES CAESAR

Did he wrong her? That's what I want to know!

SARAH FERGUSON

Oh, will we never have comfort in the world! John, does she mean that he harmed her . . . *harmed* her? (*Wildly to the others.*) One of you do something! Andrew! Jimmy!!

JAMES CAESAR

I've swore many's a time to have his life and never done it. I was a poor, trembling creature, but I'll tremble no more! (*He goes to the door.*) Good-night to you all!

JOHN FERGUSON

Where are you going, Jimmy?

JAMES CAESAR

I'm going—somewhere!

JOHN FERGUSON

Sit down, Jimmy . . .

JAMES CAESAR

It's no good you talking to me, John! (*He opens the door violently and goes out.*)

JOHN FERGUSON

Andrew, go after him and bring him back. There's enough harm done already. Go and stop him, son!
(ANDREW *goes unwillingly to the door. He stands there looking up the dark "loanie."*)

ANDREW FERGUSON

I can't see him!

JOHN FERGUSON

You must be able to see him. He can't be that far! Go after him, man, and bring him back here.

ANDREW FERGUSON

No, da, I won't! (*He shuts the door and returns to his seat.*) The man has a right to be left to himself.

JOHN FERGUSON

Andrew! (*He tries to get up from his chair, but* HANNAH'S *weight prevents him.*) Here, Sarah, take Hannah and put her to her bed. Get up, daughter!

HANNAH FERGUSON

(*Clinging to him*). Da, da!

JOHN FERGUSON

Ay, daughter, ay! God's scourged us hard, and it isn't easy to bear. We must just . . . just try and be patient. (*Kissing her.*) Go to your ma, dear, and let her take care of you!

SARAH FERGUSON

Come to your bed, Hannah!
(HANNAH'S *anguish unbalances her, and she becomes hysterical, and stands clinging to her father and weeping bitterly.*)

JOHN FERGUSON

(*Comforting her*). You must control yourself, daughter. Go with your ma, now, like a good girl. Take her, Sarah!
(MRS. FERGUSON *leads her daughter towards the stairs. They go out.*)

ANDREW FERGUSON

I hope Jimmy'll kill him.

JOHN FERGUSON

(*Weakly*). Son, son, don't talk that way!

ANDREW FERGUSON

I can't help it, da. He ought to be killed. He's not fit to live.

JOHN FERGUSON

Are you setting yourself up to judge God's work?

ANDREW FERGUSON

An eye for an eye, da, and a tooth for a tooth!

JOHN FERGUSON

That's not the spirit that lives now, son! That's the spirit that was destroyed on the Cross. If a man does an injury to you, and you injure him back, you're as bad as he is. You have your own work to do in the world, and you must leave God to do His; it's His work to judge, not ours! (*His utterance exhausts him a little, and he staggers back into his chair. His voice changes to a pleading note.*) Ah, Andrew, son, don't never talk that way again! I meant you for the ministry, to teach people how to live for God! You can't go into the ministry now, son, but you can teach people just the same. Just the same! I would rather you were dead nor hear you speak about Jimmy Caesar the way you're doing . . . (*He gets up from his chair and goes to his son, taking him by the shoulder.*) Will you not go out and look for him, son? He has suffered enough, poor man, without him damning his soul!

ANDREW FERGUSON

He can bear God's strokes as well as we can!

JOHN FERGUSON

Your heart's bitter, son! I wish I could go! (*He staggers towards the door.*) I haven't the strength I used to have . . . Andrew, will you not do as I bid you?

ANDREW FERGUSON

No, da, I won't interfere between them.

JOHN FERGUSON

I must go myself, then. I must try and find him . . .
(MRS. FERGUSON *comes down the stairs into the kitchen.*)

SARAH FERGUSON

John!

JOHN FERGUSON

Ay, woman!

SARAH FERGUSON

Hannah wants you. She'll not be quiet without you near her.

JOHN FERGUSON

I can't go up to her yet, Sarah. I'm going to look for Jimmy Caesar. I can't let him be wandering about wild in the night. If he finds Witherow he'll mebbe do him an injury. (*He turns towards the door again.*) Andrew won't go, so I must. I can't let the man destroy himself.

SARAH FERGUSON

What way's that to be talking and you the sick you are? Is it your death you're wanting? And no coat on or nothing. (*To her son.*) Andrew, think shame of yourself to be letting your da go out in the dark and damp! (*To her husband.*) You must come to Hannah. She won't keep still without you! (*To* ANDREW.) You go and look for Jimmy, Andrew. The poor creature's near distracted mad, and dear knows in that state he might do something fearful.

ANDREW FERGUSON

I'm not going, ma. I've told my da that already.

SARAH FERGUSON

Ah, aren't you headstrong? (*To her husband.*) Come up to Hannah first, John!

JOHN FERGUSON

She must wait till I come back. It's Jimmy Caesar that's in the greatest danger now. I'll come to her when I get back, tell her!

SARAH FERGUSON

You'll rue this night, the pair of you, but you must have your own way, I suppose!

JOHN FERGUSON

Give me my coat, woman! (MRS. FERGUSON *goes to get his coat for him.*) Andrew, will you not come with me and help me to find him?

ANDREW FERGUSON

I'll not budge out of the door, da. I wouldn't lift a finger to stop him from doing anything he wants to do. (MRS. FERGUSON *returns to the kitchen carrying a jacket, a topcoat, and a muffler.*) It's no business of mine to interfere between them.

SARAH FERGUSON

(*Helping her husband into his coat*). Muffle yourself up well, John. It's cold the night.

JOHN FERGUSON

Ay, Sarah, thank you.
(*He puts the muffler round his throat.*)

ANDREW FERGUSON

I only hope Jimmy'll have the manhood to kill Witherow!

JOHN FERGUSON

(*In pain*). Wheesht, wheesht, son! Wheesht, adear! (*He recovers himself, and turns to his wife.*) Tell Hannah where I'm gone, Sarah! That'll mebbe keep her quiet till I get back! (*He opens the door.*) I'll come as soon as I can!
(*He goes out, closing the door behind him.*)

SARAH FERGUSON

It'll kill him, this night's work! Andrew, how can you stand there and see your da going out in the wet and dark, and you knowing well the sick and feeble he is!

ANDREW FERGUSON

I can't stop him from going, can I?

SARAH FERGUSON

You could have gone yourself.

ANDREW FERGUSON

(*Turning to her and speaking fiercely*). I tell you I don't want to stop Jimmy from killing Witherow if he's going to do it. It's right that he should kill him. The man's bad from head to foot. Everything about him shows that! It isn't only the way he's treated us, but others too. You've told me yourself many's a time, and my da's told me too, of the cuts and insults Jimmy's had to bear from him! Isn't this greater nor the lot of them put together? Hasn't Jimmy a right to turn on him now if he never had the right before? I don't care what my da says! Jimmy has the right to turn on him and kill him if he can.

SARAH FERGUSON

(*Bewildered by the catastrophe in which she is involved*). I'm all moidhered by it. I don't understand what's happening. Your da says it's the will of God, but I . . . I can't make it out . . . (*She goes towards the stairs.*) I'll mebbe not come down again, Andrew. Good-night, son!

ANDREW FERGUSON

Good-night, ma!
(MRS. FERGUSON *goes upstairs.* ANDREW *walks across the room and opens the door. He looks out for a moment or two. Then he shuts the door and walks back to the fireplace.*)

"CLUTIE" JOHN

Your da's a forgiving man, Andrew!

ANDREW FERGUSON

(*Absently*). Eh?

"CLUTIE" JOHN

I say, your da's a forgiving man!

ANDREW FERGUSON

(*Carelessly*). Oh, ay. Ay!
(*He walks across the room and back again.*)

"CLUTIE" JOHN

You're not a forgiving man, are you, Andrew?
(ANDREW *sits down at the table, with his face to the audience. He does not reply to* "CLUTIE" JOHN.)

"CLUTIE" JOHN

You're not a forgiving man, are you, Andrew? (*He gets up and comes to the table.*) You wouldn't forgive till seventy times seven, would you?

ANDREW FERGUSON

(*Impatiently*). Ah, quit!

"CLUTIE" JOHN

Your da has a quare good nature. He always says you should turn the other cheek to the man that harms you. That's a great spirit to have, that, isn't it?

ANDREW FERGUSON

(*Who has not been listening*). Eh? What's that you say?

"CLUTIE" JOHN

I was talking about your da, Andrew, and him having the great fine spirit of forgiveness in him.

ANDREW FERGUSON

(*Indifferently*). Oh, ay! Ay!

"CLUTIE" JOHN

I could never be as forgiving as your da if I lived to be a thousand years old. (*He pauses for a moment, and then says eagerly.*) Will I play something to you? (ANDREW *does not make any movement.*) Are you not listening to me?

ANDREW FERGUSON

(*Crossly*). Ah, what is it? What's the matter with you?

"CLUTIE" JOHN

Will I not play something to you? It's a great comfort when you're in trouble to hear a man playing a tune . . .

ANDREW FERGUSON

(*Sharply*). Quit blethering!

"CLUTIE" JOHN

(*Going back to his seat at the fire*). I was only wondering could I do anything to please you, Andrew? But I'll keep still and quiet. I'll not disturb you at all.
(*They sit in silence for a few moments.*)

"CLUTIE" JOHN

He's a bad man, that man Witherow! That's what he is! He has a sour nature in him. Whenever he meets me he makes a mock of me and says, "When are they going to put you in the asylum, 'Clutie'?" Sometimes he hits me with his stick or a whip mebbe. He done that the day there fornent your own door, Andrew! He couped me into the hedge and near broke my whistle on me. That shows the bad-natured man he is to be hurting a poor fellow like myself that has to beg his bread from door to door!

ANDREW FERGUSON

Hold your tongue, will you?

"CLUTIE" JOHN

(*Meekly*). All right, Andrew! I was only saying what he done to me, but, sure, it doesn't matter what he does to the like of me, a poor senseless fellow that wanders the world with a whistle! It's quare and different, Andrew, when he does harm to a girl like Hannah . . .

ANDREW FERGUSON

(*Turning to him and speaking quickly*). Ay, it is different, "Clutie"! You're right there. My sister is the finest girl in the County Down . . .

"CLUTIE" JOHN

(*Eagerly*). Ay, she is, Andrew. She is in sang. There isn't her equal in the province of Ulster. There is not. I've oftentimes heard people talking about her, and saying what a fine match she'll make for some man, and one time I tried to make up a song about her to be singing on the roads, but I couldn't do it with any satisfaction to myself. I'm no hand at making up poetry. She's a fine young girl and a great companion she'll be to anyone.

ANDREW FERGUSON

It's only a fine man that's fit for her.

"CLUTIE" JOHN

That's true! (*He gets up and comes to the table and leans across* it.) It would never have done if she'd married Jimmy Caesar. The mountains can never consort with the hills.

ANDREW FERGUSON

No! No!! I wasn't best pleased about the match when I heard of it.

"CLUTIE" JOHN

He's not much of a man, Jimmy Caesar!

ANDREW FERGUSON

No, he isn't, indeed!

"CLUTIE" JOHN

He's a poor-natured man, that's what he is. He'd be worse nor Witherow if he had the pluck. Mebbe he is worse nor him, for he has no pluck at all. He's a mean man.

ANDREW FERGUSON

I daresay you're right.
(*He goes to the fire and stands with his back to it.*)

"CLUTIE" JOHN

Ay, I am. He'd beat you on the ground, that lad would, but he would run away from you if you were to stand up to him. That's the kind he is.

ANDREW FERGUSON

Ah, well, he's had a poor life of it.

"CLUTIE" JOHN

He'd have been mean-natured whatever kind of a life he had, Andrew! I've seen men like him before in my time. They think I'm a fool and see nothing, but when I'm playing my whistle, Andrew, I see them when they're not thinking I'm looking at them—and there's plenty of them, high up and low down, that are crawling when they're at your feet and are ready to crawl when they're standing up. That's the way of them. A man like Jimmy Caesar would be a poor defender for Hannah!

ANDREW FERGUSON

Mebbe he would!

"CLUTIE" JOHN

I'd be afeard to trust myself to him if I was in need of a person to take care of me. I would so.

ANDREW FERGUSON

Ah, you can take care of yourself! Quit talking now, or if you can't keep quiet, go out to the hayloft and talk to yourself.
(*He goes half-way across the room and then returns to the fire. He stands with his face to it.*)

"CLUTIE" JOHN

(*After a pause*). I wonder will Jimmy Caesar kill Witherow!

ANDREW FERGUSON

What makes you wonder that?

"CLUTIE" JOHN

I was just wondering! (*He turns towards the door.*) I'd better be going to my bed. It was kind of your ma to give me leave to sleep in the loft. It'll be nice and comfortable to stretch myself out on the hay.

ANDREW FERGUSON

Ay. Good-night.

"CLUTIE" JOHN

Good-night to you, Andrew. (*He looks back to his seat.*) Ah, dear bless us, I was near forgetting my whistle! (*He goes to his seat and picks up the whistle.*) It's not a great deal to look at, but it can play a grand tune! (*He puts it in his pocket.*) I wouldn't be surprised but Caesar doesn't do it!

ANDREW FERGUSON

(*Abstractedly*). Doesn't do what?

"CLUTIE" JOHN

Kill Witherow.

ANDREW FERGUSON

What makes you think that?

"CLUTIE" JOHN

It's the way of him to be talking and not doing.

ANDREW FERGUSON

Ah, man, but this is different.

"CLUTIE" JOHN

You can't help your nature, Andrew. No one can. Jimmy Caesar's always been afeard of Henry Witherow and it's likely he always will be. He can't help it, God be good to him!

ANDREW FERGUSON

(*Thinking this over for a second, and then turning away contemptuously*). Ah, you don't know what you're talking about!

"CLUTIE" JOHN

No. No, Andrew, that's true! I have no sense in my head at all. I've oftentimes been told that. Good-night again to you, Andrew!

ANDREW FERGUSON

Good-night!

"CLUTIE" JOHN

(*Before he reaches the door*). Mind you, Jimmy Caesar'll mean to kill him! I daresay he will. And mebbe he would have killed him if he had been standing fornent him that minute, with his back turned, but . . . he had to go out and find him, Andrew! It's a good step from here to Witherow's farm, and he had to get a gun . . . or something. You have time to think when you're going that length.

ANDREW FERGUSON

Ay.

"CLUTIE" JOHN

I wouldn't doubt but he went home. I daresay he's lying huddled up in his bed this minute, Andrew, and your poor old da hunting for him in the dark, and your sister up there weeping her eyes out . . .

ANDREW FERGUSON

Ah, quit, man, quit! You're tormenting me with your talk.

"CLUTIE" JOHN

A fine girl like Hannah to be depending on Jimmy Caesar for a man . . .

ANDREW FERGUSON

Go on with you, go on!

"CLUTIE" JOHN

And him mebbe at home all the time, snuggled up in his bed!

ANDREW FERGUSON

What do you mean, "Clutie"? What are you trying to prove?

"CLUTIE" JOHN

Prove! Me? Sure, I couldn't prove anything if I was paid to do it. I'm no hand at proving things. That's why I haven't got any sense.

ANDREW FERGUSON

(*Going to him and taking hold of his shoulder*). What's all this talk about Jimmy Caesar mean? You have some meaning in your mind?

"CLUTIE" JOHN

I wish I had, but sure I'll never be right, never. I'll always be quare.

ANDREW FERGUSON

(*Turning away from him in disgust*). Och, away with you! (*He goes back to the fire, standing with his face to it.*) You have as much talk as Jimmy Caesar himself! ("CLUTIE" JOHN *stands still for a few moments. Then he steps lightly across the floor to where* ANDREW *is standing and taps him on the shoulder.*)

"CLUTIE" JOHN

Andrew!

ANDREW FERGUSON

What ails you now?

"CLUTIE" JOHN

Supposing Jimmy Caesar doesn't kill Witherow?

ANDREW FERGUSON

Well? Well, well?

"CLUTIE" JOHN

That 'ud be fearful, wouldn't it? Can't you picture Witherow sitting up there in his hungry house laughing to himself . . .

ANDREW FERGUSON

My God, "Clutie"!

"CLUTIE" JOHN

And mebbe saying he'll look out for Hannah again!

ANDREW FERGUSON

Aw, my God, my God!

"CLUTIE" JOHN

And making a mock of Jimmy Caesar, the way he always does, and calling him an old Jenny-Jo that'll stand by and let another man do harm to his girl . . .

ANDREW FERGUSON

Ah, wheesht with you, wheesht!

"CLUTIE" JOHN

And telling people about it! Ay, telling people about it! You can see him with his great jaw hanging down and him roaring with laughter and telling them all in Jefferson's public-house on the fair-day!

ANDREW FERGUSON

Ay, indeed, that's what he'd do!

"CLUTIE" JOHN

That's what he done over the head of Martha Foley that had the child to him. Didn't I hear him myself, telling them all about it, and them splitting their sides and calling him the great lad and the gallous boy and the terrible man for women? . . . And then mebbe him to be telling them how your da, that's near his death, went out to try and stop Jimmy from killing him, and all the while your da was tumbling over the dark fields Jimmy was lying trembling with fright in his bed, afeard to move . . .

ANDREW FERGUSON

He'd never be such a collie as that, "Clutie." He couldn't for shame.

"CLUTIE" JOHN

(*Coming nearer to him*). If I was Hannah's brother I'd make sure!

ANDREW FERGUSON

Make sure! What do you mean?

"CLUTIE" JOHN

Ah, what do I mean? Sure, I don't know what I'm saying half my time! I'm all throughother. I don't know what I mean, Andrew; I don't know. God reward you, and I'll bid you good-night. I'll go up to the loft and play a while to myself. Sure, I'll disturb no one there but the cows mebbe in the byre, and God knows the poor beasts'll not complain if a poor fellow like myself has a small diversion. And when I lie down and stretch myself in the hay, I can be thinking, mebbe Jimmy Caesar is lying in a fine warm bed, and be pitying your da that's out looking for him, and be cursing Henry Witherow that's mebbe laughing now and making up great stories to be telling on the fair-day . . .

ANDREW FERGUSON

Are you trying to drive me demented?

"CLUTIE" JOHN

Wheesht, wheesht!

(MRS. FERGUSON *comes down the stairs.*)

SARAH FERGUSON

Will you not keep quiet, the pair of you? I'm trying hard to get Hannah asleep, but the clatter you're making would wake the dead! Is your da not back yet, Andrew?

ANDREW FERGUSON

No, ma, not yet!

SARAH FERGUSON

(*Picking up* JIMMY CAESAR'S *coat*). Dear bless us, Jimmy left his coat behind him. He'll be sure to get his death of cold, for he always had a delicate chest. (*She puts the coat aside.*) I wish you'd go and find your da, Andrew, and bring him home. It's no time of the night for him to be wandering about in the cold air. Hannah'll never rest without him near her. Will you not go now and find him, son?

ANDREW FERGUSON

All right, ma!

SARAH FERGUSON

That's a good son. Tell him to come home as quick as he can. "Clutie" John'll stay here while you look for him. (*She listens for a moment.*) That's Hannah crying again! I can't leave her for a minute but she begins lamenting . . .

(*She goes hurriedly upstairs again.* ANDREW *goes to the door and looks out. He is followed by* "CLUTIE" JOHN.)

"CLUTIE" JOHN

Look, Andrew, there's a light in Witherow's window. Do you see it over there on the side of the hill? It shines down the valley a long way. Do you see it, Andrew?

ANDREW FERGUSON

Ay.

"CLUTIE" JOHN

It doesn't look as if Jimmy'd got there, does it? The light's still shining.

ANDREW FERGUSON

He might be there for all that.

"CLUTIE" JOHN

Mebbe! Ay, mebbe! Well, I'll away on now to my bed. The night's turned sharp, and I feel tired and sleepy. (*He stands in the doorway, gazing up at the sky.*) There's a lot of wee stars out the night, Andrew, but no moon.

ANDREW FERGUSON

Ay.

"CLUTIE" JOHN

I oftentimes think it must be quare and lonely up in the sky. Good-night to you, Andrew!

ANDREW FERGUSON

Good-night, "Clutie."

("CLUTIE" JOHN *goes out.* ANDREW FERGUSON *stands still, watching the light in* WITHEROW'S *window. Then a great anger goes over him. He mutters something to himself, and turns suddenly into the kitchen. He takes down the gun and, after examining it to see if it is loaded, he goes out. In a few moments* SARAH FERGUSON *is heard calling to him from the top of the stairs.*)

SARAH FERGUSON

Andrew! Andrew!! Are you there? (*She comes down part of the staircase and looks over the banister.*) Are you there, Andrew? "Clutie"! (*She comes into the kitchen and looks about her.*) "Clutie"! (*She goes to the foot of the stairs and calls up to* HANNAH.) It's all right, Hannah, dear! Andrew's away to fetch your da!

(*She goes to the door and looks out for a few moments. Then she closes the door and goes up the stairs again.*)

ACT THREE

IT *is early morning of the following day. The room is bright and cheery because a fine sunshine pours in at the window and open door. There is nothing in the appearance of the kitchen to indicate that any unusual thing has happened; the gun is again suspended over the fire-place.* MRS. FERGUSON *is bending over the fire, settling a kettle on the coals and turf, when her husband comes into the kitchen from the staircase.*

SARAH FERGUSON

Is that you, John?

JOHN FERGUSON

Ay. (*He seats himself by the fire.*) Where's Andrew?

SARAH FERGUSON

He's away out to the byre. Will I call him?

JOHN FERGUSON

Ay, do!

(MRS. FERGUSON *goes to the door and calls out "Andrew! Andrew!!"* ANDREW *is heard to shout, "What do you want, ma?" and* MRS. FERGUSON *replies, "Your da wants you a minute!"* ANDREW *shouts back, "I'll be in in a wee while."* MRS. FERGUSON *returns to the fire.*

SARAH FERGUSON

He says he'll be in in a minute! Did you get your rest, John?

JOHN FERGUSON

I couldn't sleep at all! I lay still and closed my eyes, but my mind was working all the time. I kept on wondering where Jimmy went to last night. I suppose no one has come up the "loanie" with news?

SARAH FERGUSON

There's been no one next or near this place this morning but ourselves and "Clutie" John. I gave him his breakfast and sent him packing. He was in a quare wild mood, that lad, and could hardly contain himself for excitement.

JOHN FERGUSON

I daresay he was greatly disturbed in his mind after what happened yesterday. Them people is quare and easily excited. I wish Andrew would come! Is Hannah up yet?

SARAH FERGUSON

Indeed I don't know. I didn't call her this morning. She was a long while getting her sleep, and so I just let her lie on. She'll be all the better for the rest!

JOHN FERGUSON

Ay. I can't make out where Jimmy went to last night. I thought mebbe he'd go straight to Witherow from here, and so I went there first, but I didn't see him.

SARAH FERGUSON

Did you see Witherow?

JOHN FERGUSON

Ay. I warned him about Jimmy.

SARAH FERGUSON

You warned him?

JOHN FERGUSON

Ay.

SARAH FERGUSON

And you never laid a finger on him?

JOHN FERGUSON

No.

SARAH FERGUSON

Well, indeed, I can't make you out, John! There's a man's harmed your daughter, and you didn't as much as lift your hand to him! You went and warned him about Jimmy! . . . Oh, John, I can't understand you! It doesn't seem right someway to be acting like that!

JOHN FERGUSON

God's Word says I must love my enemies, Sarah. That is my guide in all I do. It's hard to obey that commandment, and when I was standing there in front of Witherow I was tempted to take a hold of him and do him an injury . . . but I resisted the temptation, and I did what God bid me. I wasn't able to love him, but I warned him. I could do no more than that . . . but God'll mebbe understand!

SARAH FERGUSON

(*Sighing*). Ah, well! It's a quare way to look at things. If any one was to hurt me, I'd do my best to hurt them back, and hurt them harder nor they hurt me. That would learn them!

JOHN FERGUSON

Would it? Men's been hitting back since the beginning of the world, but hitting back has learned no one anything but hatred and bitterness.

SARAH FERGUSON

What did you do after you saw Witherow?

JOHN FERGUSON

I went down to Jimmy's shop, but he wasn't there. I dundhered on the door, but I could get no answer. Matt Kerr put his head out of his window, but he couldn't tell me a thing about Jimmy. I didn't know what to do after that! I wandered about in the dark for a while, and then I went back to the shop, but he still wasn't there! I was feeling tired, and I sat down for a wee while thinking mebbe Jimmy would turn up while I was waiting, but he didn't, and so I came home.

SARAH FERGUSON

You might have got your death of cold sitting there in the damp. It's a wonder to me you never knocked against Andrew!

JOHN FERGUSON

Ay, it is, but sure it's easy to miss people when it isn't light.

(ANDREW FERGUSON *enters by the door. There is a somber look on his face. It is not the darkness of a man who is horrified by his own deed, but the darkness of a man who has set himself willingly to do some desperate work that must be done.*)

ANDREW FERGUSON

You were wanting me, da?

JOHN FERGUSON

Ay, Andrew! (*Regarding his son closely.*) You're looking tired, son!

ANDREW FERGUSON

I am tired, but sure we all are. Da, you ought not to have got up this morning. You're not strong, and you must nearly be worn out.

JOHN FERGUSON

I couldn't rest, son. Andrew, I want you to go and inquire about Jimmy Caesar. I'll not be easy in my mind till I see him safe and sound. I feel my own responsibility, son. I'll admit to you I was hoping Hannah'd marry him, and I didn't discourage her from saying "yes" to him when he asked her, for all I knew she was only doing it for the farm. I knew the girl couldn't bear him, but I pretended to myself it would all come right in the end. I . . . I love this house, Andrew! That's the excuse I have for not being honest with Hannah.

SARAH FERGUSON

Ah, sure, you left it to her own free will.

JOHN FERGUSON

Ay, I tried to salve my conscience that way, but I said it in a way that showed plain what my desire was. If I had been firm, there would have been none of this bother now. You understand me, son, don't you? I feel I won't be happy till I see Jimmy safe and sound from harm, because I put him in danger. God knows what would happen if he was to meet Witherow in the temper he was in last night.

ANDREW FERGUSON

I daresay he's all right, da!

JOHN FERGUSON

I'd be glad if you'd go all the same and search for him, Andrew.

SARAH FERGUSON

Just go to please him, Andrew. His mind's upset about Jimmy, and there'll be no contenting him till he sees him.

ANDREW FERGUSON

It'll put the work on the farm behind, da.

JOHN FERGUSON

That doesn't matter, son!

ANDREW FERGUSON

. . . but I'll go to please you!

JOHN FERGUSON

Thank you, son!

ANDREW FERGUSON

There's no need for you to be uneasy about him, though. You may be sure Jimmy's come to no harm. We all know rightly the kind he is. Mebbe he's lying snug in his bed this minute, moaning and groaning, and saying what he'll do to Witherow one of these days, but you know as well as you're living he'll never do it.

JOHN FERGUSON

I'd liefer he was a collie a thousand times over nor have him take a man's life.

ANDREW FERGUSON

Even after what Witherow's done?

JOHN FERGUSON

Ay, son. Witherow will have to make his answer to God, and God will deal justly with him. We can't do that. No one can do justice to a man that's done an injury to them. We'd be thinking all the time of our trouble and wanting revenge. We wouldn't be striving hard, the way God would, to understand everything.

ANDREW FERGUSON

There's no need to be striving to understand everything, da. It's a plain matter that a child can understand. The man done wrong, and he has a right to suffer for it.

JOHN FERGUSON

Ay, son, he'll suffer for it, but that's the work of his Maker, and not the work of Jimmy Caesar or you or me or any man. You're wrong, Andrew, when you say there's nothing to understand. There's everything to understand. There's the man himself to understand. Do you think that Jimmy Caesar can judge Henry Witherow when he doesn't know him as God knows him?

ANDREW FERGUSON

(*Impatiently*). I've no time or patience for that kind of talk. If Jimmy Caesar . . . killed him . . . he was right to kill him . . . only I don't suppose he did.

JOHN FERGUSON

Don't you see now, Andrew, that you're not fit to judge Henry Witherow either? You can't judge a man if you have anger in your heart against him. You must love him before you can do justly by him.

ANDREW FERGUSON

Och, quit, da!

JOHN FERGUSON

And that's what God does, Andrew! God's something that sees inside you and knows every bit of you and never has no spite against you. Do you understand me, son? He judges you, but He doesn't punish you. He just gives knowledge to you so that you see yourself as He sees you, and that's your punishment, Andrew, if you've done wrong. It's knowing yourself as God knows you that hurts you harder nor anything else in the world. Do you think Henry Witherow'll be happy when he sees himself with God's eyes? I wouldn't be that man on the last day for the wealth of the world! . . . I'm all moidhered, Andrew, and I'm a poor hand at saying what's in my mind, but I know well that if Henry Witherow wronged me a thousand times more nor he has, I'd be doing God's will if I knelt down and kissed his feet.

ANDREW FERGUSON

I don't understand that kind of religion.

SARAH FERGUSON

Here's some one coming up the "loanie." I can hear their steps. (*She goes to the door as she speaks.*) It's Jimmy!

JOHN FERGUSON

Jimmy Caesar?

SARAH FERGUSON

Ay.

JOHN FERGUSON

Oh, thank God, thank God, he's come at last!
(JAMES CAESAR *enters. The look of assurance has completely gone, and so, too, has some of the meanness. He has the look of a man who has suffered great shame and humiliation, and although he feels mean, he does not look so mean as he did at the beginning of the play.*)

SARAH FERGUSON

Come in, Jimmy, come in! Sure, we're all right and glad to see you again!

JOHN FERGUSON

(*Going to him and wringing his hand*). Ay, Jimmy, we are, indeed. I'm glad this minute to see you safe from harm. Sit down, man! (*He leads* CAESAR *to a chair, and* CAESAR *sits down.*) You must be worn out. (JAMES CAESAR *glances about the room for a moment. Then he bows his head on the table and begins to cry hysterically.*) Ay, man, you'll want to cry after the trouble you've had.

ANDREW FERGUSON

(*Contemptuously*). My God, what a man!

JOHN FERGUSON

It's the reaction, son, that's what it is. He can't help himself. Nobody could.

SARAH FERGUSON

A drink of tea 'll do him a world of good. The kettle's on, and I'll have the tea wet in no time at all. (*She goes to* CAESAR *and pats him on the back.*) There, there, Jimmy, keep your heart up! Sure, we all know the troubles you've had to bear. Just put a good face on it, and you'll be as happy as you like.

JAMES CAESAR

I'm a disgraced man!

JOHN FERGUSON

No, no, no, Jimmy!

JAMES CAESAR

(*Raising his head*). Ay, I am, John. I'm a disgraced man! I heard what Andrew said to you a minute ago, and he was right. "My God," he said, "what a man!"

SARAH FERGUSON

Ah, sure, Andrew didn't mean it, Jimmy. Don't be paying no heed to him.

ANDREW FERGUSON

(*Angrily*). I did mean it.

JOHN FERGUSON

That's poor comfort, Andrew, to be offering to a broken man. I'd be ashamed to say that to any one.

JAMES CAESAR

(*As if eager to make little of himself*). But it's true, John, for all that. I've failed another time.

JOHN FERGUSON

It was God that checked you, Jimmy.

JAMES CAESAR

I went out of this house last night with my mind set on killing Witherow. If I'd met him in the "loanie" I'd 'a' throttled him there and then . . .

JOHN FERGUSON

I'm thankful you didn't meet him!

JAMES CAESAR

(*Rambling on*). . . . I was near demented with rage, and I hardly knew what I was doing. I started off for his farm. I could see the light in his front room shining down the glen, and it drew me towards it. I was that mad I didn't care what I done. I scrambled through the hedges and tore my hands and face with the thorns. Look at the cuts on my hands!
(*He holds out his hands for inspection.*)

JOHN FERGUSON

Ay, ay.

JAMES CAESAR

But I didn't care what happened to me. I felt nothing but the desire to get Witherow dead. I went across the fields, tumbling over stooks of corn, and slipping in puddles and drains till I come near the farm, and then I remembered I had nothing to kill him with . . .

ANDREW FERGUSON

(*Sneering*). Ha!

JAMES CAESAR

(*Turning to* ANDREW). I'm no match for him, Andrew, and if I'd gone into the house then, he'd have thrown me into the yard before I could have lifted a finger on him. (*Insisting on his weakness.*) I haven't the strength, Andrew, and I've a poor spirit. It wouldn't have been a fair fight if I'd gone in then and me with no weapon, would it, Andrew? Would it, John? I hadn't even a sally rod in my hands!

SARAH FERGUSON

He's stronger nor you by a good piece, Jimmy.

JAMES CAESAR

Yes, Mrs. Ferguson! That's what I said to myself. I said, "I'll have no chance against him if I go without a weapon!" That's what I said to myself. I made up my mind I'd go back to the shop to get my gun, and then I'd come back again to the farm and I'd shoot him dead.

JOHN FERGUSON

Aw, horrible, horrible!

ANDREW FERGUSON

And why didn't you go back again?

JAMES CAESAR

(*Miserably*). You've guessed right, Andrew. I never went near the place again. I got to the shop and I went in quietly and got the gun, and then I come out again. I had hardly got across the doorstep when I began to feel afeard, and I could feel the gun shaking in my hands as I gripped it. I went a bit of the way along the road, and I kept thinking some one was watching me, and then all of a sudden I started to run, and I run and I run till I come to the planting. I went in among the trees, and before I knew where I was I tripped over something on the ground and the gun went off in my hands. I was scared of my life for fear any one would hear it, and I got up and left the gun on the ground, and I run on through the trees like a wild thing till I could run no more. Then I crawled in under a whinbush and I hid there till this morning. I lay there cursing myself for a collie, and trying to stir myself up to go and kill him in the daylight . . . but I couldn't do it. I kept on making excuses. That's the sort of me, John! I'm always imagining myself doing grand things, and seeing people clapping me and making speeches about me, and printing things in the papers because of my greatness and my gallantry; but if a cow was to make a run at me in the fields, I'd be near scared to death of it. It's bad enough, Andrew, to know that other people are ashamed of you, but it's hell to be ashamed of yourself, the way I am this minute, and it's hell to have dreams of yourself doing big things, and you knowing rightly you'll never have the pluck to do a wee thing, let alone a big one.

JOHN FERGUSON

There's many a thing that a lad like Andrew might think was big, but it's quare and small.

JAMES CAESAR

It's kind of you to talk the way you do, John, but it's poor comfort to a man that knows he's as poor-spirited as myself. If Hannah was married on me now, I feel I would leave her in the lurch if she needed my help any time. That's the way of me, and I knew it well last night when I was hiding under the whinbush. I'm not like you, John Ferguson, that has no hatred in your heart, and can forgive a man that does an injury to you. I'm full of hate, and I want to hurt them that hurts me, but I haven't the courage to do it.

ANDREW FERGUSON

Well, there's no use in sitting here talking about it.

JAMES CAESAR

No, Andrew, there isn't. I come here this morning to excuse myself to Hannah and all of you. I thought that was the least I could do.

JOHN FERGUSON

No, no, Jimmy, no, no! I'm right and glad you didn't harm Witherow. I'd have been sore-hearted if you had.

SARAH FERGUSON

He went out to search for you last night, Jimmy.

JAMES CAESAR

Who? John?

SARAH FERGUSON

Ay.

ANDREW FERGUSON

He searched the place for you. A sick man went out to try and prevent a strong, able-bodied man from doing what he ought to have done; and while the sick man was wearing himself out with the search, the strong man was hiding underneath a whin-bush in mortal fear of his life!
(ANDREW'S *voice grows in anger and contempt as he speaks.*)

JAMES CAESAR

(*Miserably*). Oh, my God, my God!

JOHN FERGUSON

Wheesht, Andrew, wheesht! Jimmy, man, it's not like the thing for you to give way in that fashion! Control yourself, man! I'm as happy this minute as ever I've been in my life because I know God's saved you from sinning your soul with a murder. I'm proud to think you wouldn't kill Witherow . . .

JAMES CAESAR

(*In a misery of self-abasement*). But I'm not saved from sin, John. I didn't leave Witherow alone because I didn't want to kill him. I did want to kill him. I left him alone because I was afeard to touch him. My mind's the same now as it was when I went out of this house last night with murder in my heart. I want Witherow to be dead. I'd be glad this minute if some one come in the door there and told me he was dead. But I'd be afeard to lay a finger on him myself. That's the cowardliest thing of all, to want to commit a sin and not have the courage to do it. Do you think God 'll be gratified when He thinks I didn't kill Witherow because I was too big a collie to do it?

SARAH FERGUSON

Well, quit talking about it anyway. Make yourself content while I get you a bite to eat.

JAMES CAESAR

I couldn't taste it. It 'ud choke me.

SARAH FERGUSON

Now, a drop of tea never choked no one. The kettle's boiling, and it'll not take me a minute to make a cup of good warm tea for you. You must be perished with the cold, and you lying out on the damp grass all night. Just content yourself while I spread the table.
(*She sets about preparing the meal.*)

JAMES CAESAR

(*In whom confession has now grown to something like a craving*). I know rightly you have contempt for me, Andrew (ANDREW *stands at the window with his back to the others. He does not answer.*) I know you have. Anybody would. (*To* JOHN FERGUSON.) Hannah 'll have the quare contempt for me too. There'll be plenty will, and they'll be pointing at me and making remarks about me. It'll be quare and hard for me to hold up my head again after this. It will, in sang. (*His voice changes its note slightly as he begins to speculate on his conduct.*) You know, it's quare the way things turn out! Yesterday, after Hannah said she'd have me, I was having the great notions of myself and her. I imagined myself prospering greatly, and Andrew here doing well in the branch I was going to open at Ballymaclurg, and then I thought to myself I'd mebbe get made a magistrate . . .

ANDREW FERGUSON

(*Scornfully*). Ha! Ha, ha!

JAMES CAESAR

Well, Andrew, there's many that's not so well reared as myself that are made magistrates this day, and can send fellows like "Clutie" John to jail for a month and more for being without visible means of subsistence . . .

ANDREW FERGUSON

Ay, indeed, that sort of a job would suit you rightly! You could be doing an injury to other people without running any risk yourself! By my sang, Jimmy, you ought to be a magistrate! Mebbe if you were one now you'd fine Witherow forty shillings for what he done to Hannah! (*In great fury.*) Ah, you make me feel sick! I'll go out in the air a while and be quit of you. I'm near stifled in here!
(*He goes out violently.*)

JAMES CAESAR

There you are, John! That's the kind of contempt I'll have to thole from people after this. Hannah's tongue is bitterer nor Andrew's, and she'll be harder to bear nor him.

SARAH FERGUSON

(*Completing the arrangements for the meal*). Well, indeed, it's easy enough to bear the weight of a person's tongue. You'll come to small harm, Jimmy Caesar, if that's all the trouble you have. Sit up, now, and take your breakfast!

JAMES CAESAR

(*Drawing his chair closer to the table*). It's kind and thoughtful of you, Mrs. Ferguson, but I've no appetite at all.

SARAH FERGUSON

Ah, wheesht with you!

JAMES CAESAR

I'll only take the tea.
(*He begins to eat his breakfast.*)

SARAH FERGUSON

Draw up, John, to the table! I wonder ought I to call Andrew in or let him have his after a wee while.

JOHN FERGUSON

(*Coming to the table*). Leave him for the present. His mind's disturbed.

SARAH FERGUSON

Very well. (*She goes to the foot of the stairs.*) Hannah! (*She pauses, and then calls again.*) Hannah!

JAMES CAESAR

You're not bringing her down, are you?

SARAH FERGUSON

She has to have her food the same as yourself. (*She calls again.*) Are you up yet, Hannah!

HANNAH FERGUSON

(*Upstairs*). Ay, ma.

SARAH FERGUSON

Well, come down and have your breakfast.
(*She returns to the table and sits down.*)

JOHN FERGUSON

Mebbe she'd better have hers upstairs.

SARAH FERGUSON

No, indeed, she won't have it upstairs. There's no good of her sitting up there crying her eyes out. The world has to go on just the same as ever, no matter what happens. What'll you have, Jimmy? A piece of soda or a piece of wheaten farl? I baked the soda yesterday.

JAMES CAESAR

Ah, I couldn't touch it.

SARAH FERGUSON

(*Putting bread on his plate*). Well, just take it on your plate anyway, and if you have a fancy for it after a while it'll be convenient to you. John, what'll you have? (HANNAH *descends the stairs.*) Ah, is that you at last, Hannah? Come on here and have your breakfast! Do you see Jimmy Caesar?

HANNAH FERGUSON

Ay, ma. Good-morning, Jimmy!
(*She sits down beside her father*).

JAMES CAESAR

Good-morning to you, Hannah.

JOHN FERGUSON

(*Kissing* HANNAH *affectionately*). How're you, daughter?

JAMES CAESAR

Hannah, I've come here this morning to make a confession to you!

SARAH FERGUSON

Well, eat your breakfast first.

JAMES CAESAR

I must tell her, Mrs. Ferguson, before I take another bite. Hannah, I went out last night to kill Henry Witherow, but when I was getting ready to kill him I got afeard and I run away and hid myself. I come here this morning to tell you the poor sort of a man I am. I daresay you're thankful you broke your word to me, for I'm not much of a support for any woman.

HANNAH FERGUSON

I don't want you to make no confession to me.

JAMES CAESAR

Ah, but I must. Sure, I must tell people the way I feel. That's the only thing that's left to me now. Hannah, will you forgive me for not killing Witherow?

HANNAH FERGUSON

I didn't ask you to kill him. I had no call to ask you.

JAMES CAESAR

(*On whom the mean manner has gradually been gaining control*). If you're not angry with me, Hannah, then I'm glad I didn't do an injury to him. If I had killed him, mebbe it would have done no good! I daresay your da's right! Sure, if I'd done anything to Witherow I'd 'a' been put in jail, and my business that I've built up this long while would 'a' been sold on me, and mebbe I'd be hanged, and there'd be no good in that at all. I wonder now is it not better to forget and forgive! Of course, if a man does wrong he ought to be made to suffer for it. That's only right, and if Witherow was brought before the magistrates . . . (HANNAH *gets up suddenly in distress*).

HANNAH FERGUSON

Oh, quit talking about it, quit talking! (*She goes to the sofa and throws herself prone on it.*)

SARAH FERGUSON

(*Going to her*). There, there, Hannah, don't be upsetting yourself! (*She comforts* HANNAH.)

JAMES CAESAR

That's the way of me again, John! I'm always raking things up! I wish now I had killed Witherow. There'd be some satisfaction in that! Do you think Hannah 'd marry me if I was to ask her again? I'd be willing to marry her just the same! (*He turns to* HANNAH.) Hi, Hannah, do you hear that? I'm willing to marry you just the same if you'll have me! Will you? (HANNAH, *still sobbing, does not reply.*)

SARAH FERGUSON

Hannah, dear, do you not hear Jimmy speaking to you?

JAMES CAESAR

(*Getting up and going to* HANNAH). Listen Hannah! I was thinking as I was coming along that mebbe you'd have a poor opinion of me when you heard the way I'd behaved, but mebbe after all things has turned out for the best, and if you'll marry me I daresay we'll be as happy as any one. (*To* MRS. FERGUSON.) Dear bless us, Mrs. Ferguson, it's quare the way my mind alters every wee minute or so! I think one time I ought to have killed Witherow, and then I think another time I was right not to kill him, and one minute I'm ashamed of myself and another minute I'm near satisfied. (*To* HANNAH.) Are you listening to me, Hannah?

JOHN FERGUSON

Don't trouble her now, Jimmy! Come and finish your breakfast.

JAMES CAESAR

Well, we can discuss it later. (*He returns to the table and begins his meal again.*) When I come in here this morning I felt as if I could never put another bite of food in my mouth, and now I'm eating my breakfast as easy as anything. How would you account for the like of that, John?

JOHN FERGUSON

I can account for nothing, Jimmy, outside God's will.

JAMES CAESAR

(*Unctuously*). Ah, that's true. "God moves in a mysterious way His wonders to perform."

("CLUTIE" JOHN *enters in a state of great excitement.*)

"CLUTIE" JOHN

Mr. Ferguson! Mr. Ferguson!!

SARAH FERGUSON

(*Starting up in alarm*). Ah, "Clutie" John, go 'long with you! You near startled me out of my wits! What do you want to come running in like that for? Go 'long with you, man! We don't want you here the day again!

"CLUTIE" JOHN

(*Tensely*). I must tell you, I must tell you! Mr. Ferguson! . . . (*He sees* JAMES CAESAR.) Oh, there's Mr. Caesar!

JAMES CAESAR

Have you never seen me before, you great gumph, you, that you're standing there gaping at me like that?

JOHN FERGUSON

What is it, "Clutie"? (*To* JAMES CAESAR.) Don't be harsh with him, Jimmy! He's greatly upset after what happened yesterday.

JAMES CAESAR

All right!

(*He goes on with his meal*).

"CLUTIE" JOHN

I've fearful news for you, Mr. Ferguson! It's quare Mr. Caesar should be here!

JAMES CAESAR

What's quare about it?

"CLUTIE" JOHN

(*Looking at him in an odd manner*). Didn't you kill Mr. Witherow?

JAMES CAESAR

(*Rising in a fury*). Quit out of the place, damn you . . .

"CLUTIE" JOHN

(*Shrinking from* CAESAR *and running to* JOHN FERGUSON). Don't let him strike me, Mr. Ferguson! I'm afeard of my life of him!

JOHN FERGUSON

(*Quietening him*). He'll not harm you, "Clutie." Sit down somewhere and control yourself! And don't be talking about killing anybody!

"CLUTIE" JOHN

But he's dead, Mr. Ferguson!

JOHN FERGUSON

Dead!

SARAH FERGUSON

Who's dead?

"CLUTIE" JOHN

Henry Witherow!

JOHN FERGUSON

My God!

"CLUTIE" JOHN

He was found this morning in the farmyard shot through the heart.

JOHN FERGUSON

Shot!

"CLUTIE" JOHN

Ay, shot he was! The peelers is up at the farm now. Sergeant Kernaghan and two constables is there . . .

SARAH FERGUSON

Aw, it's not true, it's not true! The poor creature's demented and doesn't know what he's saying!

HANNAH FERGUSON

"Clutie," are you sure? . . .

"CLUTIE" JOHN

Ay, Hannah, I am. Certain sure! (*To* MRS. FERGUSON.) It is true. It is indeed, and 'deed and doubles! I wouldn't tell you a lie for the world. I saw his corpse myself, stretched out in the yard. It was quare to think of him lying there, and me could hit him if I liked and him couldn't hit back!

JAMES CAESAR

But . . . but who killed him? (JOHN FERGUSON *turns to look at him, and* JAMES CAESAR *sees accusation in his eyes.*) I didn't do it, John! It wasn't me that killed him! I swear to God it wasn't me! I'll take my oath on the Bible! . . .

JOHN FERGUSON

Jimmy! . . .

JAMES CAESAR

I tell you I didn't do it. How do you know he's dead? You only have "Clutie" John's word for it, and you know rightly he's away in the mind!

HANNAH FERGUSON

Oh, he's dead, thank God, he's dead!

JAMES CAESAR

(*Turning to her*). It's mebbe not true, Hannah . . .

"CLUTIE" JOHN

It's as true as death, Hannah! I tell you I saw him myself, and the peelers were asking a wheen of questions . . .

JAMES CAESAR

(*In a panic*). Did they ask anything about me, "Clutie"? (*He does not wait for an answer, but sitting down at the table buries his face in his hands.*) Oh, my God, they'll be blaming me for it, and I never did it at all! (*He gets up and goes to* JOHN FERGUSON, *plucking his arm.*) John, listen to me! You know the sort I am, don't you? You know rightly I couldn't have done it myself! I came here this morning and told you I was afeard to do it! Oh, my God, won't you believe me?

HANNAH FERGUSON

Jimmy!

JAMES CAESAR

(*Miserably*). Ay, Hannah.

HANNAH FERGUSON

Don't deny it if you did it.

JAMES CAESAR

I wouldn't deny it! (*He goes to* HANNAH.) Hannah, make your da believe me! Tell him you don't think I did it. You don't, do you?

HANNAH FERGUSON

You say you didn't, Jimmy!

JAMES CAESAR

But you think I did do it! I know you do! I can see it in your eyes!

HANNAH FERGUSON

I'd be proud if you had done it, Jimmy!

JAMES CAESAR

(*Miserably*). Every one 'll think I did it, the peelers and every one!
(*He subsides again at the table.*)

"CLUTIE" JOHN

It's a fearful thing to take a man's life. It is, in sang! There was many a song made up in Ireland about the like of a thing of that sort. I wonder, now, could I make up a song about Henry Witherow to be singing on the fair-days!

SARAH FERGUSON

Wheesht with you, "Clutie"!

JAMES CAESAR

(*Starting up and addressing* "CLUTIE" JOHN). What sort of questions were the peelers asking, "Clutie"? Did they make any mention of me, did you hear?

"CLUTIE" JOHN

I couldn't hear a word they were saying, Mr. Caesar, but whatever questions they were asking, they were putting the answers down in their wee books.

JAMES CAESAR

If they get to know I had a grudge against Witherow over the head of Hannah, they'll be after me. They know rightly I never cared for him any time of my life, but then I never done any harm to him for all my talk, and if they didn't know about Hannah mebbe they'd never think of me. (*Going to* JOHN FERGUSON.) John, you'll never let on anything, will you? (*He turns, without waiting for an answer, and speaks to* MRS. FERGUSON *and* HANNAH.) You two won't either, will you? And "Clutie" John? I'm sorry, "Clutie," for all I said to you. I wasn't thinking, that's why I said it. And if you'll not let on to the peelers about me, I'll give you something for yourself.

"CLUTIE" JOHN

What'll you give me, Mr. Caesar?

JAMES CAESAR

I don't know yet. I'll give you something. I'll give you your dinner whenever you want it, and I'll let you sleep in my loft. (*To* JOHN FERGUSON.) John, make him promise not to clash on me! You have more influence over him nor any one. Where's Andrew? We must make him promise too! Call him in, Mrs. Ferguson, and bid him promise he won't tell!

JOHN FERGUSON

We can't make any promises, Jimmy.

JAMES CAESAR

You'll not promise! Oh, you'll never go and tell the peelers, will you, and have them suspecting me, and me didn't do it?

JOHN FERGUSON

You must answer to the law, Jimmy . . .

JAMES CAESAR

But I didn't do it, I tell you! I'll take my oath I didn't! Where's the Bible? I'll swear on the Bible!
(ANDREW FERGUSON *enters from the door.*)

ANDREW FERGUSON

What ails you all?

JOHN FERGUSON

Henry Witherow's dead!
(ANDREW *pauses for a few moments before he replies. When he speaks his voice is very strained.*)

ANDREW FERGUSON

Oh!

JOHN FERGUSON

He was found in his yard this morning, shot!

ANDREW FERGUSON

Shot!

JOHN FERGUSON

Ay!

ANDREW FERGUSON

That's . . . quare!

JAMES CAESAR

(*Wildly*). Your da thinks it was me that shot him, Andrew, and so does your ma and Hannah, but I tell you I didn't. You know me, Andrew, don't you? You guessed that I wouldn't have the courage to kill Witherow, didn't you? . . .

ANDREW FERGUSON

(*Turning away from him.*) Ay.

JAMES CAESAR

There, you hear what your son says, John Ferguson! You hear him, don't you? Andrew doesn't believe I did it. I feel happier in my mind now. Mebbe the peelers 'll believe me when I tell them I didn't do it. Sergeant Kernaghan knows me well. Him and me was at the same school together . . .

ANDREW FERGUSON

You ought to try and get away, Jimmy . . .

JAMES CAESAR

Get away! . . . Do you not believe me either, Andrew? Do you think I killed him?

ANDREW FERGUSON

No, I don't believe you did, but it's likely other people 'll think it.

JOHN FERGUSON

Jimmy, why don't you ease your mind? There's no boundary to the love of God, and if you confess your sin, He'll forgive you for it.

JAMES CAESAR

Will I never satisfy you, John? Will you never believe I didn't do it?

JOHN FERGUSON

I wish I could believe you.

ANDREW FERGUSON

If you can prove where you were . . .

JAMES CAESAR

How can I prove it when no one seen me? ("CLUTIE" JOHN *goes to the door and looks down the "loanie."*)

"CLUTIE" JOHN

Here's the peelers coming!

JAMES CAESAR

(*In terror*). Oh, my God!

"CLUTIE" JOHN

There's the sergeant and the constables and a crowd of people running after them!

JAMES CAESAR

They're coming for me! I know rightly they are! They'll take me up . . . John, for the love of God, help me to hide somewhere!

JOHN FERGUSON

I can't, Jimmy, I can't. If you've broke the law, the law must have its reckoning.

ANDREW FERGUSON

Have you changed your mind, then, da! You were all for love and forgiveness a while ago.

JOHN FERGUSON

Ay, son, I was, and I am still, but Jimmy must redeem himself. A man should submit to punishment of his own free will, not be dragged to it. I know I'm not thinking clear, but I'm certain that Jimmy should submit to the law, whether he killed Witherow or not. It'll tell again' him if he runs away.
(*The noise of the approaching crowd is heard.*)

JAMES CAESAR

I must hide, I must hide! I can't face them! (*He gazes wildly round the room.*) Hannah, tell your da to let me hide!

JOHN FERGUSON

There's no use in hiding, Jimmy. You can't hide from yourself, can you?

JAMES CAESAR

Hide me, Hannah, and God'll reward you!

HANNAH FERGUSON

(*Appealingly*). Da! . . .

JOHN FERGUSON

I can't, daughter. He must submit himself to the will of God. There's no other way for a man to save himself.
(*The crowd comes to the door.* SERGEANT KERNAGHAN *and the two constables step inside the kitchen. The Sergeant advances while the constables keep back the murmuring crowd which surges round the door.*)

SERGEANT KERNAGHAN

I'm sorry to put you to any bother. (*He sees* JAMES CAESAR.) Ah, James Caesar, I arrest you on the suspicion of murdering Henry Witherow, and I warn you that anything you say will be taken down in writing and used as evidence against you!

JAMES CAESAR

(*Shrinking*). I didn't do it. I tell you, I didn't do it! Sergeant, for the love of God don't take me up! You and me attended the same school together . . .

SERGEANT KERNAGHAN

I'm heartsore at having to do it, Jimmy, but I can't help myself.
(*He beckons to the constables, who come forward and put handcuffs on* CAESAR'S *wrists. The crowd penetrates into the room, and the Sergeant goes and pushes it back.*)

JAMES CAESAR

(*More calmly*). I meant to kill him. I admit that. (*The crowd tosses this admission from lip to lip.*) But I didn't do it. If I should never speak again, that's the God's truth! I'm not sorry he's dead, but it wasn't me that killed him.

SERGEANT KERNAGHAN

Come along, now.

JAMES CAESAR

Good-bye to you all!

JOHN FERGUSON

God give you peace, Jimmy!

HANNAH FERGUSON

(*Going to* CAESAR *and touching his arm*). Good-bye, Jimmy!

JAMES CAESAR

I wish for your sake I had killed him. I'd be a happier man nor I am.

SERGEANT KERNAGHAN

I must ask you to come along now. (*To the constables.*) Just clear the crowd away from the door!
(*The constables push the people away from the door, and then they and the Sergeant close about* JIMMY CAESAR *and take him away. The crowd surges round them and slowly disappears, murmuring loudly as it goes.* HANNAH *closes the door behind them and then goes and sits down on the sofa beside her mother, who is weeping. There is silence for a moment.*)

JOHN FERGUSON

God knows His own ways best!
(ANDREW *stands staring in front of him. Then he goes to the door and opens it, and stands gazing down the "loanie" after the retreating crowd.* "CLUTIE" JOHN *sits down on the seat in the fireplace and takes out his whistle. He begins to play "Willie Reilly and his Colleen Bawn."*)

ANDREW FERGUSON

(*Fiercely*). Quit that damned whistle, will you?
("CLUTIE" JOHN *looks up at him questioningly, and then puts the whistle away.* ANDREW *stands still for a moment longer. Then he closes the door and walks towards the fire and holds his hands in front of the blaze.*)

ANDREW FERGUSON

It's colder the day nor it was yesterday!

JOHN FERGUSON

Ay, son!

ACT FOUR

IT *is the late afternoon of a day a fortnight later.* JOHN FERGUSON, *who has become feebler in the interval, but at the same time more deeply religious, is sitting in the attitude in which he was seen at the beginning of the play. His chair is drawn up to the fire, and he has his Bible open in his hands. He is reading the eighteenth chapter of the second book of Samuel. It is clear from his look of fragility that he is dying.* MRS. FERGUSON *is standing at the door, looking down the "loanie."*

JOHN FERGUSON

(*Reading aloud*). "And the king said, Is the young man Absalom safe? And Ahimaaz answered, When Joab sent the king's servant, and me thy servant, I saw a great tumult, but I knew not what it was. And the king said unto him, Turn aside and stand there. And he turned aside and stood still. And, behold, Cushi came; and Cushi said, Tidings, my lord, the king: for the Lord hath avenged thee this day of all them that rose up against thee. And the king said unto Cushi, Is the young man Absalom safe? . . ."

SARAH FERGUSON

Here's Hannah now, John! She's just turned the corner of the "loanie."

JOHN FERGUSON

(*Looking up from the Bible*). Ay, wife, it'll be about her time.

SARAH FERGUSON

(*Entering the kitchen and settling a kettle on the fire*). I don't know how she can bear to go and see Jimmy the way she does when she minds everything. If it hadn't been for her changing her mind, Witherow would be living now!

JOHN FERGUSON

(*Putting the Bible down on the table beside him, and turning to his wife*). You must never say the like of that to her, Sarah! The girl couldn't see in front of her. No one could.

SARAH FERGUSON

She would have nothing to do with him before he killed Witherow, and now she goes to see him whenever they'll let her in the jail! You would near think she was in love with him over the head of the crime, though I don't believe she is myself for all she visits him. (*She sits down on the sofa and takes up some darning on which she begins to work.*) There's been a quare change in her this last fortnight! She's quieter on it, and not so headstrong and set on herself as she used to be. Indeed, sometimes I near think she's in a decline.

JOHN FERGUSON

(*Sighing as he speaks*). Ay, she's been through a mort of sorrow, that girl! She's young to be feeling the weight of the world already.

SARAH FERGUSON

Ay, indeed! And there's Andrew hasn't a word to say to any one since it happened. Sometimes I try to talk to him about Jimmy, but sure I might as well hold my tongue. All I can get out of him is "Ay, ma!" or "No," or mebbe he'll just nod his head. (*She sighs.*) Ah, dear, our children seem to be slipping away from us, John!

JOHN FERGUSON

Mebbe they're going past us, Sarah. It's natural, that! You and your children can't keep pace with each other all your life. They must get ahead of you some time. It hurts you when you feel them outstripping you, but it's the way God works, and sure He doesn't leave you without a consolation of some sort. God never hits you with both hands at the one time, Sarah, and if we're losing our children, we're finding ourselves. You and me's drawing closer to one another, woman!
(*He holds out his hand to her.*)

SARAH FERGUSON

(*Taking his hand*). Ay, John, we are. We were always good comrades since ever we were married, you and me, for all the trouble we've had.

JOHN FERGUSON

Ay, wife, ay!
(*He takes up the Bible again and reads it to himself. As he does so,* HANNAH *enters the kitchen. Her manner is more restrained than it was when the play began, and she seems to be older in manner. Her actions appear to be independent of her thoughts.*)

SARAH FERGUSON

You're back again, Hannah?

HANNAH FERGUSON

Ay, ma!
(*She takes off her outdoor garments and lays them aside.*)

JOHN FERGUSON

Well, Hannah, how is Jimmy the day?

HANNAH FERGUSON

He seemed quieter in his mind, da.

JOHN FERGUSON

Has he confessed the truth yet?

HANNAH FERGUSON

No. I didn't like to mention it to him, and he didn't say anything to me. But I know he hasn't confessed, because I went to Mulhern, the solicitor, afterwards, and he

told me Jimmy still makes out that he didn't do it.
(*She comes and sits at the table, facing the audience.*)

JOHN FERGUSON

I wish he'd unburden his mind. It's no good him keeping it up like that. What does Mulhern say about it?

HANNAH FERGUSON

He doesn't know what to think. He says that when he's by himself he feels sure Jimmy did it, but when he's with Jimmy he begins to be doubtful.

JOHN FERGUSON

Doubtful.

HANNAH FERGUSON

Ay. There's something about the way Jimmy denies it that near makes you believe him. All the same, Mulhern thinks he did it, and he says that if he was to confess, it would be better for him. There are extenuating circumstances . . .

JOHN FERGUSON

Nothing can extenuate a murder, Hannah! God's Word is clear. "But I say unto you which hear, Love your enemies, do good to them that hate you. Bless them that curse you, and pray for them that despitefully use you. And unto him that smiteth thee on the one cheek offer also the other; and him that taketh away thy cloak forbid him not to take thy coat also." Them words is plain enough. You can't twist them out of their meaning. There can be no excuse, Hannah, for a bad deed: there can only be repentance and forgiveness.

HANNAH FERGUSON

We all have our natures, da!

JOHN FERGUSON

Ay, daughter, we have, but there's the one duty for the whole of us.

HANNAH FERGUSON

I met John Comber on the road, and he's set on getting up a petition for Jimmy. He says the judge is sure to sentence him to death . . .

SARAH FERGUSON

God save us!

HANNAH FERGUSON

. . . and so we'd better be prepared to do all that's needful.

SARAH FERGUSON

Ah, sure, they'll never hang him when they know all the facts. It wouldn't be honest or fair, and there's many says Witherow should have been shot long ago. They'll mebbe give Jimmy penal servitude for life.

HANNAH FERGUSON

That's worse nor hanging. They take your life, but they don't give you death.

SARAH FERGUSON

(*Sighing*). Ah, I daresay you're right! Dear knows, when you think of what they do to you, you'd wonder anybody ever killed a person at all.
(SAM MAWHINNEY, *the postman, comes to the door.*)

SAM MAWHINNEY

I'm not empty-handed this time, Mrs. Ferguson. I've a letter for you the day.

SARAH FERGUSON

A letter?

SAM MAWHINNEY

Ay, from America. The mail's in the day!

SARAH FERGUSON

(*Going to him and taking the letter from him*). A letter from America!

SAM MAWHINNEY

Ay! Don't you mind the last time the mail come in you were expecting a letter from America, and you were quare and cut up because you didn't get it? I declare to my goodness it was the very day Witherow was shot. A fortnight the day! I never thought of that now!

SARAH FERGUSON

(*Absently*). Thank you, Sam!

SAM MAWHINNEY

Ah, not at all. I only hope it's good news for you. Are you keeping your health, Mr. Ferguson?

JOHN FERGUSON

I'm bravely, thank you, Sam!

SAM MAWHINNEY

That's right. Good-evening to you, Hannah! Well, I must be going. Good-night to you all!

SARAH FERGUSON

Good-night to you, Sam!
(SAM MAWHINNEY *goes off.*)

SARAH FERGUSON

(*Standing in the center of the kitchen, gazing vacantly at the letter*). It's from Andrew, John! Will I open it?

JOHN FERGUSON

Ay!
(*She opens the envelope and takes out the letter and an order for money which are inside.*)

SARAH FERGUSON

Oh, he's sent the money to pay the mortgage!
(*She holds the order in her fingers and gazes stupidly at it for a few moments. They are all silent for a while.*)

HANNAH FERGUSON

(*Bitterly*). God's late, da!

JOHN FERGUSON

(*Feeling the blow to his faith*). Don't daughter, don't.

HANNAH FERGUSON

(*Getting up and going to the window*). Oh, it's wicked, it's wicked!

SARAH FERGUSON

If it had only come by the last mail!

JOHN FERGUSON

There *must* be some meaning in it. There *must* be! God doesn't make mistakes.

SARAH FERGUSON

Will I read the letter to you, John?

JOHN FERGUSON

Ay! Ay, do!

SARAH FERGUSON

(*Sitting down at the table*). There's not much in it. (*She peers at the letter.*) I can't understand his writing without my specs.!

HANNAH FERGUSON

(*Coming to her and taking the letter from her*). I'll read it, ma! (*She, too, sits down at the table, and she reads the letter aloud.*) "Dear Brother, I received your letter safe, and am sorry to hear about your trouble, but am glad to see that you are better in yourself and that Sarah and Andrew and Hannah are keeping their health as I am, too, thank God. It is a great deal of money to send, and I have had a lot of bother to raise it, but I could not let the farm go out of the family without making an effort, so I send the money to you with this letter. If I am well-spared I will mebbe come home and see you all. I am getting tired of America. It is no place for an old man that wasn't born here. Remember me to all my friends and acquaintances, and with my best love and respect to all at home, I am, your affectionate brother, Andrew. *P.S.*—Write soon." (*She turns the letter over.*) There's a piece on the other side. "*P.S.*—I am sorry I missed the mail yesterday. I made a mistake in the day, but I daresay this will reach you in time.—Andrew!"
(*She puts the letter down. They sit in silence. Then* HANNAH *begins to laugh hysterically.*)

HANNAH FERGUSON

Isn't it quare and funny, da? Isn't it funny? . . .

SARAH FERGUSON

(*Going to her and shaking her*). Hannah, Hannah, for dear sake, control yourself!

HANNAH FERGUSON

(*Lapsing from laughter to tears*). Where's the right in it, da? Where's the right in it? It's not just! It's not fair!

SARAH FERGUSON

Ah, quit, Hannah!

HANNAH FERGUSON

There would have been none of this if he hadn't forgotten the right day, none of it . . . Oh, da, da!
(ANDREW FERGUSON *enters.*)

ANDREW FERGUSON

Is anything the matter?

HANNAH FERGUSON

No, no, Andrew! Nothing's the matter! Nothing! Your uncle Andrew forgot the mail-day, that's all! . . .

ANDREW FERGUSON

(*To his father*). What's up, da?

JOHN FERGUSON

(*Feebly*). It's . . . it's your uncle . . . (*He becomes incoherent.*)

SARAH FERGUSON

Your uncle Andrew's sent the money to pay the mortgage, son. He forgot the mail-day, and just missed it. If he hadn't forgot, the money would have been here before . . . before Jimmy killed Witherow!

HANNAH FERGUSON

Ay! Ay! Before—before Jimmy killed Witherow! And then my da says it was all planned! . . .

ANDREW FERGUSON

(*With a queer wrinkled smile on his face, as he takes up the letter and fingers it*). Huh! Uncle Andrew never had a good memory, had he? (*No one speaks.*)

HANNAH FERGUSON

Ay, the farm's safe!

JOHN FERGUSON

We can't understand everything. It's no good trying to puzzle it all out. We must just have faith . . . that's all! Just have faith!

HANNAH FERGUSON

One man's dead and another's in jail in danger of his life because my uncle Andrew forgot the mail-day . . .

ANDREW FERGUSON

It's . . . it's a quare set-out!

JOHN FERGUSON

(*Sighing heavily*). Ay!

ANDREW FERGUSON

(*Hysterically*). Ha! Ha, ha! Ha, ha, ha! . . .

JOHN FERGUSON

Andrew, Andrew, son, don't you give way, too! Set an example to your sister of self-control!

ANDREW FERGUSON

(*Recovering himself*). Ay! Ay, da, I will. (*He sits down.*)

SARAH FERGUSON

Hannah's just come back from seeing Jimmy, Andrew!

ANDREW FERGUSON

Oh! Oh! Oh, yes, I remember, she was going to see him the day, wasn't she? (*His voice is very hard and strained.*) What was he like, Hannah?
(HANNAH *does not answer.*)

SARAH FERGUSON

She says he was quieter in his mind . . .

ANDREW FERGUSON

That's good. It's good to be quiet in your mind! It's well for him.

JOHN FERGUSON

It's not well for him, Andrew. He still denies that he killed Witherow . . .

ANDREW FERGUSON

Mebbe he didn't kill him, da!

JOHN FERGUSON

I would like to believe that, but I can't.

ANDREW FERGUSON

He ought to have killed him. (*More emphatically.*) He ought to have killed him . . . but he didn't.

JOHN FERGUSON

Ah, son, what's the good of talking that way? You and Hannah's overstrung, and you hardly know what you're saying or doing, the pair of you. I've noticed how quiet you've been lately, and I believe you've been brooding over Jimmy till now you can't think clearly about him.

ANDREW FERGUSON

He didn't kill Witherow, da. He hadn't the pluck to kill him. It was me that done it!

SARAH FERGUSON

(*Starting up*). You!

JOHN FERGUSON

(*Quietly*). Sit down, Sarah! The lad's beside himself. (MRS. FERGUSON *resumes her seat.*) Andrew, you must not give way to your fancies like that! (*He rises and faces him.*) Come to bed, son, and rest yourself. You look tired and exhausted.
(*He takes hold of* ANDREW'S *arm and tries to lead him to the stairs.*)

ANDREW FERGUSON

(*Eluding his father's grasp*). No, da, I'm not away in the mind, as you think. I know rightly what I'm saying. It was me that killed Witherow!
(*Now that he has confessed his deed his voice becomes quite calm.*)

JOHN FERGUSON

You're demented, son!

ANDREW FERGUSON

No, da, I'm not. I killed him. With that gun there.
(*He points to the gun over the mantelshelf.*)

SARAH FERGUSON

(*In terrible alarm*). Son-a-dear, do you know what you're saying?

ANDREW FERGUSON

I know rightly, ma.

SARAH FERGUSON

It's not true, it's not true.
(JOHN FERGUSON *has been standing gaping at his son as if he cannot understand what he is saying. Then, as comprehension comes to him, he goes to* ANDREW *and grips him by the shoulder.*)

JOHN FERGUSON

(*Almost harshly*). Andrew!

ANDREW FERGUSON

(*Quietly*). Ay, da!

JOHN FERGUSON

Do you mean . . . do you mean you killed Witherow?

ANDREW FERGUSON

I do, da!

JOHN FERGUSON

(*Releasing his grip and staggering back a little*). Oh, my God, my God!

SARAH FERGUSON

It's not true, John, it's not true. The poor lad's mind is turned with trouble.

ANDREW FERGUSON

It is true. I knew that Jimmy wouldn't kill him, so I made up my mind I'd kill him myself . . .

JOHN FERGUSON

(*Wildly*). Quit, quit, quit! I must think . . . I must think!
(*He goes back to his chair and sinks into it. As he does so, his hand touches his Bible. He pushes it away from him.*)

HANNAH FERGUSON

(*Going to her brother and putting her arms about him*). Andrew, dear!

ANDREW FERGUSON

I'm not sorry I killed him, Hannah!

HANNAH FERGUSON

No, Andrew, I know you're not.

ANDREW FERGUSON

But I'm ashamed to think I let Jimmy bear the blame for it. That's as bad as him hiding under the whinbush when he should have been killing Witherow himself. It's been on my mind ever since the peelers took him up. That's the only thing that disturbs me. I lie awake at night, and I say to myself, "You took Jimmy's place of your own free will, but you made him take your place against his will!" Mind you, I felt no more remorse when I killed Witherow nor a terrier feels when it kills a rat.

HANNAH FERGUSON

No, Andrew, why would you?

ANDREW FERGUSON

I went up to his farm, and when I got there the dog begun to bark, and Witherow come to the door. "Is that you, Jimmy Caesar?" he shouted. "Have you come to kill me?" He let a big coarse laugh out of him when he said that, and I could feel my heart jumping mad inside me. "It's not Jimmy Caesar!" I shouted back at him; "it's me!" I could see him straining to look at me, and his features was puzzled. Then I put my gun up to my shoulder, and I took aim at him. "Away home out of that!" he shouted. And then I pulled the trigger, and he let a yell out of him and fell in a lump on the ground. The dog was barking and straining at its chain . . .

HANNAH FERGUSON

Poor beast!

ANDREW FERGUSON

But I didn't mind that. I shouted at it to lie down, and then I come straight home. I mind when I was half-way home, I said to myself, "Mebbe you've not killed him," and I was near turning back to make sure. But I just didn't . . . There was no one in the kitchen when I come in, and I put the gun back where I found it, and no one knew . . . except me. It never entered no one's mind that it was me killed him. I was safe enough, and at first I didn't care whether Jimmy got hung or not. I said to myself it would serve him right if he was hung for being a collie. And then I tried to comfort myself by saying he wouldn't be hung at all when the people knew the way he'd been provoked. But it wasn't any good. I got more and more ashamed, and I couldn't sit still in the house with you all, and my da saying Jimmy ought to confess. I couldn't rest nowhere. The only consolation I had was to go into the fields and listen to "Clutie" playing his whistle. He knew it was me done it for all he didn't say anything . . .

(JOHN FERGUSON *rouses himself from the lethargy into which he sank when he heard his son's confession. He gets up from his chair and takes hold of* ANDREW *as if he were protecting him from some danger.*)

JOHN FERGUSON

We must hide him somewhere. That's what we must do. We'll send you to America, Andrew, to live with your uncle. Ay, ay! That's what the money was for! You may be certain sure that was what it come for! You'll be safe when you're out of the country, son! No one 'll harm you in America! (*To his wife.*) Stir yourself, Sarah, woman, stir yourself! We've no time to lose. The peelers might hear about it and come any minute. (*To* ANDREW.) Come on, son, and get ready! You must quit the place the night . . .

ANDREW FERGUSON

No, da . . .

JOHN FERGUSON

Ay, son, you must! You can go up to Belfast by the next train, and we'll send the money to you there. You'd better change your name, son! . . . (*He puts his hands to his head as if he were dazed.*) I'm all moidhered! Sarah, Sarah, woman!

SARAH FERGUSON

Ay, John?

JOHN FERGUSON

We must hide him the night. Do you understand me? Mebbe some one heard him telling us about it. You never know who's listening, and the world's full of clashbags! . . .

ANDREW FERGUSON

I can't go, da, and leave Jimmy in the wrong.

JOHN FERGUSON

Yes, yes, son! That'll be all right! We'll think about Jimmy afterwards. Come and get ready now, son!
(*He tries to lead* ANDREW *to the staircase, but* ANDREW *resists him.*)

SARAH FERGUSON

Go with your da, son, and get ready!

ANDREW FERGUSON

(*Freeing himself from them and sitting down again*). I must do right by Jimmy for my peace' sake.

JOHN FERGUSON

No, son, you must save yourself first.

ANDREW FERGUSON

You're asking me to do what you wouldn't let Jimmy do for all he begged you!

JOHN FERGUSON

(*Fiercely*). You're my son, Andrew, and Jimmy's not! He always meant to kill Witherow. Many's a time you all heard him say he would do it! Didn't you? You mocked him yourselves over the head of it. He killed the man many's a while in his mind, and the Bible says if you think a sin you commit a sin. (*He takes hold of* ANDREW *again.*) Come away, son! Hannah, persuade him . . .

HANNAH FERGUSON

I can't, da. Andrew knows what's best for himself.

SARAH FERGUSON

Do you want your brother hanged, Hannah? Is that what you want?

HANNAH FERGUSON

What peace will Andrew have if Jimmy suffers for him?

ANDREW FERGUSON

That's what I say to myself many's a time, Hannah! You see that yourself, da, don't you?

JOHN FERGUSON

(*Feebly going to his chair*). I've suffered enough! I've suffered enough, Andrew! It's not just or right to put more trouble on me now. I've lost my health . . . and then there was the mortgage, and . . . Hannah . . . and Jimmy . . . and now! . . . Oh, I've bore enough, and it's not fair to ask me to bear any more.

HANNAH FERGUSON

We all have to make our own peace, da. We can't have it made for us. You used always to say that.

ANDREW FERGUSON

Hannah's right, da. There'll be no content for me till I content myself. (*He rises.*) I'll go down now to the barracks and tell the sergeant.

JOHN FERGUSON

(*Turning to him and speaking brokenly*). Son, son! . . .

SARAH FERGUSON

I'll not have him made suffer! (*Going to* ANDREW *and holding him tightly.*) I'll not let you go, Andrew, I'll not let you go!

ANDREW FERGUSON

I must go, ma, for my peace' sake. Every minute that Jimmy's locked in jail is a burden on my mind. I've mocked the man times and times for a coward, though he couldn't help his nature, but I'm worse nor him a hundred times.

SARAH FERGUSON

Be wheesht with you, son, be wheesht!

ANDREW FERGUSON

Eating the heart out of me, it is. Gnawing and gnawing! . . . I never get the picture of Jimmy out of my mind! I run for miles this morning to try and tire myself out so's I could sleep and rest myself, but I can't get content nohow. That's the way of it, ma. You understand me, da, don't you?

JOHN FERGUSON

Ay, son, I understand you.

SARAH FERGUSON

You can go to America, Andrew, the way your da said you could, and when you're safe you can send home a confession to save Jimmy. That would do, wouldn't it?

JOHN FERGUSON

(*Eagerly clutching at the straw*). Ay, ay, that would do, Andrew.

SARAH FERGUSON

Or we could go ourselves and tell the peelers when you were safely out of it.

HANNAH FERGUSON

They might think it was a made-up thing . . .

SARAH FERGUSON

(*Rounding on her*). Quit, you! It doesn't become you, Hannah, to be telling your brother what to do when it's your fault he's in the trouble he is.

HANNAH FERGUSON

Ma, ma, don't say it . . .

SARAH FERGUSON

Ay, you can cry well enough, but that'll not save you from the blame. If you'd taken Jimmy at the start . . .

JOHN FERGUSON

Sarah, woman, don't . . . don't talk to her that way!

SARAH FERGUSON

I will talk to her. It was her that killed Witherow, and no one else. It's her that ought to be hanged . . .

ANDREW FERGUSON

(*Standing up and shouting at his mother*). Ma!

SARAH FERGUSON

(*Collapsing*). Am I to see my own son sent to the gallows? Am I to sit still and let you hang him between you? John, are you going to let Hannah drive Andrew to the jail? . . .

ANDREW FERGUSON

She's not driving me, ma. No one could.

SARAH FERGUSON

(*Ignoring her son*). John, will you be content to let her . . .

JOHN FERGUSON

(*Patiently*). I'm trying to discover God's will, Sarah.

SARAH FERGUSON

(*Passionately*). I don't want God's will! I want my son! It's nothing to me what he done—he's my son! I don't care if he killed a hundred men—he's my son! I'll not let him go to the jail. I'll take him away myself to some place where he'll be safe. (*She goes over to* ANDREW.) Get ready, Andrew, and we'll go away together the night. Your da wanted you to go a minute since. (*She tries to draw him away from his seat.*) Come with me, son, and don't be heeding Hannah.

ANDREW FERGUSON

(*Resisting her*). Don't, ma. (*He turns to his father.*) Da!

JOHN FERGUSON

I can't advise you, son. Don't ask me. I was weak a minute ago. I forgot God's will. Mebbe you're right, son . . . but don't ask me to advise you. I'm getting old, and I haven't the strength of mind I had one time . . .

SARAH FERGUSON

You'll never let him go and give himself up, will you? Oh, have you no nature at all, none of you? I thought you took pride in him, John! . . .

JOHN FERGUSON

I did take pride in him, but I take no pride in anything now. I must have sinned bitterly against God to be punished this way. It must have been something I done that's brought calamity on us. I'd be willing to pay whatever price was demanded of me . . . but Andrew! . . .

ANDREW FERGUSON

Da, a man must clean himself, mustn't he?

JOHN FERGUSON

Ay. Ay, son!

ANDREW FERGUSON

It's no good other people doing things for him. He must do them himself.

JOHN FERGUSON

Yes, yes.

ANDREW FERGUSON

And it's no good any one doing anything for me. I must do it myself, da. Jimmy can't pay for me. He can only pay for himself.

SARAH FERGUSON

I won't let you go, son! . . .

ANDREW FERGUSON

If they were to hang Jimmy, ma, or to keep him in jail for the rest of his life, do you think would I be happy?

SARAH FERGUSON

Ah, but you could forget, son, in a new place. We'd go where no one knew anything about us and begin all over again.

ANDREW FERGUSON

We'd know, ma. Oh, don't you mind what my da said to Jimmy: "You can't hide from yourself"? There's nothing truer nor that.

SARAH FERGUSON

(*Beating her breast*). Oh, will no one help me to keep my son safe? Will you all take him from me?
(ANDREW *goes to her and kisses her hair.*)

ANDREW FERGUSON

It's best this way, ma. You'll see that yourself some day.
(MRS. FERGUSON *clutches him to her.*)

SARAH FERGUSON

Don't leave me, son!

ANDREW FERGUSON

I must, ma, for my peace' sake! (*He kisses her and then releases himself from her embrace. She buries her face on the table and sobs without restraint.*) Will you come to the barracks with me, da?

(JOHN FERGUSON *looks up piteously at his son. His will fails him, and he puts out his hands in supplication to* ANDREW, *and then, recovering himself, draws them in again.*)

JOHN FERGUSON

Don't ask me, son; I couldn't bear it.

ANDREW FERGUSON

It'll be lonely going there by myself. Will you come, Hannah?

HANNAH FERGUSON

(*Quietly*). Ay, Andrew.

ANDREW FERGUSON

Thank you, Hannah.
(*He puts on his coat and cap.* HANNAH *picks up the garments which she threw aside when she first came into the kitchen, and puts them on. There is silence, save for* MRS. FERGUSON'S *sobs, while they do so.*)

ANDREW FERGUSON

Good-night, da!

JOHN FERGUSON

(*Without looking up*). Good-night, Andrew!
(ANDREW *bends down to kiss his father, who draws him close to him.*)

JOHN FERGUSON

(*Brokenly*). My son, my son!

ANDREW FERGUSON

(*Chokingly*). Da!
(*He releases himself and goes to his mother.*)

ANDREW FERGUSON

Good-night, ma!

SARAH FERGUSON

(*Starting up and clinging to him*). No, no, Andrew, no!

ANDREW FERGUSON

(*Firmly*). Good-night, ma!
(*He kisses her, and then gently releases himself from her clasp and puts her back into her chair.*)

ANDREW FERGUSON

(*To his father*). I think John Luke 'll be able to take care of the farm for a day or two, but I wouldn't trust him longer, da. He's bone idle, that man, and you'd better get some one else as soon as you can. If you were to get some one that understood management, he would do rightly as a laborer if he was watched well. Arthur Carnduff heard of a suitable person a while ago that might do.

JOHN FERGUSON

Ay, son, ay.

ANDREW FERGUSON

And Kerr, the butcher, 'll give you a good price for the bullock. (*To* HANNAH.) Are you ready, Hannah?

HANNAH FERGUSON

Ay, Andrew!

ANDREW FERGUSON

(*Vaguely*). Well, I'll bid you all good-night.

JOHN FERGUSON

Good-night, son.

ANDREW FERGUSON

I'll . . . I'll mebbe see you again . . . some day!
(*He pauses for a moment, but his father does not reply.* HANNAH *opens the door and* ANDREW *goes out.*)

ANDREW FERGUSON

(*In the doorway.*) The air's turned cold.

HANNAH FERGUSON

(*To her father*). I'll be back as soon as I can, da!
(*She goes out, closing the door behind her. The sound rouses* MRS. FERGUSON, *who sits up and gazes dazedly about her.*)

SARAH FERGUSON

Where are they? They're not gone?

JOHN FERGUSON

Ay, they've gone. Sit down, wife.

SARAH FERGUSON

Oh, why did you let them go? I can't let him go, John, I can't let him go!

JOHN FERGUSON

You must, Sarah. God has some purpose with us, and there's no use in holding out against God, for He knows, and we don't.

SARAH FERGUSON

I won't let him go! (*She goes to the door and opens it.*) I'll bring him back!
(*She goes out, shouting "Andrew! Andrew!!" and leaves the door open.* JOHN FERGUSON *sits brooding before the fire for a few moments. Then he gets up, moving feebly, and goes across the room and shuts the door. When he has done so he stands for a moment or two gazing helplessly about the room. Then he goes back to his seat. As he sits down, his hand comes in contact with the open Bible. Almost mechanically he picks it up and begins to read where he left off when the Act began. His lips move as he reads to himself. Then he slowly reads aloud.*)

JOHN FERGUSON

"And the king said unto Cushi, Is the young man Absalom safe? . . ."
(*The door opens, and* MRS. FERGUSON, *weeping, enters.*)

SARAH FERGUSON

They've gone! They wouldn't come back! It's not right to be sending him away like that! He's my only son, and I'm an old woman. You had no call to be sending him away.

JOHN FERGUSON

Isn't he the only son I have too? Is it any easier for a father to give up his son nor it is for a mother? Has a man no pride in his child, and no grief when it dies or does wrong? Is it women only that can feel hurt? Woman, woman, your sorrow is no more nor mine, and mine is no more nor yours. We're just stricken together. Come here, Sarah! (*She comes to him.*) Sit down, woman, here by the side of me, and give me a hold of your hand. (*She sits down on the stool beside him.*) We've been married a long while, Sarah, and shared our good fortune and our bad. We've had our pride and our humiliation. God's been good to us and He's been bitter hard. But whatever it was we've bore it together, haven't we?

SARAH FERGUSON

Ay, John.

JOHN FERGUSON

And we'll bear this together too, woman, won't we?

SARAH FERGUSON

It's a hard thing for any one to bear. Your own son to be taken from you . . .

JOHN FERGUSON

Ay, wife, it is, but we must just bear it, for God knows better nor we do what's right to be done. (*He takes up the Bible again.*) Listen to God's Word, Sarah, and that'll strengthen you. (*He continues his reading.*) 'And the king said unto Cushi, Is the young man Absalom safe? And Cushi answered, The enemies of my lord the king, and all that rise against thee to do thee hurt, be as that young man is. And the king was much moved, and went up to the chamber over the gate, and wept: and as he went (*his voice begins to break as he reads the following passages*), thus he said, O my son Absalom, my son, my son Absalom! Would God I had died for thee, O Absalom, my son . . . my son."

(*His voice ends in a sob. The Bible falls from his hands on to his lap. He sits staring into the fire. There is a low moan from his wife.*)

A. A. Milne

MR. PIM PASSES BY

ALAN ALEXANDER MILNE

In 1894, when he was twelve years old, A. A. Milne was already writing verses, parodies and short prose pieces for his school paper. At Cambridge he became editor of *The Granta,* the undergraduate periodical. From 1903 to 1906, he tried his hand at free-lance writing and then became an assistant editor of *Punch.* He remained in that post until 1914. He served in the World War with the Royal Warwickshire Regiment. In 1913 he was married to Dorothy de Selincourt, and their son, the hero of *When We Were Very Young,* Christopher Robin, is known, by name at least, to more people than almost any lad of his years in the world. Certainly their son's favorite nicknames for his toys, especially "Pooh," have come into international usage. Mr. Milne has written three volumes of plays, of which *Mr. Pim Passes By* is, by general agreement, his best. Other plays that have won wide favor are *The Dover Road* and *The Truth About Blayds.* His novels and his verse reach an enormous public.

CHARACTERS

GEORGE MARDEN, J. P.

OLIVIA, his wife.

DINAH, his niece.

LADY MARDEN, his aunt.

BRIAN STRANGE.

CARRAWAY PIM.

ANNE.

MR. PIM PASSES BY

ACT ONE

THE *morning-room at Marden House (Buckinghamshire) decided more than a hundred years ago that it was all right, and has not bothered about itself since. Visitors to the house have called the result such different adjectives as "mellow," "old-fashioned," "charming"—even "baronial" and "antique"; but nobody ever said it was "exciting." Sometimes* OLIVIA *wants it to be more exciting, and last week she let herself go over some new curtains. At present they are folded up and waiting for her; she still has the rings to put on. It is obvious that the curtains alone will overdo the excitement; they will have to be harmonised with a new carpet and cushions.* OLIVIA *has her eye on just the things, but one has to go carefully with* GEORGE. *What was good enough for his great-great-grandfather is good enough for him. However, we can trust* OLIVIA *to see him through it, although it may take time.*

There are two ways of coming into the room: by the open windows leading from the terrace or by the door. On this pleasant July morning MR. PIM *chooses the latter way—or rather* ANNE *chooses it for him; and old* MR. PIM, *wistful, kindly, gentle, little* MR. PIM, *living in some world of his own whither we cannot follow, ambles after her.*

ANNE

I'll tell Mr. Marden you're here, sir. Mr. Pim, isn't it?

PIM

(*Coming back to this world*). Yes—er—Mr. Carraway Pim. He doesn't know me, you understand, but if he could just see me for a moment—er—— (*He fumbles in his pockets.*) I gave you that letter?

ANNE

Yes, sir, I'll give it to him.

PIM

(*Bringing out a letter which is not the one he was looking for, but which reminds him of something else he has forgotten*). Dear me!

ANNE

Yes, sir?

PIM

I ought to have sent a telegram, but I can do it on my way back. You have a telegraph office in the village?

ANNE

Oh, yes, sir. If you turn to the left when you get outside the gates, it isn't more than a hundred yards down the hill.

PIM

Thank you, thank you. Very stupid of me to have forgotten.

(ANNE *goes out.* MR. PIM *wanders about the room humming to himself, and looking vaguely at the pictures. He has his back to the door as* DINAH *comes in. She is nineteen, very pretty, very happy, and full of boyish high spirits and conversation.*)

DINAH

Hullo!

PIM

(*Turning round*). Ah, good morning, Mrs. Marden. You must forgive my—er——

DINAH

Oh, I say, I'm not Mrs. Marden. I'm Dinah.

PIM

(*With a bow*). Then I will say, Good morning, Miss Diana.

DINAH

(*Reproachfully*). Now, look here, if you and I are going to be friends you mustn't do that. Dinah *not* Diana. Do remember it, there's a good man, because I get so tired of correcting people. Have you come to stay with us?

PIM

Well no, Miss—er—Dinah.

DINAH

(*Nodding*). That's right. I can see I shan't have to speak to *you* again. Now tell me *your* name, and I bet you I get it right first time. And do sit down.

PIM

(*Sitting down*). Thank you. My name is —er—Pim, Carraway Pim——

DINAH

Pim, that's easy.

PIM

And I have a letter of introduction to your father——

DINAH

Oh, no; now you're going wrong again, Mr. Pim. George isn't my father; he's my uncle. *Uncle* George—he doesn't like me calling him George. Olivia doesn't mind—I mean she doesn't mind being called Olivia, but George is rather touchy. You see, he's been my guardian since I was about two, and then about five years ago he married a widow called Mrs. Telworthy—that's Olivia—so she became my Aunt Olivia, only she lets me drop the Aunt. Got that?

PIM

(*A little alarmed*). I think so, Miss Marden.

DINAH

(*Admiringly*). I say, you *are* quick, Mr. Pim. Well, if you take my advice, when you've finished your business with George, you will hang about a bit and see if you can't see Olivia. She's simply devastating. I don't wonder George fell in love with her.

PIM

It's only the merest matter of business—just a few minutes with your uncle—I'm afraid I shall hardly——

DINAH

Well, you must please yourself, Mr. Pim. I'm just giving you a friendly word of advice. Naturally, I was awfully glad to get such a magnificent aunt, because, of course, marriage *is* rather a toss up, isn't it, and George might have gone off with anybody. It's different on the stage, where guardians always marry their wards, but George couldn't marry *me* because I'm his niece. Mind you, I don't say that I should have had him, because between ourselves he's a little bit old-fashioned.

PIM

So he married—er—Mrs. Marden instead.

DINAH

Mrs. Telworthy—don't say you've forgotten already, just when you were getting so good at names. Mrs. Telworthy. You see, Olivia married the Telworthy man and went to Australia with him, and he drank himself to death in the bush, or wherever you drink yourself to death out there, and Olivia came home to England, and met my uncle, and he fell in love with her and proposed to her, and he came into my room that night—I was about fourteen—and turned on the light and said, "Dinah, how would you like to have a beautiful aunt of your very own?" And I said: "Congratulations, George." That was the first time I called him George. Of course, I'd seen it coming for *weeks*. Telworthy, isn't it a funny name?

PIM

Very singular. From Australia, you say?

DINAH

Yes, I always say that he's probably still alive, and will turn up here one morning and annoy George, because that's what first husbands always do in books, but I'm afraid there's not much chance.

PIM

(*Shocked*). Miss Marden!

DINAH

Well, of course, I don't really *want* it to happen, but it *would* be rather exciting, wouldn't it? However, things like that never seem to occur down here, somehow. There was a hay-rick burnt last year about a mile away, but that isn't quite the same thing, is it?

PIM

No, I should say that that was certainly different.

DINAH

Of course, something very, very wonderful did happen last night, but I'm not sure if I know you well enough—— (*She looks at him hesitatingly.*)

PIM

(*Uncomfortably*). Really, Miss Marden, I am only a—a passer-by, here to-day and gone to-morrow. You really mustn't——

DINAH

And yet there's something about you, Mr. Pim, which inspires confidence. The fact is —(*in a stage whisper*)—I got engaged last night!

PIM

Dear me, let me congratulate you.

DINAH

I expect that's why George is keeping you such a long time. Brian, my young man, the well-known painter—only nobody has ever heard of him—he's smoking a pipe with George in the library and asking for his niece's hand. Isn't it exciting? You're really rather lucky, Mr. Pim—I mean being told so soon. Even Olivia doesn't know yet.

PIM

(*Rising*). Yes, yes. I congratulate you, Miss Marden. Perhaps it would be better—— (ANNE *comes in.*)

ANNE

Mr. Marden is out at the moment, sir—— Oh, I didn't see you, Miss Dinah.

DINAH

It's all right, Anne. *I'm* looking after Mr. Pim.

ANNE

Yes, Miss.
(*She goes out.*)

DINAH

(*Excitedly*). That's me. They can't discuss me in the library without breaking down, so they're walking up and down outside, and slashing at the thistles in order to conceal their emotion. *You* know. I expect Brian——

PIM

(*Looking at his watch*). Yes, I think, Miss Marden, I had better go now and return a little later. I have a telegram which I want to send, and perhaps by the time I came back——

DINAH

Oh, but how disappointing of you, when we were getting on together so nicely. And it was just going to be your turn to tell me all about *your*self.

PIM

I have really nothing to tell, Miss Marden. I have a letter of introduction to Mr. Marden, who in turn will give me, I hope, a letter to a certain distinguished man whom it is necessary for me to meet. That is all. (*Holding out his hand.*) And now, Miss Marden——

DINAH

Oh, I'll start you on your way to the post office. I want to know if you're married, and all that sort of thing. You've got heaps to tell me, Mr. Pim. Have you got your hat? That's right. Then we'll—hullo, here's Brian.

(BRIAN STRANGE *comes in at the windows. He is what* GEORGE *calls a damned futuristic painter-chap, aged twenty-four. To look at, he is a very pleasant boy, rather untidily dressed.*)

BRIAN

(*Nodding*). How do you do?

DINAH

(*Seizing him*). Brian, this is Mr. Pim. Mr. Carraway Pim. He's been telling me all about himself. It's so interesting. He's just going to send a telegram, and then he's coming back again. Mr. Pim, this is Brian —*you* know.

BRIAN

(*Smiling and shaking hands*). How do you do?

DINAH

(*Pleadingly*). You *won't* mind going to the post office by yourself, will you, because, you see, Brian and I—(*She looks lovingly at* BRIAN.)

PIM

(*Because they are so young*). Miss Dinah and Mr.—er—Brian, I have only come into your lives for a moment, and it is probable that I shall now pass out of them for ever, but you will allow an old man——

DINAH

Oh, not old!

PIM

(*Chuckling happily*). Well, a middle-aged man—to wish you both every happiness in the years that you have before you. Good-bye, good-bye.
(*He disappears gently through the windows.*)

DINAH

Brian, he'll get lost if he goes that way.

BRIAN

(*Going to the windows and calling after him*). Round to the left, sir. . . . That's right. (*He comes back into the room.*) Rum old bird. Who is he?

DINAH

Darling, you haven't kissed me yet.

BRIAN

(*Taking her in his arms*). I oughtn't to, but then one never ought to do the nice things.

DINAH

Why oughtn't you?
(*They sit on the sofa together.*)

BRIAN

Well, we said we'd be good until we'd told your uncle and aunt all about it. You see, being a guest in their house——

DINAH

But, darling child, what *have* you been doing all this morning *except* telling George?

BRIAN

Trying to tell George.

DINAH

(*Nodding*). Yes, of course, there's a difference.

BRIAN

I think he guessed there was something up, and he took me down to see the pigs—he said he had to see the pigs at once—I don't know why; an appointment perhaps. And we talked about pigs all the way, and I couldn't say, "Talking about pigs, I want to marry your niece——"

DINAH

(*With mock indignation*). Of course you couldn't.

BRIAN

No. Well, you see how it was. And then when we'd finished talking about pigs, we started talking *to* the pigs——

DINAH

(*Eagerly*). Oh, *how* is Arnold?

BRIAN

The little black-and-white one? He's very jolly, I believe, but naturally I wasn't thinking about him much. I was wondering how to begin. And then Lumsden came up, and wanted to talk pig-food, and the atmosphere grew less and less romantic, and —and I gradually drifted away.

DINAH

Poor darling. Well, we shall have to approach him through Olivia.

BRIAN

But I always wanted to tell her first; she's so much easier. Only you wouldn't let me.

DINAH

That's your fault, Brian. You would tell Olivia that she ought to have orange-and-black curtains.

BRIAN

But she *wants* orange-and-black curtains.

DINAH

Yes, but George says he's not going to have any futuristic nonsense in an honest English country house, which has been good enough for his father and his grandfather and his great-grandfather, and—and all the rest of them. So there's a sort of strained feeling between Olivia and George just now, and if Olivia were to—sort of recommend you, well, it wouldn't do you much good.

BRIAN

(*Looking at her*). I see. Of course I know what *you* want, Dinah.

DINAH

What do I want?

BRIAN

You want a secret engagement, and notes left under door-mats, and meetings by the withered thorn, when all the household is asleep. *I* know you.

DINAH

Oh, but it is such fun! I love meeting people by withered thorns.

BRIAN

Well, I'm not going to have it.

DINAH

(*Childishly*). Oh, George! Look at us being husbandy!

BRIAN

You babe! I adore you. (*He kisses her and holds her away from him and looks at her.*) You know, you're rather throwing yourself away on me. Do you mind?

DINAH

Not a bit.

BRIAN

We shall never be rich, but we shall have lots of fun, and meet interesting people, and feel that we're doing something worth doing, and not getting paid nearly enough for it, and we can curse the Academy together and the British Public, and—oh, it's an exciting life.

DINAH

(*Seeing it*). I shall love it.

BRIAN

I'll make you love it. You shan't be sorry, Dinah.

DINAH

You shan't be sorry either, Brian.

BRIAN

(*Looking at her lovingly*). Oh, I know I shan't. . . . What will Olivia think about it? Will she be surprised?

DINAH

She's never surprised. She always seems to have thought of things about a week before they happen. George just begins to get hold of them about a week *after* they've happened. (*Considering him.*) After all, there's no reason why George *shouldn't* like you, darling.

BRIAN

I'm not his sort, you know.

DINAH

You're more Olivia's sort. Well, we'll tell Olivia this morning.

OLIVIA

(*Coming in*). And what are you going to tell Olivia this morning? (*She looks at them with a smile.*) Oh, well, I think I can guess.
(*Shall be describe* OLIVIA? *But you will know all about her before the day is over.*)

DINAH

(*Jumping up*). Olivia, darling!

BRIAN

(*Following*). Say you understand, Mrs. Marden.

OLIVIA

Mrs. Marden, I am afraid, is a very dense person, Brian, but I think if you asked Olivia if she understood——

BRIAN

Bless you, Olivia, I knew you'd be on our side.

DINAH

Of course she would.

OLIVIA

I don't know if it's usual to kiss an aunt-in-law, Brian, but Dinah is such a very special sort of niece that—(*She inclines her cheek and* BRIAN *kisses it.*)

DINAH

I say, you *are* in luck to-day, Brian.

OLIVIA

(*Going over to her chair by the work-table and getting to business with the curtains*). And how many people have been told the good news?

BRIAN

Nobody yet.

DINAH

Except Mr. Pim.

BRIAN

Oh, does *he*——

OLIVIA

Who's Mr. Pim?

DINAH

Oh, he just happened—I say, are those *the* curtains? Then you're going to have them after all?

OLIVIA

(*With an air of surprise*). After all what? But I decided on them long ago. (*To* BRIAN) You haven't told George yet?

BRIAN

I began to, you know, but I never got any farther than "Er—there's just—er——"

DINAH

George *would* talk about pigs all the time.

OLIVIA

Well, I suppose you want me to help you.

DINAH

Do, darling.

BRIAN

It would be awfully decent of you. Of course, I'm not quite his sort really——

DINAH

You're *my* sort.

BRIAN

But I don't think he objects to me, and——

(GEORGE *comes in, a typical, narrow-minded, honest country gentleman of forty-odd.*)

GEORGE

(*At the windows*). What's all this about a Mr. Pim? (*He kicks some of the mud off his boots.*) Who is he? Where is he? I had most important business with Lumsden, and the girl comes down and cackles about a Mr. Pim, or Ping, or something. Where did I put his card? (*Bringing it out.*) Carraway Pim. Never heard of him in my life.

DINAH

He said he had a letter of introduction, Uncle George.

GEORGE

Oh, *you* saw him, did you? Yes, that reminds me, there was a letter— (*He brings it out and reads it.*)

DINAH

He had to send a telegram. He's coming back.

OLIVIA

Pass me those scissors, Brian.

BRIAN

These? (*He picks them up and comes close to her.*)

OLIVIA

Thank you. (*She indicates* GEORGE'S *back. "Now?" says* BRIAN *with his eyebrows. She nods.*)

GEORGE

(*Reading*). Ah, well, a friend of Brymer's. Glad to oblige him. Yes, I know the man he wants. Coming back, you say, Dinah? Then I'll be going back. Send him down to the farm, Olivia, when he comes. (*To* BRIAN) Hallo, what happened to *you?*

OLIVIA

Don't go, George, there something we want to talk about.

GEORGE

Hallo, what's this?

BRIAN

(*To* OLIVIA). Shall I——?

OLIVIA

Yes.

BRIAN

(*Stepping out*). I've been wanting to tell you all this morning, sir, only I didn't seem to have an opportunity of getting it out.

GEORGE

Well, what is it?

BRIAN

I want to marry Dinah, sir.

GEORGE

You want to marry Dinah? God bless my soul!

DINAH

(*Rushing to him and putting her cheek against his coat*). Oh, do say you like the idea, Uncle George.

GEORGE

Like the idea! Have you heard of this nonsense, Olivia?

OLIVIA

They've just this moment told me, George. I think they would be happy together.

GEORGE

(*To* BRIAN). And what do you propose to be happy together *on?*

BRIAN

Well, of course, it doesn't amount to much at present, but we shan't starve.

DINAH

Brian got fifty pounds for a picture last March!

GEORGE

(*A little upset by this*). Oh! (*Recovering gamely.*) And how many pictures have you sold since?

BRIAN

Well, none, but——

GEORGE

None! And I don't wonder. Who the devil is going to buy pictures with triangular clouds and square sheep? And they call that Art nowadays! Good God, man, (*waving him to the windows*) go outside and *look* at the clouds!

OLIVIA

If he draws round clouds in future, George, will you let him marry Dinah?

GEORGE

What—what? Yes, of course, you *would* be on his side—all this Futuristic nonsense. I'm just taking these clouds as an example. I suppose I can see as well as any man in the county, and I say that clouds *aren't* triangular.

BRIAN

After all, sir, at my age one is naturally experimenting, and trying to find one's (*with a laugh*)—well, it sounds priggish, but one's medium of expression. I shall find out what I want to do directly, but I think I shall always be able to earn enough to live on. Well, I have for the last three years.

GEORGE

I see, and now you want to experiment with a wife, and you propose to start experimenting with *my* niece?

BRIAN

(*With a shrug*). Well, of course, if you——

OLIVIA

You could help the experiment, darling, by giving Dinah a good allowance until she's twenty-one.

GEORGE

Help the experiment! I don't *want* to help the experiment.

OLIVIA

(*Apologetically*). Oh, I thought you did.

GEORGE

You will talk as if I was made of money. What with taxes always going up and rents always going down, it's as much as we can do to rub along as we are, without making allowances to everybody who thinks she wants to get married. (*To* BRIAN) And that's thanks to you, my friend.

BRIAN

(*Surprised*). To me?

OLIVIA

You never told me, darling. What's Brian been doing?

DINAH

(*Indignantly*). He hasn't been doing anything.

GEORGE

He's one of your Socialists who go turning the country upside down.

OLIVIA

But even Socialists must get married sometimes.

GEORGE

I don't see any necessity.

OLIVIA

But you'd have nobody to damn after dinner, darling, if they all died out.

BRIAN

Really, sir, I don't see what my politics and my art have got to do with it. I'm perfectly ready not to talk about either when I'm in your house, and as Dinah doesn't seem to object to them——

DINAH

I should think she doesn't.

GEORGE

Oh, you can get round the women, I daresay.

BRIAN

Well, it's Dinah I want to marry and live with. So what it really comes to is that you don't think I can support a wife.

GEORGE

Well, if you're going to do it by selling pictures, I don't think you can.

BRIAN

All right, tell me how much you want me to earn in a year, and I'll earn it.

GEORGE

(*Hedging*). It isn't merely a question of money. I just mention that as one thing—one of the important things. In addition to that, I think you are both too young to marry. I don't think you know your own minds, and I am not at all persuaded that, with what I venture to call your outrageous tastes, you and my niece will live happily together. Just because she thinks she loves you, Dinah may persuade herself now that she agrees with all you say and do, but she has been properly brought up in an honest English country household, and—er—she—well, in short, I cannot at all approve of any engagement between you. (*Getting up.*) Olivia, if this Mr.—er—Pim comes, I shall be down at the farm. You might send him along to me.
(*He walks towards the windows.*)

BRIAN

(*Indignantly*). Is there any reason why I shouldn't marry a girl who has been properly brought up?

GEORGE

I think you know my views, Strange.

OLIVIA

George, wait a moment, dear. We can't quite leave it like this.

GEORGE

I have said all I want to say on the subject.

OLIVIA

Yes, darling, but I haven't begun to say all that *I* want to say on the subject.

GEORGE

Of course, if you have anything to say, Olivia, I will listen to it; but I don't know that this is quite the time, or that you have chosen—(*looking darkly at the curtains*) —quite the occupation likely to—er—endear your views to me.

DINAH

(*Mutinously*). I may as well tell you, Uncle George, that *I* have got a good deal to say, too.

OLIVIA

I can guess what you are going to say, Dinah, and I think you had better keep it for the moment.

DINAH

(*Meekly*). Yes, Aunt Ollivia.

OLIVIA

Brian, you might take her outside for a walk. I expect you have plenty to talk about.

GEORGE

Now mind, Strange, no love-making. I put you on your honor about that.

BRIAN

I'll do my best to avoid it, sir.

DINAH

(*Cheekily*). May I take his arm if we go up a hill?

OLIVIA

I'm sure you'll know how to behave—both of you.

BRIAN

Come on, then, Dinah.

DINAH

Righto.

GEORGE

(*As they go*). And if you do see any clouds, Strange, take a good look at them. (*He chuckles to himself.*) Triangular clouds—I never heard of such nonsense. (*He goes back to his chair at the writing-table.*) Futuristic rubbish. . . . Well, Olivia?

OLIVIA

Well, George?

GEORGE

What are you doing?

OLIVIA

Making curtains, George. Won't they be rather sweet? Oh, but I forgot—you don't like them.

GEORGE

I don't like them, and what is more, I don't mean to have them in my house. As I told you yesterday, this is the house of a simple country gentleman, and I don't want any of these new-fangled ideas in it.

OLIVIA

Is marrying for love a new-fangled idea?

GEORGE

We'll come to that directly. None of you women can keep to the point. What I am saying now is that the house of my fathers and forefathers is good enough for me.

OLIVIA

Do you know, George, I can hear one of your ancestors saying that to his wife in their smelly old cave, when the new-fangled idea of building houses was first suggested. "The Cave of my Fathers is——"

GEORGE

That's ridiculous. Naturally we must have progress. But that's just the point. (*Indicating the curtains.*) I don't call this sort of thing progress. It's—ah—retrogression.

OLIVIA

Well, anyhow, it's pretty.

GEORGE

There I disagree with you. And I must say once more that I will not have them hanging in my house.

OLIVIA

Very well, George. (*But she goes on working.*)

GEORGE

That being so, I don't see the necessity of going on with them.

OLIVIA

Well, I must do something with them now I've got the material. I thought perhaps I could sell them when they're finished—as we're so poor.

GEORGE

What do you mean—so poor?

OLIVIA

Well, you said just now that you couldn't give Dinah an allowance because rents had gone down.

GEORGE

(*Annoyed*). Confound it, Olivia! Keep to the point! We'll talk about Dinah's affairs directly. We're discussing our own affairs at the moment.

OLIVIA

But what is there to discuss?

GEORGE

Those ridiculous things.

OLIVIA

But we've finished that. You've said you wouldn't have them hanging in your house, and I've said, "Very well, George." Now we can go on to Dinah and Brian.

GEORGE

(*Shouting*). But put these beastly things away.

OLIVIA

(*Rising and gathering up the curtains*). Very well, George. (*She puts them away, slowly, gracefully. There is an uncomfortable silence. Evidently somebody ought to apologize.*)

GEORGE

(*Realizing that he is the one*). Er—look here, Olivia, old girl, you've been a jolly good wife to me, and we don't often have rows, and if I've been rude to you about this—lost my temper a bit perhaps, what? —I'll say I'm sorry. May I have a kiss?

OLIVIA

(*Holding up her face*). George darling! (*He kisses her.*) Do you love me?

GEORGE

You know I do, old girl.

OLIVIA

As much as Brian loves Dinah?

GEORGE

(*Stiffly*). I've said all I want to say about that. (*He goes away from her.*)

OLIVIA

Oh, but there must be lots you want to say—and perhaps don't like to. Do tell me, darling.

GEORGE

What it comes to is this. I consider that Dinah is too young to choose a husband for herself, and that Strange isn't the husband I should choose for her.

OLIVIA

You were calling him Brian yesterday.

GEORGE

Yesterday I regarded him as a boy; now he wants me to look upon him as a man.

OLIVIA

He's twenty-four.

GEORGE

And Dinah's nineteen. Ridiculous!

OLIVIA

If he'd been a Conservative, and thought that clouds were round, I suppose he'd have seemed older, somehow.

GEORGE

That's a different point altogether. That has nothing to do with his age.

OLIVIA

(*Innocently*). Oh, I thought it had.

GEORGE

What I am objecting to is these ridiculously early marriages before either party knows its own mind, much less the mind of the other party. Such marriages invariably lead to unhappiness.

OLIVIA

Of course, my marriage wasn't a happy one.

GEORGE

As you know, Olivia, I dislike speaking about your first marriage at all, and I had no intention of bringing it up now, but since you mention it—well, that is a case in point.

OLIVIA

(*Looking back at it*). When I was eighteen, I was in love. Or perhaps I only thought I was, and I don't know if I should have been happy or not if I had married him. But my father made me marry a man called Jacob Telworthy; and when things were too hot for him in England—"too hot for him"—I think that was the expression we used in those days—then we went to Australia, and I left him there, and the only happy moment I had in all my married life was on the morning when I saw in the papers that he was dead.

GEORGE

(*Very uncomfortable*). Yes, yes, my dear, I know. You must have had a terrible time. I can hardly bear to think about it. My only hope is that I have made up to you for it in some degree. But I don't see what bearing it has upon Dinah's case.

OLIVIA

Oh, none, except that *my* father *liked* Jacob's political opinions and his views on art. I expect that that was why he chose him for me.

GEORGE

You seem to think that I wish to choose a husband for Dinah. I don't at all. Let her choose whom she likes as long as he can support her and there's a chance of their being happy together. Now, with regard to this fellow——

OLIVIA

You mean Brian?

GEORGE

He's got no money, and he's been brought up in quite a different way from Dinah. Dinah may be prepared to believe that—er—all cows are blue, and that—er—waves are square, but she won't go on believing it for ever.

OLIVIA

Neither will Brian.

GEORGE

Well, that's what I keep telling him, only he won't see it. Just as I keep telling you about those ridiculous curtains. It seems to me that I am the only person in the house with any eyesight left.

OLIVIA

Perhaps you are, darling; but you must let us find out our own mistakes for ourselves. At any rate, Brian is a gentleman; he loves Dinah, Dinah loves him; he's earning enough to support himself, and you are earning enough to support Dinah. I think it's worth risking, George.

GEORGE

(*Stiffly*). I can only say the whole question demands much more anxious thought than you seem to have given it. You say that he is a gentleman. He knows how to behave, I admit; but if his morals are as topsy-turvy as his tastes and—er—politics, as I've no doubt they are, then—er—— In short, I do *not* approve of Brian Strange as a husband for my niece and ward.

OLIVIA

(*Looking at him thoughtfully*). You *are* a curious mixture, George. You were so very unconventional when you married me, and you're so very conventional when Brian wants to marry Dinah. . . . George Marden to marry the widow of a convict!

GEORGE

Convict! What do you mean?

OLIVIA

Jacob Telworthy, convict—I forget his number—surely I told you all this, dear, when we got engaged?

GEORGE

Never!

OLIVIA

I told you how he carelessly put the wrong signature to a cheque for a thousand pounds in England; how he made a little mistake about two or three companies he'd promoted in Australia; and how——

GEORGE

Yes, yes, but you never told me he was *convicted!*

OLIVIA

What difference does it make?

GEORGE

My dear Olivia, if you can't see that—a convict!

OLIVIA

So, you see, we needn't be too particular about our niece, need we?

GEORGE

I think we had better leave your first husband out of the conversation altogether. I never wished to refer to him; I never wish to hear about him again. I certainly had not realized that he was actually—er—*convicted* for his—er——

OLIVIA

Mistakes.

GEORGE

Well, we needn't go into that. As for this other matter, I don't for a moment take it seriously. Dinah is an exceptionally pretty girl, and young Strange is a good-looking boy. If they are attracted to each other, it is a mere outward attraction which I am convinced will not lead to any lasting happiness. That must be regarded as my last word in the matter, Olivia. If this Mr.—er—what was his name, comes, I shall be down at the farm.

(*He goes out by the door.*)

(*Left alone,* OLIVIA *brings out her curtains again, and gets calmly to work upon them.*)

(DINAH *and* BRIAN *come in by the windows.*)

DINAH

Finished?

OLIVIA

Oh no, I've got all these rings to put on.

DINAH

I meant talking to George.

BRIAN

We walked about outside——

DINAH

Until we heard him *not* talking to you any more——

BRIAN

And we didn't kiss each other once.

DINAH

Brian was very George-like. He wouldn't even let me tickle the back of his neck. (*She goes up suddenly to* OLIVIA *and kneels by her and kisses her.*) Darling, being George-like is a very nice thing to be—I mean a nice thing for other people to be—I mean—oh, you know what I mean. But say that he's going to be decent about it.

OLIVIA

Of course he is, Dinah.

BRIAN

You mean he'll let me come here as——

DINAH

As my young man?

OLIVIA

Oh, I think so.

DINAH

Olivia, you're a wonder. Have you really talked him round?

OLIVIA

I haven't said anything yet. But I daresay I shall think of something.

DINAH

(*Disappointedly*). Oh!

BRIAN

(*Making the best of it*). After all, Dinah, I'm going back to London to-morrow——

OLIVIA

You can be good for one more day, Dinah, and then when Brian isn't here, we'll see what we can do.

DINAH

Yes, but I didn't want him to go back to-morrow.

BRIAN

(*Sternly*). Must. Hard work before me. Earn thousands a year. Paint the Mayor and Corporation of Pudsey, life-size, including chains of office; paint slice of haddock on plate. Copy Landseer for old gentleman in Bayswater. Design antimacassar for middle-aged sofa in Streatham. Earn a living for you, Dinah.

DINAH

(*Giggling*). Oh, Brian, you're heavenly. What fun we shall have when we're married.

BRIAN

(*Stiffly*). Sir Brian Strange, R.A., if you please, Miss Marden. Sir Brian Strange, R. A., writes: "Your Sanogene has proved a most excellent tonic. After completing the third acre of my Academy picture 'The Mayor and Corporation of Pudsey' I was completely exhausted, but one bottle of Sanogene revived me, and I finished the remaining seven acres at a single sitting."

OLIVIA

(*Looking about her*). Brian, find my scissors for me.

BRIAN

Scissors. (*Looking for them.*) Sir Brian Strange, R.A., looks for scissors. (*Finding them.*) Aha! Once more we must record an unqualified success for the eminent Academician. Your scissors.

OLIVIA

Thank you so much.

DINAH

Come on, Brian, let's go out. I feel open-airy.

OLIVIA

Don't be late for lunch, there's good people. Lady Marden is coming.

DINAH

Aunt Juli-ah! Help! (*She faints in* BRIAN'S *arms.*) That means a clean pinafore. Brian, you'll jolly well have to brush your hair.

BRIAN

(*Feeling it*). I suppose there's no time now to go up to London and get it cut?

(*Enter* ANNE, *followed by* PIM.)

ANNE

Mr. Pim!

DINAH

(*Delighted*). Hullo, Mr. Pim! Here we are again! You can't get rid of us so easily, you see.

PIM

I—er—dear Miss Marden——

OLIVIA

How do you do, Mr. Pim? I can't get up, but do come and sit down. My husband will be here in a minute. Anne, send somebody down to the farm——

ANNE

I think I heard the Master in the library, madam.

OLIVIA

Oh, will you tell him then?

ANNE

Yes, madam.

(ANNE *goes out.*)

OLIVIA

You'll stay to lunch, of course, Mr. Pim?

DINAH

Oh, do!

PIM

It's very kind of you, Mrs. Marden, but——

DINAH

Oh, you simply must, Mr. Pim. You haven't told us half enough about yourself yet. I want to hear all about your early life.

OLIVIA

Dinah!

PIM

Oh, we are almost, I might say, old friends, Mrs. Marden.

DINAH

Of course we are. He knows Brian, too. There's more in Mr. Pim than you think. You *will* stay to lunch, won't you?

PIM

It's very kind of you to ask me, Mrs. Marden, but I am lunching with the Trevors.

OLIVIA

Oh, well, you must come to lunch another day.

DINAH

The reason why we like Mr. Pim so much is that he was the first person to congratulate us. We feel that he is going to have a great influence on our lives.

PIM

(*To* OLIVIA). I, so to speak, stumbled on the engagement this morning and—er——

OLIVIA

I see. Children, you must go and tidy yourselves up. Run along.

BRIAN

Sir Brian and Lady Strange never run; they walk. (*Offering his arm.*) Madam!

DINAH

(*Taking it*). Au revoir, Mr. Pim. (*Dramatically.*) We——shall——meet——*again!*

PIM

(*Chuckling*). Good morning, Miss Dinah.

BRIAN

Good morning.
(*He and* DINAH *go out.*)

OLIVIA

You must forgive them, Mr. Pim. They're such children. And naturally they're rather excited just now.

PIM

Oh, not at all, Mrs. Marden.

OLIVIA

Of course you won't say anything about their engagement. We only heard about it five minutes ago, and nothing has been settled yet.

PIM

Of course, of course!
(*Enter* GEORGE.)

GEORGE

Ah, Mr. Pim, we meet at last. Sorry to have kept you waiting before.

PIM

The apology should come from me, Mr. Marden, for having—er——

GEORGE

Not at all. Very glad to meet you now. Any friend of Brymer's. You want a letter to this man Fanshawe?

OLIVIA

Shall I be in your way at all?

PIM

Oh, no, no, please don't.

GEORGE

It's only just a question of a letter. (*Going to his desk.*) Fanshawe will put you in the way of seeing all that you want to see. He's a very old friend of mine. (*Taking a sheet of notepaper.*) You'll stay to lunch, of course?

PIM

I'm afraid I am lunching with the Trevors.

GEORGE

Oh, well, they'll look after you all right. Good chap, Trevor.

PIM

(*To* OLIVIA). You see, Mrs. Marden, I have only recently arrived from Australia after travelling about the world for some years, and I'm rather out of touch with my—er—fellow-workers in London.

OLIVIA

Oh yes. You've been in Australia, Mr. Pim?

GEORGE

(*Disliking Australia*). I shan't be a moment, Mr. Pim. (*He frowns at* OLIVIA.)

PIM

Oh, that's all right, thank you. (*To* OLIVIA) Oh yes, I have been in Australia more than once in the last few years.

OLIVIA

Really? I used to live at Sydney many years ago. Do you know Sydney at all?

GEORGE

(*Detesting Sydney*). H'r'm! Perhaps I'd better mention that you are a friend of the Trevors?

PIM

Thank you, thank you. (*To* OLIVIA.) Indeed yes, I spent several months in Sydney.

OLIVIA

How curious. I wonder if we have any friends in common there.

GEORGE

(*Hastily*). Extremely unlikely, I should think. Sydney is a very big place.

PIM

True, but the world is a very small place, Mr. Marden. I had a remarkable instance of that, coming over on the boat this last time.

GEORGE

Ah! (*Feeling that the conversation is now safe, he resumes his letter.*)

PIM

Yes. There was a man I used to employ in Sydney some years ago, a bad fellow, I'm afraid, Mrs. Marden, who had been in prison for some kind of fraudulent company-promoting and had taken to drink and—and so on.

OLIVIA

Yes, yes, I understand.

PIM

Drinking himself to death, I should have said. I gave him at the most another year to live. Yet to my amazement the first person I saw as I stepped on board the boat that brought me to England last week was this fellow. There was no mistaking him. I spoke to him, in fact; we recognized each other.

OLIVIA

Really?

PIM

He was travelling steerage; we didn't meet again on board, and as it happened at Marseilles, this poor fellow—er—now what *was* his name? A very unusual one. Began with a—a T, I think.

OLIVIA

(*With suppressed feeling*). Yes, Mr. Pim, yes? (*She puts out a hand to* GEORGE.)

GEORGE

(*In an undertone*). Nonsense, dear!

PIM

(*Triumphantly*). I've got it! Telworthy!

OLIVIA

Telworthy!

GEORGE

Good God!

PIM

(*A little surprised at the success of his story*). An unusual name, is it not? Not a name you could forget when once you had heard it.

OLIVIA

(*With feeling*). No, it is not a name you could forget when once you had heard it.

GEORGE

(*Hastily coming over to* PIM). Quite so, Mr. Pim, a most remarkable name, a most odd story altogether. Well, well, here's your letter, and if you're sure you won't stay to lunch——

PIM

I'm afraid not, thank you. You see, I——

GEORGE

The Trevors, yes. I'll just see you on your way——(*To* OLIVIA) Er—my dear——

OLIVIA

(*Holding out her hand, but not looking at him*). Good-bye, Mr. Pim.

PIM

Good-bye, good-bye!

GEORGE

(*Leading the way through the windows*) This way, this way. Quicker for you.

PIM

Thank you, thank you.

(GEORGE *hurries* MR. PIM *out.*)

(OLIVIA *sits there and looks into the past. Now and then she shudders.*)

(GEORGE *comes back.*)

GEORGE

Good God! Telworthy! Is it possible?

(*Before* OLIVIA *can answer,* LADY MARDEN *is announced. They pull themselves together and greet her.*)

ACT TWO

LUNCH *is over and coffee has been served on the terrace. Conversation drags on, to the satisfaction of* LADY MARDEN, *but of nobody else.* GEORGE *and* OLIVIA *want to be alone; so do* BRIAN *and* DINAH. *At last* BRIAN *murmurs something about a cigarette-case; and, catching* DINAH'*s eye, comes into the house. He leans against the sofa and waits for* DINAH.

DINAH

(*Loudly as she comes in*). Have you found it?

BRIAN

Found what?

DINAH

(*In her ordinary voice*). That was just for *their* benefit. I said I'd help you find it. It *is* your cigarette-case we're looking for, isn't it?

BRIAN

(*Taking it out*). Yes. Have one?

DINAH

No, thank you, darling. Aunt Juli-ah still thinks it's unladylike. . . . Have you ever seen her beagling?

BRIAN

No. Is that very ladylike?

DINAH

Very. . . . I say, what has happened, do you think?

BRIAN

Everything. I love you, and you love me.

DINAH

Silly! I meant between George and Olivia. Didn't you notice them at lunch?

BRIAN

I noticed that you seemed to be doing most of the talking. But then I've noticed that before sometimes. Do you think Olivia and your uncle have quarrelled because of *us?*

DINAH

Of course not. George may *think* he has quarrelled, but I'm quite sure Olivia hasn't. No, I believe Mr. Pim's at the bottom of it. He's brought some terribly sad news about George's investments. The old home will have to be sold up.

BRIAN

Good. Then your uncle won't mind your marrying me.

DINAH

Yes, darling, but you must be more dramatic about it than that. "George," you must say, with tears in your eyes, "I cannot pay off the whole of the mortgage for you. I have only two and ninepence; but at least let me take your niece off your hands." Then George will thump you on the back and say gruffly, "You're a good fellow, Brian, a damn good fellow," and he'll blow his nose very loudly, and say, "Confound this cigar, it won't draw properly." (*She gives a rough impression of* GEORGE *doing it.*)

BRIAN

Dinah, you're a heavenly idiot. And you've simply got to marry me, uncles or no uncles.

DINAH

It will have to be "uncles," I'm afraid, because, you see, I'm his ward, and I can get sent to Chancery or Coventry or somewhere beastly, if I marry without his consent. Haven't *you* got anybody who objects to your marrying *me?*

BRIAN

Nobody, thank Heaven.

DINAH

Well, that's rather disappointing of you. I saw myself fascinating your aged father at the same time that you were fascinating George. I should have done it much better than you. As a George-fascinator you aren't very successful, sweetheart.

BRIAN

What am I like as a Dinah-fascinator?

DINAH

Plus six, darling.

BRIAN

Then I'll stick to that and leave George to Olivia.

DINAH

I expect she'll manage him all right. I have great faith in Olivia. But you'll marry me, anyhow, won't you, Brian?

BRIAN

I will.

DINAH

Even if we have to wait till I'm twenty-one?

BRIAN

Even if we have to wait till you're fifty-one.

DINAH

(*Holding out her hands to him*). Darling!

BRIAN

(*Uneasily*). I say, don't do that.

DINAH

Why not?

BRIAN

Well, I promised I wouldn't kiss you.

DINAH

Oh! . . . Well, you might just *send* me a kiss. You can look the other way as if you didn't know I was here.

BRIAN

Like this?
(*He looks the other way, kisses the tips of his fingers, and flicks it carelessly in her direction.*)

DINAH

That was a lovely one. Now here's one coming for you.
(*He catches it gracefully and conveys it to his mouth.*)

BRIAN

(*With a low bow*). Madam, I thank you.

DINAH

(*Curtseying*). Your servant, Mr. Strange.

OLIVIA

(*From outside*). Dinah!

DINAH

(*Jumping up*). Hullo!
(OLIVIA *comes in through the windows, followed by* GEORGE *and* LADY MARDEN, *the latter a vigorous young woman of sixty-odd, who always looks as if she were beagling.*)

OLIVIA

Aunt Julia wants to see the pigs, dear. I wish you'd take her down. I'm rather tired, and your uncle has some business to attend to.

LADY MARDEN

I've always said that you don't take enough exercise, Olivia. Look at me—sixty-five and proud of it.

OLIVIA

Yes, Aunt Julia, you're wonderful.

DINAH

How old would Olivia be if she took exercise?

GEORGE

Don't stand about asking silly questions, Dinah. Your aunt hasn't much time.

BRIAN

May I come, too, Lady Marden?

LADY MARDEN

Well, a little exercise wouldn't do *you* any harm, Mr. Strange. You're an artist, ain't you?

BRIAN

Well, I try to paint.

DINAH

He sold a picture last March for——

GEORGE

Yes, yes, never mind that now.

LADY MARDEN

Unhealthy life. Well, come along.
(*She strides out, followed by* DINAH *and* BRIAN.)
(GEORGE *sits down at his desk with his head in his hand, and stabs the blotting-paper with a pen.* OLIVIA *takes the curtains with her to the sofa and begins to work on them.*)

GEORGE

(*Looking up and seeing them*). Really, Olivia, we've got something more important, more vital to us than curtains, to discuss, now that we *are* alone at last.

OLIVIA

I wasn't going to discuss them, dear.

GEORGE

I'm always glad to see Aunt Julia in my house, but I wish she hadn't chosen this day of all days to come to lunch.

OLIVIA

It wasn't Aunt Julia's fault. It was really Mr. Pim who chose the wrong day.

GEORGE

(*Fiercely*). Good Heavens, is it true?

OLIVIA

About Jacob Telworthy?

GEORGE

You told me he was dead. You always said that he was dead. You—you——

OLIVIA

Well, I always thought that he was dead. He was as dead as anybody could be. All the papers said he was dead.

GEORGE

(*Scornfully*). The papers!

OLIVIA

(*As if this would settle it for* GEORGE). The *Times* said he was dead. There was a paragraph about him. Apparently even his death was fraudulent.

GEORGE

Yes, yes, I'm not blaming you, Olivia, but what are we going to do, that's the question, what are we going to do? My God, it's horrible! You've never been married to me at all! You don't seem to understand.

OLIVIA

It is a little difficult to realize. You see, it doesn't seem to have made any difference to our happiness.

GEORGE

No, that's what's so terrible. I mean—well, of course, we were quite innocent in the matter. But, at the same time, nothing can get over the fact that we—we had no right to—to be happy.

OLIVIA

Would you rather we had been miserable?

GEORGE

You're Telworthy's wife, that's what you don't seem to understand. You're Telworthy's wife. You—er—forgive me, Olivia, but it's the horrible truth—you committed bigamy when you married me. (*In horror*) Bigamy!

OLIVIA

It is an ugly word, isn't it?

GEORGE

Yes, but don't you understand—— (*He jumps up and comes over to her.*) Look here, Olivia, old girl, the whole thing is nonsense, eh? It isn't your husband, it's some other Telworthy that this fellow met. That's right, isn't it? Some other shady swindler who turned up on the boat, eh? This sort of thing doesn't happen to people like *us*—committing bigamy and all that. Some other fellow.

OLIVIA

(*Shaking her head*). I knew all the shady swindlers in Sydney, George. . . . They came to dinner. . . . There were no others called Telworthy.

(GEORGE *goes back despondently to his seat.*)

GEORGE

Well, what are we going to do?

OLIVIA

You sent Mr. Pim away so quickly. He might have told us things. Telworthy's plans. Where he is now. You hurried him away so quickly.

GEORGE

I've sent a note round to ask him to come back. My one idea at the moment was to get him out of the house—to hush things up.

OLIVIA

You can't hush up two husbands.

GEORGE

(*In despair*). You can't. Everybody will know. Everybody!

OLIVIA

The children, Aunt Julia, they may as well know now as later. Mr. Pim must, of course.

GEORGE

I do not propose to discuss my private affairs with Mr. Pim——

OLIVIA

But he's mixed himself up in them rather, hasn't he, and if you're going to ask him questions——

GEORGE

I only propose to ask him one question. I shall ask him if he is absolutely certain of the man's name. I can do that quite easily without letting him know the reason for my inquiry.

OLIVIA

You couldn't make a mistake about a name like Telworthy. But he might tell us something about Telworthy's plans. Perhaps he's going back to Australia at once. Perhaps he thinks I'm dead, too. Perhaps—oh, there are so many things I want to know.

GEORGE

Yes, yes, dear. It would be interesting to—that is, one naturally wants to know these things, but of course it doesn't make any real difference.

OLIVIA

(*Surprised*). No difference?

GEORGE

Well, that is to say, you're as much his wife if he's in Australia as you are if he's in England.

OLIVIA

I am not his wife at all.

GEORGE

But, Olivia, surely you understand the position——

OLIVIA

(*Shaking her head*). Jacob Telworthy may be alive, but I am not his wife. I ceased to be his wife when I became yours.

GEORGE

You never *were* my wife. That is the terrible part of it. Our union—you make me say it, Olivia—has been unhallowed by the Church. Unhallowed even by the Law. Legally, we have been living in—living in—well, the point is, how does the Law stand? I imagine that Telworthy could get a—a divorce. . . . Oh, it seems impossible that things like this can be happening to *us*.

OLIVIA

(*Joyfully*). A divorce?

GEORGE

I—I imagine so.

OLIVIA

But then we could *really* get married, and we shouldn't be living in—living in—whatever we were living in before.

GEORGE

I can't understand you, Olivia. You talk about it so calmly, as if there was nothing blameworthy in being divorced, as if there was nothing unusual in my marrying a divorced woman, as if there was nothing wrong in our having lived together for years without having been married.

OLIVIA

What seems wrong to me is that I lived for five years with a bad man whom I hated. What seems right to me is that I lived for five years with a good man whom I love.

GEORGE

Yes, yes, my dear, I know. But right and wrong don't settle themselves as easily as that. We've been living together when you were Telworthy's wife. That's *wrong*.

OLIVIA

Do you mean wicked?

GEORGE

Well, no doubt the Court would consider that we acted in perfect innocence——

OLIVIA

What Court?

GEORGE

These things have to be done legally, of course. I believe the proper method is a nullity suit, declaring our marriage null and—er—void. It would, so to speak, wipe out these years of—er——

OLIVIA

Wickedness?

GEORGE

Of irregular union, and—er—then——

OLIVIA

Then I could go back to Jacob. . . . Do you really mean that, George?

GEORGE

(*Uneasily*). Well, dear, you see—that's how things are—one can't get away from—er——

OLIVIA

What you feel is that Telworthy has the greater claim? You are prepared to—make way for him?

GEORGE

Both the Church and the Law would say that I had no claim at all, I'm afraid. I—I suppose I haven't.

OLIVIA

I see. (*She looks at him curiously.*) Thank you for making it so clear, George.

GEORGE

Of course, whether or not you go back to —er—Telworthy is another matter altogether. That would naturally be for you to decide.

OLIVIA

(*Cheerfully*). For me and Jacko to decide.

GEORGE

Er—Jacko?

OLIVIA

I used to call my first husband—I mean my only husband—Jacko. I didn't like the name of Jacob, and Jacko seemed to suit him somehow. . . . He had very long arms. Dear Jacko.

GEORGE

(*Annoyed*). You don't seem to realize that this is not a joke, Olivia.

OLIVIA

(*A trifle hysterically*). It may not be a joke, but it *is* funny, isn't it?

GEORGE

I must say I don't see anything funny in a tragedy that has wrecked two lives.

OLIVIA

Two? Oh, but Jacko's life isn't wrecked. It has just been miraculously restored to him. And a wife, too. There's nothing tragic for Jacko in it.

GEORGE

(*Stiffly*). I was referring to *our* two lives—yours and mine.

OLIVIA

Yours, George? Your life isn't wrecked. The Court will absolve you of all blame; your friends will sympathize with you, and tell you I was a designing woman who deliberately took you in; your Aunt Julia——

GEORGE

(*Overwrought*). Stop it! What do you mean? Have you no heart? Do you think I *want* to lose you, Olivia? Do you think I *want* my home broken up like this? Haven't you been happy with me these last five years?

OLIVIA

Very happy.

GEORGE

Well then, how can you talk like that?

OLIVIA

(*Pathetically*). But you want to send me away.

GEORGE

There you go again. I don't *want* to. I have hardly had time to realize just what it will mean to me when you go. The fact is I simply daren't realize it. I daren't think about it.

OLIVIA

(*Earnestly*). Try thinking about it, George.

GEORGE

And you talk as if I *wanted* to send you away!

OLIVIA

Try thinking about it, George.

GEORGE

You don't seem to understand that I'm not *sending* you away. You simply aren't mine to keep.

OLIVIA

Whose am I?

GEORGE

Your husband's. Telworthy's.

OLIVIA

(*Gently*). If I belong to anybody but myself, I think I belong to you.

GEORGE

Not in the eyes of the Law. Not in the eyes of the Church. Not even in the eyes of —er——

OLIVIA

The County?

GEORGE

(*Annoyed*). I was about to say "Heaven."

OLIVIA

(*Unimpressed*). Oh!

GEORGE

That this should happen to *us!*
(*He gets up and walks about the room, wondering when he will wake up from his impossible dream.* OLIVIA *works in silence. Then she stands up and shakes out her curtains.*)

OLIVIA

(*Looking at them*). I do hope Jacko will like these.

GEORGE

What! You—— (*Going up to her.*) Olivia, Olivia, have you no heart?

OLIVIA

Ought you to talk like that to another man's wife?

GEORGE

Confound it, is this just a joke to you?

OLIVIA

You must forgive me, George; I am a little over-excited—at the thought of returning to Jacob, I suppose.

GEORGE

Do you *want* to return to him?

OLIVIA

One wants to do what is right. In the eyes of—er—Heaven.

GEORGE

Seeing what sort of man he is, I have no doubt that you could get a separation, supposing that he didn't—er—divorce you. I don't know *what* is best. I must consult my solicitor. The whole position has been sprung on us, and—(*miserably*) I don't know, I don't know. I can't take it all in.

OLIVIA

Wouldn't you like to consult your Aunt Julia too? She could tell you what the County—I mean what Heaven really thought about it.

GEORGE

Yes, yes. Aunt Julia has plenty of common sense. You're quite right, Olivia. This isn't a thing we can keep from the family.

OLIVIA

Do I still call her *Aunt* Julia?

GEORGE

(*Looking up from his pacings*). What? What? (ANNE *comes in.*) Well, what is it?

ANNE

Mr. Pim says he will come down at once, sir.

GEORGE

Oh, thank you, thank you.
(ANNE *goes out.*)

OLIVIA

George, Mr. Pim has got to know.

GEORGE

I don't see the necessity.

OLIVIA

Not even for me? When a woman suddenly hears that her long-lost husband is restored to her, don't you think she wants to ask questions? Where is he living, and how is he looking, and——

GEORGE

(*Coldly*). Of course, if you are interested in these things——

OLIVIA

How can I help being? Don't be so silly, George. We *must* know what Jacko——

GEORGE

(*Annoyed*). I wish you wouldn't call him by that ridiculous name.

OLIVIA

My husband——

GEORGE

(*Wincing*). Yes, well—your husband?

OLIVIA

Well, we must know his plans—where we can communicate with him, and so on.

GEORGE

I have no wish to communicate with him.

OLIVIA

I'm afraid you'll have to, dear.

GEORGE

I don't see the necessity.

OLIVIA

Well, you'll want to—to apologize to him for living with his wife for so long. And as I belong to him, he ought to be told where he can—call for me.

GEORGE

(*After a struggle*). You put it in a very peculiar way, but I see your point. (*With a shudder.*) Oh, the horrible publicity of it all!

OLIVIA

(*Going up to him and comforting him*). Poor George. Dear, don't think I don't sympathize with you. I understand so exactly what you are feeling. The publicity! It's terrible.

GEORGE

(*Miserably*). I want to do what's right, Olivia. You believe that?

OLIVIA

Of course I do. It's only that we don't quite agree as to what is right and what is wrong.

GEORGE

It isn't a question of agreeing. Right is right, and wrong is wrong, all the world over.

OLIVIA

(*With a sad little smile*). But more particularly in Buckinghamshire, I think.

GEORGE

If I only considered myself, I should say: "Let us pack this man Telworthy back to Australia. He would make no claim. He would accept money to go away and say nothing about it." If I consulted simply my own happiness, Olivia, that is what I should say. But when I consult—er——

OLIVIA

(*Surprised*). Mine?

GEORGE

My conscience——

OLIVIA

Oh!

GEORGE

Then I can't do it. It's wrong. (*He is at the window as he says this.*)

OLIVIA

(*Making her first and last appeal*). George, aren't I worth a little——

GEORGE

(*Turning round*). H'sh! Dinah! (*Loudly for* DINAH'S *benefit.*) Well, then I'll write to him and——Ah, Dinah, where's Aunt Julia?

DINAH

(*Coming in*). We've seen the pigs, and now she's discussing the Art of Landseer with Brian. I just came to ask——

OLIVIA

Dinah, dear, bring Aunt Julia here. And Brian too. We have things we want to talk about with you all.

GEORGE

(*Outraged*). Olivia!

DINAH

Righto. What fun!
(*Exit* DINAH.)

GEORGE

Olivia, you don't seriously suggest that we should discuss these things with a child like Dinah and a young man like Strange, a mere acquaintance.

OLIVIA

Dinah will have to know. I'm very fond of her, George. You can't send me away without telling Dinah. And Brian is my friend. You have your solicitor and your aunt and your conscience to consult—mayn't I even have Brian?

GEORGE

(*Forgetting*). I should have thought that your *husband*——

OLIVIA

Yes, but we don't know where Jacko is.

GEORGE

I was not referring to—er—Telworthy.

OLIVIA

Well then?

GEORGE

Well, naturally I—you mustn't—— Oh, this is horrible!
(*He comes back to his desk as the others come in.*)

OLIVIA

(*Getting up*). George and I have had some rather bad news, Aunt Julia. We wanted your advice. Where will you sit?

LADY MARDEN

Thank you, Olivia. I can sit down by myself. (*She does so, near* GEORGE. DINAH *sits on the sofa with* OLIVIA, *and* BRIAN *half leans against the back of it. There is a hush of expectation. . . .*) What is it? Money, I suppose. Nobody's safe nowadays.

GEORGE

(*Signalling for help*). Olivia——

OLIVIA

We've just heard that my first husband is still alive.

DINAH

Telworthy!

BRIAN

Good Lord!

LADY MARDEN

George!

DINAH

(*Excitedly*). And only this morning I was saying that nothing ever happened in this house! (*Remorsefully to* OLIVIA.) Darling, I don't mean that. Darling one!

LADY MARDEN

What does this mean, George? I leave you for ten minutes—barely ten minutes—to go and look at the pigs, and when I come back you tell me that Olivia is a bigamist.

BRIAN

(*Indignantly*). I say——

OLIVIA

(*Restraining him*). H'sh!

BRIAN

(*To* OLIVIA). If this is a row, I'm on your side.

LADY MARDEN

Well, George?

GEORGE

I'm afraid it's true, Aunt Julia. We heard the news just before lunch—just before you came. We've only this moment had an opportunity of talking about it, of wondering what to do.

LADY MARDEN

What was his name—Tel—something——

OLIVIA

Jacob Telworthy.

LADY MARDEN

So he's alive still?

GEORGE

Apparently. There seems to be no doubt about it.

LADY MARDEN

(*To* OLIVIA). Didn't you see him die? I should always want to *see* my husband die before I married again. Not that I approve of second marriages, anyhow. I told you so at the time, George.

OLIVIA

And me, Aunt Julia.

LADY MARDEN

Did I? Well, I generally say what I think.

GEORGE

I ought to tell you, Aunt Julia, that no blame attaches to Olivia over this. Of that I am perfectly satisfied. It's nobody's fault, except——

LADY MARDEN

Except Telworthy's. *He* seems to have been rather careless. Well, what are you going to do about it?

GEORGE

That's just it. It's a terrible situation. There's bound to be so much publicity. Not only all this, but—but Telworthy's past and—and everything.

LADY MARDEN

I should have said that it was Telworthy's present which was the trouble. Had he a past as well?

OLIVIA

He was a fraudulent company promoter. He went to prison a good deal.

LADY MARDEN

George, you never told me this!

GEORGE

I—er——

OLIVIA

I don't see why he should want to talk about it.

DINAH

(*Indignantly*). What's it got to do with Olivia, anyhow? It's not *her* fault.

LADY MARDEN

(*Sarcastically*). Oh, no, I daresay it's mine.

OLIVIA

(*To* GEORGE). You wanted to ask Aunt Julia what was the right thing to do.

BRIAN

(*Bursting out*). Good Heavens, what *is* there to do except the one and only thing? (*They all look at him and he becomes embarrassed.*) I'm sorry. You don't want *me* to——

OLIVIA

I do, Brian.

LADY MARDEN

Well, go on, Mr. Strange. What would *you* do in George's position?

BRIAN

Do? Say to the woman I loved, "You're *mine*, and let this other damned fellow come and take you from me if he can!" And he couldn't—how could he?—not if the woman chose *me*.

(LADY MARDEN *gazes at* BRIAN *in amazement,* GEORGE *in anger.* OLIVIA *presses his hand gratefully. He has said what she has been waiting—oh, so eagerly—for* GEORGE *to say.*)

DINAH

(*Adoringly*). Oh, Brian! (*In a whisper.*) It is me, isn't it, and not Olivia?

BRIAN

You baby, of course!

LADY MARDEN

I'm afraid, Mr. Strange, your morals are as peculiar as your views on art. If you had led a more healthy life——

BRIAN

This is not a question of morals or of art, it's a question of love.

DINAH

Hear, hear!

LADY MARDEN

(*To* GEORGE). Isn't it that girl's bedtime yet?

OLIVIA

(*To* DINAH). We'll let her sit up a little longer if she's good.

DINAH

I will be good, Olivia, only I thought anybody, however important a debate was, was allowed to say "Hear, hear!"

GEORGE

(*Coldly*). I really think we could discuss this better if Mr. Strange took Dinah out for a walk. Strange, if you—er——

OLIVIA

Tell them what you have settled first, George.

LADY MARDEN

Settled? What is there to be settled? It settles itself.

GEORGE

(*Sadly*). That's just it.

LADY MARDEN

The marriage must be annulled—is that the word, George?

GEORGE

I presume so.

LADY MARDEN

One's solicitor will know all about that of course.

BRIAN

And when the marriage has been annulled, what then?

LADY MARDEN

Presumably Olivia will return to her husband.

BRIAN

(*Bitterly*). And that's morality! As expounded by Bishop Landseer!

GEORGE

(*Angered*). I don't know what you mean by Bishop Landseer. Morality is acting in accordance with the Laws of the Land and the Laws of the Church. I am quite prepared to believe that *your* creed embraces neither marriage nor monogamy, but my creed is different.

BRIAN

(*Fiercely*). My creed includes both marriage *and* monogamy, and monogamy means sticking to the woman you love, as long as she wants you.

LADY MARDEN

(*Calmly*). You suggest that George and Olivia should go on living together, although they have never been legally married, and wait for this Telworthy man to divorce her, and then—bless the man, what do you think the County would say?

BRIAN

(*Scornfully*). Does it matter?

DINAH

Well, if you really want to know, the men would say, "Gad, she's a fine woman; I don't wonder he sticks to her," and the women would say, "I can't *think* what he sees in her to stick to her like that," and they'd both say, "After all, he may be a damn fool, but you can't deny he's a sportsman." That's what the County would say.

GEORGE

(*Indignantly*). Was it for this sort of thing, Olivia, that you insisted on having Dinah and Mr. Strange in here? To insult me in my own house?

LADY MARDEN

I can't think what young people are coming to nowadays.

OLIVIA

I think, dear, you and Brian had better go.

DINAH

(*Getting up*). We will go. But I'm just going to say one thing, Uncle George. Brian and I *are* going to marry each other,

and when we are married we'll stick to each other, how*ever* many of our dead husbands and wives turn up!
(*She goes out indignantly, followed by* BRIAN.)

GEORGE

Upon my word, this is a pleasant discussion.

OLIVIA

I think the discussion is over, George. It is only a question of where I shall go, while you are bringing your—what sort of suit did you call it?

LADY MARDEN

(*To* GEORGE). Nullity suit. I suppose that *is* the best thing?

GEORGE

It's horrible. The awful publicity. That it should be happening to us, that's what I can't get over.

LADY MARDEN

I don't remember anything of the sort in the Marden Family before, ever.

GEORGE

(*Absently*). Lady Fanny.

LADY MARDEN

(*Recollecting*). Yes, of course; but that was two hundred years ago. The standards were different then. Besides, it wasn't quite the same, anyhow.

GEORGE

(*Absently*). No, it wasn't quite the same.

LADY MARDEN

No. We shall all feel it. Terribly.

GEORGE

(*His apology*). If there were any other way! Olivia, what *can* I do? It *is* the only way, isn't it? All that that fellow said—of course, it sounds very well—but as things are. . . . *Is* there anything in marriage, or isn't there? You believe that there is, don't you? You aren't one of these Socialists. Well, then, *can* we go on living together when you're another man's wife? It isn't only what people will say, but it *is* wrong, isn't it? . . . And supposing he doesn't divorce you, are we to go on living together, unmarried, for *ever?* Olivia, you seem to think that I'm just thinking of the publicity—what people will say. I'm not. I'm not. That comes in any way. But I want to do what's right, what's best. I don't mean what's best for *us*, what makes us happiest, I mean what's really best, what's rightest. What anybody else would do in my place. *I* don't know. It's so unfair. You're not my wife at all, but I want to do what's right. . . . Oh, Olivia, Olivia, you do understand, don't you?
(*They have both forgotten* LADY MARDEN. OLIVIA *has never taken her eyes off him as he makes his last attempt to convince himself.*)

OLIVIA

(*Almost tenderly*). So very very well, George. Oh, I understand just what you are feeling. And oh, I do so wish that you could—(*with a little sigh*)—but then it wouldn't be George, not the George I married—(*with a rueful little laugh*)—or didn't quite marry.

LADY MARDEN

I must say, I think you are both talking a little wildly.

OLIVIA

(*Repeating it, oh, so tenderly*). Or didn't —quite—marry. (*She looks at him with all her heart in her eyes. She is giving him his last chance to say "Damn Telworthy; you're mine!" He struggles desperately with himself. . . . Will he?—will he? . . . But we shall never know, for at that moment* ANNE *comes in.*)

ANNE

Mr. Pim is here, sir.

GEORGE

(*Emerging from the struggle with an effort*). Pim? Pim? Oh, ah, yes, of course. Mr. Pim. (*Looking up.*) Where have you put him?

OLIVIA

I want to see Mr. Pim, too, George.

LADY MARDEN

Who on earth is Mr. Pim?

OLIVIA

Show him in here, Anne.

ANNE

Yes, madam.
(*She goes out.*)

OLIVIA

It was Mr. Pim who told us about my husband. He came across with him in the boat, and recognized him as the Telworthy he knew in Australia.

LADY MARDEN

Oh! Shall I be in the way?

GEORGE

No, no. It doesn't matter, does it, Olivia?

OLIVIA

Please stay.
(ANNE *enters followed by* MR. PIM.)

ANNE

Mr. Pim.

GEORGE

(*Pulling himself together*). Ah, Mr. Pim! Very good of you to come. The fact is—er—— (*It is too much for him; he looks despairingly at* OLIVIA.)

OLIVIA

We're so sorry to trouble you, Mr. Pim. By the way, do you know Lady Marden? (MR. PIM *and* LADY MARDEN *bow to each other.*) Do come and sit down, won't you? (*She makes room for him on the sofa next to her.*) The fact is, Mr. Pim, you gave us rather a surprise this morning, and before we had time to realize what it all meant, you had gone.

MR. PIM

A surprise, Mrs. Marden? Dear me, not an unpleasant one, I hope?

OLIVIA

Well, rather a—surprising one.

GEORGE

Olivia, allow me a moment. Mr. Pim, you mentioned a man called Telworthy this morning. My wife used to—that is to say, I used to—that is, there are reasons——

OLIVIA

I think we had better be perfectly frank, George.

LADY MARDEN

I am sixty-five years of age, Mr. Pim, and I can say that I've never had a moment's uneasiness by telling the truth.

MR. PIM

(*After a desperate effort to keep up with the conversation*). Oh! . . . I—er—I'm afraid I am rather at sea. Have I—er—left anything unsaid in presenting my credentials to you this morning? This Telworthy whom you mention—I seem to remember the name——

OLIVIA

Mr. Pim, you told us this morning of a man whom you had met on the boat, a man who had come down in the world, whom you had known in Sydney. A man called Telworthy.

MR. PIM

(*Relieved*). Ah yes, yes, of course. I did say Telworthy, didn't I? Most curious coincidence, Lady Marden. Poor man, poor man! Let me see, it must have been ten years ago——

GEORGE

Just a moment, Mr. Pim. You're quite sure that his name was Telworthy?

MR. PIM

Telworthy—Telworthy—didn't I say Telworthy? Yes, that was it—Telworthy. Poor fellow!

OLIVIA

I'm going to be perfectly frank with you, Mr. Pim. I feel quite sure that I can trust you. This man Telworthy whom you met is my husband.

MR. PIM

Your husband? (*He looks in mild surprise at* GEORGE.) But—er——

OLIVIA

My first husband. His death was announced six years ago. I had left him some years before that, but there seems no doubt from your story that he's still alive. His record—the country he comes from—above all, the very unusual name—Telworthy.

MR. PIM

Telworthy—yes—certainly a most peculiar name. I remember saying so. Your first husband? Dear me! Dear me!

GEORGE

You understand, Mr. Pim, that all this is in absolute confidence.

MR. PIM

Of course, of course.

OLIVIA

Well, since he is my husband, we naturally want to know something about him. Where is he now, for instance?

MR. PIM

(*Surprised*). Where is he now? But surely I told you? I told you what happened at Marseilles?

GEORGE

At Marseilles?

MR. PIM

Yes, yes, poor fellow, it was most unfortunate. (*Quite happy again.*) You must understand, Lady Marden, that although I had met the poor fellow before in Australia, I was never in any way intimate——

GEORGE

(*Thumping the desk*). Where is he *now*, that's what we want to know?
(MR. PIM *turns to him with a start.*)

OLIVIA

Please, Mr. Pim!

PIM

Where is he now? But—but didn't I tell you of the curious fatality at Marseilles—poor fellow—the fish-bone?

ALL

Fish-bone?

MR. PIM

Yes, yes, a herring, I understand.

OLIVIA

(*Understanding first*). Do you mean he's dead?

MR. PIM

Dead—of course—didn't I——?

OLIVIA

(*Laughing hysterically*). Oh, Mr. Pim, you—oh, what a husband to have—oh, I —— (*But that is all she can say for the moment.*)

LADY MARDEN

Pull yourself together, Olivia. This is so unhealthy for you. (*To* PIM.) So he really *is* dead this time?

MR. PIM

Oh, undoubtedly, undoubtedly. A fish-bone lodged in his throat.

GEORGE

(*Trying to realize it*). Dead!

OLIVIA

(*Struggling with her laughter*). I think you must excuse me, Mr. Pim—I can never thank you enough—a herring—there's something about a herring—morality depends on such little things—George, you —— (*Shaking her head at him in a weak state of laughter, she hurries out of the room.*)

MR. PIM

Dear me! Dear me!

GEORGE

Now, let us have this quite clear, Mr. Pim. You say that the man, Telworthy, Jacob Telworthy, is dead?

MR. PIM

Telworthy, yes—didn't I say Telworthy? This man I was telling you about——

GEORGE

He's dead?

MR. PIM

Yes, yes, he died at Marseilles.

LADY MARDEN

A dispensation of Providence, George. One can look at it in no other light.

GEORGE

Dead! (*Suddenly annoyed.*) Really, Mr. Pim, I think you might have told us before.

MR. PIM

But I—I *was* telling you—I——

GEORGE

If you had only told us the whole story at once, instead of in two—two instalments like this, you would have saved us all a good deal of anxiety.

MR. PIM

Really, I——

LADY MARDEN

I am sure Mr. Pim meant well, George, but it seems a pity he couldn't have said so before. If the man was dead, *why* try to hush it up?

MR. PIM

(*Lost again*). Really, Lady Marden, I——

GEORGE

(*Getting up*). Well, well, at any rate, I am much obliged to you, Mr. Pim, for having come down to us this afternoon. Dead! *De mortuis,* and so forth, but the situation would have been impossible had he lived. Good-bye! (*Holding out his hand.*) Good-bye!

LADY MARDEN

Good-bye, Mr. Pim.

MR. PIM

Good-bye, good-bye! (GEORGE *takes him to the door.*) Of course, if I had—(*to himself*) Telworthy—I *think* that was the name. (*He goes out, still wondering.*)

GEORGE

(*With a sigh of thankfulness*). Well! This is wonderful news, Aunt Julia.

LADY MARDEN

Most providential! . . . You understand, of course, that you are not married to Olivia?

GEORGE

(*Who didn't*). Not married?

LADY MARDEN

If her first husband only died at Marseilles a few days ago——

GEORGE

Good Heavens!

LADY MARDEN

Not that it matters. You can get married quietly again. Nobody need know.

GEORGE

(*Considering it*). Yes . . . yes. Then all these years we have been—er—— Yes.

LADY MARDEN

Who's going to know?

GEORGE

Yes, yes, that's true. . . . And in perfect innocence, too.

LADY MARDEN

I should suggest a Registry Office in London.

GEORGE

A Registry Office, yes.

LADY MARDEN

Better go up to town this afternoon. Can't do it too quickly.

GEORGE

Yes, yes. We can stay at an hotel——

LADY MARDEN

(*Surprised*). George!

GEORGE

What?

LADY MARDEN

You will stay at your club.

GEORGE

Oh—ah—yes, of course, Aunt Julia.

LADY MARDEN

Better take your solicitor with you to be on the safe side. . . . To the Registry Office, I mean.

GEORGE

Yes.

LADY MARDEN

(*Getting up*). Well, I must be getting along, George. Say good-bye to Olivia for me. And those children. Of course, you won't allow this absurd love-business between them to come to anything?

GEORGE

Most certainly not. Good-bye, Aunt Julia!

LADY MARDEN

(*Indicating the windows*). I'll go *this* way. (*As she goes.*) And get Olivia out more, George. I don't like these hysterics. You want to be firm with her.

GEORGE

(*Firmly*). Yes, yes! Good-bye!
(*He waves to her and then goes back to his seat.*)
(OLIVIA *comes in, and stands in the middle of the room looking at him. He comes to her eagerly.*)

GEORGE

(*Holding out his hands*). Olivia! Olivia!
(*But it is not so easy at that.*)

OLIVIA

(*Drawing herself up proudly*). Mrs. Telworthy!

ACT THREE

OLIVIA *is standing where we left her at the end of the last act.*

GEORGE

(*Taken aback*). Olivia, I—I don't understand.

OLIVIA

(*Leaving melodrama with a little laugh and coming down to him*). Poor George! Did I frighten you rather?

GEORGE

You're so strange today. I don't understand you. You're not like the Olivia I know.
(*They sit down on the sofa together.*)

OLIVIA

Perhaps you don't know me very well after all.

GEORGE

(*Affectionately*). Oh, that's nonsense, old girl. You're just my Olivia.

OLIVIA

And yet it seemed as though I wasn't going to be your Olivia half an hour ago.

GEORGE

(*With a shudder*). Don't talk about it. It doesn't bear thinking about. Well, thank Heaven that's over. Now we can get married again quietly and nobody will be any the wiser.

OLIVIA

Married again?

GEORGE

Yes, dear. As you—er—(*he laughs uneasily*) said just now, you are Mrs. Telworthy. Just for the moment. But we can soon put that right. My idea was to go up this evening and—er—make arrangements, and if you come up tomorrow morning, if we can manage it by then, we could get quietly married at a Registry office, and—er—nobody any the wiser.

OLIVIA

Yes, I see. You want me to marry you at a Registry Office tomorrow?

GEORGE

If we can arrange it by then. I don't know how long these things take, but I should imagine there would be no difficulty.

OLIVIA

Oh, no, that part ought to be quite easy. But—— (*She hesitates.*)

GEORGE

But what?

OLIVIA

Well, if you want to marry me tomorrow, George, oughtn't you to propose to me first?

GEORGE

(*Amazed*). Propose?

OLIVIA

Yes. It is usual, isn't it, to propose to a person before you marry her, and—and we want to do the usual thing, don't we?

GEORGE

(*Upset*). But you—but we . . .

OLIVIA

You see, dear, you're George Marden, and I'm Olivia Telworthy, and you—you're attracted by me, and think I would make you a good wife, and you want to marry me. Well, naturally you propose to me first, and—tell me how much you are attracted by me, and what a good wife you think I shall make, and how badly you want to marry me.

GEORGE

(*Falling into the humor of it, as he thinks*). The baby! Did she want to be proposed to all over again?

OLIVIA

Well, she did rather.

GEORGE

(*Rather fancying himself as an actor*). She shall then. (*He adopts what he considers to be an appropriate attitude.*) Mrs. Telworthy, I have long admired you in silence, and the time has now come to put my admiration into words. Er—— (*But apparently he finds a difficulty.*)

OLIVIA

(*Hopefully*). Into words.

GEORGE

Er——

OLIVIA

(*With the idea of helping*). Oh, Mr. Marden!

GEORGE

Er—may I call you Olivia?

OLIVIA

Yes, George.

GEORGE

(*Taking her hands*). Olivia—I—— (*He hesitates.*)

OLIVIA

I don't want to interrupt, but oughtn't you to be on your knees? It is—usual, I believe. If one of the servants came in, you could say you were looking for my scissors.

GEORGE

Really, Olivia, you must allow me to manage my own proposal in my own way.

OLIVIA

(*Meekly*). I'm sorry. Do go on.

GEORGE

Well, er—confound it, Olivia, I love you. Will you marry me?

OLIVIA

Thank you, George, I will think it over.

GEORGE

(*Laughing*). Silly girl! Well then, tomorrow morning. No wedding-cake, I'm afraid, Olivia. (*He laughs again.*) But we'll go and have a good lunch somewhere.

OLIVIA

I will think it over, George.

GEORGE

(*Good-humoredly*). Well, give us a kiss while you're thinking.

OLIVIA

I'm afraid you mustn't kiss me until we are actually engaged.

GEORGE

(*Laughing uneasily*). Oh, we needn't take it as seriously as all that.

OLIVIA

But a woman must take a proposal seriously.

GEORGE

(*Alarmed at last*). What do you mean?

OLIVIA

I mean that the whole question, as I heard somebody say once, demands much more anxious thought than either of us has given it. These hasty marriages——

GEORGE

Hasty!

OLIVIA

Well, you've only just proposed to me, and you want to marry me tomorrow.

GEORGE

Now you're talking perfect nonsense, Olivia. You know quite well that our case is utterly different from—from any other.

OLIVIA

All the same, one has to ask oneself questions. With a young girl like—well, with a young girl, love may well seem to be all that matters. But with a woman of my age, it is different. I have to ask myself if you can afford to support a wife.

GEORGE

(*Coldly*). Fortunately that is a question that you can very easily answer for yourself.

OLIVIA

Well, but I have been hearing rather bad reports lately. What with taxes always going up, and rents always going down, some of our landowners are getting into rather straitened circumstances. At least, so I'm told.

GEORGE

I don't know what you're talking about.

OLIVIA

(*Surprised*). Oh, isn't it true? I heard of a case only this morning—a landowner who always seemed to be very comfortably off, but who couldn't afford an allowance for his only niece when she wanted to get married. It made me think that one oughtn't to judge by appearances.

GEORGE

You know perfectly well that I can afford to support a wife as my wife *should* be supported.

OLIVIA

I'm so glad, dear. Then your income—you aren't getting anxious at all?

GEORGE

(*Stiffly*). You know perfectly well what my income is. I see no reason for anxiety in the future.

OLIVIA

Ah, well, then we needn't think about that any more. Well, then, there is another thing to be considered.

GEORGE

I can't make out what you're up to. Don't you want to get married; to—er—legalize this extraordinary situation in which we are placed?

OLIVIA

I want to be sure that I am going to be happy, George. I can't just jump at the very first offer I have had since my husband died, without considering the whole question very carefully.

GEORGE

So I'm under consideration, eh?

OLIVIA

Every suitor is.

GEORGE

(*Sarcastically, as he thinks*). Well, go on.

OLIVIA

Well, then, there's your niece. You have a niece who lives with you. Of course Dinah is a delightful girl, but one doesn't like marrying into a household in which there is another grown-up woman. But perhaps she will be getting married herself soon?

GEORGE

I see no prospect of it.

OLIVIA

I think it would make it much easier if she did.

GEORGE

Is this a threat, Olivia? Are you telling me that if I do not allow young Strange to marry Dinah, you will not marry me?

OLIVIA

A threat? Oh, no, George.

GEORGE

Then what does it mean?

OLIVIA

I'm just wondering if you love me as much as Brian loves Dinah. You *do* love me?

GEORGE

(*From his heart*). You know I do, old girl. (*He comes to her.*)

OLIVIA

You're not just attracted by my pretty face? . . . *Is* it a pretty face?

GEORGE

It's an adorable one. (*He tries to kiss it, but she turns away.*)

OLIVIA

How can I be sure that it is not *only* my face which makes you think that you care for me? Love which rests upon a mere outward attraction cannot lead to any lasting happiness—as one of our thinkers has observed.

GEORGE

What's come over you, Olivia? I don't understand what you're driving at. Why should you doubt my love?

OLIVIA

Ah!—why?

GEORGE

You can't pretend that we haven't been happy together. I've—I've been a good pal to you, eh? We—we suit each other, old girl.

OLIVIA

Do we?

GEORGE

Of course we do.

OLIVIA

I wonder. When two people of our age think of getting married, one wants to be very sure that there is real community of ideas between them. Whether it is a comparatively trivial matter, like the right color for a curtain, or some very much more serious question of conduct which arises, one wants to feel that there is some chance of agreement between husband and wife.

GEORGE

We—we love each other, old girl.

OLIVIA

We do now, yes. But what shall we be like in five years' time? Supposing that after we have been married five years, we found ourselves estranged from each other upon such questions as Dinah's future, or the decorations of the drawing-room, or even the advice to give to a friend who had innocently contracted a bigamous marriage? How bitterly we should regret then our hasty plunge into a matrimony which was no true partnership, whether of tastes, or of ideas, or even of consciences! (*With a sigh.*) Ah me!

GEORGE

(*Nastily*). Unfortunately for your argument, Olivia, I can answer you out of your own mouth. You seem to have forgotten what you said this morning in the case of—er—young Strange.

OLIVIA

(*Reproachfully*). Is it quite fair, George, to drag up what was said this morning?

GEORGE

You've brought it on yourself.

OLIVIA

I? . . . Well, and what did I say this morning?

GEORGE

You said that it was quite enough that Strange was a gentleman and in love with Dinah for me to let them marry each other.

OLIVIA

Oh! . . . *Is* that enough, George?

GEORGE

(*Triumphantly*). You said so.

OLIVIA

(*Meekly*). Well, if you think so, too, I—I don't mind risking it.

GEORGE

(*Kindly*). Aha, my dear! You see!

OLIVIA

Then you do think it's enough?

GEORGE

I—er—— Yes, yes, I—I think so.

OLIVIA

(*Going to him*). My darling one! Then we can have a double wedding. How jolly!

GEORGE

(*Astounded*). A double one!

OLIVIA

Yes. You and me, Brian and Dinah.

GEORGE

(*Firmly*). Now look here, Olivia, understand once and for all, I am not to be blackmailed into giving my consent to Dinah's engagement. Neither blackmailed nor tricked. Our marriage has nothing whatever to do with Dinah's.

OLIVIA

No, dear. I quite understand. They may take place about the same time, but they have nothing to do with each other.

GEORGE

I see no prospect of Dinah's marriage taking place for many years.

OLIVIA

No, dear, that was what I said.

GEORGE

(*Not understanding for the moment*). You said . . . ? I see. Now, Olivia, let us have this perfectly clear. You apparently insist on treating my—er—proposal as serious.

OLIVIA

(*Surprised*). Wasn't it serious? Were you trifling with me?

GEORGE

You know quite well what I mean. You treat it as an ordinary proposal from a man to a woman who have never been more than acquaintances before. Very well then. Will you tell me what you propose to do, if you decide to—ah—refuse me? You do not suggest that we should go on living together—unmarried?

OLIVIA

(*Shocked*). Of course not, George! What would the County—I mean Heaven—I mean the Law—I mean, of *course* not! Besides, it's so unnecessary. If I decide to accept you, of *course* I shall marry you.

GEORGE

Quite so. And if you—ah—decide to refuse me? What will you do?

OLIVIA

Nothing.

GEORGE

Meaning by that?

OLIVIA

Just that, George. I shall stay here—just as before. I like this house. It wants a little re-decorating perhaps, but I do like it, George. . . . Yes, I shall be quite happy here.

GEORGE

I see. You will continue to live down here—in spite of what you said just now about the immorality of it.

OLIVIA

(*Surprised*). But there's nothing immoral in a widow living alone in a big country house, with perhaps the niece of a friend of hers staying with her, just to keep her company.

GEORGE

(*Sarcastic*). And what shall *I* be doing, when you've so very kindly taken possession of my house for me?

OLIVIA

I don't know, George. Travelling, I expect. You could come down sometimes with a chaperone. I suppose there would be nothing wrong in that.

GEORGE

(*Indignant*). Thank you! And what if I refuse to be turned out of my house?

OLIVIA

Then, seeing that we can't *both* be in it, it looks as though you'd have to turn *me* out. (*Casually.*) I suppose there are legal ways of doing these things. You'd have to consult your solicitor again.

GEORGE

(*Amazed*). Legal ways?

OLIVIA

Well, you couldn't *throw* me out, could you? You'd have to get an injunction against me—or prosecute me for trespass—or something. It would make an awfully unusual case, wouldn't it? The papers would be full of it.

GEORGE

You must be mad!

OLIVIA

(*Dreamily*). Widow of well-known ex-convict takes possession of J.P.'s house. Popular country gentleman denied entrance to his own home. Doomed to travel.

GEORGE

(*Angrily*). I've had enough of this. Do you mean all this nonsense?

OLIVIA

I do mean, George, that I am in no hurry to go up to London and get married. I love the country just now, and (*with a sigh*) after this morning, I'm—rather tired of husbands.

GEORGE

(*In a rage*). I've never heard so much—damned nonsense in my life. I will leave you to come to your senses. (*He goes out indignantly.*)

(OLIVIA, *who has forgiven him already, throws a loving kiss after him, and then turns triumphantly to her dear curtains. She takes them, smiling, to the sofa, and has just got to work again, when* MR. PIM *appears at the open windows.*)

PIM

(*In a whisper*). Er, may I come in, Mrs. Marden?

OLIVIA

(*Turning round in surprise*). Mr. Pim!

PIM

(*Anxiously*). Mr. Marden is—er—not here?

OLIVIA

(*Getting up*). Do you want to see him? I will tell him.

PIM

No, no, no! Not for the world! (*He comes in and looks anxiously at the door.*) There is no immediate danger of his returning, Mrs. Marden?

OLIVIA

(*Surprised*). No, I don't think so. What is it? You——

PIM

I took the liberty of returning by the window in the hope of—er—coming upon you alone, Mrs. Marden.

OLIVIA

Yes?

PIM

(*Still rather nervous*). I—er—Mr. Marden will be very angry with me. Quite rightly. I blame myself entirely. I do not know how I can have been so stupid.

OLIVIA

What is it, Mr. Pim? Has my husband come to life again?

PIM

Mrs. Marden, I throw myself on your mercy entirely. The fact is—his name was Polwittle.

OLIVIA

(*At a loss*). Whose? My husband's?

PIM

Yes, yes. The name came back to me suddenly, just as I reached the gate. Polwittle, poor fellow.

OLIVIA

But, Mr. Pim, my husband's name was Telworthy.

PIM

No, no, Polwittle.

OLIVIA

But, really I ought to . . .

PIM

(*Firmly*). Polwittle. It came back to me suddenly just as I reached the gate. For the moment, I had thoughts of conveying the news by letter. I was naturally disinclined to return in person, and—— Polwittle. (*Proudly.*) If you remember, I always said it was a curious name.

OLIVIA

But who *is* Polwittle?

PIM

(*In surprise at her stupidity*). The man I have been telling you about, who met with the sad fatality at Marseilles. Henry Polwittle—or was it Ernest? No, Henry, I think. Poor fellow.

OLIVIA

(*Indignantly*). But you said his name was Telworthy! How *could* you?

PIM

Yes, yes, I blame myself entirely.

OLIVIA

But how could you *think* of a name like Telworthy, if it wasn't Telworthy?

PIM

(*Eagerly*). Ah, that is the really interesting thing about the whole matter.

OLIVIA

Mr. Pim, all your visits here today have been interesting.

PIM

Yes, but you see, on my first appearance here this morning, I was received by—er—Miss Diana.

OLIVIA

Dinah.

PIM

Miss Dinah, yes. She was in—er—rather a communicative mood, and she happened to mention, by way of passing the time, that before your marriage to Mr. Marden you had been a Mrs.—er——

OLIVIA

Telworthy.

PIM

Yes, yes, Telworthy, of course. She mentioned also Australia. By some process of the brain—which strikes me as decidedly curious—when I was trying to recollect the name of the poor fellow on the boat, whom you remember I had also met in Australia, the fact that this other name was also stored in my memory, a name equally peculiar—this fact I say . . .

OLIVIA

(*Seeing that the sentence is rapidly going to pieces*). Yes, I understand.

PIM

I blame myself, I blame myself entirely.

OLIVIA

Oh, you mustn't do that, Mr. Pim. It was really Dinah's fault for inflicting all our family history on you.

PIM

Oh, but a charming young woman. I assure you I was very much interested in all that she told me. (*Getting up.*) Well, Mrs. —er—Marden, I can only hope that you will forgive me for the needless distress I have caused you today.

OLIVIA

Oh, you mustn't worry about that—please.

PIM

And you will tell your husband—you will break the news to him?

OLIVIA

(*Smiling to herself*). I will—break the news to him.

PIM

You understand how it is that I thought it better to come to you in the first place?

OLIVIA

I am very glad you did.

PIM

(*Holding out his hand*). Then I will say good-bye, and—er——

OLIVIA

Just a moment, Mr. Pim. Let us have it quite clear this time. You never knew my husband, Jacob Telworthy, you never met him in Australia, you never saw him on the boat, and nothing whatever happened to him at Marseilles. Is that right?

PIM

Yes, yes, that is so.

OLIVIA

So that, since he was supposed to have died in Australia six years ago, he is presumably still dead?

PIM

Yes, yes, undoubtedly.

OLIVIA

(*Holding out her hand with a charming smile*). Then good-bye, Mr. Pim, and thank you so much for—for all your trouble.

PIM

Not at all, Mrs. Marden. I can only assure you I——

DINAH

(*From the window*). Hullo, here's Mr. Pim! (*She comes in, followed by* BRIAN.)

PIM

(*Anxiously looking at the door in case* MR. MARDEN *should come in*). Yes, yes, I—er——

DINAH

Oh, Mr. Pim, you mustn't run away without even saying how do you do. Such old friends as we are. Why, it is ages since I saw you? Are you staying to tea?

PIM

I'm afraid I——

OLIVIA

Mr. Pim has to hurry away, Dinah. You mustn't keep him.

DINAH

Well, but you'll come back again?

PIM

I fear that I am only a passer-by, Miss—er—Dinah.

OLIVIA

You can walk with him to the gate, dear.

PIM

(*Gratefully to* OLIVIA). Thank you. (*He edges towards the window.*) If you would be so kind, Miss Dinah——

BRIAN

I'll catch you up.

DINAH

Come along then, Mr. Pim. (*As they go out.*) I want to hear all about your *first* wife. You haven't really told me anything yet.

(OLIVIA *resumes her work, and* BRIAN *sits on the back of the sofa looking at her.*)

BRIAN

(*Awkwardly*). I just wanted to say, if you don't think it cheek, that I'm—I'm on your side, if I may be, and if I can help you at all I should be very proud of being allowed to.

OLIVIA

(*Looking up at him*). Brian, you dear. That's sweet of you. . . . But it's quite all right now, you know.

BRIAN

Oh, I'm so glad.

OLIVIA

Yes, that's what Mr. Pim came back to say. He'd made a mistake about the name. (*Smiling.*) George is the only husband I have.

BRIAN

(*Surprised*). What? You mean that the whole thing—that Pim— (*With conviction.*) Silly ass!

OLIVIA

(*Kindly*). Oh, well, he didn't mean to be. (*After a pause.*) Brian, do you know anything about the Law?

BRIAN

I'm afraid not. I hate the Law. Why?

OLIVIA

(*Casually*). Oh, I just—I was wondering —thinking about all the shocks we've been through today. Second marriages, and all that.

BRIAN

Oh! It's a rotten business.

OLIVIA

I suppose there's nothing wrong in getting married to the *same* person twice?

BRIAN

A hundred times if you like, I should think.

OLIVIA

Oh?

BRIAN

After all, in France, they always go through it twice, don't they? Once before the Mayor or somebody, and once in church.

OLIVIA

Of course they do! How silly of me. . . . I think it's rather a nice idea. They ought to do it in England more.

BRIAN

Well, once will be enough for Dinah and me, if you can work it. (*Anxiously.*) D'you think there's any chance, Olivia?

OLIVIA

(*Smiling*). Every chance, dear.

BRIAN

(*Jumping up*). I say, do you really? Have you squared him? I mean, has he——

OLIVIA

Go and catch them up now. We'll talk about it later on.

BRIAN

Bless you. Righto.

(*As he goes out by the windows,* GEORGE *comes in at the door.* GEORGE *stands looking after him, and then turns to* OLIVIA, *who is absorbed in her curtains. He walks up and down the room, fidgeting with things, waiting for her to speak. As she says nothing, he begins to talk himself, but in an obviously unconcerned way. There is a pause after each answer of hers, before he gets out his next remark.*)

GEORGE

(*Casually*). Good-looking fellow, Strange.

OLIVIA

(*Equally casually*). Brian—yes, isn't he? And such a nice boy. . . .

GEORGE

Got fifty pounds for a picture the other day, didn't he? Hey?

OLIVIA

Yes. Of course he has only just begun. . . .

GEORGE

Critics think well of him, what?

OLIVIA

They all say he has genius. Oh, I don't think there's any doubt about it. . . .

GEORGE

Of course, I don't profess to know anything about painting.

OLIVIA

You've never had time to take it up, dear.

GEORGE

I know what I like, of course. Can't say I see much in this new-fangled stuff. If a man can paint, why can't he paint like—like Rubens or—or Reynolds?

OLIVIA

I suppose we all have our own styles. Brian will find his directly. Of course, he's only just beginning. . . .

GEORGE

But they think a lot of him, what?

OLIVIA

Oh, yes!

GEORGE

H'm! . . . Good-looking fellow.
(*There is rather a longer silence this time.* GEORGE *continues to hope that he is appearing casual and unconcerned. He stands looking at* OLIVIA'*s work for a moment.*)

GEORGE

Nearly finished 'em?

OLIVIA

Very nearly. Are my scissors there?

GEORGE

(*Looking round*). Scissors?

OLIVIA

Ah, here they are. . . .

GEORGE

Where are you going to put 'em?

OLIVIA

(*As if really wondering*). I don't quite know. . . . I *had* thought of this room, but —I'm not quite sure.

GEORGE

Brighten the room up a bit.

OLIVIA

Yes. . . .

GEORGE

(*Walking over to the present curtains*). H'm. They *are* a bit faded.

OLIVIA

(*Shaking out hers, and looking at them critically*). Sometimes I think I love them, and sometimes I'm not quite sure.

GEORGE

Best way is to hang 'em up and see how you like 'em then. Always take 'em down again.

OLIVIA

That's rather a good idea, George!

GEORGE

Best way.

OLIVIA

Yes. . . . I think we might do that. . . . The only thing is—— (*she hesitates*).

GEORGE

What?

OLIVIA

Well, the carpet and the chairs, and the cushions and things——

GEORGE

What about 'em?

OLIVIA

Well, if we had new curtains——

GEORGE

You'd want a new carpet, eh?

OLIVIA

(*Doubtfully*). Y—yes. Well, new chair-covers anyhow.

GEORGE

H'm. . . . Well, why not?

OLIVIA

Oh, but——

GEORGE

(*With an awkward laugh*). We're not so hard up as all that, you know.

OLIVIA

No, I suppose not. (*Thoughtfully.*) I suppose it would mean that I should have to go up to London for them. That's rather a nuisance.

GEORGE

(*Extremely casual*). Oh, I don't know. We might go up together one day.

OLIVIA

Well, of course if we *were* up—for anything else—we could just look about us, and see if we could find what we want.

GEORGE

That's what I meant.
(*There is another silence.* GEORGE *is wondering whether to come to closer quarters with the great question.*)

OLIVIA

Oh, by the way, George——

GEORGE

Yes?

OLIVIA

(*Innocently*). I told Brian, and I expect he'll tell Dinah, that Mr. Pim had made a mistake about the name.

GEORGE

(*Astonished*). You told Brian that Mr. Pim——

OLIVIA

Yes—I told him that the whole thing was a mistake. It seemed the simplest way.

GEORGE

Olivia! Then you mean that Brian and Dinah think that—that we have been married all the time?

OLIVIA

Yes. . . . They both think so now.

GEORGE

(*Coming close to her*). Olivia, does that mean that you *are* thinking of marrying me?

OLIVIA

At your old Registry Office?

GEORGE

(*Eagerly*). Yes!

OLIVIA

Tomorrow?

GEORGE

Yes!

OLIVIA

Do you want me to *very* much?

GEORGE

My darling, you know I do!

OLIVIA

(*A little apprehensive*). We should have to do it very quietly.

GEORGE

Of course, darling. Nobody need know at all. We don't *want* anybody to know. And now that you've put Brian and Dinah off the scent, by telling them that Mr. Pim made a mistake—— (*He breaks off, and says admiringly.*) That was very clever of you, Olivia. I should never have thought of that.

OLIVIA

(*Innocently*). No, darling. . . . You don't think it was wrong, George?

GEORGE

(*His verdict*). An innocent deception . . . perfectly harmless.

OLIVIA

Yes, dear, that was what I thought about—about what I was doing.

GEORGE

Then you will come tomorrow? (*She nods.*) And if we happen to see the carpet, or anything that you want——

OLIVIA

Oh, what fun!

GEORGE

(*Beaming*). And a wedding lunch at the Carlton, what? (*She nods eagerly.*) And—and a bit of a honeymoon in Paris?

OLIVIA

Oh, George!

GEORGE

(*Hungrily*). Give us a kiss, old girl.

OLIVIA

(*Lovingly*). George!
(*She holds up her cheek to him. He kisses it, and then suddenly takes her in his arms.*)

GEORGE

Don't ever leave me, old girl.

OLIVIA

(*Affectionately*). Don't ever send me away, old boy.

GEORGE

(*Fervently*). I won't. . . . (*Awkwardly.*) I—I don't think I would have, you know. I—I——

(DINAH *and* BRIAN *appear at the windows, having seen* MR. PIM *safely off.*)

DINAH

(*Surprised*). Oo, I say!
(GEORGE *hastily moves away.*)

GEORGE

Hallo!

DINAH

(*Going up impetuously to him*). Give *me* one, too, George; Brian won't mind.

BRIAN

Really, Dinah, you are the limit.

GEORGE

(*Formally, but enjoying it*). Do you mind, Mr. Strange?

BRIAN

(*A little uncomfortably*). Oh, I say, sir——

GEORGE

We'll risk it, Dinah. (*He kisses her.*)

DINAH

(*Triumphantly to* BRIAN). Did you notice that one? That wasn't just an ordinary affectionate kiss. It was a special bless-you-my-children one. (*To* GEORGE.) Wasn't it?

OLIVIA

You do talk nonsense, darling.

DINAH

Well, I'm so happy, now that Mr. Pim has relented about your first husband——
(GEORGE *catches* OLIVIA'S *eye and smiles; she smiles back; but they are different smiles.*)

GEORGE

(*The actor*). Yes, yes, stupid fellow Pim, what?

BRIAN

Absolute idiot.

DINAH

—And now that George has relented about *my* first husband.

GEORGE

You get on much too quickly, young woman. (*To* BRIAN.) So you want to marry my Dinah, eh?

BRIAN

(*With a smile*). Well, I do rather, sir.

DINAH

(*Hastily*). Not at once, of course, George. We want to be engaged for a long time first, and write letters to each other, and tell each other how much we love each other, and sit next to each other when we go out to dinner.

GEORGE

(*To* OLIVIA). Well, *that* sounds fairly harmless, I think.

OLIVIA

(*Smiling*). I think so . . .

GEORGE

(*To* BRIAN). Then you'd better have a talk with me—er—Brian.

BRIAN

Thank you very much, sir.

GEORGE

Well, come along then. (*Looking at his watch.*) I am going up to town after tea, so we'd better——

DINAH

I say! Are you going to London?

GEORGE

(*With the smile of the conspirator*). A little business. Never you mind, young lady.

DINAH

(*Calmly*). All right. Only, bring me back something nice.

GEORGE

(*To* BRIAN). Shall we walk down and look at the pigs?

BRIAN

Righto!

OLIVIA

Don't go far, dear. I may want you in a moment.

GEORGE

All right, darling, we'll be on the terrace. (*They go out together.*)

DINAH

Brian and George always try to discuss me in front of the pigs. So tactless of them. Are you going to London, too, darling?

OLIVIA

Tomorrow morning.

DINAH

What are you going to do in London?

OLIVIA

Oh, shopping, and—one or two little things.

DINAH

With George?

OLIVIA

Yes. . . .

DINAH

I say, wasn't it lovely about Pim?

OLIVIA

Lovely?

DINAH

Yes; he told me all about it. Making such a hash of things, I mean.

OLIVIA

(*Innocently*). Did he make a hash of things?

DINAH

Well, I mean keeping on coming like that. And if you look at it all round—well, for all he had to say, he needn't really have come at all.

OLIVIA

(*Smiling to herself*). I shouldn't quite say that, Dinah. (*She stands up and shakes out the curtains.*)

DINAH

I say, aren't they jolly?

OLIVIA

(*Demurely*). I'm so glad everybody likes them. Tell George I'm ready, will you?

DINAH

I say, is *he* going to hang them up for you?

OLIVIA

Well, I thought he could reach best.

DINAH

Righto! What fun! (*At the windows.*) George! George! (*To* OLIVIA.) Brian is just telling George about the five shillings he's got in the Post Office. . . . George!

GEORGE

(*From the terrace.*) Coming!
(*He hurries in, the model husband.* BRIAN *follows.*)

OLIVIA

Oh, George, just hang these up for me, will you?

GEORGE

Of course, darling. I'll get the steps from the library.
(*He hurries out.*)
(BRIAN *takes out his sketching block. It is obvious that his five shillings has turned the scale. He bows to* DINAH. *He kisses* OLIVIA'S *hand with an air. He motions to* DINAH *to be seated.*)

DINAH

(*Impressed*). What is it?

BRIAN

(*Beginning to draw*). Portrait of Lady Strange.
(GEORGE *hurries in with the steps, and gets to work. There is a great deal of curtain, and for the moment he becomes slightly involved in it. However, by draping it over his head and shoulders, he manages to get successfully up the steps. There we may leave him. But we have not quite finished with* MR. PIM. *It is a matter of honor with him now that he should get his little story quite accurate before passing out of the* MARDENS' *life forever. So he comes back for the last time; for the last time we see his head at the window. He whispers to* OLIVIA.)

MR. PIM

Mrs. Marden! I've just remembered. His name was *Ernest* Polwittle—*not* Henry.
(*He goes off happily. A curious family the* MARDENS. *Perhaps somebody else would have committed bigamy if he had not remembered in time that it was Ernest. . . . Ernest. . . . Yes. . . . Now he can go back with an easy conscience to the Trevors.*)

Ferenc Molnar

LILIOM

A Legend in Seven Scenes

and a Prologue

English Text by Benjamin F. Glazer

FERENC MOLNAR

In Budapest, the city whose spirit he so completely embodies and portrays, Ferenc Molnar was born on January 12th, 1878. Trained in his youth for the legal profession, his first opus was a learned paper on criminal law and statistics. There followed in great profusion short stories, novels, plays and witty feuilletons. In 1907, his play, *The Devil,* was written and shortly afterward became an American sensation. When Molnar was thirty-one, *Liliom* was produced and his international reputation was even more firmly established. As a correspondent during the World War, his articles had the distinction of being syndicated not only in his native land, but also in such enemy newspapers as the *London Morning Post* and the *New York Times.* After the War, Molnar wrote *The Swan* and won with it the French Cross of the Legion of Honor. Other plays that have added lustre to his name are *The Guardsman, The Play's the Thing, Fashions for Men,* and *One, Two, Three.* Madame Molnar (Lili Darvas) is one of the most celebrated beauties and most accomplished actresses of the Hungarian stage.

CHARACTERS

MARIE
JULIE
MRS. MUSKAT
"LILIOM"*
FOUR SERVANT GIRLS
POLICEMEN
CAPTAIN
PLAINCLOTHES MAN
MOTHER HOLLUNDER
"THE SPARROW"
WOLF BERKOWITZ
YOUNG HOLLUNDER
LINZMAN
FIRST MOUNTED POLICEMAN
SECOND MOUNTED POLICEMAN
THE DOCTOR
THE CARPENTER
FIRST POLICEMAN OF THE BEYOND
SECOND POLICEMAN OF THE BEYOND
THE RICHLY DRESSED MAN
THE POORLY DRESSED MAN
THE OLD GUARD
THE MAGISTRATE
LOUISE
PEASANTS, TOWNSPEOPLE, ETC.

* Liliom is the Hungarian for lily, and the slang term for "a tough."

SCENES

PROLOGUE: An Amusement Park on the Outskirts of Budapest.
SCENE I: A Lonely Place in the Park.
SCENE II: The Tin Type Shop of the HOLLUNDERS.
SCENE III: The Same.
SCENE IV: A Railroad Embankment Outside the City.
SCENE V: Same as Scene Two.
SCENE VI: A Courtroom in the Beyond.
SCENE VII: Before JULIE's Door.

LILIOM

THE PROLOGUE

AN *amusement park on the outskirts of Budapest on a late afternoon in Spring. Barkers stand before the booths of the sideshows haranguing the passing crowd. The strident music of a calliope is heard; laughter, shouts, the scuffle of feet, the signal bells of merry-go-round.*

The merry-go-round is at center. LILIOM *stands at the entrance, a cigarette in his mouth, coaxing the people in. The girls regard him with idolizing glances and screech with pleasure as he playfully pushes them through entrance. Now and then some girl's escort resents the familiarity, whereupon* LILIOM'S *demeanor becomes ugly and menacing, and the cowed escort slinks through the entrance behind his girl or contents himself with a muttered resentful comment.*

One girl hands LILIOM *a red carnation; he rewards her with a bow and a smile. When the soldier who accompanies her protests,* LILIOM *cows him with a fierce glance and a threatening gesture.* MARIE *and* JULIE *come out of the crowd and* LILIOM *favors them with particular notice as they pass into the merry-go-round.*

MRS. MUSKAT *comes out of the merry-go-round, bringing* LILIOM *coffee and rolls.* LILIOM *mounts the barker's stand at the entrance, where he is elevated over every one on the stage. Here he begins his harangue. Everybody turns towards him. The other booths are gradually deserted. The tumult makes it impossible for the audience to hear what he is saying, but every now and then some witticism of his provokes a storm of laughter which is audible above the din. Many people enter the merry-go-round. Here and there one catches a phrase "Room for one more on the zebra's back," "Which of you ladies?" "Ten heller for adults, five for children," "Step right up"——*

It is growing darker. A lamplighter crosses the stage, and begins unperturbedly lighting the colored gas-lamps. The whistle of a distant locomotive is heard. Suddenly the tumult ceases, the lights go out, and the curtain falls in darkness.

SCENE I

SCENE: *A lonely place in the park, half hidden by trees and shrubbery. Under a flowering acacia tree stands a painted wooden bench. From the distance, faintly, comes the tumult of the amusement park. It is the sunset of the same day.*

When the curtain rises the stage is empty.

MARIE *enters quickly, pauses at center, and looks back.*

MARIE

Julie, Julie! (*There is no answer.*) Do you hear me, Julie? Let her be! Come on. Let her be. (*Starts to go back.* JULIE *enters, looks back angrily.*)

JULIE

Did you ever hear of such a thing? What's the matter with the woman anyway?

MARIE

(*Looking back again*). Here she comes again.

JULIE

Let her come. I didn't do anything to her. All of a sudden she comes up to me and begins to raise a row.

MARIE

Here she is. Come on, let's run. (*Tries to urge her off.*)

JULIE

Run? I should say not. What would I want to run for? I'm not afraid of her.

MARIE

Oh, come on. She'll only start a fight.

JULIE

I'm going to stay right here. Let her *start* a fight.

MRS. MUSKAT

(*Entering*). What do you want to run away for? (*To* JULIE.) Don't worry. I won't eat you. But there's one thing I want to tell you, my dear. Don't let me catch you in my carousel again. I stand for a whole lot; I have to in my business. It makes no difference to me whether my customers are ladies or the likes of you—as long as they pay their money. But when a girl misbehaves herself on my carousel—out she goes. Do you understand?

JULIE

Are you talking to me?

MRS. MUSKAT

Yes, you! You—chamber-maid, you! In my carousel——

JULIE

Who did anything in your old carousel? I paid my fare and took my seat and never said a word, except to my friend here.

MARIE

No, she never opened her mouth. Liliom came over to her of his own accord.

MRS. MUSKAT

It's all the same. I'm not going to get in trouble with the police, and lose my license on account of you—you shabby kitchen maid!

JULIE

Shabby yourself.

MRS. MUSKAT

You stay out of my carousel! Letting my barker fool with you! Aren't you ashamed of yourself?

JULIE

What? What did you say?

MRS. MUSKAT

I suppose you think I have no eyes in my head. I see everything that goes on in my carousel. During the whole ride she let Liliom fool with her—the shameless hussy!

JULIE

He did not fool with me! I don't let any man fool with me!

MRS. MUSKAT

He leaned against you all through the ride!

JULIE

He leaned against the panther. He always leans against something, doesn't he? Everybody leans where he wants. I couldn't tell him not to lean, if he always leans, could I? But he didn't lay a hand on me.

MRS. MUSKAT

Oh, didn't he? And I suppose he didn't put his hand around your waist, either?

MARIE

And if he did? What of it?

MRS. MUSKAT

You hold your tongue! No one's asking you—just you keep out of it.

JULIE

He put his arm around my waist—just the same as he does to all the girls. He always does that.

MRS. MUSKAT

I'll teach him not to do it any more, my dear. No carryings on in my carousel! If you are looking for that sort of thing, you'd better go to the circus! You'll find lots of soldiers there to carry on with!

JULIE

You keep your soldiers for yourself!

MARIE

Soldiers! As if we wanted soldiers!

MRS. MUSKAT

Well, I only want to tell you this, my dear, so that we understand each other perfectly. If you ever stick your nose in my carousel again, you'll wish you hadn't! I'm not going to lose my license on account of the likes of you! People who don't know how to behave, have got to stay out!

JULIE

You're wasting your breath. If I feel like riding on your carousel I'll pay my ten heller and I'll ride. I'd like to see any one try to stop me!

MRS. MUSKAT

Just come and try it, my dear—just come and try it.

MARIE

We'll see what'll happen.

MRS. MUSKAT

Yes, you will see something happen that never happened before in this park.

JULIE

Perhaps you think you could throw me out!

MRS. MUSKAT

I'm sure of it, my dear.

JULIE

And suppose I'm stronger than you?

MRS. MUSKAT

I'd think twice before I'd dirty my hands on a common servant girl. I'll have Liliom throw you out. He knows how to handle your kind.

JULIE

You think Liliom would throw me out.

MRS. MUSKAT

Yes, my dear, so fast that you won't know what happened to you!

JULIE

He'd throw me— (*Stops suddenly, for* MRS. MUSKAT *has turned away. Both look off stage until* LILIOM *enters, surrounded by four giggling servant girls.*)

LILIOM

Go away! Stop following me, or I'll smack your face!

A LITTLE SERVANT GIRL

Well, give me back my handkerchief.

LILIOM

Go on now—

THE FOUR SERVANT GIRLS

(*Simultaneously*). What do you think of him?—My handkerchief!—Give it back to her!—That's a nice thing to do!

THE LITTLE SERVANT GIRL

(*To* MRS. MUSKAT). Please, lady, make him—

MRS. MUSKAT

Oh, shut up!

LILIOM

Will you get out of here? (*Makes a threatening gesture—the four servant girls exit in voluble but fearful haste.*)

MRS. MUSKAT

What have you been doing now?

LILIOM

None of your business. (*Glances at* JULIE.) Have you been starting with her again?

JULIE

Mister Liliom, please—

LILIOM

(*Steps threateningly towards her*). Don't yell!

JULIE

(*Timidly*). I didn't yell.

LILIOM

Well, don't. (*To* MRS. MUSKAT.) What's the matter? What has she done to you?

MRS. MUSKAT

What has she done? She's been impudent to me. Just as impudent as she could be! I put her out of the carousel. Take a good look at this innocent thing, Liliom. She's never to be allowed in my carousel again!

LILIOM

(*To* JULIE). You heard that. Run home, now.

MARIE

Come on. Don't waste your time with such people. (*Tries to lead* JULIE *away*).

JULIE

No, I won't—

MRS. MUSKAT

If she ever comes again, you're not to let her in. And if she gets in before you see her, throw her out. Understand?

LILIOM

What has she done, anyhow?

JULIE

(*Agitated and very earnest*). Mister Liliom—tell me please—honest and truly—if I come into the carousel, will you throw me out?

MRS. MUSKAT

Of course he'll throw you out.

MARIE

She wasn't talking to you.

JULIE

Tell me straight to my face, Mister Liliom, would you throw me out? (*They face each other. There is a brief pause.*)

LILIOM

Yes, little girl, if there was a reason—but if there was no reason, why should I throw you out?

MARIE

(*To* MRS. MUSKAT). There, you see!

JULIE

Thank you, Mister Liliom.

MRS. MUSKAT

And I tell you again, if this little slut dares to set her foot in my carousel, she's to be thrown out! I'll stand for no indecency in my establishment.

LILIOM

What do you mean—indecency?

MRS. MUSKAT

I saw it all. There's no use denying it.

JULIE

She says you put your arm around my waist.

LILIOM

Me?

MRS. MUSKAT

Yes, you! I saw you. Don't play the innocent.

LILIOM

Here's something new! I'm not to put my arm around a girl's waist any more! I suppose I'm to ask your permission before I touch another girl!

MRS. MUSKAT

You can touch as many girls as you want and as often as you want—for my part you can go as far as you like with any of them—but not this one—I permit no indecency in my carousel. (*There is a long pause.*)

LILIOM

(*To* MRS. MUSKAT). And now I'll ask you please to shut your mouth.

MRS. MUSKAT

What?

LILIOM

Shut your mouth quick, and go back to your carousel.

MRS. MUSKAT

What?

LILIOM

What did she do to you, anyhow? Tryin' to start a fight with a little pigeon like that . . . just because I touched her?—You come to the carousel as often as you want to, little girl. Come every afternoon, and sit on the panther's back, and if you haven't got the price, Liliom will pay for you. And if any one dares to bother you, you come and tell *me*.

MRS. MUSKAT

You reprobate!

LILIOM

Old witch!

JULIE

Thank you, Mister Liliom.

MRS. MUSKAT

You seem to think that I can't throw you out, too. What's the reason I can't? Because you are the best barker in the park? Well, you are very much mistaken. In fact, you can consider yourself thrown out already. You're discharged!

LILIOM

Very good.

MRS. MUSKAT

(*Weakening a little*). I can discharge you any time I feel like it.

LILIOM

Very good, you feel like discharging me. I'm discharged. That settles it.

MRS. MUSKAT

Playing the high and mighty, are you? Conceited pig! Good-for-nothing!

LILIOM

You said you'd throw me out, didn't you? Well, that suits me; I'm thrown out.

MRS. MUSKAT

(*Softening*). Do you have to take up every word I say?

LILIOM

It's all right; it's all settled. I'm a good-for-nothing. And a conceited pig. And I'm discharged.

MRS. MUSKAT

Do you want to ruin my business?

LILIOM

A good-for-nothing? Now I know! And I'm discharged! Very good.

MRS. MUSKAT

You're a devil, you are . . . and that woman—

LILIOM

Keep away from her!

MRS. MUSKAT

I'll get Hollinger to give you such a beating that you'll hear all the angels sing . . . and it won't be the first time, either.

LILIOM

Get out of here. I'm discharged. And you get out of here.

JULIE

(*Timidly*). Mister Liliom, if she's willing to say that she hasn't discharged you—

LILIOM

You keep out of this.

JULIE

(*Timidly*). I don't want this to happen on account of me.

LILIOM

(*To* MRS. MUSKAT, *pointing to* JULIE). Apologize to her!

MARIE

A-ha!

MRS. MUSKAT

Apologize? To who?

LILIOM

To this little pigeon. Well—are you going to do it?

MRS. MUSKAT

If you give me this whole park on a silver plate, and all the gold of the Rothschilds on top of it—I'd—I'd— Let her dare to come into my carousel again and she'll get thrown out so hard that she'll see stars in daylight!

LILIOM

In that case, dear lady (*takes off his cap with a flourish*), you are respectfully requested to get out o' here as fast as your legs will carry you—I never beat up a woman yet—except that Holzer woman who I sent to the hospital for three weeks —but—if you don't get out o' here this minute, and let this little squab be, I'll give you the prettiest slap in the jaw you ever had in your life.

MRS. MUSKAT

Very good, my son. Now you *can* go to the devil. Good-bye. You're discharged, and you needn't try to come back, either. (*She exits. It is beginning to grow dark*.)

MARIE

(*With grave concern*). Mister Liliom—

LILIOM

Don't you pity me or I'll give *you* a slap in the jaw. (*To* JULIE.) And don't you pity me, either.

JULIE

(*In alarm*). I don't pity you, Mister Liliom.

LILIOM

You're a liar, you *are* pitying me. I can see it in your face. You're thinking, now that Madame Muskat has thrown him out, Liliom will have to go begging. Huh! Look at me. I'm big enough to get along without a Madame Muskat. I have been thrown out of better jobs than hers.

JULIE

What will you do now, Mister Liliom?

LILIOM

Now? First of all, I'll go and get myself—a glass of beer. You see, when something happens to annoy me, I always drink a glass of beer.

JULIE

Then you *are* annoyed about losing your job.

LILIOM

No, only about where I'm going to get the beer.

MARIE

Well—eh—

LILIOM

Well—eh—what?

MARIE

Well—eh—are you going to stay with us, Mister Liliom?

LILIOM

Will you pay for the beer? (MARIE *looks doubtful; he turns to* JULIE.) Will you? (*She does not answer*.) How much money have you got?

JULIE

(*Bashfully*). Eight heller.

LILIOM

And you? (MARIE *casts down her eyes and does not reply.* LILIOM *continues sternly.*) I asked you how much you've got? (MARIE *begins to weep softly.*) I understand. Well, you needn't cry about it. You girls stay here, while I go back to the carousel and get my clothes and things. And when I come back, we'll go to the Hungarian beer-garden. It's all right, I'll pay. Keep your money. (*He exits.* MARIE *and* JULIE *stand silent, watching him until he has gone.*)

MARIE

Are you sorry for him?

JULIE

Are you?

MARIE

Yes, a little. Why are you looking after him in that funny way?

JULIE

(*Sits down*). Nothing—except I'm sorry he lost his job.

MARIE

(*With a touch of pride*). It was on our account he lost his job. Because he's fallen in love with you.

JULIE

He hasn't at all.

MARIE

(*Confidently*). Oh, yes! he is in love with you. (*Hesitantly, romantically.*) There is some one in love with me, too.

JULIE

There is? Who?

MARIE

I—I never mentioned it before, because you hadn't a lover of your own—but now you have—and I'm free to speak. (*Very grandiloquently.*) My heart has found its mate.

JULIE

You're only making it up.

MARIE

No, it's true—my heart's true love—

JULIE

Who? Who is he?

MARIE

A soldier.

JULIE

What kind of a soldier?

MARIE

I don't know. Just a soldier. Are there different kinds?

JULIE

Many different kinds. There are hussars, artillerymen, engineers, infantry—that's the kind that walks—and—

MARIE

How can you tell which is which?

JULIE

By their uniforms.

MARIE

(*After trying to puzzle it out*). The conductors on the street cars—are they soldiers?

JULIE

Certainly not. They're conductors.

MARIE

Well, they have uniforms.

JULIE

But they don't carry swords or guns.

MARIE

Oh! (*Thinks it over again; then.*) Well, policemen—are they?

JULIE

(*With a touch of exasperation*). Are they what?

MARIE

Soldiers.

JULIE

Certainly not. They're just policemen.

MARIE

(*Triumphantly*). But they have uniforms —and they carry weapons, too.

JULIE

You're just as dumb as you can be. You don't go by their uniforms.

MARIE

But you said—

JULIE

No, I didn't. A letter-carrier wears a uniform, too, but that doesn't make him a soldier.

MARIE

But if he carried a gun or a sword, would he be—

JULIE

No, he'd still be a letter-carrier. You can't go by guns or swords, either.

MARIE

Well, if you don't go by the uniforms or the weapons, what *do* you go by?

JULIE

By— (*Tries to put it into words; fails; then breaks off suddenly.*) Oh, you'll get to know when you've lived in the city long enough. You're nothing but a country girl. When you've lived in the city a year, like I have, you'll know all about it.

MARIE

(*Half angrily*). Well, how *do* you know when *you* see a real soldier?

JULIE

By one thing.

MARIE

What?

JULIE

One thing— (*She pauses.* MARIE *starts to cry.*) Oh, what are you crying about?

MARIE

Because you're making fun of me. . . . You're a city girl, and I'm just fresh from the country . . . and how am I expected to know a soldier when I see one? . . . You, you ought to tell me, instead of making fun of me—

JULIE

All right. Listen then, cry-baby. There's only one way to tell a soldier: by his salute! That's the only way.

MARIE

(*Joyfully; with a sigh of relief*). Ah—that's good.

JULIE

What?

MARIE

I say—it's all right then—because Wolf—Wolf— (JULIE *laughs derisively.*) Wolf—that's his name. (*She weeps again.*)

JULIE

Crying again? What now?

MARIE

You're making fun of me again.

JULIE

I'm not. But when you say, "Wolf—Wolf—" like that, I have to laugh, don't I? (*Archly.*) What's his name again?

MARIE

I won't tell you.

JULIE

All right. If you won't say it, then he's no soldier.

MARIE

I'll say it.

JULIE

Go on.

MARIE

No, I won't. (*She weeps again.*)

JULIE

Then he's not a soldier. I guess he's a letter-carrier—

MARIE

No—no—I'd rather say it.

JULIE

Well, then.

MARIE

(*Giggling*). But you mustn't look at me. You look the other way, and I'll say it. (JULIE *looks away.* MARIE *can hardly restrain her own laughter.*) Wolf! (*She laughs.*) That's his real name. Wolf, Wolf, Soldier—Wolf!

JULIE

What kind of a uniform does he wear?

MARIE

Red.

JULIE

Red trousers?

MARIE

No.

JULIE

Red coat?

MARIE

No.

JULIE

What then?

MARIE

(*Triumphantly*). His cap!

JULIE

(*After a long pause*). He's just a porter, you dunce. Red cap . . . that's a porter—and he doesn't carry a gun or a sword, either.

MARIE

(*Triumphantly*). But he salutes. You said yourself that was the only way to tell a soldier—

JULIE

He doesn't salute at all. He only greets people—

MARIE

He salutes me. . . . And if his name *is* Wolf, that doesn't prove he ain't a soldier—he salutes, and he wears a red cap and he stands on guard all day long outside a big building—

JULIE

What does he do there?

MARIE

(*Seriously*). He spits.

JULIE

(*With contempt*). He's nothing—nothing but a common porter.

MARIE

What's Liliom?

JULIE

(*Indignantly*). Why speak of him? What has he to do with me?

MARIE

The same as Wolf has to do with me. If you can talk to me like that about Wolf, I can talk to you about Liliom.

JULIE

He's nothing to me. He put his arm around me in the carousel. I couldn't tell him not to put his arm around me after he had done it, could I?

MARIE

I suppose you didn't like him to do it?

JULIE

No.

MARIE

Then why are you waiting for him? Why don't you go home?

JULIE

Why—eh—he *said* we were to wait for him. (LILIOM *enters. There is a long silence.*)

LILIOM

Are you still here? What are you waiting for?

MARIE

You told us to wait.

LILIOM

Must you always interfere? No one is talking to you.

MARIE

You asked us—why we—

LILIOM

Will you keep your mouth shut? What do you suppose I want with two of you? I meant that one of you was to wait. The other can go home.

MARIE

All right.

JULIE

All right. (*Neither starts to go.*)

LILIOM

One of you goes home. (*To* MARIE.) Where do you work?

MARIE

At the Breier's, Damjanovitsch Street, Number 20.

LILIOM

And you?

JULIE

I work there, too.

LILIOM

Well, one of you goes home. Which of you wants to stay. (*There is no answer.*) Come on, speak up, which of you stays?

MARIE

(*Officiously*). She'll lose her job if she stays.

LILIOM

Who will?

MARIE

Julie. She has to be back by seven o'clock.

LILIOM

Is that true? Will they discharge you if you're not back on time?

JULIE

Yes.

LILIOM

Well, wasn't I discharged?

JULIE

Yes—you were discharged, too.

MARIE

Julie, shall I go?

JULIE

I—can't tell you what to do.

MARIE

All right—stay if you like.

LILIOM

You'll be discharged if you do?

MARIE

Shall I go, Julie?

JULIE

(*Embarrassed*). Why do you keep asking me that?

MARIE

You know best what to do.

JULIE

(*Profoundly moved; slowly*). It's all right, Marie, you can go home.

MARIE

(*Exits reluctantly, but comes back, and says uncertainly*). Good night. (*She waits a moment to see if* JULIE *will follow her.* JULIE *does not move.* MARIE *exits. Meantime it has grown quite dark. During the following scene the gas-lamps far in the distance are lighted one by one.* LILIOM *and* JULIE *sit on the bench. From afar, very faintly, comes the music of a calliope. But the music is intermittently heard; now it breaks off, now it resumes again, as if it came down on a fitful wind. Blending with it are the sounds of human voices, now loud, now soft; the blare of a toy trumpet; the confused noises of the show-booths. It grows progressively darker until the end of the scene. There is no moonlight. The spring iridescence glows in the deep blue sky.*)

LILIOM

Now we're both discharged. (*She does not answer. From now on they speak gradually lower and lower until the end of the scene, which is played almost in whispers. Whistles softly, then.*) Have you had your supper?

JULIE

No.

LILIOM

Want to go eat something at the Garden?

JULIE

No.

LILIOM

Anywhere else?

JULIE

No.

LILIOM

(*Whistles softly, then*). You don't come to this park very often, do you? I've only seen you three times. Been here oftener than that?

JULIE

Oh, yes.

LILIOM

Did you see me?

JULIE

Yes.

LILIOM

And did you know I was Liliom?

JULIE

They told me.

LILIOM

(*Whistles softly, then*). Have you got a sweetheart?

JULIE

No.

LILIOM

Don't lie to me.

JULIE

I haven't. If I had, I'd tell you. I've never had one.

LILIOM

What an awful liar you are. I've got a good mind to go away and leave you here.

JULIE

I've never had one.

LILIOM

Tell that to some one else.

JULIE

(*Reproachfully*). Why do you insist I have?

LILIOM

Because you stayed here with me the first time I asked you to. You know your way around, you do.

JULIE

No, I don't, Mister Liliom.

LILIOM

I suppose you'll tell me you don't know why you're sitting here—like this, in the dark, alone with me—You wouldn't 'a' stayed so quick, if you hadn't done it before—with some soldier, maybe. This isn't the first time. You wouldn't have been so ready to stay if it was—what *did* you stay for, anyhow?

JULIE

So you wouldn't be left alone.

LILIOM

Alone! God, you're dumb! I don't need to be alone. I can have all the girls I want. Not only servant girls like you, but cooks and governesses, even French girls. I could have twenty of them if I wanted to.

JULIE

I know, Mister Liliom.

LILIOM

What do you know?

JULIE

That all the girls are in love with you. But that's not why *I* stayed. I stayed because you've been so good to me.

LILIOM

Well, then you can go home.

JULIE

I don't want to go home now.

LILIOM

And what if I go away and leave you sitting here?

JULIE

If you did, I wouldn't go home.

LILIOM

Do you know what you remind me of? A sweetheart I had once—I'll tell you how I met her—One night, at closing time, we had put out the lights in the carousel, and just as I was— (*He is interrupted by the entrance of two plainclothes policemen. They take their stations on either side of the bench. They are police, searching the park for vagabonds.*)

FIRST POLICEMAN

What are you doing there?

LILIOM

Me?

SECOND POLICEMAN

Stand up when you're spoken to! (*He taps* LILIOM *imperatively on the shoulder.*)

FIRST POLICEMAN

What's your name?

LILIOM

Andreas Zaboczki. (JULIE *begins to weep softly.*)

SECOND POLICEMAN

Stop your bawling. We're not goin' to eat you. We are only making our rounds.

FIRST POLICEMAN

See that he doesn't get away. (THE SECOND POLICEMAN *steps closer to* LILIOM.) What's your business?

LILIOM

Barker and bouncer.

SECOND POLICEMAN

They call him Liliom, Chief. We've had him up a couple of times.

FIRST POLICEMAN

So that's who you are! Who do you work for now?

LILIOM

I work for the widow Muskat.

FIRST POLICEMAN

What are you hanging around here for?

LILIOM

We're just sitting here—me and this girl.

FIRST POLICEMAN

Your sweetheart?

LILIOM

No.

FIRST POLICEMAN

(*To* JULIE). And who are you?

JULIE

Julie Zeller.

FIRST POLICEMAN

Servant girl?

JULIE

Maid of All Work for Mister Georg Breier, Number Twenty Damjanovitsch Street.

FIRST POLICEMAN

Show your hands.

SECOND POLICEMAN

(*After examining* JULIE's *hand*). Servant girl.

FIRST POLICEMAN

Why aren't you at home? What are you doing out here with him?

JULIE

This is my day out, sir.

FIRST POLICEMAN

It would be better for you if you didn't spend it sitting around with a fellow like this.

SECOND POLICEMAN

They'll be disappearing in the bushes as soon as we turn our backs.

FIRST POLICEMAN

He's only after your money. We know this fine fellow. He picks up you silly servant girls and takes what money you have. To-morrow you'll probably be coming around to report him. If you do, I'll throw you out.

JULIE

I haven't any money, sir.

FIRST POLICEMAN

Do you hear that, Liliom?

LILIOM

I'm not looking for her money.

SECOND POLICEMAN

(*Nudging him warningly*). Keep your mouth shut.

FIRST POLICEMAN

It is my duty to warn you, my child, what kind of company you're in. He makes a specialty of servant girls. That's why he works in a carousel. He gets hold of a girl, promises to marry her, then he takes her money and her ring.

JULIE

But I haven't got a ring.

SECOND POLICEMAN

You're not to talk unless you're asked a question.

FIRST POLICEMAN

You be thankful that I'm warning you. It's nothing to me what you do. I'm not your father, thank God. But I'm telling you what kind of a fellow he is. By to-morrow morning you'll be coming around to us to report him. Now you be sensible and go home. You needn't be afraid of him. This officer will take you home if you're afraid.

JULIE

Do I *have* to go?

FIRST POLICEMAN

No, you don't *have* to go.

JULIE

Then I'll stay, sir.

FIRST POLICEMAN

Well, you've been warned.

JULIE

Yes, sir. Thank you, sir.

FIRST POLICEMAN

Come on, Berkovics. (*The* POLICEMEN *exit.* JULIE *and* LILIOM *sit on the bench again. There is a brief pause*).

JULIE

Well, and what then?

LILIOM

(*Fails to understand*). Huh?

JULIE

You were beginning to tell me a story.

LILIOM

Me?

JULIE

Yes, about a sweetheart. You said, one night, just as they were putting out the lights of the carousel— That's as far as you got.

LILIOM

Oh, yes, yes, just as the lights were going out, some one came along—a little girl with a big shawl—you know— She came—eh—from— Say—tell me—ain't you—that is, ain't you at all—afraid of me? The officer told you what kind of a fellow I am—and that I'd take your money away from you—

JULIE

You couldn't take it away—I haven't got any. But if I had—I'd—I'd give it to you—I'd give it all to you.

LILIOM

You would?

JULIE

If you asked me for it.

LILIOM

Have you ever had a fellow you gave money to?

JULIE

No.

LILIOM

Haven't you ever had a sweetheart?

JULIE

No.

LILIOM

Some one you used to go walking with. You've had one like that?

JULIE

Yes.

LILIOM

A soldier?

JULIE

He came from the same village I did.

LILIOM

That's what all the soldiers say. Where *do* you come from, anyway?

JULIE

Not far from here. (*There is a pause.*)

LILIOM

Were you in love with him?

JULIE

Why do you keep asking me that all the time, Mister Liliom? I wasn't in love with him. We only went walking together.

LILIOM

Where did you walk?

JULIE

In the park.

LILIOM

And your virtue? Where did you lose that?

JULIE

I haven't got any virtue.

LILIOM

Well, you had once.

JULIE

No, I never had. I'm a respectable girl.

LILIOM

Yes, but you gave the soldier something.

JULIE

Why do you question me like that, Mister Liliom?

LILIOM

Did you give him something?

JULIE

You have to. But I didn't love him.

LILIOM

Do you love me?

JULIE

No, Mister Liliom.

LILIOM

Then why do you stay here with me?

JULIE

Um—nothing. (*There is a pause. The music from afar is plainly heard.*)

LILIOM

Want to dance?

JULIE

No. I have to be very careful.

LILIOM

Of what?

JULIE

My—character.

LILIOM

Why?

JULIE

Because I'm never going to marry. If I was going to marry, it would be different. Then I wouldn't need to worry so much about my character. It doesn't make any difference if you're married. But I shan't marry—and that's why I've got to take care to be a respectable girl.

LILIOM

Suppose I were to say to you—I'll marry you.

JULIE

You?

LILIOM

That frightens you, doesn't it? You're thinking of what the officer said and you're afraid.

JULIE

No, I'm not, Mister Liliom. I don't pay any attention to what he said.

LILIOM

But you wouldn't dare to marry any one like me, would you?

JULIE

I know that—that—if I loved any one—it wouldn't make any difference to me what he—even if I died for it.

LILIOM

But you wouldn't marry a rough guy like me—that is, er—if you loved me—

JULIE

Yes, I would—if I loved you, Mister Liliom. (*There is a pause.*)

LILIOM

(*Whispers*). Well—you just said—didn't you?—that you don't love me. Well, why don't you go home then?

JULIE

It's too late now, they'd all be asleep.

LILIOM

Locked out?

JULIE

Certainly. (*They are silent a while.*)

LILIOM

I think—that even a low-down good-for-nothing—can make a man of himself.

JULIE

Certainly. (*They are silent again. A lamp-lighter crosses the stage, lights the lamp over the bench, and exits.*)

LILIOM

Are you hungry?

JULIE

No. (*Another pause.*)

LILIOM

Suppose—you had some money—and I took it from you?

JULIE

Then you could take it, that's all.

LILIOM

(*After another brief silence*). All I have to do—is go back to her—that Muskat woman—she'll be glad to get me back—then I'd be earning my wages again. (*She is silent. The twilight folds darker about them.*)

JULIE

(*Very softly*). Don't go back—to her—(*Pause.*)

LILIOM

There are a lot of acacia trees around here. (*Pause.*)

JULIE

Don't go back to her— (*Pause.*)

LILIOM

She'd take me back the minute I asked her. I know why—she knows, too— (*Pause.*)

JULIE

I can smell them, too—acacia blossoms—(*There is a pause. Some blossoms drift down from the treetop to the bench.* LILIOM *picks one up and smells it.*)

LILIOM

White acacias!

JULIE

(*After a brief pause*). The wind brings them down. (*They are silent. There is a long pause before*

THE CURTAIN FALLS

SCENE II

SCENE: *A photographer's "studio," operated by the* HOLLUNDERS, *on the fringe of the park. It is a dilapidated hovel. The general entrance is Back Left. Back Right there is a window with a sofa before it. The outlook is on the amusement park with perhaps a small ferris-wheel or the scaffolding of a "scenic-railway" in the background.*

The door to the kitchen is up Left and a black-curtained entrance to the dark-room is down Left. Just in front of the dark-room stands the camera on its tripod. Against the back wall, between the door and window, stands the inevitable photographer's background-screen, ready to be wheeled into place.

It is forenoon. When the curtain rises, MARIE *and* JULIE *are discovered.*

MARIE

And *he* beat up Hollinger?

JULIE

Yes, he gave him an awful licking.

MARIE

But Hollinger is bigger than he is.

JULIE

He licked him just the same. It isn't size that counts, you know, it's cleverness. And Liliom's awful quick.

MARIE

And then he was arrested?

JULIE

Yes, they arrested him, but they let him go the next day. That makes twice in the two months we've been living here that Liliom's been arrested and let go again.

MARIE

Why do they let him go?

JULIE

Because he is innocent.

(MOTHER HOLLUNDER, *a very old woman, sharp-tongued, but in reality quite warm-hearted beneath her formidable exterior, enters at back carrying a few sticks of firewood, and scolding, half to herself.*)

MOTHER HOLLUNDER

Always wanting something, but never willing to work for it. He won't work, and he won't steal, but he'll use up a poor old widow's last bit of firewood. He'll do that cheerfully enough! A big, strong lout like that lying around all day resting his lazy bones! He ought to be ashamed to look decent people in the face.

JULIE

I'm sorry, Mother Hollunder. . . .

MOTHER HOLLUNDER

Sorry! Better be sorry the lazy good-for-nothing ain't in jail where he belongs instead of in the way of honest, hard-working people. (*She exits into the kitchen.*)

MARIE

Who's that?

JULIE

Mrs. Hollunder—my aunt. This is her (*with a sweeping gesture that takes in the camera, dark-room and screen*) studio. She lets us live here for nothing.

MARIE

What's she fetching the wood for?

JULIE

She brings us everything we need. If it weren't for her I don't know what would become of us. She's a good-hearted soul even if her tongue is sharp. (*There is a pause.*)

MARIE

(*Shyly*). Do you know—I've found out He's not a soldier.

JULIE

Do you still see him?

MARIE

Oh, yes.

JULIE

Often?

MARIE

Very often. He's asked me—

MARIE

To marry you?

MARIE

To marry me.

JULIE

You see—that proves he isn't a soldier. (*There is another pause.*)

MARIE

(*Abashed, yet a bit boastfully*). Do you know what I'm doing—I'm flirting with him.

JULIE

Flirting?

MARIE

Yes. He asks me to go to the park—and I say I can't go. Then he coaxes me, and promises me a new scarf for my head if I go. But I don't go—even then. . . . So then he walks all the way home with me—and I bid him good-night at the door.

JULIE

Is that what you call flirting?

MARIE

Um-hm! It's sinful, but it's so *thrilling*.

JULIE

Do you ever quarrel?

MARIE

(*Grandly*). Only when our Passionate Love surges up.

JULIE

Your passionate love?

MARIE

Yes. . . . He takes my hand and we walk along together. Then he wants to swing hands, but I won't let him. I say: "Don't swing my hand"; and he says, "Don't be so stubborn." And then he tries to swing my hand again, but still I don't let him. And for a long time I don't let him—until in the end I let him. Then we walk along swinging hands—up and down, up and down—just like this. *That* is Passionate Love. It's sinful, but it's awfully *thrilling.*

JULIE

You're happy, aren't you?

MARIE

Happier than—anything— But the most beautiful thing on earth is Ideal Love.

JULIE

What kind is that?

MARIE

Daylight comes about three in the morning this time of the year. When we've been up that long we're all through with flirting and Passionate Love—and then our Ideal Love comes to the surface. It comes like this: I'll be sitting on the bench and Wolf, he holds my hand tight—and he puts his cheek against my cheek and we don't talk . . . we just sit there very quiet. . . . And after a while he gets sleepy, and his head sinks down, and he falls asleep . . . but even in his sleep he holds tight to my hand. And I—I sit perfectly still just looking around me and taking long, deep breaths—for by that time it's morning and the trees and flowers are fresh with dew. But Wolf doesn't smell anything because he's so fast asleep. And I get awfully sleepy myself, but I don't sleep. And we sit like that for a long time. That is Ideal Love—(*There is a long pause.*)

JULIE

(*Regretfully; uneasily*). He went out last night and he hasn't come home yet.

MARIE

Here are sixteen Kreuzer. It was supposed to be carfare to take my young lady to the conservatory—eight there and eight back—but I made her walk. Here—save it with the rest.

JULIE

This makes three gulden, forty-six.

MARIE

Three gulden, forty-six.

JULIE

He won't work at all.

MARIE

Too lazy?

JULIE

No. He never learned a trade, you see, and he can't just go and be a day-laborer—so he does nothing.

MARIE

That ain't right.

JULIE

No. Have the Breiers got a new maid yet?

MARIE

They've had three since you left. You know, Wolf's going to take a new job. He's going to work for the city. He'll get rent free, too.

JULIE

He won't go back to work at the carousel either. I ask him why, but he won't tell me— Last Monday he hit me.

MARIE

Did you hit him back?

JULIE

No.

MARIE

Why don't you leave him?

JULIE

I don't want to.

MARIE

I would. I'd leave him. (*There is a strained silence.*)

MOTHER HOLLUNDER

(*Enters, carrying a pot of water; muttering aloud*). He can play cards, all right. He can fight, too; and take money from poor servant girls. And the police turn their heads the other way—The carpenter was here.

JULIE

Is that water for the soup?

MOTHER HOLLUNDER

The carpenter was here. There's a *man* for you! Dark, handsome, lots of hair, a respectable widower with two children—and money, and a good paying business.

JULIE

(*To* MARIE). It's three gulden sixty-six, not forty-six.

MARIE

Yes, that's what I make it—sixty-six.

MOTHER HOLLUNDER

He wants to take her out of this and marry her. This is the fifth time he's been here. He has two children, but—

JULIE

Please don't bother, Aunt Hollunder, I'll get the water myself.

MOTHER HOLLUNDER

He's waiting outside now.

JULIE

Send him away.

MOTHER HOLLUNDER

He'll only come back again—and first thing you know that vagabond will get jealous and there'll be a fight. (*Goes out, muttering.*) Oh, he's ready enough to fight, he is. Strike a poor little girl like that! Ought to be ashamed of himself! And the police just let him go on doing as he pleases. (*Still scolding, she exits at back.*)

MARIE

A carpenter wants to marry you?

JULIE

Yes.

MARIE

Why don't you?

JULIE

Because—

MARIE

Liliom doesn't support you, and he beats you—he thinks he can do whatever he likes just because he's Liliom. He's a bad one.

JULIE

He's not really bad.

MARIE

That night you sat on the bench together—he was gentle then.

JULIE

Yes, he was gentle.

MARIE

And afterwards he got wild again.

JULIE

Afterwards he got wild—sometimes. But that night on the bench . . . he was gentle. He's gentle now, sometimes, very gentle. After supper, when he stands there and listens to the music of the carousel, something comes over him—and he is gentle.

MARIE

Does he say anything?

JULIE

He doesn't say anything. He gets thoughtful and very quiet, and his big eyes stare straight ahead of him.

MARIE

Into your eyes?

JULIE

Not exactly. He's unhappy because he isn't working. That's really why he hit me on Monday.

MARIE

That's a fine reason for hitting you! Beats his wife because he isn't working, the ruffian!

JULIE

It preys on his mind—

MARIE

Did he hurt you?

JULIE

(*Very eagerly*). Oh, no.

MRS. MUSKAT

(*Enters haughtily*). Good morning. Is Liliom home?

JULIE

No.

MRS. MUSKAT

Gone out?

JULIE

He hasn't come home yet.

MRS. MUSKAT

I'll wait for him. (*She sits down.*)

MARIE

You've got a lot of gall—to come here.

MRS. MUSKAT

Are you the lady of the house, my dear? Better look out or you'll get a slap in the mouth.

MARIE

How dare you set foot in Julie's house?

MRS. MUSKAT

(*To* JULIE). Pay no attention to her, my child. You know what brings me here. That vagabond, that good-for-nothing, I've come to give him his bread and butter back.

MARIE

He's not dependent on you for his bread.

MRS. MUSKAT

(*To* JULIE). Just ignore her, my child. She's just ignorant.

MARIE

(*Going*). Good-bye.

JULIE

Good-bye.

MARIE

(*In the doorway, calling back*). Sixty-six.

JULIE

Yes, sixty-six.

MARIE

Good-bye. (*She exits.* JULIE *starts to go towards the kitchen.*)

MRS. MUSKAT

I paid him a krone a day, and on Sunday a gulden. And he got all the beer and cigars he wanted from the customers. (JULIE *pauses on the threshold, but does not answer.*) And he'd rather starve than beg my pardon. Well, I don't insist on that. I'll take him back without it. (JULIE *does not answer.*) The fact is the people ask for him —and, you see, I've got to consider business first. It's nothing to me if he starves. I wouldn't be here at all, if it wasn't for business— (*She pauses, for* LILIOM *and* FICSUR *have entered.*)

JULIE

Mrs. Muskat is here.

LILIOM

I see she is.

JULIE

You might say good-morning.

LILIOM

What for? And what do *you* want, anyhow?

JULIE

I don't want anything.

LILIOM

Then keep your mouth shut. Next thing you'll be starting to nag again about my being out all night and out of work and living on your relations—

JULIE

I'm not saying anything.

LILIOM

But it's all on the tip of your tongue—I know you—now don't start or you'll get another. (*He paces angrily up and down. They are all a bit afraid of him, and shrink and look away as he passes them.* FICSUR *shambles from place to place, his eyes cast down as if he were searching for something on the floor.*)

MRS. MUSKAT

(*Suddenly, to* FICSUR). You're always dragging him out to play cards and drink with you. I'll have you locked up, I will.

FICSUR

I don't want to talk to you. You're too common. (*He goes out by the door at back and lingers there in plain view. There is a pause.*)

JULIE

Mrs. Muskat is here.

LILIOM

Well, why doesn't she open her mouth, if she has anything to say?

MRS. MUSKAT

Why do you go around with this man Ficsur? He'll get you mixed up in one of his robberies first thing you know.

LILIOM

What's it to you who I go with? I do what I please. What do you want?

MRS. MUSKAT

You know what I want.

LILIOM

No, I don't.

MRS. MUSKAT

What do you suppose I want? Think I've come just to pay a social call?

LILIOM

Do I owe you anything?

MRS. MUSKAT

Yes, you do—but that's not what I came for. You're a fine one to come to for money! You earn so much these days! You know very well what I'm here for.

LILIOM

You've got Hollinger at the carousel, haven't you?

MRS. MUSKAT

Sure I have.

LILIOM

Well, what else do you want? He's as good as I am.

MRS. MUSKAT

You're quite right, my boy. He's every bit as good as you are. I'd not dream of letting him go. But one isn't enough any more. There's work enough for two—

LILIOM

One was enough when *I* was there.

MRS. MUSKAT

Well, I might let Hollinger go—

LILIOM

Why let him go, if he's so good?

MRS. MUSKAT

(*Shrugs her shoulders*). Yes, he's good. (*Not once until now has she looked at* LILIOM.)

LILIOM

(*To* JULIE). Ask your aunt if I can have a cup of coffee. (JULIE *exits into the kitchen.*) So Hollinger is good, is he?

MRS. MUSKAT

(*Crosses to him and looks him in the face*). Why don't you stay home and sleep at night? You're a sight to look at.

LILIOM

He's good, is he?

MRS. MUSKAT

Push your hair back from your forehead.

LILIOM

Let my hair be. It's nothing to you.

MRS. MUSKAT

All right. But if I'd told you to let it hang down over your eyes you'd have pushed it back—I hear you've been beating her, this—this—

LILIOM

None of your business.

MRS. MUSKAT

You're a fine fellow! Beating a skinny little thing like that! If you're tired of her, leave her, but there's no use beating the poor—

LILIOM

Leave her, eh? You'd like that, wouldn't you?

MRS. MUSKAT

Don't flatter yourself. (*Quite embarrassed.*) Serves me right, too. If I had any sense I wouldn't have run after you— My God, the things one must do for the sake of business! If I could only sell the carousel I wouldn't be sitting here. . . . Come, Liliom, if you have any sense, you'll come back. I'll pay you well.

LILIOM

The carousel is crowded just the same . . . *without me?*

MRS. MUSKAT

Crowded, yes—but it's not the same.

LILIOM

Then you admit that you *do* miss me.

MRS. MUSKAT

Miss you? Not I. But the silly girls miss you. They're always asking for you. Well, are you going to be sensible and come back?

LILIOM

And leave—her?

MRS. MUSKAT

You beat her, don't you?

LILIOM

No, I don't beat her. What's all this damn fool talk about beating her? I hit her once—that was all—and now the whole city seems to be talking about it. You don't call that beating her, do you?

MRS. MUSKAT

All right, all right. I take it back. I don't want to get mixed up in it.

LILIOM

Beating her! As if I'd beat her—

MRS. MUSKAT

I can't make out why you're so concerned about her. You've been married to her two months—it's plain to see that you're sick of it—and out there is the carousel—and the show booths—and money—and you'd throw it all away. For what? Heavens, how can any one be such a fool? (*Looks at him appraisingly.*) Where have you been all night? You look awful.

LILIOM

It's no business of yours.

MRS. MUSKAT

You never used to look like that. This life is telling on you. (*Pauses.*) Do you know—I've got a new organ.

LILIOM

(*Softly*). I know.

MRS. MUSKAT

How did you know?

LILIOM

You can hear it—from here.

MRS. MUSKAT

It's a good one, eh?

LILIOM

(*Wistfully*). Very good. Fine. It roars and snorts—so fine.

MRS. MUSKAT

You should hear it close by—it's heavenly. Even the carousel seems to know . . . it goes quicker. I got rid of those two horses—you know, the ones with the broken ears?

LILIOM

What have you put in their place?

MRS. MUSKAT

Guess.

LILIOM

Zebras?

MRS MUSKAT

No—an automobile.

LILIOM

(*Transported*). An automobile—

MRS. MUSKAT

Yes. If you've got any sense you'll come back. What good are you doing here? Out there is your *art*, the only thing you're fit for. You are an artist, not a respectable married man.

LILIOM

Leave her—this little—

MRS. MUSKAT

She'll be better off. She'll go back and be a servant girl again. As for you—you're an artist and you belong among artists. All the beer you want, cigars, a krone a day and a gulden on Sunday, and the girls, Liliom, the girls—I've always treated you right, haven't I? I bought you a watch, and—

LILIOM

She's not that kind. She'd never be a servant girl again.

MRS. MUSKAT

I suppose you think she'd kill herself. Don't worry. Heavens, if every girl was to commit suicide just because her— (*Finishes with a gesture.*)

LILIOM

(*Stares at her a moment, considering, then with sudden, smiling animation*). So the people don't like Hollinger?

MRS. MUSKAT

You know very well they don't, you rascal.

LILIOM

Well—

MRS. MUSKAT

You've always been happy at the carousel. It's a great life—pretty girls and beer and cigars and music—a great life and an easy one. I'll tell you what—come back and I'll give you a ring that used to belong to my dear departed husband. Well, will you come?

LILIOM

She's not that kind. She'd never be a servant girl again. But—but—for my part—if I decide—that needn't make any difference. I can go on living with her even if I do go back to my art—

MRS. MUSKAT

My God!

LILIOM

What's the matter?

MRS. MUSKAT

Who ever heard of a married man—I suppose you think all girls would be pleased to know that you were running home to your wife every night. It's ridiculous! When the people found out they'd laugh themselves sick—

LILIOM

I know what you want.

MRS. MUSKAT

(*Refuses to meet his gaze*). You flatter yourself.

LILIOM

You'll give me that ring, too?

MRS. MUSKAT

(*Pushes the hair back from his forehead*). Yes.

LILIOM

I'm not happy in this house.

MRS. MUSKAT

(*Still stroking his hair*). Nobody takes care of you. (*They are silent.* JULIE *enters, carrying a cup of coffee.* MRS. MUSKAT *removes her hand from* LILIOM'*s head. There is a pause.*)

LILIOM

Do you want anything?

JULIE

No. (*There is a pause. She exits slowly into the kitchen.*)

MRS. MUSKAT

The old woman says there is a carpenter, a widower, who—

LILIOM

I know—I know—

JULIE

(*Reëntering*). Liliom, before I forget, I have something to tell you.

LILIOM

All right.

JULIE

I've been wanting to tell you—in fact, I was going to tell you yesterday—

LILIOM

Go ahead.

JULIE

But I must tell you alone—if you'll come in—it will only take a minute.

LILIOM

Don't you see I'm busy now? Here I am talking business and you interrupt with—

JULIE

It'll only take a minute.

LILIOM

Get out of here, or—

JULIE

But I tell you it will only take a minute—

LILIOM

Will you get out of here?

JULIE

(*Courageously*). No.

LILIOM

(*Rising*). What's that!

JULIE

No.

MRS. MUSKAT

(*Rises, too*). Now don't start fighting. I'll go out and look at the photographs in the show-case a while and come back later for your answer. (*She exits at back.*)

JULIE

You can hit me again if you like—don't look at me like that. I'm not afraid of you. . . . I'm not afraid of any one. I told you I had something to tell you.

LILIOM

Well, out with it—quick.

JULIE

I can't tell you so quick. Why don't you drink your coffee?

LILIOM

Is that what you wanted to tell me?

JULIE

No. By the time you've drunk your coffee I'll have told you.

LILIOM

(*Gets the coffee and sips it*). Well?

JULIE

Yesterday my head ached—and you asked me—

LILIOM

Yes—

JULIE

Well—you see—that's what it is—

LILIOM

Are you sick?

JULIE

No. . . . But you wanted to know what my headaches came from—and you said I seemed changed.

LILIOM

Did I? I guess I meant the carpenter.

JULIE

I've been—what? The carpenter? No. It's something entirely different—it's awful hard to tell—but you'll have to know sooner or later—I'm not a bit—scared—because it's a perfectly natural thing—

LILIOM

(*Puts the coffee cup on the table*). What?

JULIE

When—when a man and woman—live together—

LILIOM

Yes.

JULIE

I'm going to have a baby. (*She exits swiftly at back. There is a pause.* FICSUR *appears at the open window and looks in.*)

LILIOM

Ficsur! (FICSUR *sticks his head in.*) Say, Ficsur—Julie is going to have a baby.

FICSUR

Yes? What of it?

LILIOM

Nothing. (*Suddenly.*) Get out of here. (FICSUR'S *head is quickly withdrawn.* MRS. MUSKAT *reënters.*)

MRS. MUSKAT

Has she gone?

LILIOM

Yes.

MRS. MUSKAT

I might as well give you ten kronen in advance. (*Opens her purse.* LILIOM *takes up his coffee cup.*) Here you are. (*She proffers some coins.* LILIOM *ignores her.*) Why don't you take it?

LILIOM

(*Very nonchalantly, his cup poised ready to drink*). Go home, Mrs. Muskat.

MRS. MUSKAT

What's the matter with you?

LILIOM

Go home (*sips his coffee*) and let me finish my coffee in peace. Don't you see I'm at breakfast?

MRS. MUSKAT

Have you gone crazy?

LILIOM

Will you get out of here? (*Turns to her threateningly.*)

MRS. MUSKAT

(*Restoring the coins to her purse*). I'll never speak to you again as long as you live.

LILIOM

That worries me a lot.

MRS. MUSKAT

Good-bye!

LILIOM

Good-bye. (*As she exits, he calls.*) Ficsur! (FICSUR *enters.*) Tell me, Ficsur. You said you knew a way to get a whole lot of money—

FICSUR

Sure I do.

LILIOM

How much?

FICSUR

More than you ever had in your life before. You leave it to an old hand like me.

MOTHER HOLLUNDER

(*Enters from the kitchen*). In the morning he must have his coffee, and at noon his soup, and in the evening coffee again—and plenty of firewood—and I'm expected to furnish it all. Give me back my cup and saucer.
(*The show booths of the amusement-park have opened for business. The familiar noises begin to sound; clear above them all, but far in the distance, sounds the organ of the carousel.*)

LILIOM

Now, Aunt Hollunder. (*From now until the fall of the curtain it is apparent that the sound of the organ makes him more and more uneasy.*)

MOTHER HOLLUNDER

And you, you vagabond, get out of here this minute or I'll call my son—

FICSUR

I have nothing to do with the likes of him. He's too common. (*But he slinks out at back.*)

LILIOM

Aunt Hollunder!

MOTHER HOLLUNDER

What now?

LILIOM

When your son was born—when you brought him into the world—

MOTHER HOLLUNDER

Well?

LILIOM

Nothing.

MOTHER HOLLUNDER

(*Muttering as she exits*). Sleep it off, you good-for-nothing lout. Drink and play cards all night long—that's all you know how to do—and take the bread out of poor peoples' mouths—you can do that, too. (*She exits.*)

LILIOM

Ficsur!

FICSUR

(*At the window*). Julie's going to have a baby. You told me before.

LILIOM

This scheme—about the cashier of the leather factory—there's money in it—

FICSUR

Lots of money—but—it takes two to pull it off.

LILIOM

(*Meditatively*). Yes. (*Uneasily.*) All right, Ficsur. Go away—and come back later.
(FICSUR *vanishes. The organ in the distant carousel drones incessantly.* LILIOM *listens a while, then goes to the door and calls.*)

LILIOM

Aunt Hollunder! (*With naïve joy.*) Julie's

going to have a baby. (*Then he goes to the window, jumps on the sofa, looks out. Suddenly, in a voice that overtops the droning of the organ, he shouts as if addressing the far-off carousel.*) I'm going to be a father.

JULIE

(*Enters from the kitchen*). Liliom! What's the matter? What's happened?

LILIOM

(*Coming down from the sofa*). Nothing. (*Throws himself on the sofa, buries his face in the cushion.* JULIE *watches him a moment, comes over to him and covers him with a shawl. Then she goes on tip-toe to the door at back and remains standing in the doorway, looking out and listening to the droning of the organ.*)

THE CURTAIN FALLS

SCENE III

SCENE: *The setting is the same, later that afternoon.* LILIOM *is sitting opposite* FICSUR, *who is teaching him a song.* JULIE *hovers in the background, engaged in some household task.*

FICSUR

Listen now. Here's the third verse. (*Sings hoarsely.*)
"Look out, look out, my pretty lad,
The damn police are on your trail;
The nicest girl you ever had
Has now commenced to weep and wail:
Look out here comes the damn police,
The damn police,
The damn police,
Look out here comes the damn police,
They'll get you every time."

LILIOM

(*Sings*).
"Look out, look out, my pretty lad,
The damn police—"

FICSUR, LILIOM

(*Sing together*).
"Are on your trail
The nicest girl you ever had
Has now commenced to weep and wail."

LILIOM

(*Alone*).
"Look out here comes the damn police,
The damn police,
The damn police—"
(JULIE, *troubled and uneasy, looks from one to the other, then exits into the kitchen.*)

FICSUR

(*When she has gone, comes quickly over to* LILIOM *and speaks furtively*). As you go down Franzen Street you come to the railroad embankment. Beyond that—all the way to the leather factory—there's not a thing in sight, not even a watchman's hut.

LILIOM

And does he always come that way?

FICSUR

Yes. Not along the embankment, but down below along the path across the fields. Since last year he's been going alone. Before that he always used to have some one with him.

LILIOM

Every Saturday?

FICSUR

Every Saturday.

LILIOM

And the money? Where does he keep it?

FICSUR

In a leather bag. The whole week's pay for the workmen at the factory.

LILIOM

Much?

FICSUR

Sixteen thousand kronen. Quite a haul, what?

LILIOM

What's his name?

FICSUR

Linzman. He's a Jew.

LILIOM

The cashier?

FICSUR

Yes—but when he gets a knife between his ribs—or if I smash his skull for him—he won't be a cashier any more.

LILIOM

Does he have to be killed?

FICSUR

No, he doesn't *have* to be. He can give up the money *without* being killed—but most of these cashiers are peculiar—they'd rather be killed.
(JULIE *reënters, pretends to get something on the other side of the room, then exits at back. During the ensuing dialogue she keeps coming in and out in the same way, showing plainly that she is suspicious and anxious. She attempts to overhear what they are saying and, in spite of their caution, does catch a word here and there, which adds to her disquiet.* FICSUR, *catching sight of her, abruptly changes the conversation.*)

FICSUR

And the next verse is:
"And when you're in the prison cell
They'll feed you bread and water."

FICSUR AND LILIOM

(*Sing together*).
"They'll make your little sweetheart tell
Them all the things you brought her.
Look out here comes the damn police,
The damn police,
The damn police.
Look out here comes the damn police
They'll get you every time."

LILIOM

(*Sings alone*).
"And when you're in the prison cell
They'll feed you bread and water—"
(*Breaks off as* JULIE *exits.*)
And when it's done, do we start right off for America?

FICSUR

No.

LILIOM

What then?

FICSUR

We bury the money for six months. That's the usual time. And after the sixth month we dig it up again.

LILIOM

And then?

FICSUR

Then you go on living just as usual for six months more—you don't touch a heller of the money.

LILIOM

In six months the baby will be born.

FICSUR

Then we'll take the baby with us, too. Three months before the time you'll go to work so as to be able to say you saved up your wages to get to America.

LILIOM

Which of us goes up and talks to him?

FICSUR

One of us talks to him with his mouth and the other talks with his knife. Depends on which you'd rather do. I'll tell you what—you talk to him with your mouth.

LILIOM

Do you hear that?

FICSUR

What?

LILIOM

Outside . . . like the rattle of swords. (FICSUR *listens. After a pause,* LILIOM *continues.*) What do I say to him?

FICSUR

You say good evening to him and: "Excuse me, sir; can you tell me the time?"

LILIOM

And then what?

FICSUR

By that time I'll have stuck him—and then you take *your* knife— (*He stops as a* POLICEMAN *enters at back.*)

POLICEMAN

Good-day!

LILIOM, FICSUR

(*In unison*). Good-day!

FICSUR

(*Calling toward the kitchen*). Hey, photographer, come out. . . . Here's a customer. (*There is a pause. The* POLICEMAN *waits.* FICSUR *sings softly.*)
"And when you're in the prison cell
They'll feed you bread and water
They'll make your little sweetheart tell. . . ."

LILIOM, FICSUR

(*Sing together, low*).
"Them all the things you brought her.
Look out here comes the—"
(*They hum the rest so as not to let the* POLICEMAN *hear the words "the damn police." As they sing,* MRS. HOLLUNDER *and her son enter.*)

POLICEMAN

Do you make cabinet photographs?

YOUNG HOLLUNDER

Certainly, sir. (*Points to a rack of photographs on the wall.*) Take your choice, sir. Would you like one full length?

POLICEMAN

Yes, full length. (MOTHER HOLLUNDER *pushes out the camera while her son poses the* POLICEMAN, *runs from him to the camera and back again, now altering the pose, now ducking under the black cloth and pushing the camera nearer. Meanwhile* MOTHER HOLLUNDER *has fetched a plate from the dark room and thrust it in the camera. While this is going on,* LILIOM *and* FICSUR, *their heads together, speak in very low tones.*)

LILIOM

Belong around here?

FICSUR

Not around here.

LILIOM

Where, then?

FICSUR

Suburban. (*There is a pause.*)

LILIOM

(*Bursts out suddenly in a rather grotesquely childish and overstrained lament*). O God, what a dirty life I'm leading—God, God!

FICSUR

(*Reassuring him benevolently*). Over in America it will be better, all right.

LILIOM

What's over there?

FICSUR

(*Virtuously*). Factories . . . industries—

YOUNG HOLLUNDER

(*To the* POLICEMAN). Now, quite still, please. One, two, three. (*Deftly removes the cover of the lens and in a few seconds restores it.*) Thank you.

MOTHER HOLLUNDER

The picture will be ready in five minutes.

POLICEMAN

Good. I'll come back in five minutes. How much do I owe you?

YOUNG HOLLUNDER

(*With exaggerated deference*). You don't need to pay in advance, Mr. Commissioner. (*The* POLICEMAN *salutes condescendingly and exits at back.* MOTHER HOLLUNDER *carries the plate into the dark-room.* YOUNG HOLLUNDER, *after pushing the camera back in place, follows her.*)

MOTHER HOLLUNDER

(*Muttering angrily as she passes* FICSUR *and* LILIOM). You hang around and dirty the whole place up! Why don't you go take a walk? Things are going so well with you that you have to sing, eh? (*Confronting* FICSUR *suddenly.*) Weren't you frightened sick when you saw the policeman?

FICSUR

(*With loathing*). Go 'way, or I'll step on you. (*She exits into the dark-room.*)

LILIOM

They like Hollinger at the carousel?

FICSUR

I should say they do.

LILIOM

Did you see the Muskat woman, too?

FICSUR

Sure. She takes care of Hollinger's hair.

LILIOM

Combs his hair?

FICSUR

She fixes him all up.

LILIOM

Let her fix him all she likes.

FICSUR

(*Urging him towards the kitchen door*). Go on. Now's your chance.

LILIOM

What for?

FICSUR

To get the knife.

LILIOM

What knife?

FICSUR

The kitchen knife. I've got a pocket-knife, but if he shows fight, we'll let him have the big knife.

LILIOM

What for? If he gets ugly, I'll bat him one over the head that'll make him squint for the rest of his life.

FICSUR

You've got to have something on you. You can't slit his throat with a bat over the head.

LILIOM

Must his throat be slit?

FICSUR

No, it *mustn't*. But if he asks for it. (*There is a pause.*) You'd like to sail on the big steamer, wouldn't you? And you want to see the factories over there, don't you? But you're not willing to inconvenience yourself a little for them.

LILIOM

If I take the knife, Julie will see me.

FICSUR

Take it so she won't see you.

LILIOM

(*Advances a few paces towards the kitchen. The* POLICEMAN *enters at back.* LILIOM *knocks on the door of the dark-room.*) Here's the policeman!

MOTHER HOLLUNDER

(*Coming out*). One minute more, please. Just a minute. (*She reënters the dark-room.* LILIOM *hesitates a moment, then exits into the kitchen. The* POLICEMAN *scrutinizes* FICSUR *mockingly.* FICSUR *returns his stare, walks a few paces towards him, then deliberately turns his back. Suddenly he wheels around, points at the* POLICEMAN *and addresses him in a teasing, childish tone.*) Christiana Street at the corner of Retti!

POLICEMAN

(*Amazed, self-conscious*). How do you know that?

FICSUR

I used to practise my profession in that neighborhood.

POLICEMAN

What is your profession?

FICSUR

Professor of pianola— (*The* POLICEMAN *glares, aware that the man is joking with him, twirls his moustache indignantly.* YOUNG HOLLUNDER *comes out of the dark room and gives him the finished pictures.*)

YOUNG HOLLUNDER

Here you are, sir. (*The* POLICEMAN *examines the photographs, pays for them, starts to go, stops, glares at* FICSUR *and exits. When he is gone,* FICSUR *goes to the doorway and looks out after him.* YOUNG HOLLUNDER *exits.* LILIOM *reënters, buttoning his coat.*)

FICSUR

(*Turns, sees* LILIOM). What are you staring at?

LILIOM

I'm not staring.

FICSUR

What then are you doing?

LILIOM

I'm thinking it over.

FICSUR

(*Comes very close to him*). Tell me then—what will you say to him?

LILIOM

(*Unsteadily*). I'll say—"Good evening—Excuse me, sir—Can you tell me the time?" And suppose he answers me, what do I say to him?

FICSUR

He won't answer you.

LILIOM

Don't you think so?

FICSUR

No. (*Feeling for the knife under* LILIOM'S *coat.*) Where is it? Where did you put it?

LILIOM

(*Stonily*). Left side.

FICSUR

That's right—over your heart. (*Feels it.*) Ah—there it is—there—there's the blade—quite a big fellow, isn't it—ah, here it begins to get narrower. (*Reaches the tip of the knife.*) And here is its eye—that's what it sees with. (JULIE *enters from the kitchen, passes them slowly, watching them in silent terror, then stops.* FICSUR *nudges* LILIOM.) Sing, come on, sing!

LILIOM

(*In a quavering voice*). "Look out for the damn police."

FICSUR

(*Joining in, cheerily, loudly, marking time with the swaying of his body*). "Look out, look out, my pretty lad."

LILIOM

"—look out, my pretty lad." (JULIE *goes out at back.* LILIOM'S *glance follows her. When she has gone, he turns to* FICSUR.) At night—in my dreams—if his ghost comes back—what will I do then?

FICSUR

His ghost won't never come back.

LILIOM

Why not?

FICSUR

A Jew's ghost don't come back.

LILIOM

Well then—afterwards——

FICSUR

(*Impatiently*). What do you mean—afterwards?

LILIOM

In the next world—when I come up before the Lord God—what'll I say then?

FICSUR

The likes of you will never come up before Him.

LILIOM

Why not?

FICSUR

Have you ever come up before the high court?

LILIOM

No.

FICSUR

Our kind comes up before the police magistrate—and the highest we *ever* get is the criminal court.

LILIOM

Will it be the same in the next world?

FICSUR

Just the same. We'll come up before a police magistrate, same as we did in this world.

LILIOM

A police magistrate?

FICSUR

Sure. For the rich folks—the Heavenly Court. For us poor people—only a police magistrate. For the rich folks—fine music and angels. For us——

LILIOM

For us?

FICSUR

For us, my son, there's only justice. In the next world there'll be lots of justice, yes, nothing but justice. And where there's justice there must be police magistrates; and where there're police magistrates, people like us get——

LILIOM

(*Interrupting*). Good evening. Excuse me, sir, can you tell me the time? (*Lays his hand over his heart.*)

FICSUR

What do you put your hand there for?

LILIOM

My heart is jumping—under the knife.

FICSUR

Put it on the other side then. (*Looks out at the sky.*) It's time we started—we'll walk slow——

LILIOM

It's too early.

FICSUR

Come on. (*As they are about to go,* JULIE *appears in the doorway at back, obstructing the way.*)

JULIE

Where are you going with him?

LILIOM

Where am I going with him?

JULIE

Stay home.

LILIOM

No.

JULIE

Stay home. It's going to rain soon, and you'll get wet.

FICSUR

It won't rain.

JULIE

How do you know?

FICSUR

I always get notice in advance.

JULIE

Stay home. This evening the carpenter's coming. I've asked him to give you work.

LILIOM

I'm not a carpenter.

JULIE

(*More and more anxious, though she tries to conceal it*). Stay home. Marie's coming with her intended to have their picture taken. She wants to introduce us to her intended husband.

LILIOM

I've seen enough intended husbands——

JULIE

Stay home. Marie's bringing some money, and I'll give it all to you.

LILIOM

(*Approaching the door*). I'm going—for a walk—with Ficsur. We'll be right back.

JULIE

(*Forcing a smile to keep back her tears*). If you stay home, I'll get you a glass of beer—or wine, if you prefer.

FICSUR

Coming or not?

JULIE

I'm not angry with you any more for hitting me.

LILIOM

(*Gruffly, but his gruffness is simulated to hide the fact that he cannot bear the sight of her suffering*). Stand out of the way—or I'll—— (*He clenches his fist.*) Let me out!

JULIE

(*Trembling*). What have you got under your coat?

LILIOM

(*Produces from his pocket a greasy pack of cards*). Cards.

JULIE

(*Trembling, speaks very low*). What's under your coat?

LILIOM

Let me out!

JULIE

(*Obstructing the way. Speaks quickly, eagerly, in a last effort to detain him*). Marie's intended knows about a place for a married couple without children to be caretakers of a house on Arader Street. Rent free, a kitchen of your own, and the privilege of keeping chickens——

LILIOM

Get out of the way! (JULIE *stands aside.* LILIOM *exits.* FICSUR *follows him.* JULIE *remains standing meditatively in the doorway.* MOTHER HOLLUNDER *comes out of the kitchen.*)

MOTHER HOLLUNDER

I can't find my kitchen knife anywhere. Have you seen anything of it?

JULIE

(*Horrified*). No.

MOTHER HOLLUNDER

It was on the kitchen table just a few minutes ago. No one was in there except Liliom.

JULIE

He didn't take it.

MOTHER HOLLUNDER

No one else was in there.

JULIE

What would Liliom want with a kitchen knife?

MOTHER HOLLUNDER

He'd sell it and spend the money on drink.

JULIE

It just so happens—see how unjust you are to him—it just so happens that I went through all of Liliom's pockets just now—I wanted to see if he had any money on him. But he had nothing but a pack of cards.

MOTHER HOLLUNDER

(*Returns to the kitchen, grumbling*). Cards in his pocket—cards! The fine gentlemen have evidently gone off to their club to play a little game. (*She exits. After a pause* MARIE, *happy and beaming, appears in the doorway at back, and enters, followed by* WOLF.)

MARIE

Here we are! (*She takes* WOLF *by the hand and leads him, grinning shyly, to* JULIE, *who has turned at her call.*) Hello!

JULIE

Hello.

MARIE

Well, we're here.

JULIE

Yes.

WOLF

(*Bows awkwardly and extends his hand*). My name is Wolf Beifeld.

JULIE

My name is Julie Zeller. (*They shake hands. There is an embarrassed silence. Then, to relieve the situation,* WOLF *takes* JULIE'S *hand again and shakes it vigorously.*)

MARIE

Well—this is Wolf.

WOLF

Yes.

JULIE

Yes. (*Another awkward silence.*)

MARIE

Where is Liliom?

WOLF

Yes, where is your husband?

JULIE

He's out.

MARIE

Where?

JULIE

Just for a walk.

MARIE

Is he?

JULIE

Yes.

WOLF

Oh! (*Another silence.*)

MARIE

Wolf's got a new place. After the first of the month he won't have to stand outside any more. He's going to work in a club after the first of the month.

WOLF

(*Apologetically*). She don't know yet how to explain these things just right—hehehe —— Beginning the first I'm to be second steward at the Burger Club—a good job, if one conducts oneself properly.

JULIE

Yes?

WOLF

The pay—is quite good—but the main thing is the tips. When they play cards there's always a bit for the steward. The tips, I may say, amount to twenty, even thirty kronen every night.

MARIE

Yes.

WOLF

We've rented two rooms for ourselves to start with—and if things go well——

MARIE

Then we'll buy a house in the country.

WOLF

If one only tends to business and keeps honest. Of course, in the country we'll miss the city life, but if the good Lord sends us children—it's much healthier for children in the country. (*There is a brief pause.*)

MARIE

Wolf's nice-looking, isn't he?

JULIE

Yes.

MARIE

And he's a good boy, Wolf.

JULIE

Yes.

MARIE

The only thing is—he's a Jew.

JULIE

Oh, well, you can get used to that.

MARIE

Well, aren't you going to wish us luck?

JULIE

Of course I do. (*She embraces* MARIE.)

MARIE

And aren't you going to kiss Wolf, too?

JULIE

Him, too. (*She embraces* WOLF, *remains quite still a moment, her head resting on his shoulder.*)

WOLF

Why are you crying, my dear Mrs.—— (*He looks questioningly at* MARIE *over* JULIE'S *shoulder.*)

MARIE

Because she has such a good heart. (*She becomes sentimental, too.*)

WOLF

(*Touched*). We thank you for your heartfelt sympathy—— (*He cannot restrain his own tears. There is a pause before* MOTHER HOLLUNDER *and her son enter.* YOUNG HOLLUNDER *immediately busies himself with the camera.*)

MOTHER HOLLUNDER

Now if you don't mind, we'll do it right away, before it gets too dark. (*She leads* MARIE *and* WOLF *into position before the background-screen. Here they immediately fall into an awkward pose, smiling mechanically.*) Full length?

MARIE

Please. Both figures full length.

MOTHER HOLLUNDER

Bride and groom?

MARIE

Yes.

MOTHER HOLLUNDER, YOUNG HOLLUNDER

(*Speak in unison, in loud professionally expressionless tones*). The lady looks at the gentleman and the gentleman looks straight into the camera.

MOTHER HOLLUNDER

(*Poses first* MARIE, *then* WOLF). Now, if you please.

YOUNG HOLLUNDER

(*Who has crept under the black cloth, calls in muffled tones*). That's good—that's very good!

MARIE

(*Stonily rigid, but very happy, trying to speak without altering her expression*). Julie, dear, do we look all right?

JULIE

Yes, dear.

YOUNG HOLLUNDER

Now, if you please, hold still. I'll count up to three, and then you must hold perfectly still. (*Grasps the cover of the lens and calls threateningly.*) One—two—three! (*He removes the cover; there is utter silence. But as he speaks the word "one" there is heard, very faintly in the distance, the refrain of the thieves' song which* FICSUR *and* LILIOM *have been singing. The refrain continues until the fall of the curtain. As he speaks the word "three" everybody is perfectly rigid save* JULIE, *who lets her head sink slowly to the table. The distant refrain dies out.*)

THE CURTAIN FALLS

SCENE IV

SCENE: *In the fields on the outskirts of the city. At back a railroad embankment crosses the stage obliquely. At center of the embankment stands a red and white signal flag, and near it a little red signal lamp which is not yet lighted. Here also a wooden stairway leads up to the embankment.*

At the foot of the embankment to the right is a pile of used railroad ties. In the background a telegraph pole, beyond it a view of trees, fences and fields; still further back a factory building and a cluster of little dwellings.

It is six o'clock of the same afternoon. Dusk has begun to fall.

LILIOM *and* FICSUR *are discovered on the stairway looking after the train which has just passed.*

LILIOM

Can you still hear it snort?

FICSUR

Listen! (*They watch the vanishing train.*)

LILIOM

If you put your ear on the tracks you can hear it go all the way to Vienna.

FICSUR

Huh!

LILIOM

The one that just puffed past us—it goes all the way to Vienna.

FICSUR

No further?

LILIOM

Yes—further, too. (*There is a pause.*)

FICSUR

It must be near six. (*As* LILIOM *ascends the steps.*) Where are you going?

LILIOM

Don't be afraid. I'm not giving you the slip.

FICSUR

Why should you give me the slip? That cashier has sixteen thousand kronen on him. Just be patient till he comes, then you can talk to him, nice and polite.

LILIOM

I say, "Good evening—excuse me, sir; what time is it?"

FICSUR

Then he tells you what time it is.

LILIOM

Suppose he don't come?

FICSUR

(*Coming down the steps*). Nonsense! He's got to come. He pays off the workmen every Saturday. And this is Saturday, ain't it? (LILIOM *has ascended to the top of the stairway and is gazing along the tracks.*) What are you looking at up there?

LILIOM

The tracks go on and on—there's no end to them.

FICSUR

What's that to stare about?

LILIOM

Nothing—only I always look after the train. When you stand down there at night it snorts past you, and spits down.

FICSUR

Spits?

LILIOM

Yes, the engine. It spits down. And then the whole train rattles past and away—and you stand there—spat on—but it draws your eyes along with it.

FICSUR

Draws your eyes along?

LILIOM

Yes—whether you want to or not, you've got to look after it—as long as the tiniest bit of it is in sight.

FICSUR

Swell people sit in it.

LILIOM

And read newspapers.

FICSUR

And smoke cigars.

LILIOM

And inhale the smoke. (*There is a short silence.*)

FICSUR

Is he coming?

LILIOM

Not yet. (*Silence again.* LILIOM *comes down, speaks low, confidentially.*) Do you hear the telegraph wires?

FICSUR

I hear them when the wind blows.

LILIOM

Even when the wind doesn't blow you can hear them humming, humming—— People talk through them.

FICSUR

Who?

LILIOM

Jews.

FICSUR

No—they telegraph.

LILIOM

They talk through them and from some other place they get answered. And it all goes through the iron strings—that's why they hum like that—they hum-m——

FICSUR

What do they hum?

LILIOM

They hum! ninety-nine, ninety-nine. Just listen.

FICSUR

What for?

LILIOM

That sparrow's listening, too. He's cocked one eye and looks at me as if to say: "I'd like to know what they're talking about."

FICSUR

You're looking at a bird?

LILIOM

He's looking at me, too.

FICSUR

Listen, you're sick. There's something the matter with you. Do you know what it is? Money. That bird has no money, either; that's why he cocks his eye.

LILIOM

Maybe.

FICSUR

Whoever has money don't cock his eye.

LILIOM

What then does he do?

FICSUR

He does most anything he wants. But nobody works unless he has money. We'll soon have money ourselves.

LILIOM

I say, "Good evening. Excuse me, sir, can you tell me what time it is!"

FICSUR

He's not coming yet. Got the cards? (LILIOM *gives him the pack of cards.*) Got any money?

LILIOM

(*Takes some coins from his trousers pocket and counts*). Eleven.

FICSUR

(*Sits astride on the pile of ties and looks off left*). All right—eleven.

LILIOM

(*Sitting astride on the ties facing him*). Put it up.

FICSUR

(*Puts the money on the ties; rapidly shuffles the cards*). We'll play twenty-one. I'll bank. (*He deals deftly.*)

LILIOM

(*Looks at his card.*) Good. I'll bet the bank.

FICSUR

Must have an ace! (*Deals him a second card.*)

LILIOM

Another one. (*He gets another card.*) Another. (*Gets still another.*) Over! (*Throws down his cards.* FICSUR *gathers in the money.*) Come on!

FICSUR

Come on what? Got no more money, have you?

LILIOM

No.

FICSUR

Then the game's over—unless you want to——

LILIOM

What?

FICSUR

Play on credit.

LILIOM

You'll trust me?

FICSUR

No—but—I'll deduct it.

LILIOM

Deduct it from what?

FICSUR

From your share of the money. If *you* win you deduct from my share.

LILIOM

(*Looks over his shoulder to see if the cashier is coming; nervous and ashamed*). All right. How much is bank?

FICSUR

That cashier is bringing us sixteen thousand kronen. Eight thousand of that is mine. Well, then, the bank is eight thousand.

LILIOM

Good.

FICSUR

Whoever has the most luck will have the most money. (*He deals.*)

LILIOM

Six hundred kronen. (FICSUR *gives him another card.*) Enough.

FICSUR

(*Laying out his own cards*). Twenty-one. (*He shuffles rapidly.*)

LILIOM

(*Moves excitedly nearer to* FICSUR). Well, then, double or nothing.

FICSUR

(*Dealing*). Double or nothing.

LILIOM

(*Gets a card*). Enough.

FICSUR

(*Laying out his own cards*). Twenty-one. (*Shuffles rapidly again.*)

LILIOM

(*In alarm*). You're not—cheating?

FICSUR

Me? Do I look like a cheat? (*Deals the cards again.*)

LILIOM

(*Glances nervously over his shoulder*). A thousand.

FICSUR

(*Nonchalantly*). Kronen?

LILIOM

Kronen. (*He gets a card.*) Another one. (*Gets another card.*) Over again! (LIKE *an inexperienced gambler who is losing heavily,* LILIOM *is very nervous. He plays dazedly, wildly, irrationally. From now on it is apparent that his only thought is to win his money back.*)

FICSUR

That makes twelve hundred you owe.

LILIOM

Double or nothing. (*He gets a card. He is greatly excited.*) Another one. (*Gets another card.*) Another. (*Throws down three cards.*)

FICSUR

(*Bends over and adds up the sum on the ground*). Ten—fourteen—twenty-three— — You owe two thousand, four hundred.

LILIOM

Now what?

FICSUR

(*Takes a card out of the deck and gives it to him.*) Here's the red ace. You can play double or nothing again.

LILIOM

(*Eagerly*). Good. (*Gets another card.*) Enough.

FICSUR

(*Turns up his own cards*). Nineteen.

LILIOM

You win again. (*Almost imploring.*) Give me an ace again. Give me the green one. (*Takes a card.*) Double or nothing.

FICSUR

Not any more.

LILIOM

Why not?

FICSUR

Because if you lose you won't be able to pay. Double would be nine thousand six hundred. And you've only got eight thousand altogether.

LILIOM

(*Greatly excited*). That—that—I call that —a dirty trick!

FICSUR

Three thousand, two hundred. That's all you can put up.

LILIOM

(*Eagerly*). All right, then—three thousand, two hundred. (FICSUR *deals him a card.*) Enough.

FICSUR

I've got an ace myself. Now we'll have to take our time and squeeze 'em. (LILIOM *pushes closer to him as he takes up his cards and slowly, intently unfolds them.*) Twenty-one. (*He quickly puts the cards in his pocket. There is a pause.*)

LILIOM

Now—now—I'll tell you now—you're a crook, a low-down——(*Now* LINZMAN *enters at Right. He is a strong, robust, red-bearded Jew about 40 years of age. At his side he carries a leather bag slung by a strap from his shoulder.* FICSUR *coughs warningly, moves to the right between* LINZMAN *and the embankment, pauses just behind* LINZMAN *and follows him.* LILIOM *stands bewildered a few paces to the left of the railroad ties. He finds himself facing* LINZMAN. *Trembling in every limb.*) Good evening. Excuse me, sir, can you tell me the time? (FICSUR *springs silently at* LINZMAN, *the little knife in his right hand. But* LINZMAN *catches* FICSUR'S *right hand with his own left and forces* FICSUR *to his knees. Simultaneously* LINZMAN *thrusts his right hand into his coat pocket and produces a revolver which he points at* LILIOM'S *breast.* LILIOM *is standing two paces away from the revolver. There is a long pause.*)

LINZMAN

(*In a low, even voice*). It is twenty-five minutes past six. (*Pauses, looks ironically down at* FICSUR.) It's lucky I grabbed the hand with the knife instead of the other one. (*Pauses again, looks appraisingly from one to the other.*) Two fine birds! (*To* FICSUR.) I should live so—Rothschild has more luck than you. (*To* LILIOM.) I'd advise you to keep nice and quiet. If you make one move, you'll get two bullets in you. Just look into the barrel. You'll see some little things in there made of lead.

FICSUR

Let me go. I didn't do anything.

LINZMAN

(*Mockingly shakes the hand which still holds the knife*). And this? What do you call this? Oh, yes, I know. You thought I had an apple in my pocket, and you wanted to peel it. That's it. Forgive me for my error. I beg your pardon, sir.

LILIOM

But I—I——

LINZMAN

Yes, my son, I know. It's so simple. You only asked what time it is. Well, it's twenty-five minutes after six.

FICSUR

Let us go, honorable sir. We didn't do anything to you.

LINZMAN

In the first place, my son, I'm not an honorable sir. In the second place, for the same money, you could have said Your Excellency. But in the third place, you'll find it very hard to beg off by flattering me.

LILIOM

But I—*I* really didn't do anything to you.

LINZMAN

Look behind you, my boy. Don't be afraid. Look behind you, but don't run away or I'll have to shoot you down. (LILIOM *turns his head slowly around.*) Who's coming up there?

LILIOM

(*Looking at* LINZMAN). Policemen.

LINZMAN

(*To* FICSUR). You hold still, or—— (*To* LILIOM *teasingly.*) How many policemen are there?

LILIOM

(*His eyes cast down*). Two.

LINZMAN

And what are the policemen sitting on?

LILIOM

Horses.

LINZMAN

And which can run faster, a horse or a man?

LILIOM

A horse.

LINZMAN

There, you see. It would be hard to get away now. (*Laughs.*) I never saw such an unlucky pair of highway robbers. I can't imagine worse luck. Just today I had to put a pistol in my pocket. And even if I hadn't—old Linzman is a match for four like you. But even that isn't all. Did you happen to notice, you oxen, what direction I came from? From the factory, didn't I? When I *went* there I had a nice bit of money with me. Sixteen thousand crowns! But now—not a heller. (*Calls off left.*) Hey, come quicker, will you? This fellow is pulling pretty strong. (FICSUR *frees himself with a mighty wrench and darts rapidly off. As* LINZMAN *aims his pistol at the vanishing* FICSUR, LILIOM *runs up the steps of the embankment.* LINZMAN *hesitates, perceives that* LILIOM *is the better target, points the pistol at him.*) Stop, or I'll shoot! (*Calls off left to the* POLICEMEN.) Why don't you come down off your horses? (*His pistol is leveled at* LILIOM, *who stands on the embankment, facing the audience. From the left on the embankment a* POLICEMAN *appears, revolver in hand.*)

FIRST POLICEMAN

Stop!

LINZMAN

Well, my boy, do you still want to know what time it is? From ten to twelve years in prison!

LILIOM

You won't get me! (LINZMAN *laughs derisively.* LILIOM *is now three or four paces from the* POLICEMAN *and equally distant from* LINZMAN. *His face is uplifted to the sky. He bursts into laughter, half defiant, half self-pitying, and takes the kitchen knife from under his coat.*) Julie—— (*The ring of farewell is in the word. He turns sideways, thrusts the knife deep in his breast, sways, falls and rolls down the far side of the embankment. There is a long pause. From the left up on the embankment come the* TWO POLICEMEN.)

LINZMAN

What's the matter? (*The* FIRST POLICEMAN *comes along the embankment as far as the steps, looks down on the opposite side, then climbs down at about the spot where* LILIOM *disappeared.* LINZMAN *and the other* POLICEMAN *mount the embankment and look down on him.*) Stabbed himself?

VOICE OF FIRST POLICEMAN

Yes—and he seems to have made a thorough job of it.

LINZMAN

(*Excitedly to the* SECOND POLICEMAN.) I'll go and telephone to the hospital. (*He runs down the steps and exits at left.*)

SECOND POLICEMAN

Go to Eisler's grocery store and telephone to the factory from there. They've a doctor there, too. (*Calling down to the other* POLICEMAN.) I'm going to tie up the horses. (*Comes down the steps and exits at left. The stage is empty. There is a pause. The little red signal lamp is lit.*)

VOICE OF FIRST POLICEMAN

Hey, Stephan!

VOICE OF SECOND POLICEMAN

What?

VOICE OF FIRST POLICEMAN

Shall I pull the knife out of his chest?

VOICE OF SECOND POLICEMAN

Better not, or he may bleed to death. (*There is a pause.*)

VOICE OF FIRST POLICEMAN

Stephan!

VOICE OF SECOND POLICEMAN

Yes.

VOICE OF FIRST POLICEMAN

Lot of mosquitoes around here.

VOICE OF SECOND POLICEMAN

Yes.

VOICE OF FIRST POLICEMAN

Got a cigar?

VOICE OF SECOND POLICEMAN

No. (*There is a pause. The* FIRST POLICEMAN *appears over the opposite side of the embankment.*)

FIRST POLICEMAN

A lot of good the new pay-schedule's done us—made things worse than they used to be—we *get* more but we *have* less than we ever had. If the Government could be made to realize that. It's a thankless job at best. You work hard year after year, you get gray in the service, and slowly you die—yes.

SECOND POLICEMAN

That's right.

FIRST POLICEMAN

Yes. (*In the distance is heard the bell of the signal tower.*)

THE CURTAIN FALLS

SCENE V

SCENE: *The photographic "studio" a half hour later that same evening.*

MOTHER HOLLUNDER, *her son,* MARIE *and* WOLF *stand in a group back right, their heads together.* JULIE *stands apart from them, a few paces to the left.*

YOUNG HOLLUNDER

(*Who has just come in, tells his story excitedly*). They're bringing him now. Two workmen from the factory are carrying him on a stretcher.

WOLF

Where is the doctor?

YOUNG HOLLUNDER

A policeman telephoned to headquarters. The police-surgeon ought to be here any minute.

MARIE

Maybe they'll pull him through after all.

YOUNG HOLLUNDER

He stabbed himself too deep in his chest. But he's still breathing. He can still talk, too, but very faintly. At first he lay there unconscious, but when they put him on the stretcher he came to.

WOLF

That was from the shaking.

MARIE

We'd better make room. (*They make room. Two workmen carry in* LILIOM *on a stretcher which has four legs and stands about as high as a bed. They put the stretcher at left directly in front of the sofa, so that the head is at right and the foot at left. Then they unobtrusively join the group at the door. Later, they go out.* JULIE *is standing at the side of the stretcher, where, without moving, she can see* LILIOM'*s face. The others crowd emotionally together near the door. The* FIRST POLICEMAN *enters.*)

FIRST POLICEMAN

Are you his wife?

JULIE

Yes.

FIRST POLICEMAN

The doctor at the factory who bandaged him up forbade us to take him to the hospital.—Dangerous to move him that far. What he needs now is rest. Just let him be until the police-surgeon comes. (*To the group near the door.*) He's not to be disturbed. (*They make way for him. He exits. There is a pause.*)

WOLF

(*Gently urging the others out*). Please—it's best if we all get out of here now. We'll only be in the way.

MARIE

(*To* JULIE). Julie, what do you think? (JULIE *looks at her without answering.*) Julie, can I do anything to help? (JULIE *does not answer.*) We'll be just outside on the bench if you want us. (MOTHER HOLLUNDER *and her son have gone out when first requested. Now* MARIE *and* WOLF *exit, too.* JULIE *sits on the edge of the stretcher and looks at* LILIOM. *He stretches his hand out to her. She clasps it. It is not quite dark yet. Both of them can still be plainly seen.*)

LILIOM

(*Raises himself with difficulty; speaks lightly at first, but later soberly, defiantly*). Little—Julie—there's something—I want to tell you—like when you go to a restaurant—and you've finished eating—and it's time—to pay—then you have to count up everything—everything you owe—well—I beat you—not because I was mad at you—no—only because I can't bear to see any one crying. You always cried—on my account—and, well, you see—I never learned a trade—what kind of a caretaker would I make? But anyhow—I wasn't going back to the carousel to fool with the girls. No, I spit on them all—understand?

JULIE

Yes.

LILIOM

And—as for Hollinger—he's good enough—Mrs. Muskat can get along all right with him. The jokes he tells are mine—and the people laugh when he tells them—but I don't care—I didn't give you anything—no home—not even the food you ate—but you don't understand.—It's true I'm not much good—but I couldn't be a caretaker—and so I thought maybe it would be better over there—in America—do you see?

JULIE

Yes.

LILIOM

I'm not asking—forgiveness—I don't do that—I don't. Tell the baby—if you like.

JULIE

Yes.

LILIOM

Tell the baby—I wasn't much good—but tell him—if you ever talk about me—tell him—I thought—perhaps—over in America—but that's no affair of yours. I'm not asking forgiveness. For my part the police can come now.—If it's a boy—if it's a girl.—Perhaps I'll see the Lord God today.—Do you think I'll see Him?

JULIE

Yes.

LILIOM

I'm not afraid—of the police Up There—if they'll only let me come up in front of the Lord God Himself—not like down here where an officer stops you at the door. If the carpenter asks you—yes—be his wife—marry him. And the child—tell him he's his father.—He'll believe you—won't he?

JULIE

Yes.

LILIOM

When I beat you—I was right.—You mustn't always think—you mustn't always be right.—Liliom can be right once, too.—It's all the same to me who was right.—It's so dumb. Nobody's right—but they all think they are right.—A lot they know!

JULIE

Yes.

LILIOM

Julie—come—hold my hand tight.

JULIE

I'm holding it tight—all the time.

LILIOM

Tighter, still tighter—I'm going——(*Pauses.*) Julie——

JULIE

Good-bye. (LILIOM *sinks slowly back and dies.* JULIE *frees her hand.* THE DOCTOR *enters with the* FIRST POLICEMAN.)

DOCTOR

Good evening. His wife?

JULIE

Yes, sir. (*Behind the* DOCTOR *and* POLICEMAN *enter* MARIE, WOLF, MOTHER HOLLUNDER, YOUNG HOLLUNDER *and* MRS. MUSKAT. *They remain respectfully at the doorway. The* DOCTOR *bends over* LILIOM *and examines him.*)

DOCTOR

A light, if you please. (JULIE *fetches a burning candle from the dark room. The* DOCTOR *examines* LILIOM *briefly in the candle-light, then turns suddenly away.*) Have you pen and ink?

WOLF

(*Proffering a pen*). A fountain-pen—American——

DOCTOR

(*Takes a printed form from his pocket; speaks as he writes out the death-certificate at the little table*). My poor woman, your husband is dead—there's nothing to be done for him—the good God will help him now—I'll leave this certificate with you. You will give it to the people from the hospital when they come—I'll arrange for the body to be removed at once. (*Rises.*) Please give me a towel and soap.

POLICEMAN

I've got them for you out here, sir. (*Points to door at back.*)

DOCTOR

God be with you, my good woman.

JULIE

Thank you, sir. (*The* DOCTOR *and* POLICEMAN *exit. The others slowly draw nearer.*)

MARIE

Poor Julie. May he rest in peace, poor man, but as for you—please don't be angry with me for saying it—but you're better off this way.

MOTHER HOLLUNDER

He is better off, the poor fellow, and so are you.

MARIE

Much better, Julie . . . you are young . . and one of these days some good man will come along. Am I right?

WOLF

She's right.

MARIE

Julie, tell me, am I right?

JULIE

You are right, dear; you are very good.

YOUNG HOLLUNDER

There's a good man—the carpenter. Oh, I can speak of it now. He comes here every day on some excuse or other—and he never fails to ask for you.

MARIE

A widower—with two children.

MOTHER HOLLUNDER

He's better off, poor fellow—and so are you. He was a bad man.

MARIE

He wasn't good-hearted. Was he, Wolf?

WOLF

No, I must say, he really wasn't. No, Liliom wasn't a good man. A good man doesn't strike a woman.

MARIE

Am I right? Tell me, Julie, am I right?

JULIE

You are right, dear.

YOUNG HOLLUNDER

It's really a good thing for her it happened.

MOTHER HOLLUNDER

He's better off—and so is she.

WOLF

Now you have your freedom again. How old are you?

JULIE

Eighteen.

WOLF

Eighteen. A mere child! Am I right?

JULIE

You are right, Wolf. You are kind.

YOUNG HOLLUNDER

Lucky for you it happened, isn't it?

JULIE

Yes.

YOUNG HOLLUNDER

All you had before was bad luck. If it weren't for my mother you wouldn't have had a roof over your head or a bite to eat—and now Autumn's coming and Winter. You couldn't have lived in this shack in the Winter time, could you?

MARIE

Certainly not! You'd have frozen like the birds in the fields. Am I right, Julie?

JULIE

Yes, Marie.

MARIE

A year from now you will have forgotten all about him, won't you?

JULIE

You are right, Marie.

WOLF

If you need anything, count on us. We'll go now. But tomorrow morning we'll be back. Come, Marie. God be with you. (*Offers* JULIE *his hand.*)

JULIE

God be with you.

MARIE

(*Embracing* JULIE, *weeping*). It's the best thing that could have happened to you, Julie, the best thing.

JULIE

Don't cry, Marie. (MARIE *and* WOLF *exit.*)

MOTHER HOLLUNDER

I'll make a little black coffee. You haven't had a thing to eat today. Then you'll come home with us. (MOTHER HOLLUNDER *and her son exit.* MRS. MUSKAT *comes over to* JULIE.)

MRS. MUSKAT

Would you mind if I—looked at him?

JULIE

He used to work for you.

MRS. MUSKAT

(*Contemplates the body; turns to* JULIE). Won't you make up with me?

JULIE

I wasn't angry with you.

MRS. MUSKAT

But you were. Let's make it up.

JULIE

(*Raising her voice eagerly, almost triumphantly*). I've nothing to make up with *you.*

MRS. MUSKAT

But I have with you. Every one says hard things against the poor dead boy—except us two. You don't say he was bad.

JULIE

(*Raising her voice yet higher, this time on a defiant, wholly triumphant note*). Yes, I *do.*

MRS. MUSKAT

I understand, my child. But he beat me, too. What does that matter? I've forgotten it.

JULIE

(*From now on answers her coldly, drily, without looking at her*). That's your own affair.

MRS. MUSKAT

If I can help you in any way——

JULIE

There's nothing I need.

MRS. MUSKAT

I still owe him two kronen, back pay.

JULIE

You should have paid him.

MRS. MUSKAT

Now that the poor fellow is dead I thought perhaps it would be the same if I paid you.

JULIE

I've nothing to do with it.

MRS. MUSKAT

All right. Please don't think I'm trying to force myself on you. I stayed because we two are the only ones on earth who loved him. That's why I thought we ought to stick together.

JULIE

No, thank you.

MRS. MUSKAT

Then you couldn't have loved him as I did.

JULIE

No.

MRS. MUSKAT

I loved him better.

JULIE

Yes.

MRS. MUSKAT

Good-bye.

JULIE

Good-bye. (MRS. MUSKAT *exits.* JULIE *puts the candle on the table near* LILIOM's *head, sits on the edge of the stretcher, looks into the dead man's face and caresses it tenderly.*) Sleep, Liliom, sleep—it's no business of hers—I never even told you—but now I'll tell you—you bad, quick-tempered, rough, unhappy, wicked—*dear* boy—sleep peacefully, Liliom—they can't understand how I feel—I can't even explain to you—not even to you—how I feel—you'd only laugh at me—but you can't hear me any more. (*Between tender motherliness and reproach, yet with great love in her voice.*) It was wicked of you to beat me—on the breast and on the head and face—but you're gone now.—You treated me badly—that was wicked of you—but sleep peacefully, Liliom—you bad, bad boy, you—I love you—I never told you before—I was ashamed—but now I've told you—I love you. Liliom—sleep—my boy—sleep. (*She rises, gets a Bible, sits down near the candle and reads softly to herself, so that, not the words, but an inarticulate murmur is heard. The* CARPENTER *enters at back.*)

CARPENTER

(*Stands near the door; in the dimness of the room he can scarcely be seen*). Miss Julie——

JULIE

(*Without alarm*). Who is that?

CARPENTER

(*Very slowly*). The carpenter.

JULIE

What does the carpenter want?

CARPENTER

Can I be of help to you in any way? Shall I stay here with you?

JULIE

(*Gratefully, but firmly*). Don't stay, carpenter.

CARPENTER

Shall I come back tomorrow?

JULIE

Not tomorrow, either.

CARPENTER

Don't be offended, Miss Julie, but I'd like to know—you see, I'm not a young man any more—I have two children—and if I'm to come back any more—I'd like to know—if there's any use——

JULIE

No use, carpenter.

CARPENTER

(*As he exits*). God be with you. (JULIE *resumes her reading.* FICSUR *enters, slinks furtively sideways to the stretcher, looks at* LILIOM, *shakes his head.* JULIE *looks up from her reading.* FICSUR *takes fright, slinks away from the stretcher, sits down at right, biting his nails.* JULIE *rises.* FICSUR *rises, too, and looks at her half fearfully. With her piercing glance upon him he slinks to the doorway at back, where he pauses and speaks.*)

FICSUR

The old woman asked me to tell you that coffee is ready, and you are to come in. (JULIE *goes to the kitchen door.* FICSUR *withdraws until she has closed the door behind her. Then he reappears in the doorway, stands on tiptoes, looks at* LILIOM, *then exits. Now the body lies alone. After a brief silence music is heard, distant at first, but gradually coming nearer. It is very much like the music of the carousel, but slower, graver, more exalted. The melody, too, is the same, yet the tempo is altered and contrapuntal measures of the thieves' song are intertwined in it. Two men in black, with heavy sticks, soft black hats and black gloves, appear in the doorway at back and stride slowly into the room. Their faces are beardless, marble white, grave and benign. One stops in front of the stretcher, the other a pace to the right. From above a dim violet light illuminates their faces.*)

THE FIRST

(*To* LILIOM). Rise and come with us.

THE SECOND

(*Politely*). You're under arrest.

THE FIRST

(*Somewhat louder, but always in a gentle, low, resonant voice*). Do you hear? Rise. Don't you hear?

THE SECOND

We are the police.

THE FIRST

(*Bends down, touches* LILIOM'S *shoulder*). Get up and come with us. (LILIOM *slowly sits up.*)

THE SECOND

Come along.

THE FIRST

(*Paternally*). These people suppose that when they die all their difficulties are solved for them.

THE SECOND

(*Raising his voice sternly*). That simply by thrusting a knife in your heart and making it stop beating you can leave your wife behind with a child in her womb——

THE FIRST

It is not as simple as that.

THE SECOND

Such things are not settled so easily.

THE FIRST

Come along. You will have to give an account of yourself. (*As both bow their heads, he continues softly.*) We are God's police. (*An expression of glad relief lights upon* LILIOM'S *face. He rises from the stretcher.*) Come.

THE SECOND

You mortals don't get off quite as easy as that.

THE FIRST

(*Softly*). Come. (LILIOM *starts to walk ahead of them, then stops and looks at them.*) The end is not as abrupt as that. Your name is still spoken. Your face is still remembered. And what you said, and what you did, and what you failed to do—these are still remembered. Remembered, too, are the manner of your glance, the ring of your voice, the clasp of your hand and how your step sounded—as long as one is left who remembers you, so long is the matter unended. Before the end there is much to be undone. Until you are quite forgotten, my son, you will not be finished with the earth—even though you *are* dead.

THE SECOND

(*Very gently*). Come. (*The music begins again. All three exit at back,* LILIOM *leading, the others following. The stage is empty and quite dark save for the candle which burns by the stretcher, on which, in the shadows, the covers are so arranged that one cannot quite be sure that a body is not still lying. The music dies out in the distance as if it had followed* LILIOM *and the two* POLICEMEN. *The candle flickers and goes out. There is a brief interval of silence and total darkness before*

THE CURTAIN FALLS

SCENE VI

SCENE: *In the Beyond. A whitewashed courtroom. There is a green-topped table; behind it a bench. Back Center is a door with a bell over it. Next to this door is a window through which can be seen a vista of rose-tinted clouds.*

Down right there is a grated iron door. Down left another door.

Two men are on the bench when the curtain rises. One is richly, the other poorly dressed.

From a great distance is heard a fanfare of trumpets playing the refrain of the thieves' song in slow, altered tempo.

Passing the window at back appear LILIOM *and the two policemen.*

The bell rings.

An old guard enters at right. He is bald and has a long white beard. He wears the conventional police uniform.

He goes to the door at back, opens it, exchanges silent greetings with the two policemen and closes the door again.

LILIOM *looks wonderingly around.*

THE FIRST

(*To the old guard*). Announce us. (*The guard exits at left.*)

LILIOM

Is this it?

THE SECOND

Yes, my son.

LILIOM

This is the police court?

THE SECOND

Yes, my son. The part for suicide cases.

LILIOM

And what happens here?

THE FIRST

Here justice is done. Sit down. (LILIOM *sits next to the two men. The two policemen stand silent near the table.*)

THE RICHLY DRESSED MAN

(*Whispers*). Suicide, too?

LILIOM

Yes.

THE RICHLY DRESSED MAN

(*Points to the* POORLY DRESSED MAN). So's he. (*Introducing himself.*) My name is Reich.

THE POORLY DRESSED MAN

(*Whispers, too*). My name is Stephen Kadar. (LILIOM *only looks at them.*)

THE POORLY DRESSED MAN

And you? What's your name?

LILIOM

None of your business. (*Both move a bit away from him.*)

THE POORLY DRESSED MAN

I did it by jumping out of a window.

THE RICHLY DRESSED MAN

I did it with a pistol—and you?

LILIOM

With a knife. (*They move a bit further away from him.*)

THE RICHLY DRESSED MAN

A pistol is cleaner.

LILIOM

If I had the price of a pistol——

THE SECOND

Silence!

(*The* POLICE MAGISTRATE *enters. He has a long white beard, is bald, but only in profile can be seen on his head a single tuft of snow-white hair. The* GUARD *reënters behind him and sits on the bench with the dead men. As the* MAGISTRATE *enters, all rise, except* LILIOM, *who remains surlily seated. When the* MAGISTRATE *sits down, so do the others.*)

THE GUARD

Yesterday's cases, your honor. The numbers are entered in the docket.

THE MAGISTRATE

Number 16,472.

THE FIRST

(*Looks in his notebook, beckons the* RICHLY DRESSED MAN). Stand up, please. (THE RICHLY DRESSED MAN *rises.*)

THE MAGISTRATE

Your name?

THE RICHLY DRESSED MAN

Doctor Reich.

THE MAGISTRATE

Age?

THE RICHLY DRESSED MAN

Forty-two, married, Jew.

THE MAGISTRATE

(*With a gesture of dismissal*). Religion does not interest us here—why did you kill yourself?

THE RICHLY DRESSED MAN

On account of debts.

THE MAGISTRATE

What good did you do on earth?

THE RICHLY DRESSED MAN

I was a lawyer——

THE MAGISTRATE

(*Coughs significantly*). Yes—we'll discuss that later. For the present I shall only ask you: Would you like to go back to earth once more before sunrise? I advise you that you have the right to go if you choose. Do you understand?

THE RICHLY DRESSED MAN

Yes, sir.

THE MAGISTRATE

He who takes his life is apt, in his haste and his excitement, to forget something. Is there anything important down there you have left undone? Something to tell some one? Something to undo?

THE RICHLY DRESSED MAN

My debts——

THE MAGISTRATE

They do not matter here. Here we are concerned only with the affairs of the soul.

THE RICHLY DRESSED MAN

Then—if you please—when I left—the house — my youngest son, Oscar — was asleep. I didn't trust myself to wake him—and bid him good-bye. I would have liked—to kiss him good-bye.

THE MAGISTRATE

(*To* THE SECOND). You will take Dr. Reich back and let him kiss his son Oscar.

THE SECOND

Come with me, please.

THE RICHLY DRESSED MAN

(*To* THE MAGISTRATE). I thank you. (*He bows and exits at back with* THE SECOND.)

THE MAGISTRATE

(*After making an entry in the docket*). Number 16,473.

THE FIRST

(*Looks in his notebook, then beckons* LILIOM). Stand up.

LILIOM

You said *please* to him. (*He rises.*)

THE MAGISTRATE

Your name?

LILIOM

Liliom.

THE MAGISTRATE

Isn't that your nickname?

LILIOM

Yes.

THE MAGISTRATE

What is your right name?

LILIOM

Andreas.

THE MAGISTRATE

And your last name?

LILIOM

Zavocki—after my mother.

THE MAGISTRATE

Your age?

LILIOM

Twenty-four.

THE MAGISTRATE

What good did *you* do on earth? (LILIOM *is silent.*) Why did you take your life? (LILIOM *does not answer.* THE MAGISTRATE *addresses* THE FIRST.) Take that knife away from him. (THE FIRST *does so.*) It will be returned to you, if you go back to earth.

LILIOM

Do I go back to earth again?

THE MAGISTRATE

Just answer my questions.

LILIOM

I wasn't answering then, I was asking if—

THE MAGISTRATE

You don't ask questions here. You only answer. Only answer, Andreas Zavocki! I ask you whether there is anything on earth you neglected to accomplish? Anything down there you would like to do?

LILIOM

Yes.

THE MAGISTRATE

What is it?

LILIOM

I'd like to break Ficsur's head for him.

THE MAGISTRATE

Punishment is our office. Is there nothing else on earth you'd like to do?

LILIOM

I don't know—I guess, as long as I'm here, I'll not go back.

THE MAGISTRATE

(*To* THE FIRST). Note that. He waives his right. (LILIOM *starts back to the bench.*) Stay where you are. You are aware that you left your wife without food or shelter?

LILIOM

Yes.

THE MAGISTRATE

Don't you regret it?

LILIOM

No.

THE MAGISTRATE

You are aware that your wife is pregnant, and that in six months a child will be born?

LILIOM

I know.

THE MAGISTRATE

And that the child, too, will be without food or shelter? Do you regret that?

LILIOM

As long as I won't be there, what's it got to do with me?

THE MAGISTRATE

Don't try to deceive us, Andreas Zavocki. We see through you as through a pane of glass.

LILIOM

If you see so much, what do you want to ask me for? Why don't you let me rest—in peace?

THE MAGISTRATE

First you must earn your rest.

LILIOM

I want—only—to sleep.

THE MAGISTRATE

Your obstinacy won't help you. Here patience is endless as time. We can wait.

LILIOM

Can I ask something—I'd like to know—if Your Honor will tell me—whether the baby will be a boy or a girl.

THE MAGISTRATE

You shall see that for yourself.

LILIOM

(*Excitedly*). I'll see the baby?

THE MAGISTRATE

When you do it won't be a baby any more. But we haven't reached that question yet.

LILIOM

I'll see it?

THE MAGISTRATE

Again I ask you: Do you not regret that you deserted your wife and child; that you were a bad husband, a bad father?

LILIOM

A bad husband?

THE MAGISTRATE

Yes.

LILIOM

And a bad father?

THE MAGISTRATE

That, too.

LILIOM

I couldn't get work—and I couldn't bear to see Julie—all the time—all the time——

THE MAGISTRATE

Weeping! Why are you ashamed to say it? You couldn't bear to see her weeping. Why are you afraid of that word? And why are you ashamed that you loved her?

LILIOM

(*Shrugs his shoulders*). Who's ashamed? But I couldn't bear to see her—and that's why I was bad to her. You see, it wouldn't do to go back to the carousel—and Ficsur came along with his talk about—that other thing—and all of a sudden it happened, I don't know how. The police and the Jew with the pistol—and there I stood—and I'd lost the money playing cards—and I didn't want to be put in prison. (*Demanding justification.*) Maybe I was wrong not to go out and steal when there was nothing to eat in the house? Should I have gone out to steal for Julie?

THE MAGISTRATE

(*Emphatically*). Yes.

LILIOM

(*After an astounded pause*). The police down there never said that.

THE MAGISTRATE

You beat that poor, frail girl; you beat her because she loved you. How could you do that?

LILIOM

We argued with each other—she said this and I said that—and because she was right I couldn't answer her—and I got mad—and the anger rose up in me—until it reached here (*points to his throat*) and then I beat her.

THE MAGISTRATE

Are you sorry?

LILIOM

(*Shakes his head, but cannot utter the word "no"; continues softly*). When I touched her slender throat—then—if you like—you might say—— (*Falters, looks embarrassed at* THE MAGISTRATE.)

THE MAGISTRATE

(*Confidently expectant*). Are you sorry?

LILIOM

(*With a stare*). I'm not sorry for anything.

THE MAGISTRATE

Liliom, Liliom, it will be difficult to help you.

LILIOM

I'm not asking any help.

THE MAGISTRATE

You were offered employment as a caretaker on Arader Street. (*To* THE FIRST.) Where is that entered?

THE FIRST

In the small docket. (*Hands him the open book.* THE MAGISTRATE *looks in it.*)

THE MAGISTRATE

Rooms, kitchen, quarterly wages, the privilege of keeping poultry. Why didn't you accept it?

LILIOM

I'm not a caretaker. I'm no good at caretaking. To be a caretaker—you have to be a caretaker——

THE MAGISTRATE

If I said to you now: Liliom, go back on your stretcher. Tomorrow morning you will arise alive and well again. Would you be a caretaker then?

LILIOM

No.

THE MAGISTRATE

Why not?

LILIOM

Because—because that's just why I died.

THE MAGISTRATE

That is not true, my son. You died because you loved little Julie and the child she is bearing under her heart.

LILIOM

No.

THE MAGISTRATE

Look me in the eye.

LILIOM

(*Looks him in the eye*). No.

THE MAGISTRATE

(*Stroking his beard*). Liliom, Liliom, if it were not for our Heavenly patience—— Go back to your seat. Number 16,474.

THE FIRST

(*Looks in his note book*). Stephan Kadar. (THE POORLY DRESSED MAN *rises.*)

THE MAGISTRATE

You came out today?

THE POORLY DRESSED MAN

Today.

THE MAGISTRATE

(*Indicating the crimson sea of clouds*). How long were you in there?

THE POORLY DRESSED MAN

Thirteen years.

THE MAGISTRATE

Officer, you went to earth with him?

THE FIRST

Yes, sir.

THE MAGISTRATE

Stephan Kadar, after thirteen years of purification by fire you returned to earth to give proof that your soul had been burned clean. What good deed did you perform?

THE POORLY DRESSED MAN

When I came to the village and looked in the window of our cottage I saw my poor little orphans sleeping peacefully. But it was raining and the rain beat into the room through a hole in the roof. So I went and fixed the roof so it wouldn't rain in any more. My hammering woke them up and they were afraid. But their mother came in to them and comforted them. She said to them: "Don't cry! It's your poor, dear father hammering up there. He's come back from the other world to fix the roof for us."

THE MAGISTRATE

Officer?

THE FIRST

That's what happened.

THE MAGISTRATE

Stephan Kadar, you have done a good deed. What you did will be written in books to gladden the hearts of children who read them. (*Indicates the door at left.*) The door is open to you. The eternal light awaits you. (THE FIRST *escorts the* POORLY DRESSED MAN *out at left with great deference.*) Liliom! (LILIOM *rises.*) You have heard?

LILIOM

Yes.

THE MAGISTRATE

When this man first appeared before us he was as stubborn as you. But now he has purified himself and withstood the test. He has done a good deed.

LILIOM

What's he done, anyhow? Any roofer can fix a roof. It's much harder to be a barker in an amusement park.

THE MAGISTRATE

Liliom, you shall remain for sixteen years in the crimson fire until your child is full grown. By that time your pride and your stubbornness will have been burnt out of you. And when your daughter——

LILIOM

My daughter!

THE MAGISTRATE

When your daughter has reached the age of sixteen—— (LILIOM *bows his head, covers his eyes with his hands, and to keep from weeping laughs defiantly, sadly.*)

THE MAGISTRATE

When your daughter has reached the age of sixteen you will be sent for one day back to earth.

LILIOM

Me?

THE MAGISTRATE

Yes—just as you may have read in the legends of how the dead reappear on earth for a time.

LILIOM

I never believed them.

THE MAGISTRATE

Now you see they are true. You will go back to earth one day to show how far the purification of your soul has progressed.

LILIOM

Then I must show what I can do—like when you apply for a job—as a coachman?

THE MAGISTRATE

Yes—it is a test.

LILIOM

And will I be told what I have to do?

THE MAGISTRATE

No.

LILIOM

How will I know, then?

THE MAGISTRATE

You must decide that for yourself. That's what you burn sixteen years for. And if you do something good, something splendid for your child, then——

LILIOM

(*Laughs sadly*). Then? (*All stand up and bow their heads reverently. There is a pause.*) Then?

THE MAGISTRATE

Now I'll bid you farewell, Liliom. Sixteen years and a day shall pass before I see you again. When you have returned from earth you will come up before me again. Take heed and think well of some good deed to do for your child. On that will depend which door shall be opened to you up here. Now go, Liliom. (*He exits at left.* THE GUARD *stands at attention. There is a pause.*)

THE FIRST

(*Approaches* LILIOM). Come along, my son. (*He goes to the door at right; pulls open the bolt and waits.*)

LILIOM

(*To the old* GUARD, *softly*). Say, officer.

THE GUARD

What do you want?

LILIOM

Please—can I get—have you got——?

THE GUARD

What?

LILIOM

(*Whispers*). A cigarette? (*The old* GUARD *stares at him, goes a few paces to the left, shakes his head disapprovingly. Then his expression softens. He takes a cigarette from his pocket and, crossing to* LILIOM—*who has gone over to the door at right—gives him the cigarette.* THE FIRST *throws open the door. An intense rose-colored light streams in. The glow of it is so strong that it blinds* LILIOM *and he takes a step backward and bows his head and covers his eyes with his hand before he steps forward into the light.*)

THE CURTAIN FALLS

SCENE VII

SCENE: *Sixteen years later. A small, tumble-down house on a bare, unenclosed plot of ground. Before the house is a tiny garden enclosed by a hip-high hedge.*

At back a wooden fence crosses the stage; in the center of it is a door large enough to admit a wagon. Beyond the fence is a view of a suburban street which blends into a broad vista of tilled fields.

It is a bright Sunday in Spring.

In the garden a table for two is laid.

JULIE, *her daughter* LOUISE, WOLF *and* MARIE *are discovered in the garden.* WOLF *is prosperously dressed,* MARIE *somewhat elaborately, with a huge hat.*

JULIE

You could stay for lunch.

MARIE

Impossible, dear. Since he became the proprietor of the Café Sorrento, Wolf simply has to be there all the time.

JULIE

But you needn't stay there all day, too.

MARIE

Oh, yes. I sit near the cashier's cage, read the papers, keep an eye on the waiters and drink in the bustle and excitement of the great city.

JULIE

And what about the children?

MARIE

You know what modern families are like. Parents scarcely ever see their children these days. The four girls are with their governess, the three boys with their tutor.

LOUISE

Auntie, dear, do stay and eat with us.

MARIE

(*Importantly*). Impossible today, dear child, impossible. Perhaps some other time. Come, Mr. Beifeld.

JULIE

Since when do you call your husband mister?

WOLF

I'd rather she did, dear lady. When we used to be very familiar we quarreled all the time. Now we are formal with each other and get along like society folk. I kiss your hand, dear lady.

JULIE

Good-bye, Wolf.

MARIE

Adieu, my dear. (*They embrace.*) Adieu, my dear child.

LOUISE

Good-bye, Aunt Marie. Good-bye, Uncle Wolf. (WOLF *and* MARIE *exit.*)

JULIE

You can get the soup now, Louise dear. (LOUISE *goes into the house and reënters with the soup. They sit at the table.*)

LOUISE

Mother, is it true we're not going to work at the jute factory any more?

JULIE

Yes, dear.

LOUISE

Where then?

JULIE

Uncle Wolf has gotten us a place in a big establishment where they make all kinds of fittings for cafés. We're to make big curtains, you know, the kind they hang in the windows, with lettering on them.

LOUISE

It'll be nicer there than at the jute factory.

JULIE

Yes, dear. The work isn't as dirty and pays better, too. A poor widow like your mother is lucky to get it. (*They eat.* LILIOM *and the two* HEAVENLY POLICEMEN *appear in the big doorway at back. The* POLICEMEN *pass slowly by.* LILIOM *stands there alone a moment, then comes slowly down and pauses at the opening of the hedge. He is dressed as he was on the day of his death. He is very pale, but otherwise unaltered.* JULIE, *at the table, has her back to him.* LOUISE *sits facing the audience.*)

LILIOM

Good day.

LOUISE

Good day.

JULIE

Another beggar! What is it you want, my poor man?

LILIOM

Nothing.

JULIE

We have no money to give, but if you care for a plate of soup—— (LOUISE *goes into the house.*) Have you come far today?

LILIOM

Yes—very far.

JULIE

Are you tired?

LILIOM

Very tired.

JULIE

Over there at the gate is a stone. Sit down and rest. My daughter is bringing you the soup. (LOUISE *comes out of the house.*)

LILIOM

Is that your daughter?

JULIE

Yes.

LILIOM

(*To* LOUISE). You are the daughter?

LOUISE

Yes, sir.

LILIOM

A fine, healthy girl. (*Takes the soup plate from her with one hand, while with the other he touches her arm.* LOUISE *draws back quickly.*)

LOUISE

(*Crosses to* JULIE). Mother!

JULIE

What, my child?

LOUISE

The man tried to take me by the arm.

JULIE

Nonsense! You only imagined it, dear. The poor, hungry man has other things to think about than fooling with young girls. Sit down and eat your soup. (*They eat.*)

LILIOM

(*Eats, too, but keeps looking at them*). You work at the factory, eh?

JULIE

Yes.

LILIOM

Your daughter, too?

LOUISE

Yes.

LILIOM

And your husband?

JULIE

(*After a pause*). I have no husband. I'm a widow.

LILIOM

A widow?

JULIE

Yes.

LILIOM

Your husband—I suppose he's been dead a long time. (JULIE *does not answer.*) I say—has your husband been dead a long time?

JULIE

A long time.

LILIOM

What did he die of? (JULIE *is silent.*)

LOUISE

No one knows. He went to America to work and he died there—in the hospital. Poor father, I never knew him.

LILIOM

He went to America?

LOUISE

Yes, before I was born.

LILIOM

To America?

JULIE

Why do you ask so many questions? Did you know him, perhaps?

LILIOM

(*Puts the plate down*). Heaven knows! I've known so many people. Maybe I knew him, too.

JULIE

Well, if you knew him, leave him and us in peace with your questions. He went to America and died there. That's all there is to tell.

LILIOM

All right. All right. Don't be angry with me. I didn't mean any harm. (*There is a pause.*)

LOUISE

My father was a very handsome man.

JULIE

Don't talk so much.

LOUISE

Did I say anything——?

LILIOM

Surely the little orphan can say that about her father.

LOUISE

My father could juggle so beautifully with three ivory balls that people used to advise him to go on the stage.

JULIE

Who told you that?

LOUISE

Uncle Wolf.

LILIOM

Who is that?

LOUISE

Mr. Wolf Beifeld, who owns the Café Sorrento.

LILIOM

The one who used to be a porter?

JULIE

(*Astonished*). Do you know him, too? It seems that you know all Budapest.

LILIOM

Wolf Beifeld is a long way from being all Budapest. But I do know a lot of people. Why shouldn't I know Wolf Beifeld?

LOUISE

He was a friend of my father.

JULIE

He was not his friend. No one was.

LILIOM

You speak of your husband so sternly.

JULIE

What's that to you? Doesn't it suit you? I can speak of my husband any way I like. It's nobody's business but mine.

LILIOM

Certainly, certainly—it's your own business. (*Takes up his soup plate again. All three eat.*)

LOUISE

(*To* JULIE). Perhaps he knew father, too.

JULIE

Ask him, if you like.

LOUISE

(*Crosses to* LILIOM. *He stands up*). Did you know my father? (LILIOM *nods.* LOUISE *addresses her mother.*) Yes, he knew him.

JULIE

(*Rises*). You knew Andreas Zavocki?

LILIOM

Liliom? Yes.

LOUISE

Was he really a very handsome man?

LILIOM

I wouldn't exactly say handsome.

LOUISE

(*Confidently*). But he was an awfully good man, wasn't he?

LILIOM

He wasn't so good, either. As far as I know he was what they called a clown, a barker in a carousel.

LOUISE

(*Pleased*). Did he tell funny jokes?

LILIOM

Lots of 'em. And he sang funny songs, too.

LOUISE

In the carousel?

LILIOM

Yes—but he was something of a bully, too. He'd fight any one. He even hit your dear little mother.

JULIE

That's a lie.

LILIOM

It's true.

JULIE

Aren't you ashamed to tell the child such awful things about her father? Get out of here, you shameless liar. Eats our soup and our bread and has the impudence to slander our dead!

LILIOM

I didn't mean—I——

JULIE

What right have you to tell lies to the child? Take that plate, Louise, and let him be on his way. If he wasn't such a hungry-looking beggar, I'd put him out myself. (LOUISE *takes the plate out of his hand.*)

LILIOM

So he didn't hit you?

JULIE

No, never. He was always good to me.

LOUISE

(*Whispers*). Did he tell funny stories, too?

LILIOM

Yes, and *such* funny ones.

JULIE

Don't speak to him any more. In God's name, go.

LOUISE

In God's name. (JULIE *resumes her seat at the table and eats.*)

LILIOM

If you please, Miss—I have a pack of cards in my pocket. And if you like, I'll show you some tricks that'll make you split your sides laughing. (LOUISE *holds* LILIOM'*s plate in her left hand. With her right she reaches out and holds the garden gate shut.*) Let me in, just a little way, Miss, and I'll do the tricks for you.

LOUISE

Go, in God's name, and let us be. Why are you making those ugly faces?

LILIOM

Don't chase me away, Miss; let me come in for just a minute—just for a minute—just long enough to let me show you something pretty, something wonderful. (*Opens the gate.*) Miss, I've something to give you. (*Takes from his pocket a big red handkerchief in which is wrapped a glittering star from Heaven. He looks furtively about him to make sure that the* POLICE *are not watching.*)

LOUISE

What's that?

LILIOM

Pst! A star! (*With a gesture he indicates that he has stolen it out of the sky.*)

JULIE

(*Sternly*). Don't take anything from him. He's probably stolen it somewhere. (*To* LILIOM.) In God's name, be off with you.

LOUISE

Yes, be off with you. Be off. (*She slams the gate.*)

LILIOM

Miss—please, Miss—I've got to do something good—or—do something good—a good deed——

LOUISE

(*Pointing with her right hand*). That's the way out.

LILIOM

Miss——

LOUISE

Get out!

LILIOM

Miss! (*Looks up at her suddenly and slaps her extended hand, so that the slap resounds loudly.*)

LOUISE

Mother! (*Looks dazedly at* LILIOM, *who bows his head dismayed, forlorn.* JULIE *rises and looks at* LILIOM *in astonishment. There is a long pause.*)

JULIE

(*Comes over to them slowly*). What's the matter here?

LOUISE

(*Bewildered, does not take her eyes off* LILIOM). Mother—the man—he hit me—on the hand—hard—I heard the sound of it—but it didn't hurt—Mother—it didn't hurt—it was like a caress—as if he had just touched my hand tenderly. (*She hides behind* JULIE. LILIOM *sulkily raises his head and looks at* JULIE.)

JULIE

(*Softly*). Go, my child. Go into the house. Go.

LOUISE

(*Going*). But Mother — I'm afraid — it sounded so loud—— (*Weepingly.*) And it didn't hurt at all—just as if he'd—kissed my hand instead—Mother! (*She hides her face.*)

JULIE

Go in, my child, go in. (LOUISE *goes slowly into the house.* JULIE *watches her until she has disappeared, then turns slowly to* LILIOM.)

JULIE

You struck my child.

LILIOM

Yes—I struck her.

JULIE

Is that what you came for, to strike my child?

LILIOM

No—I didn't come for that—but I did strike her—and now I'm going back.

JULIE

In the name of the Lord Jesus, who are you?

LILIOM

(*Simply*). A poor, tired beggar who came a long way and who was hungry. And I took your soup and bread and I struck your child. Are you angry with me?

JULIE

(*Her hand on her heart; fearfully, wonderingly*). Jesus protect me—I don't understand it—I'm *not* angry—not angry at all —— (LILIOM *goes to the doorway and leans against the doorpost, his back to the audience.* JULIE *goes to the table and sits.*)

JULIE

Louise! (LOUISE *comes out of the house.*) Sit down, dear, we'll finish eating.

LOUISE

Has he gone?

JULIE

Yes. (*They are both seated at the table.* LOUISE, *her head in her hands, is staring into space.*) Why don't you eat, dear?

LOUISE

What has happened, Mother?

JULIE

Nothing, my child. (*The* HEAVENLY POLICEMEN *appear outside.* LILIOM *walks slowly off at left. The* FIRST POLICEMAN *makes a deploring gesture. Both shake their heads deploringly and follow* LILIOM *slowly off at left.*)

LOUISE

Mother, dear, why won't you tell me?

JULIE

What is there to tell you, child? Nothing has happened. We were peacefully eating, and a beggar came who talked of bygone days, and then I thought of your father.

LOUISE

My father?

JULIE

Your father—Liliom. (*There is a pause.*)

LOUISE

Mother—tell me—has it ever happened to you—has any one ever hit you—without hurting you in the least?

JULIE

Yes, my child. It has happened to me, too. (*There is a pause.*)

LOUISE

Is it possible for some one to hit you—hard like that—real loud and hard—and not hurt you at all?

JULIE

It is possible, dear—that some one may beat you and beat you and beat you,—and not hurt you at all.—— (*There is a pause. Near by an organ-grinder has stopped. The music of his organ begins.*)

THE CURTAIN FALLS

Leonid Andreyev

HE WHO GETS SLAPPED

Translated from the Russian by

Gregory Zilboorg

LEONID ANDREYEV

Born in Orel in Central Russia, in 1871, Leonid Andreyev's life from early youth to his death was one of fierce vicissitudes and violent literary conflicts. Poverty drove him from home to Petrograd where, as a law student, he attempted suicide three times. Moving to Moscow, he took up painting and revealed considerable talent. As a free-lance journalist, he eked out a bare living. Thanks to Maxim Gorky, Andreyev became a contributor to the leading papers. His stories, brutally frank for that time, made his name known. His anti-war writings won an enthusiastic response immediately after the Russo-Japanese War. When the World War broke out, Andreyev became a Russian propagandist and severed relations with his revolutionary colleagues. He became identified with Kerensky and went into exile after the collapse of the provisional government. The breach between Gorky and Andreyev grew wider. He died in August 1919, estranged from his own land and denounced by his former confreres. Among his prose works those best known in translation are *The Seven That Were Hanged, The Red Laugh, Silence, The Life of Man, Sava, King Hunger, The Sabine Women* and *He Who Gets Slapped.*

CHARACTERS

CONSUELO, a bareback rider in a circus. Billed as "The Bareback Tango Queen"

MANCINI, Consuelo's father

HE, a clown in Briquet's circus. Billed as "HE Who Gets Slapped"

BRIQUET, Manager of the circus

ZINIDA, a lion tamer, Briquet's wife

ALFRED BEZANO, a bareback rider

A GENTLEMAN

BARON REGNARD

JACKSON, a clown

TILLY } musical clowns
POLLY }

THOMAS, ANGELICA, and other actors and actresses of Briquet's circus

The action takes place in one of the large cities of France.

HE WHO GETS SLAPPED

ACT ONE

A VERY LARGE, rather dirty room, with whitewashed walls. To the left, in a niche, is a window, the only outside window in the room, opening on a court-yard. The light from it is so dim that even by day the electricity has to be turned on.

At the very top of the center-back wall is a row of small dusty windows. They open on the circus hall. At night, when the performance is going on, a bright light shines through. By day they are dark. In the same wall is a large white door, reached by two stone steps, and nailed fast.

On the right, almost in the corner, is a high, wide, arched doorway which leads to the stables and the ring. By day it opens into pale darkness, at night into pale light.

The room is used for many purposes. It is the office of PAPA BRIQUET, *manager of the circus; here he keeps his little desk. It is the cloak-room of some of the actors. It is also the room where the cast gathers between calls, during rehearsals or performances. Again, it is a check-room for used circus property, such as gilt armchairs, scenery for pantomimes, and other wares of the circus household. The walls are covered with circus announcements and glaring posters.*

The time is morning. In the circus hall a rehearsal is going on, and preparations are being made for the evening performance. As the curtain goes up, the cracking whip and the shouts of the riding-master are heard from the ring. The stage is empty for a few seconds, then enter TILLY *and* POLLY, *the musical clowns, practising a new march. Playing on tiny pipes, they step from the dark doorway to the window. Their music is agreeable to the ear, but small, mincing, artificially clown-like, like their mincing steps; they wear jackets and resemble each other; same smooth-shaven face, same height;* TILLY, *the younger, has a scarf around his neck; both have their derbies on the backs of their heads.* TILLY *glances through the window, then they turn about, still marching.*

POLLY

(*Interrupting the march*). Stop, you're out again! Now, listen—(*He stands close to* TILLY *and plays into his face.* TILLY *absent-mindedly listens, scratching his nose.*) There! Come on now! (*They resume their music and marching. As they reach the door they meet the manager and* MANCINI; *the latter walks behind the manager, and is gnawing at the knob of his gold-mounted cane.* COUNT MANCINI *is tall and slight. The seams of his clothes are worn and he keeps his coat buttoned tight. He assumes extremely graceful manners, takes affected poses, and has a special fondness for toying with his cane, with aristocratic stylishness. When he laughs, which happens often, his thin sharp face takes on a marked resemblance to a satyr. The manager,* PAPA BRIQUET, *is a stout quiet man of average height. His bearing is hesitant. The clowns make room for the gentlemen. The manager looks questioningly at the older man.*)

POLLY

(*With an affected accent*). Our moosic for the pantomime! The March of the Ants!

BRIQUET

Ha! Yes!
(*The gentlemen walk in. The clowns resume their music,* POLLY *marching on, then turning, the younger following.*)

POLLY

Papa Briquet, Jack is working very badly today.

BRIQUET

What's the matter with him?

POLLY

He has a sore throat. You'd better take a look at him.

BRIQUET

All right. Come on, Jack. Open your mouth! Wider—wider. (*Turns clown's face to the light near the window and examines him closely and seriously.*) Just smear it with iodine.

POLLY

I told him so. I said it was nothing! Oh! Come on. (*They go away playing, marching, practising their funny mincing steps. The manager sits down.* MANCINI *strikes a pose by the wall, smiling ironically.*)

MANCINI

So. You give them medical treatment, too! Look out, Papa Briquet, you have no license.

BRIQUET

Just a little advice. They're all so afraid for their lives.

MANCINI

His throat is simply burnt with whiskey. These two fellows get drunk every night. I am amazed, Papa Briquet, to see you pay so little attention to their morals. (*He laughs.*)

BRIQUET

You make me sick, Mancini.

MANCINI

Count Mancini is at your service!

BRIQUET

You make me sick, Count Mancini. You poke your nose into everything, you disturb the artists in their work. Some day you'll get a thrashing, and I warn you that I shan't interfere.

MANCINI

As a man of superior associations and education I cannot be expected to treat your actors as my equals! What more can you ask, Briquet? You see that I do you the honor of speaking with you quite familiarly, quite simply.

BRIQUET

Ha! ha! ha! (*Slightly threatening.*) Really!

MANCINI

Never mind my joke. What if they did dare attack me—ever seen this, Briquet? (*He draws a stiletto out of his cane and advances it silently.*) Useful little thing. By the way, you have no idea of the discovery I made yesterday in a suburb. Such a girl! (*Laughs.*) Oh, well! all right, all right—I know you don't like that sort of sport. But look here, you must give me a hundred francs!

BRIQUET

Not a sou.

MANCINI

Then I'll take away Consuelo—that's all——

BRIQUET

Your daily threat!

MANCINI

Yes, my threat! And you would do the same, if you were as shamefully hard up as I am. Now look here, you know as well as I do that I have to live up to my name somehow, keep up the family reputation. Just because the tide of ill-fortune which struck my ancestors compelled me to make my daughter, the Countess Veronica, a bareback rider—to keep us from starving—do you understand—you heartless idiot!

BRIQUET

You chase the girls too much! Some day you'll land in jail, Mancini!

MANCINI

In jail? Oh, no! Why, I have to uphold our *name*, the splendor of my family (*laughs*) haven't I? The Mancinis are known all over Italy for their love of girls —just girls! Is it my fault if I must pay such crazy prices for what my ancestors got free of charge? You're nothing but an ass, a *parvenu* ass. How can you understand family traditions? I don't drink—I stopped playing cards after that accident —no, you need not smile. Now if I give up the girls, what will be left of Mancini? Only a coat of arms, that's all—— In the name of family traditions, give me a hundred francs!

BRIQUET

I told you no, I won't.

MANCINI

You know that I leave half of the salary for Consuelo—but—perhaps you think I do not love my child—my only daughter, all that remains to me as a memory of her sainted mother—what cruelty! (*Pretends to cry, wipes his eyes with a small and dirty lace handkerchief, embroidered with a coronet.*)

BRIQUET

Why don't you say, rather, that she is foolish enough to give you half her salary. You make me sick——

(*Enter* ZINIDA, *the lion tamer; burningly beautiful, her self-confident, commanding gestures at first glance give an impression of languor. She is* BRIQUET'S *unmarried wife.*)

ZINIDA

(*To* MANCINI). Good morning.

MANCINI

Madame Zinida! This barbarian, this brute may pierce me with his dagger, but I cannot control the expression of my love! (*Kneels facetiously before her.*) Madame! Count Mancini has the honor of asking you to be his wife. . . .

ZINIDA

(*To* BRIQUET). Money?

BRIQUET

Yes.

ZINIDA

Don't give him any. (*Sits down wearily on a torn sofa, shuts her eyes.* MANCINI *gets up and wipes his knees.*)

MANCINI

Duchess! Don't be cruel. I am no lion, no tiger, no savage beast which you are accustomed to tame. I am merely a poor domestic animal, who wants, miaow, miaow, a little green grass.

ZINIDA

(*Without opening her eyes*). Jim tells me you have a teacher for Consuelo. What for?

MANCINI

The solicitude of a father, duchess, the solicitude and the tireless anxiety of a loving heart. The extreme misfortunes of our family, when I was a child, have left some flaws in her education. Friends, the daughter of Count Mancini, Countess Veronica, can barely read! Is that admissible? And you, Briquet, heartless brute, you still ask why I need money!

ZINIDA

Artful!

BRIQUET

What are you teaching her?

MANCINI

Everything. A student had been giving her lessons, but I threw him out yesterday. He had the nerve to fall in love with Consuelo and stood there miaowing at the door like a cat. Everything, Briquet, that you don't know—literature, mythology, orthography—— (*Two young actresses appear, with small fur coats thrown over their light dresses. They are tired and sit down in the corner.*)

MANCINI

I do not wish my daughter——

ZINIDA

Artful!

BRIQUET

You are stupid, Mancini. What do you do it for? (*In a didactic tone.*) You are fearfully stupid, Mancini. Why does she need to learn? Since she is here she need never know anything about that life. Don't you understand? What is geography? If I were the government I would forbid artists to read books. Let them read the posters, that's enough.

(*During* BRIQUET'S *speech, the two clowns and another actor enter. They sit down wearily.*)

BRIQUET

Right now, your Consuelo is an excellent artist, but just as soon as you teach her mythology, and she begins to read, she'll become a nuisance, she'll be corrupted, and then she'll go and poison herself. I know those books, I've read 'em myself. All they teach is corruption, and how to kill oneself.

FIRST ACTRESS

I love the novels that come out in the newspaper.

BRIQUET

That shows what a foolish girl you are. You'll be done for in no time. Believe me, my friends, we must forget entirely what is happening out there. How can we understand all that goes on there?

MANCINI

You are an enemy of enlightenment, you are an obscurantist, Briquet.

BRIQUET

And you are stupid. You are from out there. What has it taught you? (*The actors laugh.*) If you'd been born in a circus as I was, you'd *know* something. Enlightenment is plain nonsense—nothing else. Ask Zinida. She knows everything they teach out there — geography, mythology —— Does it make her any happier? You tell them, dear.

ZINIDA

Leave me alone, Louis.

MANCINI

(*Angrily*). Oh! Go to the devil! When I listen to your asinine philosophy, I'd like to skin you for more than a paltry hundred francs—for two hundred—for a thousand. Great God! What an ass of a manager! Yes, right before everyone of them I want to say that you are a stingy old skinflint—that you pay starvation wages. I'll make you give Consuelo a raise of a hundred francs. Listen, all you honest vagabonds, tell me—who is it draws the crowd that fills the circus every night? You? a couple of musical donkeys? Tigers, lions? Nobody cares for those hungry cats!

ZINIDA

Leave the tigers alone.

MANCINI

Beg your pardon, Zinida. I did not mean to hurt your feelings—honestly. I really marvel at your furious audacity—at your grace —you are a heroine—I kiss your tiny hands. But what do they understand about heroism? (*An orchestra softly plays the Tango in the circus. He continues with enthusiasm.*) Hear! hear! Now tell me, honest vagabonds, who but Consuelo and Bezano draws the crowds! That Tango on horseback—it is—it is—— Oh, the devil! Even his fatuousness the Pope could not withstand its lure.

POLLY

True! It's a great trick—wasn't the idea Bezano's?

MANCINI

Idea! Idea! The lad's in love, like a cat—that's the idea. What's the good of an idea without a woman! You wouldn't dance very far with your idea alone, eh, Papa Briquet?

BRIQUET

We have a contract.

MANCINI

Such base formalities.

ZINIDA

Give him ten francs and let him go.

MANCINI

Ten! Never! *Fifteen!* Don't be stubborn, Papa. For the traditions of my house—twenty. I swear—on my honor—I can't do with less. (BRIQUET *hands him twenty francs. Nonchalantly.*) *Merci.* Thanks.

ZINIDA

Why don't you take it from your baron?

MANCINI

(*Raising his eyebrows haughtily, quite indignant*). From the Baron? Woman! who do you think I am that I should be beholden to a stranger?

ZINIDA

You're plotting something artful. I know you very little, but I guess you're an awful scoundrel.

MANCINI

(*Laughs*). Such an insult from such beautiful lips.
(*Enter an "artist," apparently an athlete.*)

ATHLETE

Papa Briquet, there's a gentleman from beyond the grave asking for you.

ACTRESS

A ghost?

ATHLETE

No. He seems alive. Did you ever see a drunken ghost?

BRIQUET

If he's drunk, tell him I'm out, Thomas. Does he want to see me or the Count?

ATHLETE

No, you. Maybe he's not drunk, but just a ghost.

MANCINI

(*Draws himself together, puffs up*). A society man?

ATHLETE

Yes. I'll tell him to come in.
(*One hears the whip cracking in the ring. The Tango sounds very low and distant—then comes nearer—louder. Silence.*)

BRIQUET

(*Touching* ZINIDA's *arm*). Tired?

ZINIDA

(*Drawing back a little*). No.

POLLY

Your red lion is nervous today, Zinida!

ZINIDA

You shouldn't tease him.

POLLY

I played a melody from Traviata for him. And he sang with me. Wouldn't that be a good trick to stage, Papa Briquet?
(THOMAS *brings in the gentleman, points out the manager, and goes heavily away. The gentleman is not young, and he is ugly, but his rather strange face is bold and lively. He wears an expensive overcoat, with a fur collar, and holds his hat and gloves in his hand.*)

GENTLEMAN

(*Bowing and smiling*). Have I the pleasure of addressing the manager?

BRIQUET

Yes. Won't you sit down, please? Tilly, bring a chair.

GENTLEMAN

Oh! Don't trouble! (*Looks around.*) These are your artists? Very glad——

MANCINI

(*Straightening and bowing slightly*). Count Mancini.

GENTLEMAN

(*Surprised*). Count?

BRIQUET

(*Indignantly*). Yes, Count. And whom have I the honor of——

GENTLEMAN

I don't quite know myself—yet. As a rule you choose your own names, don't you? I have not chosen yet. Later you might advise me about it. I have an idea already, but I am afraid it sounds too much like literature—you know.

BRIQUET

Literature?

GENTLEMAN

Yes! Too sophisticated. (*They all look surprised.*) I presume these two gentlemen are clowns? I am so glad. May I shake hands with them? (*Stands up and shakes hands with clowns, who make silly faces.*)

BRIQUET

Excuse me—but what can I do for you?

GENTLEMAN

(*With the same pleasant, confident smile*). Oh. You do something for me? No. I want to do something for you, Papa Briquet.

BRIQUET

Papa Briquet? But you don't look like——

GENTLEMAN

(*Reassuringly*). It's all right. I shall become "like." These two gentlemen just made remarkable faces. Would you like to see me imitate them? Look! (*He makes the same silly faces as the clowns.*)

BRIQUET

Yes! (*Involuntarily.*) You are not drunk, sir?

GENTLEMAN

No. I don't drink as a rule. Do I look drunk?

POLLY

A little.

GENTLEMAN

No—I don't drink. It is a peculiarity of my talent.

BRIQUET

(*Familiarly*). Where did you work before? Juggler?

GENTLEMAN

No. But I am glad you feel in me a comrade, Papa Briquet. Unfortunately I am not a juggler, and have worked nowhere—I am—just so.

MANCINI

But you look like a society man.

GENTLEMAN

Oh, you flatter me, Count. I am just so.

BRIQUET

Well, what do you want? You see I am obliged to tell you that everything is taken.

GENTLEMAN

That's immaterial. I want to be a clown, if you will allow me. (*Some of the actors smile,* BRIQUET *begins to grow angry.*)

BRIQUET

But what can you do? You're asking too much. What can you do?

GENTLEMAN

Why! Nothing! Isn't that funny! I can't do a thing.

BRIQUET

No, it's not funny. Any scoundrel knows that much.

GENTLEMAN

(*Rather helpless, but still smiling and looking around*). We can invent something—

BRIQUET

(*Ironically*). From literature?

(*The clown* JACKSON *enters slowly without being noticed by the others. He stands behind the gentlemen.*)

GENTLEMAN

Yes, one can find something literary, too. A nice little speech for instance on, let's say, a religious topic. Something like a debate among the clowns.

BRIQUET

A debate! The devil! This is no academy.

GENTLEMAN

(*Sadly*). I am very sorry. Something else then. Perhaps a joke about the creation of the world and its rulers?

BRIQUET

What about the police? No, no—nothing like that!

JACKSON

(*Coming forward*). The rulers of the world? You don't like them? I don't either. Shake.

BRIQUET

(*Introducing*). Our chief clown, the famous Jackson.

GENTLEMAN

(*Enthusiastically*). Great heavens — you! Allow me to shake hands with you heartily! You, with your genius, you have given me so much joy!

JACKSON

I'm glad indeed!

BRIQUET

(*Shrugs his shoulders; to* JACKSON). He wants to be a clown! Look him over, Jim. (JACKSON *makes a motion at which the gentleman hurriedly removes his coat and throws it on a chair. He is ready for the examination.* JACKSON *turns him round, looking him over critically.*)

JACKSON

Clown? Hm! Turn round then. Clown? Yes? Now smile. Wider—broader—do you call that a smile? So—that's better. There is something, yes—but for full developments—— (*Sadly.*) Probably you can't even turn a somersault?

GENTLEMAN

(*Sighs*). No.

JACKSON

How old are you?

GENTLEMAN

Thirty-nine. Too late? (JACKSON *moves away with a whistle. There is a silence.*)

ZINIDA

(*Softly*). Take him.

BRIQUET

(*Indignant*). What the hell shall I do with him if he doesn't know a thing? He's drunk!

GENTLEMAN

Honestly I am not. Thank you for your support, Madame. Are you not the famous Zinida, the lion tamer, whose regal beauty and audacity——

ZINIDA

Yes. But I do not like flattery.

GENTLEMAN

It is not flattery.

MANCINI

You are evidently not accustomed to good society, my dear. Flattery? This gentleman expresses his admiration in sincere and beautiful words—and you—you are not educated, Zinida. As for myself——
(*Enter* CONSUELO *and* BEZANO *in circus costume.*)

CONSUELO

You here, Daddy?

MANCINI

Yes, my child, you are not tired? (*Kisses her on the forehead.*) My daughter, sir, Countess Veronica. Known on the stage as Consuelo, The Bareback Tango Queen. Did you ever see her?

GENTLEMAN

I have enjoyed her work. It is marvellous!

MANCINI

Yes! Of course. Everyone admits it. And how do you like the name, Consuelo? I took it from the novel of George Sand. It means "Consolation."

GENTLEMAN

What a wonderful knowledge of books!

MANCINI

A small thing. Despite your strange intention, I can see, sir, that you are a gentleman. My peer! Let me explain to you, that only the strange and fatal misfortunes of our ancient family—"*sic transit gloria mundi*," sir.

CONSUELO

It's a bore, Daddy—— Where's my handkerchief, Alfred?

BEZANO

Here it is.

CONSUELO

(*Showing the handkerchief to the gentleman*). Genuine Venetian. Do you like it?

GENTLEMAN

(*Again bowing*). My eyes are dazzled: how beautiful! Papa Briquet, the more I look around me the more I want to stay with you. (*Makes a face of a simpleton.*) On the one hand a count, on the other——

JACKSON

(*Nods approval*). That's not bad. Look here, think a bit—find something. Everyone here thinks for himself.
(*Silence. The* GENTLEMAN *stands with a finger on his forehead, thinking.*)

GENTLEMAN

Find something—find something . . . Eureka!

POLLY

That means *found*. Come!

GENTLEMAN

Eureka—— I shall be among you, he who gets slapped. (*General laughter. Even* BRIQUET smiles.)

GENTLEMAN

(*Looks at them smiling*). You see I made even you laugh—is that easy? (*All grow serious.* POLLY *sighs.*)

TILLY

No, it's not easy. Did you laugh, Polly?

POLLY

Sure, a lot. Did you?

TILLY

I did. (*Imitating an instrument, he plays with his lips a melody at once sad and gay.*)

JACKSON

"He Who Gets Slapped," that's not bad.

GENTLEMAN

It's not, is it? I rather like it myself. It suits my talent. And comrades, I have even found a name—you'll call me "HE." Is that all right?

JACKSON

(*Thinking*). "HE"—Not bad.

CONSUELO

(*In a singing, melodic voice*). "HE" is so funny—"HE"—like a dog. Daddy, are there such dogs?
(JACKSON *suddenly gives a circus slap to the gentleman.* HE *steps back and grows pale.*)

GENTLEMAN

What!—(*General laughter covers his exclamation.*)

JACKSON

HE Who Gets Slapped. Or didn't you get it?

POLLY

(*Comically*). He says he wants more——
(*The gentleman smiles, rubbing his cheek.*)

GENTLEMAN

So sudden — Without waiting — How funny—you didn't hurt me, and yet my cheek burns.
(*Again there is loud laughter. The clowns cackle like ducks, hens, cocks; they bark.* ZENIDA *says something to* BRIQUET, *casts a glance toward* BEZANO, *and goes out.* MANCINI *assumes a bored air and looks at his watch. The two actresses go out.*)

JACKSON

Take him, Papa Briquet—he will push us.

MANCINI

(*Again looking at his watch*). But bear in mind, that Papa Briquet is as close as Harpagon. If you expect to get good money here you are mistaken. (HE *laughs.*) A slap? What's a slap? Worth only small change, a franc and a half a dozen. Better go back to society; you will make more money there. Why for one slap, just a light tap, you might say, my friend, Marquis Justi, was paid fifty thousand lire!

BRIQUET

Shut up, Mancini. Will you take care of him, Jackson?

JACKSON

I can.

POLLY

Do you like music? A Beethoven sonata played on a broom, for instance, or Mozart on a bottle?

HE

Alas! No. But I will be exceedingly grateful if you will teach me. A clown! My childhood's dream. When all my school friends were thrilled by Plutarch's heroes, or the light of science—I dreamed of clowns. Beethoven on a broom, Mozart on bottles! Just what I have sought all my life! Friends, I must have a costume!

JACKSON

I see you don't know much! A costume (*putting his finger on his forehead*) is a thing which calls for deep thought. Have you seen my Sun here? (*Strikes his posterior.*) I looked for it two years.

HE

(*Enthusiastically*). I shall think.

MANCINI

It is time for me to go. Consuelo, my child, you must get dressed. (*To* HE.) We are lunching with Baron Regnard, a friend of mine, a banker.

CONSUELO

But I don't want to go, Daddy. Alfred says I must rehearse today.

MANCINI

(*Horrified, holding up his hands*). Child, think of me, and what a situation you put me in! I promised the Baron, the Baron expects us. Why, it is impossible! Oh, I am in a cold sweat.

CONSUELO

Alfred says——

BEZANO

(*Drily*). She has to work. Are you rested? Then come on.

MANCINI

But—the devil take me if I know what to make of it. Hey, Bezano, bareback rider! Are you crazy? I gave you permission for Art's sake, to exercise my daughter's talent —and you——

CONSUELO

Go along, Papa, and don't be so silly. We've got to work, haven't we? Have lunch along with your Baron. And Daddy, you forgot to take a clean handkerchief again, and I washed two for you yesterday. Where did you put them?

MANCINI

(*Ashamed, blushing*). Why, my linen is washed by the laundress, and you, Consuelo, are still playing with toys. It is stupid! You're a chatter-box. You don't think. These gentlemen might imagine Heaven knows what. How stupid. I'm off.

CONSUELO

Do you want me to write him a little note?

MANCINI

(*Angrily*). A little note? Your little notes would make a horse laugh! Good-bye. (*He goes out toying angrily with his cane. The clowns follow him respectfully, playing a funeral march.* HE *and* JACKSON *laugh. The actors disappear one by one.*)

CONSUELO

(*Laughing*). Do I really write so badly? And I love so to write. Did you like my note, Alfred—or did you laugh, too?

BEZANO

(*Blushing*). No, I did not. Come on, Consuelo. (*They go, and meet* ZINIDA, *entering.* CONSUELO *passes on.*)

ZINIDA

Are you going back to work, Bezano?

BEZANO

(*Politely*). Yes. Today is a very bad day. How are your lions, Zinida? I think the weather affects them.

CONSUELO

(*From the ring*). Alfred!

ZINIDA

Yes. Someone is calling you. You'd better go. (ALFRED *goes out. To* BRIQUET.) Are you finished?

BRIQUET

Right away.

JACKSON

Then good-bye till evening. Think about your costume, HE, and I shall look for some idea, too. Be here at ten tomorrow. Don't be late, or you'll get another slap. And I'll work with you.

HE

I shall not be late. (*He looks after* JACKSON *who goes out.*) Must be a nice man. All the people about you are so nice, Papa Briquet. I suppose that good-looking bareback rider is in love with Consuelo, isn't he? (*Laughs.*)

ZINIDA

It's none of your business. For a newcomer you go poking your nose too far. How much does he want, Papa?

BRIQUET

Just a minute. See here, HE. I don't want to make a contract with you.

HE

Just as you please. Do you know what? Don't let us talk about money. You are an honest fellow, Briquet; you will see what my work is worth to you, and then——

BRIQUET

(*Pleased*). Now that's very nice of you. Zinida, the man really doesn't know anything.

ZINIDA

Well, do as he suggests. Now we must write it down. Where's the book?

BRIQUET

Here. (*To* HE.) I don't like to write (*gives book to* ZINIDA), but we have to put down the names of the actors, you know—it's police regulations. Then if any one kills himself, or——

(*Again comes the sound of the Tango, and calls from the ring.*)

ZINIDA

What is your name?

HE

(*Smiling*). HE. I chose it, you know. Or don't you like it?

BRIQUET

We like it all right—but we have to have your real name. Have you a passport?

HE

(*Confused*). A passport? No, I have none. Or, rather, yes. I have something of the kind, but I had no idea the rules were strictly enforced here. What do you need papers for?

(ZINIDA *and* BRIQUET *look at each other.* ZINIDA *pushes the book aside.*)

ZINIDA

Then we can't take you. We cannot quarrel with the police, just on your account.

BRIQUET

She is my wife. I hadn't told you. She's right. You might get hurt by a horse, or hurt yourself—or do something. We don't know you, you see. I personally don't care, but out there, it's different, you see. For me a corpse is just a corpse—and I don't ask anything about him. It's up to God or the Devil. But they—they're too curious. Well, I suppose it's necessary for order. I don't know—— Got a card?

HE

(*Rubs his head, thinking*). What shall I do? I have my card, but (*smiles*) you understand that I don't want my name to be known.

BRIQUET

Some story, hey?

HE

Yes, something like that. Why can't you imagine that I have no name? Can't I lose it as I might lose my hat? Or let someone else take it by mistake? When a stray dog comes to you, you don't ask his name—you simply give him another. Let me be that dog. (*Laughing.*) HE—the Dog!

ZINIDA

Why don't you tell us your name, just the two of us. Nobody else need know it. Unless you should break your neck——

HE

(*Hesitates*). Honestly? (ZINIDA *shrugs her shoulders.*)

BRIQUET

Where people are honest, their word is good. One sees you come from *out there.*

HE

All right. But please, don't be surprised. (*Gives* ZINIDA *his card. She looks at it, then hands it to* BRIQUET, *then both look at* HE.)

BRIQUET

If it is true, sir, that you are really what is written here——

HE

For heaven's sake—for heaven's sake—this does not exist, but was lost long ago; it is just a check for an old hat. I pray you to forget it, as I have. I am HE Who Gets Slapped—nothing else. (*Silence.*)

BRIQUET

I beg your pardon, sir, but I must ask you again, I must humbly ask you—are you not drunk, sir? There is something in your eye—something——

HE

No, no. I am HE Who Gets Slapped. Since when do you speak to me like this, Papa Briquet? You offend me.

ZINIDA

After all, it's his business, Briquet. (*She hides the card.*) Truly you are a strange man. (*Smiles.*) And you have already noticed that Bezano is in love with the horse-girl? And that I love my Briquet, did you notice that, too?

HE

(*Also smiling*). Oh, yes. You adore him.

ZINIDA

I adore him. Now go with him, Briquet, show him the ring and the stables—I have something to write.

HE

Yes, yes, please. I am so happy. At last you have taken me, haven't you? It is true—you're not joking. The circus, the tan-bark, the ring in which I shall run getting my slaps. Yes, yes, Briquet, let's go. Until I feel the sawdust under my feet, I shall not believe it.

BRIQUET

All right then. (*Kisses* ZINIDA.) Come on.

ZINIDA

Just a minute—HE! Answer me a question. I have a man who takes care of the cages, a plain fellow whom nobody knows. He just cleans the cages you know; walks in and out whenever he wants to, without even looking at the lions, as if he were perfectly at home. Why is that so? Nobody knows him, everybody knows me, everyone is afraid for me, while—— And he is such a silly man—you will see him. (*Laughs.*) But don't you think of entering the cage yourself! My red one would give you such a slap!

BRIQUET

(*Displeased*). There you are again, Zinida—stop it.

ZINIDA

(*Laughs*). All right—go. Oh yes, Louis, send me Bezano. I have to settle an account with him.

(HE *and the director go out.* ZINIDA *looks at the card once more, then hides it. She gets up and walks quickly up and down the room. She stops to listen to the Tango, which ends abruptly. Then she stands motionless, looking straight at the dark opening of the door through which* BEZANO *comes.*)

BEZANO

(*Entering*). You called me, Zinida? What do you want? Tell me quickly, I have no time——
(ZINIDA *looks at him silently.* BEZANO *flushes with anger, and knits his eyebrows. He turns to the door to go.*)

ZINIDA

Bezano!

BEZANO

(*Stops, without looking up*). What do you want? I have no time.

ZINIDA

Bezano! I keep hearing people say that you are in love with Consuelo. Is it true?

BEZANO

(*Shrugging his shoulders*). We work well together.

ZINIDA

(*Takes a step forward*). No—— Tell me, Alfred, do you love her?

BEZANO

(*Flushes like a boy, but looks straight into* ZINIDA'S *eyes. Proudly*). I do not love anybody. No, I love nobody. How can I? Consuelo? She is here today, gone tomorrow, if her father should take her away. And I? Who am I? An acrobat, the son of a Milanese shoemaker—— She! I cannot even talk about it. Like my horses I have no words. Who am I to love?

ZINIDA

Do you love me? A little?

BEZANO

No. I told you before.

ZINIDA

Still no? Not even a little?

BEZANO

(*After a silence*). I am afraid of you.

ZINIDA

(*Wants to cry out, indignantly, but masters herself and lowers her eyes, as if in an effort to shut out their light; turns pale*). Am I . . . so terrifying a woman——

BEZANO

You are beautiful, like a queen. You are almost as beautiful as Consuelo. But I don't like your eyes. Your eyes command me to love you—and I don't like to be commanded. I am afraid of you.

ZINIDA

Do I command, Bezano? No—only implore.

BEZANO

Then why not look at me straight? Now I have it. You know yourself that your eyes cannot implore. (*Laughs.*) Your lions have spoiled you.

ZINIDA

My red lion loves me——

BEZANO

Never! If he loves you, why is he so sad?

ZINIDA

Yesterday he was licking my hands like a dog.

BEZANO

And this morning he was looking for you to devour you. He thrusts out his muzzle and looks out, as if he sees only you. He is afraid of you, and he hates you. Or do you want me to lick your hands too, like a dog?

ZINIDA

No, Alfred, but I—I want to kiss *your* hand. (*With passion.*) Give it to me!

BEZANO

(*Severely*). I am ashamed to listen to you when you speak like that.

ZINIDA

(*Controlling herself*). One should not torture another as you torture me. Alfred, I love you. No, I do not command. Look into my eyes—— *I love you.* (*Silence.*)

BEZANO

(*Turns to go*). Good-bye.

ZINIDA

Alfred——
(HE *appears in the doorway, and stops.*)

BEZANO

Please never tell me any more that you love me. I don't want it. Otherwise I will quit. You pronounce the word love as if you were cracking me with your whip. You know it is disgusting——
(*He turns brusquely and goes. Both notice* HE; BEZANO, *frowning, passes out quickly.* ZINIDA *returns to her place at the desk, with a proudly indifferent expression.*)

HE

(*Coming in*). I beg your pardon, but I——

ZINIDA

There you are again, poking your nose into everything, HE. Do you really want a slap?

HE

(*Laughing*). No. I simply forgot my overcoat. I didn't hear anything.

ZINIDA

I don't care whether you did or not.

HE

May I take my coat?

ZINIDA

Take it, if it's yours. Sit down, HE.

HE

I am sitting down.

ZINIDA

Now tell me HE, could you love me?

HE

(*Laughing*). I? I and Love! Look at me, Zinida. Did you ever see a lover with such a face?

ZINIDA

One can succeed with such a face——

HE

That's because I am happy—because I lost my hat—because I am drunk—or perhaps I am not drunk. But I feel as dizzy as a young girl at her first ball. It is so nice here—slap me, I want to play my part. Perhaps it will awaken love in my heart, too. Love—(*as if listening to his own heart with pretended terror*) do you know—I feel it!
(*In the circus the Tango is played again.*)

ZINIDA

(*Listening too*). For me?

HE

No. I don't know. For everyone. (*Listens to the music.*) Yes, they are dancing—how beautiful Consuelo is—and how beautiful is the youth. He has the body of a Greek God; he looks as if he had been modeled by Praxiteles. Love! Love! (*Silence, music.*)

ZINIDA

Tell me, HE——

HE

At your service, Queen!

ZINIDA

HE, what shall I do, to make my lions love me?

CURTAIN

ACT TWO

THE SAME ROOM, *during the evening performance. Occasional music, laughter, shrieks, and applause are audible. Through the small windows, back center, the light is shining.*

Consuelo and Baron Regnard occupy the stage; Consuelo wears her stage costume; she sits with her feet on the sofa, a small shawl covering her shoulders. Before her stands the Baron, a tall stout man in evening dress, a rose in his buttonhole; grasping the ground with feet well apart, he gazes at her with convex spider-like eyes.

BARON

Is it true that your father, the Count, has introduced you to a certain Marquis Justi, a very rich man?

CONSUELO

(*Surprised*). No, he is only joking. I have often heard him speak of a Marquis Justi but I have never seen him——

BARON

And do you know that your father is just a charlatan?

CONSUELO

Oh! Don't say that—Father is such a dear.

BARON

Did you like the jewels?

CONSUELO

Yes, very much. I was very sorry when Father told me I must return them. He said it would not be nice for me to keep them. I even cried a little about it.

BARON

Your father is only a beggar and a charlatan.

CONSUELO

Oh, no, don't scold him—he loves you so much.

BARON

Let me kiss your hand——

CONSUELO

Oh, no, it isn't proper! One may kiss the hand only when one says how do you do or good-bye. But in the meantime you can't.

BARON

Everybody is in love with you, that is why you and your father make such a fuss about yourselves. Who is that new clown they call HE? I don't like him, he's too shrewd a beast. . . . Is he in love with you, too? I noticed the way he looked at you. . . .

CONSUELO

(*Laughing*). Nothing of the kind. He is so funny! He got fifty-two slaps yesterday. We counted them. Think of it, fifty-two slaps! Father said, "if they had only been gold pieces."

BARON

And Bezano, Consuelo. . . . Do you like him?

CONSUELO

Yes, very much. He is so good-looking. He says that Bezano and I are the most beautiful couple in the world. HE calls him Adam, and me Eve. But that's improper, isn't it? HE is *so* improper.

BARON

And does HE speak to you very often?

CONSUELO

Yes, often. . . . But I don't understand him. It seems as if he were drunk.

BARON

"Consuelo!" . . . It means in Spanish . . . Consolation. Your father is an ass. . . . Consuelo, I love you.

CONSUELO

Talk it over with Father.

BARON

(*Angry*). Your father is a swindler and a charlatan. He should be turned over to the police. Don't you understand that I *cannot* marry you?

CONSUELO

But Father says you can. . . .

BARON

No, I cannot. And what if I shoot myself? Consuelo, silly girl, I love you unbearably . . . unbearably, do you understand? I am probably mad . . . and must be taken to a doctor, yanked about, beaten with sticks. Why do I love you so much, Consuelo?

CONSUELO

Then, you'd better marry.

BARON

I have had a hundred women, beauties, but I didn't see them. You are the first and I don't see any one else. Who strikes man with love, God or the Devil? The Devil struck me. Let me kiss your hand.

CONSUELO

No. (*She thinks a while and sighs.*)

BARON

Do you think sometimes? What are you thinking about now, Consuelo?

CONSUELO

(*With another sigh*). I don't know why, I just felt sorry for Bezano. (*Sighs again.*) He is so nice to me when he teaches me . . . and he has such a tiny little room.

BARON

(*Indignant*). You were there?

CONSUELO

No. He told me about it. (*Smiling.*) Do you hear the noise in there? That's HE getting slapped. Poor thing . . . although I know it doesn't hurt, it's only make-believe. The intermission is coming soon. (*The* BARON *throws away his cigar, takes two quick steps forward, and falls on his knees before the girl.*)

BARON

Consuelo——

CONSUELO

Please, don't. Get up. Please leave my hand alone.

BARON

Consuelo!

CONSUELO

(*Disgusted*). Get up please, it's disgusting —you're so fat.

(*The* BARON *gets up. Voices are heard near the door and in the ring. It is the intermission. The clowns come first, talking cheerfully and excitedly.* HE *leads them, in his clown's dress, with painted eyebrows and white nose; the others are applauding him. Voices of the actors calling: "Bravo!* HE." *Then come the actors and actresses, riding-masters, and the rest, all in costume.* ZINIDA *is not among them.* PAPA BRIQUET *comes a little later.*)

POLLY

A hundred slaps! Bravo, HE!

JACKSON

Not bad, not bad at all. You'll make a career.

TILLY

He was the Professor today, and we were the students. Here goes another! (*Gives him a clown's slap. Laughter. All bid good evening to the* BARON. *He is politely rude to these vagabonds who bore him, and remains silent. They seem quite used to it. Enter* MANCINI. *He is the same, and with the same cane.*)

MANCINI

(*Shaking hands*). What a success, Baron—and think of it—how the crowd does love slaps. (*Whispering.*) Your knees are dusty, Baron, brush them off. The floor is very dirty in here. (*Aloud.*) Consuelo, dear child, how do you feel? (*Goes over to his daughter. Sound of laughing, chattering. The waiters from the buffet in the lobby bring in soda and wine. Consuelo's voice is heard.*)

CONSUELO

And where is Bezano?

HE

(*Bows before the* BARON, *affecting intimacy*). *You* do not recognize me, Baron?

BARON

Yes, I do. You are the clown, HE.

HE

Yes, I am HE Who Gets Slapped. May I presume to ask you, Baron, did you get your jewels back?

BARON

What!

HE

I was asked to return some jewels to you, and I take the liberty of—— (*The* BARON *turns his back on him*—HE *laughs loudly*.)

JACKSON

Whiskey and soda! Believe me, ladies and gents, HE will surely make a career. I am an old clown, and I know the crowd. Why today, he even eclipsed *me*—and clouds have covered my Sun. (*Striking it.*) They do not like puzzles, they want slaps! They are longing for them and dreaming about them in their homes. Your health, HE! Another whiskey and soda! HE got so many slaps today, there would be enough to go round the whole orchestra!

TILLY

I bet there wouldn't! (*To* JACKSON.) Shake!

POLLY

I bet there wouldn't—I'll go and count the old mugs.

A VOICE

The orchestra did not laugh——

JACKSON

Because they were getting it, but the galleries did, because they were looking at the orchestra getting slapped. Your health, HE!

HE

Yours, Jim! Tell me, why didn't you let me finish my speech—I was just getting a good start.

JACKSON

(*Seriously*). My friend, because your speech was a sacrilege. Politics—all right. Manners—as much as you want. But Providence—leave it in peace. And believe me, friend, I shut your mouth in time. Didn't I, Papa Briquet?

BRIQUET

(*Coming nearer*). Yes. It was too much like literature. This is not an academy. You forget yourself, HE.

TILLY

But to shut one's mouth—faugh. . . .

BRIQUET

(*In a didactic tone*). Whenever one shuts one's mouth, it is always high time to shut it, unless one is drinking. Hey, whiskey and soda!

VOICES

Whiskey and soda for the Manager!

MANCINI

But this is obscurantism. Philosophizing again, Briquet?

BRIQUET

I am not satisfied with you today, HE. Why do you tease them? They don't like it. Your health! A good slap must be clean like a crystal—fft-fft! right side, left side, and done with it. They will like it; they will laugh, and love you. But in your slaps there is a certain bite, you understand, a certain smell——

HE

But they laughed, nevertheless!

BRIQUET

But without pleasure, without pleasure, HE. You pay, and immediately draw a draft on their bank; it's not the right game—they won't like you.

JACKSON

That's what *I* tell him. He had already begun to make them angry.

BEZANO

(*Entering*). Consuelo, where are you? I have been looking for you—come on. (*Both go out. The* BARON, *after hesitating a while, follows them.* MANCINI *accompanies him respectfully to the door.*)

HE

(*Sighs*). You don't understand, my dear friends; you are simply old, and have forgotten the smell of the stage.

JACKSON

Aha! Who is old, my young man?

HE

Don't be angry, Jim. It's a play, don't you understand? I become happy when I enter the ring and hear the music. I wear a mask and I feel humorous. There is a mask on my face, and I play. I may say *anything* like a drunkard. Do you understand? Yesterday when I, with this stupid face, was playing the great man, the philosopher (*he assumes a proud monumental pose, and repeats the gesture of the play—general laughter*) I was walking this way, and was telling how great, how wise, how incomparable I was—how God lived in me, how high I stood above the earth—how glory shone above my head (*his voice changes and he is speaking faster*) then you, Jim, you hit me for the first time. And I asked you, "What is it, they're applauding me?" Then, at the tenth slap, I said: "It seems to me that they sent for me from the Academy?" (*Acts, looking around him with an air of unconquerable pride and splendor. Laughter.* JACKSON *gives him a real slap.*)

HE

(*Holding his face*). Why?

JACKSON

Because you're a fool, and play for nothing. Waiter, the check. (*Laughter. The bell calls them to the ring. The actors go out in haste, some running. The waiters collect their money.*)

BRIQUET

(*In a sing-song*). To the ring—to the ring—

MANCINI

I want to tell you something, HE. You are not going yet?

HE

No. I'll take a rest.

BRIQUET

To the ring—to the ring—
(*The clowns as they go sing in shrill, squeaky voices. Little by little they all disappear, and loud music begins.* HE *seats himself on the sofa with his legs crossed, and yawns.*)

MANCINI

HE, you have something none of my ancestors ever had—money. Let's have a nice bottle on you. Waiter, please—(*The waiter who was taking up dishes, brings a bottle of wine and glasses and goes out.*)

HE

You're blue, Mancini. (*Stretches.*) Well, at my age, a hundred slaps—it seems pretty hard. So you're blue. How are things getting on with your girl?

MANCINI

Tss! Bad! Complications—parents—(*shudders*) Agh—

HE

Prison!

MANCINI

(*Laughing*). Prison! Mustn't I uphold the glory of my name now, eh? HE, I'm joking—but there is Hell in my heart. You're the only one who understands me. But tell me how to explain this passion? It will turn my hair grey, it'll bring me to prison, to the grave. I am a tragic man. HE—(*Wipes his eyes with a dirty handkerchief.*) Why don't I like things which are not forbidden? Why, at all moments, even at the very moment of ecstasy, must I be reminded of some law—it is stupid. HE, I am becoming an anarchist. Good God!—Count Mancini, an anarchist. That's the only thing I've missed.

HE

Isn't there a way of settling it somehow?

MANCINI

Is there a way of getting money, somehow?

HE

And the Baron?

MANCINI

Oh, yes! He's just waiting for it, the bloodsucker! He'll get what he's after. Some day, you'll see me give him Consuelo for ten thousand francs, perhaps for five!

HE

Cheap.

MANCINI

Did I say it was anything else? Do I want to do it? But these bourgeois are strangling me, they've got me by the throat. HE, one can easily see that you're a gentleman, and of good society, you understand me—I showed you the jewels which I sent back to him—damn honesty—I didn't even dare change the stones, put false ones—

HE

Why?

MANCINI

It would have queered the game. Do you think he didn't weigh the diamonds when he got them back?

HE

He will not marry her.

MANCINI

Yes, he will. You don't understand. (*Laughs.*) The first half of his life, this man had only appetites—now love's got him. If he does not get Consuelo, he is lost, he is—like a withered narcissus. Plague take him with his automobiles. Did you see his car?

HE

I did. . . . Give Consuelo to the Jockey—

MANCINI

To Bezano? (*Laughs.*) What nonsense you do talk! Oh, I know. It's your joke about Adam and Eve. But please stop it. It's clever, but it compromises the child. She told me about it.

HE

Or give her to me.

MANCINI

Have you a billion? (*Laughs.*) Ah, HE, I'm not in the proper mood to listen to your clownish jokes—They say there are terrible jails in this country, and no discriminations are being made between people of my kind, and plain scoundrels. Why do you look at me like that? You're making fun of me?

HE

No.

MANCINI

I'll never get accustomed to those faces. You're so disgustingly made up.

HE

He will not marry her. You can be as proud as you please, Mancini, but he'll not marry her. What *is* Consuelo? She is not educated. When she is off her horse, any good housemaid from a decent house has nicer manners, and speaks better. (*Nonchalantly.*) Don't *you* think she's stupid?

MANCINI

No, she's not stupid. And you, HE, are a fool. What need has a woman of intelligence? Why, HE, you astonish me. Consuelo is an unpolished jewel, and only a real donkey does not notice her sparkle. Do you know what happened? I tried to begin to polish her—

HE

Yes, you took a teacher. And what happened?

MANCINI

(*Nodding his head*). I was frightened—it went too fast—I had to dismiss him. Another month or two, and *she* would have kicked *me* out. (*Laughs.*) The clever old diamond merchants of Amsterdam keep their precious stones unpolished, and fool the thieves. My father taught me that.

HE

The sleep of a diamond. It is only sleeping, then. You are wise, Mancini.

MANCINI

Do you know what blood flows in the veins of an Italian woman? The blood of Hannibal and Corsini—of a Borgia—and of a dirty Lombardi peasant—and of a Moor. Oh! an Italian woman is not of a lower race, with only peasants and gypsies behind her. All possibilities, all forms are included in her, as in our marvelous sculpture. Do you understand that, you fool? Strike here —out springs a washerwoman, or a cheap street girl whom you want to throw out, because she is sloppy and has a screechy voice. Strike there—but carefully and gently, for there stands a queen, a goddess, the Venus of the Capitol, who sings like a Stradivarius and makes you cry, idiot! An Italian woman—

HE

You're quite a poet, Mancini! But what will the Baron make of her?

MANCINI

What? What? Make of *her?* A baroness, you fool! What are you laughing at? I don't get you? But I am happy that this lovesick beast is neither a duke nor a prince—or she would be a princess and I —what would become of me? A year after the wedding they would not let me even into the kitchen (*laughing*) not even into the kitchen! I, Count Mancini, and she a—a simple—

HE

(*Jumping up*). What did you say? You are not her father, Mancini?

MANCINI

Tss—the devil—I am so nervous today! Heavens, who do you think I am? "Her father?" Of course (*tries to laugh*) how silly you are—haven't you noticed the family resemblance? Just look, the nose, the eyes— (*Suddenly sighs deeply.*) Ah, HE! How unhappy I am! Think of it. Here I am, a gentleman, nearly beaten in my struggle to keep up the honor of my name, of an old house, while there in the parquet —there sits that beast, an elephant with the eyes of a spider . . . and he looks at Consuelo . . . and . . .

HE

Yes, yes, he has the motionless stare of a spider—you're right!

MANCINI

Just what I say—a spider! But I must, I shall compel him to marry her. You'll see— (*Walking excitedly up and down, playing with his cane.*) You'll see! All my life I've been getting ready for this battle. (*He continues to walk up and down. Silence. Outside, great stillness.*)

HE

(*Listening*). Why is it so quiet out there? What a strange silence!

MANCINI

(*Disgusted*). I don't know. Out there it is quiet—but here (*touching his forehead with his cane*) here is storm, whirlwind. (*Bends over the clown.*) HE, shall I tell you a strange thing—an unusual trick of nature? (*Laughs, and looks very important.*) For three centuries the Counts Mancini have had no children! (*Laughs.*)

HE

Then how were you born?

MANCINI

Sh! Silence! That is the secret of our sainted mothers! Ha-ha! We are too ancient a stock—too exquisitely refined to trouble ourselves with such things—matters in which a peasant is more competent than ourselves. (*Enter an usher.*) What do you want? The manager is on the stage.

THE USHER

Yes, sir. Baron Regnard wished me to give you this letter.

MANCINI

The Baron? Is he there?

THE USHER

Baron Regnard has left. There is no an swer.

MANCINI

(*Opening the envelope, his hand shaking*) The devil—the devil! (*The usher is going.*)

HE

Just a minute. Why is there no music? This silence . . .

THE USHER

It is the act with Madame Zinida and her lions. (*He goes.* MANCINI *is reading the* BARON'S *note for the second time.*)

HE

What's the matter, Mancini? You shine like Jackson's sun.

MANCINI

What's the matter, did you ask? What's the matter? What's the matter? (*Balancing his cane, he takes steps like a ballet-dancer.*)

HE

Mancini! (MANCINI *rolls his eyes, makes faces, dances.*) Speak, you beast!

MANCINI

(*Holds out his hand*). Give me ten francs! Quick—ten francs—here, come on. (*Puts it automatically into his vest pocket.* Listen, HE! If in a month I don't have a car of my own, you may give me one of your slaps!

HE

What! He's going to marry? He's decided?

MANCINI

What do you mean by "decided?" (*Laughs.*) When a man has the rope about his neck, you don't ask him about his health! Baron—(*Stops suddenly, startled.* BRIQUET *is staggering in like a drunken man, his hand over his eyes.*)

HE

(*Goes to him, touches his shoulder gently*). What is the matter, Papa Briquet? Tell me!

BRIQUET

(*Groaning*). Oh, oh, I can't . . . I can't . . . Ah—

HE

Something has happened? You are ill? Please speak.

BRIQUET

I can't look at it! (*Takes his hands from his eyes, opens them wide.*) Why does she do it? Ah, ah, why does she do it? She must be taken away; she is insane. I couldn't look at it. (*Shivers.*) They will tear her to pieces. HE—her lions—they will tear her—

MANCINI

Go on, Briquet. She is always like that. You act like a child. You ought to be ashamed.

BRIQUET

No— Today she is mad! And what is the matter with the crowd? They are all like dead people—they're not even breathing. I couldn't stand it. Listen—what's that? (*All listen. There is the same silence.*)

MANCINI

(*Disturbed*). I'll go and see.

BRIQUET

(*Yelling*). No! Don't! You can't look—damned profession! Don't go. You will scorch her—every pair of eyes that looks at her—at her lions—no, no. It is impossible—it is a sacrilege. I ran away. . . . HE, they will tear her——

HE

(*Tries to be cheerful*). Keep cool, Papa Briquet—I had no idea you were such a coward. You ought to be ashamed. Have a drink. Mancini, give him some wine.

BRIQUET

I don't want any. Heavens, if it were only over— (*All listen.*) I have seen many things in my life, but this . . . Oh, she is crazy. (*All still listen. Suddenly the silence breaks, like a huge stone wall crashing. There is a thunder of applause, mixed with shouts, music, wild screams—half bestial, half human. The men give way, relieved. Briquet sinks to a seat.*)

MANCINI

(*Nervous*). You see—you see—you old fool!

BRIQUET

(*Sobs and laughs*). I am not going to allow it any more!

HE

Here she is!
(ZINIDA *walks in, alone. She looks like a drunken bacchante, or like a mad woman. Her hair falls over her shoulders disheveled, one shoulder is uncovered. She walks unseeing, though her eyes glow. She is like the living statue of a mad Victory. Behind her comes an actor, very pale, then two clowns, and a little later* CONSUELO *and* BEZANO. *All look at* ZINIDA *fearfully, as if they were afraid of a touch of her hand, or her great eyes.*)

BRIQUET

(*Shouting*). You are crazy—you're a mad woman!

ZINIDA

I? No. Did you see? Did you see? Well? (*She stands smiling, with the expression of a mad Victory.*)

TILLY

(*Plaintively*). Cut it out, Zinida. Go to the devil!

ZINIDA

You saw, too! And! . . . what—

BRIQUET

Come home—come home. (*To the others.*) You can do what you like here. Zinida, come home.

POLLY

You can't go, Papa. There's still your number.

ZINIDA

(*Her eyes meet those of* BEZANO). Ah! Bezano. (*Laughs long and happily.*) Bezano! Alfred! Did you see? My lions *do* love me! (BEZANO, *without answering, leaves the stage.* ZINIDA *seems to wither and grow dim, as a light being extinguished. Her smile fades, her eyes and face grow pale.* BRIQUET *anxiously bends over her.*)

BRIQUET

(*In a slow voice*). A chair! (ZINIDA *sits. Her head drops on her shoulder, her arms fall, she begins to shiver and tremble. Some one calls, "Cognac"—an actor runs to get it.*)

BRIQUET

(*Helpless*). What is the matter, Zinida, darling?

MANCINI

(*Running about*). She must quiet down. Get out, get out—vagabonds! I'll fix everything, Papa Briquet. The wrap—where's the wrap? She's cold. (*A clown hands it to him; they cover her.*)

TILLY

(*Timidly*). Wouldn't you like some moosic?

MANCINI

(*Giving her some cognac*). Drink, Duchess, drink! Drink it all—that's it. (ZINIDA *drinks it like water, evidently not noticing the taste. She shivers. The clowns disappear one by one.* CONSUELO, *with a sudden flexible movement, falls on her knees before* ZINIDA *and kisses her hands, warming them between her own.*)

CONSUELO

Dear, dear, you are cold! Poor little hands, dear good one, beloved one——

ZINIDA

(*Pushes her away, gently*). Ho— home. It will soon be over. It's nothing . . . I am ver—very . . . home. . . . You stay here, Briquet—you must. I'm all right.

CONSUELO

You are cold? Here is my shawl.

ZINIDA

No—let me. . . . (CONSUELO *gets up, and moves aside.*)

BRIQUET

And it's all because of your books, Zinida—your mythology. Now tell me, why do you want those beasts to love you? Beasts! Do you understand, HE? You too, you're from that world. She'll listen more to you. Explain it to her. Whom can those beasts love? Those hairy monsters, with diabolic eyes?

HE

(*Genially*). I believe—only their equals. You are right, Papa Briquet—there must be the same race.

BRIQUET

Of course, and this is all nonsense—literature. Explain it to her, HE.

HE

(*Takes on a meditative air*). Yes, you are right, Briquet.

BRIQUET

You see, dear, silly woman—everybody agrees. . . .

MANCINI

Oh! Briquet, you make me sick; you are an absolute despot, an Asiatic.

ZINIDA

(*With the shadow of a smile, gives her hand to be kissed*). Calm yourself, Louis. It is over—I am going home. (*She stands up, shaking, still chilled.*)

BRIQUET

But how? alone, dear?

MANCINI

What! fool! Did you imagine that Count Mancini would leave a woman when she needed help? *I* shall take her home—let your brutal heart be at rest—I shall take her home. Thomas, run for an automobile. Don't push me Briquet, you are as awkward as a unicorn . . . that's the way, that's the way——(*They are holding her, guiding her slowly toward the door.* CONSUELO, *her chin resting in her hand, is following them with her eyes. Unconsciously she assumes a somewhat affected pose.*)

MANCINI

I'll come back for you, child——

(*Only* HE *and* CONSUELO *are left on the stage. In the ring, music, shrieks, and laughter begin again.*)

HE

Consuelo——

CONSUELO

Is that you, HE, dear?

HE

Where did you learn that pose? I have seen it only in marble. You look like Psyche.

CONSUELO

I don't know, HE. (*She sighs and sits on the sofa, keeping in her pose the same artificiality and beauty.*) It's all so sad here, today. HE, are you sorry for Zinida?

HE

What did she do?

CONSUELO

I didn't see. I had closed my eyes, and didn't open them. Alfred says she is a wicked woman, but that isn't true. She has such nice eyes, and what tiny cold hands—as if she were dead. What does she do it for? Alfred says she should be audacious, beautiful, but quiet, otherwise what she does is only disgusting. It isn't true, is it, HE?

HE

She loves Alfred.

CONSUELO

Alfred? My Bezano? (*Shrugging her shoulders, and surprised.*) How does she love him? The same as everyone loves?

HE

Yes—as everyone loves—or still more.

CONSUELO

Bezano? Bezano? No—it's nonsense. (*Pause; silence.*) What a beautiful costume you have, HE. You invented it yourself?

HE

Jim helped me.

CONSUELO

Jim is so nice! All clowns are nice.

HE

I am wicked.

CONSUELO

(*Laughs*). You? You are the nicest of all. Oh, goodness! Three acts more! This is the second on now. Alfred and I are in the third. Are you coming to see me?

HE

I always do. How beautiful you are, Consuelo!

CONSUELO

Like Eve? (*Smiles.*)

HE

Yes, Consuelo. And if the Baron asks you to be his wife, will you accept?

CONSUELO

Certainly, HE. That's all Father and I are waiting for. Father told me yesterday that the Baron will not hesitate very long. Of course I do not love him. But I will be his honest, faithful wife. Father wants to teach me to play the piano.

HE

Are those your own words—"his honest, faithful wife?"

CONSUELO

Certainly they are mine. Whose could they be? He loves me so much, the poor thing. Dear HE, what does "love" mean? Everybody speaks of love—love—Zinida, too! Poor Zinida! What a boring evening this has been! HE, did you paint the laughter on your face yourself?

HE

My own self, dear little Consuelo——

CONSUELO

How do you do it, all of you? I tried once, but couldn't do a thing. Why are there no women clowns? Why are you so silent, HE? You, too, are sad, tonight.

HE

No, I am happy tonight. Give me your hand, Consuelo, I want to see what it says.

CONSUELO

Do you know how? What a talented man you are! Read it, but don't *lie*, like a gypsy.

(*He goes down on one knee and takes her hand. Both bend over it.*) Am I lucky?

HE

Yes, lucky. But wait a minute—this line here—funny. Ah, Consuelo, what does it say, here! (*Acting.*) I tremble, my eyes do not dare to read the strange, fatal signs. Consuelo—

CONSUELO

The stars are talking.

HE

Yes, the stars are talking. Their voices are distant and terrible; their rays are pale, and their shadows slip by, like the ghosts of dead virgins—their spell is upon thee, Consuelo, beautiful Consuelo. Thou standest at the door of Eternity.

CONSUELO

I don't understand. Does it mean that I will live long?

HE

This line—how far it goes. Strange! Thou wilt live eternally, Consuelo.

CONSUELO

You see, HE, you did tell me a lie, just like a gypsy!

HE

But it is written—here, silly—and here. Now think of what the stars are saying. Here you have eternal life, love, and glory; and here, listen to what Jupiter says. He says: "Goddess, thou must not belong to any one born on earth," and if you marry the Baron—you'll perish, you'll die, Consuelo. (CONSUELO *laughs.*)

CONSUELO

Will he eat me?

HE

No. But you will die before he has time to eat you.

CONSUELO

And what will become of Father? Is there nothing about him here? (*Laughing, she softly sings the melody of the waltz, which is playing in the distance.*)

HE

Don't laugh, Consuelo, at the voice of the stars. They are far away, their rays are light and pale, and we can barely see their sleeping shadows, but their sorcery is stern and dark. You stand at the gates of eternity. Your die is cast; you are *doomed*—and your Alfred, whom you love in your heart, even though your mind is not aware of it, your Alfred cannot save you. He, too, is a stranger on this earth. He is submerged in a deep sleep. He, too, is a little god who has lost himself, and Consuelo, never, never will he find his way to Heaven again. Forget Bezano——

CONSUELO

I don't understand a word. Do the gods really exist? My teacher told me about them. But I thought it was all tales! (*Laughs.*) And my Bezano is a god?

HE

Forget Bezano! Consuelo, do you know who can save you? The only one who can save you? I.

CONSUELO

(*Laughing*). You, HE?

HE

Yes, but don't laugh! Look. Here is the letter H. It is I, HE.

CONSUELO

HE Who Gets Slapped? Is that written here, too?

HE

That, too. The stars know everything. But look here, what more is written about him. Consuelo, welcome him. HE is an old god in disguise, who came down to earth only to love you, foolish little Consuelo.

CONSUELO

(*Laughing and singing*). Some god!

HE

Don't mock! The gods don't like such empty laughter from beautiful lips. The gods grow lonely and die, when they are not recognized. Oh, Consuelo! Oh, great joy and love! Do recognize this god, and accept him. Think a moment, one day a god suddenly went crazy!

CONSUELO

Gods go crazy, too?

HE

Yes, when they are half man, then they often go mad. Suddenly he saw his own sublimity, and shuddered with horror, with infinite solitude, with superhuman anguish. It is terrible, when anguish touches the divine soul!

CONSUELO

I don't like it. What language are you speaking? I don't understand——

HE

I speak the language of thy awakening. Consuelo, recognize and accept thy god, who was thrown down from the summit like a stone. Accept the god who fell to the earth in order to live, to play, and to be infinitely drunk with joy. Evoë Goddess!

CONSUELO

(*Tortured*). HE— I cannot understand. Let my hand alone.

HE

(*Stands up*). Sleep. Then wake again, Consuelo! And when thou wakest—remember that hour when, covered with snow-white sea-foam, thou didst emerge from the sky-blue waters. Remember heaven, and the slow eastern wind, and the whisper of the foam at thy marble feet.

CONSUELO

(*Her eyes are closed*). I believe—wait—I remember. Remind me further——

(HE *is bowed over* CONSUELO, *with lifted arms; he speaks slowly, but in a commanding voice, as if conjuring.*)

HE

You see the waves playing. Remember the song of the sirens, their sorrowless song of joy. Their white bodies, shining blue through the blue waters. Or can you hear the sun, singing? Like the strings of a divine harp, spread the golden rays— Do you not see the hand of God, which gives harmony, light, and love to the world? Do not the mountains, in the blue cloud of incense, sing their hymn of glory? Remember, O Consuelo, remember the prayer of the mountains, the prayer of the sea. (*Silence.*)

HE

(*Commandingly*). Remember—Consuelo!

CONSUELO

(*Opening her eyes*). No! HE, I was feeling so happy, and suddenly I forgot it all. Yet something of it all is still in my heart. Help me again, HE, remind me. It hurts, I hear so many voices. They all sing "Consuelo—Consuelo." What comes after? (*Silence; pause.*) What comes after? It hurts. Remind me, HE. (*Silence—in the ring, the music suddenly bursts forth in a tempestuous circus gallop. Silence.*) HE, (*opens her eyes and smiles*) that's Alfred galloping. Do you recognize his music?

HE

(*With rage*). Leave the boy alone! (*Suddenly falls on his knees before* CONSUELO.) I love you, Consuelo, revelation of my heart, light of my nights, I love you, Consuelo. (*Looks at her in ecstasy and tears—and gets a slap; starting back.*) What's this?

CONSUELO

A slap! You forget who you are. (*Stands up, with anger in her eyes.*) You are HE Who Gets Slapped! Did you forget it? Some god! With such a face—slapped face! Was it with slaps they threw you down from heaven, god?

HE

Wait! Don't stand up! I—did not finish the play!

CONSUELO

(*Sits*). Then you were playing?

HE

Wait! One minute.

CONSUELO

You lied to me. Why did you play so that I believed you?

HE

I am HE Who Gets Slapped!

CONSUELO

You are not angry because I struck you? I did not want to really, but you were so—disgusting. And now you are so funny again. You have great talent, HE—or are you drunk?

HE

Strike me again.

CONSUELO

No.

HE

I need it for my play. Strike!

CONSUELO

(*Laughs, and touches his cheek with her fingertips*). Here, then!

HE

Didn't you understand that you are a queen, and I a fool who is in love with his queen? Don't you know, Consuelo, that every queen has a fool, and he is always in love with her, and they always beat him for it. HE Who Gets Slapped.

CONSUELO

No. I didn't know.

HE

Yes, every queen. Beauty has her fool. Wisdom, too. Oh, how many fools she has! Her court is overcrowded with enamored fools, and the sound of slaps does not cease, even through the night. But I never received such a sweet slap as the one given by my little queen. (*Someone appears at the door.* HE *notices it, and continues to play, making many faces.*) Clown HE can have no rival! Who is there who could stand such a deluge of slaps, such a hailstorm of slaps, and not get soaked? (*Feigns to cry aloud.*) "Have pity on me. I am but a poor fool!"

(*Enter two men: an actor, dressed as a bareback rider, and a gentleman from the audience. He is spare, dressed in black, very respectable. He carries his hat in his hand.*)

CONSUELO

(*Laughing, embarrassed*). HE, there is someone here. Stop!

HE

(*Gets up*). Who is it? Who dares to intrude in the castle of my queen?
(HE *stops, suddenly.* CONSUELO, *laughing, jumps up and runs away, after a quick glance at the* GENTLEMAN.)

CONSUELO

You cheered me up, HE. Good-bye. (*At the door.*) You shall get a note tomorrow.

THE BAREBACK RIDER

(*Laughing*). A jolly fellow, sir. You wanted to see him? There he is. HE, the gentleman wants to see you.

HE

(*In a depressed voice*). What can I do for you? (*The actor bows, and goes away, smiling. Both men take a step toward each other.*)

GENTLEMAN

Is this you?

HE

Yes! It is I. And you? (*Silence.*)

GENTLEMAN

Must I believe my eyes? Is this *you*, Mr.—

HE

(*In a rage*). My name here is HE. I have no other name, do you hear? HE Who Gets Slapped. And if you want to stay here, don't forget it.

GENTLEMAN

You are so familiar. As far as I can remember——

HE

We are all familiar, here. (*Contemptuously.*) Besides, that's all you deserve, anywhere.

GENTLEMAN

(*Humbly*). You have not forgiven me, HE? (*Silence.*)

HE

Are you here with my wife? Is she, too, in the circus?

GENTLEMAN

(*Quickly*). Oh, no! I am alone. She stayed there!

HE

You've left her already?

GENTLEMAN

(*Humbly*). No—we have—a son. After your sudden and mysterious disappearance —when you left that strange and insulting letter——

HE

(*Laughs*). Insulting? You are still able to feel insults? What are you doing here? Were you looking for me, or is it an accident?

GENTLEMAN

I have been looking for you, for half a year—through many countries. And suddenly, today—by accident, indeed—I had no acquaintances here, and I went to the circus. We must talk things over . . . HE, I implore you. (*Silence.*)

HE

Here is a shadow I cannot lose! To talk things over! Do you really think we still have something to talk over? All right. Leave your address with the porter, and I will let you know when you can see me. Now get out. (*Proudly.*) I am busy.
(*The* GENTLEMAN *bows, and leaves.* HE *does not return his bow, but stands with outstretched hand, in the pose of a great man, who shows a boring visitor the door.*)

CURTAIN

ACT THREE

THE SAME ROOM. *Morning, before the rehearsal.* HE *is striding thoughtfully up and down the room. He wears a broad, parti-colored coat, and a prismatic tie. His derby is on the back of his head, and his face is clean-shaven like that of an actor. His eyebrows are drawn, lips pressed together energetically, his whole appearance severe and somber. After the entrance of the* GENTLEMAN *he changes. His face becomes clown-like, mobile—a living mask.*

The GENTLEMAN *comes in. He is dressed in black, and has an extremely well-bred appearance. His thin face is yellowish, like an invalid's. When he is upset, his colorless, dull eyes often twitch.* HE *does not notice him.*

GENTLEMAN

Good morning, sir.

HE

(*Turning around and looking at him absent-mindedly*). Ah! It's you.

GENTLEMAN

I am not late? You look as if you did not expect me. I hope I am not disturbing you? You fixed this time yourself however, and I took the liberty——

HE

No manners, please. What do you want? Tell me quickly, I have no time.

GENTLEMAN

(*Looking around with distaste*). I expected you would invite me to some other place . . . to your home.

HE

I have no other home. This is my home.

GENTLEMAN

But people may disturb us here.

HE

So much the worse for you. Talk faster! (*Silence.*)

GENTLEMAN

Will you allow me to sit down?

HE

Sit down. Look out! That chair is broken. (*The* GENTLEMAN, *afraid, pushes away the chair and looks helplessly around. Everything here seems to him dangerous and strange. He chooses an apparently solid little gilded divan, and sits down; puts his silk hat aside, slowly takes off his gloves, which stick to his fingers.* HE *observes him indifferently.*)

GENTLEMAN

In this suit, and with this face, you make a still stranger impression. Yesterday it seemed to me that it was all a dream; today . . . *you* . . .

HE

You have forgotten my name again? My name is HE.

GENTLEMAN

You are determined to continue talking to me like this?

HE

Decidedly! But you are squandering your time like a millionaire. Hurry up!

GENTLEMAN

I really don't know . . . Everything here strikes me so . . . These posters, horses, animals, which I passed when I was looking for you . . . And finally, *you*, a clown in a circus! (*With a slight, deprecating smile.*) Could I expect it? It is true, when everybody there decided that you were dead, I was the only man who did not agree with them. I felt that you were still alive. But to find you among such surroundings—I can't understand it.

HE

You said you have a son, now. Doesn't he look like me?

GENTLEMAN

I don't understand?

HE

Don't you know that widows or divorced women often have children by the new husband, which resemble the old one? This misfortune did not befall you? (*Laughs.*) And your book, too, is a big success, I hear.

GENTLEMAN

You want to insult me again?

HE

(*Laughing*). What a restless, touchy faker you are! Please sit still; be quiet. It is the custom here to speak this way. Why were you trying to find me?

GENTLEMAN

My conscience . . .

HE

You have no conscience. Or were you afraid that you hadn't robbed me of *everything* I possessed, and you came for the rest? But what more could you take from me now? My fool's cap with its bells? You wouldn't take it. It's too big for your bald head! Crawl back, you book-worm!

GENTLEMAN

You cannot forgive the fact your wife. . .

HE

To the devil with my wife! (*The* GENTLEMAN *is startled and raises his eyebrows.* HE *laughs.*)

GENTLEMAN

I don't know. . . . But such language! I confess I find difficulty in expressing my thoughts in such an atmosphere, but if you are so . . . indifferent to your wife, who, I shall allow myself to emphasize the fact, loved you and thought you were a saint—(HE *laughs.*) Then *what* brought you to such a . . . step? Or is it that you cannot forgive me my success? A success, it is true, not entirely deserved. And now you want to take vengeance, with your humbleness, on those who misunderstood you. But you always were so indifferent to glory. Or your indifference was only hypocrisy. And when I, a more lucky rival . . .

HE

(*With a burst of laughter*). Rival! You—a rival!

GENTLEMAN

(*Growing pale*). But my book!

HE

You are talking to me about *your* book? To me? (*The* GENTLEMAN *is very pale.* HE *looks at him with curiosity and mockery.*)

GENTLEMAN

(*Raising his eyes*). I am a very unhappy man.

HE

Why?

GENTLEMAN

I am a very unhappy man. You must forgive me. I am deeply, irreparably, and infinitely unhappy.

HE

But why? Explain it to me. (*Starts walking up and down.*) You say yourself that your book is a tremendous success, you are famous, you have glory; there is not a yellow newspaper in which *you* and *your* thoughts are not mentioned. Who knows *me?* Who cares about my heavy abstractions, from which it was difficult for them to derive a single thought? You—you are the great vulgarizer! You have made my thoughts comprehensible even to horses! With the art of a great vulgarizer, a tailor of ideas, you dressed my Apollo in a barber's jacket, you handed my Venus a yellow ticket, and to my bright hero you gave the ears of an ass. And then your career is made, as Jackson says. And wherever I go, the whole street looks at me with thousands of faces, in which—what mockery—I recognize the traits of my own children. Oh! How ugly your son must be, if he resembles me! Why then are you unhappy, you poor devil? (*The* GENTLEMAN *bows his head, plucking at his gloves.*) The police haven't caught you, as yet. What am I talking about? Is it possible to catch you? You always keep within the limits of the law. You have been torturing yourself up to now because you are not married to my wife. A notary public is always present at your thefts. What is the use of this self-torture, my friend? Get married. I died. You are not satisfied with having taken only my wife? Let my glory remain in your possession. It is yours. Accept my ideas. Assume all the rights, my most lawful heir! I died! And when I was dying (*making a stupidly pious face*) I forgave thee! (*Bursts out laughing. The* GENTLEMAN *raises his head, and bending forward, looks straight into* HE'*s eyes.*)

GENTLEMAN

And my pride?

HE

Have you any pride? (*The* GENTLEMAN *straightens up, and nods his head silently.*) Yes! But please stand off a little. I don't like to look at you. Think of it. There was a time when I loved you a little, even thought you a little gifted! You—my empty shadow.

GENTLEMAN

(*Nodding his head*). I am your shadow. (HE *keeps on walking, and looks over his shoulder at the* GENTLEMAN, *with a smile.*)

HE

Oh, you are marvellous! What a comedy! What a touching comedy! Listen. Tell me frankly if you can; do you hate me very much?

GENTLEMAN

Yes! With all the hate there is in the world! Sit down here.

HE

You order me?

GENTLEMAN

Sit down here. Thank you. (*Bows.*) I am respected and I am famous, yes? I have a wife and a son, yes. (*Laughs slowly.*) My wife still loves you: our favorite discussion is about your genius. She supposes you are a genius. We, I and she, love you even when we are in bed. Tss! It is I who must make faces. My son—yes, he'll resemble you. And when, in order to have a little rest, I go to my desk, to my ink-pot, my books—there, too, I find you. Always you! Everywhere you! And I am never alone—never myself and alone. And when at night—you, sir, should understand this—when at night I go to my lonely thoughts, to my sleepless contemplations, even then I find your image in my head, in my unfortunate brain, your damned and hateful image! (*Silence. The* GENTLEMAN'*s eyes twitch.*)

HE

(*Speaking slowly*). What a comedy! How marvelously everything is turned about in this world: the robbed proves to be a robber, and the robber is complaining of theft, and cursing! (*Laughs.*) Listen, I was mistaken. You are not my shadow. You are the crowd. If you live by my creations, you hate me; if you breathe my breath, you are choking with anger. And choking with anger, hating me, you still walk slowly on the trail of my ideas. But you are advancing backward, advancing backward, comrade. Oh, what a marvelous comedy! (*Walking and smiling.*) Tell me, would you be relieved if I really had died?

GENTLEMAN

Yes! I think so. Death augments distance and dulls the memory. Death reconciles. But you do not look like a man who——

HE

Yes, yes! Death, *certainly!*

GENTLEMAN

Sit down here.

HE

Your obedient servant. Yes?

GENTLEMAN

Certainly, I do not dare to ask you—(*makes a grimace*) to ask you to die, but tell me: you'll never come back there? No, don't laugh. If you want me to, I'll kiss your hand. Don't grimace! I would have done so if you had died.

HE

(*Slowly*). Get out, vermin!

(*Enter* TILLY *and* POLLY *as in the first act, playing. For a long time they do not see the two men.*)

HE

Jack!

TILLY

Ah! Good morning, HE. We are rehearsing. You know it is very hard. Jack has just about as much music in his head as my pig.

HE

(*Introducing, nonchalantly*). My friend . . . For the benefit performance? (*The clowns bow to the* GENTLEMAN, *making idiotic faces.*)

POLLY

Yes. What are you preparing? You are cunning, HE! Consuelo told me what you are preparing for the benefit performance. She leaves us soon, you know?

HE

Is that so?

TILLY

Zinida told us. Do you think she would get a benefit performance otherwise? She is a nice girl.

POLLY

(*Taking his small flute-pipe*). Here! Don't walk as if you were an elephant. Don't forget you are an ant! Come on! (*They go off, playing.*)

GENTLEMAN

(*Smiling*). These are your new comrades? How strange they are!

HE

Everything here is strange.

GENTLEMAN

This suit of yours. Black used to be very becoming to you. This one hurts the eyes.

HE

(*Looking himself over*). Why? It looks very nice. The rehearsal has begun. You must go away. You are disturbing us.

GENTLEMAN

You did not answer my question.

(*Slow strains of the Tango from a small orchestra in the ring.*)

HE

(*Listening absent-mindedly to the music*). What question?

GENTLEMAN

(*Who does not hear the music*). I pray you to tell me: will you ever come back?

HE

(*Listening to the music*). Never, never, never!

GENTLEMAN

(*Getting up*). Thank you. I am going.

HE

Never, never, never! Yes, run along. And don't come back. There you were still bearable and useful for something, but here you are superfluous.

GENTLEMAN

But if something should happen to you . . . you are a healthy man, but in this environment, these people . . . how will I know? They don't know your name here?

HE

My name here is unknown, but *you will know*. Anything else?

GENTLEMAN

I can be at peace? On your word of honor? Of course I mean, comparatively, at peace?

HE

Yes, you may be comparatively at peace. Never! (*They walk to the door, the* GENTLEMAN *stops.*)

GENTLEMAN

May I come to the circus? You will allow me?

HE

Certainly. You are the audience! (*Laughs.*) But I shan't give you my card for a pass. But why do you want to come? Or do you like the circus so much, and since when?

GENTLEMAN

I want to look at you some more, and to understand, perhaps. Such a transformation! Knowing you as I do, I cannot admit that you are here without any *idea*. But what idea? (*Looks short-sightedly at* HE. HE *grimaces and thumbs his nose.*)

GENTLEMAN

What is that?

HE

My idea! Good-bye, Prince! My regards to your respected wife, your Highness' wonderful son!

(*Enter* MANCINI.)

MANCINI

You positively live in the circus, HE. Whenever I come, you are here. You are a fanatic in your work, sir.

HE

(*Introducing*). Prince Poniatovsky, Count Mancini.

MANCINI

(*Drawing himself up*). Very, very glad. And you too, Prince, you know my queer fellow? What a nice face he has, hasn't he? (*He touches* HE's *shoulder patronizingly, with the tip of his cane.*)

GENTLEMAN

(*Awkwardly*). Yes, I have the pleasure . . . certainly. Good-bye, Count.

MANCINI

Good-day, Prince.

HE

(*Accompanying him*). Look out, your Highness, for the dark passages: the steps are so rotten. Unfortunately I cannot usher you out to the street.

GENTLEMAN

(*In a low voice*). You will not give me your hand when we say good-bye? We are parting for ever.

HE

Unnecessary, Prince. I shall still hope to meet you in the Kingdom of Heaven. I trust you will be there, too?

GENTLEMAN

(*With disgust*). How you did succeed! You have so much of the clown in you!

HE

I am HE Who is Getting Slapped. Good-bye, Prince. (*They take another step.*)

GENTLEMAN

(*Looking* HE *in the eyes; in a very low voice*). Tell me, you are not mad?

HE

(*Just as low, his eyes wide open*). I am afraid, I am afraid you are right, Prince. (*Still low*) Ass! Never in your life did you use such a precise expression. I am mad! (*Playing the clown again, he shows him to the stair with a big, affected gesture, a sweep of the hand and arm from his head to the floor, the fingers moving, to represent the steps.*)

HE

(*Laughing*). He is down! *Au revoir*, Prince. (*The* GENTLEMAN *goes out.* HE *comes skipping back, and takes a pose.*) Mancini! Let us dance the Tango! Mancini, I adore you!

MANCINI

(*Sitting back comfortably and playing with his cane*). Don't forget yourself, HE. But you're hiding something, my boy. I always said you used to belong to society. It is so easy to talk to you. And who is this Prince? A genuine one?

HE

Genuine. A first-rater. Like you!

MANCINI

A sympathetic face. Although at first I thought he was an undertaker who came for an order. Ah, HE! When shall I finally depart from these dirty walls, from Papa Briquet, stupid posters, and brutal jockeys!

HE

Very soon, Mancini.

MANCINI

Yes. soon. I am simply exhausted in these surroundings, HE! I begin to feel myself a horse. You are from society, still you don't yet know what high society means. To be at least decently dressed, to attend receptions, to display the splendor of wit; from time to time to have a game of baccarat (*laughing*) without tricks or cheating——

HE

And when evening comes, go to a suburb, where you are considered an honest father, who loves his children and——

MANCINI

And get hold of something, eh? (*Laughs.*) I shall wear a silk mask and two butlers shall follow me, thus protecting me from the dirty crowd. Ah, HE! The blood of my ancestors boils in me. Look at this stiletto. What do you think? Do you think that it was ever stained with blood?

HE

You frighten me, Count!

MANCINI

(*Laughing, and putting the stiletto back into its sheath*). Fool!

HE

And what about the girl?

MANCINI

Tss! I give those bourgeois absolute satisfaction, and they glorify my name. (*Laughs.*) The splendor of my name is beginning to shine with a force unknown. By the way, do you know what automobile firms are the best? Money is no object. (*Laughs.*) Ah! Papa Briquet!
(*Enter* BRIQUET *in his overcoat and silk hat. They shake hands.*)

BRIQUET

So, Mancini, you have obtained a benefit performance for your daughter, Consuelo! I only want to tell you, that if it were not for Zinida . . .

MANCINI

Listen, Briquet. Decidedly you are a donkey. What are you complaining of? The Baron has bought all the parquet seats for Consuelo's benefit performance. Isn't that enough for you, you miser?

BRIQUET

I love your daughter, Mancini, and I am sorry to let her go. What more does she need here? She has an honest job, wonderful comrades, and the atmosphere—?

MANCINI

Not *she*, but *I* need something. You understand? (*Laughs.*) I asked you to increase her salary, Harpagon! and now, Mr. Manager, wouldn't you like to change me a thousand franc note?

BRIQUET

(*With a sigh*). Give it to me.

MANCINI

(*Nonchalantly*). To-morrow. I left it at home. (*All three laugh.*) Laugh, laugh! To-day we are going with the Baron to his villa in the country; people say a very nice villa.

HE

What for?

MANCINI

You know, HE, the crazes of these billionaires. He wants to show Consuelo some winter roses, and me his wine cellars. He will come for us here. What is the matter, my little Consuelo?
(*Enter* CONSUELO, *almost crying.*)

CONSUELO

I can't, Father! Tell him! What right has he to yell at me? He almost hit me with his whip!

MANCINI

(*Straightening up*). Briquet! I beg of you, as the Manager, what is this—a stable? To hit my daughter with a whip! I'll show this cub . . . a mere jockey. . . . No, the devil knows what it is, devil knows, I swear. . . .

CONSUELO

Father . . .

BRIQUET

I will tell him.

CONSUELO

Please don't. Alfred didn't hit me. It's a silly thing, what I told you. What an idea! He is so sorry himself. . . .

BRIQUET

I shall tell him anyhow that——

CONSUELO

Don't you dare. You mustn't tell him anything. He didn't do a thing.

MANCINI

(*Still excited*). He must beg her pardon, the brat.

CONSUELO

He's already asked me to forgive him. How silly you all are! I simply cannot work to-day and I got nervous. What nonsense! The silly boy asked me to forgive him, but I didn't want to. HE, dear, good morning! I didn't notice you. How becoming your tie is! Where are you going, Briquet? To Alfred?

BRIQUET

No, I am going home, dear child. Zinida asked me to give you her love. She will not be here to-day, either. (*He goes out.*)

CONSUELO

Zinida is so nice, so good. Father, why is it that everybody seems so nice to me? Probably because I am going away soon. HE, did you hear the march that Tilly and Polly will play? (*Laughs.*) Such a cheerful one.

HE

Yes. I heard it. Your benefit performance will be remarkable.

CONSUELO

I think so, too. Father, I am hungry. Have them bring me a sandwich.

HE

I'll run for it, my Queen.

CONSUELO

Please do, HE. (*Loudly.*) But not cheese. I don't like it.

(MANCINI *and* CONSUELO *are alone.* MANCINI, *lying back comfortably in an armchair, scrutinizes his daughter with a searching eye.*)

MANCINI

I find something particular in you to-day, my child. I don't know whether it is something better or worse. You cried?

CONSUELO

Yes, a little. Oh, I am so hungry.

MANCINI

But you had your breakfast?

CONSUELO

No, I didn't. That's why I am so hungry. You again forgot to leave me some money this morning, and without money . . .

MANCINI

Oh, the devil . . . what a memory I have. (*Laughs.*) But we shall have a very nice meal to-day. Don't eat very many sandwiches. . . . Yes, positively I like you. You must cry more often, my child; it washes off your superfluous simplicity. You become more of a woman.

CONSUELO

Am I so simple, Father?

MANCINI

Very. . . . Too much. I like it in others, but not in you. Besides, the Baron . . .

CONSUELO

Nonsense. I am not simple. But you know, Bezano scolded me so much, that even you would have cried. The devil knows . . .

MANCINI

Tsss. . . . Never say "the devil knows." It isn't decent.

CONSUELO

I say it only when I am with you.

MANCINI

You must not say it when you are with me, either. I know it without you. (*Laughs.*)

CONSUELO

Ha! Listen, Father! It's a new number of Alfred's. He makes such a jump! Jim says he's bound to break his neck. Poor fish. . . .

MANCINI

(*Indifferently*). Or his leg, or his back; they all have to break something. (*Laughs.*) They are breakable toys.

CONSUELO

(*Listening to the music*). I'll be lonesome without them, Father! The Baron promised to make a ring for me to gallop over as much as I want. He's not lying?

MANCINI

A ring? (*Laughs.*) No, it's not a lie. By the way, child, when speaking of Barons, you must say, "he does not tell the truth," and not, "he lies."

CONSUELO

It's just the same. It's nice to be wealthy, Father; you can do what you want, then.

MANCINI

(*With enthusiasm*). Everything you want. Everything, my child. Ah! Our fate is being decided to-day. Pray our clement God, Consuelo. The Baron is hanging on a thread.

CONSUELO

(*Indifferently*). Yes?

MANCINI

(*Making the gesture with his fingers*). On a very thin, silk thread. I am almost sure that he will make his proposal to-day. (*Laughs.*) Winter roses, and the web of a spider amongst the roses, in order that my dear little fly . . . He is such a spider.

CONSUELO

(*Indifferently*). Yes, a terrible spider. Father, oughtn't I to let him kiss my hand yet?

MANCINI

By no means. You don't know yet, darling, what these men are.

CONSUELO

Alfred never kisses.

MANCINI

Alfred! Your Alfred is a cub, and he mustn't dare. But with men of that sort, you must be extremely careful, my child. To-day he would kiss your little finger, to-morrow your hand, and after to-morrow you would be on his lap.

CONSUELO

Foui! Father, what are you talking about? You should be ashamed!

MANCINI

But I know. . . .

CONSUELO

Don't you dare! I don't want to hear such dirty things. I shall give the Baron such a slap! A better one than HE—let him only try.

MANCINI

(*With a deprecating gesture*). All men are like that, child.

CONSUELO

It isn't true. Alfred is not. Ah! But where is HE? He said he'd run, and he hasn't come back.

MANCINI

The buffet here is closed, and he has to get the sandwiches somewhere else. Consuelo, as your father, I want to warn you about HE. Don't trust him. He knows something. (*Twirls his finger close to his forehead.*) His game is not fair.

CONSUELO

You say it about everybody. I know HE; he is such a nice man, and he loves me so much.

MANCINI

Believe me, there is something in it.

CONSUELO

Father, you make me sick with your advice. Ah! HE, thank you.
(HE, *breathing somewhat heavily, enters and gives her the sandwiches.*)

HE

Eat, Consuelo.

CONSUELO

A hot one. . . . But you were running, HE? I am so grateful. (*Eats.*) HE, do you love me?

HE

I do, my Queen. I am your court fool.

CONSUELO

(*Eating*). And when I leave, will you find another queen?

HE

(*Making a ceremonious bow*). I shall follow after you, my incomparable one. I shall carry the train of your dress and wipe away my tears with it. (*Pretends to cry.*)

MANCINI

Idiot! (*Laughs.*) How sorry I am, HE, that those wonderful times have passed, when, in the court of the Counts Mancini, there were scores of motley fools who were given gold and kicks. . . . Now, Mancini is compelled to go to this dirty circus in order to see a good fool; and still, whose fool is he? Mine? No. He belongs to everybody who pays a franc. We shall very soon be unable to breathe because of Democracy. Democracy, too, needs fools! Think of it, HE; what an unexampled impertinence.

HE

We are the servants of those who pay. But how can we help it, Count?

MANCINI

But is that not sad? Imagine: we are in my castle. I, near the fireplace with my glass of wine, you, at my feet chatting your nonsense, jingling your little bells—diverting me. Sometimes you pinch me too with your jokes: it is allowed by the traditions and necessary for the circulation of the blood. After a while—I am sick of you, I want another one. . . . Then I give you a kick and . . . Ah, HE, how wonderful it would be!

HE

It would be marvelous, Mancini!

MANCINI

Yes. Certainly! You would be getting gold coins, those wonderfully little yellow things. . . . Well, when I become rich, I shall take you. That's settled.

CONSUELO

Take him, Father . . .

HE

And when the count, tired of my chattering, will give me a kick with his Highness's foot, then I shall lie down at the little feet of my queen, and shall . . .

CONSUELO

(*Laughing*). Wait for another kick? I'm finished. Father, give me your handkerchief, I want to wipe my hands. You have another one in your pocket. Oh, my goodness, I must work some more!

MANCINI

(*Uneasy*). But don't forget, my child!

CONSUELO

No, to-day I won't forget! Go on!

MANCINI

(*Looking at his watch*). Yes, it is time. . . . He asked me to come over when you were ready. You must change your dress before I come back. (*Laughing.*) *Signori, miei complimenti.*
(*He goes out, playing with his cane.* CONSUELO *sits on the corner of the divan, and covers herself with her shawl.*)

CONSUELO

Hello, HE! Come and lie down at my feet, and tell me something cheerful. . . . You know, when you paint the laughter on your face, you are very good looking, but now, too, you are very, very nice. Come on, HE, why don't you lie down?

HE

Consuelo! Are you going to marry the Baron?

CONSUELO

(*Indifferently*). It seems so. The Baron is hanging by a thread! HE, there is one little sandwich left. Eat it.

HE

Thank you my queen. (*Eats.*) And do you remember my prediction?

CONSUELO

What prediction? How quickly you swallow! Does it taste good?

HE

Very good. That if you marry the Baron, you . . .

CONSUELO

Oh, that's what you're talking about. . . . But you were making fun.

HE

Nobody can tell, my Queen. Sometimes one makes fun, and suddenly it turns out to be true; the stars never talk in vain. If sometimes it is difficult for a human being to open his mouth and to say a word, how difficult it must be for a star. Think of it.

CONSUELO

(*Laughing*). I should say. Such a mouth! (*Makes a tiny mouth.*)

HE

No, my dear little girl, were I in your place, I would think it over. And suppose suddenly you should die? Don't marry the Baron, Consuelo!

CONSUELO

(*Thinking*). And what is—death?

HE

I do not know, my Queen. Nobody knows. Like love! Nobody knows. But your little hands will become cold, and your dear little eyes will be closed. You will be away from here. And the music will play without you, and without you the crazy Bezano will be galloping, and Tilly and Polly will be playing on their pipes without you: tilly-polly, tilly-polly . . . tilly-tilly, polly-polly . . .

CONSUELO

Please don't, HE darling—— I am so sad, anyway . . . tilly-tilly, polly-polly . . . (*Silence.* HE *looks at* CONSUELO.)

HE

You were crying, my little Consuelo?

CONSUELO

Yes, a little. Alfred made me nervous. But tell me, is it my fault that I can't do anythink to-day? I tried to, but I couldn't.

HE

Why?

CONSUELO

Ah, I don't know. There is something here. (*Presses her hand against her heart.*) I don't know. HE, I must be sick. What is sickness? Does it hurt very much?

HE

It is not sickness. It is the charm of the far off stars, Consuelo. It is the voice of your fate, my little Queen.

CONSUELO

Don't talk nonsense, please. What should the stars care about me? I am so small. Nonsense, HE! Tell me rather another tale which you know: about the blue sea and those gods, you know . . . who are so beautiful. Did they all die?

HE

They are all alive, but they hide themselves, my goddess.

CONSUELO

In the woods or mountains? Can one come across them? Ah, imagine HE . . . I come across a god, and he suddenly takes a look at me! I'd run away. (*Laughs.*) This morning when I went without breakfast, I became so sad, so disgusted, and I thought: if a god should come, and give me something to eat! And as I thought it, I suddenly heard, honestly it's true, I heard: "Consuelo, somebody's calling you." (*Angrily.*) Don't you dare laugh!

HE

Am I laughing?

CONSUELO

Honestly, it's true. Ah, HE, but he didn't come. He only called me and disappeared, and how can you find him? It hurt me so much, and hurts even now. Why did you remind me of my childhood? I'd forgotten it entirely. There was the sea . . . and something . . . many, many . . . (*closes her eyes, smiling.*)

HE

Remember, Consuelo.

CONSUELO

No. (*Opening her eyes.*) I forget everything about it. (*Looks around the room.*) HE, do you see what a poster they made for my benefit performance? It's Father's idea. The Baron liked it. (HE *laughs. Silence.*)

HE

(*Slowly*). Consuelo, my Queen! Don't go to the Baron to-day.

CONSUELO

Why? (*After a silence.*) How fresh you are, HE.

HE

(*Lowering his head, slowly*). I don't want it.

CONSUELO

(*Getting up*). What? You don't want it?

HE

(*Bowing his head still lower*). I do not want you to marry the Baron (*Imploring.*) I . . . I shall not allow it . . . I beg you!

CONSUELO

Whom, then, would you ask me to marry? You, perhaps, you fool? (*With a rancorous laugh.*) Are you crazy, my darling? "I shall not allow." HE! HE will not allow me! But it is unbearable! What business is it of yours? (*Walking up and down the room, looks over her shoulder at* HE, *with anger.*) Some fool clown, whom they can kick out of here any minute. You make me sick with your stupid tales. Or you like slaps so much. Fool, you couldn't invent anything better than a slap!

HE

(*Without lifting his head*). Forgive me, my Queen.

CONSUELO

He is glad when they laugh at him. Some god! No, I shan't forgive. I know you. (*Makes same gesture as* MANCINI.) You have something there! Laughs . . . so nicely . . . plays, plays, and then suddenly—hop! *Obey him!* No, darling, I am not that kind! Carry my train, that is your business —fool!

HE

I shall carry your train, my Queen. Forgive me. Give me back the image of my beautiful, piteous goddess.

CONSUELO

(*Quieting down*). You're playing again?

HE

I am.

CONSUELO

(*Laughing*). You see! (*Sits down.*) Foolish HE.

HE

I see everything, my Queen. I see how beautiful you are, and how low under your feet your poor court fool is lying. Somewhere in the abyss his little bells are ringing. He kneels before you and prays; forgive and pity him, my divine one. He was too impudent; he played so cheerfully that he went too far and lost his tiny little mind, the last bit of understanding he had saved up. Forgive me!

CONSUELO

All right. I forgive you. (*Laughs.*) And now will you allow me to marry the Baron?

HE

(*Also laughing*). And nevertheless I will not allow it. But what does a queen care about the permission of her enamored fool?

CONSUELO

Get up. You are forgiven. And do you know why? You think because of your words? You are a cunning beast, HE! No, because of the *sandwiches*. That's why. You were so lovely, you panted so when you brought them. Poor darling HE. From to-morrow you may be at my feet again. And as soon as I whistle, "tuwhooo"——

HE

I shall instantly lie down at thy feet, Consuelo. It is settled! But all my little bells fell off to-day and——
(BEZANO *appears, confused*.)

CONSUELO

Alfred! You came for me?

BEZANO

Yes. Will you work some more, Consuelo?

CONSUELO

Certainly. As much as you want. But I thought, Alfred, you were mad at me? I shan't dawdle any more.

BEZANO

No. You didn't dawdle. Don't be offended, because I yelled so much. You know when one has to teach, and——

CONSUELO

My goodness, do you think I don't understand? You are too nice, unbearably nice, to like teaching such a fool as me. Do you think I don't understand? Come on!

BEZANO

Come on! Hello, HE! I haven't seen you yet to-day. How are you?

HE

How are you, Bezano? Wait, wait a minute—stay here a minute, both of you—that way. Yes!
(CONSUELO *and* BEZANO *stand side by side, the jockey scowling,* CONSUELO *laughing and flushing*.)

CONSUELO

Like Adam and Eve? How foolish you are! Terribly. (*She runs away*.) I shall only change my slippers, Alfred.

HE

Consuelo! And how about Father and the Baron? They will come soon, to take you with them.

CONSUELO

Let them come. They can wait. Not very important people. (*Runs away.* BEZANO *hesitatingly follows her*.)

HE

Stay here for a while, Bezano. Sit down.

BEZANO

What more do you want? I have no time for your nonsense.

HE

You can remain standing if you want. Bezano—you love her? (*Silence*.)

BEZANO

I shall allow nobody to interfere with my affairs. You allow yourself too many liberties, HE. I don't know you. You came from the street, and why should I trust you?

HE

But you know the Baron? Listen. It is painful for me to pronounce these words: she loves you. Save her from the spider! Or are you blind, and don't see the web, which is woven in every dark corner. Get out of the vicious circle in which you are turning around, like a blind man. Take her away, steal her, do what you want . . . kill her even, and take her to the heavens or to the devil! But don't give her to this man! He is a defiler of love. And if you are timid, if you are afraid to lift your hand against her —kill the Baron! Kill!

BEZANO

(*With a smile*). And who will kill the others, to come?

HE

She loves you.

BEZANO

Did she tell you that herself?

HE

What a pretty, what a stupid, what a human pride! But *you* are a little god! A god, youth! Why don't you want to believe me? Or does the street, from which I have come, bother you? But look, look yourself. Look in my eyes, do such eyes lie? Yes, my face is ugly, I make faces and grimaces, I am surrounded by laughter, but don't you see the god behind all this, a god, like you? Look, look at me! (BEZANO *bursts out laughing.*) What are you laughing at, youth?

BEZANO

You look now as you did that evening in the ring. You remember? When you were a great man, and they sent for you from the Academy, and suddenly—Hup! HE Who Gets Slapped!

HE

(*Laughing the same way*). Yes, yes, you are right, Bezano. There is a resemblance. (*With a strained expression, taking a pose.*) "It seems to me they sent for me from the Academy!"

BEZANO

(*Displeased*). But I don't like this play. You can present *your* face for slaps if you want to, but don't dare to expose mine. (*Turns to go.*)

HE

Bezano!

BEZANO

(*Turning round*). And never let me hear any more about Consuelo, and don't dare to tell me again that I am a god! It is disgusting.

(BEZANO *goes out angrily, striking his boot with his whip.* HE *is alone. Wrathfully with a tortured expression, he makes a step towards the jockey, then stops, with soundless laughter, his head thrown backwards. The* BARON *and* MANCINI *find him in this position, when they enter.*)

MANCINI

(*Laughing*). What a cheerful chap you are, HE! You laugh when you are alone. (HE *laughs aloud.*) Stop it fool! How can you stand it?

HE

(*Bowing low, with a large gesture*). How do you do, Baron? My humblest respects to you, Count. I beg your pardon, Count, but you found the clown at work. These are, so to speak, Baron, his every-day pleasures.

MANCINI

(*Lifting his eyebrows*). Tsss. But you are a clever man, HE. I shall ask Papa Briquet to give you a benefit performance. Shall I, HE?

HE

Please do me the favor, Count.

MANCINI

Don't overdo. Be more simple, HE. (*Laughs.*) But how many slaps will you get at your benefit performance, when even on weekdays they ring you like a gong! A funny profession, isn't it, Baron?

BARON

Very strange. But where is the Countess?

MANCINI

Yes, yes. I shall go for her at once. Dear child, she is so absorbed in her benefit performance and her work. They call this jumping *work*, Baron.

BARON

I can wait a little. (*Sits down, with his silk hat on his head.*)

MANCINI

But why? I shall hurry her up. I shall be back at once. And you, HE, be a nice host, and entertain our dear guest. You will not be bored in his company, Baron.

(*He goes out.* HE *strides about the stage, smiling and glancing from time to time at the* BARON. *The latter sits with his legs spread apart and his chin on the top of his cane. The silk hat remains on his head. He is silent.*)

HE

In what way would you like me to entertain you, Baron?

BARON

In no way! I don't like clowns.

HE

Nor I Barons.

(*Silence.* HE *puts on his derby hat, takes a chair with a large gesture, and puts it down heavily, in front of the* BARON. HE *sits astride it, imitating the pose of the* BARON, *and looks him in the eyes. Silence.*)

HE

Can you be silent very long?

BARON

Very long.

HE

(*Taps on the floor with his foot*). And can you wait very long?

BARON

Very long.

HE

Until you get it?

BARON

Until I get it. And you?

HE

I too.

(*Both look at each other, silently, their heads close together. From the ring one hears the strains of the Tango.*)

CURTAIN

ACT FOUR

MUSIC *in the ring. More disorder in the room than usual. All kinds of actors' costumes hanging on pegs and lying in the corners. On the table a bouquet of fiery-red roses, put there by some careless hand. At the entrance, near the arch, three bareback riders are smoking and chattering; they are all minor actors. All part their hair the same way; two wear small moustaches; the third one is clean-shaven with a face like a bull-dog.*

THE CLEAN-SHAVEN ONE

Go on, Henry! Ten thousand francs! It's too much even for the Baron.

THE SECOND

How much are roses now?

THE SHAVEN

I don't know. In winter they are certainly more expensive, but still Henry talks nonsense. Ten thousand!

THE SECOND

The Baron has his own hothouse. They don't cost him anything.

HENRY

(*Throwing away his cigar, which has burned the tips of his fingers*). No, Grab, you're silly. There's a whole car-load full! One can smell the roses a mile away. They're to cover the entire arena.

THE SHAVEN

Only the ring.

HENRY

It's all the same. In order to cover the ring, you must have thousands and thousands of roses. You'll see what it looks like, when they've covered everything like a carpet. He ordered them to make it like a carpet! Do you see, Grab?

THE SECOND

What a Baron's craze! Isn't it time yet?

HENRY

No, we have time enough. I rather like it: a fiery-red tango on a fiery-red cover of winter roses!

THE SHAVEN

Consuelo will be galloping on roses. And Bezano?

THE SECOND

And Bezano on thorns. (*Smiles.*)

THE SHAVEN

That youngster has no self-respect. I'd have refused.

HENRY

But it is his job. He's got to do it. (*Laughs.*) Talk to him about self-respect. He's as angry and proud as a little Satan.

THE SECOND

No, you may say what you like, it's an excellent benefit performance. It's a joy to look at the crowd. They're so excited.

HENRY

Tss! (*All throw away their cigars and cigarettes, like school boys who are caught, and make way for* ZINIDA, *who enters with* HE.)

ZINIDA

What are you doing here, gentlemen? Your place is at the entrance.

HENRY

(*With a respectful smile*). We are here just for a minute, Madame Zinida. We are going. What a successful evening! And what a glory for Papa Briquet!

ZINIDA

Yes. Go, and please don't leave your places. (*They go.* ZINIDA *pulls a drawer out of the desk, and puts in some papers. She is in her lion tamer's costume.*) HE, what were you doing near my lions? You frightened me.

HE

Why, Duchess, I merely wanted to hear what the beasts were saying about the benefit performance. They are pacing in their cages, and growling.

ZINIDA

The music makes them nervous. Sit down, HE. An excellent evening, and I am so glad that Consuelo is leaving us. Have you heard about the Baron's roses?

HE

Everybody is talking about them. The Hymeneal roses!

ZINIDA

Here are some, too. (*Pushes away the bouquet.*) You find them everywhere. Yes, I am glad. She is superfluous here, and disturbs our work. It is a misfortune for a cast to have in it such a beautiful and such an . . . accessible girl.

HE

But it is an honest marriage, Duchess, is it not?

ZINIDA

I don't care what it is.

HE

Spiders, too need an improvement in their breed! Can't you imagine, Zinida, what charming little spiders this couple will create! They will have the face of their mother, Consuelo, and the stomach of their father, the Baron, and thus could be an ornament for any circus-ring.

ZINIDA

You are malicious to-day, HE. You are morose.

HE

I laugh.

ZINIDA

You do, but without joy. Why are you without make-up?

HE

I am in the third act. I have time. And how does Bezano feel about this evening? Is he glad?

ZINIDA

I didn't talk to Bezano. You know what I think, my friend? You, too, are superfluous here. (*Silence.*)

HE

How do you want me to take that, Zinida?

ZINIDA

Just as I said. In fact, Consuelo sold herself for nothing. What is the Baron worth, with his poor millions? People say that you are clever, too clever perhaps; tell me then, for how much could one buy me?

HE

(*Looking as if he were pricing her*). Only for a crown.

ZINIDA

A baron's crown?

HE

No, a royal one.

ZINIDA

You are far from being stupid. And you guessed that Consuelo is not Mancini's daughter?

HE

(*Startled*). What! And she knows it?

ZINIDA

Hardly. Why should she know it? Yes, she is a girl from Corsica whose parents are unknown. He preferred to use her for business rather than . . . But according to the law, she is his daughter, Countess Veronica Mancini.

HE

It is nice, to have everything done according to law, isn't it, Zinida? But it is curious there is more blue blood in her than in this Mancini. One would say that it was she who found him on the street, and made him a count and her father. Count Mancini! (*Laughs.*)

ZINIDA

Yes, you are gloomy, HE. I changed my mind, you'd better stay.

HE

Will I not be superfluous?

ZINIDA

When she is gone, you will not. Oh! You don't know yet, how nice it is to be with us. What a rest for the body and mind. I understand you. I am clever, too. Like you, I brought with me from out there my inclination for chains, and for a long time I chained myself to whatever I could, in order to feel firm.

HE

Bezano?

ZINIDA

Bezano and others; there were many, there will be many more. My red lion, with whom I am desperately in love, is still more terrible than Bezano. But it is all nonsense; old habits, which we are sorry to let go, like old servants who steal things. Leave Consuelo alone. She has her own way.

HE

Automobiles and diamonds?

ZINIDA

When did you see a beauty clad in simple cotton? If this one does not buy her, another will. They buy off everything that is beautiful. Yes, I know. For the first ten years she will be a sad beauty, who will attract the eyes of the poor man on the sidewalk: afterward she will begin to paint a little around her eyes and smile, and then will take——

HE

Her *chauffeur* or butler as a lover? You're not guessing badly, Zinida!

ZINIDA

Am I not right? I don't want to intrude on your confidence, but to-day I am sorry for you, HE. What can you do against Fate? Don't be offended, my friend, by the words of a woman. I like you; you are not beautiful, nor young, nor rich, and your place is——

HE

On the side-walk, from which one looks at the beauties. (*Laughs.*) And if I don't want to?

ZINIDA

What does it matter, your "want" or "don't want?" I am sorry for you, my poor friend, but if you are a strong man, and I think you are, then there is only one way for you. To forget.

HE

You think that that's being strong? And you are saying this, you, Queen Zinida, who want to awake the feeling of love, even in the heart of a lion? For one second of an illusory possession, you are ready to pay with your life, and still you advise me to forget! Give me your strong hand, my beautiful lady; see how much strength there is in this pressure, and don't pity me. (*Enter* BRIQUET *and* MANCINI. *The latter is reserved, and self-consciously imposing. He has a new suit, but the same cane, and the same noiseless smile of a satyr.*)

ZINIDA

(*Whispering*). Will you stay?

HE

Yes. I shan't go away.

MANCINI

How are you, my dear? But you are dazzling, my dear! I swear you are marvelous! Your lion would be an ass, if he did not kiss your hand, as I do. . . . (*Kisses her hand.*)

ZINIDA

May I congratulate you, Count?

MANCINI

Yes, *merci.* (*To* HE) How are you, my dear?

HE

Good evening, Count!

BRIQUET

Zinida, the Count wants to pay immediately for the breach of contract with Consuelo . . . the Countess's contract. Don't you remember, Mother, how much it is?

ZINIDA

I'll look it up, Papa.

MANCINI

Yes, please. Consuelo will not return here any more. We leave to-morrow.
(ZINIDA *and* BRIQUET *search among the papers.* HE *takes* MANCINI *roughly by the elbow, and draws him aside.*)

HE

(*In a low voice*). How are your girls, Mancini?

MANCINI

What girls? What is this, stupidity or blackmail? Look out, sir, be careful, the policeman is not far.

HE

You are much too severe, Mancini. I assumed, that since we are *tête-à-tête* . . .

MANCINI

But tell me, what kind of *tête-à-tête* is possible, between a clown and me? (*Laughs.*) You are stupid, HE. You should say what you want, and not ask questions!

BRIQUET

Three thousand francs, Count.

MANCINI

Is that all? For Consuelo? All right. I'll tell the Baron.

ZINIDA

You took——

BRIQUET

Don't, Mother, don't.

ZINIDA

Count, you drew in advance, I have it written down, eighty francs and twenty centimes. Will you pay this money, too?

MANCINI

Certainly, certainly. You will get three thousand and one hundred. (*Laughing.*) Twenty centimes! I never thought I could be so accurate. (*Seriously.*) Yes, my friends. My daughter Consuelo—the Countess—and the Baron, expressed their desire to bid farewell to the whole cast.

HE

The Baron, too?

MANCINI

Yes, Auguste, too. They want to do it during the intermission. Therefore, I ask you to gather here . . . the more decent ones . . . but please don't make it too crowded! HE, will you, sir, be kind enough to run into the buffet and tell them to bring right away a basket of champagne, bottles and glasses—you understand?

HE

Yes, Count.

MANCINI

Wait a minute, what's the hurry—what is this, a new costume? You are all burning like the devils in hell!

HE

You do me too much honor, Count, I am not a devil. I am merely a poor sinner whom the devils are frying a little. (*He goes out, bowing like a clown.*)

MANCINI

A gifted chap, but too cunning.

BRIQUET

It's the Tango color, in honor of your daughter, Count. He needs it for a new stunt, which he doesn't want to tell in advance. Don't you want to sit down, Count?

MANCINI

Auguste is waiting for me, but . . . it's all right. (*Takes a seat.*) Nevertheless I am sorry to leave you, my friend. High society, certainly, prerogatives of the title, castles of exalted noblemen, but where could I find such freedom, and . . . such simplicity. . . . And besides, these announcements, these burning posters, which take your breath in the morning, they had something which summoned, which encouraged. . . . *There,* my friends, I shall become old.

BRIQUET

But pleasures of a higher kind, Count. Why are you silent, Zinida?

ZINIDA

I'm listening.

MANCINI

By the way, my dear, how do you like my suit? You have wonderful taste. (*Spreads out his lace tie and lace cuffs.*)

ZINIDA

I like it. You look like a nobleman of the courts of long ago.

MANCINI

Yes? But don't you think it is too conspicuous? Who wears lace and satin now? This dirty democracy will soon make us dress ourselves in sack cloth. (*With a sigh.*) Auguste told me that this jabot was out of place.

ZINIDA

The Baron is too severe.

MANCINI

Yes, but it seems to me he is right. I am a little infected with your fancy. (HE *returns. Two waiters follow him, carrying a basket of champagne and glasses. They prepare everything on the table.*)

MANCINI

Ah! *merci,* HE. But, please, none of this bourgeois exploding of corks; be slower and more modest. Send the bill to Baron Regnard. Then, we will be here, Briquet. I must go.

ZINIDA

(*Looks at her watch*). Yes, the act is going to end soon.

MANCINI

Heavens! (*Disappears in a hurry.*)

BRIQUET

The devil take him!

ZINIDA

(*Pointing to the waiter*). Not so loud, Louis!

BRIQUET

No! The devil take him! And why couldn't you help me, Mother? You left me alone to talk to him. High Society! High pleasures! Swindler! (HE *and* ZINIDA *laugh. The waiters smile.*)

BRIQUET

(*To the waiters*). What are you laughing about? You can go. We will help ourselves. Whiskey and soda, Jean! (*In a low and angry voice.*) Champagne! (*Enter* JACKSON, *in his clown's costume.*)

JACKSON

A whiskey and soda for me, too! At least I hear some laughter here. Those idiots have simply forgotten how to laugh. My sun was rising and setting and crawling all over the ring——and not a smile! Look at my bottom, shines like a mirror! (*Turns around quickly.*) Beg your pardon, Zinida. And you don't look badly to-night, HE. Look out for your cheeks. I hate beauties.

BRIQUET

A benefit performance crowd!

JACKSON

(*Looking in a hand mirror, correcting his make-up*). In the orchestra there are some Barons and Egyptian mummies. I got a belly-ache from fright. I am an honest clown. I can't stand it when they look at me as if I had stolen a handkerchief. HE, please give them a good many slaps to-night.

HE

Be quiet, Jim. I shall avenge you. (*He goes out.*)

ZINIDA

And how is Bezano?

JACKSON

(*Grumbling*). Bezano! A crazy success. But he is crazy, he will break his neck to-morrow. Why does he run such a risk? Or perhaps he has wings, like a god? Devil take it. It's disgusting to look at him. It's not work any more.

BRIQUET

You are right, Jim! It is not work any more. To your health, old comrade, Jackson.

JACKSON

To yours, Louis.

BRIQUET

It is not work any more, since these Barons came here! Do you hear? They are laughing. But I am indignant, I am indignant, Jim! What do they want here, these Barons? Let them steal hens in other hen roosts, and leave us in peace. Ah! Had I been Secretary of the Interior, I should have made an iron fence between us and those people.

JACKSON

I am very sorry myself for our dear little Consuelo. I don't know why, but it seems to me that we all look to-day more like swindlers than honest artists. Don't you think so, Zinida?

ZINIDA

Everybody does what he wants. It's Consuelo's business and her father's.

BRIQUET

No, Mother, that's not true! Not everybody does what he wants, but it turns out this way . . . devil knows why.
(*Enter* ANGELICA *and* THOMAS, *an athlete.*)

ANGELICA

Is this where we're going to have champagne?

BRIQUET

And you're glad already?

THOMAS

There it is! Oh, oh, what a lot!

ANGELICA

The Count told me to come here. I met him.

BRIQUET

(*Angrily*). All right, if he said so, but there is no reason to enjoy it. Look out, Angelica, you will have a bad end. I see you through and through. How does she work, Thomas?

THOMAS

Very well.

ANGELICA

(*In a low voice*). How angry Papa Briquet is tonight.
(*Enter* HE, TILLY, POLLY, *and other actors, all in their costumes.*)

TILLY

Do you really want champagne?

POLLY

I don't want it at all. Do you, Tilly?

TILLY

And I don't want it. HE, did you see how the Count walks? (*Walks, imitating* MANCINI. *Laughter.*)

POLLY

Let me be the Baron. Take my arm. Look out, ass, you stepped on my beloved family tree!

ANGELICA

It'll soon be finished. Consuelo is galloping now. It is her waltz. What a success she is having!
(*All listen to the waltz.* TILLY *and* POLLY *are singing it softly.*)

ANGELICA

She is so beautiful! Are those her flowers? (*They listen. Suddenly, a crash as if a broken wall were tumbling down: applause, shouting, screaming; much motion on the stage. The actors are pouring champagne. New ones come in, talking and laughing. When they notice the director and the champagne, they become quiet and modest.*)

VOICES

They're coming! What a success! I should say, since all the orchestra seats . . . And what will it be when they see the Tango? Don't be envious, Alphonse.

BRIQUET

Silence! Not so much noise, please! Zinida, look here, don't be so quiet! High society! (*Enter* CONSUELO, *on the arm of the* BARON *who is stiff and erect. She is happy.* MANCINI, *serious and happy. Behind them, riders, actors, actresses. The* BARON *has in his button-hole a fiery-red rose. All applaud and cry: "Bravo, bravo!"*)

CONSUELO

Friends . . . my dears . . . Father, I can't . . . (*Throws herself into* MANCINI's *arms, and hides her face on his shoulders.* MANCINI *looks with a smile over her head at the* BARON. BARON *smiles slightly, but remains earnest and motionless. A new burst of applause.*)

BRIQUET

Enough, children! Enough!

MANCINI

Calm yourself, calm yourself, my child. How they all love you! (*Taking a step forward.*) Ladies and gentlemen, Baron Regnard did me the honor yesterday, to ask for the hand of my daughter, the Countess Veronica, whom you knew under the name of Consuelo. Please take your glasses.

CONSUELO

No, I am still Consuelo, tonight, and I shall always be Consuelo! Zinida, dear! (*Falls on the neck of* ZINIDA. *Fresh applause.*)

BRIQUET

Stop it! Silence! Take your glasses. What are you standing here for? If you came, then take the glasses.

TILLY

(*Trembling*). They are frightened. You take yours first, Papa, and we will follow. (*They take the glasses.* CONSUELO *is near the* BARON, *holding the sleeve of his dress coat with her left hand. In her right hand, she has a glass of champagne, which spills over.*)

BARON

You are spilling your wine, Consuelo.

CONSUELO

Ah! It is nothing! I am frightened, too. Are you, Father?

MANCINI

Silly child. (*An awkward silence.*)

BRIQUET

(*With a step forward*). Countess! As the director of the circus, who was happy enough . . . to witness . . . many times . . . your successes . . .

CONSUELO

I do not *like* this, Papa Briquet! I am Consuelo. What do you want to do with me? I shall cry. I don't want this "Countess." Give me a kiss, Briquet!

BRIQUET

Ah, Consuelo! Books have killed you.
(*Kisses her with tears. Laughter, applause. The clowns cluck like hens, bark, and express their emotions in many other ways. The motley crowd of clowns, which is ready for the pantomime, becomes more and more lively. The* BARON *is motionless, there is a wide space around him; the people touch glasses with him in a hurry, and go off to one side. With* CONSUELO *they clink willingly and cheerfully. She kisses the women.*)

JACKSON

Silence! Consuelo, from today on, I extinguish my sun. Let the dark night come after you leave us. You were a nice comrade and worker, we all loved you and will love the traces of your little feet on the sand. Nothing remains to us!

CONSUELO

You are so good, so good, Jim. So good that there is no one better. And your sun is better than all the other suns. I laughed so much at it. Alfred, dear, why don't you come? I was looking for you.

BEZANO

My congratulations, Countess.

CONSUELO

Alfred, I am Consuelo!

BEZANO

When you are on horseback; but here—I congratulate you, Countess. (*He passes, only slightly touching* CONSUELO's *glass.* CONSUELO *still holds it.* MANCINI *looks at the* BARON *with a smile. The latter is motionless.*)

BRIQUET

Nonsense, Bezano. You are making Consuelo unhappy. She is a good comrade.

CONSUELO

No, it's all right.

ANGELICA

You'll dance the Tango with her tonight, so how is she a countess?

TILLY

May I clink glasses with you, Consuelo? You know Polly has died of grief already, and I am going to die. I have such a weak stomach.
(*Laughter;* BARON *shows slight displeasure. General motion.*)

MANCINI

Enough, enough! The intermission is over.

CONSUELO

Already? It's so nice here.

BRIQUET

I shall prolong it. They can wait. Tell them, Thomas.

MANCINI

Auguste, the musicians of the orchestra, too, ask permission to congratulate you and Consuelo. Do you . . . ?

BARON

Certainly, certainly.
(*Enter crowd of musicians. The conductor, an old Italian, lifts his glass solemnly and without looking at the* BARON.)

THE CONDUCTOR

Consuelo! They call you Countess here, but for me you were and are *Consuelo.*

CONSUELO

Certainly!

THE CONDUCTOR

Consuelo! My violins and bassoons, my trumpets and drums, all are drinking your health. Be happy, dear child, as you were happy here. And we shall conserve for ever in our hearts the fair memory of our light-winged fairy, who guided our bows so long. I have finished! Give my love to our beautiful Italy, Consuelo.
(*Applause, compliments. The musicians one after another clink glasses and go out into the corridor.* CONSUELO *is almost crying.*)

MANCINI

Don't be so sensitive, my child, it is indecent. Had I known that you would respond this way to this comedy—Auguste, look how touched this little heart is!

BARON

Calm yourself, Consuelo.

CONSUELO

It is all right. Ah, Father, listen!
(*The musicians are playing the Tango in the corridor. Exclamations.*)

MANCINI

You see. It is for you.

CONSUELO

They are so nice. My Tango! I want to dance. Who is going to dance with me? (*Looks around, seeking* BEZANO, *who turns away sadly.*) Who, then?

VOICES

Baron! Let the Baron dance! Baron!

BARON

All right. (*Takes* CONSUELO's *arm, and stands in the centre of a circle which is formed.*) I do not know how to dance the Tango, but I shall hold tight. Dance, Consuelo. (*He stands with legs spread, heavily and awkwardly, like an iron-molded man, holding* CONSUELO's *arm firmly and seriously.*)

MANCINI

(*Applauding*). Bravo! Bravo! (CONSUELO *makes a few restless movements, and pulls her arm away.*)

CONSUELO

No, I can't this way. How stupid! Let me go! (*She goes to* ZINIDA *and embraces her, as if hiding herself. The music still plays. The* BARON *goes off quietly to the side. There is an unfriendly silence among the cast. They shrug their shoulders.*)

MANCINI

(*Alone*). Bravo! Bravo! It is charming, it is exquisite!

JACKSON

Not entirely, Count.
(TILLY *and* POLLY *imitate the* BARON *and* CONSUELO *without moving from their places.*)

TILLY

(*Shrieking*). Let me go!

POLLY

No, I'll not. Dance!
(*The music stops abruptly. General, too loud laughter; the clowns bark and roar. Papa* BRIQUET *gesticulates, in order to reestablish silence. The* BARON *is apparently as indifferent as before.*)

MANCINI

Really these vagabonds are becoming too impertinent. (*Shrugging his shoulders.*) It smells of the stable. You cannot help it, Auguste!

BARON

Don't be upset, Count.

HE

(*Holding his glass, approaches the* BARON). Baron. Will you permit me to make a toast?

BARON

Make it.

HE

To your dance! (*Slight laughter in the crowd.*)

BARON

I don't dance!

HE

Then another one, Baron. Let us drink to those who know how to wait longer, until they get it.

BARON

I do not accept any toasts which I do not understand. Say it more simply.
(*Voice of a woman: "Bravo,* HE*!" Slight laughter.* MANCINI *says something hastily to* BRIQUET; *the latter spreads his arms in gesture of helplessness.* JACKSON *takes* HE *by the arm.*)

JACKSON

Beat it, HE! The Baron doesn't like jokes.

HE

But I want to drink with the Baron. What can be simpler? Simpler? Baron, let us drink to the very small distance which will always remain 'twixt the cup and the lip! (*Spills his wine, and laughs.*)

(*The* BARON *turns his back on him, indifferently. The music plays in the ring. The bell rings.*)

BRIQUET

(*Relieved*). There! To the ring, ladies and gentlemen, to the ring, to the ring!

(*The actresses run out. The crowd becomes smaller; laughter and voices.*)

MANCINI

(*Much excited, whispers to the* BARON). "Auguste, Auguste——"

BRIQUET

(*To* ZINIDA). Thank heaven they're beginning. Ah, Mother, I asked you . . . but you want a scandal by all means, and you always——

ZINIDA

Let me alone, Louis.

(HE *approaches* CONSUELO, *who is alone.*)

CONSUELO

HE, deary, how are you? I thought you didn't want even to come near me. (*In a low voice.*) Did you notice Bezano?

HE

I was waiting for my turn, Queen. It was so difficult to get through the crowd to approach you.

CONSUELO

Through the crowd? (*With a sad smile.*) I am quite alone. What do you want, Father?

MANCINI

Child! Auguste . . .

CONSUELO

(*Pulling away her hand*). Let me alone! I'll soon be— Come here, HE. What did you say to him? They all laughed. I couldn't understand. What?

HE

I joked, Consuelo.

CONSUELO

Please don't, HE, don't make him angry; he is so terrible. Did you see how he pressed my arm? I wanted to scream. (*With tears in her eyes.*) He hurt me!

HE

It's not too late yet. Refuse him.

CONSUELO

It *is* too late, HE. Don't talk about it.

HE

Do you want it? I will take you away from here.

CONSUELO

Where to? (*Laughs.*) Ah, my dear little silly boy, where could you take me to? All right, be quiet. How pale you are! You too, love me? Don't HE, please don't! Why do they all love me?

HE

You are so beautiful!

CONSUELO

No, no. It's not true. They must not love me. I was still a little cheerful, but when they began to speak . . . so nicely . . . and about Italy . . . and to bid farewell, as if I were dying, I thought I should begin to cry. Don't talk, don't talk, but drink to . . . my happiness. (*With a sad smile.*) To my happiness, HE. What are you doing?

HE

I am throwing away the glass from which you drank with the others. I shall give you another one. Wait a minute. (*Goes to pour champagne.* CONSUELO *walks about thoughtfully. Almost all are gone. Only the principal figures are left.*)

MANCINI

(*Coming to her*). But it is really becoming indecent, Veronica. Auguste is so nice, he is waiting for you, and you talk here with this clown. Some stupid secrets. They're looking at you—it is becoming noticeable. It is high time, Veronica, to get rid of these habits.

CONSUELO

(*Loudly*). Let me alone, Father! I want to do so, and will do so. They are all my friends. Do you hear? Let me alone!

BARON

Don't, Count. Please, Consuelo, talk to whomever you please and as much as you want. Would you like a cigar, Count? Dear Briquet, please order them to prolong the intermission a little more.

BRIQUET

With pleasure, Baron. The orchestra crowd can be a little angry. (*Goes, and returns shortly.* HE *gives a glass to* CONSUELO.)

HE

Here is your glass. To your happiness, to your freedom, Consuelo!

CONSUELO

And where is yours? We must touch our glasses.

HE

You leave half.

CONSUELO

Must I drink so much? HE, deary, I shall become drunk. I still have to ride.

HE

No, you will not be drunk. Dear little girl, did you forget that I am your magician? Be quiet and drink. I charmed the wine. My witchery is in it. Drink, goddess.

CONSUELO

(*Lingeringly*). What kind eyes you have. But why are you so pale?

HE

Because I love you. Look at my kind eyes and drink; give yourself up to my charms, goddess! You shall fall asleep, and wake again, as before. Do you remember? And you shall see your country, your sky . . .

CONSUELO

(*Bringing the glass to her lips*). I shall see all this; is that true?

HE

(*Growing paler*). Yes! Awake, goddess, and remember the time when, covered with snow-white sea-foam, thou didst emerge from the sky blue waters. Remember heaven, and the low eastern wind, and the whisper of the foam at thy marble feet. . . .

CONSUELO

(*Drinking*). There! Look! Just a half! Take it. But what is the matter with you? Are you laughing or crying?

HE

I am laughing and crying.

MANCINI

(*Pushing* HE *away, slightly*). Enough, Countess, my patience is exhausted. If Auguste is good enough to allow it, then I, your Father—Your arm, Countess! Will you step aside, sir?

CONSUELO

I am tired.

MANCINI

You are not too tired to chatter and drink wine with a clown, and when your duty calls you—Briquet! Tell them to ring the bell. It is time.

CONSUELO

I am tired, Father.

ZINIDA

Count, it is cruel. Don't you see how pale she has become?

BARON

What is the matter with you, dear little Consuelo?

CONSUELO

Nothing.

ZINIDA

She simply needs a rest, Baron. She hasn't sat down yet . . . and so much excitement. . . . Sit down here, dear child. Cover yourself and rest a little. Men are so cruel!

CONSUELO

I still have to work. (*Closing her eyes.*) And the roses, are they ready?

ZINIDA

Ready, dear, ready. You will have such an extraordinary carpet. You will gallop as if on air. Rest.

POLLY

Do you want some moosic? We will play you a song; do you want it?

CONSUELO

(*Smiling, eyes closed*). Yes, I do.
(*The clowns play a soft and naïve song: tilly-polly, tilly-polly. General silence.* HE *sits in the corner with his face turned away.* JACKSON *watches him out of the corner of his eye, and drinks wine, lazily. The* BARON, *in his usual pose, wide and heavily spread legs, looks at the pale face of* CONSUELO, *with his bulging motionless eyes.*)

CONSUELO

(*With a sudden cry*). Ah! Pain!

ZINIDA

What is it, Consuelo?

MANCINI

My child! Are you sick? Calm yourself.

BARON

(*Growing pale*). Wait a moment. . . . She was too much excited. . . . Consuelo!

CONSUELO

(*Gets up, looking before her with wide-open eyes, as if she were listening to something within herself*). Ah! I feel pain. Here at the heart. Father, what is it? I am afraid. What is it? My feet too . . . I can't stand. . . . (*Falls on divan, her eyes wide open.*)

MANCINI

(*Running about*). Bring a doctor! Heavens, it is terrible! Auguste, Baron . . . It never happened to her. It is nerves, nerves. . . . Calm yourself, calm, child——

BRIQUET

Bring a doctor! (*Somebody runs for a doctor.*)

JACKSON

(*In a voice full of fear*). HE, what is the matter with you?

HE

It is death, Consuelo, my little Queen. I killed you. You are dying.
(*He cries, loudly and bitterly.* CONSUELO *with a scream, closes her eyes, and becomes silent and quiet. All are in terrible agitation. The* BARON *is motionless, and sees only* CONSUELO.)

MANCINI

(*Furious*). You are lying, rascal! Damned clown! What did you give her? You poisoned her! Murderer! Bring a doctor!

HE

A doctor will not help. You are dying, my little Queen. Consuelo! Consuelo!
(BEZANO *rushes in, cries:* "BRIQUET!" *becomes silent and looks with horror at* CONSUELO. *Somebody else come in.* BRIQUET *is making gestures for someone to close the door.*)

CONSUELO

(*In a dull and distant voice*). You are joking, HE? Don't frighten me. I am so frightened. Is that death? I don't want it. Ah, HE, my darling HE, tell me that you are joking, I am afraid, my dear, golden HE!
(HE *pushes away the* BARON, *with a commanding gesture, and stands in his place near* CONSUELO. *The* BARON *stands as before, seeing only* CONSUELO.)

HE

Yes, I am joking. Don't you hear how I laugh, Consuelo? They all laugh at you here, my silly child. Don't laugh, Jim. She is tired, and wants to sleep. How can you laugh, Jim! Sleep my dear, sleep my heart, sleep my love.

CONSUELO

Yes, I have no more pain. Why did you joke that way, and frighten me? Now I laugh at myself. You told me, didn't you, that I . . . should . . . live . . . eternally?

HE

Yes, Consuelo! You shall live eternally. Sleep. Be calm. (*Lifts up his arms, as if straining with all his forces to lift her soul higher.*) How easy it is now! How much light, how many lights are burning about you. . . . The light is blinding you.

CONSUELO

Yes, light . . . Is that the ring?

HE

No, it is the sea and the sun . . . what a sun! Don't you feel that you are the foam, white sea-foam, and you are flying to the sun? You feel light, you have no body, you are flying higher, my love!

CONSUELO

I am flying. I am the sea-foam, and this is the sun, it shines . . . so strong. . . . I feel well.

(*She dies. Silence.* HE *stays a moment with lifted arms, then takes a long look, lets his arms fall, and shakingly goes off to one side. He stands still for a moment, then sits down, drops his head on his hands, and struggles lonesomely with the torpidity of coming death.*)

BRIQUET

(*Slowly*). She has fallen asleep, Mother?

ZINIDA

(*Dropping the dead hand*). I am afraid not. . . . Step aside, Louis. Baron, it is better for you to step aside. Baron! Do you hear me? (*Weeps.*) She is dead, Louis.

(*The clowns and* BRIQUET *are crying.* MANCINI *is overwhelmed. The* BARON *and* HE *are motionless, each in his place.*)

JACKSON

(*Drawing out a large prismatic clown's handkerchief to wipe away his tears*). Faded, like a flower. Sleep, little Consuelo! The only thing that remains of you is the trace of your little feet on the sand. (*Cries.*) Ah, what did you do, what did you do, HE! . . . It would have been better if you had never come to us.

(*There is music in the ring.*)

BRIQUET

(*Gesticulating*). The music! Stop the music! They are crazy there. What a misfortune!

(*Someone runs off.* ZINIDA *approaches the crying* BEZANO *and strokes his bowed, pomaded head. When he notices her, he catches her hand and presses it to his eyes. The* BARON *takes the rose from his buttonhole, tears off the petals, and drops it, grinding it with his foot. A few pale faces peer through the door, the same masquerade crowd.*)

ZINIDA

(*Over the head of* BEZANO). Louis, we must call the police.

MANCINI

(*Awakening from his stupor, screams*). The police! Call the police! It's a murder! I am Count Mancini, I am Count Mancini! They will cut off your head, murderer, damned clown, thief! I myself will kill you, rascal! Ah, you! (HE *lifts his heavy head with difficulty.*)

HE

They will cut off my head? And what more . . . Your Excellency?

BARON

Sir! Listen, sir! I am going for the police. Stop it, sir. (*He suddenly takes a step forward, and looking* HE *in the eyes, speaks in a hoarse voice, with a cough, holding one hand at his throat.*) I am the witness. I saw. I am a witness. I saw how he put poison . . . I——

(*He leaves the room, suddenly, with the same straight, heavy steps. All move away from him, frightened.* HE *drops his head again. From time to time a tremor shakes his body.*)

JACKSON

(*Clasping his hands*). Then it is all true? Poisoned! What a vile man you are, HE. Is this the way to play? Now wait for the last slap of the executioner! (*Makes the gesture around his neck, of the guillotine.* TILLY *and* POLLY *repeat the gesture.*)

ZINIDA

Leave his soul alone, Jim. He was a man, and he loved. Happy Consuelo!

(*A shot is heard in the corridor.* THOMAS, *frightened, runs in and points to his head.*)

THOMAS

Baron . . . Baron . . . his head . . . He shot himself . . .

BRIQUET

(*Throwing his arms up*). God! What is it? The Baron? What a calamity for our circus.

MANCINI

The Baron? The Baron? No. What are you standing here for? Ah!

BRIQUET

Calm down, Count. Who would have believed it? Such a respectable . . . gentleman!

HE

(*Lifting his head with difficulty; he sees only dimly with his dulled eyes*). What more? What happened?

THOMAS

The Baron shot himself. Honestly. Straight here! He's lying out yonder.

HE

(*Thinking it over*). Baron? (*Laughs.*) Then the Baron burst?

JACKSON

Stop it! It's shameless. A man died and you . . . What's the matter with you, HE?

HE

(*Stands up, lifted to his feet by the last gleam of consciousness and life, speaks strongly and indignantly*). You loved her so much, Baron? So much? My Consuelo? And you want to be ahead of me even *there*? No! I am coming. We shall prove then whose she is to be forever. . . .
(*He catches at his throat, falls on his back. People run to him. General agitation.*)

Curtain

Elmer Rice

THE ADDING MACHINE

ELMER RICE

Born in New York City, in 1892, Elmer Rice received his early education in the public schools and won his LL.B. degree *cum laude* from the New York Law School in 1912. He was admitted to the Bar in 1913 and pursued the practice of Law for a short time. The enormous success of his first play, *On Trial,* induced him to forsake the legal profession for a career as a playwright. This play anticipated the motion-picture device of the flash-back in time and in action. *The Adding Machine* won for him further distinction as an innovator who employed the expressionistic technique to a drama with an American background. In 1924, *Street Scene* was produced and was awarded the Pulitzer Prize for the drama. Since then he has written many successful plays and a single novel, *A Voyage to Purilia,* a biting satire on motion pictures. Mr. Rice was married in 1915 to Hazel Levy. He is a member of the governing boards of the Authors' League of America, the American Dramatists, the American Civil Liberties Union, the League of British Dramatists and is active in many other organizations.

CHARACTERS

MR. ZERO
MRS. ZERO
DAISY DIANA DOROTHEA DEVORE
THE BOSS
MR. ONE
MRS. ONE
MR. TWO
MRS. TWO
MR. THREE
MRS. THREE
MR. FOUR
MRS. FOUR
MR. FIVE
MRS. FIVE
MR. SIX
MRS. SIX
POLICEMAN
JUDY O'GRADY
YOUNG MAN
SHRDLU
A HEAD
LIEUTENANT CHARLES
JOE

SCENE I: A bedroom
SCENE II: An office
SCENE III: A living room
SCENE IV: A place of justice
SCENE V: A graveyard
SCENE VI: A pleasant place
SCENE VII: Another office

THE ADDING MACHINE

SCENE I

SCENE: *A bedroom. A small room containing an "instalment-plan" bed, dresser, and chairs. An ugly electric-light fixture over the bed with a single glaring naked lamp. One small window with the shade drawn. The walls are papered with sheets of foolscap covered with columns of figures.*

MR. ZERO *is lying in the bed, facing the audience, his head and shoulders visible. He is thin, sallow, under-sized, and partially bald.* MRS. ZERO *is standing before the dresser arranging her hair for the night. She is forty-five, sharp-featured, gray streaks in her hair. She is shapeless in her long-sleeved cotton nightgown. She is wearing her shoes, over which sag her ungartered stockings.*

MRS. ZERO

(*As she takes down her hair*). I'm gettin' sick o' them Westerns. All them cowboys ridin' around an' foolin' with them ropes. I don't care nothin' about that. I'm sick of 'em. I don't see why they don't have more of them stories like "For Love's Sweet Sake." I like them sweet little love stories. They're nice an' wholesome. Mrs. Twelve was sayin' to me only yesterday, "Mrs. Zero," says she, "what I like is one of them wholesome stories, with just a sweet, simple little love story." "You're right, Mrs. Twelve," I says. "That's what I like, too." They're showin' too many Westerns at the Rosebud. I'm gettin' sick of them. I think we'll start goin' to the Peter Stuyvesant. They got a good bill there Wednesday night. There's a Chubby Delano comedy called "Sea-Sick." Mrs. Twelve was tellin' me about it. She says it's a scream. They're havin' a picnic in the country and they sit Chubby next to an old maid with a great big mouth. So he gets sore an' when she ain't lookin' he goes and catches a frog and drops it in her clam chowder. An' when she goes to eat the chowder the frog jumps out of it an' right into her mouth. Talk about laugh! Mrs. Twelve was tellin' me she laughed so she nearly passed out. He sure can pull some funny ones. An' they got that big Grace Darling feature, "A Mother's Tears." She's sweet. But I don't like her clothes. There's no style to them. Mrs. Nine was tellin' me she read in *Pictureland* that she ain't livin' with her husband. He's her second, too. I don't know whether they're divorced or just separated. You wouldn't think it to see her on the screen. She looks so sweet and innocent. Maybe it ain't true. You can't believe all you read. They say some Pittsburgh millionaire is crazy about her and that's why she ain't livin' with her husband. Mrs. Seven was tellin' me her brother-in-law has a friend that used to go to school with Grace Darling. He says her name ain't Grace Darling at all. Her right name is Elizabeth Dugan, he says, an' all them stories about her gettin' five thousand a week is the bunk, he says. She's sweet, though. Mrs. Eight was tellin' me that "A Mother's Tears" is the best picture she ever made. "Don't miss it, Mrs. Zero," she says. "It's sweet," she says. "Just sweet and wholesome. Cry!" she says, "I nearly cried my eyes out." There's one part in it where this big bum of an Englishman—he's a married man, too—an' she's this little simple country girl. An' she nearly falls for him, too. But she's sittin' out in the garden one day, and she looks up and there's her mother lookin' at her, right out of the clouds. So that night she locks the door of her room. An' sure enough, when everybody's in bed, along comes this big bum of an Englishman an' when she won't let him in what does he do but go an' kick open the door. "Don't miss it, Mrs. Zero," Mrs. Eight was tellin' me. It's at the Peter Stuyvesant Wednesday night, so don't be tellin' me you want to go to the Rosebud. The Eights seen it downtown at the Strand. They go downtown all the time. Just like us—nit! I guess by the time it gets to the Peter Stuyvesant all that part about kickin' in the door will be cut out. Just like they cut out that big cabaret scene in "The Price of Virtue." They sure are pullin' some rough stuff in the pictures nowadays. "It's no place for a young girl," I was tellin' Mrs. Eleven, only the other day. An' by the time they get uptown half of it is cut out. But you wouldn't go downtown—not if wild horses was to drag you. You can wait till they come uptown! Well, I don't want to wait, see? I want to see 'em when everybody else is seein' them an' not a month later. Now don't go tellin' me you ain't got the price. You could dig up the price all right, all right, if you wanted to. I notice you always got the price to go to the ball game. But when it comes to me havin' a good time then it's always: "I ain't got the price, I gotta start savin'." A fat lot you'll ever save! I got all I can do now makin' both ends meet an' you talkin' about savin'. (*She seats herself on a chair and begins removing her shoes and stockings.*) An' don't go pullin' that stuff about bein' tired. "I been workin' hard all day. Twice a day in the subway's enough for me." Tired! Where do you get that tired stuff, anyhow? What about me? Where do I come in? Scrubbin' floors an' cookin' your meals an' washin' your dirty clothes. An' you sittin' on a chair all day, just addin' figgers an' waitin' for five-thirty. There's no five-thirty for me. I don't wait for no whistle. I don't get no vacations neither. And what's more I don't get no pay envelope every Saturday night neither. I'd like to know where you'd be without me. An' what have I got to show for it?—slavin' my life away to give you a home. What's in it for me, I'd like to know? But it's my own fault, I guess. I was a fool for marryin' you. If I'd 'a' had any sense, I'd 'a' known what you were from the start. I wish I had it to do over again, I hope to tell you. You was goin' to do wonders, you was! You wasn't goin' to be a bookkeeper long—oh, no, not you. Wait till you got started—you was goin' to show 'em. There wasn't no job in the store that was too big for you. Well, I've been waitin'—waitin' for you to get started—see? It's been a good long wait, too. Twenty-five years! An' I ain't seen nothin' happen. Twenty-five years in the same job. Twenty-five years tomorrow! You're proud of it, ain't you? Twenty-five years in the same job an' never missed a day! That's somethin' to be proud of, ain't it? Sittin' for twenty-five years on the same chair, addin' up figures. What about bein' store-manager? I guess you forgot about that, didn't you? An' me at home here lookin' at the same four walls an' workin' my fingers to the bone to make both ends meet. Seven years since you got a raise! An' if you don't get one tomorrow, I'll bet a nickel you won't have the guts to go an' ask for one. I didn't pick much when I picked you, I'll tell the world. You ain't much to be proud of. (*She rises, goes to the window, and raises the shade. A few lighted windows are visible on the other side of the closed court. Looking out for a moment.*) She ain't walkin' around tonight, you can bet your sweet life on that. An' she won't be walkin' around any more nights, neither. Not in this house, anyhow. (*She turns away from the window.*) The dirty bum! The idea of her comin' to live in a house with respectable people. They should 'a' gave her six years, not six months. If I was the judge I'd of gave her life. A bum like that. (*She approaches the bed and stands there a moment.*) I guess you're sorry she's gone. I guess you'd like to sit home every night an' watch her goin's-on. You're somethin' to be proud of, you are! (*She stands on the bed and turns out the light. . . . A thin stream of moonlight filters in from the court. The two figures are dimly visible.* MRS. ZERO *gets into bed.*)

You'd better not start nothin' with women, if you know what's good for you. I've put up with a lot, but I won't put up with that. I've been slavin' away for twenty-five years, makin' a home for you an' nothin' to show for it. If you was any kind of a man you'd have a decent job by now an' I'd be gettin' some comfort out of life—instead of bein' just a slave, washin' pots an' standin' over the hot stove. I've stood it for twenty-five years an' I guess I'll have to stand it twenty-five more. But don't you go startin' nothin' with women—— (*She goes on talking as the curtain falls.*)

SCENE II

SCENE: *An office in a department store. Wood and glass partitions. In the middle of the room, two tall desks back to back. At one desk on a high stool is* ZERO. *Opposite him at the other desk, also on a high stool, is* DAISY DIANA DOROTHEA DEVORE, *a plain, middle-aged woman. Both wear green eye shades and paper sleeve protectors. A pendent electric lamp throws light upon both desks.* DAISY *reads aloud figures from a pile of slips which lie before her. As she reads the figures,* ZERO *enters them upon a large square sheet of ruled paper which lies before him.*

DAISY

(*Reading aloud*). Three ninety-eight. Forty-two cents. A dollar fifty. A dollar fifty. A dollar twenty-five. Two dollars. Thirty-nine cents. Twenty-seven fifty.

ZERO

(*Petulantly*). Speed it up a little, cancha?

DAISY

What's the rush? Tomorrer's another day.

ZERO

Aw, you make me sick.

DAISY

An' you make me sicker.

ZERO

Go on. Go on. We're losin' time.

DAISY

Then quit bein' so bossy. (*She reads.*) Three dollars. Two sixty-nine. Eighty-one fifty. Forty dollars. Eight seventy-five. Who do you think you are, anyhow?

ZERO

Never mind who I think I am. You tend to your work.

DAISY

Aw, don't be givin' me so many orders. Sixty cents. Twenty-four cents. Seventy-five cents. A dollar fifty. Two fifty. One fifty. One fifty. Two fifty. I don't have to take it from you and what's more I won't.

ZERO

Aw, quit talkin'.

DAISY

I'll talk all I want. Three dollars. Fifty cents. Fifty cents. Seven dollars. Fifty cents. Two fifty. Three fifty. Fifty cents. One fifty. Fifty cents.
(*She goes on, bending over the slips and transferring them from one pile to another.* ZERO *bends over his desk, busily entering the figures.*)

ZERO

(*Without looking up*). You make me sick. Always shootin' off your face about somethin'. Talk, talk, talk. Just like all the other women. Women make me sick.

DAISY

(*Busily fingering the slips*). Who do you think you are, anyhow? Bossin' me around. I don't have to take it from you, and what's more I won't.
(*They both attend closely to their work, neither looking up.*)

ZERO

Women make me sick. They're all alike. The judge gave her six months. I wonder what they do in the workhouse. Peel potatoes. I'll bet she's sore at me. Maybe she'll try to kill me when she gets out. I better be careful. Hello. Girl Slays Betrayer. Jealous Wife Slays Rival. You can't tell what a woman's liable to do. I better be careful.

DAISY

I'm gettin' sick of it. Always pickin' on me about somethin'. Never a decent word out of you. Not even the time o' day.

ZERO

I guess she wouldn't have the nerve at that. Maybe she don't even know it's me. They didn't even put my name in the paper, the big bums. Maybe she's been in the workhouse before. A bum like that. She didn't have nothin' on that one time—nothin' but a shirt. (*He glances up quickly, then bends over again.*) You make me sick. I'm sick of lookin' at your face.

DAISY

Gee, ain't that whistle ever goin' to blow? You didn't used to be like that. Not even good mornin' or good evenin'. I ain't done nothin' to you. It's the young girls. Goin' around without corsets.

ZERO

Your face is gettin' all yeller. Why don't you put some paint on it? She was puttin' on paint that time. On her cheeks and on her lips. And that blue stuff on her eyes. Just sittin' there in a shimmy puttin' on the paint. An' walkin' around the room with her legs all bare.

DAISY

I wish I was dead.

ZERO

I was a goddam fool to let the wife get on to me. She oughta get six months at that. The dirty bum. Livin' in a house with respectable people. She'd be livin' there yet, if the wife hadn't o' got on to me. Damn her!

DAISY

I wish I was dead.

ZERO

Maybe another one'll move in. Gee, that would be great. But the wife's got her eye on me now.

DAISY

I'm scared to do it, though.

ZERO

You oughta move into that room. It's cheaper than where you're livin' now. I better tell you about it. I don't mean to be always pickin' on you.

DAISY

Gas. The smell of it makes me sick.
(ZERO *looks up and clears his throat.*)
(*Looking up, startled.*) Whadja say?

ZERO

I didn't say nothin'.

DAISY

I thought you did.

ZERO

You thought wrong.
(*They bend over their work again.*)

DAISY

A dollar sixty. A dollar fifty. Two ninety. One sixty-two.

ZERO

Why the hell should I tell you? Fat chance of you forgettin' to pull down the shade!

DAISY

If I asked for carbolic they might get on to me.

ZERO

Your hair's gettin' gray. You don't wear them shirt waists any more with the low collars. When you'd bend down to pick somethin' up——

DAISY

I wish I knew what to ask for. Girl Takes Mercury After All-Night Party. Woman In Ten-Story Death Leap.

ZERO

I wonder where'll she go when she gets out. Gee, I'd like to make a date with her. Why didn't I go over there the night my wife went to Brooklyn? She never woulda found out.

DAISY

I seen Pauline Frederick do it once. Where could I get a pistol though?

ZERO

I guess I didn't have the nerve.

DAISY

I'll bet you'd be sorry then that you been so mean to me. How do I know, though? Maybe you wouldn't.

ZERO

Nerve! I got as much nerve as anybody. I'm on the level, that's all. I'm a married man and I'm on the level.

DAISY

Anyhow, why ain't I got a right to live? I'm as good as anybody else. I'm too refined, I guess. That's the whole trouble.

ZERO

The time the wife had pneumonia I thought she was goin' to pass out. But she didn't. The doctor's bill was eighty-seven dollars. (*Looking up.*) Hey, wait a minute! Didn't you say eighty-seven dollars?

DAISY

(*Looking up*). What?

ZERO

Was the last you said eighty-seven dollars?

DAISY

(*Consulting the slip*). Forty-two fifty.

ZERO

Well, I made a mistake. Wait a minute. (*He busies himself with an eraser.*) All right. Shoot.

DAISY

Six dollars. Three fifteen. Two twenty-five. Sixty-five cents. A dollar twenty. You talk to me as if I was dirt.

ZERO

I wonder if I could kill the wife without anybody findin' out. In bed some night. With a pillow.

DAISY

I used to think you was stuck on me.

ZERO

I'd get found out, though. They always have ways.

DAISY

We used to be so nice and friendly together when I first came here. You used to talk to me then.

ZERO

Maybe she'll die soon. I noticed she was coughin' this mornin'.

DAISY

You used to tell me all kinds o' things. You were goin' to show them all. Just the same, you're still sittin' here.

ZERO

Then I could do what I damn please. Oh, boy!

DAISY

Maybe it ain't all your fault neither. Maybe if you'd had the right kind of wife—somebody with a lot of common-sense, somebody refined—me!

ZERO

At that, I guess I'd get tired of bummin' around. A feller wants some place to hang his hat.

DAISY

I wish she would die.

ZERO

And when you start goin' with women you're liable to get into trouble. And lose your job maybe.

DAISY

Maybe you'd marry me.

ZERO

Gee, I wish I'd gone over there that night.

DAISY

Then I could quit workin'.

ZERO

Lots o' women would be glad to get me.

DAISY

You could look a long time before you'd find a sensible, refined girl like me.

ZERO

Yes, sir, they could look a long time before they'd find a steady meal-ticket like me.

DAISY

I guess I'd be too old to have any kids. They say it ain't safe after thirty-five.

ZERO

Maybe I'd marry you. You might be all right, at that.

DAISY

I wonder—if you don't want kids—whether—if there's any way——

ZERO

(*Looking up*). Hey! Hey! Can't you slow up? What do you think I am—a machine?

DAISY

(*Looking up*). Say, what do you want, anyhow? First it's too slow an' then it's too fast. I guess you don't know what you want.

ZERO

Well, never mind about that. Just you slow up.

DAISY

I'm gettin' sick o' this. I'm goin' to ask to be transferred.

ZERO

Go ahead. You can't make me mad.

DAISY

Aw, keep quiet. (*She reads.*) Two forty-five. A dollar twenty. A dollar fifty. Ninety cents. Sixty-three cents.

ZERO

Marry you! I guess not! You'd be as bad as the one I got.

DAISY

You wouldn't care if I did ask. I got a good mind to ask.

ZERO

I was a fool to get married.

DAISY

Then I'd never see you at all.

ZERO

What chance has a guy got with a woman tied around his neck?

DAISY

That time at the store picnic—the year your wife couldn't come—you were nice to me then.

ZERO

Twenty-five years holdin' down the same job!

DAISY

We were together all day—just sittin' around under the trees.

ZERO

I wonder if the boss remembers about it bein' twenty-five years.

DAISY

And comin' home that night—you sat next to me in the big delivery wagon.

ZERO

I got a hunch there's a big raise comin' to me.

DAISY

I wonder what it feels like to be really kissed. Men—dirty pigs! They want the bold ones.

ZERO

If he don't come across I'm goin' right up to the front office and tell him where he gets off.

DAISY

I wish I was dead.

ZERO

"Boss," I'll say, "I want to have a talk with you." "Sure," he'll say, "sit down. Have a Corona Corona." "No," I'll say, "I don't smoke." "How's that?" he'll say. "Well, boss," I'll say, "it's this way. Every time I feel like smokin' I just take a nickel and put it in the old sock. A penny saved is a penny earned, that's the way I look at it." "Damn sensible," he'll say. "You got a wise head on you, Zero."

DAISY

I can't stand the smell of gas. It makes me sick. You coulda kissed me if you wanted to.

ZERO

"Boss," I'll say, "I ain't quite satisfied. I been on the job twenty-five years now and if I'm gonna stay I gotta see a future ahead of me." "Zero," he'll say, "I'm glad you came in. I've had my eye on you, Zero! Nothin' gets by me." "Oh, I know that, boss," I'll say. That'll hand him a good laugh, that will. "You're a valuable man, Zero," he'll say, "and I want you right up here with me in the front office. You're done addin' figgers. Monday mornin' you move up here."

DAISY

Them kisses in the movies—them long ones—right on the mouth——

ZERO

I'll keep a-goin' right on up after that. I'll show some of them birds where they get off.

DAISY

That one the other night—"The Devil's Alibi"—he put his arms around her—and her head fell back and her eyes closed—like she was in a daze.

ZERO

Just give me about two years and I'll show them birds where they get off.

DAISY

I guess that's what it's like—a kinda daze—when I see them like that, I just seem to forget everything.

ZERO

Then me for a place in Jersey. And maybe a little Buick. No tin Lizzie for mine. Wait till I get started—I'll show 'em.

DAISY

I can see it now when I kinda half-close my eyes. The way her head fell back. And his mouth pressed right up against hers. Oh, Gawd! it must be grand!
(*There is a sudden shrill blast from a steam whistle.*)

DAISY AND ZERO

(*Together*). The whistle!
(*With great agility they get off their stools, remove their eye shades and sleeve protectors and put them on the desks. Then each produces from behind the desk a hat—* ZERO, *a dusty derby,* DAISY, *a frowsy straw. . . .* DAISY *puts on her hat and turns towards* ZERO *as though she were about to speak to him. But he is busy cleaning his pen and pays no attention to her. She sighs and goes towards the door at the left.*)

ZERO

(*Looking up*). G'night, Miss Devore.
(*But she does not hear him and exits.* ZERO *takes up his hat and goes left. The door at the right opens and the* BOSS *enters—middle-aged, stoutish, bald, well dressed.*)

THE BOSS

(*Calling*). Oh—er—Mister—er——
(ZERO *turns in surprise, sees who it is and trembles nervously.*)

ZERO

(*Obsequiously*). Yes, sir. Do you want me, sir?

BOSS

Yes. Just come here a moment, will you?

ZERO

Yes, sir. Right away, sir. (*He fumbles his hat, picks it up, stumbles, recovers himself, and approaches the* BOSS, *every fiber quivering.*)

BOSS

Mister—er—er——

ZERO

Zero.

BOSS

Yes, Mr. Zero. I wanted to have a little talk with you.

ZERO

(*With a nervous grin*). Yes sir, I been kinda expectin' it.

BOSS

(*Staring at him*). Oh, have you?

ZERO

Yes, sir.

BOSS

How long have you been with us, Mister —er—Mister——

ZERO

Zero.

BOSS

Yes, Mister Zero.

ZERO

Twenty-five years today.

BOSS

Twenty-five years! That's a long time.

ZERO

Never missed a day.

BOSS

And you've been doing the same work all the time?

ZERO

Yes, sir. Right here at this desk.

BOSS

Then, in that case, a change probably won't be unwelcome to you.

ZERO

No, sir, it won't. And that's the truth.

BOSS

We've been planning a change in this department for some time.

ZERO

I kinda thought you had your eye on me.

BOSS

You were right. The fact is that my efficiency experts have recommended the installation of adding machines.

ZERO

(*Staring at him*). Addin' machines?

BOSS

Yes, you've probably seen them. A mechanical device that adds automatically.

ZERO

Sure. I've seen them. Keys—and a handle that you pull. (*He goes through the motions in the air.*)

BOSS

That's it. They do the work in half the time and a high-school girl can operate them. Now, of course, I'm sorry to lose an old and faithful employee——

ZERO

Excuse me, but would you mind sayin' that again?

BOSS

I say I'm sorry to lose an employee who's been with me for so many years——
(*Soft music is heard—the sound of the mechanical player of a distant merry-go-round. The part of the floor upon which the desk and stools are standing begins to revolve very slowly.*)
But, of course, in an organization like this, efficiency must be the first consideration—
(*The music becomes gradually louder and the revolutions more rapid.*)
You will draw your salary for the full month. And I'll direct my secretary to give you a letter of recommendation——

ZERO

Wait a minute, boss. Let me get this right. You mean I'm canned?

BOSS

(*Barely making himself heard above the increasing volume of sound*). I'm sorry—no other alternative—greatly regret—old employee — efficiency — economy — business—*business*—BUSINESS——
(*His voice is drowned by the music. The platform is revolving rapidly now.* ZERO *and the* BOSS *face each other. They are entirely motionless save for the* BOSS*'s jaws, which open and close incessantly. But the words are inaudible. The music swells and swells. To it is added every off-stage effect of the theatre: the wind, the waves, the galloping horses, the locomotive whistle, the sleigh bells, the automobile siren, the glass-crash. New Year's Eve, Election Night, Armistice Day, and the Mardi-Gras. The noise is deafening, maddening, unendurable. Suddenly it culminates in a terrific peal of thunder. For an instant there is a flash of red and then everything is plunged into blackness.*)

Curtain

SCENE III

SCENE: *The* ZERO *dining room. Entrance door at right. Doors to kitchen and bedroom at left. The walls, as in the first scene, are paper with foolscap sheets covered with columns of figures. In the middle of the room, upstage, a table set for two. Along each side wall seven chairs are ranged in symmetrical rows.*

At the rise of the curtain MRS. ZERO *is seen seated at the table looking alternately at the entrance door and a clock on the wall. She wears a bungalow apron over her best dress.*

After a few moments, the entrance door opens and ZERO *enters. He hangs his hat on a rack behind the door and coming over to the table seats himself at the vacant place. His movements throughout are quiet and abstracted.*

MRS. ZERO

(*Breaking the silence*). Well, it was nice of you to come home. You're only an hour late and that ain't very much. The supper don't get very cold in an hour. An' of course the part about our havin' a lot of company tonight don't matter.

(*They begin to eat.*)

Ain't you even got sense enough to come home on time? Didn't I tell you we're goin' to have a lot o' company tonight? Didn't you know the Ones are comin'? An' the Twos? An' the Threes? An' the Fours? An' the Fives? And the Sixes? Didn't I tell you to be home on time? I might as well talk to a stone wall.

(*They eat for a few moments in silence.*)

I guess you musta had some important business to attend to. Like watchin' the score-board. Or was two kids havin' a fight an' you was the referee? You sure do have a lot of business to attend to. It's a wonder you have time to come home at all. You gotta tough life, you have. Walk in, hang up your hat, an' put on the nose-bag. An' me in the hot kitchen all day, cookin' your supper an' waitin' for you to get good an' ready to come home!

(*Again they eat in silence.*)

Maybe the boss kept you late tonight. Tellin' you what a big noise you are and how the store couldn't 'a' got along if you hadn't been pushin' a pen for twenty-five years. Where's the gold medal he pinned on you? Did some blind old lady take it away from you or did you leave it on the seat of the boss's limousine when he brought you home?

(*Again a few moment of silence.*)

I'll bet he gave you a big raise, didn't he? Promoted you from the third floor to the fourth, maybe. Raise? A fat chance you got o' gettin' a raise. All they gotta do is put an ad in the paper. There's ten thousand like you layin' around the streets. You'll be holdin' down the same job at the end of another twenty-five years—if you ain't forgot how to add by that time.

(*A noise is heard off-stage, a sharp clicking such as is made by the operation of the keys and levers of an adding machine.* ZERO *raises his head for a moment, but lowers it almost instantly.*)

There's the door-bell. The company's here already. And we ain't hardly finished supper.

(*She rises.*)

But I'm goin' to clear off the table whether you're finished or not. If you want your supper, you got a right to be home on time. Not standin' around lookin' at score-boards.

(*As she piles up the dishes,* ZERO *rises and goes towards the entrance door.*)

Wait a minute! Don't open the door yet. Do you want the company to see all the mess? An' go an' put on a clean collar. You got red ink all over it.

(ZERO *goes towards bedroom door.*)

I should think after pushin' a pen for twenty-five years, you'd learn how to do it without gettin' ink on your collar.

(ZERO *exits to bedroom.* MRS. ZERO *takes dishes to kitchen, talking as she goes.*)

I guess I can stay up all night now washin' dishes. You should worry! That's what a man's got a wife for, ain't it? Don't he buy her her clothes an' let her eat with him at the same table? An' all she's gotta do is cook the meals an' do the washin' an' scrub the floor, an' wash the dishes, when the company goes. But, believe me, you're goin' to sling a mean dish-towel when the company goes tonight!

(*While she is talking* ZERO *enters from bedroom. He wears a clean collar and is cramming the soiled one furtively into his pocket.* MRS. ZERO *enters from kitchen. She has removed her apron and carries a table cover which she spreads hastily over the table. The clicking noise is heard again.*) There's the bell again. Open the door, cancha?

(ZERO *goes to the entrance door and opens it. Six men and six women file into the room in a double column. The men are all shapes and sizes, but their dress is identical with that of* ZERO *in every detail. Each, however, wears a wig of a different color. The women are all dressed alike, too, except that the dress of each is of a different color.*)

(*Taking the first woman's hand.*) How de do, Mrs. One.

MRS. ONE

How de do, Mrs. Zero.

(MRS. ZERO *repeats this formula with each woman in turn.* ZERO *does the same with the men except that he is silent throughout. The files now separate, each man taking a chair from the right wall and each woman one from the left wall. Each sex forms a circle with the chairs very close together. The men—all except* ZERO—*smoke cigars. The women munch chocolates.*)

SIX

Some rain we're havin'.

FIVE

Never saw the like of it.

FOUR

Worst in fourteen years, paper says.

THREE

Y' can't always go by the papers.

TWO

No, that's right, too.

ONE

We're liable to forget from year to year.

SIX

Yeh, come t' think, last year was pretty bad, too.

FIVE

An' how about two years ago?

FOUR

Still this year's pretty bad.

THREE

Yeh, no gettin' away from that.

TWO

Might be a whole lot worse.

ONE

Yeh, it's all the way you look at it. Some rain, though.

MRS. SIX

I like them little organdie dresses.

MRS. FIVE

Yeh, with a little lace trimmin' on the sleeves.

MRS. FOUR

Well, I like 'em plain myself.

MRS. THREE

Yeh, what I always say is the plainer the more refined.

MRS. TWO

Well, I don't think a little lace does any harm.

MRS. ONE

No, it kinda dresses it up.

MRS. ZERO

Well, I always say it's all a matter of taste.

MRS. SIX

I saw you at the Rosebud Movie Thursday night, Mr. One.

ONE

Pretty punk show, I'll say.

TWO

They're gettin' worse all the time.

MRS. SIX

But who was the charming lady, Mr. One?

ONE

Now don't you go makin' trouble for me. That was my sister.

MRS. FIVE

Oho! That's what they all say.

MRS. FOUR

Never mind! I'll bet Mrs. One knows what's what, all right.

MRS. ONE

Oh, well, he can do what he likes—'slong as he behaves himself.

THREE

You're in luck at that, One. Fat chance I got of gettin' away from the frau even with my sister.

MRS. THREE

You oughta be glad you got a good wife to look after you.

THE OTHER WOMEN

(*In unison*). That's right, Mrs. Three.

FIVE

I guess I know who wears the pants in your house, Three.

MRS. ZERO

Never mind. I saw them holdin' hands at the movie the other night.

THREE

She musta been tryin' to get some money away from me.

MRS. THREE

Swell chance anybody'd have of gettin' any money away from you.
(*General laughter.*)

FOUR

They sure are a loving couple.

MRS. TWO

Well, I think we oughta change the subject.

MRS. ONE

Yes, let's change the subject.

SIX

(*Sotto voce*). Did you hear the one about the travellin' salesman?

FIVE

It seems this guy was in a sleeper.

FOUR

Goin' from Albany to San Diego.

THREE

And in the next berth was an old maid.

TWO

With a wooden leg.

ONE

Well, along about midnight——
(*They all put their heads together and whisper.*)

MRS. SIX

(*Sotto voce*). Did you hear about the Sevens?

MRS. FIVE

They're gettin' a divorce.

MRS. FOUR

It's the second time for him.

MRS. THREE

They're two of a kind, if you ask me.

MRS. TWO

One's as bad as the other.

MRS. ONE

Worse.

MRS. ZERO

They say that she——
(*They all put their heads together and whisper.*)

SIX

I think this woman suffrage is the bunk.

FIVE

It sure is! Politics is a man's business.

FOUR

Woman's place is in the home.

THREE

That's it! Lookin' after the kids, 'stead of hangin' around the streets.

TWO

You hit the nail on the head that time.

ONE

The trouble is they don't know what they want.

MRS. SIX

Men sure get me tired.

MRS. FIVE

They sure are a lazy lot.

MRS. FOUR

And dirty.

MRS. THREE

Always grumblin' about somethin'.

MRS. TWO

When they're not lyin'!

MRS. ONE

Or messin' up the house.

MRS. ZERO

Well, believe me, I tell mine where he gets off.

SIX

Business conditions are sure bad.

FIVE

Never been worse.

FOUR

I don't know what we're comin' to.

THREE

I look for a big smash-up in about three months.

TWO

Wouldn't surprise me a bit.

ONE

We're sure headin' for trouble.

MRS. SIX

My aunt has gall-stones.

MRS. FIVE

My husband has bunions.

MRS. FOUR

My sister expects next month.

MRS. THREE

My cousin's husband has erysipelas.

MRS. TWO

My niece has St. Vitus's dance.

MRS. ONE

My boy has fits.

MRS. ZERO

I never felt better in my life. Knock wood!

SIX

Too damn much agitation, that's at the bottom of it.

FIVE

That's it! Too damn many strikes.

FOUR

Foreign agitators, that's what it is.

THREE

They ought to be run outa the country.

TWO

What the hell do they want, anyhow?

ONE

They don't know what they want, if you ask me.

SIX

America for the Americans is what I say!

ALL

(*In unison*). That's it! Damn foreigners! Damn dagoes! Damn Catholics! Damn sheenies! Damn niggers! Jail 'em! shoot 'em! hang 'em! lynch 'em! burn 'em!
(*They all rise.*)
(*Sing in unison.*)

"My country 'tis of thee,
Sweet land of liberty!"

MRS. FOUR

Why so pensive, Mr. Zero?

ZERO

(*Speaking for the first time*). I'm thinkin'.

MRS. FOUR

Well, be careful not to sprain your mind.
(*Laughter.*)

MRS. ZERO

Look at the poor men all by themselves. We ain't very sociable.

ONE

Looks like we're neglectin' the ladies.
(*The women cross the room and join the men, all chattering loudly. The door-bell rings.*)

MRS. FOUR

Sh! The door-bell!
(*The volume of sound slowly diminishes. Again the door-bell.*)

ZERO

(*Quietly*). I'll go. It's for me.
(*They watch curiously as* ZERO *goes to the door and opens it, admitting a policeman. There is a murmur of surprise and excitement.*)

POLICEMAN

I'm lookin' for Mr. Zero.
(*They all point to* ZERO.)

ZERO

I've been expectin' you.

POLICEMAN

Come along!

ZERO

Just a minute. (*He puts his hand in his pocket.*)

POLICEMAN

What's he tryin' to pull? (*He draws a revolver.*) I got you covered.

ZERO

Sure, that's all right. I just want to give you somethin'. (*He takes the collar from his pocket and gives it to the policeman.*)

POLICEMAN

(*Suspiciously*). What's that?

ZERO

The collar I wore.

POLICEMAN

What do I want it for?

ZERO

It's got blood-stains on it.

POLICEMAN

(*Pocketing it*). All right, come along!

ZERO

(*Turning to* MRS. ZERO). I gotta go with him. You'll have to dry the dishes yourself.

MRS. ZERO

(*Rushing forward*). What are they takin' you for?

ZERO

(*Calmly*). I killed the boss this afternoon.

(*Quick Curtain as the* POLICEMAN *takes him off.*)

SCENE IV

SCENE: *A court of justice. Three bare white walls without door or windows except for a single door in the right wall. At the right is a jury-box in which are seated* MESSRS. ONE, TWO, THREE, FOUR, FIVE, *and* SIX, *and their respective wives. On either side of the jury-box stands a uniformed* OFFICER. *Opposite the jury-box is a long, bare oak table piled high with law books. Behind the books* ZERO *is seated, his face buried in his hands. There is no other furniture in the room. A moment after the rise of the curtain, one of the officers rises and, going around the table, taps* ZERO *on the shoulder.* ZERO *rises and accompanies the officer. The* OFFICER *escorts him to the great empty space in the middle of the court-room, facing the jury. He motions to* ZERO *to stop, then points to the jury and resumes his place beside the jury-box.* ZERO *stands there looking at the jury, bewildered and half afraid. The* JURORS *give no sign of having seen him. Throughout they sit with folded arms, staring stolidly before them.*

ZERO

(*Beginning to speak; haltingly*). Sure I killed him. I ain't sayin' I didn't, am I? Sure I killed him. Them lawyers! They give me a good stiff pain, that's what they give me. Half the time I don't know what the hell they're talkin' about. Objection sustained. Objection over-ruled. What's the big idea, anyhow? You ain't heard me do any objectin', have you? Sure not! What's the idea of objectin'? You got a right to know. What I say is if one bird kills another bird, why you got a right to call him for it. That's what I say. I know all about that. I been on the jury, too. Them lawyers! Don't let 'em fill you full of bunk. All that bull about it bein' red ink on the bill-file. Red ink nothin'! It was blood, see? I want you to get that right. I killed him, see? Right through the heart with the bill-file, see? I want you to get that right—all of you. One, two, three, four, five six, seven, eight, nine, ten, eleven, twelve. Twelve of you. Six and six. That makes twelve. I figgered it up often enough. Six and six makes twelve. And five is seventeen. And eight is twenty-five. And three is twenty-eight. Eight and carry two. Aw, cut it out! Them damn figgers! I can't forget 'em. Twenty-five years, see? Eight hours a day, exceptin' Sundays. And July and August half-day Saturday. One week's vacation with pay. And another week without pay if you want it. Who the hell wants it? Layin' around the house listenin' to the wife tellin' you where you get off. Nix! An' legal holidays. I nearly forgot them. New Year's, Washington's Birthday, Decoration Day, Fourth o' July, Labor Day, Election Day, Thanksgivin', Christmas. Good Friday if you want it. An' if you're a Jew, Young Kipper an' the other one—I forget what they call it. The dirty sheenies—always gettin' two to the other bird's one. An' when a holiday comes on Sunday, you get Monday off. So that's fair enough. But when the Fourth o' July comes on Saturday, why you're out of luck on account of Saturday bein' a half-day anyhow. Get me? Twenty-five years—I'll tell you somethin' funny. Decoration Day an' the Fourth o' July are always on the same day o' the week. Twenty-five years. Never missed a day, and never more'n five minutes late. Look at my time card if you don't believe me. Eight twenty-seven, eight thirty, eight twenty-nine, eight twenty-seven, eight thirty-two. Eight an' thirty-two's forty an'—Goddam them figgers! I can't forget 'em. They're funny things, them figgers. They look like people sometimes. The eights, see? Two dots for the eyes and a dot for the nose. An' a line. That's the mouth, see? An' there's others remind you of other things—but I can't talk about them, on account of there bein' ladies here.

Sure I killed him. Why didn't he shut up? If he'd only shut up! Instead o' talkin' an' talkin' about how sorry he was an' what a good guy I was an' this an' that. I felt like sayin' to him: "For Christ's sake, shut up!" But I didn't have the nerve, see? I didn't have the nerve to say that to the boss. An' he went on talkin', sayin' how sorry he was, see? He was standin' right close to me. An' his coat only had two buttons on it. Two an' two makes four an'—aw, can it! An' there was the bill-file on the desk. Right where I could touch it. It ain't right to kill a guy. I know that. When I read all about him in the paper an' about his three kids I felt like a cheap skate, I tell you. They had the kids' pictures in the paper, right next to mine. An' his wife, too. Gee, it must be swell to have a wife like that. Some guys sure is lucky. An' he left fifty thousand dollars just for a rest-room for the girls in the store. He was a good guy, at that. Fifty thousand. That's more'n twice as much as I'd have if I saved every nickel I ever made. Let's see. Twenty-five an' twenty-five an' twenty-five an'—aw, cut it out! An' the ads had a big, black border around 'em; an' all it said was that the store would be closed for three days on account of the boss bein' dead. That nearly handed me a laugh, that did. All them floor-walkers an' buyers an' high-muck-a-mucks havin' me to thank for gettin' three days off. I hadn't oughta killed him. I ain't sayin' nothin' about that. But I thought he was goin' to give me a raise, see? On account of bein' there twenty-five years. He never talked to me before, see? Except one mornin' we happened to come in the store together and I held the door open for him and he said "Thanks." Just like that, see? "Thanks!" That was the only time he ever talked to me. An' when I see him comin' up to my desk, I didn't know where I got off. A big guy like that comin' up to my desk. I felt like I was chokin' like and all of a sudden I got a kind o' bad taste in my mouth like when you get up in the mornin'. I didn't have no right to kill him. The district attorney is right about that. He read the law to you right out o' the book. Killin' a bird—that's wrong. But there was that girl, see? Six months they gave her. It was a dirty trick tellin' the cops on her like that. I shouldn't 'a' done that. But what was I gonna do? The wife wouldn't let up on me. I hadda do it. She used to walk around the room, just in her undershirt, see? Nothin' else on. Just her undershirt. An' they gave her six months. That's the last I'll ever see of her. Them birds—how do they get away with it? Just grabbin' women, the way you see 'em do in the pictures. I've seen lots I'd like to grab like that, but I ain't got the nerve—in the subway an' on the street an' in the store buyin' things. Pretty soft for them shoe-salesmen, I'll say, lookin' at women's legs all day. Them lawyers! They give me a pain, I tell you—a pain! Sayin' the same thing over an' over again. I never said I didn't kill him. But that ain't the same as bein' a regular murderer. What good did it do me to kill him? I didn't make nothin' out of it. Answer yes or no! Yes or no, me elbow! There's some things you can't answer yes or no. Give me the once-over, you guys. Do I look like a murderer? Do I? I never did no harm to nobody. Ask the wife. She'll tell you. Ask anybody. I never got into trouble. You wouldn't count that one time at the Polo Grounds. That was just fun like. Everybody was yellin', "Kill the umpire! Kill the umpire!" An' before I knew what I was doin' I fired the pop bottle. It was on account of everybody yellin' like that. Just in fun like, see? The yeller dog! Callin' that one a strike—a mile away from the plate. Anyhow, the bottle didn't hit him. An' when I seen the cop comin' up the aisle, I beat it. That didn't hurt nobody. It was just in fun like, see? An' that time in the subway. I was readin' about a lynchin', see? Down in Georgia. They took the nigger an' they tied him to a tree. An' they poured kerosene on him and lit a big fire under him. The dirty nigger! Boy, I'd of liked to been there, with a gat in each hand, pumpin' him full of lead. I was readin' about it in the subway, see? Right at Times Square where the big crowd gets on. An' all of a sudden this big nigger steps right on my foot. It was lucky for him I didn't have a gun on me. I'd of killed him sure, I guess. I guess he couldn't help it all right on account of the crowd, but a nigger's got no right to step on a white man's foot. I told him where he got off all right. The dirty nigger. But that didn't hurt nobody, either. I'm a pretty steady guy, you gotta admit that. Twenty-five years in one job an' I never missed a day. Fifty-two weeks in a year. Fifty-two an' fifty-two an' fifty-two an'— They didn't have t' look for me, did they? I didn't try to run away, did I? Where was I goin' to run to! I wasn't thinkin' about it at all, see? I'll tell you what I was thinkin' about—how I was goin' to break it to the wife about bein' canned. He canned me after twenty-five years, see? Did the lawyers tell you about that? I forget. All that talk gives me a headache. Objection sustained. Objection overruled. Answer yes or no. It gives me a headache. And I can't get the figgers outta my head. But that's what I was thinkin' about—how I was goin' t' break it to the wife about bein' canned. An' what Miss Devore would think when she heard about me killin' him. I bet she never thought I had the nerve to do it. I'd of married her if the wife had passed out. I'd be holdin' down my job yet, if he hadn't o' canned me. But he kept talkin' an' talkin'. An' there was the bill-file right where I could reach it. Do you get me? I'm just a regular guy like anybody else. Like you birds, now.

(*For the first time the* JURORS *relax, looking indignantly at each other and whispering.*)

Suppose you was me, now. Maybe you'd 'a' done the same thing. That's the way you oughta look at it, see? Suppose you was me——

THE JURORS

(*Rising as one and shouting in unison*). *GUILTY!*

(ZERO *falls back, stunned for a moment by their vociferousness. The* JURORS *right-face in their places and file quickly out of the jury-box and towards the door in a double column.*)

ZERO

(*Recovering speech as the* JURORS *pass out at the door*). Wait a minute. Jest a minute. You don't get me right. Jest give me a chance an' I'll tell you how it was. I'm all mixed up, see? On account of them lawyers. And the figgers in my head. But I'm goin' to tell you how it was. I was there twenty-five years, see? An' they gave her six months, see?

(*He goes on haranguing the empty jury-box as the curtain falls.*)

SCENE V

SCENE: *A grave-yard in full moonlight. It is a second-rate grave-yard—no elaborate tombstones or monuments—just simple headstones and here and there a cross. At the back is an iron fence with a gate in the middle. At first no one is visible, but there are occasional sounds throughout: the hooting of an owl, the whistle of a distant whippoorwill, the croaking of a bull-frog, and the yowling of a serenading cat. After a few moments two figures appear outside the gate—a man and a woman. She pushes the gate and it opens with a rusty creak. The couple enter. They are now fully visible in the moonlight—*JUDY O'GRADY *and a* YOUNG MAN.

JUDY

(*Advancing*). Come on, this is the place.

YOUNG MAN

(*Hanging back*). This! Why this here is a cemetery.

JUDY

Aw, quit yer kiddin'!

YOUNG MAN

You don't mean to say——

JUDY

What's the matter with this place?

YOUNG MAN

A cemetery!

JUDY

Sure. What of it?

YOUNG MAN

You must be crazy.

JUDY

This place is all right, I tell you. I been here lots o' times.

YOUNG MAN

Nix on this place for me!

JUDY

Ain't this place as good as another? Whaddya afraid of? They're all dead ones here! They don't bother you.
(*With sudden interest.*)
Oh, look, here's a new one.

YOUNG MAN

Come on out of here.

JUDY

Wait a minute. Let's see what it says.
(*She kneels on a grave in the foreground and putting her face close to headstone spells out the inscription.*)
Z-E-R-O. Z-e-r-o. Zero! Say, that's the guy——

YOUNG MAN

Zero? He's the guy killed his boss, ain't he?

JUDY

Yeh, that's him, all right. But what I'm thinkin' of is that I went to the hoosegow on account of him.

YOUNG MAN

What for?

JUDY

You know, same old stuff. Tenement House Law. (*Mincingly.*) Section blaa-blaa of the Penal Code. Third offence. Six months.

YOUNG MAN

And this bird——

JUDY

(*Contemptuously*). Hm? He was mamma's white-haired boy. We lived in the same house. Across the airshaft, see? I used to see him lookin' in my window. I guess his wife musta seen him, too. Anyhow, they went and turned the bulls on me. And now I'm out and he's in. (*Suddenly.*) Say —say—(*She bursts into a peal of laughter.*)

YOUNG MAN

(*Nervously*). What's so funny?

JUDY

(*Rocking with laughter*). Say, wouldn't it be funny—if—if— (*She explodes again.*) That would be a good joke on him, all right. He can't do nothin' about it now, can he?

YOUNG MAN

Come on out of here. I don't like this place.

JUDY

Aw, you're a bum sport. What do you want to spoil my joke for?
(*A cat yammers mellifluously.*)

YOUNG MAN

(*Half hysterically*). What's that?

JUDY

It's only the cats. They seem to like it here all right. But come on if you're afraid. (*They go towards the gate. As they go out.*) You nervous men sure are the limit. (*They go out through the gate. As they disappear* ZERO'*s grave opens suddenly and his head appears.*)

ZERO

(*Looking about*). That's funny! I thought I heard her talkin' and laughin'. But I don't see nobody. Anyhow, what would she be doin' here? I guess I must 'a' been dreamin'. But how could I be dreamin' when I ain't been asleep? (*He looks about again.*) Well, no use goin' back. I can't sleep, anyhow. I might as well walk around a little.
(*He rises out of the ground, very rigidly. He wears a full-dress suit of very antiquated cut and his hands are folded stiffly across his breast.*)
(*Walking woodenly.*) Gee! I'm stiff! (*He slowly walks a few steps, then stops.*) Gee,

it's lonesome here! (*He shivers and walks on aimlessly.*) I should 'a' stayed where I was. But I thought I heard her laughin'. (*A loud sneeze is heard.* ZERO *stands motionless, quaking with terror. The sneeze is repeated.*)
(*Hoarsely.*) What's that?

A MILD VOICE

It's all right. Nothing to be afraid of.
(*From behind a headstone* SHRDLU *appears. He is dressed in a shabby and ill-fitting cutaway. He wears silver-rimmed spectacles and is smoking a cigarette.*)

SHRDLU

I hope I didn't frighten you.

ZERO

(*Still badly shaken*). No-o. It's all right. You see, I wasn't expectin' to see anybody.

SHRDLU

You're a newcomer, aren't you?

ZERO

Yeh, this is my first night. I couldn't seem to get to sleep.

SHRDLU

I can't sleep either. Suppose we keep each other company, shall we?

ZERO

(*Eagerly*). Yeh, that would be great. I been feelin' awful lonesome.

SHRDLU

(*Nodding*). I know. Let's make ourselves comfortable.
(*He seats himself easily on a grave.* ZERO *tries to follow his example but he is stiff in every joint and groans with pain.*)

ZERO

I'm kinda stiff.

SHRDLU

You mustn't mind the stiffness. It wears off in a few days. (*He seats himself on the grave beside* ZERO *and produces a package of cigarettes.*) Will you have a Camel?

ZERO

No, I don't smoke.

SHRDLU

I find it helps keep the mosquitoes away. (*He lights a cigarette. Suddenly taking the cigarette out of his mouth*). Do you mind if I smoke, Mr.—Mr.——?

ZERO

No, go right ahead.

SHRDLU

(*Replacing the cigarette*). Thank you. I didn't catch your name.
(ZERO *does not reply.*)
(*Mildly.*) I say I didn't catch your name.

ZERO

I heard you the first time. (*Hesitantly.*) I'm scared if I tell you who I am and what I done, you'll be off me.

SHRDLU

(*Sadly*). No matter what your sins may be, they are as snow compared to mine.

ZERO

You got another guess comin'. (*He pauses dramatically.*) My name's Zero. I'm a murderer.

SHRDLU

(*Nodding calmly*). Oh, yes, I remember reading about you, Mr. Zero.

ZERO

(*A little piqued*). And you still think you're worse than me?

SHRDLU

(*Throwing away his cigarette*). Oh, a thousand times worse, Mr. Zero—a million times worse.

ZERO

What did you do?

SHRDLU

I, too, am a murderer.

ZERO

(*Looking at him in amazement*). Go on! You're kiddin' me!

SHRDLU

Every word I speak is the truth, Mr. Zero. I am the foulest, the most sinful of murderers! You only murdered your employer, Mr. Zero. But I—I murdered my mother. (*He covers his face with his hands and sobs.*)

ZERO

(*Horrified*). The hell yer say!

SHRDLU

(*Sobbing*). Yes, my mother!—my beloved mother!

ZERO

(*Suddenly*). Say, you don't mean to say you're Mr.——

SHRDLU

(*Nodding*). Yes. (*He wipes his eyes, still quivering with emotion.*)

ZERO

I remember readin' about you in the papers.

SHRDLU

Yes, my guilt has been proclaimed to all the world. But that would be a trifle if only I could wash the stain of sin from my soul.

ZERO

I never heard of a guy killin' his mother before. What did you do it for?

SHRDLU

Because I have a sinful heart—there is no other reason.

ZERO

Did she always treat you square and all like that?

SHRDLU

She was a saint—a saint, I tell you. She cared for me and watched over me as only a mother can.

ZERO

You mean to say you didn't have a scrap or nothin'?

SHRDLU

Never a harsh or an unkind word. Nothing except loving care and good advice. From my infancy she devoted herself to guiding me on the right path. She taught me to be thrifty, to be devout, to be unselfish, to shun evil companions and to shut my ears to all the temptations of the flesh—in short, to become a virtuous, respectable, and God-fearing man. (*He groans.*) But it was a hopeless task. At fourteen I began to show evidence of my sinful nature.

ZERO

(*Breathlessly*). You didn't kill anybody else, did you?

SHRDLU

No, thank God, there is only one murder on my soul. But I ran away from home.

ZERO

You did!

SHRDLU

Yes. A companion lent me a profane book—the only profane book I have ever read, I'm thankful to say. It was called *Treasure Island*. Have you ever read it?

ZERO

No, I never was much on readin' books.

SHRDLU

It is a wicked book—a lurid tale of adventure. But it kindled in my sinful heart a desire to go to sea. And so I ran away from home.

ZERO

What did you do—get a job as a sailor?

SHRDLU

I never saw the sea—not to the day of my death. Luckily, my mother's loving intuition warned her of my intention and I was sent back home. She welcomed me with open arms. Not an angry word, not a look of reproach. But I could read the mute suffering in her eyes as we prayed together all through the night.

ZERO

(*Sympathetically*). Gee, that must 'a' been tough. Gee, the mosquitoes are bad, ain't they? (*He tries awkwardly to slap at them with his stiff hands.*)

SHRDLU

(*Absorbed in his narrative*). I thought that experience had cured me of evil and I began to think about a career. I wanted to go in foreign missions at first, but we couldn't bear the thought of the separation. So we finally decided that I should become a proofreader.

ZERO

Say, slip me one o' them Camels, will you? I'm gettin' all bit up.

SHRDLU

Certainly. (*He hands* ZERO *cigarettes and matches.*)

ZERO

(*Lighting up*). Go ahead. I'm listenin'.

SHRDLU

By the time I was twenty I had a good job reading proof for a firm that printed catalogues. After a year they promoted me and let me specialize in shoe catalogues.

ZERO

Yeh? That must 'a' been a good job.

SHRDLU

It was a very good job. I was on the shoe catalogues for thirteen years. I'd been on them yet, if I hadn't—— (*He chokes back a sob.*)

ZERO

They oughta put a shot o' citronella in that embalmin'-fluid.

SHRDLU

(*He sighs*). We were so happy together. I had my steady job. And Sundays we would go to morning, afternoon, and evening service. It was an honest and moral mode of life.

ZERO

It sure was.

SHRDLU

Then came that fatal Sunday. Dr. Amaranth, our minister, was having dinner with us—one of the few pure spirits on earth. When he had finished saying grace, we had our soup. Everything was going along as usual—we were eating our soup and discussing the sermon, just like every other Sunday I could remember. Then came the leg of lamb—— (*He breaks off, then resumes in a choking voice.*) I see the whole scene before me so plainly—it never leaves me—Dr. Amaranth at my right, my mother at my left, the leg of lamb on the table in front of me and the cuckoo clock on the little shelf between the windows. (*He stops and wipes his eyes.*)

ZERO

Yeh, but what happened?

SHRDLU

Well, as I started to carve the lamb—— Did you ever carve a leg of lamb?

ZERO

No, corned beef was our speed.

SHRDLU

It's very difficult on account of the bone. And when there's gravy in the dish there's danger of spilling it. So Mother always used to hold the dish for me. She leaned forward, just as she always did, and I could see the gold locket around her neck. It had my picture in it and one of my baby curls. Well, I raised my knife to carve the leg of lamb—and instead I cut my mother's throat! (*He sobs.*)

ZERO

You must 'a' been crazy!

SHRDLU

(*Raising his head, vehemently*). No! Don't try to justify me. I wasn't crazy. They tried to prove at the trial that I was crazy. But Dr. Amaranth saw the truth! He saw it from the first! He knew that it was my sinful nature—and he told me what was in store for me.

ZERO

(*Trying to be comforting*). Well, your troubles are over now.

SHRDLU

(*His voice rising*). Over! Do you think this is the end?

ZERO

Sure. What more can they do to us?

SHRDLU

(*His tones growing shriller and shriller*). Do you think there can ever be any peace for such as we are—murderers, sinners? Don't you know what awaits us—flames, eternal flames!

ZERO

(*Nervously*). Keep your shirt on, Buddy—they wouldn't do that to us.

SHRDLU

There's no escape—no escape for us, I tell you. We're doomed! We're doomed to suffer unspeakable torments through all eternity. (*His voice rises higher and higher.*)
(*A grave opens suddenly and a head appears.*)

THE HEAD

Hey, you birds! Can't you shut up and let a guy sleep?
(ZERO *scrambles painfully to his feet.*)

ZERO

(*To* SHRDLU). Hey, put on the soft pedal.

SHRDLU

(*Too wrought up to attend*). It won't be long now! We'll receive our summons soon.

THE HEAD

Are you goin' to beat it or not? (*He calls into the grave.*) Hey, Bill, lend me your head a minute.
(*A moment later his arm appears holding a skull.*)

ZERO

(*Warningly*). Look out! (*He seizes* SHRDLU *and drags him away just as* THE HEAD *throws the skull.*)

THE HEAD

(*Disgustedly*). Missed 'em. Damn old tabby cats! I'll get 'em next time. (*A prodigious yawn.*) No-hum! Me for the worms!

(THE HEAD *disappears as the curtain falls.*)

SCENE VI

SCENE: *A pleasant place. A scene of pastoral loveliness. A meadow dotted with fine old trees and carpeted with rich grass and field flowers. In the background are seen a number of tents fashioned of gay-striped silks and beyond gleams a meandering river. Clear air and a fleckless sky. Sweet distant music throughout.*

At the rise of the curtain, SHRDLU *is seen seated under a tree in the foreground in an attitude of deep dejection. His knees are drawn up and his head is buried in his arms. He is dressed as in the preceding scene.*

A few minutes later, ZERO *enters at right. He walks slowly and looks about him with an air of half-suspicious curiosity. He, too, is dressed as in the preceding scene. Suddenly he sees* SHRDLU *seated under the tree. He stands still and looks at him half fearfully. Then, seeing something familiar in him, goes closer.* SHRDLU *is unaware of his presence. At last* ZERO *recognizes him and grins in pleased surprise.*

ZERO

Well, if it ain't——! (*He claps* SHRDLU *on the shoulder.*) Hello, Buddy!

(SHRDLU *looks up slowly, then recognizing* ZERO, *he rises gravely and extends his hand courteously.*)

SHRDLU

How do you do, Mr. Zero? I'm very glad to see you again.

ZERO

Same here. I wasn't expectin' to see you, either. (*Looking about.*) This is a kinda nice place. I wouldn't mind restin' here a while.

SHRDLU

You may if you wish.

ZERO

I'm kinda tired. I ain't used to bein' outdoors. I ain't walked so much in years.

SHRDLU

Sit down here, under the tree.

ZERO

Do they let you sit on the grass?

SHRDLU

Oh, yes.

ZERO

(*Seating himself*). Boy, this feels good. I'll tell the world my feet are sore. I ain't used to so much walkin'. Say, I wonder would it be all right if I took my shoes off; my feet are tired.

SHRDLU

Yes. Some of the people here go barefoot.

ZERO

Yeh? They sure must be nuts. But I'm goin' t' leave 'em off for a while. So long as it's all right. The grass feels nice and cool. (*He stretches out comfortably.*) Say, this is the life of Riley all right, all right. This sure is a nice place. What do they call this place, anyhow?

SHRDLU

The Elysian Fields.

ZERO

The which?

SHRDLU

The Elysian Fields.

ZERO

(*Dubiously*). Oh! Well, it's a nice place, all right.

SHRDLU

They say that this is the most desirable of all places. Only the most favored remain here.

ZERO

Yeh? Well, that let's me out, I guess. (*Suddenly.*) But what are you doin' here? I thought you'd be burned by now.

SHRDLU

(*Sadly*). Mr. Zero, I am the most unhappy of men.

ZERO

(*In mild astonishment*). Why, because you ain't bein' roasted alive?

SHRDLU

(*Nodding*). Nothing is turning out as I expected. I saw everything so clearly—the flames, the tortures, an eternity of suffering as the just punishment for my unspeakable crime. And it has all turned out so differently.

ZERO

Well, that's pretty soft for you, ain't it?

SHRDLU

(*Wailingly*). No, no, no! It's right and just that I should be punished. I could have endured it stoically. All through those endless ages of indescribable torment I should have exulted in the magnificence of divine justice. But this—this is maddening! What becomes of justice? What becomes of morality? What becomes of right and wrong? It's maddening—simply maddening! Oh, if Dr. Amaranth were only here to advise me! (*He buries his face and groans.*)

ZERO

(*Trying to puzzle it out*). You mean to say they ain't called you for cuttin' your mother's throat?

SHRDLU

No! It's terrible—terrible! I was prepared for anything—anything but this.

ZERO

Well, what did they say to you?

SHRDLU

(*Looking up*). Only that I was to come here and remain until I understood.

ZERO

I don't get it. What do they want you to understand?

SHRDLU

(*Despairingly*). I don't know—I don't know! If I only had an inkling of what they meant—— (*Interrupting him.*) Just listen quietly for a moment; do you hear anything?
(*They are both silent, straining their ears.*)

ZERO

(*At length*). Nope.

SHRDLU

You don't hear any music? Do you?

ZERO

Music? No, I don't hear nothin'.

SHRDLU

The people here say that the music never stops.

ZERO

They're kiddin' you.

SHRDLU

Do you think so?

ZERO

Sure thing. There ain't a sound.

SHRDLU

Perhaps. They're capable of anything. But I haven't told you of the bitterest of my disappointments.

ZERO

Well, spill it. I'm gettin' used to hearin' bad news.

SHRDLU

When I came to this place, my first thought was to find my dear mother. I wanted to ask her forgiveness. And I wanted her to help me to understand.

ZERO

An' she couldn't do it?

SHRDLU

(*With a deep groan*). She's not here! Mr. Zero! Here where only the most favored dwell, that wisest and purest of spirits is nowhere to be found. I don't understand it.

A WOMAN'S VOICE

(*In the distance*). Mr. Zero! Oh, Mr. Zero! (ZERO *raises his head and listens attentively.*)

SHRDLU

(*Going on, unheedingly*). If you were to see some of the people here—the things they do——

ZERO

(*Interrupting*). Wait a minute, will you? I think somebody's callin' me.

THE VOICE

(*Somewhat nearer*). Mr. Ze-ro! Oh! Mr. Ze-ro!

ZERO

Who the hell's that now? I wonder if the wife's on my trail already. That would be swell, wouldn't it? An' I figured on her bein' good for another twenty years, anyhow.

THE VOICE

(*Nearer*). Mr. Ze-ro! Yoo-hoo!

ZERO

No. That ain't her voice. (*Calling, savagely.*) Yoo-hoo. (*To* SHRDLU) Ain't that always the way? Just when a guy is takin' life easy an' havin' a good time! (*He rises and looks off left.*) Here she comes, whoever she is. (*In sudden amazement.*) Well, I'll be——! Well, what do you know about that!

(*He stands looking in wonderment, as* DAISY DIANA DOROTHEA DEVORE *enters. She wears a much-beruffled white muslin dress which is a size too small and fifteen years too youthful for her. She is red-faced and breathless.*)

DAISY

(*Panting*). Oh! I thought I'd never catch up to you. I've been followin' you for days —callin' an' callin'. Didn't you hear me?

ZERO

Not till just now. You look kinda winded.

DAISY

I sure am. I can't hardly catch my breath.

Well, sit down an' take a load off your feet. (*He leads her to the tree.*)

(DAISY *sees* SHRDLU *for the first time and shrinks back a little.*)

It's all right, he's a friend of mine. (*To* SHRDLU) Buddy, I want you to meet my friend, Miss Devore.

SHRDLU

(*Rising and extending his hand courteously*). How do you do, Miss Devore?

DAISY

(*Self-consciously*). How do!

ZERO

(*To* DAISY). He's a friend of mine. (*To* SHRDLU) I guess you don't mind if she sits here a while an' cools off, do you?

SHRDLU

No, no, certainly not.

(*They all seat themselves under the tree.* ZERO *and* DAISY *are a little self-conscious.* SHRDLU *gradually becomes absorbed in his own thoughts.*)

ZERO

I was just takin' a rest myself. I took my shoes off on account of my feet bein' so sore.

DAISY

Yeh, I'm kinda tired, too. (*Looking about.*) Say, ain't it pretty here, though?

ZERO

Yeh, it is at that.

DAISY

What do they call this place?

ZERO

Why—er—let's see. He was tellin' me just a minute ago. The—er—I don't know. Some kind o' fields. I forget now. (*To* SHRDLU) Say, Buddy, what do they call this place again? (SHRDLU, *absorbed in his thoughts, does not hear him. To* DAISY) He don't hear me. He's thinkin' again.

DAISY

(*Sotto voce*). What's the matter with him?

ZERO

Why, he's the guy that murdered his mother—remember?

DAISY

(*Interested*). Oh, yeh! Is that him?

ZERO

Yeh. An' he had it all figgered out how they was goin' t' roast him or somethin'. And now they ain't goin' to do nothin' to him an' it's kinda got his goat.

DAISY

(*Sympathetically*). Poor feller!

ZERO

Yeh. He takes it kinda hard.

DAISY

He looks like a nice young feller.

ZERO

Well, you sure are good for sore eyes. I never expected to see you here.

DAISY

I thought maybe you'd be kinda surprised.

ZERO

Surprised is right. I thought you was alive an' kickin'. When did you pass out?

DAISY

Oh, right after you did—a coupla days.

ZERO

(*Interested*). Yeh? What happened? Get hit by a truck or somethin'?

DAISY

No. (*Hesitantly.*) You see—it's this way. I blew out the gas.

ZERO

(*Astonished*). Go on! What was the big idea?

DAISY

(*Falteringly*). Oh, I don't know. You see, I lost my job.

ZERO

I'll bet you're sorry you did it now, ain't you?

DAISY

(*With conviction*). No, I ain't sorry. Not a bit. (*Then hesitantly.*) Say, Mr. Zero, I been thinkin'—— (*She stops.*)

ZERO

What?

DAISY

(*Plucking up courage*). I been thinkin' it would be kinda nice—if you an' me—if we could kinda talk things over.

ZERO

Yeh. Sure. What do you want to talk about?

DAISY

Well—I don't know—but you and me—we ain't really ever talked things over, have we?

ZERO

No, that's right, we ain't. Well, let's go to it.

DAISY

I was thinkin' if we could be alone—just the two of us, see?

ZERO

Oh, yeh! Yeh, I get you. (*He turns to* SHRDLU *and coughs loudly.* SHRDLU *does not stir.*)

ZERO

(*To* DAISY) He's dead to the world. (*He turns to* SHRDLU) Say, Buddy! (*No answer.*) Say, Buddy!

SHRDLU

(*Looking up with a start*). Were you speaking to me?

ZERO

Yeh. How'd you guess it? I was thinkin' that maybe you'd like to walk around a little and look for your mother.

SHRDLU

(*Shaking his head*). It's no use. I've looked everywhere. (*He relapses into thought again.*)

ZERO

Maybe over there they might know.

SHRDLU

No, no! I've searched everywhere. She's not here.

(ZERO *and* DAISY *look at each other in despair.*)

ZERO

Listen, old shirt, my friend here and me—see?—we used to work in the same store. An' we got some things to talk over—business, see?—kinda confidential. So if it ain't askin' too much——

SHRDLU

(*Springing to his feet*). Why, certainly! Excuse me!

(*He bows politely to* DAISY *and walks off.* DAISY *and* ZERO *watch him until he has disappeared.*)

ZERO

(*With a forced laugh*). He's a good guy at that.

(*Now that they are alone, both are very self-conscious, and for a time they sit in silence.*)

DAISY

(*Breaking the silence*). It sure is pretty here, ain't it?

ZERO

Sure is.

DAISY

Look at the flowers! Ain't they just perfect! Why, you'd think they was artificial, wouldn't you?

ZERO

Yeh, you would.

DAISY

And the smell of them. Like perfume.

ZERO

Yeh.

DAISY

I'm crazy about the country, ain't you?

ZERO

Yeh. It's nice for a change.

DAISY

Them store picnics—remember?

ZERO

You bet. They sure was fun.

DAISY

One time—I guess you don't remember—the two of us—me and you—we sat down on the grass together under a tree—just like we're doin' now.

ZERO

Sure I remember.

DAISY

Go on! I'll bet you don't.

ZERO

I'll bet I do. It was the year the wife didn't go.

DAISY

(*Her face brightening*). That's right! I didn't think you'd remember.

ZERO

An' comin' home we sat together in the truck.

DAISY

(*Eagerly, rather shamefacedly*). Yeh! There's somethin' I've always wanted to ask you.

ZERO

Well, why didn't you?

DAISY

I don't know. It didn't seem refined. But I'm goin' to ask you now, anyhow.

ZERO

Go ahead. Shoot.

DAISY

(*Falteringly*). Well—while we was comin' home—you put your arm up on the bench behind me—and I could feel your knee kinda pressin' against mine. (*She stops.*)

ZERO

(*Becoming more and more interested*). Yeh—well—what about it?

DAISY

What I wanted to ask you was—was it just kinda accidental?

ZERO

(*With a laugh*). Sure it was accidental. Accidental on purpose.

DAISY

(*Eagerly*). Do you mean it?

ZERO

Sure I mean it. You mean to say you didn't know it?

DAISY

No. I've been wantin' to ask you——

ZERO

Then why did you get sore at me?

DAISY

Sore? I wasn't sore! When was I sore?

ZERO

That night. Sure you was sore. If you wasn't sore why did you move away?

DAISY

Just to see if you meant it. I thought if you meant it you'd move up closer. An' then when you took your arm away I was sure you didn't mean it.

ZERO

An' I thought all the time you was sore. That's why I took my arm away. I thought if I moved up you'd holler and then I'd be in a jam, like you read in the paper all the time about guys gettin' pulled in for annoyin' women.

DAISY

An' I was wishin' you'd put your arm around me—just sittin' there wishin' all the way home.

ZERO

What do you know about that? That sure is hard luck, that is. If I'd 'a' only knew! You know what I felt like doin'—only I didn't have the nerve?

DAISY

What?

ZERO

I felt like kissin' you.

DAISY

(*Fervently*). I wanted you to.

ZERO

(*Astonished*). You would 'a' let me?

DAISY

I wanted you to! I wanted you to! Oh, why didn't you—why didn't you?

ZERO

I didn't have the nerve. I sure was a dumbbell.

DAISY

I would 'a' let you all you wanted to. I wouldn't 'a' cared. I know it would 'a' been wrong but I wouldn't 'a' cared. I wasn't thinkin' about right an' wrong at all. I didn't care—see? I just wanted you to kiss me.

ZERO

(*Feelingly*). If I'd only knew. I wanted to do it, I swear I did. But I didn't think you cared nothin' about me.

DAISY

(*Passionately*). I never cared nothin' about nobody else.

ZERO

Do you mean it—on the level? You ain't kiddin' me, are you?

DAISY

No, I ain't kiddin'. I mean it. I'm tellin' you the truth. I ain't never had the nerve to tell you before—but now I don't care. It don't make no difference now. I mean it—every word of it.

ZERO

(*Dejectedly*). If I'd only knew it.

DAISY

Listen to me. There's somethin' else I want to tell you. I may as well tell you everything now. It don't make no difference now. About my blowin' out the gas—see? Do you know why I done it?

ZERO

Yeh, you told me—on account o' bein' canned.

DAISY

I just told you that. That ain't the real reason. The real reason is on account o' you.

ZERO

You mean to say on account o' me passin' out——?

DAISY

Yeh. That's it. I didn't want to go on livin'. What for? What did I want to go on livin' for? I didn't have nothin' to live for with you gone. I often thought of doin' it before. But I never had the nerve. An' anyhow I didn't want to leave you.

ZERO

An' me bawlin' you out, about readin' too fast an' readin' too slow.

DAISY

(*Reproachfully*). Why did you do it?

ZERO

I don't know, I swear I don't. I was always stuck on you. An' while I'd be addin' them figgers, I'd be thinkin' how if the wife died, you an' me could get married.

DAISY

I used to think o' that, too.

ZERO

An' then before I knew it, I was bawlin' you out.

DAISY

Them was the times I'd think o' blowin' out the gas. But I never did till you was gone. There wasn't nothin' to live for then. But it wasn't so easy to do, anyhow. I never could stand the smell o' gas. An' all the while I was gettin' ready, you know, stuffin' up all the cracks, the way you read about in the paper—I was thinkin' of you and hopin' that maybe I'd meet you again. An' I made up my mind if I ever did see you, I'd tell you.

ZERO

(*Taking her hand*). I'm sure glad you did. I'm sure glad. (*Ruefully.*) But it don't do much good now, does it?

DAISY

No, I guess it don't. (*Summoning courage.*) But there's one thing I'm goin' to ask you.

ZERO

What's that?

DAISY

(*In a low voice*). I want you to kiss me.

ZERO

You bet I will! (*He leans over and kisses her cheek.*)

DAISY

Not like that. I don't mean like that. I mean really kiss me. On the mouth. I ain't never been kissed like that.
(ZERO *puts his arms about her and presses his lips to hers. A long embrace. At last they separate and sit side by side in silence.*)
(*Putting her hands to her cheeks.*) So that's what it's like. I didn't know it could be like that. I didn't know anythin' could be like that.

ZERO

(*Fondling her hand*). Your cheeks are red. They're all red. And your eyes are shinin'. I never seen your eyes shinin' like that before.

DAISY

(*Holding up her hand*). Listen—do you hear it? Do you hear the music?

ZERO

No, I don't hear nothin'!

DAISY

Yeh—music. Listen an' you'll hear it.
(*They are both silent for a moment.*)

ZERO

(*Excitedly*). Yeh! I hear it! He said there was music, but I didn't hear it till just now.

DAISY

Ain't it grand?

ZERO

Swell! Say, do you know what?

DAISY

What?

ZERO

It makes me feel like dancin'.

DAISY

Yeh? Me, too.

ZERO

(*Springing to his feet*). Come on! Let's dance!
(*He seizes her hands and tries to pull her up.*)

DAISY

(*Resisting laughingly*). I can't dance. I ain't danced in twenty years.

ZERO

That's nothin'. I ain't, neither. Come on! I feel just like a kid!
(*He pulls her to her feet and seizes her about the waist.*)

DAISY

Wait a minute! Wait till I fix my skirt. (*She turns back her skirts and pins them above the ankles.*)
(ZERO *seizes her about the waist. They dance clumsily but with gay abandon.* DAISY's *hair becomes loosened and tumbles over her shoulders. She lends herself more and more to the spirit of the dance. But* ZERO *soon begins to tire and dances with less and less zest.*)

ZERO

(*Stopping at last, panting for breath*). Wait a minute! I'm all winded.
(*He releases* DAISY, *but before he can turn away, she throws her arms about him and presses her lips to his.*)
Wait a minute! Let me get my wind!
(*He limps to the tree and seats himself under it, gasping for breath.* DAISY *looks after him, her spirits rather dampened.*)
Whew! I sure am winded! I ain't used to dancin'.
(*He takes off his collar and tie and opens the neckband of his shirt.* DAISY *sits under the tree near him, looking at him longingly. But he is busy catching his breath.*)
Gee, my heart's goin' a mile a minute.

DAISY

Why don't you lay down an' rest? You could put your head on my lap.

ZERO

That ain't a bad idea.
(*He stretches out, his head in* DAISY's *lap.*)

DAISY

(*Fondling his hair*). It was swell, wasn't it?

ZERO

Yeh. But you gotta be used to it.

DAISY

Just imagine if we could stay here all the time—you an' me together—wouldn't it be swell?

ZERO

Yeh. But there ain't a chance.

DAISY

Won't they let us stay?

ZERO

No. This place is only for the good ones.

DAISY

Well, we ain't so bad, are we?

ZERO

Go on! Me a murderer an' you committin' suicide. Anyway, they wouldn't stand for this—the way we been goin' on.

DAISY

I don't see why.

ZERO

You don't! You know it ain't right. Ain't I got a wife?

DAISY

Not any more you ain't. When you're dead that ends it. Don't they always say "until death do us part?"

ZERO

Well, maybe you're right about that, but they wouldn't stand for us here.

DAISY

It would be swell—the two of us together—we could make up for all them years.

ZERO

Yeh, I wish we could.

DAISY

We sure were fools. But I don't care. I've got you now. (*She kisses his forehead and cheeks and mouth.*)

ZERO

I'm sure crazy about you. I never saw you lookin' so pretty before, with your cheeks all red. An' your hair hangin' down. You got swell hair. (*He fondles and kisses her hair.*)

DAISY

(*Ecstatically*). We got each other now, ain't we?

ZERO

Yeh. I'm crazy about you. Daisy! That's a pretty name. It's a flower, ain't it? Well—that's what you are—just a flower.

DAISY

(*Happily*). We can always be together now, can't we?

ZERO

As long as they'll let us. I sure am crazy about you. (*Suddenly he sits upright.*) Watch your step!

DAISY

(*Alarmed*). What's the matter?

ZERO

(*Nervously*). He's comin' back.

DAISY

Oh, is that all? Well, what about it?

ZERO

You don't want him to see us layin' around like this, do you?

DAISY

I don't care if he does.

ZERO

Well, you oughta care. You don't want him to think you ain't a refined girl, do you? He's an awful moral bird, he is.

DAISY

I don't care nothin' about him. I don't care nothin' about anybody but you.

ZERO

Sure, I know. But we don't want people talkin' about us. You better fix your hair an' pull down your skirts.
(DAISY *complies rather sadly. They are both silent as* SHRDLU *enters.*)
(*With feigned nonchalance.*) Well, you got back all right, didn't you?

SHRDLU

I hope I haven't returned too soon.

ZERO

No, that's all right. We were just havin' a little talk. You know—about business an' things.

DAISY

(*Boldly*). We were wishin' we could stay here all the time.

SHRDLU

You may if you like.

ZERO AND DAISY

(*In astonishment*). What!

SHRDLU

Yes. Any one who likes may remain——

ZERO

But I thought you were tellin' me——

SHRDLU

Just as I told you, only the most favored do remain. But any one may.

ZERO

I don't get it. There's a catch in it somewheres.

DAISY

It doesn't matter as long as we can stay.

ZERO

(*To* SHRDLU) We were thinkin' about gettin' married, see?

SHRDLU

You may or not, just as you like.

ZERO

You don't mean to say we could stay if we didn't, do you?

SHRDLU

Yes. They don't care.

ZERO

An' there's some here that ain't married?

SHRDLU

Yes.

ZERO

(*To* DAISY) I don't know about this place, at that. They must be kind of a mixed crowd.

DAISY

It don't matter, so long as we got each other.

ZERO

Yeh, I know, but you don't want to mix with people that ain't respectable.

DAISY

(*To* SHRDLU) Can we get married right away? I guess there must be a lot of ministers here, ain't there?

SHRDLU

Not as many as I had hoped to find. The two who seem most beloved are Dean Swift and the Abbé Rabelais. They are both much admired for some indecent tales which they have written.

ZERO

(*Shocked*). What! Ministers writin' smutty stories! Say, what kind of a dump is this, anyway?

SHRDLU

(*Despairingly*). I don't know, Mr. Zero. All these people here are so strange, so unlike the good people I've known. They seem to think of nothing but enjoyment or of wasting their time in profitless occupations. Some paint pictures from morning until night, or carve blocks of stone. Others write songs or put words together, day in and day out. Still others do nothing but lie under the trees and look at the sky. There are men who spend all their time reading books and women who think only of adorning themselves. And for ever they are telling stories and laughing and singing and drinking and dancing. There are drunkards, thieves, vagabonds, blasphemers, adulterers. There is one——

ZERO

That's enough. I heard enough. (*He seats himself and begins putting on his shoes.*)

DAISY

(*Anxiously*). What are you goin' to do?

ZERO

I'm goin' to beat it, that's what I'm goin' to do.

DAISY

You said you liked it here.

ZERO

(*Looking at her in amazement*). Liked it! Say, you don't mean to say you want to stay here, do you, with a lot of rummies an' loafers an' bums?

DAISY

We don't have to bother with them. We can just sit here together an' look at the flowers an' listen to the music.

SHRDLU

(*Eagerly*). Music! Did you hear music?

DAISY

Sure. Don't you hear it?

SHRDLU

No, they say it never stops. But I've never heard it.

ZERO

(*Listening*). I thought I heard it before but I don't hear nothin' now. I guess I must 'a' been dreamin'. (*Looking about.*) What's the quickest way out of this place?

DAISY

(*Pleadingly*). Won't you stay just a little longer?

ZERO

Didn't yer hear me say I'm goin'? Goodbye, Miss Devore. I'm goin' to beat it. (*He limps off at the right.* DAISY *follows him slowly.*)

DAISY

(*To* SHRDLU) I won't ever see him again.

SHRDLU

Are you goin' to stay here?

DAISY

It don't make no difference now. Without him I might as well be alive. (*She goes off right.* SHRDLU *watches her a moment, then sighs and, seating himself under the tree, buries his head on his arm. Curtain falls.*)

SCENE VII

SCENE: *Before the curtain rises the clicking of an adding machine is heard. The curtain rises upon an office similar in appearance to that in Scene II except that there is a door in the back wall through which can be seen a glimpse of the corridor outside. In the middle of the room* ZERO *is seated completely absorbed in the operation of an adding machine. He presses the keys and pulls the lever with mechanical precision. He still wears his full-dress suit but he has added to it sleeve protectors and a green eye shade. A strip of white paper-tape flows steadily from the machine as* ZERO *operates. The room is filled with this tape—streamers, festoons, billows of it everywhere. It covers the floor and the furniture, it climbs the walls and chokes the doorways. A few moments later,* LIEUTENANT CHARLES *and* JOE *enter at the left.* LIEUTENANT CHARLES *is middle-aged and inclined to corpulence. He has an air of world-weariness. He is bare-footed, wears a Panama hat, and is dressed in bright red tights which are a very bad fit—too tight in some places, badly wrinkled in others.* JOE *is a youth with a smutty face dressed in dirty blue overalls.*

CHARLES

(*After contemplating* ZERO *for a few moments*). All right, Zero, cease firing.

ZERO

(*Looking up, surprised*). Whaddja say?

CHARLES

I said stop punching that machine.

ZERO

(*Bewildered*). Stop? (*He goes on working mechanically.*)

CHARLES

(*Impatiently*). Yes. Can't you stop? Here, Joe, give me a hand. He can't stop.
(JOE *and* CHARLES *each take one of* ZERO'S *arms and with enormous effort detach him from the machine. He resists passively—mere inertia. Finally they succeed and swing him around on his stool.* CHARLES *and* JOE *mop their foreheads.*)

ZERO

(*Querulously*). What's the idea? Can't you lemme alone?

CHARLES

(*Ignoring the question*). How long have you been here?

ZERO

Jes' twenty-five years. Three hundred months, ninety-one hundred thirty-one days, one hundred thirty-six thousand——

CHARLES

(*Impatiently*). That'll do! That'll do!

ZERO

(*Proudly*). I ain't missed a day, not an hour, not a minute. Look at all I got done. (*He points to the maze of paper.*)

CHARLES

It's time to quit.

ZERO

Quit? Whaddye mean quit? I ain't goin' to quit!

CHARLES

You've got to.

ZERO

What for? What do I have to quit for?

CHARLES

It's time for you to go back.

ZERO

Go back where? Whaddya talkin' about?

CHARLES

Back to earth, you dub. Where do you think?

ZERO

Aw, go on, Cap, who are you kiddin'?

CHARLES

I'm not kidding anybody. And don't call me Cap. I'm a lieutenant.

ZERO

All right, Lieutenant, all right. But what's this you're tryin' to tell me about goin' back?

CHARLES

Your time's up. I'm telling you. You must be pretty thick. How many times do you want to be told a thing?

ZERO

This is the first time I heard about goin' back. Nobody ever said nothin' to me about it before.

CHARLES

You didn't think you were going to stay here for ever, did you?

ZERO

Sure. Why not? I did my bit, didn't I? Forty-five years of it. Twenty-five years in the store. Then the boss canned me and I knocked him cold. I guess you ain't heard about that——

CHARLES

(*Interrupting*). I know all about that. But what's that got to do with it?

ZERO

Well, I done my bit, didn't I? That oughta let me out.

CHARLES

(*Jeeringly*). So you think you're all through, do you?

ZERO

Sure, I do. I did the best I could while I was there and then I passed out. And now I'm sittin' pretty here.

CHARLES

You've got a fine idea of the way they run things, you have. Do you think they're going to all the trouble of making a soul just to use it once?

ZERO

Once is often enough, it seems to me.

CHARLES

It seems to you, does it? Well, who are you? And what do you know about it? Why, man, they use a soul over and over again—over and over until it's worn out.

ZERO

Nobody ever told me.

CHARLES

So you thought you were all through, did you? Well, that's a hot one, that is.

ZERO

(*Sullenly*). How was I to know?

CHARLES

Use your brains! Where would we put them all! We're crowded enough as it is. Why, this place is nothing but a kind of repair and service station—a sort of cosmic laundry, you might say. We get the souls in here by the bushelful. Then we get busy and clean them up. And you ought to see some of them. The muck and the slime. Phoo! And as full of holes as a flour-sifter. But we fix them up. We disinfect them and give them a kerosene rub and mend the holes and back they go—practically as good as new.

ZERO

You mean to say I've been here before—before the last time, I mean?

CHARLES

Been here before! Why, you poor boob—you've been here thousands of times—fifty thousand, at least.

ZERO

(*Suspiciously*). How is it I don't remember nothin' about it?

CHARLES

Well—that's partly because you're stupid. But it's mostly because that's the way they fix it. (*Musingly.*) They're funny that way—every now and then they'll do something white like that—when you'd least expect it. I guess economy's at the bottom of it, though. They figure that the souls would get worn out quicker if they remembered.

ZERO

And don't any of 'em remember?

CHARLES

Oh, some do. You see there's different types: there's the type that gets a little better each time it goes back—we just give them a wash and send them right through. Then there's another type—the type that gets a little worse each time. That's where you belong!

ZERO

(*Offended*). Me? You mean to say I'm gettin' worse all the time?

CHARLES

(*Nodding*). Yes. A little worse each time.

ZERO

Well—what was I when I started? Somethin' big?—A king or somethin'?

CHARLES

(*Laughing derisively*). A king! That's a good one! I'll tell you what you were the first time—if you want to know so much—a monkey.

ZERO

(*Shocked and offended*). A monkey!

CHARLES

Yes, sir—just a hairy, chattering, long-tailed monkey.

ZERO

That musta been a long time ago.

CHARLES

Oh, not so long. A million years or so. Seems like yesterday to me.

ZERO

Then look here, whaddya mean by sayin' I'm gettin' worse all the time?

CHARLES

Just what I said. You weren't so bad as a monkey. Of course, you did just what all the other monkeys did, but still it kept you out in the open air. And you weren't women shy—there was one little red-headed monkey—— Well, never mind. Yes, sir, you weren't so bad then. But even in those days there must have been some bigger and brainier monkey that you kowtowed to. The mark of the slave was on you from the start.

ZERO

(*Sullenly*). You ain't very particular about what you call people, are you?

CHARLES

You wanted the truth, didn't you? If there ever was a soul in the world that was labelled slave it's yours. Why, all the bosses and kings that there ever were have left their trademarks on your backside.

ZERO

It ain't fair, if you ask me.

CHARLES

(*Shrugging his shoulders*). Don't tell me about it. I don't make the rules. All I know is you've been getting worse—worse each time. Why, even six thousand years ago you weren't so bad. That was the time you were hauling stones for one of those big pyramids in a place they call Africa. Ever hear of the pyramids?

ZERO

Them big pointy things?

CHARLES

(*Nodding*). That's it.

ZERO

I seen a picture of them in the movies.

CHARLES

Well, you helped build them. It was a long step down from the happy days in the jungle, but it was a good job—even though you didn't know what you were doing and your back was striped by the foreman's whip. But you've been going down, down. Two thousand years ago you were a Roman galley-slave. You were on one of the triremes that knocked the Carthaginian fleet for a goal. Again the whip. But you had muscles then—chest muscles, back muscles, biceps. (*He feels* ZERO's *arm gingerly and turns away in disgust.*) Phoo! a bunch of mush! (*He notices that* JOE *has fallen asleep. Walking over, he kicks him in the shin.*)

CHARLES

Wake up, you mutt! Where do you think you are! (*He turns to* ZERO *again.*) And then another thousand years and you were a serf—a lump of clay digging up other lumps of clay. You wore an iron collar then—white ones hadn't been invented yet. Another long step down. But where you dug, potatoes grew and that helped fatten the pigs. Which was something. And now—well, I don't want to rub it in——

ZERO

Rub it in is right! Seems to me I got a pretty healthy kick comin'. I ain't had a square deal! Hard work! That's all I've ever had!

CHARLES

(*Callously*). What else were you ever good for?

ZERO

Well, that ain't the point. The point is I'm through! I had enough! Let 'em find somebody else to do the dirty work. I'm sick of bein' the goat! I quit right here and now! (*He glares about defiantly. There is a thunderclap and a bright flash of lightning.*)

ZERO

(*Screaming*). Ooh! What's that? (*He clings to* CHARLES.)

CHARLES

It's all right. Nobody's going to hurt you. It's just their way of telling you that they don't like you to talk that way. Pull yourself together and calm down. You can't change the rules—nobody can—they've got it all fixed. It's a rotten system—but what are you going to do about it?

ZERO

Why can't they stop pickin' on me? I'm satisfied here—doin' my day's work. I don't want to go back.

CHARLES

You've got to, I tell you. There's no way out of it.

ZERO

What chance have I got—at my age? Who'll give me a job?

CHARLES

You big boob, you don't think you're going back the way you are, do you?

ZERO

Sure, how then?

CHARLES

Why, you've got to start all over.

ZERO

All over?

CHARLES

(*Nodding*). You'll be a baby again—a bald, red-faced little animal, and then you'll go through it all again. There'll be millions of others like you—all with their mouths open, squawling for food. And then when you get a little older you'll begin to learn things—and you'll learn all the wrong things and learn them all in the wrong way. You'll eat the wrong food and wear the wrong clothes and you'll live in swarming dens where there's no light and no air! You'll learn to be a liar and a bully and a braggart and a coward and a sneak. You'll learn to fear the sunlight and to hate beauty. By that time you'll be ready for school. There they'll tell you the truth about a great many things that you don't give a damn about and they'll tell you lies about all the things you ought to know—and about all the things you want to know they'll tell you nothing at all. When you get through you'll be equipped for your life-work. You'll be ready to take a job.

ZERO

(*Eagerly*). What'll my job be? Another adding machine?

CHARLES

Yes. But not one of these antiquated adding machines. It will be a superb, super-hyper-adding machine, as far from this old piece of junk as you are from God. It will be something to make you sit up and take notice, that adding machine. It will be an adding machine which will be installed in a coal mine and which will record the individual output of each miner. As each miner down in the lower galleries takes up a shovelful of coal, the impact of his shovel will automatically set in motion a graphite pencil in your gallery. The pencil will make a mark in white upon a blackened, sensitised drum. Then your work comes in. With the great toe of your right foot you release a lever which focuses a violet ray on the drum. The ray playing upon and through the white mark, falls upon a selenium cell which in turn sets the keys of the adding apparatus in motion. In this way the individual output of each miner is recorded without any human effort except the slight pressure of the great toe of your right foot.

ZERO

(*In breathless, round-eyed wonder*). Say, that'll be some machine, won't it?

CHARLES

Some machine is right. It will be the culmination of human effort—the final triumph of the evolutionary process. For millions of years the nebulous gases swirled in space. For more millions of years the gases cooled and then through inconceivable ages they hardened into rocks. And then came life. Floating green things on the waters that covered the earth. More millions of years and a step upward—an animate organism in the ancient slime. And so on—step by step, down through the ages—a gain here, a gain there—the mollusc, the fish, the reptile, then mammal, man! And all so that you might sit in the gallery of a coal mine and operate the super-hyper-adding machine with the great toe of your right foot!

ZERO

Well, then—I ain't so bad, after all.

CHARLES

You're a failure, Zero, a failure. A waste product. A slave to a contraption of steel and iron. The animal's instincts, but not his strength and skill. The animal's appetites, but not his unashamed indulgence of them. True, you move and eat and digest and excrete and reproduce. But any microscopic organism can do as much. Well—time's up! Back you go—back to your sunless groove—the raw material of slums and wars—the ready prey of the first jingo or demagogue or political adventurer who takes the trouble to play upon your ignorance and credulity and provincialism. You poor, spineless, brainless boob—I'm sorry for you!

ZERO

(*Falling to his knees*). Then keep me here! Don't send me back! Let me stay!

CHARLES

Get up. Didn't I tell you I can't do anything for you? Come on, time's up!

ZERO

I can't! I can't! I'm afraid to go through it all again.

CHARLES

You've got to, I tell you. Come on, now!

ZERO

What did you tell me so much for? Couldn't you just let me go, thinkin' everythin' was goin' to be all right?

CHARLES

You wanted to know, didn't you?

ZERO

How did I know what you were goin' to tell me? Now I can't stop thinkin' about it! I can't stop thinkin'! I'll be thinkin' about it all the time.

CHARLES

All right! I'll do the best I can for you. I'll send a girl with you to keep you company.

ZERO

A girl? What for? What good will a girl do me?

CHARLES

She'll help make you forget.

ZERO

(*Eagerly*). She will? Where is she?

CHARLES

Wait a minute, I'll call her. (*He calls in a loud voice.*) Oh! Hope! Yoo-hoo! (*He turns his head aside and says in the manner of a ventriloquist imitating a distant feminine voice.*) Ye-es. (*Then in his own voice.*) Come here, will you? There's a fellow who wants you to take him back. (*Ventriloquously again.*) All right. I'll be right over, Charlie dear. (*He turns to* ZERO.) Kind of familiar, isn't she? Charlie dear!

ZERO

What did you say her name is?

CHARLES

Hope. H-o-p-e.

ZERO

Is she good-lookin'?

CHARLES

Is she good-looking! Oh, boy, wait until you see her! She's a blonde with big blue eyes, red lips, little white teeth and——

ZERO

Say, that listens good to me. Will she be long?

CHARLES

She'll be here right away. There she is now! Do you see her?

ZERO

No. Where?

CHARLES

Out in the corridor. No, not there. Over farther. To the right. Don't you see her blue dress? And the sunlight on her hair?

ZERO

Oh, sure! Now I see her! What's the matter with me, anyhow? Say, she's some jane! Oh, you baby vamp!

CHARLES

She'll make you forget your troubles.

ZERO

What troubles are you talkin' about?

CHARLES

Nothing. Go on. Don't keep her waiting.

ZERO

You bet I won't! Oh, Hope! Wait for me! I'll be right with you! I'm on my way! (*He stumbles out eagerly.*)
(JOE *bursts into uproarious laughter.*)

CHARLES

(*Eyeing him in surprise and anger*). What in hell's the matter with you?

JOE

(*Shaking with laughter*). Did you get that? He thinks he saw somebody and he's following her! (*He rocks with laughter.*)

CHARLES

(*Punching him in the jaw*). Shut your face!

JOE

(*Nursing his jaw*). What's the idea? Can't I even laugh when I see something funny?

CHARLES

Funny! You keep your mouth shut or I'll show you something funny. Go on, hustle out of here and get something to clean up this mess with. There's another fellow moving in. Hurry now.
(*He makes a threatening gesture.* JOE *exits hastily.* CHARLES *goes to chair and seats himself. He looks weary and dispirited.*)

CHARLES

(*Shaking his head*). Hell, I'll tell the world this is a lousy job! (*He takes a flask from his pocket, uncorks it, and slowly drains it.*)

Curtain.

Bernard Shaw

SAINT JOAN

A Chronicle Play
in Six Scenes and an Epilogue

BERNARD SHAW

On July 26, 1936, Bernard Shaw celebrated his eightieth birthday. The activities of his four-score years embrace his championship of the cause of Fabianism, his early brilliant career as a musical critic, his novels, which he termed works of his "nonage," his essays, of which his prefaces stand unique in literature, and, finally, his plays, by far his most lasting contribution to the world's dramatic treasures. To single out his most important works would be to encourage a storm of protest from Shaw enthusiasts who stand by their own preferences. Let it suffice to list the fourteen plays produced by the Theatre Guild, which are, in their order: *Heartbreak House, Back to Methuselah, The Devil's Disciple, Saint Joan, Caesar and Cleopatra, Arms and the Man, Androcles and the Lion, Pygmalion, The Doctor's Dilemma, Major Barbara, The Apple Cart, Getting Married, Too True to Be Good,* and *The Simpleton from the Unexpected Isles.* In 1925, Bernard Shaw was awarded the Nobel Prize for Literature.

CHARACTERS

JOAN

CAPTAIN ROBERT DE BAUDRICOURT

BERTRAND DE POULENGEY

THE ARCHBISHOP OF RHEIMS

MONSEIGNEUR DE LA TRÉMOUILLE

GILLES DE RAIS (BLUEBEARD)

CAPTAIN LA HIRE

KING CHARLES VII (THE DAUPHIN)

THE DUCHESS DE LA TRÉMOUILLE

THE DUKE OF VENDÔME

DUNOIS

RICHARD DE BEAUCHAMP, EARL OF WARWICK

JOHN DE STOGUMBER

MONSEIGNEUR CAUCHON, BISHOP OF BEAUVAIS

BROTHER JOHN LEMAÎTRE (THE INQUISITOR)

CANON JOHN D'ESTIVET

CANON DE COURCELLES

BROTHER MARTIN LADVENU

THE EXECUTIONER

Steward, Pages, Dominican monks, Doctors of Law, Scribes, Canons, Assessors, Executioner's assistants, English soldiers.

SCENES

SCENE I

The castle of Vaucouleurs, on the River Meuse, between Lorraine and Champagne. 1429.

SCENE II

The throne-room in the castle. Chinon, in Touraine. Late afternoon, March 8th, 1429.

SCENE III

On the bank of the River Loire. Orleans, May 29th, 1429.

SCENE IV

A tent in the English camp.

SCENE V

The ambulatory in the cathedral of Rheims.

SCENE VI

A stone hall in the castle at Rouen. May 30th, 1431.

EPILOGUE

Bedroom in a chateau of King Charles VII. June, 1456.

PREFACE TO SAINT JOAN

18 pages
preface

Joan the Original and Presumptuous

Joan of Arc, a village girl from the Vosges, was born about 1412; burnt for heresy, witchcraft, and sorcery in 1431; rehabilitated after a fashion in 1456; designated Venerable in 1904; declared Blessed in 1908; and finally canonized in 1920. She is the most notable Warrior Saint in the Christian calendar, and the queerest fish among the eccentric worthies of the Middle Ages. Though a professed and most pious Catholic, and the projector of a Crusade against the Husites, she was in fact one of the first Protestant martyrs. She was also one of the first apostles of Nationalism, and the first French practitioner of Napoleonic realism in warfare as distinguished from the sporting ransom-gambling chivalry of her time. She was a pioneer of rational dressing for women, and, like Queen Christina of Sweden two centuries later, to say nothing of the Chevalier D'Eon and innumerable obscure heroines who have disguised themselves as men to serve as soldiers and sailors, she refused to accept the specific woman's lot, and dressed and fought and lived as men did.

As she contrived to assert herself in all these ways with such force that she was famous throughout Western Europe before she was out of her teens (indeed she never got out of them), it is hardly surprising that she was judicially burnt, ostensibly for a number of capital crimes which we no longer punish as such, but essentially for what we call unwomanly and insufferable presumption. At eighteen Joan's pretensions were beyond those of the proudest Pope or the haughtiest emperor. She claimed to be the ambassador and plenipotentiary of God, and to be in effect, a member of the Church Triumphant whilst still in the flesh on earth. She patronized her own king, and summoned the English king to repentance and obedience to her commands. She lectured, talked down, and overruled statesmen and prelates. She poohpoohed the plans of generals, leading their troops to victory on plans of her own. She had an unbounded and quite unconcealed contempt for official opinion, judgment, and authority, and for War Office tactics and strategy. Had she been a sage and monarch in whom the most venerable hierarchy and the most illustrious dynasty converged, her pretensions and proceedings would have been as trying to the official mind as the pretensions of Caesar were to Cassius. As her actual condition was pure upstart, there were only two opinions about her. One was that she was miraculous: the other that she was unbearable.

Joan and Socrates

If Joan had been malicious, selfish, cowardly or stupid, she would have been one of the most odious persons known to history instead of one of the most attractive. If she had been old enough to know the effect she was producing on the men whom she humiliated by being right when they were wrong, and had learned to flatter and manage them, she might have lived as long as Queen Elizabeth. But she was too young and rustical and inexperienced to have any such arts. When she was thwarted by men whom she thought fools, she made no secret of her opinion of them or her impatience with their folly; and she was naïve enough to expect them to be obliged to her for setting them right and keeping them out of mischief. Now it is always hard for superior wits to understand the fury roused by their exposures of the stupidities of comparative dullards. Even Socrates, for all his age and experience, did not defend himself at his trial like a man who understood the long accumulated fury that had burst on him, and was clamoring for his death. His accuser, if born 2300 years later, might have been picked out of any first-class carriage on a suburban railway during the evening or morning rush from or to the City; for he had really nothing to say except that he and his like could not endure being shown up as idiots every time Socrates opened his mouth. Socrates, unconscious of this, was paralyzed by his sense that somehow he was missing the point of the attack. He petered out after he had established the fact that he was an old soldier and a man of honorable life, and that his accuser was a silly snob. He had no suspicion of the extent to which his mental superiority had roused fear and hatred against him in the hearts of men towards whom he was conscious of nothing but good will and good service.

Contrast with Napoleon

If Socrates was as innocent as this at the age of seventy, it may be imagined how innocent Joan was at the age of seventeen. Now Socrates was a man of argument, operating slowly and peacefully on men's minds, whereas Joan was a woman of action, operating with impetuous violence on their bodies. That, no doubt, is why the contemporaries of Socrates endured him so long, and why Joan was destroyed before she was fully grown. But both of them combined terrifying ability with a frankness, personal modesty, and benevolence which made the furious dislike to which they fell victims absolutely unreasonable, and therefore inapprehensible by themselves. Napoleon, also possessed of terrifying ability, but neither frank nor disinterested, had no illusions as to the nature of his popularity. When he was asked how the world would take his death, he said it would give a gasp of relief. But it is not so easy for mental giants who neither hate nor intend to injure their fellows to realize that nevertheless their fellows hate mental giants and would like to destroy them, not only enviously because the juxtaposition of a superior wounds their vanity, but quite humbly and honestly because it frightens them. Fear will drive men to any extreme; and the fear inspired by a superior being is a mystery which cannot be reasoned away. Being immeasurable it is unbearable when there is no presumption or guarantee of its benevolence and moral responsibility: in other words, when it has no official status. The legal and conventional superiority of Herod and Pilate, and of Annas and Caiphas, inspires fear; but the fear, being a reasonable fear of measurable and avoidable consequences which seem salutary and protective is bearable; whilst the strange superiority of Christ and the fear it inspires elicit a shriek of Crucify Him from all who cannot divine its benevolence. Socrates has to drink the hemlock, Christ to hang on the cross, and Joan to burn at the stake, whilst Napoleon, though he ends in St. Helena, at least dies in his bed there; and many terrifying but quite comprehensible official scoundrels die natural deaths in all the glory of the kingdoms of this world, proving that it is far more dangerous to be a saint than to be a conqueror. Those who have been both, like Mahomet and Joan, have found that it is the conqueror who must save the saint, and that defeat and capture mean martyrdom. Joan was burnt without a hand lifted on her own side to save her. The comrades she had led to victory and the enemies she had disgraced and defeated, the French king she had crowned and the English king whose crown she had kicked into the Loire, were equally glad to be rid of her.

Was Joan Innocent or Guilty?

As this result could have been produced by a crapulous inferiority as well as by a sublime superiority, the question which of the two was operative in Joan's case has to be faced. It was decided against her by her contemporaries after a very careful and conscientious trial, and the reversal of the verdict twenty-five years later, in form a rehabilitation of Joan, was really only a confirmation of the validity of the coronation of Charles VII. It is the more impressive reversal by a unanimous Posterity, culminating in her canonization, that has quashed the original proceedings, and put her judges on their trial, which, so far, has been much more unfair than their trial of her. Nevertheless, the rehabilitation of 1456, corrupt job as it was, really did produce evidence enough to satisfy all reasonable critics that Joan was not a common termagant, not a harlot, not a witch, not a blasphemer, no more an idolater than the Pope himself, and not ill conducted in any sense apart from her soldiering, her wearing of men's clothes, and her audacity, but on the contrary good-humored, an intact virgin, very pious, very temperate (we should call her meal of bread soaked in the common wine which is the drinking water of France ascetic), very kindly, and, though a brave and hardy soldier, unable to endure loose language or licentious conduct. She went to the stake without a stain on her character except the overweening presumption, the superbity as they called it, that led her thither. It would therefore be waste of time now to prove that the Joan of the first part of the Elizabethan chronicle play of Henry VI (supposed to have been tinkered by Shakespear) grossly libels her in its concluding scenes in deference to Jingo patriotism. The mud that was thrown at her has dropped off by this time so completely that there is no need for any modern writer to wash up after it. What is far more difficult to get rid of is the mud that is being thrown at her judges, and the whitewash which disfigures her beyond recognition. When Jingo scurrility had done its worst to her, sectarian scurrility (in this case Protestant scurrility) used her stake to beat the Roman Catholic Church and the Inquisition. The easiest way to make these institutions the villains of a melodrama was to make The Maid its heroine. That melodrama may be dismissed as rubbish. Joan got a far fairer trial from the Church and the Inquisition than any prisoner of her type and in her situation gets nowadays in any official secular court; and the decision was strictly according to law. And she was not a melodramatic heroine: that is, a physically beautiful lovelorn parasite on an equally beautiful hero, but a genius and a saint, about as completely the opposite of a melodramatic heroine as it is possible for a human being to be.

Let us be clear about the meaning of the terms. A genius is a person who, seeing farther and probing deeper than other people, has a different set of ethical valuations from theirs, and has energy enough to give effect to this extra vision and its valuations in whatever manner best suits his or her specific talents. A saint is one who having practised heroic virtues, and enjoyed revelations or powers of the order which the Church classes technically as supernatural, is eligible for canonization. If a historian is an Anti-Feminist, and does not believe women to be capable of genius in the traditional masculine departments, he will never make anything of Joan, whose genius was turned to practical account mainly in soldiering and politics. If he is Rationalist enough to deny that saints exist, and to hold that new ideas cannot come otherwise than by conscious ratiocination, he will never catch Joan's likeness. Her ideal biographer must be free from nineteenth-century prejudices and biases; must understand the Middle Ages, the Roman Catholic Church, and the Holy Roman Empire much more intimately than our Whig historians have ever understood them; and must be capable of throwing off sex partialities and their romance, and regarding woman as the female of the human species, and not as a different kind of animal with specific charms and specific imbecilities.

Joan's Good Looks

To put the last point roughly, any book about Joan which begins by describing her as a beauty may be at once classed as a romance. Not one of Joan's comrades, in village, court, or camp, even when they were straining themselves to please the king by praising her, ever claimed that she was pretty. All the men who alluded to the matter declared most emphatically that she was unattractive sexually to a degree that seemed to them miraculous, considering that she was in the bloom of youth, and neither ugly, awkward, deformed, nor unpleasant in her person. The evident truth is that like most women of her hardy managing type she seemed neutral in the conflict of sex because men were too much afraid of her to fall in love with her. She herself was not sexless: in spite of the virginity she had vowed up to a point, and preserved to her death, she never excluded the possibility of marriage for herself. But marriage, with its preliminary of the attraction, pursuit, and capture of a husband, was not her business: she had something else to do. Byron's formula, "Man's love is of man's life a thing apart: 'tis woman's whole existence" did not apply to her any more than to George Washington or any other masculine worker on the heroic scale. Had she lived in our time, picture postcards might have been sold of her as a general: they would not have been sold of her as a sultana. Nevertheless there is one reason for crediting her with a very remarkable face. A sculptor of her time in Orleans made a statue of a helmeted young woman with a face that is unique in art in point of being evidently not an ideal face but a portrait, and yet so uncommon as to be unlike any real woman one has ever seen. It is surmised that Joan served unconsciously as the sculptor's model. There is no proof of this; but those extraordinarily spaced eyes raise so powerfully the question "If this woman be not Joan, who is she?" that I dispense with further evidence, and challenge those who disagree with me to prove a negative. It is a wonderful face, but quite neutral from the point of view of the operatic beauty fancier.

Such a fancier may perhaps be finally chilled by the prosaic fact that Joan was the defendant in a suit for breach of promise of marriage, and that she conducted her own case and won it.

Joan's Social Position

By class Joan was the daughter of a working farmer who was one of the headmen of his village, and transacted its feudal business for it with the neighboring squires and their lawyers. When the castle in which the villagers were entitled to take refuge from raids became derelict, he organized a combination of half a dozen farmers to obtain possession of it so as to occupy it when there was any danger of invasion. As a child, Joan could please herself at times with being the young lady of this castle. Her mother and brothers were able to follow and share her fortune at court without making themselves notably ridiculous. These facts leave us no excuse for the popular romance that turns every heroine into either a princess or a beggarmaid. In the somewhat similar case of Shakespear a whole inverted pyramid of wasted research has been based on the assumption that he was an illiterate laborer, in the face of the plainest evidence that his father was a man of business, and at one time a very prosperous one, married to a woman of some social pretensions. There is the same tendency to drive Joan into the position of a hired shepherd girl, though a hired shepherd girl in Domrémy would have deferred to her as the young lady of the farm.

The difference between Joan's case and Shakespear's is that Shakespear was not illiterate. He had been to school, and knew as much Latin and Greek as most university passmen retain: that is, for practical purposes, none at all. Joan was absolutely illiterate. "I do not know A from B" she said. But many princesses at that time and for long after might have said the same. Marie Antoinette, for instance, at Joan's age could not spell her own name correctly. But this does not mean that Joan was an ignorant person, or that she suffered from the diffidence and sense of social disadvantage now felt by people who cannot read or write. If she could not write letters, she could and did dictate them and attach full and indeed excessive importance to them. When she was called a shepherd lass to her face she very warmly resented it, and challenged any woman to compete with her in the household arts of the mistresses of well-furnished houses. She understood the political and military situation in France much better than most of our newspaper-fed university women-graduates understand the corresponding situation of their own country today. Her first convert was the neighboring commandant at Vaucouleurs; and she converted him by telling him about the defeat of the Dauphin's troops at the Battle of Herrings so long before he had official news of it that he concluded she must have had a divine revelation. This knowledge of and interest in public affairs was nothing extraordinary among farmers in a war-swept countryside. Politicians came to the door too often sword in hand to be disregarded: Joan's people could not afford to be ignorant of what was going on in the feudal world. They were not rich; and Joan worked on the farm as her father did, driving the sheep to pasture and so forth; but there is no evidence or suggestion of sordid poverty, and no reason to believe that Joan had to work as a hired servant works, or indeed to work at all when she preferred to go to confession, or dawdle about waiting for visions and listening to the church bells to hear voices in them. In short, much more of a young lady, and even of an intellectual, than most of the daughters of our petty bourgeoisie.

Joan's Voices and Visions

Joan's voices and visions have played many tricks with her reputation. They have been held to prove that she was mad, that she was a liar and impostor, that she was a sorceress (she was burnt for this), and finally that she was a saint. They do not prove any of these things; but the variety of the conclusions reached shew how little our matter-of-fact historians know about other people's minds, or even about their own. There are people in the world whose imagination is so vivid that when they have an idea it comes to them as an audible voice, sometimes uttered by a visible figure. Criminal lunatic asylums are occupied largely by murderers who have obeyed voices. Thus a woman may hear voices telling her that she must cut her husband's throat and strangle her child as they lie asleep; and she may feel obliged to do what she is told. By a medico-legal superstition it is held in our courts that criminals whose temptations present themselves under these illusions are not responsible for their actions, and must be treated as insane. But the seers of visions and the hearers of revelations are not always criminals. The inspirations and institutions and unconsciously reasoned conclusions of genius sometimes assume similar illusions. Socrates, Luther, Swedenborg, Blake saw visions and heard voices just as Saint Francis and Saint Joan did. If Newton's imagination had been of the same vividly dramatic kind he might have seen the ghost of Pythagoras walk into the orchard and explain why the apples were falling. Such an illusion would have invalidated neither the theory of gravitation nor Newton's general sanity. What is more, the visionary method of making the discovery would not be a whit more miraculous than the normal method. The test of sanity is not the normality of the method but the reasonableness of the discovery. If Newton had been informed by Pythagoras that the moon was made of green cheese, then Newton would have been locked up. Gravitation, being a reasoned hypothesis which fitted remarkably well into the Copernican version of the observed physical facts of the universe, established Newton's reputation for extraordinary intelligence, and would have done so no matter how fantastically he had arrived at it. Yet his theory of gravitation is not so impressive a mental feat as his astounding chronology, which establishes him as the king of mental conjurors, but a Bedlamite king whose authority no one now accepts. On the subject of the eleventh horn of the beast seen by the prophet Daniel he was more fantastic than Joan, because his imagination was not dramatic but mathematical and therefore extraordinarily susceptible to numbers: indeed if all his works were lost except his chronology we should say that he was as mad as a hatter. As it is, who dares diagnose Newton as a madman?

In the same way Joan must be judged a sane woman in spite of her voices because they never gave her any advice that might not have come to her from her mother wit exactly as gravitation came to Newton. We can all see now, especially since the late war threw so many of our women into military life, that Joan's campaigning could not have been carried on in petticoats. This was not only because she did a man's work, but because it was morally necessary that sex should be left out of the question as between her and her comrades-in-arms. She gave this reason herself when she was pressed on the subject; and the fact that this entirely reasonable necessity came to her imagination first as an order from God delivered through the mouth of Saint Catherine does not prove that she was mad. The soundness of the order proves that she was unusually sane; but its form proves that her dramatic imagination played tricks with her senses. Her policy was also quite sound: nobody disputes that the relief of Orleans, followed up by the coronation at Rheims of the Dauphin as a counterblow to the suspicions then current of his legitimacy and consequently of his title, were military and political masterstrokes that saved France. They might have been planned by Napoleon or any other illusion-proof genius. They came to Joan as an instruction from her Counsel, as she called her visionary saints; but she was none the less an able leader of men for imagining her ideas in this way.

The Evolutionary Appetite

What then is the modern view of Joan's voices and visions and messages from God? The nineteenth century said that they were delusions, but that as she was a pretty girl, and had been abominably ill-treated and finally done to death by a superstitious rabble of medieval priests hounded on by a corrupt political bishop, it must be assumed that she was the innocent dupe of these delusions. The twentieth century finds this explanation too vapidly commonplace, and demands something more mystic. I think the twentieth century is right, because an explanation which amounts to Joan being mentally defective instead of, as she obviously was, mentally excessive, will not wash. I cannot believe, nor, if I could, could I expect all my readers to believe, as Joan did, that three ocularly visible well-dressed persons, named respectively Saint Catherine, Saint Margaret, and Saint Michael, came down from heaven and gave her certain instructions with which they were charged by God for her. Not that such a belief would be more improbable or fantastic than some modern beliefs which we all swallow; but there are fashions and family habits in belief, and it happens that, my fashion being Victorian and my family habit Protestant, I find myself unable to attach any such objective validity to the form of Joan's visions.

But that there are forces at work which use individuals for purposes far transcending the purpose of keeping these individuals alive and prosperous and respectable and safe and happy in the middle station in life, which is all any good bourgeois can reasonably require, is established by the fact that men will, in the pursuit of knowledge and of social readjustments for which they will not be a penny the better, and are indeed often many pence the worse, face poverty, infamy, exile, imprisonment, dreadful hardship, and death. Even the selfish pursuit of personal power does not nerve men to the efforts and sacrifices which are eagerly made in pursuit of extensions of our power over nature, though these extensions may not touch the personal life of the seeker at any point. There is no more mystery about this appetite for knowledge and power than about the appetite for food: both are known as facts and as facts only, the difference between them being that the appetite for food is necessary to the life of the hungry man and is therefore a personal appetite, whereas the other is an appetite for evolution, and therefore a superpersonal need.

The diverse manners in which our imaginations dramatize the approach of the superpersonal forces is a problem for the psychologist, not for the historian. Only, the historian must understand that visionaries are neither impostors nor lunatics. It is one thing to say that the figure Joan recognized as St Catherine was not really St Catherine, but the dramatization by Joan's imagination of that pressure upon her of the driving force that is behind evolution which I have just called the evolutionary appetite. It is quite another to class her visions with the vision of two moons seen by a drunken person, or with Brocken spectres, echoes and the like. Saint Catherine's instructions were far too cogent for that; and the simplest French peasant who believes in apparitions of celestial personages to favored mortals is nearer to the scientific truth about Joan than the Rationalist and Materialist historians and essayists who feel obliged to set down a girl who saw saints and heard them talking to her as either crazy or mendacious. If Joan was mad, all Christendom was mad too; for people who believe devoutly in the existence of celestial personages are every whit as mad in that sense as the people who think they see them. Luther, when he threw his inkhorn at the devil, was no more mad than any other Augustinian monk: he had a more vivid imagination, and had perhaps eaten and slept less: that was all.

The Mere Iconography Does Not Matter

All the popular religions in the world are made apprehensible by an array of legendary personages, with an Almighty Father, and sometimes a mother and divine child, as the central figures. These are presented to the mind's eye in childhood; and the result is a hallucination which persists strongly throughout life when it has been well impressed. Thus all the thinking of the hallucinated adult about the fountain of inspiration which is continually flowing in the universe, or about the promptings of virtue and the revulsions of shame: in short, about aspiration and conscience, both of which forces are matters of fact more obvious than electromagnetism is thinking in terms of the celestial vision. And when in the case of exceptionally imaginative persons, especially those practising certain appropriate austerities, the hallucination extends from the mind's eye to the body's, the visionary sees Krishna or the Buddha or the Blessed Virgin or St Catherine as the case may be.

The Modern Education Which Joan Escaped

It is important to every one nowadays to understand this, because modern science is making short work of the hallucinations without regard to the vital importance of the things they symbolize. If Joan were reborn today she would be sent, first to a convent school in which she would be mildly taught to connect inspiration and conscience with St Catherine and St Michael exactly as she was in the fifteenth century, and then finished up with a very energetic training in the gospel of Saints Louis Pasteur and Paul Bert, who would tell her (possibly in visions but more probably in pamphlets) not to be a superstitious little fool, and to empty out St Catherine and the rest of the Catholic hagiology as an obsolete iconography of exploded myths. It would be rubbed into her that Galileo was a martyr, and his persecutors incorrigible ignoramuses, and that St Teresa's hormones had gone astray and left her incurably hyperpituitary or hyperadrenal or hysteroid or epileptoid or anything but asteroid. She would have been convinced by precept and experiment that baptism and receiving the body of her Lord were contemptible superstitions, and that vaccination and vivisection were enlightened practices. Behind her new Saints Louis and Paul there would be not only Science purifying Religion and being purified by it, but hypochondria, melancholia, cowardice, stupidity, cruelty, muckraking curiosity, knowledge without wisdom, and everything that the eternal soul in Nature loathes, instead of the virtues of which St Catherine was the figure head. As to the new rites, which would be the saner Joan? the one who carried little children to be baptized of water and the spirit, or the one who sent the police to force their parents to have the most villainous racial poison we know thrust into their veins? the one who told them the story of the angel and Mary, or the one who questioned them as to their experiences of the Edipus complex? the one to whom the consecrated wafer was the very body of the virtue that was her salvation, or the one who looked forward to a precise and convenient regulation of her health and her desires by a nicely calculated diet of thyroid extract, adrenalin, thymin, pituitrin, and insulin, with pick-me-ups of hormone stimulants, the blood being first carefully fortified with anti-bodies against all possible infections by inoculations of infected bacteria and serum from infected animals, and against old age by surgical extirpation of the reproductive ducts or weekly doses of monkey gland?

It is true that behind all these quackeries there is a certain body of genuine scientific physiology. But was there any the less a certain body of genuine psychology behind St Catherine and the Holy Ghost? And which is the healthier mind? the saintly mind or the monkey gland mind? Does not the present cry of Back to the Middle Ages, which has been incubating ever since the pre-Raphaelite movement began, mean that it is no longer our Academy pictures that are intolerable, but our credulities that have not the excuse of being superstitions, our cruelties that have not the excuse of barbarism, our persecutions that have not the excuse of religious faith, our shameless substitution of successful swindlers and scoundrels and quacks for saints as objects of worship, and our deafness and blindness to the calls and visions of the inexorable power that made us, and will destroy us if we disregard it? To Joan and her contemporaries we should appear as a drove of Gadarene swine, possessed by all the unclean spirits cast out by the faith and civilization of the Middle Ages, running violently down a steep place into a hell of high explosives. For us to set up our condition as a standard of sanity, and declare Joan mad because she never condescended to it, is to prove that we are not only lost but irredeemable. Let us then once for all drop all nonsense about Joan being cracked, and accept her as at least as sane as Florence Nightingale, who also combined a very simple iconography of religious belief with a mind so exceptionally powerful that it kept her in continual trouble with the medical and military panjandrums of her time.

Failures of the Voices

That the voices and visions were illusory, and their wisdom all Joan's own, is shewn by the occasions on which they failed her, notably during her trial, when they assured her that she would be rescued. Here her hopes flattered her; but they were not unreasonable: her military colleague La Hire was in command of a considerable force not so very far off; and if the Armagnacs, as her party was called, had really wanted to rescue her, and had put anything like her own vigor into the enterprise, they could have attempted it with very fair chances of success. She did not understand that they were glad to be rid of her, nor that the rescue of a prisoner from the hands of the Church was a much more serious business for a medieval captain, or even a medieval king, than its mere physical difficulty as a military exploit suggested. According to her lights her expectation of a rescue was reasonable; therefore she heard Madame Saint Catherine assuring her it would happen, that being her way of finding out and making up her own mind. When it became evident that she had miscalculated: when she was led to the stake, and La Hire was not thundering at the gates of Rouen nor charging Warwick's men at arms, she threw over Saint Catherine at once, and recanted. Nothing could be more sane or practical. It was not until she discovered that she had gained nothing by her recantation but close imprisonment for life that she withdrew it, and deliberately and explicitly chose burning instead: a decision which shewed not only the extraordinary decision of her character, but also a Rationalism carried to its ultimate human tests of suicide. Yet even in this the illusion persisted; and she announced her relapse as dictated to her by her voices.

Joan a Galtonic Visualizer

The most sceptical scientific reader may therefore accept as a flat fact, carrying no implication of unsoundness of mind, that Joan was what Francis Galton and other modern investigators of human faculty call a visualizer. She saw imaginary saints just as some other people see imaginary diagrams and landscapes with numbers dotted about them, and are thereby able to perform feats of memory and arithmetic impossible to non-visualizers. Visualizers will understand this at once. Non-visualizers who have never read Galton will be puzzled and incredulous. But a very little inquiry among their acquaintances will reveal to them that the mind's eye is more or less a magic lantern, and that the street is full of normally sane people who have hallucinations of all sorts which they believe to be part of the normal permanent equipment of all human beings.

Joan's Manliness and Militarism

Joan's other abnormality, too common among uncommon things to be properly called a peculiarity, was her craze for soldiering and the masculine life. Her father tried to frighten her out of it by threatening to drown her if she ran away with the soldiers, and ordering her brothers to drown her if he were not on the spot. This extravagance was clearly not serious: it must have been addressed to a child young enough to imagine that he was in earnest. Joan must therefore as a child have wanted to run away and be a soldier. The awful prospect of being thrown into the Meuse and drowned by a terrible father and her big brothers kept her quiet until the father had lost his terrors and the brothers yielded to her natural leadership; and by that time she had sense enough to know that the masculine and military life was not a mere matter of running away from home. But the taste for it never left her, and was fundamental in determining her career.

If any one doubts this, let him ask himself why a maid charged with a special mission from heaven to the Dauphin (this was how Joan saw her very able plan for retrieving the desperate situation of the uncrowned king) should not have simply gone to the court as a maid, in woman's dress, and urged her counsel upon him in a woman's way, as other women with similar missions had come to his mad father and his wise grandfather. Why did she insist on having a soldier's dress and arms and sword and horse and equipment, and on treating her escort of soldiers as comrades, sleeping side by side with them on the floor at night as if there were no difference of sex between them? It may be answered that this was the safest way of travelling through a country infested with hostile troops and bands of marauding deserters from both sides. Such an answer has no weight, because it applies to all the women who travelled in France at that time, and who never dreamt of travelling otherwise than as women. But even if we accept it, how does it account for the fact that when the danger was over, and she could present herself at court in feminine attire with perfect safety and obviously with greater propriety, she presented herself in her man's dress, and instead of urging Charles, like Queen Victoria urging the War Office to send Roberts to the Transvaal, to send D'Alençon, De Rais, La Hire and the rest to the relief of Dunois at Orleans, insisted that she must go herself and lead the assault in person? Why did she give exhibitions of her dexterity in handling a lance, and of her seat as a rider? Why did she accept presents of armor and chargers and masculine surcoats, and in every action repudiate the conventional character of a woman? The simple answer to all these questions is that she was the sort of woman that wants to lead a man's life. They are to be found wherever there are armies on foot or navies on the seas, serving in male disguise, eluding detection for astonishingly long periods, and sometimes, no doubt, escaping it entirely. When they are in a position to defy public opinion they throw off all concealment. You have your Rosa Bonheur painting in male blouse and trousers, and George Sand living a man's life and almost compelling her Chopins and De Mussets to live women's lives to amuse her. Had Joan not been one of those "unwomanly women," she might have been canonized much sooner.

But it is not necessary to wear trousers and smoke big cigars to live a man's life any more than it is necessary to wear petticoats to live a woman's. There are plenty of gowned and bodiced women in ordinary civil life who manage their own affairs and other people's, including those of their menfolk, and are entirely masculine in their tastes and pursuits. There always were such women, even in the Victorian days when women had fewer legal rights than men, and our modern women magistrates, mayors, and members of Parliament were unknown. In reactionary Russia in our own century a woman soldier organized an effective regiment of amazons, which disappeared only because it was Aldershottian enough to be against the Revolution. The exemption of women from military service is founded, not on any natural inaptitude that men do not share, but on the fact that communities cannot reproduce themselves without plenty of women. Men are more largely dispensable, and are sacrificed accordingly.

Was Joan Suicidal?

These two abnormalities were the only ones that were irresistibly prepotent in Joan; and they brought her to the stake. Neither of them was peculiar to her. There was nothing peculiar about her except the vigor and scope of her mind and character, and the intensity of her vital energy. She was accused of a suicidal tendency; and it is a fact that when she attempted to escape from Beaurevoir Castle by jumping from a tower said to be sixty feet high, she took a risk beyond reason, though she recovered from the crash after a few days fasting. Her death was deliberately chosen as an alternative to life without liberty. In battle she challenged death as Wellington did at Waterloo, and as Nelson habitually did when he walked his quarter deck during his battles with all his decorations in full blaze. As neither Nelson nor Wellington nor any of those who have performed desperate feats, and preferred death to captivity, have been accused of suicidal mania, Joan need not be suspected of it. In the Beaurevoir affair there was more at stake than her freedom. She was distracted by the news that Compiègne was about to fall; and she was convinced that she could save it if only she could get free. Still, the leap was so perilous that her conscience was not quite easy about it; and she expressed this, as usual, by saying that Saint Catherine had forbidden her to do it, but forgave her afterwards for her disobedience.

Joan Summed Up

We may accept and admire Joan, then, as a sane and shrewd country girl of extraordinary strength of mind and hardihood of body. Everything she did was thoroughly calculated; and though the process was so rapid that she was hardly conscious of it, and ascribed it all to her voices, she was a woman of policy and not of blind impulse. In war she was as much a realist as Napoleon: she had his eye for artillery and his knowledge of what it could do. She did not expect besieged cities to fall Jerichowise at the sound of her trumpet, but, like Wellington, adapted her methods of attack to the peculiarities of the defence; and she anticipated the Napoleonic calculation that if you only hold on long enough the other fellow will give in: for example, her final triumph at Orleans was achieved after her commander Dunois had sounded the retreat at the end of a day's fighting without a decision. She was never for a moment what so many romancers and playwrights have pretended: a romantic young lady. She was a thorough daughter of the soil in her peasantlike matter-of-factness and doggedness, and her acceptance of great lords and kings and prelates as such without idolatry or snobbery, seeing at a glance how much they were individually good for. She had the respectable countrywoman's sense of the value of public decency, and would not tolerate foul language and neglect of religious observances, nor allow disreputable women to hang about her soldiers. She had one pious ejaculation *"En nom Dé!"* and one meaningless oath *"Par mon martin;"* and this much swearing she allowed to the incorrigibly blasphemous La Hire equally with herself. The value of this prudery was so great in restoring the self-respect of the badly demoralized army that, like most of her policy, it justified itself as soundly calculated. She talked to and dealt with people of all classes, from laborers to kings, without embarrassment or affectation, and got them to do what she wanted when they were not afraid or corrupt. She could coax and she could hustle, her tongue having a soft side and a sharp edge. She was very capable: a born boss.

Joan's Immaturity and Ignorance

All this, however, must be taken with one heavy qualification. She was only a girl in her teens. If we could think of her as a managing woman of fifty we should seize her type at once; for we have plenty of managing women among us of that age who illustrate perfectly the sort of person she would have become had she lived. But she, being only a lass when all is said, lacked their knowledge of men's vanities and of the weight and proportion of social forces. She knew nothing of iron hands in velvet gloves: she just used her fists. She thought political changes much easier than they are, and, like Mahomet in his innocence of any world but the tribal world, wrote letters to kings calling on them to make millennial rearrangements. Consequently it was only in the enterprises that were really simple and compassable by swift physical force, like the coronation and the Orleans campaign, that she was successful.

Her want of academic education disabled her when she had to deal with such elaborately artificial structures as the great ecclesiastical and social institutions of the Middle Ages. She had a horror of heretics without suspecting that she was herself a heresiarch, one of the precursors of a schism that rent Europe in two, and cost centuries of bloodshed that is not yet staunched. She objected to foreigners on the sensible ground that they were not in their proper place in France; but she had no notion of how this brought her into conflict with Catholicism and Feudalism, both essentially international. She worked by commonsense; and where scholarship was the only clue to institutions she was in the dark and broke her shins against them, all the more rudely because of her enormous self-confidence, which made her the least cautious of human beings in civil affairs.

This combination of inept youth and academic ignorance with great natural capacity, push, courage, devotion, originality and oddity, fully accounts for all the facts in Joan's career, and makes her a credible historical and human phenomenon; but it clashes most discordantly both with the idolatrous romance that has grown up round her, and the belittling scepticism that reacts against that romance.

The Maid in Literature

English readers would probably like to know how these idolizations and reactions have affected the books they are most familiar with about Joan. There is the first part of the Shakesperean, or pseudo-Shakesperean trilogy of Henry VI, in which Joan is one of the leading characters. This portrait of Joan is not more authentic than the descriptions in the London papers of George Washington in 1780, of Napoleon in 1803, of the German Crown Prince in 1917, or of Lenin in 1917. It ends in mere scurrility. The impression left by it is that the playwright, having begun by an attempt to make Joan a beautiful and romantic figure, was told by his scandalized company that English patriotism would never stand a sympathetic representation of a French conqueror of English troops, and that unless he at once introduced all the old charges against Joan of being a sorceress and a harlot, and assumed her to be guilty of all of them, his play could not be produced. As likely as not, this is what actually happened: indeed there is only one other apparent way of accounting for the sympathetic representation of Joan as a heroine culminating in her eloquent appeal to the Duke of Burgundy, followed by the blackguardly scurrility of the concluding scenes. That other way is to assume that the original play was wholly scurrilous, and that Shakespear touched up the earlier scenes. As the work belongs to a period at which he was only beginning his practice as a tinker of old works, before his own style was fully formed and hardened, it is impossible to verify this guess. His finger is not unmistakably evident in the play, which is poor and base in its moral tone; but he may have tried to redeem it from downright infamy by shedding a momentary glamor on the figure of The Maid.

When we jump over two centuries to Schiller, we find Die Jungfrau von Orleans drowned in a witch's caldron of raging romance. Schiller's Joan has not a single point of contact with the real Joan, nor indeed with any mortal woman that ever walked this earth. There is really nothing to be said of his play but that it is not about Joan at all, and can hardly be said to pretend to be; for he makes her die on the battlefield, finding her burning unbearable. Before Schiller came Voltaire, who burlesqued Homer in a mock epic called La Pucelle. It is the fashion to dismiss this with virtuous indignation as an obscene libel; and I certainly cannot defend it against the charge of extravagant indecorum. But its purpose was not to depict Joan, but to kill with ridicule everything that Voltaire righteously hated in the institutions and fashions of his own day. He made Joan ridiculous, but not contemptible nor (comparatively) unchaste; and as he also made Homer and St Peter and St Denis and the brave Dunois ridiculous, and the other heroines of the poem very unchaste indeed, he may be said to have let Joan off very easily. But indeed the personal adventures of the characters are so outrageous, and so Homerically free from any pretence at or even possibility of historical veracity, that those who affect to take them seriously only make themselves Pecksniffian. Samuel Butler believed The Iliad to be a burlesque of Greek Jingoism and Greek religion, written by a hostage or a slave; and La Pucelle makes Butler's theory almost convincing. Voltaire represents Agnes Sorel, the Dauphin's mistress, whom Joan never met, as a woman with a consuming passion for the chastest concubinal fidelity, whose fate it was to be continually falling into the hands of licentious foes and suffering the worst extremities of rapine. The combats in which Joan rides a flying donkey, or in which, taken unaware with no clothes on, she defends Agnes with her sword, and inflicts appropriate mutilations on her assailants, can be laughed at as they are intended to be without scruple; for no sane person could mistake them for sober history; and it may be that their ribald irreverence is more wholesome than the beglamored sentimentality of Schiller. Certainly Voltaire should not have asserted that Joan's father was a priest; but when he was out to *écraser l'infâme* (the French Church) he stuck at nothing.

So far, the literary representations of The Maid were legendary. But the publication by Quicherat in 1841 of the reports of her trial and rehabilitation placed the subject on a new footing. These entirely realistic documents created a living interest in Joan which Voltaire's mock Homerics and Schiller's romantic nonsense missed. Typical products of that interest in America and England are the histories of Joan by Mark Twain and Andrew Lang. Mark Twain was converted to downright worship of Joan directly by Quicherat. Later on, another man of genius, Anatole France, reacted against the Quicheratic wave of enthusiasm, and wrote a Life of Joan in which he attributed Joan's ideas to clerical prompting and her military success to an adroit use of her by Dunois as a *mascotte*: in short, he denied that she had any serious military or political ability. At this Andrew saw red, and went for Anatole's scalp in a rival Life of her which should be read as a corrective to the other. Lang had no difficulty in showing that Joan's ability was not an unnatural fiction to be explained away as an illusion manufactured by priests and soldiers, but a straightforward fact.

It has been lightly pleaded in explanation that Anatole France is a Parisian of the art world, into whose scheme of things the able, hardheaded, hardhanded female, though she dominates provincial France and business Paris, does not enter; whereas Lang was a Scot, and every Scot knows that the gray mare is as likely as not to be the better horse. But this explanation does not convince me. I cannot believe that Anatole France does not know what everybody knows. I wish everybody knew all that he knows. One feels antipathies at work in his book. He is not anti-Joan; but he is anti-clerical, anti-mystic, and fundamentally unable to believe that there ever was any such person as the real Joan.

Mark Twain's Joan, skirted to the ground, and with as many petticoats as Noah's wife in a toy ark, is an attempt to combine Bayard with Esther Summerson from Bleak House into an unimpeachable American school teacher in armor. Like Esther Summerson she makes her creator ridiculous, and yet, being the work of a man of genius, remains a credible human goodygoody in spite of her creator's infatuation. It is the description rather than the valuation that is wrong. Andrew Lang and Mark Twain are equally determined to make Joan a beautiful and most ladylike Victorian; but both of them recognize and insist on her capacity for leadership, though the Scots scholar is less romantic about it than the Mississippi pilot

But then Lang was, by lifelong professional habit, a critic of biographies rather than a biographer, whereas Mark Twain writes his biography frankly in the form of a romance.

Protestant Misunderstandings of the Middle Ages

They had, however, one disability in common. To understand Joan's history it is not enough to understand her character: you must understand her environment as well. Joan in a nineteenth-twentieth-century environment is as incongruous a figure as she would appear were she to walk down Piccadilly today in her fifteenth-century armor. To see her in her proper perspective you must understand Christendom and the Catholic Church, the Holy Roman Empire and the Feudal System, as they existed and were understood in the Middle Ages. If you confuse the Middle Ages with the Dark Ages, and are in the habit of ridiculing your aunt for wearing "medieval clothes," meaning those in vogue in the eighteen-nineties, and are quite convinced that the world has progressed enormously, both morally and mechanically, since Joan's time, then you will never understand why Joan was burnt, much less feel that you might have voted for burning her yourself if you had been a member of the court that tried her; and until you feel that you know nothing essential about her.

That the Mississippi pilot should have broken down on this misunderstanding is natural enough. Mark Twain, the Innocent Abroad, who saw the lovely churches of the Middle Ages without a throb of emotion, author of A Yankee at the Court of King Arthur, in which the heroes and heroines of medieval chivalry are guys seen through the eyes of a street arab, was clearly out of court from the beginning. Andrew Lang was better read; but, like Walter Scott, he enjoyed medieval history as a string of border romances rather than as the record of a high European civilization based on a catholic faith. Both of them were baptized as Protestants, and impressed by all their schooling and most of their reading with the belief that Catholic bishops who burnt heretics were persecutors capable of any villainy; that all heretics were Albigensians or Husites or Jews or Protestants of the highest character; and that the Inquisition was a Chamber of Horrors invented expressly and exclusively for such burnings. Accordingly we find them representing Peter Cauchon, Bishop of Beauvais, the judge who sent Joan to the stake, as an unconscionable scoundrel, and all the questions put to her as "traps" to ensnare and destroy her. And they assume unhesitatingly that the two or three score of canons and doctors of law and divinity who sat with Cauchon as assessors, were exact reproductions of him on slightly less elevated chairs and with a different headdress.

Comparative Fairness of Joan's Trial

The truth is that Cauchon was threatened and insulted by the English for being too considerate to Joan. A recent French writer denies that Joan was burnt, and holds that Cauchon spirited her away and burnt somebody or something else in her place, and that the pretender who subsequently personated her at Orleans and elsewhere was not a pretender but the real authentic Joan. He is able to cite Cauchon's pro-Joan partiality in support of his view. As to the assessors, the objection to them is not that they were a row of uniform rascals, but that they were political partisans of Joan's enemies. This is a valid objection to all such trials; but in the absence of neutral tribunals they are unavoidable. A trial by Joan's French partisans would have been as unfair as the trial by her French opponents; and an equally mixed tribunal would have produced a deadlock. Such recent trials as those of Edith Cavell by a German tribunal and Roger Casement by an English one were open to the same objection; but they went forward to the death nevertheless, because neutral tribunals were not available. Edith, like Joan, was an arch heretic: in the middle of the war she declared before the world that "Patriotism is not enough." She nursed enemies back to health, and assisted their prisoners to escape, making it abundantly clear that she would help any fugitive or distressed person without asking whose side he was on, and acknowledging no distinction before Christ between Tommy and Jerry and Pitou the *poilu*. Well might Edith have wished that she could bring the Middle Ages back, and have fifty civilians learned in the law or vowed to the service of God, to support two skilled judges in trying her case according to the Catholic law of Christendom, and to argue it out with her at sitting after sitting for many weeks. The modern military Inquisition was not so squeamish. It shot her out of hand; and her countrymen, seeing in this a good opportunity for lecturing the enemy on his intolerance, put up a statue to her, but took particular care not to inscribe on the pedestal "Patriotism is not enough," for which omission, and the lie it implies, they will need Edith's intercession when they are themselves brought to judgment, if any heavenly power thinks such moral cowards capable of pleading to an intelligible indictment.

The point need be no further labored. Joan was persecuted essentially as she would be persecuted today. The change from burning to hanging or shooting may strike us as a change for the better. The change from careful trial under ordinary law to recklessly summary military terrorism may strike us as a change for the worse. But as far as toleration is concerned the trial and execution in Rouen in 1431 might have been an event of today; and we may charge our consciences accordingly. If Joan had to be dealt with by us in London she would be treated with no more toleration than Miss Sylvia Pankhurst, or the Peculiar People, or the parents who keep their children from the elementary school, or any of the others who cross the line we have to draw, rightly or wrongly, between the tolerable and the intolerable.

Joan Not Tried as a Political Offender

Besides, Joan's trial was not, like Casement's, a national political trial. Ecclesiastical courts and the courts of the Inquisition (Joan was tried by a combination of the two) were Courts Christian: that is, international courts; and she was tried, not as a traitress, but as a heretic, blasphemer, sorceress and idolater. Her alleged offences were not political offences against England, nor against the Burgundian faction in France, but against God and against the common morality of Christendom. And although the idea we call Nationalism was so foreign to the medieval conception of Christian society that it might almost have been directly charged against Joan as an additional heresy, yet it was not so charged; and it is unreasonable to suppose that the political bias of a body of Frenchmen like the assessors would on this point have run strongly in favor of the English foreigners (even if they had been making themselves particularly agreeable in France instead of just the contrary) against a Frenchwoman who had vanquished them.

The tragic part of the trial was that Joan, like most prisoners tried for anything but the simplest breaches of the ten commandments, did not understand what they were accusing her of. She was much more like Mark Twain than like Peter Cauchon. Her attachment to the Church was very different from the Bishop's, and does not, in fact, bear close examination from his point of view. She delighted in the solaces the Church offers to sensitive souls: to her, confession and communion were luxuries beside which the vulgar pleasures of the senses were trash. Her prayers were wonderful conversations with her three saints. Her piety seemed superhuman to the formally dutiful people whose religion was only a task to them. But when the Church was not offering her her favorite luxuries, but calling on her to accept its interpretation of God's will, and to sacrifice her own, she flatly refused, and made it clear that her notion of a Catholic Church was one in which the Pope was Pope Joan. How could the Church tolerate that, when it had just destroyed Hus, and had watched the career of Wycliffe with a growing anger that would have brought him, too, to the stake, had he not died a natural death before the wrath fell on him in his grave? Neither Hus nor Wycliffe was as bluntly defiant as Joan: both were reformers of the Church like Luther; whilst Joan, like Mrs. Eddy, was quite prepared to supersede St Peter as the rock on which the Church was built, and, like Mahomet, was always ready with a private revelation from God to settle every question and fit every occasion.

The enormity of Joan's pretension was proved by her own unconsciousness of it, which we call her innocence, and her friends called her simplicity. Her solutions of the problems presented to her seemed, and indeed mostly were, the plainest commonsense, and their revelation to her by her Voices was to her a simple matter of fact. How could plain commonsense and simple fact seem to her to be that hideous thing, heresy? When rival prophetesses came into the field, she was down on them at once for liars and humbugs; but she never thought of them as heretics. She was in a state of invincible ignorance as to the Church's view; and the Church could not tolerate her pretensions without either waiving its authority or giving her a place beside the Trinity during her lifetime and in her teens, which was unthinkable. Thus an irresistible force met an immovable obstacle, and developed the heat that consumed poor Joan.

Mark and Andrew would have shared her innocence and her fate had they been dealt with by the Inquisition: that is why their accounts of the trial are as absurd as hers might have been could she have written one. All that can be said for their assumption that Cauchon was a vulgar villain, and that the questions put to Joan were traps, is that it has the support of the inquiry which rehabilitated her twenty-five years later. But this rehabilitation was as corrupt as the contrary proceeding applied to Cromwell by our Restoration reactionaries. Cauchon had been dug up, and his body thrown into the common sewer. Nothing was easier than to accuse him of cozenage, and declare the whole trial void on that account. That was what everybody wanted, from Charles the Victorious, whose credit was bound up with The Maid's, to the patriotic Nationalist populace, who idolized Joan's memory. The English were gone; and a verdict in their favor would have been an outrage on the throne and on the patriotism which Joan had set on foot.

We have none of these overwhelming motives of political convenience and popularity to bias us. For us the first trial stands valid; and the rehabilitation would be negligible but for the mass of sincere testimony it produced as to Joan's engaging personal character. The question then arises: how did the Church get over the verdict at the first trial when it canonized Joan five hundred years later?

The Church Uncompromised by Its Amends

Easily enough. In the Catholic Church, far more than in law, there is no wrong without a remedy. It does not defer to Joanesque private judgment as such, the supremacy of private judgment for the individual being the quintessence of Protestantism; nevertheless it finds a place for private judgment *in excelsis* by admitting that the highest wisdom may come as a divine revelation to an individual. On sufficient evidence it will declare that individual a saint. Thus, as revelation may come by way of an enlightenment of the private judgment no less than by words of a celestial personage appearing in a vision, a saint may be defined as a person of heroic virtue whose private judgment is privileged. Many innovating saints, notably Francis and Clare, have been in conflict with the Church during their lives, and have thus raised the question whether they were heretics or saints. Francis might have gone to the stake had he lived longer. It is therefore by no means impossible for a person to be excommunicated as a heretic, and on further consideration canonized as a saint. Excommunication by a provincial ecclesiastical court is not one of the acts for which the Church claims infallibility. Perhaps I had better inform my Protestant readers that the famous Dogma of Papal Infallibility is by far the most modest pretension of the kind in existence. Compared to our infallible democracies, our infallible medical councils, our infallible astronomers, our infallible judges, and our infallible parliaments, the Pope is on his knees in the dust confessing his ignorance before the throne of God, asking only that as to certain historical matters on which he has clearly more sources of information open to him than any one else his decision shall be taken as final. The Church may, and perhaps some day will, canonize Galileo without compromising such infallibility as it claims for the Pope, if not without compromising the infallibility claimed for the Book of Joshua by simple souls whose rational faith in more important things has become bound up with a quite irrational faith in the chronicle of Joshua's campaigns as a treatise on physics. Therefore the Church will probably not canonize Galileo yet awhile, though it might do worse. But it has been able to canonize Joan without any compromise at all. She never doubted that the sun went round the earth: she had seen it do so too often.

Still, there was a great wrong done to Joan and to the conscience of the world by her burning. *Tout comprendre, c'est tout pardonner,* which is the Devil's sentimentality, cannot excuse it. When we have admitted that the tribunal was not only honest and legal, but exceptionally merciful in respect of sparing Joan the torture which was customary when she was obdurate as to taking the oath, and that Cauchon was far more self-disciplined and conscientious both as priest and lawyer than any English judge ever dreams of being in a political case in which his party and class prejudices are involved, the human fact remains that the burning of Joan of Arc was a horror, and that a historian who would defend it would defend anything. The final criticism of its physical side is implied on the refusal of the Marquesas islanders to be persuaded that the English did not eat Joan. Why, they ask, should any one take the trouble to roast a human being except with that object? They cannot conceive its being a pleasure. As we have no answer for them that is not shameful to us, let us blush for our more complicated and pretentious savagery before we proceed to unravel the business further, and see what other lessons it contains for us.

Cruelty, Modern and Medieval

First, let us get rid of the notion that the mere physical cruelty of the burning has any special significance. Joan was burnt just as dozens of less interesting heretics were burnt in her time. Christ, in being crucified, only shared the fate of thousands of forgotten malefactors. They have no pre-eminence in mere physical pain: much more horrible executions than theirs are on record, to say nothing of the agonies of so-called natural death at its worst.

Joan was burnt more than five hundred years ago. More than three hundred years later: that is, only about a hundred years before I was born, a woman was burnt on Stephen's Green in my native city of Dublin for coining, which was held to be treason. In my preface to the recent volume on English Prisons under Local Government, by Sidney and Beatrice Webb, I have mentioned that when I was already a grown man I saw Richard Wagner conduct two concerts, and that when Richard Wagner was a young man he saw and avoided a crowd of people hastening to see a soldier broken on the wheel by the more cruel of the two ways of carrying out that hideous method of execution. Also that the penalty of hanging, drawing and quartering, unmentionable in its details, was abolished so recently that there are men living who have been sentenced to it. We are still flogging criminals, and clamoring for more flogging. Not even the most sensationally frightful of these atrocities inflicted on its victim the misery, degradation, and conscious waste and loss of life suffered in our modern prisons, especially the model ones, without, as far as I can see, rousing any more compunction than the burning of heretics did in the Middle Ages. We have not even the excuse of getting some fun out of our prisons as the Middle Ages did out of their stakes and wheels and gibbets. Joan herself judged this matter when she had to choose between imprisonment and the stake, and chose the stake. And thereby she deprived the Church of the plea that it was guiltless of her death, which was the work of the secular arm. The Church should have confined itself to excommunicating her. There it was within its rights: she had refused to accept its authority or comply with its conditions; and it could say with truth "You are not one of us: go forth and find the religion that suits you, or found one for yourself." It had no right to say "You may return to us now that you have recanted; but you shall stay in a dungeon all the rest of your life." Unfortunately, the Church did not believe that there was any genuine soul-saving religion outside itself; and it was deeply corrupted, as all the churches were and still are, by primitive Calibanism (in Browning's sense), or the propitiation of a dreaded deity by suffering and sacrifice. Its method was not cruelty for cruelty's sake, but cruelty for the salvation of Joan's soul. Joan, however, believed that the saving of her soul was her own business, and not that of *les gens d'église*. By using that term as she did, mistrustfully and contemptuously, she announced herself as, in germ, an anti-Clerical as thoroughgoing as Voltaire or Anatole France. Had she said in so many words "To the dustbin with the Church Militant and its black-coated officials: I recognize only the Church Triumphant in heaven," she would hardly have put her view more plainly.

Catholic Anti-Clericalism

I must not leave it to be inferred here than one cannot be an anti-Clerical and a good Catholic too. All the reforming Popes have been vehement anti-Clericals, veritable scourges of the clergy. All the great Orders arose from dissatisfaction with the priests: that of the Franciscans with priestly snobbery, that of the Dominicans with priestly laziness and Laodiceanism, that of the Jesuits with priestly apathy and ignorance and indiscipline. The most bigoted Ulster Orangeman or Leicester Low Church bourgeois (as described by Mr. Henry Nevinson) is a mere Gallio compared to Machiavelli, who, though no Protestant, was a fierce anti-Clerical. Any Catholic may, and many Catholics do, denounce any priest or body of priests, as lazy, drunken, idle, dissolute, and unworthy of their great Church and their function as the pastors of their flocks of human souls. But to say that the souls of the people are no business of the Churchmen is to go a step further, a step across the Rubicon. Joan virtually took that step.

Catholicism not yet Catholic Enough

And so, if we admit, as we must, that the burning of Joan was a mistake, we must broaden Catholicism sufficiently to include her in its charter. Our Churches must admit that no official organization of mortal men whose vocation does not carry with it extraordinary mental powers (and this is all that any Church Militant can in the face of fact and history pretend to be), can keep pace with the private judgment of persons of genius except when, by a very rare accident, the genius happens to be Pope, and not even then unless he is an exceedingly overbearing Pope. The Churches must learn humility as well as teach it. The Apostolic Succession cannot be secured or confined by the laying on of hands: the tongues of fire have descended on heathens and outcasts too often for that, leaving anointed Churchmen to scandalize History as worldly rascals. When the Church Militant behaves as if it were already the Church Triumphant, it makes these appalling blunders about Joan and Bruno and Galileo and the rest which make it so difficult for a Freethinker to join it; and a Church which has no place for Freethinkers: nay, which does not inculcate and encourage freethinking with a complete belief that thought, when really free, must by its own law take the path that leads to the Church's bosom, not only has no future in modern culture, but obviously has no faith in the valid science of its own tenets, and is guilty of the heresy that theology and science are two different and opposite impulses, rivals for human allegiance.

I have before me the letter of a Catholic priest. "In your play," he writes, "I see the dramatic presentation of the conflict of the Regal, sacerdotal, and Prophetical powers, in which Joan was crushed. To me it is not the victory of any one of them over the others that will bring peace and the Reign of the Saints in the Kingdom of God, but their fruitful interaction in a costly but noble state of tension." The Pope himself could not put it better; nor can I. We must accept the tension, and maintain it nobly without letting ourselves be tempted to relieve it by burning the thread. This is Joan's lesson to the Church; and its formulation by the hand of a priest emboldens me to claim that her canonization was a magnificently Catholic gesture as the canonization of a Protestant saint by the Church of Rome. But its special value and virtue cannot be apparent until it is known and understood as such. If any simple priest for whom this is too hard a saying tells me that it was not so intended, I shall remind him that the Church is in the hands of God, and not, as simple priests imagine, God in the hands of the Church; so if he answers too confidently for God's intentions he may be asked "Hast thou entered into the springs of the sea? or hast thou walked in the recesses of the deep?" And Joan's own answer is also the answer of old: "Though He slay me, yet will I trust in Him; *but I will maintain my own ways before Him.*"

The Law of Change is the Law of God

When Joan maintained her own ways she claimed, like Job, that there was not only God and the Church to be considered, but the Word made Flesh: that is, the unaveraged individual, representing life possibly at its highest actual human evolution and possibly at its lowest, but never at its merely mathematical average. Now there is no deification of the democratic average in the theory of the Church: it is an avowed hierarchy in which the members are sifted until at the end of the process an individual stands supreme as the Vicar of Christ. But when the process is examined it appears that its successive steps of selection and election are of the superior by the inferior (the cardinal vice of democracy), with the result that great popes are as rare and accidental as great kings, and that it has sometimes been safer for an aspirant to the Chair and the Keys to pass as a moribund dotard than as an energetic saint. At best very few popes have been canonized, or could be without letting down the standard of sanctity set by the self-elected saints.

No other result could have been reasonably expected; for it is not possible that an official organization of the spiritual needs of millions of men and women, mostly poor and ignorant, should compete successfully in the selection of its principals with the direct choice of the Holy Ghost as it flashes with unerring aim upon the individual. Nor can any College of Cardinals pray effectively that its choice may be inspired. The conscious prayer of the inferior may be that his choice may light on a greater than himself; but the sub-conscious intention of his self-preserving individuality must be to find a trustworthy servant for his own purposes. The saints and prophets, though they may be accidentally in this or that official position or ranks, are always really self-selected, like Joan. And since neither Church nor State, by the secular necessities of its constitution, can guarantee even the recognition of such self-chosen missions, there is nothing for us but to make it a point of honor to privilege heresy to the last bearable degree on the simple ground that all evolution in thought and conduct must at first appear as heresy and misconduct. In short, though all society is founded on intolerance, all improvement is founded on tolerance, or the recognition of the fact that the law of evolution is Ibsen's law of change. And as the law of God, in any sense of the word which can now command a faith proof against science is a law of evolution, it follows that the law of God is a law of change, and that when the Churches set themselves against change as such, they are setting themselves against the law of God.

Credulity, Modern and Medieval

When Abernethy, the famous doctor, was asked why he indulged himself with all the habits he warned his patients against as unhealthy, he replied that his business was that of a direction post, which points out the way to a place, but does not go thither itself. He might have added that neither does it compel the traveller to go thither, nor prevent him from seeking some other way. Unfortunately our clerical direction posts always do coerce the traveller when they have the political power to do so. When the Church was a temporal as well as a spiritual power, and for long after to the full extent to which it could control or influence the temporal power, it enforced conformity by persecutions that were all the more ruthless because their intention was so excellent. Today, when the doctor has succeeded to the priest, and can do practically what he likes with parliament and the press through the blind faith in him which has succeeded to the far more critical faith in the parson, legal compulsion to take the doctor's prescription, however poisonous, is carried to an extent that would have horrified the Inquisition and staggered Archbishop Laud. Our credulity is grosser than that of the Middle Ages, because the priest had no such direct pecuniary interest in our sins as the doctor has in our diseases: he did not starve when all was well with his flock, nor prosper when they were perishing, as our private commercial doctors must. Also the medieval cleric believed that something extremely unpleasant would happen to him after death if he was unscrupulous, a belief now practically extinct among persons receiving a dogmatically materialist education. Our professional corporations are Trade Unions without souls to be damned! and they will soon drive us to remind them that they have bodies to be kicked. The Vatican was never soulless: at worst it was a political conspiracy to make the Church supreme temporally as well as spiritually. Therefore the question raised by Joan's burning is a burning question still, though the penalties involved are not so sensational. That is why I am probing it. If it were only an historical curiosity I would not waste my reader's time and my own on it for five minutes.

Toleration, Modern and Medieval

The more closely we grapple with it the more difficult it becomes. At first sight we are disposed to repeat that Joan should have been excommunicated and then left to go her own way, though she would have protested vehemently against so cruel a deprivation of her spiritual food; for confession, absolution, and the body of her Lord were first necessities of life to her. Such a spirit as Joan's might have got over that difficulty as the Church of England got over the Bulls of Pope Leo, by making a church of her own, and affirming it to be the temple of the true and original faith from which her persecutors had strayed. But as such a proceeding was, in the eyes of both Church and State at that time, a spreading of damnation and anarchy, its toleration involved a greater strain on faith in freedom than political and ecclesiastical human nature could bear. It is easy to say that the Church should have waited for the alleged evil results instead of assuming that they would occur, and what they would be. That sounds simple enough; but if a modern

Public Health Authority were to leave people entirely to their own devices in the matter of sanitation, saying, "We have nothing to do with drainage or your views about drainage; but if you catch smallpox or typhus we will prosecute you and have you punished very severely like the authorities in Butler's Erewhon," it would either be removed to the County Asylum or reminded that A's neglect of sanitation may kill the child of B two miles off, or start an epidemic in which the most conscientious sanitarians may perish.

We must face the fact that society is founded on intolerance. There are glaring cases of the abuse of intolerance; but they are quite as characteristic of our own age as of the Middle Ages. The typical modern example and contrast is compulsory inoculation replacing what was virtually compulsory baptism. But compulsion to inoculate is objected to as a crudely unscientific and mischievous anti-sanitary quackery, not in the least because we think it wrong to compel people to protect their children from disease. Its opponents would make it a crime, and will probably succeed in doing so; and that will be just as intolerant as making it compulsory. Neither the Pasteurians nor their opponents the Sanitarians would leave parents free to bring up their children naked, though that course also has some plausible advocates. We may prate of toleration as we will; but society must always draw a line somewhere between allowable conduct and insanity or crime, in spite of the risk of mistaking sages for lunatics and saviors for blasphemers. We must persecute, even to the death; and all we can do to mitigate the danger of persecution is, first, to be very careful what we persecute, and second, to bear in mind that unless there is a large liberty to shock conventional people, and a well-informed sense of the value of originality, individuality, and eccentricity, the result will be apparent stagnation covering a repression of evolutionary forces which will eventually explode with extravagant and probably destructive violence.

Variability of Toleration

The degree of tolerance attainable at any moment depends on the strain under which society is maintaining its cohesion. In war, for instance, we suppress the gospels and put Quakers in prison, muzzle the newspapers, and make it a serious offence to shew a light at night. Under the strain of invasion the French Government in 1792 struck off 4000 heads, mostly on grounds that would not in time of settled peace have provoked any Government to chloroform a dog; and in 1920 the British Government slaughtered and burnt in Ireland to persecute the advocates of a constitutional change which it had presently to effect itself. Later on the Fascisti in Italy did everything that the Black and Tans did in Ireland, with some grotesquely ferocious variations, under the strain of an unskilled attempt at industrial revolution by Socialists who understood Socialism even less than Capitalists understand Capitalism. In the United States an incredibly savage persecution of Russians took place during the scare spread by the Russian Bolshevik revolution after 1917. These instances could easily be multiplied; but they are enough to shew that between a maximum of indulgent toleration and a ruthlessly intolerant Terrorism there is a scale through which toleration is continually rising or falling, and that there was not the smallest ground for the self-complacent conviction of the nineteenth century that it was more tolerant than the fifteenth, or that such an event as the execution of Joan could not possibly occur in what we call our own more enlightened times. Thousands of women, each of them a thousand times less dangerous and terrifying to our Governments than Joan was to the Government of her day, have within the last ten years been slaughtered, starved to death, burnt out of house and home, and what not that Persecution and Terror could do to them, in the course of Crusades far more tyrannically pretentious than the medieval Crusades which proposed nothing more hyperbolical than the rescue of the Holy Sepulchre from the Saracens. The Inquisition, with its English equivalent the Star Chamber, are gone in the sense that their names are now disused; but can any of the modern substitutes for the Inquisition, the Special Tribunals and Commissions, the punitive expeditions, the suspensions of the Habeas Corpus Act, the proclamations of martial law and of minor states of siege, and the rest of them, claim that their victims have as fair a trial, as well considered a body of law to govern their cases, or as conscientious a judge to insist on strict legality of procedure as Joan had from the Inquisition and from the spirit of the Middle Ages even when her country was under the heaviest strain of civil and foreign war? From us she would have had no trial and no law except a Defense of the Realm Act suspending all law; and for judge she would have had, at best, a bothered major, and at worst a promoted advocate in ermine and scarlet to whom the scruples of a trained ecclesiastic like Cauchon would seem ridiculous and ungentlemanly.

The Conflict between Genius and Discipline

Having thus brought the matter home to ourselves, we may now consider the special feature of Joan's mental constitution which made her so unmanageable. What is to be done on the one hand with rulers who will not give any reason for their orders, and on the other with people who cannot understand the reasons when they are given? The government of the world, political, industrial, and domestic, has to be carried on mostly by the giving and obeying of orders under just these conditions. "Don't argue: do as you are told" has to be said not only to children and soldiers, but practically to everybody. Fortunately most people do not want to argue: they are only too glad to be saved the trouble of thinking for themselves. And the ablest and most independent thinkers are content to understand their own special department. In other departments they will unhesitatingly ask for and accept the instructions of a policeman or the advice of a tailor without demanding or desiring explanations.

Nevertheless, there must be some ground for attaching authority to an order. A child will obey its parents, a soldier his officer, a philosopher a railway porter, and a workman a foreman, all without question, because it is generally accepted that those who give the orders understand what they are about, and are duly authorized and even obliged to give them, and because, in the practical emergencies of daily life, there is no time for lessons and explanations, or for arguments as to their validity. Such obediences are as necessary to the continuous operation of our social system as the revolutions of the earth are to the succession of night and day. But they are not so spontaneous as they seem: they have to be very carefully arranged and maintained. A bishop will defer to and obey a king; but let a curate venture to give him an order, however necessary and sensible, and the bishop will forget his cloth and damn the curate's impudence. The more obedient a man is to accredited authority the more jealous he is of allowing any unauthorized person to order him about.

With all this in mind, consider the career of Joan. She was a village girl, in authority over sheep and pigs, dogs and chickens, and to some extent over her father's hired laborers when he hired any, but over no one else on earth. Outside the farm she had no authority, no prestige, no claim to the smallest deference. Yet she ordered everybody about, from her uncle to the king, the archbishop, and the military General Staff. Her uncle obeyed her like a sheep, and took her to the castle of the local commander, who, on being ordered about, tried to assert himself, but soon collapsed and obeyed. And so on up to the king, as we have seen. This would have been unbearably irritating even if her orders had been offered as rational solutions of the desperate difficulties in which her social superiors found themselves just then. But they were not so offered. Nor were they offered as the expression of Joan's arbitrary will. It was never "I say so," but always "God says so."

Joan as Theocrat

Leaders who take that line have no trouble with some people, and no end of trouble with others. They need never fear a lukewarm reception. Either they are messengers of God, or they are blasphemous impostors. In the Middle Ages the general belief in witchcraft greatly intensified this contrast, because when an apparent miracle happened (as in the case of the wind changing at Orleans) it proved the divine mission to the credulous, and proved a contract with the devil to the sceptical. All through, Joan had to depend on those who accepted her as an incarnate angel against those who added to an intense resentment of her presumption a bigoted abhorrence of her as a witch. To this abhorrence we must add the extreme irritation of those who did not believe in the voices, and regarded her as a liar and impostor. It is hard to conceive anything more infuriating to a statesman or a military commander, or to a court favorite, than to be overruled at every turn, or to be robbed of the ear of the reigning sovereign, by an impudent young upstart practising on the credulity of the populace and the vanity and silliness of an immature prince by exploiting a few of those lucky coincidences which pass as miracles with uncritical people. Not only were the envy, snobbery, and competitive ambition of the baser natures exacerbated by Joan's success, but among the friendly ones that were clever enough to be critical a quite reasonable scepticism and mistrust of her ability, founded on a fair observation of her obvious ignorance and temerity, were at work against her. And as she met all remonstrances and all criticisms, not with arguments or persuasion, but with a flat appeal to the authority of God and a claim to be in God's special confidence, she must have seemed, to all who were not infatuated by her, so insufferable that nothing but an unbroken chain of overwhelming successes in the military and political field could have saved her from the wrath that finally destroyed her.

Unbroken Success Essential in Theocracy

To forge such a chain she needed to be the king, the Archbishop of Rheims, the Bastard of Orleans, and herself into the bargain; and that was impossible. From the moment when she failed to stimulate Charles to follow up his coronation with a swoop on Paris she was lost. The fact that she insisted on this while the king and the rest timidly and foolishly thought they could square the Duke of Burgundy, and effect a combination with him against the English, made her a terrifying nuisance to them; and from that time onward she could do nothing but prowl about the battlefields waiting for some lucky chance to sweep the captains into a big move. But it was to the enemy that the chance came: she was taken prisoner by the Burgundians fighting before Compiègne, and at once discovered that she had not a friend in the political world. Had she escaped she would probably have fought on until the English were gone, and then had to shake the dust of the court off her feet, and retire to Domrémy as Garibaldi had to retire to Caprera.

Modern Distortions of Joan's History

This, I think, is all that we can now pretend to say about the prose of Joan's career. The romance of her rise, the tragedy of her execution, and the comedy of the attempts of posterity to make amends for that execution, belong to my play and not to my preface, which must be confined to a sober essay on the facts. That such an essay is badly needed can be ascertained by examining any of our standard works of reference. They give accurately enough the facts about the visit to Vaucouleurs, the annunciation to Charles at Chinon, the raising of the siege of Orleans and the subsequent battles, the coronation at Rheims, the capture at Compiègne, and the trial and execution at Rouen, with their dates and the names of the people concerned; but they all break down on the melodramatic legend of the wicked bishop and the entrapped maiden and the rest of it. It would be far less misleading if they were wrong as to the facts, and right in their view of the facts. As it is, they illustrate the too little considered truth that the fashion in which we think changes like the fashion of our clothes, and that it is difficult, if not impossible, for most people to think otherwise than in the fashion of their own period.

History Always out of Date

This, by the way, is why children are never taught contemporary history. Their history books deal with periods of which the thinking has passed out of fashion, and the circumstances no longer apply to active life. For example, they are taught history about Washington, and told lies about Lenin. In Washington's time they were told lies (the same lies) about Washington, and taught history about Cromwell. In the fifteenth and sixteenth centuries they were told lies about Joan, and by this time might very well be told the truth about her. Unfortunately the lies did not cease when the political circumstances became obsolete. The Reformation, which Joan had unconsciously anticipated, kept the questions which arose in her case burning up to our own day (you can see plenty of the burnt houses still in Ireland), with the result that Joan has remained the subject of anti-Clerical lies, of specifically Protestant lies, and of Roman Catholic evasions of her unconscious Protestantism. The truth sticks in our throats with all the sauces it is served with: it will never go down until we take it without any sauce at all.

The Real Joan not Marvelous Enough for Us

But even in its simplicity, the faith demanded by Joan is one which the anti-metaphysical temper of nineteenth-century civilization, which remains powerful in England and America, and is tyrannical in France, contemptuously refuses her. We do not, like her contemporaries, rush to the opposite extreme in a recoil from her as from a witch self-sold to the devil, because we do not believe in the devil nor in the possibility of commercial contracts with him. Our credulity, though enormous, is not boundless; and our stock of it is quite used up by our mediums, clairvoyants, hand readers, slate writers, Christian Scientists, psycho-analysts, electronic vibration diviners, therapeutists of all schools registered and unregistered, astrologers, astronomers who tell us that the sun is nearly a hundred million miles away and that Betelgeuse is ten times as big as the whole universe, physicists who balance Betelgeuse by describing the incredible smallness of the atom, and a host of other marvel mongers whose credulity would have dissolved the Middle Ages in a roar of sceptical merriment. In the Middle Ages people believed that the earth was flat, for which they had at least the evidence of their senses: we believe it to be round, not because as many as one per cent of us could give the physical reasons for so quaint a belief, but because modern science has convinced us that nothing that is obvious is true, and that everything that is magical, improbable, extraordinary, gigantic, microscopic, heartless, or outrageous is scientific.

I must not, by the way, be taken as implying that the earth is flat, or that all or any of our amazing credulities are delusions or impostures. I am only defending my own age against the charge of being less imaginative than the Middle Ages. I affirm that the nineteenth century, and still more the twentieth, can knock the fifteenth into a cocked hat in point of susceptibility to marvels and miracles and saints and prophets and magicians and monsters and fairy tales of all kinds. The proportion of marvel to immediately credible statement in the latest edition of the Encyclopædia Britannica is enormously greater than in the Bible. The medieval doctors of divinity who did not pretend to settle how many angels could dance on the point of a needle cut a very poor figure as far as romantic credulity is concerned beside the modern physicists who have settled to the billionth of a millimeter every movement and position in the dance of the electrons. Not for worlds would I question the precise accuracy of these calculations or the existence of electrons (whatever they may be). The fate of Joan is a warning to me against such heresy. But why the men who believe in electrons should regard themselves as less credulous than the men who believed in angels is not apparent to me. If they refuse to believe, with the Rouen assessors of 1431, that Joan was a witch, it is not because that explanation is too marvelous, but because it is not marvelous enough.

The Stage Limits of Historical Representation

For the story of Joan I refer the reader to the play which follows. It contains all that need be known about her; but as it is for stage use I have had to condense into three and a half hours a series of events which in their historical happening were spread over four times as many months; for the theatre imposes unities of time and place from which Nature in her boundless wastefulness is free. Therefore the reader must not suppose that Joan really put Robert de Baudricourt in her pocket in fifteen minutes, nor that her excommunication, recantation, relapse, and death at the stake were a matter of half an hour or so. Neither do I claim more for my dramatizations of Joan's contemporaries than that some of them are probably slightly more like the originals than those imaginary portraits of all the Popes from Saint Peter onward through the Dark Ages which are still gravely exhibited in the Uffizi in Florence (or were when I was there last). My Dunois would do equally well for the Duc d'Alençon. Both left descriptions of Joan so similar that, as a man always describes himself unconsciously whenever he describes any one else, I have inferred that these good-natured young men were very like one another in mind, so I have lumped the twain into a single figure, thereby saving the theatre manager a salary and a suit of armor. Dunois' face, still on record at Châteaudun, is a suggestive help. But I really know no more about these men and their circle than Shakespear knew about Falconbridge and the Duke of Austria, or about Macbeth and Macduff. In view of the things they did in history, and have to do again in the play, I can only invent appropriate characters for them in Shakespear's manner.

A Void in the Elizabethan Drama

I have, however, one advantage over the Elizabethans. I write in full view of the Middle Ages, which may be said to have been rediscovered in the middle of the nineteenth century after an eclipse of about four hundred and fifty years. The Renascence of antique literature and art in the sixteenth century, and the lusty growth of Capitalism, between them buried the Middle Ages; and their resurrection is a second Renascence. Now there is not a breath of medieval atmosphere in Shakespear's histories. His John of Gaunt is like a study of the old age of Drake. Although he was a Catholic by family tradition, his figures are all intensely Protestant, individualist, sceptical, self-centered in everything but their love affairs, and completely personal and selfish even in them. His kings are not statesmen: his cardinals have no religion: a novice can read his plays from one end to the other without learning that the world is finally governed by forces expressing themselves in religions and laws which make epochs rather than by vulgarly ambitious individuals who make rows. The divinity which shapes our ends, rough hew them how we will, is mentioned fatalistically only to be forgotten immediately like a passing vague apprehension. To Shakespear as to Mark Twain, Cauchon would have been a tyrant and a bully instead of a Catholic, and the inquisitor Lemaître would have been a Sadist instead of a lawyer. Warwick would have had no more feudal quality than his successor the King Maker has in the play of Henry VI. We should have seen them all completely satisfied that if they would only to their own selves be true they could not then be false to any man (a precept which represents the reaction against medievalism at its intensest) as if they were beings in the air, without public responsibilities of any kind. All Shakespear's characters are so: that is why they seem natural to our middle classes, who are comfortable and irresponsible at other people's expense, and are neither ashamed of that condition nor even conscious of it. Nature abhors this vacuum in Shakespear; and I have taken care to let the medieval atmosphere blow through my play freely. Those who see it performed will not mistake the startling event it records for a mere personal accident. They will have before them not only the visible and human puppets, but the Church, the Inquisition, the Feudal System, with divine inspiration always beating against their too inelastic limits: all more terrible in their dramatic force than any of the little mortal figures clanking about in plate armor or moving silently in the frocks and hoods of the order of St Dominic.

Tragedy not Melodrama

There are no villains in the piece. Crime, like disease, is not interesting: it is something to be done away with by general consent, and that is all about it. It is what men do at their best, with good intentions, and what normal men and women find that they must and will do in spite of their intentions, that really concern us. The rascally bishop and the cruel inquisitor of Mark Twain and Andrew Lang are as dull as pickpockets; and they reduce Joan to the level of the even less interesting person whose pocket is picked. I have represented both of them as capable and eloquent exponents of the Church Militant and the Church Litigant, because only by doing so can I maintain my drama on the level of high tragedy and save it from becoming a mere police court sensation. A villain in a play can never be anything more than a *diabolus ex machina,* possibly a more exciting expedient than a *deus ex machina,* but both equally mechanical, and therefore interesting only as mechanism.

It is, I repeat, what normally innocent people do that concerns us; and if Joan had not been burnt by normally innocent people in the energy of their righteousness her death at their hands would have no more significance than the Tokyo earthquake, which burnt a great many maidens. The tragedy of such murders is that they are not committed by murderers. They are judicial murders, pious murders; and this contradiction at once brings an element of comedy into the tragedy: the angels may weep at the murder, but the gods laugh at the murderers.

The Inevitable Flatteries of Tragedy

Here then we have a reason why my drama of Saint Joan's career, though it may give the essential truth of it, gives an inexact picture of some accidental facts. It goes almost without saying that the old Jeanne d'Arc melodramas, reducing everything to a conflict of villain and hero, or in Joan's case villain and heroine, not only miss the point entirely, but falsify the characters, making Cauchon a scoundrel, Joan a prima donna, and Dunois a lover. But the writer of high tragedy and comedy, aiming at the innermost attainable truth, must needs flatter Cauchon nearly as much as the melodramatist vilifies him. Although there is, as far as I have been able to discover, nothing against Cauchon that convicts him of bad faith or exceptional severity in his judicial relations with Joan, or of as much anti-prisoner, pro-police, class and sectarian bias as we now take for granted in our own courts, yet there is hardly more warrant for classing him as a great Catholic churchman, completely proof against the passions aroused by the temporal situation. Neither does the inquisitor Lemaître, in such scanty accounts of him as are now recoverable, appear quite so able a master of his duties and of the case before him as I have given him credit for being. But it is the business of the stage to make its figures more intelligible to themselves than they would be in real life; for by no other means can they be made intelligible to the audience. And in this case Cauchon and Lemaître have to make intelligible not only themselves but the Church and the Inquisition, just as Warwick has to make the feudal system intelligible, the three between them having thus to make a twentieth-century audience conscious of an epoch fundamentally different from its own. Obviously the real Cauchon, Lemaître, and Warwick could not have done this: they were part of the Middle Ages themselves, and therefore as unconscious of its peculiarities as of the atomic formula of the air they breathed. But the play would be unintelligible if I had not endowed them with enough of this consciousness to enable them to explain their attitude to the twentieth century. All I claim is that by this inevitable sacrifice of verisimilitude I have secured in the only possible way sufficient veracity to justify me in claiming that as far as I can gather from the available documentation, and from such powers of divination as I possess, the things I represent these three exponents of the drama as saying are the things they actually would have said if they had known what they were really doing. And beyond this neither drama nor history can go in my hands.

Some Well-meant Proposals for the Improvement of the Play

I have to thank several critics on both sides of the Atlantic, including some whose admiration for my play is most generously enthusiastic, for their heartfelt instructions as to how it can be improved. They point out that by the excision of the epilogue and all the references to such undramatic and tedious matters as the Church, the feudal system, the Inquisition, the theory of heresy and so forth, all of which, they point out, would be ruthlessly blue pencilled by any experienced manager, the play could be considerably shortened. I think they are mistaken. The experienced knights of the blue pencil, having saved an hour and a half by disemboweling the play, would at once proceed to waste two hours in building elaborate scenery, having real water in the river Loire and a real bridge across it, and staging an obviously sham fight for possession of it, with the victorious French led by Joan on a real horse. The coronation would eclipse all previous theatrical displays, showing, first, the procession through the streets of Rheims, and then the service in the cathedral, with special music written for both. Joan would be burnt on the stage, as Mr. Matheson Lang always is in The Wandering Jew, on the principle that it does not matter in the least why a woman is burnt provided she is burnt, and people can pay to see it done. The intervals between the acts while these splendors were being built up and then demolished by the stage carpenters would seem eternal, to the great profit of the refreshment bars. And the weary and demoralized audience would lose their last trains and curse me for writing such inordinately long and intolerably dreary and meaningless plays. But the applause of the press would be unanimous. Nobody who knows the stage history of Shakespear will doubt that this is what would happen if I knew my business so little as to listen to these well-intentioned but disastrous counsellors: indeed it probably will happen when I am no longer in control of the performing rights. So perhaps it will be as well for the public to see the play while I am still alive.

The Epilogue

As to the epilogue, I could hardly be expected to stultify myself by implying that Joan's history in the world ended unhappily with her execution, instead of beginning there. It was necessary by hook or crook to show the canonized Joan as well as the incinerated one; for many a woman has got herself burnt by carelessly whisking a muslin skirt into the drawing-room fireplace, but getting canonized is a different matter, and a more important one. So I am afraid the epilogue must stand.

To the Critics, Lest They Should Feel Ignored

To a professional critic (I have been one myself) theatre-going is the curse of Adam. The play is the evil he is paid to endure in the sweat of his brow; and the sooner it is over, the better. This would seem to place him in irreconcilable opposition to the paying playgoer, from whose point of view the longer the play, the more entertainment he gets for his money. It does in fact so place him, especially in the provinces, where the playgoer goes to the theatre for the sake of the play solely, and insists so effectively on a certain number of hours' entertainment that touring managers are sometimes seriously embarrassed by the brevity of the London plays they have to deal in.

For in London the critics are reinforced by a considerable body of persons who go to the theatre as many others go to church, to display their best clothes and compare them with other people's; to be in the fashion, and have something to talk about at dinner parties; to adore a pet performer; to pass the evening anywhere rather than at home: in short, for any or every reason except interest in dramatic art as such. In fashionable centers the number of irreligious people who go to church, of unmusical people who go to concerts and operas, and of undramatic people who go to the theatre, is so prodigious that sermons have been cut down to ten minutes and plays to two hours; and, even at that, congregations sit longing for the benediction and audiences for the final curtain, so that they may get away to the lunch or supper they really crave for, after arriving as late as (or later than) the hour of beginning can possibly be made for them.

Thus from the stalls and in the Press an atmosphere of hypocrisy spreads. Nobody says straight out that genuine drama is a tedious nuisance, and that to ask people to endure more than two hours of it (with two long intervals of relief) is an intolerable imposition. Nobody says "I hate classical tragedy and comedy as I hate sermons and symphonies; but I like police news and divorce news and any kind of dancing or decoration that has an aphrodisiac effect on me or on my wife or husband. And whatever superior people may pretend, I cannot associate pleasure with any sort of intellectual activity; and I don't believe any one else can either." Such things are not said; yet nine-tenths of what is offered as criticism of the drama in the metropolitan Press of Europe and America is nothing but a muddled paraphrase of it. If it does not mean that, it means nothing.

I do not complain of this, though it complains very unreasonably of me. But I can take no more notice of it than Einstein of the people who are incapable of mathematics. I write in the classical manner for those who pay for admission to a theatre because they like classical comedy or tragedy for its own sake, and like it so much when it is good of its kind and well done that they tear themselves away from it with reluctance to catch the very latest train or omnibus that will take them home. Far from arriving late from an eight or half-past eight o'clock dinner so as to escape at least the first half-hour of the performance, they stand in queues outside the theatre doors for hours beforehand in bitingly cold weather to secure a seat. In countries where a play lasts a week, they bring baskets of provisions and sit it out. These are the patrons on whom I depend for my bread. I do not give them performances twelve hours long, because circumstances do not at present make such entertainments feasible; though a performance beginning after breakfast and ending at sunset is as possible physically and artistically in Surrey or Middlesex as in Ober-Ammergau; and an all-night sitting in a theatre would be at least as enjoyable as an all-night sitting in the House of Commons, and much more useful. But in St. Joan I have done my best by going to the well-established classical limit of three and a half hours practically continuous playing, barring the one interval imposed by considerations which have nothing to do with art. I know that this is hard on the pseudo-critics and on the fashionable people whose playing is a hypocrisy. I cannot help feeling some compassion for them when they assure me that my play, though a great play, must fail hopelessly, because it does not begin at a quarter to nine and end at eleven. The facts are overwhelmingly against them. They forget that all men are not as they are. Still, I am sorry for them; and though I cannot for their sakes undo my work and help the people who hate the theatre to drive out the people who love it, yet I may point out to them that they have several remedies in their own hands. They can escape the first part of the play by their usual practice of arriving late. They can escape the epilogue by not waiting for it. And if the irreducible minimum thus attained is still too painful, they can stay away altogether. But I deprecate this extreme course, because it is good neither for my pocket nor for their own souls. Already a few of them, noticing that what matters is not the absolute length of time occupied by a play, but the speed with which that time passes, are discovering that the theatre, though purgatorial in its Aristotelian moments, is not necessarily always the dull place they have so often found it. What do its discomforts matter when the play makes us forget them?

AYOT ST. LAWRENCE,
May 1924.

SAINT JOAN

SCENE I

A FINE *spring morning on the river Meuse, between Lorraine and Champagne, in the year* 1429 A.D., *in the castle of Vaucouleurs.*

CAPTAIN ROBERT DE BAUDRICOURT, *a military squire, handsome and physically energetic, but with no will of his own, is disguising that defect in his usual fashion by storming terribly at his steward, a trodden worm, scanty of flesh, scanty of hair, who might be any age from* 18 *to* 55, *being the sort of man whom age cannot wither because he has never bloomed.*

The two are in a sunny stone chamber on the first floor of the castle. At a plain strong oak table, seated in chair to match, the captain presents his left profile. The steward stands facing him at the other side of the table, if so deprecatory a stance as his can be called standing. The mullioned thirteenth-century window is open behind him. Near it in the corner is a turret with a narrow arched doorway leading to a winding stair which descends to the courtyard. There is a stout fourlegged stool under the table, and a wooden chest under the window.

ROBERT

No eggs! No eggs!! Thousand thunders, man, what do you mean by no eggs?

STEWARD

Sir: it is not my fault. It is the act of God.

ROBERT

Blasphemy. You tell me there are no eggs; and you blame your Maker for it.

STEWARD

Sir: what can I do? I cannot lay eggs.

ROBERT

(*Sarcastic*). Ha! You jest about it.

STEWARD

No, sir, God knows. We all have to go without eggs just as you have, sir. The hens will not lay.

ROBERT

Indeed! (*Rising.*) Now listen to me, you.

STEWARD

(*Humbly*). Yes, sir.

ROBERT

What am I?

STEWARD

What are you, sir?

ROBERT

(*Coming at him*). Yes: what am I? Am I Robert, squire of Baudricourt and captain of this castle of Vaucouleurs: or am I a cowboy?

STEWARD

Oh, sir, you know you are a greater man here than the king himself.

ROBERT

Precisely. And now, do you know what you are?

STEWARD

I am nobody, sir, except that I have the honor to be your steward.

ROBERT

(*Driving him to the wall, adjective by adjective*). You have not only the honor of being my steward, but the privilege of being the worst, most incompetent, drivelling snivelling jibbering jabbering idiot of a steward in France. (*He strides back to the table.*)

STEWARD

(*Cowering on the chest*). Yes, sir: to a great man like you I must seem like that.

ROBERT

(*Turning*). My fault, I suppose. Eh?

STEWARD

(*Coming to him deprecatingly*). Oh, sir: you always give my most innocent words such a turn!

ROBERT

I will give your neck a turn if you dare tell me, when I ask you how many eggs there are, that you cannot lay any.

STEWARD

(*Protesting*). Oh, sir, oh, sir—

ROBERT

No: not oh, sir, oh, sir, but no, sir, no, sir. My three Barbary hens and the black are the best layers in Champagne. And you come and tell me that there are no eggs! Who stole them? Tell me that, before I kick you out through the castle gate for a liar and a seller of my goods to thieves. The milk was short yesterday, too: do not forget that.

STEWARD

(*Desperate*). I know, sir. I know only too well. There is no milk: there are no eggs: tomorrow there will be nothing.

ROBERT

Nothing! You will steal the lot: eh?

STEWARD

No, sir: nobody will steal anything. But there is a spell on us: we are bewitched.

ROBERT

That story is not good enough for me. Robert de Baudricourt burns witches and hangs thieves. Go. Bring me four dozen eggs and two gallons of milk here in this room before noon, or Heaven have mercy on your bones! I will teach you to make a fool of me. (*He resumes his seat with an air of finality.*)

STEWARD

Sir: I tell you there are no eggs. There will be none—not if you were to kill me for it—as long as The Maid is at the door.

ROBERT

The Maid! What maid? What are you talking about?

STEWARD

The girl from Lorraine, sir. From Domremy.

ROBERT

(*Rising in fearful wrath*). Thirty thousand thunders! Fifty thousand devils! Do you mean to say that that girl, who had the impudence to ask to see me two days ago, and whom I told you to send back to her father with my orders that he was to give her a good hiding, is here still?

STEWARD

I have told her to go, sir. She won't.

ROBERT

I did not tell you to tell her to go: I told you to throw her out. You have fifty men-at-arms and a dozen lumps of able-bodied servants to carry out my orders. Are they afraid of her?

STEWARD

She is so positive, sir.

ROBERT

(*Seizing him by the scruff of the neck*). Positive! Now see here. I am going to throw you downstairs.

STEWARD

No, sir. Please.

ROBERT

Well, stop me by being positive. It's quite easy: any slut of a girl can do it.

STEWARD

(*Hanging limp in his hands*). Sir, sir: you cannot get rid of her by throwing me out. (ROBERT *has to let him drop. He squats on his knees on the floor, contemplating his master resignedly.*) You see, sir, you are much more positive than I am. But so is she.

ROBERT

I am stronger than you are, you fool.

STEWARD

No, sir: it isn't that: it's your strong character, sir. She is weaker than we are: she is only a slip of a girl; but we cannot make her go.

ROBERT

You parcel of curs: you are afraid of her.

STEWARD

(*Rising cautiously*). No, sir: we are afraid of you; but she puts courage into us. She really doesn't seem to be afraid of anything. Perhaps you could frighten her, sir.

ROBERT

(*Grimly*). Perhaps. Where is she now?

STEWARD

Down in the courtyard, sir, talking to the soldiers as usual. She is always talking to the soldiers except when she is praying.

ROBERT

Praying! Ha! You believe she prays, you idiot. I know the sort of girl that is always talking to soldiers. She shall talk to me a bit. (*He goes to the window and shouts fiercely through it.*) Hallo, you there!

A GIRL'S VOICE

(*Bright, strong and rough*). Is it me, sir?

ROBERT

Yes, you.

THE VOICE

Be you captain?

ROBERT

Yes, damn your impudence, I be captain. Come up here. (*To the soldiers in the yard.*) Shew her the way, you. And shove her along quick. (*He leaves the window and returns to his place at the table, where he sits magisterially.*)

STEWARD

(*Whispering*). She wants to go and be a soldier herself. She wants you to give her soldier's clothes. Armor, sir! And a sword! Actually! (*He steals behind* ROBERT.)

(JOAN *appears in the turret doorway. She is an able-bodied country girl of 17 or 18, respectably dressed in red, with an uncommon face; eyes very wide apart and bulging as they often do in very imaginative people, a long well-shaped nose with wide nostrils, a short upper lip, resolute but full-lipped mouth, and handsome fighting chin. She comes eagerly to the table, delighted at having penetrated to* BAUDRICOURT'S *presence at last, and full of hope as to the result. His scowl does not check or frighten her in the least. Her voice is normally a hearty coaxing voice, very confident, very appealing, very hard to resist.*)

JOAN

(*Bobbing a curtsey*). Good morning, captain squire. Captain: you are to give me a horse and armor and some soldiers, and send me to the Dauphin. Those are your orders from my Lord.

ROBERT

(*Outraged*). Orders from your lord! And who the devil may your lord be? Go back to him, and tell him that I am neither duke nor peer at his orders: I am squire of Baudricourt; and I take no orders except from the king.

JOAN

(*Reassuringly*). Yes, squire: that is all right. My Lord is the King of Heaven.

ROBERT

Why, the girl's mad. (*To the* STEWARD.) Why didn't you tell me so, you blockhead?

STEWARD

Sir: do not anger her: give her what she wants.

JOAN

(*Impatient, but friendly*). They all say I am mad until I talk to them, squire. But you see that it is the will of God that you are to do what He has put into my mind.

ROBERT

It is the will of God that I shall send you back to your father with orders to put you under lock and key and thrash the madness out of you. What have you to say to that?

JOAN

You think you will, squire; but you will find it all coming quite different. You said you would not see me; but here I am.

STEWARD

(*Appealing*). Yes, sir. You see, sir.

ROBERT

Hold your tongue, you.

STEWARD

(*Abjectly*). Yes sir.

ROBERT

(*To* JOAN, *with a sour loss of confidence*). So you are presuming on my seeing you, are you?

JOAN

(*Sweetly*). Yes, squire.

ROBERT

(*Feeling that he has lost ground, brings down his two fists squarely on the table, and inflates his chest imposingly to cure the unwelcome and only too familiar sensation*). Now listen to me. I am going to assert myself.

JOAN

(*Busily*). Please do, squire. The horse will cost sixteen francs. It is a good deal of money; but I can save it on the armor. I can find a soldier's armor that will fit me well enough: I am very hardy; and I do not need beautiful armor made to my measure like you wear. I shall not want many soldiers: the Dauphin will give me all I need to raise the siege of Orleans.

ROBERT

(*Flabbergasted*). To raise the siege of Orleans!

JOAN

(*Simply*). Yes, squire: that is what God is sending me to do. Three men will be enough for you to send with me if they are good men and gentle to me. They have promised to come with me. Polly and Jack and—

ROBERT

Polly!! You impudent baggage, do you dare call squire Bertrand de Poulengey Polly to my face?

JOAN

His friends call him so, squire: I did not know he had any other name. Jack—

ROBERT

That is Monsieur John of Metz, I suppose?

JOAN

Yes, squire. Jack will come willingly: he is a very kind gentleman, and gives me money to give to the poor. I think John Godsave will come, and Dick the Archer, and their servants John of Honecourt and Julian. There will be no trouble for you, squire: I have arranged it all: you have only to give the order.

ROBERT

(*Contemplating her in a stupor of amazement*). Well, I am damned!

JOAN

(*With muffled sweetness*). No, squire: God is very merciful; and the blessed saints Catherine and Margaret, who speak to me every day (*he gapes*), will intercede for you. You will go to paradise; and your name will be remembered forever as my first helper.

ROBERT

(*To the* STEWARD, *still much bothered, but changing his tone as he pursues a new clue*). Is this true about Monsieur de Poulengey?

STEWARD

(*Eagerly*). Yes, sir, and about Monsieur de Metz too. They both want to go with her.

ROBERT

(*Thoughtful*). Mf! (*He goes to the window, and shouts into the courtyard.*) Hallo! You there: send Monsieur de Poulengey to me, will you? (*He turns to* JOAN.) Get out; and wait in the yard.

JOAN

(*Smiling brightly at him*). Right, squire. (*She goes out.*)

ROBERT

(*To the* STEWARD). Go with her, you, you dithering imbecile. Stay within call: and keep your eye on her. I shall have her up here again.

STEWARD

Do so, in God's name, sir. Think of those hens, the best layers in Champagne; and—

ROBERT

Think of my boot; and take your backside out of reach of it.

(*The* STEWARD *retreats hastily and finds himself confronted in the doorway by* BERTRAND DE POULENGEY, *a lymphatic French gentleman-at-arms, aged 36 or thereabout, employed in the department of the provost-marshal, dreamily absent-minded, seldom speaking unless spoken to, and then slow and obstinate in reply: altogether in contrast to the self-assertive, loud-mouthed, superficially energetic, fundamentally will-less* ROBERT. *The* STEWARD *makes way for him, and vanishes.*)

(POULENGEY *salutes, and stands awaiting orders.*)

ROBERT

(*Genially*). It isn't service, Polly. A friendly talk. Sit down. (*He hooks the stool from under the table with his instep.*)

(POULENGEY, *relaxing, comes into the room; places the stool between the table and the window; and sits down ruminatively.* ROBERT, *half sitting on the end of the table, begins the friendly talk.*)

ROBERT

Now listen to me, Polly. I must talk to you like a father.

(POULENGEY *looks up at him gravely for a moment, but says nothing.*)

ROBERT

It's about this girl you are interested in. Now, I have seen her. I have talked to her. First, she's mad. That doesn't matter. Second, she's not a farm wench. She's a bourgeoise. That matters a good deal. I know her class exactly. Her father came here last year to represent his village in a law-suit: he is one of their notables. A farmer. Not a gentleman farmer: he makes money by it, and lives by it. Still, not a laborer. Not a mechanic. He might have a cousin a lawyer, or in the Church. These sort of people may be of no account socially; but they can give a lot of bother to the authorities. That is to say, to me. Now no doubt it seems to you a very simple thing to take this girl away, humbugging her into the belief that you are taking her to the Dauphin. But if you get her into trouble, you may get me into no end of a mess, as I am her father's lord, and responsible for her protection. So friends or no friends, Polly, hands off her.

POULENGEY

(*With deliberate impressiveness*). I should as soon think of the Blessed Virgin herself in that way, as of this girl.

ROBERT

(*Coming off the table*). But she says you and Jack and Dick have offered to go with her. What for? You are not going to tell me that you take her crazy notion of going to the Dauphin seriously, are you?

POULENGEY

(*Slowly*). There is something about her. They are pretty foul-mouthed and foul-minded down there in the guardroom, some of them. But there hasn't been a word that has anything to do with her being a woman. They have stopped swearing before her. There is something. Something. It may be worth trying.

ROBERT

Oh, come, Polly! Pull yourself together. Commonsense was never your strong point; but this is a little too much. (*He retreats disgustedly.*)

POULENGEY

(*Unmoved*). What is the good of commonsense? If we had any commonsense we should join the Duke of Burgundy and the English king. They hold half the country, right down to the Loire. They have Paris. They have this castle: you know very well that we had to surrender it to the Duke of Bedford, and that you are only holding it on parole. The Dauphin is in Chinon, like a rat in a corner, except that he won't fight. We don't even know that he is the Dauphin: his mother says he isn't; and she ought to know. Think of that! the queen denying the legitimacy of her own son!

ROBERT

Well, she married her daughter to the English king. Can you blame the woman?

POULENGEY

I blame nobody. But thanks to her the Dauphin is down and out; and we may as well face it. The English will take Orleans: the Bastard will not be able to stop them.

ROBERT

He beat the English the year before last at Montargis. I was with him.

POULENGEY

No matter: his men are cowed now; and he can't work miracles. And I tell you that nothing can save our side now but a miracle.

ROBERT

Miracles are all right, Polly. The only difficulty about them is that they don't happen nowadays.

POULENGEY

I used to think so. I am not so sure now. (*Rising and moving ruminatively towards the window.*) At all events this is not a time to leave any stone unturned. There is something about the girl.

ROBERT

Oh! You think the girl can work miracles, do you?

POULENGEY

I think the girl herself is a bit of a miracle. Anyhow, she is the last card left in our hand. Better play her than throw up the game. (*He wanders to the turret.*)

ROBERT

(*Wavering*). You really think that?

POULENGEY

(*Turning*). Is there anything else left for us to think?

ROBERT

(*Going to him*). Look here, Polly. If you were in my place would you let a girl like that do you out of sixteen francs for a horse?

POULENGEY

I will pay for the horse.

ROBERT

You will!

POULENGEY

Yes: I will back my opinion.

ROBERT

You will really gamble on a forlorn hope to the tune of sixteen francs?

POULENGEY

It is not a gamble.

ROBERT

What else is it?

POULENGEY

It is a certainty. Her words, and her ardent faith in God have put fire into me.

ROBERT

(*Giving him up*). Whew! you are as mad as she is.

POULENGEY

(*Obstinately*). We want a few mad people now. See where the sane ones have landed us!

ROBERT

(*His irresoluteness now openly swamping his affected decisiveness*). I shall feel like a precious fool. Still, if you feel sure—?

POULENGEY

I feel sure enough to take her to Chinon—unless you stop me.

ROBERT

This is not fair. You are putting the responsibility on me.

POULENGEY

It is on you whichever way you decide.

ROBERT

Yes: that's just it. Which way am I to decide? You don't see how awkward this is for me. (*Snatching at a dilatory step with an unconscious hope that* JOAN *will make up his mind for him.*) Do you think I ought to have another talk to her?

POULENGEY

(*Rising*). Yes. (*He goes to the window and calls.*) Joan!

JOAN'S VOICE

Will he let us go, Polly?

POULENGEY

Come up. Come in. (*Turning to* ROBERT.) Shall I leave you with her?

ROBERT

No: stay here; and back me up.

(POULENGEY *sits down on the chest.* ROBERT *goes back to his magisterial chair, but remains standing to inflate himself more imposingly.* JOAN *comes in, full of good news.*)

JOAN

Jack will go halves for the horse.

ROBERT

Well!! (*He sits, deflated.*)

POULENGEY

(*Gravely*). Sit down, Joan.

JOAN

(*Checked a little, and looking to* ROBERT). May I?

ROBERT

Do what you are told.

(JOAN *curtsies and sits down on the stool between them.* ROBERT *outfaces his perplexity with his most peremptory air.*)

ROBERT

What is your name?

JOAN

(*Chattily*). They always call me Jenny in Lorraine. Here in France I am Joan. The soldiers call me The Maid.

ROBERT

What is your surname?

JOAN

Surname? What is that? My father sometimes calls himself d'Arc; but I know nothing about it. You met my father. He—

ROBERT

Yes, yes; I remember. You come from Domremy in Lorraine, I think.

JOAN

Yes; but what does it matter? we all speak French.

ROBERT

Don't ask questions: answer them. How old are you?

JOAN

Seventeen: so they tell me. It might be nineteen. I don't remember.

ROBERT

What did you mean when you said that St. Catherine and St. Margaret talked to you every day?

JOAN

They do.

ROBERT

What are they like?

JOAN

(*Suddenly obstinate*). I will tell you nothing about that: they have not given me leave.

ROBERT

But you actually see them; and they talk to you just as I am talking to you?

JOAN

No: it is quite different. I cannot tell you: you must not talk to me about my voices.

ROBERT

How do you mean? voices?

JOAN

I hear voices telling me what to do. They come from God.

ROBERT

They come from your imagination.

JOAN

Of course. That is how the messages of God come to us.

POULENGEY

Checkmate.

ROBERT

No fear! (*To* JOAN) So God says you are to raise the siege of Orleans?

JOAN

And to crown the Dauphin in Rheims Cathedral.

ROBERT

(*Gasping*). Crown the D——! Gosh!

JOAN

And to make the English leave France.

ROBERT

(*Sarcastic*). Anything else?

JOAN

(*Charming*). Not just at present, thank you, squire.

ROBERT

I suppose you think raising a siege is as easy as chasing a cow out of a meadow. You think soldiering is anybody's job?

JOAN

I do not think it can be very difficult if God is on your side, and you are willing to put your life in His hand. But many soldiers are very simple.

ROBERT

(*Grimly*). Simple! Did you ever see English soldiers fighting?

JOAN

They are only men. God made them just like us; but He gave them their own country and their own language; and it is not His will that they should come into our country and try to speak our language.

ROBERT

Who has been putting such nonsense into your head? Don't you know that soldiers are subject to their feudal lord, and that it is nothing to them or to you whether he is the duke of Burgundy or the king of England or the king of France? What has their language to do with it?

JOAN

I do not understand that a bit. We are all subject to the King of Heaven; and He gave us our countries and our languages, and meant us to keep them. If it were not so it would be murder to kill an Englishman in battle; and you, squire, would be in great danger of hell fire. You must not think about your duty to your feudal lord, but about your duty to God.

POULENGEY

It's no use, Robert: she can choke you like that every time.

ROBERT

Can she, by Saint Dennis! We shall see. (*To* JOAN) We are not talking about God: we are talking about practical affairs. I ask you again, girl, have you ever seen English soldiers fighting? Have you ever seen them plundering, burning, turning the countryside into a desert? Have you heard no tales of their Black Prince who was blacker than the devil himself, or of the English king's father?

JOAN

You must not be afraid, Robert—

ROBERT

Damn you, I am not afraid. And who gave you leave to call me Robert?

JOAN

You were called so in church in the name of our Lord. All the other names are your father's or your brother's or anybody's.

ROBERT

Tcha!

JOAN

Listen to me, squire. At Domremy we had to fly to the next village to escape from the English soldiers. Three of them were left behind, wounded. I came to know these three poor goddams quite well. They had not half my strength.

ROBERT

Do you know why they are called goddams?

JOAN

No. Every one calls them goddams.

ROBERT

It is because they are always calling on their God to condemn their souls to perdition. That is what goddam means in their language. How do you like it?

JOAN

God will be merciful to them; and they will act like His good children when they go back to the country He made for them, and made them for. I have heard the tales of the Black Prince. The moment he touched the soil of our country the devil entered into him and made him a black fiend. But at home, in the place made for him by God, he was good. It is always so. If I went into England against the will of God to conquer England, and tried to live there and speak its language, the devil would enter into me; and when I was old I should shudder to remember the wickedness I did.

ROBERT

Perhaps. But the more devil you were the better you might fight. That is why the goddams will take Orleans. And you cannot stop them, nor ten thousand like you.

JOAN

One thousand like me can stop them. Ten like me can stop them with God on our side. (*She rises impetuously, and goes at him, unable to sit quiet any longer.*) You do not understand, squire. Our soldiers are always beaten because they are fighting only to save their skins; and the shortest way to save your skin is to run away. Our knights are thinking only of the money they will make in ransoms: it is not kill or be killed with them, but pay or be paid. But I will teach them all to fight that the will of God may be done in France; and then they will drive the poor goddams before them like sheep. You and Polly will live to see the day when there will not be an English soldier on the soil of France; and there will be but one king there: not the feudal English king, but God's French one.

ROBERT

(*To* POULENGEY). This may be all rot, Polly; but the troops might swallow it, though nothing that we can say seems able to put any fight into them. Even the Dauphin might swallow it. And if she can put fight into him, she can put it into anybody.

POULENGEY

I can see no harm in trying. Can you? And there is something about the girl—

ROBERT

(*Turning to* JOAN). Now listen you to me; and (*desperately.*) don't cut in before I have time to think.

JOAN

(*Plumping down on the stool again, like an obedient schoolgirl*). Yes, squire.

ROBERT

Your orders are, that you are to go to Chinon under the escort of this gentleman and three of his friends.

JOAN

(*Radiant, clasping her hands*). Oh, squire! Your head is all circled with light, like a saint's.

POULENGEY

How is she to get into the royal presence?

ROBERT

(*Who has looked up for his halo rather apprehensively*). I don't know: how did she get into my presence? If the Dauphin can keep her out he is a better man than I take him for. (*Rising.*) I will send her to Chinon; and she can say I sent her. Then let come what may: I can do no more.

JOAN

And the dress? I may have a soldier's dress, mayn't I, squire?

ROBERT

Have what you please. I wash my hands of it.

JOAN

(*Wildly excited by her success*). Come, Polly. (*She dashes out.*)

ROBERT

(*Shaking* POULENGEY'S *hand*). Good-bye, old man, I am taking a big chance. Few other men would have done it. But as you say, there is something about her.

POULENGEY

Yes: there is something about her. Good-bye. (*He goes out.*)

(ROBERT *still very doubtful whether he has not been made a fool of by a crazy female, and a social inferior to boot, scratches his head and slowly comes back from the door. The* STEWARD *runs in with a basket.*)

STEWARD

Sir, sir—

ROBERT

What now?

STEWARD

The hens are laying like mad, sir. Five dozen eggs!

ROBERT

(*Stiffens convulsively; crosses himself; and forms with his pale lips the words*). Christ in heaven! (*Aloud but breathless.*) She did come from God.

SCENE II

Chinon, in Touraine. An end of the throne-room in the castle, curtained off to make an antechamber. THE ARCHBISHOP OF RHEIMS, *close on 50, a full-fed political prelate with nothing of the ecclesiastic about him except his imposing bearing, and the Lord Chamberlain,* MONSEIGNEUR DE LA TRÉMOUILLE, *a monstrous arrogant wineskin of a man, are waiting for the Dauphin. There is a door in the wall to the right of the two men. It is late in the afternoon on the 8th of March,* 1429. THE ARCHBISHOP *stands with dignity whilst the Chamberlain, on his left, fumes about in the worst of tempers.*

LA TRÉMOUILLE

What the devil does the Dauphin mean by keeping us waiting like this? I don't know how you have the patience to stand there like a stone idol.

THE ARCHBISHOP

You see, I am an archbishop; and an archbishop is a sort of idol. At any rate he has to learn to keep still and suffer fools patiently. Besides, my dear Lord Chamberlain, it is the Dauphin's royal privilege to keep you waiting, is it not?

LA TRÉMOUILLE

Dauphin be damned! saving your reverence. Do you know how much money he owes me?

THE ARCHBISHOP

Much more than he owes me, I have no doubt, because you are a much richer man. But I take it he owes you all you could afford to lend him. That is what he owes me.

LA TRÉMOUILLE

Twenty-seven thousand: that was his last haul. A cool twenty-seven thousand!

THE ARCHBISHOP

What becomes of it all? He never has a suit of clothes that I would throw to a curate.

LA TRÉMOUILLE

He dines on a chicken or a scrap of mutton. He borrows my last penny; and there is nothing to shew for it. (*A page appears in the doorway.*) At last!

THE PAGE

No, my lord: it is not His Majesty. Monsieur de Rais is approaching.

LA TRÉMOUILLE

Young Bluebeard! Why announce him?

THE PAGE

Captain La Hire is with him. Something has happened, I think.
(GILLES DE RAIS, *a young man of 25, very smart and self-possessed, and sporting the extravagance of a little curled beard dyed blue at a clean-shaven court, comes in. He is determined to make himself agreeable, but lacks natural joyousness, and is not really pleasant. In fact when he defies the Church some eleven years later he is accused of trying to extract pleasure from horrible cruelties, and hanged. So far, however, there is no shadow of the gallows on him. He advances gaily to the* ARCHBISHOP. *The* PAGE *withdraws.*)

BLUEBEARD

Your faithful lamb, Archbishop. Good day, my lord. Do you know what has happened to La Hire?

LA TRÉMOUILLE

He has sworn himself into a fit, perhaps.

BLUEBEARD

No: just the opposite. Foul Mouthed Frank, the only man in Touraine who could beat him at swearing, was told by a soldier that he shouldn't use such language when he was at the point of death.

THE ARCHBISHOP

Nor at any other point. But was Foul Mouthed Frank on the point of death?

BLUEBEARD

Yes: he has just fallen into a well and been drowned. La Hire is frightened out of his wits.
(*Captain* LA HIRE *comes in: a war dog with no court manners and pronounced camp ones.*)

BLUEBEARD

I have just been telling the Chamberlain and the Archbishop. The Archbishop says you are a lost man.

LA HIRE

(*Striding past* BLUEBEARD, *and planting himself between* THE ARCHBISHOP *and* LA TRÉMOUILLE). This is nothing to joke about. It is worse than we thought. It was not a soldier, but an angel dressed as a soldier.

THE ARCHBISHOP

THE CONSTABLE

BLUEBEARD

(*Exclaiming all together*). An angel!

LA HIRE

Yes, an angel. She has made her way from Champagne with half a dozen men through the thick of everything: Burgundians, Goddams, deserters, robbers, and Lord knows who; and they never met a soul except the country folk. I know one of them: de Poulengey. He says she's an angel. If ever I utter an oath again may my soul be blasted to eternal damnation.

THE ARCHBISHOP

A very pious beginning, Captain.
(BLUEBEARD *and* LA TRÉMOUILLE *laugh at him. The* PAGE *returns.*)

THE PAGE

His Majesty.

(*They stand perfunctorily at court attention. The Dauphin, aged 26, really* KING CHARLES THE SEVENTH *since the death of his father, but as yet uncrowned, comes in through the curtains with a paper in his hands. He is a poor creature physically; and the current fashion of shaving closely, and hiding every scrap of hair under the head-covering or headdress, both by women and men, makes the worst of his appearance. He has little narrow eyes, near together, a long pendulous nose that droops over his thick short upper lip, and the expression of a young dog accustomed to be kicked, yet incorrigible and irrepressible. But he is neither vulgar nor stupid; and he has a cheeky humor which enables him to hold his own in conversation. Just at present he is excited, like a child with a new toy. He comes to the* ARCHBISHOP'S *left hand.* BLUEBEARD *and* LA HIRE *retire towards the curtains.*)

CHARLES

Oh, Archbishop, do you know what Robert de Baudricourt is sending me from Vaucouleurs?

THE ARCHBISHOP

(*Contemptuously*). I am not interested in the newest toys.

CHARLES

(*Indignantly*). It isn't a toy. (*Sulkily.*) However, I can get on very well without your interest.

THE ARCHBISHOP

Your Highness is taking offence very unnecessarily.

CHARLES

Thank you. You are always ready with a lecture, aren't you?

LA TRÉMOUILLE

(*Roughly*). Enough grumbling. What have you got there?

CHARLES

What is that to you?

LA TRÉMOUILLE

It is my business to know what is passing between you and the garrison at Vaucouleurs. (*He snatches the paper from the Dauphin's hand, and begins reading it with some difficulty, following the words with his finger and spelling them out syllable by syllable.*)

CHARLES

(*Mortified*). You all think you can treat me as you please because I owe you money, and because I am no good at fighting. But I have the blood royal in my veins.

THE ARCHBISHOP

Even that has been questioned, your Highness. One hardly recognizes in you the grandson of Charles the Wise.

CHARLES

I want to hear no more of my grandfather. He was so wise that he used up the whole family stock of wisdom for five generations, and left me the poor fool I am, bullied and insulted by all of you.

THE ARCHBISHOP

Control yourself, sir. These outbursts of petulance are not seemly.

CHARLES

Another lecture! Thank you. What a pity it is that though you are an archbishop saints and angels don't come to see you!

THE ARCHBISHOP

What do you mean?

CHARLES

Aha! Ask that bully there (*pointing to* LA TRÉMOUILLE.).

LA TRÉMOUILLE

(*Furious*). Hold your tongue. Do you hear?

CHARLES

Oh, I hear. You needn't shout. The whole castle can hear. Why don't you go and shout at the English, and beat them for me?

LA TRÉMOUILLE

(*Raising his fist*). You young—

CHARLES

(*Running behind the* ARCHBISHOP). Don't you raise your hand to me. It's high treason.

LA HIRE

Steady, Duke! Steady!

THE ARCHBISHOP

(*Resolutely*). Come, come! this will not do. My lord Chamberlain; please! please! we must keep some sort of order. (*To the Dauphin.*) And you, sir: if you cannot rule your kingdom, at least try to rule yourself.

CHARLES

Another lecture! Thank you.

LA TRÉMOUILLE

(*Handing the paper to the* ARCHBISHOP). Here: read the accursed thing for me. He has sent the blood boiling into my head: I can't distinguish the letters.

CHARLES

(*Coming back and peering round* LA TRÉMOUILLE'S *left shoulder*). I will read it for you if you like. I can read, you know.

LA TRÉMOUILLE

(*With intense contempt, not at all stung by the taunt*). Yes: reading is about all you are fit for. Can you make it out, Archbishop?

THE ARCHBISHOP

I should have expected more commonsense from De Baudricourt. He is sending some cracked country lass here—

CHARLES

(*Interrupting*). No: he is sending a saint: an angel. And she is coming to me: to me, the king, and not to you, Archbishop, holy as you are. She knows the blood royal if you don't. (*He struts up to the curtains between* BLUEBEARD *and* LA HIRE.)

THE ARCHBISHOP

You cannot be allowed to see this crazy wench.

CHARLES

(*Turning*). But I am the king; and I will.

LA TRÉMOUILLE

(*Brutally*). Then she cannot be allowed to see you. Now!

CHARLES

I tell you I will. I am going to put my foot down—

BLUEBEARD

(*Laughing at him*). Naughty! What would your wise gradfather say?

CHARLES

That just shews your ignorance, Bluebeard. My grandfather had a saint who used to float in the air when she was praying, and told him everything he wanted to know. My poor father had two saints, Marie de Maillé and the Gasque of Avignon. It is in our family; and I don't care what you say: I will have my saint too.

THE ARCHBISHOP

This creature is not a saint. She is not even a respectable woman. She does not wear women's clothes. She is dressed like a soldier, and rides round the country with soldiers. Do you suppose such a person can be admitted to your Highness's court?

LA HIRE

Stop. (*Going to the* ARCHBISHOP.) Did you say a girl in armor, like a soldier?

THE ARCHBISHOP

So De Baudricourt describes her.

LA HIRE

But by all the devils in hell—Oh, God forgive me, what am I saying?—by Our Lady and all the saints, this must be the angel that struck Foul Mouthed Frank dead for swearing.

CHARLES

(*Triumphantly*). You see! A miracle.

LA HIRE

She may strike the lot of us dead if we cross her. For Heaven's sake, Archbishop, be careful what you are doing.

THE ARCHBISHOP

(*Severely*). Rubbish! Nobody has been struck dead. A drunken blackguard who has been rebuked a hundred times for swearing has fallen into a well, and been drowned. A mere coincidence.

LA HIRE

I do not know what a coincidence is. I do know that the man is dead, and that she told him he was going to die.

THE ARCHBISHOP

We are all going to die, Captain.

LA HIRE

(*Crossing himself*). I hope not. (*He backs out of the conversation.*)

BLUEBEARD

We can easily find out whether she is an angel or not. Let us arrange when she comes that I shall be the Dauphin, and see whether she will find me out.

CHARLES

Yes: I agree to that. If she cannot find the blood royal I will have nothing to do with her.

THE ARCHBISHOP

It is for the Church to make saints: let De Baudricourt mind his own business, and not dare usurp the function of his priest. I say the girl shall not be admitted.

BLUEBEARD

But, Archbishop—

THE ARCHBISHOP

(*Sternly*). I speak in the Church's name. (*To the Dauphin.*) Do you dare say she shall?

CHARLES

(*Intimidated but sulky*). Oh, if you make it an excommunication matter, I have nothing more to say, of course. But you haven't read the end of the letter. De Baudricourt says she will raise the siege of Orleans, and beat the English for us.

LA TRÉMOUILLE

Rot!

CHARLES

Well, will you save Orleans for us, with all your bullying?

LA TRÉMOUILLE

(*Savagely*). Do not throw that in my face again: do you hear? I have done more fighting than you ever did or ever will. But I cannot be everywhere.

THE DAUPHIN

Well, that's something.

BLUEBEARD

(*Coming between the* ARCHBISHOP *and* CHARLES). You have Jack Dunois at the head of your troops in Orleans: the brave Dunois, the handsome Dunois, the wonderful invincible Dunois, the darling of all the ladies, the beautiful bastard. Is it likely that the country lass can do what he cannot do?

CHARLES

Why doesn't he raise the siege, then?

LA HIRE

The wind is against him.

BLUEBEARD

How can the wind hurt him at Orleans? It is not on the Channel.

LA HIRE

It is on the river Loire; and the English hold the bridgehead. He must ship his men across the river and upstream, if he is to take them in the rear. Well, he cannot, because there is a devil of a wind blowing the other way. He is tired of paying the priests to pray for a west wind. What he needs is a miracle. You tell me that what the girl did to Foul Mouthed Frank was no miracle. No matter: it finished Frank. If she changes the wind for Dunois, that may not be a miracle either; but it may finish the English. What harm is there in trying?

THE ARCHBISHOP

(*Who has read the end of the letter and become more thoughtful*). It is true that De Baudricourt seems extraordinarily impressed.

LA HIRE

De Baudricourt is a blazing ass; but he is a soldier; and if he thinks she can beat the English, all the rest of the army will think so too.

LA TRÉMOUILLE

(*To the* ARCHBISHOP, *who is hesitating*). Oh, let them have their way. Dunois' men will give up the town in spite of him if somebody does not put some fresh spunk into them.

THE ARCHBISHOP

The Church must examine the girl before anything decisive is done about her. However, since his Highness desires it, let her attend the Court.

LA HIRE

I will find her and tell her. (*He goes out.*)

CHARLES

Come with me, Bluebeard; and let us arrange so that she will not know who I am. You will pretend to be me. (*He goes out through the curtains.*)

BLUEBEARD

Pretend to be that thing! Holy Michael! (*He follows the Dauphin.*)

LA TRÉMOUILLE

I wonder will she pick him out!

THE ARCHBISHOP

Of course she will.

LA TRÉMOUILLE

Why? How is she to know?

THE ARCHBISHOP

She will know what everybody in Chinon knows: that the Dauphin is the meanest-looking and worst-dressed figure in the Court, and that the man with the blue beard is Gilles de Rais.

LA TRÉMOUILLE

I never thought of that.

THE ARCHBISHOP

You are not so accustomed to miracles as I am. It is part of my profession.

LA TRÉMOUILLE

(*Puzzled and a little scandalized*). But that would not be a miracle at all.

THE ARCHBISHOP

(*Calmly*). Why not?

LA TRÉMOUILLE

Well, come; what is a miracle?

THE ARCHBISHOP

A miracle, my friend, is an event which creates faith. That is the purpose and nature of miracles. They may seem very wonderful to the people who witness them, and very simple to those who perform them. That does not matter: if they confirm or create faith they are true miracles.

LA TRÉMOUILLE

Even when they are frauds, do you mean?

THE ARCHBISHOP

Frauds deceive. An event which creates faith does not deceive: therefore it is not a fraud, but a miracle.

LA TRÉMOUILLE

(*Scratching his neck in his perplexity*). Well, I suppose as you are an archbishop you must be right. It seems a bit fishy to me. But I am no churchman, and don't understand these matters.

THE ARCHBISHOP

You are not a churchman; but you are a diplomatist and a soldier. Could you make our citizens pay war taxes, or our soldiers sacrifice their lives, if they knew what is really happening instead of what seems to them to be happening?

LA TRÉMOUILLE

No, by Saint Dennis: the fat would be in the fire before sundown.

THE ARCHBISHOP

Would it not be quite easy to tell them the truth?

LA TRÉMOUILLE

Man alive, they wouldn't believe it.

THE ARCHBISHOP

Just so. Well, the Church has to rule men for the good of their souls as you have to rule them for the good of their bodies. To do that, the Church must do as you do: nourish their faith by poetry.

LA TRÉMOUILLE

Poetry! I should call it humbug.

THE ARCHBISHOP

You would be wrong, my friend. Parables are not lies because they describe events that have never happened. Miracles are not frauds because they are often—I do not say always—very simple and innocent contrivances by which the priest fortifies the faith of his flock. When this girl picks out the Dauphin among his courtiers, it will not be a miracle for me, because I shall know how it has been done, and my faith will not be increased. But as for the others, if they feel the thrill of the supernatural, and forget their sinful clay in a sudden sense of the glory of God, it will be a miracle and a blessed one. And you will find that the girl herself will be more affected than any one else. She will forget how she really picked him out. So, perhaps, will you.

LA TRÉMOUILLE

Well, I wish I were clever enough to know how much of you is God's archbishop and how much the most artful fox in Touraine. Come on, or we shall be late for the fun; and I want to see it, miracle or no miracle.

THE ARCHBISHOP

(*Detaining him a moment*). Do not think that I am a lover of crooked ways. There is a new spirit rising in men: we are at the dawning of a wider epoch. If I were a simple monk, and had not to rule men, I should seek peace for my spirit with Aristotle and Pythagoras rather than with the saints and their miracles.

LA TRÉMOUILLE

And who the deuce was Pythagoras?

THE ARCHBISHOP

A sage who held that the earth is round, and that it moves round the sun.

LA TRÉMOUILLE

What an utter fool! Couldn't he use his eyes?

(*They go out together through the curtains, which are presently withdrawn, revealing the full depth of the throne-room with the Court assembled. On the right are two Chairs of State on a dais.* BLUEBEARD *is standing theatrically on the dais, playing the king, and, like the courtiers, enjoying the joke rather obviously. There is a curtained arch in the wall behind the dais; but the main door, guarded by men-at-arms, is at the other side of the room; and a clear path across is kept and lined by the courtiers.* CHARLES *is in this path in the middle of the room.* LA HIRE *is on his right. The* ARCHBISHOP, *on his left, has taken his place by the dais:* LA TRÉMOUILLE *at the other side of it. The* DUCHESS DE LA TRÉMOUILLE, *pretending to be the Queen, sits in the Consort's chair, with a group of ladies in waiting close by, behind the* ARCHBISHOP.)

(*The chatter of the courtiers makes such a noise that nobody notices the appearance of the page at the door.*)

THE PAGE

The Duke of—(*Nobody listens.*) The Duke of—(*The chatter continues. Indignant at his failure to command a hearing, he snatches the halberd of the nearest man-at-arms, and thumps the floor with it. The chatter ceases; and everybody looks at him in silence.*) Attention! (*He restores the halberd to the man-at-arms.*) The Duke of Vendôme presents Joan the Maid to his Majesty.

CHARLES

(*Putting his finger on his lip*). Ssh! (*He hides behind the nearest courtier, peering out to see what happens.*)

BLUEBEARD

(*Majestically*). Let her approach the throne.

(JOAN, *dressed as a soldier, with her hair bobbed and hanging thickly round her face, is led in by a bashful and speechless nobleman, from whom she detaches herself to stop and look round eagerly for the Dauphin.*)

THE DUCHESS

(*To the nearest lady in waiting*). My dear! Her hair!
(*All the ladies explode in uncontrollable laughter.*)

BLUEBEARD

(*Trying not to laugh, and waving his hand in deprecation of their merriment*). Ssh—ssh! Ladies! Ladies!!

JOAN

(*Not at all embarrassed*). I wear it like this because I am a soldier. Where be Dauphin?
(*A titter runs through the Court as she walks to the dais.*)

BLUEBEARD

(*Condescendingly*). You are in the presence of the Dauphin.
(JOAN *looks at him sceptically for a moment, scanning him hard up and down to make sure. Dead silence, all watching her. Fun dawns in her face.*)

JOAN

Coom, Bluebeard! Thou canst not fool me. Where be Dauphin?
(*A roar of laughter breaks out as* GILLES, *with a gesture of surrender, joins in the laugh, and jumps down from the dais beside* LA TRÉMOUILLE. JOAN, *also on the broad grin, turns back, searching along the row of courtiers, and presently makes a dive, and drags out* CHARLES *by the arm.*)

JOAN

(*Releasing him and bobbing him a little curtsey*). Gentle little Dauphin, I am sent to you to drive the English away from Orleans and from France, and to crown you king in the cathedral at Rheims, where all true kings of France are crowned.

CHARLES

(*Triumphant, to the Court*). You see, all of you: she knew the blood royal. Who dare say now that I am not my father's son? (*To* JOAN) But if you want me to be crowned at Rheims you must talk to the Archbishop, not to me. There he is (*he is standing behind her*)!

JOAN

(*Turning quickly, overwhelmed with emotion*). Oh, my lord! (*She falls on both knees before him, with bowed head, not daring to look up.*) My lord: I am only a poor country girl; and you are filled with the blessedness and glory of God Himself; but you will touch me with your hands, and give me your blessing, won't you?

BLUEBEARD

(*Whispering to* LA TRÉMOUILLE). The old fox blushes.

LA TRÉMOUILLE

Another miracle!

THE ARCHBISHOP

(*Touched, putting his hand on her head*). Child: you are in love with religion.

JOAN

(*Startled: looking up at him*). Am I? I never thought of that. Is there any harm in it?

THE ARCHBISHOP

There is no harm in it, my child. But there is danger.

JOAN

(*Rising, with a sunflush of reckless happiness irradiating her face*). There is always danger, except in Heaven. Oh, my lord, you have given me such strength, such courage. It must be a most wonderful thing to be Archbishop.
(*The Court smiles broadly: even titters a little.*)

THE ARCHBISHOP

(*Drawing himself up sensitively*). Gentlemen: your levity is rebuked by this maid's faith. I am, God help me, all unworthy; but your mirth is a deadly sin.
(*Their faces fall. Dead silence.*)

BLUEBEARD

My lord: we were laughing at her, not at you.

THE ARCHBISHOP

What? Not at my unworthiness but at her faith! Gilles de Rais: this maid prophesied that the blasphemer should be drowned in his sin——

JOAN

(*Distressed*). No!

THE ARCHBISHOP

(*Silencing her by a gesture*). I prophesy now that you will be hanged in yours if you do not learn when to laugh and when to pray.

BLUEBEARD

My lord: I stand rebuked. I am sorry: I can say no more. But if you prophesy that I shall be hanged, I shall never be able to resist temptation, because I shall always be telling myself that I may as well be hanged for a sheep as a lamb.
(*The courtiers take heart at this. There is more tittering.*)

JOAN

(*Scandalized*). You are an idle fellow, Bluebeard; and you have great impudence to answer the Archbishop.

LA HIRE

(*With a huge chuckle*). Well said, lass! Well said!

JOAN

(*Impatiently to the* ARCHBISHOP). Oh, my lord, will you send all these silly folks away so that I may speak to the Dauphin alone?

LA HIRE

(*Good-humoredly*). I can take a hint. (*He salutes; turns on his heel; and goes out.*)

THE ARCHBISHOP

Come, gentlemen. The Maid comes with God's blessing, and must be obeyed.
(*The courtiers withdraw, some through the arch, others at the opposite side. The* ARCHBISHOP *marches across to the door, followed by the* DUCHESS *and* LA TRÉMOUILLE. *As the* ARCHBISHOP *passes* JOAN, *she falls on her knees, and kisses the hem of his robe fervently. He shakes his head in instinctive remonstrance; gathers the robe from her; and goes out. She is left kneeling directly in the* DUCHESS's *way.*)

THE DUCHESS

(*Coldly*). Will you allow me to pass, please?

JOAN

(*Hastily rising, and standing back*). Beg pardon, ma'am, I am sure.
(*The* DUCHESS *passes on.* JOAN *stares after her; then whispers to the Dauphin.*)

JOAN

Be that Queen?

CHARLES

No. She thinks she is.

JOAN

(*Again staring after the* DUCHESS). Oo-oo-ooh! (*Her awe-struck amazement at the figure cut by the magnificently dressed lady is not wholly complimentary.*)

LA TRÉMOUILLE

(*Very surly*). I'll trouble your Highness not to gibe at my wife. (*He goes out. The others have already gone.*)

JOAN

(*To the Dauphin*). Who be old Gruff-and-Grum?

CHARLES

He is the Duke de la Trémouille.

JOAN

What be his job?

CHARLES

He pretends to command the army. And whenever I find a friend I can care for, he kills him.

JOAN

Why dost let him?

CHARLES

(*Petulantly moving to the throne side of the room to escape from her magnetic field*). How can I prevent him? He bullies me. They all bully me.

JOAN

Art afraid?

CHARLES

Yes: I am afraid. It's no use preaching to me about it. It's all very well for these big men with their armor that is too heavy for me, and their swords that I can hardly lift, and their muscle and their shouting and their bad tempers. They like fighting: most of them are making fools of themselves all the time they are not fighting; but I am quiet and sensible; and I don't want to kill people: I only want to be left alone to enjoy myself in my own way. I never asked to be a king: it was pushed on me. So if you are going to say "Son of St. Louis: gird on the sword of your ancestors, and lead us to victory," you may spare your breath to cool your porridge; for I cannot do it. I am not built that way; and there is an end of it.

JOAN

(*Trenchant and masterful*). Blethers! We are all like that to begin with. I shall put courage into thee.

CHARLES

But I don't want to have courage put into me. I want to sleep in a comfortable bed, and not live in continual terror of being killed or wounded. Put courage into the others, and let them have their bellyful of fighting; but let me alone.

JOAN

It's no use, Charlie: thou must face what God puts on thee. If thou fail to make thyself king, thoult be a beggar: what else art fit for? Come! Let me see thee sitting on the throne. I have looked forward to that.

CHARLES

What is the good of sitting on the throne when the other fellows give all the orders? However! (*he sits enthroned, a piteous figure*) here is the king for you! Look your fill at the poor devil.

JOAN

Thou 'rt not king yet, lad: thou 'rt but Dauphin. Be not led away by them around thee. Dressing up don't fill empty noddle. I know the people: the real people that make thy bread for thee; and I tell thee they count no man king of France until the holy oil has been poured on his hair, and himself consecrated and crowned in Rheims Cathedral. And thou needs new clothes, Charlie. Why does not Queen look after thee properly?

CHARLES

We're too poor. She wants all the money we can spare to put on her own back. Besides, I like to see her beautifully dressed; and I don't care what I wear myself; I should look ugly anyhow.

JOAN

There is some good in thee, Charlie; but it is not yet a king's good.

CHARLES

We shall see. I am not such a fool as I look. I have my eyes open; and I can tell you that one good treaty is worth ten good fights. These fighting fellows lose all on the treaties that they gain on the fights. If we can only have a treaty, the English are sure to have the worst of it, because they are better at fighting than at thinking.

JOAN

If the English win, it is they that will make the treaty; and then God help poor France! Thou must fight, Charlie, whether thou will or no. I will go first to hearten thee. We must take our courage in both hands: aye, and pray for it with both hands too.

CHARLES

(*Descending from his throne and again crossing the room to escape from her dominating urgency*). Oh, do stop talking about God and praying. I can't bear people who are always praying. Isn't it bad enough to have to do it at the proper times?

JOAN

(*Pitying him*). Thou poor child, thou hast never prayed in thy life. I must teach thee from the beginning.

CHARLES

I am not a child: I am a grown man and a father; and I will not be taught any more.

JOAN

Aye, you have a little son. He that will be Louis the Eleventh when you die. Would you not fight for him?

CHARLES

No: a horrid boy. He hates me. He hates everybody, selfish little beast! I don't want to be bothered with children. I don't want to be a father; and I don't want to be a son: especially a son of St. Louis. I don't want to be any of these fine things you all have your heads full of: I want to be just what I am. Why can't you mind your own business, and let me mind mine?

JOAN

(*Again contemptuous*). Minding your own business is like minding your own body: it's the shortest way to make yourself sick. What is my business? Helping mother at home. What is thine? Petting lapdogs and sucking sugarsticks. I call that muck. I tell thee it is God's business we are here to do: not our own. I have a message to thee from God; and thou must listen to it, though thy heart break with the terror of it.

CHARLES

I don't want a message; but can you tell me any secrets? Can you do any cures? Can you turn lead into gold, or anything of that sort?

JOAN

I can turn thee into a king, in Rheims Cathedral; and that is a miracle that will take some doing, it seems.

CHARLES

If we go to Rheims, and have a coronation, Anne will want new dresses. We can't afford them. I am all right as I am.

JOAN

As you are! And what is that? Less than my father's poorest shepherd. Thourt not lawful owner of thy own land of France till thou be consecrated.

CHARLES

But I shall not be lawful owner of my own land anyhow. Will the consecration pay off my mortgages? I have pledged my last acre to the Archbishop and that fat bully. I owe money even to Bluebeard.

JOAN

(*Earnestly*). Charlie: I come from the land, and have gotten my strength working on the land; and I tell thee that the land is thine to rule righteously and keep God's peace in, and not to pledge at the pawnshop as a drunken woman pledges her children's clothes. And I come from God to tell thee to kneel in the cathedral and solemnly give thy kingdom to Him for ever and ever, and become the greatest king in the world as His steward and His bailiff, His soldier and His servant. The very clay of France will become holy: her soldiers will be the soldiers of God: the rebel dukes will be rebels against God: the English will fall on their knees and beg thee let them return to their lawful homes in peace. Wilt be a poor little Judas, and betray me and Him that sent me?

CHARLES

(*Tempted at last*). Oh, if I only dare!

JOAN

I shall dare, dare, and dare again, in God's name! Art for or against me?

CHARLES

(*Excited*). I'll risk it. I warn you I shan't be able to keep it up; but I'll risk it. You shall see. (*Running to the main door and shouting.*) Hallo! Come back, everybody. (*To* JOAN, *as he runs back to the arch opposite.*) Mind you stand by and don't let me be bullied. (*Through the arch.*) Come along, will you: the whole Court. (*He sits down in the royal chair as they all hurry in to their former places, chattering and wondering.*) Now I'm in for it; but no matter: here goes! (*To the* PAGE.) Call for silence, you little beast, will you?

THE PAGE

(*Snatching a halberd as before and thumping with it repeatedly*). Silence for His Majesty the King. The King speaks. (*Peremptorily.*) Will you be silent there? (*Silence.*)

CHARLES

(*Rising*). I have given the command of the army to The Maid. The Maid is to do as she likes with it. (*He descends from the dais.*)

(*General amazement.* LA HIRE, *delighted, slaps his steel thigh-piece with his gauntlet.*)

LA TRÉMOUILLE

(*Turning threateningly towards* CHARLES). What is this? *I* command the army.

JOAN *quickly puts her hand on* CHARLES'S *shoulder as he instinctively recoils.* CHARLES, *with a grotesque effort, culminating in an extravagant gesture, snaps his fingers in the Chamberlain's face.*)

JOAN

Thou'rt answered, old Gruff-and-Grum. (*Suddenly flashing out her sword as she divines that her moment has come.*) Who is for God and His Maid? Who is for Orleans with me?

LA HIRE

(*Carried away, drawing also*). For God and His Maid! To Orleans!

ALL THE KNIGHTS

(*Following his lead with enthusiasm*). To Orleans!

(JOAN, *radiant, falls on her knees in thanksgiving to God. They all kneel, except the* ARCHBISHOP, *who gives his benediction with a sign, and* LA TRÉMOUILLE, *who collapses, cursing.*)

SCENE III

Orleans, May 29th, 1429. DUNOIS, *aged 26, is pacing up and down a patch of ground on the south bank of the silver Loire, commanding a long view of the river in both directions. He has had his lance stuck up with a pennon, which streams in a strong east wind. His shield with its bend sinister lies beside it. He has his commander's baton in his hand. He is well built, carrying his armor easily. His broad brow and pointed chin give him an equilaterally triangular face, already marked by active service and responsibility, with the expression of a good-natured and capable man who has no affectations and no foolish illusions. His page is sitting on the ground, elbows on knees, cheeks on fists, idly watching the water. It is evening; and both man and boy are affected by the loveliness of the Loire.*

DUNOIS

(*Halting for a moment to glance up at the streaming pennon and shake his head wearily before he resumes his pacing*). West wind, west wind, west wind. Strumpet: steadfast when you should be wanton, wanton when you should be steadfast. West wind on the silver Loire: what rhymes to Loire? (*He looks again at the pennon, and shakes his fist at it.*) Change, curse you, change, English harlot of a wind, change. West, west, I tell you. (*With a growl he resumes his march in silence, but soon begins again.*) West wind, wanton wind, wilful wind, womanish wind, false wind from over the water, will you never blow again?

THE PAGE

(*Bounding to his feet*). See! There! There she goes!

DUNOIS

(*Startled from his reverie: eagerly*). Where? Who? The Maid?

THE PAGE

No: the kingfisher. Like blue lightning. She went into that bush.

DUNOIS

(*Furiously disappointed*). Is that all? You infernal young idiot: I have a mind to pitch you into the river.

THE PAGE

(*Not afraid, knowing his man*). It looked frightfully jolly, that flash of blue. Look! There goes the other!

DUNOIS

(*Running eagerly to the river brim*). Where? Where?

THE PAGE

(*Pointing*). Passing the reeds.

DUNOIS

(*Delighted*). I see.
(*They follow the flight until the bird takes cover.*)

THE PAGE

You blew me up because you were not in time to see them yesterday.

DUNOIS

You knew I was expecting The Maid when you set up your yelping. I will give you something to yelp for next time.

THE PAGE

Aren't they lovely? I wish I could catch them.

DUNOIS

Let me catch you trying to trap them, and I will put you in the iron cage for a month to teach you what a cage feels like. You are an abominable boy.
(THE PAGE *laughs, and squats down as before.*)

DUNOIS

(*Pacing*). Blue bird, blue bird, since I am friend to thee, change thou the wind for me. No: it does not rhyme. He who has sinned for thee: that's better. No sense in it, though. (*He finds himself close to the* PAGE.) You abominable boy! (*He turns away from him.*) Mary in the blue snood, kingfisher color: will you grudge me a west wind?

A SENTRY'S VOICE WESTWARD

Halt! Who goes there?

JOAN'S VOICE

The Maid.

DUNOIS

Let her pass. Hither, Maid! To me!
(JOAN, *in splendid armor, rushes in in a blazing rage. The wind drops; and the pennon flaps idly down the lance; but* DUNOIS *is too much occupied with* JOAN *to notice it.*)

JOAN

(*Bluntly*). Be you Bastard of Orleans?

DUNOIS

(*Cool and stern, pointing to his shield*). You see the bend sinister. Are you Joan the Maid?

JOAN

Sure.

DUNOIS

Where are your troops?

JOAN

Miles behind. They have cheated me. They have brought me to the wrong side of the river.

DUNOIS

I told them to.

JOAN

Why did you? The English are on the other side!

DUNOIS

The English are on both sides.

JOAN

But Orleans is on the other side. We must fight the English there. How can we cross the river?

DUNOIS

(*Grimly*). There is a bridge.

JOAN

In God's name, then, let us cross the bridge, and fall on them.

DUNOIS

It seems simple; but it cannot be done.

JOAN

Who says so?

DUNOIS

I say so; and older and wiser heads than mine are of the same opinion.

JOAN

(*Roundly*). Then your older and wiser heads are fatheads: they have made a fool of you; and now they want to make a fool of me too, bringing me to the wrong side of the river. Do you not know that I bring you better help than ever came to any general or any town?

DUNOIS

(*Smiling patiently*). Your own?

JOAN

No: the help and counsel of the King of Heaven. Which is the way to the bridge?

DUNOIS

You are impatient, Maid.

JOAN

Is this a time for patience? Our enemy is at our gates; and here we stand doing nothing. Oh, why are you not fighting? Listen to me: I will deliver you from fear. I——

DUNOIS

(*Laughing heartily, and waving her off*). No, no, my girl: if you delivered me from fear I should be a good knight for a story book, but a very bad commander for the army. Come! let me begin to make a soldier of you. (*He takes her to the water's edge.*) Do you see those two forts at this end of the bridge? the big ones?

JOAN

Yes. Are they ours or the goddams'?

DUNOIS

Be quiet, and listen to me. If I were in either of those forts with only ten men I could hold it against an army. The English have more than ten times ten goddams in those forts to hold them against us.

JOAN

They cannot hold them against God. God did not give them the land under those forts: they stole it from Him. He gave it to us. I will take those forts.

DUNOIS

Single-handed?

JOAN

Our men will take them. I will lead them.

DUNOIS

Not a man will follow you.

JOAN

I will not look back to see whether any one is following me.

DUNOIS

(*Recognizing her mettle, and clapping her heartily on the shoulder*). Good. You have the makings of a soldier in you. You are in love with war.

JOAN

(*Startled*). Oh! And the Archbishop said I was in love with religion.

DUNOIS

I, God forgive me, am a little in love with war myself, the ugly devil! I am like a man with two wives. Do you want to be like a woman with two husbands?

JOAN

(*Matter-of-factly*). I will never take a husband. A man in Toul took an action against me for breach of promise; but I never promised him. I am a soldier: I do not want to be thought of as a woman. I will not dress as a woman. I do not care for the things women care for. They dream of lovers, and of money. I dream of leading a charge, and of placing the big guns. You soldiers do not know how to use the big guns: you think you can win battles with a great noise and smoke.

DUNOIS

(*With a shrug*). True. Half the time the artillery is more trouble than it is worth.

JOAN

Aye, lad; but you cannot fight stone walls with horses: you must have guns, and much bigger guns too.

DUNOIS

(*Grinning at her familiarity, and echoing it*). Aye, lass; but a good heart and a stout ladder will get over the stoniest wall.

JOAN

I will be first up the ladder when we reach the fort, Bastard. I dare you to follow me.

DUNOIS

You must not dare a staff officer, Joan; only company officers are allowed to indulge in displays of personal courage. Besides, you must know that I welcome you as a saint, not as a soldier. I have daredevils enough at my call, if they could help me.

JOAN

I am not a daredevil: I am a servant of God. My sword is sacred: I found it behind the altar in the church of St. Catherine, where God hid it for me; and I may not strike a blow with it. My heart is full of courage, not of anger. I will lead; and your men will follow: that is all I can do. But I must do it: you shall not stop me.

DUNOIS

All in good time. Our men cannot take those forts by a sally across the bridge. They must come by water, and take the English in the rear on this side.

JOAN

(*Her military sense asserting itself*). Then make rafts and put big guns on them; and let your men cross to us.

DUNOIS

The rafts are ready; and the men are embarked. But they must wait for God.

JOAN

What do you mean? God is waiting for them.

DUNOIS

Let Him send us a wind then. My boats are downstream: they cannot come up against both wind and current. We must wait until God changes the wind. Come: let me take you to the church.

JOAN

No. I love church; but the English will not yield to prayers: they understand nothing but hard knocks and slashes. I will not go to church until we have beaten them.

DUNOIS

You must: I have business for you there.

JOAN

What business?

DUNOIS

To pray for a west wind. I have prayed; and I have given two silver candlesticks; but my prayers are not answered. Yours may be: you are young and innocent.

JOAN

Oh, yes: you are right. I will pray: I will tell St. Catherine: she will make God give me a west wind. Quick: shew me the way to the church.

THE PAGE

(*Sneezes violently*). At-cha!!!

JOAN

God bless you, child! Coom, Bastard.

(*They go out. The* PAGE *rises to follow. He picks up the shield, and is taking the spear as well when he notices the pennon, which is now streaming eastward.*)

THE PAGE

(*Dropping the shield and calling excitedly after them*). Seigneur! Seigneur! Mademoiselle!

DUNOIS

(*Running back*). What is it? The kingfisher? (*He looks eagerly for it up the river.*)

JOAN

(*Joining them*). Oh, a kingfisher! Where?

THE PAGE

No: the wind, the wind, the wind. (*Pointing to the pennon.*) That is what made me sneeze.

DUNOIS

(*Looking at the pennon*). The wind has changed. (*He crosses himself.*) God has spoken. (*Kneeling and handing his baton to* JOAN.) You command the king's army. I am your soldier.

THE PAGE

(*Looking down the river*). The boats have put off. They are ripping upstream like anything.

DUNOIS

(*Rising*). Now for the forts. You dared me to follow. Dare you lead?

JOAN

(*Bursting into tears and flinging her arms round* DUNOIS, *kissing him on both cheeks*). Dunois, dear comrade in arms, help me. My eyes are blinded with tears. Set my foot on the ladder, and say "Up, Joan."

DUNOIS

(*Dragging her out*). Never mind the tears: make for the flash of the guns.

JOAN

(*In a blaze of courage*). Ah!

DUNOIS

(*Dragging her along with him*). For God and Saint Dennis!

THE PAGE

(*Shrilly*). The Maid! The Maid! God and The Maid! Hurray-ay-ay! (*He snatches up the shield and lance, and capers out after them, mad with excitement.*)

SCENE IV

A TENT *in the English camp. A bullnecked English chaplain of* 50 *is sitting on a stool at a table, hard at work writing. At the other side of the table an imposing nobleman, aged* 46, *is seated in a handsome chair turning over the leaves of an illuminated Book of Hours. The nobleman is enjoying himself: the chaplain is struggling with suppressed wrath. There is an unoccupied leather stool on the nobleman's left. The table is on his right.*

THE NOBLEMAN

Now this is what I call workmanship. There is nothing on earth more exquisite than a bonny book, with well-placed columns of rich black writing in beautiful borders, and illuminated pictures cunningly inset. But nowadays, instead of looking at books, people read them. A book might as well be one of those orders for bacon and bran that you are scribbling.

THE CHAPLAIN

I must say, my lord, you take our situation very coolly. Very coolly indeed.

THE NOBLEMAN

(*Supercilious*). What is the matter?

THE CHAPLAIN

The matter, my lord, is that we English have been defeated.

THE NOBLEMAN

That happens, you know. It is only in history books and ballads that the enemy is always defeated.

THE CHAPLAIN

But we are being defeated over and over again. First, Orleans——

THE NOBLEMAN

(*Poohpoohing*). Oh, Orleans!

THE CHAPLAIN

I know what you are going to say, my lord: that was a clear case of witchcraft and sorcery. But we are still being defeated. Jargeau, Meung, Beugency, just like Orleans. And now we have been butchered at Patay, and Sir John Talbot taken prisoner. (*He throws down his pen, almost in tears.*) I feel it, my lord: I feel it very deeply. I cannot bear to see my countrymen defeated by a parcel of foreigners.

THE NOBLEMAN

Oh! you are an Englishman, are you?

THE CHAPLAIN

Certainly not, my lord: I am a gentleman. Still, like your lordship, I was born in England; and it makes a difference.

THE NOBLEMAN

You are attached to the soil, eh?

THE CHAPLAIN

It pleases your lordship to be satirical at my expense: your greatness privileges you to be so with impunity. But your lordship knows very well that I am not attached to the soil in a vulgar manner, like a serf. Still, I have a feeling about it; (*with growing agitation*) and I am not ashamed of it; and (*rising wildly*) by God, if this goes on any longer I will fling my cassock to the devil, and take arms myself, and strangle the accursed witch with my own hands.

THE NOBLEMAN

(*Laughing at him good-naturedly*). So you shall, chaplain: so you shall, if we can do nothing better. But not yet, not quite yet. (THE CHAPLAIN *resumes his seat very sulkily*).

THE NOBLEMAN

(*Airily*). I should not care very much about the witch—you see, I have made my pilgrimage to the Holy Land; and the Heavenly Powers, for their own credit, can hardly allow me to be worsted by a village sorceress—but the Bastard of Orleans is a harder nut to crack; and as he has been to the Holy Land too, honors are easy between us as far as that goes.

THE CHAPLAIN

He is only a Frenchman, my lord.

THE NOBLEMAN

A Frenchman! Where did you pick up that expression? Are these Burgundians and Bretons and Picards and Gascons beginning to call themselves Frenchmen, just as our fellows are beginning to call themselves Englishmen? They actually talk of France and England as their countries. Theirs, if you please! What is to become of me and you if that way of thinking comes into fashion?

THE CHAPLAIN

Why, my lord? Can it hurt us?

THE NOBLEMAN

Men cannot serve two masters. If this cant of serving their country once takes hold of them, good-bye to the authority of their feudal lords, and good-bye to the authority of the Church. That is, good-bye to you and me.

THE CHAPLAIN

I hope I am a faithful servant of the Church; ond there are only six cousins between me and the barony of Stogumber, which was created by the Conqueror. But is that any reason why I should stand by and see Englishmen beaten by a French bastard and a witch from Lousy Champagne?

THE NOBLEMAN

Easy, man, easy: we shall burn the witch and beat the bastard all in good time. Indeed I am waiting at present for the Bishop of Beauvais, to arrange the burning with him. He has been turned out of his diocese by her faction.

THE CHAPLAIN

You have first to catch her, my lord.

THE NOBLEMAN

Or buy her. I will offer a king's ransom.

THE CHAPLAIN

A king's ransom! For that slut!

THE NOBLEMAN

One has to leave a margin. Some of Charles's people will sell her to the Burgundians; the Burgundians will sell her to us; and there will probably be three or four middlemen who will expect their little commissions.

THE CHAPLAIN

Monstrous. It is all those scoundrels of Jews: they get in every time money changes hands. I would not leave a Jew alive in Christendom if I had my way.

THE NOBLEMAN

Why not? The Jews generally give value. They make you pay; but they deliver the goods. In my experience the men who want something for nothing are invariably Christians.

(*A page appears.*)

THE PAGE

The Right Reverend the Bishop of Beauvais: Monseigneur Cauchon.

(CAUCHON, *aged about 60, comes in. The* PAGE *withdraws. The two Englishmen rise.*)

THE NOBLEMAN

(*With effusive courtesy*). My dear Bishop, how good of you to come! Allow me to introduce myself: Richard de Beauchamp, Earl of Warwick, at your service.

CAUCHON

Your lordship's fame is will known to me.

WARWICK

This reverend cleric is Master John de Stogumber.

THE CHAPLAIN

(*Glibly*). John Bowyer Spenser Neville de Stogumber, at your service, my lord: Bachelor of Theology, and Keeper of the Private Seal to His Eminence the Cardinal of Winchester.

WARWICK

(*To* CAUCHON). You call him the Cardinal of England, I believe. Our king's uncle.

CAUCHON

Messire John de Stogumber: I am always the very good friend of His Eminence. (*He extends his hand to the chaplain, who kisses his ring.*)

WARWICK

Do me the honor to be seated. (*He gives* CAUCHON *his chair, placing it at the head of the table.*)

(CAUCHON *accepts the place of honor with a grave inclination.* WARWICK *fetches the leather stool carelessly, and sits in his former place. The* CHAPLAIN *goes back to his chair.*)

(*Though* WARWICK *has taken second place in calculated deference to the* BISHOP, *he assumes the lead in opening the proceedings as a matter of course. He is still cordial and expansive; but there is a new note in his voice which means that he is coming to business.*)

WARWICK

Well, my Lord Bishop, you find us in one of our unlucky moments. Charles is to be crowned at Rheims, practically by the young woman from Lorraine; and—I must not deceive you, nor flatter your hopes—we cannot prevent it. I suppose it will make a great difference to Charles's position.

CAUCHON

Undoubtedly. It is a masterstroke of The Maid's.

THE CHAPLAIN

(*Again agitated*). We were not fairly beaten, my lord. No Englishman is ever fairly beaten.

(CAUCHON *raises his eyebrow slightly, then quickly composes his face.*)

WARWICK

Our friend here takes the view that the young woman is a sorceress. It would, I presume, be the duty of your reverend lordship to denounce her to the Inquisition, and have her burnt for that offense.

CAUCHON

If she were captured in my diocese: yes.

WARWICK

(*Feeling that they are getting on capitally*). Just so. Now I suppose there can be no reasonable doubt that she is a sorceress.

THE CHAPLAIN

Not the least. An arrant witch.

WARWICK

(*Gently reproving the interruption*). We are asking for the Bishop's opinion, Messire John.

CAUCHON

We shall have to consider not merely our own opinions here, but the opinions—the prejudices, if you like—of a French court.

WARWICK

(*Correcting*). A Catholic court, my lord.

CAUCHON

Catholic courts are composed of mortal men, like other courts, however sacred their function and inspiration may be. And if the men are Frenchmen, as the modern fashion calls them, I am afraid the bare fact that an English army has been defeated by a French one will not convince them that there is any sorcery in the matter.

THE CHAPLAIN

What! Not when the famous Sir John Talbot himself has been defeated and actually taken prisoner by a drab from the ditches of Lorraine!

CAUCHON

Sir John Talbot, we all know, is a fierce and formidable soldier, Messire; but I have yet to learn that he is an able general. And though it pleases you to say that he has been defeated by this girl, some of us may be disposed to give a little of the credit to Dunois.

THE CHAPLAIN

(*Contemptuously*). The Bastard of Orleans!

CAUCHON

Let me remind——

WARWICK

(*Interposing*). I know what you are going to say, my lord. Dunois defeated me at Montargis.

CAUCHON

(*Bowing*). I take that as evidence that the Seigneur Dunois is a very able commander indeed.

WARWICK

Your lordship is the flower of courtesy. I admit, on our side, that Talbot is a mere fighting animal, and that it probably served him right to be taken at Patay.

THE CHAPLAIN

(*Chafing*). My lord: at Orleans this woman had her throat pierced by an English arrow, and was seen to cry like a child from the pain of it. It was a death wound; yet she fought all day; and when our men had repulsed all her attacks like true Englishmen, she walked alone to the wall of our fort with a white banner in her hand; and our men were paralyzed, and could neither shoot nor strike whilst the French fell on them and drove them on to the bridge, which immediately burst into flames and crumbled under them, letting them down into the river, where they were drowned in heaps. Was this your bastard's generalship? or were those flames the flames of hell, conjured up by witchcraft?

WARWICK

You will forgive Messire John's vehemence, my lord; but he has put our case. Dunois is a great captain, we admit; but why could he do nothing until the witch came?

CAUCHON

I do not say that there were no supernatural powers on her side. But the names on that white banner were not the names of Satan and Beelzebub, but the blessed names of our Lord and His holy mother. And your commander who was drowned—Clahz-da I think you call him——

WARWICK

Glasdale. Sir William Glasdale.

CAUCHON

Glass-dell, thank you. He was no saint; and many of our people think that he was drowned for his blasphemies against The Maid.

WARWICK

(*Beginning to look very dubious*). Well, what are we to infer from all this, my lord? Has The Maid converted you?

CAUCHON

If she had, my lord, I should have known better than to have trusted myself here within your grasp.

WARWICK

(*Blandly deprecating*). Oh! oh! My lord!

CAUCHON

If the devil is making use of this girl—and I believe he is——

WARWICK

(*Reassured*). Ah! You hear, Messire John? I knew your lordship would not fail us. Pardon my interruption. Proceed.

CAUCHON

If it be so, the devil has longer views than you give him credit for.

WARWICK

Indeed? In what way? Listen to this, Messire John.

CAUCHON

If the devil wanted to damn a country girl, do you think so easy a task would cost him the winning of half a dozen battles? No, my lord: any trumpery imp could do that much if the girl could be damned at all. The Prince of Darkness does not condescend to such cheap drudgery. When he strikes, he strikes at the Catholic Church, whose realm is the whole spiritual world. When he damns, he damns the souls of the entire human race. Against that dreadful design the Church stands ever on guard. And it is as one of the instruments of that design that I see this girl. She is inspired, but diabolically inspired.

THE CHAPLAIN

I told you she was a witch.

CAUCHON

(*Fiercely*). She is not a witch. She is a heretic.

THE CHAPLAIN

What difference does that make?

CAUCHON

You, a priest, ask me that! You English are strangely blunt in the mind. All these things that you call witchcraft are capable of a natural explanation. The woman's miracles would not impose on a rabbit: she does not claim them as miracles herself. What do her victories prove but that she has a better head on her shoulders than your swearing Glass-dells and mad bull Talbots, and that the courage of faith, even though it be a false faith, will always outstay the courage of wrath?

THE CHAPLAIN

(*Hardly able to believe his ears*). Does your lordship compare Sir John Talbot, the heir to the earldom of Shrewsbury, to a mad bull? ! ! !

WARWICK

It would not be seemly for you to do so, Messire John, as you are still six removes from a barony. But as I am an earl, and Talbot is only a knight, I may make bold to accept the comparison. (*To the* BISHOP.) My lord: I wipe the slate as far as the witchcraft goes. None the less, we must burn the woman.

CAUCHON

I cannot burn her. The Church cannot take life. And my first duty is to seek this girl's salvation.

WARWICK

No doubt. But you do burn people occasionally.

CAUCHON

No. When the Church cuts off an obstinate heretic as a dead branch from the tree of life, the heretic is handed over to the secular arm. The Church has no part in what the secular arm may see fit to do.

WARWICK

Precisely. And I shall be the secular arm in this case. Well, my lord, hand over your dead branch; and I will see that the fire is ready for it. If you will answer for the Church's part, I will answer for the secular part.

CAUCHON

(*With smouldering anger*). I can answer for nothing. You great lords are too prone to treat the Church as a mere political convenience.

WARWICK

(*Smiling and propitiatory*). Not in England, I assure you.

CAUCHON

In England more than anywhere else. No, my lord: the soul of this village girl is of equal value with yours or your king's before the throne of God; and my first duty is to save it. I will not suffer your lordship to smile at me as if I were repeating a meaningless form of words, and it were well understood between us that I should betray the girl to you. I am no mere political bishop: my faith is to me what your honor is to you; and if there be a loophole through which this baptized child of God can creep to her salvation, I shall guide her to it.

THE CHAPLAIN

(*Rising in a fury*). You are a traitor.

CAUCHON

(*Springing up*). You lie, priest. (*Trembling with rage.*) If you dare do what this woman has done—set your country above the holy Catholic Church—you shall go to the fire with her.

THE CHAPLAIN

My lord: I—I went too far. I—(*He sits down with a submissive gesture.*)

WARWICK

(*Who has risen apprehensively*). My lord: I apologize to you for the word used by Messire John de Stogumber. It does not mean in England what it does in France. In your language traitor means betrayer: one who is perfidious, treacherous, unfaithful, disloyal. In our country it means simply one who is not wholly devoted to our English interests.

CAUCHON

I am sorry: I did not understand. (*He subsides into his chair with dignity.*)

WARWICK

(*Resuming his seat, much relieved*). I must apologize on my own account if I have seemed to take the burning of this poor girl too lightly. When one has seen whole countrysides burnt over and over again as mere items in military routine, one has to grow a very thick skin. Otherwise one might go mad: at all events, I should. May I venture to assume that your lordship also, having to see so many heretics burnt from time to time, is compelled to take—shall I say a professional view of what would otherwise be a very horrible incident?

CAUCHON

Yes: it is a painful duty: even, as you say, a horrible one. But in comparison with the horror of heresy it is less than nothing. I am not thinking of this girl's body, which will suffer for a few moments only, and which must in any event die in some more or less painful manner, but of her soul, which may suffer to all eternity.

WARWICK

Just so; and God grant that her soul may be saved! But the practical problem would seem to be how to save her soul without saving her body. For we must face it, my lord: if this cult of The Maid goes on, our cause is lost.

THE CHAPLAIN

(*His voice broken like that of a man who has been crying*). May I speak, my lord?

WARWICK

Really, Messire John, I had rather you did not, unless you can keep your temper.

THE CHAPLAIN

It is only this. I speak under correction; but The Maid is full of deceit: she pretends to be devout. Her prayers and confessions are endless. How can she be accused of heresy when she neglects no observance of a faithful daughter of the Church?

CAUCHON

(*Flaming up*). A faithful daughter of the Church! The Pope himself at his proudest dare not presume as this woman presumes. She acts as if she herself were the Church. She brings the message of God to Charles; and the Church must stand aside. She will crown him in the cathedral of Rheims: she, not the Church! She sends letters to the king of England giving him God's command through her to return to his island on pain of God's vengeance, which she will execute. Let me tell you that the writing of such letters was the practice of the accursed Mahomet, the anti-Christ. Has she ever in all her utterances said one word of the Church? Never. It is always God and herself.

WARWICK

What can you expect? A beggar on horse-back! Her head is turned.

CAUCHON

Who has turned it? The devil. And for a mighty purpose. He is spreading this heresy everywhere. The man Hus, burnt only thirteen years ago at Constance, infected all Bohemia with it. A man named WcLeef, himself an anointed priest, spread the pestilence in England; and to your shame you let him die in his bed. We have such people here in France too: I know the breed. It is cancerous: if it be not cut out, stamped out, burnt out, it will not stop until it has brought the whole body of human society into sin and corruption, into waste and ruin. By it an Arab camel driver drove Christ and His Church out of Jerusalem, and ravaged his way west like a wild beast until at last there stood only the Pyrenees and God's mercy between France and damnation. Yet what did the camel driver do at the beginning more than this shepherd girl is doing? He had his voices from the angel Gabriel: she has her voices from St. Catherine and St. Margaret and the Blessed Michael. He declared himself the messenger of God, and wrote in God's name to the kings of the earth. Her letters to them are going forth daily. It is not the Mother of God now to whom we must look for intercession, but to Joan the Maid. What will the world be like when the Church's accumulated wisdom and knowledge and experience, its councils of learned, venerable pious men, are thrust into the kennel by every ignorant laborer or dairymaid whom the devil can puff up with the monstrous self-conceit of being directly inspired from heaven? It will be a world of blood, of fury, of devastation, of each man striving for his own hand: in the end a world wrecked back into barbarism. For now you have only Mahomet and his dupes, and The Maid and her dupes; but what will it be when every girl thinks herself a Joan and every man a Mahomet? I shudder to the very marrow of my bones when I think of it. I have fought it all my life; and I will fight it to the end. Let all this woman's sins be forgiven her except only this sin; for it is the sin against the Holy Ghost; and if she does not recant in the dust before the world, and submit herself to the last inch of her soul to her Church, to the fire she shall go if she once falls into my hand.

WARWICK

(*Unimpressed*). You feel strongly about it, naturally.

CAUCHON

Do not you?

WARWICK

I am a soldier, not a churchman. As a pilgrim I saw something of the Mahometans. They were not so ill-bred as I had been led to believe. In some respects their conduct compared favorably with ours.

CAUCHON

(*Displeased*). I have noticed this before. Men go to the East to convert the infidels. And the infidels pervert them. The Crusader comes back more than half a Saracen. Not to mention that all Englishmen are born heretics.

THE CHAPLAIN

Englishmen heretics!!! (*Appealing to* WARWICK.) My lord: must we endure this? His lordship is beside himself. How can what an Englishman believes be heresy? It is a contradiction in terms.

CAUCHON

I absolve you, Messire de Stogumber, on the ground of invincible ignorance. The thick air of your country does not breed theologians.

WARWICK

You would not say so if you heard us quarreling about religion, my lord! I am sorry you think I must be either a heretic or a blockhead because, as a traveled man, I know that the followers of Mahomet profess great respect for our Lord, and are more ready to forgive St. Peter for being a fisherman than your lordship is to forgive Mahomet for being a camel driver. But at least we can proceed in this matter without bigotry.

CAUCHON

When men call the zeal of the Christian Church bigotry I know what to think.

WARWICK

They are only east and west views of the same thing.

CAUCHON

(*Bitterly ironical*). Only east and west! Only!!

WARWICK

Oh, my Lord Bishop, I am not gain-saying you. You will carry the Church with you; but you have to carry the nobles also. To my mind there is a stronger case against The Maid than the one you have so forcibly put. Frankly, I am not afraid of this girl becoming another Mahomet, and superseding the Church by a great heresy. I think you exaggerate that risk. But have you noticed that in these letters of hers, she proposes to all the kings of Europe, as she has already pressed on Charles, a transaction which would wreck the whole social structure of Christendom?

CAUCHON

Wreck the Church. I tell you so.

WARWICK

(*Whose patience is wearing out*). My lord: pray get the Church out of your head for a moment; and remember that there are temporal institutions in the world as well as spiritual ones. I and my peers represent the feudal aristocracy as you represent the Church. We are the temporal power. Well, do you not see how this girl's idea strikes at us?

CAUCHON

How does her idea strike at you, except as it strikes at all of us, through the Church?

WARWICK

Her idea is that the kings should give their realms to God, and then reign as God's bailiffs.

CAUCHON

(*Not interested*). Quite sound theologically, my lord. But the king will hardly care, provided he reign. It is an abstract idea: a mere form of words.

WARWICK

By no means. It is a cunning device to supersede the aristocracy, and make the king sole and absolute autocrat. Instead of the king being merely the first among his peers, he becomes their master. That we cannot suffer: we call no man master. Nominally we hold our lands and dignities from the king, because there must be a keystone to the arch of human society; but we hold our lands in our own hands, and defend them with our own swords and those of our own tenants. Now by The Maid's doctrine the king will take our lands—our lands!—and make them a present to God; and God will then vest them wholly in the king.

CAUCHON

Need you fear that? You are the maker of kings after all. York or Lancaster in England, Lancaster or Valois in France: they reign according to your pleasure.

WARWICK

Yes: but only as long as the people follow their feudal lords, and know the king only as a traveling show, owning nothing but the highway that belongs to everybody. If the people's thoughts and hearts were turned to the king, and their lords became only the king's servants in their eyes, the king could break us across his knee one by one; and then what should we be but liveried courtiers in his halls?

CAUCHON

Still you need not fear, my lord. Some men are born kings; and some are born statesmen, the two are seldom the same. Where would the king find counsellors to plan and carry out such a policy for him?

WARWICK

(*With a not too friendly smile*). Perhaps in the Church, my lord.

(CAUCHON, *with an equally sour smile, shrugs his shoulders, and does not contradict him.*)

WARWICK

Strike down the barons; and the cardinals will have it all their own way.

CAUCHON

(*Conciliatory, dropping his polemical tone*). My lord: we shall not defeat The Maid if we strike against one another. I know well that there is a Will to Power in the world. I know that while it lasts there will be a struggle between the Emperor and the Pope, between the dukes and the political cardinals, between the barons and the kings. The devil divides us and governs. I see you are no friend to the Church: you are an earl first and last, as I am a churchman first and last. But can we not sink our differences in the face of a common enemy? I see now that what is in your mind is not that this girl has never once mentioned the Church, and thinks only of God and herself, but that she has never once mentioned the peerage, and thinks only of the king and herself.

WARWICK

Quite so. These two ideas of hers are the same idea at bottom. It goes deep, my lord. It is the protest of the individual soul against the interference of priest or peer between the private man and his God. I should call it Protestantism if I had to find a name for it.

CAUCHON

(*Looking hard at him*). You understand it wonderfully well, my lord. Scratch an Englishman, and find a Protestant.

WARWICK

(*Playing the pink of courtesy*). I think you are not entirely void of sympathy with The Maid's secular heresy, my lord. I leave you to find a name for it.

CAUCHON

You mistake me, my lord. I have no sympathy with her political presumptions. But as a priest I have gained a knowledge of the minds of the common people; and there you will find yet another most dangerous idea. I can express it only by such phrases as France for the French, England for the English, Italy for the Italians, Spain for the Spanish, and so forth. It is sometimes so narrow and bitter in country folk that it surprises me that this country girl can rise above the idea of her village for its villagers. But she can. She does. When she threatens to drive the English from the soil of France she is undoubtedly thinking of the whole extent of country in which French is spoken. To her the French-speaking people are what the Holy Scriptures describe as a nation. Call this side of her heresy Nationalism if you will: I can find you no better name for it. I can only tell you that it is essentially anti-Catholic and anti-Christian; for the Catholic Church knows only one realm, and that is the realm of Christ's kingdom. Divide that kingdom into nations, and you dethrone Christ. Dethrone Christ, and who will stand between our throats and the sword? The world will perish in a welter of war.

WARWICK

Well, if you will burn the Protestant, I will burn the Nationalist, though perhaps I shall not carry Messire John with me there. England for the English will appeal to him.

THE CHAPLAIN

Certainly England for the English goes without saying: it is the simple law of nature. But this woman denies to England her legitimate conquests, given her by God because of her peculiar fitness to rule over less civilized races for their own good. I do not understand what your lordship means by Protestant and Nationalist: you are too learned and subtle for a poor clerk like myself. But I know as a matter of plain commonsense that the woman is a rebel; and that is enough for me. She rebels against Nature by wearing man's clothes, and fighting. She rebels against the Church by usurping the divine authority of the Pope. She rebels against God by her damnable league with Satan and his evil spirits against our army. And all these rebellions are only excuses for her great rebellion against England. That is not to be endured.

Let her perish. Let her burn. Let her not infect the whole flock. It is expedient that one woman die for the people.

WARWICK

(*Rising*). My lord: we seem to be agreed.

CAUCHON

(*Rising also, but in protest*). I will not imperil my soul. I will uphold the justice of the Church. I will strive to the utmost for this woman's salvation.

WARWICK

I am sorry for the poor girl. I hate these severities. I will spare her if I can.

THE CHAPLAIN

(*Implacably*). I would burn her with my own hands.

CAUCHON

(*Blessing him*). Sancta simplicitas!

SCENE V

THE *ambulatory in the cathedral of Rheims, near the door of the vestry. A pillar bears one of the stations of the cross. The organ is playing the people out of the nave after the coronation.* JOAN *is kneeling in prayer before the station. She is beautifully dressed, but still in male attire. The organ ceases as* DUNOIS, *also splendidly arrayed, comes into the ambulatory from the vestry.*

DUNOIS

Come, Joan! you have had enough praying. After that fit of crying you will catch a chill if you stay here any longer. It is all over: the cathedral is empty; and the streets are full. They are calling for The Maid. We have told them you are staying here alone to pray: but they want to see you again.

JOAN

No: let the king have all the glory.

DUNOIS

He only spoils the show, poor devil. No, Joan: you have crowned him; and you must go through with it.
(JOAN *shakes her head reluctantly.*)

DUNOIS

(*Raising her*). Come come! it will be over in a couple of hours. It's better than the bridge at Orleans, eh?

JOAN

Oh, dear Dunois, how I wish it were the bridge at Orleans again! We lived at that bridge.

DUNOIS

Yes, faith, and died too: some of us.

JOAN

Isn't it strange, Jack? I am such a coward: I am frightened beyond words before a battle; but it is so dull afterwards when there is no danger: oh, so dull! dull! dull!

DUNOIS

You must learn to be abstemious in war, just as you are in your food and drink, my little saint.

JOAN

Dear Jack: I think you like me as a soldier likes his comrade.

DUNOIS

You need it, poor innocent child of God. You have not many friends at court.

JOAN

Why do all these courtiers and knights and churchmen hate me? What have I done to them? I have asked nothing for myself except that my village shall not be taxed; for we cannot afford war taxes. I have brought them luck and victory: I have set them right when they were doing all sorts of stupid things: I have crowned Charles and made him a real king; and all the honors he is handing out have gone to them. Then why do they not love me?

DUNOIS

(*Rallying her*). Sim-ple-ton! Do you expect stupid people to love you for shewing them up? Do blundering old military dug-outs love the successful young captains who supersede them? Do ambitious politicians love the climbers who take the front seats from them? Do archbishops enjoy being played off their own altars, even by saints? Why, I should be jealous of you myself if I were ambitious enough.

JOAN

You are the pick of the basket here, Jack: the only friend I have among all these nobles. I'll wager your mother was from the country. I will go back to the farm when I have taken Paris.

DUNOIS

I am not so sure that they will let you take Paris.

JOAN

(*Startled*). What!

DUNOIS

I should have taken it myself before this if they had all been sound about it. Some of them would rather Paris took you, I think. So take care.

JOAN

Jack: the world is too wicked for me. If the goddams and the Burgundians do not make an end of me, the French will. Only for my voices I should lose all heart. That is why I had to steal away to pray here alone after the coronation. I'll tell you something, Jack. It is in the bells I hear my voices. Not today, when they all rang: that was nothing but jangling. But here in this corner, where the bells come down from heaven, and the echoes linger, or in the fields, where they come from a distance through the quiet of the countryside, my voices are in them. (*The cathedral clock chimes the quarter.*) Hark! (*She becomes rapt.*) Do you hear? "Dear-child-of-God:" just what you said. At the half-hour they will say "Be-brave-go-on." At the three-quarters they will say "I-am-thy-Help." But it is at the hour, when the great bell goes after "God-will-save-France:" it is then that St Margaret and St Catherine and sometimes even the blessed Michael will say things that I cannot tell beforehand. Then, oh then—

DUNOIS

(*Interrupting her kindly but not sympathetically*). Then, Joan, we shall hear whatever we fancy in the booming of the bell. You make me uneasy when you talk about your voices: I should think you were a bit cracked if I hadn't noticed that you give me very sensible reasons for what you do, though I hear you telling others you are only obeying Madame Saint Catherine.

JOAN

(*Crossly*). Well, I have to find reasons for you, because you do not believe in my voices. But the voices come first; and I find the reasons after: whatever you may choose to believe.

DUNOIS

Are you angry, Joan?

JOAN

Yes. (*Smiling.*) No: not with you. I wish you were one of the village babies.

DUNOIS

Why?

JOAN

I could nurse you for awhile.

DUNOIS

You are a bit of a woman after all.

JOAN

No: not a bit: I am a soldier and nothing else. Soldiers always nurse children when they get a chance.

DUNOIS

That is true. (*He laughs.*)

(KING CHARLES, *with* BLUEBEARD *on his left and* LA HIRE *on his right, comes from the vestry, where he has been disrobing.* JOAN *shrinks away behind the pillar.* DUNOIS *is left between* CHARLES *and* LA HIRE.)

DUNOIS

Well, your Majesty is an anointed king at last. How do you like it?

CHARLES

I would not go through it again to be emperor of the sun and moon. The weight of those robes! I thought I should have dropped when they loaded that crown on to me. And the famous holy oil they talked so much about was rancid: phew! The Archbishop must be nearly dead: his robes must have weighed a ton: they are stripping him still in the vestry.

DUNOIS

(*Drily*). Your Majesty should wear armor oftener. That would accustom you to heavy dressing.

CHARLES

Yes: the old jibe! Well, I am not going to wear armor: fighting is not my job. Where is The Maid?

JOAN

(*Coming forward between* CHARLES *and* BLUEBEARD, *and falling on her knee*). Sire: I have made you king: my work is done. I am going back to my father's farm.

CHARLES

(*Surprised, but relieved*). Oh, are you? Well, that will be very nice.
(JOAN *rises, deeply discouraged*.)

CHARLES

(*Continuing heedlessly*). A healthy life, you know.

DUNOIS

But a dull one.

BLUEBEARD

You will find the petticoats tripping you up after leaving them off for so long.

LA HIRE

You will miss the fighting. It's a bad habit, but a grand one, and the hardest of all to break yourself of.

CHARLES

(*Anxiously*). Still, we don't want you to stay if you would really rather go home.

JOAN

(*Bitterly*). I know well that none of you will be sorry to see me go. (*She turns her shoulder to* CHARLES *and walks past him to the more congenial neighborhood of* DUNOIS *and* LA HIRE.)

LA HIRE

Well, I shall be able to swear when I want to. But I shall miss you at times.

JOAN

La Hire: in spite of all your sins and swears we shall meet in heaven; for I love you as I love Pitou, my old sheep dog. Pitou could kill a wolf. You will kill the English wolves until they go back to their country and become good dogs of God, will you not?

LA HIRE

You and I together: yes.

JOAN

No: I shall last only a year from the beginning.

ALL THE OTHERS

What!

JOAN

I know it somehow.

DUNOIS

Nonsense!

JOAN

Jack: do you think you will be able to drive them out?

DUNOIS

(*With quiet conviction*). Yes: I shall drive them out. They beat us because we thought battles were tournaments and ransom markets. We played the fool while the goddams took war seriously. But I have learnt my lesson, and taken their measure. They have no roots here. I have beaten them before; and I shall beat them again.

JOAN

You will not be cruel to them, Jack?

DUNOIS

The goddams will not yield to tender handling. We did not begin it.

JOAN

(*Suddenly*). Jack: before I go home, let us take Paris.

CHARLES

(*Terrified*). Oh, no, no. We shall lose everything we have gained. Oh, don't let us have any more fighting. We can make a very good treaty with the Duke of Burgundy.

JOAN

Treaty! (*She stamps with impatience.*)

CHARLES

Well, why not, now that I am crowned and anointed? Oh, that oil!

(*The* ARCHBISHOP *comes from the vestry, and joins the group between* CHARLES *and* BLUEBEARD.)

Archbishop, The Maid wants to start fighting again.

THE ARCHBISHOP

Have we ceased fighting, then? Are we at peace?

CHARLES

No: I suppose not; but let us be content with what we have done. Let us make a treaty. Our luck is too good to last; and now is our chance to stop before it turns.

JOAN

Luck! God has fought for us; and you call it luck! And you would stop while there are still Englishmen on this holy earth of dear France!

THE ARCHBISHOP

(*Sternly*). Maid: the king addressed himself to me, not to you. You forget yourself. You very often forget yourself.

JOAN

(*Unabashed, and rather roughly*). Then speak, you; and tell him that it is not God's will that he should take his hand from the plough.

THE ARCHBISHOP

If I am not so glib with the name of God as you are, it is because I interpret His will with the authority of the Church and of my sacred office. When you first came you respected it, and would not have dared to speak as you are now speaking. You came clothed with the virtue of humility; and because God blessed your enterprises accordingly, you have stained yourself with the sin of pride. The old Greek tragedy is rising among us. It is the chastisement of hubris.

CHARLES

Yes: she thinks she knows better than every one else.

JOAN

(*Distressed, but naïvely incapable of seeing the effect she is producing*). But I do know better than any of you seem to. And I am not proud: I never speak unless I know I am right.

CHARLES

BLUEBEARD

(*Exclaiming together*). Ha ha! Just so.

THE ARCHBISHOP

How do you know you are right?

JOAN

I always know. My voices—

CHARLES

Oh, your voices, your voices. Why don't the voices come to me? I am king, not you.

JOAN

They do come to you; but you do not hear them. You have not sat in the field in the evening listening for them. When the angelus rings you cross yourself and have done with it; but if you prayed from your heart, and listened to the thrilling of the bells in the air after they stop ringing, you would hear the voices as well as I do. (*Turning brusquely from him.*) But what voices do you need to tell you what the blacksmith can tell you: that you must strike while the iron is hot? I tell you we must make a dash at Compiègne and relieve it as we relieved Orleans. Then Paris will open its gates; or if not, we will break through them. What is your crown worth without your capital?

LA HIRE

That is what I say too. We shall go through them like a red-hot shot through a pound of butter. What do you say, Bastard?

DUNOIS

If our cannon balls were all as hot as your head, and we had enough of them, we should conquer the earth, no doubt. Pluck and impetuosity are good servants in war, but bad masters; they have delivered us into the hands of the English every time we have trusted to them. We never know when we are beaten: that is our great fault.

JOAN

You never know when you are victorious: that is a worse fault. I shall have to make you carry looking-glasses in battle to convince you that the English have not cut off all your noses. You would have been besieged in Orleans still, you and your councils of war, if I had not made you attack. You should always attack; and if you only hold on long enough the enemy will stop first. You don't know how to begin a battle; and you don't know how to use your cannons. And I do.
(*She squats down on the flags with crossed ankles, pouting.*)

DUNOIS

I know what you think of us, General Joan.

JOAN

Never mind that, Jack. Tell them what you think of me.

DUNOIS

I think that God was on your side; for I have not forgotten how the wind changed, and how our hearts changed when you came; and by my faith I shall never deny that it was in your sign that we conquered. But I tell you as a soldier that God is no man's daily drudge, and no maid's either. If you are worthy of it He will sometimes snatch you out of the jaws of death and set you on your feet again; but that is all; once on your feet you must fight with all your might and all your craft. For He has to be fair to your enemy too: don't forget that. Well, He set us on our feet through you at Orleans; and the glory of it has carried us through a few good battles here to the coronation. But if we presume on it further, and trust to God to do the work we should do ourselves, we shall be defeated; and serve us right!

JOAN

But—

DUNOIS

Sh! I have not finished. Do not think, any of you, that these victories of ours were won without generalship. King Charles: you have said no word in your proclamations of my part in this campaign; and I make no complaint of that; for the people will run after The Maid and her miracles and not after the Bastard's hard work finding troops for her and feeding them. But I know exactly how much God did for us through The Maid, and how much He left me to do by my own wits; and I tell you that your little hour of miracles is over, and that from this time on he who plays the war game best will win—if the luck is on his side.

JOAN

Ah! if, if, if, if! If ifs and ans were pots and pans there'd be no need of tinkers. (*Rising impetuously.*) I tell you, Bastard, your art of war is no use, because your knights are no good for real fighting. War is only a game to them, like tennis and all their other games; they make rules as to what is fair and what is not fair, and heap armor on themselves and on their poor horses to keep out the arrows; and when they fall they can't get up, and have to wait for their squires to come and lift them to arrange about the ransom with the man that has poked them off their horse. Can't you see that all the like of that is gone by and done with? What use is armor against gunpowder? And if it was, do you think men that are fighting for France and for God will stop to bargain about ransoms, as half your knights live by doing? No: they will fight to win; and they will give up their lives out of their own hand into the hand of God when they go into battle, as I do. Common folks understand this. They cannot afford armor and cannot pay ransoms; but they follow me half naked into the moat and up the ladder and over the wall. With them it is my life or thine, and God defend the right! You may shake your head, Jack; and Bluebeard may twirl his billygoat's beard and cock his nose at me; but remember the day your knights and captains refused to follow me to attack the English at Orleans! You locked the gates to keep me in; and it was the townsfolk and the common people that followed me and forced the gate, and shewed you the way to fight in earnest.

BLUEBEARD

(*Offended*). Not content with being Pope Joan, you must be Caesar and Alexander as well.

THE ARCHBISHOP

Pride will have a fall, Joan.

JOAN

Oh, never mind whether it is pride or not: is it true? is it commonsense?

LA HIRE

It is true. Half of us are afraid of having our handsome noses broken; and the other half are out for paying off their mortgages. Let her have her way, Dunois: she does not know everything; but she has got hold of the right end of the stock. Fighting is not what it was; and those who know least about it often make the best job of it.

DUNOIS

I know all that. I do not fight in the old way: I have learnt the lesson of Agincourt, of Poitiers and Crecy. I know how many lives any move of mine will cost; and if the move is worth the cost I make it and pay the cost. But Joan never counts the cost at all: she goes ahead and trusts to God: she thinks she has God in her pocket. Up to now she has had the numbers on her side; and she has won. But I know Joan; and I see that some day she will go ahead when she has only ten men to do the work of a hundred. And then she will find that God is on the side of the big battalions. She will be taken by the enemy. And the lucky man that makes the capture will receive sixteen thousand pounds from the Earl of Ouareek.

JOAN

(*Flattered*). Sixteen thousand pounds! Eh, laddie, have they offered that for me? There cannot be so much money in the world.

DUNOIS

There is, in England. And now tell me, all of you, which of you will lift a finger to save Joan once the English have got her? I speak first, for the army. The day after she has been dragged from her horse by a goddam or a Burgundian, and he is not struck dead: the day after she is locked in a dungeon, and the bars and bolts do not fly open at the touch of St. Peter's angel: the day when the enemy finds out that she is as vulnerable as I am and not a bit more invincible, she will not be worth the life of a single soldier to us; and I will not risk that life, much as I cherish her as a companion-in-arms.

JOAN

I don't blame you, Jack: you are right. I am not worth one soldier's life if God lets me be beaten; but France may think me worth my ransom after what God has done for her through me.

CHARLES

I tell you I have no money; and this coronation, which is all your fault, has cost me the last farthing I can borrow.

JOAN

The Church is richer than you. I put my trust in the Church.

THE ARCHBISHOP

Woman: they will drag you through the streets, and burn you as a witch.

JOAN

(*Running to him*). Oh, my lord, do not say that. It is impossible. I a witch!

THE ARCHBISHOP

Peter Cauchon knows his business. The University of Paris has burnt a woman for saying that what you have done was well done, and according to God.

JOAN

(*Bewildered*). But why? What sense is there in it? What I have done is according to God. They could not burn a woman for speaking the truth.

THE ARCHBISHOP

They did.

JOAN

But you know that she was speaking the truth. You would not let them burn me.

THE ARCHBISHOP

How could I prevent them?

JOAN

You would speak in the name of the Church. You are a great prince of the Church. I would go anywhere with your blessing to protect me.

THE ARCHBISHOP

I have no blessing for you while you are proud and disobedient.

JOAN

Oh, why will you go on saying things like that? I am not proud and disobedient. I am a poor girl, and so ignorant that I do not know A from B. How could I be proud? And how can you say that I am disobedient when I always obey my voices, because they come from God.

THE ARCHBISHOP

The voice of God on earth is the voice of the Church Militant; and all the voices that come to you are the echoes of your own wilfulness.

JOAN

It is not true.

THE ARCHBISHOP

(*Flushing angrily*). You tell the Archbishop in his cathedral that he lies; and yet you say you are not proud and disobedient.

JOAN

I never said you lied. It was you that as good as said my voices lied. When have they ever lied? If you will not believe in them: even if they are only the echoes of my own commonsense, are they not always right? and are not your earthly counsels always wrong?

THE ARCHBISHOP

(*Indignantly*). It is waste of time admonishing you.

CHARLES

It always comes back to the same thing. She is right, and every one else is wrong.

THE ARCHBISHOP

Take this as your last warning. If you perish through setting your private judgment above the instructions of your spiritual directors, the Church disowns you, and leaves you to whatever fate your presumption may bring upon you. The Bastard has told you that if you persist in setting up your military conceit above the counsels of your commanders—

DUNOIS

(*Interposing*). To put it quite exactly, if you attempt to relieve the garrison in Compiègne without the same superiority in numbers you had at Orleans—

THE ARCHBISHOP

The army will disown you, and will not rescue you. And His Majesty the King has told you that the throne has not the means of ransoming you.

CHARLES

Not a penny.

THE ARCHBISHOP

You stand alone: absolutely alone, trusting to your own conceit, your own ignorance, your own headstrong presumption, your own impiety in hiding all these sins under the cloak of a trust in God. When you pass through these doors into the sunlight, the crowd will cheer you. They will bring you their little children and their invalids to heal: they will kiss your hands and feet, and do what they can, poor simple souls, to turn your head, and madden you with the self-confidence that is leading you to your destruction. But you will be none the less alone: they cannot save you. We and we only can stand between you and the stake at which our enemies have burnt that wretched woman in Paris.

JOAN

(*Her eyes skyward*). I have better friends and better counsel than yours.

THE ARCHBISHOP

I see that I am speaking in vain to a hardened heart. You reject our protection, and are determined to turn us all against you. In future, then, fend for yourself; and if you fail, God have mercy on your soul.

DUNOIS

That is the truth, Joan. Heed it.

JOAN

Where would you all have been now if I had heeded that sort of truth? There is no help, no counsel, in any of you. Yes: I am alone on earth: I have always been alone. My father told my brothers to drown me if I would not stay to mind his sheep while France was bleeding to death: France might perish if only our lambs were safe. I thought France would have friends at the court of the king of France; and I find only wolves fighting for pieces of her poor torn body. I thought God would have friends everywhere, because He is the friend of every one; and in my innocence I believed that you who now cast me out would be like strong towers to keep harm from me. But I am wiser now; and nobody is any the worse for being wiser. Do you think you can frighten me by telling me that I am alone? France is alone; and God is alone; and what is my loneliness before the loneliness of my country and my God? I see now that the loneliness of God is His strength: what would He be if He listened to your jealous little counsels? Well, my loneliness shall be my strength too: it is better to be alone with God: His friendship will not fail me, nor His counsel, nor His love. In His strength I will dare, and dare, and dare, until I die. I will go out now to the common people, and let the love in their eyes comfort me for the hate in yours. You will all be glad to see me burnt; but if I go through the fire I shall go through it to their hearts for ever and ever. And so, God be with me!

(*She goes from them. They stare after her in glum silence for a moment. Then* GILLES DE RAIS *twirls his beard*.)

BLUEBEARD

You know, the woman is quite impossible. I don't dislike her, really; but what are you to do with such a character?

DUNOIS

As God is my judge, if she fell into the Loire I would jump in in full armor to fish her out. But if she plays the fool at Compiègne, and gets caught, I must leave her to her doom.

LA HIRE

Then you had better chain me up; for I could follow her to hell when the spirit rises in her like that.

THE ARCHBISHOP

She disturbs my judgment too: there is a dangerous power in her outbursts. But the pit is open at her feet; and for good or evil we cannot turn her from it.

CHARLES

If only she would keep quiet, or go home!

(*They follow her dispiritedly*.)

SCENE VI

Rouen, 30th May 1431. A great stone hall in the castle, arranged for a trial-at-law, but not a trial-by-jury, the court being the BISHOP'S *court with the Inquisition participating: hence there are two raised chairs side by side for the* BISHOP *and the* INQUISITOR *as judges. Rows of chairs radiating from them at an obtuse angle are for the canons, the doctors of law and theology, and the Dominican monks, who acts as assessors. In the angle is a table for the scribes, with stools. There is also a heavy rough wooden stool for the prisoner. All these are at the inner end of the hall. The further end is open to the courtyard through a row of arches. The court is shielded from the weather by screens and curtains.*

Looking down the great hall from the middle of the inner end, the judicial chairs and scribes' table are to the right. The prisoner's stool is to the left. There are arched doors right and left. It is a fine sunshiny May morning.

WARWICK *comes in through the arched doorway on the judges' side, followed by his page.*

THE PAGE

(*Pertly*). I suppose your lordship is aware that we have no business here. This is an ecclesiastical court; and we are only the secular arm.

WARWICK

I am aware of that fact. Will it please your impudence to find the Bishop of Beauvais for me, and give him a hint that he can have a word with me here before the trial, if he wishes?

THE PAGE

(*Going*). Yes, my lord.

WARWICK

And mind you behave yourself. Do not address him as Pious Peter.

THE PAGE

No, my lord. I shall be kind to him, because, when The Maid is brought in, Pious Peter will have to pick a peck of pickled pepper.

(CAUCHON *enters through the same door with a Dominican monk and a canon, the latter carrying a brief.*)

THE PAGE

The Right Reverend his lordship the Bishop of Beauvais. And two other reverend gentlemen.

WARWICK

Get out; and see that we are not interrupted.

THE PAGE

Right, my lord. (*He vanishes airily.*)

CAUCHON

I wish your lordship good-morrow.

WARWICK

Good-morrow to your lordship. Have I had the pleasure of meeting your friends before? I think not.

CAUCHON

(*Introducing the monk, who is on his right*). This, my lord, is Brother John Lemaître, of the order of St. Dominic. He is acting as deputy for the Chief Inquisitor into the evil of heresy in France. Brother John: the Earl of Warwick.

WARWICK

Your Reverence is most welcome. We have no Inquisitor in England, unfortunately; though we miss him greatly, especially on occasions like the present.

(THE INQUISITOR *smiles patiently, and bows. He is a mild elderly gentleman, but has evident reserves of authority and firmness.*)

CAUCHON

(*Introducing the Canon, who is on his left.*) This gentleman is Canon John D'Estivet, of the Chapter of Bayeux. He is acting as Promoter.

WARWICK

Promoter?

CAUCHON

Prosecutor, you would call him in civil law.

WARWICK

Ah! prosecutor. Quite, quite. I am very glad to make your acquaintance, Canon D'Estivet.
(D'ESTIVET *bows. He is on the young side of middle age, well mannered, but vulpine beneath his veneer.*)

WARWICK

May I ask what stage the proceedings have reached? It is now more than nine months since The Maid was captured at Compiègne by the Burgundians. It is fully four months since I bought her from the Burgundians for a very handsome sum, solely that she might be brought to justice. It is very nearly three months since I delivered her up to you, my Lord Bishop, as a person suspected of heresy. May I suggest that you are taking a rather unconscionable time to make up your minds about a very plain case? Is this trial never going to end?

THE INQUISITOR

(*Smiling*). It has not yet begun, my lord.

WARWICK

Not yet begun! Why, you have been at it eleven weeks!

CAUCHON

We have not been idle, my lord. We have held fifteen examinations of The Maid: six public and nine private.

THE INQUISITOR

(*Always patiently smiling*). You see, my lord, I have been present at only two of these examinations. They were proceedings of the Bishop's court solely, and not of the Holy Office. I have only just decided to associate myself—that is, to associate the Holy Inquisition—with the Bishop's court. I did not at first think that this was a case of heresy at all. I regarded it as a political case, and The Maid as a prisoner of war. But having now been present at two of the examinations, I must admit that this seems to be one of the gravest cases of heresy within my experience. Therefore everything is now in order; and we proceed to trial this morning. (*He moves towards the judicial chairs.*)

CAUCHON

This moment, if your lordship's convenience allows.

WARWICK

(*Graciously*). Well, that is good news, gentlemen. I will not attempt to conceal from you that our patience was becoming strained.

CAUCHON

So I gathered from the threats of your soldiers to drown those of our people who favor The Maid.

WARWICK

Dear me! At all events their intentions were friendly to you, my lord.

CAUCHON

(*Sternly*). I hope not. I am determined that the woman shall have a fair hearing. The justice of the Church is not a mockery, my lord.

THE INQUISITOR

(*Returning*). Never has there been a fairer examination within my experience, my lord. The Maid needs no lawyers to take her part: she will be tried by her most faithful friends, all ardently desirous to save her soul from perdition.

D'ESTIVET

Sir: I am the Promoter; and it has been my painful duty to present the case against the girl; but believe me, I would throw up my case today and hasten to her defence if I did not know that men far my superiors in learning and piety, in eloquence and persuasiveness, have been sent to reason with her, to explain to her the danger she is running, and the ease with which she may avoid it. (*Suddenly bursting into forensic eloquence, to the disgust of* CAUCHON *and* THE INQUISITOR, *who have listened to him so far with patronizing approval.*) Men have dared to say that we are acting from hate; but God is our witness that they lie. Have we tortured her? No. Have we ceased to exhort her; to implore her to have pity on herself; to come to the bosom of her Church as an erring but beloved child? Have we—

CAUCHON

(*Interrupting drily*). Take care, Canon. All that you say is true; but if you make his lordship believe it I will not answer for your life, and hardly for my own.

WARWICK

(*Deprecating, but by no means denying*). Oh, my lord, you are very hard on us poor English. But we certainly do not share your pious desire to save The Maid: in fact I tell you now plainly that her death is a political necessity which I regret but cannot help. If the Church lets her go—

CAUCHON

(*With fierce and menacing pride*). If the Church lets her go, woe to the man, were he the Emperor himself, who dares lay a finger on her! The Church is not subject to political necessity, my lord!

THE INQUISITOR

(*Interposing smoothly*). You need have no anxiety about the result, my lord. You have an invincible ally in the matter: one who is far more determined than you that she shall burn.

WARWICK

And who is this very convenient partisan, may I ask?

THE INQUISITOR

The Maid herself. Unless you put a gag in her mouth you cannot prevent her from convicting herself ten times over every time she opens it.

D'ESTIVET

That is perfectly true, my lord. My hair bristles on my head when I hear so young a creature utter such blasphemies.

WARWICK

Well, by all means do your best for her if you are quite sure it will be of no avail. (*Looking hard at* CAUCHON.) I should be sorry to have to act without the blessing of the Church.

CAUCHON

(*With a mixture of cynical admiration and contempt*). And yet they say Englishmen are hypocrites! You play for your side, my lord, even at the peril of your soul. I cannot but admire such devotion; but I dare not go so far myself. I fear damnation.

WARWICK

If we feared anything we could never govern England, my lord. Shall I send your people in to you?

CAUCHON

Yes: it will be very good of your lordship to withdraw and allow the court to assemble.

(WARWICK *turns on his heel, and goes out through the courtyard.* CAUCHON *takes one of the judicial seats; and* D'ESTIVET *sits at the scribes' table, studying his brief.*)

CAUCHON

(*Casually, as he makes himself comfortable*). What scoundrels these English nobles are!

THE INQUISITOR

(*Taking the other judicial chair on* CAUCHON'S *left*). All secular power makes men scoundrels. They are not trained for the work; and they have not the Apostolic Succession. Our own nobles are just as bad. (*The* BISHOP'S *assessors hurry into the hall, headed by* CHAPLAIN DE STOGUMBER *and* CANON DE COURCELLES, *a young priest of* 30. *The scribes sit at the table, leaving a chair vacant opposite* D'ESTIVET. *Some of the assessors take their seats: others stand chatting, waiting for the proceedings to begin formally.* DE STOGUMBER, *aggrieved and obstinate will not take his seat: neither will the Canon, who stands on his right.*)

CAUCHON

Good morning, Master de Stogumber. (*To the* INQUISITOR) Chaplain to the Cardinal of England.

THE CHAPLAIN

(*Correcting him*). Of Winchester, my lord. I have to make a protest, my lord.

CAUCHON

You make a great many.

THE CHAPLAIN

I am not without support, my lord. Here is Master de Courcelles, Canon of Paris, who associates himself with me in my protest.

CAUCHON

Well, what is the matter?

THE CHAPLAIN

(*Sulkily*). Speak you, Master de Courcelles, since I do not seem to enjoy his lordship's confidence. (*He sits down in dudgeon next to* CAUCHON, *on his right.*)

COURCELLES

My lord: we have been at great pains to draw up an indictment of The Maid on sixty-four counts. We are now told that they have been reduced, without consulting us.

THE INQUISITOR

Master de Courcelles: I am the culprit. I am overwhelmed with admiration for the zeal displayed in your sixty-four counts; but in accusing a heretic, as in other things, enough is enough. Also you must remember that all the members of the court are not so subtle and profound as you, and that some of your very great learning might appear to them to be very great nonsense. Therefore I have thought it well to have your sixty-four articles cut down to twelve.

COURCELLES

(*Thunderstruck*). Twelve!!!

THE INQUISITOR

Twelve will, believe me, be quite enough for your purpose.

THE CHAPLAIN

But some of the most important points have been reduced almost to nothing. For instance, The Maid has actually declared that the blessed saints Margaret and Catherine, and the holy Archangel Michael, spoke to her in French. That is a vital point.

THE INQUISITOR

You think, doubtless, that they should have spoken in Latin?

CAUCHON

No: he thinks they should have spoken in English.

THE CHAPLAIN

Naturally, my lord.

THE INQUISITOR

Well, as we are all here agreed, I think, that these voices of The Maid are the voices of evil spirits tempting her to her damnation, it would not be very courteous to you, Master de Stogumber, or to the King of England, to assume that English is the devil's native language. So let it pass. The matter is not wholly omitted from the twelve articles. Pray take your places, gentlemen; and let us proceed to business. (*All who have not taken their seats, do so.*)

THE CHAPLAIN

Well, I protest. That is all.

COURCELLES

I think it hard that all our work should go for nothing. It is only another example of the diabolical influence which this woman exercises over the court. (*He takes his chair, which is on* THE CHAPLAIN'S *right.*)

CAUCHON

Do you suggest that I am under diabolical influence?

COURCELLES

I suggest nothing, my lord. But it seems to me that there is a conspiracy here to hush up the fact that The Maid stole the Bishop of Senlis's horse.

CAUCHON

(*Keeping his temper with difficulty*). This is not a police court. Are we to waste our time on such rubbish?

COURCELLES

(*Rising, shocked*). My lord: do you call the Bishop's horse rubbish?

THE INQUISITOR

(*Blandly*). Master de Courcelles: The Maid alleges that she paid handsomely for the Bishop's horse, and that if he did not get the money the fault was not hers. As that may be true, the point is one on which The Maid may well be acquitted.

COURCELLES

Yes, if it were an ordinary horse. But the Bishop's horse! How can she be acquitted for that? (*He sits down again, bewildered and discouraged.*)

THE INQUISITOR

I submit to you, with great respect, that if we persist in trying The Maid on trumpery issues on which we may have to declare her innocent, she may escape us on the great main issue of heresy, on which she seems so far to insist on her own guilt. I will ask you, therefore, to say nothing, when The Maid is brought before us, of these stealings of horses, and dancing round fairy trees with the village children, and prayings at haunted wells, and a dozen other things which you were diligently inquiring into until my arrival. There is not a village girl in France against whom you could not prove such things: they all dance round haunted trees, and pray at magic wells. Some of them would steal the Pope's horse if they got the chance. Heresy, gentlemen, heresy is the charge we have to try. The detection and suppression of heresy is my peculiar business: I am here as an inquisitor, not as an ordinary magistrate. Stick to the heresy, gentlemen; and leave the other matters alone.

CAUCHON

I may say that we have sent to the girl's village to make inquiries about her; and there is practically nothing serious against her.

THE CHAPLAIN

COURCELLES

(*Rising and clamoring together*).
Nothing serious, my lord—
What! The fairy tree not—

CAUCHON

(*Out of patience*). Be silent, gentlemen; or speak one at a time.

(COURCELLES *collapses into his chair, intimidated.*)

THE CHAPLAIN

(*Sulkily resuming his seat*). That is what The Maid said to us last Friday.

CAUCHON

I wish you had followed her counsel, sir. When I say nothing serious, I mean nothing that men of sufficiently large mind to conduct an inquiry like this would consider serious. I agree with my colleague the Inquisitor that it is on the count of heresy that we must proceed.

LADVENU

(*A young but ascetically fine-drawn Dominican who is sitting next* COURCELLES, *on his right*). But is there any great harm in the girl's heresy? Is it not merely her simplicity? Many saints have said as much as Joan.

THE INQUISITOR

(*Dropping his blandness and speaking very gravely*). Brother Martin: if you had seen what I have seen of heresy, you would not think it a light thing even in its most apparently harmless and even lovable and pious origins. Heresy begins with people who are to all appearance better than their neighbors. A gentle and pious girl, or a young man who has obeyed the command of our Lord by giving all his riches to the poor, and putting on the garb of poverty, the life of austerity, and the rule of humility and charity, may be the founder of a heresy that will wreck both Church and Empire if not ruthlessly stamped out in time. The records of the holy Inquisition are full of histories we dare not give to the world, because they are beyond the belief of honest men and innocent women; yet they all began with saintly simpletons. I have seen this again and again. Mark what I say: the woman who quarrels with her clothes, and puts on the dress of a man, is like the man who throws off his fur gown and dresses like John the Baptist: they are followed, as surely as the night follows the day, by bands of wild women and men who refuse to wear any clothes at all. When maids will neither marry nor take regular vows, and men reject marriage and exalt their lusts into divine inspirations, then, as surely as the summer follows the spring, they begin with polygamy, and end by incest. Heresy at first seems innocent and even laudable; but it ends in such a monstrous horror of unnatural wickedness that the most tender-hearted among you, if you saw it at work as I have seen it, would clamor against the mercy of the Church in dealing with it. For two hundred years the Holy Office has striven with these diabolical madnesses; and it knows that they begin always by vain and ignorant persons setting up their own judgment against the Church, and taking it upon themselves to be the interpreters of God's will. You must not fall into the common error of mistaking these simpletons for liars and hypocrites. They believe honestly and sincerely that their diabolical inspiration is divine. Therefore you must be on your guard against your natural compassion. You are all, I hope, merciful men: how else could you have devoted your lives to the service of our gentle Savior? You are going to see before you a young girl, pious and chaste; for I must tell you, gentlemen, that the things said of her by our English friends are supported by no evidence, whilst there is abundant testimony that her excesses have been excesses of religion and charity and not of worldliness and wantonness. This girl is not one of those whose hard features are the sign of hard hearts, and whose brazen looks and lewd demeanor condemn them before they are accused. The devilish pride that has led her into her present peril has left no mark on her countenance. Strange as it may seem to you, it has even left no mark on her character outside those special matters in which she is proud; so that you will see a diabolical pride and a natural humility seated side by side in the selfsame soul. Therefore be on your guard. God forbid that I should tell you to harden your hearts; for her punishment if we condemn her will be so cruel that we should forfeit our own hope of divine mercy were there one grain of malice against her in our hearts. But if you hate cruelty—and if any man here does not hate it I command him on his soul's salvation to quit this holy court—I say, if you hate cruelty, remember that nothing is so cruel in its consequences as the toleration of heresy. Remember also that no court of law can be so cruel as the common people are to those whom they suspect of heresy. The heretic in the hands of the Holy Office is safe from violence, is assured of a fair trial, and cannot suffer death, even when guilty, if repentance follows sin. Innumerable lives of heretics have been saved because the Holy Office has taken them out of the hands of the people, and because the people have yielded them up, knowing that the Holy Office would deal with them. Before the Holy Inquisition existed, and even now when its officers are not within reach, the unfortunate wretch suspected of heresy, perhaps quite ignorantly and unjustly, is stoned, torn in pieces, drowned, burned in his house with all his innocent children, without a trial, unshriven, unburied save as a dog is buried: all of them deeds hateful to God and most cruel to man. Gentlemen: I am compassionate by nature as well as by my profession; and though the work I have to do may seem cruel to those who do not know how much more cruel it would be to leave it undone, I would go to the stake myself sooner than do it if I did not know its righteousness, its necessity, its essential mercy. I ask you to address yourself to this trial in that conviction. Anger is a bad counsellor: cast out anger. Pity is sometimes a worse: cast out pity. But do not cast out mercy. Remember only that justice comes first. Have you anything to say, my lord, before we proceed to trial?

CAUCHON

You have spoken for me, and spoken better than I could. I do not see how any sane man could disagree with a word that has fallen from you. But this I will add. The crude heresies of which you have told us are horrible; but their horror is like that of the black death: they rage for a while and then die out, because sound and sensible men will not under any incitement be reconciled to nakedness and incest and polygamy and the like. But we are confronted today throughout Europe with a heresy that is spreading among men not weak in mind nor diseased in brain: nay, the stronger the mind, the more obstinate the heretic. It is neither discredited by fantastic extremes nor corrupted by the common lusts of the flesh; but it, too, sets up the private judgment of the single erring mortal against the considered wisdom and experience of the Church. The mighty structure of Catholic Christendom will never be shaken by naked madmen or by the sins of Moab and Ammon. But it may be betrayed from within, and brought to barbarous ruin and desolation, by this arch heresy which the English Commander calls Protestantism.

THE ASSESSORS

(*Whispering*). Protestantism! What was that? What does the Bishop mean? Is it a new heresy? The English Commander, he said. Did you ever hear of Protestantism? etc., etc.

CAUCHON

(*Continuing*). And that reminds me. What provision has the Earl of Warwick made for the defence of the secular arm should The Maid prove obdurate, and the people be moved to pity her?

THE CHAPLAIN

Have no fear on that score, my lord. The noble earl has eight hundred men-at-arms at the gates. She will not slip through our English fingers even if the whole city be on her side.

CAUCHON

(*Revolted*). Will you not add, God grant that she repent and purge her sin?

THE CHAPLAIN

That does not seem to me to be consistent; but of course I agree with your lordship.

CAUCHON

(*Giving him up with a shrug of contempt*). The court sits.

THE INQUISITOR

Let the accused be brought in.

LADVENU

(*Calling*). The accused. Let her be brought in.

(JOAN, *chained by the ankles, is brought in through the arched door behind the prisoner's stool by a guard of English soldiers. With them is the* EXECUTIONER *and his assistants. They lead her to the prisoner's stool, and place themselves behind it after taking off the chain. She wears a page's black suit. Her long imprisonment and the strain of the examinations which have preceded the trial have left their mark on her; but her vitality still holds: she confronts the court unabashed, without a trace of the awe which their formal solemnity seems to require for the complete success of its impressiveness.*)

THE INQUISITOR

(*Kindly*). Sit down, Joan. (*She sits on the prisoner's stool.*) You look very pale today. Are you not well?

JOAN

Thank you kindly: I am well enough. But the Bishop sent me some carp; and it made me ill.

CAUCHON

I am sorry. I told them to see that it was fresh.

JOAN

You meant to be good to me, I know; but it is a fish that does not agree with me. The English thought you were trying to poison me—

CAUCHON
THE CHAPLAIN

(*Together*). What! No, my lord.

JOAN

(*Continuing*). They are determined that I shall be burnt as a witch; and they sent their doctor to cure me; but he was forbidden to bleed me because the silly people believe that a witch's witchery leaves her if she is bled; so he only called me filthy names. Why do you leave me in the hands of the English? I should be in the hands of the Church. And why must I be chained by the feet to a log of wood? Are you afraid I will fly away?

D'ESTIVET

(*Harshly*). Woman: it is not for you to question the court: it is for us to question you.

COURCELLES

When you were left unchained, did you not try to escape by jumping from a tower sixty feet high? If you cannot fly like a witch, how is it that you are still alive?

JOAN

I suppose because the tower was not so high then. It has grown higher every day since you began asking me questions about it.

D'ESTIVET

Why did you jump from the tower?

JOAN

How do you know that I jumped?

D'ESTIVET

You were found lying in the moat. Why did you leave the tower?

JOAN

Why would anybody leave a prison if they could get out?

D'ESTIVET

You tried to escape.

JOAN

Of course I did; and not for the first time either. If you leave the door of the cage open the bird will fly out.

D'ESTIVET

(*Rising*). That is a confession of heresy. I call the attention of the court to it.

JOAN

Heresy, he calls it! Am I a heretic because I try to escape from prison?

D'ESTIVET

Assuredly, if you are in the hands of the Church, and you wilfully take yourself out of its hands, you are deserting the Church; and that is heresy.

JOAN

It is great nonsense. Nobody could be such a fool as to think that.

D'ESTIVET

You hear, my lord, how I am reviled in the execution of my duty by this woman. (*He sits down indignantly.*)

CAUCHON

I have warned you before, Joan, that you are doing yourself no good by these pert answers.

JOAN

But you will not talk sense to me. I am reasonable if you will be reasonable.

THE INQUISITOR

(*Interposing*). This is not yet in order. You forget, Master Promoter, that the proceedings have not been formally opened. The time for questions is after she has sworn on the Gospels to tell us the whole truth.

JOAN

You say this to me every time. I have said again and again that I will tell you all that concerns this trial. But I cannot tell you the whole truth: God does not allow the whole truth to be told. You do not understand it when I tell it. It is an old saying that he who tells too much truth is sure to be hanged. I am weary of this argument: we have been over it nine times already. I have sworn as much as I will swear; and I will swear no more.

COURCELLES

My lord: she should be put to the torture.

THE INQUISITOR

You hear, Joan? That is what happens to the obdurate. Think before you answer. Has she been shewn the instruments?

THE EXECUTIONER

They are ready, my lord. She has seen them.

JOAN

If you tear me limb from limb until you separate my soul from my body you will get nothing out of me beyond what I have told you. What more is there to tell that you could understand? Besides, I cannot bear to be hurt; and if you hurt me I will say anything you like to stop the pain. But I will take it all back afterwards; so what is the use of it?

LADVENU

There is much in that. We should proceed mercifully.

COURCELLES

But the torture is customary.

THE INQUISITOR

It must not be applied wantonly. If the accused will confess voluntarily, then its use cannot be justified.

COURCELLES

But this is unusual and irregular. She refuses to take the oath.

LADVENU

(*Disgusted*). Do you want to torture the girl for the mere pleasure of it?

COURCELLES

(*Bewildered*). But it is not a pleasure. It is the law. It is customary. It is always done.

THE INQUISITOR

That is not so, Master, except when the inquiries are carried on by people who do not know their legal business.

COURCELLES

But the woman is a heretic. I assure you it is always done.

CAUCHON

(*Decisively*). It will not be done today if it is not necessary. Let there be an end of this. I will not have it said that we proceeded on forced confessions. We have sent our best preachers and doctors to this woman to exhort and implore her to save her soul and body from the fire: we shall not now send the executioner to thrust her into it.

COURCELLES

Your lordship is merciful, of course. But it is a great responsibility to depart from the usual practice.

JOAN

Thou art a rare noodle, Master. Do what was done last time is thy rule, eh?

COURCELLES

(*Rising*). Thou wanton: dost thou dare call me noodle?

THE INQUISITOR

Patience. Master, patience: I fear you will soon be only too terribly avenged.

COURCELLES

(*Mutters*). Noodle indeed! (*He sits down, much discontented.*)

THE INQUISITOR

Meanwhile, let us not be moved by the rough side of a shepherd lass's tongue.

JOAN

Nay: I am no shepherd lass, though I have helped with the sheep like any one else. I will do a lady's work in the house—spin or weave—against any woman in Rouen.

THE INQUISITOR

This is not a time for vanity, Joan. You stand in great peril.

JOAN

I know it: have I not been punished for my vanity? If I had not worn my cloth of gold surcoat in battle like a fool, that Burgundian soldier would never have pulled me backwards off my horse; and I should not have been here.

THE CHAPLAIN

If you are so clever at woman's work why do you not stay at home and do it?

JOAN

There are plenty of other women to do it; but there is nobody to do my work.

CAUCHON

Come! we are wasting time on trifles. Joan: I am going to put a most solemn question to you. Take care how you answer; for your life and salvation are at stake on it. Will you for all you have said and done, be it good or bad, accept the judgment of God's Church on earth? More especially as to the acts and words that are imputed to you in this trial by the Promoter here, will you submit your case to the inspired interpretation of the Church Militant?

JOAN

I am a faithful child of the Church. I will obey the Church—

CAUCHON

(*Hopefully leaning forward*). You will?

JOAN

—Provided it does not command anything impossible.

(CAUCHON *sinks back in his chair with a heavy sigh. The* INQUISITOR *purses his lips and frowns.* LADVENU *shakes his head pitifully.*)

D'ESTIVET

She imputes to the Church the error and folly of commanding the impossible.

JOAN

If you command me to declare that all that I have done and said, and all the visions and revelations I have had, were not from God, then that is impossible: I will not declare it for anything in the world. What God made me do I will never go back on; and what He has commanded or shall command I will not fail to do in spite of any man alive. That is what I mean by impossible. And in case the Church should bid me do anything contrary to the command I have from God, I will not consent to it, no matter what it may be.

THE ASSESSORS

(*Shocked and indignant*). Oh! The Church contrary to God! What do you say now? Flat heresy. This is beyond everything, etc., etc.

D'ESTIVET

(*Throwing down his brief*). My lord: do you need anything more than this?

CAUCHON

Woman: you have said enough to burn ten heretics. Will you not be warned? Will you not understand?

THE INQUISITOR

If the Church Militant tells you that your revelations and visions are sent by the devil to tempt you to your damnation, will you not believe that the Church is wiser than you?

JOAN

I believe that God is wiser than I; and it is His commands that I will do. All the things that you call my crimes have come to me by the command of God. I say that I have done them by the order of God: it is impossible for me to say anything else. If any Churchman says the contrary I shall not mind him: I shall mind God alone, whose command I always follow.

LADVENU

(*Pleading with her urgently*). You do not know what you are saying, child. Do you want to kill yourself? Listen. Do you not believe that you are subject to the Church of God on earth?

JOAN

Yes. When have I ever denied it?

LADVENU

Good. That means, does it not, that you are subject to our Lord the Pope, to the cardinals, the archbishops, and the bishops for whom his lordship stands here today?

JOAN

God must be served first.

D'ESTIVET

Then your voices command you not to submit yourself to the Church Militant?

JOAN

My voices do not tell me to disobey the Church; but God must be served first.

CAUCHON

And you, and not the Church, are to be the judge?

JOAN

What other judgment can I judge by but my own?

THE ASSESSORS

(*Scandalized*). Oh! (*They cannot find words.*)

CAUCHON

Out of your own mouth you have condemned yourself. We have striven for your salvation to the verge of sinning ourselves: we have opened the door to you again and again; and you have shut it in our faces and in the face of God. Dare you pretend, after what you have said, that you are in a state of grace?

JOAN

If I am not, may God bring me to it: if I am, may God keep me in it!

LADVENU

That is a very good reply, my lord.

COURCELLES

Were you in a state of grace when you stole the Bishop's horse?

CAUCHON

(*Rising in a fury*). Oh, devil take the Bishop's horse and you too! We are here to try a case of heresy; and no sooner do we come to the root of the matter than we are thrown back by idiots who understand nothing but horses. (*Trembling with rage, he forces himself to sit down.*)

THE INQUISITOR

Gentlemen, gentlemen: in clinging to these small issues you are The Maid's best advocates. I am not surprised that his lordship has lost patience with you. What does the Promoter say? Does he press these trumpery matters?

D'ESTIVET

I am bound by my office to press everything; but when the woman confesses a heresy that must bring upon her the doom of excommunication, of what consequence is it that she has been guilty also of offences which expose her to minor penances? I share the impatience of his lordship as to these minor charges. Only, with great respect I must emphasize the gravity of two very horrible and blasphemous crimes which she does not deny. First, she has intercourse with evil spirits, and is therefore a sorceress. Second, she wears men's clothes, which is indecent, unnatural, and abominable; and in spite of our most earnest remonstrances and entreaties, she will not change them even to receive the sacrament.

JOAN

Is the blessed St Catherine an evil spirit? Is St Margaret? Is Michael the Archangel?

COURCELLES

How do you know that the spirit which appears to you is an archangel? Does he not appear to you as a naked man?

JOAN

Do you think God cannot afford clothes for him?

(*The assessors cannot help smiling, especially as the joke is against* COURCELLES.)

LADVENU

Well answered, Joan.

THE INQUISITOR

It is, in effect, well answered. But no evil spirit would be so simple as to appear to a young girl in a guise that would scandalize her when he meant her to take him for a messenger from the Most High? Joan: the Church instructs you that these apparitions are demons seeking your soul's perdition. Do you accept the instruction of the Church?

JOAN

I accept the messenger of God. How could any faithful believer in the Church refuse him?

CAUCHON

Wretched woman: again I ask you, do you know what you are saying?

THE INQUISITOR

You wrestle in vain with the devil for her soul, my lord: she will not be saved. Now as to this matter of the man's dress. For the last time, will you put off that impudent attire, and dress as becomes your sex?

JOAN

I will not.

D'ESTIVET

(*Pouncing*). The sin of disobedience, my lord.

JOAN

(*Distressed*). But my voices tell me I must dress as a soldier.

LADVENU

Joan, Joan: does not that prove to you that the voices are the voices of evil spirits? Can you suggest to us one good reason why an angel of God should give you such shameless advice?

JOAN

Why, yes: what can be plainer commonsense? I was a soldier living among soldiers. I am a prisoner guarded by soldiers. If I were to dress as a woman they would think of me as a woman; and then what would become of me? If I dress as a soldier they think of me as a soldier, and I can live with them as I do at home with my brothers. That is why St Catherine tells me I must not dress as a woman until she gives me leave.

COURCELLES

When will she give you leave?

JOAN

When you take me out of the hands of the English soldiers. I have told you that I should be in the hands of the Church, and not left night and day with four soldiers of the Earl of Warwick. Do you want me to live with them in petticoats?

LADVENU

My lord: what she says is, God knows, very wrong and shocking; but there is a grain of worldly sense in it such as might impose on a simple village maiden.

JOAN

If we were as simple in the village as you are in your courts and palaces, there would soon be no wheat to make bread for you.

CAUCHON

That is the thanks you get for trying to save her, Brother Martin.

LADVENU

Joan: we are all trying to save you. His lordship is trying to save you. The Inquisitor could not be more just to you if you were his own daughter. But you are blinded by a terrible pride and self-sufficiency.

JOAN

Why do you say that? I have said nothing wrong. I cannot understand.

THE INQUISITOR

The blessed St. Athanasius has laid it down in his creed that those who cannot understand are damned. It is not enough to be simple. It is not enough even to be what simple people call good. The simplicity of a darkened mind is no better than the simplicity of a beast.

JOAN

There is great wisdom in the simplicity of a beast, let me tell you; and sometimes great foolishness in the wisdom of scholars.

LADVENU

We know that, Joan: we are not so foolish as you think us. Try to resist the temptation to make pert replies to us. Do you see that man who stands behind you? (*He indicates the* EXECUTIONER.)

JOAN

(*Turning and looking at the man*). Your torturer? But the Bishop said I was not to be tortured.

LADVENU

You are not to be tortured because you have confessed everything that is necessary to your condemnation. That man is not only the torturer: he is also the Executioner. Executioner: let The Maid hear your answers to my questions. Are you prepared for the burning of a heretic this day?

THE EXECUTIONER

Yes, Master.

LADVENU

Is the stake ready?

THE EXECUTIONER

It is. In the market-place. The English have built it too high for me to get near her and make the death easier. It will be a cruel death.

JOAN

(*Horrified*). But you are not going to burn me now?

THE INQUISITOR

You realize it at last.

LADVENU

There are eight hundred English soldiers waiting to take you to the market-place the moment the sentence of excommunication has passed the lips of your judges. You are within a few short moments of that doom.

JOAN

(*Looking round desperately for rescue*). Oh, God!

LADVENU

Do not despair, Joan. The Church is merciful. You can save yourself.

JOAN

(*Hopefully*). Yes: my voices promised me I should not be burnt. St Catherine bade me be bold.

CAUCHON

Woman: are you quite mad? Do you not yet see that your voices have deceived you?

JOAN

Oh, no: that is impossible.

CAUCHON

Impossible! They have led you straight to your excommunication, and to the stake which is there waiting for you.

LADVENU

(*Pressing the point hard*). Have they kept a single promise to you since you were taken at Compiègne? The devil has betrayed you. The Church holds out its arms to you.

JOAN

(*Despairing*). Oh, it is true: it is true: my voices have deceived me. I have been mocked by devils: my faith is broken. I have dared and dared; but only a fool will walk into a fire: God, who gave me my commonsense, cannot will me to do that.

LADVENU

Now God be praised that He has saved you at the eleventh hour! (*He hurries to the vacant seat at the scribes' table, and snatches a sheet of paper, on which he sets to work writing eagerly.*)

CAUCHON

Amen!

JOAN

What must I do?

CAUCHON

You must sign a solemn recantation of your heresy.

JOAN

Sign? That means to write my name. I cannot write.

CAUCHON

You have signed many letters before.

JOAN

Yes; but some one held my hand and guided the pen. I can make my mark.

THE CHAPLAIN

(*Who has been listening with growing alarm and indignation*). My lord: do you mean that you are going to allow this woman to escape us?

THE INQUISITOR

The law must takes its course, Master de Stogumber. And you know the law.

THE CHAPLAIN

(*Rising, purple with fury*). I know that there is no faith in a Frenchman. (*Tumult, which he shouts down.*) I know what my lord the Cardinal of Winchester will say when he hears of this. I know what the Earl of Warwick will do when he learns that you intend to betray him. There are eight hundred men at the gate who will see that this abominable witch is burnt in spite of your teeth.

THE ASSESSORS

(*Meanwhile*). What is this? What did he say? He accuses us of treachery! This is past bearing. No faith in a Frenchman! Did you hear that? This is an intolerable fellow. Who is he? Is this what English Churchmen are like? He must be mad or drunk, etc., etc.

THE INQUISITOR

(*Rising*). Silence, pray! Gentlemen: pray silence! Master Chaplain: bethink you a moment of your holy office: of what you are, and where you are. I direct you to sit down.

THE CHAPLAIN

(*Folding his arms doggedly, his face working convulsively*). I will NOT sit down.

CAUCHON

Master Inquisitor; this man has called me a traitor to my face before now.

THE CHAPLAIN

So you are a traitor. You are all traitors. You have been doing nothing but begging this damnable witch on your knees to recant all through this trial.

THE INQUISITOR

(*Placidly resuming his seat*). If you will not sit, you must stand: that is all.

THE CHAPLAIN

I will NOT stand. (*He flings himself back into his chair.*)

LADVENU

(*Rising with the paper in his hand*). My lord: here is the form of recantation for The Maid to sign.

CAUCHON

Read it to her.

JOAN

Do not trouble. I will sign it.

THE INQUISITOR

Woman: you must know what you are putting your hand to. Read it to her, Brother Martin. And let all be silent.

LADVENU

(*Reading quietly*). "I, Joan, commonly called The Maid, a miserable sinner, do confess that I have most grievously sinned in the following articles. I have pretended to have revelations from God and the angels and the blessed saints, and perversely rejected the Church's warnings that these were temptations by demons. I have blasphemed abominably by wearing an immodest dress, contrary to the Holy Scripture and the canons of the Church. Also I have clipped my hair in the style of a man, and, against all the duties which have made my sex specially acceptable in heaven, have taken up the sword, even to the shedding of human blood, inciting men to slay each other, invoking evil spirits to delude them, and stubbornly and most blasphemously imputing these sins to Almighty God. I confess to the sin of sedition, to the sin of idolatry, to the sin of disobedience, to the sin of pride, and to the sin of heresy. All of which sins I now renounce and abjure and depart from, humbly thanking you Doctors and Masters who have brought me back to the truth and into the grace of our Lord. And I will never return to my errors, but will remain in communion with our Holy Church and in obedience to our Holy Father the Pope of Rome. All this I swear by God Almighty and the Holy Gospels, in witness whereto I sign my name to this recantation."

THE INQUISITOR

You understand this, Joan?

JOAN

(*Listless*). It is plain enough, sir.

THE INQUISITOR

And it is true?

JOAN

It may be true. If it were not true, the fire would not be ready for me in the marketplace.

LADVENU

(*Taking up his pen and a book, and going to her quickly lest she should compromise herself again*). Come, child: let me guide your hand. Take the pen. (*She does so; and they begin to write, using the book as a desk.*) J.E.H.A.N.E. So. Now make your mark by yourself.

JOAN

(*Makes her mark, and gives him back the pen, tormented by the rebellion of her soul against her mind and body*). There!

LADVENU

(*Replacing the pen on the table, and handing the recantation to* CAUCHON *with a rev-*

erence). Praise be to God, my brothers, the lamb has returned to the flock; and the shepherd rejoices in her more than in ninety and nine just persons. (*He returns to his seat.*)

THE INQUISITOR

(*Taking the paper from* CAUCHON). We declare thee by this act set free from the danger of excommunication in which thou stoodest. (*He throws the paper down to the table.*)

JOAN

I thank you.

THE INQUISITOR

But because thou hast sinned most presumptuously against God and the Holy Church, and that thou mayest repent thy errors in solitary contemplation, and be shielded from all temptation to return to them, we, for the good of thy soul, and for a penance that may wipe out thy sins and bring thee finally unspotted to the throne of grace, do condemn thee to eat the bread of sorrow and drink the water of affliction to the end of thy earthly days in perpetual imprisonment.

JOAN

(*Rising in consternation and terrible anger*). Perpetual imprisonment? Am I not then to be set free?

LADVENU

(*Mildly shocked*). Set free, child, after such wickedness as yours! What are you dreaming of?

JOAN

Give me that writing. (*She rushes to the table; snatches up the paper; and tears it into fragments.*) Light your fire: do you think I dread it as much as the life of a rat in a hole? My voices were right.

LADVENU

Joan! Joan!

JOAN

Yes: they told me you were fools (*the word gives great offence*), and that I was not to listen to your fine words nor trust to your charity. You promised me my life; but you lied. (*Indignant exclamations.*) You think that life is nothing but not being stone dead. It is not the bread and water I fear: I can live on bread: when have I asked for more? It is no hardship to drink water if the water be clean. Bread has no sorrow for me, and water no affliction. But to shut me from the light of the sky and the sight of the fields and flowers; to chain my feet so that I can never again ride with the soldiers nor climb the hills; to make me breathe foul damp darkness, and keep from me everything that brings me back to the love of God when your wickedness and foolishness tempt me to hate Him: all this is worse than the furnace in the Bible that was heated seven times. I could do without my war horse; I could drag about in a skirt; I could let the banners and the trumpets and the knights and soldiers pass me and leave me behind as they leave the other women, if only I could still hear the wind in the trees, the larks in the sunshine, the young lambs crying through the healthy frost, and the blessed blessed church bells that send my angel voices to me on the wind. But without these things I cannot live; and by your wanting to take them away from me, or from any human creature, I know that your counsel is of the devil, and that mine is of God.

THE ASSESSORS

(*In great commotion*). Blasphemy! blasphemy! She is possessed. She said our counsel was of the devil. And hers of God. Monstrous! The devil is in our midst, etc., etc.

D'ESTIVET

(*Shouting above the din*). She is a relapsed heretic, obstinate, incorrigible, and altogether unworthy of the mercy we have shewn her. I call for her excommunication.

THE CHAPLAIN

(*To the* EXECUTIONER). Light your fire, man. To the stake with her.

(*The* EXECUTIONER *and his assistants hurry out through the courtyard.*)

LADVENU

You wicked girl: if your counsel were of God would He not deliver you?

JOAN

His ways are not your ways. He wills that I go through the fire to His bosom; for I am His child, and you are not fit that I should live among you. That is my last word to you.
(*The soldiers seize her.*)

CAUCHON

(*Rising*). Not yet.
(*They wait. There is a dead silence.* CAUCHON *turns to the* INQUISITOR *with an inquiring look. The* INQUISITOR *nods affirmatively. They rise solemnly, and intone the sentence antiphonally.*)

CAUCHON

We decree that thou art a relapsed heretic.

THE INQUISITOR

Cast out from the unity of the Church.

CAUCHON

Sundered from her body.

THE INQUISITOR

Infected with the leprosy of heresy.

CAUCHON

A member of Satan.

THE INQUISITOR

We declare that thou must be excommunicate.

CAUCHON

And now we do cast thee out, segregate thee, and abandon thee to the secular power.

THE INQUISITOR

Admonishing the same secular power that it moderate its judgment of thee in respect of death and division of the limbs. (*He resumes his seat.*)

CAUCHON

And if any true sign of penitence appear in thee, to permit our Brother Martin to administer to thee the sacrament of penance.

THE CHAPLAIN

Into the fire with the witch. (*He rushes at her, and helps the soldiers to push her out.*)

(JOAN *is taken away through the courtyard. The assessors rise in disorder, and follow the soldiers, except* LADVENU, *who has hidden his face in his hands.*)

CAUCHON

(*Rising again in the act of sitting down*). No, no; this is irregular. The representative of the secular arm should be here to receive her from us.

THE INQUISITOR

(*Also on his feet again*). That man is an incorrigible fool.

CAUCHON

Brother Martin: see that everything is done in order.

LADVENU

My place is at her side, my lord. You must exercise your own authority. (*He hurries out.*)

CAUCHON

These English are impossible: they will thrust her straight into the fire. Look!
(*He points to the courtyard, in which the glow and flicker of fire can now be seen reddening the May daylight. Only the* BISHOP *and the* INQUISITOR *are left in the Court.*)

CAUCHON

(*Turning to go*). We must stop that.

THE INQUISITOR

(*Calmly*). Yes; but not too fast, my lord.

CAUCHON

(*Halting*). But there is not a moment to lose.

THE INQUISITOR

We have proceeded in perfect order. If the English choose to put themselves in the wrong, it is not our business to put them in the right. A flaw in the procedure may be useful later on: one never knows. And the sooner it is over, the better for that poor girl.

CAUCHON

(*Relaxing*). That is true. But I suppose we must see this dreadful thing through.

THE INQUISITOR

One gets used to it. Habit is everything. I am accustomed to the fire: it is soon over. But it is a terrible thing to see a young and innocent creature crushed between these mighty forces, the Church and the Law.

CAUCHON

You call her innocent!

THE INQUISITOR

Oh, quite innocent. What does she know of the Church and the Law? She did not understand a word we were saying. It is the ignorant who suffer. Come, or we shall be late for the end.

CAUCHON

(*Going with him*). I shall not be sorry if we are: I am not so accustomed as you.
(*They are going out when* WARWICK *comes in, meeting them.*)

WARWICK

Oh, I am intruding. I thought it was all over. (*He makes a feint of retiring.*)

CAUCHON

Do not go, my lord. It is all over.

THE INQUISITOR

The execution is not in our hands, my lord; but it is desirable that we should witness the end. So by your leave—(*He bows, and goes out through the courtyard.*)

CAUCHON

There is some doubt whether your people have observed the forms of law, my lord.

WARWICK

I am told that there is some doubt whether your authority runs in this city, my lord. It is not in your diocese. However, if you will answer for that I will answer for the rest.

CAUCHON

It is to God that we both must answer. Good morning, my lord.

WARWICK

My lord: good morning.
(*They look at one another for a moment with unconcealed hostility. Then* CAUCHON *follows* THE INQUISITOR *out.* WARWICK *looks round. Finding himself alone, he calls for attendance.*)

WARWICK

Hallo: some attendance here! (*Silence.*) Hallo, there! (*Silence.*) Hallo! Brian, you young blackguard, where are you? (*Silence.*) Guard! (*Silence.*) They have all gone to see the burning: even that child.
(*The silence is broken by some one frantically howling and sobbing.*)

WARWICK

What in the devil's name——?
(THE CHAPLAIN *staggers in from the courtyard like a demented creature, his face streaming with tears, making the piteous sounds that* WARWICK *has heard. He stumbles to the prisoner's stool, and throws himself upon it with heartrending sobs.*)

WARWICK

(*Going to him and patting him on the shoulder*). What is it, Master John? What is the matter?

THE CHAPLAIN

(*Clutching at his hands*). My lord, my lord: for Christ's sake pray for my wretched guilty soul.

WARWICK

(*Soothing him*). Yes, yes: of course I will. Calmly, gently——

THE CHAPLAIN

(*Blubbering miserably*). I am not a bad man, my lord.

WARWICK

No, no: not at all.

THE CHAPLAIN

I meant no harm. I did not know what it would be like.

WARWICK

(*Hardening*). Oh! You saw it, then?

THE CHAPLAIN

I did not know what I was doing. I am a hotheaded fool; and I shall be damned to all eternity for it.

WARWICK

Nonsense! Very distressing, no doubt; but it was not your doing.

THE CHAPLAIN

(*Lamentably*). I let them do it. If I had known, I would have torn her from their hands. You don't know: you haven't seen: it is so easy to talk when you don't know. You madden yourself with words: you damn yourself because it feels grand to throw oil on the flaming hell of your own temper. But when it is brought home to you; when you see the thing you have done; when it is blinding your eyes, stifling your nostrils, tearing your heart, then—then—(*Falling on his knees.*) O God, take away this sight from me! O Christ, deliver me from this fire that is consuming me! She cried to Thee in the midst of it: Jesus! Jesus! Jesus! She is in Thy bosom; and I am in hell for evermore.

WARWICK

(*Summarily hauling him to his feet*). Come come, man! you must pull yourself together. We shall have the whole town talking of this. (*He throws him not too gently into a chair at the table.*) If you have not the nerve to see these things, why do you not do as I do, and stay away?

THE CHAPLAIN

(*Bewildered and submissive*). She asked for a cross. A soldier gave her two sticks tied together. Thank God he was an Englishman! I might have done it; but I did not: I am a coward, a mad dog, a fool. But he was an Englishman too.

WARWICK

The fool! They will burn him too if the priests get hold of him.

THE CHAPLAIN

(*Shaken with convulsion*). Some of the people laughed at her. They would have laughed at Christ. They were French people, my lord: I know they were French.

WARWICK

Hush: some one's coming. Control yourself. (LADVENU *comes back through the courtyard to* WARWICK*'s right hand, carrying a bishop's cross which he has taken from the church. He is very grave and composed.*)

WARWICK

I am informed that it is all over, Brother Martin.

LADVENU

(*Enigmatically*). We do not know, my lord. It may have only just begun.

WARWICK

What does that mean, exactly?

LADVENU

I took this cross from the church for her that she might see it to the last: she had only two sticks that she put into her bosom. When the fire crept round us, and she saw that if I held the cross before her I should be burnt myself, she warned me to get down and save myself. My lord: a girl who could think of another's danger in such a moment was not inspired by the devil. When I had to snatch the cross from her sight, she looked up to heaven. And I do not believe that the heavens were empty. I firmly believe that her Savior appeared to her then in His tenderest glory. She called to Him and died. This is not the end for her, but the beginning.

WARWICK

I am afraid it will have a bad effect on the people.

LADVENU

It had, my lord, on some of them. I heard laughter. Forgive me for saying that I hope and believe it was English laughter.

THE CHAPLAIN

(*Rising frantically*). No: it was not. There was only one Englishman there that disgraced his country; and that was the mad dog de Stogumber. (*He rushes wildly out, shrieking.*) Let them torture him. Let them burn him. I will go pray among her ashes. I am no better than Judas: I will hang myself.

WARWICK

Quick, Brother Martin: follow him: he will do himself some mischief. After him, quick.

(LADVENU *hurries out,* WARWICK *urging him. The* EXECUTIONER *comes in by the door behind the judges' chairs; and* WARWICK, *returning, finds himself face to face with him.*)

WARWICK

Well, fellow: who are you?

THE EXECUTIONER

(*With dignity*). I am not addressed as fellow, my lord. I am the Master Executioner of Rouen: it is a highly skilled mystery. I am come to tell your lordship that your orders have been obeyed.

WARWICK

I crave your pardon, Master Executioner; and I will see that you lose nothing by having no relics to sell. I have your word, have I, that nothing remains, not a bone, not a nail, not a hair?

THE EXECUTIONER

Her heart would not burn, my lord; but everything that was left is at the bottom of the river. You have heard the last of her.

WARWICK

(*With a wry smile, thinking of what* LADVENU *said*). The last of her? Hm? I wonder!

25 years later

EPILOGUE

A RESTLESS *fitfully windy night in June 1456, full of summer lightning after many days of heat.* KING CHARLES THE SEVENTH *of France, formerly* JOAN'S *Dauphin, now Charles the Victorious, aged 51, is in bed in one of his royal chateaux. The bed, raised on a dais of two steps, is towards the side of the room so as to avoid blocking a tall lancet window in the middle. Its canopy bears the royal arms in embroidery. Except for the canopy and the huge down pillows there is nothing to distinguish it from a broad settee with bed-clothes and a valance. Thus its occupant is in full view from the foot.*

CHARLES *is not asleep: he is reading in bed, or rather looking at the pictures in Fouquet's Boccaccio with his knees doubled up to make a reading desk. Beside the bed on his left is a little table with a picture of the Virgin, lighted by candles of painted wax. The walls are hung from ceiling to floor with painted curtains which stir at times in the draughts. At first glance the prevailing yellow and red in these hanging pictures is somewhat flame-like when the folds breathe in the wind.*

The door is on CHARLES'S *left, but in front of him close to the corner fartherest from him. A large watchman's rattle, handsomely designed and gaily painted, is in the bed under his hand.*

CHARLES *turns a leaf. A distant clock strikes the half-hour softly.* CHARLES *shuts the book with a clap; throws it aside; snatches up the rattle; and whirls it energetically, making a deafening clatter.* LADVENU *enters, 25 years older, strange and stark in bearing, and still carrying the cross from Rouen.* CHARLES *evidently does not expect him; for he springs out of bed on the farther side from the door.*

CHARLES

Who are you? Where is my gentleman of the bedchamber? What do you want?

LADVENU

(*Solemnly*). I bring you glad tidings of great joy. Rejoice, O king; for the taint is removed from your blood, and the stain from your crown. Justice, long delayed, is at last triumphant.

CHARLES

What are you talking about? Who are you?

LADVENU

I am Brother Martin.

CHARLES

And who, saving your reverence, may Brother Martin be?

LADVENU

I held this cross when The Maid perished in the fire. Twenty-five years have passed since then: nearly ten thousand days. And on every one of those days I have prayed God to justify His daughter on earth as she is justified in heaven.

CHARLES

(*Reassured, sitting down on the foot of the bed*). Oh, I remember now. I have heard of you. You have a bee in your bonnet about The Maid. Have you been at the inquiry?

LADVENU

I have given my testimony.

CHARLES

Is it over?

LADVENU

It is over.

CHARLES

Satisfactorily?

LADVENU

The ways of God are very strange.

CHARLES

How so?

LADVENU

At the trial which sent a saint to the stake as a heretic and a sorceress, the truth was told; the law was upheld; mercy was shewn beyond all custom; no wrong was done but the final and dreadful wrong of the lying sentence and the pitiless fire. At this inquiry from which I have just come, there was shameless perjury, courtly corruption, calumny of the dead who did their duty according to their lights, cowardly evasion of the issue, testimony made of idle tales that could not impose on a ploughboy. Yet out of this insult to justice, this defamation of the Church, this orgy of lying and foolishness, the truth is set in the noonday sun on the hilltop; the white robe of innocence is cleansed from the smirch of the burning faggots; the holy life is sanctified; the true heart that lived through the flames is consecrated; a great lie is silenced forever; and a great wrong is set right before all men.

CHARLES

My friend: provided they can no longer say that I was crowned by a witch and a heretic, I shall not fuss about how the trick has been done. Joan would not have fussed about it if it came all right in the end: she was not that sort: I knew her. Is her rehabilitation complete? I made it pretty clear that there was to be no nonsense about it.

LADVENU

It is solemnly declared that her judges were full of corruption, cozenage, fraud and malice. Four falsehoods.

CHARLES

Never mind the falsehoods: her judges are dead.

LADVENU

The sentence on her is broken, annulled, annihilated, set aside as non-existent, without value or effect.

CHARLES

Good, nobody can challenge my consecration now, can they?

LADVENU

Not Charlemagne nor King David himself was more sacredly crowned.

CHARLES

(*Rising*). Excellent. Think of what that means to me!

LADVENU

I think of what it means to her!

CHARLES

You cannot. None of us ever knew what anything meant to her. She was like nobody else; and she must take care of herself wherever she is; for *I* cannot take care of her; and neither can you, whatever you may think: you are not big enough. But I will tell you this about her. If you could bring her back to life, they would burn her again within six months, for all their present adoration of her. And you would hold up the cross, too, just the same. So (*crossing himself*) let her rest; and let you and I mind our own business, and not meddle with hers.

LADVENU

God forbid that I should have no share in her, nor she in me! (*He turns and strides out as he came, saying.*) Henceforth my path will not lie through palaces, nor my conversation be with kings.

CHARLES

(*Following him towards the door, and shouting after him*). Much good may it do you, holy man! (*He returns to the middle of the chamber, where he halts, and says quizzically to himself.*) That was a funny chap. How did he get in? Where are my people? (*He goes impatiently to the bed, and swings the rattle. A rush of wind through the open door sets the walls swaying agitatedly. The candles go out. He calls in the darkness.*) Hallo! Some one come and shut the windows: everything is being blown all over the place. (*A flash of summer lightning shows up the lancet windows. A figure is seen in silhouette against it.*) Who is there? Who is that? Help! Murder! (*Thunder. He jumps into bed, and hides under the clothes.*)

JOAN'S VOICE

Easy, Charlie, easy. What art making all that noise for? No one can hear thee. Thou'rt asleep. (*She is dimly seen in a pallid greenish light by the bedside.*)

CHARLES

(*Peeping out*). Joan! Are you a ghost, Joan?

JOAN

Hardly even that, lad. Can a poor burnt-up lass have a ghost? I am but a dream that thou'rt dreaming. (*The light increases: they become plainly visible as he sits up.*) Thou looks older, lad.

CHARLES

I am older. Am I really asleep?

JOAN

Fallen asleep over thy silly book.

CHARLES

That's funny.

JOAN

Not so funny as that I am dead, is it?

CHARLES

Are you really dead?

JOAN

As dead as anybody ever is, laddie. I am out of the body.

CHARLES

Just fancy! Did it hurt much?

JOAN

Did what hurt much?

CHARLES

Being burnt.

JOAN

Oh, that! I cannot remember very well. I think it did at first; but then it all got mixed up; and I was not in my right mind until I was free of the body. But do not thou go handling fire and thinking it will not hurt thee. How hast been ever since?

CHARLES

Oh, not so bad. Do you know, I actually lead my army out and win battles? Down into the moat up to my waist in mud and blood. Up the ladders with the stones and hot pitch raining down. Like you.

JOAN

No! Did I make a man of thee after all, Charlie?

CHARLES

I am Charles the Victorious now. I had to be brave because you were. Agnes put a little pluck into me too.

JOAN

Agnes! Who was Agnes?

CHARLES

Agnes Sorel. A woman I fell in love with. I dream of her often. I never dreamed of you before.

JOAN

Is she dead, like me?

CHARLES

Yes. But she was not like you. She was very beautiful.

JOAN

(*Laughing heartily*). Ha ha! I was no beauty: I was always a rough one: a regular soldier. I might almost as well have been a man. Pity I wasn't: I should not have bothered you all so much then. But my head was in the skies; and the glory of God was upon me; and, man or woman, I should have bothered you as long as your noses were in the mud. Now tell me what has happened since you wise men knew no better than to make a heap of cinders of me?

CHARLES

Your mother and brothers have sued the courts to have your case tried over again. And the courts have declared that your judges were full of corruption and cozenage, fraud and malice.

JOAN

Not they. They were as honest a lot of poor fools as ever burned their betters.

CHARLES

The sentence on you is broken, annihilated, annulled; null, non-existent, without value or effect.

JOAN

I was burnt all the same. Can they unburn me?

CHARLES

If they could, they would think twice before they did it. But they have decreed that a beautiful cross be placed where the stake stood, for your perpetual memory and for your salvation.

JOAN

It is the memory and the salvation that sanctify the cross, not the cross that sanctifies the memory and the salvation. (*She turns away, forgetting him.*) I shall outlast that cross. I shall be remembered when men will have forgotten where Rouen stood.

CHARLES

There you go with your self-conceit, the same as ever! I think you might say a word of thanks to me for having had justice done at last.

CAUCHON

(*Appearing at the window between them*). Liar!

CHARLES

Thank you.

JOAN

Why, if it isn't Peter Cauchon! How are you, Peter? What luck have you had since you burnt me?

CAUCHON

None. I arraign the justice of Man. It is not the justice of God.

JOAN

Still dreaming of justice, Peter? See what justice came to with me! But what has happened to thee? Art dead or alive?

CAUCHON

Dead. Dishonored. They pursued me beyond the grave. They excommunicated my dead body: they dug it up and flung it into the common sewer.

JOAN

Your dead body did not feel the spade and the sewer as my live body felt the fire.

CAUCHON

But this thing that they have done against me hurts justice; destroys faith; saps the foundation of the Church. The solid earth sways like the treacherous sea beneath the feet of men and spirits alike when the innocent are slain in the name of law, and their wrongs are undone by slandering the pure of heart.

JOAN

Well, well, Peter, I hope men will be the better for remembering me; and they would not remember me so well if you had not burnt me.

CAUCHON

They will be the worse for remembering me: they will see in me evil triumphing over good, falsehood over truth, cruelty over mercy, hell over heaven. Their courage will rise as they think of you, only to faint as they think of me. Yet God is my witness I was just: I was merciful: I was faithful to my light: I could do no other than I did.

CHARLES

(*Scrambling out of the sheets and enthroning himself on the side of the bed*). Yes: it is always you good men that do the big mischiefs. Look at me! I am not Charles the Good, nor Charles the Wise, nor Charles the Bold. Joan's worshippers may even call me Charles the Coward because I did not pull her out of the fire. But I have done less harm than any of you. You people with your heads in the sky spend all your time trying to turn the world upside down; but I take the world as it is, and say that top-side-up is right-side-up; and I keep my nose pretty close to the ground. And I ask you, what king of France has done better, or been a better fellow in his little way?

JOAN

Art really king of France, Charlie? Be the English gone?

DUNOIS

(*Coming through the tapestry on* JOAN'*s left, the candles relighting themselves at the same moment, and illuminating his armor and surcoat cheerfully*). I have kept my word: the English are gone.

JOAN

Praised be God! now is fair France a province in heaven. Tell me all about the fighting, Jack. Was it thou that led them? Wert thou God's captain to thy death?

DUNOIS

I am not dead. My body is very comfortably asleep in my bed at Chateaudun; but my spirit is called here by yours.

JOAN

And you fought them my way, Jack: eh? Not the old way, chaffering for ransoms; but The Maid's way: staking life against death, with the heart high and humble and void of malice, and nothing counting under God but France free and French. Was it my way, Jack?

DUNOIS

Faith, it was any way that would win. But the way that won was always your way. I give you best, lassie. I wrote a fine letter to set you right at the new trial. Perhaps I should never have let the priests burn you; but I was busy fighting; and it was the Church's business, not mine. There was no use in both of us being burnt, was there?

CAUCHON

Ay! put the blame on the priests. But I, who am beyond praise and blame, tell you that the world is saved neither by its priests nor its soldiers, but by God and His Saints. The Church Militant sent this woman to the fire; but even as she burnt, the flames whitened into the radiance of the Church Triumphant.

(*The clock strikes the third quarter. A rough male voice is heard trolling an improvised tune.*)

Rum tum trumpledum,
Bacon fat and rumpledum,
Old Saint mumpledum,
Pull his tail and stumpledum,
O my Ma-ry Ann!

(*A ruffianly English soldier comes through the curtain and marches between* DUNOIS *and* JOAN.)

DUNOIS

What villainous troubadour taught you that doggerel?

THE SOLDIER

No troubadour. We made it up ourselves as we marched. We were not gentlefolks and troubadours. Music straight out of the heart of the people, as you might say. Rum tum trumpledum, Bacon fat and rumpledum, Old Saint mumpledum, Pull his tail and stumpledum: that don't mean anything, you know; but it keeps you marching. Your servant, ladies and gentleman. Who asked for a saint?

JOAN

Be you a saint?

THE SOLDIER

Yes, lady, straight from hell.

DUNOIS

A saint, and from hell!

THE SOLDIER

Yes, noble captain: I have a day off. Every year, you know. That's my allowance for my one good action.

CAUCHON

Wretch! In all the years of your life did you do only one good action?

THE SOLDIER

I never thought about it: it came natural like. But they scored it up for me.

CHARLES

What was it?

THE SOLDIER

Why, the silliest thing you ever heard of. I——

JOAN

(*Interrupting him by strolling across to the bed, where she sits beside* CHARLES). He tied two sticks together, and gave them to a poor lass that was going to be burnt.

THE SOLDIER

Right. Who told you that?

JOAN

Never mind. Would you know her if you saw her again?

THE SOLDIER

Not I. There are so many girls! And they all expect you to remember them as if there was only one in the world. This one must have been a prime sort; for I have a day off every year for her; and so, until twelve o'clock punctually, I am a saint, at your service, noble lords and lovely ladies.

CHARLES

And after twelve?

THE SOLDIER

After twelve, back to the only place fit for the likes of me.

JOAN

(*Rising*). Back there; You! that gave the lass the cross!

THE SOLDIER

(*Excusing his unsoldierly conduct*). Well, she asked for it; and they were going to burn her. She had as good a right to a cross as they had; and they had dozens of them. It was her funeral, not theirs. Where was the harm in it?

JOAN

Man: I am not reproaching you. But I cannot bear to think of you in torment.

THE SOLDIER

(*Cheerfully*). No great torment, lady. You see I was used to worse.

CHARLES

What! worse than hell?

THE SOLDIER

Fifteen years' service in the French wars. Hell was a treat after that.

(JOAN *throws up her arms, and takes refuge from despair of humanity before the picture of the Virgin.*)

THE SOLDIER

(*Continuing*). Suits me somehow. The day off was dull at first, like a wet Sunday. I don't mind it so much now. They tell me I can have as many as I like as soon as I want them.

CHARLES

What is hell like?

THE SOLDIER

You won't find it so bad, sir. Jolly. Like as if you were always drunk without the trouble and expense of drinking. Tip top company too: emperors and popes and kings and all sorts. They chip me about giving that young judy the cross; but I don't care: I stand up to them proper, and tell them that if she hadn't a better right to it than they, she'd be where they are. That dumbfounds them, that does. All they can do is gnash their teeth, hell fashion; and I just laugh, and go off singing the old chanty: Rum tum trumple—Hullo! Who's that knocking at the door?

(*They listen. A long gentle knocking is heard.*)

CHARLES

Come in.

(*The door opens; and an old priest, white-haired, bent, with a silly but benevolent smile, comes in and trots over to* JOAN.)

THE NEWCOMER

Excuse me, gentle lords and ladies. Do not let me disturb you. Only a poor old harmless English rector. Formerly chaplain to the cardinal: to my lord of Winchester. John de Stogumber, at your service. (*He looks at them inquiringly.*) Did you say anything? I am a little deaf, unfortunately. Also a little—well, not always in my right mind, perhaps; but still, it is a small village with a few simple people. I suffice: I suffice: they love me there; and I am able to do a little good. I am well connected, you see; and they indulge me.

JOAN

Poor old John! What brought thee to this state?

DE STOGUMBER

I tell my folks they must be very careful. I say to them, "If you only saw what you think about you would think quite differently about it. It would give you a great shock. Oh, a great shock." And they all say "Yes, parson: we all know you are a kind man, and would not harm a fly." That is a great comfort to me. For I am not cruel by nature, you know.

THE SOLDIER

Who said you were?

DE STOGUMBER

Well, you see, I did a very cruel thing once because I did not know what cruelty was like. I had not seen it, you know. That is the great thing: you must see it. And then you are redeemed and saved.

CAUCHON

Were not the sufferings of our Lord Christ enough for you?

DE STOGUMBER

No. Oh, no: not at all. I had seen them in pictures, and read of them in books, and been greatly moved by them, as I thought. But it was no use: it was not our Lord that redeemed me, but a young woman whom I saw actually burnt to death. It was dreadful: oh, most dreadful. But it saved me. I have been a different man ever since, though a little astray in my wits sometimes.

CAUCHON

Must then a Christ perish in torment in every age to save those that have no imagination?

JOAN

Well, if I saved all those he would have been cruel to if he had not been cruel to me, I was not burnt for nothing, was I?

DE STOGUMBER

Oh, no; it was not you. My sight is bad: I cannot distinguish your features: but you are not she: oh, no: she was burnt to a cinder: dead and gone, dead and gone.

THE EXECUTIONER

(*Stepping from behind the bed curtains on* CHARLES's *right, the bed being between them*). She is more alive than you, old man. Her heart would not burn; and it would not drown. I was a master at my craft: better than the master of Paris, better than the master of Toulouse; but I could not kill The Maid. She is up and alive everywhere.

THE EARL OF WARWICK

(*Sallying from the bed curtains on the other side, and coming to* JOAN's *left hand*). Madame: my congratulations on your rehabilitation. I feel that I owe you an apology.

JOAN

Oh, please don't mention it.

WARWICK

(*Pleasantly*). The burning was purely political. There was no personal feeling against you, I assure you.

JOAN

I bear no malice, my lord.

WARWICK

Just so. Very kind of you to meet me in that way: a touch of true breeding. But I must insist on apologizing very amply. The truth is, these political necessities sometimes turn out to be political mistakes; and this one was a veritable howler; for your spirit conquered us, madame, in spite of our faggots. History will remember me for your sake, though the incidents of the connection were perhaps a little unfortunate.

JOAN

Ay, perhaps just a little, you funny man.

WARWICK

Still, when they make you a saint, you will owe your halo to me, just as this lucky monarch owes his crown to you.

JOAN

(*Turning from him*). I shall owe nothing to any man: I owe everything to the spirit of God that was within me. But fancy me a saint! What would St Catherine and St Margaret say if the farm girl was cocked up beside them!

(*A clerical-looking gentleman in black frockcoat and trousers, and tall hat, in the fashion of the year* 1920, *suddenly appears before them in the corner on their right. They all stare at him. Then they burst into uncontrollable laughter.*)

THE GENTLEMAN

Why this mirth, gentlemen?

WARWICK

I congratulate you on having invented a most extraordinary comic dress.

THE GENTLEMAN

I do not understand. You are all in fancy dress: I am properly dressed.

DUNOIS

All dress is fancy dress, is it not, except our natural skins?

THE GENTLEMAN

Pardon me: I am here on serious business, and cannot engage in frivolous discussions. (*He takes out a paper, and assumes a dry official manner.*) I am sent to announce to you that Joan of Arc, formerly known as The Maid, having been the subject of an inquiry instituted by the Bishop of Orleans——

JOAN

(*Interrupting*). Ah! They remember me still in Orleans.

THE GENTLEMAN

(*Emphatically, to mark his indignation at the interruption*).—by the Bishop of Orleans into the claim of the said Joan of Arc to be canonized as a saint——

JOAN

(*Again interrupting*). But I never made any such claim.

THE GENTLEMAN

(*As before*).—the Church has examined the claim exhaustively in the usual course, and, having admitted the said Joan successively to the ranks of Venerable and Blessed——

JOAN

(*Chuckling*). Me venerable!

THE GENTLEMAN

—has finally declared her to have been endowed with heroic virtues and favored with private revelations, and calls the said Venerable and Blessed Joan to the communion of the Church Triumphant as Saint Joan.

JOAN

(*Rapt*). Saint Joan!

THE GENTLEMAN

On every thirtieth day of May, being the anniversary of the death of the said most blessed daughter of God, there shall in every Catholic church to the end of time be celebrated a special office in commemoration of her; and it shall be lawful to dedicate a special chapel to her, and to place her image on its altar in every such church. And it shall be lawful and laudable for the faithful to kneel and address their prayers through her to the Mercy Seat.

JOAN

Oh, no. It is for the saint to kneel. (*She falls on her knees, still rapt.*)

THE GENTLEMAN

(*Putting up his paper, and retiring beside the* EXECUTIONER). In Basilica Vaticana, the sixteenth day of May, nineteen hundred and twenty.

DUNOIS

(*Raising* JOAN). Half an hour to burn you, dear saint; and four centuries to find out the truth about you!

DE STOGUMBER

Sir: I was chaplain to the Cardinal of Winchester once. They always would call him the Cardinal of England. It would be a great comfort to me and to my master to see a fair statute to The Maid in Winchester Cathedral. Will they put one there, do you think?

THE GENTLEMAN

As the building is temporarily in the hands of the Anglican heresy, I cannot answer for that.

(*A vision of the statue in Winchester Cathedral is seen through the window.*)

DE STOGUMBER

Oh, look! look! that is Winchester.

JOAN

Is that meant to be me? I was stiffer on my feet.

(*The vision fades.*)

THE GENTLEMAN

I have been requested by the temporal authorities of France to mention that the multiplication of public statues to The Maid threatens to become an obstruction to traffic. I do so as a matter of courtesy to the said authorities, but must point out on behalf of the Church that The Maid's horse is no greater obstruction to traffic than any other horse.

JOAN

Eh! I am glad they have not forgotten my horse.

(*A vision of the statue before Rheims Cathedral appears.*)

JOAN

Is that funny little thing me too?

CHARLES

That is Rheims Cathedral where you had me crowned. It must be you.

JOAN

Who has broken my sword? My sword was never broken. It is the sword of France.

DUNOIS

Never mind. Swords can be mended. Your soul is unbroken; and you are the soul of France.

(*The vision fades. The* ARCHBISHOP *and the* INQUISITOR *are now seen on the right and left of* CAUCHON.)

JOAN

My sword shall conquer yet: the sword that never struck a blow. Though men destroyed my body, yet in my soul I have seen God.

CAUCHON

(*Kneeling to her*). The girls in the field praise thee; for thou hast raised their eyes; and they see that there is nothing between them and heaven.

DUNOIS

(*Kneeling to her*). The dying soldiers praise thee, because thou art a shield of glory between them and the judgment.

THE ARCHBISHOP

(*Kneeling to her*). The princes of the Church praise thee, because thou hast redeemed the faith their wordlinesses have dragged through the mire.

WARWICK

(*Kneeling to her*). The cunning counsellors praise thee, because thou hast cut the knots in which they have tied their own souls.

DE STOGUMBER

(*Kneeling to her*). The foolish old men on their deathbeds praise thee, because their sins against thee are turned into blessings.

THE INQUISITOR

(*Kneeling to her*). The judges in the blindness and bondage of the law praise thee, because thou hast vindicated the vision and the freedom of the living soul.

THE SOLDIER

(*Kneeling to her*). The wicked out of hell praise thee, because thou hast shewn them that the fire that is not quenched is a holy fire.

THE EXECUTIONER

(*Kneeling to her*). The tormentors and executioners praise thee, because thou hast shown that their hands are guiltless of the death of the soul.

CHARLES

(*Kneeling to her*). The unpretending praise thee, because thou hast taken upon thyself the heroic burdens that are too heavy for them.

JOAN

Woe unto me when all men praise me! I bid you remember that I am a saint, and that saints can work miracles. And now tell me: shall I rise from the dead, and come back to you a living woman?

(*A sudden darkness blots out the walls of the room as they all spring to their feet in consternation. Only the figures and the bed remain visible.*)

JOAN

What! Must I burn again? Are none of you ready to receive me?

CAUCHON

The heretic is always better dead. And mortal eyes cannot distinguish the saint from the heretic. Spare them. (*He goes out as he came.*)

DUNOIS

Forgive us, Joan: we are not yet good enough for you. I shall go back to my bed. (*He also goes.*)

WARWICK

We sincerely regret our little mistake; but political necessities, though occasionally erroneous, are still imperative; so if you will be good enough to excuse me—— (*He steals discreetly away.*)

THE ARCHBISHOP

Your return would not make me the man you once thought me. The utmost I can say is that though I dare not bless you, I hope I may one day enter into your blessedness. Meanwhile, however—— (*He goes.*)

THE INQUISITOR

I who am of the dead, testified that day that you were innocent. But I do not see how The Inquisition could possibly be dispensed with under existing circumstances. Therefore—— (*He goes.*)

DE STOGUMBER

Oh, do not come back: you must not come back. I must die in peace. Give us peace in our time, O Lord! (*He goes.*)

THE GENTLEMAN

The possibility of your resurrection was not contemplated in the recent proceedings for your canonization. I must return to Rome for fresh instructions. (*He bows formally, and withdraws.*)

THE EXECUTIONER

As a master in my profession I have to consider its interest. And, after all, my first duty is to my wife and children. I must have time to think over this. (*He goes.*)

CHARLES

Poor old Joan! They have all run away from you except this blackguard who has to go back to hell at twelve o'clock. And what can I do but follow Jack Dunois' example, and go back to bed too? (*He does so.*)

JOAN

(*Sadly*). Good night, Charlie.

CHARLES

(*Mumbling in his pillows*). Goo ni. (*He sleeps. The darkness envelops the bed.*)

JOAN

(*To the soldier*). And you, my one faithful? What comfort have you for Saint Joan?

THE SOLDIER

Well, what do they all amount to, these kings and captains and bishops and lawyers and such like? They just leave you in the ditch to bleed to death; and the next thing is, you meet them down there, for all the airs they give themselves. What I say is, you have as good a right to your notions as they have to theirs, and perhaps better. (*Settling himself for a lecture on the subject.*) You see, it's like this. If—(*The first stroke of midnight is heard softly from a distant bell.*) Excuse me: a pressing appointment—— (*He goes on tiptoe.*)

(*The last remaining rays of light gather into a white radiance descending on* JOAN. *The hour continues to strike.*)

JOAN

O God that madest this beautiful earth, when will it be ready to receive Thy saints? How long, O Lord, how long?

Franz Werfel

GOAT SONG

(BOCKSGESANG)

Translated from the German by

Ruth Langner

FRANZ WERFEL

Franz Werfel was born on September 10, 1890, at Prague in Czechoslovakia. His education, begun at the Prague Gymnasium, was continued at Leipzig and Hamburg, where he devoted himself to the study of philosophy. In 1915 he became a lecturer in philosophy at the University of Leipzig, only to have his work interrupted by the World War, in which he served with the German army on the Russian front. His first honors in literature were won as a poet. Among his plays, *Goat Song* and *Juarez and Maximilian* were produced by the Theatre Guild. More recently, he achieved international fame as the author of the novel *The Forty Days of Musa Dagh.* Franz Werfel is now a distinguished exile from the land of his adoption, Germany.

CHARACTERS

GOSPODAR (SQUIRE) STEVAN MILIC
MIRKO, his son
MIRKO'S MOTHER
GOSPODAR JEVREM VESILIC
STANJA, his daughter
STANJA'S MOTHER
STARSINA
THE OLD MAN OF KRASNOKRAJ
THE OLD MAN OF MODRYGOR
THE OLD MAN OF MEDEGYA
THE OTHER OLD MEN
THE CLERK
BABKA
A SERVANT
A POPE (Greek Orthodox Priest)
THE PHYSICIAN
A MESSENGER
BOGOBOJ WITH THE WHITE BEARD
JUVAN, the student
TEITERLIK, an acrobat
THE AMERICAN
FEIWEL
KRUNA
THE OTHER RETURNED WANDERERS, UNLANDED MEN, AND VAGABONDS
AN INNKEEPER
A BASHI BAZOOK
SOLDIERS IN THE REGIMENT OF JANISSARIES
THE DRUNKEN BUTCHER

The action of the play takes place in a Slavic countryside beyond the Danube, at the close of the eighteenth century.

GOAT SONG

ACT ONE

The big farm kitchen of GOSPODAR STEVAN MILIC'S *house. Left, near the door, the oven with a bench running around it. . . . Right, many little windows lighted by a late March afternoon. In the darkening background a stair leads left, and in an alcove is the shrine of the holy pictures. A deserted table.*

SCENE I

GOSPODAR STEVAN MILIC, MIRKO, MIRKO'S MOTHER, GOSPODAR JEVREM VESILIC, STANJA, STANJA'S MOTHER, BABKA, A MAID.

The two families stand in a stiff and solemn row before the oven. BABKA *and the* MAID *hand them little wooden cups of prune brandy under the watchful housewife's eye of* MIRKO'S MOTHER.

STEVAN

One more little swallow before you go! Your health, my dear guests.
(*They drink.*)

JEVREM

(*Wiping his mouth*). You make a stiff drink here.

MIRKO'S MOTHER

I hope it brings you good health.

STANJA'S MOTHER

We thank you.
(BABKA *and the* MAID *exit.*)

STEVAN

Now we've talked it over to our heart's content and everything is signed and sealed. We are happy to see your little Stanja as the betrothed of our son, our son Mirko. Why is your daughter so silent? She hasn't said a word all day—the pretty one.

STANJA'S MOTHER

(*Nudges her daughter*). Go on, talk, say something.

STANJA

(*Stands motionless. Only her bridal wreath of flowers and ribbon trembles lightly.*)

JEVREM

A silent one she is. Silent at home, as well. Don't think her stupid. I tell you, brother, she's cleverer than we old ones.

STEVAN

Other days, other ways. When our fathers gave me and Mother to each other no one asked us anything and no one would have listened to us anyway. Other days, other ways. Therefore I ask you, Stanjoschka, is there anything on your mind against Mirko here for a husband?

STANJA

Nothing!

JEVREM

Nothing, you hear?

STANJA'S MOTHER

Nothing, you hear?

MIRKO

(*Angrily*). Why these questions, Father? It's not for you to ask her that.

STEVAN

Son, you know nothing of the ways of women. (*To* STANJA.) Well, then you are invited, dear Stanja, to stay here in the house until the fourth Sunday, as is the custom, and learn to know your new home. Look about the household, make the servants trust you. Mother will tell you whatever you want to know. But no work for you during these happy days. Enjoy your life with us to the full. Are you content?

STANJA

I am, and I thank you.

JEVREM AND HIS WIFE

We, too, thank you.

STEVAN

This is solemn talk for young folks. Run along, children, no need to stand there before us old people shifting from one foot to the other. Go, and God be with you.

MIRKO

Come, Stanja!
(*They exit.*)

SCENE II

JEVREM

(*Shakes hands cordially with* STEVAN). Ah! Today I'm truly happy.

STANJA'S MOTHER

A young couple such as God smiles on.

MIRKO'S MOTHER

—And folks will envy.

JEVREM

We are both rich, dear kinsman and neighbor, and masters of many souls. Each of us gives as good as he gets. We need not hate each other like some fathers-in-law, for neither your child nor mine gets the worst of it. God grant you're as happy as I am.

STEVAN

I am, I am.

JEVREM

What a future for us both!

STEVAN

Yes, our paths go upward.

JEVREM

Our fathers were still tenant farmers and vassals to the Turk. But the Spahi has grown old and sits puffing his nargileh in the stone houses of the Vilajet, or looking wearily down from his battle towers into the rippling stream.

STEVAN

We have taken what was ours.

JEVREM

And the Moslem; God protect him. His soldiers will defend us, for there is murmuring aplenty among the peasants against us, their masters and the owners of the land.

STEVAN

Let him fear who has evil on his mind. Once our farmers, servants, tenants, barnyards, dairies, and vineyards are united, they will truly make a lord's estate.

JEVREM

You know, that has been my thought for a long while. If a man gathers and multiplies his wealth and bows to the authorities he's sure of their help to guard his land. Are there many vagrants in your part of the country?

STEVAN

All too many. And especially this year when such a lot of people have come home from beyond the Danube. It means trouble enough for me and the council of elders. (*He sighs.*)

JEVREM

It might be wise to be neighborly and allow them a bit of land for farming. Unused woods eat up the fruitlands and cry for tilling. . . . (STEVAN *nods.*) And better still—your son, our son, the future master will raise him a regiment of followers out of these landless men. Such things have happened.

STEVAN

That would please his vanity. (JEVREM *ostentatiously takes out a fat watch;* STEVAN *opens his eyes wide.*)

JEVREM

This comes from Vienna.

STEVAN

Yes. We are beginning to live in the world again.

JEVREM

God of my fathers! It's high time we went. We've long outstayed our welcome.

STEVAN

Don't say that! Stay a little longer.

JEVREM

Impossible! We'd get home late at night.

STEVAN

I will have your horses hitched, then. (*Goes to the door.*)

JEVREM

I'll go with you.

STEVAN

The women can wait here for us till then. (*Both exit.*)

SCENE III

STANJA'S MOTHER

I envy your house, my dear. Everything shining—dishes, silver, ornaments. And even the food you put before us. They can't bake or stew more tastily at the Emperor's in Vienna. I will tremble when you come to us. We poor people! And I envy my daughter Stanja, too, with the chance to copy your recipes; although the bad girl has no mind for those things.

MIRKO'S MOTHER

I'll find everything at your house just the same as mine. (*Politely.*) They say that you weave better than we can here. (*Pause.*)

STANJA'S MOTHER

Pardon me, my dear. You won't take offence if I say something? You look sad—not happy. . . . I say this only because I'm so fond of you.

MIRKO'S MOTHER

Forgive me! I am happy. God didn't bless me. I cannot show my happiness.

STANJA'S MOTHER

God *has* blessed you! Aren't you proud of your boy?

MIRKO'S MOTHER

Of my son? Of Mirko? Oh, I am proud of him.

STANJA'S MOTHER

A son is always different from a daughter. The men are never satisfied with daughters. My old man . . . he's not near so good tempered as he seems . . . Many's the beating I've had because I bore a girl. That you've been spared. When the only child is a son there's joy in the house, and the fault findings are silenced. But (forgive me, my love talks), perhaps some old, old sorrow clouds your joy. . . . I remember. . . . (*She shifts inquisitively on her chair.*) Two years before our fine boy came along . . . didn't you go the full nine months? (MIRKO'S MOTHER *is silent.*)

STANJA'S MOTHER

(*Sympathetically watchful*). The baby died quite young, eh? Even women who have ten or twelve and mix the children's names never forget little ones like that. My love talks . . .

MIRKO'S MOTHER

The baby died at birth.

STANJA'S MOTHER

A boy?

MIRKO'S MOTHER

No.

STANJA'S MOTHER

Oh, a girl?

MIRKO'S MOTHER

No.

STANJA'S MOTHER

What? How so?

MIRKO'S MOTHER

(*Quickly*). How stupid! Forgive me! It was a boy. Of course, a boy.

THE MEN'S VOICES

(*Through the window*). Hey! You women!

MIRKO'S MOTHER

(*Rising swiftly*). Let us not keep our old men waiting.
(*Both off.*)

SCENE IV

(*Enter* BABKA *with dishes, the* YOUNG SERVING MAN *following.*)

MAN

Babka! It is hollering for you.

BABKA

What's hollering?

MAN

Or was it singing? Maybe it's singing! Hahaha! Haha . . .

BABKA

Fool, what are you talking about, and laughing at?

MAN

Oh, I'm a fool, am I? But just the same . . .

BABKA

(*Interrupting*). What?

MAN

That!

BABKA

It won't be long before you've eaten your last spoonful of rice soup here.

MAN

(*Sings*). "If you have eyes to see
A wanderer you will be."

BABKA

You have a mouth, too—to shut.

MAN

I know another song:
"And the little house of stone
Has a fire of its own."

BABKA

You go sing your songs to the sheep.

MAN

You can't make me stop. (*Sings.*)
"Iron hinges on the door
Seven locks and seven more—
Who carries all those keys?"

BABKA

Rascal! Get out of the master's room. They're coming.
(MAN *withdraws mockingly.*)

SCENE V

(MIRKO *and* STANJA *enter,* BABKA *exits.*)

MIRKO

Your parents are gone now. Are you sad?

STANJA

No, I am not sad.

MIRKO

Then you don't love your parents?

STANJA

I love them.

MIRKO

Then you must be sad. Doesn't it hurt you when something is over? The axle creaks, the horses draw up, the whip. . . . And then, something is ended.

STANJA

I never ache for what is past.

MIRKO

Oh, I often do. I can lie in the meadow hour after hour longing for the games I played there on the grass.

STANJA

That is because you are a man. (*Short pause.*)

MIRKO

Do the house and the farm please you?

STANJA

Why shouldn't they? House, rooms, chimneys, stables, pigsties, and hencoops and dovecots, same as everywhere.

MIRKO

And do I please you?

STANJA

Why shouldn't you please me?

MIRKO

Do you know, Stanja, I would have liked it better if you had cried before, when they left you. . . . (*Suddenly turns on her.*) You! What if you've loved someone before! Tell me! Have you loved someone else?

STANJA

(*Hesitatingly*). No.

MIRKO

(*Slowly, his eyes closed*). I think, when we're married, I will beat you.

STANJA

That's what all husbands do.

MIRKO

Did you tell me the truth?

STANJA

No.

MIRKO

Ah! You did love another before me, before me . . .

STANJA

Did I love him? Just once, I dreamed of him in the night. He'd been our guest for an hour. He wore a scholar's cap on his head and a laced coat. He was a student.

MIRKO

(*Presses her hand*). Did he speak to you? Did you see him again? Or dream of him?

STANJA

Never again.

MIRKO

(*Lets her hand fall, brusquely*). A student? Ho! You want to show me you're a smart one.

STANJA

(*Flashing*). That takes no showing.

MIRKO

Damn!

STANJA

You led me through the rooms and closets up to the attic. We looked at all the stalls, the cattle, the dairies, the storehouse, the threshing floors, wine-presses, everything. But I have eyes . . .

MIRKO

(*Excited, tries to embrace her*). Blue eyes, sharp, bad, sweet. . . .

STANJA

(*Thrusts him from her*). But mighty quick you slipped by that little house of stone, and by that rusty iron door. You wouldn't look, and pushed me away. (*Triumphant.*) What does the smoking chimney of that big kennel mean? You light no fire for animals. That rising smoke is human. . . . I have eyes!

MIRKO

(*Stroking his forehead in helpless bewilderment*). I do not know, Stanja. Believe me, I do not know. Ever since I was a little child that was the forbidden place that we hurried by in fear, with downcast eyes. I dared not ask my mother or my father. I love my—father—not as you love yours. So I kept still and let my father bear the secret. I got used to it as a child and never gave it thought. But now! For twenty years, day after day, I have passed it—and always with my foreboding heart, yet never thinking of it. And now, all of a sudden, after so many years, I'm forced to think. . . . Yes, true enough! A fire's there each spring and winter. (*Seized by an obscure horror.*) Stanja! I will not ask my father. I'll never ask.

STANJA

Now do you see who is the smart one? For twenty years you never thought or asked. But a woman comes to the house and asks you the first hour.

SCENE VI

(STEVAN *enters.*)

STEVAN

Still in the house, children? Away with you. They are finishing the dancing on the village green. The folks want to see you. It's only right the master's son and daughter should lead the dancers. (*To* MIRKO.) What's the matter?

MIRKO

(*Urgently*). Father!

STEVAN

You are your own master now. Here is some money. Make merry with your betrothed and treat your friends.
(MIRKO *hesitates.*)
Off with you. (*Impatiently.*) Go! (MIRKO *and* STANJA *go to the door.*) And call Babka for me.
(MIRKO *and* STANJA *exit.* STEVAN *quickly takes a long gun with a jointed butt down from the wall and loads it. Then he stands rigid for a few moments and hangs the weapon up again as hastily as he took it down.*)

SCENE VII

(BABKA *enters.*)

BABKA

Peace to you, master, peace at last.

STEVAN

(*Rousing from his abstraction, suddenly, hoarsely*). His sickness?

BABKA

Master, he's getting better. The poor thing ate, drank and slept for the first time in many days.

STEVAN

(*Clenching his fists*). Christ, why do you not help?

BABKA

His eyes roll again . . . round the walls . . . without stopping.

STEVAN

(*Almost screaming*). On two feet or four, Babka?

BABKA

(*Quietly*). On two and four—both.

STEVAN

Do you see to him daily?

BABKA

Daily at twilight, at the hour of the evening meal.

STEVAN

(*Looks at her in horror*). You . . .

BABKA

Can I shun what I have suckled, shun him, the wild big thing that once was tiny with a greedy mouth?

STEVAN

He screamed today, the second time in his cursed life.

BABKA

He screamed for the joy of health with his ever silent voice.

STEVAN

Does he never greet you?

BABKA

No, but he knows his old Babka.

STEVAN

Did anybody hear the cry?

BABKA

Oh, yes, they heard him.

STEVAN

Heard? Satan . . .

BABKA

(*Interrupting him*). That's what many say.

STEVAN

The people. . . . Get them all out of the house, you hear? To play games or to dance on the green—not a man or woman home before midnight. You hear?

BABKA

I knew your will, master. They are gone. Do nothing evil. (STEVAN *motions her to go.* BABKA, *at the door.*) Do nothing evil. (*Turns to go.*)

STEVAN

Babka, has he a human face?

BABKA

The face of a man, of an old man, a hundred years old, a face shrewd and knowing.

STEVAN

Give me the key.

BABKA

Why, master? Turn from such thoughts. Your life is happy now.

STEVAN

The key. (BABKA *takes out a key and hands it to him.*) You do not let it rust.

BABKA

You have the key now, master. (*Exits slowly.*)

STEVAN

(*Slowly, to himself*). Shame, shame! Pain, shame! (*Groans. Collapses over the table.*)

SCENE VIII

(MIRKO'S MOTHER *enters.*)

MOTHER

The people are gone. We are alone now. It is terrible.

STEVAN

(*Turns to her wildly*). Tell me, tell me at last, tell me your awful secret. What you hid from me and then bore to our shame.

MOTHER

I had no secret from you but my pain at knowing that while I was heavy with child you lay with all the wenches.

STEVAN

Twisting my words again, with your woman's tongue!

MOTHER

You're brave enough to handle wild steers with your naked fists, but you'll lie to me till death, you coward.

STEVAN

You twister of words, you sly one. Who begot him in you? He cannot be my child. Sound stock, sound to the tenth generation, my seed.

MOTHER

Don't lie about yourself, you waster. How you must have filthied your seed that it could so lower me. Sound as I was, and clean when you took me.

STEVAN

There is much of you I do not know.

MOTHER

There is much of you I do not know.

STEVAN

But this I know. My first born was not baptised.

MOTHER

Who was it mocked the sacrament? Not I —not I.

STEVAN

Would you have had the courage to be a thing of loathing to the world?

MOTHER

Now the poor thing, unbaptised, will drag us with him down to hell.

STEVAN

Not us. You, you! This shame to me grew in your body.

MOTHER

(*On a scream*). Oh, stop, stop . . .

STEVAN

(*Pleading*). Don't cry, don't cry . . . Mother . . . don't cry.

MOTHER

A child after the night of pain, seven hours old, when the dawn came . . . rosy, sweet as milk, lying there in its basket with the little cap already on its downy head. . . . No! That morning you did not look at him . . . nor I.

STEVAN

It is my fault?

MOTHER

(*Even more wearily than he*). Is it mine?

STEVAN

(*Bitter*). Well-formed babies who have smiled up at their fathers die. Many, many. He is alive, has lived for three and twenty years. What does God mean?

MOTHER

Can't you ever stop thinking of it?

STEVAN

No. Everywhere I go I drag the secret, drag the secret with me.

MOTHER

Why do you never go in to him?

STEVAN

You ask that, you, his mother, his loving mother? Why have you never dared to look at that which you so love?

MOTHER

(*Trembling*). Because I love so. . . . (*A knock, the* PHYSICIAN *enters.*)

SCENE IX

PHYSICIAN

A good evening to you, Stevan Milic, a good evening to you, dear mistress of the house. I hear there has been a betrothal in this house. I give you my best wishes. Yes, money flows to money as water does to water. And I in my little wagon have grown to be sixty with no second nag to make up my team. How long is it, Gospodar, since I last visited you?

STEVAN

I can tell you to the day, Master Physician. It's twelve years.

PHYSICIAN

Gracious heavens. I used to come this way more often. Everything gone well with you?

STEVAN

As well as God wills.

PHYSICIAN

God, God!! Are you still harping upon Him? I, for my part carry Voltaire with me. And your . . . what is his name:—Marko,—Mirko? The little fellow's grown, I wager, into a strapping bridegroom.

MOTHER

So he has, with the help of God.

PHYSICIAN

And then . . . the other? The bio-anatomical-morphophysiological wonder? Pardon the heartless phrases of science!

STEVAN

Still living.

PHYSICIAN

On this farm? Still hidden in the little stall? (*An acquiescent silence.* PHYSICIAN *paces up and down with huge strides, then remains standing close in front of* STEVAN.) Stevan Milic, you are the head of a family and a big farm, a councillor of the town, one of the gentry, and even if this blue-blood talk is all nonsense, you still owe it to your position to be a little broadminded. I know, yes, yes, I know, you believe that the Evil One in person became the fruit of your loins, and that you must forever hide the shame of your fatherhood. Why do you make a deformed half creature more unhappy than need be? Puny man, you who measure all creation in your image, what is there that you do not consider monstrous and deformed? (*Emphatically.*) Nature, the gambling dreamer, rules everywhere, and fulfills her own divine intention with joy more holy than all your scribbled revelations. Listen to me: (*In the tone of a teacher.*) In the womb on our way from seed to sense we pass through all the stages of plant and animal life. We are one by one and all in one the pollen and the lily, the gnat and the reptile, fish, fowl, and man. Many and many an obstacle must the child outgrow to become a child. Is that not natural? Well, in your wife's body the child was not able to overcome these obstacles which the lower forms imposed on him. For each form wants to be supreme and undying. It is like the ravening ambition of a king. And these earlier forms have left their mark upon this creature which could not fit itself for human life. But neither is it fit for death. Is that not natural?

STEVAN

It may be natural.

PHYSICIAN

(*Gruffly*). It is very natural. Three out of every hundred children born are warped like yours, though to my recollection this case somewhat exceeds the common. But who can curb the pranks of nature? The universe itself, eternally a child, plays, plays, plays. God and Satan have no hand in the game.

MOTHER

How can you know that?

PHYSICIAN

You fools, fools, fools. You cherish the horror here in your house. You are all black with lies, excuses, slyness and reserves. And so little's needed to release you. In the big city, there on the other side of the river, are homes for crippled humans, for monsters of this sort, homes where the unhappy creatures are kept clean and guarded, and allowed to savor their poor twilit lives. The spider has its pleasure, the otter and the eel, why not a half-man? But seriously . . . give me (I have asked you so many times) give me this sport of nature. I will take him to the city, to that home. The journey will not cost you dear. For when science stands to gain I gladly trim my bills.

STEVAN

That will not do. People would hear of it.

MOTHER

He would be seen. No night would be black enough to hide such a journey.

PHYSICIAN

Right! I would be at no pains to hide him.

MOTHER

(*Quickly*). I'll never, never let him go.

STEVAN

Tell me! When he's entered in this house will his name, which is mine as well, be written down?

PHYSICIAN

Yes, indeed, Stevan Milic.

STEVAN

Never! No! Never!

PHYSICIAN

Oh, you . . . (*Swallows the insult.*) Why not?

STEVAN

Sir—we are ashamed.

PHYSICIAN

Did you make the world?

STEVAN

You are a bachelor and a bookworm. You cannot understand us.

PHYSICIAN

You cannot be helped. Never again will I say another word. But be warned! Your neighbors have noses.

STEVAN

My secret is well guarded.

PHYSICIAN

Very well. Then give me the key to his stall. I'm more than a little eager to see how the wonder has grown up. (STEVAN *hesitates.*) Have no fear. I would be no scientist if I could pass by such a wonder. It is years ago but I remember the place well.

STEVAN

(*Gives him the key*). Take care of yourself when you're with him.

PHYSICIAN

A doctor is a soldier. Many's the giant madman these old bones have tamed. Wait for me.
(*Exit.*)

STEVAN

Mother, bring a light.
(MOTHER *goes.*)

PHYSICIAN

(*Sticks his head in at the door*). Did you give me that key before?

STEVAN

You just took it.

PHYSICIAN

(*Searching his pockets*). Did I? My taper . . . my flint. . . . Ah, here it is. Oh, I am getting old. I'm getting old.

STEVAN

Take care of yourself, Master. It's getting dark. (PHYSICIAN *disappears.*)

SCENE X

(*The* MOTHER *brings the light, then silence.*)

STEVAN

As soon as the wedding's over I shall go on a pilgrimage to Mount Athos.

MOTHER

And leave me?

STEVAN

I will keep nothing. Mirko is old enough. When I return he shall take over the whole place and my position, as my heir.

MOTHER

And we?

STEVAN

Will flee . . .

MOTHER

(*Laughs maliciously*). With him?

STEVAN

Perhaps I'll gather strength enough upon the pilgrimage to talk to Mirko. I must find the strength to tell him everything.

MOTHER

You will leave your son an evil house with pious speeches.

STEVAN

That is true. But sooner or later he must know. I'd rather journey to the monks of Temesvar.

MOTHER

Oh, husband! Cowardly as ever. Must your son, who still lives happily, carry the burden you've thrown down?

STEVAN

You are right. I will be silent.

MOTHER

(*Quickly*). And what's to happen when we die?

STEVAN

We daren't die.

MOTHER

Death might come to me this very hour.

STEVAN

(*Clinging tightly to her*). No, my companion. I need you—to share my secret.

MOTHER

And I need you for the sake of the child that is your child too. If you were to die and leave me I'd go mad.

STEVAN

We are no longer human. . . .

MOTHER

Because we no longer need each other for each other's sake.

STEVAN

There's no way out.

MOTHER

No. Not even if we both should kill ourselves this hour. Mirko, the unsuspecting, would have to find out everything tomorrow.

STEVAN

(*Agonized*). I will speak to him tonight.

MOTHER

Speak . . . keep silent . . . speak. . . . To what end? I can see Mirko's face. And she? She's a smart one. I hate her already.

STEVAN

Not even death my refuge. (*Softly, to the mother.*) Accursed!

SCENE XI

(*A* MESSENGER *enters.*)

MESSENGER

The old men are assembled in the big house in council. They ask the Gospodar if they are still to wait.

STEVAN

Let them wait a little longer. But if I take too long, let them begin the meeting. Say that to the Starsina. (MESSENGER *exits.*)

MOTHER

The joy in your eyes, the joy at not having to be in the house tonight near him, with me . . .

STEVAN

Yes, joy, joy indeed. I breathe, I breathe relief because I do not have to be here all this evening.

MOTHER

(*Whimpering*). Don't leave me alone, Father, take me with you, don't leave me alone here in the house. (STEVAN *stands rigid for a moment intensely thinking.*) . . . Ah, you are not listening to me.

STEVAN

(*Very curtly*). Go now. The doctor. I want to be alone with him.
(MOTHER *goes off slowly rear.* PHYSICIAN *enters.*)

SCENE XII

PHYSICIAN

(*Shaken*). It almost makes you turn to God again. Cool-headed as I am, I dripped with sweat. (*Has to sit down.*) Nature is boundless and imagination nothing. Milic, I do not envy you.

STEVAN

The braggart's trembling now.

PHYSICIAN

You have not seen him since birth?

STEVAN

A servant brought him up.

PHYSICIAN

Well! Formerly I still could comprehend it. But now! The ancients believed that at high noon something could spring from quivering nature, formless but visible, horrible and full of majesty, blasting all that crossed it, like the vision of the Whole compressed into a second. . . . Understand me or not—I saw something like that just now.

STEVAN

Have you ever spoken of my misfortune to anyone, Master?

PHYSICIAN

Never. That goes without saying. I am a physician.

STEVAN

(*Painfully*). I must speak to you, Master.

PHYSICIAN

That I can well imagine.

STEVAN

(*Struggling for breath*). Master! He . . . he . . . must go away.

PHYSICIAN

Of course. And you can thank me for it. Listen. Give me a big wagon with a team of your best horses. It's a troublesome business, but I'll bring the creature to the place where it belongs. (*Scratches himself under his wig.*) Wonder if they'll accept it? Well, that's my affair.

STEVAN

That's . . . not what I want.

PHYSICIAN

What do you want?

STEVAN

He must go differently.

PHYSICIAN

Differently?

STEVAN

You must have something in your pocket, something . . . that you can't give much of to sick people . . .

PHYSICIAN

Poison?

STEVAN

(*Relieved*). Poison.

PHYSICIAN

And you want me, just like that, to make away with a creature I did not create; something which breathes, eager for life? Such an extraordinary, if you will allow me, master prank of nature, into the bargain?

STEVAN

(*Suddenly the humbly stupid peasant*). Yes, yes, do that!

PHYSICIAN

Sir, I am a physician. I am here to lengthen life.

STEVAN

Poison . . . in . . . his . . . food!

PHYSICIAN

I understand you. So that's what you want. But we doctors have our superstitions too, and hold with many of Mohammed's maxims. I think, you see, that we are reborn in all the patients we help from life to death. Salaam Aleikum!
(*Exit.*)

STEVAN

(*Screaming*). Mother! Mother!

SCENE XIII

(MOTHER *enters swiftly.*)

STEVAN

The Bible! The Bible! (MOTHER *moves the desk with the church calendar to the light.* STEVAN *leafs it through with mad fingers.*) Abraham, Isaac, Abraham, Isaac . . .

MOTHER

(*Totters to him, screaming*). No! Mother Mary! Not that! Not that!

STEVAN

Yes! That! That! That! (*Savoring the words.*) And you will hold the light.

MOTHER

Agh . . . I carried him without knowing and now . . . woe, woe. . . .

STEVAN

My house must be made over. I must do it for Mirko, for his future and his children. Way for Mirko!

MOTHER

Mirko . . . no! (*Beaming.*) It's him . . . him . . . him I love.

STEVAN

Quiet!

MOTHER

Never seen . . .

STEVAN

You'll see him now.

MOTHER

(*Rigid, slowly*). Unloved . . .

STEVAN

(*Grabs the gun from the wall*). Take the lamp.

MOTHER

(*Looks into the distance*). His little heart . . . a human heart.

STEVAN

(*Stamps*). Keep still!

MOTHER

His blood . . . my blood. . . .

STEVAN

Mine. I gave it. I take it.

MOTHER

(*Tenderly—tenderly*). Mine . . . Mine! And so. . . .

STEVAN

Come! (*Suddenly* BABKA *appears in the shadows.*) Not you! Babka, take the light!

BABKA

(*Quietly*). I suckled him, but I obey the master. (*Holds the lamp high.*)

STEVAN

(*At the door*). Lord of life! I do not know what your plan is, but I am of it.
(*Off.* BABKA *off.* MOTHER *alone in the dark.*)

MOTHER

Nothing. . . . No remembrance. . . . Never seen. . . . Nothing. . . . Nothing left. Was in me. Now, now . . . his heart . . . beats in mine. (*She listens, listens. Awaking.*) The shot! Why is there no shot? Mother of God! . . .
(*She falls in a faint.*)

SCENE XIV

(*Quick steps outside.* STEVAN *holds to the doorpost, swaying.* BABKA, *with the lamp, behind him.*)

STEVAN

The key, the key! The old man left the door unlocked. He's gone, broken loose, escaped! Ah, ah! (*Shakes the unconscious mother.*) Mother, do you hear? He's free! Free!

Curtain.

ACT TWO

SCENE: *Council Room. A low ceiling. In the background a long table stretching all the way across the stage with a corresponding bench behind it. Right, a little table for the presiding officer and the clerk. Left, an oven with an oven bench. The ten* ELDERS *have already gathered. Some sit on the long bench with their jugs, some walk back and forth talking, or change their seats. The* STARSINA *sits at the little table and watches the* CLERK *cutting a pen.* KRASNOKRAJ *and* MODRYGOR *as "Elders" sit on the oven bench talking. The little oil lamp hanging above the presiding officer's table is the only light.*

SCENE I

STARSINA

(*Raps on the table*). Are we going to wait any longer?

SEVERAL VOICES

(*From the long table*). The bell in the linden has not rung yet.
(*The conversations continue.*)

ELDER OF KRASNOKRAJ

Can you remember a meeting when he hasn't kept us waiting?

ELDER OF MODRYGOR

It is usually unhappiness that keeps us men at home.

KRASNOKRAJ

He? He hasn't a wish in the world. Today he betrothed his son to the daughter of the rich man of Kouxelni vrh.

MODRYGOR

But they say the bride is a trouble-maker.

KRASNOKRAJ

He was given cattle from the land of the Magyars for breeding. His stock is better than ours.

MODRYGOR

But it is always suffering from worms and sore feet.

KRASNOKRAJ

He has cut timber and floated his long logs down our stream to the Danube.

MODRYGOR

But the merchant from the north still owes him for them.

KRASNOKRAJ

Yes, that is true. There's always a "but" for him. What his right hand wins his left hand loses. Always a curse on the play.

MODRYGOR

Not master enough to my mind. He might be a real master. He has the brains.

KRASNOKRAJ

It is his eyes, I tell you. That's where the trouble lies. He is forever hiding something. A dog hides the stolen bone. He has an evil treasure hidden somewhere.

MODRYGOR

Eyes that roam—trouble at home.

KRASNOKRAJ

Things are not going too well for us, either. All this trouble these last years with the landless and the returning emigrants. The flies settle thickly on the carcass.

MODRYGOR

We will take council upon that today.

KRASNOKRAJ

You can't go peacefully cross-country any more. Out of the grainfield, out from behind tree shadows, out of the ditches, suddenly you see an unknown face with its eager, hungry eyes. Eh! An honest man shudders at all the shadowy dancers.

MODRYGOR

The Turk has grown sleepy. We who were once weak, miserable, and oppressed by him are grown great. But the children of the men who had to fear his vengeance, the exiles and the refugees, have also smelt the green tang of our air. They have a claim on it.

KRASNOKRAJ

If they turn against Mahomet, they will turn against us. We are too well off. Stevan Milic's fists are much too soft.

MODRYGOR

He has troubles enough in his own precinct. His own people, so they say, don't stand behind him.

ELDER OF MEDEGYA

(*Coming over to the others*). Have you heard the strange things our brother of Pozar has been telling us? In their town a dead man goes about sucking the blood of the living in the night. Next morning there is a little mark no larger than a mole on the breasts of those he attacks. (The Emperor has sent out a commission.) They pricked the corpse with flowering thorn. Fresh red blood burst from the heart, the eyes glowed and there was no stench to the flesh.

KRASNOKRAJ

Yes, witches and vampires are breeding. A were-wolf from the mountains of Woljo . . . has . . . (*Distant bell rings.*)

STARSINA

(*Raps three times*). The meeting will begin. (*All take their places.*) Clerk, read the order of the day.

CLERK

(*Reads*). The business of this evening's meeting, ad punctum, primum, et ultimum is as follows: The cases of the landless, the returned natives and vagabonds, the question being whether they shall be ordered on or allowed to settle, or what legal measures shall be taken. Further, audience is to be given to three of their members, men whom they have chosen as spokesmen, to wit: the American who does not know his father's name, Teiterlik, a tumbler and acrobat, and finally the Jew, Reb Feiwel, born here. The said three persons are outside the door. Finally a vote and decision on the above-mentioned case.
(*Sits.*)

STARSINA

Has anyone an objection to this procedure? (*Silence.*) To the procedure? (*Silence.*) You elders know that it has been unsafe for a year and a day to travel on the streets, paths, and by-roads leading from village to village. When the herdsman goes his rounds of a morning it is not uncommon for him to come on a cold corpse by the hedgerow. It is not the fox that steals all the fowl, nor the hawk that lifts all the lambs from the fold. We know the guilty persons well. The Turkish Bassa in his mercy and wisdom has appointed honorable and well born men of our race for our governors, and the peasants no longer pay tribute to the turban, but to a Christian landowner. Well we know the men who sneak in to poison their minds. Let us decide wisely so as not to lose the good will of the peasants. And now I propose that we let in the men who wait outside the door. (*All the* ELDERS *raise their hands in approval.*) Let them in.
(CLERK *off.*)

SCENE II

(*The* AMERICAN, TEITERLIK, *and* FEIWEL *enter; the* CLERK *comes back to his former place. The* AMERICAN *is pockmarked, dressed in ragged farm clothes with long leather boots and a sombrero.* TEITERLIK *has one upstanding clown's curl on his otherwise bald head, his nose is snub, eaten away, his body is emaciated in his stage tights, with one red, one yellow leg.* FEIWEL *has a full head, red cheeks, kaftan, and fur cap. All three bow before the* STARSINA *and the* ELDERS, *the* AMERICAN *slightly, the* ROPE-WALKER *and the* JEW *to the ground.*)

STARSINA

The fool speaks first.

TEITERLIK

(*Makes a few forced, stiff, pirouetting steps*). Highly honored, excellent, and landed sirs! The world is big, the heart little; a little mill of flesh that grinds and grinds yet never grinds out the last grain of our hope.

FEIWEL

(*Maliciously*). He he! He he!

TEITERLIK

There are many cities. There is London, and the Thames flows through it, the stream from which the fogs come and where the state drowns criminals and heretics. Then there is Vienna with its Prater. There the Emperor rides in a golden wagon and ten thousand riders follow him. And Naples, too, known awhile back as Babylon, which is another city than Lisbon. In this here Naples is the mountain called Vesuvius, the chimney of hell . . .

FEIWEL

Oi, the stupid. In the newspapers I read of that mountain.

AMERICAN

Pah, you never swallowed salt water, that's why your tongue wags so fast.

STARSINA

Let the tumbler talk.

TEITERLIK

Worshipful landowners. You landed gentlemen! I have been in all these cities and a thousand cities, markets, and towns more, good and bad. We always halted, whether I was master or apprenticed to the troupe, at the edge of the town where the commons are gray and shaggy like the pelt of an old dog. On Sunday, at sunset, the silver would rain on our plates, but on weekdays we often went to sleep without a bite. Of course later on I was not alone, for I found my woman—but in my trade you can't enjoy the women much. It weakens supple joints and makes the eyes see the tight-rope double and triple. Many's the comrades I lost that couldn't say no to them.

AMERICAN

Make it shorter, man.

TEITERLIK

How fine it all is when you're young. You get up early from under the leaves—a-cracking your joints, and sling a stone at the sun. But suddenly, worshipful landowners, this feeling, this awful feeling, comes over you. When your joints are too stiff for the job, you feel the shame of smirking and bowing, and—not being able to sit at a Christian table. At night the cough gnaws at your back like a wolf and you can knock your heart out at the hospital and there's no welcome for you. Yes, the pain was there and would not let go. And I thought of my old folks and how they tilled their fields in this place, and I called to mind the doorstep of their home, here, where as a little boy I used to sit. A piece of land—for the love of God! It is like sleep to the weary. Weary am I, and those with me are weary. You worshipful landowners, you are rich, with many unused acres, hills and bottomlands that you leave fallow. Give us, the children who have come back—give us of your plenty. (*Softly.*) We are weary.

FEIWEL

(*Very loudly, to the* STARSINA). I am the Jew Feiwel. I should think you know that. Who does not know me?

AMERICAN

(*Pushes him away*). No one asked you to speak.

FEIWEL

And who asked you to speak?

STARSINA

The Jew comes last.

FEIWEL

(*With a deliberate, ironical gesture of mouth and hand*). Don't I know it.

AMERICAN

Mesch'schurs and Señores. America is a wonderful country. It is called the new world and the men there talk little. Therefore, I will talk briefly but to the point. Across the great water, there was a war between the new men and the old English. The new men,—(I fought on their side), —won. And that is well. Their land is monstrous, huge. The Indians, brave fighters, were conquered by the firewater. The new men were not born there but came from the whole world, to settle inland and on the coast. They are free and obey no one. The stranger knocks at the blockhouse at night and the head of the house asks him no questions about who, whither, or whence, but pushes him up a chair to the fire and they smoke great cigars, these self-reliant souls. No man thinks himself better than the rest, and the son of the hanged and the daughter of the whore have nothing to fear there. They know nothing of high and low, landowners and landless men. The government gives away land with both hands to all men, and they grow grain, cut timber, pasture flocks, become rich, and no one is downtrodden.

I was one of them, and I did well. Then this cursed sneaking homesickness came over me, and now I have come back here and am ashamed to name my father's name. I who was rich lie with the beggars, a beggar myself, with hate in my heart. I tell you this so you may act like the Americans, and put aside your greed and give each of your countrymen some of the waste land. Then a new race may grow here, rich in experience and goods, and no one live in misery. We that have nothing to eat and no place to sleep have a claim on you, you farmers! Beware of our hatred!

MURMUR OF THE ELDERS

Who dares threaten us?

AMERICAN

I—I who have travelled far and know the world much better than you left-behinds. If you knew anything of business, you would not let new sources of revenue escape you.

TEITERLIK

See our weariness! Only a patch of ground and place for the beggar's hut.

FEIWEL

(*Stepping before the table, fumbles the question*). I?

STARSINA

(*Contemptuously*). Jew!

FEIWEL

(*Waving his hands about for silence*). Ssh now!—Am I or am I not the important person that I am? Do I belong with these beggars here, with whom do I belong? Who brings the women needles, thread, yarn, wool, buttons, cotton, handkerchiefs, kerchief silks? Who buys the toys for the children, the tools you need for house and kitchen, wick lamps, and oiled paper? Who brings your mousetraps, bracelets, pipes? Who travels into the world for you? Who runs the life out of his body for love of you? Who brings you the latest news and gossip? But for me who would know that in France they have kicked out their king and that the Messiah will arise there? The *Turks* are a good people. The Jews may live among them. They can come home *Erev Shabbos* and light their candles without fear. But *you!* I was born here, as my father, *Olav Hasholom,* was born here. But my grandchildren yet will have to live with the gallows-birds. That's you! You! You!

SCENE III

(STEVAN *enters quickly. He carries the gun in his hand. Three of the* ELDERS *rise and the* STARSINA *leaves his place.*)

FEIWEL

(*Resigned*). May a Jew only say two words?

STEVAN

(*Taking the* STARSINA's *place*). Clerk, send a rider after the Physician, to catch up with his wagon outside the city. Tell him I want him to come back. (CLERK *off*. STEVAN *stares into the air, long. The* ELDERS *shake their heads and mutter.*)

ELDERS

What is the matter with him?

STEVAN

(*To the three delegates*). You?

TEITERLIK

(*Bows low, his arms crossed*). Land, Excellency, a bit of land from your overflow, for us, the miserable, who have come home. It's time to settle down and be human.

AMERICAN

(*Gruffly*). Rich man! Give of your waste land to the beggars. Give them their share. They're sturdy people. It's not a charity, but an investment.

STEVAN

How many are you?

FEIWEL

Excellence, I have the count. In round numbers, four hundred: men, women, children, Jew, Gipsy, and Christian.

STEVAN

What do the Elders say?

KRASNOKRAJ

Never ground and land to the worthless.

MODRYGOR

We must weigh the matter.

STEVAN

(*In an uncontrollable outburst of rage*). Nothing's to be weighed. (*He presses toward the three. Trembling, they retreat.*) Damn you! Have you human faces? No, not human faces.

Ha, pockmarks, nose, missing teeth, popeyes, foxbeard. The face of the ageless, shrewd, goatlike ape; his face, the face that must stay hidden. There, there's where it broke loose. Our ancestors covered up there secret sin, but now, no cloth is thick enough to smother it, and it walks abroad. Oh, you sons of the blood sin, would you settle among us to whom the land belongs, who have bettered and built it? Among us sons of light, us? By day and by night shall these scarecrows surround us in church and inn? Do you want to walk upright or on all fours among us? Away, away! Go, go!

KRASNOKRAJ

I don't understand all the Gospodar is saying there, but one thing is true. You are not peasants and never will be, for none of you is fit to till, lazy as you are, and practised in nothing but thieving. You're neither clean nor decent, just a vain and worthless lot who want to hurt your betters, and that's us.

MODRYGOR

Do not be too hasty.

TEITERLIK

I have worked much, in danger of my life, to satisfy your love of wonders. None of you graybeards has dared as much as I, no, not if there's a king among you.

AMERICAN

Sir! Over there I was one of you! And over there a man who throws insults at decent men is dead a long time.
(CLERK *enters again.*)

FEIWEL

(*Persuading the* ELDERS, *vehemently*). Can't you see it? Milic is drunk!

STEVAN

(*In a mighty voice*). Away. Out of our country by to-morrow. Let no landless man show himself here after three days' time. Ten pair of bloodhounds will track on you. And those who resist will be tied to a tree and flogged.

A FEW VOICES

We're here too. This is not decided on.

STEVAN

It has been ordered. Clerk, write the order. Who dares to rise, to stir? Still I am I! I am not yet beaten. Write the order!

AMERICAN

Man! Such an order befits no one but the Pasha of the Kaimakamluks. Where shall we poor devils go?

STEVAN

To the mines, to the harbors, to foreign lands. Only let me be free again. (*Slowly.*) Oh, you outcasts who call nothing your own, if you knew how happy you are. (*Beside himself, swings the gun to hit the three.*) Away with you.

(ELDERS, *near the madman in great excitement.*)

SCENE IV

(*Enter* BABKA *with a lantern. She stands at the door.*)

STEVAN

(*Screams to her*). Where?

BABKA

Nowhere.

STEVAN

No trace?

BABKA

None!

STEVAN

Speak!

BABKA

Looked . . . nothing.

STEVAN

Screams?

BABKA

None! Vanished!

STEVAN

With whose aid?

BABKA

The devil's!

STEVAN

Elders! The meeting is over. I must go hunting. (STEVAN *tears the lantern out of* BABKA'S *hand and runs off.*)

ELDERS

(*Scared, huddled, confusedly*). He is mad.

Curtain.

ACT THREE

SCENE I

Garden of a decayed inn. Left a shed which serves as a residence and inn. Right front a table surrounded by benches, further to the back a second, wholly worm-eaten table without a bench. In the distance, rear, screened by trees and shrubbery, the glare of campfires and many shadows moving here and there. Distant, thin music and the stamping of feet on the dance-floor. A full moon.

In the foreground, surrounded by a crowd of children and listeners among them fifteen year old KRUNA, *stands white-bearded* BOGOBOJ. *At the table front, alone, sits* JUVAN, *the student.*

BOGOBOJ

(*His eyes closed, as if in a trance*). On these clear moonlit nights they ride over the backs of the hills and lie on the ledges, the summits, the plateaus. Their sheepboys, shepherds, and milk-maids, and herdsmen roam with them and guard the flocks. But the serving folk are not immortal like them. They only live a thousand years. The animals they herd are mostly roe and goats; no matter how high they climb and how wildly they frolic they never stray off to the haunts of men.

KRUNA

Why do they have only goats, father?

BOGOBOJ

They live on goatmilk. But what they prepare in their big cauldrons when the mountain fires burn, that no one knows.

KRUNA

Will they ever come back again?

BOGOBOJ

Oh, their hearts are trembling now with the joy of return. They hug the trees in monstrous glee and they listen to the pulsing sap of the pine. They kiss the hardy blossoms of the mountain-tops and feel bittersweet on their lips the taste of their own immortality. With loving hands they fondle the fur of the sacred untamed herds. The goats bleat and they answer the song from the depths of their souls. (*Weaving his head rhythmically.*) I hear in the wind the song of the goats.

KRUNA

And mortals?

BOGOBOJ

Some of them have come down from the hills and loved a mortal. So they have children, outposts, in many places. And in their eyes a diamond burns. (*To* JUVAN.) Hear, son of the sorceress.

KRUNA

And have they messengers?

BOGOBOJ

The devils who serve them. (*To* JUVAN.) Hear, son of the sorceress.

JUVAN

(*Beating his fist wildly on the table*). Don't call me that, old idiot. The midwife was my mother. Not even the money for her coffin could her magic win her.

BOGOBOJ

And your father, unbeliever?

JUVAN

I do not know my father. You know that.

BOGOBOJ

Indeed you do not know your father, son of the sorceress.

JUVAN

Be still! General of the billygoats. You're crazy.

KRUNA

Don't cross the old man. He is a prophet.

JUVAN

A gabbler, that's what he is.

BOGOBOJ

You cannot cross me, student. I alone know your mission.

JUVAN

(*Carried away, to himself*). Mission? I, of all men in that monstrous, strange city the lowest? Bed on the benches. Winter. Women gliding by. They and their rustling, God rot them. Sitting at the oven in the classroom, jealous of those seated closer, hearing nothing in my hunger and exhaustion. Cheekbones jutting. Hammering Greek into flabby rich children for one gulden a month. . . . No! That was not all. They learned to know *me*. . . . And now I am here. Among you. Among you.

BOGOBOJ

It was ordained that you should come.

KRUNA

Once they chose a man like you.

A VERY OLD WOMAN

"And purple the slippers of our Prince."

AN OLD MAN

Strong youth, you, a writer and a reader, are the man to help us.

KRUNA

(*Comes closer to the table*). Why do you stay with us?

JUVAN

(*After a pause*). Because I hate the others and you mean nothing to me. I hate them. Perhaps I hate you too.

KRUNA

You always sit apart.

JUVAN

Lucky for you. I'd spoil your fun.

KRUNA

You haven't had much fun, have you?

JUVAN

(*Slowly, simply*). True. Perhaps I've only had one joy in all my life, the time I saw a forest burn . . .

BOGOBOJ

(*Softly*). Rulers of our people. He is your son.

JUVAN

(*To himself*). And that's no lie. (*Aloud*.) And why should I not sit apart? The biggest fools among you are gone to the potato diggers to beg them for a bit of land. Soon you will all be farmers and farmers' women, stingy eaters of prune mash and lovers of stuffy rooms. Soon you will have forgotten how to steal.
(*Spits*.)

A MAN

Spit at us, do you? What do you want?

JUVAN

I want nothing. Nothing of you, nothing of myself. Only to lie on a cliff, smoking, staring at the treetops, drinking.

BOGOBOJ

(*Softly*). Empty must be the jar into which they pour their milk. (JUVAN *laughs*.)

KRUNA

Why do you laugh, student?

JUVAN

That is my greatest talent. I can laugh because I'm bored. You bore me. Perhaps that's why I stay with you.

BOGOBOJ

That is a lie, you crafty one. Know that you wait.

JUVAN

(*Struck*). I wait! Yes! Since childhood! I wait.

BOGOBOJ

And they have ordained . . .

JUVAN

Innkeeper! Ljuben!

BOGOBOJ

. . . They are agreed.

JUVAN

(*Loudly*). Innkeeper! Ljuben!

BOGOBOJ

And it shall come to pass. . . .

JUVAN

(*Bellows*). Innkeeper!

BOGOBOJ

And it must come . . .

JUVAN

(*Sharply, excited*). What?

BOGOBOJ

You know.

JUVAN

(*Jumping up*). Then woe. . . . (INNKEEPER *enters,* JUVAN *laughs*.) Woe to the innkeeper.

INNKEEPER

Hey?

JUVAN

A bottle.

INNKEEPER

Money first . . . you know that.

JUVAN

(*Throws down three silver gulden*). Dog! (INNKEEPER *whistles through his teeth*.) Just for that you'll have to crawl for it. (INNKEEPER *off hastily*. JUVAN *declaims gravely*.)

If I've not a farthing
I'll ride in a coach
And if I've a million
I'll starve with the pack.

(INNKEEPER *brings the bottle*.)

SCENE II

(TEITERLIK, *the* AMERICAN, FEIWEL. *Behind them a crowd of motley vagabonds.* BOGOBOJ *and his audience go to meet them.*)

AMERICAN

All's lost, you people.

CHORUS

Curse them. Curse them!

AMERICAN

Your packs and beggar's traps up on the wagons quickly.

YOUNG MAN

Why do we yield?

OLD MAN

The powderhorn hangs by their hearthstones.

AMERICAN

To-morrow they will drive us from our home land with their dogs.

JUVAN

Good! That's right!

CHORUS

Where can we go?

TEITERLIK

Who's playing still and dancing? (*Distant bass rhythms stop.*) You poor things! We poor things! Whither to-morrow?

CHORUS

Whither to-morrow? No one to lead us—no one to help us.

FEIWEL

What's that? No one leads? No one helps? I made a speech for you before the council. You should have heard me. They ought to write my speech down and put it in the papers. Hey, Mr. Ropedancer? Hey, Mr. American? How was my speech? What kind of lawyer am I? (*To the many who now come from the dance floor.*) All honor, says I, to the needy and they shook their fists in my face and their knives, and still I spoke on for your rights.

AMERICAN

That's a lie, man.

FEIWEL

(*Softly*). Ssh, Mr. American, that's politics! (*Loudly.*) And now I speak to you! I have connections in the highest circles. The king of Sweden is my friend. I'll write him a petition. Sure! I'm a Jew, and brave. Why are you frightened? You are so many? Why do you let yourselves be chased? Is man an animal?
(*He has grown moody.*)

JUVAN

(*Very loudly*). Light on the table, Ljuben!

FEIWEL

(*Suddenly breaks off, afraid*). Always at your service.
(*Dives into the crowd.*)

TEITERLIK

(*To* JUVAN). You in the laced coat and scholar's cap, help us now.

AMERICAN

You didn't get your learnng in a Sunday school.

TEITERLIK

You are learned. They will fear you.

JUVAN

(*Turns brusquely*). What do you want?

AMERICAN

To have you talk to them.

JUVAN

I? With them? With them? It bores me.

TEITERLIK

Beg him, the Gospodar, in our behalf.

JUVAN

(*Slowly, sharply*). It bores me.
(INNKEEPER *lights a lamp.*)

AMERICAN

Ask them to give us more time.

JUVAN

You were born upon this land but there's no land left for you.

TEITERLIK

Think of the children wandering forever; no church, no teaching!

JUVAN

You teach them to dance on the tightrope and stand on their heads.

AMERICAN

Comrade! Why talk like that? Something must be done. You can help. I'll help too.

JUVAN

I will help you if the devil helps you. (BOGOBOJ *murmurs strange words.*)

AMERICAN

Well at least give us some advice, man, if you're so brainy.

JUVAN

(*Almost phlegmatic*). Advice enough. Steal. Steal ducks, pigs, calves, but don't forget the iron things you kill with. And do you want some fine advice? Disguise yourselves as mendicant monks; steal in, ruin the women, pervert the children. Pretend you're doctors, give out tinctures, sell henbane juice as a love-philtre; or pour brandy on their open wounds. (*Suddenly in earnest.*) And here's the best advice of all. Rip the big limbs from off the trees, strip them, and dip them in pitch.

AMERICAN

I'll follow that last advice, man!

FEIWEL

(*Close to* JUVAN's *ear*). I know a good place. Mehmet Muchlis in the town. He rents weapons. (JUVAN *brusquely turns his back on them all.*)

BOGOBOJ

(*Rising*). Will you be awake when the hour comes, son of the unknown father?

JUVAN

(*Over his shoulder*). You know I sleep only by day. (*The crowd withdraws to the rear.*)

SCENE III

(STANJA *and* MIRKO *enter.*)

MIRKO

This is damned unreasonable, Stanjoschka! What are these vagabonds to us? They own nothing, they are dirty, they do not go to communion. Our fathers are fighting them. Let's go back.

STANJA

But I don't like your friends on the dancing green tinkling their silver chains.

MIRKO

How can you talk so? Duko Petkovic is there: he was one of the Emperor's Hussars at Temesvar for a whole year, and his old man has put by a good ten thousand. And young Trifunovic who inherited the bakery and knows the great Pasha. (STANJA's *expression stops him in midsentence.*) You cat! You woman! I know you want to take my friends from me; comrades I've known since I was a child, who understand me if I so much as blink at them.

MIRKO

Woe to me that I am in love with you, sniffing the odor of your body like a hound. I love, so I must bend to you, you cold one.

STANJA

Go to your friends.

MIRKO

I can't because you tell me to. But if I weren't such a coward . . . Jesus—Jesus. I would leave you standing here.

STANJA

But I am tired. I want to sit down.

MIRKO

That table with the candle! No . . . there's a man sitting there.

STANJA

The table's all right. Come.

MIRKO

A man is sitting there, I told you.

STANJA

What does it matter? Aren't you my betrothed? Can't you protect me?

MIRKO

(*Whimpering*). Oh . . . I don't want to . . . oh!

STANJA

Don't stand there looking stupid. Come. (*Both go to* JUVAN's *table.*)

MIRKO

(*Very stiffly*). We came along the road very late. Hm . . . hm . . . (JUVAN *stares at him in silent calm.*) You will allow us . . . (JUVAN *stares, without answering, at* MIRKO. MIRKO *confused.*) We don't disturb you?

JUVAN

(*After a pause*). This is an inn for all comers. And you are noble guests such as do not come every day.

MIRKO

(*Vaguely oppressed, to* STANJA). Come away! (JUVAN *moves to one side,* MIRKO *and* STANJA *sit so that* STANJA *is behind the light, with a man on either side of her and almost in darkness.* MIRKO *whispers.*) His scholar's cap and laced coat! Is it the student?

STANJA

He? I never saw him before.

MIRKO

(*To himself*). Suppose she's lying!

MIRKO

(*To* JUVAN). We're here because we lost our way, brother. You can't help roaming about, festival time.

JUVAN

Now none of your silly tricks, Mirko Milic.

MIRKO

He knows me! Damn it! (*In flattered tones, to* STANJA.) I'm not the Gospodar's son for nothing! (*To* JUVAN.) And now! We'll have a drink together! (*Takes coins from his pocket.*) I'll treat.

JUVAN

One minute, friend! Who sat here first? I! Therefore I am the host, the land owner, the king, and you are guests. You are my guests! He! Ho! Ljuben!

MIRKO

Allow me——
(INNKEEPER *comes.*)

JUVAN

Two of the same!
(INNKEEPER *off.*)

MIRKO

Allow me, and forgive me. You are respectable, a follower of the arts, with your laced coat, but . . .

JUVAN

But . . .

MIRKO

Poor! Anyone can see that. You belong to the crowd over there by the fires. (*Enter* INNKEEPER *with two bottles.* MIRKO *counts the coins into his own hand ringingly.*) You'd just as soon have me pay, wouldn't you?

JUVAN

(*Takes* MIRKO's *hand as it lies on the table and closes it*). Don't worry. Even if it's stolen my money's good. (*To the* INNKEEPER.) The ruby glasses, you ass, for guests like these.

INNKEEPER

Knew that.

MIRKO

I meant no offence.

JUVAN

No matter. (INNKEEPER *places Bohemian glasses on the table.*) These glasses are stolen, too.

STANJA

You're an awkward boor. You'll never do anything but shame me. You can learn from him what manners are.

MIRKO

(*In hurt tones*). Stanjoschka, you!
(JUVAN *pours.*)

STANJA

(*Slightly exaggerated*). I like this place. Air that tastes like honey floats down from the hills. The new mown hay has a different smell than the dry grass heaped in your meadows.
(*She laughs up the scale.*)

JUVAN

(*Gravely*). Why are you cooing, daughter of the rich?

STANJA

I laugh at the burning moths. At the bats up there I laugh . . .

MIRKO

(*Between his teeth*). You've found your tongue, silent one!

STANJA

If I was silent with you, I speak now, grumbler, and laugh.

JUVAN

I know well how to laugh. But I am never merry.

STANJA

I drink to the man who is never merry, to make him so.

JUVAN

(*Quietly*). Do not touch my glass, rich woman.

MIRKO

Shameless . . . you see? Shameless . . .

STANJA

Do what you like! (*Drains her glass, laughing.*) It pleases me to sit between two men, one a well brought up son who sees only the things he's meant to see, and the other you, you poacher laced in the laced coat. (*Pointing to the background.*) And all these motley ragged men; they please me, too.

JUVAN

The same men, daughter of the rich, that you are going to chase out with your dogs to-morrow.

STANJA

That shall not be. I say so.

JUVAN

(*Emphatically*). It shall be—I say so. It shall be your chase until they turn on you. Then let it turn again.

MIRKO

(*Rises*). Stanja, come now. We're going.

STANJA

Go if you like. You can't order me. I'm still free.

MIRKO

(*Sits*). You don't know what you're doing. You're playing with fire.

JUVAN

Mirko Milic, drink. Drink, my guest!

MIRKO

That I will do, student, I am not afraid.
(*Drinks two glasses full, one after the other.*)

STANJA

Don't drink so much. You know you cannot stand it, mother's boy!
(MIRKO *groans.*)

JUVAN

Laugh at her, Milic, she's nothing but a woman!

MIRKO

(*Speaking thickly*). Can't . . . think . . . any more. . . .

JUVAN

Why do you look at me so, bride?

STANJA

Did I look at you? Well, I didn't see you then.

JUVAN

What are you thinking?

STANJA

I was just thinking I hate blondes and like the swarthy lads. (MIRKO *shatters his glass.*) Fool!

JUVAN

(*Gravely*). A guest's privilege.
(*To* STANJA.) You are mistaken, girl, I am your enemy.

STANJA

If you only were.

JUVAN

You are right. I used too big a word. I do not love possession, but I love to steal possessions. I do not love the booty, but I love to fling it from me.

STANJA

Those who know the merchant's fingers bless the robber's hand.

JUVAN

(*Leans toward her*). You're beautiful enough.

STANJA

Enemy!

JUVAN

With your glistening hair.

STANJA

(*In quiet triumph*). Enemy!

JUVAN

I am no bed-robber.

MIRKO

(*Starting up in mad rage*). Ah! Ah! Ah! You insulted my betrothed. Draw your knife.
(*Stands with his knife raised.*)

JUVAN

(*Leisurely*). I have not even touched your betrothed, Mirko Milic.

MIRKO

Whether you have or haven't, come on!

JUVAN

Go your way! Too early yet for bloodshed.

SCENE IV

(TEITERLIK, AMERICAN, FEIWEL, KRUNA, *the crowd, group about the three.*)

VOICES

The son of the Gospodar. The little fellow. They're going to fight . . .

MIRKO

Ah! Everything is over now. If you live, I must take her like a beggar at your hands. So you must die, die, because I love her. Come on!

JUVAN

Is it your will, daughter of the rich? Shall we spill blood?

STANJA

It is my will. And may you fall.

JUVAN

Come on, then, Mirko Milic! The moon is shining for us.
(*Opens his knife. Brilliant growing moonlight. Confusion of voices dies down.* MIRKO *and* JUVAN *stand in position with blades bared.*)

SCENE V

(*Lightning, then quick darkening of the stage. Total darkness for the space of three pulse-beats. Equally quick lighting of the stage. It seems as though a giant shadow had passed above them. Endless pause of panic-stricken numbness. Every one—each petrified in a different attitude, looks in a different direction. Only the knife falls from* JUVAN's *hand as he stands in a listening attitude as if some one had called him. At the sound the paralysis breaks into a nameless, hysterical confession.)*

MIRKO

(*In the foreground, his knife still raised*). Come! Or I'll kill *you*.
(*Tears* STANJA *away with him. Fluttering laugh of fear from the crowd. It is repeated on all hands.*)

FEIWEL

Shma Ysroel!

TEITERLIK

Did you . . . oh, oh, oh . . . did you see the shadow?

CRIES

We saw! . . . We didn't see.

AMERICAN

Quiet, children. The shadow won't eat you.

FIRST VOICE

I saw him. It was a man.

SECOND VOICE

It was no man.

THIRD VOICE

A goat . . . a giant goat.

FOURTH VOICE

No, a man!

FIFTH VOICE

Where did he go? The goat, the goat!

SIXTH VOICE

Turning handsprings down the road.

TEITERLIK

No, no . . . into the house!

SCENE VI

(*The* INNKEEPER *rushes out of the house howling, his eyes wild, sinks on his knees.*)

INNKEEPER

Holy Mary, pray for us! Holy Anna, pray for us! Holy Joseph, pray for us!

AMERICAN

(*Shakes him*). Speak Ljuben! Calm yourself! What did you see?

INNKEEPER

Holy Chrysostome, pray for us! Holy Athanasius, pray for us! Cyril and Methodius, intercede for us!

AMERICAN

(*Shakes him wildly*). Man alive—what's the matter?

INNKEEPER

(*Stumbling over his words*). Beneficent hermits, pray for us! Oh, he . . . oh, it . . . (*Falls unconscious.*)

SCENE VII

(*Whitebearded* BOGOBOJ *in a white, fantastically mysterious robe, hair and beard decorated with flowers, enters. He carries panpipes in his hand.*)

BOGOBOJ

The terror has been sent to us. They send the terror before them. I slept, but now I am awake. The terror has been sent to us. Where is their son, where is he?
(*Blows on the pipes.* JUVAN *rouses with a fearful start and runs through the avenue of frightened people to the house.*)

TEITERLIK

He is a dead man now.

AMERICAN

Great God! What courage!

KRUNA

(*Enchanted*). Juvan, our leader! Now he begins to live!
(*Long pause of listening suspense. A shrill, penetrating laugh in the crowd.*)

FEIWEL

Stop that laughing, God of my Fathers!

BOGOBOJ

Gather, children, gather and prepare! They will command you. The son is with the messenger. Gather!
(*He blows on the pipes.*)

SCENE VIII

(JUVAN, *deadly pale, steps out of the door. Closes it with widespread arms.*)

JUVAN

The hour has struck. Seize whatever weapons you can find; pitchforks, axes, knives, and fire. Juvan, the man of many conspiracies, the son of this mountain soil, commands you. The doom of the rich is at hand. For he has come to us—the one who has been denied. He has escaped. Now has the secret given itself into my hands.

Curtain.

ACT FOUR

SCENE: *Interior of a wooden village church: Greek Orthodox. The room is dominated by the Ikonostas, the gay wall of gold, silver, and colored pictures which guards the holy of holies. The Ikonostas is broken by two small side doors, and the big central door, called the "royal gate." These three doors, used during the sacred performance for the exits and entrances of the priests and diakons, are now shut. A few scattered tapers are burning.*

SCENE I

Front stage before the Ikonostas, JUVAN *and the* PRIEST. *Two armed* REVOLUTIONARIES *stand guard at the church door.*

PRIEST

(*His teeth chattering*). The last day! The high altar no longer protects, nor the gracious place of the communion. Let me go. Let me die outside.

JUVAN

(*Points to the royal gate*). Did you see him in there?

PRIEST

See? Him? Did I dare to look at him? Eh, eh! He laughs at his bonds, the shaggy one.

JUVAN

And do you know who he is?

PRIEST

Do not say his name! Do not name him! You . . . you! Let me out! Let me out!

JUVAN

So you do not doubt? You believe he is what he is?

PRIEST

I believe in the death of the world. Leave me.

JUVAN

(*Takes him by the throat*). If you believe, then name his name.

PRIEST

(*Groaningly*). His given name's uprising, murder, arson, and heresy . . .

JUVAN

(*Lets him go*). Go!

PRIEST

(*Quickly takes the big Bible and a silver paten out of hiding*). I want to save the holy vessels.

JUVAN

(*Knocks the two things out of the* PRIEST's *hand with his weapon*). Jewels, gold and silver, those are what you want to save, my shrewd priest.

PRIEST

(*Running off*). I believe it is he. I believe!

SCENE II

(TEITERLIK *comes in drunk, clad half in a remarkable uniform, half in his clown's costume.*)

TEITERLIK

Captain! . . . A clean sweep! . . . Captain! We're in clover! We wallow in brandy in the barrooms. Beg to announce army growing. Serfs, tenants, yeomen, farmhands, all with us. The charcoal burners from the wood, the smugglers, and many bearded strangers forming gangs. Beg to announce sky is red. You're to be king, so they say. And I get promotion, too, if doing and dying's deserving. Captain, I'll make a good lieutenant. I'll walk before them on my hands. Think I'm not young enough? Look.
(*Tries to turn a Catherine wheel.*)

JUVAN

You shall be lieutenant as long as you are drunk. But as soon as I see you sober, you're going to be shot.

TEITERLIK

Orders're orders.

JUVAN

How big is the army, lieutenant?

TEITERLIK

A thousand of us, they say. And all those weapons! Swords, guns, and one little cannon that won't shoot. (*He falls on his knees and crosses himself.*) The one in there has brought the weapons here by magic.

SCENE III

(FEIWEL *enters stormily.*)

JUVAN

Your news!

FEIWEL

Well, Mr. General, now look here! (*To himself.*) . . . Me in a church! (*To* JUVAN.) Why are you looking at me so?

JUVAN

Insolence! You are not my equal to speak to me so!

FEIWEL

Ts, ts. Christian stays Christian. Fine revolutionaries, the *Goyim*. Give them a sabre and they strut around and play soldiers.

FEIWEL

Well, Mr. General, I thought this was to be the hour of justice and freedom. But what must I see? Murder, Mr. General! Everywhere the drunkards, the fanatics, are murdering. Nobody resisting, yet they murder. Blood of men, Mr. General, human blood, flowing under the doors, over the threshold, down the steps. . . . "Oh, woe, woe to us!" everywhere in my ears. You must stop it, you must order them back. I cannot see blood. And he in there—if he really is in there—what would he want that for?

JUVAN

Jew! Do you know why you are the lowest of all men?

FEIWEL

Everyone has a different reason.

JUVAN

Because you cannot understand bloodlust.

FEIWEL

Look at that. I thought that was what made us the chosen people!

SCENE IV

(AMERICAN *enters.*)

AMERICAN

Man, I put order in that crowd. Divided and drilled them in squads, like I learnt to in war, and each has its orders. The farms to the southward are all blazing, and now the people have broken out against the Gospodar. But there's no holding them any longer, especially the women. They want to see him.

JUVAN

They will see him.

AMERICAN

Congratulations, student. You know people. You did a good job not to show the hidden one, but to bring him here tight in a covered cage.

JUVAN

Fear death, if you cannot believe.

AMERICAN

Don't let's fool ourselves, sir. I see straight. I wasn't born yesterday. I learned a lot across the water. There are great settlements there, and suddenly the spirit comes over these sons of Adam; they pray wildly, journey over the land, murdering and burning in religious frenzy, tearing the clothes from their bodies, and practicing vice in the name of the Lord. But there's something to be learned by a man with brains, from both God and madness.

JUVAN

I lived a prisoner in my body. Then came the vision, fever broke loose in me, and seized you all. I will do my work because I believe. And you, American, must believe too!

AMERICAN

Like you I will believe in revenge. My father ended very high. Five feet above ground.

TEITERLIK

The crowd's outside!

SCENE V

(*Enter* BOGOBOJ, *dressed as at the end of Act Three.*)

BOGOBOJ

Prince of the people! Son of the unknown! You are to prophesy and show him to us.

JUVAN

How strong is your madness, how high your faith?

BOGOBOJ

Of blood we have drunken that was wine. And of wine that was blood.

JUVAN

Are you ready, then, for the service?

BOGOBOJ

We are thirsty unto death for the mass, we are ravening for the liturgy.

SCENE VI

(*The crowd flows into the room, drunk and lusting for miracles. Men and women carry all sorts of weapons, scythes and threshing flails, and a few tar torches.*)

CHORUS

Let us see him . . . see him . . . see him!

KRUNA

(*At* JUVAN's *feet*). You our lord, exalt us!

JUVAN

You are not yet fit to worship his presence.

KRUNA

Teach us!

JUVAN

If you can grasp hs meaning you may redeem the world.

KRUNA

And you our ruler.

BOGOBOJ

Many centuries have you slept. Now you are awake.

JUVAN

What are you all?

KRUNA

Men!

JUVAN

That is just it. He says unto you, "Be men no more."

KRUNA

What are we to be?

JUVAN

Look into your soul and find the answer. (KRUNA *looks at* JUVAN *with a curious expression, then slowly loosens her long hair, and shakes her head so that it floats about her.*) Have you seen and understood?

KRUNA

Release!

CHORUS

(*On a scream*). Release——!

JUVAN

Yes, release! For man is knotted, man is cramped——

CHORUS

Break through our torment——
(JUVAN *breaks a great cross over his knee and throws it into the crowd.*)

FEIWEL

Oi, my poor brother!

JUVAN

Man is the animal crucified.

BOGOBOJ

Did you hear the word?

KRUNA

Lord, take us from the cross!

JUVAN

I will give you back to the fields, you doe with the dancing eyes! All of you! In your eyes I see the struggle of animals in death. I am wide awake. I see the beasts. There! Look of the murdered stallion! There! Look of the strangled wild cat. There! Last glint from the eyes of a dying wolf.
(*The vision of the faces is too strong. He closes his eyes for a moment.*)

KRUNA

Free the poor animal!

CHORUS

Free the beast!

JUVAN

(*Gesturing toward the royal door of the Ikonostasis*). The sight of him will free you!

CHORUS

Show us the holy god!
(*The people start a wild milling. The women shake out their unbound hair and be-*

gin to tear their clothes. The men have hard work to keep on their faces the expression of sullen brooding embarrassment which is the lightning that precedes a frightful mass outbreak.)

JUVAN

He is the way back, the way home. We broke out of the ancient forests of night, blinking in the sunlight. Let us return to the forest. Our eyes will become big and quiet again. He will lead us home to the night when our task is done, when nothing built by man is left standing; when the hereditary lie is wiped out and vengeance wreaked on man; when the last plow lies rotting in a bloody ditch.

BOGOBOJ

(*Holds an embroidered vestment before him.*) So, with three fingers, I grasp the narrow stola of the diakon and hurry down through the temple, flying with the drunken flight of the heavenly spirits. . . . (*Moves tottering through the church.*) To the services, you believers! Come, rouse your sense to the surge of the mass, to the flow of the ritual.
(*Turns back to the Ikonostas. Chorus turns, as one, to the altar.*)

JUVAN

Begin your service, Diakon.

BOGOBOJ

So be it.

JUVAN

What light is fitting to receive him?

BOGOBOJ

Darkness.

JUVAN

What color for his greeting?

BOGOBOJ

Color of flesh slain in lust.

JUVAN

What music to acclaim him?

BOGOBOJ

Swelling and deafening.

JUVAN

Where are the musicians?

BOGOBOJ

You grimy ones. Begin!
(*Charcoal burners group at one side of the altar. They wear fur clothing and horn ornaments on their heads. Their instruments are drums, bag-pipes, tambourine, and two-sided guzla. Candles go out.*)

AMERICAN

(*To* JUVAN). Enough of this madness! Are you bent on destruction?
(*The charcoal burners start, softly, at first, to play their monotonous music which repeats one rhythmic figure again and again.* JUVAN *steps into the shadow.*)

BOGOBOJ

(*Enchanted*). Beloved, sing the litany with me! (*Psalm-wise.*)

Tragos Lyaios Oikoloi
Venga Venga Chaire moi
Pomiluj Nas Pomiluj!

(*Music becomes louder and quicker.*)

CHORUS

(*On their knees*).

Tragos Lyaios Oikoloi
Venga Venga Chaire moi
Pomiluj Nas Pomiluj!

(*The women start screaming, the men cry out gaspingly.*)

FEIWEL

(*In the grip of his eternal difference, prays*). *Shma ysroel, adonoi, elohenu adonoi echod.*

AMERICAN

(*Fighting the hypnosis in vain*). I have a clear head, but it's got me. (*Throws himself down howling.*) Pomiluj Nas Pomiluj!

ALL

(*In a rhythmic daze*). Pomiluj Nas Pomiluj! (JUVAN *steps forth.*)

SCENE VII

(STEVAN, *the* MOTHER, MIRKO, STANJA, BABKA, *the* ELDERS *of* MODRYGOR *and* KRASNOKRAJ, *a few farm-hands with lanterns, make a path for themselves through the throng, which gives way before them, suddenly dumb. Music breaks off.*)

STEVAN

(*His foot on the altar step, to* JUVAN). Rioters! Blasphemers, murderers! I come unarmed, with the women of my household, bringing you the message of the Elders.

CHORUS

Beat them to death!

JUVAN

Not a sound from you! (*To* STEVAN.) And what do you wish?

STEVAN

You have burned down our villages, more ruthless than the Turkish hordes. You have murdered and maimed men, women and children, dazed and defenceless. If I wished to act according to the word of men and God I would not be standing here.

JUVAN

What do you want?

STEVAN

My heart was always too soft. Do you think I sent riders to the city to the Turkish governor, for soldiers to trample down your madmen? No, I did not send, you bloodsuckers. Understand that!

AMERICAN

We're not crazy enough to swallow that!

JUVAN

And what do you wish?

STEVAN

I wish to bargain with you. You destroyer in a scholar's coat!

JUVAN

What do you want us to do?

STEVAN

Drop your weapons, your plunder, your torches, and disband.

JUVAN

What do you offer in return?

STEVAN

Is it not enough that you go free and unpunished?

JUVAN

That is not the sort of bargain you bargainers are in the habit of making.

STEVAN

Kneel before me, all of you and hear the merciful decision of the council of Elders. If you submit immediately, all the bloodshed will be forgotten, and . . . kneel, weep, you murderers . . . and every landless, wandering immigrant will receive some of our waste land and seed for its sowing.
(CHORUS *silent and sullen.*)

TEITERLIK

(*Whimpering*). Though I'm a lieutenant . . . land . . . my land . . .

JUVAN

You have not told us all your demands.

STEVAN

(*Softly*). You must surrender him—instantly.

JUVAN

Whom?

STEVAN

(*Shamefaced, between his teeth*). The unbaptised!

JUVAN

His name!

STEVAN

(*Writhing with shame*). Don't pretend, you fiend! There—in the holy of holies . . .

JUVAN

Name him!

STEVAN

(*Loudly, tonelessly*). His name? I do not know his name. He is my son.

MIRKO

Father! You!

BOGOBOJ

A God was born to the poor in a stable.

MAN'S VOICE

But this one was born to the rich.

WOMAN'S VOICE

Hehehahaha! The rich people's secret!

BOGOBOJ

Who dares say: "He is my son?"

JUVAN

Gospodar! Your demand is refused.
He, who is our victory remains.

STEVAN

Who stands in a father's way?
(*Tries to advance, but armed men who have gathered about* JUVAN *hold their weapons towards him.*)

MOTHER

(*Stepping forward*). This father hates his son. But no man knows what my life has been since that day. Let me go to him. . . .

BABKA

Back, woman. (*Pushes* MOTHER *aside.*) His parents denied him. But I suckled him, I nursed him, his only servant till this day. I alone have power over him. He went to sleep to my songs. (*To* JUVAN.) Devil! I warn you. Let me coax him.

JUVAN

There is another woman with you!

MIRKO

(*Seizes* STANJA *in an iron grip*). Hide!

JUVAN

Gospodar! See, I'll show you what Juvan is. Suddenly he changes his mind. He spits now on what was precious and holy to him. Your terms are accepted and I will close with you.

CHORUS

Traitor.

AMERICAN

I never understood him. . . .

BOGOBOJ

Bow to the will. It does not come from him.

JUVAN

(*Very emphatically*). I close with you. You shall have him. He returns if she, the pretty one, there—Mirko's bride, if . . . if she goes in and leads him to you.

STEVAN

The face that its father did not dare to look on, year after year . . . she, a maiden?

JUVAN

She can save you.

STEVAN

(*Softly, horrified*). Away from here, my daughter!

MIRKO

(*Slackly, with infinite sadness*). For the second time we must flee from him, Stanja. The student is stronger than we. And . . . we bring no happiness for each other . . . I shall die without you. . . . I release you.

ELDERS OF KRASNOKRAJ AND MODRYGOR

(*Whispering to* STANJA). Do not be afraid. We'll arm ourselves and take you back secretly to your parents.

STEVAN'S FAMILY AND THE ELDERS

(*Speaking all together to* STANJA, *softly*). Away! Softly! Unnoticed! Escape!

JUVAN

What answer?

STANJA

(*Slowly ascending the altar steps*). This! (STANJA *and* JUVAN *look long into each other's eyes.*)

BOGOBOJ

(*Seized by a fit of trembling*). Children! The secret of the mass is at hand!

CHORUS

(*Moved, melodious*).
The fair one is fair,
A wreath of ribbon in her hair,
And bridal clothes, and bridal clothes.

KRUNA

(*Wraps herself in her hair*). Weep!
(*Russian music, softly, in a different rhythm.*)

MOTHER

Never has he seen a young woman. She goes to her death.

MIRKO

To my brother.

JUVAN

Stanja. Am I your enemy now?

STANJA

Not as much as I am yours.

JUVAN

Are you doing this to save your people?

STANJA

Mine? They are not mine.

JUVAN

Why are you doing it then, Stanja?

STANJA

Robber! I fling away your booty!

JUVAN

(*Haughtily concealing his defeat*). Step down. You shall not be my sacrifice.

STANJA

Your sacrifice? Who are you? Did I ever know you? I do not know. (*She bends before the Ikonostas.*) Here I have already stood to receive God. (*Rising above her triumph.*) Go, servant! Open!

JUVAN

Here is a knife for you.
You understand? A knife.

STANJA

(*Takes the knife*). I will cut through his bonds. But for myself I will not use it. Open!
(JUVAN *raises his hand, but cannot move.* STANJA, *without looking back, disappears through the royal gate. Music ceases.*)

SCENE VIII

(MIRKO *has taken the half of the broken cross with the two silver-set arms and throws himself on* JUVAN.)

MIRKO

For the second time I meet you! (*He falls upon the outstretched steel of one of the guards.*) Oh . . . oh . . . oh . . . Father . . . oh . . . oh . . . oh.
(*Dies.*)

STEVAN

(*Kneeling by the dead man, after a long pause*). He is not breathing (*With a hoarse cry.*) But he. . . .

MOTHER

(*Who cannot hide the crazy light of sinful joy in her eyes*). Justice! O Justice!
(*Throws herself upon the corpse.*)

BABKA

(*Coldly, seeng the mother's conflicting emotions*). Woman! Stand up!

STEVAN

(*Rises. In a hard voice, to a farmhand*). Take hold of the dead man and lift him.

MODRYGOR

Brother! Are you going to desert the girl?

STEVAN

Her betrothed is dead. She is no longer ours. Pass.

(*Men with the corpse move toward the door,* STEVAN, MOTHER, BABKA *following.*)

KRASNOKRAJ

(*To* MODRYGOR). Kinsman! Let us hide and wait for the daughter of Kauzelni vrh.

STEVAN

(*Calling into the room from the church door*). If you want to destroy us, hurry. I deceived you. The Janissaries have been on the march for hours.
(*He and his family off.*)

SCENE IX

BOGOBOJ

I feel the holy approach. Prepare! Pray! A moment more, and you will see him.

CHORUS

(*Drowning their rising fear in song*). Pomiluj Nas Pomiluj.
(JUVAN *suddenly, starting up, in haggard triumph.*)

JUVAN

Jew, out to the green. To the linden bell! Ring, Jew, ring the bells, the wedding bells.

FEIWEL

Hei! Hei! The Jew is going to ring the Christian bells, the Jew, the Jew!
(*Runs off.*)

AMERICAN

It seemed to me just now that I heard distant trumpets.

TEITERLIK

Damn! I'd rather be on a rope stretched between two roofs. The chill of dawn is in my bones. Who wants my job?

JUVAN

What have I done?
(*A monstrous cry of joy sings on, descending chromatically, not human, inhumanly superhuman, sounding from the holy of holies. The bells chime in wildly.*)

BOGOBOJ

Lo, the miracle!

KRUNA

Why did you not sacrifice me?

CHORUS

She is dead.
(JUVAN, *with a hollow cry, throws himself against the royal gate.* BOGOBOJ *bars his way with outstretched arms.*)

JUVAN

Save her. . . .

BOGOBOJ

Stay not the sacrifice.

JUVAN

Back, old man.

BOGOBOJ

Endure the holy moment.
(*He clings to* JUVAN *with monstrous strength.*)

JUVAN

I suffer.
(*They struggle. The bells cease. The two* ELDERS *appear by the altar rail.*)

KRASNOKRAJ

Hold me! My knees are trembling.

MODRYGOR

There! Ah, I saw something! Now! There! Behind that last window. A girl's shadow. Quick! Through the little door.
(*They disappear through a secret door.*)

FEIWEL

(*Appears at the rail, his teeth chattering, softly*). Horns! Horns sound from all the hills——
(*Makes off.*)

JUVAN

(*Has overcome the giant old man, who totters aside*). Stanja!
(*Scarcely has he taken the first wild step to-

ward the holy of holies when he becomes rigid.)

CHORUS

He is coming!
(Everyone on the stage retreats, a dark mass. The great royal gate of the Ikonostas slowly opens of its own accord. Behind it the great high altar becomes visible, blindingly radiant with a thousand candles.)

BOGOBOJ

(On his face). I see.

CHORUS

(Prostrate). We see him.
(The high altar is tremulous with flame. Before the audience can see anything else clearly the curtain falls.)

Curtain.

ACT FIVE

The ruins of STEVAN'S *farm, the courtyard. In the background the walls of the outbuildings. The big courtyard door alone stands open and unharmed, and behind it the devastated fields are visible.*

Left, the blackened but not crumbled farmhouse, with the door, to which three steps lead. At either side of the door a rough bench. In the middle a spring. Right foreground a small grassy rise in the ground, rising off into the wings, indicates that a street leads through the courtyard. Late morning.

SCENE I

STEVAN *and the* PHYSICIAN *step out of the door.*

PHYSICIAN

(Playing with the key). Your secret, this key to it, and my absent-mindedness, have sufficed, and a whole little world has been destroyed. Oh, marvelously complete chain of causation which needs no superhuman agency to fulfill its inevitable wonders. God himself, as Voltaire says, would have to convert himself to atheism.

STEVAN

What's all that you're saying?

PHYSICIAN

Ah, yes, I know. The secret was the primal cause that started it. But what, at bottom, is your secret? Nothing but leftover fears, the dregs, the undigested food in the belly of evolution. Ah, you ought to learn to read French.

STEVAN

Sir!

PHYSICIAN

Superstition, Stevan Milic, that's all it was —yours and theirs. You cannot blame me. I always warned you. I offered over and over again to take the fearful changeling to a home. But vanity with its serpent eye froze all of you in terror. A day had to come when the stench would be discovered, even in the house of the mighty. . . . Now it has been hideously brought to light.

STEVAN

Yes, and in all my misery I thank God for it.

PHYSICIAN

The superstition of those poor people is more justifiable than yours. For need and suffering crave redemption, and they easily see God or His opposite in a human monster.

STEVAN

Now I, too, am as poor as the poorest.

PHYSICIAN

(*Claps him on the shoulder, heartily*). You won't be for long. For a man is born to poverty or riches just as he is to prophecy. It is simply a certain arrangement of the human tissues. The rabble have shed much blood, but the soldiers have shed even more blood of theirs. The poor pay double. Did you lose your son?

STEVAN

Both sons, Master.

PHYSICIAN

The other, they say, ran off into the burning woods and died there.

STEVAN

Stifled or burned to death, who knows?

PHYSICIAN

Did they find him?

STEVAN

I have asked no one.

PHYSICIAN

Well, life still lies before you.

STEVAN

I feel as if I had lived many lives.

PHYSICIAN

You are only fifty.

STEVAN

And now for the first time I feel as though that age were really youth.

PHYSICIAN

I wish I were made of your mettle. (*Looks at the house-walls.*) Traces of the Janissaries' bullets here, too. After all, the best of them was the student. What do you know of him?

STEVAN

Not a lad of us but knew his pretty mother once.

PHYSICIAN

He was a great man. He was well known to the authorities, an arch-schemer, slippery as an eel. My diagnosis is a plain case of religious mania. They will never let him off with a flogging.

STEVAN

I hate no one any more.

PHYSICIAN

And that crazy graybeard, the prophet, nothing could be done for him, either. They buried him yesterday.

STEVAN

Tell me, Doctor, how could all these things happen in so short a time?

PHYSICIAN

The world of men, my friend, no less than that of nature, has, I regret to say, its unplumbed seasons, eclipses, northern lights, and magnetic storms; convulsions of the established order. Original chaos surges to the surface. The animal hidden in us takes possession.

STEVAN

I do not understand what you are saying. But it may well be. For all my sorrow my heart feels so light, so light!

PHYSICIAN

That is a noble sentiment, Stevan Milic! Haha! See how catastrophes, like everything else, are only there to be gabbled about. And over there in the shed lies a poor patient shot through the lung. A poor rope-dancer, who cannot live out the day. I must steal a march on that damned priest. (*Raises his tricorn.*) You can always find me, if you want me. Excuse me now.
(*Off.*)

SCENE II

(MOTHER *appears in the doorway.*)

STEVAN

Mother! (*Takes her by the hand.*) Have you come out of that black room at last, and dressed in this lovely old dress I like so well?

MOTHER

Yes, Father. This morning dawned so blue . . . I . . . I . . . I . . . Come sit down with me, Father!
(*They sit on the bench by the door.*)

STEVAN

What are you hiding from me?

MOTHER

I am lost. I must tell you something terrible, something mortally sinful.

STEVAN

I know. Say it!

MOTHER

Mortal sin, Father.

STEVAN

Say the word, Mother.

MOTHER

(*Softly*). I am happy.

STEVAN

I understand. I, too . . . I too . . . (*Buries his head in his hands.*) . . . am happy.

MOTHER

Our children are dead.

STEVAN

The wellformed and the other.

MOTHER

Our pride and our shame.

STEVAN

One could not live without the other. That was fate.

MOTHER

Eternal bliss is barred to me . . . for, Father . . . as Mirko lay bleeding . . . happiness welled up in my heart, happiness for the other one.

STEVAN

He was the one you really loved.

MOTHER

I never looked upon his face. So he was my pain day in and day out. And yet I worshipped him, the poor accursed one. Now he has gone in flaming death . . . I suffer . . . and yet I am released.

STEVAN

Released! Children do not make men happy.

MOTHER

Only women, as long as the milk is in their breasts.

STEVAN

But children and rooftree grow and crowd out man's heaven.

MOTHER

And his love.

STEVAN

Do you know, Mother, there is something else that makes me happy and young.

MOTHER

Tell me.

STEVAN

(*With a gesture toward the ruins*). This destruction.

MOTHER

Yes, we are poor. The barns and dairies are burned down, the pens empty, the storehouses stripped . . .

STEVAN

But our hidden shame is gone. This I have discovered: Possession is concealment and in all order grins the hidden thing. And as our secrets wax, so wanes our youth. But to shoulder each day, boldly carefree, singing, that . . . that is youth. (*Stretches out his arms.*) And I have it again.

MOTHER

Father!

STEVAN

Mother!

MOTHER

What are you saying? We are no longer father and mother.

STEVAN

True, father and mother no longer. But what are we?

MOTHER

Don't you know the word?

STEVAN

(*Looks at her long*). Wife!

MOTHER

(*Her voice trembling*). Husband!

STEVAN

So long since I used that word——

MOTHER

(*Tears streaming*). So long . . . and where was I?

STEVAN

By my side. But awakening from all this fever I see you now, you . . . for the first time I see you again.

MOTHER

But this is no longer I——

STEVAN

I had to lose everything to find you.

MOTHER

I am no longer I.

STEVAN

Lovelier, lovelier, than ever I find you. The sun, this golden sun on your face—what matter if it is the light of your sunset?

MOTHER

You never looked at me when I was beautiful.

STEVAN

The ripened years are best. This gray in your hair moves me, moves me so, so deeply. (*Hovering over her.*) Holy—sweet—mysterious.

MOTHER

(*Her voice fails*). You . . .

STEVAN

No silver wedding will I seal with you but our second betrothal . . . (MOTHER *sinks into his arms.*) . . . with this kiss! (*They kiss long and deeply. He rises, stamps his feet wide apart, loudly.*) Ah! He! Ho! Haha! Wife! You! Mine! I am new, all new. Do you hear? Bold, unthinking, whistling, to meet the day. (*After a little pause.*) An old lame horse is all that's left, but we can harness him and start again singing . . . hahaha . . . singing!

(*Goes off to the fields through the courtyard door.* MOTHER *looks after him, her arms timidly stretched toward him.*)

SCENE III

(STANJA *enters slowly, sits on the edge of the well and remains rigid, impenetrable.*)

MOTHER

Still here!

STANJA

Always here. Why do you distrust me, Mother?

MOTHER

Our son is dead. Nothing more binds you to us.

STANJA

I stay true to your son, Mother.

MOTHER

Your people have sent for you.

STANJA

My people! Always my people. Who are my people! Let me stay with you.

MOTHER

You see there is no longer any home here. Your place is where wealth and happiness are, at home where the new suitors are already standing at the door. Here there is room for nothing but hard hands that want to work.

STANJA

My hands want to work, Mother.

MOTHER

Why should you wear out your days with us old folk that have worn out our own?

STANJA

Because I am true to your son.

MOTHER

You never loved him, you strange girl, and now he is dead.

STANJA

Why do you distrust me?

MOTHER

I don't distrust you any more. When you came to us, young, pretty, silent, my haughty daughter-in-law, with your youthful breasts, a stranger, then I did hate you. I do not know what happened to you that night. Let me see your face. (STANJA *turns her face away.*) Child! I no longer hate you. No, I trust you now.

STANJA

Then let me stay here.

MOTHER

Why do you not tell——

STANJA

(*From a distance*). Tell——

MOTHER

No, don't tell me. Ah, when I look at you I cannot believe you are so much younger than I, daughter. Now I begin to love you.

STANJA

I know you are not my enemy any longer.

MOTHER

That is just why it is that, with a heavy heart, I tell you . . . go, go. What do you want here? Everything is soon over for a woman. She has only one day, one hour, on which to build her power. You will find a new man, you are so pretty; perhaps a better man.

STANJA

I am true to your son. Let me stay. I am not afraid to work. Let me help you, Mother.

SCENE IV

(FEIWEL, *his peddler's pack on his back, comes along the road.*)

FEIWEL

(*From a distance, in great excitement*). God, how much has happened! God, what I have had to see! Almighty, what I am still living through! This lovely courtyard, this princely courtyard, this royal courtyard. Eijajajei! Such a fortune. Gone! (*Clenching his fists.*) The blood hounds.

MOTHER

You cannot have lost much, Feiwel. You carry your wealth on your back.

FEIWEL

Is sympathy nothing, and sleepless nights? It is true my fortune is all moveable, but that's just why I mix with so many people. With my soft heart . . . how can I—help myself? . . . I have to live everyone's sorrows, his bankruptcies, his misfortunes. God, what don't I have to bear? The Christians are wonderful beings, but they don't know what sympathy is.

MOTHER

And yet you egged them on and spoke for them.

FEIWEL

(*Answers with an exaggerated start*). God of Justice, who put that lie on me? My enemies, the godless in Mizraim. I am an educated man. I can read the German newspapers, and I know what politics is. And because I'm a born speaker I made a speech to the Elders. What good did it do me? I spoke up for the starving out of sympathy. The greatest statesmen make speeches pro and con. And that is why, God of Justice, they call me a man who egged them on? But of course, when the hail falls, the Jew is stoned.

MOTHER

Weren't you one of the wildest, Feiwel?

FEIWEL

I? Woe! I must sit down. (*Sits on the bench.*) That is my fate. I am in it but not in it and not in it but in it. I was coming along the road just like now. Feiwel is weak—Feiwel is timid. Feiwel would never make trouble, but they swept me along. Why did I go? Why? To calm the wild *Goyim*. I was only a Kibbitzer. Out of sympathy for you. But I know, you want to accuse me, ruin me . . .

MOTHER

No, not that, Jew. I accuse no one.

FEIWEL

That is a speech that God will write down in His golden book. All those whom He would smite—He has smitten. The American is dead. The rope-dancer—he's dying, and the leader of the rabble——

STANJA

(*Nonchalantly*). The leader?

FEIWEL

(*Shades his eyes, peering into the distance*). Wait, perhaps we can see it from here.

STANJA

What?

FEIWEL

(*Grinning*). Ah, miss, nothing for you. Still, I must say, with all respects for the young miss . . .

STANJA

What are you looking at?

FEIWEL

You can't see it from here.

STANJA

What can't be seen?

FEIWEL

What they've fixed on the hill for the student.

STANJA

(*Quietly*). Then it is all over?

FEIWEL

No! It takes place at noon. But the crowd is gathering now. Something else only Christians can stand. (*Takes his pack off.*) But I'm forgetting business. I'll show you what kind of a man I am. I am the only one who fitted himself to what has happened. In the midst of the fighting, (oh, my cramps), I got hold of all the things that are needed for building homes again. (*Peddler's whine.*) Nails of all sizes, practical tools for sale, lime, real gold cheap collar-buttons, Christian holy pictures, guaranteed durable, sweet-tasting laxative . . .

MOTHER

Go, Feiwel.

FEIWEL

I stay where I'm not wanted? Your servant, ladies. (*Zigzags off.*)

STANJA

(*Takes* MOTHER'S *hand*). Mother?

MOTHER

I do not understand you, but . . . (*Kisses her.*) . . . live with us from now on, bride of my son. I will tell my husband.

(STANJA *sinks her head on her breast,* MOTHER *goes into the house.* STANJA *sits on the edge of the well again.*)

SCENE V

(*Enter* GOSPODAR JEVREM VESILIC *and* STANJA'S MOTHER.)

JEVREM

We have come ourselves. You paid no attention to all our messengers and the wagon that was to have fetched you came back empty.

STANJA'S MOTHER

So we toiled along the hard road ourselves, child, and we have come to take you home.

STANJA

(*As if she had not heard*). How are you, Father and Mother?

JEVREM

Heaven destroys only Sodom.

STANJA'S MOTHER

But he spares the righteous.

JEVREM

We have no evil secret.

STANJA'S MOTHER

And we hide no sin in our house.

JEVREM

Pride goes before a fall.

STANJA'S MOTHER

A pitcher at the edge of a table is ready to be smashed.

JEVREM

It is well that they are not here so we need speak no false words.

STANJA'S MOTHER

The souls of the righteous shun the godless. . . .

JEVREM

And we are glad nothing came of it.

STANJA'S MOTHER

The dead man was a rag in the wind. Sorrow and shame has been all our portion.

JEVREM

Such a match. We are highly respected, but it is almost a stain on us.

STANJA'S MOTHER

We will burn candles.

JEVREM

And we have just the man for you.

STANJA'S MOTHER

A better man. . . .

JEVREM

With a family such as you don't get every day.

STANJA'S MOTHER

And they are richer than these here were.

JEVREM

Be happy, then, you wicked girl, and say a word to us.

STANJA

I am Milic's betrothed, Father.

JEVREM

(*Overcome by excitement against his daughter*). Don't cross me, girl. I came. But I am full of wrath.

STANJA'S MOTHER

You are not the same to us after all this business.

STANJA

What harm did I do you?

JEVREM

Everybody is to blame for his own misfortunes.

STANJA'S MOTHER

You always were one for not wanting to obey, you sly cat. That brings misfortune.

JEVREM

All your friends bring their parents happiness. All of them well married. Misfortune is a disgrace.

STANJA

I obeyed you, my parents.

JEVREM

Yes, but unwillingly, and with the bit between your teeth. We do not understand you. I beat you too little.

STANJA

Why do you abuse me now?

JEVREM

Bad results deserve the stick.

STANJA

You brought me to this house yourselves.

JEVREM

Don't contradict your father. The gall is rising in me. Come now.

STANJA

I stay here, my parents, in my widowhood.

STANJA'S MOTHER

Widowhood, you crazy thing? You are a virgin, and that is the only thing left to you that pays.

JEVREM

For the last time I tell you, come.

STANJA

Go back home, Father and Mother.

JEVREM

(*Furious, raises his stick at her*). Ah! Woe! You belong to me. Get up, you bitch. The devil knows what you've been up to.

STANJA'S MOTHER

Jesus! Can't you see what you're doing to your father? Don't anger him any more. He is old.

JEVREM

(*Gasping*). My heart, my heart . . .

STANJA'S MOTHER

(*Shrieks*). If anything happens to him, you killed him.

STANJA

Father and Mother, go away from here, go.

JEVREM

I go, go. I won't drag you away, I won't see you again, you are no longer my daughter. But one last word. If by tomorrow sundown you have not crept home hugging the cross, you will die of my curse. (*Bellowing.*) My curse!
(*Quickly off.*)

STANJA'S MOTHER

(*Hurrying after him*). Vesilic, don't! Don't Jevrem Vesilic. (*She calls back menacingly.*) You! You——

STANJA

(*Alone*). Not of this curse will I die. (*Choked.*) Where? . . . Where? Where? (*Looks in the same direction as* FEIWEL *did, then suddenly turns to find* JUVAN, *in chains, before her. Behind him is an escort consisting of the* BASHI BAZOOK *and two soldiers.*)

SCENE VI

JUVAN

Bashi Bazook! Did I take advantage of the privilege of the condemned?

BASHI

You waved aside the food and left the wine standing.

JUVAN

Then you still owe me the fulfillment of a wish.

BASHI

That is not written in my orders.

JUVAN

Nor is it written in your orders that if you deny me I can still escape. It would not be the first time.

BASHI

I will have your feet shackled.

JUVAN

There is no need. See the truth in my eyes. You have my word. Let me talk to this woman, only for a moment. I will give you no trouble.

BASHI

Will you keep your word?

JUVAN

See the truth in my eyes!

BASHI

Then for your sake I will overstep my orders, even though you do eat unclean meat. (*Commanding the two Janissaries.*) About face. Ten paces forward. March! Halt. Turn. (*Soldiers posted outside audience's line of vision.* BASHI *commands them.*) Shoulder arms. Hup, hup, hup. (*To* JUVAN.) Make one move and you will both be shot. I shall stand over there and count several times to a hundred.
(*Off to the soldiers.*)

SCENE VII

JUVAN

You know where I am going. (STANJA *silent.*) I knew that I would meet you on this road. So I went with my eyes closed.

STANJA

I waited.

JUVAN

You know the fearful question burning in me, Stanja.

STANJA

(*Very tenderly*). I know it. Go in peace, in peace, Juvan.

JUVAN

But he screamed, a scream of love!

STANJA

Clean I am and yours, until death. Go in peace, Juvan.

JUVAN

How is it, beloved? This is the first time I have spoken to you. And yet how many paths we have walked together hand in hand.

STANJA

This is not the first time I speak to you. I have heard this new voice of yours in many dreams.

JUVAN

Speak, speak, speak! Back there a man is counting.

STANJA

One rainy night you came into the house for shelter. You sat on the bench and I passed through the room, once, twice . . .

JUVAN

I have . . . forgotten.

STANJA

I have not forgotten.

JUVAN

Wait! I have not forgotten. In my darkness, searching—a gleam of light beneath the door.

STANJA

And though you did not recognize me when I sat at the table with my betrothed, I know you knew me.

JUVAN

Yes. That is so. Why else should I have had to wound you? And then the secret leaped between us.

STANJA

(*Very softly*). The animal.

JUVAN

See! Now I feel as if the secret had broken loose from us. (*Grasping her hand.*) No, no. Not from you . . . me!

STANJA

(*Low, as if comforted*). Was it you?

JUVAN

But I threw you before him.

STANJA

(*A flash of bitterness in her pride*). That is not true. I conquered you. I went in myself, of my free will.

JUVAN

You conquered me. As I gave you the knife, trembling, I was lost, my cause was lost, and that of my people, and the Turkish crescent threatened from the hill.

STANJA

(*Mothering*). You, . . . now you have come to me.

JUVAN

Madness! Who was I! Who! Lying on my back I stared at the dead sky without thoughts, full only of a passion for vengeance on something I had never known, perhaps my unknown father. Hate for the secure, the righteous, the smug, and pious. Longing to return to animal eyes and breath. Only one lust in me, the lust for ruin. Only one happiness, to bellow into the storm, only one light, the light of a great fire. Forever joined to my companions in my thirst for the ecstasy of destruction. But then . . .

STANJA

Then, my love?

JUVAN

Then came day after all those burning nights, and I woke under this spring sky. It is my last day. Because I hated, a woman had to shatter and wake me. Oh, the miracle of the morning came to me. For the first time I heard the lark, a burning song against the sun, and a shout broke from me because of the wonder of the world. Then I knew you, you, everywhere.

STANJA

Speak, speak, speak. A man is counting over there.

JUVAN

Loving you, I loved. My chained hand was softly hollowed to gather, to caress. Oh, woman, with your clear strong limbs! Love . . . first love . . . is so strong . . . so strong. . . .
(*Tears run down his cheeks.*)

STANJA

Then tell me, mouth that is still alive, why, if we were made for one another, it was not to be?

JUVAN

Because everything eternal fears fulfillment.

STANJA

(*Screaming*). I want you, forever, forever. Do not go from me, now. I must tell you.

JUVAN

(*Tearing at his chains*). Stanja! Speak! He . . .

STANJA

(*In a shining voice*). No, my beloved. No! This life is yours.

JUVAN

Are you saying that just to make my dying easier?

STANJA

(*Clings to him*). How can I live when you no longer live?

JUVAN

(*Suddenly*). I feel he has stopped counting.

STANJA

Listen and act quickly, while there is time. If you love me, let us die together. One step and they will kill us both.

JUVAN

Tell me again that you escaped unharmed.

STANJA

You know the truth. And now, my life, just a few steps. They will shoot and all will be well.

JUVAN

(*After a pause*). No!

STANJA

(*Trembling*). There is yet time.

JUVAN

No, you must live. I must know that you, my wife, are still in the world like light and like warmth and that I leave a hearth behind me.

STANJA

(*Sliding down to his feet*). Again you deny me. Again!

SCENE VIII

(BASHI BAZOOK *and soldiers appear.*)

BASHI

I have graciously counted. Now come, student!
(*Lays his hand on him.*)

JUVAN

(*Shakes off the hand*). You are only the last link in the chain of my destiny. Death is the climax of my life's fulfillment.
(*Quickly off, followed by the escort.*)

STANJA

(*Alone*). A mere moment longer for him. But I must bear out my life—all my life—accursed.

MOTHER

(*Stepping out of the house*). I have cooked a meal. We must call your father. Who is coming?

NINTH AND LAST SCENE

(*Drunken* HANGMAN-*trapper comes in his rude wagon drawn by a miserable donkey.*)

HANGMAN

Huah! Prr! Prr!
Hey! You women of the house! Have you a little brandy left? (*Women silent in horror.*) What, no one here? The inn gone? Well! I have enough for now. Do you know me?

MOTHER

Go away. . . . Hangman!

HANGMAN

Ow, what, what a name. I'm a state . . . state . . . offizhiel. But if you knew what I have today!
(*Singing a folksong.*)
The hero walks unharmed
Through fire and war before us
And lead us on to victory.
(*Snaps his whip.*)
Business is good!

MOTHER

(*Swaying*). Into the house!

STANJA

(*Holds her back*). No, stay!

HANGMAN

Ah, I knew, cu . . . curious, like all the women. But I'm always nice to pretty ladies. Today I have three spiked dogs, three drowned cats, all very good skins, in the wagon here . . . and then, . . . Cur . . . curious women are.

MOTHER

Let me go!

STANJA

(*Holds her in an iron grip*). Stay!

HANGMAN

And then something very, *very* curious. It was lying there in the charred wood, lying, lying there without a hair singed. A wonder. The priest must bless it for me. Here I have the fiend himself to whom my soul would soon belong. . . . (MOTHER *screams softly. Distant whirl of drums.*)
Go on drumming. No more gallows goods for the furrier. (STANJA *advances a little*

step.) No! Can't do it! Got to pay to see it. And not even a sip of brandy for me. Huah, aho!
(*Off with his wagon.*)

MOTHER

(*Rousing after a long rigidity*). He was in me, growing in my body. I bore and loved him. Even if I did not dare look at him, yet I listened for ten thousand anguished nights toward the place where his heart was beating, and was happy that he lived. . . . And now he will be thrown to the carrion, he, who sprang from me, and not a name, not even a trace, of the secret of my womb will be left in the world.

STANJA

You are wrong, Mother. He is still in the world. (*Coldly controlling a twitching.*) I am carrying his child.

Quick curtain.

Sidney Howard

THE SILVER CORD

To My Wife

SIDNEY HOWARD

The first play produced by the Theatre Guild to win the Pulitzer Prize was Sidney Howard's *They Knew What They Wanted.* This was for the season of 1924-1925. Eight years before it was written, Sidney Howard was a student at Professor George Pierce Baker's 47 Workshop at Harvard University. His work there was not completed because he left in mid-term to serve with the American Ambulance on the Western front and in the Balkans during the early part of the World War. Subsequently he became a captain of the United States Army Aviation Service. After the Armistice, he joined the editorial staff of the magazine *Life* and soon became its literary editor. As a special investigator and feature writer for the *New Republic* and *Hearst's International Magazine,* Mr. Howard's articles attracted national attention. His plays include many adaptations and collaborations with such men as Sinclair Lewis, Charles MacArthur and Edward Sheldon. Of those that appear under his own name, the best known are *The Silver Cord, Lucky Sam McCarver, Yellowjack, Alien Corn,* and *The Late Christopher Bean.* Mr. Howard has been active in behalf of authors and has been one of the leading spirits in organizing the scattered writers of America. He is a member of the Society of American Dramatists and Composers, National Institute of Arts and Letters, Authors' League of America and other writers' guilds.

"Demon—with the highest respect for you—behold your work!"

GEORGE SAMPSON TO MRS. R. W.

CHARACTERS

MRS. PHELPS
DAVID, her son
ROBERT, her younger son
CHRISTINA, David's wife
HESTER, Robert's fiancée
MAID (Mute)

SCENES

The action occurs in the present day in Mrs. Phelps's house, which it situated in one of the more mature residential developments of an Eastern American city.

First in the living-room on Sunday afternoon.

Then in the living-room again, early that same evening.

Then in David's bedroom, later that same evening.

Then in the living-room, the Monday morning after.

THE SILVER CORD

ACT ONE

A LIVING-ROOM, *built and decorated in the best manner of 1905, and cluttered with the souvenirs of maternal love, European travel, and an orthodox enthusiasm for the arts. There is a vast quantity of Braun Clement and Arundel Society reproduction of the Renaissance Italian masters. The piano features Grieg, Sibelius and Macdowell. A door gives on a spacious hallway. Windows look out over a snow-covered garden.*

The rise of the curtain discloses HESTER *lost in the rotogravure sections of the Sunday papers. She is a lovely, frail phantom of a girl with a look of recent illness about her. She wears the simplest and most charming of house frocks. The door-bell rings. There is the least sound of commotion in the hall.* HESTER *looks up. In a moment, the door opens and* DAVID *enters. He is a personable young man, well enough dressed, and a gentleman. He belongs to the somewhat stolid or unimaginative type which is generally characterized, in this country, as "steady." His smile is slow and wide, his speech slow and to the point. His principal quality is a rare and most charming amiability, but he is clearly lacking in many of the more sophisticated perceptions and he is clearly of a conventional bent in his attitude toward life. The door, as he leaves it open, shows* CHRISTINA, *in the act of shedding her fur coat with the assistance of the maid. She, as* DAVID'S *wife, presents something of a contrast to her husband. She is tall, slender, grave, honest, shy, intelligent, most trusting and, when need be, courageous. She has a scientist's detachment and curiosity and these serve oddly to emphasize a very individual womanliness which is far removed from the accepted feminine. One suspects that, where* DAVID *is stubborn, she is open-minded, where he is blind, she is amazingly clear-sighted. That is the difference which makes one the complement of the other. The common quality which brought them together in the holy bonds of matrimony is their mutual candor.* DAVID *is incapable of subtlety;* CHRISTINA *will not bother with it. The result is congeniality. So much for* DAVID *and* CHRISTINA. HESTER *rises.*

HESTER

Hello!

DAVID

Eh? . . . Oh, I beg your pardon! The maid said there wasn't anybody home.

HESTER

You're David, aren't you? (*She advances to meet him.*) I'm Hester.

DAVID

You're *not!* (*He goes quickly toward her and shakes hands as* CHRISTINA *enters.*) Well! (*He turns; smiling broadly to* CHRISTINA.) Look, Chris! Here's Hester who's going to marry my brother Rob.

CHRISTINA

(*With the most charming warmth*). Isn't she lovely!

HESTER

Oh, I think you're dears, both of you! (*The two women kiss.*) Aren't you hours ahead of time?

CHRISTINA

We caught the one o'clock instead of whatever the other was.

DAVID

Where are Mother and Rob?

HESTER

Your mother's drinking tea at . . . Aren't there some people named Donohue?

DAVID

Great friends of Mother's. Why aren't you there?

HESTER

Not allowed. I'm having a breakdown.

CHRISTINA

Why don't you telephone her, Dave? She'll want to know that you're here.

DAVID

She'll find out soon enough. Where's Rob?

HESTER

Gone skating.

DAVID

(*Turns to the window*). On the pond? No. There's no one on the pond.

HESTER

Somewhere else, then.

CHRISTINA

(*Hovering over the fire*). Dave, do you suppose I could get some tea? I'm half frozen.

DAVID

Of course you can. I'll order it. (*To* HESTER.) What's the maid's name?

HESTER

Delia.

DAVID

Delia. It used to be Hannah and before that it was Stacia who got married to our old coachman, Fred. Well, it's not so bad to be home again!

(ROBERT *enters, very much dressed for skating, and carrying his skates.* ROBERT *only faintly suggests his brother. He is more volatile and stammers slightly.*)

ROBERT

(*A shout*). Dave!

DAVID

Hello, Robert! (*They shake hands vigorously.*) We were just wondering when you'd come in and Hester said . . .

HESTER

(*Speaking at the same time*). Wasn't it lucky I was here to receive them?

ROBERT

(*As he shakes* CHRISTINA'S *hand*). I think this is simply magnificent! (*As he strips off his skating things.*) How did you get here so soon? We weren't expecting you for . . .

DAVID

We caught the one o'clock.

CHRISTINA

Just.

DAVID

We thought it would be fun to surprise you.

ROBERT

Mother'll drop dead in her tracks.

DAVID

How *is* she?

ROBERT

Oh, she's in fine form . . . (*To* CHRISTINA.) You'll adore her.

CHRISTINA

I'm sure I shall.

ROBERT

She *is* marvellous, isn't she, Hester?

HESTER

She is indeed. . . . Perfectly marvellous!

DAVID

Mother's immense. And I'm glad, for Chris's sake, that things worked out this way. First Chris sees the old house. Then she meets Hester. Then Rob comes breezing in, full of health. And, last of all, Mother comes.

ROBERT

It's like a play. I always want things to be like a play. Don't you, Hester?

HESTER

I dunno. Why?

ROBERT

Don't you, Christina? (*But he does not wait for an answer—a habit with him in his better humored moments.*) You have to tell us you like this old house, you know. Mother and I wouldn't change it for the world.

CHRISTINA

(*Smiling as she looks around her*). How about that tea, Dave?

DAVID

Excuse me, Chris! I forgot. . . .

CHRISTINA

(*To* ROBERT). I've been here three minutes and I'm ordering food already!

ROBERT

Well, let me "do the honors."

DAVID

Honors, hell! Isn't Julia still in the kitchen?

ROBERT

Sure she is.

DAVID

Well, I *must* see Julia! (*He goes.*)

ROBERT

(*To* CHRISTINA). Julia'll drop dead, too. I expect half the town'll be dropping dead. Dave's always been the Greek god around this place, you know.

HESTER

He should be.

ROBERT

I can remember the time I didn't think so. (*A door slams. In the hall,* MRS. PHELPS *is heard talking, excitedly.*)

MRS. PHELPS

Those bags! Have they come, Delia?

HESTER

Here's your mother now.

CHRISTINA

So soon? How nice!
(MRS. PHELPS *enters. She is pretty, distinguished, stoutish, soft, disarming and, in short, has everything one could possibly ask including a real gift for looking years younger than her age, which is well past fifty. She boasts a reasonable amount of conventional culture, no great amount of intellect, a superabundant vitality, perfect health and a prattling spirit. At the moment she is still wearing her hat and furs and she looks wildly about her.*)

MRS. PHELPS

Dave! Dave, boy! Where are you, Dave? Where are you? It's Mother, Dave! (*She does not see him in the room and she is already turning back to the hall without a word or a look for anybody else.*) Where are you, Dave? Come here this minute! Don't you hear me, Dave? It's Mother! (*Then* DAVID *appears in the hall.*) Oh, Dave!

DAVID

(*A little abashed by the vigor of this welcome*). Hello, Mother.

MRS. PHELPS

Dave, is it really you?

DAVID

Guess it must be, Mother.

MRS. PHELPS

Dave, dear! (*She envelops as much of him as she can possibly reach.*)

DAVID

(*Prying loose*). Well! Glad to see us, Mother?

MRS. PHELPS

Glad!

DAVID

You certainly seem to be glad. . . . But you haven't spoken to . . . (CHRISTINA, *at his look, steps forward.*)

MRS. PHELPS

(*Still not seeing her*). To think I wasn't here!

DAVID

We're ahead of time, you know. Christina . . .

MRS. PHELPS

I must have known somehow. Something just made me put down my cup and rush home. But you're not looking badly. You *are* well, aren't you? I do believe you've put on weight. You must be careful, though, not to take cold this weather. Was the crossing awfully rough? Were you seasick? You haven't been working too hard, have you, Dave boy?

CHRISTINA

(*Unable to stand on one foot any longer*). He hasn't been working at all. Not for weeks!

MRS. PHELPS

(*She turns at the sound of the strange voice*). Eh? Oh!

DAVID

I've been trying to make you take notice of Christina, Mother.

MRS. PHELPS

(*With the utmost warmth*). Oh, my dear Christina, I *am* sorry. (*She kisses* CHRISTINA *on both cheeks.*) Seeing this big boy again quite took me off my feet. Let me look at *you,* now. Why, Dave, she's splendid. Perfectly splendid! I always knew Dave would choose only the best. Didn't I always say so, Dave, boy? (*Which takes her back to* DAVID.) Dave, you *have* been working too hard. I don't like those circles under your eyes.

DAVID

Nonsense, Mother!

CHRISTINA

I think he looks pretty well.

MRS. PHELPS

But only pretty well. I can't help worrying about these big boys of mine. (*Her emotion stops here. She turns gallantly to* ROBERT.) Did you skate, Rob?

ROBERT

As a matter of fact, I couldn't. They've been cutting ice on the pond and it's full of holes.

MRS. PHELPS

I must have signs put up tomorrow. Remember that, everybody. If any of you do go out in this freezing cold, don't take the short cut across the pond. . . . Dave, boy, this is too good to be true. After two whole years away and five, nearly six months married.
(*The maid brings tea.*)

DAVID

Here's tea.

MRS. PHELPS

Sit down here beside me, dear, dear Christina. And, Dave, boy, sit over there where I can see you. Just take my furs, Delia, so I can do my duty in comfort. My boy, my boy, you don't know . . . you don't know how happy I am to have you home again! Just hand me my salts, will you, Robin? This excitement has laid me out. Christina, my dear, how do you take your tea?
(*She sits at the table.* ROBERT *has fetched her bottle of "Crown Lavender" from somewhere. She motions him to put it down and proceeds to pour tea.*)

CHRISTINA

Just tea, please. As it comes and nothing in it.

MRS. PHELPS

A real tea drinker! I hope my tea stands the test. (*She passes* CHRISTINA *her cup and ceases to take any notice of her whatsoever.*) Tea, Dave, boy?

DAVID

Please, Mother.

MRS. PHELPS

The same old way?

DAVID

Yes.

MRS. PHELPS

Tea, Robin? (*She hands* DAVID *his cup.*)

ROBERT

(*Busy passing sandwiches and such*). As usual, please.

MRS. PHELPS

(*Very absent-minded about the salts*). Who do you suppose was asking after you yesterday, Dave, boy? Old George, the doorman, down at the bank. You remember old George? He's so thrilled about your coming back! And Mrs. Donohue's so thrilled! Such a sweet woman! You know, I'm afraid he's drinking again. You must run right over early tomorrow morning and let her have a look at you. I must have some people in to meet you. Some very nice new people who've come here since you went away. Named Clay. He used to be a publisher in Boston, but he gave it up because he says nobody really cares about good books any more. Of course, this house has been a real godsend to him. I must give a big dinner for you, Dave, and ask all our old friends. I do need your cool head, too, on my business. Robin does his best, but he isn't really a business man. You remember the American Telephone I bought? Mr. Curtin, at the bank, advises me to sell and take my profit, but I don't think so. What do you think, Dave, boy?

HESTER

May I have a cup, please, Mrs. Phelps?

MRS. PHELPS

Hester, my dear, how forgetful of me! How will you have it?

HESTER

As usual.

MRS. PHELPS

Let me see, that's cream and sugar?

HESTER

Only cream. No sugar.

MRS. PHELPS

Of course. Robin, will you give Hester her tea?

ROBERT

(*As he gives* HESTER *the cup*). You see, we have to take a back seat now.

MRS. PHELPS

A back seat, Robin?

ROBERT

I'm only warning Hester. She's got to know what to expect in this family when Dave's around.

DAVID

Oh, shut up, Rob!

MRS. PHELPS

(*Smiling*). My two beaux! My two jealous beaux!

ROBERT

Oh, well! Dave's out in the great world now and I'm still the same old homebody I always was. Look at him, Mother!

MRS. PHELPS

(*Looking*). Oh, my boy, my boy, if you knew what it means to me to see all my plans and hopes for you fulfilled. I've dreamed of your being an architect ever since . . . ever since . . .

ROBERT

Ever since he first showed an interest in his blocks.

MRS. PHELPS

I have those blocks still, Dave. Do you remember them?

DAVID

Do I remember those blocks!

MRS. PHELPS

(*Solemnly*). You must never forget them, because it's quite true what Robin says and, some day, when you have children of your own, I shall show them the foundation stones of their father's great career. If I

have one gift it's the ability to see what people have in them and to bring it out. I saw what David had in him, even then. And I brought it out.
(*She smiles benignly. There is a brief pause. A quizzical frown contracts* CHRISTINA'S *brow.*)

CHRISTINA

It seems a risky business.

MRS. PHELPS

(*Turning with that same start which* CHRISTINA'S *voice caused before*). What seems a risky business?

CHRISTINA

The way families have of doing that.

MRS. PHELPS

(*Setting her tea-cup down a little too deliberately*). What could be more natural?

HESTER

(*Coming to* CHRISTINA'S *rescue from an abyss of boredom*). I see what Christina means. From blocks to architecture *is* a long guess. You might very easily have guessed wrong, you know. I had some rabbits, once, and I loved 'em. Suppose my family had seen what I had in me, then, and brought me up to be a lion tamer?

MRS. PHELPS

(*Offended*). Really, Hester!

HESTER

Isn't that just what happens to most of us? Christina's job doesn't sound like the kind parents usually pick out for a girl, though.

ROBERT

I'll say it doesn't.

CHRISTINA

My parents did pick it out, though. I'm just like the rest.

HESTER

Well, it only goes to prove what I was saying. Christina might have been a homebody instead of a scientist. I might have been a lion tamer. If only our parents hadn't had ideas about us!

DAVID

One guess is as good as another. I daresay I wanted to be a fireman. What do little girls want to be?

HESTER

Queens.

CHRISTINA

Wouldn't it be a pleasant world with nothing but queens and firemen in it!

ROBERT

I guess Mother knew. She always does know.

HESTER

What I say about children is this: Have 'em. Love 'em. And then leave 'em be.

CHRISTINA

(*Amused*). I'm not sure that isn't a very profound remark.

MRS. PHELPS

(*She makes up her mind to investigate this daughter-in-law more closely and, with sudden briskness, takes back the conversation*). Why don't you two great things take the bags upstairs out of the hall?

DAVID

That's an idea.

MRS. PHELPS

Dear Christina's in the little front room, and Dave, you're in the back in your old room.

DAVID

(*Surprised*). I say, Mother . . . can't we . . .

HESTER

Don't they want to be together, Mrs. Phelps? Let me move out of the guest room and then . . .

MRS. PHELPS

Indeed, I'll do nothing of the sort. Hester's here for a rest and I won't upset her. Dave can be perfectly comfortable in his old room and so can Christina in front and it won't hurt them a bit.

CHRISTINA

Of course not. . . .

HESTER

But, Mrs. Phelps . . .

MRS. PHELPS

Not another word, my dear. (*To* CHRISTINA.) This child has danced herself into a decline and she's got to be taken care of.

DAVID

Right!

ROBERT

Come along, Dave.

MRS. PHELPS

Go and supervise, Hester, and leave me to . . . to visit with my new daughter. (DAVE *and* ROB *go.* HESTER *following.*)

HESTER

(*As she goes*). But really , David, I might just as well move. I didn't think. And if you and Christina . . .

MRS. PHELPS

(*A broad smile to* CHRISTINA). Now, my dear, let me give you another cup of tea.

CHRISTINA

Thank you.

MRS. PHELPS

And take your hat off so that I can really see you. I've never seen a lady scientist before.

CHRISTINA

I hope I'm not so very different from other women.

MRS. PHELPS

I've quite got over being afraid of you.

CHRISTINA

Afraid of me, Mrs. Phelps?

MRS. PHELPS

Can't you understand that? My big boy sends me a curt cable to say that he's marrying a charming and talented research geologist.

CHRISTINA

Biologist.

MRS. PHELPS

Biologist. It did sound just the least bit in the world improbable.

CHRISTINA

Yes. . . . I can see that.

MRS. PHELPS

Now that I know you, though, I'm very proud to have you for a daughter. Every woman wants a daughter, you know!

CHRISTINA

You're being very nice to me, Mrs. Phelps.

MRS. PHELPS

It isn't at all hard to be nice to you, my dear. Tell me about your tour. You went to Sicily?

CHRISTINA

We did, indeed.

MRS. PHELPS

Sicily, the home of . . . (*She gives herself up to Sicilian emotion.*) . . . of all those great ancient . . . poets and . . . poets. To think of your taking my boy to Sicily where I'd always planned to take him! I've never been, you see. How many opportunities we miss! That's what we're always saying of dead people, isn't it? Though, of course, I shouldn't think of calling David dead merely because he's got married. I do hope you read "Glorious Apollo" before you went to Venice. When I read it, I felt that I had made a new friend. I always make such close friends of my books and, you know, there's no friend like a really good book. And there's nothing like a good historical novel to make a city vivid and interesting. They do bring things back to one. "Glorious Apollo!" What a despicable character that man Byron was! Though I daresay he couldn't have been as bad as he was painted. People do exaggerate so. Especially writers. Do you know "The Little Flowers of St. Francis?"

CHRISTINA

I'm afraid not. Are they exaggerated?

MRS. PHELPS

Well, of course, they're really fairy tales. Only to one with a profoundly religious point of view . . . and, if there's one thing I pride myself on it *is* my profoundly religious point of view . . . I always keep the "Little Flowers" on the table beside my bed. And read *in* them, you know? I quite brought Robin up on them. Dave never took to them. Though Dave loved his regular fairy tales. His Grimm and his Hans Christian. You read, I hope?

CHRISTINA

I can. I sometimes have to.

MRS. PHELPS

Oh, my dear, I only meant that I think it's so important, for David's happiness, that you should be what *I* call "a reader." Both my boys learned their classics at their mother's knee. Their Scott and their Thackeray. *And* their Dickens. Lighter things too, of course. "Treasure Island" and "Little Lord Fauntleroy." And you went to Prague, too. Dave wrote me from Prague. Such interesting letters, Dave writes! I wondered why you stayed so long in Prague.

CHRISTINA

It's a charming city, and an architect's paradise. Dave and I thought he ought to look at something besides cathedrals and temples. . . . There *is* domestic architecture, you know.

MRS. PHELPS

Yes. I suppose there is.

CHRISTINA

People *do* want houses. I'm inclined to think houses are more interesting than churches nowadays.

MRS. PHELPS

Oh, nowadays! I'm afraid I've very little use for nowadays. I've always thought it a pity that Dave and Rob couldn't have grown up in Italy in the Renaissance and known such men as . . . well, as Cellini.

CHRISTINA

I'm not sure Cellini would have been the ideal companion for a growing boy.

MRS. PHELPS

No? Well, perhaps not. I must certainly take in Prague my next trip abroad. It's really been very hard for me to stay home these last two years. But I said to myself: Dave must have his fling. I don't like mothers who keep their sons tied to their apron strings. I said: Dave will come home to me a complete man. Though I didn't actually look for his bringing you with him, my dear, and coming home a married man. Still . . . So I stayed home with Robin. And I was glad to. I'm not sure I haven't sometimes neglected Robin for David. Given myself too much to the one, not enough to the other. The first born, you know. We mothers are human, however much we may try not to be. Tell me, Christina, you think David *is* well, don't you?

CHRISTINA

Yes, perfectly.

MRS. PHELPS

He didn't seem quite himself just now.

CHRISTINA

Perhaps he was embarrassed.

MRS. PHELPS

With me? His own mother?

CHRISTINA

Wouldn't I have accounted for it?

MRS. PHELPS

How silly of me not to remember that! Tell me what your plans are—if you have any plans, which I hope you haven't, because I've been making so many for you and such perfect ones.

CHRISTINA

Well, as a matter of fact, we haven't many, but what we have are pretty definite.

MRS. PHELPS

Really! Are they really? What are they?

CHRISTINA

Well, we're going to live in New York, of course.

MRS. PHELPS

Why "New York of course?" It seems to me that you might choose a pleasanter place to live than New York.

CHRISTINA

No doubt of that, Mrs. Phelps. But it does seem a good place for Dave to work and . . .

MRS. PHELPS

Oh, I can't agree with you!

CHRISTINA

I shouldn't have thought there could be two ways about New York for Dave any more than for me.

MRS. PHELPS

For you?

CHRISTINA

It's where my appointment is.

MRS. PHELPS

Your appointment?

CHRISTINA

At the Rockefeller Institute.

MRS. PHELPS

So that's what takes Dave and you to New York? Your geology.

CHRISTINA

Partly. Only it isn't geology. It's biology.

MRS. PHELPS

Of course. Geology's about rocks, isn't it?

CHRISTINA

Largely.

MRS. PHELPS

And biology?

CHRISTINA

Well—about Life.

MRS. PHELPS

(*Getting it clear*). So you're a student of Life, my dear. I do wish David had called you that instead of the other.

CHRISTINA

I understand how you felt, Mrs. Phelps. I hope you don't hold my job against me.

MRS. PHELPS

(*With deep feeling*). My dearest Christina, I don't! Oh, if you thought that, I should be heart-broken. You've made my darling David happy, my dear, and for that I'm prepared to love everything about you. Even your job. Do you smoke?

CHRISTINA

Yes, thank you. May I?

MRS. PHELPS

Please. And I shall, too. . . . (*They light cigarettes.*) Don't you like my lighter?

CHRISTINA

It's sweet. And very handy, I should think.

MRS. PHELPS

A friend sent it me from London. Let me give it to you.

CHRISTINA

Oh, no.

MRS. PHELPS

Please? I've not had a chance yet to give my new daughter anything. My dearest Christina . . . please?

CHRISTINA

Thank you. I shall always keep it and use it.

MRS. PHELPS

I like the little ceremonial gift. . . . Now, about your job . . .

CHRISTINA

My job?

MRS. PHELPS

As you call it. I don't like to say "profession" because that has such a sinister sound for a woman. And then science is hardly a profession, is it? Rather more of a hobby. You're planning to continue?

CHRISTINA

With my job? Oh, yes.

MRS. PHELPS

Just as though you hadn't married, I mean?

CHRISTINA

I have to, don't I? To earn my right to call myself a biologist . . .

MRS. PHELPS

Do people call you that?

CHRISTINA

I guess they call me "doctor."

MRS. PHELPS

You're *not* a doctor?

CHRISTINA

Technically, I am.

MRS. PHELPS

Oh, I can never agree with you that women make good doctors!

CHRISTINA

We shan't have to argue that point. I've no intention of practicing.

MRS. PHELPS

Not at all? Above all, not on David?

CHRISTINA

I shouldn't think of it.

MRS. PHELPS

I remember hearing that doctors never do practice on their own families. I remember that when our doctor here had a baby . . . of course, his wife had the baby . . . he called in quite an outsider to deliver the child. I remember how that struck me at the time. Tell me more about yourself, my dear. When Dave cabled me about meeting you and marrying you so suddenly . . .

CHRISTINA

It wasn't so sudden, Mrs. Phelps. I spent a good six or seven months turning him down flat.

MRS. PHELPS

(*Offended*). Indeed?

CHRISTINA

Dave and I met in Rome last winter. Then he came to Heidelberg where I was working and I accepted him. . . . I'd never given him the least encouragement before.

MRS. PHELPS

(*As before*). Indeed?

CHRISTINA

We were married straight off . . . and went to Sicily.

MRS. PHELPS

I didn't know about the preliminaries. Dave never told me. And now you're taking him off to New York!

CHRISTINA

Please don't put it that way.

MRS. PHELPS

I'm stating a fact, my dear girl. After all, you *have* got your—(*She gets it right this time.*)—biology to think of.

CHRISTINA

You can't blame me for that, dear Mrs. Phelps, so long as I think of Dave's work, too.

MRS. PHELPS

No. . . . So long as you do that. . . . How did you come to select your career?

CHRISTINA

My father was a doctor. I grew up in his hospital. Everything followed quite naturally.

MRS. PHELPS

Your father—is he living?

CHRISTINA

He died two years ago. Tragically, but rather splendidly.

MRS. PHELPS

How?

CHRISTINA

He'd been experimenting for years on infantile paralysis and . . .

MRS. PHELPS

And he died of that? (CHRISTINA *nods rather solemnly.*) Is your mother living?

CHRISTINA

Oh, yes; at home.

MRS. PHELPS

At home?

CHRISTINA

In Omaha.

MRS. PHELPS

(*Meditatively*). Omaha . . .

CHRISTINA

Yes.

MRS. PHELPS

Hm . . . And you'll go on with your father's experiments?

CHRISTINA

Oh, no! That's not at all in my line.

MRS. PHELPS

What *is* your line?

CHRISTINA

It's hard to say. I did some rather hard work this last year at Heidelberg on the embryos of chickens. In the egg, you know.

MRS. PHELPS

For heaven's sake, what for?

CHRISTINA

Trying to find out something about what makes growth stop.

MRS. PHELPS

Why . . . ?

CHRISTINA

Curiosity, I guess. Now I'm admitting what low people we scientists are. I think that curiosity's all we have. And a little training.

MRS. PHELPS

Does David follow your work?

CHRISTINA

No. And I don't expect him to.

MRS. PHELPS

Quite right. David wouldn't be appealed to by rotten eggs. . . . Not that he couldn't understand them if they did appeal to him.

CHRISTINA

Of course.

MRS. PHELPS

Isn't the Rockefeller Institute one of those places where they practice vivisection?

CHRISTINA

One of many. Yes. . . .

MRS. PHELPS

Have you . . .

CHRISTINA

What?

MRS. PHELPS

Experimented on animals?

CHRISTINA

Isn't it a part of my job? Dave understands that. You must try to understand it.

MRS. PHELPS

Very well, I shall try, my dear. Now you must listen to me and try to understand me. . . . Look at me. What do you see? Simply—David's mother. I can't say of you that you're simply David's wife, because, clearly, you're many things beside that. But I am simply his mother. . . . I think, as I talk to you, that I belong to a dead age. I wonder if you think that? In my day, we considered a girl immensely courageous and independent who taught school or gave music lessons. Nowadays, girls sell real estate and become scientists and think nothing of it. Give us our due, Christina. We weren't entirely bustles and smelling salts, we girls who did not go into the world. We made a great profession which I fear may be in some danger of vanishing from the face of the earth. We made a profession of motherhood. That may sound old-fashioned to you. Believe me, it had its value. I was trained to be a wife that I might become a mother. (CHRISTINA *is about to protest.* MRS. PHELPS *stops her.*) Your father died of his investigations of a dangerous disease. You called that splendid of him, didn't you? Would you say less of us who gave our lives to being mothers? Mothers of sons, particularly. Listen to me, Christina. David was five, Rob only a little baby, when my husband died. I'd been married six years, not so very happily. I was pretty, as a girl, too. Very pretty. (*This thought holds her for a second.*) For twenty-fours years, since my husband died, I've given all my life, all my strength to Dave and Rob. They've been my life and my job. They've taken the place of husband and friends both, for me. Where do I stand, now? Rob is marrying. Dave is married already. This is the end of my life and my job. . . . Oh, I'm not asking for credit or praise. I'm asking for something more substantial. I'm asking you, my dear, dear Christina, not to take all my boy's heart. Leave me, I beg you, a little, little part of it. I've earned that much. I'm not sure I couldn't say that you owe me that much—as David's mother. I believe I've deserved it. Don't you think I have?

CHRISTINA

(*Deeply moved*). My dear, dear Mrs. Phelps!

MRS. PHELPS

It's agreed then, isn't it, that I'm not to be shut out?

CHRISTINA

Of course you're not!

MRS. PHELPS

Not by you, Christina. Nor by your work?

CHRISTINA

No! No!

MRS. PHELPS

Nor by anything?

CHRISTINA

You must know that I should never come between a mother and her son. You must know that I appreciate what you've done for Dave and all you've always been and meant to him. You *must* know that!

MRS. PHELPS

Christina, my dear, you're a very disarming person. You are indeed. I've known you ten minutes and unloaded my whole heart to you.

CHRISTINA

I'm proud that you trust me.

MRS. PHELPS

(*Patting her hand*). Thank you, my dear. And now . . . now that you know how I feel . . . now you won't go to New York, will you? You won't take Dave to New York?

CHRISTINA

(*Drawing back in alarm*). But, Mrs. Phelps!

MRS. PHELPS

Because that *would* be coming between mother and son as you just now said. That could mean only one thing—crowding me out, setting me aside, robbing me. . . .

CHRISTINA

(*Completely baffled*). You're quite mistaken, Mrs. Phelps! You've no reason to think any such thing!

MRS. PHELPS

Well, it's nice of you to reassure me, and we don't have to worry about it for some time yet. You'll have plenty of time to see how carefully I've worked everything out for David—and for you, too, my dear. You've a nice, long visit ahead and . . .

CHRISTINA

I only wish we *had* a nice long visit, Mrs. Phelps.

MRS. PHELPS

What do you mean?

CHRISTINA

I start work at the Institute a week from tomorrow.

MRS. PHELPS

(*Staggered*). What *are* you saying, child?

CHRISTINA

We didn't even bring our trunks up, you know.

MRS. PHELPS

(*Recovering herself*). I'll not hear of it! A week of David after two years without him? What *are* you thinking of? Don't you realize that David has practically been my sole companion for nearly twenty-five years?

CHRISTINA

You've had Robert, too.

MRS. PHELPS

I'm not thinking so much of Robert, now. He isn't threatened as David is.

CHRISTINA

Threatened, Mrs. Phelps?

MRS. PHELPS

I don't want to see David's career sacrificed.

CHRISTINA

But, I'm not planning to sacrifice it.

MRS. PHELPS

You make the word sound disagreeable. I admire your work, Christina, but I am very clearly of the impression that it may easily obliterate David's work.

CHRISTINA

I don't see any conflict.

MRS. PHELPS

Aren't you taking him to New York, which he simply loathes? To live in a stuffy tenement . . . well, an apartment. . . . They're the same thing. . . . Without proper heat or sunshine or food? I told you I'd made plans. I've arranged everything for David's best interest. I can't believe that a girl of your intelligence won't realize how good my arrangements are. I happen to own a very large tract of land here. A very beautiful tract, most desirable for residences. To the north of the Country Club just beside the links. Hilly and wooded. You can see it, off there to the left of the pond. I've had many offers for it, most advantageous offers. But I've held on to it, ever since Dave chose his profession. Pleasant Valley, it's called. I shall change the name to Phelps Manor and open it. David will have charge. David will lay out the streets, design the gateways, build the houses and make his fortune, his reputation and his place in the world out of it.

CHRISTINA

(*Pause, then*). Don't you mean his place in this part of the world, Mrs. Phelps?

MRS. PHELPS

(*Positively*). As well this as any. With me to back him, he's certain of a proper start here, and there can't be any doubt about the outcome. His success is assured here and his happiness and prosperity with it. And yours, too. Don't you see that?

CHRISTINA

It certainly sounds safe enough.

MRS. PHELPS

I knew you'd see. Furthermore, he's never happy in New York.

CHRISTINA

Happiness is very important. Only different people have different ideas of it.

MRS. PHELPS

David's always had my ideas. And they're very sound ones.

CHRISTINA

(*Politely*). I'm sure of it. But perhaps they aren't sound for David. I mean, from what I know of him. . . .

MRS. PHELPS

I'm David's mother, my dear. I know him better than you do.

CHRISTINA

I wonder!

MRS. PHELPS

Oh, I do! And I know how little New York has to offer. I know the competition there. I know what the struggle would be.

Look at the choice. On the one hand obscurity, a desk in some other man's office, years of hack work and discouragement. On the other, immediate prominence, unquestionable success . . .

CHRISTINA

With his mother behind him.

MRS. PHELPS

Who better?

CHRISTINA

Oh, I see the difference!

MRS. PHELPS

Yes, don't you! And as to your work, my dear, I'm sure we can keep you busy and contented.

CHRISTINA

(*Smiling in spite of herself*). How will you do that?

MRS. PHELPS

Well, it's hard to say, off-hand. But if we really set our minds to it. . . . I know! I'm the chairman of our hospital here, and I have a great deal of influence with the doctors. We've a beautiful laboratory. You couldn't ask for anything nicer or cleaner or more comfortable than that laboratory. You do your work in a laboratory, I suppose?

CHRISTINA

Usually.

MRS. PHELPS

I'll take you down in the morning and introduce you to Dr. McClintock, homeopathic, but very agreeable, and he'll show you our laboratory. We've just got in a new microscope, too. Oh, a very fine one! One the High School didn't want any more. You'll simply love our laboratory. Oh, you will! It has a splendid new sink with hot and cold running water and quite a good gas stove because it's also the nurses' washroom and diet kitchen. And you'll be allowed to putter around as much as you like whenever it isn't in use by the nurses or the real doctors. I can arrange everything perfectly, my dear. I'm certain that, when you see our laboratory, you'll sit right down and write to Mr. Rockerfeller, who, I'm told, is a very kind old man at heart, and won't misunderstand in the least, that you've found an opening here that's ever so much more desirable than his old Institute, where you won't be obliged to cut up cats and dogs. You will think it over, won't you? Going to New York, I mean. Taking Dave to New York and ruining all his prospects?

CHRISTINA

(*After a pause, in all sincere kindliness*). Mrs. Phelps, the third time I refused Dave, he asked me for a reason. I told him I couldn't throw myself away on a big frog in a small puddle.

MRS. PHELPS

You don't mean that you want him to be a small frog, a mere polliwog, in a great ocean like New York?

CHRISTINA

I'm afraid that's just what I do mean. And when he came back at me three months later with some real sketches and a great deal more humility and with a real job in a real architect's office . . .

MRS. PHELPS

Has David a job? In New York?

CHRISTINA

A chance anyway. With Michaels.

MRS. PHELPS

Michaels?

CHRISTINA

He's a big man. And he's interested in Dave.

MRS. PHELPS

I don't approve at all. I think it's madness.

CHRISTINA

You may be right. But, isn't it best left to Dave and me?

MRS. PHELPS

(*Deeply hurt at the implication*). My dear Christina, if you think I'm trying to interfere, you're quite mistaken. You're very unfair. . . . Only tell me what makes you so sure Dave can succeed in New York.

CHRISTINA

I haven't given a thought to whether he'll succeed or not. That depends on his own talent, doesn't it? As to how much he makes, or how we get on, at first, I don't think that matters either . . . so long as Dave stands really on his own feet.

MRS. PHELPS

Oh, Christina, be honest with yourself. You *are* sacrificing David!

CHRISTINA

How?

MRS. PHELPS

By thinking only of yourself, of course.

CHRISTINA

Won't you believe that I'm thinking of both of us?

MRS. PHELPS

How can I? It's too bad of you, really. It means—(*In despair.*)—It means that it's all been for nothing!

CHRISTINA

What has?

MRS. PHELPS

(*Crescendo, as she walks about*). All, all that I've done for David and given up for him and meant to him!

CHRISTINA

How can you say that?

MRS. PHELPS

I did so want to be friendly with David's wife. If you knew how I've wished and dreamt and prayed for that!

CHRISTINA

(*Rising herself*). But can't we be friends?

MRS. PHELPS

Some day you'll have a child of your own and then you may know what I mean, if . . .

CHRISTINA

If what?

MRS. PHELPS

(*The last volley*). If you don't sacrifice your child, too, to this work of yours.

CHRISTINA

(*Deeply distressed*). Mrs. Phelps, I wish you wouldn't feel that. It makes me feel that I've got off on a very wrong foot here. (ROBERT *enters.*)

ROBERT

Christina!

CHRISTINA

Yes?

ROBERT

Dave says, if you want a bath before dinner, you'd better be quick about it.

CHRISTINA

I didn't know it was so late. Thanks. (*She goes to* MRS. PHELPS.) You'll see that I do understand, dear Mrs. Phelps. You'll see that it all comes straight somehow and turns out for the best. Life takes care of such things. All we have to do is to keep out of life's way and make the best of things as *healthily* as possible.

MRS. PHELPS

You think I'm selfish.

CHRISTINA

Oh, no! I don't think anything of the sort!

MRS. PHELPS

Because if there's one thing I pride myself on, I may have many faults, but I am not selfish. I haven't a selfish hair in my head.

CHRISTINA

I tell you, I understand.
(*She kisses her quickly and goes out.*)

ROBERT

(*Looking curiously after* CHRISTINA). Mother!

MRS. PHELPS

(*Wildly*). Oh, Robin! I'm so lonely! So lonely!

ROBERT

(*Startled*). Mother!

MRS. PHELPS

I'm afraid I'm a dreadful coward!

ROBERT

You, Mother?

MRS. PHELPS

I ought to have been prepared to lose my two great, splendid sons. I've told myself over and over again that the time would come, and now that it *has* come, I can't face it! She's taking Dave away to New York, away from me, away from all the wonderful plans I've made for him here!

ROBERT

Well, if Dave's fool enough to go!

MRS. PHELPS

I shouldn't do to any woman on earth what she's doing to me!

ROBERT

Of course you wouldn't. But then, Christina isn't your sort, is she?

MRS. PHELPS

You've noticed that, too?

ROBERT

Who *is* your sort, Mother? . . . Oh, it's a wonderful gift you've given us.

MRS. PHELPS

What's that, Robin?

ROBERT

A wonderful ideal of womanhood. You know what I mean.

MRS. PHELPS

No. What?

ROBERT

Your own marvelous self, Mother!

MRS. PHELPS

Dave didn't stop to think of any such ideal, did he?

ROBERT

Oh, Dave!

MRS. PHELPS

Perhaps I shouldn't be hurt. But you can't know what it is to be a mother. I nearly died when Dave was born. Hours and hours I suffered for him, trapped in agony. He was a twelve-pound baby, you know. If I could be sure of his happiness!

ROBERT

You mustn't ask too much.

MRS. PHELPS

You're right. No mother should expect any woman to love her son as she loves him.

ROBERT

Your sons don't expect any woman to love them as you do.

MRS. PHELPS

Oh, Robin! Is that how you feel?

ROBERT

I think it must be. (*She looks at him, watching him think it all out.*) It's a funny business, isn't it? After a woman like you has suffered the tortures of the damned bringing us into the world, and worked like a slave to help us grow up in it, we can't wait to cut loose and give up the one thing we can be sure of! And for what? To run every known risk of disillusion and disappointment.

MRS. PHELPS

(*Struck by this*). What *is* the one thing you can be sure of, Robin?

ROBERT

You are. Don't you know that? Why can't we leave well enough alone?

MRS. PHELPS

Presently you'll be going too, Rob.

ROBERT

Yes . . . I know I shall. . . . But nothing will ever come between us, Mother.

MRS. PHELPS

Come over here by the fire, Robin, and let's forget all these unpleasant things. (*She goes to sit by the fire.*) Let's have a real old-time talk about nothing at all. Sit down. (*He sits as directed on a stool at her feet.*) Head in my lap! (*He obeys.*) So! This has shown me something I've always suspected. That you are *my* son. David takes after his father.

ROBERT

Mother!

MRS. PHELPS

Tell me, Robin, what you meant just now when you said that about the one thing you can be sure of. Did you mean that you've had dark thoughts about *your* future?

ROBERT

I must have meant something of the sort.

MRS. PHELPS

Hm. . . . It was dear of you, my great Robin, to say what you did about my being your ideal. You know my dream has always been to see my two boys married and settled down. But happily! Happily! Has Hester come to any decision about where she wants to spend her honeymoon?

ROBERT

Abroad.

MRS. PHELPS

Nothing more definite than just "abroad?"

ROBERT

No. She doesn't care where we go.

MRS. PHELPS

That seems very odd to me. I took such an interest in my honeymoon. Why, your father and I had every day of it planned, weeks before we were married. . . . Hester hasn't picked out her flat silver yet, either, has she?

ROBERT

I don't think so.

MRS. PHELPS

I can't understand it!

ROBERT

What?

MRS. PHELPS

Her indifference. It rather shocks me. (*She notices that* ROBERT *is shocked, too.*) But I suppose I'm old-fashioned. Like this room. You must give me a little of your time and taste, Robin, before you're married, and advise me about doing this room over.

ROBERT

(*Eagerly*). Have you come to that at last?

MRS. PHELPS

I'm afraid so. How's Hester planning to do your new home?

ROBERT

(*His spirits subsiding at once*). Oh, I don't know.

MRS. PHELPS

You don't mean to say she hasn't made *any* plans?

ROBERT

I've been trying to get her interested in house-hunting.

MRS. PHELPS

And she doesn't care about that either?

ROBERT

She says anything will suit her.

MRS. PHELPS

Does she, indeed! Most girls . . . most *normal* girls, that is, look forward so to having their homes to receive their friends in.

ROBERT

She leaves it all to me. She says I know much more about such things than she does.

MRS. PHELPS

How little she understands my poor Robin who ought never to be bothered!

ROBERT

Oh, well!

MRS. PHELPS

Do you happen to know if Hester *has* many friends? I mean, many men friends? Did she have lots of suitors beside you?

ROBERT

I daresay she had loads.

MRS. PHELPS

Do you *know* that she had?

ROBERT

She never told me so. Why?

MRS. PHELPS

I was wondering. She's been out two years. One does wonder how much a girl has been sought after. But, then, why should she have bothered with others when she thought she could land you? You are rather a catch, you know.

ROBERT

I, Mother?

MRS. PHELPS

Any girl would set her cap for you.

ROBERT

I don't believe Hester did that.

MRS. PHELPS

My dear, I wasn't saying that she did! But why shouldn't she? Only . . .

ROBERT

Only what?

MRS. PHELPS

I can't help wondering if Hester's feeling for you is as strong as you think it is. (ROBERT *wonders, too.*) I've been wondering for some time, Robin. I've hesitated to speak to you about it. But after what you've just told me . . .

ROBERT

Well, it's too late to worry now.

MRS. PHELPS

I can't help worrying, though. Marriage is such an important step and you're such a sensitive, shrinking character. It would be too terrible if you had to go through what you were just speaking of—the disillusionment and disappointment. . . . I'm only trying to find out what it is that's come between you two young people.

ROBERT

Nothing has, Mother. Hester isn't you, that's all!

MRS. PHELPS

Nonsense, Robin! . . . It isn't that awful woman I was so worried about when you were at Harvard?

ROBERT

I'm not raising a second crop of wild oats.

MRS. PHELPS

Then it *must* be that risk you were speaking of! Oh, why do boys run that risk! Why will they break away!

ROBERT

I wish I knew!

MRS. PHELPS

Perhaps your trouble is that—(*A pause. Then, very low.*)—that you don't love Hester.

ROBERT

Oh, love! I must love her or I wouldn't have asked her to marry me. I guess she loves me in her way. Is her way enough? I'll find that out in time. A man ought to marry.

MRS. PHELPS

(*A little more positively*). You *don't* love Hester, and it isn't fair to her!

ROBERT

Yes, I do love her! Only I wonder if I'm the marrying kind. Failing the possibility of marrying you. I mean your double.

MRS. PHELPS

(*Always increasing*). You don't love Hester.

ROBERT

I do, I tell you! Who could help loving her? I mean . . . Good God, what do I mean?

MRS. PHELPS

Either you don't love Hester or Hester doesn't love you.

ROBERT

She does love me.

MRS. PHELPS

She may say she does, but I haven't seen her showing it.

ROBERT

Mother!

MRS. PHELPS

You don't love Hester and Hester doesn't love you. It's as simple as that, Robin, and you're making a very grave mistake to go on with this. These things may be painful, but they're better faced before than after. Children come after, Robin, and then it's too late! Think, Robin! Think before it's too late! And remember, the happiness of three people is at stake!

ROBERT

Hester's and mine and . . .

MRS. PHELPS

And mine! And mine! . . . Only, I was wrong to say that! You must put my fate out of your mind just as Dave has done. Let Dave find out for himself what he's done. She won't be able to hold him. She won't have time for a home and children. She won't take any more interest in him than Hester takes in you. But you, Robin, *you* can still be saved! I want to save you from throwing yourself away as Dave has. You will face the facts, won't you?

ROBERT

You mean . . . I'm to . . . to break with Hester?

MRS. PHELPS

You will be a man?

ROBERT

(*Pause, then*). Well . . . I'll . . . I'll try, Mother.

MRS. PHELPS

(*Pause, then*). When?

ROBERT

Well . . . the . . . the first chance I get.

MRS. PHELPS

(*Trying not to appear eager*). Tonight? . . . You'll have your chance tonight, Robin. I'll see that you get it. Promise me to take it?

ROBERT

(*Pause*). All right. . . . If you think I'd better. . . . All right. . . .

MRS. PHELPS

Oh, thank God for this confidence between us! Thank God I've saved my boy one more tumble! You'll see it won't be so bad to put up with your mother a little longer! You'll see I've still plenty to give you and to do for you!

ROBERT

My blessed, blessed mother!

MRS. PHELPS

(*Unable to repress her triumph*). And I won't have to be lonely now! I won't have to be lonely!

ROBERT

No, Mother! No!
(*He takes her in his arms.*)

MRS. PHELPS

Kiss me.
(*He does; on the lips, fervently.* DAVID *comes in, dressed for dinner.*)

DAVID

Hello! That's a pretty picture! . . . Chris'll be down in a minute.

ROBERT

Where's Hester?

DAVID

In Chris's room. I heard them giggling in there. Isn't it grand they've hit it off so well?

ROBERT

(*Meeting his mother's eyes*). Isn't it? I'll make a cocktail.
(*He goes.*)

DAVID

You like Christina, don't you, Mother?

MRS. PHELPS

Didn't you know I should?

DAVID

Sure I did! After all, I couldn't have gone far wrong on a wife, could I? I mean, having you for a mother would make most girls look pretty cheesey. I waited a long time. And all the time I was waiting for Chris! You'll see how wonderful Chris is. Why, she gets better every day. I don't know how I ever pulled it off. I swear I don't. I certainly had luck.

MRS. PHELPS

You're happy?

DAVID

You bet I'm happy!

MRS. PHELPS

You're not going to let your happiness crowd me out entirely, are you, Dave boy?

DAVID

(*Amiably irritated*). Oh, Mother! Lay off! (ROBERT *returns with shaker and cocktail glasses.*)

ROBERT

This is just a preliminary, Mother. We both need it, before we dress.

MRS. PHELPS

Perhaps we do.

DAVID

Shan't we call Chris and Hester?

MRS. PHELPS

No! Just we three!

ROBERT

It'll never be we three any more. I heard them coming as I crossed the hall.
(*He pours the cocktail into the glasses and goes about passing them.*)

MRS. PHELPS

My two boys! My big one and my little one!

DAVID

(*Calls out*). Hurry up, Chris!

MRS. PHELPS

If I can keep the little corner Christina doesn't need, Dave . . . that's all I ask . . .

DAVID

Don't you worry, Mother. (CHRISTINA *and* HESTER *enter. They are both dressed appropriately for the evening.* CHRISTINA *is particularly lovely.*) Here we are!

CHRISTINA

Thank you, Robert.
(*They sip their cocktails.*)

DAVID

Chris!

CHRISTINA

Yes?

DAVID

Let's tell Mother.

CHRISTINA

Now? In front of everybody?

DAVID

It won't hurt 'em to hear.

CHRISTINA

I don't mind, if they don't.

ROBERT

Mind what?

DAVID

It'll make Mother so happy.

MRS. PHELPS

What will?

DAVID

A surprise Chris and I have got to spring on you!

MRS. PHELPS

How nice! What is it?

CHRISTINA

(*A smiling pause—then*). In about four months I'm going to have a baby.

HESTER

Oh, Christina, how wonderful!

ROBERT

Are you really!

DAVID

Isn't that a grand surprise, Mother?

MRS. PHELPS

(*Recovering as from a body blow*). Of course . . . David. I'm very glad, my dear. Very glad. . . . Have you a napkin there, Robin? I've spilled my cocktail all over my dress.

CURTAIN

ACT TWO

SCENE I

THE *living-room again. It is the same evening, after supper. The lamps are lighted.* MRS. PHELPS, HESTER, CHRISTINA, DAVID *and* ROB *are all present.* CHRISTINA, HESTER *and* DAVID *are dressed as we saw them at the end of the first act.* ROB *wears his dinner coat and his mother has changed to a simple evening dress. They have only just finished their coffee and* MRS. PHELPS *is busily showing a collection of photographs which she has in a great Indian basket beside her chair.*

CHRISTINA

What were you doing in the sailor suit, Dave?

DAVID

Dancing the hornpipe, I believe.

MRS. PHELPS

(*Fondly*). That was at Miss Briggs's dancing school. Do you remember Miss Briggs, David?

DAVID

Do I! The hornpipe must have been something special, Mother.

MRS. PHELPS

I see that I've marked it "Masonic Temple, April 6th, 1904."

DAVID

It must have been special. They don't usually dance hornpipes in Masonic Temples.

CHRISTINA

Did Miss Briggs teach you to be graceful, Dave?

DAVID

She did indeed. As a boy I was a gazelle. But I got over it.

CHRISTINA

I'm just as glad. I've known one or two adult gazelles.

MRS. PHELPS

Both David and Robin danced beautifully.

DAVID

I haven't thought of Miss Briggs for years. I remember her so well. She seemed so old to me. She must have been old, too. A good deal older than God. She looked it, in spite of her red hair and her castanets. Spain, she used to say, is the land of the dance.

MRS. PHELPS

She had all the nicest children.

DAVID

Castanets and Spanish shawls . . . *and* a police whistle. She blew the whistle at the boys for running and sliding. God knows what dances she taught us. Very different from the steps you indulge in, Hester, with your low modern tastes.

HESTER

Running and sliding sounds very pleasant.

DAVID

We thought that up for ourselves.

MRS. PHELPS

How long ago that all seems! (*She shows another photograph.*) This is David when he was ten weeks old.

CHRISTINA

Oh, David!

HESTER

Let me see. (CHRISTINA *shows her.*) What a darling baby! Did they always sit them in shells in those days?

MRS. PHELPS

(*Just a little coldly*). It was a fashion like any other.

CHRISTINA

David on the half shell!

HESTER

Have you ever noticed how much all babies look like Chief Justice Taft?

MRS. PHELPS

(*She takes the photographs back in ill-concealed irritation*). David was a beautiful child.

DAVID

I didn't always sit in shells. Mother's got one of me on a white fur rug.

MRS. PHELPS

It hangs over my bed to this day.

CHRISTINA

In the nude?

DAVID

No. In an undershirt.
(HESTER *giggles.*)

MRS. PHELPS

Fashions change.

CHRISTINA

I suppose they must. David wouldn't think of being photographed in his undershirt, now. Let me see the picture again, Mrs. Phelps.

MRS. PHELPS

I think that's enough for this evening.
(*She rises, in great dignity, to put the photographs aside.*)

CHRISTINA

Dear Mrs. Phelps, please don't be angry. We were only teasing David. They're awfully interesting pictures.

MRS. PHELPS

Only interesting to me, I'm afraid.

CHRISTINA

Not at all. I loved them. Do show me some more, Mrs. Phelps. Are there many more?

MRS. PHELPS

(*Still stern about them*). Dave and Robin were photographed twice every month until they were twelve years old.

HESTER

(*Calculating rapidly*). Good Lord! That makes over two hundred and fifty of each!

MRS. PHELPS

I never counted. I used to study their photographs, month by month, just as I did their weight. I wasn't satisfied to watch only their bodies grow. I wanted a record of the development of their little minds and souls as well. I could compare the expression of Dave's eyes, for instance, at nine, with their expression at eight and a half, and see the increased depth. And I was never disappointed.

HESTER

I knew a mother once who called her son "her beautiful black swan."

MRS. PHELPS

I should never have called either of my sons by such a name!

ROBERT

I can remember when you used to call us your Arab steeds!

MRS. PHELPS

(*Furious*). Only in fun. Will you put them away, Robin?
(ROBERT *takes the photographs.*)

ROBERT

Sure you don't want to go through the rest, Mother?

MRS. PHELPS

I'm afraid of boring Christina. Christina has other interests, of course. Higher interests than her husband. Higher even than children, I suspect.
(*There is an abashed, awful pause, at this.* CHRISTINA *looks hurt and baffled.* HESTER *is horrified.* DAVID, *puzzled, rises and goes to the window.* ROBERT *smiles to himself as he stows the photographs away.*)

HESTER

(*Breaking out*). Well, of all the . . .
(CHRISTINA, *catching her eye, stops her.*)

MRS. PHELPS

(*Polite, but dangerous*). What was it you were about to say, Hester?

HESTER

(*Recovering herself none too expertly*). I was just looking at Christina's dress. I was just going to say: "Well, of all the lovely dresses I ever saw, that's the loveliest."

CHRISTINA

It *is* nice, isn't it? I got it in Paris. From Poiret. Dave made me.

MRS. PHELPS

(*As she studies the dress*). I've a little woman right here in town who does well enough for me. I know who that dress *would* look well on! Dave, you remember Clara Judd? Such an exquisite figure, Clara had, and such distinction! That dress *wants* distinction and a figure. You might wear it, too, Hester.
(*There is another painful pause.* CHRISTINA *is really crushed.*)

DAVID

(*Desperately snatching for a change of subject*). Look, Chris! The moon's up. You can see the kids coasting down the long hill.

CHRISTINA

(*Joining him at the window gratefully*). If I weren't all dressed up, I'd join them!

HESTER

Don't you love coasting?

CHRISTINA

(*She nods*). Once last winter we had a big snowfall at Heidelberg. I'd been all day in the laboratory, I remember, straining my eyes out at a scarlet fever culture for our bacteriology man. Krauss, his name was. They called him "The Demon of the Neckar." The theory was that he used to walk along the river bank, thinking up cruel things to say to his students. I never knew such a terrifying man. . . . Well, this day I'm talking about, I came out of Krauss's laboratory into the snow. Into Grimm's fairy tales, as Dave knows, because Dave's seen Heidelberg. Another bacteriologist, a dear boy from Marburg, came with me. We looked at the snow and we wanted to coast. . . . We found a small boy with a very large sled and we rented it, *with* the boy, who wouldn't trust us not to steal it. We certainly coasted. We got so ardent, we took the funicular up the Schlossberg and coasted down from there. The lights came out along the Neckar and the snow turned all the colors snow *can* turn and still we coasted. . . . Presently, we had an accident. A bob turned over in front of us with an old man on it. We couldn't stop and so we just hit the bob and the old man and you know how that is when you're going fast! . . . We picked ourselves up—or, rather, dug ourselves out—and went to see if we'd hurt the old fellow and, God save us, it was Krauss himself! . . . I don't mind telling you our hearts sank. We stood there petrified. But we needn't have worried. Krauss didn't mind. He smiled the sweetest smile—you'd *never* have suspected he had it in him!—and touched his cap like a little boy and apologized for his clumsiness. "My age hasn't improved my skill," he said. . . . I could have kissed him. I wasn't quite sure how he'd have taken that, so, instead, I asked him to join us. He was delighted. We kept it up for another hour, we two students and the great god Krauss. "Jugend ist Trunkenheit ohne Wein!" he said. I daresay he was quoting a poem. . . . He couldn't have been a day under seventy. Three months later, he died of an inoperable internal tumor. In his notes, they found an observation he had written on his condition that very day we coasted. Think of a man who could write observations on his approaching death and then go off to coast afterwards! It's what life can be and should be. It's the difference between life and self.

MRS. PHELPS

Hm! . .

HESTER

I think that's the most marvelous story I've ever heard!

ROBERT

Isn't it marvelous?

HESTER

I wish I'd known such a man!

CHRISTINA

Do you remember the night *we* coasted in Heidelberg, Dave?

DAVID

Do I? (*To his mother.*) Chris means the night she accepted me!

MRS. PHELPS

Does she really?

DAVID

(*Dashed and giving it up*). Yeah. . . . Let's go outside and watch the kids, Chris. It'll do us good.

CHRISTINA

(*Seeing his point*). Right! I'd love to! (*They go.*)

MRS. PHELPS

I'm beginning to wonder if Christina's studies at Heidelberg haven't made her just the least little bit in the world pro-German.

HESTER

Mrs. Phelps, how *can* you say such a thing! (HESTER *looks from* ROBERT *to his mother in amazement.* MRS. PHELPS *sits down at the piano and begins to play the easier portions of one of Chopin's nocturnes.*) I think that was simply inspiring!

MRS. PHELPS

I can't play Chopin if you interrupt me, Hester.

HESTER

I'm sorry. I simply can't get Christina out of my mind.

MRS. PHELPS

What do you mean?

HESTER

I mean that I think she's the most perfect person I've ever seen.

MRS. PHELPS

Do you really? Which way did they go, Robin?

ROBERT

(*At the window*). Down the front.

MRS. PHELPS

Can you see them?

ROBERT

They're just standing in the road. Now they're moving down under the trees.

MRS. PHELPS

But they can't even *see* the long hill from the trees.

ROBERT

They're not looking at the long hill.

MRS. PHELPS

What *are* they looking at?

ROBERT

Each other. It's quite a romantic picture. Now she's put her head on his shoulder. His arm is around her waist. . . .

MRS. PHELPS

Faugh! Call them in!
(*Her irritation produces a discord in the nocturne.* ROBERT *moves to go.*)

HESTER

Oh, don't, Rob! It's the first chance they've had to be alone together.

MRS. PHELPS

They can be alone without David's catching pneumonia, can't they? She drags him out of doors at night in freezing weather to spoon in the road like a couple of mill hands! I should think she might have some consideration for her husband's health, let alone for my feelings.

HESTER

(*A little hotly*). In the first place, it was David who dragged *her* out. In the second, they *are* in love and *do* want to be alone. In the third, I don't see any reason for worrying over the health of any man who looks as husky as David does. And in the fourth, if there *is* any worrying to be done, let me remind you that it's Christina and *not* David who is going to have a baby. (MRS. PHELPS *breaks off her playing in the middle of a phrase.*) I'm sorry if I've shocked you, but the truth is, you've both shocked me.

ROBERT

How have we shocked you?

HESTER

By not being a great deal more thrilled over Christina's baby. When I drank my cocktail to it before dinner, neither of you drank yours. When I wanted to talk about it during dinner, you both changed the subject. You haven't mentioned that baby since dinner, except once, and that was catty! You've known about that baby for over two hours and you aren't excited about it yet! Not what *I* call excited.

MRS. PHELPS

If you'll forgive my saying so, Hester, I'm not sure that an unborn baby is quite the most suitable subject for . . .

HESTER

I'm blessed if I see anything bad form about a baby!

ROBERT

No more does Mother—after it's born.

HESTER

I can't wait for that. I *love* thinking about them. And wondering what they're going to be—I mean, boy or girl. Why, we had bets on my sister's baby for months before he was born.

MRS. PHELPS

I'm not ashamed to be old-fashioned.

HESTER

You ought to be. This is going to be a very remarkable baby. There aren't many born with such parents. And I intend to go right on talking about it with anyone who'll listen to me. Christina doesn't mind. She's just as interested as I am. I've already made her promise to have my sister's obstetrician.

MRS. PHELPS

Really, Hester!

HESTER

I'd go to the ends of the earth for that man. Christina's baby has put me in a very maternal frame of mind.

MRS. PHELPS

Maternal!

HESTER

What I say is: I'm as good as married. I might as well make the best of my opportunities to get used to the idea. Because I intend to have as many babies as possible.

MRS. PHELPS

(*Glancing at* ROBERT). Is that why you're marrying Rob, Hester?

HESTER

What better reason could I have? I'm sorry if I've shocked you, but, as I said before, you've shocked me and that's that.
(*Coolly,* MRS. PHELPS *goes for the coffee tray. Her eyes meet* ROBERT'S *and there is no mistaking the intention of the look they give him. Then, without a word, she leaves* ROBERT *and* HESTER *alone together.*)

ROBERT

(*Starting after her*). Mother! . . . Hester didn't mean. . . . Oh. . . . (*He turns back to* HESTER.) Hester, how could you?

HESTER

I don't know. . . . But I don't care if I did!

ROBERT

It doesn't make things any easier for me.

HESTER

Oh, Rob, dear, I *am* sorry!

ROBERT

You've got Mother all ruffled and upset. Now we'll have to smooth her down and have all kinds of explanations and everything. Really, it was too bad of you.

HESTER

I know. I lost my temper. . . . You understand, don't you?

ROBERT

I understand that you're a guest in Mother's house.

HESTER

Is that *all* you understand? Oh, Rob!

ROBERT

I'm sorry, Hester. But, for the moment, I'm thinking of Mother.

HESTER

I see. . . . I'll apologize.

ROBERT

That's up to you.

HESTER

I suppose she'll never forgive me. It isn't this, though.

ROBERT

This?

HESTER

The scene I made.

ROBERT

What do you mean?

HESTER

I don't know. . . . Some mothers like the girls their sons marry.

ROBERT

Doesn't that depend on the girls?

HESTER

Not entirely.

ROBERT

You mustn't be unjust to Mother.

HESTER

Rob, I'm a little tired of hearing about your mother. . . . (*Suddenly penitent again.*) Oh, I didn't mean to say that! I didn't mean it a bit! I'm sorry, Rob. . . . Now I'm apologizing to you. Don't you hear me?

ROBERT

Yes, I hear you. What then?

HESTER

Oh, what difference does it make? I'm not marrying your mother. I'm marrying you. And I love you, Rob! I love you!

ROBERT

Yes, my dear.

HESTER

I'll never be bad again.

ROBERT

I'm willing to take your word for it.

HESTER

You'd better be. Oh, you are angry with me, Rob!

ROBERT

No. I'm not.

HESTER

You're a queer one.

ROBERT

Think so? How?

HESTER

As a lover. I've never seen another like you.

ROBERT

Haven't you? (*A thought strikes him.*) Tell me something, Hester.

HESTER

What?

ROBERT

Have you had many?

HESTER

Many what?

ROBERT

Lovers.

HESTER

Oh, Robert, what a thing to say to a lady!

ROBERT

You know what I mean.

HESTER

I'm not quite sure I want to answer.

ROBERT

I'm not asking for their names.

HESTER

Oh, I shouldn't mind that . . . the truth is . . . I don't know . . .

ROBERT

You must.

HESTER

I don't really. I used to think . . . oh, quite often . . . that one of my beaux was coming to the point . . . but . . .

ROBERT

Yes?

HESTER

But none of them ever did.

ROBERT

That surprises me. Why not?

HESTER

I don't think it was entirely lack of allure, Rob.

ROBERT

Of course it wasn't!

HESTER

I think it was because I always laughed.

ROBERT

You didn't laugh at me.

HESTER

You looked foolish enough, now that I think of it.

ROBERT

Yes. I daresay. . . . So I *was* the only one.

HESTER

Say the only one I didn't laugh at, please. You make me sound so undesirable.

ROBERT

I didn't mean to. Tell me, Hester . . .

HESTER

Anything.

ROBERT

Have you thought what it will mean to be my wife?

HESTER

A very pleasant life.

ROBERT

For you?

HESTER

I certainly hope so.

ROBERT

I don't know that I quite share your enthusiasm for children.

HESTER

You will.

ROBERT

They don't exactly help a career, you know.

HESTER

Have you got a career?

ROBERT

I fully intend to have one.

HESTER

I'm glad to hear it.

ROBERT

I've got just as much talent as Dave has.

HESTER

What kind of talent?

ROBERT

I haven't decided. I can draw pretty well. I'm not a bad musician. I might decide to compose. I might even write. I've often thought of it. And children, you see . . .

HESTER

I don't know much about careers, but Lincoln had children and adored 'em, and if you can do half as well as he did . . .

ROBERT

Then my preferences aren't to be considered?

HESTER

You just leave things to me. If we're poor, I'll cook and scrub floors. I'll bring up our children. I'll take care of you whether we live in New York or Kamchatka. This business is up to me, Rob. Don't let it worry you.

ROBERT

(*Crushed*). I only wanted to make sure you understood my point of view.

HESTER

If I don't, I shall, so let's cut this short. (*She goes a little huffily to the window,* ROBERT *watching her uneasily.*) Hello!

ROBERT

What is it?

HESTER

There goes your mother down the road.

ROBERT

(*He joins her*). So it is! What can she be doing?

HESTER

She's fetching her darling David in out of the cold. I knew she would.

ROBERT

Hester, would you mind not speaking that way of Mother?

HESTER

Can't she leave them alone for a minute?

ROBERT

She's the worrying kind.

HESTER

Oh, rot!

ROBERT

Evidently you're bent on making things as difficult as possible for me.

HESTER

I'm sorry you feel that.
(*A long irritable pause, then.*)

ROBERT

Hester?

HESTER

Yes?

ROBERT

Have you thought any more about our honeymoon?

HESTER

Didn't we decide to go abroad?

ROBERT

Abroad's a pretty general term. You were to think *where* you wanted to be taken.

HESTER

I left that to you.

ROBERT

You said you "didn't care."

HESTER

I don't.

ROBERT

Nor where we live after . . . nor how.

HESTER

I don't . . . I don't . . . I want to live with *you*. (*Suddenly warming*.) What's the use of this, Rob?

ROBERT

We've never talked seriously about our marriage before.

HESTER

What is there to say about it?

ROBERT

A great deal.

HESTER

I don't agree. Marriages are things of feeling. They'd better *not* be talked about.

ROBERT

Real marriages can stand discussion!

HESTER

Rob!

ROBERT

What?

HESTER

That wasn't nice.

ROBERT

Wasn't it?

HESTER

(*Suddenly frightened*). What's the matter, Rob? I'll talk as seriously as you please. Do I love you? Yes. Am I going to make you a good wife? I hope so, though I *am* only twenty and may make mistakes. Are you going to be happy with me? I hope that, too, but you'll have to answer it for yourself.

ROBERT

I can't answer it.

HESTER

Why can't you?

ROBERT

Because I'm not sure of it.

HESTER

Aren't you, Rob?

ROBERT

These things are better faced before than after.

HESTER

What is it you're trying to say?

ROBERT

If only we could be sure!

HESTER

(*Stunned*). So that's it!

ROBERT

Are you so sure you want to marry me?

HESTER

How can I be—now?

ROBERT

Marriage is such a serious thing. You don't realize how serious.

HESTER

Don't I?

ROBERT

No. . . . I hope you won't think harshly of me. . . . And, mind you, I haven't said I wanted to break things off. . . . I only want . . .

HESTER

Please, Rob!

ROBERT

No. You've got to hear me out.

HESTER

I've heard enough, thank you!

ROBERT

I'm only trying to look at this thing . . .

HESTER

Seriously. . . . I know. . . .

ROBERT

Because, after all, the happiness of three people is affected by it.

HESTER

Three?

ROBERT

As Mother said, before dinner.

HESTER

So you talked this over with your mother?

ROBERT

Isn't that natural?

HESTER

Is your mother the third?

ROBERT

Wouldn't she be?

HESTER

Yes, I suppose she would. . . . I think you might tell me what else she had to say.

ROBERT

It was all wise and kind. You may be as hard as you like on me, but you mustn't be hard on poor splendid lonely Mother.

HESTER

(*Savage—under her breath*). So she's lonely, too!

ROBERT

You *will* twist my meaning!

HESTER

You *said* "lonely."

ROBERT

Perhaps I did. But Mother didn't. You know, she never talks about herself.

HESTER

I see. What else did she say about us?

ROBERT

Well, you haven't been very interested in planning our future. She notices such things.

HESTER

What else?

ROBERT

She sees through people, you know.

HESTER

Through me?

ROBERT

She thought, as I must say I do, that we didn't love each other quite enough to . . . At least, she thought we ought to think very carefully before we . . .

HESTER

(*Gripping his two arms with all her strength, she stops him*). If you really want to be free . . . if you really want that, Rob, it's all right. It's perfectly all right. . . . I'll set you free. . . . Don't worry. . . . Only you've got to say so. You've *got* to. . . . Answer me, Rob. *Do* you want to be rid of me? (*There is a pause.* ROBERT *cannot hold her gaze and his eyes fall. She takes the blow.*) I guess that's answer enough. (*She draws a little back from him and pulls the engagement ring from her finger.*) Here's your ring.

ROBERT

Hester! Don't do anything you'll be sorry for afterwards! Don't, please! I can't take it yet!

HESTER

(*Without any sign of emotion, she drops it on a table*). I shall have an easier time of it, if you keep away from me. I want to save my face . . . if I can.

ROBERT

Hester, please!

HESTER

All right, if you won't go, I will.

ROBERT

I'm sorry. Of course I'll go.

HESTER

And take your ring with you.
(*He goes to the table, picks up the ring, pockets it and has just got to the door when* HESTER *breaks into furious, hysterical sobbing. Her sobs rack her and seem, at the same time, to strike* ROBERT *like the blows of a whip.*)

ROBERT

For God's sake, Hester. . . . (*She drops into a chair and sits, staring straight before her, shaken by her sobs of outraged fury and wretchedness.*) Mother! Christina! Come here! Hester . . . (CHRISTINA *appears in the door.* MRS. PHELPS *follows her.* DAVID *appears.* ROBERT *returns to* HESTER.) Can't you pull yourself together? (*She motions him away.*)

CHRISTINA

What's the matter?

ROBERT

It's Hester. Can't you stop her?

MRS. PHELPS

Good heavens, Robin! What's wrong with the child?

ROBERT

She's . . . upset . . . you see, I was just . . . you know . . .

MRS. PHELPS

I see! . . . She's taking it badly.
(HESTER'S *sobs only increase.*)

CHRISTINA

Hester, stop it!

HESTER

I'm all right. . . . I can't . . . I . . . Christina . . . please . . .

CHRISTINA

Open a window, Dave. . . . Haven't you any smelling salts in the house, Mrs. Phelps?
(MRS. PHELPS *goes for them where she left them at tea-time.*)

HESTER

Tell Rob to go away! Tell Rob to go away!

CHRISTINA

Never mind Rob! . . . Get me some aromatic spirits, one of you! Hurry up!
(ROBERT *goes.*)

MRS. PHELPS

Here are my salts.

CHRISTINA

(*Peremptorily*). Hester! (*She holds the salts for* HESTER *to smell.*) Now, stop it! Stop it, do you hear me?

HESTER

I'm trying to stop. If you'd only send these awful people out! Take me away, Christina! Take me back to New York! I've got to get away from here. I can't face them! I can't! I can't!

CHRISTINA

Now, *stop* it!

DAVID

(*Comes forward from a window*). Here's some snow in my handkerchief. Rub it on her wrists and temples.

CHRISTINA

Thanks, Dave.
(*She applies it.* HESTER, *by dint of great effort, gradually overcomes her sobs.* ROBERT *returns with a tumbler partly filled with a milky solution of aromatic spirits.*)

MRS. PHELPS

(*Speaking at the same time, in unfeigned wonderment to* DAVID). Really, I do wonder at what happens to girls nowadays! When I was Hester's age I danced less and saved a little of my strength for self-control.

ROBERT

(*Speaking through*). Here, Dave. Take this.
(DAVID *takes it.* ROBERT *goes again.* DAVID *gives the tumbler to* CHRISTINA.)

CHRISTINA

Good! Can you drink this now, Hester?

HESTER

Thank you, Christina. I'm all right now. It was only . . .

CHRISTINA

Never mind what it was. Drink this. (HESTER *drinks it.*) There, now. That's better. Just sit still and relax.

DAVID

What on earth brought it on?

MRS. PHELPS

(*Shrugging her shoulders*). Rob and she must have had a falling out.

DAVID

No ordinary one. . . . Rob! He's gone. . . . That's funny.

MRS. PHELPS

He'd naturally be distressed.

HESTER

I'm really all right, now, Christina . . . and frightfully ashamed. . . .

MRS. PHELPS

You'd better see how Rob is, Dave. His nerves are none too stout. Such scenes aren't good for him.

HESTER

(*In a high, strained voice*). No, isn't that so, Mrs. Phelps?

MRS. PHELPS

Did you speak to me, Hester?

HESTER

Take the smelling salts to Rob with my love. . . . Oh God, Christina!

CHRISTINA

Now, never *mind,* Hester. You'll go to pieces again.

HESTER

But I've got to mind! And I'm all right! It won't hurt me. . . I wish you'd go, David.

CHRISTINA

Yes, Dave, do. I'll come up in a jiffy.

MRS. PHELPS

When Hester's quieted down. (*To* DAVID.) We'd better both go and see how Rob is. (*She is just going.*)

HESTER

Mrs. Phelps. There's something I want to ask you before we part.

MRS. PHELPS

Tomorrow, my dear girl. . . .

HESTER

There isn't going to be any tomorrow.

MRS. PHELPS

What?

HESTER

Rob has just broken our engagement.

MRS. PHELPS

Not really!

CHRISTINA

(*Staggered*). Hester, what do you mean?

HESTER

I mean what I say. Rob's just broken our engagement.
(CHRISTINA *motions to* DAVE *to go. He obeys.*)

MRS. PHELPS

I'm immensely distressed, of course.

HESTER

(*Shaking her head doggedly*). He talked it all over with you before dinner. He told me that much, so it won't do you the least bit of good to pretend to be surprised.

MRS. PHELPS

Aren't you forgetting yourself, Hester?

HESTER

You made him do it. Why did you make him do it, Mrs. Phelps?
(CHRISTINA, *amazed, draws back to observe the pair of them.*)

MRS. PHELPS

(*Perfect dignity*). I don't intend to stand here, Hester, and allow any hysterical girl to be rude to me.

HESTER

(*Driving on querulously*). I'm not being rude! All I want to know is why you talked Rob into jilting me. Will you answer me, please?

MRS. PHELPS

Such things may be painful, my dear girl, but they're far less painful before than after.

HESTER

He quoted that much.

CHRISTINA

What's the good of this, Hester?

HESTER

I'm only trying to make her tell me why she did it.

MRS. PHELPS

But, Hester! Really! This is absurd!

HESTER

You've got to! You've got to explain!

MRS. PHELPS

I had nothing to do with Robin's change of heart.

HESTER

You must have had, Mrs. Phelps, and I'm demanding an explanation of why you talked Rob into . . .

MRS. PHELPS

Isn't it enough that he found out in time that you weren't the wife for him?

HESTER

That isn't the truth!

CHRISTINA

Hester, darling!

HESTER

Can you tell me what he meant when he said that the happiness of *three* people was at stake?

MRS. PHELPS

He must have been thinking of your happiness as well as his own and mine.

HESTER

What about your loneliness?

MRS. PHELPS

This *is* contemptible of you!

CHRISTINA

Really, Hester, this *can't* do any good!

HESTER

I'm going to make her admit that she made Rob . . .

MRS. PHELPS

(*Exploding*). Very well, then, since you insist! I did advise my son to break with you. Do you want to know why?

HESTER

Yes!

MRS. PHELPS

Because of your indifference. . . .

HESTER

Oh!

MRS. PHELPS

Because he came to me to say that you neither love him nor make any pretense of loving him . . .

HESTER

Rob said that?

MRS. PHELPS

He even said that you must have misconstrued his friendship and that he never wanted to marry you . . .

HESTER

No!

MRS. PHELPS

And I told him to risk anything . . . anything, rather than such an appalling marriage . . .

HESTER

I don't believe a word of it!

MRS. PHELPS

You may believe it or not!

CHRISTINA

Mrs. Phelps, you had really better let me handle this.

MRS. PHELPS

Willingly.

HESTER

Do you believe I took advantage of Rob, Christina?

CHRISTINA

Of course not!

MRS. PHELPS

So you take her side, Christina!

CHRISTINA

I don't believe *that,* Mrs. Phelps.

MRS. PHELPS

(*She realizes that she has gone too far*). No? Well, perhaps . . .

CHRISTINA

Whatever Robert may think, I can't believe that he said . . .

MRS. PHELPS

(*Frightened*). Perhaps he didn't say quite that, in so many words . . . but he certainly meant . . .

HESTER

I'm going. I'm going now. Right this minute.

MRS. PHELPS

There's a train at nine in the morning. It gets you to New York at twelve. I shall have the car for you at eight-thirty.

HESTER

May I have the car now, please, Mrs. Phelps?

MRS. PHELPS

There's no train tonight.

HESTER

It doesn't matter. I won't stay here. Not another minute. I'll go to the hotel in town.

MRS. PHELPS

You'll do nothing of the sort!

HESTER

You see if I don't!

MRS. PHELPS

You've got to think of appearances!

HESTER

Appearances are your concern. Yours and Rob's. I'm going to the hotel. I don't care what people say! I don't care about anything. I won't stay here!

MRS. PHELPS

Can't you talk to her, Christina? Surely you see . . . for all our sakes!

HESTER

If you won't let me have the car, I'll call a taxi. . . . (*She plunges towards the telephone.*)

MRS. PHELPS

I forbid you!

HESTER

(*Seizing the instrument*). I want a taxi . . . a taxi. . . . What *is* the number? . . . Well, give it to me. . . . Locust 4000? Give me Locust 4000!

(MRS. PHELPS *hesitates an instant, then, with terrible coolness, steps forward and jerks the telephone cord from the wall. Except for a startled exclamation, very low, from* CHRISTINA, *there is not a sound.* HESTER *hangs up the receiver and sets down the dead instrument.*)

MRS. PHELPS

(*After an interminable silence*). You are the only person in the world who has ever forced me to do an undignified thing. I shall not forget it.

(*She goes nobly.*)

HESTER

(*Weakly, turning to* CHRISTINA). Christina, it isn't true what she said. . . . He did. . . . He did want to marry me! Really, he did! He did!

CHRISTINA

Of course he did, darling!

HESTER

I won't stay! I won't stay under that woman's roof!

CHRISTINA

Hester, darling!

HESTER

I'll walk to town!

CHRISTINA

Don't, Hester!

HESTER

That wasn't true, what she said!

CHRISTINA

Of course not!

HESTER

I still love him. . . . Let me go, Christina, I'll walk . . .

CHRISTINA

You can't, at this time of night! It wouldn't be safe!

HESTER

I don't care! I won't stay!

CHRISTINA

There! There! You'll come to bed now, won't you!

HESTER

No! No! I can't! I'd rather die! I'll walk to town.

CHRISTINA

You'll force me to come with you, Hester. I can't let you go alone.

HESTER

I won't stay another minute!

CHRISTINA

Do you want to make me walk with you? Think, Hester! Think what I told you before dinner! Do you want to make me walk all that way in the cold?

HESTER

(*Awed by this*). Oh, your baby! I didn't mean to forget your baby! Oh, Christina, you mustn't stay, either! This is a dreadful house! You've got to get your baby away from this house, Christina! Awful things happen here!

CHRISTINA

Hester, darling! Won't you please be sensible and come up to bed?

HESTER

(*Speaking at the same time as her nerves begin to go again*). Awful things, Christina. . . . You'll see if you don't come away! You'll see! . . . She'll do the same thing to you that she's done to me. You'll see! You'll see!

CURTAIN

ACT TWO

SCENE II

SCENE: *The curtan rises again, as soon as possible, upon* DAVID'S *little bedroom, untouched since the day when* DAVID *went away to Harvard and scorned to take his prep school trophies and souvenirs with him. The furniture is rather more than simple. The bed is single. There is a dresser. There are only a couple of chairs. The curtains at the single window have been freshly laundered and put back in their old state by* MRS. PHELPS *in a spirit of maternal archeology. Insignificant loving cups, won at tennis, stand about the dresser. No pennants, no banners. There might be some tennis racquets, golf sticks, crossed skis, a pair of snow-shoes, class photographs and framed diplomas. There must also be a fairly important reproduction of Velasquez' Don Balthazar Carlos on horseback, selected by* MRS. PHELPS *as* DAVID'S *favorite Old Master. A final touch is* DAVID'S *baby pillow.*

DAVID *stands in his pajamas and socks, about to enter upon the last stages of his preparations to retire for the night. The room has been strewn with clothing during the preliminary stages. Now he is in the ambulatory state of mind. A series of crosses and circumnavigations produces several empty packs of cigarettes from several pockets, corners of the suitcase, etc. This frustration brings on baffled scratchings of the head and legs. Then he gives up the cigarette problem, turns again to the suitcase, spills out several dirty shirts and finally, apparently from the very bottom, extracts a dressing-gown, a pair of slippers, a tooth-brush and some tooth-paste. He sheds the socks, dons the slippers and dressing-gown and sallies forth with brush and paste to do up his teeth in the bathroom. He goes by the door which gives on the hall at the head of the stairs.*

After he has been gone a few seconds, a tiny scratching sound is heard on the other side of the other door to the room and that is opened from without. We see the scratcher at work conveying the impression that a wee mousie wants to come in. The wee mousie is none other than MRS. PHELPS, *all smiles in her best negligée, the most effective garment she wears in the course of the entire play, carrying the largest eiderdown comforter ever seen on any stage.*

The smile fades a little when she discovers that the room is empty. Then its untidiness catches her eye and she shakes her head reprovingly, as who should say: "What creatures these big boys are!" She goes to work at once, true mother that she is, to pick things up. She loves her work and puts her whole heart into it. The trousers are neatly hung over the back of the chair, the coat and waistcoat hung over them. The shirts, socks and underwear are folded and laid chastely on the seat. One or two of the garments receive devout maternal kisses and hugs. Then she goes to the bed, lifts off the suitcase, pushes it underneath, adjusts the eiderdown, smooths the pillow and kisses that. Last, all smiles again, she sits, carefully disposing her laces and ribbons, to await DAVID'S *return. She yearns for it and she has not long to wait.*

DAVID *returns. His mother's beaming smile, as he opens the door, arouses his usual distaste for filial sentimentality. It is intensified, now—and very ill-concealed—by the hour, his costume and recent events. He hesitates in the doorway.*

MRS. PHELPS

Why do you look so startled? It's only Mother!

DAVID

(*Laconic*). Hello, Mother!

MRS. PHELPS

I came in to ask if you needed anything and . . .

DAVID

Not a thing, thanks.

MRS. PHELPS

And to warn you against opening the window in this weather. Oh, and I brought you that extra cover. I've been picking up after you, too!

DAVID

(*Looking gloomily about*). You needn't have troubled.

MRS. PHELPS

It took me back to the old days when I used to tuck you up in that same little bed . . .

DAVID

(*A strong hint*). Yeah. . . . I'm just turning in, Mother.

MRS. PHELPS

(*Regardless*). . . . And then sit in this very chair and talk over all my problems with you. I feel that I must talk to my big boy tonight. . . . I must get acquainted with my Dave again.

DAVID

(*An even stronger hint*). We're not exactly strangers, are we? And besides, it's getting late.

MRS. PHELPS

(*Even more persistent*). It was always in these late hours that we had our talks in the old days when we were still comrades. Oh, are those days gone forever? Don't you remember how we used to play that we had an imaginary kingdom where we were king and queen?

DAVID

(*Moribund*). Did we? I wish Chris 'ud come up.

MRS. PHELPS

(*A frown and she speaks quickly*). Have you noticed, Dave boy, that your room is just as you left it? I've made a little shrine of it. The same curtains, the same . . .

DAVID

(*Breaking in*). I suppose Chris is still trying to get Hester quiet?

MRS. PHELPS

I suppose so. . . . And every day I dusted in here myself and every night I prayed in here for . . .

DAVID

(*A little too dryly for good manners*). Thanks.

MRS. PHELPS

(*Reproachfully*). Oh, David, you can't get that horrid scene downstairs out of your mind!

DAVID

No.

MRS. PHELPS

Try! I need my big boy so! Because I'm facing the gravest problem of my life, Dave. And you've got to help me.

DAVID

What is it?

MRS. PHELPS

Is it true that I'm of no more use to my two sons?

DAVID

Whatever put such an idea in your head?

MRS. PHELPS

You did.

DAVID

(*Shocked*). I?

MRS. PHELPS

(*Nodding*). You weren't really glad to see me this afternoon.

DAVID

(*In all sincerity*). I was. . . . I was delighted!

MRS. PHELPS

(*Bravely stopping him*). Not glad as I was to see you. I noticed, Dave! . . . And that made me wonder whether this scientific age—because it is a scientific age, Dave—isn't making more than one boy forget that the bond between mother and son is the strongest bond on earth. . . .

DAVID

(*Not quite sure of the superlative*). Well, it's certainly strong.

MRS. PHELPS

Do you realize how sinful any boy would be to want to loosen it?

DAVID

Sure I realize that!

MRS. PHELPS

I see so many poor mothers, no less deserving of love and loyalty than I, neglected and discarded by their children, set aside for other interests.

DAVID

What interests?

MRS. PHELPS

All kinds of things. . . . Wives. . . .

DAVID

(*Shying*). Nonsense, Mother!

MRS. PHELPS

The Chinese never set any relationship above their filial piety. They'd be the greatest people on earth if only they'd stop smoking opium.

DAVID

You haven't any kick, have you? I mean: Rob and I haven't let you down?

MRS. PHELPS

Not yet, Dave. But, you know the old saying?

DAVID

What old saying?

MRS. PHELPS

That a boy's mother is his best friend.

DAVID

Oh! Bet I do!

MRS. PHELPS

Do you think of *your* mother as *your* best friend?

DAVID

None better, certainly.

MRS. PHELPS

None better! Hm! You *can* say, though, that you haven't entirely outgrown me?

DAVID

Of course I haven't! Why, I'd hate to have you think that just because I'm a grown man, I . . .

MRS. PHELPS

No son is ever a grown man to his mother! (*A knock at the door.*) Who can that be at this hour?

DAVID

I hope it's Chris.
(*He starts for the door.*)

MRS. PHELPS

(*Freezing suddenly as she rises*). Dave!

DAVID

(*Turning*). What?

MRS. PHELPS

Wait. . . . I mustn't intrude. . . . Goodnight. . . .

DAVID

(*Calling out*). Just a minute! (*To his mother, politely.*) You wouldn't be intruding!

MRS. PHELPS

Not on you, I know. But . . .

DAVID

Not on Chris either!

MRS. PHELPS

I know best. Kiss me goodnight.

DAVID

Goodnight, Mother.
(*He kisses her cheek.*)

MRS. PHELPS

(*A quick hug*). God bless my big boy!
(*She goes as she came.* DAVID'S *look, as he watches her door close behind her, is baffled. He goes quickly to the other door.* ROBERT *is standing outside.*)

DAVID

For Pete's sake, Rob! I thought it was Chris! . . . Why didn't you walk in?

ROBERT

I thought Mother was in here.

DAVID

She was. She just went to bed.

ROBERT

(*Entering*). She must have thought it was Chris, too!

DAVID

How do you mean?

ROBERT

I shouldn't rush things if I were you.

DAVID

Maybe you're right. Women are too deep for me.

ROBERT

I came in for a smoke. I had to talk to you. I've been sitting in my room wondering what you think of all this.

DAVID

(*Cigarette business*). I don't think much and that's the truth!

ROBERT

Good God, Dave, can't you be a little easier on me? Didn't you ever feel any doubts when you were engaged? Were you always so sure of Christina that you . . .

DAVID

The first time I asked Chris to marry me, she made it perfectly clear that, as far as she was concerned, I was to consider myself dripping wet. After that I was too damn scared I wouldn't get her to think whether she loved me or not.

ROBERT

(*Darkly*). And I never had one comfortable moment from the time Hester accepted me.

DAVID

Oh, being in love's like everything else. You've got to put some guts in it.

ROBERT

(*Bitter anger*). You think I haven't got any guts. You want to make me look like a callous cad! All right, I'll *be* a cad. I don't care what people think about me! But I'll tell you one thing! I'm damned if I'm going to let you turn Mother against me!

DAVID

Do *what?*

ROBERT

You heard me!

DAVID

My God, haven't you outgrown that old stuff yet?

ROBERT

I know from experience what to expect when you and Mother get together. I used to listen at that door, night after night, night after night, while you and Mother sat in here and talked me over. Then I'd watch for the change in her next morning at breakfast when I hadn't slept a wink all night. The way you used to own the earth at those breakfasts! Well, if you try any of that old stuff tonight, I'll lose the only prop I've got left.

DAVID

Isn't it about time you let go of Mother's apron-strings?

ROBERT

You would say that! You don't realize that I'm desperate.

DAVID

Desperate, hell! You're crazy! Mother's gone to bed and . . . (*The wee mousie scratches at the door again.*) What's that?

MRS. PHELPS

(*Entering*). It's only Mother. Are my two beaux quarreling? Jealous, jealous Robin! What's the matter?

DAVID

Nothing.

MRS. PHELPS

A fine man is a frank man, David! Do you think I didn't hear every word you said? Surely you must know that Hester wasn't worthy of your brother?

DAVID

Wasn't she? Well, let's not talk any more about it.

MRS. PHELPS

Oh, but we must. For all our sakes, we must clear the air. *I* have always taken the stand that my boys could do absolutely no wrong and that is the proper stand for a mother to take. Didn't I always side with you in your school scrapes? Even against the masters? Even when you were clearly in the wrong? Of course, I did! And I shall not permit one word of criticism against your brother now. Loyalty, Dave! Loyalty! Come, now! Tell Mother all about it!

DAVID

But if you overheard every word we said!

MRS. PHELPS

"Overheard," David? Am I given to eavesdropping?

DAVID

I didn't say so.

MRS. PHELPS

I simply want to make sure I didn't miss anything while I was in my bath.

DAVID

I don't misunderstand him. I'm sorry for Hester, that's all.

ROBERT

We're all sorry for Hester.

DAVID

I don't think it's your place to be too sorry.

ROBERT

Let's drop it, Mother.

MRS. PHELPS

No. I've got to know what's on Dave's mind. My whole life may hang on it. What is it, Dave? (*Carefully sounding.*) If Robin's not to blame, perhaps I am?

ROBERT

(*Horrified*). Mother!

DAVID

What's the use of getting so worked up over nothing?

MRS. PHELPS

Nothing! Can you say "nothing" after what *we* were talking about a few minutes ago?

DAVID

(*Cornered*). I only think . . .

MRS. PHELPS

What?

DAVID

Well, that you've both handed Hester a somewhat dirty deal. And Chris must think so, too!

MRS. PHELPS

(*Wary*). Indeed! And how, please?

DAVID

Well, it comes of what Chris calls "mythologizing."

MRS. PHELPS

(*Frightened*). Does Christina discuss our family affairs already?

DAVID

No. It's one of her old ideas about people in general. You mythologize Rob into a little tin god. Rob thinks he is a little tin god. Along comes Hester and falls in love with the real Rob. She never heard of your little tin god Rob. She doesn't deliver the incense and tom-toms. That makes you and Rob sore and the whole works goes to hell. That's mythologizing. Believe me, it can make plenty of trouble.

MRS. PHELPS

(*Relieved that the criticism is so general*). If that's all I'm to blame for, I don't know that I can object. Expecting the best of everyone is, at least, a worthy fault. Still, if I may venture an older woman's opinion on one of Christina's ideas?

DAVID

I wish to God I hadn't started this.

MRS. PHELPS

So do I. But perhaps you'll tell me what Christina would say to the true reason for Robin's break with Hester?

DAVID

What is the true reason?

MRS. PHELPS

Do you want to tell him, Robin?

ROBERT

(*Inspired*). I broke with Hester because of an idea, the ideal of womankind Mother gave us both by being the great woman that she is. *I* knew *I* couldn't be happy with any woman who fell short of her.

MRS. PHELPS

What becomes of your "dirty deal" now, David?

DAVID

But I'm not going against that ideal, Mother. That's another thing.

ROBERT

You couldn't have troubled much about it when you married!

MRS. PHELPS

You shouldn't have said that, Robin. I haven't had Christina's advantages. I wasn't given a German education.

DAVID

Now, don't take this out on Chris, Mother.

MRS. PHELPS

I think I know a little of a mother's duty toward her daughter-in-law. Goodnight, Robin. I must talk with your brother alone, now. And before you quarrel again, stop to think that you are all I have, you two, and try to consider me. It isn't much to ask and it won't be for long. You both know what the doctors think about my heart! Dr. McClintock tells me I may go at any moment. (*Pause, then.*) Goodnight, Robin.

ROBERT

(*Frightened*). Goodnight, Mother.

MRS. PHELPS

You may come into my room later, if you like. I may need you to comfort me after . . . (*She waves her hand. He leaves. She has never taken her eyes off* DAVID. *When the door closes behind* ROBERT, *she speaks.*) David, in this moment, when your brother and I most needed your loyalty, you have hurt me more than I have ever been hurt in my life before, even by your father.

DAVID

I never meant to hurt you.

MRS. PHELPS

(*Working it up*). You have been wicked, David! Wicked! Wicked!

DAVID

How?

MRS. PHELPS

You have shown me too clearly that what I most dreaded has already come to pass!

DAVID

What, Mother?

MRS. PHELPS

You *have* loosened the bond between us. You have discarded me.

DAVID

(*Horrified*). But I haven't done any such thing!

MRS. PHELPS

Don't say any more! Act upon your treachery, if you will, but don't, please, don't say another thing. Remember!
"The brave man does it with a sword,
The coward with a word!"
(*And she sweeps out, slamming her door after her.*)

DAVID

(*Speaking through her door*). But I didn't mean anything. . . . Won't you let me explain? . . . I didn't know what I was talking about!
(*There is no answer. He rattles the door. It is locked. He comes away, swearing softly under his breath. Then, manfully, he*

takes refuge in sulks. He kicks off his slippers and throws his dressing-gown aside. He lights a cigarette and flounces into bed, snatching up a book or magazine en route. Just as he is settled, his mother's door opens again very slowly. MRS. PHELPS *presents a tear-stained face to view and comes in.*)

MRS. PHELPS

Smoking in bed, Dave boy?

DAVID

(*Starting up*). Eh?

MRS. PHELPS

It's only Mother. . . . No, don't get up. . . . Let me sit here as I used to in the old days.

DAVID

(*Sitting up*). Mother, I didn't mean . . .

MRS. PHELPS

Never mind. I was wrong to be hurt.

DAVID

But you had me all wrong. I mean . . . You and I . . . We're just the same as we always were. . . . Believe me, we are. . . . Why, if anything came to spoil things between us . . .

MRS. PHELPS

(*The first objective conquered*). That's what I wanted you to say! Now talk to me about Christina.

DAVID

(*Taken aback without knowing why*). Huh?

MRS. PHELPS

Give me your hand in mine and tell me all about her.

DAVID

(*Obeying rather reluctantly*). What is there to tell?

MRS. PHELPS

Well, for one thing, tell me you think she's going to like me!

DAVID

(*Warmly*). She does already!

MRS. PHELPS

Doesn't think I'm an old-fashioned frump?

DAVID

I should say not! How could she?

MRS. PHELPS

She's such a modern young lady. So lovely, but so very up-to-date. You must tell me everything I can do to win her to me. And I'll do it. Though I'm afraid of her, Dave.

DAVID

(*Amused*). Afraid of Chris? Why?

MRS. PHELPS

She's so much cleverer than I am. She makes me realize that I'm just a timid old lady of the old school.

DAVID

(*Nice indignation*). You old!

MRS. PHELPS

(*Archly so brave about it*). Yes, I am!

DAVID

Well, you and Chris are going to be the best friends ever.

MRS. PHELPS

You *are* happy, aren't you?

DAVID

You bet I am!

MRS. PHELPS

Really happy?

DAVID

Couldn't be happier!

MRS. PHELPS

I'm so glad! And I thank God that when your hour struck it didn't strike falsely as it did for Robin. Because any one can see the difference between Christina and Hester. Of course, that's a little the difference between you and Rob. You know what I've always said. You are *my* son. Robert takes after his father. But you mustn't be impatient with Christina if she seems at first, a little slow, a little resentful of our family. We've always been so close, we three. She's bound to feel a little out of it, at first. A little jealous . . .

DAVID

Not Chris!

MRS. PHELPS

Oh, come now, Dave! I'm sure she's perfect, but you mustn't try to tell me she isn't human. Young wives are sure to be a little bit possessive and exacting and . . . selfish at first.

DAVID

We needn't worry about that.

MRS. PHELPS

No. . . . At first I thought Christina was going to be hard and cold. I didn't expect her to have our sense of humor and I don't believe she has much of that. But we've more than we need already. If only she will learn to care for me as I care for her, we can be so happy, all four of us together, can't we?

DAVID

You bet we can!

MRS. PHELPS

(*Dreamily*). Building our houses in Phelps Manor. . . . Deciding to put an Italian Villa here and a little bungalow there. . . . (*As* DAVID *grows restive*.) But the important thing for you, Dave boy, is a sense of proportion about your marriage. I'm going to lecture you, now, for your own good. If, at first, Christina does seem a little exacting or unreasonable, particularly about us, remember that she has to adjust herself to a whole new world here, a very different world from her friends in Omaha. And you must never be impatient with her. Because, if you are, I shall take her side against you.

DAVID

You *are* a great woman, Mother!

MRS. PHELPS

You're the great one! How many boys of your age let their wives undermine all their old associations and loosen all their old ties!

DAVID

Chris wouldn't try that!

MRS. PHELPS

She might not *want* to. But jealous girls think things that aren't so and say things that aren't true. Morbid things.

DAVID

Morbid things? Chris?

MRS. PHELPS

Only you won't pay too much attention or take her too seriously. I know that, because you would no more let anyone strike at me than I would let anyone strike at you.

DAVID

But Chris wouldn't . . .

MRS. PHELPS

As I said to Christina this afternoon: "Christina," I said, "I cannot allow you to sacrifice David!"

DAVID

Chris sacrifice me! How?

MRS. PHELPS

Why, by taking you away from your magnificent opportunity here.

DAVID

Oh!

MRS. PHELPS

Be master in your own house. Meet her selfishness with firmness, her jealousy with fairness and her . . . her exaggerations with a grain of salt. . . .

DAVID

What exaggerations?

MRS. PHELPS

Well, you know . . . a girl . . . a young wife, like Christina . . . *might* possibly make the mistake of . . . well, of taking sides . . . in what happened downstairs, for instance . . . and without fully understanding. . . . You can see how fatal *that* would be. . . . But, if you face the facts always, Dave boy, and nothing *but* the facts, your marriage will be a happy one. And, when you want advice, come to your mother always.

DAVID

Thanks.

MRS. PHELPS

Now, isn't your mother your best friend?

DAVID

You bet you are, Mummy!

MRS. PHELPS

How long it is since you've called me that! Bless you, my dear, dear boy!
(*She leans over to seal her triumph with a kiss.* CHRISTINA'S *entrance follows so closely upon her knock that the picture is still undisturbed for her to see. She has changed her dress for a very simple negligée. Her mood is dangerous.*)

CHRISTINA

Oh, I beg your pardon!

MRS. PHELPS

(*So sweetly, after the very briefest pause*). Come in, Christina. I was only saying goodnight to Dave. Nothing private! You're one of the family now. You must feel free to come and go as you like in the house.

CHRISTINA

Thank you.

MRS. PHELPS

We can accustom ourselves to it, can't we, Dave?

DAVID

Yeah. . . .

CHRISTINA

Dave and I have got so used to sharing the same room, I came in here quite naturally and . . .

MRS. PHELPS

Here's your dressing-gown, Dave boy. We won't look while you slip it on.
(*Confusedly* DAVE *gets out of bed and robes himself.* CHRISTINA'S *eyes meet his mother's.* CHRISTINA'S *eyes have the least flash of scorn in them,* MRS. PHELPS' *the least quaver of fear. In that glance, the two women agree on undying enmity.*)

DAVID

You can . . . you can look now.

CHRISTINA

Are you quite sure *I* may, Mrs. Phelps?

MRS. PHELPS

Whatever else you may have taken from me, Christina, you *cannot* take from me the joy of feeling my son here, once more, in his old room, beside me.

CHRISTINA

(*Marking up the first score*). I haven't meant to take anything from you, Mrs. Phelps.

MRS. PHELPS

(*So sweetly again*). You know I was only joking. (*She is routed, though.*) Good-night. (*The two women kiss.*) Don't keep Dave up too late. He's very tired. (*She pats* DAVE, *as she passes him on her way to her door.*) You must be tired, too, Christina. How *is* Hester, now?

CHRISTINA

Quite all right, thank you.

MRS. PHELPS

Thank *you!*
(*She blows a kiss to* DAVID *from the door and goes.* CHRISTINA *stands motionless.* DAVID *reaches for a cigarette.*)

DAVID

You look pretty stern, Chris.

CHRISTINA

Do I?

DAVID

You've been a brick.

CHRISTINA

Thanks.

DAVID

Hester *is* all right, isn't she?

CHRISTINA

Yes, poor youngster! I shouldn't be surprised if she were really in luck, Dave.

DAVID

You may be right. But it isn't exactly up to me to say so, is it?
(*He lights his cigarette. Her eyes burn him up.*)

CHRISTINA

Dave. . . .

DAVID

Yes?

CHRISTINA

Whom do you love?

DAVID

You. Why?

CHRISTINA

I wondered, that's all. I want to be kissed.

DAVID

That's easy.
(*He takes her in his arms.*)

CHRISTINA

Such a tired girl, Dave. . . . I want to be held on to and made much of. . . . I want to feel all safe and warm. . . . I want you to tell me that you're in love with me and that you enjoy being in love with me. Because just loving isn't enough and it's being in love that really matters. . . . Will you tell me all that, please, Dave?

DAVID

(*Hugging her*). Darling!

CHRISTINA

You haven't kissed me yet.

DAVID

(*Complying, a trifle absent-mindedly*). There!

CHRISTINA

(*As she draws back from him*). That isn't what I call making love in a big way.

DAVID

(*Repeating the kiss with more energy*). Is that better?

CHRISTINA

There's still something lacking. . . . What's the matter? There's nobody watching us.

DAVID

That's a funny thing to say.

CHRISTINA

You take me right back to my first beau in Germany. He never got very far, either. All the English he knew was "water closet."

DAVID

Chris! Shame on you!

CHRISTINA

Shame on *you*, making me take to low jokes to amuse you. . . . I love you.

DAVID

Darling, darling, Chris!

CHRISTINA

I love you! I love you! (*For a moment she clings to him wildly.*) I hate being so far from you tonight, Dave. 'Way off there at the other end of the hall!

DAVID

I'm none too pleased myself. It's just one of Mother's fool ideas.
(*He lowers his voice whenever he mentions his mother.*)

CHRISTINA

She naturally wanted you near *her!*

DAVID

That's it. (*His eyes fall beneath her steady gaze.*) We mustn't talk so loud. We'll keep Mother awake. She can hear every sound we make.

CHRISTINA

Let her hear! It'll do her good!

DAVID

That's no way to talk, Chris!

CHRISTINA

Excuse me. I didn't mean to snap. I've been fearfully shaken up tonight.

DAVID

I know you have.

CHRISTINA

And I'm awfully tired.

DAVID

Poor girl!

CHRISTINA

Poor Hester! . . . I don't feel like going to bed yet. I want to talk. Do you mind?

DAVID

Go to it.

CHRISTINA

I've never come up against anything like this before, I've heard of it, but I've never met it. I don't know what to do about it. And it scares me.

DAVID

What does?

CHRISTINA

I don't know how to tell you. (*Then with sudden force.*) But I've got to tell you, Dave. I've got to tell you. There are no two ways about that.

DAVID

What are you driving at?

CHRISTINA

Well . . . (*But she changes her mind.*) May I ask you a question? Rather an intimate one?

DAVID

If you must!

CHRISTINA

Being your wife, I thought I might.

DAVID

Shoot!

CHRISTINA

Do you look on me as apart from all other women? I mean, do you think of all the women in the world and then think of me quite, quite differently? Do you, Dave?

DAVID

I'll bite. Do I?

CHRISTINA

Please answer me. It's awfully important to me just now.

DAVID

Of course I do. . . . Why is it so important just now?

CHRISTINA

Because that's how I feel about you and all the other men in the world. Because that's what being in love must mean and being properly and happily married. Two people, a man and a woman, together by themselves, miles and miles from everybody, from *everybody* else, glancing around, now and then, at all the rest of mankind, at *all* the rest, Dave, and saying: "Are you still there? And getting along all right? Sure there's nothing we can do to help?"

DAVID

Only we do help, don't we?

CHRISTINA

Only really if we feel that way about one another. Only *by* feeling that way.

DAVID

That's pretty deep! You do go off on the damnedest tacks!

CHRISTINA

Don't you see how that feeling between a man and a woman is what keeps life going?

DAVID

Is it?

CHRISTINA

What else could be strong enough?

DAVID

Perhaps you're right. (*Then, unaccountably, he shies.*) But what's the idea in getting so worked up about it?

CHRISTINA

Because it matters so much, Dave . . . just now . . . that you and I feel that way about each other and that we go on feeling that way and exclude everybody, *everybody* else. Tell me you think so, too?

DAVID

Sure, I think so. . . . (*Then, again, he shies from her inner meaning.*) You're getting the worst habit of working yourself up over nothing!

CHRISTINA

Do you realize, Dave, that the blackest sinner on earth is the man . . . or woman . . . who breaks in on that feeling? Or tampers with it in any way? Or perverts it?

DAVID

If you say so, I'll say he is.

CHRISTINA

He!

DAVID

Huh?

CHRISTINA

Never mind. . . . Your brother didn't feel that way about poor Hester, did he?

DAVID

Rob always was a funny egg.

CHRISTINA

Your mother calls him Robin! "Tweet! Tweet! What does the Birdie say?"

DAVID

From all I can gather, Hester didn't feel much of *any* way about him.

CHRISTINA

I know better than that. . . . I've had that child on my hands for the past hour. I've learned an awful lot, Dave. About her, and *from* her.

DAVID

Look here, Chris. . . . Don't you get mixed up in this business, will you?

CHRISTINA

I wonder if I'm not mixed up in it already.

DAVID

Well, don't "take sides."

CHRISTINA

I wonder if I can help taking sides.

DAVID

It's none of our business.

CHRISTINA

I wish I were sure of that. (*Baffled, she again shifts her approach.*) Poor little Hester goes tomorrow morning. How long are we staying?

DAVID

Oh, I dunno.

CHRISTINA

A week?

DAVID

We can't do less, can we?

CHRISTINA

Can't we?

DAVID

Don't you want to? (*There is another pause before* CHRISTINA *shakes her head.* DAVID *frowns.*) You see what comes of taking things so hard? I'm just as distressed over what's happened as you are. Maybe more. But I certainly don't want to run away. It wouldn't be right. Mother'd never understand. I'd feel like a bum going off and leaving her in the lurch after this. Think what Rob's put her through today and what she'll have to go through with Hester's family and all her friends and everybody else before she's done!

CHRISTINA

She seems to be bearing up.

DAVID

You can't be sure with Mother.

CHRISTINA

Can't you?

DAVID

She's so damned game.

CHRISTINA

Is she?

DAVID

Can't you see that? And, anyway, I've got to look around.

CHRISTINA

What at? The houses in Phelps Manor?

DAVID

I know how you feel, Chris, about Mother's helping hand. But I can't be *throwing* away opportunities, now, can I? With the baby coming?

CHRISTINA

(*Gravely*). No, Dave. Of course, you can't. Neither can I.

DAVID

How do you mean?

CHRISTINA

Forgotten all about *my* opportunities, haven't you?

DAVID

What opportunities?

CHRISTINA

My appointment.

DAVID

Didn't Mother say she could scare up something for you here?

CHRISTINA

She thought she might "scare up" a place where I could "putter around" and keep myself "happy and contented" when the "real doctors" weren't working.

DAVID

She didn't mean anything unkind, Chris. Just give Mother a chance and . . . What are you crying for?

CHRISTINA

(*Hotly untruthful*). I'm not crying.

DAVID

You are!

CHRISTINA

I can't help it. . . .

DAVID

But what's the matter?

CHRISTINA

It doesn't look as if I'm to have much of a show for my eight years of hard work, does it?

DAVID

Mother and I'll dope out something. I couldn't leave her now. You know that. And anyway, I've got to stay till I get my shirts washed. I've only got two left.

CHRISTINA

Then we stay, of course.

DAVID

And I must say, Chris, that I don't think you're quite playing ball to judge my home and my family entirely on what you've seen tonight. Besides, the whole purpose of this visit was to bring you and Mother together and to show Mother that a lady scientist mayn't be as bad as she sounds. Because you and Mother have just got to hit it off, you know.

CHRISTINA

Have we?

DAVID

You're apt to be impatient, Chris, and I'm afraid you're intolerant.

CHRISTINA

Those are bad faults in a scientist.

DAVID

They're bad faults in anybody. . . . Now, you just give me time and you'll see how things straighten out.

CHRISTINA

Aren't you satisfied with the way our meeting has come off?

DAVID

There's no use pretending it was ideal. I believe in facing the facts always. But don't you worry. Mother gets on *my* nerves sometimes. You just have to remember what a hard life she's had.

CHRISTINA

How has it been hard?

DAVID

Oh, lots of ways. My father wasn't much, you know.

CHRISTINA

I didn't know. You've never mentioned him.

DAVID

He died when I was five.

CHRISTINA

What was the matter with him? Women or drink?

DAVID

Nothing like that. He just didn't amount to much.

CHRISTINA

Made a lot of money, didn't he?

DAVID

Lots.

CHRISTINA

And left your mother rich. What other troubles has she had?

DAVID

Well, her health.

CHRISTINA

It doesn't seem so bad.

DAVID

It is, though. Heart. And I wish I could tell you half of what she's gone through for Rob and me.

CHRISTINA

Go on and tell me. I'd like to hear.

DAVID

I've heard her say she was born without a selfish hair in her head.

CHRISTINA

No!

DAVID

And that's about true. Why, I've seen her nurse Rob through one thing after another when she'd admit to me that she was twice as sick as he was. I've seen her come in here from taking care of him and she'd be half fainting with her bad heart, but there'd be nothing doing when I'd beg her to get him a nurse. She said we were her job and she just wouldn't give in. And the way she always took interest in everything we did. Why, when she used to come up to school, all the boys went just crazy about her.

CHRISTINA

I'm sure they did. (*But she turns the enquiry into more significant channels.*) How did your girl friends get on with her?

DAVID

Oh, they loved her, too! Mother used to give us dances here.

CHRISTINA

Did she invite the girls you were in love with?

DAVID

I never fell in love! Not really. Not till I met you.

CHRISTINA

Darling! (*She smiles rather absently.*) What was the name of the one your mother thought could wear my dress?

DAVID

Clara Judd?

CHRISTINA

Weren't you sweet on Clara?

DAVID

I dunno. What made you ask that?

CHRISTINA

Just something in the way your mother spoke of her this evening. It came back to me. Weren't you?

DAVID

Mother thought so.

CHRISTINA

Used to pester you about Clara, didn't she?

DAVID

She was afraid I was going to marry Clara.

CHRISTINA

I see. Anything wrong with her?

DAVID

With Clara? No. Damn nice girl. You'll meet her.

CHRISTINA

Then why didn't your mother want you to marry her?

DAVID

Thought I was too young.

CHRISTINA

When was it?

DAVID

Summer after the war.

CHRISTINA

You weren't so young, were you?

DAVID

You know Mother.

CHRISTINA

How about your brother? Did he used to fall in love a great deal?

DAVID

I don't know that I'd call it "in love."

CHRISTINA

Why not?

DAVID

It's the family skeleton. She was a chorus girl, my dear. She cost Mother twelve thousand berries.

CHRISTINA

That must have been jolly! Was she the only one or were there others?

DAVID

There were plenty of others. Only they didn't have lawyers.

CHRISTINA

And then Hester?

DAVID

Right.

CHRISTINA

Well, that's all very interesting.

DAVID

What are you trying to prove?

CHRISTINA

An idea this affair of Hester's put into my head. And I must say, it fits in rather extraordinarily.

DAVID

What does?

CHRISTINA

You're being too young to marry after the war and Robert's taking to wild women. . . . And you had to be three thousand miles from home to fall in love with me! Never mind. . . . That's enough of that! Now let me tell *you* something. Only you must promise not to get mad.

DAVID

I won't get mad.

CHRISTINA

Promise?

DAVID

Promise.

CHRISTINA

(*A deep breath, then*). Shirts or no shirts, we've got to get out of here tomorrow.

DAVID

(*As though she had stuck him with a pin*). Now, Chris! Haven't we been over all that?

CHRISTINA

Yes. But not to the bottom of it.

DAVID

What more is there to say?

CHRISTINA

(*With sudden violence*). That a defenseless, trusting, little girl has been cruelly treated! We've got to "take sides" with her, Dave!

DAVID

What's the matter with Hester's own family? This is their business, not ours!

CHRISTINA

We owe it to ourselves to *make* it our business.

DAVID

I don't see it.

CHRISTINA

Why don't you see it? What have you put over your eyes that keeps you from seeing it? Do you dare answer that?

DAVID

Dare? What do you mean?

CHRISTINA

"Face the facts," Dave! "Face the facts!"

DAVID

Rot! You're making a mountain out of a mole-hill!

CHRISTINA

Cruelty to children isn't a mole-hill!

DAVID

You're exaggerating! Hester's engagement isn't the first that was ever broken.

CHRISTINA

Think how it was broken and by whom!

DAVID

You just said she was in luck to be rid of Rob. I'll grant you that. I haven't any more use for Rob than you have.

CHRISTINA

Who stands behind Rob?

DAVID

I don't know what you mean.

CHRISTINA

Don't you?

DAVID

No.

CHRISTINA

All right, I'll tell you.

DAVID

(*Quickly*). You needn't. . . . Are you trying to pick a fight with me?

CHRISTINA

On the contrary. I'm asking you to stand by me. (*Her eyes corner him.*)

DAVID

I won't go away and leave Mother in the lurch.

CHRISTINA

You see? You do know what I mean!

DAVID

I don't! I'm just telling you I won't let Mother down.

CHRISTINA

You'd rather stand by your mother than by the right, wouldn't you?

DAVID

Oh, the right?

CHRISTINA

Isn't Hester the right?

DAVID

(*Cornered again*). I can't help it if she is. I won't let Mother down.

CHRISTINA

You'll let *me* down.

DAVID

Oh, Chris! It's late. Come on. Let's turn in.

CHRISTINA

You'd rather stand by your mother than by me, wouldn't you?

DAVID

No, I wouldn't. I tell you Hester's none of our business.

CHRISTINA

You'll admit *this* is?

DAVID

What is?

CHRISTINA

This! . . . Who comes first with you? Your mother or me?

DAVID

Now what's the good of putting things that way?

CHRISTINA

That's what things come to! If your mother and I ever quarreled about anything, if it ever came up to you to choose between sticking by me and sticking by her, which would you stick by?

DAVID

I'd . . . I'd try to do the right thing. . . .

CHRISTINA

That isn't an answer. That's another evasion.

DAVID

But why ask such a question?

CHRISTINA

Because I love you. Because I've got to find out if you love me. And I'm afraid . . . I'm afraid. . . .

DAVID

Why?

CHRISTINA

Because you won't see the facts behind all this. I'm trying to tell you what they are and you won't listen. You can't even hear me.

DAVID

I *can* hear you. And a worse line of hooey I've never listened to in my life.

CHRISTINA

(*Gravely, but with steadily increasing fervor*). Have you ever thought what it would be like to be trapped in a submarine in an accident? I've learned tonight what that kind of panic would be like. I'm in that kind of a panic now, this minute. I've been through the most awful experience of my life tonight. And I've been through it alone. I'm still going through it alone. It's pretty awful to have to face such things alone. . . . No, don't interrupt me. I've got to get this off my chest. Ever since we've been married I've been coming across queer rifts in your feeling for me, like arid places in your heart. Such vast ones, too! I mean, you'll be my perfect lover one day and the next, I'll find myself floundering in sand, and alone, and you nowhere to be seen. We've never been really married, Dave. Only now and then, for a little while at a time, between your retirements into your arid places. . . . I used to wonder what you did there. At first, I thought you did your work there. But you don't. Your work's in my part of your heart, what there is of my part. Then I decided the other was just No-Man's Land. And I thought: little by little, I'll encroach upon it and pour my love upon it, like water on the western desert, and make it flower here and bear fruit there. I thought: then he'll be all alive, all free and all himself; not partly dead and tied and blind; not partly someone else—or nothing. You see, our marriage and your architecture were suffering from the same thing. They only worked a little of the time. I meant them both to work all the time. I meant you to work all the time and to win your way, *all* your way, Dave, to complete manhood. And that's a good deal farther than you've got so far. . . . Then we came here and this happened with Hester and your brother and you just stepped aside and did nothing about it! You went to bed. You did worse than that. You retired into your private wastes and sat tight. . . . I've shown you what you should do and you won't see it. I've called to you to come out to me, and you won't come. So now I've discovered what keeps you. Your mother keeps you. It isn't No-Man's Land at all. It's your mother's land. Arid, sterile, and your mother's! You won't let me get in there. Worse than that, you won't let life get in there! Or she won't! . . . That's what I'm afraid of, Dave: your mother's hold on you. And that's what kept me from getting anywhere with you, all these months. I've seen what she can do with Robert. And what she's done to Hester. I can't help wondering what she may not do with you and to me and to the baby. That's why I'm asking you to take a stand on this business of Hester's, Dave. You'll never find the right any clearer than it is here. It's a kind of test case for me. Don't you see? What you decide about this is what you may, eventually, be expected to decide about . . . about our marriage.

DAVID

(*A pause, then, with sullen violence*). No! I'm damned if I see!

CHRISTINA

(*Breaking*). Then I can't hope for much, can I? . . . I feel awfully like a lost soul, right now. . . . Oh, my God, what am I going to do! What am I going to do!

DAVID

I hope you're going to behave. You ought to be ashamed. Just as I was bringing Mother around to you and . . .

CHRISTINA

(*Violently*). You'd better think a little about bringing me around to your mother!

DAVID

Chris!

CHRISTINA

Why should your mother and I get on?

DAVID

Because you should, that's why. Because she's an older woman and my mother. And you know, just as well as I do . . .

CHRISTINA

I know a great deal better than you that your mother dislikes me fully as much as I dislike her. You're wasting your time trying to bring your mother and me together, because we won't be brought. You say you believe in facing the facts. Well, let's see you face that one!

DAVID

I've never heard anything so outrageous. When you know what Mother means to me and what . . .

CHRISTINA

(*Desperate*). Your mother! Your mother! Always your mother! She's got you back! Dave, her big boy, who ran off and got married! She's got you back!

DAVID

I won't stand for any more of this. A man's mother is his mother.

CHRISTINA

(*Crescendo*). And what's his wife, may I ask? Or doesn't she count?

DAVID

This is morbid rot! She warned me you'd be jealous of her!

CHRISTINA

Did she?

DAVID

But I never expected anything like this!

CHRISTINA

What's going to become of me?

DAVID

I won't stand for any more. . . .

CHRISTINA

Hester's escaped, but I'm caught! I can't go back and be the old Christina again. She's done for. And Christina, your wife, doesn't even exist! That's the fact I've got to face! I'm going to have a baby by a man who belongs to another woman!

DAVID

Damn it, Chris! Do you want Mother to hear you?

CHRISTINA

Do I not!
(MRS. PHELPS *stands in her door, white, but steady.*)

DAVID

(*Turning, sees her*). Oh . . . You *did* hear!

MRS. PHELPS

How could I help hearing every word that Christina said?

DAVID

Oh, this is awful!

MRS. PHELPS

We know, now, where we stand, all three of us.

DAVID

Chris, can't you tell her you didn't mean it?

MRS. PHELPS

(*Heroic sarcasm*). Christina isn't one to say things she doesn't mean. And I have no intention of defending myself.

DAVID

Mother, please! . . . Chris, you'd better beat it.

MRS. PHELPS

I ask her to stay. She has made me afraid ever to be alone with you again. She must have made you afraid to be alone with me.

DAVID

Nonsense, Mother! She hasn't done anything of the sort. You'd better go, Chris. It's the least you can do after what you've said.

CHRISTINA

The very least. I belong with Hester now. (*She goes quickly.*)

DAVID

(*Turning wildly to his mother*). I'll straighten everything out in the morning. I swear I will!

MRS. PHELPS

(*A very different, very noble tone*). This is an old story, Dave boy, and I'm on Christina's side just as I said I should be.

DAVID

I can't have you talking like that, Mother!

MRS. PHELPS

I accept my fate. You have your own life to live with the woman you have chosen. No boy could have given me back the love I gave you. Go to Christina! Make your life with her! No bond binds you to me any longer.

DAVID

That isn't true!

MRS. PHELPS

I'm not complaining. I'm only sorry for one thing. I'm only sorry to see you throw away your chance here, your great chance!

DAVID

But I haven't thrown it away. I'll stay here and work for you, if you want me to.

MRS. PHELPS

Christina won't let you. You know that!

DAVID

She's my wife, isn't she?

MRS. PHELPS

Think what that means, Dave! Think what that means!

DAVID

And you're my mother. I'm thinking what that means, too!

MRS. PHELPS

Then it *isn't* good-bye? Then I've still got my big boy, after all?

DAVID

You bet you've got him!

MRS. PHELPS

(*Triumph*). Oh, Dave! Dave! Dave!

DAVID

Now, Mummy! (*But a sound downstairs distracts him.*) Hello! What's that? (*She listens, too.*)

MRS. PHELPS

Heavens, it isn't a fire, is it?

DAVID

Wait . . . I'll see. . . .
(*He opens the door into the hall and stands listening.*)

CHRISTINA

(*Off-stage and below*). I went into her room and she wasn't there and then I looked for her and I found the dining-room window open.

ROBERT

(*Off-stage and below*). What do you think has happened?

CHRISTINA

(*Off-stage and below*). I don't like to imagine things, but . . .

ROBERT

(*Off-stage and below*). Hester, where are you?

CHRISTINA

(*Off-stage and below*). She's got away! I tell you, she's got away! I shouldn't have left her. . . .

DAVID

(*Speaking during the above*). What?

MRS. PHELPS

It's Christina and Robert.

DAVID

Something's happened to Hester.

MRS. PHELPS

No!

DAVID

Chris! What's going on?

ROBERT

(*Off-stage*). Hester! Where are you, Hester?

CHRISTINA

(*Appearing in the hall*). Hester's got away, Dave. Out by the dining-room window. You'll have to get dressed and find her. She can't get to town tonight in this cold.

DAVID

All right. We'll have a look.

MRS. PHELPS

The little fool! Let her go, Dave!

CHRISTINA

But, Mrs. Phelps, she isn't properly dressed. She didn't even take her coat. . . .

ROBERT

(*Still calling off-stage and below*). Hester! Where are you Hester? Hester! . . . Oh, my God!
(CHRISTINA *has walked to the window to look out. She utters an inarticulate scream.*)

DAVID

What is it, Chris?

MRS. PHELPS

Good heavens!

CHRISTINA

(*Strangled with horror*). It's the pond! The holes in the pond! Quick, Dave, for heaven's sake!

DAVID

What? . . . Oh! . . .
(*He runs out as* CHRISTINA *opens the window.*)

MRS. PHELPS

Dave! . . . (*To* CHRISTINA.) What is it you say?

ROBERT

(*Off-stage and below*). Dave! For God's sake! Hold on, Hester! Don't struggle!
(DAVID'S *shouts join his.*)

CHRISTINA

(*As she collapses on the bed*). The pond! . . . I can't look. . . .

MRS. PHELPS

Oh, I've no patience with people who have hysterics!

CHRISTINA

Mrs. Phelps, the girl's drowning!

MRS. PHELPS

Oh, no! . . . Not that! (*She, too, goes to the window, but recoils in horror from what she sees.*) They'll save her, won't they? They must . . . they must save her . . . If only . . . (*Then a new fear overwhelms her.*) If only those two boys don't catch pneumonia! (*And she leaps to the window to call after her sons as they race, shouting, across the snow.*) Robin, you're not dresssed! Dave, get your coat! Are you crazy? Do you *want* to catch pneumonia?

CURTAIN.

ACT THREE

THE *living-room again, and the next morning.* MRS. PHELPS *is wearing a simple house dress and busily fixing a great many flowers which she takes from boxes strewn about the stage. After she has been so occupied for a few seconds,* ROBERT *enters.*

ROBERT

The doctor's gone.

MRS. PHELPS

(*Surprised*). Without seeing me?

ROBERT

It seems so.

MRS. PHELPS

Doesn't that seem very strange to you, Robin? Of course, I thought it best not to go up to Hester's room with him. In view of the perfectly unreasonable attitude she's taken toward me. But, I should have supposed, naturally, that he'd have made his report to me.

ROBERT

He says she may as well go today. He says traveling won't be as bad for her as staying here.

MRS. PHELPS

Did he say that to you?

ROBERT

I couldn't face him. *They* told him the whole story.

MRS. PHELPS

Christina and Hester? (ROBERT *nods.*) I might have known they would. . . . And he listened to them and never so much as asked for me?

ROBERT

What of it!

MRS. PHELPS

He'll never enter this house again!

ROBERT

So *he* said! He also said there's nothing the matter with your heart and never has been anything the matter with it. He said it would take a stick of dynamite to kill you.

MRS. PHELPS

Damned homeopath!

ROBERT

And that isn't the worst.

MRS. PHELPS

What more?

ROBERT

He said that I'd always been a rotter.

MRS. PHELPS

Oh?

ROBERT

And that I couldn't have been anything else—with such a mother.
(*There is venom in this last.* MRS. PHELPS's *lips stiffen under it.*)

MRS. PHELPS

I think you might have spared me that, Robin.

ROBERT

I didn't mean to be nasty.

MRS. PHELPS

No. Still, there are things one doesn't repeat to sensitive people. (*But a dark foreboding will not be downed.*) Somehow, though, I can't help feeling that . . . (*She does not say what she sees in the future.*)

ROBERT

Neither can I.
(*She looks at him in quick fear. Then she returns to her flowers with a shrug.*)

MRS. PHELPS

Oh, well! There can't have been much wrong with the girl if she's able to go this morning.

ROBERT

Thank God for that. (*Then with level-eyed cruelty.*) It might have been serious, though, after what you did to the telephone. Because we couldn't have reached a soul, you know. And without Christina in the house . . .

MRS. PHELPS

How was I to know the little fool wanted to drown herself?

ROBERT

(*Shuddering*). For heaven's sake, don't put it that way!

MRS. PHELPS

How do *you* put it?

ROBERT

She tried to get away, that's all. And she got lost in the dark and . . .

MRS. PHELPS

I tell you, she tried to kill herself. I've always suspected there was insanity in her family. She had a brother who was an aviator in the war. Everybody knows that aviators are lunatics. Her own conduct has never been what I should call normal. Everything points to insanity. That's another reason why you shouldn't have married her. Because we've never had any of that in our family. Except your father's Bright's Disease. I shall certainly tell everyone that Hester is insane.

ROBERT

Perhaps that *will* make things simpler.

MRS. PHELPS

As to the telephone, it's the only thing I've ever done to be ashamed of, and I said as much when I did it. She made me angry with her wanton attacks on you.

ROBERT

I didn't hear any wanton attacks.

MRS. PHELPS

Where were you?

ROBERT

Out there in the hall.

MRS. PHELPS

You couldn't have heard the things she muttered under her breath.

ROBERT

(*An incredulous sneer*). No! (*There is a pause, sullen on his part, troubled on hers.*) We're just like Macbeth and Lady Macbeth, aren't we?

MRS. PHELPS

For heaven's sakes, how?

ROBERT

We've got into a mess we can't ever get out of. We'll have to get in deeper and deeper until *we* go mad and . . .

MRS. PHELPS

Don't be ridiculous.

ROBERT

I'm sorry, Mother, but I can't help regretting.

MRS. PHELPS

Regretting what?

ROBERT

(*Low*). Hester.

MRS. PHELPS

Nonsense, Robin! I tell you . . .

ROBERT

What do you know about it? Do you understand me any better than Hester did?

MRS. PHELPS

How *can* you, Robin? I not understand you? Haven't I always told you that however David may take after his father, you are *my* son?

ROBERT

What's that got to do with it?

MRS. PHELPS

Robin!

ROBERT

If I wasn't sure that I *loved* Hester, how on earth can I be sure that I *didn't* love her? I don't know this minute whether I loved her or not. I only know that I'll regret losing her all my life long. (*A movement of exasperation from his mother stops him. Then he concludes.*) Maybe Dave's right about me. Maybe I *am* too weak to love any one.

MRS. PHELPS

(*Frightened—to herself*). Dave didn't say *that!*

ROBERT

He said I hadn't any guts.

MRS. PHELPS

Ugh! That horrible word! No, Robin. You must put all such thoughts aside.

ROBERT

I suppose I'll have to take your word for it. (*Then with sudden, cold fury.*) But I won't next time!

MRS. PHELPS

Robin! You're not holding *me* responsible?

ROBERT

Who put the idea in my head? Who persuaded me? Who made me promise?

MRS. PHELPS

Are you implying that *I* came between you?

ROBERT

Well, if you didn't, who did?

MRS. PHELPS

Robin! You ought to be ashamed!

ROBERT

Think so?

MRS. PHELPS

That *you* should turn on me! Some day you'll regret this. It won't be Hester, but *this* that you'll regret. . . . When it's too late.
(*And from force of habit her hand steals to her heart.*)

ROBERT

I daresay I've got a life full of regrets ahead of me. (*He walks sullenly to the window.*)

MRS. PHELPS

You frighten me, Robin! I don't know you like this.

ROBERT

Don't you?
(*There is a pause.* MRS. PHELPS *stares at him in growing horror. He looks out of the window.*)

MRS. PHELPS

No.

ROBERT

(*Looking out, his back to her*). That's too bad. . . . There's Dave putting up danger signs all around the pond! Isn't that like him! After it's too late. (*She turns away from him and dully goes on with her flowers, carrying a bowl of them over to the piano.* ROBERT *watches her coldly. Then a sudden frown contracts his brow and he moves toward her.*) Mother!

MRS. PHELPS

What?

ROBERT

Don't put those flowers there! They're too low!

MRS. PHELPS

Fix them yourself.

ROBERT

(*Changing them with a jar of something else*). Isn't that better?

MRS. PHELPS

Much. What an eye you have!

ROBERT

Perhaps I'll develop it some day.

MRS. PHELPS

Would you like to?

ROBERT

I've got to do something.

MRS. PHELPS

(*Darkly*). I quite agree. Every young man should have some profession.
(*Then, suddenly and involuntarily, the boy reverts and is a child again.*)

ROBERT

What are we going to do, Mother?

MRS. PHELPS

(*Low*). Do?

ROBERT

What are we going to do, you and I? We're in the same boat, you know.

MRS. PHELPS

(*Lower*). I don't know what you mean.

ROBERT

Well, what am I going to do, then? I can't stay here and face people after this!

MRS. PHELPS

What will there be to face?

ROBERT

(*Crescendo*). You know as well as I do. This story'll be all over this damn town. And Hester's people aren't going to keep quiet in New York. Her brothers go everywhere I go. My friends will begin cutting me in the street.

MRS. PHELPS

If we say she's insane?

ROBERT

What difference will that make?

MRS. PHELPS

(*Very low*). The *Paris* sails on Saturday.

ROBERT

(*Pause, then, tremulously*). What of it?

MRS. PHELPS

We might go to Washington to hurry our passports.

ROBERT

Could we get passage, though?

MRS. PHELPS

(*Slowly*). I've already wired for it. This morning.

ROBERT

I see. . . . Then we're to sneak away like two guilty fugitives!

MRS. PHELPS

(*Avoiding his eye*). Sh! Don't say such things! (DAVID *enters, his cheeks stung crimson by the cold.*)

DAVID

Phew, it's cold. The pond'll be frozen again by to-morrow if this keeps up. What's the doc say about Hester?

ROBERT

She's leaving us today.

DAVID

I'm glad she's well enough.

MRS. PHELPS

There never was anything the matter with her.

DAVID

It's easy to see, Mother, that you don't often bathe in that pond in zero weather.

MRS. PHELPS

I hope I have more self-control. Robin, will you see, please, that the car is ready for Hester?

ROBERT

Yes.
(*He goes.*)

DAVID

Anybody seen Chris?

MRS. PHELPS

Not I.

DAVID

No. I suppose not. . . . What's the idea in the floral display?

MRS. PHELPS

I felt I had to have flowers about me.

DAVID

That sounds pretty Green Hattish. . . . It has a festive look, too. I don't see what there is to celebrate.

MRS. PHELPS

(*Noble tragedienne that she is*). Last night, at a single blow, beauty was stricken out of my life. I can't live without beauty, Dave. You must know that. So I went to the florist this morning and bought these. They comfort me . . . a little.

DAVID

(*That worried look again*). I've been thinking, Mother, that maybe, all things considered, after last night, it will be as well for me to take Chris away on Wednesday, say.

MRS. PHELPS

If you like.

DAVID

We can come back later. After things have cooled down.

MRS. PHELPS

Later, I hope, and often.

DAVID

Time does make things easier, doesn't it?

MRS. PHELPS

They say so.

DAVID

When scientists get these wild ideas and fly off the handle, they're just as embarrassed afterwards as any one else would be.

MRS. PHELPS

Naturally.

DAVID

And then Hester's running away and the telephone being busted and all. . . .

MRS. PHELPS

I quite understand.

DAVID

I knew you would.

MRS. PHELPS

(*The boxes and papers all stowed away, she sits down to business*). What I'm wondering now, though, is what I'm to do with Robin? And I'm afraid you've got to help me with him.

DAVID

I'll do anything I can.

MRS. PHELPS

If I were well and able to stand the things I used to stand before my heart went back on me—because it *has* gone back on me—and before my blood pressure got so high . . . I shouldn't trouble you. But as I am, and with Robin on the verge of a complete breakdown . . .

DAVID

But Rob isn't . . .

MRS. PHELPS

Oh, yes, he is, Dave! He said things to me before you came in that no son of mine would dream of saying unless he had something the matter with him. I've got to get him away.

DAVID

Send him abroad.

MRS. PHELPS

I don't think he ought to go alone. He can't face things alone. He's like his father, in that. You're *my* son, you know. That's why I always turn to you.

DAVID

Why not go with him?

MRS. PHELPS

Because I'm really not well enough in case anything should happen. . . . And, I don't know what to do. Oh, Dave, boy, do you think . . .

DAVID

What?

MRS. PHELPS

That Christina could spare you for a little? Just a few weeks? Just long enough to get Rob and me settled in some restful place? Do you think she would?

DAVID

There's no need of that!

MRS. PHELPS

Of course. I'd love to have Christina, too. Only I'm afraid that *would* be asking too much. I mean, making her put off her work when she's so set on it.

DAVID

But Rob isn't going to give you any trouble.

MRS. PHELPS

Do you think I'd ask such a sacrifice of you . . . and Christina, if I weren't sure that it's absolutely necessary? Oh, I'm not thinking of myself. I no longer matter. Except that I shouldn't want to die abroad with only Robin there, in his present condition.

DAVID

Don't talk that way, Mother!

MRS. PHELPS

Why not? I'm not asking you to be sorry for me. It's Robin I'm thinking of. Because we haven't done all that we should for Robin. And now that I'm old . . . and sick . . . dying . . .
(*She breaks down.*)

DAVID

You're not, Mother!

MRS. PHELPS

(*Weeping hysterically*). I can't cope with him. He'll slip back again to drinking and fast women . . .

DAVID

Get hold of yourself, Mother!

MRS. PHELPS

(*More hysterical*). And when I think of what I might have done for him and realize that it's too late, that I haven't any more time . . . only a few months . . . or weeks . . . I don't know . . . I . . .
(*She really becomes quite faint.*)

DAVID

(*Snatching her hand in terror*). Mother, what's the matter? Are you ill?

MRS. PHELPS

(*Recovering by inches as she gasps for breath*). No! It's nothing . . . I . . . Just give me a minute . . . Don't call any one . . . I'll be all right. . . . There! . . . That's better!

DAVID

You scared me to death.

MRS. PHELPS

I scare myself sometimes. You see I do need *somebody's* help.

DAVID

Yes, I see you do.

MRS. PHELPS

And so I thought: well, since Dave *is* going to build my houses in Phelps Manor. . . . You're not going to disappoint me there, I hope?

DAVID

Oh, no!

MRS. PHELPS

Well, then you won't want to start in that New York office.

DAVID

Why not?

MRS. PHELPS

When you'll be leaving so soon to begin here? They wouldn't want you.

DAVID

I hadn't thought of that.

MRS. PHELPS

And so I thought: Well, he can't begin here until April anyway and that leaves him with two idle months on his hands when he might be drawing plans and getting ideas abroad. Think it over, Dave, boy.

DAVID

You certainly are a great planner, Mother.

MRS. PHELPS

I make such good plans!

DAVID

When would you be sailing?

MRS. PHELPS

Well, I . . . I *had* thought . . . vaguely . . . of sailing on the *Paris* . . . Saturday . . .

DAVID

Good Lord! Give a man time to think! I want to do the right thing, but I couldn't leave Chris . . . Not with the baby coming, you know.

MRS. PHELPS

But you'll be home in plenty of time for that.

DAVID

That may all be, but, just the same, I wouldn't feel right to leave her.
(ROBERT *returns.*)

MRS. PHELPS

I've just been telling Dave about our wonderful plans, Robin, and he's so enthusiastic! I shouldn't wonder if he came along with us.
(*A sign to* DAVID *to play up.*)

ROBERT

What *are* the plans?

MRS. PHELPS

Why, your going abroad to study interior decorating, of course.
(ROBERT *looks surprised.*)

DAVID

Oh, is Rob going to do that?

ROBERT

Any objections?

DAVID

I think it's just the job for you. Painting rosebuds on bath-tubs.

ROBERT

I can make your houses look like something after you've finished with them.

MRS. PHELPS

(*Ecstatically*). My two boys in partnership! Oh, that's always been my dream! Oh, how simply things come straight when people are willing to cooperate and make little sacrifices! If there's one thing I pride myself on, it's my willingness to make little sacrifices. Here we are, we three, a moment ago all at odds with life and with each other; now united and of a single mind . . .

DAVID

This is all very fine. But don't you forget that I've got to talk to Christina . . .
(*But* CHRISTINA *has opened the door upon his very words. She is dressed as she was when she first came to the house. She wears her hat and her fur coat and carries her bag in her hand.*)

CHRISTINA

(*Speaking as she enters*). Well, now's your chance, Dave. What have you got to talk to me about?

DAVID

(*Staring at her*). What's the idea, Chris?

CHRISTINA

(*Setting the bag down by the door*). I'm going away with Hester. Are you coming, too?

DAVID

(*Staggered*). Now?

CHRISTINA

In a few minutes. I came down ahead. No, don't go, Mrs. Phelps. And won't you stay, too, Robert? I think it's best that we should thrash this question out together, here and now, for good and all.

MRS. PHELPS

What question, Christina?

CHRISTINA

The David question, Mrs. Phelps. Whether David is going on from this point as your son or as my husband.

ROBERT

What?

CHRISTINA

Isn't that the issue?
(*She asks the question less of* DAVID *than of* MRS. PHELPS, *who turns to her sons in terror.*)

MRS. PHELPS

I can't go through this a second time!

DAVID

(*Quieting her with a gesture*). No one expects you to. . . . (*To* CHRISTINA, *pleading almost pathetically.*) You're not going to begin all that again, Chris?

CHRISTINA

I'm afraid I am.

DAVID

But, just as I was getting everything all straightened out . . .

CHRISTINA

Were you doing that?

DAVID

If only you'll leave things be, they'll be all right. You may believe it or not . . .

CHRISTINA

I can't believe it and I can't leave things be. Oh, I'd walk out without a word, even loving you as I do, if I thought this state of affairs made any one of you happy.

ROBERT

What state of affairs?

CHRISTINA

The state of affairs you've all been living in and suffering from, for so long.

MRS. PHELPS

You might let us judge our own happiness.

CHRISTINA

I might, if you had any. But you haven't.

ROBERT

You're quite sure of that?

CHRISTINA

Quite, Robert. You're all of you perfectly miserable! Am I wrong?

MRS. PHELPS

Christina! Please!

ROBERT

Thank you for being sorry for us!

CHRISTINA

You give me such good reason, Robert. Such awfully good reason! Because you're really not bad people, you know. You're just wrong, all wrong, terribly, pitifully, all of you, and you're trapped . . .

MRS. PHELPS

What we say in anger, we sometimes regret, Christina. . . .

CHRISTINA

Oh, I'm not angry. I was, but I've got over it. I rather fancy myself, now, as a sort of scientific Nemesis. I mean to strip this house and show it up for what it really is. I mean to show you up, Mrs. Phelps. Then Dave can use his own judgment.

MRS. PHELPS

(*Blank terror at this attack*). Oh! Dave, I . . .

DAVID

Now, Mother! Chris! Haven't you any consideration for our feelings? Are they nothing to you?

CHRISTINA

I'm trying to save my love, my home, my husband and my baby's father. Are they nothing to you?

DAVID

But surely I can be both a good son and a good husband!

CHRISTINA

Not if your mother knows it, you can't!

MRS. PHELPS

(*A last desperate snatch at dignity*). If you'll excuse me, I'd rather not stay to be insulted again.
(*She is going.*)

CHRISTINA

You'll probably lose him if you don't stay, Mrs. Phelps! (MRS. PHELPS *stays.* CHRISTINA *turns to* DAVID.) No, Dave. There's no good in any more pretending. Your mother won't allow you to divide your affections and I refuse to go on living with you on any basis she will allow.

MRS. PHELPS

I cannot see that this is necessary.

CHRISTINA

It's a question a great many young wives leave unsettled, Mrs. Phelps. I'm not going to make that mistake. (*Back to* DAVE *again.*) You see, Dave, I'm not beating about the bush. I'm not persuading you or wasting any time on tact. Do you want your chance or don't you? Because, if you don't, I'll have to get over being in love with you as best I can and . . .

DAVID

I wish you wouldn't talk this way, Chris!

CHRISTINA

Are you coming with me? On the understanding that, for the present, until your affections are definitely settled on your wife and child, you avoid your mother's society entirely. Well? What do you say?

DAVID

I don't know what to say.

CHRISTINA

You never do, Dave darling.

DAVID

I'm too shocked. I've never been so shocked in my life.

CHRISTINA

(*A glance at her wrist watch*). Just take your time and think before you speak.

DAVID

I don't mean that I don't know what to say about taking my chance, as you call it. I can answer that by reminding you of your duty to me. I can answer that by calling all this what I called it last night. Morbid rot! But I *am* shocked at your talking this way about my mother and to her face, too!

CHRISTINA

Is that your answer?

DAVID

No, it isn't! But a man's mother *is* his mother.

CHRISTINA

So you said last night. I'm not impressed. An embryological accident is no grounds for honor. Neither is a painful confinement, for I understand, Mrs. Phelps, that you're very proud of the way you bore your children. I know all about the legend of yourself as a great woman that you've built up these thirty years for your sons to worship. It hasn't taken me long to see that you're not fit to be any one's mother.

DAVID

Chris!

ROBERT

(*Speaking at the same time*). See here, now!

MRS. PHELPS

Let her go on! Let her go on! She will explain that or retract it!

CHRISTINA

I'm only too glad to explain. It's just what I've been leading up to. And I'll begin by saying that if my baby ever feels about me as your sons feel about you, I hope that somebody will take a little enameled pistol and shoot me, because I'll deserve it.

MRS. PHELPS

(*Going again*). I've been insulted once too often.

CHRISTINA

I don't mean to insult you. I'm being as scientific and impersonal as possible.

ROBERT

Good God!

CHRISTINA

(*Regardless*). Speaking of insults, though, what explanation can *you* offer *me* for your rudeness to me as a guest in your house?

MRS. PHELPS

I have not been rude to you.

CHRISTINA

You have been appallingly rude. Second question: Why do you resent the fact that I am going to have a baby?

MRS. PHELPS

I don't resent it.

CHRISTINA

Then why are you so churlish about it?

MRS. PHELPS

Your indelicacy about it would have . . .

CHRISTINA

That's another evasion. You're afraid that baby will give me another and stronger hold on David and you mean to separate David and me if it's humanly possible.

MRS. PHELPS

I do not! I do not!

CHRISTINA

Did you or did you not bend every effort to separate Hester and Robert?

MRS. PHELPS

I most certainly did not!

CHRISTINA

Then how do you account for the deliberate and brutal lies you told Hester about Robert? Because she did lie to Hester about you, Robert. She told Hester that you never wanted to marry her.

ROBERT

(*Aghast*). Mother, you didn't!

MRS. PHELPS

Of course, I didn't!

CHRISTINA

(*Joan of Arc raising the siege of Orleans*). I heard her. And I heard her call both of you back, last night, when you ran out to save Hester from drowning. I heard her call you back from saving a drowning girl for fear of your catching cold. I heard her. I heard her.

DAVID

(*Shaken*). You shouldn't have called us, Mother!

CHRISTINA

Can she deny that her one idea is to keep her sons dependent on her? Can she deny that she opposes any move that either one of you makes toward independence? Can she deny that she is outraged by your natural impulses toward other women?

MRS. PHELPS

(*Furious*). I deny all of it!

CHRISTINA

You may deny it until you're black in the face; every accusation I make is true! You belong to a type that's very common in this country, Mrs. Phelps—a type of self-centered, self-pitying, son-devouring tigress, with unmentionable proclivities suppressed on the side.

DAVID

Chris!

CHRISTINA

I'm not at all sure it wouldn't be a good idea, just as an example to the rest of the tribe, to hang one of your kind every now and then!

ROBERT

Really!

CHRISTINA

Oh, there are normal mothers around; mothers who *want* their children to be men and women and take care of themselves; mothers who are people, too, and don't have to be afraid of loneliness after they've outlived their motherhood; mothers who can look on their children as people and enjoy them as people and not be forever holding on to them and pawing them and fussing about their health and singing them lullabies and tucking them up as though they were everlasting babies. But you're *not* one of the normal ones, Mrs. Phelps! Look at your sons, if you don't believe me. You've destroyed Robert. You've swallowed him up until there's nothing left of him but an effete make-believe. Now he's gone melancholy mad and disgraced himself. And Dave! Poor Dave! The best he can do is dodge the more desperate kinds of unhappiness by pretending! How he survived at all is beyond me. If you're choking a bit on David, now, that's my fault because you'd have swallowed him up, too, if I hadn't come along to save him! Talk about cannibals! You and your kind beat any cannibals I've ever heard of! And what makes you doubly deadly and dangerous is that people admire you and your kind. They actually admire you! You professional mothers! . . . You see, I'm taking this differently from that poor child upstairs. She's luckier than I am, too. She isn't married to one of your sons. Do you remember what she said about children yesterday? "Have 'em. Love 'em. And leave 'em be."

MRS. PHELPS

You are entitled to your opinions, Christina, just as I am to mine and David is to his. I only hope that he sees the kind of woman he's married. I hope he sees the sordidness, the hardness, the nastiness she offers him for his life.

CHRISTINA

(*An involuntary cry of pain*). I'm not nasty! I'm not!

MRS. PHELPS

What have you to offer David?

CHRISTINA

A hard time. A chance to work on his own. A chance to *be* on his own. Very little money on which to share with me the burden of raising his child. The pleasure of my society. The solace of my love. The enjoyment of my body. To which I have reason to believe he is not indifferent.

MRS. PHELPS

(*Revolted*). Ugh!

CHRISTINA

Can you offer so much?

MRS. PHELPS

I offer a mother's love. Or perhaps you scoff at that?

CHRISTINA

Not if it's kept within bounds. I hope my baby loves me. I'm practically certain I'm going to love my baby. But within bounds.

MRS. PHELPS

And what do you mean by within bounds?

CHRISTINA

To love my baby with as much and as deep respect as I hope my baby will feel for me if I deserve its respect. To love my baby unpossessively; above all, unromantically.

MRS. PHELPS

I suppose that's biology! You don't know the difference between good and evil!

CHRISTINA

As a biologist, though, I do know the difference between life and death. And I know sterility when I see it. I doubt if evil is any more than a fancy name for sterility. And sterility, of course, is what you offer Dave. Sterility for his mind as well as for his body. That's your professional mother's stock in trade. Only we've been over that, haven't we? Well, Dave! How about it?

ROBERT

I think this has gone far enough!

MRS. PHELPS

No! This woman has got to answer me one question.

CHRISTINA

Willingly. What is it?

MRS. PHELPS

How old were you when you married?

CHRISTINA

The same age I am now. Twenty-nine.

MRS. PHELPS

I was twenty.

CHRISTINA

Just Hester's age.

MRS. PHELPS

(*Riding over her*). I was twenty and my husband was fifteen years older than I. Oh, thirty-five isn't old, but he was a widower, too, and an invalid. Everyone told me I'd made a great match. And I thought I had. But before we'd been married a week, I saw my illusions shattered. I knew at the end of the week how miserable and empty my marriage was. He was good to me. He made very few demands on me. But he never dreamed of bringing the least atom of happiness into my life. Or of romance. . . . Only a woman who has lived without romance knows how to value it. . . . That isn't true of my life either. I didn't live without romance. I found it . . . and I'm proud to have found it where you say it doesn't belong . . . in motherhood. I found it in my two babies. In Dave first and in Robin four years later. I found it in doing for them myself all those things which, nowadays, nurses and governesses are hired to do. To spare mothers! I never asked to be spared. . . . Their father died. The night he died, Robin had croup and I had to make the final choice between my duties. I stayed with Robin. You, with your modern ideas and your science, Christina, would have chosen differently? I knew the difference between life and death that night. And I've known it for every step of the way I battled for Robin's health, every step as I taught Dave his gentleness and his generosity. . . . If I made my mistakes, and I'm only human . . . I'm sorry for them. But I can point to my two sons and say that my mistakes could not have been serious ones. . . . Think! I was a widow, rich and very pretty, at twenty-five. Think what that means! But I had found my duty and I never swerved from it. . . . There was one man in particular. A fine man. But I resisted. I knew that second marriage was not for me. Not when I had my sons. I put them first, always. . . . I shall not stoop to answer any of the foulnesses you have charged me with. They are beneath my dignity as a woman and my contempt as a mother. No, there is one I cannot leave unanswered. That word "sterility." Sterility is what I offer David, you say. I wonder, is sterility David's word for all he has had of me these thirty years? Let him answer that for himself. All my life I have saved to launch my two boys on their careers, saved in vision as well as in money. I don't offer my sons a love half dedicated to selfish, personal ambition. I don't offer them careers limited by the demands of other careers. I offer David a clear field ahead and a complete love to sustain him, a mother's love, until a real marriage, a suitable marriage may be possible for him. And I do *not* deny that I would cut off my right hand and burn the sight out of my eyes to rid my son of you! . . . That is how I answer your impersonal science, Christina.

CHRISTINA

(*Before either of the boys can speak*). I see! . . . Well. . . . It's a very plausible and effective answer. And I'm sure you mean it and I believe it's sincere. But it *is* the answer of a woman whose husband let her down pretty hard and who turned for satisfaction to her sons. . . . I'm almost sorry I can't say more for it, but I can't. . . . (*She turns from* MRS. PHELPS *to the two sons.*) It's a pity she didn't marry again. Things would have been so much better for both of you if she had. (*Then, with an increasing force, to* DAVID.) But the fact remains, Dave, that she did separate you and me last night and that she separated us because she couldn't bear the thought of our sleeping together. (*They flinch at this, but she downs them.*) And she couldn't bear that because she refuses to believe that you're a grown man and capable of desiring a woman. And that's because, grown man that you are, down, down in the depths of her, she still wants to suckle you at her breast!

DAVID

(*A cry of horror*). Chris!

ROBERT

(*At the same time*). Good God!

MRS. PHELPS

(*At the same time*). No!

CHRISTINA

You find that picture revolting, do you? Well, so it is. . . . I can't wait any longer for your answer, Dave.

DAVID

I don't think you've any sense of decency left in you. Of all the filthy, vile . . .

CHRISTINA

I'm sorry you feel that way.

DAVID

How else *can* I feel?

CHRISTINA

Is that your answer?

DAVID

I want to do the right thing, but . . .

CHRISTINA

Remember me, won't you, on Mother's Day! (*Then she calls out.*) Are you ready, Hester?

DAVID

You make things mighty hard, Chris, for a man who knows what fair play is and gratitude and all those other things I naturally feel for my mother.

CHRISTINA

Do I?

DAVID

What do you expect me to say?

CHRISTINA

I don't know. I've never known. That's been the thrill of it. (HESTER, *dressed for her journey, appears in the door and stands beside* CHRISTINA. CHRISTINA'S *arm encircles the younger girl's shoulders.*) It's time, Hester.

HESTER

Isn't David coming with us?

CHRISTINA

I'm afraid not.

HESTER

Oh, Christina!

CHRISTINA

Sssh! Never mind. It can't be helped.

ROBERT

(*Breaking out*). Hester! Hester! Couldn't we try again? Couldn't you . . .

HESTER

What?

ROBERT

I mean . . . what are you going to do . . . now?

HESTER

I don't know. (*Then a smile comes through.*) Yes, I do, too, know. I'm going to marry an orphan.

CHRISTINA

(*A long look at* DAVID). Good-bye, Dave.

DAVID

(*Desperately pleading*). Chris, you can't! It isn't fair to me!

CHRISTINA

(*Still looking at him*). I'm sorry it's come to this. . . . It might easily have been so . . . (*Her voice chokes with crying. She picks up her bag where she put it down beside the door and goes quickly out.* HESTER, *with a reproachful glance at* DAVID, *follows her.* DAVID *stands rigid.* MRS. PHELPS *watches him.* ROBERT *covers his face with his hands. Then the front door slams and* DAVID *comes suddenly to life.*)

DAVID

(*A frantic cry*). Chris! (*He turns excitedly to his mother.*) I'm sorry, Mother, but I guess I'll have to go.

MRS. PHELPS

(*Reeling*). No, Dave! No! No!

DAVID

I guess she's right.

MRS. PHELPS

Oh, no!! You mustn't say that! You mustn't say that!

DAVID

(*Holding her off from him*). I can't help it. She said we were trapped. We *are* trapped. I'm trapped.

MRS. PHELPS

(*Absolutely beyond herself*). No! No! She isn't right! She can't be right! I won't believe it!

DAVID

(*Breaking loose from her*). I can't help that!

MRS. PHELPS

(*Speaking at the same time*). For God's sake, Dave, don't go with her! Not with that awful woman, Dave! That wicked woman! For God's sake don't leave me for her, Dave! (*She turns wildly to* ROBERT.) You know it isn't true, Robin! You know it was vile, what she said! Tell him! Tell him! (*But he is gone.*) Dave! My boy! My boy! My boy! Oh, my God! Dave! She isn't right! She isn't, Dave! Dave! Dave! (*The front door slams a second time. An awful pause, then.*) He's gone.

ROBERT

(*Uncovering his face*). Who? Dave?

MRS. PHELPS

Can you see them from the window?

ROBERT

(*Looking out*). Yes. . . . They're talking. . . . Now he's kissed her and taken the suitcase. . . . Now he's helping Hester . . . Hester into the car. . . . Now he's getting in. . . . Now they're starting.

MRS. PHELPS

I loved him too much. I've been too happy. Troubles had to come. I must be brave. I must bear my troubles bravely.

ROBERT

(*Turning to her*). Poor Mother!

MRS. PHELPS

I must remember that I still have one of my great sons. I must keep my mind on that.

ROBERT

(*A step or two toward her*). That's right, Mother.

MRS. PHELPS

And we'll go abroad, my great Robin and I, and stay as long as ever we please.

ROBERT

(*As he kneels beside her*). Yes, Mother.

MRS. PHELPS

(*Her voice growing stronger as that deeply religious point of view of hers comes to her rescue*). And you must remember that David, in his blindness, has forgotten. That mother love suffereth long and is kind; envieth not, is not puffed up, is not easily provoked; beareth all things; believeth all things; hopeth all things; endureth all things. . . . At least, I think *my* love does?

ROBERT

(*Engulfed forever*). Yes, Mother.

CURTAIN.

Dorothy Heyward and DuBose Heyward

PORGY

From the Novel by DuBose Heyward

DUBOSE HEYWARD

DuBose Heyward's first ventures in verse and all his later prose have their origin and being in Charleston, South Carolina, where he was born on August 31, 1885. Heyward left school at fourteen and drifted from job to job along the waterfront, sometimes with a steamboat line and again as a checker in a cotton shed. It was only after he had grown to manhood and had made a success in the insurance business that he could afford the leisure to write of the city whose pulse was his own. In 1923, DuBose Heyward was married to Dorothy Hartzell Kuhns, a student in Professor Baker's 47 Workshop at Harvard and collaborator with him in the dramatic version of *Porgy*. When *Porgy* was published as a novel its success only foreshadowed the triumph it was to have under the aegis of the Theatre Guild. In its third incarnation, *Porgy* emerged as an opera, re-entitled *Porgy and Bess,* also under the management of the Theatre Guild, with a score by the gifted American composer, George Gershwin.

CHARACTERS

MARIA, keeper of the cookshop
JAKE, captain of the fishing fleet
LILY
MINGO
ANNIE
SPORTING LIFE
SERENA, Robbins's wife
ROBBINS, a young stevedore
JIM
CLARA, Jake's wife
PETER, the honey-man
PORGY, a crippled beggar
CROWN, a stevedore
CROWN'S BESS
A DETECTIVE
TWO POLICEMEN
UNDERTAKER
SCIPIO
SIMON FRAZIER, a lawyer
NELSON, a fisherman
ALAN ARCHDALE
THE CRAB MAN
THE CORONER
RESIDENTS OF CATFISH ROW, FISHERMEN, CHILDREN, STEVEDORES, ETC.

The action of the play takes place in Charleston, S. C., at the present time.

PORGY

ACT ONE

SCENE I

BEFORE *the rise of each curtain, the bells of St. Michael's, adjacent to the Negro quarter of old Charleston, chime the hour. The chimes are heard occasionally throughout the play.*

Before the rise of first curtain, St. Michael's chimes the quarters and strikes eight.

The curtain rises on the court of Catfish Row, now a Negro tenement in a fallen quarter of Charleston, but in Colonial days one of the finest buildings of the aristocracy. The walls rise around a court, except a part of the rear wall of the old house, which breaks to leave a section of lower wall pierced at its center by a massive wrought-iron gate of great beauty which hangs unsteadily between brick pillars surmounted by pineapples carved of Italian marble.

By day, the walls of the entire structure present a mottled color effect of varying pastel shades, caused by the atmospheric action of many layers of color wash. A brilliant note is added by rows of blooming flame-colored geraniums in old vegetable tins on narrow shelves attached to each window sill. All of the windows are equipped with dilapidated slat shutters, some of which are open, others closed, but with the slats turned so that any one inside could look out without being seen. The floor of the spacious court is paved with large flagstones, and these gleam in faintly varying colors under their accumulated grime.

Beyond the gate and above the wall, one sees a littered cobbled street, an old gas street lamp, and, beyond that again, the blue expanse of the bay, with Fort Sumter showing on the horizon. Over the wall can be seen masts and spars of fishing boats lying on the beach.

By night, the court depends for its illumination upon the wheezing gas lamp, and the kerosene lamps and lanterns that come and go in the hands of the occupants of the Row.

At left front is PORGY'S *room (door and window), and beyond it, an arch letting on an inside yard. The pump stands against the wall right back; then, on around right wall,* SERENA'S *doorway, with her window above it, two more doors, then the door to* MARIA'S *cookshop. Center right is seen* SERENA'S *wash bench, and near right wall, well down front, is table on which* MARIA *serves her meals during the warm weather.*

As the curtain rises, revealing Catfish Row on a summer evening, the court reëchoes with African laughter and friendly banter in "Gullah," the language of the Charleston Negro, which still retains many African words. The audience understands none of it. Like the laughter and movement, the twanging of a guitar from an upper window, the dancing of an urchin with a loose, shuffling step, it is a part of the picture of Catfish

Row as it really is—an alien scene, a people as little known to most Americans as the people of the Congo.

Gradually, it seems to the audience that they are beginning to understand this foreign language. In reality, the "Gullah" is being tempered to their ears, spoken more distinctly with the African words omitted.

It is Saturday night, and most of the residents of Catfish Row are out in the court, sitting watching the crap shooters or moving to and fro to visit with one neighbor, then another. Among those present are:

MARIA, matriarch of the court, massive in proportions and decisive in action.

ANNIE, middle-aged, quiet, and sedate.

LILY, loud, good-natured, the court hoyden.

CLARA, who has her baby in her arms. She is scarcely more than a girl and has a sweet, wistful face.

JAKE, CLARA's husband. A successful captain of the fishing fleet; good-looking, good-natured.

"SPORTING LIFE," bootlegger to Catfish Row; a slender, overdressed, high-yellow Negro.

MINGO, young and lazy.

JIM and NELSON, fishermen.

SCIPIO, a boy of twelve, one of the numerous offspring of ROBBINS and SERENA.

ROBBINS *and* SERENA *are still in their room on the second floor.* SERENA *is seen occasionally as she moves back and forth past her lighted window. She is a self-respecting "white folks" Negress, of about thirty.*

The men are gathering for their Saturday-night crap game. They are grouped between gate and PORGY'S *room.* JAKE *is squatting right,* MINGO *center rear, and* SPORTING LIFE *is left, forming triangle. A smoking kerosene lamp is in center of group, and the men are tossing and retrieving their dice in the circle of light.*

JAKE

(*Rolling*). Seems like dese bones don't gib me nuttin' but box cars tonight. It was de same two weeks ago, an' de game broke me. I ain't likes dat luck.

(SPORTING LIFE *produces his own dice, and throws with a loud grunt and snap of his fingers.* MINGO *snatches the dice and balances them in his hand.*)

SPORTING LIFE

Damn yu', gib me dem bones.

(MINGO *holds him off with one hand while he hands the dice to* JAKE.)

MINGO

Whut yo' say to dese, Jake?

JAKE

(*Examining them*). Dem's de same cock-eye bones whut clean de gang out las' week. Ef dey rolls in dis game, I rolls out. (*Hands the dice back to* SPORTING LIFE.) Eberybody rolls de same bones in dis game, Sportin' Life—take 'em or leabe 'em.

(ROBBINS *comes from door, rear right. He is a well-set-up Negro of about thirty. The window above him opens, and* SERENA *leans from sill.*)

SERENA

(*Pleadingly*). Honey-boy!

ROBBINS

Now, fuh Gawd's sake, don't start dat again. I goin' play—git dat.

SERENA

Ef yo' didn't hab licker in yo' right now, yo' wouldn't talk like dat. Yo' know whut yo' done promise' me las' week.

ROBBINS

All right, den, I wouldn't shoot no more dan fifty cents. (*Joins the group.*)

(CLARA *paces up and down the court, singing softly to her baby.*)

Dat ole lady ob mine hell on joinin' de buryin' lodge. I says, spen' um while yo' is still alibe an' kickin'. (*Picks up dice. Throws them with a loud grunt.*) I ain't see no buzzard 'round her yit.

(JIM, *a big, strong-looking fellow, saunters over to the group of crap players. A cotton hook swings from his belt.*)

JIM

Lor', I is tire' dis night. I'm t'inkin' ob gettin' out ob de cotton business. Mebby it all right fo' a nigger like Crown dat Gawd start to make into a bull, den change He min'. But it ain't no work fo' a man.

JAKE

Better come 'long on de *Sea Gull*. I gots place fo' nudder fishermans.

JIM

Dat suit me. Dis cotton hook hab swung he las' bale ob cotton. Here, Scipio, yo' wants a cotton hook?

(*Throws the hook to* SCIPIO, *who takes it eagerly, fastens it at his waist, and goes about court playing that he is a stevedore, lifting objects with the hook and pretending that they are of tremendous weight.* CLARA *passes the group, crooning softly.*)

CLARA

"Hush, li'l baby, don' yo' cry.
Fadder an' mudder born to die."

JAKE

(*Standing up*). Whut! dat chile ain't 'sleep yit. Gib 'um to me. I'll fix um fo' yo'. (*Takes baby from* CLARA, *rocks it in his arms, sings.*)

"My mammy tells me, long time ago,
Son, don' yo' marry no gal yo' know.
Spen' all yo' money—eat all yo' bread,
Gone to Savannah, lef' yo' fo' dead."

(*Several of the men join in on the last line.* JAKE *rocks the baby more violently and begins to shuffle.* CLARA *watches anxiously.*)

"Spen all yo' money. Steal all yo' clothes.
Whut will become of yo', Gawd only knows."

(*The light leaves* SERENA'*s window.* JAKE *swings the baby back to* CLARA.)

Dere now! Whut I tells yo'. He 'sleep already.

(*The baby wails. The men laugh.* CLARA *carries baby to her room. Closes door.* SERENA *comes from her door with a lamp which she sets on her wash bench. She sits beside it and looks anxiously toward crap players.*)

MARIA

(*To* SERENA). Whut worryin' yo', Serena? Yo' gots one ob de bes' mens in Catfish Row. Why yo' ain't let um play widout pickin' on um?

SERENA

He gots licker in um tonight, an' Robbins ain't de same man wid licker.

(MINGO *is rolling and retrieving the dice. While he does so, he looks and laughs at* ROBBINS, *then sings at him.*)

MINGO

(*Singing*).

"My mammy tell me, long time ago,
Son don't yo' marry no gal yo' know."

(*Speaking to* ROBBINS.) Ought to be single like Porgy an' me. Den yo' kin shoot bones widout git pick on.

ROBBINS

Oh, my lady all right; only 'cep' she don' like craps. She born a w'ite folks nigger. She people b'long to Gob'nor Rutledge. Ain't yo' see Miss Rutledge come to see she when she sick?

MARIA

(*Overhearing, to* SERENA). Oh, dat Miss Rutledge come to see yuh?

SERENA

Sho! yo' ain' know dat?

MARIA

She eber sell any ob she ole clothes?

SERENA

Not she. But sometime she gib 'em away to de nigger'.

MARIA

(*Sighing*). I wish I could git a dress off she. She de firs' pusson I eber see whut hipped an' busted 'zac'ly like me.

ROBBINS

(*Boasting*). Yes, suh! my lady——
Yo' bes' sabe yo' talk fo' dem dice. Bones ain't got no patience wid 'omen.

MINGO

Dat's de trut'. Course dey can't git along togedder. Dey is all two atter de same nigger money.

JAKE

Annie dere likes de single life, ain't it, Annie? Whut become ob dat ole fisherman used to come fo' see yo'?

ANNIE

He ain't fisherman.

JAKE

Whut he do?

ANNIE

Him ain't do nuttin' mos' all de time. Odder time, him is a shoe carpenter.
(*The voice of* PETER, *the old "honey man," is heard in the street, drawing nearer and nearer.*)

PETER

Here comes de honey man. Yo' gots honey?—Yes, ma'am, I gots honey.—Yo' gots honey in de comb?—Yes, ma'am, I gots honey in de comb.—Yo' gots honey cheap?—Yes, ma'am, my honey cheap.

(PETER *enters gate and closes it behind him. He is a gentle, kindly Negro, verging on senility. A large wooden tray covered with a white cloth is balanced on his head.*)

LILY

(*Going to meet him*). Well, here come my ole man. (*Takes tray from his head and shouts in his ear.*) Now gimme de money. (*He hands her some coins. She points to bench.*)
Now go sit an' res'.
(*He does as he is told. She places tray in her room and returns to circle.*)

MARIA

Yo', Scipio! Here come Porgy! Open de gate fo' uh!
(PORGY *drives up to the gate in his soapbox chariot. He is a crippled beggar of the Charleston streets, who has done much to overcome his handicap of almost powerless legs by supplying himself with a patriarchal and very dirty goat, which draws a cart made of an upturned soap box, on two lopsided wheels, which bears the inscription,* "WILD ROSE SOAP, PURE AND FRAGRANT."
PORGY *is no longer young, and yet not old. There is a suggestion of the mystic in his thoughtful, sensitive face. He is black, with the almost purple blackness of unadulterated Congo blood.*
SCIPIO *reluctantly interrupts his performance on a mouth organ, shuffles across court, and opens one side of the ponderous gate.*
PORGY *drives through and pulls up beside the crap ring.*)

JAKE

Here de ole crap shark.

PORGY

All right, Mingo! Jake! Gib' me a han' out dis wagon. I gots a pocket full ob de buckra money, an' he goin' to any man whut gots de guts fo' shoot 'em off me!
(MINGO *and* JAKE *help* PORGY *from wagon to a seat on ground at left front of circle.* SCIPIO *leads goat away through arch at rear left.*)
(JIM *saunters to gate and looks out.*)

ROBBINS

All right, mens! Roll 'em! We done wait long 'nough.

JIM

(*Returning to group*). Yo' bes' wait for Crown. I seen um comin', takin' de whole sidewalk, an' he look like he ain't goin' stan' no foolin'.

PORGY

Is Bess wid um?

JAKE

Listen to Porgy! I t'ink he sof' on Crown's Bess! (*All the men laugh.*)

PORGY

Gawd make cripple to be lonely. T'ain't no use for um to be sof' on a 'oman.

MARIA

Porgy gots too good sense to look twice at dat licker-guzzlin' slut.

LILY

Licker-guzzlin'! It takes more'n licker fo' sati'fy Crown's Bess.

SERENA

Happy dus'! Dat's what it take! Dat gal Bess ain't fit for Gawd-fearin' ladies to 'sociate wid!

SPORTING LIFE

Sistuhs! You needn't worry! Gawd-fearin' ladies is de las' t'ing on eart' Bess is a-wantin' for 'sociate wid.

PORGY

Can't yo' keep yo' mout' off Bess! Between de Gawd-fearin' ladies an' de Gawd-damnin' men, dat gal ain't gots no chance.

JAKE

Ain't I tells yo' Porgy sof' on um? (*More laughter.*)

PORGY

I ain't neber swap one word wid she. (CROWN *and* BESS *appear at gate.* CROWN *is lurching slightly and* BESS *is piloting him through the entrance.*

CROWN *is a huge Negro of magnificent physique, a stevedore on the cotton wharfs. He is wearing blue denim pants and tan shirt with a bright bandanna about his neck. From his belt hangs a long gleaming cotton hook.*

BESS *is slender, but sinewy; very black, wide nostrils, and large, but well-formed mouth. She flaunts a typical, but debased, Negro beauty.*

From the occupants of Catfish Row there are cries of, "Here comes Big Boy!" "'Low, Crown!" "'Low Bess," etc.)

CROWN

(*To* SPORTING LIFE). All right, high stepper. Gib us a pint, an make it damn' quick. (SPORTING LIFE *pulls a flask from his hip pocket and hands it to* CROWN. CROWN *jerks out cork and takes a long pull.*)

(*To* BESS.) Pay um, Bess!

(BESS *settles for the bottle, then takes her seat by* CROWN, *ignoring the women of the court.*

CROWN *hands her the flask, from which she takes a long pull. She meets* SERENA'S *eyes, laughs at their hostility, and at once extends the bottle to* ROBBINS.)

BESS

Hab one to de Gawd-fearin' ladies. Dere's nuttin' else like 'em—t'ank Gawd!

(ROBBINS *tries to resist, but the fumes of raw liquor are too much for him. He takes a deep drink.*

CROWN *snatches the bottle from him, gulps the entire remaining contents, and shatters it on the flags behind him.*

The crap circle is now complete. The positions are as follows:

Rear

X BESS   X CROWN

X DADDY PETER

X MINGO   X SPORTING LIFE

X JAKE

X ROBBINS   X PORGY

Footlights

(CROWN *throws coin down before him.*)

CROWN

I'm talkin' to yo' mans. Anybody answerin' me?
(*They all throw down money.*)

ROBBINS

(*To* JAKE). An' dem fine chillen ob mine!

CROWN

Shet yo' damn mout' an' t'row.

ROBBINS

(*Taken aback and rolling hastily*). Box cars again! (*They all roar with laughter.*)

MINGO

Cover 'em, brudder, cover 'em.

ROBBINS

Cover hell! I goin' pass 'em along an' see ef I kin break my luck.

MINGO

He lady ain't 'low um but fifty cent, an' he can't take no chance wid bad luck.
(*All laugh at* ROBBINS.)

BESS

(*With a provocative look at* SERENA). Dat all right, Honey-boy, I'll stake yo' when yo' four bits done gone.

SERENA

(*To* ROBBINS). Go ahead an' play, yo' ain't need no charity off no she-devils.

BESS

(*To* ROBBINS). See whut I git fuh yo'. De she-gawds is easy when yo' knows de way.
(CROWN *claps his hand over* BESS'S *mouth.*)

CROWN

Shet yo' damn mout'. Yo' don' gib Mingo no chance to talk to de bones.
(JAKE *has cast and lost, and the dice are now with* MINGO, *who is swinging them back and forth in his hand. Sings.*)

MINGO

"Ole snake-eye, go off an' die.
Ole man seben, come down from Heaben."
(*Grunts, throws, and snaps fingers.*) Seben! (*Scoops up dice.*)

CROWN

I ain't see dat seben yit. (*Snatches* MINGO'S *hand and opens fingers. Looks at dice.*) Yo' done tu'n um ober.

MINGO

(*To Circle*). Whut I t'row?
(*Cries of "Seben," "Jus' as he say," etc.* MINGO *pulls in pot.*)

CROWN

Well, dere's more'n one nigger done meet he Gawd fuh pullin' 'em in 'fore I reads 'em. See? An' I'm a-sayin' it ober tonight.
(*All ante again.*)

MINGO

Come home again to yo' pappy. (*Shoots.*) Four to make! Come four! (*Shoots.*)
(*Cries of "Seben," "Crapped out," etc.* MINGO *passes dice to* CROWN.)

CROWN

Come clean, yo' little black-eyed bitches! (*Shoots. Cries of "Six," "Six to make," etc.* CROWN *takes up bones and produces rabbit foot from pocket. He touches dice with it.*)
Kiss rabbit foot. (*Shoots.*)

SPORTING LIFE

(*Reaching for dice*). Crapped out! Come to your pappy.
(CROWN *extends a huge arm and brushes him back. He tries to focus his eyes on dice.*)

ROBBINS

Crown too cock-eyed drunk to read um. What he is say, Bess?

BESS

Seben.

CROWN

(*Scowls at* ROBBINS, *then turns to* SPORTING LIFE). I ain't drunk 'nough to read 'em, dat's de trouble. Licker ain't strong 'nough. Gimme a pinch ob happy dus', Sportin' Life.
(SPORTING LIFE *takes from his pocket a small folded paper.*)

BESS

Don' gib' um dat stuff, Sportin' Life. He's ugly drunk already.

CROWN

Yo' is a good one to talk! Pay um and shut up.
(*Takes the paper from* SPORTING LIFE, *unfolds it, and inhales the powder.*
BESS *pays* SPORTING LIFE. DADDY PETER *takes his pipe from his mouth and crowds in between* CROWN *and* SPORTING LIFE, *putting a hand on the arm of each.*)

PETER

Frien' an' dice an' happy dus' ain't meant to 'sociate. Yo' mens bes' go slow.
(CROWN *draws back his fist. Cries of "Leabe Uncle Peter be!" "He ain't mean no harm!" etc.* CROWN *relaxes.* SPORTING LIFE *picks up the dice.*)

SPORTING LIFE

Huh, seben! Huh, seben! Huh, seben! (*Shoots.*) 'Leben! Come home, Fido! (*Whistles, snaps fingers, and pulls in pot.*) (*All ante.*)

CROWN

Gawd damn it. I ain't read um yet.
(*All laugh at him. Cries of "Crown cockeye drunk." "Can't tell dice from watermillion," etc.*)

CROWN

(*Growling*). All right. I'm tellin' yo'.

SPORTING LIFE

(*Shooting*). Six to make! Get um again! (*Shoots.*) (*Cries of "Seben," "Crapped out," etc.* PORGY *takes up dice and commences to sway, with his eyes half closed. He apostrophizes dice in a sort of singsong chant.*)

PORGY

Oh, little stars, roll me some light. (*Shoots.*) 'Leben little stars, come home.
(*Pulls in pot.*)
(*All ante.*)
Roll dis poor beggar a sun an' moon! (*Shoots.*)

MINGO

Snake eyes!

PORGY

Dem ain't no snake eyes. Dey is a flock ob mornin' an' ebenin' star. An' jus' yo' watch um rise for dis po' beggar. (*Shoots.*)
(*Cries of "Made um," "Dat's he point," etc.* PORGY *pulls in pot.*)

CROWN

Roll up dat nigger sleeve.
(PORGY *rolls up his sleeves.*)
Well, yo' gots dem damn dice conjer den.
(*All ante.* PORGY *rolls. Cries of "Snake eyes," "Crapped out!" All ante.* ROBBINS *takes up bones, whistles, shoots, snaps them back up very rapidly.*)

ROBBINS

Nine to make! (*Whistles, shoots, snaps fingers.*) Read um! Nine spot! (*Sweeps them up, and reaches for money.* CROWN *seizes his wrist.*)

CROWN

Tech dat money an' meet yo' Gawd.

ROBBINS

Take yo' han' off me, yo' lousy houn'! (*Turns to* JAKE.) Han' me dat brick behin' yo'.
(JAKE *reaches brickbat and puts it in his free hand.* CROWN *jerks his cotton hook out of his belt and lunges forward, bowling* ROBBINS *over, and knocking brick from his hand.* CROWN *then steps back and kicks over lamp, extinguishing it.*
The stage is now dark except for the small lamp at SERENA'S *wash bench. This lights up the woman's terrified face as she strains her gaze into the darkness.*
MARIA, CLARA *and the others of her group stand behind her.*
From the crap ring come cries and curses. Suddenly, shutters are thrown open in right and left walls of building, and forms strain from the sills. As the shutters are banged open, shafts of light from them flash across the court, latticing it with a cross play of light.
CROWN *and* ROBBINS *are revealed facing each other:* CROWN *crouched for a spring with gleaming cotton hook extended;* ROBBINS *defenceless, his back to the wall.*
Then ROBBINS *lunges under the hook and they clinch. The fight proceeds with no distinguishable words from the combatants, but with bestial growls and breath that sobs and catches in their throats. In*

and out of the cross-play of light they sway —now revealed, now in darkness. The watchers move back and stand around the wall. They commence a weird, high-keyed moaning that rises as the figures take the light, and subsides almost to silence when they are obscured.
Suddenly, out of the dark, CROWN *swings* ROBBINS *into a shaft of light.* CROWN *is facing the audience and is holding* ROBBINS *by the throat at arms' length. With a triumphant snarl, he swings the hook downward.* ROBBINS *drops back toward audience into darkness, and* CROWN *stands in high light. There is dead silence now. In it* CROWN *looks down at his hands, opening and closing them. Then he draws his arm across his eyes.*
The silence is shattered by a piercing scream, and SERENA *runs across the court and throws herself on the body.*
BESS *appears in the light beside* CROWN. *She shakes him violently by the arm.)*

BESS

Wake up an' hit it out. Yo' ain't got no time to lose.

CROWN

(*Looking stupidly into the gloom at* SERENA *and the body of her man*). Whut de matter?

BESS

(*Hysterically*). Yo' done kill Robbins, an' de police'll be comin'. (*She starts to pull him toward the gate.*)

CROWN

Whar yo' goin' hide? Dey knows you an' me pulls togedder.
(*In the half light, it can now be seen that the court has been deserted, except for* SERENA, *who sits beside the body with her head bowed, and sways from side to side with a low, steady moaning.*
A match is scratched and held in PORGY'S *hand. He is crouched on his doorstep. He looks toward* ROBBINS'S *body, and his face shows horror and fear. He gives a whimpering moan, and as the match burns out, he drags himself over his threshold and closes the door.*)

BESS

Dey wouldn't look fuh me here. I'll stay here an' hide. Somebody always willin' to take care ob Bess.

CROWN

(*Now at gate*). Well, git dis: he's temporary. I'se comin' back when de hell dies down.

BESS

All right. Only git out now. Here, take dis. (*Thrusts the money into his hand. She pushes him out of gate. He disappears into the shadows. She turns around and faces the court. It is silent and empty except for the body and* SERENA. SPORTING LIFE *steps out of the shadows under* SERENA'S *steps, startling her.*)
Dat yo', Sportin' Life? Fo' Gawd's sake, gib' me a little touch happy dus'. I shakin' so I can hardly stan'. (*Suddenly remembering.*) Oh, I done gib' all de money to Crown. I can't pay fo' um. But, for Gawd's sake, gib me jus' a touch!

SPORTING LIFE

Yo' ain't needs to pay fo' um, Bess. (*Pours powder into her hand.*) Sportin' Life ain't go back on a frien' in trouble like dese odder low-life nigger'.
(BESS *quickly inhales the powder. Sighs with relief.*)
Listen! I'll be goin' back up to Noo Yo'k soon. All yo' gots to do is to come wid me now. I'll hide yo' out an' take yo' on wid me when I go. Why, yo' an' me'll be a swell team! Wid yo looks an' all de frien's I gots dere, it'll be ebery night an' all night —licker, dus', bright lights, an' de sky de limit! (*He looks apprehensively toward gate. Takes her arm.*) Come 'long! We gots to beat it while de beatin's good.
(BESS *draws away sharply from his grasp.*)
Nobody 'round here's goin' to take in Crown's Bess. Yo' bes' go wid yo' only frien'.

BESS

I ain't come to dat yet.

SPORTING LIFE

Well, de cops ain't goin' find me here fo' no 'oman! (*Slinks out gate.*)

(BESS *looks desperately about for shelter. She advances timidly and takes up lamp from the wash bench. She starts at rear left, and tries all of the doors as she goes. They are either locked, or slammed in her face as she reaches out to them. She comes to* MARIA'S *shop door, and as she reaches it, it is jerked open and* MARIA *confronts her.*)

MARIA

(*In a tense voice*). Yo' done bring trouble 'nough. Git out 'fore de police comes.

BESS

Yo' wouldn't hab' a heart, an' let me in?

MARIA

Not till hell freeze!

(*A light is lit in* PORGY'S *room, showing at window and crack in door.*)

BESS

(*Indicating* PORGY'S *room*). Who lib ober dere?

MARIA

He ain't no use to yo' kin'. Dat's Porgy. He a cripple an' a beggar.

(BESS *seems to agree with* MARIA *that* PORGY *is of no use to her. Crosses to gate, hesitates. Then she turns slowly toward* PORGY'S *room and crosses, shuddering away from* SERENA *and the body, which she must pass on the way. She reaches the door, puts her hand on the knob, hesitates, then slowly she opens it, enters, and closes it behind her.*)

CURTAIN

SCENE II

ST. MICHAEL'S *chimes the quarters and strikes seven.*

The curtain rises on SERENA'S *room, a second story room in Catfish Row, which still bears traces of its ancient beauty in its high panelled walls and tall, slender mantel with Grecian frieze and intricate scroll work. The door is in left wall at back. Near the center of back wall a window looks toward the sea. The fireplace is in right wall. Over the mantel is a gaudy lithograph of Lincoln striking chains from the slaves.*

The room is vaguely lighted by several kerosene lamps, and is scantily furnished: a bed against the back wall at left, and a few chairs.

ROBBINS'S *body lies upon the bed, completely covered by a white sheet. On its chest is a large blue saucer. Standing about the bed or seated on the floor are Negroes, all singing and swaying and patting with their large feet.*

SERENA *sits at the foot of the bed swaying dismally to the rhythm.*

They have been singing for hours. The monotony of the dirge and the steady beat of the patting has lulled several into a state of coma.

"Deat', ain't yuh gots no shame, shame?
Deat', ain't yuh gots no shame, shame?
Deat', ain't yuh gots no shame, shame?
Deat', ain't yuh gots no shame?

"Teck dis man an' gone, gone,
Teck dis man an' gone, gone,
Teck dis man an' gone, gone,
Deat', ain't yuh gots no shame?

"Leabe dis 'oman lone, lone,
Leabe dis 'oman lone, lone,
Leabe dis 'oman lone, lone,
Deat', ain't yuh gots no shame?"

(*The door opens and* PETER *comes in. Doffs his old hat, crosses, and puts coins in saucer. The singing and swaying continue. He finds a seat at right front and begins to sway and pat with the others.*

SERENA *reaches over, gets saucer, and counts coins. Replaces saucer with a hopeless expression.*)

JAKE

How de saucer stan', Sistuh?

(*The singing dies gradually as, one by one, the Negroes stop to listen, but the rhythm continues.*)

SERENA

(*Dully*). Fourteen dolluh and thirty-six cent.

MARIA

(*Encouragingly*). Dat's a-comin' on Sistuh. Yo' can bury him soon.

SERENA

De Boa'd ob Healt' say he gots to git buried tomorruh.

CLARA

It cost thirty-four dolluh for bury my grandmudder, but she gots de three carriage'.

SERENA

What I goin' to do ef I ain't gots de money?

PETER

(*Understanding that they refer to saucer*). Gawd gots plenty coin' fo' de saucer.

SERENA

Bless de Lo'd.

PETER

An' He goin' soften dese nigger heart' fo' fill de saucer till he spill ober.

SERENA

Amen, my Jedus!

PETER

De Lord will provide a grabe fo' He chillun.

CLARA

Bless de Lo'd!
(*The swaying gradually changes to the rhythm of* PETER'S *prayer.*)

PETER

An' he gots comfort fo' de widder.

SERENA

Oh, my Jedus!

PETER

An' food fo' de fadderless.

SERENA

Yes, Lo'd!

PETER

An' he goin' raise dis poor nigger out de grabe.

JAKE

Allelujah!

PETER

An' set him in de seat of de righteous, Amen.

SERENA

Amen, my brudder.
(*They all sway in silence.*)

ANNIE

(*Looking toward door*). What dat?

CLARA

I hear somebody comin' up de steps now bringing much penny fo' de saucer.
(MARIA *opens the door and looks out.*)

SERENA

Who dat?

MARIA

It's Porgy comin' up de steps.

JAKE

(*Starting to rise*). Somebody bes' go help um.

MARIA

He gots help. Crown's Bess is a-helpin' um.

SERENA

(*Spring to her feet*). What's she a-comin' here fo'?
(*They are all silent, looking toward door.* PORGY *and* BESS *enter.* PORGY *looks about; makes a movement toward corpse.* BESS *starts to lead him across room.* SERENA *stands defiant, silent, till they have gone half the way.*)
What yo' bring dat 'oman here fo'?

PORGY

She want to come help sing. She's a good shouter.
(BESS, *self-possessed, leads* PORGY *on toward saucer. He deposits his coins. Then* BESS *stretches her hand toward saucer.*)

SERENA

I don' need yo' money fo' bury my man.
(BESS *hesitates.*)
I ain't takin' money off he murderer.

PORGY

Dat ain't Crown's money. I gib um to Bess fo' put in de saucer.

SERENA

All right. Yo' can put um in.
(BESS *drops the money in saucer and leads* PORGY *to a place at left front. They sit side by side on the floor.* SERENA *stands glaring after them.*)

PETER

(*Trying to make peace*). Sing, Sistuh, sing! Time is passin', an' de saucer ain't full.

SERENA

(*To* PORGY). She can sit ober dere in de corner, ef she want to. But she can't sing!
(BESS *sits with quiet dignity; seeming scarcely to notice* SERENA's *tone and words.*)

PORGY

Dat all right. Bess don' want fo' sing, anyway.
(*The spiritual begins again.*)

"Leabe dese chillun starve, starve,
Leabe dese chillun starve, starve,
Leabe dese chillun starve, starve,
Deat', ain't yuh gots no shame?"

MINGO

(*Looking upward*). Dat rain on de roof?

JAKE

Yes, rainin' hard out.

PORGY

Dat's all right now fo' Robbins. Gawd done send He rain already fo' wash he feet-steps offen dis eart'.

LILY

Oh, yes, Brudder!

SERENA

Amen, my Jedus!
(*The spiritual continues. The swaying and patting begin gradually and grow. Slowly* BESS *begins to sway with the others, but she makes no sound.*
The door is burst suddenly open and the DETECTIVE *enters.* TWO POLICEMEN *wait in the doorway.*
The spiritual ceases abruptly. All the Negroes' eyes are riveted on the white man and filled with fear. He strides over to the corpse, looks down at it.)

DETECTIVE

Um! A saucer-buried nigger, I see! (*To* SERENA.) You're his widow?

SERENA

Yes, suh.

DETECTIVE

He didn't leave any burial insurance?

SERENA

No, boss. He didn't leabe nuttin'.

DETECTIVE

Well, see to it that he's buried to-morrow.
(*Turns away from her. Slowly circles room, looking fixedly at each Negro in turn. Each quails under his gaze. He pauses abruptly before* PETER. *Suddenly shouts at him.*) You killed Robbins, and I'm going to hang you for it!
(PETER *is almost paralyzed by terror, his panic heightened by the fact that he cannot hear what the* DETECTIVE *says. His mouth opens and he cannot find his voice.*)

LILY

(*To* DETECTIVE). He ain't done um.

PETER

(*Helplessly*). What he say?

LILY

(*Shouting in* PETER's *ear*). He say yo' kill Robbins.

DETECTIVE

(*Laying his hand on* PETER's *shoulder*). Come along now!

PETER

'Fore Gawd, boss, I ain't neber done um!
(*The* DETECTIVE *whips out his revolver and points it between* PETER's *eyes.*)

DETECTIVE

Who did it, then? (*Shouting.*) You heard me! Who did it?

PETER

(*Wildly*). Crown done um, boss. I done see him do um.

DETECTIVE

(*Shouting*). You're sure you saw him?

PETER

I swear to Gawd, boss. I was right dere, close beside um.

DETECTIVE

(*With satisfied grunt*). Umph! I thought as much. (*Swings suddenly on* PORGY *and points the pistol in his face.*) You saw it, too!
(PORGY *trembles but does not speak. He lowers his eyes.*)
Come! Out with it! I don't want to have to put the law on you!
(PORGY *sits silent. The* DETECTIVE *shouts with fury.*) Look at me, you damned nigger!
(PORGY *slowly raises his eyes to the* DETECTIVE's *face.*)

PORGY

I ain't know nuttin' 'bout um, boss.

DETECTIVE

(*Angrily*). That's your room in the corner, isn't it? (*Points downward toward left.*)

PORGY

Yes, boss. Dat's my room.

DETECTIVE

The door opens on the court, don't it?

PORGY

Yes, boss, my door open on de cou't.

DETECTIVE

And yet you didn't see or hear anything?

PORGY

I ain't know nuttin' 'bout um. I been inside asleep on my bed wid de door closed.

DETECTIVE

(*Exasperated*). You're a damned liar. (*Turns away disgusted. Saunters toward door. To* POLICEMEN, *indicating* PETER.) He saw the killing. Take him along and lock him up as a material witness.
(FIRST POLICEMAN *crosses to* PETER.)

FIRST POLICEMAN

(*Helping* PETER *to his feet*). Come along, Uncle.

PETER

(*Shaking with terror*). I ain't neber done um, boss.

POLICEMAN

Nobody says you did it. We're just taking you along as a witness.
(*But* PETER *does not understand.*)

SERENA

What yo' goin' to do wid um?

POLICEMAN

Lock him up. Come along. It ain't going to be so bad for you as for Crown, anyway.

SECOND POLICEMAN

(*To* DETECTIVE). How about the cripple?

DETECTIVE

(*Sourly*). He couldn't have helped seeing it, but I can't make him come through. But it don't matter. One's enough to hang Crown (*with a short laugh*)—if we ever get him.

MARIA

(*To* FIRST POLICEMAN). How long yo' goin' lock um up fo'?

FIRST POLICEMAN

Till we catch Crown.

PORGY

(*Sadly*). I reckon Crown done loose now in de palmetto thickets, an' de rope ain't neber made fo' hang um.

DETECTIVE

Then the old man's out of luck. (*To* SERENA.) Remember! You've got to bury that nigger tomorrow or the Board of Health will take him and turn him over to the medical students.

PETER

I ain't neber done um, boss.

DETECTIVE

(*To* FIRST POLICEMAN). Come on! Get the old man in the wagon.

(PETER, *shaking in every limb, is led out. The* DETECTIVE *and* SECOND POLICEMAN *follow. A moment of desolated silence.*)

MARIA

It sho' pay nigger to go blin' in dis world.

JAKE

Porgy ain't got much leg, but he sho' got sense in dealin' wid de w'ite folks.

PORGY

(*Slowly, as though half to himself*). I can't puzzle dis t'ing out. Peter war a good man. An' dat nigger Crown war a killer an' fo'eber gettin' into trouble. But dere go Peter fo' be lock up like t'ief, an he're lie Robbins wid he wife an fadderless chillun. An Crown done gone he was fo' do de same t'ing ober again somewheres else.
(*The Negroes begin to sway and moan.*)

CLARA

Gone fo' true! Yes, Jedus!
(*A voice raises the spiritual, "What de Matter, Chillun?" It swells slowly. One voice joins in after another. The swaying and patting begin and grow slowly in tempo and emphasis. As before,* BESS *sways in silence.*)

"What' de mattuh, chillun?
What' de mattuh, chillun?
What' de mattuh, chillun?
Yuh can't stan' still.
Pain gots de body.
Pain gots de body.
Pain gots de body.
An' I can't stan' still.

"What de mattuh, Sistuh?
What de mattuh, Sistuh?
What de mattuh, Sistuh?
Yuh can't stan' still.
Jedus gots our brudder,
Jedus gots our brudder,
Jedus gots our brudder,
An' I can't stan' still."

(*The door opens and the* UNDERTAKER *bustles into the room with an air of great importance. He is a short, yellow Negro with a low, oily voice. He is dressed entirely in black. He crosses to* SERENA. *The song dies away, but the swaying continues to its rhythm.*)

UNDERTAKER

How de saucer stan' now, my sistuh? (*Glances appraisingly at saucer.*)

SERENA

(*In a flat, despairing voice*). Dere ain't but fifteen dollah.

UNDERTAKER

Umph! Can't bury um fo' fifteen dollah.

JAKE

He gots to git buried tomorruh or de Boa'd ob Healt' 'll take um an' gib um to de students.

SERENA

(*Wildly*). Oh, fo' Gawd's sake bury um in de grabeyahd. (*She rises to her knees and seizes the* UNDERTAKER'S *hand in both hers. Imploringly.*) Don' let de students hab um. I goin' to work Monday, an' I swear to Gawd I gon' to pay yo' ebery cent.
(*Even the swaying ceases now. The Negroes all wait tensely, their eyes riveted on the* UNDERTAKER'S *face, pleading silently. After a moment's hesitation, the* UNDERTAKER'S *professional manner slips from him.*)

UNDERTAKER

(*Simply*). All right, Sistuh. Wid de box an' one carriage, it's cost me more'n twenty-five. But I'll see yo' t'rough.
(*An expression of vast relief sweeps into every face.* SERENA *silently relaxes across the foot of the bed, her head between her outstretched arms.*)
Yo' can all be ready at eight tomorruh. It's a long trip to de cemetery.
(*The* UNDERTAKER *goes out door. The Negroes gaze silently after him with eyes filled with gratitude. There is a moment of silence after his departure. Then, carried out of herself by sympathy and gratitude,* BESS, *forgetful of the ban laid upon her. lifts her strong, beautiful voice triumphantly.*)

BESS

"Oh, I gots a little brudder in de new grabeyahd

What outshine de sun,
Outshine de sun,"

(PORGY'S *voice joins hers.*)

"Outshine de sun."

(*By the fourth line, many of the Negro voices have joined in, and the song grows steadily in volume and fervor.*)

"Oh, I gots a little brudder in de new grabeyahd
What outshine de sun,
An' I'll meet um in de Primus Lan'."

(BESS'S *voice is heard again for one brief moment alone as it rises high and clear on the first line of the chorus*).

"I will meet um in de Primus Lan'!"

(*Then a full chorus, with deep basses predominating, crashes in on the second line of the refrain.* SERENA, *last of all, joins enthusiastically in the chorus.*)

"Oh, I'll meet um in de Primus Lan'!
I will meet um, meet um, meet um,
I will meet um, meet um, meet um,
I will meet um in de Primus Lan'!

"Oh, I gots a mansion up on high
What ain't make wid' han',
Ain't make wid han',
Ain't make wid han',
Oh, I gots a mansion up on high
What ain't make wid' han',
An' I'll meet um in de Primus Lan'!"

(*The beautiful old spiritual beats triumphantly through the narrow room, steadily gaining in speed.*
SERENA *is the first to leap to her feet and begin to "shout."* * *One by one, as the spirit moves them, the Negroes follow her example till they are all on their feet, swaying, shuffling, clapping their hands.*
BESS *leads the "shouting" as she has the singing, throwing her whole soul into an intricate shuffle and complete turn. Each Negro "shouts" in his own individual way, some dancing in place, others merely swaying and patting their hands.*
"Allelujahs" and cries of "Yes, Lord" are interjected into the singing. And the rhythm swells till the old walls seem to rock and surge with the sweep of it.)

CURTAIN

*"Shouting" is the term given by the Carolina Negroes to the body rhythms and steps with which they accompany their emotional songs.

ACT TWO

SCENE I

ST. MICHAEL'S *chimes the quarters and strikes one. Morning.*

The court is full of movement, the Negroes going about their tasks. At right front, a group of fishermen are rigging their lines. They are working leisurely with much noisy laughter and banter. Occasionally, a snatch of song is heard.

PORGY *is sitting at his window. The soap-box car stands by his door, the goat is inside the room. Occasionally looks out door.*

JAKE

Fish runnin' well outside de bar dese days.

MINGO

(*An onlooker*). Hear tell de Bufort mens bring in such a catch yesterday dat de boat look like he gots floor ob silber.

JIM

I hears dey gots to t'row away half de catch so as not glut de market.

JAKE

Yes, suh! Fish runnin' well, an' we mens bes' make de mores ob it.

JIM

Dats de trut'. Dem Septembuh storm due soon, an' fish don' like eas' win' an' muddy watuh.

ANNIE

(*Calling across court*). Mus' be you mens forget 'bout picnic. Ain't yo' know de parade start up de block at ten o'clock?

MINGO

Dat's de trut', Sistuh.
(*The men begin to gather up their fishing gear.*)

PORGY

(*At window. Solicitously*). Bess, ain't you wants to go to de picnic after all? Yo' know I is membuh in good standin' ob "De Sons and Daughters ob Repent Ye Saith de Lord."

BESS

(*Unseen within room*). I radder stay home wid yo'.

PORGY

Yo' gots jus' as much right to go as any 'oman in Catfish Row.

BESS

(*In unconvincing voice*). I ain't care much 'bout picnic.
(PORGY *is troubled. Sits in silence.*)

SPORTING LIFE

(*Who has sauntered over to group of fishermen*). All yo' mens goin' to de picnic?

JAKE

Goin' fo' sho'. How come yo' t'ink we ain't goin'?

SPORTING LIFE

I jus' ask. Don' hab no picnic in Noo Yo'k. Yo' folks still hab yo' picnic on Kittiwah Islan'?

JIM

Listen to Sporting Life. He been six mont' in Noo Yo'k, an' he want to know ef we still hab we picnic on Kittiwah! (*They laugh.*)

(SPORTING LIFE *moves off. Sits at* MARIA'S *table.* LILY *joins the group of men.*)

JAKE

All right, mens. I'm all fuh ridin' luck fur as he will tote me. Turn out at four tomorruh mornin', an' we'll push de *Sea Gull* clean to de Blackfish Banks 'fore we wets de anchor. I gots a feelin' we goin' be gunnels under wid de pure fish when we comes in at night.

LILY

Yuh goin' fuh take de *Sea Gull* out beyond bah? (*She laughs. Calls out to* NELSON, *who is on far side of court.*) Heah dis, Nelson. Dese mens aimin' fuh take de *Sea Gull* to de Blackfish Banks!
(NELSON *joins the group.* CLARA, *overhearing, slowly approaches, her baby in her arms.* LILY *turns to the others.*)
Yo' mens bes' keep yo' ole washtub close to home. Wait till yo' gets a good boat like de *Mosquito* 'fore yo' trabble.
(*All the men and* LILY *laugh delightedly.*)

JAKE

Mosquito born in de water, but he can drown jus' de same.
(*All laugh,* LILY *slapping* NELSON'S *shoulder in her appreciation.*
CLARA *has stood silently beside them with anxious eyes.*)

CLARA

Jake! Yo' ain't plannin' to take de *Sea Gull* to de Blackfish Bank? It's time fuh de Septembuh storms.

JAKE

(*Laughing reassuringly*). Ain't yo' know we had one stiff gale las' yeah, an' he nebber come two yeah han' runnin'.

CLARA

Jake, I don' want yo' fuh go outside de bah!

JAKE

How yo' t'ink we goin' gib dat man child college edication?
(*They all laugh, except* CLARA.)

CLARA

Deys odder way fuh make money 'sides fish.

JAKE

Hear de 'oman! Mebbe yo' like me to be a cotton nigger! Huh?
(*The men laugh.* SCIPIO *is playing about the court with a broad red sash pinned across his breast from shoulder to waist. It bears the legend, "Repent Ye Saith the Lord." From the boy's breast flutters a yellow ribbon with the word "Marshal." He struts about court leading an imaginary parade.* JAKE, *looking about for change of subject, see* SCIPIO *and starts to his feet.*)
Heah, Scipio! Who sash dat yo' gots?
(SCIPIO *backs away.* JAKE *pursues.*)
Come heah, yo'! Jus' as I t'ought. Dat's my sash!
(*Not watching where he is going,* SCIPIO, *in his flight from* JAKE, *runs straight into* MARIA, *who delivers him to* JAKE.)

MARIA

Heah yo' is, Jake.

JAKE

T'ank yo' kindly Sistuh. (*To* SCIPIO, *while he rescues his sash and badge.*) How yo' t'ink I goin' lead dis picnic parade atter yo' been ruin my sash? (*Pins ribbons on his own breast. Sits on washing bench. Lights pipe.*)
(*The crowd begins to break up with noisy laughter and joking.*
SERENA *comes in at gate, wearing a neat white apron and a hat. Crosses to* PORGY'S *door, greeting her friends as she passes them.*)

SERENA

(*To the men*). Fine day fuh de picnic.

JIM

Fine fuh true, Sistuh.
(SERENA *knocks at* PORGY'S *door.* BESS *opens it.* SERENA *pays no attention to her.*)

SERENA

(*Looking through* BESS). Porgy! (*Sees him at window. Crosses to him.*) Oh, dere yo' is. I gots news. I done been to see my white folks 'bout Peter.

PORGY

What dey say?

SERENA

Dey say dey gots a white gentleman frien', name ob Mistah Archdale, who is lawyer an' he can get um out. I tells um yo' is de pusson fo' um to talk to 'cause yo' gots so much sense when yo' talks to w'ite folks. An' dey say he'll come fo' see yo' 'cause he pass right by here ebery day, an' yo' is cripple. (*Turns away, ignoring* BESS. *Crosses, sits beside* JAKE, *takes out and lights her pipe.*)
(MARIA *is serving a late breakfast to* SPORTING LIFE. JIM *and* MINGO *have joined him at table. St. Michael's chimes the quarter hour.* MARIA *crosses to pump to fill kettle. After a few puffs,* SERENA *whispers loudly to* JAKE.)
It's a shame when good Christian 'omans got to lib under de same roof wid a murderin' she-debil like dat Crown's Bess.

JAKE

She don' seem to harm nobody, an' Porgy seem to like to hab she 'roun'.

MARIA

Porgy change since dat 'oman go to lib' wid he.

SERENA

How he change?

MARIA

I tell yo' dat nigger happy now.

SERENA

Go 'long wid yo'. Dat 'oman ain't de kin' fo' make cripple happy. It take a killer like Crown to hol' she down.

MARIA

Dat may be so, but Porgy don't know dat yet. An', 'sides, ef a man is de kin' what need a 'oman, he goin' be happy regahdless.

JAKE

Dat's de trut', Sistuh. Him dress she up in he own eye, till she stan' like de Queen ob Sheba to he.

MARIA

Porgy t'ink right now dat he gots a shegawd in he room.

SERENA

Well, dere is gawds and gawds, an' Porgy sho' got de kin' what goin' gib um hell. Much as I likes Porgy, I wouldn't swap a word wid she.

MARIA

Dat all so, Sistuh. But yo' keep yo' eye on Porgy. He use to hate all dese chillen, but now he nebber come home widout candy ball fuh de crowd.

JAKE

I tells yo' dat 'oman——
(BESS *crosses to pump with bucket.*)

SERENA

Sh!
(*The three are silent watching* BESS. *She is neatly dressed, walks with queenly dignity, passes them as though they did not exist, fills her bucket, swings it easily to her head, turns from them with an air of cool scorn, and recrosses to her own door. The three look after her with varying expressions:* MARIA *interested,* SERENA *indignant,* JAKE *admiring.*)

JAKE

Dat's de t'ing. She sho' ain't askin' no visit ofen none ob she neighbors.

SERENA

Yo' poor sof'-headed nigger! Ain't yo' shame to set dere 'fore me an' talk sweet-mout' 'bout dat murderin' Crown's Bess? (*Making eyes at him.*) Now, ef I was a man, I'd sabe my sof' wo'd fuh de God-fearin' 'omans.

JAKE

Ef yo' was a man—— (*Pauses, looking thoughtfully at her, then shakes his head.*) No, it ain't no use. Yo' wouldn't understan'. Dat's somethin' shemale sense ain't goin' help yo' none wid. (*Knocks ashes from his pipe.*)
(MARIA *has turned toward her table. She suddenly puts down her kettle, strides to the table, seizes* SPORTING LIFE'S *hand, opens the fingers before he has time to resist, and blows a white powder from his palm.*)

SPORTING LIFE

(*Furiously*). What yo' t'ink yo' doin'! Dat stuff cos' money.

(MARIA *stands back, arms akimbo, staring down at him for a moment in silence.* SPORTING LIFE *shifts uneasily in his chair.*)

MARIA

(*In stentorian tones*). Nigger! I jus' tryin' to figger out wedder I better kill yuh decent now, wid yo' frien' about yo'—or leabe yo' fuh de white folks to hang atter a while. I ain't say nuttin' no matter how drunk yo' gets dese boys on you' rot-gut whisky. But nobody ain't goin' peddle happy dus' roun' my shop. Yo' heah what I say?

SPORTING LIFE

Come now, ole lady, don't talk like dese ole-fashioned, lamp-oil niggers. Why, up in Noo Yo'k, where I been waitin' in a—hotel——

MARIA

Hotel, eh? I suppose dese gal' yo' tryin' to get to go back to Noo Yo'k wid yo' is goin' to be bordahs! (*Shouting*). Don' yo' try any ob yo' Noo Yo'kin' roun' dis town. Ef I had my way, I'd go down to dat Noo Yo'k boat an' take ebery Gawd's nigger what come up de gangplank wid a Joseph coat on he back an' a glass headlight on he buzzum an' drap um to de catfish 'fore he foot hit decent groun'. Yes! my belly fair ache wid dis Noo Yo'k talk.
(*Bangs table so violently with her fist that* SPORTING LIFE *leaps from his chair and extends a propitiating hand toward her.*)

SPORTING LIFE

Dat's all right, Auntie. Le's you an' me be frien'.

MARIA

Frien' wid you'! One ob dese day I might lie down wid rattlesnake, an' when dat time come, yo' kin come right 'long an' git in de bed. But till den, keep yo' shiny carcass in Noo Yo'k til de debble ready to take cha'ge ob um.
(SIMON FRAZIER, *an elderly Negro dressed in black frock coat, comes in at the gate, looks about, crosses to* MARIA'S *table.* MARIA *is still glaring at* SPORTING LIFE *so ferociously that* FRAZIER *hesitates.* MARIA *looks up and sees him. She is suddenly all smiles.*)

MARIA

Mornin', lawyer. Lookin' fuh somebody?

FRAZIER

Porgy live here, don't he?

MARIA

Sho' he do. Right ober dere he room.

FRAZIER

T'ank yo', Sistuh. (*Crosses toward* PORGY'S *door.*)

LILY

(*Who is near* PORGY'S *door*). Porgy! Lawyer Frazier to see yo'.
(MARIA *gives* SPORTING LIFE *final glare and enters shop.* BESS *helps* PORGY *on to door-step and returns to room.*)

FRAZIER

Mornin', Porgy.

PORGY

Mornin', lawyer.

FRAZIER

I come to see yo' on business fo' one ob my w'ite client'.

PORGY

Huh?

FRAZIER

I been in to see Mistah Alan Archdale yesterday an' he gib' me message fo' yo'.

PORGY

Who he?

FRAZIER

(*In disgust*). Who he? Yo' ain't know who is Mistah Alan Archdale? He lawyer, same as me.

PORGY

(*Uneasily*). Whut he wants wid me?

FRAZIER

I been in to see um on private business like we lawyers always has togedder. An' he say to me, "Mistah Frazier, do yo' know dat black scoundrel dat hitches his boat outside my window ebery mornin'?" I sez: "Yes, Misteh Archdale, I knows um." An' he say: "Well, when yo' goes out, tell um to mobe on." When I comes out, yo' is gone, so I come heah fo' tell yo'. *Mobe on.*

PORGY

Why he don't tell me heself?

FRAZIER

Yo' t'ink Misteh Alan Archdale gots time fo' tell nigger to mobe on? No, suh! He put he case in my han', an' I is authorize fo' tell yo' yo' gots to fin' nudder hitchin' place.

PORGY

(*Unhappily*). I been hitch on dat corner mos' a mont' now. Why he don't want me 'roun'?

FRAZIER

(*Scratching his head*). I ain't quite make dat out. He say sompen 'bout de goat an' de commodity advertise on de chariot. (*Pointing to cart.*) "Pure an' fragrant." Dat's soap, ain't it? I gather dat he t'ink yo' goat need soap.

PORGY

(*Astonished*). Whut a goat want wid soap?

FRAZIER

(*Also puzzled*). I ain't know ezac'ly.
(BESS *comes to doorway and stands behind* PORGY. FRAZIER *resumes his authoritative tone.*)
All I knows is yuh gots to *mobe on!*
(FRAZIER *looks up and sees* BESS.) How yo' do?
(*Looks at her, scrutinizing.*) Ain't yo' Crown's Bess?

PORGY

No, suh, she ain't. She's Porgy's Bess.

FRAZIER

(*Sensing business*). Oh! I guess den yo' goin' be wantin' divorce.

PORGY

Huh?

FRAZIER

Ef de 'oman goin' stay wid' yo', she gots to hab divorce from Crown or else it ain't legal.
(*Takes legal-looking document from pocket. Shows it to* PORGY. PORGY *looks at it, much impressed. Passes it to* BESS.)

PORGY

How much it cos'?

FRAZIER

One dollah, ef dere ain't no complications.
(PORGY *looks dubious.* FRAZIER *quickly takes huge seal from his coat-tail pocket. Shows it to* PORGY.)

FRAZIER

When yo' gits divorce, I puts dis seal on de paper to show you has paid cash.

PORGY

Bess, yo' likes to hab divorce?

BESS

(*With longing*). Whut yo' t'ink, Porgy?
(*The other Negroes are gradually edging nearer to listen.*)

PORGY

I goin' buy yo' divorce. Bring me my pocketbook.
(BESS *goes into room and returns immediately with a number of small coins tied up in a rag, hands it to* PORGY. *He laboriously counts out a dollar in nickels and pennies. In the meantime,* FRAZIER *is filling in document with fountain pen. Group of Negroes now listening frankly.* FRAZIER *takes coins from* PORGY. *Counts them.* BESS *holds out her hand for document.*)

FRAZIER

(*Pocketing coins*). Wait a minute. 'Tain't legal yet. (*Holding paper in hands, lowers glasses on his nose. Begins in solemn tones.*) Yo' name?

BESS

Bess.
(FRAZIER *makes note.*)

FRAZIER

Yo' age?

BESS

Twenty-six yeah.

FRAZIER

Yo' desire to be divorce from dis man Crown?

BESS

Yas, boss.

FRAZIER

Address de co't as Yo' Honor.

BESS

Yas, Yo' Honor.

FRAZIER

When was yo' an Crown marry?
(BESS *hesitates.*)

BESS

I don' rightly 'member, boss—Yo' Honor.

FRAZIER

One yeah? Ten yeah?

BESS

Ain't I done tell yo' I don' remember?

LILY

She ain't neber been marry.

FRAZIER

(*To* BESS). Dat de trut'?

BESS

Yas, Yo' Honor.

FRAZIER

(*Triumphantly*). Ah, dat's a complication.

BESS

I ain't know dat mattered.

PORGY

Yo' can't gib she divorce? Gib me back my dollah.

FRAZIER

Who say I can't gib she divorce? But, under circumstances, dis divorce cos' two dollah. It take expert fuh divorce 'oman whut ain't marry.

BESS

Don't yuh pay um no two dollah, Porgy. It ain't wuth it.

FRAZIER

Berry well, den, ef yo' wants to go on libbin' in sin. (*Takes coins from pocket and begins to count. Seeing that they do not weaken, he pauses abruptly in his counting.*) Seein' that we is ole frien', I goin' make dis divo'ce dollah an' er half.
(*Again takes out impressive seal.* PORGY *eyes seal, greatly impressed. Begins counting out more pennies.* FRAZIER *affixes seal. Hands it to* PORGY. *Pockets extra money.*)

FRAZIER

Dat ain't much money considerin' whut yo' gets. One dollah an er half to change from a 'oman to a lady.

BESS

(*Happily*). T'ank yo' kindly, Yo' Honor.

FRAZIER

Glad to serbe yo'. When yo' ready to buy license, come to me.

PORGY

Whut she want wid license? She gots divorce, ain't she?

FRAZIER

Well, yo' ought to be stylish like de white folks, an' follow up divorce wid marriage license.
(PORGY *and* BESS *look quite depressed at prospect of further complications.*)
Well, good mornin', Missus Porgy. (*Turns to go. To* MARIA.) Yo' gots de cup coffee fo' sweeten my mout'?

MARIA

Sho' I is. Step right ober.
(*She and* FRAZIER *enter cookshop.*
The court is alive with noisy laughter and action. A fish vendor is calling his wares. St. Michael's is chiming the half hour. MARIA *is bustling back and forth serving the men at her table.* SERENA *is pumping water and calling to her friends.* ANNIE *is holding* CLARA'S *baby, rocking and tossing it.* CLARA *is rearranging sash with motto "Repent Ye Saith the Lord" across* JAKE'S *breast, and consulting the others as to the proper angle. The sash adjusted,* JAKE *bursts into song. "Brer Rabbit, whut yo' da do dey!"* LILY *answers with second line of song. The duet continues.*
SCIPIO *runs in at gate. Runs to* SERENA.)

SCIPIO

Dey's a buckra comin'. I heah um axin' outside ef dis Catfish Row.
(*The Negroes suddenly break off in their tasks.* JAKE *ceases to sing.*)

NELSON

(*Calling to* SERENA). Whut he say?

SERENA

(*In guarded voice, but addressing the court in general*). W'ite gen'man.
(*There is a sudden deep silence, contrasting strangely with noise and movement that preceded it.* ANNIE *gives* CLARA *her baby, goes quickly inside her own door.* JAKE *removes sash, puts it in pocket.* SERENA *retreats behind her tubs. The men at table give absorbed attention to their food.* MARIA *serves them in silence without looking up.* SCIPIO *becomes engrossed in tinkering with an old barrel hoop.* BESS *goes inside.* PORGY *feigns sleep.*
ALAN ARCHDALE, *a tall, kindly man in early middle age, whose bearing at once stamps him the aristocrat, enters the court, looks about at the Negroes, all ostensibly oblivious of his presence.*)

ARCHDALE

(*Calling to* SCIPIO). Boy!
(SCIPIO *approaches, reluctant, shuffling.*)
I'm looking for a man by the name of Porgy. Which is his room?
(SCIPIO *shuffles and is silent.*)
Don't you know Porgy?

SCIPIO

(*His eyes on the ground*). No, suh.

ARCHDALE

He lives here, doesn't he?

SCIPIO

I ain't know, boss.

(CLARA *is nearest.* ARCHDALE *crosses to her. She listens submissively, her eyes lowered.*)

ARCHDALE

I'm looking for a man named Porgy. Can you direct me to his room?

CLARA

(*Polite, but utterly negative*). Porgy? (*Repeats the name slowly as though trying to remember.*) No, boss, I ain't nebber heah ob nobody 'roun' dese parts name Porgy.

ARCHDALE

Come, you must know him. I am sure he lives in Catfish Row.

CLARA

(*Raising her voice*). Anybody heah know a man by de name Porgy?
(*Several of the Negroes repeat the name to one another, with shakes of their heads.*)

ARCHDALE

(*Laughing reassuringly*). I'm a friend of his, Mr. Alan Archdale, and I want to help him.
(SERENA *approaches. Looks keenly at* ARCHDALE.)

SERENA

Go 'long an' wake Porgy. Can't yo' tell *folks* when yo' see um?
(*A light of understanding breaks over* CLARA'S *face.*)

CLARA

Oh, yo' means *Porgy!* I ain't understan' whut name yo' say, boss.
(VOICES *all about the court: "Oh, de gen'-man mean Porgy. How come we ain't onderstan'!"*
CLARA *crosses to* PORGY'S *door, all smiles.*)
A gen'man come fuh see Porgy.
(PORGY *appears to awake.* ARCHDALE *crosses to him.*)

PORGY

How yo' does, boss?

ARCHDALE

You're Porgy? Oh, you're the fellow who rides in the goat cart. (*Sits on step.*)

PORGY

Yes, boss, I gots goat.

ARCHDALE

Tell me about your friend who got locked up on account of the Robbins murder.

PORGY

(*His face inscrutable*). How come yo' to care, boss?

ARCHDALE

Why, I'm the Rutledge's lawyer, and I look after their colored folks for them. Serena Robbins is the daughter of their old coachman, and she asked them to help out her friend.

PORGY

(*A shade of suspicion still in his voice*). Peter ain't gots no money, yo' know, boss; an' I jus' begs from do' to do'!

ARCHDALE

(*Reassuringly*). It will not take any money. At least, not much. And I am sure that Mrs. Rutledge will take care of that. So you can go right ahead and tell me all about it.
(PORGY'S *suspicions vanish.*)

PORGY

It like dis, boss. Crown kill Robbins, an' Peter see um do it. Now Crown gone he ways, an' dey done gots ole Peter lock up.

ARCHDALE

I see, as a witness.

PORGY

Till dey catch Crown, dey say, but ef dey keep um lock up till den, dat ole man gots er life sentence.

ARCHDALE

(*Under his breath*). The dirty hounds!
(*He is silent for a moment, his face set and stern.* PORGY *waits.* ARCHDALE *turns wearily to him.*)
Of course, we can go to law about this, but it will take no end of time. There is an easier way.
(*Across the sunlit walls of Catfish Row*

falls the shadow of a great bird flying low, evidently just out of range of vision of audience. There is a sudden great commotion in the court. Cries of "Drive um away," "Don't let um light," "T'row dis brick." Brooms are waved at the bird overhead. Bricks thrown. PORGY *looks up in anxiety.* BESS *comes to door with broom.* ARCHDALE *rises in perplexity.*)

PORGY

Dribe um off, Bess! Don't let um light.

ARCHDALE

What is it? What's the matter?
(*The shadow rises high. The commotion dies down.*)

PORGY

Dat's a buzzard. Yo' don' know dat bird like fo' eat dead folks?

ARCHDALE

But there's no one dead here, is there?

PORGY

Boss, dat bird mean trouble. Once de buzzard fold he wing an' light ober yo' do', yo' know all yo' happiness done dead.
(*With relief, the Negroes stand watching the bird disappear in the distance.* ARCHDALE *also looks after it.*)

SERENA

(*Leaning from her window and surveying court*). It sho' make me 'shamed to see all dese superstitious nigger' makin' spectacle ob demself befo' de w'ite gentlemans. Ain't we all see dat buzzard sit smack on Maria's table day fo' yesterday? An' whut happen? Nuttin'! No bad luck 'tall.

MARIA

(*Indignantly*). Bad luck! Whut dat 'oman call bad luck? Ain't I had more drunk customer' yesterday dan any day dis mont'? Dey fair bus' up my shop. (*Goes into shop muttering indignantly.*)

ARCHDALE

(*Turning back to* PORGY). Now, listen. Peter must have someone to go his bond. Do you know a man by the name of Huysenberg who keeps a corner shop over by the East End wharf?

PORGY

(*His face darkening*). Yes, boss, I knows um. He rob ebery nigger he git he han' on.

ARCHDALE

I see you know him. Well, take him this ten dollars and tell him that you want him to go Peter's bond. He hasn't any money of his own, and his shop is in his wife's name, but he has an arrangement with the magistrate that makes him entirely satisfactory. (*Hands* PORGY *a ten-dollar bill.*) Do you understand?

PORGY

Yes, boss. T'ank yo', boss.
(ARCHDALE, *about to go, hesitates, looks at goat-cart.*)

ARCHDALE

Porgy, there's another little matter I want to speak to you about. The last few weeks you've been begging right under my office window. I wish you'd find another place. (*Noticing* PORGY'S *troubled expression.*) There are lots of other street corners.

PORGY

(*Sadly*). I done try all de oder corner, boss. Ebery time I stop fo' beg, somebody tell' me to keep mobin'. But I been beggin' under yo' window fo' t'ree week' now, an' I beginnin to say to myself, "Porgy, yo' is fix fo' life. Mus' be yo' is found a gentlemans whut got place in de heart fo' de poor cripple."

ARCHDALE

I have a place in my heart for the cripple but not for the goat.

PORGY

Dis bery nice goat, boss. Lawyer Frazier say yo' t'ink he need soap. But I don't see how dat can be, boss. Two week han' runnin' now dat goat eat up Serena's washin' soap.

ARCHDALE

He doesn't need it inside.

PORGY

(*Mystified*). Whut goat want wid soap outside? (*Suddenly enlightened.*) Oh, yo' don' like to smell um? (FRAZIER *comes from shop. Sees* ARCHDALE. *Approaches. Stands waiting, hat in hand.* PORGY *is now all smiles.*)
Dat all right, boss. By tumorroh I goin' hab' dis goat wash till yo' can't tell um from one ob dose rose bush in de park.

ARCHDALE

I'm sorry, Porgy. But you must find another place.

FRAZIER

Good-mornin', Misteh Archdale. I done gib' dis nigger yo' message. (*Sternly to* PORGY.) 'Membuh what I tell yo'—*Mobe on!*

ARCHDALE

All right, Frazier. (*To* PORGY). If Peter isn't out in a week, let me know.
(*Turning to take leave*): I suppose you're all going to the picnic today.
(*The Negroes nod and smile.* PORGY *looks wistfully at* BESS, *who stands behind him in the doorway.* ARCHDALE *is crossing toward gate.*)

JAKE

Yas, boss. We goin'.

PORGY

Bess, ain't yo' change yo' mind 'bout picnic now yo' gots divo'ce?
(ARCHDALE *catches word "divorce," turns.*)

ARCHDALE

Divorce?

PORGY

(*Proudly*). Yas, boss, Misteh Frazier jus' sell my 'oman a divo'ce. She an honest 'oman now.

ARCHDALE

(*Sternly, to* FRAZIER, *who is looking guilty*). Didn't the judge tell you that if you sold any more divorces he'd put you in jail? I've a good mind to report you.

FRAZIER

Mus' be dat judge fergit dat I votes de Democratic ticket.

ARCHDALE

That won't help you now. The gentleman from the North, who has come down to better moral conditions among the Negroes, says you are a menace to morals. He's going to have you indicted if you don't quit.

PORGY

(*Suspiciously; handing paper to* ARCHDALE). Ain't dis no good as he stan', boss? 'Cause I ain't goin' pay um fo' no more complications.
(*As* ARCHDALE *glances over the paper,* PORGY *glares vindictively at* FRAZIER.)
Dat nigger come 'round heah in he By-God coat, an' fo' yo' can crack yo' teet', he gone wid yo' las' cent.

ARCHDALE

(*Reading*). "I, Simon Frazier, hereby divorce Bess and Crown for a charge of one dollar and fifty cents cash. Signed, SIMON FRAZIER." Well, that's simple enough. (*Examines seal.*) "Sealed—Charleston Steamboat Company." Where did you get this seal?

FRAZIER

I done buy um from de junk-shop Jew, boss.

ARCHDALE

Don't you know that there is no such thing as divorce in this state?

FRAZIER

I heah tell dere ain't no such er t'ing fuh de w'ite folks; but de nigger need um so bad, I ain't see no reason why I can't make one up whut sattify de nigger. (*His voice breaks.*) Dem divo'ce is keepin' me alibe, boss, an' whut mo', he is keepin' de nigger straight.

ARCHDALE

How's that?

FRAZIER

Dat jedge say de gots to lib togedder anyhow till dey done dead. Dat's de law, he say. But nigger ain't make dat way. I done get my black folks all properly moralize, an' now he say he goin' jail me. Ef I stops now de nigger leabe each odder anyway.

Ef it don't cos' de nigger nuttin' to leabe he wife, het ain't goin' keep she er mont'. But when he gots fuh pay dolluh to get way, he goin' t'ink twice 'fore he trabble.
(ARCHDALE *keeps from laughing with difficulty.*)

BESS

Ain't mah divo'ce no good, boss? Porgy done pay one dolluh an' er half fuh it.

ARCHDALE

(*Looking at paper*). I could hardly say that it is legal.

BESS

Legal! Dat wo'd mean good?

ARCHDALE

Well, sometimes.

PORGY

Plenty ob our frien' is divo'ce', boss.

ARCHDALE

(*With accusing look at* FRAZIER, *who cringes*). So I hear. (*Again consults paper.*) You've left this man, Crown, and intend to stay with Porgy?

BESS

Yes, suh.

ARCHDALE

I suppose this makes a respectable woman of you. Um—on the whole—I'd keep it. I imagine that respectability at one-fifty would be a bargain anywhere. (*Hands paper to* BESS. *Turns back to* FRAZIER.) But remember, Frazier: *No more divorces!* Or to jail you go. I won't report you this time. (*The goat sticks its head out door.* PORGY *throws his arm around its neck.* ARCHDALE *turns to go.*) Good morning. (*Crosses toward gate.*)

FRAZIER

(*Close by* PORGY'S *door. Recovering from his emotion enough to speak*). Gawd bless yo', boss. Good mornin', boss.

PORGY

(*Imitating* FRAZIER'S *professional manner*). Mobe on, please. Mobe on! I gots er bery polite goat heah whut object to de smell ob de jail bird.
(ARCHDALE, *overhearing, laughs suddenly. Goes out gate, his shoulders shaking with laughter.* FRAZIER *moves off, talks to Negroes in background, and soon leaves the court.* BESS *sits by* PORGY *on step.*)
Ain't yo' hear de boss laugh?

BESS

Fo' sho' I heah um laugh.

PORGY

(*Hugging goat*). No, no, bruddah, we ain't goin' mobe on. When de nigger make de buckra laugh, he done win. We goin' spend we life under Misteh Archdale's window. Yo' watch!
(*Draws himself up by door frame, goes inside.* BESS *remains on step. St. Michael's chimes the three-quarter hour. Preparations for the picnic are now at their height. One by one the women, when not on stage, have changed to their most gorgeously colored dresses. Men and women are now wearing sashes all bearing the legend: "Repent Ye Saith the Lord." The leaders have also badges denoting their various ranks: "Marshal," etc. Baskets are being assembled in the court. The court is full of bustle and confusion.* SPORTING LIFE *saunters over to* BESS, *who is sitting on step wistfully watching the picnic preparations.*)

SPORTING LIFE

'Lo, Bess! Goin' to picnic?

BESS

No, guess I'll stay home.

SPORTING LIFE

Picnics all right fo' dese small-town nigger', but we is used to de high life. Yo' an' me onderstan' each odder. I can't see fo' de life ob me what yo' hangin' 'round dis place for! Wid yo' looks, Bess, an' yo' way wid de boys, dere's big money fo' yo' an' me in Noo Yo'k.

BESS

(*Quietly*). I can't remembuh eber meet a nigger I likes less dan I does yo'.

SPORTING LIFE

(*Laughingly*). Oh, come on, now! How 'bout a little touch happy dus' fo' de ole time' sake?

BESS

I t'rough wid dat stuff.

SPORTING LIFE

Come on! Gib me yo' hand.
(*Reaches out and takes her hand, draws it toward him, and with other hand unfolds paper ready to pour powder.*)

BESS

(*Wavering*). I tells yo' I t'rough!

SPORTING LIFE

Jus' a pinch. Not 'nough to hurt a flea.
(BESS *snatches her hand away.*)

BESS

I done gib' up happy dus'.

SPORTING LIFE

Tell dat to somebody else! Nobody *eber* gib' up happy dus'.
(*Again he takes her hand and she does not resist. Gazes fascinated at the powder.* PORGY'S *hand reaches suddenly into the open space of the door; seizes* SPORTING LIFE'S *wrist in an iron grip.* SPORTING LIFE *looks at the hand in astonishment mixed with a sort of horror.*)
Leggo, yo' damn cripple!
(*The hand twists* SPORTING LIFE'S *wrist till he relinquishes* BESS'S *hand and grunts with pain. Then* PORGY'S *hand is silently withdrawn.*)
Gawd, what a grip fo' a piece ob a man!

BESS

(*Rising*). Go 'long now.

SPORTING LIFE

(*Regaining his swagger*). All right! Yo' men friend' come an' dey go. But 'membuh, ole Sportin' Life an' de happy dus' here all along. (*Saunters along—goes out gate.*)
(*From the distance is heard the blare of a discordant band. It is playing "Ain't It Hard to Be a Nigger," though the tune is scarcely recognizable to the audience. The Negroes, however, are untroubled by the discords. One or another sings a line or two of the song. A jumble of voices rises above the music: "Here come de orphans!" "Dere de orphan band down de block!" "Le's we go!" etc.*
A man passes outside the gate, stopping long enough to call in to the occupants of Catfish Row: "Eberybody gettin' in line up de block. You nigger' bes' hurry."
PORGY *comes out on doorstep to watch. Sits.* BESS *stands beside him absorbed in the gay scene.* PORGY *looks at her keenly, troubled.*)

JAKE

(*In the midst of his preparations*). Come 'long to de picnic, Bess! (*Does not wait for reply.*)

PORGY

(*Triumphantly*). Dere! Don' yo' hear Jake ask yo' fo' go? Go 'long!

BESS

Plenty ob de mens ask me. Yo' ain't hear none ob de ladies sayin' nuttin'.

PORGY

Bess, yo' can put on my lodge sash an' be just as good as any 'oman in dat crowd.

BESS

(*With a little laugh*). Yo' an' me know it take more'n sash.
(*The confusion grows. Picnickers once started on their way come scurrying back for forgotten bundles.* SCIPIO *runs in at gate in high excitement.*)

SCIPIO

(*Breathless; to* SERENA). Ma, I gots good news fo' yo'.

SERENA

What dat?

SCIPIO

De bandmaster say I can be a orphan!
(*The song breaks out in greater volume.*)

"Ain't it hahd to be a nigger!
Ain't it hahd to be a nigger!
Ain't it hahd to be a nigger!

Cause yo' can't git yo' rights when yo' do.
I was sleepin' on a pile ob lumbah
Jus' as happy as a man could be
When a w'ite man woke me from my slumbah
An' he say, 'Yo' gots fo' work now cause yo' free.'"

(*Other voices are calling back and forth: "How dem little nigger' can play!" "Ain't yo' ready! Time fo' go!" "We off fo' Kittiwah!"*
The band plays with more abandon. BESS *wears the expression of a dreamer who sees herself in the midst of the merrymakers. Her feet begin to shuffle in time to the music.* PORGY *does not look up, but his eyes watch the shuffling feet.*)

PORGY

(*Mournfully*). Yo' can't tell me yo' ain't wants to go.
(*The Negroes troop across the court all carrying their baskets. In twos and threes they go out at the gate. Among the last to go,* MARIA *comes hurrying from her shop carrying a gigantic basket. Turns to follow the others. Sees* PORGY *and* BESS. *Hesitates. As though afraid of being left behind, turns again toward gate. Then resolutely sets down her basket.*)

MARIA

What de mattuh wid yo', Sistuh? Ain't yo' know yo' late fo' de picnic?
(*A sudden wave of happiness breaks over* BESS's *face. She is too surprised to answer.*)

PORGY

Bess says she ain't figgerin' to go.

MARIA

(*Crosses rapidly to them*). Sho' she goin'! Eberybody goin'. She gots to help me wid my basket. I gots 'nough fo' six. Where yo' hat? (*Reaches hat just inside door and puts it on* BESS's *head.*)

PORGY

(*Taking sash from pocket and holding it out to* BESS). Here my sash, Bess.
(MARIA *unties* BESS's *apron. Throws it through door. Takes sash from* PORGY, *pins it across* BESS's *breast, jerking her peremptorily about to save time. Then starts for her basket.*)

MARIA

Come 'long now!

BESS

(*Hesitating*). I hate fo' leabe yo,' Porgy.

PORGY

(*Happily*). I too happy fo' hab' yo' go.

MARIA

Ain't yo' goin' help me wid dis basket?
(BESS *hurries to her and takes one handle of basket.*) See yo' some mo', Porgy!
(MARIA *crosses rapidly to gate. To keep her hold on the basket,* BESS *is forced to hurry.*)
(*Looking back*). Good-bye, Porgy!
(MARIA, *apparently seeing the others far ahead and anxious not to be left behind, breaks into a lumbering run, dragging* BESS *after her.* BESS *is waving to* PORGY *as she goes.*
The voices of the Negroes grow fainter. Then the last distant crashes of the band are heard, and the court is quiet.
PORGY *sits on his doorstep dreaming, gazing happily into space, rocking a little. Takes pipe from his pocket, knocks out ashes; lights it.*
Across the sunlit walls falls the shadow of the buzzard flying lazily over the court. PORGY *remains in happy abstraction, oblivious of the bird. Puffs leisurely at his pipe.*
The shadow hovers over his door; then falls across his face. He looks up suddenly and sees the bird. Swift terror sweeps into his face.)

PORGY

(*Frantically*). Get out ob here! Don' yo' light! Lef' it! Yo' hear me! Lef' it! (*He waves futile arms at it. The bird continues to hover above him.*) Get out! Somebody bring broom! Don' yo' light on my door, yo' debil! Help! Somebody help me! Oh, Gawd!
(*He struggles down the steps and at last reaches the brick.*
The shadow wings of the bird close as it comes to rest directly over PORGY's *door.*

Grasping the brick, he again looks up to take aim. His fingers slowly relax, and the brick falls to the ground.)
'Tain't no use now. 'Tain't no use. He done lit.

(PORGY *regains his seat on step and sits looking up at the bird with an expression of hopelessness as the curtain falls.*)

CURTAIN

SCENE II

Kittiwah Island. Moonlight revealing a narrow strip of sand backed by a tangled palmetto thicket. In the distance (right) the band is playing "Ain't It Hard to Be a Nigger." JAKE, MINGO, *and several others troop across stage from left to right, swinging apparently empty baskets.*

MINGO

Dis been some picnic, but, Lor', I tired!

JAKE

(*Swinging his basket in a circle*). Dis basket some lighter fo' carry dan when we come out.
(*Breaks into song: "Ain't It Hard," etc. The others join in. They go off right, their song growing fainter in distance.*
SERENA *and* LILY *enter, followed a moment later by* BESS *and* MARIA. MARIA *is puffing, out of breath.*)

MARIA

I ain't no han' fo' walk so fas' on a full stomach. (*Stops abruptly. Looks about her on ground.*)

SERENA

Yo' goin' miss de boat ef yo' ain't hurry, Sistuh.

MARIA

It was jus' about heah I los' my pipe. I 'membuh dere was palmetto sort ob twisted like dat.

LILY

How come yo' lose yo' pipe?

MARIA

(*Searching ground. The others help her*). I was sittin' under de tree a-smokin', an' I see a Plat-eye ha'nt a-lookin' at me t'rough de palmetto leaf. An', 'fo yo' can crack yo' teet', I is gone from heah, but my pipe ain't gone wid me.

LILY

Plat-eye ha'nt! What was he like?

MARIA

Two big eye' like fireball a-watchin' me.

SERENA

(*Scornfully*). Plat-eye ha'nt! Yo' ain't read nuttin' in de Bible 'bout Plat-eye is yo'?

MARIA

I ain't needs to read 'bout 'em. I sees 'em lookin' at me t'rough de palmetto leaf.

SERENA

Jus' like yo' hab' buzzard set on yo' table two day ago, an' yo' hab' mighty ha'd time a-thinkin' up some bad luck to lay to um.

MARIA

Bad luck! Aint I lose my pipe dat I smoke dese twenty yeah', an' my mudder smoke um befo' me?

LILY

I ain't partial to sleepin' out wid de rattlesnake'. Les' we go or de boat go widout us.

MARIA

Ef dat boat go widout me, dey's goin' to be some sick nigger' in Catfish Row when I gets back.
(*Steamboat whistles off right.* MARIA *answers it.*)
Hold yo' halt! I ain't goin' till I gets my pipe.

BESS

Yo' bes' go along, Maria, and le's we whut is de fas' walker' look fo' um a bit.

MARIA

(*Pointing left*). It might hab' been a little farder back dat way I lose um.
(BESS *begins to search at left and wanders off left, her eyes combing the ground.*)
An' it might hab' been a little farder dese way.
(*Goes off right searching.* LILY *follows.* SERENA *continues her search on stage.*)

LILY

(*Off right*). I ain't see um nowheres. Le's we go.

MARIA

(*Farther in distance*). I goin' fin' um.
(*From the blackness of the thicket two eyes can be seen watching* SERENA. *As she turns in her quest, she sees them. For a moment, she is motionless; then her breath catches in a shuddering gasp of horror, and she flees swiftly off right. A snatch of the song rises suddenly in distance and quickly dies down again.* BESS *comes on from left, her head bent, still searching.*
A great black hand creeps slowly out among the palmetto branches and draws them aside. BESS *hears the sound. Straightens, stands rigid, listening.*)

BESS

(*In a low, breathless voice*). Crown?

CROWN

Yo' know bery well dis Crown.
(*She turns and looks at him. He partly emerges from the thicket, naked to the waist, his cotton trousers frayed away to the knees.*)
I seen yo' land, an' I been waitin' all day fo' yo'. I mos' dead on dis damn islan'!

BESS

(*Looks at him slowly*). Yo' ain't look mos' dead. Yo' bigger'n eber.

CROWN

Oh, plenty bird' egg, oyster, an' t'ing. But I mos' dead ob lonesome wid not a Gawd's person fo' swap a word wid. Lor' I'se glad yo' come!

BESS

I can't stay, Crown, or de boat go widout me.

CROWN

Got any happy dus' wid you'?

BESS

No.

CROWN

Come on! Ain't yo' gots jus' a little?

BESS

No, I ain't. I done gib up dope.
(CROWN *laughs loudly.*)

CROWN

It sho' do a lonesome man good to hab' he 'oman come an' swap a couple joke wid um.

BESS

Dat's de Gawd's trut'. An' 'sides—I gots sompen fo' tell yo'.

CROWN

Yo' bes' listen to whut I gots fo' tell yo'. I waitin' here til de cotton begin comin' in. Den libin' 'll be easy. Davy 'll hide yo' an' me on de ribber boat fur as Savannah. Who yo' libin' wid now?

BESS

I libin' wid de cripple Porgy.

CROWN

(*Laughing*). Yo' gots de funny tas' in men. But dats yo' business. I ain't care who yo' takes up wid while I'm away. But 'membuh whut I tol' yo'! He's temporary! I guess it be jus' couple ob week' now 'fo' I comes fo' yo'!

BESS

(*With an effort*). Crown, I got sompen fo' tell yo'.

CROWN

What dat?

BESS

I—I sort ob change' my way'.

CROWN

How yo' change'?

BESS

I—I libin' wid Porgy now—an' I libin' decent.

CROWN

Yo' heah whut I tol' yo'? I say in couple week I comin' fo' yo', an' yo' goin' tote fair 'less yo' wants to meet yo' Gawd. Yo' gits dat?

BESS

Crown, I tells yo' I change'. I stayin' wid Porgy fo' good.
(*He seizes her by the arm and draws her savagely toward him. The steamboat whistles.*)
Take yo' han' off me. I goin' miss dat boat!

CROWN

Dere's anudder boat day atter tomorruh.

BESS

I tells yo' I means what I says. Porgy my man now.

CROWN

(*Jeering at her*). I ain't had a laugh in weeks.

BESS

Take yo' hot han' off me. I tells yo' I stayin' wid Porgy for keeps.

CROWN

Yo' is tellin' me yo' radder hab' dat crawlin' cripple dan Crown?

BESS

(*Taking a propitiatory tone*). It like dis, Crown—I de only 'oman Porgy eber hab'. An' I thinkin' how it goin' be if all dese odder nigger' goes back to Catfish Row tonight, an' I ain't come home to um. He be like a little chil' dat los' its ma.
(CROWN, *still holding her, throws back his head and laughs.* BESS *begins to be frightened.*)
Yo' can laugh, but I tells yo' I change'!

CROWN

Yo' change' all right. Yo' ain't neber been so funny.
(*The boat whistles. She tries to pull away. He stops laughing and holds her tighter with lowering look. Draws her nearer.*)

BESS

Lemme go, Crown! Yo' can get plenty odder women.

CROWN

What I wants wid odder women? I gots a 'oman. An' dats yo'. See?

BESS

(*Trying flattery*). Yo' know how it always been wid yo', Crown—yo' ain't neber want for a 'oman. Look at dis chest, an' look at dese arm' yo' got! Dere's plenty better-lookin' gal dan me. Yo' know how it always been wid yo'. Dese five year 'now I been yo' 'oman—yo' could kick me in de street, an' den, when yo' ready fo' me back, yo' could whistle fo' me, an' dere I was again a-lickin' yo' han'. What yo' wants wid Bess? She gettin' ole now. (*She sees that her flattery has failed and is terrified.*) Dat boat goin' widout me! Lemme go! Crown, I'll come back fo' see yo'. I swear to Gawd I'll come on de Friday boat. Jus' lemme go *now!* I can't stop out here all night. I 'fraid! Dere's t'ings movin' in de t'icket—rattlesnake, an' such! Lemme go, I tells yo'. Take yo' han' off me!

CROWN

(*Holding her and looking steadily at her*). No man ever take my 'oman from me. It goin' to be good joke on Crown ef he lose um to one wid no leg' an' no gizzard. (*Draws her closer.*) So yo' is change, is yo'? (*Grips her more tightly. Looks straight into her eyes.*) Whut yo' say now?

BESS

(*Summoning the last of her resolution*). I stayin' wid Porgy fo' good.
(*His jaw shoots forward, and his huge shoulder muscles bulge and set. Slowly his giant hands close round her throat. He brings his eyes still closer to hers. The boat whistles long and loud, but neither gives sign of hearing it. After a moment,* CROWN *laughs with satisfaction at what he sees in* BESS'S *eyes.*
His hands leave her throat and clasp her savagely by the shoulders. BESS *throws back her head with a wild hysterical laugh.*)

CROWN

I knows yo' ain't change'! Wid yo' an' me, it always goin' be de same. See?
(He swings her about and hurls her face forward through an opening in the thicket. Then, with a low laugh, he follows her. She regains her balance and goes on ahead of him. The band is still playing, but growing faint in the distance.)

Curtain

ACT THREE

SCENE I

ST. MICHAEL'S *chimes the half hour. Curtain. The court before dawn. Lights in a few windows:* MARIA'S, JAKE'S, PORGY'S.

The fishermen are preparing for an early departure.

JAKE

(Coming from his door). Dat all de breakfas' I time fo'. *(Calls to men in* MARIA'S *shop.)* Come on yo' mens! It almost light.
*(*CLARA *comes from their room, the baby in her arms. Her eyes are anxious and reproachful, but she says nothing.)*

JIM

(Coming from MARIA'S *shop, wiping his mouth)*. Yo' ready, Jake? We bes' be off.

JAKE

Le's we go!
*(*MARIA *appears in her doorway, wiping hands on her apron.)*

MARIA

Good-bye, boys! Hope yo' has de same good luck today!
*(*JAKE *quickly takes baby from* CLARA'S *arms, kisses it hurriedly, and returns it to* CLARA.*)*

JAKE

'Bye, big boy!
*(*BESS'S *voice is heard from her room, droning in delirium. All the Negroes stop suddenly to listen.)*

BESS

Eighteen mile to Kittiwah—eighteen mile—palmetto bush by de sho'—rattlesnake an' such.
*(*JAKE *crosses to* PORGY'S *window.)*

JAKE

How Bess dis mornin'?
*(*PORGY *appears at window.)*

PORGY

She no better.

JAKE

She still out she head?
*(*PORGY *nods.)*

BESS

Bess goin' fin' um fo' yo'. Dat all right, Maria, Bess goin' fin' um . . .
*(*JAKE *shakes his head sadly. Hurriedly recrosses to the other men. They go toward gate together,* CLARA *following.)*

JIM

I bet dat catch we made yesterday de bigges' catch eber make 'round dese parts.

NELSON

We bes' make de mores ob to-day. Look to me like de las' good day we goin' hab'. Gots a wet tas' to um.

JAKE

Don' yo' know dat ain't de kin' ob talk to talk 'fore my 'oman? Ain't yo' hears de raggin' I gits ebery day? *(Laughs.)* But, see! I gots 'er trained now. She ain't sayin' a word. So long, Clara!
*(*JAKE *gives* CLARA *a hurried, affectionate pat and follows the other men as they troop out the gate, talking and laughing. The gate clangs shut behind them.* CLARA *goes silently into her room, closes door.)*

BESS

Mus' be right heah on de groun'. Bess goin' fin' um . . . *(*BESS'S *voice drones on.)*

(MARIA, *in her doorway, listens a moment. Then crosses to* PORGY'S *door; hesitates, awed by the mystery of delirium.* SERENA *silently crosses the court and joins* MARIA. *They listen a moment longer.*)

SERENA

(*In a low voice*). She still out she head?
(MARIA *nods. They stand silent.*)

BESS

(*From the room*). Eighteen mile to Kittiwah—palmetto bush by de sho'. Eighteen mile to Kittiwah . . .
(PETER *appears outside the gate. He seems older and feebler, but his face is joyful. Pushes gate open, comes into court, looking eagerly about. Sees the two women and crosses toward them.*)

PETER

How eberybody?
(*They turn and see him.*)

MARIA

(*Joyfully*). Ef it ain't ole Peter!

SERENA

Heah Daddy Peter home again. Hey, yo' Lily! Heah yo' ole man. Lordy, we is glad fo' see yo'!
(LILY *comes running from her door. Hurries to* PETER *and greets him joyfully.*)

LILY

Ef it ain't my ole gran'daddy!

PETER

I begin fo' t'ink mebby I ain't eber see Catfish Row——
(BESS'S *voice rises in a sudden wail. The women turn awestricken faces toward* PORGY'S *door.* PETER, *who has not heard, is mystified by their expressions. His words die away. He looks questioningly from one to another.* BESS *again takes up her monotonous refrain.*)

BESS

Palmetto bush sort ob twisted like—rattlesnake an' t'ing . . .

PETER

Whut de mattuh?

MARIA

(*Shouting into his ear*). Porgy's 'oman bery sick.

LILY

(*Shouting*). She out she head.

PETER

How long she been like dat?

MARIA

More'n a week now. Eber since we hab de picnic on Kittiwah.

SERENA

She wander off by sheself an' git lost in de palmetto t'icket. She ain't come home fo' two day.

BESS

Dat's right, Maria, I goin' fin' um—eighteen mile to Kittiwah—eighteen mile . . .

PORGY

(*Within room, soothingly*). Das all right, Bess. Yo' here wid Porgy now.

BESS

(*Monotonously*). Palmetto bush by de sho' . . .
(MARIA, SERENA, *and* PETER *stand wide-eyed, looking in at the door. They do not go too near.*)

PORGY

Yo' right here wid Porgy an' nuttin' can't hurt yo'. Soon de cool wedder comin' an' chill off dese febers.

PETER

(*Shaking his head*). Dat 'oman bery sick.
(*The women nod.*)

PORGY

Ain't yo' remembuh how de cool win' come to town wid de smell ob pine tree, an' how de stars is all polishin' up like w'ite folk's silber? Den eberybody git well. Ain't yo' know? Yo' jus' keep still an' watch what Porgy say.
(*Silence in the room.* CLARA *comes from her door carrying her baby, crosses to the gate and stands looking out toward the sea. After a moment,* PORGY *comes from his door, softly closes it behind him.*)

PORGY

I t'ink mebby she goin' sleep now. (*Sinks wearily on to step.*)
(*Dully.*) Dat yo' Peter? A whole week gone, now, an' she ain't no better! What I goin' do?
(*A moment of silence.*)

PETER

Ef yo' wants to listen to me, I advise yo' to send she to de w'ite folks' hospital.
(*Blank consternation.* MARIA *is first to find her voice.*)

MARIA

(*Speaking into his ears*). Fo' Gawd's sake, Peter! Ain't yo' know dey lets nigger' die dere so dey can gib um to de student'? I say dey gib um to de student'.

PETER

De student' ain't gits um till he done dead. Ain't dat so? Den he can't hurt um none. Ain't dat so too? An' I gots dis to say. One ob my w'ite folks is a nurse to de hospital. An' dat lady is a pure angel wid de sick nigger. Ef I sick to-morruh I goin' to she, an' what she say is good wid me. I wants dis carcass took care ob w'ile he is alibe. When he done dead, I ain't keer.

LILY

(*Shouting*). Yo' ain't keer wedder yo' is cut up an' scatter, 'stead ob bein' bury in Gawd's own grabeyahd!

PETER

Well, mebby I ain't say I jus' as lief. But I t'ink Gawd onderstan' de succumstance an' make allowance.

PORGY

(*Moaning*). Oh, Gawd! Don't let um take Bess to de hospital!

SERENA

(*In injured tone*). Mus' be yo' is all fergit how I pray Clara's baby out ob de convulsion. Dey ain't nebber been a sick pusson or corpse in Catfish Row dat I has refuse' my prayers. Dey is fo' de righteous an' fo' de sinner all two.

PORGY

Dat's right, Sistuh. Yo' pray ober um. Dat can't hurt um none.

(SERENA *closes her eyes and begins to sway.*)

SERENA

Oh, Jedus who done trouble de watuh in de Sea ob Gallerie—

PORGY

Amen!

SERENA

—an' likewise who done cas' de debil out ob de afflicted time an' time again—

PETER

Oh, Jedus! (*Begins to sway.*)

SERENA

—what make yo' ain't lay yo' han' on dis sistuh' head—

LILY

Oh, my Fadder!

SERENA

—an' sen' de debil out ob she, down a steep place into de sea, like yo' used to do, time an' time again.

PORGY

Time an' time again.

SERENA

Lif' dis poor cripple up out ob de dus'—

PETER

Allelujah!

SERENA

—an' lif' up he 'oman an' make she well, time an' time again.
(*They sway a moment in silence. Then* SERENA *silently rises and departs. After a moment,* PETER *and* LILY *follow her.*)

MARIA

(*In a low voice*). Listen to me. Yo' wants dat 'oman cure up, ain't yo'?

PORGY

Yo' knows I does.

MARIA

Bery well, den. Why ain't yo' sen' to Lody?

PORGY

Fo' make conjur'?

MARIA

Yo' gots two dollah?
(PORGY *nods.*)
Den yo' bes' waste no time. Yo' go quick to Lody an' gib she de two dollah an' tell she to make conjur' fo' cas' de debil out ob Bess.
(MINGO *has sauntered in and taken a seat at the table by* MARIA'S *door.*)

PORGY

How I goin' leabe Bess?

MINGO

Hey, Maria! How 'bout a little serbice?

MARIA

Here, yo' Mingo, come here!
(*He crosses to them.*)
Yo' do little job fo' Porgy an' I gib yo' de free breakfas' when yo' gits back. Yo' know Lody, de conjur' 'oman?

MINGO

Who don't know Lody!

MARIA

Yo' go to Lody an' tell she fo' make conjur' fo' cas' de debil out ob Porgy's Bess. He goin' gib' yo' two dollah fo she.
(PORGY *has taken out his money bag and is counting out pennies.*)

MINGO

Dat long way to Lody's 'fore breakfus'.

MARIA

Listen to de nigger! Ef yo' wa'n't dead on yo' feet, yo' could get dere an' back in ten minute'.

MINGO

Whut yo' gots fo' breakfus'?

MARIA

I gots de butts meat fo' grease yo' mout', an' de corn bread an' 'lasses fo' sweet yo' mout'.

MINGO

How 'bout er little shark steak?

MARIA

Listen to me, nigger! I ain't serbe no free breakfus' alley cat.

MINGO

(*Belligerently*). Who you callin' alley cat?

MARIA

(*Despairingly*). Dis nigger ain't know nuttin'! Get dis! I decides fo' my customer' whut dey goin' hab', but ain't yo' neber been in one ob dem stylish rest'rant where de name ob all de victual' is writ up on de wall, an' you can pick an' choose 'mong um? Dat's alley cat.

PORGY

I goin' gib' yo' quarter fo' goin'.

MINGO

Ah! He ain't so far now!

PORGY

(*Handing him money*). Here de two dollah fo' Lody an' de quarter fo' yo'self.
(MINGO *starts for gate.*)

MARIA

Dat breakfas' I promise yo' goin' be on de table in ten minute'. Ef yo' ain't hurry, he'll be cold.

MINGO

I be back fo' yo' can crack yo' teet'.
(*Goes out gate and off to left. St. Michael's chimes the three-quarter hour.*)

MARIA

Quarter till five. Eben dat lazy nigger can't spend more'n ten minute' *gittin'* to Lody's. By fib o'clock sure, she goin' hab she conjur' make.

PORGY

(*Eagerly*). Yo' t'ink dat cure she?

MARIA

I ain't t'ink. I know. Yo' watch what I say, my brudder. Bess good as cure right now. Yo' gots jus' a quartuh hour to wait. Come five o'clock, dat 'oman well. (*Crosses to her shop. Goes about her work.*)
(SERENA *has gone to work at her tubs. She now calls to* CLARA, *who still stands gazing out through gate.*)

SERENA

What yo' stan' dere fo', Clara? Boats must be out ob sight by now.

CLARA

Dey been out ob sight fo' long time now.

MARIA

(*Working at her table*). Yo' ain't gots no call fo' worry 'bout yo' man. Dis goin' be a fine day.

CLARA

I neber see de watuh look so black.

MARIA

Well, has yo' eber see it look so still?

CLARA

No. He too still. An' somet'ing in my head keep a-listenin' fo' dat hurricane bell. (*Crosses to* SERENA. *Sits on bench.*) Let me sit here wid yo', an' yo' talk a lot.

MARIA

(*Who has crossed to pump with kettle*). I got a feelin'——

SERENA

What yo' gots a feelin' 'bout?

MARIA

I gots a feelin' when dat 'oman of Porgy's got lost on Kittiwah Islan' she done been wid Crown.

SERENA

(*Her face darkening*). Yo' t'ink dat nigger on Kittiwah?

MARIA

I always figger he been dere in dem deep palmettuhs, an' when I hear de t'ings dat 'oman keep sayin' in she sickness, I sure ob two t'ing'—one, dat he is dere, and two, dat she been wid um.

CLARA

Yo' beliebe she still run wid dat nigger!

MARIA

Dem sort ob mens ain't need to worry 'bout habin' women.

SERENA

Bess goin' stay wid Porgy ef she know what good fo' she!

MARIA

She know all right, an' she lobe Porgy. But, ef dat nigger come after she, dey ain't goin' be nobody 'round here but Porgy an' de goat.

(*As* MARIA *speaks,* PORGY *comes from his door. The other women sign to* MARIA *to be careful. Seeing* PORGY, *she drops the subject and returns to her shop.*)

SERENA

(*Piling clothes in basket*). Come on, Clara, lend me a han' wid dese clothes.

(CLARA, *holding baby on one arm, takes one handle of basket.* SERENA *lifts the other. They carry it through* SERENA'*s door.*

PORGY *sits on his doorstep, his face tense, waiting.*

DADDY PETER *comes from his door followed by* LILY, *who carries the honey tray. She places it on his head and returns to room, closing the door.* PETER *crosses toward gate, beginning instantly to chant.*)

PETER

I gots honey.—Has yo' gots honey?—Yes, ma'am, I gots honey.—You gots honey cheap?

(*A woman leans from an upper window and calls.*)

THE WOMAN

Oh, honey man! Honey man!

PETER

(*Going on*). Yes, ma'am, my honey cheap.

THE WOMAN

Hey, dere! I wants some honey!

(PETER *goes out gate and off to the right.*)

PETER

You gots honey in de comb?—Yes, ma'am, I gots honey in de comb.—Heah comes de honey man!—I gots honey.

(PORGY *sits waiting. St. Michael's begins to chime the hour.* PORGY *grows suddenly rigid.*

As the chimes continue, MARIA *comes to her doorway and stands motionless, also lis-*

tening. She and PORGY *gaze at each other across court with tense, expectant faces. The chimes cease.*)

PORGY

(*In a low, vibrant voice*). Now de time! Oh, Gawd!
(*St. Michael's strikes five. As* PORGY *and* MARIA *still wait motionless.* BESS'S *voice is heard, weakly.*)

BESS

Porgy!
(PORGY *and* MARIA *are both electrified by the sound. They gaze at each other with joyful faces, but for a second neither moves.*)
Porgy! Dat yo' dere, ain't it? Why yo' ain't talk to me?

PORGY

(*With a half-laugh that breaks in a sob*). T'ank Gawd! T'ank Gawd!
(BESS *appears in the doorway in her white nightgown. She is very weak.*)

BESS

I lonesome here all by myself.
(MARIA *crosses to her quickly. Gently assists her as she lowers herself to seat beside* PORGY.)

BESS

It hot in dere. Let me sit here a while in de cool.

MARIA

I'll get yo' blanket.

PORGY

Maria, ain't she ought to go back to bed?

MARIA

(*Going past them into room*). Let she be. What I done tell yo'? Ain't dat conjur' cured she?

BESS

I been sick, ain't it?

PORGY

Oh, Bess! Bess!

BESS

What de mattuh?

PORGY

(*Almost sobbing with relief*). Yo' been bery sick! T'ank Gawd de conjur' cure yo'!
(MARIA *reappears with blanket, which she wraps about* BESS.)

MARIA

I ain't goin' let yo' set here bery long. (*Returns to her shop.*)

PORGY

I got yo' back, Bess!

BESS

How long I been sick, Porgy?

PORGY

Jus' a week. Yo' come back from Kittiwah wid yo' eye like fireball, an' Maria git yo' in de bed. An' yo' ain't know me!
(BESS *suddenly catches her breath in a stifled sob.*)
What de mattuh, Bess?

BESS

I guess I ain't know nuttin' wid de feber—or I ain't come back at all!

PORGY

Yo' ain't come back to Porgy?
(*She begins to moan hysterically.*)

BESS

No, I ain't ought to come back!

PORGY

(*Soothingly*). Dat all right. Don' yo' worry none, Bess. I knows yo' been wid Crown.
(BESS *draws in her breath sharply, then speaks in a whisper.*)

BESS

How yo' know?

PORGY

Yo' been talk 'bout um while yo' out ob yo' head.

BESS

What I say?

PORGY

Yo' ain't say nuttin' 'cept crazy stuff, but

Gawd gib cripple to know many t'ing' he ain't gib strong men.

BESS

Yo' ain't want me go away?

PORGY

No, I ain't want yo' go, Bess. (*Looks at her keenly.*) (*A moment of silence.*)
Yo' neber lie to me, Bess.

BESS

No, I neber lie to yo'. Yo' gots to gib me dat. (*Another silence.*)

PORGY

How t'ings stan' 'tween yo' an' Crown?

BESS

(*After a pause*). He comin' fo' me when de cotton come to town.

PORGY

Yo' goin'?

BESS

I tell um—yes.
(PORGY *turns his head from her and sits looking straight before him. After a moment,* BESS *reaches out timidly and lays her hand on his arm. Then she tries to encircle it with her fingers.*)
Porgy! Gawd! Yo' gets de arm like stebedore! Why yo' muscle pull up like dat?
(*He looks at her, his face set and stern. She cowers, her hand still on his arm.*)
It makes me 'fraid!
(*A pause.*)

PORGY

Yo' ain't gots nuttin' fo' be 'fraid of. I ain't try to keep no 'oman what don' want to stay. Ef yo' wants to go wid Crown, dat fo' yo' to say.

BESS

I ain't wants to go, Porgy.
(PORGY *looks at her with hope.*)

BESS

But I ain't yo' kin'. When Crown put he hand on me dat day, I run to he like watuh. Some day again he goin' put he han' on my throat. It goin' be like dyin', den. But I gots to talk de trut' to yo'. When dem time come, I goin' to go.
(*Silence.*)

PORGY

(*In a whisper*). Ef dey wa'n't no Crown, Bess! Ef dey was only jus' yo' an' Porgy, what den?
(*She looks into his face with an expression of yearning. Then, suddenly, the weakness of her illness sweeps down upon her and she breaks out hysterically, trembling with fear.*)

BESS

Oh, fo' Gawd's sake, Porgy! Don' let dat man come an' handle me! Ef yo' is willin' to keep me, den lemme stay! (*Her voice rises hysterically, broken by sobs.*) Ef he jus' don' put dem hot han' on me, I can be good! I can 'membuh! I can be happy!
(*The sobs overcome her.*)

PORGY

Dere, dere, Bess.
(*Pats her arm soothingly, waiting for the storm to spend itself. She grows suddenly quiet, except for occasional silent, rending sighs.*)
Yo' ain't need to be afraid. Ain't yo' gots yo' man? Ain't yo' gots Porgy fo' take care ob yo'? What kin' ob nigger yo' tinks yo' gots anyway, fo' let anudder nigger carry he 'oman? No, suh! Yo' gots yo' man now! Yo' gots Porgy!
(BESS *has become quiet. A pause.*)
Dere, now. Yo' been set up too long. Let Porgy help yo' back to bed.
(*He draws himself up by the door frame.* BESS *rises unsteadily and, with a hand on his arm, they make their way into the room.* PORGY *closes the door behind them.* MINGO *appears outside the gate, steadies himself against it, then staggers through and crosses to* MARIA'S *table. Slumps into chair. Pounds on table, then buries head in his hands.* MARIA *comes to doorway.*)

MARIA

Oh, dat yo', Mingo! Gawd A'mighty, how yo' gits drunk so fas'! (*Goes into shop and immediately returns with breakfast things on a tray. Begins putting them before him.*)

I bet yo' drink dat rot-gut stuff straight! Ain't yo' know nuff to pollute yo' whisky wid watuh?

MINGO

(*Pushing dishes away*). Don' want dat stuff. Wants de shark steak.

MARIA

(*Hands on hips*). So yo' don' want dat stuff! Bery well! Yo' wants de shark steak! Yo' t'ink I gibin' shark steak wid de free breakfas'?

MINGO

I tells yo' I wants de shark steak. (*With uncertain movements, draws a handful of change from pocket.*)

MARIA

(*Mollified*). Ob course, ef yo' goin' pay fo' um!

(MINGO *spills the money in a pile on table. It is all pennies.* MARIA *stares at it, then at him. Her eyes are suddenly filled with suspicion.*)

Where yo' gits dat money?

(MINGO *looks up at her stupidly. She speaks in a ferocious whisper.*)

Where yo' gits dat money?

(MINGO *seems to try to recollect.*)

He all pennies—jus' like Porgy gits fo' beggin'! (*She suddenly seizes him, jerks him to his feet.*) Dats Porgy's money, I tells yo', what he gibe yo' fo' Lody! (MINGO *opens his mouth to protest, searching wildly for words.*)

MARIA

Don' yo' lie to me, nigger!

MINGO

I jus' take 'nough fo' li'l' drink.

(MARIA *gives him a savage shake which seems to spill out further words.*)

I t'ink Lody must habe move'. I can't find she. (*With weak bravado.*) Leggo me, ole lady! (*Tries to shake off her grip.*)

(MARIA *holds him tighter and brings her face close to his. His eyes suddenly meet hers, and he sees a look of such cold ferocity that he quails and sobs with terror.*)

MINGO

Oh, Jedus.

MARIA

Yo' low, crawlin' houn'! Yo' drink up de conjur' money ob a poor dyin' 'oman, an' ain't leabe she nuttin' but de Christian prayers! You listen to me, nigger! (*Slowly and impressively.*) Fo' yo' own good, I goin' lock yo' up in my coset till yo' sober nuff to keep yo' mout' shut. Den mebby I lets yo' loose. But I goin' to where I can git my han' on yo' again! Ef yo' eber tell Porgy —or any libin' pusson—dat yo' ain't deliber dat message to Lody, I goin' hab nigger blood on my soul when I stan' at de Jedgment. Now, yo', gots dat straight in yo' head?

(MINGO, *unable to speak, nods. She swings him suddenly about, hurls him into her room, and closes the door on him. Wipes her face on apron, looks with mystified expression toward* PORGY'*s closed door. Baffled.*)

Mus' hab' been Jedus done cure Bess after all. (*Considers a moment. Takes a few steps toward* PORGY'*s door. Then stops, with decision.*) No, I be damn ef He did. He ain't gots it in um. (*Goes into her room. Bangs door behind her.*)

(*For a moment, the court is empty and silent. Suddenly, the silence is broken by the deep, ominous clang of a bell, very different from the silver tone of St. Michael's. Instantly, every resident of Catfish Row, excepting* MINGO *and* BESS, *is in the court or leaning from his window. Having come, they now stand motionless, scarcely breathing, listening to the bell.*

CLARA, *with her baby, has come from* SERENA'*s door, her eyes bright with terror.*)

MARIA

Mus' be de bell fo' a hot wave. Yo' see! He ain't goin' ring more'n twelbe.

LILY

(*Who has been counting half audibly*).—ten—eleben—twelbe——

(*For a moment no one breathes. Then the bell rings on. Every face is suddenly rigid with horror.*)

CLARA

(*Wildly*). Twenty! (*She runs to the gate and looks off left.*)

SERENA

(*Following and seeking to comfort her*).

Dat bell mus' be mistake! Ain't yo' membuh de las' hurricane? How he take two day' fo' blow up?

ANNIE

Now eberyt'ing quiet. Not a breaf ob air. (*All the Negroes have gone to the gate and are gazing off to left.*)

PORGY

(*From his window*). How de Custom House flag?

SERENA

He right dere on de pole, jus' like always.

MARIA

(*Seeing it too, relieved*). Don' yo' see dat flag dere, Clara?

SERENA

(*Reassuringly to* CLARA). Dat ain't no hurricane signal, is it?

MARIA

Ain't yo' know long as de American flag wabin' ober de Custom House dat mean eberyt'ing all right, jus' like——
(*They are all gazing off left at the distant flag. Suddenly, a new wave of horror sweeps simultaneously over every face.* MARIA'*s speech breaks off with her lips still parted.*)

LILY

(*In a low, awed voice*). Gawd! Dey take um down! (*They continue to gaze, fascinated, but* CLARA *turns away, back into the court. Her terror has given way to dull hopelessness.*)

CLARA

Dey don' hab' to run up no hurricane signal to tell me nuttin'. My head stop listenin' fo' um now.

PORGY

De mens goin' see de signal an' come home quick.

CLARA

Dey can't see dat signal from de Blackfish Banks, an' dey dere by dis time.

ANNIE

(*Hysterically*). How dey goin' come back wid no win' fo' de sail?

MARIA

(*Sternly silencing her*). Dey can row in 'fo' dis storm come. He ain't here yet, is he?

PORGY

No, he ain't here yet.

LILY

I ain't fo' worryin' 'bout t'ing dat mightn't happen 'tall.
(*There is a general babble of voices: "Time 'nough fo' worry when de storm come!" "Mebby by to-morruh we habe li'l' storm!" etc.*
While they reassure themselves, the sea is darkening. The shutters of Catfish Row begin to flap back and forth in a sudden wind. CLARA *stands watching the swinging shutters.*)

Curtain

SCENE II

BEFORE *the rise of the curtain the sound of wind and water begins and swiftly swells and rises. Through the wind the chimes and bell of St. Michael's are heard, sometimes rising clear and strong as the wind lulls, then lost completely in a sudden gust.*

The curtain rises on SERENA'*s room, dim and shadowy in the light of guttering kerosene lamps. The Negroes are huddled together in groups. A few have found seats on the chairs and bed. Others sit on the floor. A small group at right, including* SERENA *and* PETER, *are on their knees, swaying and singing the monotonous chant of "The Judgment Day Spiritual."*

PORGY *and* BESS *sit together on the floor at left front.* CLARA *stands motionless at window, her baby in her arms. Every face is filled with fear. They shudder and draw closer together as the wind rises.*

THE SINGERS

"We will all sing togedduh on dat day,
We will all sing togedduh on dat day,
An' I'll fall upon my knees an' face de risin' sun,
Oh, Lord, hab' mercy on me!"

MARIA

(*Speaking above the monotonous chant*). What yo' stand ere all de time a-lookin' out fo', Clara? Yo' can't see nuttin' in de dark.

CLARA

(*Gazing out between slats of closed shutters; in a flat, dull voice*). I t'ink I see a little light now 'round de edge ob dis storm. He mus' be mos' daytime.
(*In a sudden silence of the wind, a faint, distant sound is heard.*)

ANNIE

What dat? Sound like a whinny.

CLARA

Somebody's poor horse in de watuh.

PORGY

(*Moaning*). My poor li'l' goat. He goin' to dead. Dat goat's my leg', I can't neber walk again!

MARIA

Dat's right sma't goat, Porgy. He goin' to climb on yo' bed an' keep he head out ob de watuh. Yo' watch whut I say!

PETER

Yo' bes' come sing wid me, Clara. Dat make yo' feel better.

CLARA

(*Suddenly hysterical*). I mos' lose my min' wid yo' singin'. Yo' been singin' de same speritual since daylight yesterday!

SERENA

(*Severely*). Ain't we want to be ready when de grabe gib up de dead an' Gabriel sound he trumpet?

SPORTING LIFE

I ain't so sure dis de Jedgment Day. We hab bad storm 'fore.

SERENA

Not like dis.

MINGO

I 'membuh my ma tell me, when dey hab' de earthquake here, all day de nigger' sing dat Jedgment Day speritual, waiting fo' de sound ob de trumpet. But he ain't de Jedgment Day den, an' mebby he ain't now.

SERENA

Dat may be so, but dis ain't no time fo' takin' chances. (*Bursts again into song. Her group joins her.*)
(*The shutters suddenly fly apart and flap violently in the wind, drowning out the singing. The Negroes cower and draw closer together. Some of the men struggle to capture the flying shutters.* BESS *sits calm, gazing straight ahead of her.* PORGY *is watching her thoughtfully.*)

PORGY

(*In a brief moment of quiet*). Yo' ain't 'fraid, Bess? (BESS *shakes her head. A pause.*) What make yo' ain't say nuttin'?

BESS

I jus' t'inkin'.
(*The men finally lash the shutters together with rope.*)
Yo' know whut I t'inkin' 'bout, Porgy.

PORGY

Yo' t'inkin' whut storm like dis mus' be like out on de sea islands.
(BESS *nods.*)

BESS

Wabe' like dese mus' wash clean across Kittiwah.
(*After a moment, she lays her hand on his arm.* PORGY *looks keenly into her eyes.*)

PORGY

Yo' sorry?

BESS

I sorry fo' any man lef' out in storm like dis. But I can stop a-listenin' now fo' his step a-comin'. (*Puts her hand in his.*) I guess yo' gots me fo' keeps, Porgy.

PORGY

Ain't I tells yo' dat all 'long.
(*A distant roar is heard, coming steadily nearer.*)

LILY

(*Terror-stricken*). Here he come now!

SERENA

Oh, Masteh! I is ready!
(*The crash and roar sweep by.*)

MARIA

Yo' can see um, Clara?

CLARA

He somebody's roof goin' by.

ANNIE

Gawd A'mighty!

PETER

Oh, Jedus, hab' a little pity!

SERENA

Le's we sing!
(SERENA's *group begins to sing, but before they have completed a single line* CLARA *cries out loudly.*)

CLARA

Fo' Gawd's sake, sing somet'ing else!
(*The singers are startled into silence. A blank pause. Then* BESS *begins to sing, "Somebody's Knockin' at de Door," and one by one the others join her till the whole room is singing.*)

ALL

"Dere's somebody knockin' at de do'.
Dere's somebody knockin' at de do'.
Oh, Mary, oh, Mart'a,
Somebody knockin' at de do'.

"It's a moaner, Lord,
Somebody knockin' at de do'.
It's a moaner, Lord,
Somebody knockin' at de do'.
Oh, Mary, oh, Mart'a,
Somebody knockin' at de do'.

"It's a sinnuh, Lord," etc.
"It's my preachuh, Lord," etc.
"It's my Jedus, Lord," etc.

(*The spiritual swells and gains in tempo; the rhythm of the patting and swaying grows. A few begin to shout.*)

PETER

I hear death knockin' at de door. (*Looks fearfully at door.*)
(*His haunted expression draws the attention of the others. One by one, they stop singing.*)

ANNIE

What yo' say, Daddy Peter?
(*The singing stops, but the rhythm continues.*)

PETER

I hear death knockin' at de do'.
(*A horrified silence. All eyes turn to door.*)

LILY

(*In an awed whisper*). It mus' be death, or Peter can't hear um.

MINGO

He ain't hear nuttin'. Nobody knock.

LILY

Yes, dey is! Somebody dere!

PETER

Death is knockin' at de do'.

MARIA

Open de do' an' show um nobody ain't dere.

MINGO

Open um yo'self.
(MARIA *rises and starts toward door.*)

LILY

(*Wildly*). I tells yo' dere is somebody dere! An' Peter can't hear no libbon' person!
(MARIA *hesitates. A loud knock is heard. The Negroes immediately burst into a pandemonium of terror. There are cries of "Oh, Gawd, hab' me'cy!" "Don't let um come in!"
The knock is repeated, louder. Some begin to pray, but the more energetic begin piling furniture in front of door. "Bring dat dresser!" "Wedge um under de knob," etc. The door is shaken violently.*)

BESS

Dat ain't no use. Ef he death, he comes in, anyway.

MARIA

(*Now the most terrified of all*). Oh, Gawd! Gawd! Don't let um in!
(*With a sucking sound of the wind, the door slowly opens, pushing away the flimsy furniture. Shrieks of terror and prayers fill the room.*
CROWN, *bent double against the wind, enters. As one by one they gain courage to look toward the door, the prayers die away. For a moment, the Negroes stare at him in silence. Then there are cries of "Crown!" "Gawd, it's Crown!"*
BESS *sits silent, rigid.* PORGY *gazes at her searchingly.*)

CROWN

Yo' is a nice pa'cel ob nigger! Shut a frien' out in a storm like dis!

SERENA

Who' frien' is yo'?

CROWN

I yo' frien', Sistuh. Glad fo' see yo'! Still mopin' or has yo' got anudder man?

SERENA

I prayin' Gawd to hold back my han'.

CROWN

(*Laughing*). Well, he'll hold it, all right. Better try de police.

MARIA

Yo' know bery well Serena too decent to gib' a nigger away to de w'ite folks.

CROWN

(*To* SERENA). Well, between yo' Gawd an' yo' manners, yo' sho' makes t'ings soft fo' a hard nigger! (*Sees* BESS.)
Oh, dere's who I'm lookin' fo'! Why ain't yo' come say hello to yo' man?

BESS

Yo' ain't my man.

CROWN

Its sho' time I was comin' back! Dere jus' ain't no 'oman a man can leabe! (*Looking at* PORGY.) Yo' ain't done much fo' yo'self while I been gone. Ain't dere no whole ones left?

BESS

(*Rising and facing him*). Keep yo' mout' off Porgy!

CROWN

Well, fo' Gawd's sake! Dem humn-whiners got yo' too?

BESS

I tol' yo' I ain't goin' wid yo' no more. I stayin' wid Porgy fo' good.

CROWN

'Oman! Do yo' want to meet yo' Gawd? Come here!

BESS

(*Holding her ground*). Porgy my man now.

CROWN

(*Laughing*). Yo' call dat a man! Don' yo' min'. I gots de forgivin' nature, an' I goin' take yo' back.
(*Reaches for her.* BESS *violently repulses him.*)

BESS

Keep yo' han' off me!

SERENA

(*To* CROWN). Ef yo' stick 'round here, yo' sure to get killed sooner or later. Den de w'ite folks goin' figger I done um. Dey gots it in de writin' now dat I been Robbins' wife. An' dey goin' lock me up fo' um anyway. So I might as well do um.
(BESS *returns to her seat by* PORGY.)

CROWN

(*Laughing*). What makes yo' t'ink I goin' get killed? Ef Gawd want to kill me, he got plenty ob chance 'tween here an' Kittiwah Islan'. Me an' Him been havin' it out all de way from Kittiwah; first Him on top, den me. Dere ain't nuttin' He likes better'n a scrap wid a man! Gawd an' me frien'!
(*A terrific roar of wind.*)

SERENA

(*Terror-stricken*). Yo' fool! Ain't yo' gots more sense dan talk 'bout Gawd like dat in a storm like dis! (*Another sudden gust.*)

CROWN

Gawd's laughin' at yo'!

PETER

It bery dangerous fo' we all to hab' dat blasphemin' nigger 'mong us. Le's we sing unto de Lord!
(*A woman's voice leads the spiritual, "Got to Meet de Jedgment."*)

THE WOMEN

"All I know—

SEVERAL MEN

I got to meet de Jedgment.

THE WOMEN

"All I know—

THE MEN

Got to meet de Jedgment.

THE WOMEN

"All I know—

THE MEN

Got to meet de Jedgment.

TOGETHER

All I know, All I know, All I know—

THE WOMEN

"All I moan—

THE MEN

I got to meet de Jedgment. . . ."

(*As the wind subsides, the spiritual rises strong and clear. The Negroes sing and sway for a moment uninterrupted.*)

CROWN

(*His voice rising above the singing*). Yo' folk mus' t'ink de Lord bery easy pleased ef yo' t'ink he like to listen to dat.
(*They sing on.*)
Ef it affec' Him de way it do me, yo' is gibin' um de lonesome blues.
(*They continue to sing.* CROWN *shouts above singing.*)

CROWN

Here, here! Cut dat! I didn't come all de way from Kittiwah to sit up wid no corpses! Dem as is in such a hurry fo' de Jedgment, all dey gots fo' do is to kiss demselves good-bye an' step out dat door. Yo', Uncle Peter, here's yo' chance. The Jim Crow's leabin' an' yo' don' need no ticket! (*Turning to* SERENA.) How 'bout yo', Sistuh? All abo'd! What, dey ain't no trabbelers?
(*A roar of wind.*)

CROWN

Dere go de train! An' yo' miss yo' chance! (*The wind rises above the singing.* CROWN *shouts up at ceiling.*) Dat's right, drown um out! Don' yo' listen to um sing! Dey don' gib' yo' credit fo' no taste in music. How 'bout dis one, Big Frien'? (*Sings.*)

"Rock in de mountain,
Fish in de sea,
Dere neber was a nigger
Take an 'oman from me."

LILY

Jedus! He goin' call down Gawd' wrath on we all! (*The wind rises to its highest pitch. The Negroes huddle together in terror. They begin to sway and moan.*
CROWN *stands in middle of room, his arms thrown wide. His voice rises above the wind.*)

CROWN

Don' yo' hear Gawd A'mighty—laughing up dere? Dat's right, Ole Frien'! Gawd laugh, an' Crown laugh back! (*Throws back his head and laughs. The wind shrieks above his laugh.*) Dat's right! Yo' like um, Gawd? I'll gib' yo' anudder verse! (*Sings.*)

"I ain't no doctor,
No' doctor' son,
But I can cool yo' feber
Till de doctor come."

(*While he is singing, the wind suddenly ceases. The Negroes look at one another, appalled by the suddenness of the change.*)

BESS

Mus' be de storm ober.

PORGY

He jus' takin' a res'. When de wind lull like dis, he come back soon, worse'n eber.

CROWN

Ain't I tell yo' Gawd like um? He quiet now fo' listen. (*He bursts again into song.*)

"I laugh in de country,
I laugh in de town,
'Cause a cripple t'ink he goin'
Take an 'oman from Crown."

(*Then begins to shuffle.*) Come on, Bess! Yo' ain't one ob dese spiritual-whimperin' niggers. What, ain't yo' got no guts! Come 'long! Yo' used to be de bes' dancer in Charleston. Ef yo' don' want to dance wid Crown, mebby yo' new man'll dance wid yo'!
(*Roars with laughter.* BESS *is silent. He dances a few more steps.*) Come 'long, Maria! Yo' can't tell me dese Gawd-f'arin' whiners has got yo'!
(MARIA *hesitates,* CROWN *dances on. Laughs.*)
Dis ole lady too fat fo' dance!

MARIA

(*Indignantly*).Who say I'm too fat!
(*Gets lumberingly to her feet and begins to shuffle.* MINGO *begins to clap for them.*)

CROWN

(*Dancing*). How 'bout ole Sportin' Life?
(SPORTING LIFE *joins in the dancing.* PETER *begins to clap.*)

LILY

Stop dat, yo' ole fool!

CROWN

(*Dancing near* PETER *and shouting in his ear*). Dis nigger too ole fo' dance!

PETER

(*Indignant, puffing out his chest*). Who say I too ole! (*Gets laboriously to his feet and begins a feeble shuffle.*)
(*A group are now forgetting their terror in song and dance in the middle of the room. Another group, including* SERENA, *are looking on disapprovingly and with fear in their faces.* CLARA *pays no attention to it all, gazes steadily from window.* PORGY *and* BESS *sit together, absorbed in each other. Every now and then* CROWN *cuts a pigeon wing before* BESS. *She ignores him. He laughs and dances away.*
A wild crescendo shriek cuts across the sound of merriment. The dancers stop in their places. Everyone turns to CLARA, *who is pointing from the window, her eyes wild and horror-stricken. They all rush to the window.* SERENA *and* ANNIE *are already trying to comfort* CLARA.)

ANNIE

Course it's a boat upside down, but 'tain't de *Sea Gull*.

CLARA

It got red gunnels same as *Sea Gull*.

SERENA

Don' yo' know *Sea Gull* gots bird wid spread wing on he bow.

MINGO

(*Pointing*). He goin' come up ober dere now.

SERENA

You'll see! He gots no bird! Dere! Watch um! See he——
(*She breaks off suddenly with widening eyes.* CLARA *cries out.*)

MINGO

Gawd! It de *Sea Gull* fo' true!

CLARA

(*Shaking off* SERENA'S *arm*). Lemme go!

PETER

What yo' goin' do?

SERENA

(*Holding her*). Yo' wait now, Clara!

CLARA

Lemme go! (*Breaks from* SERENA'S *hold. Runs frantically to the door. Then turns back suddenly to* BESS.) Bess, yo' keep my baby till I come back. (*Thrusts the baby into* BESS'S *arms. Wrests the door open while the Negroes call protests after her.*)

BESS

Clara! Don' go!
(CLARA *rushes out. The door bangs shut behind her. A startled moment of silence. They all stand looking at closed door.*)

MINGO

Dat 'oman t'ink she goin' find Jake *alibe!*

BESS

Clara oughtn't to be out dere by sheself.

SPORTING LIFE

Eberyt'ing quiet now.

PORGY

Dat storm comin' back any minute.

BESS

Somebody go fo' Clara. Don' leabe she out dere alone! (*No one moves.*)

SPORTING LIFE

What de fool 'oman go fo'!

MARIA

Dey ain't nobody in here got de guts ob a chicken.

MINGO

Go 'long yo'self, Auntie. Dere ain't no wabe big nough fo' drown yo'.

PETER

(*Starting for door*). Who goin' wid me?

BESS

(*Holding him back*). Yo' ain't goin', Daddy Peter! Yo' too ole. (*Looking scornfully over the room.*) Ain't dere no *man* 'round here?

CROWN

Yes! Where all dem nigger been wantin' to meet de Jedgment? Go 'long! Yo' been askin' fo' somet'ing, an' yo' ain't got de gizzards to go an' get um. Now's yo' chance. (*Laughs. Goes and stands before* BESS, *looking sideways to see effect on her.*) Porgy, what yo sittin' dere fo'? Ain't yo' hear yo' 'oman calling fo' a *man?* Yes, looks to me like only *one man* 'round here! (*Again glances toward* BESS; *then runs to door, throwing up his arms and calling. Calls the men by name: "Go 'long, Sam!" etc.*)
All right, Ole Frien' up dere! We's on fo' annudder bout! (*Jerks door open and runs out.*)
(*A moment of silence. The stage has grown perceptibly lighter. All the Negroes crowd to the window, looking over each other's shoulders through slats of the closed shutters.*)

PETER

Dere Clara almost to de wharf already.

BESS

De watuh deep?

SERENA

Almost to she waist.

SPORTING LIFE

Gawd! How Crown splash t'rough dat watuh!
(*They watch a moment in silence.*
A roar of wind and water. The stage darkens suddenly. With a swift, sucking sound, the shutters fly apart. Confused cries of "Oh, Jedus! Hab' a little me'cy!" "Gawd A'might'! De storm come back!" "Ain't I tell yo' he comin' worser'n eber.")

SERENA

(*Kneeling center*). Gawd answerin' Crown!
(*Others kneel with her, shrinking close together, moaning with terror.*)

MINGO

(*At window, his voice rising high in horror*). De wharf goin'! Gawd A'mighty!

BESS

(*Screaming futilely against the wind*). Clara! Clara!
(*Wild shrieks of horror from all the Negroes at window. Then a terrific roar, accompanied by the splintering of timber. Then a sudden awed silence in the room.* PETER *turns the women from the window, blocking further view. They huddle together in the center of the room around* SERENA'S *group.* BESS *crosses to* PORGY. *Sits beside him, the baby in her arms. All the others fall upon their knees as with one accord they begin to sing the "Jedgment Day Spiritual."*
BESS *does not sing, but sits holding the baby close, with a rapt look in her eyes.*)
"We will all pray togedduh on dat day,
We will all pray togedduh on dat day,
An' I'll fall upon my knees an' face de risin' sun.
Oh, Lord, hab' mercy on me!

"We will drink wine togedduh on dat day.
We will drink wine togedduh on dat day," etc.

"We will eat bread togedduh on dat day,
We will eat bread togedduh on dat day,
An' I'll fall upon my knees an' face de risin' sun.
Oh, Lord, hab' mercy on me!"

DADDY PETER

(*In the midst of the singing*). Allelujah! Gawd hab' mercy on de souls ob Clara an' Crown!

(BESS *turns and looks directly at* PORGY. *With an expression of awe in his face, he reaches out a timid hand and touches the baby's cheek.*
The roar increases. The shutters fly back and forth. With fear-stricken eyes, the Negroes sway and pat and sing, their voices sometimes rising above the roar of the wind and sometimes drowned by it.
BESS *continues silent, looking straight ahead of her, tenderness, yearning, and awe in her face.* PORGY *sits watching her. The shutters crash more violently. The roar of wind and water increases. The Negroes huddle closer and sing on.*)

Curtain

ACT FOUR

SCENE I

CHIMES. *St. Michael's strikes one. Curtain. The court, dark except for lights around the closed shutters of a second story room at back left and the blow from* MARIA'S *open door.*

PORGY *is at his window but is only vaguely seen in the darkness. He holds the shutters partly closed so as to screen himself, while he is able to look out.*

From the second-story room comes the sound of a spiritual muffled by the closed shutters.

Door to stairway at back left opens and SERENA *comes out. Through the open door the spiritual is heard more plainly. It is sung by women's voices—a slow, mournful dirge.*

"Nelson, Nelson, don' let yo' brudder condemn yo'.
Nelson, Nelson, don't let yo' brudder condemn yo'.
Nelson, Nelson, don't let yo' brudder condemn yo'.
Way down in dat lonesome grabeyahd."

(SERENA *closes door, muffling the chant. She crosses toward her room; sees the light from* MARIA'S *door and pauses.*)

SERENA

Yo' still up, Maria? How come yo' ain't sing wid we women fo' de dead in de storm?

MARIA

(*Coming to her doorway*). Some ob dose nigger' liable to sing all night, I too tired clearin' t'ing' up. My stove been wash' clean 'cross de street. An' 'sides, it break my heart to hear dese 'omans mourning fo' de mens dat provide um wid bread and what was dey lover' too. All dem fine, strong mens, dead in de storm! (*In lower voice.*) It gib' me de creeps, Serena, to t'ink how many ghost' must be listenin' 'round dis court to-night.

SERENA

(*Nervously*). I ain't no patience wid yo' talk 'bout ghost'.

(PORGY *softly moves his shutter.* SERENA *starts.*) What's dat?

MARIA

Jus' Porgy watchin' at he window. (*Draws* SERENA *farther from* PORGY'S *window and lowers her voice ominously.*) What's he watchin' for?

SERENA

(*Impatiently*). How I know?

MARIA

He been dere all day. He ain't gone out on de street to beg like he always does. An' he ain't gone up wid Bess to sing for de dead in de storm.

SERENA

What ob dat?

MARIA

Crown dead, ain't he? (*Lowers voice still further.*) Mus' be he t'ink Crown' ghost is a-comin' for trouble', Bess. (SERENA *gives a scornful grunt.*) Bery well, Sistuh. But I knows dis—Gawd gib' dat cripple to see many t'ing' yo' an' me can't see—an' if he is watch for sompen, den dere is sompen for watch for.

(BESS, *the baby in her arms, opens door at left back. The spiritual is again heard clearly.* BESS *does not close door, but stands listening, holding baby close.* MARIA *and* SERENA *move over to listen.*)

WOMEN'S VOICES

"Jake, Jake, don't let yo' brudder condemn yo'
Jake, Jake, don' let yo' brudder condemn yo' . . ."

BESS

Dey singin' for Jake an' Clara now. I couldn't stay. (*The three women listen a moment in silence.*)

VOICES

"Clara, Clara, don' let yo' sistuh condemn yo'
Way down in dat lonesome grabeyahd . . ."

(BESS *softly closes door, muffling the singing. Turns toward her own door.*)

SERENA

What we all goin' to do wid dat poor mudderless baby?

BESS

(*Stopping short. Turns slowly back*). Mus' be Clara has come back already.

SERENA

(*Looks fearfully about her*). What yo' means?

BESS

Mus' be Clara has come back an' say sompen to yo' I ain't hear. I ain't hear her say nuttin' 'bout "we." She say, "Bess, yo' keep dis baby for me till I comes for um."

SERENA

Somebody oughts to make sure de poor chile gets a proper Christian raisin'.

BESS

Clara ain't say nuttin' to me 'bout dat, an', until she do, I goin' stan' on she las' libbin' word an' keep she baby for she till she do come back. (*Again starts toward her door. Again turns back impulsively.*) Oh, let me be, Serena. Can't yo' see I ain't de same 'oman what used to run wid Crown? Gawd wouldn't ha' let Clara gib' me dis baby if He hadn't seen I was different inside. He wouldn't ha' gib' me Porgy if he didn't want to gib me my chance. (*Looking down at baby.*) See! He t'ink already dat I he ma. I gots de big brightness all inside me to-day. I can't stan' not to hab' ebery-body kind to me to-day! (*Holds baby out to* SERENA.) Look at um now, Serena—hold um a minute. Tell um he gots a good ma what goin' stan' by um!

(SERENA *takes the baby reluctantly, but responds when it touches her bosom. She rocks it in her arms.*)

SERENA

Yes—I reckon yo' gots a good ma now. She gots Gawd in she heart at las'. Yo' ain't gots no cause for fret. (*Hands baby back to* BESS, *who draws it close.*)

BESS

Ain't yo' see, Serena, how he scroogin' down? Dis baby know already dat he done git back home. (*Turns to go.*)

SERENA

Good-night, Sistuh.

(BESS *pauses slightly, as though taken by surprise.*)

BESS

Good-night—Sistuh.

(*Goes into her room. A dim light appears in the room. The shutters are closed from within.*

SERENA *goes to her room.* MARIA *begins to shut up her shop for the night. Several women carrying lanterns come from the funeral room, leaving the door open. They go out of the gate.*

The spiritual is again heard.)

THE SINGERS

"Ummmmm, Ummmmm, yeddy ole Egypt duh yowlin'
Way down in dat lonesome grabeyahd.

"Crown, Crown don' let yo' brudder condemn yo',
Crown, Crown, don't let yo' brudder condemn yo' . . ."

(*There is a sudden raucous laugh in the darkness.* MARIA *starts; then turns and peers into the shadows under* SERENA'S *stairs.*)

MARIA

Yo' low-live skunk! What yo' hidin' 'round here for?

SPORTING LIFE

(*Sauntering into the light from* MARIA'S *window*). Jus' listenin' to de singin'. Nice happy little tune dat. Now dey's stowin' my ole frien' Crown. (*Laughs again.*)

(MARIA *crosses quickly; closes the door, muffling the singing.*)

MARIA

(*Returning to* SPORTING LIFE). Yo' ain't gots no shame—laughin' at dem poor 'omans singin' for dere dead mens!

SPORTING LIFE

I ain't see no sense makin' such a fuss ober a man when he dead. When a gal's man done gone, dere's plenty mens still libin' what likes good-lookin' gals.

MARIA

I know it ain't dem gals yo' is atter. Ain't yo' see Bess gots no use for yo'? Ain't yo' see she gots a man?

SPORTING LIFE

I see more'n dat, Auntie. (*Laughs as though at a joke all his own.*)

MARIA

What yo' means?

SPORTING LIFE

I see she gots two mens—an' when a 'oman gots two mens—pretty soon she ain't got none at all!

MARIA

(*Threateningly*). What yo' means by dat—Bess gots two mens?

SPORTING LIFE

What make yo' all so sure Crown dead?

MARIA

Ain't we see de wharf wash' away under um?

SPORTING LIFE

Ain't he tell yo' Gawd an' he frien'?

MARIA

(*Alarmed*). Yo' is tellin' me Crown ain't dead?

SPORTING LIFE

(*Nonchalantly*). I ain't tellin' yo' nuttin', Auntie.

MARIA

(*Advancing on him threateningly*). Yas, yo' is. Yo' tellin' me eberyt'ing yo' knows, an' damn quick! (*Corners him.*)

SPORTING LIFE

Ob course he dead! Ain't we hear um singin' he funeral song?

MARIA

(*Grabbing his arm and bringing her face close to his*). Yo' has seen um?

SPORTING LIFE

How can I seen um if he dead? Mus' be he ghos' I seen hangin' 'round here.

MARIA

(*Meditatively*). So yo' has seen um. (*Menacingly.*) Well, if Bess gots two mens, dat sho' count' yo' out.

(SPORTING LIFE *laughs at her. While they talk,* PORGY'S *shutter opens inch by inch.*)

SPORTING LIFE

Dat jus' where I comes in. When a 'oman gots jus' one man, mebby she gots um for keep. But when she gots two mens—dere's mighty apt to be carvin'!—An' de cops takes de leabin's.

MARIA

(*Warningly*). Dere ain't nobody in dis court would gib' a nigger 'way to de cops.

SPORTING LIFE

Oh, no, Auntie! But dem cops is bery smart, an' dey gots it in fo' Crown, remembuh! An', when dat time comes, yo' can tell Bess for me dat little ole Sportin' Life is still on de premises.

MARIA

(*Starting for him*). Well, he ain't goin' stay bery long on my premises!

SPORTING LIFE

(*Hurriedly withdrawing, but not forgetting his swagger*). Dat's all right, ole lady! I was jus' leabin'. (*Saunters toward gate.*) (MARIA *turns back to the closing of her shop.* SPORTING LIFE *glances at her over his shoulder. Sees her engaged in barring her windows. Steps swiftly into the darkness under* SERENA'S *stairs.* MARIA *finishes her work. Looks about court. Sees its apparently empty. Goes into her shop. Locks door.*)
A child's whimper is heard from BESS'S *room, then* BESS'S *voice singing in the darkness.*)

"Hush, little baby, don' yo' cry,
Hush, little baby, don' yo' cry,
Hush, little baby, don' yo' cry,
Mother an' fadder born to die.

"Heard a thunder in de sky,
Heard a thunder in de sky,
Heard a thunder in de sky,
Mus' be Jedus passin' by.

"Heard a rumblin' in de groun',
Heard a rumblin' in de groun',
Heard a rumblin' in de groun',
Mus' be Satan turnin' 'roun'.

"Hush, little baby, don' yo' cry,
Mother an' fadder born to die."

(*Her voice trails off sleepily and is silent. During her lullaby, the last singers have come from the funeral room and crossed to their own rooms or gone out at gate. The light in the funeral room goes out.* MARIA'S *light goes out.*
A moment of complete darkness and silence in Catfish Row; then the sudden flash of a match in the darkness reveals SPORTING LIFE *about to light a cigarette. He hears something at gate and hurriedly extinguishes match, with cigarette unlit.*
Against the gray background beyond the gate a gigantic figure can be seen. The gate opens very slowly and noiselessly. CROWN *comes stealthily into court; very gently closes gate behind him. Picks his way slowly and silently across court. Stops to listen. Silence. Goes on to* PORGY'S *door. Again listens. Puts his hand on knob and softly tries door. Opens it very cautiously, inch by inch. When it is wide enough, he stealthily slips through. Inch by inch, the door closes.*
A full minute of absolute silence. MARIA *is in her wrapper; opens her door and stands listening. Satisfied, she is turning back.*
A muffled thud sounds from PORGY'S *room.* MARIA *stops short. Stands motionless. Suddenly* PORGY'S *laugh is heard, deep, swelling, lustful. The baby cries out.*)

BESS

(*Within room. Horror in her voice*). Fo' Gawd' sake, Porgy! What yo' laughin' 'bout?

PORGY

(*Triumphantly*). Dat all right, honey. Don' yo' be worryin'. Yo' gots Porgy now, an' he look atter he 'oman. Ain't I don' tell yo'? Yo' gots a *man* now!
(MARIA *crosses the court swiftly. Opens* PORGY'S *door, goes in, and closes it behind her.*
Again the flash of a match in the shadows. SPORTING LIFE *lights his cigarette and continues his vigil.*)

Curtain.

SCENE II

ST. MICHAEL'S *chimes and strikes six. The curtain rises on the court, silent and apparently deserted.*
After a moment, three white men appear outside the gate. One is the DETECTIVE *who arrested* PETER. *The second is the* CORONER, *a fat, easy-going, florid man. The third is a* POLICEMAN.

DETECTIVE

(*To* POLICEMAN, *pointing off right*). Bring the wagon 'round to the corner, Al, and wait for us there. (*The* POLICEMAN *goes off right. The* DETECTIVE *and* CORONER *come in at gate.*)
This is the joint. I'd like to get something on it this time that would justify closing it up as a public nuisance and turning the lot of 'em into the street. It's alive with crooked niggers.

CORONER

(*Looking around him*). Looks pretty dead to me.

DETECTIVE

Dead, hell! If you was on the force, 'stead of sitting down in the coroner's office, you'd know we don't make a move that isn't watched by a hundred pair of eyes. (*The* CORONER *looks exceedingly uncomfortable. Glances apprehensively about him.*)
There! Did you catch that?
(*Points at a window.* CORONER *starts.*)
They're gone now.

CORONER

Don't know as I have much business, after all. Just to get a witness to identify the body at the inquest. Maybe you'll bring one along for me when you come.

DETECTIVE

Like hell I will! You stay and get your own witness, and I'll learn you something about handling niggers, too. Now, let's see—got several leads here! The widow of Robbins, the fellow Crown killed. That's her room there. And then there's the corpse's woman. She's living with the cripple in there now.

CORONER

What makes you think the buck was killed here?

DETECTIVE

(*Pointing toward sea*). Found right out there.

CORONER

Found at flood tide. Might have been washed in from miles out.

DETECTIVE

A hell of a lot you know about niggers. Come on! I'll show you.
(CORONER *nods and follows* DETECTIVE. *They stop at door leading to* SERENA'S *room.* DETECTIVE *kicks it open, and shouts up the stairs.*)

DETECTIVE

Come on down, Serena Robbins, and make it damn quick!
(*There is silence for a moment, then the shutters of* SERENA'S *window are slowly* opened, and ANNIE *looks out.*)

ANNIE

Serena been sick in she bed three day, an' I been here wid she all dat time.

DETECTIVE

The hell she has! Tell her, if she don't come down, I'll get the wagon and run her in.

ANNIE

She bery sick, boss. She can't leabe she bed.

DETECTIVE

She'll leave it damn quick if she knows what's good for her.
(ANNIE *disappears. A loud moaning is heard. Then* ANNIE *reappears accompanied by another woman. Between them they support* SERENA. *She wears a voluminous white nightgown, and her face and head are bound in a towel. She collapses across the window sill with a loud groan.*)
Drop that racket.
(SERENA *is silent.*)
Where were you last night?

SERENA

(*Slowly and as though in great pain*). I been sick in dis bed now three day an' night.

ANNIE

We been sittin' wid she an' nursin' she all dat time.

THE OTHER WOMAN

Dat's de Gawd's trut'.

CORONER

Would you swear to that?

SERENA, ANNIE, AND OTHER WOMAN

(*In unison, as though answer had been learned by rote*). Yes, boss, we swear to dat.

CORONER

(*To* DETECTIVE). There you are—an air-tight alibi. (DETECTIVE *regards* CORONER *with scorn.*)

DETECTIVE

(*To* SERENA). You know damn well you were out yesterday. I've a good mind to send for the wagon and carry you in.
(*The women are silent.* DETECTIVE *waits, then shouts abruptly.*)
Well?

THE THREE WOMEN

(*Again in unison*). We swear to Gawd we been in dis room three day'.

DETECTIVE

(*Bluffing*). Ah-hh, that's what I wanted! So you swear you were in last night, eh?
(*The women are frightened and silent.*)
And just two months ago—right here—Crown killed your husband, didn't he?
(*No answer.*)
Answer me!
(DETECTIVE *runs halfway upstairs.*)
You'll either talk here or in jail. Get that! Did Crown kill Robbins? Yes or no!
(SERENA *nods her head.*)
Exactly. And last night Crown got his right here—didn't he?
(*Women are silent except* SERENA, *who groans as though in pain.*
DETECTIVE *pretends to construe groan as assent—triumphantly.*)
Yes, and how do you know he was killed if you didn't see it?

WOMEN

(*In unison*). We ain't see nuttin', boss. We been in here t'ree day an' night, an' de window been closed.

DETECTIVE

(*Shouting*). Look at me, Robbins! Do you mean to tell me that the man who killed your husband was bumped off right here, under your window, and you didn't know?

WOMEN

(*In unison*). We ain't see nuttin', boss. We been in here——

DETECTIVE

(*Interrupting*). —three days and nights with the window closed. You needn't do that one again. (*Turning away disgustedly.*) Oh, hell! You might as well argue with a parrot cage, but you'll never break them without your own witnesses, and you'll never get 'em.
(*The three women leave the window, closing shutters.*)
Well, come along. Let's see what's here.
(*Goes to* LILY'S *and* PETER'S *door. Throws it open.*)
Come on out here, you!
(LILY *comes to door.*)
What's your name?

LILY

(*Seeing* CORONER). Do, Lord! Ef it ain't Mr. Jennings!

CORONER

Well, Lily! So you live here? (*To* DETECTIVE.) I'll answer for this woman. She worked for us for years.

DETECTIVE

That don't prove she don't know anything about this murder, does it? (*To* LILY.) What's your name?

LILY

(*Stubbornly*). I don' know nuttin' 'bout um.

DETECTIVE

(*Shouting at her*). I didn't ask you whether——

CORONER

Let me question her. (*Kindly to* LILY.) What's your name?

LILY

Do, Mr. Jennings! You ain't 'membuh my name is Lily Holmes?

CORONER

I know your name was Lily Holmes, but you left us to get married. What's your name now?

LILY

Lord, Mr. Jennings! I de same Lily Holmes. You ain't t'ink I goin' be responsible for no ole nigger' name? No, suh! An' I ain't gib' um my name, nedder!

DETECTIVE

(*Looking through door*). That your husband? (*Calling into room.*) Come on out here, you!

LILY

I'll fetch um. (*Goes into room. Returns with* PETER.)

CORONER

Why, it's the old honey man!
(PETER *is terror-stricken at sight of* DETECTIVE.)

DETECTIVE

(*Recognizing him*). Oh, so it's you, is it? Well, Uncle, do you want to go back to jail or are you going to come clean?

LILY

(*Appealing to* CORONER). Ain't no use to ask him nuttin'. He deaf, an' 'sides, he ain't got good sense nohow.

CORONER

But, Lily, you didn't marry the old honey man?

LILY

(*Surveying* PETER). Whut wrong wid um?

CORONER

He's not a suitable age.

LILY

(*Puzzled*). Whut he ain't?

CORONER

Do you think he's the right age?

LILY

Sho he de right age. He eighty-two.

CORONER

An old man like that's apt to linger on your hands.
(DADDY PETER, *hearing nothing of conversation, but feeling that he is its subject, is nodding and smiling with self-appreciation.*)

LILY

No, boss. Ef I is marry to young man an' he took sick, mebbe *he* linger on my hand. But (*Points to* PETER, *who smiles more amiably.*) he ain't linger on my han'. He took sick—he gone.

CORONER

What did you marry him for?

LILY

Why, yo' see, boss, he like dis. Ain't yo' 'membuh how I used to hab' dem crazy fits ob misery in my stomach? I wake up in de night wid 'em. De doctor say to me, "Lily Holmes, one ob dese nights yo' goin' dead in yo' bed all by yo'self." So I t'ink I bes' marry dat nigger so as I won't go dead all by myself. But since I marry um, I gets well ob my misery, an' I ain't got no furder use for 'um.

DETECTIVE

(*To* CORONER). Say, are you investigating a murder or just paying social calls? (*To* LILY *and* PETER.) That'll do for you two. Get inside.
(LILY *and* PETER *hurriedly return to their room.*)

CORONER

Well, seems to me I get as much out of them as you do.

DETECTIVE

Come on, let's put the cripple and his woman through. I have a hunch that's where we'll find our bacon.
(*Crosses toward* PORGY'S *door.* CORONER *follows.*)

CORONER

All right. Go ahead. I'm watching you handle them.

DETECTIVE

You won't find the cripple much of a witness. I tried to break him in the Robbins case but he wouldn't come through. (*Kicks the door open with a bang.*) Come on out, both of you niggers. Step lively now!
(BESS *helps* PORGY *to seat on doorstep. Then she stands by him, the baby in her arms.* DETECTIVE *enters room.*)

CORONER

(*To* PORGY). What is your name?
(PORGY *looks at him keenly, then, reassured, smiles.*)

PORGY

Jus' Porgy. You knows me, boss. Yo' done gib' me plenty ob pennies on Meetin' Street.

CORONER

Of course! You're the goat man. I didn't know you without your wagon. Now, this nigger Crown—you knew him by sight, didn't you?

PORGY

(*As though remembering with difficulty*). Yes, boss—I 'membuh um when he used to come here, long ago.

CORONER

You could identify him, I suppose.
(PORGY *looks blank.*)
You'd know him if you saw him again, I mean.

PORGY

(*Slowly*). Yes, boss, I'd know um. (*With dawning apprehension.*) But I ain't care none 'bout see um.
(CORONER *laughs. Makes note in notebook. Puts it in pocket. Calls to* DETECTIVE.)

CORONER

Well, I'm through. Let's pull freight.

DETECTIVE

(*Appears in doorway; looks knowingly at* PORGY *and* BESS). Mighty clean floor in there. Funny it got its first scrubbing in twenty years this morning.

BESS

I scrubs my floor ebery week. You can ask these people here 'bout um.

CORONER

(*Sneering*). Oh, yes! More witnesses! (*Then triumphantly.*) But you missed the blood under the bed this time. (*Jerks out his gun, covers* PORGY, *shouts.*) Come, out with it! You killed Crown, didn't you? Speak up, or I'll hang you sure as hell!
(PORGY *and* BESS *sit silent, with eyes lowered.*)
Well?

BESS

I ain't understan', boss. Dere ain't no blood dere, an' nobody ain't kill Crown in our room.

CORONER

(*Drawing* DETECTIVE *aside*). For God's sake, Duggan, let's call it a day. The cripple couldn't kill a two-hundred-pound buck and tote him a hundred yards.

DETECTIVE

You don't know much about niggers, do you?

CORONER

(*Turning toward gate*). Anyway, *I'm* through, and I've got to get along. It's 'most time for my inquest.
(BESS *and* PORGY *go swiftly inside. Close door.*)

DETECTIVE

(*Following* CORONER *reluctantly*). Got your witness?

CORONER

Yeh.
(*They go out gate and off to left.
Again the court is deserted and silent. For a moment, there is no sound or movement. Then, in one of the rooms, a voice is raised singing.*)

VOICE

"Ain't it hard to be a nigger!
Ain't it hard to be a nigger!"

(*Another voice joins, then another. In a moment, the empty court is ringing with the song, sung mockingly, triumphantly. Another moment, and doors and shutters*

begin to fly open. The Negroes come from their doors or lean from their windows, and the court is quickly filled with life and movement. They are all singing.
SERENA's *door flies open, and she comes out singing. She is fully dressed and carries a great basket of clothes, which she begins to hang on line while she sings.*
BESS *helps* PORGY *on to the doorstep and sits beside him, the baby in her arms. Both are singing.* LILY *comes out carrying the honey tray.* PETER *follows. She balances it on his head.* SCIPIO *drives* PORGY's *goat cart in through archway.*
Then someone breaks into a wilder tune, and all the others instantly change to the new song.)

"Sit down! I can't sit down!
Sit down! I can't sit down!
My soul's so happy dat I can't sit down!"

(*A Negro near the gate looks out, suddenly gives a loud hiss and waves his arms—in a warning gesture.*
The song ceases abruptly. SERENA *grabs her wash from the line. The Negroes return swiftly and silently to their rooms. Doors and shutters close stealthily.*
BESS *attempts to help* PORGY *to his feet, but, seeing that they have no time, he sinks down again on his doorstep and pretends to doze.* BESS *goes inside, closes door.* SCIPIO *drives the goat back through archway.*
The court is again silent, and deserted by all but PORGY.
A POLICEMAN *enters from left. Comes in at gate. Looks about court. Sees* PORGY, *who is apparently oblivious of him. Crosses to* PORGY.)

POLICEMAN

Hey, you!
(PORGY *opens his eyes.*)
You're Porgy, aren't you? I've got something for you.
(*Holds out paper.* PORGY *looks at it in alarm.* POLICEMAN *speaks kindly.*)
You needn't be afraid to take it. It's just a summons as a witness at the coroner's inquest. All you've got to do is view the body and tell the coroner who it is.
(PORGY *is suddenly terror-stricken. His voice shakes.*)

PORGY

I gots to go an' look on Crown's face?

POLICEMAN

Yes, that's all.

PORGY

Wid all dem w'ite folks lookin' at me?

POLICEMAN

Oh, cheer up! I reckon you've seen a dead nigger before. It'll be all over in a few minutes.
(BESS *appears in doorway, listening, her eyes wide with horror.*)

PORGY

Dere ain't goin' be no nigger in dat room 'cept me?

POLICEMAN

Just you and Crown—if you still call him one. (*Turns away.*)

PORGY

(*Scarcely able to speak for terror*). Boss—I couldn' jus' bring a 'oman wid me? I couldn't eben carry my—my 'oman?

POLICEMAN

(*Slightly impatient*). No, you can't bring anyone. Say, you're the cripple, aren't you? I'll get the wagon and carry you down. And as soon as you've seen Crown, you can come home. (*Starts for gate.*)

PORGY

(*Desperately*). Boss——

POLICEMAN

Now, listen, I've summoned you, and you've got to go, or it's contempt of court. I'll call the wagon for you. (*Goes out gate and off to left.*)
(*As soon as he has gone, doors open stealthily. The Negroes come out and gather about* PORGY, *speaking in low, frightened tones.*)

PORGY

Oh, Gawd! Whut I goin' to do?

BESS

Yo' got to go, Porgy. Mebby yo' can jus' make like to look at um an' keep yo' eye' shut.

MARIA

Yo' goin' be all right, Porgy. Yo' jus' goin' to be a witness.

SPORTING LIFE

I ain't so sure ob dat.
(*They all look at him in alarm.*)
I don' know who done de killin'. All I knows is, when de man what done um goes in dat room, Crown' wounds begin to bleed.

PORGY

(*Terror-stricken*). Oh, Jedus!

SPORTING LIFE

Dat's one way de cops got ob tellin' who done um.

PORGY

(*In a panic, moaning*). I can't look on he face! Oh, Gawd! Whut I goin' to do!

SPORTING LIFE

(*Taking command of the situation*). Listen to me! Yo' do jus' as I say an' yo' won't hab' to look on he face.

PORGY

What I do, Sporting Life?

SPORTING LIFE

Get busy, yo' niggers. We gots to get Porgy out ob here! Get de goat, Scipio. Here, Mingo! Yo' stan' by to gib' me a han' wid Porgy.

BESS

Don' yo' go, Porgy! He can't get away!

SPORTING LIFE

He gots to get away or dey'll hang um sure.

PORGY

Oh, Gawd!
(SCIPIO *has brought the goat cart.* SPORTING LIFE *and* MINGO *are lifting* PORGY *in while he moans with terror and mutters unintelligibly.*)

SPORTING LIFE

Now, listen! Make straight for Bedens Alley. When yo' gets dere, turn in an' lie low.

MINGO

Bedens Alley too far. He'll neber make it.

SPORTING LIFE

Shut up, Mingo. I'm runnin' dis. All right, Porgy, light out!

MARIA

Quick! Start um!

BESS

Make um run!
(*The clang of the patrol wagon bell is heard approaching rapidly. The Negroes stand as though paralyzed with terror.*)

MINGO

Here dey is!

BESS

Oh, Gawd! It's too late now!

SPORTING LIFE

No, it ain't. Here, yo' niggers, get um in dere!
(*Directs them to the archway. They drive the goat through, then mass in front of archway, hiding* PORGY *from view.*
SPORTING LIFE *saunters across the court as though he had nothing to do with the affair, and awaits developments.*
The patrol bell rings more slowly as the wagon slows down, then comes to a stop at left of gate just out of view.
The POLICEMAN *again comes in at gate. Looks toward* PORGY'S *door. Crosses to it abruptly. Throws it open.*)

POLICEMAN

Hey, you there! (*Runs to gate. Calls.*) Jim! The fool's trying to make a get-away! Come on! (*Turns to the Negroes.*) Where did he go?
(*They look at him with blank faces.*)
All right! (*Starts for* PORGY'S *door.*)
(*The* SECOND POLICEMAN *enters from left.*)
You take that side, Jim. I'll take this. (*Goes into* PORGY'S *room.*)
(SECOND POLICEMAN *goes through* SERENA'S *door. As soon as both* POLICEMEN *are out of sight, the Negroes beckon to* PORGY, *who drives from archway and quickly toward gate.*
The shutters of an upper window are thrown open, and the FIRST POLICEMAN *looks out.*)

POLICEMAN

Hey, you! What d'you think you're doing? (PORGY *leans forward and wrings the goat's tail. The astonished animal leaps forward and goes out gate at a run.*)
Jim!
(*The* SECOND POLICEMAN *throws open shutters of room opposite and leans from window.*)
Look there! (*Points to* PORGY *as he disappears off left.*)
(*Both* POLICEMEN *burst into peals of laughter.*
The Negroes follow to gate, pushing it shut, looking out through bars.)

SECOND POLICEMAN

He must want to have a race.
(*The two* POLICEMEN *leave the windows and a minute later come running from doors.*)

FIRST POLICEMAN

Racing the wagon! That's good!
(*They start toward gate.*)

SECOND POLICEMAN

(*Laying a hand on the other's arm*). Say, let him get a start.
(*They double up with laughter.*)
This is going to be good!

FIRST POLICEMAN

Here, you niggers! Get away from the gate.
(*The Negroes stand back. He opens gate.*)
Come on now! We're off!
(*They run out gate, still shouting with laughter. They run off right. The Negroes press close about gate to watch.*
The clang of the patrol wagon bell is heard as the vehicle sets off at top speed.)

ANNIE

Oh, Gawd! Dey'll get um!

MARIA

Ef he can jus' git 'round de corner!——

LILY

—Mebby dey won't fin' um.

BESS

(*Turning hopelessly away*). 'Tain't no use.
(*The tension in the crowd of watchers suddenly relaxes, and their faces assume hopeless expressions.*)
Dey got um?

LILY

Yeh. Dey got um.

SERENA

Dey putting him an' de goat all two in de wagon.
(BESS *sits hopelessly on her doorstep. The other Negroes return to their various rooms and tasks.* SPORTING LIFE *saunters across court and sits down on step by* BESS.
The stage is darkening. A light appears in a window.)

BESS

Oh, Gawd! Dey goin' carry um to look on Crown' face!

SPORTING LIFE

(*Laughing*). Don' yo' worry none 'bout dat, Sistuh. Dat nigger ain't a witness now. Dey goin' lock um up in de jail.

MINGO

(*At gate*). Dat's de trut'. Dey done turn de wagon 'round toward de jail.

BESS

Well, dat better'n makin' um look on Crown. (*Fearfully.*) Not for long, Sportin' Life?

SPORTING LIFE

(*Sympathetically*). No, not for long. Jus' a yeah, mebby.

BESS

A yeah.

SPORTING LIFE

Contempt ob court—dat's a serious offence.
(BESS *drops her face into her hands.*)
Jus' like I tol' yo'. Nobody home now but Bess an' ole Sportin' Life.

BESS

I ain't gots no time fo' yo'.

SPORTING LIFE

(*Laughing*). Fo' sho' yo' has. Yo' jus' gots nice little vacation now fo' play 'round wid yo' ole frien'. Contempt ob court—dat serious offence. Dat nigger ain't be back heah fo' a yeah.

BESS

(*Alarmed*). Sportin' Life, yo' ain't t'ink dey puts Porgy up fo' a yeah?

SPORTING LIFE

A yeah for sho'. Cheer up, Sistuh! Gib' me yo' han'. (*He takes her hand. She is too preoccupied to resist.*) Ole Sportin' Life got de stuff fo' scare away de lonesome blues. (*Pours powder into her hand.* BESS *looks down at it.*)

BESS

Happy dus'! (*Gazes at the powder with fascinated horror.*) I ain't want none ob dat stuff, I tells yo'.

SPORTING LIFE

Ain't nuff ter hurt er flea.

BESS

Take dat stuff away, nigger! (*But she continues to hold it in her hand.*)

SPORTING LIFE

Jus' a little touch fo' ole time' sake.
(BESS *suddenly claps her hand over her face. When she takes it away, it is empty.* SPORTING LIFE *smiles with satisfaction.*)
Dat de t'ing, ain't it? An' 'membuh, dere's plenty more where dat come from.
Dere's a boat to Noo Yo'k to-morruh an' I'm goin'. (*Pauses significantly.* BESS *says nothing.*)
Why yo' such a fool, Bess? What yo' goin' to do a whole yeah here by yo'self? Now's yo' chance.
(BESS *leaps to her feet, her eyes blazing. She glares at* SPORTING LIFE *with contempt and hatred.*)

BESS

Yo' low, crawlin' houn'! Git 'way from my door, I tell yo'! Lef it, yo'! Rattlesnake! Dat's whut yo' is! Rattlesnake!
(*While she berates him,* SPORTING LIFE *lights a cigarette, continues to sit on step.*)

SPORTING LIFE

Rave on, Sistuh! But I'll be right here when yo' is wantin' dat second shot.
(BESS *runs suddenly past him into her room. Slams door behind her.* SPORTING LIFE *sits smiling to himself and leisurely blowing smoke rings.*
(MARIA *comes to her doorway. Sees him. Crosses to him.*)

MARIA

(*Contemptuously*). What yo' waitin' 'round here for?

SPORTING LIFE

Jus' waitin'. (*Smokes contentedly.*)

MARIA

What yo' t'ink yo' goin' to get?

SPORTING LIFE

(*With shrug of shoulders*). Uummmmmm —jus' waitin'.

MARIA

(*Turning scornfully away*). Yo' don' know Bess. (*Recrosses to her shop.*)
(SPORTING LIFE *watches her till she has reached her doorstep.*)

SPORTING LIFE

(*In a low voice, not intended for* MARIA *to hear*). You don' know happy dus'.
(MARIA *does not hear. Goes into shop; closes door.* SPORTING LIFE *continues to wait. St. Michael's chimes the half hour.*)

Curtain

SCENE III

CHIMES. *Two o'clock. The court is as usual, except that* PORGY'S *door and shutters are closed. Negroes are coming and going about their tasks.*

PETER, LILY, *and* MINGO *sit at* MARIA'S *table. She is busy serving them.* SCIPIO *is playing near the gate.* SERENA *sits near her door rocking a baby in her arms and singing, "Hush little baby, don't you cry."* MARIA *goes into her shop.*

PORGY *drives up outside the gate and calls softly to* SCIPIO. *His air is one of mystery.*

PORGY

Here, Scipio! Here Porgy back from jail. Open de gate an' don't make no noise.

(SCIPIO *goes reluctantly to gate, opens it, and leads the goat inside.* SERENA *looks up, sees* PORGY, *stops singing in the middle of a bar, and hunches over the baby as though to hide it.*

Various Negroes about the court look up, see him, and go silently into their rooms. PORGY *is too preoccupied with his secret to notice anything. He drives over and stops beside* MARIA'S *table,* LILY, PETER, *and* MINGO *half rise, then see that it is too late to escape, and resume their seats.*)

PORGY

(*In a joyous but guarded voice*). Shhh, don't nobody let on yet dat I is home again. I gots a surprise for Bess, an' I ain't want she to know till I gots eberyt'ing ready.

(*He does not notice that the others are silent and embarrassed, and, reaching into the wagon, commences to remove packages, talking volubly all the time. He unwraps a harmonica and hands it to* SCIPIO.)

Here, boy. T'row away dat ole mout' organ you gots an' start in on dis one. See, he gots picture ob brass band on um. Work on dat, an' fus' t'ing dat yo' know, yo'll be playin' wid de orphans. (*He turns to* LILY.) Here, gal, hol' up yo' head. Dat's right. I nebber did like dem ole funeral bonnet Peter buy fo' yo'. (*Unwraps a gorgeous, feather-trimmed hat and hands it to her.*) Now get underneat' dat, an' make all de red bird and de blue jay jealous.

(LILY *takes hat, but is unable to speak her thanks.* PORGY *is hurrying on, and does not notice this. He opens a package and shakes out a gay dress, then lays it on the table.*) Now, dat's de style for Bess. She is one gal what always look good in red. (*He opens a hat and places it beside the dress.*) I reckon I is de fus' nigger anybody roun' here ebber see what go to jail po', an' leabe dere rich. But Porgy' luck ridin' high now. Ain't nuttin' can stop um. When de buckra search me in de jail, I all de time gots my lucky bones in my mout'—see! an time I get settle' in my new boardin' house, I start to go right t'rough dem odder crap-shootin' nigger' like Glory Hallelujah.

(*He takes a package from the cart, opens it, and holds up a baby dress.*)

Now, ain't dis de t'ing! Course, de baby ain't really big 'nough for wear dress yet, but he goin' grow fas'. You watch, he goin' be in dat dress by de fus' frost.

(*Continues his story.*)

Yas, suh! dere warn't no stoppin' dem bones. Dey jus' gone whoopin' right t'rough dat jail, a-pullin' me after 'em. And den, on de las' day, de big buckra guard hear 'bout it, an' he come an' say I gots to gib up de bones. But I been seein' um roll wid de jailer in de watch house, an' I know he weakness. I ask dat buckra if he ain't likes me to teach um how to sing lucky to de bones 'fore I gib' dem up, an' 'fore he git 'way I done gone t'rough um for t'ree dollar an' seben cent an' dis shirt.

(*He proudly exhibits shirt that he is wearing. His purchases are now all spread out on the table, and he looks from them to the faces of the Negroes.*)

Now it time to call Bess. Oh, Bess. Here Porgy come home.

(*There is a moment of absolute silence.* LILY *gets to her feet, buries her face in her hands, and runs to her room.* PETER *starts to follow.* MINGO *rises and goes toward* MARIA'S *door.*)

Here, Lily, Peter, Mingo, where you all goin'? What de hell kin' ob a welcome dis for a man what been in jail for a week, an' for de contemp' ob court at dat. Oh, now I see. Well, yo' ain't gots to min' Bess an' me. All de time we wants to hab we frien' wid us. Eben now, we ain't wants to be jus' by weself.

(*They continue to withdraw. He looks about him in growing surprise, and discovers* SERENA *hunched up silently over the baby.*)

Why, hello! Dere's Serena. Yo' sho' work fas', Sistuh. I ain't been gone a week, an' yo' done gots a new baby. (SERENA *rises hurriedly, exposing baby for first time.*) Here, hold on. Let me see dat chile. Dat's Bess's baby, ain't it? Where yo' get um? Where Bess, anyhow? She ain't answer me.

SERENA

(*Calling*). Maria, come out dat cookshop. Here Porgy come home. *You* gots to talk wid um.

(PORGY *drives to his own door.*)

PORGY

Bess! Ain't yo' dere, Bess? (MARIA *comes to her doorway.* PORGY *turns to her, his eyes wide with alarm.*) Where's Bess? (MARIA *sits on her doorstep.* PORGY *turns his goat and drives over to her.*) Tell me quick. Where's Bess? (MARIA *does not answer.*) Where? Where?

MARIA

(*Trying to put on a bold face*). Ain't we tell yo' all along, Porgy, dat 'oman ain't fit for yo'?

PORGY

(*Frantically*). I ain't ask yo' opinion. Where' Bess? (*They all shrink from telling him. Each evades, trying to leave it to the others.*)

MARIA

Dat dirty dog Sportin' Life make us all t'ink yo' is lock up for a yeah.

PORGY

Won't somebody tell me, where Bess?

SERENA

Bess very low in she min' 'cause she t'ink yo' is gone for a yeah. (*Pauses, unable to come to the point.*)

PORGY

But I home *now*. I want to tell she I is here.

SERENA

She gone back to de happy dus' an' de red eye. She been very drunk two day'.

PORGY

But where she now? I ain't care if she was drunk. I want she now.

LILY

Dat houn' Sportin' Life was foreber hangin' 'round and gettin' she to take more dope.

PORGY

(*Driving again to his own door. Calls*). Bess! Bess! Won't nobody tell me——

MARIA

(*Following him*). Ain't we tellin' yo'? Dat Houn' Sportin' Life——

PORGY

(*Desperately*). I ain't ask 'bout Sportin' Life. Where Bess?

SERENA

She gone, Porgy. An' I done take dis chile to gib um a Christian raisin'——

PORGY

Where she gone?

SERENA

Dat gal ain't neber had Gawd in she heart, an' de debil get um at last.

MARIA

'Tain't de debil. De happy dus' done for um.

PORGY

(*Wildly*). You—Bess?—Yo' ain't means Bess dead?

SERENA

She worse dan dead.

LILY

Sportin' Life carry she away on de Noo Yo'k boat. (*They are all silent, gazing at* PORGY. *He, too, is silent for a moment.*)

PORGY

Where dat dey take she?

MINGO

Noo Yo'k.

MARIA

Dat's way up Nort'.

PORGY

(*Pointing*). It dat way?

MARIA

It take two days by de boat. Yo' can't find um.

PORGY

I ain't say I can find um. I say, where it is?

MARIA

Yo' can't go after she. Ain't yo' hear we say yo' can't find um.

ANNIE

Ain't yo' know Noo Yo'k mos' a t'ousand mile' from here?

PORGY

Which way dat?

LILY

(*Pointing*). Up Nort'—past de Custom House.
(PORGY *turns his goat and drives slowly with bowed head toward the gate.*)

MARIA

Porgy, I tells yo' it ain't no use!

LILY

Dat great big city. Yo' can't find um dere!

SERENA

Ain't we tells yo'——
(*But* PORGY *is going on toward gate as if he did not hear, and they cease to protest and stand motionless watching him.*
As PORGY *reaches the gate,* SCIPIO *silently opens it.* PORGY *drives through and turns to left, as* LILY *pointed.*
St. Michael's chimes the quarter hour. The gate clangs shut.)

Curtain

Eugene O'Neill

STRANGE INTERLUDE

EUGENE O'NEILL

Eugene Gladstone O'Neill was born in New York City in 1888, the son of James O'Neill, the popular romantic actor. His early education was acquired at two Catholic boarding schools and the Betts Academy in Stamford, Connecticut. After a year at Princeton University and a short term of employment in New York, O'Neill ventured forth on a gold-prospecting trip to Honduras. Following his return to the United States and a tour with one of his father's theatrical companies, he shipped to Buenos Aires on a Norwegian barque. Subsequently, he earned his able-bodied seaman's certificate in the trans-Atlantic service. After recovering from an illness in 1913, he began his writing career in earnest. A year of study in the famous 47 Workshop at Harvard was the next step in his development as a playwright. His first full-length play, *Beyond the Horizon,* won for him the Pulitzer Prize, an award which he has the unique distinction of having won three times. *Anna Christie* won the Pulitzer Prize for 1921-22 and *Strange Interlude* for 1927-28. The body of his work consists of some twenty-one long plays and sixteen plays in one act. Today Eugene O'Neill stands pre-eminent among the dramatists of the world.

CHARACTERS

CHARLES MARSDEN
PROFESSOR HENRY LEEDS
NINA LEEDS, his daughter
EDMUND DARRELL
SAM EVANS
MRS. AMOS EVANS, Sam's mother
GORDON EVANS
MADELINE ARNOLD

SCENES

First Part

ACT I

Library, the Leeds' home in a small university town of New England—an afternoon in late summer.

ACT II

The same. Fall of the following year. Night.

ACT III

Dining room of the Evans' homestead in Northern New York State—late spring of the next year. Morning.

ACT IV

The same as Acts One and Two. Fall of the same year. Evening.

ACT V

Sitting room of small house Evans has rented in a seashore suburb near New York. The following April. Morning.

Second Part

ACT VI

The same. A little over a year later. Evening.

ACT VII

Sitting room of the Evans' apartment on Park Avenue. Nearly eleven years later. Early afternoon.

ACT VIII

Section of afterdeck of the Evans' cruiser anchored near the finish line at Poughkeepsie. Ten years later. Afternoon.

ACT IX

A terrace on the Evans' estate on Long Island. Several months later. Late afternoon.

STRANGE INTERLUDE

ACT ONE

SCENE: *The library of* PROFESSOR LEEDS' *home in a small university town in New England. This room is at the front part of his house with windows opening on the strip of lawn between the house and the quiet residential street. It is a small room with a low ceiling. The furniture has been selected with a love for old New England pieces. The walls are lined almost to the ceiling with glassed-in bookshelves. These are packed with books, principally editions, many of them old and rare, of the ancient classics in the original Greek and Latin, of the later classics in French and German and Italian, of all the English authors who wrote while* s *was still like an* f *and a few since then, the most modern probably being Thackeray. The atmosphere of the room is that of a cosy, cultured retreat, sedulously built as a sanctuary where, secure with the culture of the past at his back, a fugitive from reality can view the present safely from a distance, as a superior with condescending disdain, pity, and even amusement.*

There is a fair-sized table, a heavy armchair, a rocker, and an old bench made comfortable with cushions. The table, with the Professor's armchair at its left, is arranged toward the left of the room, the rocker is at center, the bench at right.

There is one entrance, a door in the right wall, rear.

It is late afternoon of a day in August. Sunshine, cooled and dimmed in the shade of trees, fills the room with a soothing light.

The sound of a MAID'S VOICE—*a middle-aged woman—explaining familiarly but respectfully from the right, and* MARSDEN *enters. He is a tall thin man of thirty-five, meticulously well-dressed in tweeds of distinctly English tailoring, his appearance that of an Anglicized New England gentleman. His face is too long for its width, his nose is high and narrow, his forehead broad, his mild blue eyes those of a dreamy self-analyst, his thin lips ironical and a bit sad. There is an indefinable feminine quality about him, but it is nothing apparent in either appearance or act. His manner is cool and poised. He speaks with a careful ease as one who listens to his own conversation. He has long fragile hands, and the stoop to his shoulders of a man weak muscularly, who has never liked athletics and has always been regarded as of delicate constitution. The main point about his personality is a quiet charm, a quality of appealing, inquisitive friendliness, always willing to listen, eager to sympathize, to like and to be liked.*

MARSDEN

(*Standing just inside the door, his tall, stooped figure leaning back against the books—nodding back at the* MAID *and smiling kindly*). I'll wait in here, Mary. (*His eyes follow her for a second, then return to gaze around the room slowly with an appreciative relish for the familiar significance of the books. He smiles affectionately and his amused voice recites the words with a rhetorical resonance.*) Sanctum Sanctorum! (*His voice takes on a monotonous musing quality, his eyes stare idly at his drifting thoughts*). How perfectly the Professor's unique haven! . . . (*He smiles.*) Primly classical . . . when New Englander meets Greek! . . . (*Looking at the books now.*) He hasn't added one book in years . . . how old was I when I first came here? . . . six . . . with my father . . . father . . . how dim his face has grown! . . . he wanted to speak to me just before he died . . . the hospital . . . smell of iodoform in the cool halls . . . hot summer . . . I bent down . . . his voice had withdrawn so far away . . . I couldn't understand him . . . what son can ever understand? . . . always too near, too soon, too distant or too late! . . . (*His face has become sad with a memory of the bewildered suffering of the adolescent boy he had been at the time of his father's death. Then he shakes his head, flinging off his thoughts, and makes himself walk about the room.*) What memories on such a smiling afternoon! . . . this pleasant old town after three months . . . I won't go to Europe again . . . couldn't write a line there . . . how answer the fierce question of all those dead and maimed? . . . too big a job for me! . . . (*He sighs —then self-mockingly.*) But back here . . . it is the interlude that gently questions . . . in this town dozing . . . decorous bodies moving with circumspection through the afternoons . . . their habits affectionately chronicled . . . an excuse for weaving amusing words . . . my novels . . . not of cosmic importance, hardly . . . (*Then self-reassuringly*) but there is a public to cherish them, evidently . . . and I can write! . . . more than one can say of these modern sex-yahoos! . . . I must start work tomorrow . . . I'd like to use the Professor in a novel sometime . . . and his wife . . . seems impossible she's been dead six years . . . so aggressively his wife! . . . poor Professor! now it's Nina who bosses him . . . but that's different . . . she has bossed me, too, ever since she was a baby . . . she's a woman now . . . known love and death . . . Gordon brought down in flames . . . two days before the armistice . . . what fiendish irony! . . . his wonderful athlete's body . . . her lover . . . charred bones in a cage of twisted steel . . . no wonder she broke down . . . Mother said she's become quite queer lately . . . Mother seemed jealous of my concern . . . why have I never fallen in love with Nina? . . . could I? . . . that way . . . used to dance her on my knee . . . sit her on my lap . . . even now she'd never think anything about it . . . but sometimes the scent of her hair and skin . . . like a dreamy drug . . . dreamy! . . . there's the rub! . . . all dreams with me! . . . my sex life among the phantoms! . . . (*He grins torturedly.*) Why? . . . oh, this digging in gets nowhere . . . to the devil with sex! . . . our impotent pose of today to beat the loud drum on fornication! . . . boasters . . . eunuchs parading with the phallus! . . . giving themselves away . . . whom do they fool? . . . not even themselves! . . . (*His face suddenly full of an intense pain and disgust.*) Ugh! . . . always that memory! . . . why can't I ever forget? . . . as sickeningly clear as if it were yesterday . . . prep school . . . Easter vacation . . . Fatty Boggs and Jack Fraser . . . that house of cheap vice . . . one dollar! . . . why did I go? . . . Jack, the dead game sport . . . how I admired him! . . . afraid of his taunts . . . he pointed to the Italian girl . . . "Take her!" . . . daring me . . . I went . . . miserably frightened . . . what a pig she was! . . . pretty vicious face under caked powder and rouge . . . surly and contemptuous . . . lumpy body . . . short legs and thick ankles . . . slums of Naples . . . "What you gawkin' about? Git a move on, kid" . . . kid! . . . I *was* only a kid! . . . sixteen . . . test of manhood . . . ashamed to face Jack again unless . . . fool! . . . I might have lied to him! . . . but I honestly thought that wench would feel humiliated if I . . . oh, stupid kid! . . . back at the hotel I waited till they were asleep . . . then sobbed . . . thinking of Mother . . . feeling I had defiled her . . . and myself . . . forever! . . . (*Mocking bitterly.*) "Nothing half so sweet in life as love's young dream," what? . . . (*He gets to his feet impatiently.*) Why does my mind always have to dwell on that? . . . too silly . . . no importance really . . . an incident such as any boy of my age . . .

(*He hears someone coming quickly from the right and turns expectantly.* PROFESSOR LEEDS *enters, a pleased relieved expression fighting the flurried worry on his face. He is a small, slender man of fifty-five, his hair gray, the top of his head bald. His face, prepossessing in spite of its too-small, overrefined features, is that of a retiring, studious nature. He has intelligent eyes and a smile that can be ironical. Temperamentally timid, his defense is an assumption of his complacent, superior manner of the classroom toward the world at large. This defense is strengthened by a natural tendency toward a prim provincialism where practical present-day considerations are concerned (though he is most liberal—even radical—in his tolerant understanding of the manners and morals of Greece and Imperial Rome!). This classroom poise of his, however, he cannot quite carry off outside the classroom. There is an unconvincing quality about it that leaves his larger audience—and particularly the* PROFESSOR *himself—subtly embarrassed. As* MARSDEN *is one of his old students, whom, in addition, he has known from childhood, he is perfectly at ease with him.)*

MARSDEN

(*Holding out his hand—with unmistakable liking*). Here I am again, Professor!

PROFESSOR LEEDS

(*Shaking his hand and patting him on the back—with genuine affection*). So glad to see you, Charlie! A surprise, too! We didn't expect you back so soon! (*He sits in his chair on the left of the table while* MARSDEN *sits in the rocker.*)

(*Looking away from* MARSDEN *a moment, his face now full of selfish relief as he thinks.*) Fortunate, his coming back . . . always calming influence on Nina . . .

MARSDEN

And I never dreamed of returning so soon. But Europe, Professor, is the big casualty they were afraid to set down on the list.

PROFESSOR LEEDS

(*His face clouding*). Yes, I suppose you found everything completely changed since before the war.

(*He thinks resentfully*). The war . . . Gordon! . . .

MARSDEN

Europe has "gone west"—(*he smiles whimsically*) to America, let's hope! (*Then frowningly.*) I couldn't stand it. There were millions sitting up with the corpse already, who had a family right to be there—(*Then matter-of-factly.*) I was wasting my time, too. I couldn't write a line. (*Then gaily.*) But where's Nina? I must see Nina!

PROFESSOR LEEDS

She'll be right in. She said she wanted to finish thinking something out—You'll find Nina changed, Charlie, greatly changed!

(*He sighs—thinking with a trace of guilty alarm*). The first thing she said at breakfast . . . "I dreamed of Gordon" . . . as if she wanted to taunt me! . . . how absurd! . . . her eyes positively glared! . . .

(*Suddenly blurting out resentfully*). She dreams about Gordon.

MARSDEN

(*Looking at him with amused surprise*). Well, I'd hardly call that a change, would you?

PROFESSOR LEEDS

(*Thinking, oblivious to this remark*). But I must constantly bear in mind that she's not herself . . . that she's a sick girl . . .

MARSDEN

(*Thinking*). The morning news of Gordon's death came . . . her face like gray putty . . . beauty gone . . . no face can afford intense grief . . . it's only later when sorrow . . .

(*With concern*). Just what do you mean by changed, Professor? Before I left she seemed to be coming out of that horrible numbed calm.

PROFESSOR LEEDS

(*Slowly and carefully*). Yes, she has played a lot of golf and tennis this summer, motored around with her friends, and even danced a good deal. And she eats with a ravenous appetite.

(*Thinking frightenedly*). Breakfast . . . "dreamed of Gordon" . . . what a look of hate for me in her eyes! . . .

MARSDEN

But that sounds splendid! When I left she wouldn't see anyone or go anywhere.

(*Thinking pityingly*). Wandering from room to room . . . her thin body and pale lost face . . . gutted, love-abandoned eyes! . . .

PROFESSOR LEEDS

Well, now she's gone to the opposite extreme! Sees everyone—bores, fools—as if she'd lost all discrimination or wish to discriminate. And she talks interminably, Charlie—intentional nonsense, one would say! Refuses to be serious! Jeers at everything!

MARSDEN

(*Consolingly*). Oh, that's all undoubtedly part of the effort she's making to forget.

PROFESSOR LEEDS

(*Absent-mindedly*). Yes.

(*Arguing with himself*). Shall I tell him? . . . no . . . it might sound silly . . . but it's terrible to be so alone in this . . . if Nina's mother had lived . . . my wife . . . dead! . . . and for a time I actually felt released! . . . wife! . . . help-meet! . . . now I need help! . . . no use! . . . she's gone! . . .

MARSDEN

(*Watching him—thinking with a condescending affection*). Good little man . . . he looks worried . . . always fussing about something . . . he must get on Nina's nerves. . . .

(*Reassuringly*). No girl could forget Gordon in a hurry, especially after the shock of his tragic death.

PROFESSOR LEEDS

(*Irritably*). I realize that.

(*Thinking resentfully*). Gordon . . . always Gordon with everyone! . . .

MARSDEN

By the way, I located the spot near Sedan where Gordon's machine fell. Nina asked me to, you know.

PROFESSOR LEEDS

(*Irritated—expostulatingly*). For heaven's sake, don't remind her! Give her a chance to forget if you want to see her well again. After all, Charlie, life must be lived and Nina can't live with a corpse forever! (*Trying to control his irritation and talk in an objective tone.*) You see, I'm trying to see things through clearly and unsentimentally. If you'll remember, I was as broken up as anyone over Gordon's death. I'd become so reconciled to Nina's love for him—although, as you know, I was opposed at first, and for fair reasons, I think, for the boy, for all his good looks and prowess in sport and his courses, really came of common people and had no money of his own except as he made a career for himself.

MARSDEN

(*A trifle defensively*). I'm sure he would have had a brilliant career.

PROFESSOR LEEDS

(*Impatiently*). No doubt. Although you must acknowledge, Charlie, that college heroes rarely shine brilliantly in after life. Unfortunately, the tendency to spoil them in the university is a poor training—

MARSDEN

But Gordon was absolutely unspoiled, I should say.

PROFESSOR LEEDS

(*Heatedly*). Don't misunderstand me, Charlie! I'd be the first to acknowledge—(*A bit pathetically.*) It isn't Gordon, Charlie. It's his memory, his ghost, you might call it, haunting Nina, whose influence I have come to dread because of the terrible change in her attitude toward me.

(*His face twitches as if he were on the verge of tears—he thinks desperately*). I've got to tell him . . . he will see that I acted for the best . . . that I was justified. . . .

(*He hesitates—then blurts out*). It may sound incredible, but Nina has begun to act as if she hated me!

MARSDEN

(*Startled*). Oh, come now!

PROFESSOR LEEDS

(*Insistently*). Absolutely! I haven't wanted to admit it. I've refused to believe it, until it's become too appallingly obvious in her whole attitude toward me! (*His voice trembles.*)

MARSDEN

(*Moved—expostulating*). Oh, now you're becoming morbid! Why, Nina has always idolized you! What possible reason—?

PROFESSOR LEEDS

(*Quickly*). I can answer that, I think. She has a reason. But why she should blame me when she must know I acted for the best—You probably don't know, but just before he sailed for the front Gordon wanted their marriage to take place, and Nina consented. In fact, from the insinuations she lets drop now, she must have been most eager, but at the time—However, I felt it was ill-advised and I took Gordon aside and pointed out to him that such a precipitate marriage would be unfair to Nina, and scarcely honorable on his part.

MARSDEN

(*Staring at him wonderingly*). You said that to Gordon?

(*Thinking cynically*). A shrewd move! . . . Gordon's proud spot, fairness and honor! . . . but was it honorable of you? . . .

PROFESSOR LEEDS

(*With a touch of asperity*). Yes, I said it, and I gave him my reason. There *was* the possibility he might be killed, in the flying service rather more than a possibility, which, needless to say, I did not point out, but which Gordon undoubtedly realized, poor boy! If he were killed, he would be leaving Nina a widow, perhaps with a baby, with no resources, since he was penniless, except what pension she might get from the government; and all this while she was still at an age when a girl, especially one of Nina's charm and beauty, should have all of life before her. Decidedly, I told him, in justice to Nina, they must wait until he had come back and begun to establish his position in the world. That was the square thing. And Gordon was quick to agree with me!

MARSDEN

(*Thinking*). The square thing! . . . but we must all be crooks where happiness is concerned! . . . steal or starve! . . .

(*Then rather ironically*). And so Gordon told Nina he'd suddenly realized it wouldn't be fair to her. But I gather he didn't tell her it was your scruple originally?

PROFESSOR LEEDS

No, I asked him to keep what I said strictly confidential.

MARSDEN

(*Thinking ironically*). Trusted to his honor again! . . . old fox! . . . poor Gordon! . . .

But Nina suspects now that you—?

PROFESSOR LEEDS

(*Startled*). Yes. That's exactly it. She knows in some queer way. And she acts toward me exactly as if she thought I had deliberately destroyed her happiness, that I had hoped for Gordon's death and been secretly overjoyed when the news came! (*His voice is shaking with emotion.*) And there you have it, Charlie—the whole absurd mess!

(*Thinking with a strident accusation*). And it's true, you contemptible . . . ! (*Then miserably defending himself.*) No! . . . I acted unselfishly . . . for her sake! . . .

MARSDEN

(*Wonderingly*). You don't mean to tell me she has accused you of all this?

PROFESSOR LEEDS

Oh, no, Charlie! Only by hints—looks—innuendos. She knows she has no real grounds, but in the present state of her mind the real and the unreal become confused—

MARSDEN

(*Thinking cynically*). As always in all minds . . . or how could men live? . . .

(*Soothingly*). That's just what you ought to bear in your mind—the state of hers—and not get so worked up over what I should say is a combination of imagination on both your parts. (*He gets to his feet as he hears voices from the right.*) Buck up! This must be Nina coming.

(*The* PROFESSOR *gets to his feet, hastily*

composing his features into his bland, cultured expression.)

MARSDEN

(*Thinking self-mockingly but a bit worried about himself*). My heart pounding! . . . seeing Nina again! . . . how sentimental . . . how she'd laugh if she knew! . . . and quite rightly . . . absurd for me to react as if I loved . . . that way . . . her dear old Charlie . . . ha! . . . (*He smiles with bitter self-mockery.*)

PROFESSOR LEEDS

(*Thinking worriedly*). I hope she won't make a scene . . . she's seemed on the verge all day . . . thank God, Charlie's like one of the family . . . but what a life for me! . . . with the opening of the new term only a few weeks off! . . . I can't do it . . . I'll have to call in a nerve specialist . . . but the last one did her no good . . . his outrageous fee . . . he can take it to court . . . I absolutely refuse . . . but if he should bring suit? . . . what a scandal . . . no, I'll have to pay . . . somehow . . . borrow . . . he has me in a corner, the robber! . . .

NINA

(*Enters and stands just inside the doorway looking directly at her father with defiant eyes, her face set in an expression of stubborn resolve. She is twenty, tall with broad square shoulders, slim strong hips and long beautifully developed legs—a fine athletic girl of the swimmer, tennis player, golfer type. Her straw-blond hair, framing her sun-burned face, is bobbed. Her face is striking, handsome rather than pretty, the bone structure prominent, the forehead high, the lips of her rather large mouth clearly modelled above the firm jaw. Her eyes are beautiful and bewildering, extraordinarily large and a deep greenish blue. Since* GORDON'S *death they have a quality of continually shuddering before some terrible enigma, of being wounded to their depths and made defiant and resentful by their pain. Her whole manner, the charged atmosphere she gives off, is totally at variance with her healthy outdoor physique. It is strained, nerve-racked, hectic, a terrible tension of will alone maintaining self-possession. She is dressed in smart sport clothes. Too preoccupied with her resolve to remember or see* MARSDEN, *she speaks directly to her father in a voice tensely cold and calm*). I have made up my mind, Father.

PROFESSOR LEEDS

(*Thinking distractedly*). What does she mean? . . . oh, God help me! . . .

(*Flustered—hastily*). Don't you see Charlie, Nina?

MARSDEN

(*Troubled—thinking*). She has changed . . . what has happened? . . .

(*He comes forward toward her—a bit embarrassed but affectionately using his pet name for her*). Hello, Nina Cara Nina! Are you trying to cut me dead, young lady?

NINA

(*Turning her eyes to* MARSDEN, *holding out her hand for him to shake, in her cool, preoccupied voice*). Hello, Charlie. (*Her eyes immediately return to her father.*) Listen, Father!

MARSDEN

(*Standing near her, concealing his chagrin*). That hurts! . . . I mean nothing! . . . but she's a sick girl . . . I must make allowance . . .

PROFESSOR LEEDS

(*Thinking distractedly*). That look in her eyes! . . . hate! . . .

(*With a silly giggle*). Really, Nina, you're absolutely rude! What has Charlie done?

NINA

(*In her cool tone*). Why, nothing. Nothing at all. (*She goes to him with a detached, friendly manner.*) Did I seem rude, Charlie? I didn't mean to be. (*She kisses him with a cool, friendly smile.*) Welcome home.

(*Thinking wearily*). What has Charlie done? . . . nothing . . . and never will . . . Charlie sits beside the fierce river, immaculately timid, cool and clothed, watching the burning, frozen naked swimmers drown at last. . . .

MARSDEN

(*Thinking torturedly*). Cold lips . . . the kiss of contempt! . . . for dear old Charlie! . . .

(*Forcing a good-natured laugh*). Rude? Not a bit! (*Banteringly*) As I've often reminded you, what can I expect when the first word you ever spoke in this world was an insult to me. "Dog" you said, looking right at me—at the age of one! (*He laughs. The* PROFESSOR *laughs nervously.* NINA *smiles perfunctorily.*)

NINA

(*Thinking wearily*). The fathers laugh at little daughter Nina . . . I must get away! . . . nice Charlie doggy . . . faithful . . . fetch and carry . . . bark softly in books at the deep night. . . .

PROFESSOR LEEDS

(*Thinking*). What is she thinking? . . . I can't stand living like this! . . .

(*Giggle gone to a twitching grin*). You are a cool one, Nina! You'd think you'd just seen Charlie yesterday!

NINA

(*Slowly—coolly and reflectively*). Well, the war is over. Coming back safe from Europe isn't such an unusual feat now, is it?

MARSDEN

(*Thinking bitterly*). A taunt . . . I didn't fight . . . physically unfit . . . not like Gordon . . . Gordon in flames . . . how she must resent my living! . . . thinking of me, scribbling in press bureau . . . louder and louder lies . . . drown the guns and the screams . . . deafen the world with lies . . . hired choir of liars! . . .

(*Forcing a joking tone*). Little you know the deadly risks I ran, Nina! If you'd eaten some of the food they gave me on my renovated transport, you'd shower me with congratulations!

(*The* PROFESSOR *forces a snicker.*)

NINA

(*Coolly*). Well, you're here, and that's that. (*Then suddenly expanding in a sweet, genuinely affectionate smile.*) And I *am* glad, Charlie, always glad you're here! You know that.

MARSDEN

(*Delighted and embarrassed*). I hope so, Nina!

NINA

(*Turning on her father—determinedly*). I must finish what I started to say, Father. I've thought it all out and decided that I simply must get away from here at once—or go crazy! And I'm going on the nine-forty tonight. (*She turns to* MARSDEN *with a quick smile.*) You'll have to help me pack, Charlie!

(*Thinking with weary relief*). Now that's said . . . I'm going . . . never come back . . . oh, how I loathe this room! . . .

MARSDEN

(*Thinking with alarm*). What's this? . . . going? . . . going to whom? . . .

PROFESSOR LEEDS

(*Thinking—terrified*). Going? . . . never come back to me? . . . no! . . .

(*Desperately putting on his prim severe manner toward an unruly pupil*). This is rather a sudden decision, isn't it? You haven't mentioned before that you were considering—in fact, you've led me to believe that you were quite contented here—that is, of course I mean for the time being, and I really think—

MARSDEN

(*Looking at* NINA*—thinking with alarm*). Going away to whom? . . .

(*Then watching the* PROFESSOR *with a pitying shudder.*) He's on the wrong tack with his professor's manner . . . her eyes seeing cruelly through him . . . with what terrible recognition! . . . God, never bless me with children! . . .

NINA

(*Thinking with weary scorn*). The Professor of Dead Languages is talking again . . . a dead man lectures on the past of living . . . since I was born I have been in his class, loving-attentive, pupil-daughter Nina . . . my ears numb with spiritless messages from the dead . . . dead words droning on . . . listening because he is my cultured father . . . a little more inclined to deafness than the rest (let me be just) because he is my father . . . father? . . . what is father? . . .

PROFESSOR LEEDS

(*Thinking—terrified*). I must talk her out of it! . . . find the right words! . . . oh, I know she won't hear me! . . . oh, wife, why did you die, you would have talked to her, she would have listened to you! . . .

(*Continuing in his professor's superior manner*)—and I really think, in justice to yourself above all, you ought to consider this step with great care before you definitely commit yourself. First and foremost, there is your health to be taken into consideration. You've been very ill, Nina, how perilously so perhaps you're not completely aware, but I assure you, and Charlie can corroborate my statement, that six months ago the doctors thought it might be years before—and yet, by staying home and resting and finding healthy outdoor recreation among your old friends, and keeping your mind occupied with the routine of managing the household—(*he forces a prim playful smile*) and managing me, I might add!—you have wonderfully improved and I think it most ill-advised in the hottest part of August, while you're really still a convalescent—

NINA

(*Thinking*). Talking! . . . his voice like a fatiguing dying tune droned on a beggar's organ . . . his words arising from the tomb of a soul in puffs of ashes . . . (*Torturedly.*) Ashes! . . . oh, Gordon, my dear one! . . . oh, lips on my lips, oh, strong arms around me, oh, spirit so brave and generous and gay! . . . ashes dissolving into mud! . . . mud and ashes! . . . that's all! . . . gone! . . . gone forever from me! . . .

PROFESSOR LEEDS

(*Thinking angrily*) Her eyes . . . I know that look . . . tender, loving . . . not for me . . . damn Gordon! . . . I'm glad he's dead! . . .

(*A touch of asperity in his voice*). And at a couple of hours' notice to leave everything in the air, as it were—(*Then judicially.*) No, Nina, frankly, I can't see it. You know I'd gladly consent to anything in the world to benefit you, but—surely, you can't have reflected!

NINA

(*Thinking torturedly*). Gordon darling, I must go away where I can think of you in silence! . . .

(*She turns on her father, her voice trembling with the effort to keep it in control—icily*). It's no use talking, Father. I *have* reflected and I am going!

PROFESSOR LEEDS

(*With asperity*). But I tell you it's quite impossible! I don't like to bring up the money consideration but I couldn't possibly afford—And how will you support yourself, if I may ask? Two years in the University, I am sorry to say, won't be much use to you when applying for a job. And even if you had completely recovered from your nervous breakdown, which it's obvious to anyone you haven't, then I most decidedly think you should finish out your science course and take your degree before you attempt—

(*Thinking desperately*). No use! . . . she doesn't hear . . . thinking of Gordon . . . she'll defy me . . .

NINA

(*Thinking desperately*). I must keep calm . . . I mustn't let go or I'll tell him everything . . . and I mustn't tell him . . . he's my father . . .

(*With the same cold calculating finality*). I've already had six months' training for a nurse. I will finish my training. There's a doctor I know at a sanitarium for crippled soldiers—a friend of Gordon's. I wrote to him and he answered that he'll gladly arrange it.

PROFESSOR LEEDS

(*Thinking furiously*). Gordon's friend . . . Gordon again! . . .

(*Severely*). You seriously mean to tell me you, in your condition, want to nurse in a soldiers' hospital! Absurd!

MARSDEN

(*Thinking with indignant revulsion*). Quite right, Professor! . . . her beauty . . . all those men . . . in their beds . . . it's too revolting! . . .

(*With a persuasive quizzing tone*). Yes, I must say I can't see you as a peace-time Florence Nightingale, Nina!

NINA

(*Coolly, struggling to keep control, ignoring these remarks*). So you see, Father, I've thought of everything and there's not the slightest reason to worry about me. And I've been teaching Mary how to take care of you. So you won't need me at all. You can go along as if nothing had happened—and really, nothing will have happened that hasn't already happened.

PROFESSOR LEEDS

Why, even the manner in which you address me—the tone you take—proves conclusively that you're not yourself!

NINA

(*Her voice becoming a bit uncanny, her thoughts breaking through*). No, I'm not myself yet. That's just it. Not all myself. But I've been becoming myself. And I must finish!

PROFESSOR LEEDS

(*With angry significance—to* MARSDEN). You hear her, Charlie? She's a sick girl!

NINA

(*Slowly and strangely*). I'm not sick. I'm too well. But they are sick and I must give my health to help them to live on, and to live on myself. (*With a sudden intensity in her tone.*) I must pay for my cowardly treachery to Gordon! You should understand this, Father, you who— (*She swallows hard, catching her breath.*)

(*Thinking desperately*). I'm beginning to tell him! . . . I mustn't! . . . he's my father! . . .

PROFESSOR LEEDS

(*In a panic of guilty fear, but defiantly*). What do you mean? I am afraid you're not responsible for what you're saying.

NINA

(*Again with the strange intensity*). I must pay! It's my plain duty! Gordon is dead! What use is my life to me or anyone? But I must make it of use—by giving it! (*Fiercely.*) I must learn to give myself, do you hear—give and give until I can make that gift of myself for a man's happiness without scruple, without fear, without joy except in his joy! When I've accomplished this I'll have found myself, I'll know how to start in living my own life again! (*Appealing to them with a desperate impatience.*) Don't you see? In the name of the commonest decency and honor, I owe it to Gordon!

PROFESSOR LEEDS

(*Sharply*). No, I can't see—nor anyone else!

(*Thinking savagely*). I hope Gordon is in hell! . . .

MARSDEN

(*Thinking*). Give herself? . . . can she mean her body? . . . beautiful body . . . to cripples? . . . for Gordon's sake? . . . damn Gordon! . . .

(*Coldly*). What do you mean, you owe it to Gordon, Nina?

PROFESSOR LEEDS

(*Bitterly*). Yes, how ridiculous! It seems to me when you gave him your love, he got more than he could ever have hoped—

NINA

(*With fierce self-contempt*). I gave him? What did I give him? It's what I didn't give! That last night before he sailed—in his arms until my body ached—kisses until my lips were numb—knowing all that night—something in me knowing he would die, that he would never kiss me again—knowing this so surely yet with my cowardly brain lying, no, he'll come back and marry you, you'll be happy ever after and feel his children at your breasts looking up with eyes so much like his, possessing eyes so happy in possessing you! (*Then violently.*) But Gordon never possessed me! I'm still Gordon's silly virgin! And Gordon is muddy ashes! And I've lost my happiness forever! All that last night I knew he wanted me. I knew it was only the honorable code-bound Gordon, who kept commanding from his brain, no, you mustn't, you must respect her, you must wait till you have a marriage license! (*She gives a mocking laugh.*)

PROFESSOR LEEDS

(*Shocked*). Nina! This is really going too far!

MARSDEN

(*Repelled. With a superior sneer*). Oh, come now, Nina! You've been reading books. Those don't sound like your thoughts.

NINA

(*Without looking at him, her eyes on her father's—intensely*). Gordon wanted me! I wanted Gordon! I should have made him take me! I knew he would die and I would have no children, that there would be no big Gordon or little Gordon left to me, that happiness was calling me, never to call again if I refused! And yet I did refuse! I didn't make him take me! I lost him forever! And now I am lonely and not pregnant with anything at all, but—but loathing! (*She hurls this last at her father—fiercely.*) Why did I refuse? What was that cowardly something in me that cried, no, you mustn't, what would your father say?

PROFESSOR LEEDS

(*Thinking—furiously*). What an animal! . . . and my daughter! . . . she doesn't get it from me! . . . was her mother like that? . . .

(*Distractedly*). Nina! I really can't listen!

NINA

(*Savagely*). And that's exactly what my father did say! Wait, he told Gordon! Wait for Nina till the war's over, and you've got a good job and can afford a marriage license!

PROFESSOR LEEDS

(*Crumbling pitifully*). Nina! I—!

MARSDEN

(*Flurriedly—going to him*). Don't take her seriously, Professor!

(*Thinking with nervous repulsion*). Nina has changed . . . all flesh now . . . lust . . . who would dream she was so sensual? . . . I wish I were out of this! . . . I wish I hadn't come here today! . . .

NINA

(*Coldly and deliberately*). Don't lie any more, Father! Today I've made up my mind to face things. I know now why Gordon suddenly dropped all idea of marriage before he left, how unfair to me he suddenly decided it would be! Unfair to me! Oh, that's humorous! To think I might have had happiness, Gordon, and now Gordon's child—(*Then directly accusing him.*) You told him it'd be unfair, you put him on his honor, didn't you?

PROFESSOR LEEDS

(*Collecting himself—woodenly*). Yes. I did it for your sake, Nina.

NINA

(*In the same voice as before*). It's too late for lies!

PROFESSOR LEEDS

(*Woodenly*). Let us say then that I *persuaded* myself it was for your sake. That may be true. You are young. You think one can live with truth. Very well. It is also true I was jealous of Gordon. I was alone and I wanted to keep your love. I hated him as one hates a thief one may not accuse nor punish. I did my best to prevent your marriage. I was glad when he died. There. Is that what you wish me to say?

NINA

Yes. Now I begin to forget I've hated you. You were braver than I, at least.

PROFESSOR LEEDS

I wanted to live comforted by your love until the end. In short, I am a man who happens to be your father. (*He hides his face in his hands and weeps softly.*) Forgive that man!

MARSDEN

(*Thinking timidly*). In short, forgive us our possessing as we forgive those who possessed before us . . . Mother must be wondering what keeps me so long . . . it's time for tea . . . I must go home . . .

NINA

(*Sadly*). Oh, I forgive you. But do you understand now that I must somehow find a way to give myself to Gordon still, that I must pay my debt and learn to forgive myself?

PROFESSOR LEEDS

Yes.

NINA

Mary will look after you.

PROFESSOR LEEDS

Mary will do very well, I'm sure.

MARSDEN

(*Thinking*). Nina has changed . . . this is no place for me . . . Mother is waiting tea. . . .

(*Then venturing on an uncertain tone of pleasantry*). Quite so, you two. But isn't this all nonsense? Nina will be back with us in a month, Professor, what with the depressing heat and humidity, and the more depressing halt and the lame!

PROFESSOR LEEDS

(*Sharply*). She must stay away until she gets well. This time I do speak for her sake.

NINA

I'll take the nine-forty. (*Turning to* MARSDEN—*with a sudden girlishness.*) Come on upstairs, Charlie, and help me pack! (*She grabs him by the hand and starts to pull him away.*)

MARSDEN

(*Shrugging his shoulders—confusedly*). Well—I don't understand this!

NINA

(*With a strange smile*). But some day I'll read it all in one of your books, Charlie, and it'll be so simple and easy to understand that I won't be able to recognize it, Charlie, let alone understand it! (*She laughs teasingly.*) Dear old Charlie!

MARSDEN

(*Thinking in agony*). God damn in hell . . . dear old Charlie! . . .

(*Then with a genial grin*). I'll have to propose, Nina, if you continue to be my severest critic! I'm a stickler for these little literary conventions, you know!

NINA

All right. Propose while we pack. (*She leads him off, right.*)

PROFESSOR LEEDS

(*Blows his nose, wipes his eyes, sighs, clears his throat, squares his shoulders, pulls his coat down in front, sets his tie straight, and starts to take a brisk turn about the room. His face is washed blandly clean of all emotion*). Three weeks now . . . new term . . . I will have to be looking over my notes . . . (*He looks out of window, front.*) Grass parched in the middle . . . Tom forgotten the sprinkler . . . careless . . . ah, there goes Mr. Davis of the bank . . . bank . . . my salary will go farther now . . . books I really need . . . all bosh two can live as cheaply as one . . . there are worse things than being a trained nurse . . . good background of discipline . . . she needs it . . . she may meet rich fellow there . . . mature . . . only students here for her . . . and their fathers never approve if they have anything. . . . (*He sits down with a forced sigh of peace.*) I am glad we had it out . . . his ghost will be gone now . . . no more Gordon, Gordon, Gordon, love and praise and tears, all for Gordon! . . . Mary will do very well by me . . . I will have more leisure and peace of mind . . . and Nina will come back home . . . when she is well again . . . the old Nina! . . . my little Nina! . . . she knows and she forgave me . . . she said so . . . said! . . . but could she really? . . . don't you imagine? . . . deep in her heart? . . . she still must hate? . . . oh, God! . . . I feel cold! . . . alone! . . . this home is abandoned! . . . the house is empty and full of death! . . . there is a pain about my heart! . . .

(*He calls hoarsely, getting to his feet*). Nina!

NINA'S VOICE

(*Her voice, fresh and girlish, calls from upstairs*). Yes, Father. Do you want me?

PROFESSOR LEEDS

(*Struggling with himself—goes to door and calls with affectionate blandness*). No. Never mind. Just wanted to remind you to call for a taxi in good time.

NINA'S VOICE

I won't forget.

PROFESSOR LEEDS

(*Looks at his watch*). Five-thirty just . . . nine-forty, the train . . . then . . . Nina no more! . . . four hours more . . . she'll be packing . . . then good-bye . . . a kiss . . . nothing more ever to say to each other . . . and I'll die in here some day . . . alone . . . gasp, cry out for help . . . the president will speak at the funeral . . . Nina will be here again . . . Nina in black . . . too late! . . .
(*He calls hoarsely*). Nina!
(*There is no answer.*)
In other room . . . doesn't hear . . . just as well . . . (*He turns to the bookcase and pulls out the first volume his hands come on and opens it at random and begins to read aloud sonorously like a child whistling to keep up his courage in the dark.*)

"Stetit unus in arcem
Erectus capitis victorque ad sidera mittit
Sidereos oculos propiusque adspectat Olympum
Inquiritque Iovem;" . . .

Curtain.

ACT TWO

SCENE: *The same as Scene One,* PROFESSOR LEEDS' *study. It is about nine o'clock of a night in early fall, over a year later. The appearance of the room is unchanged except that all the shades, of the color of pale flesh, are drawn down, giving the windows a suggestion of lifeless closed eyes and making the room seem more withdrawn from life than before. The reading lamp on the table is lit. Everything on the table, papers, pencils, pens, etc., is arranged in meticulous order.*

MARSDEN *is seated on the chair at center. He is dressed carefully in an English-made suit of blue serge so dark as to seem black, and which, combined with the gloomy brooding expression of his face, strongly suggests one in mourning. His tall, thin body sags wearily in the chair, his head is sunk forward, the chin almost touching his chest, his eyes stare sadly at nothing.*

MARSDEN

(*His thoughts at ebb, without emphasis, sluggish and melancholy*). Prophetic Professor! . . . I remember he once said . . . shortly after Nina went away . . . "some day, in here, . . . you'll find me" . . . did he foresee? . . . no . . . everything in life is so contemptuously accidental! . . . God's sneer at our self-importance! . . . (*Smiling grimly.*) Poor Professor! he was horribly lonely . . . tried to hide it . . . always telling you how beneficial the training at the hospital would be for her . . . poor old chap! . . . (*His voice grows husky and uncertain—he controls it—straightens himself.*) What time is it? . . . (*He takes out his watch mechanically and looks at it.*) Ten after nine. . . . Nina ought to be here. . . . (*Then with sudden bitterness.*) Will she feel any real grief over his death, I wonder? . . . I doubt it! . . . but why am I so resentful? . . . the two times I've visited the hospital she's been pleasant enough . . . pleasantly evasive! . . . perhaps she thought her father had sent me to spy on her . . . poor Professor! . . . at least she answered his letters . . . he used to show them to me . . . pathetically overjoyed . . . newsy, loveless scripts, telling nothing whatever about herself . . . well, she won't have to compose them any more . . . she never answered mine . . . she might at least have acknowledged them. . . . Mother thinks she's behaved quite inexcusably . . . (*Then jealously.*) I suppose every single damned inmate has fallen in love with her! . . . her eyes seemed cynical . . . sick with men . . . as though I'd looked into the eyes of a prostitute . . . not that I ever have . . . except that once . . . the dollar house . . . hers were like patent-leather buttons in a saucer of blue milk! . . . (*Getting up with a movement of impatience.*) The devil! . . . what beastly incidents our memories insist on cherishing! . . . the ugly and disgusting . . . the beautiful things we have to keep diaries to remember! . . . (*He smiles with a wry amusement for a second—then bitterly.*) That last night Nina was here . . . she talked so brazenly about giving herself . . . I wish I knew the truth of what she's been doing in that house full of men . . . particularly that self-important young ass of a doctor! . . . Gordon's friend! . . . (*He frowns at himself, determinedly puts an end to his train of thought and comes and sits down again in the chair—in sneering, conversational tones as if he were this time actually addressing another person.*) Really, it's hardly a decent time, is it, for that kind of speculation . . . with her father lying dead upstairs? . . . (*A silence as if he had respectably squelched himself—then he pulls out his watch mechanically and stares at it. As he does so a noise of a car is heard approaching, stopping at the curb beyond the garden. He jumps to his feet and starts to go to door—then hesitates confusedly.*) No, let Mary go . . . I wouldn't know what to do . . . take her in my arms? . . . kiss her? . . . right now? . . . or wait until she? . . . (*A bell rings insistently from the back of the house. From the front voices are heard, first* NINA'S, *then a man's.* MARSDEN *starts, his face suddenly angry and dejected.*) Someone with her! . . . a man! . . . I thought she'd be alone! . . . (MARY *is heard shuffling to the front door which is opened. Immediately, as* MARY *sees* NINA, *she breaks down and there is the sound of her uncontrolled sobbing and choking, incoherent words drowning out* NINA'S *voice, soothing her.*)

NINA

(*As* MARY'S *grief subsides a trifle, her voice is heard, flat and toneless*). Isn't Mr. Marsden here, Mary? (*She calls.*) Charlie!

MARSDEN

(*Confused—huskily*). In here—I'm in the study, Nina. (*He moves uncertainly toward the door.*)

NINA

(*Comes in and stands just inside the doorway. She is dressed in a nurse's uniform with cap, a raglan coat over it. She appears older than in the previous scene; her face is pale and much thinner, her cheek bones stand out, her mouth is taut in hard lines of a cynical scorn. Her eyes try to armor her wounded spirit with a defensive stare of disillusionment. Her training has also tended to coarsen her fiber a trifle, to make her insensitive to suffering, to give her the nurse's professionally callous attitude. In her fight to regain control of her nerves she has over-striven after the cool and efficient poise, but she is really in a more highly strung disorganized state than ever, although she is now more capable of suppressing and concealing it. She remains strikingly handsome and her physical appeal is enhanced by her pallor and the mysterious suggestion about her of hidden experience. She stares at* MARSDEN *blankly and speaks in queer flat tones*). Hello, Charlie. He's dead, Mary says.

MARSDEN

(*Nodding his head several times—stupidly*). Yes.

NINA

(*In same tones*). It's too bad. I brought Doctor Darrell. I thought there might be a chance. (*She pauses and looks about the room.*)

(*Thinking confusedly*). His books . . . his chair . . . he always sat there . . . there's his table . . . little Nina was never allowed to touch anything . . . she used to sit on his lap . . . cuddle against him . . . dreaming into the dark beyond the windows . . . warm in his arms before the fireplace . . . dreams like sparks soaring up to die in the cold dark . . . warm in his love, safe-drifting into sleep . . . "Daddy's girl, aren't you?" . . . (*She looks around and then up and down.*) His home . . . my home . . . he was my father . . . he's dead . . . (*She shakes her head.*) Yes, I hear you, little Nina, but I don't understand one word of it. . . . (*She smiles with a cynical self-contempt.*) I'm sorry, Father! . . . you see you've been dead for me a long time . . . when Gordon died, all men died . . . what did you feel for me then? . . . nothing . . . and now I feel nothing . . . it's too bad . . .

MARSDEN

(*Thinking woundedly*). I hoped she would throw herself in my arms . . . weeping . . . hide her face on my shoulder . . . "Oh, Charlie, you're all I've got left in the world . . ." (*Then angrily.*) Why did she have to bring that Darrell with her?

NINA

(*Flatly*). When I said good-bye that night I had a premonition I'd never see him again.

MARSDEN

(*Glad of this opening for moral indignation*). You've never tried to see him, Nina! (*Then overcome by disgust with himself —contritely.*) Forgive me! It was rotten of me to say that!

NINA

(*Shaking her head—flatly*). I didn't want him to see what he would have thought was me. (*Ironically.*) That's the other side of it you couldn't dissect into words from here, Charlie! (*Then suddenly asking a necessary question in her nurse's cool, efficient tones.*) Is he upstairs? (MARSDEN *nods stupidly.*) I'll take Ned up. I might as well. (*She turns and walks out briskly.*)

MARSDEN

(*Staring after her—dully*). That isn't Nina. . . . (*Indignantly.*) They've killed her soul down there! . . . (*Tears come to his eyes suddenly and he pulls out his handkerchief and wipes them, muttering huskily.*) Poor old Professor! . . . (*Then suddenly jeering at himself.*) For God's sake, stop acting! . . . it isn't the Professor! . . . dear old Charlie is crying because she didn't weep on his shoulder . . . as he had hoped! . . .

(*He laughs harshly—then suddenly sees a man outside the doorway and stares—then calls sharply*). Who's that?

EVANS

(*His voice embarrassed and hesitating comes from the hall*). It's all right. (*He appears in the doorway, grinning bashfully.*) It's me—I, I mean—Miss Leeds told me to come in here. (*He stretches out his hand awkwardly.*) Guess you don't remember me, Mr. Marsden. Miss Leeds introduced us one day at the hospital. You were leaving just as I came in. Evans is my name.

MARSDEN

(*Who has been regarding him with waning resentment, forces a cordial smile and shakes hands*). Oh, yes. At first I couldn't place you.

EVANS

(*Awkwardly*). I sort of feel I'm butting in.

MARSDEN

(*Beginning to be taken by his likable boyish quality*). Not at all. Sit down. (*He sits in the rocker at center as* EVANS *goes to the bench at right.*)

(EVANS *sits uncomfortably hunched forward, twiddling his hat in his hands. He is above the medium height, very blond, with guileless, diffident blue eyes, his figure inclined to immature lumbering outlines. His face is fresh and red-cheeked, handsome in a boyish fashion. His manner is bashful with women or older men, coltishly playful with his friends. There is a lack of self-confidence, a lost and strayed appealing air about him, yet with a hint of some unawakened obstinate force beneath his apparent weakness. Although he is twenty-five and has been out of college three years, he still wears the latest in collegiate clothes and as he looks younger than he is, he is always mistaken for an undergraduate and likes to be. It keeps him placed in life for himself.*)

MARSDEN

(*Studying him keenly—amused*). This is certainly no giant intellect . . . overgrown boy . . . likable quality though . . .

EVANS

(*Uneasy under* MARSDEN'S *eyes*). Giving me the once-over . . . seems like good egg . . . Nina says he is . . . suppose I ought to say something about his books, but I can't even remember a title of one . . .

(*He suddenly blurts out*). You've known Nina—Miss Leeds—ever since she was a kid, haven't you?

MARSDEN

(*A bit shortly*). Yes. How long have you known her?

EVANS

Well—really only since she's been at the hospital, although I met her once years ago at a Prom with Gordon Shaw.

MARSDEN

(*Indifferently*). Oh, you knew Gordon?

EVANS

(*Proudly*). Sure thing! I was in his class! (*With admiration amounting to hero-worship.*) He sure was a wonder, wasn't he?

MARSDEN

(*Cynically*). Gordon über alles and forever! . . . I begin to appreciate the Professor's viewpoint . . .

(*Casually*). A fine boy! Did you know him well?

EVANS

No. The crowd he went with were mostly fellows who were good at sports—and I always was a dud. (*Forcing a smile.*) I was always one of the first to get bounced off the squad in any sport. (*Then with a flash of humble pride.*) But I never quit trying, anyway!

MARSDEN

(*Consolingly*). Well, the sport hero usually doesn't star after college.

EVANS

Gordon did! (*Eagerly—with intense admiration*). In the war! He was an ace! And he always fought just as cleanly as he'd played football! Even the Huns respected him!

MARSDEN

(*Thinking cynically*). This Gordon worshipper must be the apple of Nina's eye! . . .

(*Casually*). Were you in the army?

EVANS

(*Shamefacedly*). Yes—infantry—but I never got to the front—never saw anything exciting.

(*Thinking glumly*). Won't tell him I tried for flying service . . . wanted to get in Gordon's outfit . . . couldn't make the physical exam. . . . never made anything I wanted . . . suppose I'll lose out with Nina, too . . . (*Then rallying himself.*) Hey, you! . . . what's the matter with you? . . . don't quit! . . .

MARSDEN

(*Who has been staring at him inquisitively*). How did you happen to come out here tonight?

EVANS

I was calling on Nina when your wire came. Ned thought I better come along, too—might be of some use.

MARSDEN

(*Frowning*). You mean Doctor Darrell? (EVANS *nods.*) Is he a close friend of yours?

EVANS

(*Hesitatingly*). Well, sort of. Roomed in the same dorm with me at college. He was a senior when I was a freshman. Used to help me along in lots of ways. Took pity on me, I was so green. Then about a year ago when I went to the hospital to visit a fellow who'd been in my outfit I ran into him again. (*Then with a grin.*) But I wouldn't say Ned was close to anyone. He's a dyed-in-the-wool doc. He's only close to whatever's the matter with you! (*He chuckles—then hastily.*) But don't get me wrong about him. He's the best egg ever! You know him, don't you?

MARSDEN

(*Stiffly*). Barely. Nina introduced us once. (*Thinking bitterly*). He's upstairs alone with her . . . I hoped it would be I who . . .

EVANS

Don't want him to get the wrong idea of Ned . . . Ned's my best friend . . . doing all he can to help me with Nina . . . he thinks she'll marry me in the end . . . God, if she only would! . . . I wouldn't expect her to love me at first . . . be happy only to take care of her . . . cook her breakfast . . . bring it up to her in bed . . . tuck the pillows behind her . . . comb her hair for her . . . I'd be happy just to kiss her hair! . . .

MARSDEN

(*Agitated—thinking suspiciously*). What are Darrell's relations with Nina? . . . close to what's the matter with her? . . . damned thoughts! . . . why should I care? . . . I'll ask this Evans . . . pump him while I have a chance . . .

(*With forced indifference*). Is your friend, the Doctor, "close" to Miss Leeds? She's had quite a lot the matter with her since her breakdown, if that's what interests him! (*He smiles casually.*)

EVANS

(*Gives a start, awakening from his dream*). Oh—er—yes. He's always trying to bully her into taking better care of herself, but she only laughs at him. (*Soberly.*) It'd be much better if she'd take his advice.

MARSDEN

(*Suspiciously*). No doubt.

EVANS

(*Pronounces with boyish solemnity*). She isn't herself, Mr. Marsden. And I think nursing all those poor guys keeps the war before her when she ought to forget it. She ought to give up nursing and be nursed for a change, that's my idea.

MARSDEN

(*Struck by this—eagerly*). Exactly my opinion.

(*Thinking*). If she'd settle down here . . . I could come over every day . . . I'd nurse her . . . Mother home . . . Nina here . . . how I could work then! . . .

EVANS

(*Thinking*). He certainly seems all for me . . . so far! . . . (*Then in a sudden flurry.*) Shall I tell him? . . . he'll be like her guardian now . . . I've got to know how he stands . . .

(*He starts with a solemn earnestness*). Mr. Marsden, I—there's something I ought to tell you, I think. You see, Nina's talked a lot about you. I know how much she thinks of you. And now her old man—(*he hesitates in confusion*) I mean, her father's dead—

MARSDEN

(*In a sort of panic—thinking*). What's this? . . . proposal? . . . in form? . . . for her hand? . . . to me? . . . Father Charlie now, eh? . . . ha! . . . God, what a fool! . . . does he imagine she'd ever love him? . . . but she might . . . not bad-looking . . . likable, innocent . . . something to mother . . .

EVANS

(*Blundering on regardless now*). I know it's hardly the proper time—

MARSDEN

(*Interrupting—dryly*). Perhaps I can anticipate. You want to tell me you're in love with Nina?

EVANS

Yes, sir, and I've asked her to marry me.

MARSDEN

What did she say?

EVANS

(*Sheepishly*). Nothing. She just smiled.

MARSDEN

(*With relief*). Ah. (*Then harshly.*) Well, what could you expect? Surely you must know she still loves Gordon?

EVANS

(*Manfully*). Sure I know it—and I admire her for it! Most girls forget too easily. She ought to love Gordon for a long time yet. And I know I'm an awful wash-out compared to him—but I love her as much as he did, or anyone could! And I'll work my way up for her—I know I can!—so I can give her everything she wants. And I wouldn't ask for anything in return except the right to take care of her. (*Blurts out confusedly.*) I never think of her—that way—she's too beautiful and wonderful—not that I don't hope she'd come to love me in time—

MARSDEN

(*Sharply*). And just what do you expect me to do about all this?

EVANS

(*Taken aback*). Why—er—nothing, sir. I just thought you ought to know. (*Sheepishly he glances up at ceiling, then down at floor, twiddling his hat.*)

MARSDEN

(*Thinking—at first with a grudging appreciation and envy*). He thinks he means that . . . pure love! . . . it's easy to talk . . . he doesn't know life . . . but he might be good for Nina . . . if she were married to this simpleton would she be faithful? . . . and then I? . . . what a vile thought! . . . I don't mean that! . . .

(*Then forcing a kindly tone*). You see, there's really nothing I can do about it. (*With a smile.*) If Nina will, she will—and if she won't, she won't. But I can wish you good luck.

EVANS

(*Immediately all boyish gratitude*). Thanks! That's darn fine of you, Mr. Marsden!

MARSDEN

But I think we'd better let the subject drop, don't you? We're forgetting that her father—

EVANS

(*Guiltily embarrassed*). Yes—sure—I'm a damn fool! Excuse me!

(*There is the noise of steps from the hall and* DOCTOR DARRELL *enters. He is twenty-seven, short, dark, wiry, his movements rapid and sure, his manner cool and observant, his dark eyes analytical. His head is handsome and intelligent. There is a quality about him, provoking and disturbing to women, of intense passion which he has rigidly trained himself to control and set free only for the objective satisfaction of studying his own and their reactions; and so he has come to consider himself as immune to love through his scientific understanding of its real sexual nature. He sees* EVANS *and* MARSDEN, *nods at* MARSDEN *silently, who returns it coldly, goes to the table and taking a prescription pad from his pocket, hastily scratches on it.*)

MARSDEN

(*Thinking sneeringly*). Amusing, these young doctors! . . . perspire with the effort to appear cool! . . . writing a prescription . . . cough medicine for the corpse, perhaps! . . . good-looking? . . . more or less . . . attractive to women, I dare say. . . .

DARRELL

(*Tears it off—hands it to* EVANS). Here, Sam. Run along up the street and get this filled.

EVANS

(*With relief*). Sure. Glad of the chance for a walk. (*He goes out, rear.*)

DARRELL

(*Turning to* MARSDEN). It's for Nina. She's got to get some sleep tonight.

(*He sits down abruptly in the chair at center.* MARSDEN *unconsciously takes the* PROFESSOR'S *place behind the table. The two men stare at each other for a moment,* DARRELL *with a frank probing, examining look that ruffles* MARSDEN *and makes him all the more re-*

sentful toward him). This Marsden doesn't like me . . . that's evident . . . but he interests me . . . read his books . . . wanted to know his bearing on Nina's case . . . his novels just well-written surface . . . no depth, no digging underneath . . . why? . . . has the talent but doesn't dare . . . afraid he'll meet himself somewhere . . . one of those poor devils who spend their lives trying not to discover which sex they belong to! . . .

MARSDEN

Giving me the fishy, diagnosing eye they practice at medical school . . . like freshmen from Ioway cultivating broad A's at Harvard! . . . what is his specialty? . . . neurologist, I think . . . I hope not psychoanalyst . . . a lot to account for, Herr Freud! . . . punishment to fit his crimes, be forced to listen eternally during breakfast while innumerable plain ones tell him dreams about snakes . . . pah, what an easy cure-all! . . . sex the philosopher's stone . . . "O Oedipus, O my king! The world is adopting you!" . . .

DARRELL

Must pitch into him about Nina . . . have to have his help . . . damn little time to convince him . . . he's the kind you have to explode a bomb under to get them to move . . . but not too big a bomb . . . they blow to pieces easily . . . (*Brusquely*). Nina's gone to pot again! Not that her father's death is a shock in the usual sense of grief. I wish to God it were! No, it's a shock because it's finally convinced her she can't feel anything any more. That's what she's doing upstairs now—trying to goad herself into feeling something!

MARSDEN

(*Resentfully*). I think you're mistaken. She loved her father—

DARRELL

(*Shortly and dryly*). We can't waste time being sentimental, Marsden! She'll be down any minute, and I've got a lot to talk over with you. (*As* MARSDEN *seems again about to protest.*) Nina has a real affection for you and I imagine you have for her. Then you'll want as much as I do to get her straightened out. She's a corking girl. She ought to have every chance for a happy life. (*Then sharply driving his words in.*) But the way she's conditioned now, there's no chance. She's piled on too many destructive experiences. A few more and she'll dive for the gutter just to get the security that comes from knowing she's touched bottom and there's no farther to go!

MARSDEN

(*Revolted and angry, half-springs to his feet*). Look here, Darrell, I'll be damned if I'll listen to such a ridiculous statement!

DARRELL

(*Curtly—with authority*). How do you know it's ridiculous? What do you know of Nina since she left home? But she hadn't been nursing with us three days before I saw she really ought to be a patient; and ever since then I've studied her case. So I think it's up to you to listen.

MARSDEN

(*Freezingly*). I'm listening.

(*With apprehensive terror*). Gutter . . . has she . . . I wish he wouldn't tell me! . . .

DARRELL

(*Thinking*). How much need I tell him? . . . can't tell him the raw truth about her promiscuity . . . he isn't built to face reality . . . no writer is outside of his books . . . have to tone it down for him . . . but not too much! . . . Nina has been giving way more and more to a morbid longing for martyrdom. The reason for it is obvious. Gordon went away without—well, let's say marrying her. The war killed him. She was left suspended. Then she began to blame herself and to want to sacrifice herself and at the same time give happiness to various fellow war-victims by pretending to love them. It's a pretty idea but it hasn't worked out. Nina's a bad actress. She hasn't convinced the men of her love—or herself of her good intentions. And each experience of this kind has only left her more a prey to a guilty conscience than before and more determined to punish herself!

MARSDEN

(*Thinking*). What does he mean? . . . how far did she? . . . how many? . . . (*Coldly and sneeringly*). May I ask on what specific actions of hers this theory of yours is based?

DARRELL

(*Coldly in turn*). On her evident craving to make an exhibition of kissing, necking, petting—whatever you call it—spooning in general—with any patient in the institution who got a case on her!

(*Ironically—thinking*). Spooning! . . . rather a mild word for her affairs . . . but strong enough for this ladylike soul. . . .

MARSDEN

(*Bitterly*). He's lying! . . . what's he trying to hide? . . . was he one of them? . . . her lover? . . . I must get her away from him . . . get her to marry Evans! . . .

(*With authority*). Then she mustn't go back to your hospital, that's certain!

DARRELL

(*Quickly*). You're quite right. And that brings me to what I want you to urge her to do.

MARSDEN

(*Thinking suspiciously*). He doesn't want her back . . . I must have been wrong . . . but there might be many reasons why he'd wish to get rid of her . . .

(*Coldly*). I think you exaggerate my influence.

DARRELL

(*Eagerly*). Not a bit. You're the last link connecting her with the girl she used to be before Gordon's death. You're closely associated in her mind with that period of happy security, of health and peace of mind. I know that from the way she talks about you. You're the only person she still respects—and really loves. (*As* MARSDEN *starts guiltily and glances at him in confusion—with a laugh.*) Oh, you needn't look frightened. I mean the sort of love she'd feel for an uncle.

MARSDEN

(*Thinking in agony*). Frightened? . . . was I? . . . only person she loves . . . and then he said "love she'd feel for an uncle" . . . Uncle Charlie now! . . . God damn him! . . .

DARRELL

(*Eyeing him*). Looks damnably upset . . . wants to evade all responsibility for her, I suppose . . . he's that kind . . . all the better! . . . he'll be only too anxious to get her safely married. . . .

(*Bluntly*). And that's why I've done all this talking. You've got to help snap her out of this.

MARSDEN

(*Bitterly*). And how, if I may ask?

DARRELL

There's only one way I can see. Get her to marry Sam Evans.

MARSDEN

(*Astonished*). Evans? (*He makes a silly gesture toward the door.*)

(*Thinking confusedly*). Wrong again . . . why does he want her married to . . . it's some trick. . . .

DARRELL

Yes, Evans. He's in love with her. And it's one of those unselfish loves you read about. And she is fond of him. In a maternal way, of course—but that's just what she needs now, someone she cares about to mother and boss and keep her occupied. And still more important, this would give her a chance to have children. She's got to find normal outlets for her craving for sacrifice. She needs normal love objects for the emotional life Gordon's death blocked up in her. Now marrying Sam ought to do the trick. Ought to. Naturally, no one can say for certain. But I think his unselfish love, combined with her real liking for him, will gradually give her back a sense of security and a feeling of being worth something to life again, and once she's got that, she'll be saved! (*He has spoken with persuasive feeling. He asks anxiously.*) Doesn't that seem good sense to you?

MARSDEN

(*Suspicious—dryly non-committal*). I'm sorry but I'm in no position to say. I don't know anything about Evans, for one thing.

DARRELL

(*Emphatically*). Well, I do. He's a fine healthy boy, clean and unspoiled. You can take my word for that. And I'm convinced he's got the right stuff in him to succeed, once he grows up and buckles down to work. He's only a big kid now, but all he needs is a little self-confidence and a sense of responsibility. He's holding down a fair job, too, considering he's just started in the advertising game—enough to keep them living. (*With a slight smile.*) I'm prescribing for Sam, too, when I boost this wedding.

MARSDEN

(*His snobbery coming out*). Do you know his family—what sort of people?—

DARRELL

(*Bitingly*). I'm not acquainted with their social qualifications, if that's what you mean! They're upstate country folks—fruit growers and farmers, well off, I believe. Simple, healthy people, I'm sure of that although I've never met them.

MARSDEN

(*A bit shamefacedly—changing the subject hastily*). Have you suggested this match to Nina?

DARRELL

Yes, a good many times lately in a half-joking way. If I were serious she wouldn't listen, she'd say I was prescribing. But I think what I've said has planted it in her mind as a possibility.

MARSDEN

(*Thinking suspiciously*). Is this Doctor her lover? . . . trying to pull the wool over my eyes? . . . use me to arrange a convenient triangle for him? . . .

(*Harshly—but trying to force a joking tone*). Do you know what I'm inclined to suspect, Doctor? That you may be in love with Nina yourself!

DARRELL

(*Astonished*). The deuce you do! What in the devil makes you think that? Not that any man mightn't fall in love with Nina. Most of them do. But I didn't happen to. And what's more I never could. In my mind she always belongs to Gordon. It's probably a reflection of her own silly fixed idea about him. (*Suddenly, dryly and harshly.*) And I couldn't share a woman—even with a ghost!

(*Thinking cynically*). Not to mention the living who have had her! . . . Sam doesn't know about them . . . and I'll bet he couldn't believe it of her even if she confessed! . . .

MARSDEN

(*Thinking baffledly*). Wrong again! . . . he isn't lying . . . but I feel he's hiding something . . . why does he speak so resentfully of Gordon's memory? . . . why do I sympathize? . . .

(*In a strange mocking ironic tone*). I can quite appreciate your feeling about Gordon. I wouldn't care to share with a ghost-lover myself. That species of dead is so invulnerably alive! Even a doctor couldn't kill one, eh? (*He forces a laugh—then in a friendly confidential tone.*) Gordon is too egregious for a ghost. That was the way Nina's father felt about him, too. (*Suddenly reminded of the dead man—in penitently sad tones.*) You didn't know her father, did you? A charming old fellow!

DARRELL

(*Hearing a noise from the hall—warningly*). Sstt!

(NINA *enters slowly. She looks from one to the other with a queer, quick, inquisitive stare, but her face is a pale expressionless mask drained of all emotional response to human contacts. It is as if her eyes were acting on their own account as restless, prying, recording instruments. The two men have risen and stare at her anxiously.* DARRELL *moves back and to one side until he is standing in relatively the same place as* MARSDEN *had occupied in the previous scene while* MARSDEN *is in her father's place and she stops where she had been. There is a pause. Then just as each of the men is about to speak, she answers as if they had asked a question.)*

NINA

(*In a queer flat voice*). Yes, he's dead—my father—whose passion created me—who began me—he is ended. There is only his end living—his death. It lives now to draw nearer me, to draw me nearer, to become my end! (*Then with a strange twisted smile.*) How we poor monkeys hide from ourselves behind the sounds called words!

MARSDEN

(*Thinking frightenedly*). How terrible she is! . . . who is she? . . . not my Nina! . . .

(*As if to reassure himself—timidly*). Nina!

(DARRELL *makes an impatient gesture for him to let her go on. What she is saying interests him and he feels talking it out will do her good. She looks at* MARSDEN *for a moment startledly as if she couldn't recognize him.*)

NINA

What? (*Then placing him—with real affection that is like a galling goad to him.*) Dear old Charlie!

MARSDEN

Dear damned Charlie! . . . She loves to torture! . . .

(*Then forcing a smile—soothingly*). Yes, Nina Cara Nina! Right here!

NINA

(*Forcing a smile*). You look frightened, Charlie. Do I seem queer? It's because I've suddenly seen the lies in the sounds called words. You know—grief, sorrow, love, father—those sounds our lips make and our hands write. You ought to know what I mean. You work with them. Have you written another novel lately? But, stop to think, you're just the one who couldn't know what I mean. With you the lies have become the only truthful things. And I suppose that's the logical conclusion to the whole evasive mess, isn't it? Do you understand me, Charlie? Say lie—(*She says it, drawing it out.*) L-i-i-e! Now say life. L-i-i-f-e! You see! Life is just a long drawn out lie with a sniffling sigh at the end! (*She laughs.*)

MARSDEN

(*In strange agony*). She's hard! . . . like a whore! . . . tearing your heart with dirty finger nails! . . . my Nina! . . . cruel bitch! . . . some day I won't bear it! . . . I'll scream out the truth about every woman! . . . no kinder at heart than dollar tarts! . . . (*Then in a passion of remorse.*) Forgive me, Mother! . . . I didn't mean all! . . .

DARRELL

(*A bit worried himself now—persuasively*). Why not sit down, Nina, and let us two gentlemen sit down?

NINA

(*Smiling at him swiftly and mechanically*). Oh, all right, Ned. (*She sits at center. He comes and sits on the bench.* MARSDEN *sits by the table. She continues sarcastically.*) Are you prescribing for me again, Ned? This is my pet doctor, Charlie. He couldn't be happy in heaven unless God called him in because He'd caught something! Did you ever know a young scientist, Charlie? He believes if you pick a lie to pieces, the pieces are the truth! I like him because he's so inhuman. But once he kissed me—in a moment of carnal weakness! I was as startled as if a mummy had done it! And then he looked so disgusted with himself! I had to laugh! (*She smiles at him with a pitying scorn.*)

DARRELL

(*Good-naturedly smiling*). That's right! Rub it in!

(*Ruffled but amused in spite of it*). I'd forgotten about that kiss . . . I was sore at myself afterwards . . . she was so damned indifferent! . . .

NINA

(*Wanderingly*). Do you know what I was doing upstairs? I was trying to pray. I tried hard to pray to the modern science God. I thought of a million light years to a spiral nebula—one other universe among innumerable others. But how could that God care about our trifling misery of death-born-of-birth? I couldn't believe in Him, and I wouldn't if I could! I'd rather imitate His indifference and prove I had that one trait at least in common!

MARSDEN

(*Worriedly*). Nina, why don't you lie down?

NINA

(*Jeeringly*). Oh, let me talk, Charlie! They're only words, remember! So many many words have jammed up into thoughts in my poor head! You'd better let them overflow or they'll burst the dam! I wanted to believe in any God at any price—a heap of stones, a mud image, a drawing on a wall, a bird, a fish, a snake, a baboon—or even a good man preaching the simple platitudes of truth, those Gospel words we love the sound of but whose meaning we pass on to spooks to live by!

MARSDEN

(*Again—half-rising—frightenedly*). Nina! You ought to stop talking. You'll work yourself into—(*He glances angrily at* DARRELL *as if demanding that, as a doctor, he do something.*)

NINA

(*With bitter hopelessness*). Oh, all right!

DARRELL

(*Answering his look—thinking*). You poor fool! . . . it'll do her good to talk this out of her system . . . and then it'll be up to you to bring her around to Sam . . .

(*Starts toward the door*). Think I'll go out and stretch my legs.

MARSDEN

(*Thinking—in a panic*). I don't want to be alone with her! . . . I don't know her! . . . I'm afraid! . . .

(*Protestingly*). Well—but—hold on—I'm sure Nina would rather—

NINA

(*Dully*). Let him go. I've said everything I can say—to him. I want to talk to you, Charlie. (DARRELL *goes out noiselessly with a meaning look at* MARSDEN—*a pause.*)

MARSDEN

(*Thinking tremblingly*). Here . . . now . . . what I hoped . . . she and I alone . . . she will cry . . . I will comfort her . . . why am I so afraid? . . . whom do I fear? . . . is it she? . . . or I? . . .

NINA

(*Suddenly, with pity yet with scorn*). Why have you always been so timid, Charlie? Why are you always afraid? What are you afraid of?

MARSDEN

(*Thinking in a panic*). She sneaked into my soul to spy! . . . (*Then boldly.*) Well then, a little truth for once in a way! . . .

(*Timidly*). I'm afraid of—of life, Nina.

NINA

(*Nodding slowly*). I know. (*After a pause—queerly.*) The mistake began when God was created in a male image. Of course, women would see Him that way, but men should have been gentlemen enough, remembering their mothers, to make God a woman! But the God of Gods—the Boss—has always been a man. That makes life so perverted, and death so unnatural. We should have imagined life as created in the birth-pain of God the Mother. Then we would understand why we, Her children, have inherited pain, for we would know that our life's rhythm beats from Her great heart, torn with the agony of love and birth. And we would feel that death meant reunion with Her, a passing back into Her substance, blood of Her blood again, peace of Her peace! (MARSDEN *has been listening to her fascinatedly. She gives a strange little laugh.*) Now wouldn't that be more logical and satisfying than having God a male whose chest thunders with egotism and is too hard for tired heads and thoroughly comfortless? Wouldn't it, Charlie?

MARSDEN

(*With a strange passionate eagerness*). Yes! It would, indeed! It would, Nina!

NINA

(*Suddenly jumping to her feet and going to him—with a horrible moaning desolation*). Oh, God, Charlie, I want to believe in something! I want to believe so I can feel! I want to feel that he is dead—my father! And I can't feel anything, Charlie! I can't feel anything at all! (*She throws herself on her knees beside him and hides her face in her hands on his knees and begins to sob—stifled torn sounds.*)

MARSDEN

(*Bends down, pats her head with trembling hands, soothes her with uncertain trembling words*). There—there—don't —Nina, please—don't cry—you'll make yourself sick—come now—get up—do! (*His hands grasping her arms he half raises her to her feet, but, her face still hidden in her hands, sobbing, she slips on to his lap like a little girl and hides her face on his shoulder. His expression becomes transported with a great happiness.*)

(*In an ecstatic whisper*). As I dreamed . . . with a deeper sweetness! . . . (*He kisses her hair with a great reverence.*) There . . . this is all my desire . . . I am this kind of lover . . . this is my love . . . she is my girl . . . not woman . . . my little girl . . . and I am brave because of her little girl's pure love . . . and I am proud . . . no more afraid . . . no more ashamed of being pure! . . . (*He kisses her hair again tenderly and smiles at himself.*)

(*Then soothingly with a teasing incongruous gaiety*). This will never do, Nina Cara Nina—never, never do, you know—I can't permit it!

NINA

(*In a muffled voice, her sobbing beginning to ebb away into sighs—in a young girl's voice*). Oh, Charlie, you're so kind and comforting! I've wanted you so!

MARSDEN

(*Immediately disturbed*). Wanted? . . . wanted? . . . not that kind of wanted . . . can she mean? . . .

(*Questioning hesitatingly*). You've wanted me, Nina?

NINA

Yes,—awfully! I've been so homesick. I've wanted to run home and 'fess up, tell how bad I've been, and be punished! Oh, I've got to be punished, Charlie, out of mercy for me, so I can forgive myself! And now Father dead, there's only you. You will, won't you—or tell me how to punish myself? You've simply got to, if you love me!

MARSDEN

(*Thinking intensely*). If I love her! . . . oh, I do love her! . . .

(*Eagerly*). Anything you wish, Nina—anything!

NINA

(*With a comforted smile, closing her eyes and cuddling up against him*). I knew you would. Dear old Charlie! (*As he gives a wincing start.*) What is it? (*She looks up into his face.*)

MARSDEN

(*Forcing a smile—ironically*). Twinge—rheumatics—getting old, Nina.

(*Thinking with wild agony*). Dear old Charlie! . . . descended again into hell! . . .

(*Then in a flat voice*). What do you want to be punished for, Nina?

NINA

(*In a strange, far-away tone, looking up not at him but at the ceiling*). For playing the silly slut, Charlie. For giving my cool clean body to men with hot hands and greedy eyes which they called love! Ugh! (*A shiver runs over her body.*)

MARSDEN

(*Thinking with sudden agony*). Then she did! . . . the little filth! . . .

(*In his flat voice*). You mean you—(*Then pleadingly.*) But not—Darrell?

NINA

(*With simple surprise*). Ned? No, how could I? The war hadn't maimed him. There would have been no point in that. But I did with others—oh, four or five or six or seven men, Charlie. I forgot—and it doesn't matter. They were all the same. Count them all as one, and that one a ghost of nothing. That is, to me. They were important to themselves, if I remember rightly. But I forget.

MARSDEN

(*Thinking in agony*). But why? . . . the dirty little trollop! . . . why? . . .

(*In his flat voice*). Why did you do this, Nina?

NINA

(*With a sad little laugh*). God knows, Charlie! Perhaps I knew at the time but I've forgotten. It's all mixed up. There was a desire to be kind. But it's horribly hard to give anything, and frightful to receive! And to give love—oneself—not in this world! And men are difficult to please, Charlie. I seemed to feel Gordon standing against a wall with eyes bandaged and these men were a firing squad whose eyes were also bandaged—and only I could see! No, I was the blindest! I would not see! I knew it was a stupid, morbid business, that I was more maimed than they were, really, that the war had blown my heart and insides out! And I knew too that I was torturing these tortured men, morbidly supersensitive already, that they loathed the cruel mockery of my gift! Yet I kept on, from one to one, like a stupid, driven animal until one night not long ago I had a dream of Gordon diving down out of the sky in flames and he looked at me with such sad burning eyes, and all my poor maimed men, too, seemed staring out of his eyes with a burning pain, and I woke up crying, my own eyes burning. Then I saw what a fool I'd been—a guilty fool! So be kind and punish me!

MARSDEN

(*Thinking with bitter confusion*). I wish she hadn't told me this . . . it has upset me terribly! . . . I positively must run home at once . . . Mother is waiting up . . . oh, how I'd love to hate this little whore! . . . then I could punish! . . . I wish her father were alive . . . "now he's dead there's only you," she said . . . "I've wanted you," . . . (*With intense bitterness.*) Dear old Father Charlie now! . . . ha! . . . that's how she wants me! . . .

(*Then suddenly in a matter-of-fact tone that is mockingly like her father's*). Then, under the circumstances, having weighed the pros and cons, so to speak, I should say that decidedly the most desirable course—

NINA

(*Drowsily—her eyes shut*). You sound so like Father, Charlie.

MARSDEN

(*In a tone like her father's*) —is for you to marry that young Evans. He is a splendid chap, clean and boyish, with real stuff in him, too, to make a career for himself if he finds a helpmeet who will inspire him to his best efforts and bring his latent ability to the surface.

NINA

(*Drowsily*). Sam is a nice boy. Yes, it would be a career for me to bring a career to his surface. I would be busy—surface life—no more depths, please God! But I don't love him, Father.

MARSDEN

(*Blandly—in the tone like her father's*). But you like him, Nina. And he loves you devotedly. And it's time you were having children—and when children come, love comes, you know.

NINA

(*Drowsily*). I want children. I must become a mother so I can give myself. I am sick of sickness.

MARSDEN

(*Briskly*). Then it's all settled?

NINA

(*Drowsily*). Yes. (*Very sleepily.*) Thank you, Father. You've been so kind. You've let me off too easily. I don't feel as if you'd punished me hardly at all. But I'll never, never do it again, I promise—never, never!—(*She falls asleep and gives a soft little snore.*)

MARSDEN

(*Still in her father's tones—very paternally—looking down*). She's had a hard day of it, poor child! I'll carry her up to her room. (*He rises to his feet with* NINA *sleeping peacefully in his arms. At this moment* SAM EVANS *enters from the right with the package of medicine in his hand.*)

EVANS

(*Grinning respectfully*). Here's the—(*As he sees* NINA.) Oh! (*Then excitedly.*) Did she faint?

MARSDEN

(*Smiling kindly at* EVANS—*still in her father's tones*). Sssh! She's asleep. She cried and then she fell asleep—like a little girl. (*Then benignantly.*) But first we spoke a word about you, Evans, and I'm sure you have every reason to hope.

EVANS

(*Overcome, his eyes on his shuffling feet and twiddling cap*). Thanks—I—I really don't know how to thank—

MARSDEN

(*Going to door—in his own voice now*). I've got to go home. My mother is waiting up for me. I'll just carry Nina upstairs and put her on her bed and throw something over her.

EVANS

Can't I help you, Mr. Marsden?

MARSDEN

(*Dully*). No. I cannot help myself. (*As* EVANS *looks puzzled and startled he adds with an ironical, self-mocking geniality.*) You'd better call me just Charlie after this. (*He smiles bitterly to himself as he goes out.*)

EVANS

(*Looks after him for a moment—then cannot restrain a joyful, coltish caper—gleefully*). Good egg! Good old Charlie! (*As if he had heard or guessed,* MARSDEN's *bitter laugh comes back from the end of the hallway.*)

Curtain.

ACT THREE

SCENE: *Seven months or so later—the dining room of the* EVANS' *homestead in Northern New York State—about nine o'clock in the morning of a day in late spring of the following year.*

The room is one of those big, misproportioned dining rooms that are found in the large, jigsaw country houses scattered around the country as a result of the rural taste for grandeur in the eighties. There is a cumbersome hanging lamp suspended from chains over the exact center of the ugly table with its set of straight-backed chairs set back at spaced intervals against the walls. The wall paper, a repulsive brown, is stained at the ceiling line with damp blotches of mildew, and here and there has started to peel back where the strips join. The floor is carpeted in a smeary brown with a dark red design blurred into it. In the left wall is one window with starched white curtains looking out on a covered side porch, so that no sunlight ever gets to this room and the light from the window, although it is a beautiful warm day in the flower garden beyond the porch, is cheerless and sickly. There is a door in the rear, to left of center, that leads to a hall opening on the same porch. To the right of door a heavy sideboard, a part of the set, displaying some "company" china and glassware. In the right wall, a door leading to the kitchen.

NINA *is seated at the foot of the table, her back to the window, writing a letter. Her whole personality seems changed, her face has a contented expression, there is an inner calm about her. And her personal appearance has changed in kind, her face and figure have filled out, she is prettier in a conventional way and less striking and unusual; nothing remains of the strange fascination to her face except her unchangeably mysterious eyes.*

NINA

(*Reading what she has just written over to herself*). It's a queer house, Ned. There is something wrong with its psyche, I'm sure. Therefore you'd simply adore it. It's a hideous old place, a faded gingerbread with orange fixin's and numerous lightning rods. Around it are acres and acres of apple trees in full bloom, all white and pinkish and beautiful, like brides just tripping out of church with the bridegroom, Spring, by the arm.

Which reminds me, Ned, that it's over six months since Sam and I were married and we haven't seen hide nor hair of you since the ceremony. Do you think that is any nice way to act? You might at least drop me a line. But I'm only joking. I know how busy you must be now that you've got the chance you've always wanted to do research work. Did you get our joint letter of congratulation written after we read of your appointment?

But to get back to this house. I feel it has lost its soul and grown resigned to doing without it. It isn't haunted by anything at all—and ghosts of some sort are the only normal life a house has—like our minds, you know. So although last evening when we got here at first I said "obviously haunted" to myself, now that I've spent one night in it I know that whatever spooks there may once have been have packed up their manifestations a long time ago and drifted away over the grass, wisps of mist between the apple trees, without one backward glance of regret or recollection. It's incredible to think Sam was born and spent his childhood here. I'm glad he doesn't show it! We slept last night in the room he was born in. Or rather he slept, I couldn't. I lay awake and found it difficult to breathe, as if all the life in the air had long since been exhausted in keeping the dying living a little longer. It was hard to believe anyone had ever been born alive there. I know you're saying crossly "She's still morbid" but I'm not. I've never been more normal. I feel contented and placid. (*Looking up from the letter, thinking embarrassedly.*) Should I have told him? . . . no . . . my own secret . . . tell no one . . . not even Sam . . . why haven't I told Sam? . . . it'd do him so much good . . . he'd feel so proud of himself, poor dear . . . no . . . I want to keep it just my baby . . . only mine . . . as long as I can . . . and it will be time enough to let Ned know when I go to New York . . . he can suggest a good obstetrician . . . how delighted he'll be when he hears! . . . he always said it would be the best thing for me . . . well, I do feel happy when I think . . . and I love Sam now . . . in a way . . . it will be his baby too . . . (*Then with a happy sigh, turns back to letter.*) But speaking of Sam's birth, you really must meet his mother sometime. It's amazing how little she is like him, a strange woman from the bit I saw of her last night. She has been writing Sam regularly once a week ever since she's known we were married, the most urgent invitations to visit her. They were really more like commands, or prayers. I suspect she is terribly lonely all by herself in this big house. Sam's feeling toward her puzzles me. I don't believe he ever mentioned her until her letters began coming or that he'd ever have come to see the poor woman if I hadn't insisted. His attitude rather shocked me. It was just as though he'd forgotten he had a mother. And yet as soon as he saw her he was sweet enough. She seemed dreadfully upset to see Charlie with us, until we'd explained it was thanks to his kindness and in his car we were taking this deferred honeymoon. Charlie's like a fussy old woman about his car, he's afraid to let Sam or me drive it—

MARSDEN

(*Enters from the rear. He is spruce, dressed immaculately, his face a bit tired and resigned, but smiling kindly. He has a letter in his hand*). Good morning. (*She gives a start and instinctively covers the letter with her hand.*)

NINA

Good morning.

(*Thinking amusedly*). If he knew what I'd just written . . . poor old Charlie! . . .

(*Then indicating the letter he carries*). I see you're an early correspondent, too.

MARSDEN

(*With sudden jealous suspicion*). Why did she cover it up like that? . . . whom is she writing to? . . .

(*Coming toward her*). Just a line to Mother to let her know we've not all been murdered by rum-bandits. You know how she worries.

NINA

(*Thinking with a trace of pitying contempt*). Apron strings . . . still his devotion to her is touching . . . I hope if mine is a boy he will love me as much . . . oh, I hope it is a boy . . . healthy and strong and beautiful . . . like Gordon! . . .

(*Then suddenly sensing* MARSDEN'S *curiosity—perfunctorily*). I'm writing to Ned Darrell. I've owed him one for ages. (*She folds it up and puts it aside.*)

MARSDEN

(*Thinking glumly*). I thought she'd forgotten him . . . still I suppose it's just friendly . . . and it's none of my business, now she's married. . . .

(*Perfunctorily*). How did you sleep?

NINA

Not a wink. I had the strangest feeling.

MARSDEN

Sleeping in a strange bed, I suppose. (*Jokingly.*) Did you see any ghosts?

NINA

(*With a sad smile*). No. I got the feeling the ghosts had all deserted the house and left it without a soul—as the dead so often leave the living—(*she forces a little laugh*) if you get what I mean.

MARSDEN

(*Thinking worriedly*). Slipping back into that morbid tone . . . first time in a long while . . .

(*Teasingly*). Hello! Do I hear graveyards yawning from their sleep—and yet I observe it's a gorgeous morning without, the flowers are flowering, the trees are treeing with one another, and you, if I mistake not, are on your honeymoon!

NINA

(*Immediately gaily mocking*). Oh, very well, old thing! "God's in his heaven, all's right with the world!" And Pippa's cured of the pip! (*She dances up to him.*)

MARSDEN

(*Gallantly*). Pippa is certainly a pippin this morning!

NINA

(*Kisses him quickly*). You deserve one for that! All I meant was that ghosts remind me of men's smart crack about women, you can't live with them and can't live without them. (*Stands still and looks at him teasingly.*) But there you stand proving me a liar by every breath you draw! You're ghostless and womanless—and as sleek and satisfied as a pet seal! (*She sticks out her tongue at him and makes a face of superior scorn.*) Bah! That for you, 'Fraid-cat Charlie, you slacker bachelor! (*She runs to the kitchen door.*) I'm going to bum some more coffee! How about you?

MARSDEN

(*With a forced smile*). No, thank you. (*She disappears into the kitchen.*)

(*Thinking with bitter pain*). Ghostless! . . . if she only knew . . . that joking tone hides her real contempt! . . . (*Self-mockingly.*) "But when the girls began to play 'Fraid-cat Charlie ran away!" (*Then rallying himself.*) Bosh! . . . I haven't had such thoughts . . . not since their marriage . . . happy in her happiness . . . but is she happy? . . . in the first few months she was obviously playing a part . . . kissed him too much . . . as if she'd determined to make herself a loving wife . . . and then all of a sudden she became contented . . . her face filled out . . . her eyes lazily examined peace . . . pregnant . . . yes, she must be . . . I hope so. . . . why? . . . for her sake . . . my own, too . . . when she has a child I know I can entirely accept . . . forget I have lost her . . . lost her? . . . silly ass! . . . how can you lose what you never possessed? . . . except in dreams! . . . (*Shaking his head exasperatedly.*) Round and round . . . thoughts . . . damn pests! . . . mosquitoes of the soul . . . whine, sting, suck one's blood . . . why did I invite Nina and Sam on this tour . . . it's a business trip with me, really . . . I need a new setting for my next novel . . . "Mr. Marsden departs a bit from his familiar field" . . . well, there they were stuck in the Professor's house . . . couldn't afford a vacation . . . never had a honeymoon . . . I've pretended to be done up every night so they could . . . I've gone to bed right after dinner so they could be alone and . . . I wonder if she can really like him . . . that way? . . . (*The sound of* EVANS' *voice and his mother's is heard from the garden.* MARSDEN *goes over and carefully peers out.*) Same with his mother . . . peculiar woman . . . strong . . . good character for a novel . . . no, she's too somber . . . her eyes are the saddest . . . and, at the same time, the grimmest . . . they're coming in . . . I'll drive around the country a bit . . . give them a chance for a family conference . . . discuss Nina's pregnancy, I suppose . . . does Sam know? . . . he gives no indication . . . why do wives hide it from their husbands? . . . ancient shame . . . guilty of continuing life, of bringing fresh pain into the world . . .

(*He goes out, rear. The outside door in the hall is heard being opened and* EVANS *and his mother evidently meet* MARSDEN *as he is about to go out. Their voices, his voice explaining, are heard, then the outer door being opened and shut again as* MARSDEN *departs. A moment later* EVANS *and his mother enter the dining room.* SAM *looks timorously happy, as if he could not quite believe in his good fortune and had constantly to reassure himself about it, yet he is riding the crest of the wave, he radiates love and devotion and boyish adoration. He is a charming-looking fresh boy now. He wears a sweater and linen knickers, collegiate to the last degree. His mother is a tiny woman with a frail figure, her head and face, framed in iron-gray hair, seeming much too large for her body, so that at first glance she gives one the impression of a wonderfully made, lifelike doll. She is only about forty-five but she looks at least sixty. Her face with its delicate features must have once been of a romantic, tender, clinging-vine beauty, but what has happened to her has compressed its defenseless curves into planes, its mouth into the thin line around a locked door, its gentle chin has been forced out aggressively by a long reliance on clenched teeth. She is very pale. Her big dark eyes are grim with the prisoner-pain of a walled-in soul. Yet a sweet loving-kindness, the ghost of an old faith and trust in life's goodness, hovers girlishly, fleetingly, about the corners of her mouth and softens into deep sorrow the shadowy grimness of her eyes. Her voice jumps startlingly in tone from a caressing gentleness to a blunted flat assertiveness, as if what she said then was merely a voice on its own without human emotion to inspire it.*)

EVANS

(*As they come in—rattling on in the cocksure boastful way of a boy showing off his prowess before his mother, confident of thrilled adulation*). In a few years you won't have to worry one way or another about the darned old apple crop. I'll be able to take care of you then. Wait and see! Of course, I'm not making so much now. I couldn't expect to. I've only just started. But I'm making good, all right, all right—since I got married—and it's only a question of time when—Why, to show you, Cole—he's the manager and the best egg ever—called me into his office and told me he'd had his eye on me, that my stuff was exactly what they wanted, and he thought I had the makings of a real find. (*Proudly.*) How's that? That's certainly fair enough, isn't it?

MRS. EVANS

(*Vaguely—she has evidently not heard much of what he said*). That's fine, Sammy.

(*Thinking apprehensively*). I do hope I'm wrong! . . . but that old shiver of dread took me the minute she stepped in the door! . . . I don't think she's told Sammy but I got to make sure. . . .

EVANS

(*Seeing her preoccupation now—deeply hurt—testily*). I'll bet you didn't hear a word I said! Are you still worrying about how the darn old apples are going to turn out?

MRS. EVANS

(*With a guilty start—protestingly*). Yes, I did hear you, Sammy—every word! That's just what I was thinking about—how proud I am you're doing so wonderful well!

EVANS

(*Mollified but still grumbling*). You'd never guess it from the gloomy way you looked! (*But encouraged to go on.*) And Cole asked me if I was married—seemed to take a real personal interest—said he was glad to hear it because marriage was what put the right kind of ambition into a fellow—unselfish ambition—working for his wife and not just himself—(*Then embarrassedly.*) He even asked me if we were expecting an addition to the family.

MRS. EVANS

(*Seeing this is her chance—quickly—forcing a smile*). I've been meaning to ask you that myself, Sammy. (*Blurts out apprehensively.*) She—Nina—she isn't going to have a baby, is she?

EVANS

(*With an indefinable guilty air—as if he were reluctant to admit it*). I—why—you mean, is she now? I don't think so, Mother. (*He strolls over to the window whistling with an exaggeratedly casual air, and looks out.*)

MRS. EVANS

(*Thinking with grim relief*). He don't know . . . there's that much to be thankful for, anyway. . . .

EVANS

(*Thinking with intense longing*). If that'd only happen! . . . soon! . . . Nina's begin to love me . . . a little . . . I've felt it the last two months . . . God, it's made me happy! . . . before that she didn't . . . only liked me . . . that was all I asked . . . never dared hope she'd come to love me . . . even a little . . . so soon . . . sometimes I feel it's too good to be true . . . don't deserve it . . . and now . . . if that'd happen . . . then I'd feel sure . . . it'd be there . . . half Nina, half me . . . living proof! . . . (*Then an apprehensive note creeping in.*) And I know she wants a baby so much . . . one reason why she married me . . . and I know she's felt right along that then she'd love me . . . really love me . . . (*Gloomily.*) I wonder why . . . ought to have happened before this . . . hope it's nothing wrong . . . with me! . . .

(*He starts, flinging off this thought—then suddenly clutching at a straw, turns hopefully to his mother*). Why did you ask me that, Mother? D'you think—?

MRS. EVANS

(*Hastily*). No, indeed! I don't think she is! I wouldn't say so at all!

EVANS

(*Dejectedly*). Oh—I thought perhaps—(*Then changing the subject.*) I suppose I ought to go up and say hello to Aunt Bessie.

MRS. EVANS

(*Her face becoming defensive—in blunted tones, a trifle pleadingly*). I wouldn't, Sammy. She hasn't seen you since you were eight. She wouldn't know you. And you're on your honeymoon, and old age is always sad to young folks. Be happy while you can! (*Then pushing him toward door.*) Look here! You catch that friend, he's just getting his car out. You drive to town with him, give me a chance to get to know my daughter-in-law, and call her to account for how she's taking care of you! (*She laughs forcedly.*)

EVANS

(*Bursting out passionately*). Better than I deserve! She's an angel, Mother! I know you'll love her!

MRS. EVANS

(*Gently*). I do already, Sammy! She's so pretty and sweet!

EVANS

(*Kisses her—joyously*). I'll tell her that. I'm going out this way and kiss her good-bye. (*He runs out through the kitchen door.*)

MRS. EVANS

(*Looking after him—passionately*). He loves her! . . . he's happy! . . . that's all that counts! . . . being happy! . . . (*Thinking apprehensively.*) If only she isn't going to have a baby . . . if only she doesn't care so much about having one . . . I got to have it out with her . . . got to! . . . no other way . . . in mercy . . . in justice . . . this has got to end with my boy . . . and he's got to live happy! . . . (*At the sound of steps from the kitchen she straightens up in her chair stiffly.*)

NINA

(*Comes in from the kitchen, a cup of coffee in her hand, smiling happily*). Good morning—(*she hesitates—then shyly*) Mother. (*She comes over and kisses her—slips down and sits on the floor beside her.*)

MRS. EVANS

(*Flusteredly—hurriedly*). Good morning! It's a real fine day, isn't it? I ought to have been here and got your breakfast, but I was out gallivanting round the place with Sammy. I hope you found everything you wanted.

NINA

Indeed I did! And I ate so much I'm ashamed of myself! (*She nods at the cup of coffee and laughs.*) See. I'm still at it.

MRS. EVANS

Good for you!

NINA

I ought to apologize for coming down so late. Sam should have called me. But I wasn't able to get to sleep until after daylight somehow.

MRS. EVANS

(*Strangely*). You couldn't sleep? Why? Did you feel anything funny—about this house?

NINA

(*Struck by her tone—looks up*). No. Why?

(*Thinking*). How her face changes! . . . what sad eyes! . . .

MRS. EVANS

(*Thinking in an agony of apprehension*). Got to start in to tell her . . . got to . . .

NINA

(*Apprehensive herself now*). That sick dead feeling . . . when something is going to happen . . . I felt it before I got the cable about Gordon . . .

(*Then taking a sip of coffee, and trying to be pleasantly casual*). Sam said you wanted to talk to me.

MRS. EVANS

(*Dully*). Yes. You love my boy, don't you?

NINA

(*Startled—forcing a smile, quickly*). Why, of course!

(*Reassuring herself*). No, it isn't a lie . . . I do love him . . . the father of my baby . . .

MRS. EVANS

(*Blurts out*). Are you going to have a baby, Nina?

NINA

(*She presses* MRS. EVANS' *hand. Simply*). Yes, Mother.

MRS. EVANS

(*In her blunt flat tones—with a mechanical rapidity to her words*). Don't you think it's too soon? Don't you think you better wait until Sammy's making more money? Don't you think it'll be a drag on him and you? Why don't you just go on being happy together, just you two?

NINA

(*Thinking frightenedly*). What is behind what she's saying? . . . that feeling of death again! . . .

(*Moving away from her—repulsed*). No, I don't think any of those things, Mrs. Evans. I want a baby—beyond everything! We both do!

MRS. EVANS

(*Hopelessly*). I know. (*Then grimly.*) But you can't! You've got to make up your mind you can't!

(*Thinking fiercely—even with satisfaction*). Tell her! . . . make her suffer what I was made to suffer! . . . I've been too lonely! . . .

NINA

(*Thinking with terrified foreboding*). I knew it! . . . Out of a blue sky . . . black! . . .

(*Springing to her feet—bewilderedly*). What do you mean? How can you say a thing like that?

MRS. EVANS

(*Reaching out her hand tenderly, trying to touch* NINA). It's because I want Sammy—and you, too, child—to be happy. (*Then as* NINA *shrinks away from her hand—in her blunted tones.*) You just can't.

NINA

(*Defiantly*). But I can! I have already! I mean—I am, didn't you understand me?

MRS. EVANS

(*Gently*). I know it's hard. (*Then inexorably.*) But you can't go on!

NINA

(*Violently*). I don't believe you know what you're saying! It's too terrible for you—Sam's own mother—how would you have felt if someone—when you were going to have Sam—came to you and said—?

MRS. EVANS

(*Thinking fiercely*). Now's my chance! . . .

(*Tonelessly*). They did say it! Sam's own father did—my husband! And I said it to myself! And I did all I could, all my husband could think of, so's I wouldn't—but we didn't know enough. And right to the time the pains come on, I prayed Sammy'd be born dead, and Sammy's father prayed, but Sammy was born healthy and smiling, and we just had to love him, and live in fear. He doubled the torment of fear we lived in. And that's what you'd be in for. And Sammy, he'd go the way his father went. And your baby, you'd be bringing it into torment. (*A bit violently.*) I tell you it'd be a crime—a crime worse than murder! (*Then recovering—commiseratingly.*) So you just can't, Nina!

NINA

(*Who has been listening distractedly—thinking*). Don't listen to her! . . . feeling of death! . . . what is it? . . . she's trying to kill my baby! . . . oh, I hate her! . . .

(*Hysterically resentful*). What do you mean? Why don't you speak plainly? (*Violently.*) I think you're horrible! Praying your baby would be born dead! That's a lie! You couldn't!

MRS. EVANS

(*Thinking*). I know what she's doing now . . . just what I did . . . trying not to believe . . . (*Fiercely.*) But I'll make her! . . . she's got to suffer, too! . . . I been too lonely! . . . she's got to share and help me save my Sammy! . . .

(*With an even more blunted flat relentless tonelessness*). I thought I was plain, but I'll be plainer. Only remember it's a family secret, and now you're one of the family. It's the curse on the Evanses. My husband's mother—she was an only child—died in an asylum and her father before her. I know that for a fact. And my husband's sister, Sammy's aunt, she's out of her mind. She lives on the top floor of this house, hasn't been out of her room in years, I've taken care of her. She just sits, doesn't say a word, but she's happy, she laughs to herself a lot, she hasn't a care in the world. But I remember when she was all right, she was always unhappy, she never got married, most people around here were afraid of the Evanses in spite of their being rich for hereabouts. They knew about the craziness going back, I guess, for heaven knows how long. I didn't know about the Evanses until after I'd married my husband. He came to the town I lived in, no one there knew about the Evanses. He didn't tell me until after we were married. He asked me to forgive him, he said he loved me so much he'd have gone mad without me, said I was his only hope of salvation. So I forgave him. I loved him an awful lot. I said to myself, I'll be his salvation—and maybe I could have been if we hadn't had Sammy born. My husband kept real well up to then. We'd swore we'd never have children, we never forgot to be careful for two whole years. Then one night we'd both gone to a dance, we'd both had a little punch to drink, just enough—to forget—driving home in the moonlight—that moonlight!—such little things at the back of big things!

NINA

(*In a dull moan*). I don't believe you! I won't believe you!

MRS. EVANS

(*Drones on*). My husband, Sammy's father, in spite of all he and I fought against it, he finally gave in to it when Sammy was only eight, he couldn't keep up any more living in fear for Sammy, thinking any minute the curse might get him, every time he was sick, or had a headache, or bumped his head, or started crying, or had a nightmare and screamed, or said something queer like children do naturally. (*A bit stridently.*) Living like that with that fear is awful torment! I know that! I went through it by his side! It nearly drove me crazy, too—but I didn't have it in my blood! And that's why I'm telling you! You got to see you can't, Nina!

NINA

(*Suddenly breaking out—frenziedly*). I don't believe you! I don't believe Sam would ever have married me if he knew!

MRS. EVANS

(*Sharply*). Who said Sammy knew? He don't know a single thing about it! That's been the work of my life, keeping him from knowing. When his father gave up and went off into it I sent Sammy right off to boarding school. I told him his father was sick, and a little while after I sent word his father was dead, and from then on until his father did really die during Sammy's second year to college, I kept him away at school in winter and camp in summers and I went to see him, I never let him come home. (*With a sigh.*) It was hard, giving up Sammy, knowing I was making him forget he had a mother. I was glad taking care of them two kept me so busy I didn't get much chance to think then. But here's what I've come to think since, Nina: I'm certain sure my husband might have kept his mind with the help of my love if I hadn't had Sammy. And if I'd never had Sammy I'd never have loved Sammy—or missed him, would I?—and I'd have kept my husband.

NINA

(*Not heeding this last—with wild mockery*). And I thought Sam was so normal—so healthy and sane—not like me! I thought he'd give me such healthy, happy children and I'd forget myself in them and learn to love him!

MRS. EVANS

(*Horrified, jumping to her feet*). Learn to? You told me you did love Sammy!

NINA

No! Maybe I almost have—lately—but only when I thought of his baby! Now I hate him! (*She begins to weep hysterically.* MRS. EVANS *goes to her and puts her arms around her.* NINA *sobs out.*) Don't touch me! I hate you, too! Why didn't you tell him he must never marry!

MRS. EVANS

What reason could I give, without telling him everything? And I never heard about you till after you were married. Then I wanted to write to you but I was scared he might read it. And I couldn't leave her upstairs to come away to see you. I kept writing Sammy to bring you here right off, although having him come frightened me to death for fear he might get to suspect something. You got to get him right away from here, Nina! I just kept hoping you wouldn't want children right away—young folks don't nowadays—until I'd seen you and told you everything. And I thought you'd love him like I did his father, and be satisfied with him alone.

NINA

(*Lifting her head—wildly*). No! I don't! I won't! I'll leave him!

MRS. EVANS

(*Shaking her, fiercely*). You can't! He'd go crazy sure then! You'd be a devil! Don't you see how he loves you?

NINA

(*Breaking away from her—harshly*). Well, I don't love him! I only married him because he needed me—and I needed children! And now you tell me I've got to kill my—oh, yes, I see I've got to, you needn't argue any more! I love it too much to make it run that chance! And I hate it too, now, because it's sick, it's not my baby, it's his! (*With terrible ironic bitterness.*) And still you can dare to tell me I can't even leave Sam!

MRS. EVANS

(*Very sadly and bitterly*). You just said you married him because he needed you. Don't he need you now—more'n ever? But I can't tell you not to leave him, not if you don't love him. But you oughtn't to have married him when you didn't love him. And it'll be your fault, what'll happen.

NINA

(*Torturedly*). What will happen?—what do you mean?—Sam will be all right—just as he was before—and it's not my fault anyway!—it's not my fault!

(*Then thinking conscience-strickenly*). Poor Sam . . . she's right . . . it's not his fault . . . it's mine . . . I wanted to use him to save myself . . . I acted the coward again . . . as I did with Gordon . . .

MRS. EVANS

(*Grimly*). You know what'll happen to him if you leave him—after all I've told you! (*Then breaking into intense pleading.*) Oh, I'd get down on my knees to you, don't make my boy run that risk! You got to give one Evans, the last one, a chance to live in this world! And you'll learn to love him, if you give up enough for him! (*Then with a grim smile.*) Why, I even love that idiot upstairs, I've taken care of her so many years, lived her life for her with my life, you might say. You give your life to Sammy, then you'll love him same as you love yourself. You'll have to! That's sure as death! (*She laughs a queer gentle laugh full of amused bitterness.*)

NINA

(*With a sort of dull stupid wonderment*). And you've found peace?—

MRS. EVANS

(*Sardonically*). There's peace in the green fields of Eden, they say! You got to die to find out! (*Then proudly.*) But I can say I feel proud of having lived fair to them that gave me love and trusted in me!

NINA

(*Struck—confusedly*). Yes—that's true, isn't it?

(*Thinking strangely*). Lived fair . . . pride . . . trust . . . play the game! . . . who is speaking to me . . . Gordon! . . . oh, Gordon, do you mean I must give Sam the life I didn't give you? . . . Sam loved you too . . . he said, if we have a boy, we'll call him Gordon in Gordon's honor . . . Gordon's honor! . . . what must I do now in your honor, Gordon . . . yes! . . . I know! . . .

(*Speaking mechanically in a dull voice*). All right, Mother. I'll stay with Sam. There's nothing else I can do, is there, when it isn't his fault, poor boy! (*Then suddenly snapping and bursting out in a despairing cry.*) But I'll be so lonely! I'll have lost my baby! (*She sinks down on her knees at* MRS. EVANS' *feet—piteously.*) Oh, Mother, how can I keep on living?

MRS. EVANS

(*Thinking miserably*). Now she knows my suffering . . . now I got to help her . . . she's got a right to have a baby . . . another baby . . . sometime . . . somehow . . . she's giving her life to save my Sammy . . . I got to save her! . . .

(*Stammeringly*). Maybe, Nina—

NINA

(*Dully and resentfully again now*). And how about Sam? You want him to be happy, don't you? It's just as important for him as it is for me that I should have a baby! If you know anything at all about him, you ought to see that!

MRS. EVANS

(*Sadly*). I know that. I see that in him, Nina. (*Gropingly.*) There must be a way—somehow. I remember when I was carrying Sam, sometimes I'd forget I was a wife, I'd only remember the child in me. And then I used to wish I'd gone out deliberate in our first year, without my husband knowing, and picked a man, a healthy male to breed by, same's we do with stock, to give the man I loved a healthy child. And if I didn't love that other man nor him me where would be the harm? Then God would whisper: "It'd be a sin, adultery, the worst sin!" But after He'd gone I'd argue back again to myself, then we'd have a healthy child, I needn't be afraid! And maybe my husband would feel without ever knowing how he felt it, that I wasn't afraid and that child wasn't cursed and so he needn't fear and I could save him. (*Then scornfully.*) But I was too afraid of God then to have ever done it! (*Then very simply.*) He loved children so, my poor husband did, and the way they took to him, you never saw anything like it, he was a natural born father. And Sammy's the same.

NINA

(*As from a distance—strangely*). Yes, Sammy's the same. But I'm not the same as you. (*Defiantly.*) I don't believe in God the Father!

MRS. EVANS

(*Strangely*). Then it'd be easy for you. (*With a grim smile.*) And I don't believe in Him, neither, not any more. I used to be a great one for worrying about what's God and what's devil, but I got richly over it living here with poor folks that was being punished for no sins of their own, and me being punished with them for no sin but loving much. (*With decision.*) Being happy, that's the nearest we can ever come to knowing what's good! Being happy, that's good! The rest is just talk! (*She pauses — then with a strange austere sternness.*) I love my boy, Sammy. I could see how much he wants you to have a baby. Sammy's got to feel sure you love him—to be happy. Whatever you can do to make him happy is good—is good, Nina! I don't care what! You've got to have a healthy baby—sometime—so's you can both be happy! It's your rightful duty.

NINA

(*Confusedly—in a half-whisper*). Yes, Mother.

(*Thinking longingly*). I want to be happy! . . . it's my right . . . and my duty! . . . (*Then suddenly in guilty agony.*) Oh, my baby . . . my poor baby . . . I'm forgetting you . . . desiring another after you are dead! . . . I feel you beating against my heart for mercy . . . oh! . . . (*She weeps with bitter anguish.*)

MRS. EVANS

(*Gently and with deep sympathy*). I know what you're suffering. And I wouldn't say what I just said now only I know us two mustn't see each other ever again. You and Sammy have got to forget me. (*As* NINA *makes a motion of protest—grimly and inexorably.*) Oh, yes, you will—easy. People forget everything. They got to, poor people! And I'm saying what I said about a healthy baby so's you will remember it when you need to, after you've forgotten—this one.

NINA

(*Sobbing pitifully*). Don't! Please, Mother!

MRS. EVANS

(*With sudden tenderness—gathering* NINA *up in her arms, brokenly*). You poor child! You're like the daughter of my sorrow! You're closer to me now than ever Sammy could be! I want you to be happy! (*She begins to sob, too, kissing* NINA*'s bowed head.*)

Curtain.

ACT FOUR

SCENE: *An evening early in the following winter about seven months later. The* PROFESSOR's *study again. The books in the cases have never been touched, their austere array shows no gaps, but the glass separating them from the world is gray with dust, giving them a blurred ghostly quality. The table, although it is the same, is no longer the* PROFESSOR's *table, just as the other furniture in the room, by its disarrangement, betrays that the* PROFESSOR's *well-ordered mind no longer trims it to his personality. The table has become neurotic. Volumes of the Encyclopedia Britannica mixed up with popular treatises on Mind Training for Success, etc., looking startlingly modern and disturbing against the background of classics in the original, are slapped helter-skelter on top of each other on it. The titles of these books face in all directions, no one volume is placed with any relation to the one beneath it—the effect is that they have no connected meaning. The rest of the table is littered with an ink bottle, pens, pencils, erasers, a box of typewriting paper, and a typewriter at the center before the chair, which is pushed back, setting the rug askew. On the floor beside the table are an overflowing wastepaper basket, a few sheets of paper and the rubber cover for the typewriter like a collapsed tent. The rocking chair is no longer at center but has been pulled nearer the table, directly faces it with its back to the bench. This bench in turn has been drawn much closer, but is now placed more to the rear and half-faces front, its back squarely to the door in the corner.*

EVANS *is seated in the* PROFESSOR's *old chair. He has evidently been typing, or is about to type, for a sheet of paper can be seen in the machine. He smokes a pipe, which he is always relighting whether it needs it or not, and which he bites and shifts about and pulls in and out and puffs at nervously. His expression is dispirited, his eyes shift about, his shoulders are collapsed submissively. He seems much thinner, his face drawn and sallow. The collegiate clothes are no longer natty, they need pressing and look too big for him.*

EVANS

(*Turns to his typewriter and pounds out a few words with a sort of aimless desperation—then tears the sheet out of the machine with an exclamation of disgust, crumples it up and throws it violently on the floor, pushing his chair back and jumping to his feet*). Hell!

(*He begins pacing up and down the room, puffing at his pipe, thinking tormentedly*). No use . . . can't think of a darn thing . . . well, who could dope out a novel ad on another powdered milk, anyway? . . . all the stuff been used already . . . Tartars conquering on dried mare's milk . . . Metchnikoff, eminent scientist . . . been done to death . . . but simply got to work out something or . . . Cole said, what's been the matter with you lately? . . . you started off so well . . . I thought you were a real find, but your work's fallen off to nothing . . . (*He sits down on the edge of the bench nearby, his shoulders hunched—despondently.*) Couldn't deny it . . . been going stale ever since we came back from that trip home . . . no ideas . . . I'll get fired . . . sterile . . . (*with a guilty terror*) in more ways than one, I guess! . . . (*He springs to his feet as if this idea were a pin stuck in him—lighting his already lighted pipe, walks up and down again, forcing his thoughts into other channels.*) Bet the old man turns over in his grave at my writing ads in his study . . . maybe that's why I can't . . . bum influence . . . try tomorrow in my bedroom . . . sleeping alone . . . since Nina got sick . . . some woman's sickness . . . wouldn't tell me . . . too modest . . . still, there are some things a husband has a right to know . . . especially when we haven't . . . in five months . . . doctor told her she mustn't, she said . . . what doctor? . . . she's never said . . . what the hell's the matter with you, do you think Nina's lying? . . . no . . . but . . . (*Desperately.*) If I was only sure it was because she's really sick . . . not just sick of me! . . . (*He sinks down in the rocking chair despondently.*) Certainly been a big change in her . . . since that visit home . . . what happened between Mother and her? . . . she says nothing . . . they seemed to like each other . . . both of them cried when we left . . . still, Nina insisted on going that same day and Mother seemed anxious to get rid of us . . . can't make it out . . . next few weeks Nina couldn't be loving enough . . . I never was so happy . . . then she crashed . . . strain of waiting and hoping she'd get pregnant . . . and nothing happening . . . that's what did it . . . my fault! . . . how d'you know? . . . you can't tell that! . . . (*He jumps to his feet again—walks up and down again distractedly.*) God, if we'd only have a kid! . . . then I'd show them all what I could do! . . . Cole always used to say I had the stuff, and Ned certainly thought so. . . . (*With sudden relieved excitement.*) By gosh, I was forgetting! . . . Ned's coming out tonight . . . forgot to tell Nina . . . mustn't let her get wise I got him to come to look her over . . . she'd hate me for swallowing my pride after he's never been to see us . . . but I had to . . . this has got my goat . . . I've got to know what's wrong . . . and Ned's the only one I can trust . . . (*He flings himself on chair in front of desk and, picking up a fresh sheet of paper, jams it into the machine.*) Gosh, I ought to try and get a new start on this before it's time . . . (*He types a sentence or two, a strained frown of consternation on his face.* NINA *comes silently through the door and stands just inside it looking at him. She has grown thin again, her face is pale and drawn, her movements are those of extreme nervous tension.*)

NINA

(*Before she can stifle her immediate reaction of contempt and dislike*). How weak he is! . . . he'll never do anything . . . never give me my desire . . . if he'd only fall in love with someone else . . . go away . . . not be here in my father's room . . . I even have to give him a home . . . if he'd disappear . . . leave me free . . . if he'd die . . . (*Checking herself—remorsefully.*) I must stop such thoughts . . . I don't mean it . . . poor Sam! . . . trying so hard . . . loving me so much . . . I give so little in return . . . he feels I'm always watching him with scorn . . . I can't tell him it's with pity . . . how can I help watching him? . . . help worrying over his worry because of what it might lead to . . . after what his mother . . . how horrible life is! . . . he's worried now . . . he doesn't sleep . . . I hear him tossing about . . . I must sleep with him again soon . . . he's only home two nights a week . . . it isn't fair of me . . . I must try . . . I must! . . . he suspects my revulsion . . . it's hurting him . . . oh, poor dead baby I dared not bear, how I might have loved your father for your sake! . . .

EVANS

(*Suddenly feeling her presence, jerks himself to his feet—with a diffident guilty air which is noticeable about him now whenever he is in her presence*). Hello, dear. I thought you were lying down. (*Guiltily.*) Did the noise of my typing bother you? I'm terribly sorry!

NINA

(*Irritated in spite of herself*). Why is he always cringing? . . . (*She comes forward to the chair at center and sits down—forcing a smile.*)

But there's nothing to be terribly sorry about! (*As he stands awkward and confused, like a schoolboy who has been called on to recite and cannot and is being "bawled out" before the class, she forces a playful *tone.*) Goodness, Sam, how tragic you can get about nothing at all!

EVANS

(*Still forced to justify himself—contritely*). I know it isn't pleasant for you having me drag my work out here, trying to pound out rotten ads. (*With a short laugh.*) Trying to is right! (*Blurts out.*) I wouldn't do it except that Cole gave me a warning to buck up—or get out.

NINA

(*Stares at him, more annoyed, her eyes hardening, thinking*). Yes! . . . he'll always be losing one job, getting another, starting with a burst of confidence each time, then . . .

(*Cutting him with a careless sneering tone*). Well, it isn't a job to worry much about losing, is it?

EVANS

(*Wincing pitiably*). No, not much money. But I used to think there was a fine chance to rise there—but of course that's my fault, I haven't made good—(*he finishes miserably*) somehow.

NINA

(*Her antagonism giving way to remorseful pity*). What makes me so cruel? . . . he's so defenseless . . . his mother's baby . . . poor sick baby! . . . poor Sam! . . . (*She jumps to her feet and goes over to him.*)

EVANS

(*As she comes—with a defensive, boastful bravery*). Oh, I can get another job just as good, all right—maybe a lot better.

NINA

(*Reassuringly*). Certainly, you can! And I'm sure you're not going to lose this one. You're always anticipating trouble. (*She kisses him and sits on the arm of his chair, putting an arm around his neck and pulling his head on to her breast.*) And it isn't your fault, you big goose, you! It's mine. I know how hard it makes everything for you, being tied to a wife who's too sick to be a wife. You ought to have married a big strapping, motherly—

EVANS

(*In the seventh heaven now—passionately*). Bunk! All the other women in the world aren't worth your little finger! It's you who ought to have married someone worth while, not a poor fish like me! But no one could love you more than I do, no matter what he was!

NINA

(*Presses his head on her breast, avoiding his eyes, kisses him on the forehead*). And I love you, Sam.

(*Staring out over his head—with loving pity, thinking*). I almost do . . . poor unfortunate boy! . . . at these moments . . . as his mother loves him . . . but that isn't enough for him . . . I can hear his mother saying, "Sammy's got to feel sure you love him . . . to be happy." . . . I must try to make him feel sure . . .

(*Speaking gently*). I want you to be happy, Sam.

EVANS

(*His face transformed with happiness*). I am—a hundred times more than I deserve!

NINA

(*Presses his head down on her breast so he cannot see her eyes—gently*). Ssshh.

(*Thinking sadly*). I promised her . . . but I couldn't see how hard it would be to let him love me . . . after his baby . . . was gone . . . it was hard even to keep on living . . . after that operation . . . Gordon's spirit followed me from room to room . . . poor reproachful ghost! . . . (*With bitter mockery.*) Oh, Gordon, I'm afraid this is a deeper point of honor than any that was ever shot down in flames! . . . what would your honor say now? . . . "Stick to him! . . . play the game!" . . . oh, yes, I know . . . I'm sticking . . . but he isn't happy . . . I'm trying to play the game . . . then why do I keep myself from him? . . . but I was really sick . . . for a time after . . . since then, I couldn't . . . but . . . oh, I'll try . . . I'll try soon.

(*Tenderly—but having to force herself to say it*). Doesn't my boy want to sleep with me again—sometime soon?

EVANS

(*Passionately—hardly able to believe his ears*). Oh, it'd be wonderful, Nina! But are you sure you really want me to—that you'll feel well enough?

NINA

(*Repeats his words as if she were memorizing a lesson*). Yes, I want you to. Yes, I'll feel well enough. (*He seizes her hand and kisses it in a passionately grateful silence.*)

(*She thinks with resigned finality*). There, Sammy's mother and Gordon . . . I'll play the game . . . it will make him happy for a while . . . as he was in those weeks after we'd left his mother . . . when I gave myself with a mad pleasure in torturing myself for his pleasure! . . . (*Then with weary hopelessness.*) He'll be happy until he begins to feel guilty again because I'm not pregnant . . . (*With a grim bitter smile.*) Poor Sam, if he only knew the precautions . . . as if I wouldn't die rather than take the slightest chance of that happening! . . . ever again . . . what a tragic joke it was on both of us! . . . I wanted my baby so! . . . oh, God! . . . his mother said . . . "You've got to have a healthy baby . . . sometime . . . it's your rightful duty" . . . that seemed right then . . . but now . . . it seems cowardly . . . to betray poor Sam . . . and vile to give myself . . . without love or desire . . . and yet I've given myself to men before without a thought, just to give them a moment's happiness . . . can't I do that again? . . . when it's a case of Sam's happiness? . . . and my own? . . .

(*She gets up from beside him with a hunted movement*). It must be half past eight. Charlie's coming to bring his suggestions on my outline for Gordon's biography.

EVANS

(*His bliss shattered—dejectedly*). Always happens . . . just as we get close . . . something comes between . . .

(*Then confusedly*). Say, I forgot to tell you Ned's coming out tonight.

NINA

(*Astonished*). Ned Darrell?

EVANS

Sure. I happened to run into him the other day and invited him and he said Saturday evening. He couldn't tell what train. Said never mind meeting him.

NINA

(*Excitedly*). Why didn't you tell me before, you big booby! (*She kisses him.*) There, don't mind. But it's just like you. Now someone'll have to go down to the store. And I'll have to get the spare room ready. (*She hurries to the doorway. He follows her.*)

EVANS

I'll help you.

NINA

You'll do nothing of the kind! You'll stay right downstairs and bring them in here and cover up my absence. Thank heavens, Charlie won't stay long if Ned is here. (*The doorbell rings—excitedly.*) There's one of them now. I'll run upstairs. Come up and tell me if it's Ned—and get rid of Charlie. (*She kisses him playfully and hurries out.*)

EVANS

(*Looking after her—thinks*). She seems better tonight . . . happier . . . she seems to love me . . . if she'll only get all well again, then everything will . . . (*The bell rings again.*) I must give Ned a good chance to talk to her . . . (*He goes out to the outer door—returns a moment later with* MARSDEN. *The latter's manner is preoccupied and nervous. His face has an expression of anxiety which he tries to conceal. He seems a prey to some inner fear he is trying to hide even from himself and is resolutely warding off from his consciousness. His tall, thin body stoops as if part of its sustaining will had been removed.*)

EVANS

(*With a rather forced welcoming note*). Come on in, Charlie. Nina's upstairs lying down.

MARSDEN

(*With marked relief*). Then by all means don't disturb her. I just dropped in to bring back her outline with the suggestions I've made. (*He has taken some papers out of his pocket and hands them to* EVANS.) I couldn't have stayed but a minute in any event. Mother is a bit under the weather these days.

EVANS

(*Perfunctorily*). Too bad.

(*Thinking vindictively*). Serve her right, the old scandal-monger, after the way she's gossiped about Nina! . . .

MARSDEN

(*With assumed carelessness*). Just a little indigestion. Nothing serious but it annoys her terribly.

(*Thinking frightenedly*). That dull pain she complains of . . . I don't like it . . . and she won't see anyone but old Doctor Tibbetts . . . she's sixty-eight . . . I can't help fearing . . . no! . . .

EVANS

(*Bored—vaguely*). Well, I suppose you've got to be careful of every little thing when you get to her age.

MARSDEN

(*Positively bristling*). Her age? Mother isn't so old!

EVANS

(*Surprised*). Over sixty-five, isn't she?

MARSDEN

(*Indignantly*). You're quite out there! She's under sixty-five—and in health and spirits she isn't more than fifty! Everyone remarks that!

(*Annoyed at himself*). Why did I lie to him about her age? . . . I must be on edge . . . Mother is rather difficult to live with these days, getting me worried to death, when it's probably nothing . . .

EVANS

(*Annoyed in his turn—thinking*). Why all the fuss? . . . as if I gave a damn if the old girl was a million! . . . (*Indicating the papers*). I'll give these to Nina first thing in the morning.

MARSDEN

(*Mechanically*). Righto. Thank you. (*He starts to go toward door—then turns—fussily.*) But you'd better take a look while I'm here and see if it's clear. I've written on the margins. See if there's anything you can't make out. (EVANS *nods helplessly and begins reading the sheets, going back beneath the lamp.*)

MARSDEN

(*Looking around him with squeamish disapproval*). What a mess they've made of this study . . . poor Professor! . . . dead and forgotten . . . and his tomb desecrated . . . does Sam write his ads here of a week-end now? . . . the last touch! . . . and Nina labors with love at Gordon's biography . . . whom the Professor hated! . . . "life is so full of a number of things!" . . . why does everyone in the world think they can write? . . . but I've only myself to blame . . . why in the devil did I ever suggest it to her? . . . because I hoped my helping her while Sam was in the city would bring us alone together? . . . but I made the suggestion before she had that abortion performed! . . . how do you know she did? . . . because I know! . . . there are psychic affinities . . . her body confessed . . . and since then, I've felt an aversion . . . as if she were a criminal . . . she is! . . . how could she? . . . why? . . . I thought she wanted a child . . . but evidently I don't know her . . . I suppose, afraid it would spoil her figure . . . her flesh . . . her power to enslave men's senses . . . mine . . . and I had hoped . . . looked forward to her becoming a mother . . . for my peace of mind. . . . (*Catching himself—violently.*) Shut up! . . . what a base creature I'm becoming! . . . to have such thoughts when Mother is sick and I ought to be thinking only of her! . . . and it's none of my damn business, anyway! . . . (*Glaring at* EVANS *resentfully as if he were to blame.*) Look at him! . . . he'll never suspect anything! . . . what a simple-simon! . . . he adored Gordon as a newsboy does a champion pugilist! . . . and Nina writes of Gordon as if he had been a demi-god! . . . when actually he came from the commonest people! . . .

(*He suddenly speaks to* EVANS *with a really savage satisfaction*). Did I tell you I once looked up Gordon's family in Beachampton? A truly deplorable lot! When I remembered Gordon and looked at his father I had either to suspect a lover in the wood pile or to believe in an Immaculate Conception . . . that is, until I saw his mother! Then a stork became the only conceivable explanation!

EVANS

(*Who has only half-heard and hasn't understood, says vaguely*). I never saw his folks. (*Indicating the papers.*) I can make this all out all right.

MARSDEN

(*Sarcastically*). I'm glad it's understandable!

EVANS

(*Blunderingly*). I'll give it to Nina—and I hope your mother is feeling better tomorrow.

MARSDEN

(*Piqued*). Oh, I'm going. Why didn't you tell me if I was interrupting—your writing!

EVANS

(*Immediately guilty*). Oh, come on, Charlie, don't get peevish, you know I didn't mean— (*The bell rings.* EVANS *stammers in confusion, trying at a nonchalant air.*) Hello! That must be Ned. You remember Darrell. He's coming out for a little visit. Excuse me. (*He blunders out of the door.*)

MARSDEN

(*Looking after him with anger mixed with alarmed suspicion and surprise*). Darrell? . . . what's he doing here? . . . have they been meeting? . . . perhaps he was the one who performed the . . . no, his idea was she ought to have a child . . . but if she came and begged him? . . . but why should Nina beg not to have a baby? . . . (*Distractedly.*) Oh, I don't know! . . . it's all a sordid mess! . . . I ought to be going home! . . . I don't want to see Darrell! . . . (*He starts for the door—then struck by a sudden thought, stops.*) Wait . . . I could ask him about Mother . . . yes . . . good idea . . . (*He comes back to the middle of the room, front, and is standing there when* DARRELL *enters, followed by* EVANS. DARRELL *has not changed in appearance except that his expression is graver and more thoughtful. His manner is more convincingly authoritative, more mature. He takes in* MARSDEN *from head to foot with one comprehensive glance.*)

EVANS

(*Awkwardly*). Ned, you remember Charlie Marsden?

MARSDEN

(*Holding out his hand, urbanely polite*). How are you, Doctor?

DARRELL

(*Shaking his hand—briefly*). Hello.

EVANS

I'll go up and tell Nina you're here, Ned. (*He goes, casting a resentful glance at* MARSDEN.)

MARSDEN

(*Awkwardly, as* DARRELL *sits down in the chair at center, goes over and stands by the table*). I was on the point of leaving when you rang. Then I decided to stop and renew our acquaintance. (*He stoops and picks up one sheet of paper, and puts it back carefully on the table.*)

DARRELL

(*Watching him—thinking*). Neat . . . suspiciously neat . . . he's an old maid who seduces himself in his novels . . . so I suspect . . . I'd like a chance to study him more closely. . . .

MARSDEN

(*Thinking resentfully*). What a boor! . . . he might say something! . . . (*Forcing a smile*). And I wanted to ask a favor of you, a word of advice as to the best specialist, the very best, it would be possible to consult—

DARRELL

(*Sharply*). On what?

MARSDEN

(*Almost naïvely*). My mother has a pain in her stomach.

DARRELL

(*Amused—dryly*). Possibly she eats too much.

MARSDEN

(*As he bends and carefully picks another sheet from the floor to place it as carefully on the table*). She doesn't eat enough to keep a canary alive. It's a dull, constant pain, she says. She's terribly worried. She's terrified by the idea of cancer. But, of course, that's perfect rot, she's never been sick a day in her life and—

DARRELL

(*Sharply*). She's showing more intelligence about her pain than you are.

MARSDEN

(*Bending down for another sheet, his voice trembling with terror*). I don't understand—quite. Do you mean to say you think—?

DARRELL

(*Brutally*). It's possible. (*He has pulled out his pen and a card and is writing.*)

(*Thinking grimly*). Explode a bomb under him, as I did once before . . . only way to get him started doing anything. . . .

MARSDEN

(*Angrily*). But—that's nonsense!

DARRELL

(*With satisfaction—unruffledly*). People who are afraid to face unpleasant possibilities until it's too late commit more murders and suicides than— (*Holds out card.*) Doctor Schultz is your man. Take her to see him—tomorrow!

MARSDEN

(*Bursting out in anger and misery*). Damn it, you're condemning her without—! (*He breaks down chokingly.*) You've no damn right!— (*He bends down, trembling all over, to pick up another piece of paper.*)

DARRELL

(*Genuinely astonished and contrite*). And I thought he was so ingrown he didn't care a damn about anyone! . . . his mother . . . now I begin to see him. (*He jumps from his chair and going to* MARSDEN *puts a hand on his shoulder—kindly*). I beg your pardon, Marsden. I only wanted to drive it in that all delay is dangerous. Your mother's pain may be due to any number of harmless causes, but you owe it to her to make sure. Here. (*He hands out the card.*)

MARSDEN

(*Straightens up and takes it, his eyes grateful now—humbly*). Thank you. I'll take her to see him tomorrow. (EVANS *comes in.*)

EVANS

(*To* MARSDEN, *blunderingly*). Say, Charlie, I don't want to hurry you but Nina wants some things at the store before it closes, and if you'd give me a lift—

MARSDEN

(*Dully*). Of course. Come along. (*He shakes hands with* DARRELL.) Good night, Doctor—and thank you.

DARRELL

Good night. (MARSDEN *goes, followed by* EVANS.)

EVANS

(*Turns in the doorway and says meaningly*). Nina'll be right down. For Pete's sake, have a good heart-to-heart talk with her, Ned!

DARRELL

(*Frowning—impatiently*). Oh—all right! Run along. (EVANS *goes.*)

(DARRELL *remains standing near the table looking after them, thinking about* MARSDEN). Queer fellow, Marsden . . . mother's boy still . . . if she dies what will he do? . . . (*Then dismissing* MARSDEN *with a shrug of his shoulders.*) Oh, well, he can always escape life in a new book. . . . (*He moves around the table examining its disorder critically, then sits down in armchair—amused.*) Evidences of authorship . . . Sam's ads? . . . isn't making good, he said . . . was I wrong in thinking he had stuff in him? . . . hope not . . . always liked Sam, don't know why exactly . . . said Nina'd gotten into a bad state again . . . what's happened to their marriage?

. . . I felt a bit sorry for myself at their wedding . . . not that I'd ever fallen . . . but I did envy him in a way . . . she always had strong physical attraction for me . . . that time I kissed her . . . one reason I've steered clear since . . . take no chances on emotional didos . . . need all my mind on my work . . . got rid of even that slight suspicion . . . I'd forgotten all about her . . . she's a strange girl . . . interesting case . . . I should have kept in touch on that account . . . hope she'll tell me about herself . . . can't understand her not having child . . . it's so obviously the sensible thing . . . (*Cynically.*) Probably why . . . to expect common sense of people proves you're lacking in it yourself! . . .

NINA

(*Enters silently. She has fixed herself up, put on her best dress, arranged her hair, rouged, etc.—but it is principally her mood that has changed her, making her appear a younger, prettier person for the moment.* DARRELL *immediately senses her presence, and, looking up, gets to his feet with a smile of affectionate admiration. She comes quickly over to him, saying with frank pleasure*). Hello, Ned. I'm certainly glad to see you again—after all these years!

DARRELL

(*As they shake hands—smiling*). Not as long as all that, is it?

(*Thinking admiringly*). Wonderful-looking as ever . . . Sam is a lucky devil! . . .

NINA

(*Thinking*). Strong hands like Gordon's . . . take hold of you . . . not like Sam's . . . yielding fingers that let you fall back into yourself . . .

(*Teasingly*). I ought to cut you dead after the shameful way you've ignored us!

DARRELL

(*A bit embarrassedly*). I've really meant to write.

(*His eyes examining her keenly*). Been through a lot since I saw her . . . face shows it . . . nervous tension pronounced . . . hiding behind her smile.

NINA

(*Uneasy under his glance*). I hate that professional look in his eyes . . . watching symptoms . . . without seeing me.

(*With resentful mockery*). Well, what do you suspect is wrong with the patient now, Doctor? (*She laughs nervously.*) Sit down, Ned. I suppose you can't help your diagnosing stare. (*She turns from him and sits down in the rocker at center.*)

DARRELL

(*Quickly averting his eyes—sits down—jokingly*). Same old unjust accusation! You were always reading diagnosis into me, when what I was really thinking was what fine eyes you had, or what a becoming gown, or—

NINA

(*Smiling*). Or what a becoming alibi you could cook up! Oh, I know you! (*With a sudden change of mood she laughs gaily and naturally.*) But you're forgiven—that is, if you can explain why you've never been to see us.

DARRELL

Honestly, Nina, I've been so rushed with work I haven't had a chance to go anywhere.

NINA

Or an inclination!

DARRELL

(*Smiling*). Well—maybe.

NINA

Do you like the Institute so much? (*He nods gravely.*) Is it the big opportunity you wanted?

DARRELL

(*Simply*). I think it is.

NINA

(*With a smile*). Well, you're the taking kind for whom opportunities are made!

DARRELL

(*Smiling*). I hope so.

NINA

(*Sighing*). I wish that could be said of more of us—(*then quickly*)—meaning myself.

DARRELL

(*Thinking with a certain satisfaction*). Meaning Sam . . . that doesn't look hopeful for future wedded bliss! (*Teasingly*). But I heard you were "taking an opportunity" to go in for literature—collaborating with Marsden.

NINA

No, Charlie is only going to advise. He'd never deign to appear as co-author. And besides, he never appreciated the real Gordon. No one did except me.

DARRELL

(*Thinking caustically*). Gordon myth strong as ever . . . root of her trouble still . . .
(*Keenly inquisitive*). Sam certainly appreciated him, didn't he?

NINA

(*Not remembering to hide her contempt*). Sam? Why, he's the exact opposite in every way!

DARRELL

(*Caustically thinking*). These heroes die hard . . . but perhaps she can write him out of her system. . . .
(*Persuasively*). Well, you're going ahead with the biography, aren't you? I think you ought to.

NINA

(*Dryly*). For my soul, Doctor? (*Listlessly.*) I suppose I will. I don't know. I haven't much time. The duties of a wife—(*Teasingly.*) By the way, if it isn't too rude to inquire, aren't you getting yourself engaged to some fair lady or other?

DARRELL

(*Smiling—but emphatically*). Not on your life! Not until after I'm thirty-five, at least!

NINA

(*Sarcastically*). Then you don't believe in taking your own medicine? Why, Doctor! Think of how much good it would do you!—(*excitedly with a hectic sarcasm*)—if you had a nice girl to love—or was it learn to love?—and take care of—whose character you could shape and whose life you could guide and make what you pleased, in whose unselfish devotion you could find peace! (*More and more bitterly sarcastic.*) And you ought to have a baby, Doctor! You will never know what life is, you'll never be really happy until you've had a baby, Doctor—a fine, healthy baby! (*She laughs a bitter, sneering laugh.*)

DARRELL

(*After a quick, keen glance, thinking*). Good! . . . she's going to tell . . .
(*Meekly*). I recognize my arguments. Was I really wrong on every point, Nina?

NINA

(*Harshly*). On every single point, Doctor!

DARRELL

(*Glancing at her keenly*). But how? You haven't given the baby end of it a chance yet, have you?

NINA

(*Bitterly*). Oh, haven't I? (*Then bursts out with intense bitterness.*) I'll have you know I'm not destined to bear babies, Doctor!

DARRELL

(*Startledly*). What's that? . . . why not? . . . (*Again with a certain satisfaction.*) Can she mean Sam? . . . that he . . .
(*Soothingly—but plainly disturbed*). Why don't you begin at the beginning and tell me all about it? I feel responsible.

NINA

(*Fiercely*). You are! (*Then wearily.*) And you're not. No one is. You didn't know. No one could know.

DARRELL

(*In same tone*). Know what?
(*Thinking with the same eagerness to believe something he hopes*). She must mean no one could know that Sam wasn't . . . but I might have guessed it . . . from his general weakness . . . poor unlucky devil . . .
(*Then as she remains silent—urgingly*). Tell me. I want to help you, Nina.

NINA

(*Touched*). It's too late, Ned. (*Then suddenly.*) I've just thought—Sam said he happened to run into you. That isn't so, is it? He went to see you and told you how worried he was about me and asked you out to see me, didn't he? (*As* DARRELL *nods.*) Oh, I don't mind! It's even rather touching. (*Then mockingly.*) Well, since you're out here professionally, and my husband wants me to consult you, I might as well give you the whole case history! (*Wearily.*) I warn you it isn't pretty, Doctor! But then life doesn't seem to be pretty, does it? And, after all, you aided and abetted God the Father in making this mess. I hope it'll teach you not to be so cocksure in future. (*More and more bitterly.*) I must say you proceeded very unscientifically, Doctor! (*Then suddenly starts her story in a dull monotonous tone recalling that of* EVANS' *mother in the previous Act.*) When we went to visit Sam's mother I'd known for two months that I was going to have a baby.

DARRELL

(*Startled—unable to hide a trace of disappointment*). Oh, then you actually were?

(*Thinking disappointedly and ashamed of himself for being disappointed*). All wrong, what I thought . . . she was going to . . . then why didn't she? . . .

NINA

(*With a strange happy intensity*). Oh, Ned, I loved it more than I've ever loved anything in my life—even Gordon! I loved it so it seemed at times that Gordon must be its real father, that Gordon must have come to me in a dream while I was lying asleep beside Sam! And I was happy! I almost loved Sam then! I felt he was a good husband!

DARRELL

(*Instantly repelled—thinking with scornful jealousy*). Ha! . . . the hero again! . . . comes to her bed! . . . puts horns on poor Sam! . . . becomes the father of his child! . . . I'll be damned if hers isn't the most idiotic obsession I ever . . .

NINA

(*Her voice suddenly becoming flat and lifeless*). And then Sam's mother told me I couldn't have my baby. You see, Doctor, Sam's great-grandfather was insane, and Sam's grandmother died in an asylum, and Sam's father had lost his mind for years before he died, and an aunt who is still alive is crazy. So of course I had to agree it would be wrong—and I had an operation.

DARRELL

(*Who has listened with amazed horror—profoundly shocked and stunned*). Good God! Are you crazy, Nina? I simply can't believe! It would be too hellish! Poor Sam, of all people! (*Bewilderedly.*) Nina! Are you absolutely sure?

NINA

(*Immediately defensive and mocking*). Absolutely, Doctor! Why? Do you think it's I who am crazy? Sam looks so healthy and sane, doesn't he? He fooled you completely, didn't he? You thought he'd be an ideal husband for me! And poor Sam's fooling himself too because he doesn't know anything about all this—so you can't blame him, Doctor!

DARRELL

(*Thinking in a real panic of horror—and a flood of protective affection for her*). God, this is too awful! . . . on top of all the rest! . . . how did she ever stand it! . . . she'll lose her mind too! . . . and it's my fault! . . .

(*Getting up, comes to her and puts his hands on her shoulders, standing behind her—tenderly*). Nina! I'm so damned sorry! There's only one possible thing to do now. You'll have to make Sam give you a divorce.

NINA

(*Bitterly*). Yes? Then what do you suppose would be his finish? No, I've enough guilt in my memory now, thank you! I've got to stick to Sam! (*Then with a strange monotonous insistence.*) I've promised Sam's mother I'd make him happy! He's unhappy now because he thinks he isn't able to give me a child. And I'm unhappy because I've lost my child. So I must have another baby—somehow—don't you think, Doctor?—to make us both happy? (*She looks up at him pleadingly. For a moment they stare into each other's eyes—then both turn away in guilty confusion.*)

DARRELL

(*Bewilderedly thinking*). That look in her eyes . . . what does she want me to think? . . . why does she talk so much about being happy? . . . am I happy? . . . I don't know . . . what is happiness? . . .

(*Confusedly*). Nina, I don't know what to think.

NINA

(*Thinking strangely*). That look in his eyes . . . what did he mean? . . .

(*With the same monotonous insistence*). You must know what to think. I can't think it out myself any more. I need your advice—your *scientific* advice this time, if you please, Doctor. I've thought and thought about it. I've told myself it's what I ought to do. Sam's own mother urged me to do it. It's sensible and kind and just and good. I've told myself this a thousand times and yet I can't quite convince something in me that's afraid of something. I need the courage of someone who can stand outside and reason it out as if Sam and I were no more than guinea pigs. You've got to help me, Doctor! You've got to show me what's the sane—the truly sane, you understand!—thing I must do for Sam's sake, and my own.

DARRELL

(*Thinking confusedly*). What do I have to do? . . . this was all my fault . . . I owe her something in return . . . I owe Sam something . . . I owe them happiness! . . . (*Irritably.*) Damn it, there's a humming in my ears! . . . I've caught some fever . . . I swore to live coolly . . . let me see. . . .

(*In a cold, emotionless professional voice, his face like a mask of a doctor*). A doctor must be in full possession of the facts, if he is to advise. What is it precisely that Sam's wife has thought so much of doing?

NINA

(*In the same insistent tone*). Of picking out a healthy male about whom she cared nothing and having a child by him that Sam would believe was his child, whose life would give him confidence in his own living, who would be for him a living proof that his wife loved him.

(*Confusedly, strangely and purposefully*). This doctor is healthy. . . .

DARRELL

(*In his ultra-professional manner—like an automaton of a doctor*). I see. But this needs a lot of thinking over. It isn't easy to prescribe—

(*Thinking*). I have a friend who has a wife . . . I was envious at his wedding . . . but what has that to do with it? . . . damn it, my mind won't work! . . . it keeps running away to her . . . it wants to mate with her mind . . . in the interest of Science? . . . what damned rot I'm thinking! . . .

NINA

(*Thinking as before*). This doctor is nothing to me but a healthy male . . . when he was Ned he once kissed me . . . but I cared nothing about him . . . so that's all right, isn't it, Sam's mother?

DARRELL

(*Thinking*). Let me see. . . . I am in the laboratory and they are guinea pigs . . . in fact, in the interest of science, I can be for the purpose of this experiment, a healthy guinea pig myself and still remain an observer . . . I observe my pulse is high, for example, and that's obviously because I am stricken with a recurrence of an old desire . . . desire is a natural male reaction to the beauty of the female . . . her husband is my friend. . . . I have always tried to help him . . .

(*Coldly*). I've been considering what Sam's wife told me and her reasoning is quite sound. The child can't be her husband's.

NINA

Then you agree with Sam's mother? She said: "Being happy is the nearest we can ever come to knowing what good is!"

DARRELL

I agree with her decidedly. Sam's wife should find a healthy father for Sam's child at once. It is her sane duty to her husband.

(*Worriedly thinking*). Have I ever been happy? . . . I have studied to cure the body's unhappiness . . . I have watched happy smiles form on the lips of the dying . . . I have experienced pleasure with a number of women I desired but never loved . . . I have known a bit of honor and a trifle of self-satisfaction . . . this talk of happiness seems to me extraneous . . .

NINA

(*Beginning to adopt a timid, diffident, guilty tone*). This will have to be hidden from Sam so he can never know! Oh, Doctor, Sam's wife is afraid!

DARRELL

(*Sharply professional*). Nonsense! This is no time for timidity! Happiness hates the timid! So does Science! Certainly Sam's wife must conceal her action! To let Sam know would be insanely cruel of her—and stupid, for then no one could be the happier for her act!

(*Anxiously thinking*). Am I right to advise this? . . . yes, it is clearly the rational thing to do . . . but this advice betrays my friend! . . . no, it saves him! . . . it saves his wife . . . and if a third party should know a little happiness . . . is he any poorer, am I any the less his friend because I saved him? . . . no, my duty to him is plain . . . and my duty as an experimental searcher after truth . . . to observe these three guinea pigs, of which I am one . . .

NINA

(*Thinking determinedly*). I must have my baby! . . .

(*Timidly—gets from her chair and half-turns toward him—pleadingly*). You must give his wife courage, Doctor. You must free her from her feeling of guilt.

DARRELL

There can only be guilt when one deliberately neglects one's manifest duty to life. Anything else is rot! This woman's duty is to save her husband and herself by begetting a healthy child!

(*Thinking guiltily and instinctively moving away from her*). I am healthy . . . but he is my friend . . . there is such a thing as honor! . . .

NINA

(*Determinedly*). I must take my happiness! . . .

(*Frightenedly—comes after him*). But she is ashamed. It's adultery. It's wrong.

DARRELL

(*Moving away again—with a cold sneering laugh of impatience*). Wrong! Would she rather see her husband wind up in an asylum? Would she rather face the prospect of going to pot mentally, morally, physically herself through year after year of devilling herself and him? Really, Madame, if you can't throw overboard all such irrelevant moral ideas, I'll have to give up this case here and now!

(*Thinking frightenedly*). Who is talking? . . . is he suggesting me? . . . but you know very well I can't be the one, Doctor! . . . why not, you're healthy and it's a friendly act for all concerned.

NINA

(*Thinking determinedly*). I must have my baby! . . .

(*Going further toward him—she can now touch him with her hand*). Please, Doctor, you must give her strength to do this right thing that seems to her so right and then so wrong! (*She puts out her hand and takes one of his.*)

DARRELL

(*Thinking frightenedly*). Whose hand is this? . . . it burns me . . . I kissed her once . . . her lips were cold . . . now they would burn with happiness for me! . . .

NINA

(*Taking his other hand and slowly pulling him around to face her, although he does not look at her—pleadingly*). Now she feels your strength. It gives her the courage to ask you, Doctor, to suggest the father. She has changed, Doctor, since she became Sam's wife. She can't bear the thought now of giving herself to any man she could neither desire nor respect. So each time her thoughts come to the man she must select they are afraid to go on! She needs your courage to choose!

DARRELL

(*As if listening to himself*). Sam is my friend . . . well, and isn't she your friend? . . . her two hands are so warm! . . . I must not even hint at my desire! . . .

(*Judicially calm*). Well, the man must be someone who is not unattractive to her physically, of course.

NINA

Ned always attracted her.

DARRELL

(*Thinking frightenedly*). What's that she said? . . . Ned? . . . attracts? . . .

(*In same tone*). And the man should have a mind that can truly understand—a scientific mind superior to the moral scruples that cause so much human blundering and unhappiness.

NINA

She always thought Ned had a superior mind.

DARRELL

(*Thinking frightenedly*). Did she say Ned? . . . she thinks Ned . . . ?

(*In same tone*). The man should like and admire her, he should be her good friend and want to help her, but he should not love her—although he might, without harm to anyone, desire her.

NINA

Ned does not love her—but he used to like her and, I think, desire her. Does he now, Doctor?

DARRELL

(*Thinking*). Does he? . . . who is he? . . . he is Ned! . . . Ned is I! . . . I desire her! . . . I desire happiness! . . .

(*Trembling now—gently*). But, Madame, I must confess the Ned you are speaking of is I, and I am Ned.

NINA

(*Gently*). And I am Nina, who wants her baby. (*Then she reaches out and turns his head until his face faces hers but he keeps his eyes down—she bends her head meekly and submissively—softly.*) I should be so grateful, Ned. (*He starts, looks up at her wildly, makes a motion as though to take her in his arms, then remains fixed for a moment in that attitude, staring at her bowed head as she repeats submissively.*) I should be so humbly grateful.

DARRELL

(*Suddenly falling on his knees and taking her hand in both of his and kissing it humbly—with a sob*). Yes—yes, Nina—yes—for your happiness—in that spirit!

(*Thinking—fiercely triumphant*). I shall be happy for a while! . . .

NINA

(*Raising her head—thinking—proudly triumphant*). I shall be happy! . . . I shall make my husband happy! . . .

Curtain.

ACT FIVE

SCENE: *The sitting room of a small house* EVANS *has rented in a seashore suburb near New York. It is a bright morning in the following April.*

The room is a typical sitting room of the quantity-production bungalow type. Windows on the left look out on a broad porch. A double doorway in rear leads into the hall. A door on right, to the dining room. NINA *has tried to take the curse of offensive, banal newness off the room with some of her own things from her old home but the attempt has been half-hearted in the face of such overpowering commonness, and the result is a room as disorganized in character as was the* PROFESSOR'S *study in the last Act.*

The arrangement of the furniture follows the same pattern as in preceding scenes. There is a Morris chair and a round golden-oak table at left of center, an upholstered chair, covered with bright chintz at center, a sofa covered with the same chintz at right.

NINA *is sitting in the chair at center. She has been trying to read a book but has let this drop listlessly on her lap. A great change is noticeable in her face and bearing. She is again the pregnant woman of Act Three but this time there is a triumphant strength about her expression, a ruthless self-confidence in her eyes. She has grown stouter, her face has filled out. One gets no impression of neurotic strain from her now, she seems nerveless and deeply calm.*

NINA

(*As if listening for something within her—joyfully*). There! . . . that can't be my imagination . . . I felt it plainly . . . life . . . my baby . . . my only baby . . . the other never really lived . . . this is the child of my love! . . . I love Ned! . . . I've loved him ever since that first afternoon . . . when I went to him . . . so scientifically! . . . (*She laughs at herself.*) Oh, what a goose I was! . . . then love came to me . . . in his arms . . . happiness! . . . I hid it from him . . . I saw he was frightened . . . his own joy frightened him . . . I could feel him fighting with himself . . . during all those afternoons . . . our wonderful afternoons of happiness! . . . and I said nothing . . . I made myself be calculating . . . so when he finally said . . . dreadfully disturbed . . . "Look here, Nina, we've done all that is necessary, playing with fire is dangerous" . . . I said, "You're quite right, Ned, of all things I don't want to fall in love with you!" . . . (*She laughs.*) He didn't like that! . . . he looked angry . . . and afraid . . . then for weeks he never even phoned . . . I waited . . . it was prudent to wait . . . but every day I grew more terrified . . . then just as my will was breaking, his broke . . . he suddenly appeared again . . . but I held him to his aloof doctor's pose and sent him away, proud of his will power . . . and sick of himself with desire for me! . . . every week since then he's been coming out here . . . as my doctor . . . we've talked about our child wisely, dispassionately . . . as if it were Sam's child . . . we've never given in to our desire . . . and I've watched love grow in him until I'm sure . . . (*With sudden alarm.*) But am I? . . . he's never once mentioned love . . . perhaps I've been a fool to play the part I've played . . . it may have turned him against me . . . (*Suddenly with calm confidence.*) No . . . he does . . . I feel it . . . it's only when I start thinking, I begin to doubt . . . (*She settles back and stares dreamily before her—a pause.*) There . . . again . . . his child! . . . my child moving in my life . . . my life moving in my child . . . the world is whole and perfect . . . all things are each other's . . . life is . . . and the is is beyond reason . . . questions die in the silence of this peace . . . I am living a dream within the great dream of the tide . . . breathing in the tide I dream and breathe back my dream into the tide . . . suspended in the movement of the tide, I feel life move in me, suspended in me . . . no whys matter . . . there is no why . . . I am a mother . . . God is a Mother . . . (*She sighs happily, closing her eyes. A pause.*)

(EVANS *enters from the hallway in rear. He is dressed carefully but his clothes are old ones—shabby collegiate gentility—and he has forgotten to shave. His eyes look pitiably harried, his manner has become a distressingly obvious attempt to cover up a chronic state of nervous panic and guilty conscience. He stops inside the doorway and looks at her with a pitiable furtiveness, arguing with himself, trying to get up his courage.*)

EVANS

Tell her! . . . go on! . . . you made up your mind to, didn't you? . . . don't quit now! . . . tell her you've decided . . . for her sake . . . to face the truth . . . that she can't love you . . . she's tried . . . she's acted like a good sport . . . but she's beginning to hate you . . . and you can't blame her . . . she wanted children . . . and you haven't been able . . . (*Protesting feebly.*) But I don't know for certain . . . that that's my fault . . . (*Then bitterly.*) Aw, don't kid yourself, if she'd married someone else . . . if Gordon had lived and married her . . . I'll bet in the first month she'd . . . you'd better resign from the whole game . . . with a gun! . . . (*He swallows hard as if he were choking back a sob—then savagely.*) Stop whining! . . . go on and wake her up! . . . say you're willing to give her a divorce so she can marry some real guy who can give her what she ought to have! . . . (*Then with sudden terror.*) And if she says yes? . . . I couldn't bear it! . . . I'd die without her! . . . (*Then with a somber alien forcefulness.*) All right . . . good riddance! . . . I'd have the guts to bump off then, all right! . . . that'd set her free . . . come on now! . . . ask her! . . .

(*But his voice begins to tremble uncertainly again as he calls*). Nina.

NINA

(*Opens her eyes and gazes calmly, indifferently at him*). Yes?

EVANS

(*Immediately terrified and beaten—thinking*). I can't! . . . the way she looks at me! . . . she'd say yes! . . .

(*Stammering*). I hate to wake you up but —it's about time for Ned to come, isn't it?

NINA

(*Calmly*). I wasn't asleep.

(*Thinking as if she found it hard to concentrate on him, to realize his existence*). This man is my husband . . . it's hard to remember that . . . people will say he's the father of my child. . . . (*With revulsion.*) That's shameful! . . . and yet that's exactly what I wanted! . . . wanted! . . . not now! . . . now I love Ned! . . . I won't lose him! . . . Sam must give me a divorce . . . I've sacrificed enough of my life . . . what has he given me? . . . not even a home . . . I had to sell my father's home to get money so we could move near his job . . . and then he lost his job! . . . now he's depending on Ned to help him get another! . . . my love! . . . how shameless! . . . (*Then contritely.*) Oh, I'm unjust . . . poor Sam doesn't know about Ned . . . and it was I who wanted to sell the place . . . I was lonely there . . . I wanted to be near Ned.

EVANS

(*Thinking in agony*). What's she thinking? . . . probably lucky for me I don't know! . . .

(*Forcing a brisk air as he turns away from her*). I hope Ned brings that letter he promised me to the manager of the Globe company. I'm keen to get on the job again.

NINA

(*With scornful pity*). Oh, I guess Ned will bring the letter. I asked him not to forget.

EVANS

I hope they'll have an opening right off. We can use the money. (*Hanging his head.*) I feel rotten, living on you when you've got so little.

NINA

(*Indifferently but with authority, like a governess to a small boy*). Now, now!

EVANS

(*Relieved*). Well, it's true. (*Then coming to her—humbly ingratiating.*) You've felt a lot better lately, haven't you, Nina?

NINA

(*With a start—sharply*). Why?

EVANS

You look ever so much better. You're getting fat. (*He forces a grin.*)

NINA

(*Curtly*). Don't be absurd, please! As a matter of fact, I don't feel a bit better.

EVANS

(*Thinking despondently*). Lately, she jumps on me every chance she gets . . . as if everything I did disgusted her!

(*He strays over to the window and looks out listlessly*). I thought we'd get some word from Charlie this morning saying if he was coming down or not. But I suppose he's still too broken up over his mother's death to write.

NINA

(*Indifferently*). He'll probably come without bothering to write.

(*Vaguely—wonderingly*). Charlie . . . dear old Charlie . . . I've forgotten him, too. . . .

EVANS

I think that's Ned's car now. Yes. It's stopping. I'll go out and meet him. (*He starts for the door in rear.*)

NINA

(*Sharply, before she can restrain the impulse*). Don't be such a fool!

EVANS

(*Stops—stammers confusedly*). What—what's the matter?

NINA

(*Controlling herself—but irritably*). Don't mind me. I'm nervous.

(*Thinking guiltily*). One minute I feel ashamed of him for making such a fool of himself over my lover . . . the next minute something hateful urges me to drive him into doing it!

(*The maid has answered the ring and opened the outer door.* NED DARRELL *comes in from the rear. His face looks older. There is an expression of defensive bitterness and self-resentment about his mouth and eyes. This vanishes into one of desire and joy as he sees* NINA. *He starts toward her impulsively.*) Nina! (*Then stops short as he sees* EVANS.)

NINA

(*Forgetting* EVANS, *gets to her feet as if to receive* DARRELL *in her arms—with love*). Ned!

EVANS

(*Affectionately and gratefully*). Hello, Ned! (*He holds out his hand, which* DARRELL *takes mechanically.*)

DARRELL

(*Trying to overcome his guilty embarrassment*). Hello, Sam. Didn't see you. (*Hurriedly reaching in his coat pocket.*) Before I forget, here's that letter. I had a talk over the phone with Appleby yesterday. He's pretty sure there's an opening—(*with a condescension he can't help*)—but you'll have to get your nose on the grindstone to make good with him.

EVANS

(*Flushing guiltily—forcing a confident tone*). You bet I will! (*Then gratefully and humbly.*) Gosh, Ned, I can't tell you how grateful I am!

DARRELL

(*Brusquely, to hide his embarrassment*). Oh, shut up! I'm only too glad.

NINA

(*Watching* EVANS *with a contempt that is almost gloating—in a tone of curt dismissal*). You'd better go and shave, hadn't you, if you're going to town?

EVANS

(*Guiltily, passing his hand over his face—forcing a brisk, purposeful air*). Yes, of course. I forgot I hadn't. Excuse me, will you? (*This to* DARRELL. EVANS *hurries out, rear.*)

DARRELL

(*As soon as he is out of earshot—turning on* NINA *accusingly*). How can you treat him that way? It makes me feel—like a swine!

NINA

(*Flushing guiltily—protestingly*). What way? (*Then inconsequentially.*) He's always forgetting to shave lately.

DARRELL

You know what I mean, Nina!

(*Turns away from her—thinking bitterly*). What a rotten liar I've become! . . . and he trusts me absolutely! . . .

NINA

(*Thinking frightenedly*). Why doesn't he take me in his arms? . . . oh, I feel he doesn't love me now! . . . he's so bitter! . . .

(*Trying to be matter-of-fact*). I'm sorry, Ned. I don't mean to be cross but Sam does get on my nerves.

DARRELL

(*Thinking bitterly*). Sometimes I almost hate her! . . . if it wasn't for her I'd have kept my peace of mind . . . no good for anything lately, damn it! . . . but it's idiotic to feel guilty . . . if Sam only didn't trust me! . . . (*Then impatiently.*) Bosh! . . . sentimental nonsense! . . . end justifies means! . . . this will have a good end for Sam, I swear to that! . . . why doesn't she tell him she's pregnant? . . . what's she waiting for? . . .

NINA

(*Thinking passionately, looking at him*). Oh, my lover, why don't you kiss me? . . .

(*Imploringly*). Ned! Don't be cross with me, please!

DARRELL

(*Fighting to control himself—coldly*). I'm not cross, Nina. Only you must admit these triangular scenes are, to say the least, humiliating. (*Resentfully.*) I won't come out here again!

NINA

(*With a cry of pain*). Ned!

DARRELL

(*Thinking exultingly at first*). She loves me! . . . she's forgotten Gordon! . . . I'm happy! . . . do I love her? . . . no! . . . I won't! . . . I can't! . . . think what it would mean to Sam! . . . to my career! . . . be objective about it . . . you guinea pig! . . . I'm her doctor . . . and Sam's . . . I prescribed child for them . . . that's all there is to it! . . .

NINA

(*Torn between hope and fear*). What is he thinking? . . . he's fighting his love . . . oh, my lover! . . .

(*Again with longing*). Ned!

DARRELL

(*Putting on his best professional air, going to her*). How do you feel today? You look as if you might have a little fever. (*He takes her hand as if to feel her pulse. Her hand closes over his. She looks up into his face. He keeps his turned away.*)

NINA

(*Straining up toward him—with intense longing—thinking*). I love you! . . . take me! . . . what do I care for anything in the world but you! . . . let Sam die! . . .

DARRELL

(*Fighting himself—thinking*). Christ! . . . touch of her skin! . . . her nakedness! . . . those afternoons in her arms! happiness! . . . what do I care for anything else? . . . to hell with Sam! . . .

NINA

(*Breaking out passionately*). Ned! I love you! I can't hide it any more! I won't! I love you, Ned!

DARRELL

(*Suddenly taking her in his arms and kissing her frantically*). Nina! Beautiful!

NINA

(*Triumphantly—between kisses*).. You love me, don't you? Say you do, Ned!

DARRELL

(*Passionately*). Yes! Yes!

NINA

(*With a cry of triumph*). Thank God! At last you've told me! You've confessed it to yourself! Oh, Ned, you've made me so happy! (*There is a ring from the front door bell.* DARRELL *hears it. It acts like an electric shock on him. He tears himself away from her. Instinctively she gets up too and moves to the lounge at right.*)

DARRELL

(*Stupidly*). Someone—at the door.

(*He sinks down in the chair by the table at left. Thinking torturedly*). I said I loved her! . . . she won! . . . she used my desire! . . . but I don't love her! . . . I won't! . . . she can't own my life! . . .

(*Violently—almost shouts at her*). I don't, Nina! I tell you I don't!

NINA

(*The maid has just gone to the front door*). Sshh! (*Then in a triumphant whisper.*) You do, Ned! You do!

DARRELL

(*With dogged stupidity*). I don't!

(*The front door has been opened.* MARSDEN *appears in the rear, walks slowly and woodenly like a man in a trance into the room. He is dressed immaculately in deep mourning. His face is pale, drawn, haggard with loneliness and grief. His eyes have a dazed look as if he were still too stunned to comprehend clearly what has happened to him. He does not seem conscious of* DARRELL'S *presence at first. His shoulders are bowed, his whole figure droops.*)

NINA

(*Thinking—in a strange superstitious panic*). Black . . . in the midst of happiness . . . black comes . . . again . . . death . . . my father . . . comes between me and happiness! . . . (*Then recovering herself, scornfully.*) You silly coward! . . . it's only Charlie! . . . (*Then with furious resentment.*) The old fool! . . . what does he mean coming in on us without warning? . . .

MARSDEN

(*Forcing a pitiful smile to his lips*). Hello, Nina. I know it's an imposition—but—I've been in such a terrible state since Mother—(*He falters, his face becomes distorted into an ugly mask of grief, his eyes water.*)

NINA

(*Immediately sympathetic, gets up and goes to him impulsively*). There's no question of imposition, Charlie. We were expecting you. (*She has come to him and put her arms around him. He gives way and sobs, his head against her shoulder.*)

MARSDEN

(*Brokenly*). You don't know, Nina—how terrible—it's terrible!—

NINA

(*Leading him to the chair at center, soothingly*). I know, Charlie.

(*Thinking with helpless annoyance*). Oh, dear, what can I say? . . . his mother hated me . . . I'm not glad she's dead . . . but neither am I sorry . . . (*With a trace of contempt.*) Poor Charlie . . . he was so tied to her apron strings . . .

(*Then kindly but condescendingly, comforting him*). Poor old Charlie!

MARSDEN

(*The words and the tone shock his pride to life. He raises his head and half-pushes her away—resentfully, thinking*). Poor old Charlie! . . . damn it, what am I to her? . . . her old dog who's lost his mother? . . . Mother hated her . . . no, poor dear Mother was so sweet, she never hated anyone . . . she simply disapproved . . .

(*Coldly*). I'm all right, Nina. Quite all right now, thank you. I apologize for making a scene.

DARRELL

(*Has gotten up from his chair—with relief—thinking*). Thank God for Marsden . . . I feel sane again . . .

(*He comes to* MARSDEN*—cordially*). How are you, Marsden? (*Then offering conventional, consolation, pats* MARSDEN'S *shoulder.*) I'm sorry, Marsden.

MARSDEN

(*Startled, looks up at him in amazement*). Darrell! (*Then with instant hostility.*) There's nothing to be sorry about that I can discover! (*Then as they both look at him in surprise he realizes what he has said—stammeringly.*) I mean—sorry—is hardly the right word—hardly—is it?

NINA

(*Worriedly*). Sit down, Charlie. You look so tired.

(*He slumps down in the chair at center mechanically.* NINA *and* DARRELL *return to their chairs.* NINA *looks across him at* DARRELL*—triumphantly—thinking*). You do love me, Ned! . . .

DARRELL

(*Thinking—answering her look—defiantly*). I don't love you! . . .

MARSDEN

(*Stares intensely before him. Thinking suspiciously—morbidly agitated*). Darrell! . . . and Nina! . . . there's something in this room! . . . something disgusting! . . . like a brutal, hairy hand, raw and red, at my throat! . . . stench of human life! . . . heavy and rank! . . . outside it's April . . . green buds on the slim trees . . . the sadness of spring . . . my loss at peace in Nature . . . her sorrow of birth consoling my sorrow of death . . . something human and unnatural in this room! . . . love and hate and passion and possession! . . . cruelly indifferent to my loss! . . . mocking my loneliness! . . . no longer any love for me in any room! . . . lust in this room! . . . lust with a loathsome jeer taunting my sensitive timidities! . . . my purity! . . . purity? . . . ha! yes, if you say prurient purity! . . . lust ogling me for a dollar with oily shoe-button Italian eyes! . . . (*In terror.*) What thoughts! . . . what a low scoundrel you are! . . . and your mother dead only two weeks! . . . I hate Nina! . . . that Darrell in this room! . . . I feel their desires! . . . where is Sam? . . . I'll tell him! . . . no, he wouldn't believe . . . he's such a trusting fool . . . I must punish her some other way . . . (*Remorsefully.*) What? . . . punish Nina? . . . my little Nina? . . . why, I want her to be happy! . . . even with Darrell? . . . it's all so confused! . . . I must stop thinking! . . . I must talk! . . . forget! . . . say something! . . . forget everything! . . .

(*He suddenly bursts into a flood of garrulity*). Mother asked for you, Nina—three days before the end. She said, "Where is Nina Leeds now, Charlie? When is she going to marry Gordon Shaw?" Her mind was wandering, poor woman! You remember how fond she always was of Gordon. She used to love to watch the football games when he was playing. He was so handsome and graceful, she always thought. She always loved a strong, healthy body. She took such strict care of her own, she walked miles every day, she loved bathing and boating in the summer even after she was sixty, she was never sick a day in her life until—(*He turns on* DARRELL—*coldly.*) You were right, Doctor Darrell. It was cancer. (*Then angrily.*) But the doctor you sent me to, and the others he called in could do nothing for her—absolutely nothing! I might just as well have imported some witch doctors from the Solomon Islands! They at least would have diverted her in her last hours with their singing and dancing, but your specialists were a total loss! (*Suddenly with an insulting, ugly sneer, raising his voice.*) I think you doctors are a pack of God-damned ignorant liars and hypocrites!

NINA

(*Sharply*). Charlie!

MARSDEN

(*Coming to himself—with a groan—shamefacedly*). Don't mind me. I'm not myself, Nina. I've been through hell! (*He seems about to sob—then abruptly springs to his feet, wildly.*) It's this room! I can't stand this room! There's something repulsive about it!

NINA

(*Soothingly*). I know it's ugly, Charlie. I haven't had a chance to fix it up yet. We've been too broke.

MARSDEN

(*Confusedly*). Oh, it's all right. I'm ugly, too! Where's Sam?

NINA

(*Eagerly*). Right upstairs. Go on up. He'll be delighted to see you.

MARSDEN

(*Vaguely*). Very well. (*He goes to the door, then stops mournfully.*) But from what I saw on that visit to his home, he doesn't love his mother much. I don't think he'll understand, Nina. He never writes to her, does he?

NINA

(*Uneasily*). No—I don't know.

MARSDEN

She seemed lonely. He'll be sorry for it some day after she—(*He gulps.*) Well—(*He goes.*)

NINA

(*In a sudden panic—thinking*). Sam's mother! . . . "Make my boy, Sammy, happy!" . . . I promised . . . oh, why did Charlie have to remember her? . . . (*Then resolutely.*) I can't remember her now! . . . I won't! . . . I've got to be happy! . . .

DARRELL

(*Uneasily trying to force a casual conversation*). Poor Marsden is completely knocked off balance, isn't he? (*A pause.*) My mother died when I was away at school. I hadn't seen her in some time, so her death was never very real to me; but in Marsden's case—

NINA

(*With a possessive smile of tolerance*). Never mind Charlie, Ned. What do I care about Charlie? I love you! And you love me!

DARRELL

(*Apprehensively, forcing a tone of annoyed rebuke*). But I don't! And you don't! You're simply letting your romantic imagination run away with you—(*showing his jealous resentment in spite of himself.*)—as you did once before with Gordon Shaw!

NINA

(*Thinking*). He is jealous of Gordon! . . . how wonderful that is! . . .

(*With provoking calm*). I loved Gordon.

DARRELL

(*Irritably ignoring this as if he didn't want to hear it*). Romantic imagination! It has ruined more lives than all the diseases! Other diseases, I should say! It's a form of insanity! (*He gets up forcefully and begins to pace about the room.*)

(*Thinking uneasily*). Mustn't look at her . . . find an excuse and get away . . . and this time never come back! . . .

(*Avoiding looking at her, trying to argue reasonably—coldly*). You're acting foolishly, Nina—and very unfairly. The agreement we made has no more to do with love than a contract for building a house. In fact, you know we agreed it was essential that love mustn't enter into it. And it hasn't, in spite of what you say. (*A pause. He walks about. She watches him.*)

(*Thinking*). She's got to come back to earth! . . . I've got to break with her! . . . bad enough now! . . . but to go on with it! . . . what a mess it'd make of all our lives! . . .

NINA

(*Thinking tenderly*). Let his pride put all the blame on me! . . . I'll accept it gladly! . . .

DARRELL

(*Irritably*). Of course, I realize I've been to blame, too. I haven't been able to be as impersonal as I thought I could be. The trouble is there's been a dangerous physical attraction. Since I first met you, I've always desired you physically. I admit that now.

NINA

(*Smiling tenderly—thinking*). Oh, he admits that, does he? . . . poor darling! . . .

(*Enticingly*). And you still do desire me, don't you, Ned?

DARRELL

(*Keeping his back turned to her—roughly*). No! That part of it is finished! (NINA *laughs softly, possessively. He whirls around to face her—angrily.*) Look here! You're going to have the child you wanted, aren't you?

NINA

(*Implacably*). My child wants its father!

DARRELL

(*Coming a little toward her—desperately*). But you're crazy! You're forgetting Sam! It may be stupid but I've got a guilty conscience! I'm beginning to think we've wronged the very one we were trying to help!

NINA

You were trying to help me, too, Ned!

DARRELL

(*Stammering*). Well—all right—let's say that part of it was all right then. But it's got to stop! It can't go on!

NINA

(*Implacably*). Only your love can make me happy now! Sam must give me a divorce so I can marry you.

DARRELL

(*Thinking suspiciously*). Look out! . . . there it is! . . . marry! . . . own me! . . . ruin my career! . . .

(*Scornfully*). Marry? Do you think I'm a fool? Get that out of your head quick! I wouldn't marry anyone—no matter what! (*As she continues to look at him with unmoved determination—pleadingly.*) Be sensible, for God's sake! We're absolutely unsuited to each other! I don't admire your character! I don't respect you! I know too much about your past! (*Then indignantly.*) And how about Sam? Divorce him? Have you forgotten all his mother told you? Do you mean to say you'd deliberately—? And you expect me to—? What do you think I am?

NINA

(*Inflexibly*). You're my lover! Nothing else matters. Yes, I remember what Sam's mother said. She said, "being happy is the nearest we can come to knowing what good is." And I'm going to be happy! I've lost everything in life so far because I didn't have the courage to take it—and I've hurt everyone around me. There's no use trying to think of others. One human being can't think of another. It's impossible. (*Gently and caressingly.*) But this time I'm going to think of my own happiness—and that means you—and our child! That's quite enough for one human being to think of, dear, isn't it? (*She reaches out and takes his hand. A pause. With her other hand she gently pulls him around until he is forced to look into her eyes.*)

DARRELL

(*Thinking fascinatedly*). I see my happiness in her eyes . . . the touch of her soft skin! . . . those afternoons! . . . God, I was happy! . . .

(*In a strange dazed voice—as if it were forced out of him by an impulse stronger than his will*). Yes, Nina.

NINA

(*In a determined voice*). I've given Sam enough of my life! And it hasn't made him happy, not the least bit! So what's the good? And how can we really know that his thinking our child was his would do him any good? We can't! It's all guesswork. The only thing sure is that we love each other.

DARRELL

(*Dazedly*). Yes. (*A noise from the hall and* EVANS *comes in from the rear. He sees their two hands together but mistakes their meaning.*)

EVANS

(*Genially—with a forced self-confident air*). Well, Doc, how's the patient? I think she's much better, don't you—although she won't admit it.

DARRELL

(*At the first sound of* EVANS' *voice, pulls his hand from* NINA'S *as if it were a hot coal—avoiding* EVANS' *eyes, moving away from her jerkily and self-consciously*). Yes. Much better.

EVANS

Good! (*He pats* NINA *on the back. She shrinks away. His confidence vanishes in a flash.*)

(*Thinking miserably*). Why does she shrink away . . . if I even touch her? . . .

NINA

(*Matter-of-factly*). I must see how lunch is coming on. You'll stay, of course, Ned?

DARRELL

(*Struggling—shakenly*). No, I think I'd better—

(*Thinking desperately*). Got to go! . . . can't go! . . . got to go! . . .

EVANS

Oh, come on, old man!

NINA

(*Thinking*). He must stay . . . and after lunch we'll tell Sam. . . .

(*With certainty*). He'll stay. (*Meaningly.*) And we want to have a long talk with you after lunch, Sam—don't we, Ned? (DARRELL *does not answer. She goes out, right.*)

EVANS

(*Vaguely making talk*). I got Charlie to lie down. He's all in, poor guy. (*Then trying to face* DARRELL *who keeps looking away from him.*) What did Nina mean, you want a long talk with me? Or is it a secret, Ned?

DARRELL

(*Controlling an impulse toward hysterical laughter*). A secret? Yes, you bet it's a secret! (*He flings himself in the chair at left, keeping his face averted.*)

(*His thoughts bitter and desperate like a cornered fugitive's.*) This is horrible! . . . Sam thinks I'm finest fellow in world . . . and I do this to him! . . . as if he hadn't enough! . . . born under a curse! . . . I finish him! . . . a doctor! . . . God damn it! . . . I can see his end! . . . never forgive myself! . . . never forget! . . . break me! . . . ruin my career! . . . (*More desperately.*) Got to stop this! . . . while there's time! . . . she said . . . after lunch, talk . . . she meant, tell him . . . that means kill him . . . then she'll marry me! . . . (*Beginning to be angry.*) By God, I won't! . . . she'll find out! . . . smiling! . . . got me where she wants me! . . . then be as cruel to me as she is to him! . . . love me? . . . liar! . . . still loves Gordon! . . . her body is a trap! . . . I'm caught in it! . . . she touches my hand, her eyes get in mine, I lose my will! . . . (*Furiously.*) By God, she can't make a fool of me that way! . . . I'll go away some place! . . . go to Europe! . . . study! . . . forget her in work! . . . keep hidden until boat sails so she can't reach me! . . . (*He is in a state of strange elation by this time.*) Go now! . . . no! . . . got to spike her guns with Sam! . . . by God, I see! . . . tell him about baby! . . . that'll stop her! . . . when she knows I've told him that, she'll see it's hopeless! . . . she'll stick to him! . . . poor Nina! . . . I'm sorry! . . . she does love me! . . . hell! . . . she'll forget! . . . she'll have her child! . . . she'll be happy! . . . and Sam'll be happy! . . .

(*He suddenly turns to* EVANS *who has been staring at him, puzzledly—in a whisper*). Look here, Sam. I can't stay to lunch. I haven't time, I've got a million things to do. I'm sailing for Europe in a few days.

EVANS

(*Surprised*). You're sailing?

DARRELL

(*Very hurriedly*). Yes—going to study over there for a year or so. I haven't told anyone. I came out today to say good-bye. You won't be able to reach me again. I'll be out of town visiting. (*Then elatedly.*) And now for your secret! It ought to make you very happy, Sam. I know how much you've wished for it, so I'm going to tell you although Nina'll be furious with me. She was saving it to surprise you with at her own proper time—(*still more elatedly*)—but I'm selfish enough to want to see you happy before I go!

EVANS

(*Not daring to believe what he hopes—stammering*). What—what is it, Ned?

DARRELL

(*Clapping him on the back—with strange joviality*). You're going to be a father, old scout, that's the secret! (*Then as* EVANS *just stares at him dumbly in a blissful satisfaction, he rattles on.*) And now I've got to run. See you again in a year or so. I've said good-bye to Nina. Good-bye, Sam. (*He takes his hand and clasps it.*) Good luck! Buckle down to work now! You've got the stuff in you! When I get back I'll expect to hear you're on the highroad to success! And tell Nina I'll expect to find you both happy in your child—both of you, tell her!—happy in your child! Tell her that, Sam! (*He turns and goes to the door.*)

(*Thinking as he goes*). That does it! . . . honorably! . . . I'm free! . . . (*He goes out—then out the front door—a moment later his motor is heard starting—dies away.*)

EVANS

(*Stares after him dumbly in the same state of happy stupefaction—mumbles*). Thank you—Ned.

(*Thinking disjointedly*). Why did I doubt myself? . . . now she loves me . . . she's loved me right along . . . I've been a fool . . . (*He suddenly falls on his knees.*) Oh, God, I thank you!

(NINA *comes in from the kitchen. She stops in amazement when she sees him on his knees. He jumps to his feet and takes her in his arms with confident happiness and kisses her*). Oh, Nina, I love you so! And now I know you love me! I'll never be afraid of anything again!

NINA

(*Bewildered and terror-stricken, trying feebly to push him away—thinking*). Has he . . . has he gone crazy? . . .

(*Weakly*). Sam! What's come over you, Sam?

EVANS

(*Tenderly*). Ned told me—the secret—and I'm so happy, dear! (*He kisses her again.*)

NINA

(*Stammering*). Ned told you—what?

EVANS

(*Tenderly*). That we're going to have a child, dear. You mustn't be sore at him. Why did you want to keep it a secret from me? Didn't you know how happy it would make me, Nina?

NINA

He told you we—we—you, the father—? (*Then suddenly breaking from him—wildly.*) Ned! Where is Ned?

EVANS

He left a moment ago.

NINA

(*Stupidly*). Left? Call him back. Lunch is ready.

EVANS

He's gone. He couldn't stay. He's got so much to do getting ready to sail.

NINA

Sail?

EVANS

Didn't he tell you he was sailing for Europe? He's going over for a year or so to study.

NINA

A year or so! (*Wildly.*) I've got to call him up! No, I'll go in and see him right now! (*She takes a wavering step toward the door.*)

(*Thinking in anguish*). Go! . . . go to him! . . . find him! . . . my lover! . . .

EVANS

He won't be there, I'm afraid. He said we couldn't reach him, that he'd be visiting friends out of town until he sailed. (*Solicitously.*) Why, do you have to see him about something important, Nina? Perhaps I could locate—

NINA

(*Stammering and swaying*). No. (*She stifles an hysterical laugh.*) No, nothing—nothing important—nothing is important—ha—! (*She stifles another laugh—then on the verge of fainting, weakly.*) Sam! Help me—

EVANS

(*Rushes to her, supports her to sofa at right*). Poor darling! Lie down and rest. (*She remains in a sitting position, staring blankly before her. He chafes her wrists.*) Poor darling!

(*Thinking jubilantly*). Her condition . . . this weakness comes from her condition! . . .

NINA

(*Thinking in anguish*). Ned doesn't love me! . . . he's gone! . . . gone forever! . . . like Gordon! . . . no, not like Gordon! . . . like a sneak, a coward! . . . a liar! . . . oh, I hate him! . . . O Mother God, please let me hate him! . . . he must have been planning this! . . . he must have known it today when he said he loved me! . . . (*Thinking frenziedly.*) I won't bear it . . . he thinks he has palmed me off on Sam forever! . . . and his child! . . . he can't! . . . I'll tell Sam he was lying! . . . I'll make Sam hate him! . . . I'll make Sam kill him! . . . I'll promise to love Sam if he kills him! . . .

(*Suddenly turns to* EVANS—*savagely*). He lied to you!

EVANS

(*Letting her wrists drop—appalled—stammers*). You mean—Ned lied about—?

NINA

(*In same tone*). Ned lied to you!

EVANS

(*Stammers*). You're not—going to have a child—

NINA

(*Savagely*). Oh, yes! Oh, yes, I am! Nothing can keep me from that! But you're—you're—I mean, you . . .

(*Thinking in anguish*). I can't say that to him! . . . I can't tell him without Ned to help me! . . . I can't! . . . look at his face! . . . oh, poor Sammy! . . . poor little boy! . . . poor little boy! . . . (*She takes his head and presses it to her breast and begins to weep.*)

(*Weeping*). I mean, you weren't to know about it, Sammy.

EVANS

(*Immediately on the crest again—tenderly*). Why? Don't you want me to be happy, Nina?

NINA

Yes—yes, I do, Sammy.

(*Thinking strangely*). Little boy! . . . little boy! . . . one gives birth to little boys! . . . one doesn't drive them mad and kill them! . . .

EVANS

(*Thinking*). She's never called me Sammy before . . . someone used to . . . oh, yes, Mother . . .

(*Tenderly and boyishly*). And I'm going to make you happy from now on, Nina. I tell you, the moment Ned told me, something happened to me! I can't explain it, but—I'll make good now, Nina! I know I've said that before but I was only boasting. I was only trying to make myself think so. But now I say it knowing I can do it! (*Softly.*) It's because we're going to have a child, Nina. I knew that you'd never come to really love me without that. That's what I was down on my knees for when you came in. I was thanking God—for our baby!

NINA

(*Tremblingly*). Sammy! Poor boy!

EVANS

Ned said when he came back he'd expect to find us both happy—in our baby. He said to tell you that. You will be happy now, won't you, Nina?

NINA

(*Brokenly and exhaustedly*). I'll try to make you happy, Sammy. (*He kisses her, then hides his head on her breast. She stares out over his head. She seems to grow older.*)

(*Thinking as if she were repeating the words of some inner voice of life*). Not Ned's child! . . . not Sam's child! . . . mine! . . . there! . . . again! . . . I feel my child live . . . moving in my life . . . my life moving in my child . . . breathing in the tide I dream and breathe my dream back into the tide . . . God is a Mother. . . . (*Then with sudden anguish.*) Oh, afternoons . . . dear wonderful afternoons of love with you, my lover . . . you are lost . . . gone from me forever! . . .

Curtain.

ACT SIX

SCENE: *The same—an evening a little over a year later. The room has undergone a significant change. There is a comfortable, homey atmosphere as though now it definitely belonged to the type of person it was built for. It has a proud air of modest prosperity.*

It is soon after dinner—about eight o'clock. EVANS *is sitting by the table at left, glancing through a newspaper at headlines and reading an article here and there.* NINA *is in the chair at center, knitting a tiny sweater.* MARSDEN *is sitting on the sofa at right, holding a book which he pretends to be looking through, but glancing wonderingly at* EVANS *and* NINA.

There is a startling change in EVANS. *He is stouter, the haggard look of worry and self-conscious inferiority has gone from his face, it is full and healthy and satisfied. There is also, what is more remarkable, a decided look of solidity about him, of a determination moving toward ends it is confident it can achieve. He has matured, found his place in the world.*

The change in NINA *is also perceptible. She looks noticeably older, the traces of former suffering are marked on her face, but there is also an expression of present contentment and calm.*

MARSDEN *has aged greatly. His hair is gray, his expression one of a deep grief that is dying out into a resignation resentful of itself. He is dressed immaculately in dark tweed.*

NINA

(*Thinking*). I wonder if there's a draft in the baby's room? . . . maybe I'd better close the window? . . . oh, I guess it's all right . . . he needs lots of fresh air . . . little Gordon . . . he does remind me of Gordon . . . something in his eyes . . . my romantic imagination? . . . Ned said that . . . why hasn't Ned ever written? . . . it's better he hasn't . . . how he made me suffer! . . . but I forgive him . . . he gave me my baby . . . the baby certainly doesn't look like him . . . everyone says he looks like Sam . . . how absurd! . . . but Sam makes a wonderful father . . . he's become a new man in the past year . . . and I've helped him . . . he asks me about everything . . . I have a genuine respect for him now . . . I can give myself without repulsion . . . I am making him happy . . . I've written his mother I'm making him happy . . . I was proud to be able to write her that . . . how queerly things work out! . . . all for the best . . . and I don't feel wicked . . . I feel good . . . (*She smiles strangely.*)

MARSDEN

(*Thinking*). What a change! . . . the last time I was here the air was poisoned . . . Darrell . . . I was sure he was her lover . . . but I was in a morbid state . . . why did Darrell run away? . . . Nina could have got Sam to divorce her if she really loved Darrell . . . then it's evident she couldn't have loved him . . . and she was going to have Sam's baby . . . Darrell's love must have seemed like treachery . . . so she sent him away . . . that must be it . . . (*With satisfaction.*) Yes, I've got it straight now. . . . (*With contemptuous pity.*) Poor Darrell . . . I have no use for him but I did pity him when I ran across him in Munich . . . he was going the pace . . . looked desperate . . . (*Then gloomily.*) My running away was about as successful as his . . . as if one could leave one's memory behind! . . . I couldn't forget

Mother . . . she haunted me through every city of Europe . . . (*Then irritatedly.*) I must get back to work! . . . not a line written in over a year! . . . my public will be forgetting me! . . . a plot came to me yesterday . . . my mind is coming around again . . . I am beginning to forget, thank God! . . . (*Then remorsefully.*) No, I don't want to forget you, Mother! . . . but let me remember . . . without pain! . . .

EVANS

(*Turning over a page of his paper*). There's going to be the biggest boom before long this country has ever known, or I miss my guess, Nina.

NINA

(*With great seriousness*). Do you think so, Sammy?

EVANS

(*Decidedly*). I'm dead sure of it.

NINA

(*With a maternal pride and amusement*). Dear Sam . . . I can't quite believe in this self-confident business man yet . . . but I have to admit he's proved it . . . he asked for more money and they gave it without question . . . they're anxious to keep him . . . they ought to be . . . how he's slaved! . . . for me and my baby! . . .

EVANS

(*Has been looking at* MARSDEN *surreptitiously over his paper*). Charlie's mother must have hoarded up a half million . . . he'll let it rot in government bonds . . . wonder what he'd say if I proposed that he back me? . . . he's always taken a friendly interest . . . well, it's worth a bet, anyway . . . he'd be an easy partner to handle . . .

MARSDEN

(*Staring at* EVANS *wonderingly*). What a changed Sam! . . . I preferred him the old way . . . futile but he had a sensitive quality . . . now he's brash . . . a little success . . . oh, he'll succeed all right . . . his kind are inheriting the earth . . . hogging it, cramming it down their tasteless gullets! . . . and he's happy! . . . actually happy! . . . he has Nina . . . a beautiful baby . . . a comfortable home . . . no sorrow, no tragic memories . . . and I have nothing! . . . but utter loneliness! . . . (*With grieving self-pity.*) If only Mother had lived! . . . how horribly I miss her! . . . my lonely home . . . who will keep house for me now? . . . it has got to be done sympathetically or I won't be able to work . . . I must write to Jane . . . she'll probably be only too glad . . .

(*Turning to* NINA). I think I'll write to my sister in California and ask her to come on and live with me. She's alone now that her youngest daughter is married, and she has very little money. And my hands are tied as far as sharing the estate with her is concerned. According to Mother's will, I'm cut off too if I give her a penny. Mother never got over her bitter feeling about Jane's marriage. In a way, she was right. Jane's husband wasn't much—no family or position or ability—and I doubt if she was ever happy with him. (*Sarcastically.*) It was one of those love matches!

NINA

(*Smiling—teasingly*). There's no danger of your ever making a love match, is there, Charlie?

MARSDEN

(*Wincing—thinking*). She can't believe any woman could possibly love me! . . .

(*Caustically*). I trust I'll never make that kind of a fool of myself, Nina!

NINA

(*Teasingly*). Pooh! Aren't you the superior bachelor! I don't see anything to be so proud of! You're simply shirking, Charlie!

MARSDEN

(*Wincing but forcing a teasing air*). You were my only true love, Nina. I made a vow of perpetual bachelorhood when you threw me over in Sam's favor!

EVANS

(*Has listened to this last—jokingly*). Hello! What's this? I never knew you were my hated rival, Charlie!

MARSDEN

(*Dryly*). Oh—didn't you really? (*But* EVANS *has turned back to his paper.*)

(*Thinking savagely*). That fool, too! . . . he jokes about it! . . . as if I were the last one in the world he could imagine . . .

NINA

(*Teasingly*). Well, if I'm responsible, Charlie, I feel I ought to do something about it. I'll pick out a wife for you—guaranteed to suit! She must be at least ten years older than you, large and matronly and placid, and a wonderful cook and housekeeper—

MARSDEN

(*Sharply*). Don't be stupid!

(*Thinking angrily*). She picks someone beyond the age! . . . she never imagines sex could enter into it! . . .

NINA

(*Placatingly—seeing he is really angry*). Why, I was only picking out a type I thought would be good for you, Charlie—and for your work.

MARSDEN

(*Sneeringly—with a meaning emphasis*). You didn't mention chaste. I couldn't respect a woman who hadn't respected herself!

NINA

(*Thinking—stung*). He's thinking of those men in the hospital . . . what a fool I was ever to tell him! . . .

(*Cuttingly*). Oh, so you think you deserve an innocent virgin!

MARSDEN

(*Coldly—controlling his anger*). Let's drop me, if you please. (*With a look at her that is challenging and malicious.*) Did I tell you I ran into Doctor Darrell in Munich?

NINA

(*Startled—thinking frightenedly and confusedly*). Ned! . . . he saw Ned! . . . why hasn't he told me before? . . . why did he look at me like that? . . . does he suspect? . . .

(*Trying to be calm but stammering*). You saw—Ned?

MARSDEN

(*With savage satisfaction*). That struck home! . . . look at her! . . . guilty! . . . then I was right that day! . . .

(*Casually*). Yes, I chanced to run into him.

NINA

(*More calmly now*). Why on earth didn't you tell us before, Charlie?

MARSDEN

(*Coolly*). Why? Is it such important news? You knew he was there, didn't you? I supposed he'd written you.

EVANS

(*Looking up from his paper—affectionately*). How was the old scout?

MARSDEN

(*Maliciously*). He seemed in fine feather—said he was having a gay time. When I saw him he was with a startling-looking female—quite beautiful, if you like that type. I gathered they were living together.

NINA

(*Cannot restrain herself—breaks out*). I don't believe it! (*Then immediately controlling herself and forcing a laugh.*) I mean, Ned was always so serious-minded it's hard to imagine him messed up in that sort of thing.

(*Thinking in a queer state of jealous confusion*). Hard to imagine! . . . my lover! . . . oh, pain again! . . . why? . . . I don't love him now . . . be careful! . . . Charlie's staring at me. . . .

MARSDEN

(*Thinking—jealously*). Then she did love him! . . . does she still? . . . (*Hopefully.*) Or is it only pique? . . . no woman likes to lose a man even when she no longer loves him. . . .

(*With malicious insistence*). Why is that hard to imagine, Nina? Darrell never struck me as a Galahad. After all, why shouldn't he have a mistress? (*Meaningly.*) He has no tie over here to remain faithful to, has he?

NINA

(*Struggling with herself—thinking pitiably*). He's right . . . why shouldn't Ned? . . . is that why he's never written? . . .

(*Airily*). I don't know what ties he has or hasn't got. It's nothing to me if he has fifty mistresses. I suppose he's no better than the rest of you.

EVANS

(*Looking over at her—tenderly reproachful*). That isn't fair, Nina.

(*Thinking proudly*). I'm proud of that . . . never anyone before her . . .

NINA

(*Looking at him—with real gratitude*). I didn't mean you, dear.

(*Thinking—proudly*). Thank God for Sammy! . . . I know he's mine . . . no jealousy . . . no fear . . . no pain . . . I've found peace . . . (*Then distractedly.*) Oh, Ned, why haven't you written? . . . stop it! . . . what a fool I am! . . . Ned's dead for me! . . . oh, I hate Charlie! . . . why did he tell me? . . .

MARSDEN

(*Looking at* EVANS*—contemptuously thinking*). What a poor simpleton Sam is! . . . boasting of his virtue! . . . as if women loved you for that! . . . they despise it! . . . I don't want Nina to think I've had no experiences with women. . . .

(*Mockingly*). So then it's Sam who is the Galahad, eh? Really, Nina, you should have put him in the Museum among the prehistoric mammals!

EVANS

(*Pleased—comes back kiddingly*). Well, I never had your chances, Charlie! I couldn't run over to Europe and get away with murder the way you have!

MARSDEN

(*Foolishly pleased—admitting while denying*). Oh, I wasn't quite as bad as all that, Sam!

(*Scornfully ashamed of himself—thinking*). Poor sick ass that I am! . . . I want them to think I've been a Don Juan! . . . how pitiful and disgusting! . . . I wouldn't have a mistress if I could! . . . if I could? . . . of course I could! . . . I've simply never cared to degrade myself! . . .

NINA

(*Thinking — tormentedly*). The thought of that woman! . . . Ned forgetting our afternoons in nights with her! . . . stop these thoughts! . . . I won't give in to them! . . . why did Charlie want to hurt me? . . . is he jealous of Ned? . . . Charlie has always loved me in some queer way of his own . . . how ridiculous! . . . look at him! . . . he's so proud of being thought a Don Juan! . . . I'm sure he never even dared to kiss a woman except his mother! . . .

(*Mockingly*). Do tell us about all your various mistresses in foreign parts, Charlie!

MARSDEN

(*In confusion now*). I—I really don't remember, Nina!

NINA

Why, you're the most heartless person I've ever heard of, Charlie! Not remember even one! And I suppose there are little Marsdens—and you've forgotten all about them too! (*She laughs maliciously—*EVANS *laughs with her.*)

MARSDEN

(*Still more confused—with a silly idiotic smirk*). I can't say about that, Nina. It's a wise father who knows his own child, you know!

NINA

(*Frightenedly — thinking*). What does he mean? . . . does he suspect about the baby too? . . . I must be terribly careful of Charlie! . . .

EVANS

(*Looking up from his paper again*). Did Ned say anything about coming back?

NINA

(*Thinking—longingly*). Come back? . . . oh, Ned, how I wish! . . .

MARSDEN

(*Looking at her—meaningly*). No, he didn't say. I gathered he was staying over indefinitely.

EVANS

I'd sure like to see him again.

NINA

(*Thinking*). He has forgotten me . . . if he did come, he'd probably avoid me. . . .

MARSDEN

He spoke of you. He asked if I'd heard whether Nina had had her baby yet or not. I told him I hadn't.

EVANS

(*Heartily*). Too bad you didn't know. You could have told him what a world-beater we've got! Eh, Nina?

NINA

(*Mechanically*). Yes.

(*Joyfully—thinking*). Ned asked about my baby! . . . then he hadn't forgotten! . . . if he came back he'd come to see his baby! . . .

EVANS

(*Solicitously*). Isn't it time to nurse him again?

NINA

(*Starts to her feet automatically*). Yes, I'm going now.

(*She glances at* MARSDEN, *thinking calculatingly*). I must win Charlie over again . . . I don't feel safe . . . (*She stops by his chair and takes his hand and looks into his eyes gently and reproachfully.*)

MARSDEN

(*Thinking shamefacedly*). Why have I been trying to hurt her? . . . my Nina! . . . I am nearer to her than anyone! . . . I'd give my life to make her happy! . . .

NINA

(*Triumphantly*). How his hand trembles! . . . what a fool to be afraid of Charlie! . . . I can always twist him round my finger! . . .

(*She runs her hand through his hair, and speaks as though she were hiding a hurt reproach beneath a joking tone*). I shouldn't like you any more, do you know it, after you've practically admitted you've philandered all over Europe! And I thought you were absolutely true to me, Charlie!

MARSDEN

(*So pleased he can hardly believe his ears*). Then she did believe me! . . . she's actually hurt! . . . but I can't let her think . . .

(*With passionate earnestness, clasping her hand in both of his, looking into her eyes*). No, Nina! I swear to you!

NINA

(*Thinking—cruelly*). Pah! . . . how limp his hands are! . . . his eyes are so shrinking! . . . is it possible he loves me? . . . like that? . . . what a sickening idea! . . . it seems incestuous somehow! . . . no, it's too absurd! . . .

(*Smiling, gently releases her hand*). All right. I forgive you, Charlie. (*Then matter-of-factly.*) Excuse me, please, while I go up and feed my infant, or we're due to hear some lusty howling in a moment. (*She turns away, then impulsively turns back and kisses* MARSDEN *with real affection.*) You're an old dear, do you know it, Charlie? I don't know what I'd do without you!

(*Thinking*). It's true, too! . . . he's my only dependable friend . . . I must never lose him . . . never let him suspect about little Gordon . . . (*She turns to go.*)

EVANS

(*Jumping up, throwing his paper aside*). Wait a second. I'll come with you. I want to say good night to him. (*He comes, puts his arm about her waist, kisses her and they go out together.*)

MARSDEN

(*Thinking excitedly*). I almost confessed I loved her! . . . a queer expression came over her face . . . what was it? . . . was it satisfaction? . . . she didn't mind? . . . was it pleasure? . . . then I can hope? (*Then miserably.*) Hope for what . . . what do I want?

. . . If Nina were free, what would I do? . . . would I do anything? . . . would I wish to? . . . what would I offer her? . . . money? . . . she could get that from others . . . myself? (*Bitterly.*) What a prize! . . . my ugly body . . . there's nothing in me to attract her . . . my fame? . . . God, what a shoddy, pitiful! . . . but I might have done something big . . . I might still . . . if I had the courage to write the truth . . . but I was born afraid . . . afraid of myself . . . I've given my talent to making fools feel pleased with themselves in order that they'd feel pleased with me . . . and like me . . . I'm neither hated nor loved . . . I'm liked . . . women like me . . . Nina likes me! . . . (*Resentfully.*) She can't help letting the truth escape her! . . . "You're an old dear, do you know it, Charlie?" Oh, yes, I know it . . . too damned well! . . . dear old Charlie! . . . (*In anguish.*) Dear old Rover, nice old doggie, we've had him for years, he's so affectionate and faithful but he's growing old, he's getting cross, we'll have to get rid of him soon! . . . (*In a strange rage, threateningly.*) But you won't get rid of me so easily, Nina! . . . (*Then confusedly and shamefacedly.*) Good God, what's the matter with me! . . . since Mother's death I've become a regular idiot! . . .

EVANS

(*Comes back from the right, a beaming look of proud parenthood on his face*). He was sleeping so soundly an earthquake wouldn't have made him peep! (*He goes back to his chair—earnestly.*) He sure is healthy and husky, Charlie. That tickles me more than anything else. I'm going to start in training him as soon as he's old enough—so he'll be a crack athlete when he goes to college—what I wanted to be and couldn't. I want him to justify the name of Gordon and be a bigger star than Gordon ever was, if that's possible.

MARSDEN

(*With a sort of pity—thinking*). His is an adolescent mind . . . he'll never grow up . . . well, in this adolescent country, what greater blessing could he wish for? . . .

(*Forcing a smile*). How about training his mind?

EVANS

(*Confidently*). Oh, that'll take care of itself. Gordon was always near the top in his studies, wasn't he? And with Nina for a mother, his namesake ought to inherit a full set of brains.

MARSDEN

(*Amused*). You're the only genuinely modest person I know, Sam.

EVANS

(*Embarrassed*). Oh—me—I'm the boob of the family. (*Then hastily.*) Except when it comes to business. I'll make the money. (*Confidently.*) And you can bet your sweet life I will make it!

MARSDEN

I'm quite sure of that.

EVANS

(*Very seriously—in a confidential tone*). I couldn't have said that two years ago—and believed it. I've changed a hell of a lot! Since the baby was born, I've felt as if I had a shot of dynamite in each arm. They can't pile on the work fast enough. (*He grins—then seriously.*) It was about time I got hold of myself. I wasn't much for Nina to feel proud about having around the house in those days. Now—well—at least I've improved. I'm not afraid of my own shadow any more.

MARSDEN

(*Thinking strangely*). Not to be afraid of one's shadow! . . . that must be the highest happiness of heaven! . . .

(*Flatteringly*). Yes, you've done wonders in the past year.

EVANS

Oh, I haven't even started yet. Wait till I get my chance! (*Glances at* MARSDEN *sharply, makes up his mind and leans forward toward him confidentially.*) And I see my real chance, Charlie—lying right ahead, waiting for me to grab it—an agency that's been allowed to run down and go to seed.

Within a year or so they'll be willing to sell out cheap. One of their people who's become a good pal of mine told me that in confidence, put it up to me. He'd take it on himself but he's sick of the game. But I'm not! I love it! It's great sport! (*Then putting the brake on this exuberance—matter-of-factly.*) But I'll need a hundred thousand—and where will I get it? (*Looking at* MARSDEN *keenly but putting on a joking tone.*) Any suggestion you can make, Charlie, will be gratefully received.

MARSDEN

(*Thinking suspiciously*). Does he actually imagine I . . . ? and a hundred thousand, no less! . . . over one-fifth of my entire . . . by Jove, I'll have to throw cold water on that fancy! . . .

(*Shortly*). No, Sam, I can't think of anyone. Sorry.

EVANS

(*Without losing any confidence—with a grin*). Check! . . . That's that! . . . Charlie's out . . . till the next time! . . . but I'll keep after him! . . . (*Contemplating himself with pride.*) Gee, I have changed all right! I can remember when a refusal like that would have ruined my confidence for six months!

(*Heartily*). Nothing to be sorry about, old man. I only mentioned it on the off chance you might know of someone. (*Trying a bold closing stroke—jokingly.*) Why don't you be my partner, Charlie? Never mind the hundred thousand. We'll get that elsewhere. I'll bet you might have darn fine original ideas to contribute.

(*Thinking—satisfied*). There! . . . That'll keep my proposition pinned up in his mind! . . .

(*Then jumping to his feet—briskly*). What do you say to a little stroll down to the shore and back? Come on—do you good. (*Taking his arm and hustling him genially toward the door.*) What you need is exercise. You're soft as putty. Why don't you take up golf?

MARSDEN

(*With sudden resistance pulls away—determinedly*). No, I won't go, Sam. I want to think out a new plot.

EVANS

Oh, all right! If it's a case of work, go to it! See you later. (*He goes out. A moment later the front door is heard closing.*)

MARSDEN

(*Looks after him with a mixture of annoyance and scornful amusement*). What a fount of meaningless energy he's tapped! . . . always on the go . . . typical terrible child of the age . . . universal slogan, keep moving . . . moving where? . . . never mind that . . . don't think of ends . . . the means are the end . . . keep moving! . . . (*He laughs scornfully and sits down in* EVANS' *chair, picking up the paper and glancing at it sneeringly.*) It's in every headline of this daily newer testament . . . going . . . going . . . never mind the gone . . . we won't live to see it . . . and we'll be so rich, we can buy off the deluge anyway! . . . even our new God has His price! . . . must have! . . . aren't we made in His image? . . . or vice-versa? . . . (*He laughs again, letting the paper drop disdainfully—then bitterly.*) But why am I so superior? . . . where am I going? . . . to the same nowhere! . . . worse! . . . I'm not even going! . . . I'm there! . . . (*He laughs with bitter self-pity—then begins to think with amused curiosity.*) Become Sam's partner? . . . there's a grotesque notion! . . . it might revive my sense of humor about myself, at least . . . I'm the logical one to help him . . . I helped him to Nina . . . logical partner . . . partner in Nina? . . . what inane thoughts! . . . (*With a sigh.*) No use trying to think out that plot tonight . . . I'll try to read. . . . (*He sees the book he has been reading on the couch and gets up to get it. There is a ring from the front door.* MARSDEN *turns toward it uncertainly. A pause. Then* NINA'S *voice calls down the stairs.*)

NINA

The maid's out. Will you go to the door, Charlie?

MARSDEN

Surely. (*He goes out and opens the front door. A pause. Then he can be heard say-*

ing resentfully.) Hello, Darrell. (*And someone answering "Hello,* MARSDEN*" and coming in and the door closing.*)

NINA

(*From upstairs, her voice strange and excited*). Who is it, Charlie?

DARRELL

(*Comes into view in the hall, opposite the doorway, at the foot of the stairs—his voice trembling a little with suppressed emotion*). It's I, Nina—Ned Darrell.

NINA

(*With a glad cry*). Ned! (*Then in a voice which shows she is trying to control herself, and is frightened now.*) I—make yourself at home. I'll be down—in a minute or two. (DARRELL *remains standing looking up the stairs in a sort of joyous stupor.* MARSDEN *stares at him.*)

MARSDEN

(*Sharply*). Come on in and sit down. (DARRELL *starts, comes into the room, plainly getting a grip on himself.* MARSDEN *follows him, glaring at his back with enmity and suspicion.* DARRELL *moves as far away from him as possible, sitting down on the sofa at right.* MARSDEN *takes* EVANS' *chair by the table.* DARRELL *is pale, thin, nervous, unhealthy looking. There are lines of desperation in his face, puffy shadows of dissipation and sleeplessness under his restless, harried eyes. He is dressed carelessly, almost shabbily. His eyes wander about the room, greedily taking it in.*)

DARRELL

(*Thinking disjointedly*). Here again! . . . dreamed of this house . . . from here, ran away . . . I've come back . . . my turn to be happy! . . .

MARSDEN

(*Watching him—savagely*) Now I know! . . . absolutely! . . . his face! . . . her voice! . . . they did love each other! . . . they do now . . .

(*Sharply*) When did you get back from Europe?

DARRELL

(*Curtly*). This morning on the Olympic.

(*Thinking—cautiously*). Look out for this fellow . . . always had it in for me . . . like a woman . . . smells out love . . . he suspected before . . . (*Then boldly*) Well, who gives a damn now? . . . all got to come out! . . . Nina wanted to tell Sam . . . now I'll tell him myself! . . .

MARSDEN

(*Righteously indignant*). What has brought him back? . . . what a devilish, cowardly trick to play on poor unsuspecting Sam! . . . (*Revengefully.*) But I'm not unsuspecting! . . . I'm not their fool! . . .

(*Coldly*). What brought you back so soon? When I saw you in Munich you weren't intending—

DARRELL

(*Shortly*). My father died three weeks ago. I've had to come back about his estate.

(*Thinking*). Lie . . . Father's death just gave me an excuse to myself . . . wouldn't have come back for that . . . came back because I love her! . . . damn his questions! . . . I want to think . . . before I see her . . . sound of her voice . . . seemed to burn inside my head . . . God, I'm licked! . . . no use fighting it . . . I've done my damnedest . . . work . . . booze . . . other women . . . no use . . . I love her! . . . always! . . . to hell with pride! . . .

MARSDEN

(*Thinking*). He has two brothers . . . they'll probably all share equally . . . his father noted Philadelphia surgeon . . . rich, I've heard . . . (*With a bitter grin.*) Wait till Sam hears that! . . . he'll ask Darrell to back him . . . and Darrell will jump at it . . . chance to avert suspicion . . . conscience money, too! . . . it's my duty to protect Sam . . . (*As he hears* NINA *coming down the stairs.*) I must watch them . . . it's my duty to protect Nina from herself . . . Sam is a simpleton . . . I'm all she has . . .

DARRELL

(*Hearing her coming—in a panic—thinking*). Coming! . . . in a second

I'll see her! . . . (*Terrified.*) Does she still love me? . . . she may have forgotten . . . no, it's my child . . . she can never forget that! . . .

(NINA *comes in from the rear. She has put on a fresh dress, her hair is arranged, her face newly rouged and powdered, she looks extremely pretty and this is heightened by the feverish state of mind she is in—a mixture of love, of triumphant egotism in knowing her lover has come back to her, and of fear and uncertainty in feeling her new peace, her certainties, her contented absorption in her child failing her. She hesitates just inside the door, staring into* DARRELL'S *eyes, thinking a fierce question.*)

NINA

Does he still love me? . . . (*Then triumphantly as she reads him.*) Yes! . . . he does! . . . he does! . . .

DARRELL

(*Who has jumped to his feet—with a cry of longing*). Nina!

(*Thinking with alarm now*). She's changed! . . . changed! . . . can't tell if she loves!

(*He has started to go to her. Now he hesitates. His voice taking on a pleading uncertain quality*). Nina!

NINA

(*Thinking triumphantly—with a certain cruelty*). He loves me! . . . he's mine . . . now more than ever! . . . he'll never dare leave me again! . . .

(*Certain of herself now, she comes to him and speaks with confident pleasure*). Hello, Ned! This is a wonderful surprise! How are you? (*She takes his hand.*)

DARRELL

(*Taken aback—confusedly*). Oh—all right, Nina.

(*Thinking in a panic*). That tone! . . . as if she didn't care! . . . can't believe that! . . . she's playing a game to fool Marsden! . . .

MARSDEN

(*Who is watching them keenly—thinking*). She loves his love for her . . . she's cruelly confident . . . much as I hate this man I can't help feeling sorry . . . I know her cruelty . . . it's time I took a hand in this . . . what a plot for a novel! . . .

(*Almost mockingly*). Darrell's father died, Nina. He had to come home to see about the estate.

DARRELL

(*With a glare at* MARSDEN*—protestingly*). I was coming home anyway. I only intended to stay a year, and it's over that since—(*Intensely.*) I was coming back anyway, Nina!

NINA

(*Thinking with triumphant happiness*). You dear, you! . . . as if I didn't know that! . . . oh, how I'd love to take you in my arms! . . .

(*Happily*). I'm awfully glad you've come, Ned. We've missed you terribly.

DARRELL

(*Thinking—more and more at sea*). She looks glad . . . but she's changed . . . I don't understand her . . . "we've missed" . . . that means Sam . . . what does that mean? . . .

(*Intensely, pressing her hand*) And I've missed you—terribly!

MARSDEN

(*Sardonically*). Yes, indeed, Darrell, I can vouch for their missing you—Sam in particular. He was asking about you only a short while ago—how things were going with you when I saw you in Munich. (*Maliciously.*) By the way, who was the lady you were with that day? She was certainly startling looking.

NINA

(*Thinking—triumphantly mocking*). A miss, Charlie! . . . he loves me! . . . what do I care about that woman? . . .

(*Gaily*). Yes, who was the mysterious beauty, Ned? Do tell us! (*She moves away from him and sits down at center.* DARRELL *remains standing.*)

DARRELL

(*Glaring at* MARSDEN, *sullenly*). Oh, I don't remember—

(*Thinking apprehensively with a bitter resentment*). She doesn't give a damn! . . . if she loved me she'd be jealous! . . . but she doesn't give a damn! . . .

(*He blurts out resentfully at* NINA). Well, she was my mistress—for a time—I was lonely. (*Then with sudden anger turning on* MARSDEN.) But what's all this to you, Marsden?

MARSDEN

(*Coolly*). Absolutely nothing. Pardon me. It was a tactless question. (*Then with continued open malice.*) But I was starting to say how Sam had missed you, Darrell. It's really remarkable. One doesn't encounter such friendship often in these slack days. Why, he'd trust you with anything!

NINA

(*Wincing—thinking*). That hurts . . . hurts Ned . . . Charlie is being cruel! . . .

DARRELL

(*Wincing—in a forced tone*). And I'd trust Sam with anything.

MARSDEN

Of course. He is a person one can trust. They are rare. You're going to be amazed at the change in Sam, Darrell. Isn't he, Nina? He's a new man. I never saw such energy. If ever a man was bound for success Sam is. In fact, I'm so confident he is that as soon as he thinks the time is ripe to start his own firm I'm going to furnish the capital and become his silent partner.

DARRELL

(*Puzzled and irritated—thinking confusedly*). What's he driving at? . . . why doesn't he get the hell out and leave us alone? . . . but I'm glad Sam is on his feet . . . makes it easier to tell him the truth. . . .

NINA

(*Thinking — worriedly*). What's Charlie talking about? . . . it's time I talked to Ned . . . Oh, Ned, I do love you! . . . you can be my lover! . . . we won't hurt Sam! . . . he'll never know! . . .

MARSDEN

Yes, ever since the baby was born Sam's been another man—in fact, ever since he knew there was going to be a baby, isn't it, Nina?

NINA

(*Agreeing as if she had only half-heard him*). Yes.

(*Thinking*). Ned's baby! . . . I must talk to him about our baby. . . .

MARSDEN

Sam is the proudest parent I've ever seen!

NINA

(*As before*). Yes, Sam makes a wonderful father, Ned.

(*Thinking*). Ned doesn't care for children . . . I know what you're hoping, Ned . . . but if you think I'm going to take Sam's baby from him, you're mistaken! . . . or if you think I'll run away with you and leave my baby . . .

MARSDEN

(*With the same strange driving insistence*). If anything happened to that child I actually believe Sam would lose his reason! Don't you think so, Nina?

NINA

(*With emphasis*). I know I'd lose mine! Little Gordon has become my whole life.

DARRELL

(*Thinking—with a sad bitter irony*). Sam . . . wonderful father . . . lose his reason . . . little Gordon! . . . Nina called my son after Gordon! . . . romantic imagination! . . . Gordon is still her lover! . . . Gordon, Sam and Nina! . . . and my son! . . . closed corporation! . . . I'm forced out! . . . (*Then rebelling furiously.*) No! . . . not yet, by God! . . . I'll smash it up! . . . I'll tell Sam the truth no matter what! . . .

NINA

(*Thinking with a strange calculation*). I couldn't find a better husband than Sam . . . and I couldn't find a better lover than Ned . . . I need them both to be happy . . .

MARSDEN

(*With sudden despairing suspicion*). Good God . . . after all, is it Sam's child? . . . mightn't it be Darrell's! . . . why have I never thought of that? . . . No! . . . Nina couldn't be so vile! . . . to go on living with Sam pretending . . . and, after all, why should she, you fool? . . . there's no sense! . . . she could have gone off with Darrell, couldn't she? . . . Sam would have given her a divorce . . . there was no possible reason for her staying with Sam, when she loved Darrell, unless exactly because this was Sam's baby . . . for its sake . . . (*Hectically relieved.*) Of course! . . . of course! . . . that's all right! . . . I love that poor baby now! . . . I'll fight for its sake against these two! (*Smilingly gets to his feet—thinking.*) I can leave them alone now . . . for they won't be alone, thanks to me! . . . I leave Sam and his baby in this room with them . . . and their honor . . . (*Suddenly raging.*) Their honor! . . . what an obscene joke . . . the honor of a harlot and a pimp! . . . I hate them! . . . if only God would strike them dead! . . . now! . . . and I could see them die! . . . I would praise His justice . . . His kindness and mercy to me! . . .

NINA

(*Thinking—with horrified confusion*). Why doesn't Charlie go? . . . What is he thinking? . . . I suddenly feel afraid of him! . . .

(*She gets to her feet with a confused pleading cry*). Charlie!

MARSDEN

(*Immediately urbane and smiling*). It's all right. I'm going out to find Sam. When he knows you're here he'll come on the run, Darrell. (*He goes to the door. They watch him suspiciously.*) And you two probably have a lot to talk over. (*He chuckles pleasantly and goes into the hall—mockingly warning.*) We'll be back before long.

(*The front door is heard slamming.* NINA *and* DARRELL *turn and look at each other guiltily and frightenedly. Then he comes to her and takes both of her hands uncertainly.*)

DARRELL

(*Stammeringly*). Nina—I—I've come back to you—do you—do you still care—Nina?

NINA

(*Giving way to his love passionately, as if to drown her fears*). I love you, Ned!

DARRELL

(*Kisses her awkwardly—stammering*). I—I didn't know—you seemed so cold—damn Marsden—he suspects, doesn't he? —but it makes no difference now, does it? (*Then in a flood of words.*) Oh, it's been hell, Nina! I couldn't forget you! Other women—they only made me love you more! I hated them and loved you even at the moment when—that's honest! It was always you in my arms—as you used to be—those afternoons—God, how I've thought of them—lying awake—recalling every word you said, each movement, each expression on your face, smelling your hair, feeling your soft body— (*Suddenly taking her in his arms and kissing her again and again—passionately.*) Nina! I love you so!

NINA

And I've longed for you so much! Do you think I've forgotten those afternoons? (*Then in anguish.*) Oh, Ned, why did you run away? I can never forgive that! I can never trust you again!

DARRELL

(*Violently*). I was a fool! I thought of Sam! And that wasn't all! Oh, I wasn't all noble, I'll confess! I thought of myself and my career! Damn my career! A lot of good that did it! I didn't study! I didn't live! I longed for you—and suffered! I paid in full, believe me, Nina! But I know better now! I've come back. The time for lying is past! You've got to come away with me! (*He kisses her.*)

NINA

(*Letting herself go, kissing him passionately*). Yes! My lover! (*Then suddenly resisting and pushing him away.*) No! You're forgetting Sam—and Sam's baby!

DARRELL

(*Staring at her wildly*). Sam's baby? Are you joking? Ours, you mean! We'll take him with us, of course!

NINA

(*Sadly*). And Sam?

DARRELL

Damn Sam! He's got to give you a divorce! Let him be generous for a change!

NINA

(*Sadly but determinedly*). He would be. You must be just to Sam. He'd give his life for my happiness. And this would mean his life. Could we be happy then? You know we couldn't! And I've changed, Ned. You've got to realize that. I'm not your old mad Nina. I still love you. I will always love you. But now I love my baby too. His happiness comes first with me!

DARRELL

But—he's mine, too!

NINA

No! You gave him to Sam to save Sam!

DARRELL

To hell with Sam! It was to make you happy!

NINA

So I could make Sam happy! That was in it too! I was sincere in that, Ned! If I hadn't been, I could never have gone to you that first day—or if I had, I'd never have forgiven myself. But as it is I don't feel guilty or wicked. I have made Sam happy! And I'm proud! I love Sam's happiness! I love the devoted husband and father in him! And I feel it's his baby—that we've made it his baby!

DARRELL

(*Distractedly*). Nina! For God's sake! You haven't come to love Sam, have you? Then—I'll go—I'll go away again—I'll never come back—I tried not to this time—but I had to, Nina!

NINA

(*Taking him in her arms—with sudden alarm*). No, don't go away, Ned—ever again. I don't love Sam! I love you!

DARRELL

(*Miserably*). But I don't understand! Sam gets everything—and I have nothing!

NINA

You have my love! (*With a strange, self-assured smile at him.*) It seems to me you're complaining unreasonably!

DARRELL

You mean—I can be—your lover again?

NINA

(*Simply, even matter-of-factly*). Isn't that the nearest we can come to making everyone happy? That's all that counts.

DARRELL

(*With a harsh laugh*). And is that what you call playing fair to Sam?

NINA

(*Simply*). Sam will never know. The happiness I have given him has made him too sure of himself ever to suspect me now. And as long as we can love each other without danger to him, I feel he owes that to us for all we've done for him. (*With finality.*) That's the only possible solution, Ned, for all our sakes, now you've come back to me.

DARRELL

(*Repulsed*). Nina! How can you be so inhuman and calculating!

NINA

(*Stung—mockingly*). It was you who taught me the scientific approach, Doctor!

DARRELL

(*Shrinking back from her—threateningly*). Then I'll leave again! I'll go back to Europe! I won't endure—! (*Then in a queer, futile rage.*) You think I'll stay—to be your lover—watching Sam with my wife and my child—you think that's what I came back to you for? You can go to hell, Nina!

NINA

(*Calmly—sure of him*). But what else can I do, Ned? (*Then warningly.*) I hear them coming, dear. It's Sam, you know.

DARRELL

(*In a frenzy*). What else can you do? Liar! But I can do something else! I can smash your calculating game for you! I can tell Sam—and I will—right now—by God, I will!

NINA

(*Quietly*). No. you won't, Ned. You can't do that to Sam.

DARRELL

(*Savagely*). Like hell I can't!
(*The front door is opened.* EVANS' *voice is immediately heard, even before he bounds into the room. He rushes up to* NED *hilariously, shakes his hand and pounds his back, oblivious to* DARRELL'S *wild expression.*)

EVANS

You old son of a gun! Why didn't you let a guy know you were coming? We'd have met you at the dock, and brought the baby. Let me have a look at you! You look thinner. We'll fatten you up, won't we, Nina? Let us do the prescribing this time! Why didn't you let us know where you were, you old bum? We wanted to write you about the baby. And I wanted to boast about how I was getting on! You're the only person in the world—except Nina and Charlie—I would boast about that to.

NINA

(*Affectionately*). Mercy, Sam, give Ned a chance to get a word in! (*Looking at* NED *pityingly but challengingly.*) He wants to tell you something, Sam.

DARRELL

(*Crushed—stammers*). No—I mean, yes—I want to tell you how damn glad I am . . . (*He turns away, his face is screwed up in his effort to hold back his tears.*)
(*Thinking miserably*). I can't tell him! . . . God damn him, I can't! . . .

NINA

(*With a strange triumphant calm*). There! . . . that's settled for all time! . . . poor Ned! . . . how crushed he looks! . . . I mustn't let Sam look at him! . . .
(*She steps between them protectingly*). Where's Charlie, Sam?

MARSDEN

(*Appearing from the hall*). Here, Nina. Always here! (*He comes to her, smiling with assurance.*)

NINA

(*Suddenly with a strange unnatural elation—looking from one to the other with triumphant possession*). Yes, you're here, Charlie—always! And you, Sam—and Ned! (*With a strange gaiety.*) Sit down, all of you! Make yourselves at home! You are my three men! This is your home with me! (*Then in a strange half-whisper.*) Ssshh! I thought I heard the baby. You must all sit down and be very quiet. You must not wake our baby.
(*Mechanically the three sit down, careful to make no noise—*EVANS *in his old place by the table,* MARSDEN *at center,* DARRELL *on the sofa at right. They sit staring before them in silence.* NINA *remains standing, dominating them, a little behind and to the left of* MARSDEN.)

MARSDEN

(*Thinking abjectly*). I couldn't! . . . there are things one may not do and live with oneself afterwards . . . there are things one may not say . . . memory is too full of echoes! . . . there are secrets one must not reveal . . . memory is lined with mirrors! . . . he was too happy! . . . to kill happiness is a worse murder than taking life! . . . I gave him that happiness! . . . Sam deserves my happiness! . . . God bless you, Sam! . . . (*Then in a strange objective tone—thinking.*) My experiment with the guinea pigs has been a success . . . the ailing ones, Sam and the female, Nina, have been restored to health and normal function . . . only the other male, Ned, seems to have suffered deterioration. . . . (*Then bitterly humble.*) Nothing left but to accept her terms . . . I love her . . . I can help to make her happy . . . half a loaf is better . . . to a starving man. . . (*Glancing over at* EVANS*—bitterly gloating*) And your child is mine! . . . your wife is mine! . . . your happiness is mine! . . . may you enjoy my happiness, her husband! . . .

EVANS

(*Looking at* DARRELL *affectionately*). Sure good to see Ned again . . . a real friend if there ever was one . . . looks blue about something . . . oh, that's right, Charlie said his old man had kicked in . . . his old man was rich . . . that's an idea . . . I'll bet he'd put up that capital . . . (*Then ashamed of himself.*) Aw hell, what's the matter with me? . . . he's no sooner here than I start . . . he's done enough . . . forget it! . . . now anyway . . . he looks pretty dissipated . . . too many women . . . ought to get married and settle down . . . tell him that if I didn't think he'd laugh at me giving him advice . . . but he'll soon realize I'm not the old Sam he knew . . . I suppose Nina's been boasting about that already . . . she's proud . . . she's helped me . . . she's a wonderful wife and mother . . . (*Looking up to her—solicitously.*) She acted a bit nervous just now . . . queer . . . like she used to . . . haven't noticed her that way in a long time . . . suppose it's the excitement of Ned turning up . . . mustn't let her get overexcited . . . bad for the baby's milk. . . .

MARSDEN

(*Glancing furtively over his shoulder at* NINA*—broodingly thinking*). She's the old queer Nina now . . . the Nina I could never fathom . . . her three men! . . . and we are! . . . I? . . . yes, more deeply than either of the others since I serve for nothing . . . a queer kind of love, maybe . . . I am not ordinary! . . . our child . . . what could she mean by that? . . . child of us three? . . . on the surface, that's insane . . . but I felt when she said it there was something in it . . . she has strange devious intuitions that tap the hidden currents of life . . . dark intermingling currents that become the one stream of desire . . . I feel, with regard to Nina, my life queerly identified with Sam's and Darrell's . . . her child is the child of our three loves for her . . . I would like to believe that . . . I would like to be her husband in a sense . . . and the father of a child, after my fashion . . . I could forgive her everything . . . permit everything . . . (*Determinedly.*) And I do forgive! . . . and I will not meddle hereafter more than is necessary to guard her happiness, and Sam's and our baby's . . . as for Darrell, I am no longer jealous of him . . . she is only using his love for her own happiness . . . he can never take her away from me! . . .

NINA

(*More and more strangely triumphant*). My three men! . . . I feel their desires converge in me! . . . to form one complete beautiful male desire which I absorb . . . and am whole . . . they dissolve in me, their life is my life . . . I am pregnant with the three! . . . husband! . . . lover! . . . father! . . . . . . and the fourth man! . . . little Gordon! . . . he is mine too! . . . that makes it perfect! . . . (*With an extravagant suppressed exultance.*) Why, I should be the proudest woman on earth! . . . I should be the happiest woman in the world! . . . (*Then suppressing an outbreak of hysterical triumphant laughter only by a tremendous effort.*) Ha-ha . . . only I better knock wood . . . (*She raps with both knuckles in a fierce tattoo on the table.*) before God the Father hears my happiness! . . .

EVANS

(*As the three turn to her—anxiously*). Nina? What's the matter?

NINA

(*Controlling herself with a great effort comes to him—forcing a smile—puts her arms around him affectionately*). Nothing, dear. Nerves, that's all. I've gotten overtired, I guess.

EVANS

(*Bullying her—with loving authority*). Then you go right to bed, young lady! We'll excuse you.

NINA

(*Quietly and calmly now*). All right, dear. I guess I do need a rest. (*She kisses him as she might kiss a big brother she loved—affectionately.*) Good night, you bossy old thing, you!

EVANS

(*With deep tenderness*). Good night, darling.

NINA

(*She goes and kisses Charlie dutifully on the cheek as she might her father—affectionately*). Good night, Charlie.

MARSDEN

(*With a touch of her father's manner*). That's a good girl! Good night, dear.

NINA

(*She goes and kisses* DARRELL *lovingly on the lips as she would kiss her lover*). Good night, Ned.

DARRELL

(*Looks at her with grateful humility*). Thank you. Good night.

(*She turns and walks quietly out of the room. The eyes of the three men follow her.*)

Curtain.

ACT SEVEN

SCENE: *Nearly eleven years later. The sitting room of the* EVAN'S *apartment on Park Avenue, New York City—a room that is a tribute to* NINA'S *good taste. It is a large, sunny room, the furniture expensive but extremely simple. The arrangement of the furniture shown is as in previous scenes except there are more pieces. Two chairs are by the table at left. There is a smaller table at center, and a chaise longue. A large, magnificently comfortable sofa is at right.*

It is about one in the afternoon of a day in early fall. NINA *and* DARRELL *and their son,* GORDON, *are in the room.* NINA *is reclining on the chaise longue watching* GORDON *who is sitting on the floor near her, turning over the pages of a book.* DARRELL *is sitting by the table at left, watching* NINA.

NINA *is thirty-five, in the full bloom of her womanhood. She is slimmer than in the previous scene. Her skin still retains a trace of summer tan and she appears in the pink of physical condition. But as in the first act of the play, there is beneath this a sense of great mental strain. One notices the many lines in her face at second glance. Her eyes are tragically sad in repose and her expression is set and masklike.*

GORDON *is eleven—a fine boy with, even at this age, the figure of an athlete. He looks older than he is. There is a grave expression to his face. His eyes are full of a quick-tempered sensitiveness. He does not noticeably resemble his mother. He looks nothing at all like his father. He seems to have sprung from a line distinct from any of the people we have seen.*

DARRELL *has aged greatly. His hair is streaked with gray. He has grown stout. His face is a bit jowly and puffy under the eyes. The features have become blurred. He has the look of a man with no definite aim or ambition to which he can relate his living. His eyes are embittered and they hide his inner self-resentment behind a pose of cynical indifference.*

GORDON

(*Thinking as he plays—resentfully*). I wish Darrell'd get out of here! . . . why couldn't Mother let me run my own birthday? . . . I'd never had him here, you bet! . . . what's he always hanging 'round for? . . . why don't he go off on one of his old trips again . . .

last time he was gone more'n a year . . . I was hoping he'd died! . . . what makes Mother like him so much? . . . she makes me sick! . . . I'd think she'd get sick of the old fool and tell him to get out and never come back! . . . I'd kick him out if I was big enough! . . . it's good for him he didn't bring me any birthday present or I'd smash it first chance I got! . . .

NINA

(*Watching him—brooding and loving tenderness—sadly*). No longer my baby . . . my little man . . . eleven . . . I can't believe it . . . I'm thirty-five . . . five years more . . . at forty a woman has finished living . . . life passes her by . . . she rots away in peace! . . . (*Intensely.*) I want to rot away in peace! . . . I'm sick of the fight for happiness! . . . (*Smiling with a wry amusement at herself.*) What ungrateful thoughts on my son's birthday! . . . my love for him has been happiness . . . how handsome he is! . . . not at all like Ned . . . when I was carrying him I was fighting to forget Ned . . . hoping he might be like Gordon . . . and he is . . . poor Ned, I've made him suffer a great deal . . . ! (*She looks over at* DARRELL—*self-mockingly.*) My lover! . . . so very rarely now, those interludes of passion . . . what has bound us together all these years? . . . love? . . . if he could only have been contented with what I was able to give him! . . . but he has always wanted more . . . yet never had the courage to insist on all or nothing . . . proud without being proud enough! . . . he has shared me for his comfort's sake with a little gratitude and a big bitterness . . . and sharing me has corrupted him! . . . (*Then bitterly.*) No. I can't blame myself! . . . no woman can make a man happy who has no purpose in life! . . . why did he give up his career? . . . because I had made him weak? . . . (*With resentful scorn.*) No, it was I who shamed him into taking up biology and starting the station at Antigua . . . if I hadn't he'd simply have hung around me year after year, doing nothing . . . (*Irritatedly.*) Why does he stay so long? . . . over six months . . . I can't stand having him around me that long any more! . . . why doesn't he go back to the West Indies? . . . I always get a terrible feeling after he's been back a while that he's waiting for Sam to die! . . . or go insane! . . .

DARRELL

(*Thinking—with an apathetic bitterness*). What is she thinking? . . . we sit together in silence, thinking . . . thoughts that never know the other's thoughts . . . our love has become the intimate thinking together of thoughts that are strangers . . . our love! . . . well, whatever it is that has bound us together, it's strong! . . . I've broken with her, run away, tried to forget her . . . running away to come back each time more abject! . . . or, if she saw there was some chance I might break loose, she'd find some way to call me back . . . and I'd forget my longing for freedom, I'd come wagging my tail . . . no, guinea pigs have no tails . . . I hope my experiment has proved something! . . . Sam . . . happy and wealthy . . . and healthy! . . . I used to hope he'd break down . . . I'd watch him and read symptoms of insanity into every move he made . . . despicable? . . . certainly, but love makes one either noble or despicable! . . . he only grew healthier . . . now I've given up watching him . . . almost entirely . . . now I watch him grow fat and I laugh! . . . the huge joke has dawned on me! . . . Sam is the only normal one! . . . we lunatics! . . . Nina and I! . . . have made a sane life for him out of our madness! . . . (*Watching* NINA—*sadly.*) Always thinking of her son . . . well, I gave him to her . . . Gordon . . . I hate that name . . . why do I continue hanging around here? . . . each time after a few months my love changes to bitterness . . . I blame Nina for the mess I've made of life . . .

NINA

(*Suddenly turning on him*). When are you going back to the West Indies, Ned?

DARRELL

(*Determinedly*). Soon!

GORDON

(*Stops playing to listen—thinking*). Gosh, I'm glad! . . . How soon, I wonder? . . .

NINA

(*With a trace of a sneer*). I don't see how you can afford to leave your work for such long periods. Don't you grow rusty?

DARRELL

(*Looking at her meaningly*). My life work is to rust—nicely and unobtrusively! (*He smiles mockingly.*)

NINA

(*Sadly—thinking*). To rot away in peace . . . that's all he wants now, too! . . . and this is what love has done to us! . . .

DARRELL

(*Bitterly*). My work was finished twelve years ago. As I believe you know, I ended it with an experiment which resulted so successfully that any further meddling with human lives would have been superfluous!

NINA

(*Pityingly*). Ned!

DARRELL

(*Indifferent and cynical*). But you meant my present dabbling about. You know better than to call that work. It's merely my hobby. Our backing Sam has made Marsden and me so wealthy that we're forced to take up hobbies. Marsden goes in for his old one of dashing off genteel novels, while I play at biology. Sam argued that golf would be healthier and less nonsensical for me, but you insisted on biology. And give it its due, it has kept me out in the open air and been conducive to travelling and broadening my mind! (*Then forcing a smile.*) But I'm exaggerating. I really am interested, or I'd never keep financing the Station. And when I'm down there I do work hard, helping Preston. He's doing remarkable work already, and he's still in his twenties. He'll be a big man—(*his bitterness cropping up again*) at least if he takes my advice and never carries his experiments as far as human lives!

NINA

(*In a low voice*). How can you be so bitter, Ned—on Gordon's birthday?

DARRELL

(*Thinking cynically*). She expects me to love the child she deliberately took from me and gave to another man! . . . no, thank you, Nina! . . . I've been hurt enough! . . . I'll not leave myself open there! . . .

(*Regarding his son bitterly*). Every day he gets more like Sam, doesn't he?

GORDON

(*Thinking*). He's talking about me . . . he better look out! . . .

NINA

(*Resentfully*). I don't think Gordon resembles Sam at all. He reminds me a great deal of his namesake.

DARRELL

(*Touched on a sore spot—with a nasty laugh—cuttingly*). Gordon Shaw? Not the slightest bit in the world! And you ought to thank God he doesn't! It's the last thing I'd want wished on a boy of mine—to be like that rah-rah hero!

GORDON

(*Thinking contemptuously*). Boy of his! . . . He hasn't got a boy! . . .

NINA

(*Amused and pleased by his jealousy*). Poor Ned! . . . isn't he silly? . . . at his age, after all we've been through, to still feel jealous . . .

DARRELL

I'd much rather have him (*pointing to* GORDON) grow up to be an exact duplicate of the esteemed Samuel!

GORDON

(*Thinking resentfully*). He's always making fun of my father! . . . he better look out! . . .

DARRELL

(*More and more mockingly*). And what could be fairer? The good Samuel is an A One success. He has a charming wife and a darling boy, and a Park Avenue apartment and a membership in an expensive golf club. And, above all, he rests so complacently on the proud assurance that he is self-made!

NINA

(*Sharply*). Ned! You ought to be ashamed! You know how grateful Sam has always been to you!

DARRELL

(*Bitingly*). Would he be grateful if he knew how much I'd really done for him?

NINA

(*Sternly*). Ned!

GORDON

(*Suddenly jumps up and confronts* DARRELL, *his fists clenched, trembling with rage, stammers*). You—shut up—making fun of my father!

NINA

(*In dismay*). Gordon!

DARRELL

(*Mockingly*). My dear boy, I wouldn't make fun of your father for the world!

GORDON

(*Baffledly—his lips trembling*). You—you did, too! (*Then intensely.*) I hate you!

NINA

(*Shocked and indignant*). Gordon! How dare you talk like that to your Uncle Ned!

GORDON

(*Rebelliously*). He's not my uncle! He's not my anything!

NINA

Not another word or you'll be punished, whether it's your birthday or not! If you can't behave better than that, I'll have to phone to all your friends they mustn't come here this afternoon, that you've been so bad you can't have a party!

(*Thinking remorsefully*). Is this my fault? . . . I've done my best to get him to love Ned! . . . but it only makes him worse! . . . it makes him turn against me! . . . turn from me to Sam! . . .

GORDON

(*Sullenly*). I don't care! I'll tell Dad!

NINA

(*Peremptorily*). Leave the room! And don't come near me again, do you hear, until you've apologized to Uncle Ned!

(*Thinking angrily*). Dad! . . . It's always Dad with him now! . . .

DARRELL

(*Boredly*). Oh, never mind, Nina!

GORDON

(*Going out—mutters*). I won't 'pologize—never!

(*Thinking vindictively*). I hate her too when she sides with him! . . . I don't care if she is my mother! . . . she has no right! . . . (*He goes out, rear.*)

DARRELL

(*Irritably*). What if he does hate me? I don't blame him! He suspects what I know—that I've acted like a coward and a weakling toward him! I should have claimed him no matter what happened to other people! Whose fault is it if he hates me, and I dislike him because he loves another father? Ours! You gave him to Sam and I consented! All right! Then don't blame him for acting like Sam's son!

NINA

But he shouldn't say he hates you.

(*Thinking bitterly*). Sam's! . . . he's becoming all Sam's! . . . I'm getting to mean nothing! . . .

DARRELL

(*Sardonically*). Perhaps he realizes subconsciously that I am his father, his rival in your love; but I'm not his father ostensibly, there are no taboos, so he can come right out and hate me to his heart's content! (*Bitterly.*) If he realized how little you love me any more, he wouldn't bother!

NINA

(*Exasperatedly*). Oh, Ned, do shut up! I can't stand hearing those same old reproaches I've heard a thousand times before! I can't bear to hear myself making the same old bitter counter-accusations. And then there'll be the same old terrible scene of hate and you'll run away—it used to be to drink and women, now it's to the Station. Or I'll send you away, and then after a time I'll call you back, because I'll have gotten so lonely again living this lonely lie of my life, with no one to speak to except Sam's business friends and their deadly wives. (*She laughs helplessly.*) Or else you'll get lonely in your lie a little before I do and come back again of your own desire! And then we'll kiss and cry and love each other again!

DARRELL

(*With an ironical grimace*). Or I might cheat myself into believing I'd fallen in love with some nice girl and get myself engaged to be married again as I did once before! And then you'd be jealous again and have to find some way of getting me to break it off!

NINA

(*Forlornly amused*). Yes—I suppose the thought of a wife taking you away from me would be too much—again! (*Then helplessly.*) Oh, Ned, when are we ever going to learn something about each other? We act like such brainless fools—with our love. It's always so wonderful when you first come back, but you always stay too long—or I always keep you too long! You never leave before we've come to the ugly bitter stage when we blame each other! (*Then suddenly forlornly tender.*) Is it possible you can still love me, Ned?

DARRELL

(*Mournfully smiling*). I must, or I'd never act this fool way, would I?

NINA

(*Smiling back*). And I must love you. (*Then seriously.*) After all, I can never forget that Gordon is the child of your love, Ned.

DARRELL

(*Sadly*). You'd better forget that, for his sake and your own. Children have sure intuitions. He feels cheated of your love—by me. So he's concentrating his affections on Sam whose love he knows is secure, and withdrawing from you.

NINA

(*Frightened—angrily*). Don't be stupid, Ned! That isn't so at all! I hate you when you talk that way!

DARRELL

(*Cynically*). Hate me, exactly. As he does! That's what I'm advising you to do if you want to keep his love! (*He smiles grimly.*)

NINA

(*Sharply*). If Gordon doesn't love you it's because you've never made the slightest attempt to be lovable to him! There's no earthly reason why he should like you, when you come right down to it, Ned! Take today, for instance. It's his birthday but you'd forgotten, or didn't care! You never even brought him a present.

DARRELL

(*With bitter sadness*). I did bring him a present. It's out in the hall. I bought him a costly delicate one so he could get full satisfaction and yet not strain himself when he smashed it, as he's smashed every present of mine in the past! And I left it out in the hall, to be given to him after I've gone because, after all, he is my son and I'd prefer he didn't smash it before my eyes! (*Trying to mock his own emotion back—with savage bitterness.*) I'm selfish, you see! I don't want my son to be too happy at my expense, even on his birthday!

NINA

(*Tormented by love and pity and remorse*). Ned! For God's sake! How can you torture us like that! Oh, it's too dreadful—what I have done to you! Forgive me, Ned!

DARRELL

(*His expression changing to one of pity for her—goes to her and puts his hand on her head—tenderly*). I'm sorry. (*With remorseful tenderness.*) Dreadful, what you've done, Nina? Why, you've given me the only happiness I've ever known! And no matter what I may say or do in bitterness, I'm proud—and grateful, Nina!

NINA

(*Looks up at him with deep tenderness and admiration*). Dearest, it's wonderful of you to say that! (*She gets up and puts her hands on his shoulders and looks into his eyes—tenderly in a sort of pleading.*) Can't we be brave enough—for you to go away—now, on this note—sure of our love—with no ugly bitterness for once?

DARRELL

(*Joyfully*). Yes! I'll go—this minute if you wish!

NINA

(*Playfully*). Oh, you needn't go this minute! Wait and say good-bye to Sam. He'd be terribly hurt if you didn't. (*Then seriously.*) And will you promise to stay away two years—even if I call you back before then—and work this time, really work?

DARRELL

I'll try, Nina!

NINA

And then—surely come back to me!

DARRELL

(*Smiling*). Surely—again!

NINA

Then good-bye, dear! (*She kisses him.*)

DARRELL

Again! (*He smiles and she smiles and they kiss again.* GORDON *appears in the doorway at rear and stands for a moment in a passion of jealousy and rage and grief, watching them.*)

GORDON

(*Thinking with a strange tortured shame*). I mustn't see her! . . . pretend I didn't see her! . . . mustn't never let her know I saw her! . . . (*He vanishes as silently as he had come.*)

NINA

(*Suddenly moving away from* DARRELL, *looking around her uneasily*). Ned, did you see—? I had the queerest feeling just then that someone—

GORDON

(*His voice sounds from the hall with a strained casualness*). Mother! Uncle Charlie's downstairs. Shall he come right up?

NINA

(*Startled, her own voice straining to be casual*). Yes, dear—of course! (*Then worriedly.*) His voice sounded funny. Did it to you? Do you suppose he—?

DARRELL

(*With a wry smile*). It's possible. To be on the safe side, you'd better tell him you kissed me good-bye to get rid of me! (*Then angrily.*) So Marsden's here again! The damned old woman! I simply can't go him any more, Nina! Why Gordon should take such a fancy to that old sissy is beyond me!

NINA

(*Suddenly struck—thinking*). Why, he's jealous of Gordon liking Charlie! . . . (*Immediately all affectionate pity.*) Then he must love Gordon a little! . . . (*Letting her pity escape her*). Poor Ned! (*She makes a movement toward him.*)

DARRELL

(*Startled and afraid she may have guessed something he doesn't acknowledge to himself*). What? Why do you say that? (*Then rudely defensive.*) Don't be silly! (*Resentfully.*) You know well enough what I've always held against him! I wanted to put up all the money to back Sam when he started. I wanted to do it for Sam's sake—but especially for my child's sake. Why did Marsden absolutely insist on Sam letting him in equally? It isn't that I begrudge him the money he's made, but I know there was something queer in his mind and that he did it intentionally to spite me! (*From the hallway comes the sound of* MARSDEN's *voice and* GORDON's *greeting him vociferously as he lets him into the apartment. As* DARRELL *listens his expression becomes furious again. He bursts out angrily.*) You're letting that old ass spoil Gordon, you fool, you!

(MARSDEN *comes in from the rear, smiling, immaculately dressed as usual. He looks hardly any older except that his hair is grayer and his tall figure more stooped. His expression and the general atmosphere he gives out are more nearly like those of Act One. If not happy, he is at least living in comparative peace with himself and his environment.*)

MARSDEN

(*Comes straight to* NINA). Hello, Nina Cara Nina! Congratulations on your son's birthday! (*He kisses her.*) He's grown so much bigger and stronger in the two months since I've seen him. (*He turns and shakes hands with* DARRELL *coldly—with a trace of a patronizing air.*) Hello, Darrell. Last time I was here you were leaving for the West Indies in a week but I see you're still around.

DARRELL

(*Furious—with a mocking air*). And here you are around again, yourself! You're looking comfortable these days, Marsden. I hope your sister is well. It must be a great comfort, having her to take your mother's place! (*Then with a harsh laugh.*) Yes, we're two bad pennies, eh, Marsden?—counterfeits—fakes—Sam's silent partners!

NINA

(*Thinking irritably*). Ned's getting hateful again! . . . Poor Charlie! . . . I won't have him insulted! . . . he's become such a comfort . . . he understands so much . . . without my having to tell him . . .

(*Looking rebukingly at* DARRELL). Ned is sailing this week, Charlie.

MARSDEN

(*Thinking triumphantly*). He's trying to insult me . . . I know all he means . . . but what do I care what he says . . . she's sending him away! . . . intentionally before me! . . . it means he's finished! . . .

DARRELL

(*Thinking resentfully*). Is she trying to humiliate me before him? . . . I'll teach her! . . . (*Then struggling with himself—remorsefully.*) No . . . not this time . . . I promised . . . no quarrel . . . remember . . .

(*Acquiescing—with a pleasant nod to* MARSDEN). Yes, I'm going this week and I except to be gone at least two years this time—two years of hard work.

MARSDEN

(*Thinking with scornful pity*). His work! . . . what a pretense! . . . a scientific dilettante! . . . could anything be more pitiable? . . . poor chap! . . .

(*Perfunctorily*). Biology must be an interesting study. I wish I knew more about it.

DARRELL

(*Stung yet amused by the other's tone—ironically*). Yes, so do I wish you did, Marsden! Then you might write more about life and less about dear old ladies and devilish bachelors! Why don't you write a novel about life sometime, Marsden? (*He turns his back on* MARSDEN *with a glance of repulsion and walks to the window and stares out.*)

MARSDEN

(*Confusedly*). Yes—decidedly—but hardly in my line—

(*Thinking in anguish—picking up a magazine and turning over the pages aimlessly*). That . . . is . . . true! . . . he's full of poison! . . . I've never married the word to life! . . . I've been a timid bachelor of Arts, not an artist! . . . my poor pleasant books! . . . all is well! . . . is this well, the three of us? . . . Darrell has become less and less her lover . . . Nina has turned more and more to me . . . we have built up a secret life of subtle sympathies and confidences . . . she has known I have understood about her mere physical passion for Darrell . . . what woman could be expected to love Sam passionately? . . . some day she'll confide all about Darrell to me . . . now that he's finished . . . she knows that I love her without my telling . . . she even knows the sort of love it is. . . . (*Passionately—thinking.*) My love is finer than any she has known! . . . I do not lust for her! . . . I would be content if our marriage should be purely the placing of our ashes in the same tomb . . . our urns side by side and touching one another . . . could the others say as much, could they love so deeply? . . . (*Then suddenly miserably self-contemptuous.*) What! . . . platonic heroics at my age! . . . do I believe a word of that? . . . look at her beautiful eyes! . . . wouldn't I give anything in life to see them desire me? . . . and the intimacy I'm boasting about, what more does it mean than that I've been playing the dear old Charlie of her girlhood again? . . . (*Thinking in anguish.*) Damned coward and weakling! . . .

NINA

(*Looking at him—pityingly—thinking*). What does he always want of me? . . . me? . . . I am the only one who senses his deep hurt . . . I feel how life has wounded him . . . is that partly my fault, too? . . . I have wounded everyone . . . poor Charlie, what can I do for you? . . . if giving myself to you would bring you a moment's happiness, could I? . . . the idea used to be revolting . . . now, nothing about love seems important enough to be revolting . . . poor Charlie, he only thinks he ought to desire me! . . . dear Charlie, what a perfect lover he would make for one's old age! . . . what a perfect lover when one was past passion! . . . (*Then with sudden scornful revulsion.*) These men make me sick! . . . I hate all three of them! . . . they disgust me! . . . the wife and mistress in me has been killed by them! . . . thank God, I am only a mother now! . . . Gordon is my little man, my only man! . . .

(*Suddenly*). I've got a job for you, Charlie—make the salad dressing for lunch. You know, the one I'm so crazy about.

MARSDEN

(*Springs to his feet*). Righto! (*He puts his arm about her waist and they go out together laughingly, without a glance at* DARRELL.)

DARRELL

(*Thinking dully*). I mustn't stay to lunch . . . ghost at my son's feast! . . . I better go now . . . why wait for Sam? . . . what is there to say to him I can say? . . . and there's nothing about him I want to see . . . he's as healthy as a pig . . . and as sane . . . I was afraid once his mother had lied to Nina . . . I went upstate and investigated . . . true, every word of it . . . his great-grandfather, his grandmother, his father, were all insane . . . (*Moving uneasily.*) Stop it! . . . time to go when those thoughts come . . . sail on Saturday . . . not come here again . . . Nina will soon be fighting Sam for my son's love! . . . I'm better out of that! . . . O Christ, what a mess it all is! . . .

GORDON

(*Appears in the doorway in rear. He carries a small, expensive yacht's model of a sloop with the sails set. He is in a terrific state of conflicting emotions, on the verge of tears yet stubbornly determined*). I got to do it! . . . Gosh, it's awful . . . this boat is so pretty . . . why did it have to come from him? . . . I can get Dad to buy me another boat . . . but now I love this one . . . but he kissed Mother . . . she kissed him . . .

(*He walks up defiantly and confronts* DARRELL *who turns to him in surprise*). Hey—Darrell—did you—? (*He stops chokingly.*)

DARRELL

(*Immediately realizing what is coming—thinking with somber anguish*). So this has to happen! . . . what I dreaded! . . . my fate is merciless, it seems! . . .

(*With strained kindliness*). Did what?

GORDON

(*Growing hard—stammers angrily*). I found this—out in the hall. It can't be from anybody else. Is this—your present?

DARRELL

(*Hard and defiant himself*). Yes.

GORDON

(*In a rage—tremblingly*). Then—here's what—I think of you! (*Beginning to cry, he breaks off the mast, bowsprit, breaks the mast in two, tears the rigging off and throws the dismantled hull at* DARRELL'S *feet.*) There! You can keep it!

DARRELL

(*His anger overcoming him for an instant*). You—you mean little devil, you! You don't get that from me—(*He has taken a threatening step forward.* GORDON *stands white-faced, defying him.* DARRELL *pulls himself up short—then in a trem-*

bling voice of deeply wounded affection.) You shouldn't have done that, son. What difference do I make? It was never my boat. But it was your boat. You should consider the boat, not me. Don't you like boats for themselves? It was a beautiful little boat, I thought. That's why I—

GORDON

(*Sobbing miserably*). It was awful pretty! I didn't want to do it! (*He kneels down and gathers up the boat into his arms again.*) Honest I didn't. I love boats! But I hate you! (*This last with passionate intensity.*)

DARRELL

(*Dryly*). So I've observed.

(*Thinking with angry anguish*). He hurts, damn him! . . . .

GORDON

No, you don't know! More'n ever now! More'n ever! (*The secret escaping him.*) I saw you kissing Mother! I saw Mother, too!

DARRELL

(*Startled, but immediately forcing a smile*). But I was saying good-bye. We're old friends. You know that.

GORDON

You can't fool me! This was different! (*Explosively.*) It would serve you good and right—and Mother, too—if I was to tell Dad on you!

DARRELL

Why, I'm Sam's oldest friend. Don't make a little fool of yourself!

GORDON

You are not his friend. You've always been hanging around cheating him—hanging around Mother!

DARRELL

Keep still! What do you mean cheating him?

GORDON

I don't know. But I know you aren't his friend. And sometime I'm going to tell him I saw you—

DARRELL

(*With great seriousness now—deeply moved*). Listen! There are things a man of honor doesn't tell anyone—not even his mother or father. You want to be a man of honor, don't you? (*Intensely.*) There are things we don't tell, you and I!

(*He has put his hand around* GORDON's *shoulder impulsively.*) This is my son! . . . I love him! . . .

GORDON

(*Thinking—terribly torn*). Why do I like him now? . . . I like him awful! . . .

(*Crying*). We?—who d'you mean?—I've got honor!—more'n you!—you don't have to tell me!—I wasn't going to tell Dad anyway, honest I wasn't! We?—what d'you mean, we?—I'm not like you! I don't want to be ever like you! (*There is the sound of a door being flung open and shut and* EVANS' *hearty voice.*)

EVANS

(*From the entrance hall*). Hello, everybody!

DARRELL

(*Slapping* GORDON *on the back*). Buck up, son! Here he is! Hide that boat or he'll ask questions.

(GORDON *runs and hides the boat under the sofa. When* EVANS *enters,* GORDON *is entirely composed and runs to him joyfully.* EVANS *has grown stouter, his face is heavy now, he has grown executive and used to command, he automatically takes charge wherever he is. He does not look his age except that his hair has grown scanty and there is a perceptible bald spot on top. He is expensively tailored.*)

EVANS

(*Hugging* GORDON *to him—lovingly*). How's the old son? How's the birthday coming along?

GORDON

Fine, Dad!

EVANS

Hello, Ned! Isn't this kid of mine a whopper for his age, though!

DARRELL

(*Smiling strainedly*). Yes.

(*Writhing—thinking*). It hurts now! . . . to see my son his son! . . . I've had enough! . . . get out! . . . any excuse! . . . I can phone afterwards! . . . I'll yell out the whole business if I stay! . . .

I was just going, Sam. I've got to step around and see a fellow who lives near—biologist. (*He has gone to the door.*)

EVANS

(*Disappointedly*). Then you won't be here for lunch?

DARRELL

(*Thinking*). I'll yell the truth into your ears if I stay a second longer . . . you damned lunatic! . . .

Can't stay. Sorry. This is important. I'm sailing in a few days—lots to do—see you later, Sam. So long—Gordon.

GORDON

(*As he goes out with awkward haste*). Good-bye—Uncle Ned.

(*Thinking confusedly*). Why did I call him that when I said I never would! . . . I know . . . must be because he said he's sailing and I'm glad . . .

EVANS

So long, Ned.

(*Thinking—good-naturedly superior.*) Ned and his biology! . . . He takes his hobby pretty seriously! . . . (*With satisfaction.*) Well, he can afford to have hobbies now! . . . his investment with me has made him a pile. . . .

Where's Mother, son?

GORDON

Out in the kitchen with Uncle Charlie.

(*Thinking*). I hope he never comes back! . . . why did I like him then? . . . it was only for a second . . . I didn't really . . . I never could! . . . why does he always call me Gordon as if he hated to? . . .

EVANS

(*Sitting down at left*). I hope lunch is ready soon. I'm hungry as the devil, aren't you?

GORDON

(*Absent-mindedly*). Yes, Dad.

EVANS

Come over here and tell me about your birthday. (GORDON *comes over.* EVANS *pulls him up on his lap.*) How'd you like your presents? What'd you get from Uncle Ned?

GORDON

(*Evasively*). They were all dandy. (*Suddenly.*) Why was I named Gordon?

EVANS

Oh, you know all about that—all about Gordon Shaw. I've told you time and again.

GORDON

You told me once he was Mother's beau—when she was a girl.

EVANS

(*Teasingly*). What do you know about beaus? You're growing up!

GORDON

Did Mother love him a lot?

EVANS

(*Embarrassedly*). I guess so.

GORDON

(*Thinking keenly*). That's why Darrell hates me being called Gordon . . . he knows Mother loved Gordon better'n she does him . . . now I know how to get back at him . . . I'll be just like Gordon was and Mother'll love me better'n him! . . .

And then that Gordon was killed, wasn't he? Am I anything like him?

EVANS

I hope you are. If when you go to college you can play football or row like Gordon did, I'll—I'll give you anything you ask for! I mean that!

GORDON

(*Dreamily*). Tell me about him again, will you, Dad—about the time he was stroking the crew and the fellow who was Number Seven began to crack, and he couldn't see him but he felt him cracking somehow, and he began talking back to him all the time and sort of gave him his strength so that when the race was over and they'd won Gordon fainted and the other fellow didn't.

EVANS

(*With a fond laugh*). Why, you know it all by heart! What's the use of my telling you?

NINA

(*Comes in from the rear while they are talking. She comes forward slowly. Thinking resentfully*). Does he love Sam more than he does me? . . . oh, no, he can't! . . . but he trusts him more! . . . he confides in him more! . . .

GORDON

Did you ever used to fight fellows, Dad?

EVANS

(*Embarrassedly*). Oh, a little—when I had to.

GORDON

Could you lick Darrell?

NINA

(*Thinking frightenedly*). Why does he ask that? . . .

EVANS

(*Surprised*). Your Uncle Ned? What for? We've always been friends.

GORDON

I mean, if you weren't friends, could you?

EVANS

(*Boastfully*). Oh, yes, I guess so. Ned was never as strong as I was.

NINA

(*Thinking contemptuously*). Ned is weak. . . . (*Then apprehensively.*) But you're getting too strong, Sam. . . .

GORDON

But Gordon could have licked you, couldn't he?

EVANS

You bet he could!

GORDON

(*Thinking*). She must have loved Gordon better'n Dad even! . . .

NINA

(*She comes forward to the chair at center, forcing a smile*). What's all this talk about fighting? That's not nice. For heaven's sake, Sam, don't encourage him—

EVANS

(*Grinning*). Never mind the women, Gordon. You've got to know how to fight to get on in this world.

NINA

(*Thinking pityingly*). You poor booby! . . . how brave you are now! . . . (*Softly*). Perhaps you're right, dear. (*Looking around.*) Has Ned gone?

GORDON

(*Defiantly*). Yes—and he's not coming back—and he's sailing soon!

NINA

(*With a shudder*). Why does he challenge me that way? . . . and cling to Sam? . . . he must have seen Ned and me . . . he doesn't offer to come to my lap . . . he used to . . . Ned was right . . . I've got to lie to him . . . get him back . . . here . . . on my lap! . . . (*With a sneer—to* EVANS). I'm glad Ned's gone. I was afraid he was going to be on our hands all day.

GORDON

(*Eagerly, half-getting down from his father's lap*). You're glad—?

(*Then cautiously thinking*). She's cheating . . . I saw her kiss him. . . .

NINA

Ned's getting to be an awful bore. He's so weak. He can't get started on anything unless he's pushed.

GORDON

(*Moving a little nearer—searching her face—thinking*). She doesn't seem to like him so much . . . but I saw her kiss him! . . .

EVANS

(*Surprised*). Oh, come now, Nina, aren't you being a little hard on Ned? It's true he's sort of lost his grip in a way but he's our best friend.

GORDON

(*Moving away from his father again — resentfully — thinking*). What's Dad standing up for him to her for?

NINA

(*Thinking triumphantly*). That's right, Sam . . . just what I wanted you to say! . . .

(*Boredly*). Oh, I know he is but he gets on my nerves hanging around all the time. Without being too rude, I urged him to get back to his work, and made him promise me he wouldn't return for two years. Finally he promised—and then he became silly and sentimental and asked me to kiss him good-bye for good luck! So I kissed him to get rid of him! The silly fool!

GORDON

(*Thinking—overjoyed*). Then! . . . that's why! . . . that's why! . . . and he'll be gone two years! . . . oh, I'm so glad! . . .

(*He goes to her and looks up into her face with shining eyes*). Mother!

NINA

Dear! (*She takes him up on her lap and hugs him in her arms.*)

GORDON

(*Kisses her*). There!

(*Triumphantly thinking*). That makes up for his kiss! . . . That takes it off her mouth. . . .

EVANS

(*Grinning*). Ned must be falling for you—in his old age! (*Then sentimentally.*) Poor guy! He's never married, that's the trouble. He's lonely. I know how he feels. A fellow needs a little feminine encouragement to help him keep his head up.

NINA

(*Snuggling* GORDON'S *head against hers—laughing teasingly*). I think your hard-headed Dad is getting mushy and silly! What do you think, Gordon?

GORDON

(*Laughing with her*). Yes, he's mushy, Mother! He's silly! (*He kisses her and whispers.*) I'm going to be like Gordon Shaw, Mother! (*She hugs him fiercely to her, triumphantly happy.*)

EVANS

(*Grinning*). You two are getting too hard-boiled for me. (*He laughs. They all laugh happily together.*)

NINA

(*Suddenly overcome by a wave of conscience-stricken remorse and pity*). Oh, I am hard on Ned! . . . poor dear generous Ned! . . . you told me to lie to your son against you . . . for my sake . . . I'm not worthy of your love! . . . I'm low and selfish! . . . but I do love you! . . . this is the son of our love in my arms! . . . oh, Mother God, grant my prayer that some day we may tell our son the truth and he may love his father! . . .

GORDON

(*Sensing her thoughts, sits in her lap and stares into her face, while she guiltily avoids his eyes—in fear and resentment. Thinking*). She's thinking about that Darrell now! . . . I know! . . . she likes him too! . . . she can't fool me! . . . I saw her kissing! . . . she didn't think he was a silly fool then! . . . she was lying to Dad and me! . . . (*He pushes off her lap and backs away from her.*)

NINA

(*Thinking frightenedly*). He read my thoughts! . . . I mustn't even think of Ned when he's around! . . . poor Ned! . . . no, don't think of him! . . .

(*Leaning forward toward* GORDON *with her arms stretched out entreatingly but adopting a playful tone*). Why, Gordon, what's come over you? You jumped off my lap as though you'd sat on a tack! (*She forces a laugh.*)

GORDON

(*His eyes on the floor—evasively*). I'm hungry. I want to see if lunch is nearly ready. (*He turns abruptly and runs out.*)

EVANS

(*In a tone of superior manly understanding, kindly but laying down the law to womanly weakness*). He's sick of being babied, Nina. You forget he's getting to be a big boy. And we want him to grow up a real he-man and not an old lady like Charlie. (*Sagaciously.*) That's what's made Charlie like he is, I'll bet. His mother never stopped babying him.

NINA

(*Submissively—but with a look of bitter scorn at him*). Perhaps you're right, Sam.

EVANS

(*Confidently*). I know I am!

NINA

(*Thinking with a look of intense hatred*). Oh, Mother God, grant that I may some day tell this fool the truth!

Curtain.

ACT EIGHT

SCENE: *Late afternoon in late June, ten years later—the afterdeck of the* EVANS' *motor cruiser anchored in the lane of yachts near the finish line at Poughkeepsie. The bow and amidship of the cruiser are off right, pointed upstream. The portside rail is in the rear, the curve of the stern at left, the rear of the cabin with broad windows and a door is at right. Two wicker chairs are at left and a chaise longue at right. A wicker table with another chair is at center. The afterdeck is in cool shade, contrasted with the soft golden haze of late afternoon sunlight that glows on the river.*

NINA *is sitting by the table at center,* DARRELL *in the chair farthest left,* MARSDEN *in the chaise longue at right.* EVANS *is leaning over the rail directly back of* NINA, *looking up the river through a pair of binoculars.* MADELINE ARNOLD *is standing by his side.*

NINA'S *hair has turned completely white. She is desperately trying to conceal the obvious inroads of time by an over-emphasis on make-up that defeats its end by drawing attention to what it would conceal. Her face is thin, her cheeks taut, her mouth drawn with forced smiling. There is little left of her face's charm except her eyes which now seem larger and more deeply mysterious than ever. But she has kept her beautiful figure. It has the tragic effect of making her face seem older and more worn-out by contrast. Her general manner recalls instantly the* NINA *of Act Four, neurotic, passionately embittered and torn. She is dressed in a white yachting costume.*

DARRELL *seems to have "thrown back" to the young doctor we had seen at the house of* NINA'S *father in Act Two. He has again the air of the cool, detached scientist regarding himself and the people around him as interesting phenomena. In appearance, he is once more sharply defined, his face and body have grown lean and well-conditioned, the puffiness and jowls of the previous Act are gone. His skin is tanned almost black by his years in the tropics. His thick hair is iron-gray. He wears flannel pants, a blue coat, white buckskin shoes. He looks his fifty-one years, perhaps, but not a day more.* MARSDEN *has aged greatly. The stoop of his tall figure is accentuated, his hair has grown whitish. He is an older image of the* MARSDEN *of Act Five, who was so prostrated by his mother's death. Now it is his sister's death two months before that has plunged him into despair. His present grief, however, is more resigned to its fate than the old. He is dressed immaculately in black, as in Act Five.*

EVANS *is simply* EVANS, *his type logically developed by ten years of continued success and accumulating wealth, jovial and simple and good-natured as ever, but increasingly stubborn and self-opinionated. He has grown very stout. His jowly broad face has a heavy, flushed, apoplectic look. His head has grown quite bald on top. He is wearing a yachting cap, blue yachting coat, white flannel pants, buckskin shoes.*

MADELINE ARNOLD *is a pretty girl of nineteen, with dark hair and eyes. Her skin is deeply tanned, her figure tall and athletic, reminding one of* NINA'S *when we first saw her. Her personality is direct and frank. She gives the impression of a person who always knows exactly what she is after and generally gets it, but is also generous and a good loser, a good sport who is popular with her own sex as well as sought after by men. She is dressed in a bright-colored sport costume.*

EVANS

(*Nervous and excited—on pins and needles—lowering his binoculars impatiently*). Can't see anything up there! There's a damned haze on the river! (*Handing the binoculars to* MADELINE.) Here, Madeline. You've got young eyes.

MADELINE

(*Eagerly*). Thank you. (*She looks up the river through the glasses.*)

NINA

(*Thinking—bitterly*). Young eyes! . . . they look into Gordon's eyes! . . . he sees love in her young eyes! . . . mine are old now! . . .

EVANS

(*Pulling out his watch*). Soon be time for the start. (*Comes forward—exasperatedly.*) Of course, the damned radio has to pick out this time to go dead! Brand new one I had installed especially for this race, too! Just my luck! (*Coming to* NINA *and putting his hand on her shoulder.*) Gosh, I'll bet Gordon's some keyed-up right at this moment, Nina!

MADELINE

(*Without lowering the glasses*). Poor kid! I'll bet he is!

NINA

(*Thinking with intense bitterness*). That tone in her voice! . . . her love already possesses him! . . . my son! . . . (*Vindictively.*) But she won't! . . . as long as I live! . . .

(*Flatly*). Yes, he must be nervous.

EVANS

(*Taking his hand away, sharply*). I didn't mean nervous. He doesn't know what it is to have nerves. Nothing's ever got him rattled yet. (*This last with a resentful look down at her as he moves back to the rail.*)

MADELINE

(*With the calm confidence of one who knows*). Yes, you can bank on Gordon never losing his nerve.

NINA

(*Coldly*). I'm quite aware my son isn't a weakling— (*Meaningly, with a glance at* MADELINE) even though he does do weak things sometimes.

MADELINE

(*Without lowering the glasses from her eyes—thinking good-naturedly*). Ouch! . . . that was meant for me! . . . (*Then hurt.*) Why does she dislike me so? . . . I've done my best, for Gordon's sake, to be nice to her. . . .

EVANS

(*Looking back at* NINA *resentfully—thinking*). Another nasty crack at Madeline! . . . Nina's certainly become the prize bum sport! . . . I thought once her change of life was over she'd be ashamed of her crazy jealousy . . . instead of that it's got worse . . . but I'm not going to let her come between Gordon and Madeline . . . he loves her and she loves him . . . and her folks have got money and position, too . . . and I like her a lot . . . and, by God, I'm going to see to it their marriage goes through on schedule, no matter how much Nina kicks up! . . .

DARRELL

(*Keenly observant—thinking*). Nina hates this young lady . . . of course! . . . Gordon's girl . . . she'll smash their engagement if she can . . . as she did mine once . . . once! . . . thank God my slavery is over! . . . how did she know I was back in town? . . . I wasn't going to see her again . . . but her invitation was so imploring . . . my duty to Gordon, she wrote . . . what duty? . . . pretty late in the day! . . . that's better left dead, too! . . .

EVANS

(*Looking at his watch again*). They ought to be lined up at the start any minute now. (*Pounding his fist on the rail—letting his pent-up feelings explode.*) Come on, Gordon!

NINA

(*Startled—with nervous irritation*). Sam! I told you I have a splitting headache!

(*Thinking intensely*). You vulgar boor! . . . Gordon's engagement to her is all your fault! . . .

EVANS

(*Resentfully*). I'm sorry. Why don't you take some aspirin?

(*Thinking irritably*). Nina in the dumps! . . . Charlie in mourning! . . . what a pair of killjoys! . . . I wanted to bring Gordon and his friends on board to celebrate . . . no chance! . . . have to take Madeline . . . stage a party in New York . . . leave this outfit flat . . . Nina'll be sore as the devil but she'll have to like it . . .

DARRELL

(*Examining* NINA *critically—thinking*). She's gotten into a fine neurotic state . . . reminds me of when I first knew her . . . (*Then exultantly.*) Thank God, I can watch her objectively again . . . these last three years away have finally done it . . . complete cure! . . . (*Then remorsefully.*) Poor Nina! . . . we're all deserting her . . . (*Then glancing at* MARSDEN*—with a trace of a sneer.*) Even Marsden seems to have left her for the dead! . . .

MARSDEN

(*Vaguely irritated—thinking*). What am I doing here? . . . what do I care about this stupid race? . . . why did I let Nina bully me into coming? . . . I ought to be alone . . . with my memories of dear Jane . . . it will be two months ago Saturday she died . . . (*His lips tremble, tears come to his eyes.*)

MADELINE

(*With an impatient sigh, lowering the glasses*). It's no use, Mr. Evans, I can't see a thing.

EVANS

(*With angry disgust*). If only that damned radio was working!

NINA

(*Exasperatedly*). For heaven's sake, stop swearing so much!

EVANS

(*Hurt—indignantly*). What about it if I am excited? Seems to me you could show a little more interest without it hurting you, when it's Gordon's last race, his last appearance on a varsity! (*He turns away from her.*)

MADELINE

(*Thinking*). He's right . . . she's acting rotten . . . if I were Gordon's mother, I certainly wouldn't . . .

EVANS

(*Turning back to* NINA*—resentfully*). You used to cheer loud enough for Gordon Shaw! And our Gordon's got him beat a mile, as an oarsman, at least! (*Turning to* DARRELL.) And that isn't father stuff either, Ned! All the experts say so!

DARRELL

(*Cynically*). Oh, come on, Sam! Surely no one could ever touch Shaw in anything! (*He glances at* NINA *with a sneer.*)

(*Immediately angry at himself*). What an idiot! . . . that popped out of me! . . . old habit! . . . I haven't loved her in years! . . .

NINA

(*Thinking indifferently*). Ned still feels jealous . . . that no longer pleases me . . . I don't feel anything . . . except that I must get him to help me. (*She turns to* DARRELL *bitterly*). Sam said "our" Gordon. He means his. Gordon's become so like Sam, Ned, you won't recognize him!

MADELINE

(*Thinking indignantly*). She's crazy! . . . he's nothing like his father! . . . he's so strong and handsome! . . .

EVANS

(*Good-naturedly, with a trace of pride*). You flatter me, Nina. I wish I thought that. But he isn't a bit like me, luckily for him. He's a dead ringer for Gordon Shaw at his best.

MADELINE

(*Thinking*). Shaw . . . I've seen his picture in the gym . . . my Gordon is better looking . . . he once told me Shaw was an old beau of his mother's . . . they say she was beautiful once . . .

NINA

(*Shaking her head—scornfully*). Don't be modest, Sam. Gordon *is* you. He may be a fine athlete like Gordon Shaw, because you've held that out to him as your ideal, but there the resemblance ceases. He isn't really like him at all, not the slightest bit!

EVANS

(*Restraining his anger with difficulty—thinking*). I'm getting sick of this! . . . she's carrying her jealous grouch too far! . . .

(*Suddenly exploding, pounds his fists on the rail*). Damn it, Nina, if you had any feeling you couldn't—right at the moment when he's probably getting into the shell— (*He stops, trying to control himself, panting, his face red.*)

NINA

(*Staring at him with repulsion—with cool disdain*). I didn't say anything so dire, did I—merely that Gordon resembles you in character. (*With malice.*) Don't get excited. It's bad for your high blood pressure. Ask Ned if it isn't.

(*Intensely—thinking*). If he'd only die! . . . (*Thinking—immediately.*) Oh, I don't mean that . . . I mustn't.

DARRELL

(*Thinking keenly*). There's a death wish . . . things have gone pretty far . . . Sam does look as if he might have a bad pressure . . . what hope that would have given me at one time! . . . no more, thank God! . . .

(*In a joking tone*). Oh, I guess Sam's all right, Nina.

EVANS

(*Gruffly*). I never felt better. (*He jerks out his watch again.*) Time for the start. Come on in the cabin, Ned, and shoot a drink. We'll see if McCabe's getting the damned radio fixed. (*Passing by* MARSDEN *he claps him on the shoulder exasperatedly.*) Come on, Charlie! Snap out of it!

MARSDEN

(*Startled out of his trance—bewilderedly*). Eh?—what is it?—are they coming?

EVANS

(*Recovering his good nature—with a grin, taking his arm*). You're coming to shoot a drink. You need about ten, I think, to get you in the right spirit to see the finish! (*To* DARRELL *who has gotten up but is still standing by his chair.*) Come on, Ned.

NINA

(*Quickly*). No, leave Ned with me. I want to talk to him. Take Madeline—and Charlie.

MARSDEN

(*Looking at her appealingly*). But I'm perfectly contented sitting—

(*Then after a look in her eyes—thinking*). She wants to be alone with Darrell . . . all right . . . doesn't matter now . . . their love is dead . . . but there's still some secret between them she's never told me . . . never mind . . . she'll tell me sometime . . . I'm all she will have left . . . soon. . . . (*Then stricken with guilt.*) Poor dear Jane! . . . how can I think of anyone but you! . . . God, I'm contemptible! . . . I'll get drunk with that fool! . . . that's all I'm good for! . . .

MADELINE

(*Thinking resentfully*). She takes a fine do-this-little-girl tone toward me! . . . I'll give in to her now . . . but once I'm married! . . .

EVANS

Come on then, Madeline. We'll give you a small one. (*Impatiently.*) Charlie! Head up!

MARSDEN

(*With hectic joviality*). I hope it's strong poison!

EVANS

(*Laughing*). That's the spirit! We'll make a sport out of you yet!

MADELINE

(*Laughing, goes and takes* MARSDEN'S *arm*). I'll see you get home safe, Mr. Marsden!

(*They go into the cabin,* EVANS *following them.* NINA *and* DARRELL *turn and look at each other wonderingly, inquisitively, for a long moment.* DARRELL *remains standing and seems to be a little uneasy.*)

DARRELL

(*Thinking with melancholy interest*). And now? . . . what? . . . I can look into her eyes . . . strange eyes that will never grow old . . . without desire or jealousy or bitterness . . . was she ever my mistress? . . . can she be the mother of my child? . . . is there such a person as my son? . . . I can't think of these things as real any more . . . they must have happened in another life.

NINA

(*Thinking sadly*). My old lover . . . how well and young he looks . . . now we no longer love each other at all . . . our account with God the Father is settled . . . afternoons of happiness paid for with years of pain . . . love, passion, ecstasy . . . in what a far-off life were they alive! . . . the only living life is in the past and future . . . the present is an interlude . . . strange interlude in which we call on past and future to bear witness we are living!

(*With a sad smile*). Sit down, Ned. When I heard you were back I wrote you because I need a friend. It has been so long since we loved each other we can now be friends again. Don't you feel that?

DARRELL

(*Gratefully*). Yes. I do. (*He sits down in one of the chairs at the left, drawing it up closer to her.*)

(*Thinking cautiously*). I want to be her friend . . . but I will never . . .

NINA

(*Thinking cautiously*). I must keep very cool and sensible or he won't help me. . . .

(*With a friendly smile*). I haven't seen you look so young and handsome since I first knew you. Tell me your secret. (*Bitterly.*) I need it! I'm old! Look at me! And I was actually looking forward to being old! I thought it would mean peace. I've been sadly disillusioned! (*Then forcing a smile.*) So tell me what fountain of youth you've found.

DARRELL

(*Proudly*). That's easy. Work! I've become as interested in biology as I once was in medicine. And not selfishly interested, that's the difference. There's no chance of my becoming a famous biologist and I know it. I'm very much a worker in the ranks. But our Station is a "huge success," as Sam would say. We've made some damned important discoveries. I say "we." I really mean Preston. You may remember I used to write you about him with enthusiasm. He's justified it. He *is* making his name world-famous. He's what I might have been—I did have the brains, Nina!—if I'd had more guts and less vanity, if I'd hewn to the line! (*Then ,orcing a smile.*) But I'm not lamenting. I've found myself in helping him. In that way I feel I've paid my debt—that his work is partly my work. And he acknowledges it. He possesses the rare virtue of gratitude. (*With proud affection.*) He's a fine boy, Nina! I suppose I should say man now he's in his thirties.

NINA

(*Thinking with bitter sorrow*). So, Ned . . . you remember our love . . . with bitterness! . . . as a stupid mistake! . . . the proof of a gutless vanity that ruined your career! . . . oh! . . . (*Then controlling herself—thinking cynically.*) Well, after all, how do I remember our love? . . . with no emotion at all, not even bitterness! . . . (*Then with sudden alarm.*) He's forgotten Gordon for this Preston! . . . (*Thinking desperately.*) I must make him remember Gordon is his child or I can never persuade him to help me! (*Reproachfully*). So you have found a son while I was losing mine—who is yours, too!

DARRELL

(*Struck by this—impersonally interested*). That's never occurred to me but now I think of it— (*Smiling.*) Yes, perhaps unconsciously Preston is a compensating substitute. Well, it's done both of us good and hasn't harmed anyone.

NINA

(*With bitter emphasis*). Except your real son—and me—but we don't count, I suppose!

DARRELL

(*Coolly*). Harmed Gordon? How? He's all right, isn't he? (*With a sneer.*) I should say from all I've been hearing that he was your ideal of college hero—like his never-to-be-forgotten namesake!

NINA

(*Thinking resentfully*). He's sneering at his own son! . . . (*Then trying to be calculating.*) But I mustn't get angry . . . I must make him help me. . . . (*Speaking with gentle reproach*). And am I the ideal of a happy mother, Ned?

DARRELL

(*Immediately moved by pity and ashamed of himself*). Forgive me, Nina. I haven't quite buried all my bitterness, I'm afraid. (*Gently.*) I'm sorry you're unhappy, Nina.

NINA

(*Thinking with satisfaction*). He means that . . . he still does care a little . . . if only it's enough to . . . ! (*Speaking sadly*). I've lost my son, Ned! Sam has made him all his. And it was done so gradually that, although I realized what was happening, there was never any way I could interfere. What Sam advised seemed always the best thing for Gordon's future. And it was always what Gordon himself wanted, to escape from me to boarding school and then to college, to become Sam's athletic hero—

DARRELL

(*Impatiently*). Oh, come now, Nina, you know you've always longed for him to be like Gordon Shaw!

NINA

(*Bursting out in spite of herself—violently*). He's not like Gordon! He's forgotten me for that—! (*Trying to be more reasonable.*) What do I care whether he's an athlete or not? It's such nonsense, all this fuss! I'm not the slightest bit interested in this race today, for example! I wouldn't care if he came in last!

(*Stopping herself—thinking frightenedly*). Oh, if he should ever guess I said that! . . .

DARRELL

(*Thinking keenly*). Hello! . . . she said that as if she'd like to see him come last! . . . why? . . . (*Then vindictively.*) Well, so would I! . . . it's time these Gordons took a good licking from life! . . .

MADELINE

(*Suddenly appears in the door from the cabin, her face flushed with excitement*). They're off! Mr. Evans is getting something—it's terribly faint but—Navy and Washington are leading—Gordon's third! (*She disappears back in the cabin.*)

NINA

(*Looking after her with hatred*). Her Gordon! . . . she is so sure! . . . how I've come to detest her pretty face! . . .

DARRELL

(*Thinking with a sneer*). "Gordon's third"! . . . you might think there was no one else pulling the shell! . . . what idiots women make of themselves about these Gordons! . . . she's pretty, that Madeline! . . . she's got a figure like Nina's when I first loved her . .

those afternoons . . . age is beginning to tell on Nina's face . . . but she's kept her wonderful body! . . .

(*With a trace of malice—dryly*). There's a young lady who seems to care a lot whether Gordon comes in last or not!

NINA

(*Trying to be sorrowful and appealing*). Yes. Gordon is hers now, Ned. (*But she cannot bear this thought—vindictively.*) That is, they're engaged. But, of course, that doesn't necessarily mean— Can you imagine him throwing himself away on a little fool like that? I simply can't believe he really loves her! Why, she's hardly even pretty and she's deadly stupid. I thought he was only flirting with her—or merely indulging in a passing physical affair. (*She winces.*) At his age, one has to expect—even a mother must face nature. But for Gordon to take her seriously, and propose marriage—it's too idiotic for words!

DARRELL

(*Thinking cynically*). Oh, so you'll compromise on his sleeping with her . . . if you have to . . . but she must have no real claim to dispute your ownership, eh? . . . you'd like to make her the same sort of convenient slave for him that I was for you! . . .

(*Resentfully*). I can't agree with you. I find her quite charming. It seems to me if I were in Gordon's shoes I'd do exactly what he has done.

(*In confusion—thinking bitterly*). In Gordon's shoes! . . . I always was in Gordon Shaw's shoes! . . . and why am I taking this young Gordon's part? . . . what is he to me, for God's sake?

NINA

(*Unheedingly*). If he marries her, it means he'll forget me! He'll forget me as completely as Sam forgot his mother! She'll keep him away from me! Oh, I know what wives can do! She'll use her body until she persuades him to forget me! My son, Ned! And your son, too! (*She suddenly gets up and goes to him and takes one of his hands in both of hers.*) The son of our old love, Ned!

DARRELL

(*Thinking with a strange shudder of mingled attraction and fear as she touches him*). Our love . . . old love . . . old touch of her flesh . . . we're old . . . it's silly and indecent . . . does she think she still can own me? . . .

NINA

(*In the tone a mother takes in speaking to her husband about their boy*). You'll have to give Gordon a good talking to, Ned.

DARRELL

(*Still more disturbed—thinking*). Old . . . but she's kept her wonderful body . . . how many years since? . . . she has the same strange influence over me . . . touch of her flesh . . . it's dangerous . . . bosh, I'm only humoring her as a friend . . . as her doctor . . . and why shouldn't I have a talk with Gordon? . . . a father owes something to his son . . . he ought to advise him. . . . (*Then alarmed.*) But I was never going to meddle again . . .

(*Sternly*). I swore I'd never again meddle with human lives, Nina!

NINA

(*Unheedingly*). You must keep him from ruining his life.

DARRELL

(*Doggedly—struggling with himself*). I won't touch a life that has more than one cell! (*Harshly.*) And I wouldn't help you in this, anyway! You've got to give up owning people, meddling in their lives as if you were God and had created them!

NINA

(*Strangely forlorn*). I don't know what you mean, Ned. Gordon is my son, isn't he?

DARRELL

(*With a sudden strange violence*). And mine! Mine, too! (*He stops himself.*)

(*Thinking*). Shut up, you fool! . . . is that the way to humor her? . . .

NINA

(*With strange quiet*). I think I still love you a little, Ned.

DARRELL

(*In her tone*). And I still love you a little, Nina. (*Then sternly.*) But I will not meddle in your life again! (*With a harsh laugh.*) And you've meddled enough with human love, old lady! Your time for that is over! I'll send you a couple million cells you can torture without harming yourself! (*Regaining control — shamefacedly.*) Nina! Please forgive me!

NINA

(*Starts as if out of a dream—anxiously*). What were you saying, Ned? (*She lets go of his hand and goes back to her chair.*)

DARRELL

(*Dully*). Nothing.

NINA

(*Strangely*). We were talking about Sam, weren't we? How do you think he looks?

DARRELL

(*Confusedly casual*). Fine. A bit too fat, of course. He looks as though his blood pressure might be higher than it ought to be. But that's not unusual in persons of his build and age. It's nothing to hope—I meant, to worry over! (*Then violently.*) God damn it, why did you make me say hope?

NINA

(*Calmly*). It may have been in your mind, too, mayn't it?

DARRELL

No! I've nothing against Sam. I've always been his best friend. He owes his happiness to me.

NINA

(*Strangely*). There are so many curious reasons we dare not think about for thinking things!

DARRELL

(*Rudely*). Thinking doesn't matter a damn! Life is something in one cell that doesn't need to think!

NINA

(*Strangely*). I know! God the Mother!

DARRELL

(*Excitedly*). And all the rest is gutless egotism! But to hell with it! What I started to say was, what possible reason could I have for hoping for Sam's death?

NINA

(*Strangely*). We're always desiring death for ourselves or others, aren't we—while we while away our lives with the old surface ritual of coveting our neighbor's ass?

DARRELL

(*Frightenedly*). You're talking like the old Nina now—when I first loved you. Please don't! It isn't decent—at our age!

(*Thinking in terror*). The old Nina! . . . am I the old Ned? . . . then that means? . . . but we must not meddle in each other's lives again! . . .

NINA

(*Strangely*). I am the old Nina! And this time I will not let my Gordon go from me forever!

EVANS

(*Appears in the doorway of the cabin—excited and irritated*). Madeline's listening in now. It went dead on me. (*Raising the binoculars as he goes to the rail, he looks up the river.*) Last I got, Gordon third, Navy and Washington leading. They're the ones to fear, he said—Navy especially. (*Putting down the glasses—with a groan.*) Damned haze! My eyes are getting old. (*Then suddenly with a grin.*) You ought to see Charlie! He started throwing Scotch into him as if he were drinking against time. I had to take the bottle away from him. It's hit him an awful wallop. (*Then looking from one to the other—resentfully.*) What's the matter with you two? There's a race going on, don't you know it? And you sit like dead clams!

DARRELL

(*Placatingly*). I thought someone'd better stay out here and let you know when they get in sight.

EVANS

(*Relieved*). Oh, sure, that's right! Here, take the glasses. You always had good eyes.

(DARRELL *gets up and takes the glasses and goes to the rail and begins adjusting them.*)

DARRELL

Which crew was it you said Gordon feared the most?

EVANS

(*Has gone back to the cabin doorway*). Navy. (*Then proudly.*) Oh, he'll beat them! But it'll be damn close. I'll see if Madeline's getting— (*He goes back in the cabin.*)

DARRELL

(*Looking up the river—with vindictive bitterness—thinking*). Come on, Navy! . . .

NINA

(*Thinking bitterly*). Madeline's Gordon! . . . Sam's Gordon! . . . the thanks I get for saving Sam at the sacrifice of my own happiness! . . . I won't have it! . . . what do I care what happens to Sam now? . . . I hate him! . . . I'll tell him Gordon isn't his child! . . . and threaten to tell Gordon too, unless! . . . he'll be in deadly fear of that! . . . he'll soon find some excuse to break their engagement! . . . he can! . . . he has the strangest influence over Gordon! . . . but Ned must back me up or Sam won't believe me! . . . Ned must tell him too! . . . but will Ned? . . . he'll be afraid of the insanity! . . . I must make him believe Sam's in no danger . . .

(*Intensely*). Listen, Ned, I'm absolutely sure, from things she wrote me before she died, that Sam's mother must have been deliberately lying to me about the insanity that time. She was jealous because Sam loved me and she simply wanted to be revenged, I'm sure.

DARRELL

(*Without lowering glasses—dryly*). No. She told you the truth. I never mentioned it, but I went up there once and made a thorough investigation of his family.

NINA

(*With resentful disappointment*). Oh—I suppose you wanted to make sure so you could hope he'd go insane?

DARRELL

(*Simply*). I needed to be able to hope that, then. I loved you horribly at that time, Nina—horribly!

NINA

(*Putting her hands on his arm*). And you don't—any more, Ned?

(*Thinking intensely*). Oh, I must make him love me again . . . enough to make him tell Sam! . . .

DARRELL

(*Thinking strangely — struggling with himself*). She'd like to own me again . . . I wish she wouldn't touch me . . . what is this tie of old happiness between our flesh? . . .

(*Harshly—weakly struggling to shake off her hands, without lowering the glasses*). I won't meddle again with human lives, I told you!

NINA

(*Unheeding, clinging to him*). And I loved you horribly! I still do love you, Ned! I used to hope he'd go insane myself because I loved you so! But look at Sam! He's sane as a pig! There's absolutely no danger now!

DARRELL

(*Thinking—alarmed*). What is she after now—what does she want me for? . . .

(*Stiffly*). I'm no longer a doctor but I should say he's a healthy miss of Nature's. It's a thousand to one against it at this late day.

NINA

(*With sudden fierce intensity*). Then it's time to tell him the truth, isn't it? We've suffered all our lives for his sake! We've made him rich and happy! It's time he gave us back our son!

DARRELL

(*Thinking*). Aha . . . so that's it! . . . tell Sam the truth? . . . at last! . . . by God, I'd like to tell him, at that! . . .

(*With a sneer*). Our son? You mean yours, my dear! Kindly count me out of any further meddling with—

NINA

(*Unruffledly—obsessed*). But Sam won't believe me if I'm the only one to tell him! He'll think I'm lying for spite, that it's only my crazy jealousy! He'll ask you! You've got to tell him too, Ned!

DARRELL

(*Thinking*). I'd like to see his face when I told him this famous oarsman isn't his son but mine! . . . that might pay me back a little for all he's taken from me! . . .

(*Harshly*). I've stopped meddling in Sam's life, I tell you!

NINA

(*Insistently*). Think of what Sam has made us go through, of how he's made us suffer! You've got to tell him! You still love me a little, don't you, Ned? You must when you remember the happiness we've known in each other's arms! You were the only happiness I've ever known in life!

DARRELL

(*Struggling weakly—thinking*). She lies! . . . there was her old lover, Gordon! . . . he was always first! . . . then her son, Gordon! . . . (*With desperate rancor—thinking*). Come on, Navy! . . . beat her Gordons for me! . . .

NINA

(*Intensely*). Oh, if I'd only gone away with you that time when you came back from Europe! How happy we would have been, dear! How our boy would have loved you —if it hadn't been for Sam!

DARRELL

(*Thinking—weakly*). Yes, if it hadn't been for Sam I would have been happy! . . . I would have been the world's greatest neurologist! . . . my boy would have loved me and I'd have loved him! . . .

NINA

(*With a crowning intensity to break down his last resistance*). You must tell him, Ned! For my sake! Because I love you! Because you remember our afternoons—our mad happiness! Because you love me!

DARRELL

(*Beaten—dazedly*). Yes—what must I do?—meddle again?

(*The noise of* MADELINE's *excited voice cheering and clapping her hands, of* MARSDEN's *voice yelling drunkenly, of* EVANS', *all shouting "Gordon! Gordon! Come on, Gordon!" comes from the cabin.* MARSDEN *appears swaying in the cabin doorway yelling "Gordon!" He is hectically tipsy.* DARRELL *gives a violent shudder as if he were coming out of a nightmare and pushes* NINA *away from him.*)

DARRELL

(*Thinking—dazedly still, but in a tone of relief*). Marsden again! . . . thank God! . . . he's saved me! . . . from her! . . . and her Gordons! . . .

(*Turning on her triumphantly*). No, Nina—sorry—but I can't help you. I told you I'd never meddle again with human lives! (*More and more confidently.*) Besides, I'm quite sure Gordon isn't my son, if the real deep core of the truth were known! I was only a body to you. Your first Gordon used to come back to life. I was never more to you than a substitute for your dead lover! Gordon is really Gordon's son! So you see I'd be telling Sam a lie if I boasted that I—And I'm a man of honor! I've proved that, at least! (*He raises his glasses and looks up the river.*)

(*Thinking exultantly*). I'm free! . . . I've beaten her at last! . . . now come on, Navy! . . . you've got to beat her Gordons for me! . . .

NINA

(*After staring at him for a moment—walking away from him—thinking with a dull fatalism*). I've lost him . . . he'll never tell Sam now . . . is what he said right? . . . is Gordon Gordon's? . . . oh, I hope so! . . . oh, dear, dead Gordon, help me to get back your son! . . . I must find some way. . . . (*She sits down again.*)

MARSDEN

(*Who has been staring at them with a foolish grin*). Hello, you two! Why do you look so guilty? You don't love each other any more! It's all nonsense! I don't feel the slightest twinge of jealousy. That's proof enough, isn't it? (*Then blandly apologetic.*) Pardon me if I sound a bit pipped—a good bit! Sam said ten and then took the bottle away when I'd had only five! But it's enough! I've forgotten sorrow! There's nothing in life worth grieving about, I assure you, Nina! And I've gotten interested in this race now. (*He sings raucously.*) "Oh we'll row, row, row, right down the river! And we'll row, row, row—" Remember that old tune—when you were a little girl, Nina? Oh, I'm forgetting Sam said to tell you Gordon was on even terms with the leaders! A gallant spurt did it! Nip and tuck now! I don't care who wins—as long as it isn't Gordon! I don't like him since he's grown up! He thinks I'm an old woman! (*Sings.*) "Row, row, row." The field against Gordon!

DARRELL

(*Hectically*). Right! (*He looks through the glasses—excitedly.*) I see a flashing in the water way up there! Must be their oars! They're coming! I'll tell Sam! (*He hurries into the cabin.*)

NINA

(*Thinking dully*). He'll tell Sam . . . no, he doesn't mean that . . . I must find some other way . . .

MARSDEN

(*Walks a bit uncertainly to* NINA'S *chair*). Gordon really should get beaten today—for the good of his soul, Nina. That Madeline is pretty, isn't she? These Gordons are too infernally lucky—while we others—(*He almost starts to blubber—angrily*) we others have got to beat him today! (*He slumps clumsily down to a sitting position on the deck by her chair and takes her hand and pats it.*) There, there, Nina Cara Nina! Don't worry your pretty head! It will all come out all right! We'll only have a little while longer to wait and then you and I'll be quietly married!

(*Thinking frightenedly*). The devil! . . . what am I saying? . . . I'm drunk! . . . all right, all the better! . . . I've wanted all my life to tell her! . . .

Of course, I realize you've got a husband at present but, never mind, I can wait. I've waited a lifetime already; but for a long while now I've had a keen psychic intuition that I wasn't born to die before—

(EVANS *and* MADELINE *and* DARRELL *come rushing out of the cabin. They all have binoculars. They run to the rail and train their glasses up the river.*)

MADELINE

(*Excitedly*). I see them! (*Grabbing his arm and pointing.*) Look, Mr. Evans—there—don't you see?

EVANS

(*Excitedly*). No—not yet— Yes! Now I see them! (*Pounding on the rail.*) Come on, Gordon boy!

MADELINE

Come on, Gordon!

(*The whistles and sirens from the yachts up the river begin to be heard. This grows momentarily louder as one after another other yachts join in the chorus as the crews approach nearer and nearer until toward the close of the scene there is a perfect pandemonium of sound.*)

NINA

(*With bitter hatred—thinking*). How I hate her! . . . (*Then suddenly with a deadly calculation—thinking.*) Why not tell her? . . . as Sam's mother told me? . . . of the insanity? . . . she thinks Gordon is Sam's son. (*With a deadly smile of triumph.*) That will be poetic justice! . . . that will solve everything! . . . she won't marry him! . . . he will turn to me for comfort! . . . but I must plan it out carefully! . . .

MARSDEN

(*Driven on—extravagantly*). Listen, Nina! After we're married I'm going to write a novel—my first real novel! All the twenty-odd books I've written have been long-winded fairy tales for grown-ups—about dear old ladies and witty, cynical bachelors and quaint characters with dialects, and married folk who always admire and respect each other, and lovers who avoid love in hushed whispers! That's what I've been, Nina—a hush-hush whisperer of lies! Now I'm going to give an honest healthy yell—turn on the sun into the shadows of lies—shout "This is life and this is sex, and here are passion and hatred and regret and joy and pain and ecstasy, and these are men and women and sons and daughters whose hearts are weak and strong, whose blood is blood and not a soothing syrup!" Oh, I can do it, Nina! I can write the truth! I've seen it in you, your father, my mother, sister, Gordon, Sam, Darrell and myself. I'll write the book of us! But here I am talking while my last chapters are in the making—right here and now— (*Hurriedly.*) You'll excuse me, won't you, Nina? I must watch—my duty as an artist! (*He scrambles to his feet and peers about him with a hectic eagerness.* NINA *pays no attention to him.*)

EVANS

(*Exasperatedly, taking down his glasses*). You can't tell a damn thing—which is which or who's ahead—I'm going to listen in again. (*He hurries into the cabin.*)

NINA

(*With a smile of cruel triumph—thinking*). I can tell her . . . confidentially . . . I can pretend I'm forced to tell her . . . as Sam's mother did with me . . . because I feel it's due to her happiness and Gordon's . . . It will explain my objection to the engagement . . . oh, it can't help succeeding . . . my Gordon will come back! . . . I'll see he never gets away again! . . .

(*She calls*). Madeline!

MARSDEN

(*Thinking*). Why is she calling Madeline? . . . I must watch all this carefully! . . .

EVANS

(*Comes rushing out in wild alarm*). Bad news! Navy has drawn ahead—half a length—looks like Navy's race, he said—(*Then violently.*) But what does he know, that damn fool announcer—some poor boob—!

MADELINE

(*Excitedly*). He doesn't know Gordon! He's always best when he's pushed to the limit!

NINA

(*She calls more sharply*). Madeline!

DARRELL

(*Turns around to stare at her—thinking*). Why is she calling Madeline? . . . she's bound she'll meddle in their lives . . . I've got to watch her . . . well, let's see. . . .

(*He touches* MADELINE *on the shoulder*). Mrs. Evans is calling you, Miss Arnold.

MADELINE

(*Impatiently*). Yes, Mrs. Evans. But they're getting closer. Why don't you come and watch?

NINA

(*Not heeding — impressively*). There's something I must tell you.

MADELINE

(*In hopeless irritation*). But— Oh, all right. (*She hurries over to her, glancing eagerly over her shoulder towards the river.*) Yes, Mrs. Evans?

DARRELL

(*Moves from the rail toward them—thinking keenly*). I must watch this . . . she's in a desperate meddling mood! . . .

NINA

(*Impressively*). First, give me your word of honor that you'll never reveal a word of what I'm going to tell you to a living soul—above all not to Gordon!

MADELINE

(*Looking at her in amazement—soothingly*). Couldn't you tell me later, Mrs. Evans—after the race?

NINA

(*Sternly—grabbing her by the wrists*). No, now! Do you promise?

MADELINE

(*With helpless annoyance*). Yes, Mrs. Evans.

NINA

(*Sternly*). For the sake of your future happiness and my son's I've got to speak! Your engagement forces me to! You've probably wondered why I objected. It's because the marriage is impossible. You can't marry Gordon! I speak as your friend! You must break your engagement with him at once!

MADELINE

(*Cannot believe her ears—suddenly panic-stricken*). But why—why?

DARRELL

(*Who has come closer—resentfully thinking*). She wants to ruin my son's life as she ruined mine! . . .

NINA

(*Relentlessly*). Why? Because—

DARRELL

(*Steps up suddenly beside them—sharply and sternly commanding*). No, Nina! (*He taps* MADELINE *on the shoulder and draws her aside.* NINA *lets go of her wrist and stares after them in a sort of stunned stupor.*) Miss Arnold, as a doctor I feel it my duty to tell you that Mrs. Evans isn't herself. Pay no attention to anything she may say to you. She's just passed through a crucial period in a woman's life and she's morbidly jealous of you and subject to queer delusions! (*He smiles kindly at her.*) So get back to the race! And God bless you! (*He grips her hand, strangely moved.*)

MADELINE

(*Gratefully*). Thank you. I understand, I think. Poor Mrs. Evans! (*She hurries back to the rail, raising her glasses.*)

NINA

(*Springing to her feet and finding her voice—with despairing accusation*). Ned!

DARRELL

(*Steps quickly to her side*). I'm sorry, Nina, but I warned you not to meddle. (*Then affectionately.*) And Gordon is—well—sort of my stepson, isn't he? I really want him to be happy. (*Then smiling good-naturedly.*) All the same, I can't help hoping he'll be beaten in this race. As an oarsman he recalls his father, Gordon Shaw, to me. (*He turns away and raises his glasses, going back to the rail.* NINA *slumps down in her chair again.*)

EVANS

Damn! They all look even from here! Can you tell which is which, Madeline?

MADELINE

No—not yet—oh, dear, this is awful! Gordon!

NINA

(*Looking about her in the air—with a dazed question*). Gordon?

MARSDEN

(*Thinking*). Damn that Darrell! . . . if he hadn't interfered Nina would have told . . . something of infinite importance, I know! . . .

(*He comes and again sits on the deck by her chair and takes her hand*). Because what, Nina—my dear little Nina Cara Nina—because what? Let me help you!

NINA

(*Staring before her as if she were in a trance—simply, like a young girl*). Yes, Charlie. Yes, Father. Because all of Sam's father's family have been insane. His mother told me that time so I wouldn't have his baby. I was going to tell Madeline that so she wouldn't marry Gordon. But it would have been a lie because Gordon isn't really Sam's child at all, he's Ned's. Ned gave him to me and I gave him to Sam so Sam could have a healthy child and be well and happy. And Sam is well and happy, don't you think? (*Childishly.*) So I haven't been such an awfully wicked girl, have I, Father?

MARSDEN

(*Horrified and completely sobered by what he has heard—stares at her with stunned eyes*). Nina! Good God! Do you know what you're saying?

MADELINE

(*Excitedly*). There! The one on this side! I saw the color on their blades just now!

EVANS

(*Anxiously*). Are you sure? Then he's a little behind the other two!

DARRELL

(*Excitedly*). The one in the middle seems to be ahead! Is that the Navy?

(*But the others pay no attention to him. All three are leaning over the rail, their glasses glued to their eyes. looking up the *river. The noise from the whistles is now very loud. The cheering from the observation trains can be heard.)*

MARSDEN

(*Stares into her face with great pity now*). Merciful God, Nina! Then you've lived all these years—with this horror! And you and Darrell deliberately—?

NINA

(*Without looking at him—to the air*). Sam's mother said I had a right to be happy too.

MARSDEN

And you didn't love Darrell then—?

NINA

(*As before*). I did afterwards. I don't now. Ned is dead, too. (*Softly.*) Only you are alive now, Father—and Gordon.

MARSDEN

(*Gets up and bends over her paternally, stroking her hair with a strange, wild, joyous pity*). Oh, Nina—poor little Nina—my Nina—how you must have suffered! I forgive you! I forgive you everything! I forgive even your trying to tell Madeline—you wanted to keep Gordon—oh, I understand that—and I forgive you!

NINA

(*As before—affectionately and strangely*). And I forgive you, Father. It was all your fault in the beginning, wasn't it? You mustn't ever meddle with human lives again!

EVANS

(*Wildly excited*). Gordon's sprinting, isn't he? He's drawing up on that middle one!

MADELINE

Yes! Oh, come on, Gordon!

DARRELL

(*Exultantly*). Come on, Navy!

EVANS

(*Who is standing next to* NED, *whirls on him in a furious passion*). What's that? What the hell's the matter with you?

DARRELL

(*Facing him—with a strange friendliness slaps him on the back*). We've got to beat these Gordons, Sam! We've got to beat—

EVANS

(*Raging*). You—! (*He draws back his fist—then suddenly horrified at what he is doing but still angry, grabs* DARRELL *by both shoulders and shakes him.*) Wake up! What the hell's got into you? Have you gone crazy?

DARRELL

(*Mockingly*). Probably! It runs in my family! All of my father's people were happy lunatics—not healthy, country folk like yours, Sam! Ha!

EVANS

(*Staring at him*). Ned, old man, what's the trouble? You said "Navy."

DARRELL

(*Ironically—with a bitter hopeless laugh*). Slip of the tongue! I meant Gordon! Meant Gordon, of course! Gordon is always meant—meant to win! Come on, Gordon! It's fate!

MADELINE

Here they come! They're both spurting! I can see Gordon's back!

EVANS

(*Forgetting everything else, turns back to the race*). Come on, boy! Come on, son! (*The chorus of noise is now a bedlam as the crews near the finish line. The people have to yell and scream to make themselves heard.*)

NINA

(*Getting up—thinking with a strange, strident, wild passion*). I hear the Father laughing! . . . O Mother God, protect my son! . . . let Gordon fly to you in heaven! . . . quick, Gordon! . . . love is the Father's lightning! . . . Madeline will bring you down in flames! . . . I hear His screaming laughter! . . . fly back to me! . . . (*She is looking desperately up into the sky as if some race of life and death were happening there for her.*)

EVANS

(*Holding on to a stanchion and leaning far out at the imminent risk of falling in*). One spurt more will do it! Come on, boy, come on! It took death to beat Gordon Shaw! You can't be beaten either, Gordon! Lift her out of the water, son! Stroke! Stroke! He's gaining! Now! Over the line, boy! Over with her! Stroke! That's done it! He's won! He's won!

MADELINE

(*Has been shrieking at the same time*). Gordon! Gordon! He's won! Oh, he's fainted! Poor dear darling! (*She remains standing on the rail, leaning out dangerously, holding on with one hand, looking down longingly toward his shell.*)

EVANS

(*Bounding back to the deck, his face congested and purple with a frenzy of joy, dancing about*). He's won! By God, it was close! Greatest race in the history of rowing! He's the greatest oarsman God ever made! (*Embracing* NINA *and kissing her frantically.*) Aren't you happy, Nina? Our Gordon! The greatest ever!

NINA

(*Torturedly—trying incoherently to force out a last despairing protest*). No!—not yours!—mine!—and Gordon's!—Gordon is Gordon's!—he was my Gordon!—his Gordon is mine!

EVANS

(*Soothingly, humoring her—kissing her again*). Of course he's yours, dear—and a dead ringer for Gordon Shaw, too! Gordon's body! Gordon's spirit! Your body and spirit, too, Nina! He's not like me, lucky for him! I'm a poor boob! I never could row worth a damn! (*He suddenly staggers as if he were very drunk, leaning on* MARSDEN*—then gives a gasp and collapses inertly to the deck, lying on his back.*)

MARSDEN

(*Stares down at him stupidly—then thinking strangely*). I knew it! . . . I saw the end beginning! . . .

(*He touches* NINA's *arm—in a low voice*). Nina—your husband! (*Touching* DARRELL *who has stood staring straight before him with a bitter ironical smile on his lips.*) Ned—your friend! Doctor Darrell—a patient!

NINA

(*Stares down at* EVANS*—slowly, as if trying to bring her mind back to him*). My husband? (*Suddenly with a cry of pain, sinks on her knees beside the body.*) Sam!

DARRELL

(*Looking down at him—thinking yearningly*). Is her husband dead . . . at last? . . . (*Then with a shudder at his thoughts.*) No! . . . I don't hope! . . . I don't! . . .

(*He cries*). Sam! (*He kneels down, feels of his heart, pulse, looks into his face—with a change to a strictly professional manner.*) He's not dead. Only a bad stroke.

NINA

(*With a cry of grief*). Oh, Ned, did all our old secret hopes do this at last?

DARRELL

(*Professionally, staring at her coldly*). Bosh, Mrs. Evans! We're not in the Congo that we can believe in evil charms! (*Sternly.*) In his condition, Mr. Evans must have absolute quiet and peace of mind or— And perfect care! You must tend him night and day! And I will! We've got to keep him happy!

NINA

(*Dully*). Again? (*Then sternly in her turn, as if swearing a pledge to herself.*) I will never leave his side! I will never tell him anything that might disturb his peace!

MARSDEN

(*Standing above them—thinking exultantly*). I will not have long to wait now! . . . (*Then ashamed.*) How can I think such things . . . poor Sam! . . . he was . . . I mean he is my friend . . .

(*With assertive loyalty*). A rare spirit! A pure and simple soul! A good man—yes, a good man! God bless him! (*He makes a motion over the body like a priest blessing.*)

DARRELL

(*His voice suddenly breaking with a sincere human grief*). Sam, old boy! I'm so damned sorry! I will give my life to save you!

NINA

(*In dull anguish*). Save—again? (*Then lovingly, kissing* EVANS' *face.*) Dear husband, you have tried to make me happy, I will give you my happiness again! I will give you Gordon to give to Madeline!

MADELINE

(*Still standing on the rail, staring after* GORDON'S *shell*). Gordon! . . . dear lover . . . how tired . . . but you'll rest in my arms . . . your head will lie on my breast . . . soon! . . .

Curtain

ACT NINE

SCENE: *Several months later. A terrace on the* EVANS' *estate on Long Island. In the rear, the terrace overlooks a small harbor with the ocean beyond. On the right is a side entrance of the pretentious villa. On the left is a hedge with an arched gateway leading to a garden. The terrace is paved with rough stone. There is a stone bench at center, a recliner at right, a wicker table and armchair at left.*

It is late afternoon of a day in early fall. GORDON EVANS *is sitting on the stone bench, his chin propped on his hands,* MADELINE *standing behind him, her arm about his shoulders.* GORDON *is over six feet tall with the figure of a trained athlete. His sun-bronzed face is extremely handsome after the fashion of the magazine-cover American collegian. It is a strong face but of a strength wholly material in quality. He has been too thoroughly trained to progress along a certain groove to success ever to question it or be dissatisfied with its rewards. At the same time, although entirely an unimaginative code-bound gentleman of his groove, he is boyish and likable, of an even, modest, sporting disposition. His expression is boyishly forlorn, but he is making a manly effort to conceal his grief.*

MADELINE *is much the same as in the previous Act except that there is now a distinct maternal older feeling in her attitude toward* GORDON *as she endeavors to console him.*

MADELINE

(*Tenderly, smoothing his hair*). There, dear! I know how horribly hard it is for you. I loved him, too. He was so wonderful and sweet to me.

GORDON

(*His voice trembling*). I didn't really realize he was gone—until out at the cemetery—(*His voice breaks.*)

MADELINE

(*Kissing his hair*). Darling! Please don't!

GORDON

(*Rebelliously*). Damn it, I don't see why he had to die! (*With a groan.*) It was that constant grind at the office! I ought to have insisted on his taking better care of himself. But I wasn't home enough, that's the trouble. I couldn't watch him. (*Then bitterly.*) But I can't see why Mother didn't!

MADELINE

(*Reprovingly but showing she shares his feeling*). Now! You mustn't start feeling bitter toward her.

GORDON

(*Contritely*). I know I shouldn't. (*But returning to his bitter tone.*) But I can't help remembering how unreasonably she's acted about our engagement.

MADELINE

Not since your father was taken sick, she hasn't, dear. She's been wonderfully nice.

GORDON

(*In the same tone*). Nice? Indifferent, you mean! She doesn't seem to care a damn one way or the other any more!

MADELINE

You could hardly expect her to think of anyone but your father. She's been with him every minute. I never saw such devotion.

(*Thinking*). Will Gordon ever get old and sick like that? . . . oh, I hope we'll both die before! . . . but I'd nurse him just as she did his father . . . I'll always love him! . . .

GORDON

(*Consoled—proudly*). Yes, she sure was wonderful to him, all right! (*Then coming back to his old tone.*) But—this may sound rotten of me—I always had a queer feeling she was doing it as a duty. And when he died, I felt her grief was—not from love for him—at least, only the love of a friend, not a wife's love. (*As if under some urgent compulsion from within.*) I've never told you, but I've always felt, ever since I was a little kid, that she didn't really love Dad. She liked him and respected him. She was a wonderful wife. But I'm sure she didn't love him. (*Blurting it out as if he couldn't help it.*) I'll tell you, Madeline! I've always felt she cared a lot for—Darrell. (*Hastily.*) Of course, I might be wrong. (*Then bursting out.*) No, I'm not wrong! I've felt it too strongly, ever since I was a kid. And then when I was eleven—something happened. I've been sure of it since then.

MADELINE

(*Thinking in amazement, but not without a queer satisfaction*). Does he mean that she was unfaithful to his father? . . . no, he'd never believe that . . . but what else could he mean? . . . (*Wonderingly*). Gordon! Do you mean you've been sure that your mother was—

GORDON

(*Outraged by something in her tone—jumping to his feet and flinging her hand off—roughly*). Was what? What do you mean, Madeline?

MADELINE

(*Frightened—placatingly puts her arms around him*). I didn't mean anything, dear. I simply thought you meant—

GORDON

(*Still indignant*). All I meant was that she must have fallen in love with Darrell long after she was married—and then she sent him away for Dad's sake—and mine, too, I suppose. He kept coming back every couple of years. He didn't have guts enough to stay away for good! Oh, I suppose I'm unfair. I suppose it was damned hard on him. He fought it down, too, on account of his friendship for Dad. (*Then with a bitter laugh.*) I suppose they'll be getting married now! And I'll have to wish them good luck. Dad would want me to. He was game. (*With a bitter gloomy air.*) Life is damn queer, that's all I've got to say!

MADELINE

(*Thinking with a sort of tender, loving scorn for his boyish naïveté*). How little he knows her! . . . Mr. Evans was a fine man but . . . Darrell must have been fascinating once . . . if she loved anyone she isn't the kind who would hesitate . . . any more than I have with Gordon . . . oh, I'll never be unfaithful to Gordon . . . I'll love him always! . . . (*She runs her fingers through his hair caressingly—comfortingly.*) You must never blame them, dear. No one can help love. We couldn't, could we? (*She sits beside him. He takes her in his arms. They kiss each other with rising passion.* MARSDEN *comes in noiselessly from the garden, a bunch of roses and a pair of shears in his hands. He looks younger, calm and contented. He is dressed in his all-black, meticulous, perfectly tailored mourning costume. He stands looking at the two lovers, a queer agitation coming into his face.*)

MARSDEN

(*Scandalized as an old maid—thinking*). I must say! . . . his father hardly cold in his grave! . . . it's positively bestial! . . . (*Then struggling with himself—with a defensive self-mockery.*) Only it wasn't his father . . . what is Sam to Darrell's son? . . . and even if he were Sam's son, what have the living to do with the dead? . . . his duty is to love that life may keep on living . . . and what has their loving to do with me? . . . my life is cool green shade wherein comes no scorching zenith sun of passion and possession to wither the heart with bitter poisons . . . my life gathers roses, coolly crimson, in sheltered gardens, on late afternoons in love with evening . . . roses heavy with after-blooming of the long day, desiring evening . . . my life is an evening . . . Nina is a rose, my rose, exhausted by the long, hot day, leaning wearily toward peace. . . . (*He kisses one of the roses with a simple sentimental smile—then still smiling, makes a gesture toward the two lovers.*) That is on another planet, called the world . . . Nina and I have moved on to the moon. . . .

MADELINE

(*Passionately*). Dear one! Sweetheart!

GORDON

Madeline! I love you!

MARSDEN

(*Looking at them—gaily mocking—thinking*). Once I'd have felt jealous . . . cheated . . . swindled by God out of joy! . . . I would have thought bitterly, "The Gordons have all the luck!" . . . but now I know that dear old Charlie . . . yes, poor dear old Charlie!—passed beyond desire, has all the luck at last! . . . (*Then matter-of-factly.*) But I'll have to interrupt their biological preparations . . . there are many things still to be done this evening . . . Age's terms of peace, after the long interlude of war with life, have still to be concluded . . . Youth must keep decently away . . . so many old wounds may have to be unbound, and old scars pointed to with pride, to prove to ourselves we have been brave and noble! . . .

(*He lets the shears drop to the ground. They jump startledly and turn around. He smiles quietly*). Sorry to disturb you. I've been picking some roses for your mother, Gordon. Flowers really have the power to soothe grief. I suppose it was that discovery that led to their general use at funerals—and weddings! (*He hands a rose to* MADELINE.) Here, Madeline, here's a rose for you. Hail, Love, we who have died salute you! (*He smiles strangely. She takes the rose automatically, staring at him uncomprehendingly*).

MADELINE

(*Thinking suspiciously*). What a queer creature! . . . there's something uncanny! . . . oh, don't be silly! . . . it's only poor old Charlie! . . .

(*She makes him a mocking curtsey*). Thank you, Uncle Charlie!

GORDON

(*Thinking with sneering pity*). Poor old guy! . . . he means well . . . Dad liked him. . . .

(*Pretending an interest in the roses*). They're pretty. (*Then suddenly.*) Where's Mother—still in the house?

MARSDEN

She was trying to get rid of the last of the people. I'm going in. Shall I tell her you want to see her? It would give her an excuse to get away.

GORDON

Yes. Will you? (MARSDEN *goes into the house on right.*)

MADELINE

You'd better see your mother alone. I'll go down to the plane and wait for you. You want to fly back before dark, don't you?

GORDON

Yes, and we ought to get started soon. (*Moodily.*) Maybe it would be better if you weren't here. There are some things I feel I ought to say to her—and Darrell. I've got to do what I know Dad would have wanted. I've got to be fair. He always was to everyone all his life.

MADELINE

You dear, you! You couldn't be unfair to anyone if you tried! (*She kisses him.*) Don't be too long.

GORDON

(*Moodily*). You bet I won't! It won't be so pleasant I'll want to drag it out!

MADELINE

Good-bye for a while then.

GORDON

So long. (*He looks after her lovingly as she goes out right, rear, around the corner of the house.*)

(*Thinking*). Madeline's wonderful! . . . I don't deserve my luck . . . but, God, I sure do love her! . . . (*He sits down on the bench again, his chin on his hands.*) It seems rotten and selfish to be happy . . . when Dad . . . oh, he understands, he'd want me to be . . . it's funny how I got to care more for Dad than for Mother . . . I suppose it was finding out she loved Darrell . . . I can remember that day seeing her kiss him . . . it did something to me I never got over . . . but she made Dad happy . . . she gave up her own happiness for his sake . . . that was certainly damn fine . . . that was playing the game . . . I'm a hell of a one to criticize . . . my own mother! . . . (*Changing the subject of his thoughts abruptly.*) Forget it! . . . think of Madeline . . . we'll be married . . . then two months' honeymoon in Europe . . . God, that'll be great! . . . then back and dive into the business . . . Dad relied on me to carry on where he left off . . . I'll have to start at the bottom but I'll get to the top in a hurry, I promise you that, Dad! . . .

(NINA *and* DARRELL *come out of the house on the right. He hears the sound of the door and looks around.*)

(*Thinking resentfully*). Funny! . . . I can't stand it even now! . . . when I see him with Mother! . . . I'd like to beat him up! . . . (*He gets to his feet, his face unconsciously becoming older and cold and severe. He stares accusingly at them as they come slowly toward him in silence.* NINA *looks much older than in the preceding Act. Resignation has come into her face, a resignation that uses no make-up, that has given up the struggle to be sexually attractive and look younger. She is dressed in deep black.* DARRELL'S *deep sunburn of the tropics has faded, leaving his skin a Mongolian yellow. He, too, looks much older. His expression is sad and bitter.*)

NINA

(*Glancing at* GORDON *searchingly—thinking sadly*). He sent for me to say good-bye . . . really good-bye forever this time . . . he's not my son now, nor Gordon's son, nor Sam's, nor Ned's . . . he has become that stranger, another woman's lover. . . .

DARRELL

(*Also after a quick keen glance at* GORDON'S *face—thinking*). There's something up . . . some final accounting . . . (*Thinking resignedly.*) Well, let's get it over . . . then I can go back to work. . . . I've stayed too long up here . . . Preston must be wondering if I've deserted him. . . . (*Then with a wondering sadness.*) Is that my son? . . . my flesh and blood? . . . staring at me with such cold enmity? . . . how sad and idiotic this all is! . . .

NINA

(*Putting on a tone of joking annoyance*). Your message was a godsend, Gordon. Those stupid people with their social condolences were killing me. Perhaps I'm morbid but I always have the feeling that they're secretly glad someone is dead—that it flatters their vanity and makes them feel superior because they're living. (*She sits wearily on the bench.* DARRELL *sits on side of the recliner at right.*)

GORDON

(*Repelled by this idea—stiffly*). They were all good friends of Dad's. Why shouldn't they be sincerely sorry? His death ought to be a loss to everyone who knew him. (*His voice trembles. He turns away and walks to the table.*)

(*Thinking bitterly*). She doesn't care a damn! . . . she's free to marry Darrell now! . . .

NINA

(*Thinking sadly, looking at his back*). He's accusing me because I'm not weeping . . . well, I did weep . . . all I could . . . there aren't many tears left . . . it was too bad Sam had to die . . . living suited him . . . he was so contented with himself . . . but I can't feel guilty . . . I helped him to live . . . I made him believe I loved him . . . his mind was perfectly sane to the end . . . and just before he died, he smiled at me . . . so gratefully and forgivingly, I thought . . . closing our life together with that smile . . . that life is dead . . . its regrets are dead . . . I am sad but there's comfort in the thought that now I am free at last to rot away in peace . . . I'll go and live in Father's old home . . . Sam bought that back . . . I suppose he left it to me . . . Charlie will come in every day to visit . . . he'll comfort and amuse me . . . we can talk together of the old days . . . when I was a girl . . . when I was happy . . . before I fell in love with Gordon Shaw and all this tangled mess of love and hate and pain and birth began! . . .

DARRELL

(*Staring at* GORDON'S *back resentfully*). It gets under my skin to see him act so unfeelingly toward his mother! . . . if he only knew what she's suffered for his sake! . . . the Gordon Shaw ideal passed on through Sam has certainly made my son an insensitive clod! . . . (*With disgust.*) Bah, what has that young man to do with me? . . . compared to Preston he's only a well-muscled, handsome fool! . . . (*With a trace of anger.*) But I'd like to jolt his stupid self-complacency! . . . if he knew the facts about himself, he wouldn't be sobbing sentimentally about Sam . . . he'd better change his tune or I'll certainly be tempted to tell him . . . there's no reason for his not knowing now . . . (*His face is flushed. He has worked himself into a real anger.*)

GORDON

(*Suddenly, having got back his control, turns to them—coldly*). There are certain things connected with Dad's will I thought I ought to— (*With a tinge of satisfied superiority.*) I don't believe Dad told you about his will, did he, Mother?

NINA

(*Indifferently*). No.

GORDON

Well, the whole estate goes to you and me, of course. I didn't mean that. (*With a resentful look at* DARRELL.) But there is one provision that is peculiar, to say the least. It concerns you, Doctor Darrell—a half-million for your Station to be used in biological research work.

DARRELL

(*His face suddenly flushing with anger*). What's that? That's a joke, isn't it?

(*Thinking furiously*). It's worse! . . . it's a deliberate insult! . . . a last sneer of ownership! . . . of my life! . . .

GORDON

(*Coldly sneering*). I thought it must be a joke myself—but Dad insisted.

DARRELL

(*Angrily*). Well, I won't accept it—and that's final!

GORDON

(*Coldly*). It's not left to you but to the Station. Your supervision is mentioned but I suppose if you won't carry on, whoever is in real charge down there will be only too glad to accept it.

DARRELL

(*Stupefied*). That means Preston! But Sam didn't even know Preston—except from hearing me talk about him! What had Sam to do with Preston? Preston is none of his business! I'll advise Preston to refuse it!

(*Thinking torturedly*). But it's for science! . . . he has no right to refuse! . . . I have no right to ask him to! . . . God damn Sam! . . . wasn't it enough for him to own my wife, my son, in his lifetime? . . . now in death he reaches out to steal Preston! . . . to steal my work! . . .

NINA

(*Thinking bitterly*). Even in death Sam makes people suffer . . .

(*Sympathetically*). It isn't for you—nor for Preston. It's for science, Ned. You must look at it that way.

GORDON

(*Thinking resentfully*). What a tender tone she takes toward him! . . . she's forgotten Dad already! . . .

(*With a sneer*). You'd better accept. Half-millions aren't being thrown away for nothing every day.

NINA

(*In anguish—thinking*). How can Gordon insult poor Ned like that! . . . his own father! . . . Ned has suffered too much! . . .

(*Sharply*). I think you've said about enough, Gordon!

GORDON

(*Bitterly, but trying to control himself—meaningly*). I haven't said all I'm going to say, Mother!

NINA

(*Thinking—at first frightenedly*). What does he mean? . . . does he know about Ned being . . . ? (*Then with a sort of defiant relief.*) Well, what does it matter what he thinks of me? . . . he's hers now, anyway. . . .

DARRELL

(*Thinking vindictively*). I hope he knows the truth, for if he doesn't, by God, I'll tell him! . . . if only to get something back from Sam of all he's stolen from me! . . .

(*Authoritatively—as* GORDON *hesitates*). Well, what have you got to say? Your mother and I are waiting.

GORDON

(*Furiously, taking a threatening step toward him*). Shut up, you! Don't take that tone with me or I'll forget your age—(*contemptuously*) and give you a spanking!

NINA

(*Thinking hysterically*). Spanking! . . . the son spanks the father! . . .

(*Laughing hysterically*). Oh, Gordon, don't make me laugh! It's all so funny!

DARRELL

(*Jumps from his chair and goes to her—solicitously*). Nina! Don't mind him! He doesn't realize—

GORDON

(*Maddened, comes closer*). I realize a lot! I realize you've acted like a cur! (*He steps forward and slaps* DARRELL *across the face viciously.* DARRELL *staggers back from the force of the blow, his hands to his face.* NINA *screams and flings herself on* GORDON, *holding his arms.*)

NINA

(*Piteously—hysterically*). For God's sake, Gordon! What would your father say? You don't know what you're doing! You're hitting your father!

DARRELL

(*Suddenly breaking down—chokingly*). No—it's all right, son—all right—you didn't know—

GORDON

(*Crushed, overcome by remorse for his blow*). I'm sorry—sorry—you're right, Mother—Dad would feel as if I'd hit him—just as bad as if I'd hit him!

DARRELL

It's nothing, son—nothing!

GORDON

(*Brokenly*). That's damn fine, Darrell—damn fine and sporting of you! It was a rotten, dirty trick! Accept my apology, Darrell, won't you?

DARRELL

(*Staring at him stupidly—thinking*). Darrell? . . . he calls me Darrell! . . . but doesn't he know? . . . I thought she told him. . . .

NINA

(*Laughing hysterically—thinking*). I told him he hit his father . . . but he can't understand me! . . . why, of course he can't! . . . how could he? . . .

GORDON

(*Insistently holding out his hand*). I'm damned sorry! I didn't mean it! Shake hands, won't you?

DARRELL

(*Doing so mechanically—stupidly*). Only too glad—pleased to meet you—know you by reputation—the famous oarsman—great race you stroked last June—but I was hoping the Navy would give you a beating.

NINA

(*Thinking in desperate hysterical anguish*). Oh, I wish Ned would go away and stay away forever! . . . I can't bear to watch him suffer any more! . . . it's too frightful! . . . yes, God the Father, I hear you laughing . . . you see the joke . . . I'm laughing too . . . it's all so crazy, isn't it? . . .

(*Laughing hysterically*). Oh, Ned! Poor Ned! You were born unlucky!

GORDON

(*Making her sit down again—soothing her*). Mother! Stop laughing! Please! It's all right—all right between us! I've apologized! (*As she has grown calmer.*) And now I want to say what I was going to say. It wasn't anything bad. It was just that I want you to know how fine I think you've both acted. I've known ever since I was a kid that you and Darrell were in love with each other. I hated the idea on Father's account—that's only natural, isn't it?—but I knew it was unfair, that people can't help loving each other any more than Madeline and I could have helped ourselves. And I saw how fair you both were to Dad—what a good wife you were, Mother—what a true friend you were, Darrell—and how damn much he loved you both! So all I wanted to say is, now he's dead, I hope you'll get married and I hope you'll be as happy as you both deserve— (*Here he breaks down, kissing her and then breaking away.*) I've got to say good-bye—got to fly back before dark—Madeline's waiting. (*He takes* DARRELL'S *hand and shakes it again. They have both been staring at him stupidly.*) Good-bye Darrell! Good luck!

DARRELL

(*Thinking sufferingly*). Why does he keep on calling me Darrell . . . he's my boy . . . I'm his father . . . I've got to make him realize I'm his father! . . .

(*Holding* GORDON'S *hand*). Listen, son. It's my turn. I've got to tell you something—

NINA

(*Thinking torturedly*). Oh, he mustn't! . . . I feel he mustn't! . . .

(*Sharply*). Ned! First let me ask Gordon a question. (*Then looking her son in the eyes, slowly and impressively.*) Do you think I was ever unfaithful to your father, Gordon?

GORDON

(*Startled, stares at her—shocked and horrified—then suddenly he blurts out indignantly*). Mother, what do you think I am—as rotten-minded as that! (*Pleadingly.*) Please, Mother, I'm not as bad as that! I know you're the best woman that ever lived—the best of all! I don't even except Madeline!

NINA

(*With a sobbing triumphant cry*). My dear Gordon! You do love me, don't you?

GORDON

(*Kneeling beside her and kissing her*). Of course!

NINA

(*Pushing him away—tenderly*). And now go! Hurry! Madeline is waiting! Give her my love! Come to see me once in a while in the years to come! Good-bye, dear! (*Turning to* DARRELL, *who is standing with a sad resigned expression—imploringly.*) Did you still want to tell Gordon something, Ned?

DARRELL

(*Forcing a tortured smile*). Not for anything in the world! Good-bye, son.

GORDON

Good-bye, sir.

(*He hurries off around the corner of the house at left, rear, thinking troubledly*). What does she think I am? . . . I've never thought that! . . . I couldn't! . . . my own mother! I'd kill myself if I ever even caught myself thinking . . . ! (*He is gone.*)

NINA

(*Turns to* NED, *gratefully taking his hand and pressing it*). Poor dear Ned, you've always had to give! How can I ever thank you?

DARRELL

(*With an ironical smile—forcing a joking tone*). By refusing me when I ask you to marry me! For I've got to ask you! Gordon expects it! And he'll be so pleased when he knows you turned me down. (MARSDEN *comes out of the house.*) Hello, here comes Charlie. I must hurry. Will you marry me, Nina?

NINA

(*With a sad smile*). No. Certainly not. Our ghosts would torture us to death! (*Then forlornly.*) But I wish I did love you, Ned! Those were wonderful afternoons long ago! The Nina of those afternoons will always live in me, will always love her lover, Ned, the father of her baby!

DARRELL

(*Lifting her hand to his lips—tenderly*). Thank you for that! And that Ned will always adore his beautiful Nina! Remember him! Forget me! I'm going back to work. (*He laughs softly and sadly.*) I leave you to Charlie. You'd better marry him, Nina—if you want peace. And after all, I think you owe it to him for his life-long devotion.

MARSDEN

(*Thinking uneasily*). They're talking about me . . . why doesn't he go? . . . she doesn't love him any more . . . even now he's all heat and energy and the tormenting drive of noon . . . can't he see she is in love with evening? . . .

(*Clearing his throat uneasily*). Do I hear my name taken in vain?

NINA

(*Looking at* MARSDEN *with a strange yearning*). Peace! . . . yes . . . that is all I desire . . . I can no longer imagine happiness . . . Charlie has found peace . . . he will be tender . . . as my father was when I was a girl . . . when I could imagine happiness . . .

(*With a girlish coquettishness and embarrassment—making way for him on the bench beside her—strangely*). Ned's just proposed to me. I refused him, Charlie. I don't love him any more.

MARSDEN

(*Sitting down beside her*). I suspected as much. Then whom do you love, Nina Cara Nina?

NINA

(*Sadly smiling*). You, Charlie, I suppose. I have always loved your love for me. (*She kisses him—wistfully.*) Will you let me rot away in peace?

MARSDEN

(*Strongly*). All my life I've waited to bring you peace.

NINA

(*Sadly teasing*). If you've waited that long, Charlie, we'd better get married tomorrow. But I forgot. You haven't asked me yet, have you? Do you want me to marry you, Charlie?

MARSDEN

(*Humbly*). Yes, Nina.

(*Thinking with a strange ecstasy*). I knew the time would come at last when I would hear her ask that! . . . I could never have said it, never! . . . oh, russet-golden afternoon, you are a mellow fruit of happiness ripely falling!

DARRELL

(*Amused—with a sad smile*). Bless you, my children! (*He turns to go.*)

NINA

I don't suppose we'll ever see you again, Ned.

DARRELL

I hope not, Nina. A scientist shouldn't believe in ghosts. (*With a mocking smile.*) But perhaps we'll become part of cosmic positive and negative electric charges and meet again.

NINA

In our afternoons—again?

DARRELL

(*Smiling sadly*). Again. In our afternoons.

MARSDEN

(*Coming out of his day dream*). We'll be married in the afternoon, decidedly. I've already picked out the church, Nina—a gray ivied chapel, full of restful shadow, symbolical of the peace we have found. The crimsons and purples in the windows will stain our faces with faded passion. It must be in the hour before sunset when the earth dreams in afterthoughts and mystic premonitions of life's beauty. And then we'll go up to your old home to live. Mine wouldn't be suitable for us. Mother and Jane live there in memory. And I'll work in your father's old study. He won't mind me.

(*From the bay below comes the roaring hum of an airplane motor.* NINA *and* DARRELL *jump startledly and go to the rear of the terrace to watch the plane ascend from the water, standing side by side.* MARSDEN *remains oblivious.*)

NINA

(*With anguish*). Gordon! Good-bye, dear! (*Pointing as the plane climbs higher moving away off to the left—bitterly.*) See, Ned! He's leaving me without a backward look!

DARRELL

(*Joyfully*). No! He's circling. He's coming back! (*The roar of the engine grows steadily nearer now.*) He's going to pass directly over us! (*Their eyes follow the plane as it comes swiftly nearer and passes directly over them.*) See! He's waving to us!

NINA

Oh, Gordon! My dear son! (*She waves frantically.*)

DARRELL

(*With a last tortured protest*). Nina! Are you forgetting? He's my son, too! (*He shouts up at the sky.*) You're my son, Gordon! You're my— (*He controls himself abruptly—with a smile of cynical self-pity.*) He can't hear! Well, at least I've done my duty! (*Then with a grim fatalism—with a final wave of his hand at the sky.*) Good-bye, Gordon's son!

NINA

(*With tortured exultance*). Fly up to heaven, Gordon! Fly with your love to heaven! Fly always! Never crash to earth like my old Gordon! Be happy, dear! You've got to be happy!

DARRELL

(*Sardonically*). I've heard that cry for happiness before, Nina! I remember hearing myself cry it—once—it must have been long ago! I'll get back to my cells—sensible unicellular life that floats in the sea and has never learned to cry for happiness! I'm going, Nina.

(*As she remains oblivious, staring after the plane—thinking fatalistically*). She doesn't hear, either. . . . (*He laughs up at the sky.*) Oh, God, so deaf and dumb and blind! . . . teach me to be resigned to be an atom! . . . (*He walks off, right, and enters the house.*)

NINA

(*Finally lowering her eyes—confusedly*). Gone. My eyes are growing dim. Where is Ned? Gone, too. And Sam is gone. They're all dead. Where are Father and Charlie? (*With a shiver of fear she hurries over and sits on the bench beside* MARSDEN, *huddling against him.*) Gordon is dead, Father. I've just had a cable. What I mean is, he flew away to another life—my son, Gordon, Charlie. So we're alone again—just as we used to be.

MARSDEN

(*Putting his arm around her—affectionately*). Just as we used to be, dear Nina Cara Nina, before Gordon came.

NINA

(*Looking up at the sky—strangely*). My having a son was a failure, wasn't it? He couldn't give me happiness. Sons are always their fathers. They pass through the mother to become their father again. The Sons of the Father have all been failures! Failing they died for us, they flew away to other lives, they could not stay with us, they could not give us happiness!

MARSDEN

(*Paternally—in her father's tone*). You had best forget the whole affair of your association with the Gordons. After all, dear Nina, there was something unreal in all that has happened since you first met Gordon Shaw, something extravagant and fantastic, the sort of thing that isn't done, really, in our afternoons. So let's you and me forget the whole distressing episode, regard it as an interlude, of trial and preparation, say, in which our souls have been scraped clean of impure flesh and made worthy to bleach in peace.

NINA

(*With a strange smile*). Strange interlude! Yes, our lives are merely strange dark interludes in the electrical display of God the Father! (*Resting her head on his shoulder.*) You're so restful, Charlie. I feel as if I were a girl again and you were my father and the Charlie of those days made into one. I wonder is our old garden the same? We'll pick flowers together in the aging afternoons of spring and summer, won't we? It will be a comfort to get home—to be old and to be home again at last—to be in love with peace together—to love each other's peace—to sleep with peace together—! (*She kisses him—then shuts her eyes with a deep sigh of requited weariness*) —to die in peace! I'm so contentedly weary with life!

MARSDEN

(*With a serene peace*). Rest, dear Nina. (*Then tenderly.*) It has been a long day. Why don't you sleep now—as you used to, remember?—for a little while?

NINA

(*Murmurs with drowsy gratitude*). Thank you, Father—have I been wicked?—you're so good—dear old Charlie!

MARSDEN

(*Reacting automatically and wincing with pain—thinking mechanically*). God damn dear old . . . ! (*Then with a glance down at* NINA's *face, with a happy smile.*) No, God bless dear old Charlie . . . who, passed beyond desire, has all the luck at last! . . . (NINA *has fallen asleep. He watches with contented eyes the evening shadows closing in around them.*)

Curtain.

Philip Barry

HOTEL UNIVERSE

To

Rosemary and Stephen Vincent Benét

PHILIP BARRY

Philip Barry's career as a dramatist does immense credit to the training given to him, and to so many other distinguished graduates, by Professor George Pierce Baker in his 47 Workshop at Harvard. Born in Rochester, N. Y., on June 18, 1896, Philip Barry received his early education in his native city and was later graduated from Yale. Thereafter he was attached to the Department of State in Washington, D. C., and then filled a post in the American Embassy in London. In 1922, his comedy *You and I* was chosen as the Harvard Prize Play. A New York production followed. Since his first success, he has written and produced many notable plays, of which the best known are: *Hotel Universe, The Animal Kingdom, White Wings, Tomorrow and Tomorrow* and *Holiday*.

CHARACTERS

ANN FIELD
TOM AMES
HOPE AMES
LILY MALONE
NORMAN ROSE
ALICE KENDALL
PAT FARLEY
STEPHEN FIELD
FELIX

HOTEL UNIVERSE

THE *Terrace is like a spacious, out-door room, irregularly paved with flags of gray stone. The house itself forms one wall on the left, a wall from which two screened doors open —the first from a hall, the second from a sitting-room. Down Left, against this wall a flight of outside stairs, guarded by a slendor iron railing, mounts to a balcony.*

The other entrance is at Right, down from the garden by stone steps. A three-foot wall follows the back and left sides of the terrace just to where the the row of small cypresses, which screens the garden terrace, begins. Over and beyond the wall nothing is visible: sea meets sky without a line to mark the meeting. There, the angle of the terrace is like a wedge into space.

Down Right, a small but ancient fig-tree in full leaf rises from the pavement. There is a large fan-back chair beneath it. Upon the wall at Back, there are two folding-cushions. A small upright piano stands against the wall of the house. Near it, there is a table, upon which stand a carafe of brandy, a bottle of Cointreau, a bottle of champagne, and glasses. A few straw and wicker chairs and a sofa complete the furniture. It is about nine o'clock in the evening, and still quite light.

ANN FIELD *sits at a small table at Left, a silver-coffee-service before her. She is about twenty-eight, and lovely. Near her, taking their coffee, sit* TOM *and* HOPE AMES, LILY MALONE *and* NORMAN ROSE. *On the other side of the terrace, half asleep upon a cushion with a coffee-cup beside her,* ALICE KENDALL *reclines. She is twenty-six, very smart and rather pretty.* PAT FARLEY *is at the piano. He is thirty-two, medium tall, slight, likable looking.* NORMAN ROSE *is the handsomest of the men, and about thirty-eight.* TOM AMES *is forty, of amiable good looks.* HOPE, *his wife, is four years younger, in full bloom.* LILY MALONE *is small, slight and thirty. Without a feature to remark upon, she is able to impart to her small, impudent face a certain prettiness. All are browned by the sun and wear light summer clothes. The women, except* LILY, *who is in a linen day-dress, wear simple evening-dresses. The men are in flannels.*

PAT

—And this is a cheerful number from the heart of Old Provence: "Le Roy a fait battre Tambour." Yvette Guilbert used to do it.
(*He plays and sings the song, with its threatening, repeated refrain "Rat-a-plan, rat-a-plan, rat-a-plan-plan-plan-plan."*)

TOM

(*At the conclusion*).
Sad.

HOPE

Oh, isn't it!

LILY

Lovely, though.

ALICE

But Ann said to play something gay.

PAT

Yes? How gay, Ann—very gay? (*He looks at* ANN. *She meets his eyes for a moment, then averts her head sharply.*) Well, here's how the monks tried to be gay at Easter. It's Gregorian—eleventh century—rejoice, rejoice—God, how gay. (*He begins to intone the chant: "Halleluiah! Halleluiah!"*) —Can't you see the lines of them, shuffling along, heads down, hands in sleeves, rejoicing, rejoicing?

(*He continues to sing "Halleluiah! Halleluiah!" Suddenly* ANN *rises.*)

ANN

Pat!

(*But he goes on singing.* ANN *mounts the steps to the balcony and goes into the house.* HOPE *rises and goes to* PAT.)

HOPE

Pat——

PAT

What?

HOPE

Quit it!

PAT

Why?

HOPE

Why must we take our nerves out on Ann?

PAT

"Nerves" did you say?

HOPE

—You heard what I said. And you've been the worst. Knowing what you used to be to her, I suppose the torture's great fun.

PAT

Go away, Hope.

HOPE

—Then why do you suppose she suddenly leaves us this way?

PAT

It's her own house, isn't it?

HOPE

Yes—and a fine time we've been giving her in it! The wonder to me is that she's endured our bad manners as long as she has.

TOM

Oh, come now, darling——

HOPE

I mean it! All we've done for three mortal days has been to sit around and make bitter cracks about anything we could put our tongues to.—Don't you realize that we're the first Americans she's seen since she's been here? She begged us to come. It meant so much to her to have us. And now, on our very last night with her, we still behave like—oh, I'm so ashamed.

(*She returns to her chair.*)

TOM

What do you want us to do, Hope?

NORMAN

Yes, what shall we?

HOPE

I don't know—something—anything but what we have been. It must be horrible for her, living here. She had a right to expect we'd bring some breath of life with us. And what have we given her?

PAT

Say it: the breath of death.

LILY

(*To* HOPE). You know the reason for our so-called "nerves," don't you?

TOM

(*Quickly*). Now don't start that, Lily. We agreed when we left Antibes not to speak of that again.

NORMAN

Yes—Ann's got enough to depress her, without adding the sad story of a person she never knew or heard of.

LILY

Nobody's going to burden Ann with it. The point is, what it did to us. Every time I close my eyes I see him: a bright, sweet, utterly unimaginative boy of twenty-six—

HOPE

Don't——

LILY

—Standing up there, brown as a berry in a pair of blue swimming-pants on the highest rock over the sea, and—Pat, did you really hear him say that?

PAT

Of course I did. He said: "Look, Farley, I'm off for Africa!"

TOM

It was the most beautiful dive I've ever seen.

ALICE

He couldn't have meant it. I'm sure it was an accident.

PAT

Accident nothing. It was suicide.

LILY

Just five minutes before, I was rubbing his back with oil. He asked me to. He couldn't reach between the shoulders.

PAT

Little mother——

LILY

Shut up.

HOPE

He had a daisy behind his ear, the way a grocer-boy wears a pencil——

TOM

And didn't look silly, either.

LILY

Not he!

NORMAN

Of course there must have been some reason for what he did.

HOPE

Please, let's not talk about it any more. It isn't safe to dwell on things like that. It makes you morbid.

TOM

There was something grand about the way he did it.

LILY

He laughed up at me—the way his teeth gleamed from the water!—Did he have unusually white teeth?

PAT

—Brushed them night and morning. Promised nurse he would.

HOPE

Pat——

PAT

Oh, what the hell—you all make me sick. None of us gave a hang for him. We scarcely knew him.

TOM

We do now.

PAT

A neat job, I call it—no body to dispose of. You know, it's the devil getting a body out of France. The export duty's enormous. And I think there's a luxury-tax.—Do I offend you? Sorry.

LILY

Why did he do it? Why did he *do* it?

PAT

He'd just had enough, that's all. Eleven o'clock in the morning, up on a rock in the blazing sun——(*He looks away, his eyes narrowing.*) "I'm off for Africa" and that's all. Lord, it's magnificent. It's scored for drums, that. (*He sings again.*) "Rat-a-plan, rat-a-plan, rat-a-plan, plan, plan."

TOM

Look here, if we don't get that boy off our minds——

LILY

I know. There's something contagious about it. It's like having been in a room with a person with——

HOPE

Lily——

LILY

All right.

TOM

No one is to mention it again. We're here on this visit to dispense cheer to Ann, aren't we? Isn't that why we came? Well, then——

LILY

Hopeless, hopeless, hopeless.—As cheermakers I'd sell the lot of us at a nickel a pound, on the hoof.

TOM

We can keep the ball in the air until we go, at any rate.

HOPE

We've simply got to. Think of her—buried down here for three years in this fake, rootless country, dying of homesickness with a half-mad father——

ALICE

I saw him, you know.

HOPE

You did!

NORMAN

When?

TOM

Where, Alice?

ALICE

It must have been him. Last night I woke up and couldn't get back to sleep again. I thought I heard someone down here, so I came out on the balcony. It was a funny light. Everything was—I don't know—awfully pale. For instance, that fig-tree didn't seem to have any color.

TOM

But where was he? Here?

ALICE

Yes. At least there was a man—quite a nice-looking man, with gray hair. He was all in white. He was standing here at the wall, looking out over. The light-house was lit, and every now and then it would light him all up.

PAT

(*Unimpressed*). Was there a very bright star in the sky?

ALICE

I didn't notice.

LILY

You ought to look out for those things, Alice, you really ought.

ALICE

I can see it all so distinctly, even to the way a button on his coat caught the light and a lace on his shoe that was untied and dragged along after him.

PAT

Then what did he do—ride off on a unicorn?

ALICE

No, he just went up there into the garden, the rooster after him.

HOPE

The what?

ALICE

Didn't I tell you? He had a white rooster with him.—After a while I heard it crow, quite far away.

HOPE

It must have been dawn then——

ALICE

No—it was nowhere near it.

LILY

Well, it must have been dawn somewhere.

PAT

It usually is——

TOM

You dreamed all that, Alice.

ALICE

I saw it.

PAT

—While we're here he's staying down at the what-do-you-call-it—the little house—the bastide. I imagine he's sicker than he thinks. A fine end for one of the foremost electrical experts in the country, eh? A swell finish for the only first-rate physicist we've ever had.

ALICE

But hasn't he always been a little—you know?

PAT

He never seemed so to me.—Who'll have a drink?
(*He refills his glass.*)

NORMAN

But when was it he began to crack?

PAT

Only about five or six years ago.—This is a noble brandy.

TOM

I heard something about his haranguing a crowd in Central Park once——

PAT

He can't take people casually—that was part of his trouble. He's supposed to have some kind of power over them. Somebody said it's because he always seems so close to death.—It tastes like cucumbers.

LILY

I've never known anyone to seem further from it than that boy standing there on that rock, and——

HOPE

Lily!

LILY

Oh, all right.—Only I never have—not any one.

PAT

Finally Ann had to bring him here, where he doesn't see anyone but her, and seems to be all right. It's a swell deal for Ann. (*His tone changes.*) So we thought we'd come and put on a show for her, did we? We thought we'd remind her of what a big, gay, exciting life exists outside these walls —rub a little salt in, just so she'd be really content to stay on here—is that it?

TOM

Lord, you can be a louse.

PAT

You bet I can.—If Ann has any illusions about what goes on in the great big wonderful world back home, *I* haven't.

(*He goes to the wall and sits there, looking out.*)

HOPE

Just the same, Pat——

PAT

—Oh, go ahead. Do as you like. Be bright, be merry.
(*A silence.* LILY *looks about her.*)

LILY

I'm not happy in this old place. It's too violent, it's too dramatic. I know I'm an actress but hang it, I'm on a holiday. You get a sense of things being born all the time. They come bursting out of the ground. There's too much raw life about.

TOM

The house used to be a small hotel—the Hotel de l'Univers, it was called. I heard a tale or two about it down at the port today. It had been deserted for quite awhile before Ann and her father took it.

HOPE

Deserted? Why?

TOM

The boatman said things began to happen.
(PAT *laughs.*)

PAT

The man in 608 had a nightmare, and the lady in 609 rang for ice-water.

ALICE

Things! What things?

TOM

The idea seemed to be that people began to resemble other people and the place itself other places. And time went sort of funny. Their pasts kept cropping up.

LILY

—Excuse me, friends, but *I'm* taking the night-boat for Albany.

TOM

I'm only telling you what I heard at the port.

NORMAN

There may be something in it.—When *I* stepped out on this terrace the other night, it was for all the world like the Grand Central the first time I saw it, when I was fifteen. I don't mean just the way it looked. I mean——

LILY

I know—and now it's a hill-top in New Hampshire. We played Concord once. I used to climb out my window at night when Father had drunk enough to sleep—and up it, and lie on my back there.
(*She closes her eyes.*)

TOM

Maybe what you call the "raw life" here makes people children again.—Lord, I remember the way Under the Piano became as many places in as many moments: a boat to London, and then London. An airship, and a grocery-store. A circus-tent, and 'way down cellar.—And it was—for the moment it really was.
(*A silence. Then:*)

HOPE

Tom, I wonder how the children are? I'm worried. I think I'll cable.
(*Another silence. Then:*)

LILY

Dear, dear Father—how I miss him.

ALICE

Oh, she's got her father on the brain. Every theatre we went to in Paris, she did nothing but talk about how he used to play——

LILY

That's enough, Alice.

ALICE

Of course we're sorry he's dead, but why we should be bored with endless accounts of his——

LILY

I say it's enough!

TOM

This is pleasant.

HOPE

I tell you, you're all in a state.

PAT

I don't doubt that the people who used to come here were, too. Lord knows it's on the edge of the world.
(HOPE *glances toward the house.*)

HOPE

Here she is. Now for Heaven's sake——
(ANN *comes in from the house.*)

ANN

—That was foolish of me. Please don't mind. (*She goes to the coffee-table.*) More coffee, any one?

TOM

I will.

HOPE

Me too. It's so delicious.

ANN

It took me two years to discover why French coffee was so vile.

HOPE

I could have told you. They load it full of chicory.

ANN

But the real trouble is in the roasting. They roast it black, till it looks like shoe-buttons.

NORMAN

That was the spirit that won the War.

TOM

(*Reflectively*). When I was a child, I used to have a pair of button-shoes that I wore Sundays.

LILY

(*To* NORMAN). Has there been a war? I've been away——

TOM

I don't think they make them any more.

ANN

—So what did I do, but buy a roasting-

machine of my own. It makes a very fine smell of a morning. More, Pat?
(PAT *turns.*)

PAT

Thanks, I'll take another brandy.

TOM

So will Tom. I like my good things together.
(PAT *fills two glasses for them and returns to the wall with his.*)

HOPE

It stays light so late, doesn't it?

ANN

Wasn't the beach a glory today? Wasn't it? Oh, I love that beach! It's my mother.—Why do you go? Why don't you all stay on with me? I'll be good to you——

LILY

If we could——

ANN

You're really splendid, you know. You are so splendid!

LILY

Don't make me cry, Ann.

ANN

You? (*She laughs.*) Imagine! (*And turns to* PAT.) What *are* you doing there, Pat?

PAT

Me? Oh, just looking——

ANN

But I thought you didn't like views.

PAT

This isn't a view. For a view you've got to have a horizon. There's not a sign of one out there. The sea meets the sky without a line to mark the meeting. The dome begins under your feet. The arc's perfect.

ANN

But I want to see your face. I'm fond of your lean, brown face——(*He turns to her.*) That's better!—Pat, you're older. (*He turns away again.*)—But I like you better older!

LILY

(*After a slight pause*). It's fantastic, this terrace. It just hangs here. Some day it'll float off in space—and anchor there, like an island in time.—I'm full of whimsies tonight. I need a good dose at bed-time.

ANN

Lily, why do you spoil everything you say?

LILY

Do I?

ANN

Yes. What are you afraid of?

LILY

Oh—these people's gibes.

ANN

I don't understand it.

LILY

Ah, Ann—come on home with us! We do need you so.

HOPE

Yes, Ann! To Paris tonight—sail with us Wednesday. Just as a farewell-present. Oh, do!

ANN

What a grand idea!—Tied up in a box-ribbons! Lovely!

HOPE

Isn't it even possible?
(ANN *laughs.*)

ANN

No, dear, it's not—not possibly possible.
(LILY *picks up a book and begins to read it.*)

HOPE

But surely you could leave your father for a month, say. You could get a good nurse in Marseilles or Toulon, and——

ANN

Father doesn't need a nurse.

HOPE

I'm sorry, I'm stupid.

ANN

No you're not. You're sweet. You're all sweet. But I'm like that theoule tree—um, smell it!—I live here.

NORMAN

Three years is quite a while in one place.

ANN

Not here. Ever since we came my sense of time's been confined to music.
(PAT *lights a cigarette.*)

PAT

—Look, everyone: there's nothing travels so fast as light—thirty million miles a minute. But by the time they see this match on Orion we'll all have been dead fifty years, maybe more.
(FELIX*, a French butler of about fifty, in a white summer uniform, comes in from the house.*)

ANN

(*Laughing*). There's a modest man!—He thinks they're hanging out of windows on Orion, to see him light a little match! (*She turns to* FELIX.)—Oui, Felix?

FELIX

(*To* PAT). Pardon, Monsieur——

PAT

Oui?

FELIX

Il est neuf heure juste, Monsieur.

PAT

Bon. Merci.
(FELIX *traverses the terrace and goes out into the garden.*)

ALICE

—And why was that, may I ask?

PAT

We've got to leave before eleven. I told him to let me know every half-hour from nine until then.

ANN

That was perfectly dear of you, Pat. That will help. (*A moment. Then impulsively.*) Oh, I don't see why you at least can't stay on! I want you to. Pat—stay——

PAT

I wish I could, but I've got dates with mountains.
(TOM *pours himself a glass of champagne.*)

TOM

If you had any sense at all you'd know you ought to train for mountain-climbing.

PAT

I feel pretty good, thanks.—Oh, by the way, would you mail some letters for me in New York?

TOM

Sure.
(PAT*, from a book on the wall takes several small envelopes and one large one and gives them to* TOM.)

TOM

—The big one's got no address.

PAT

There are four or five others inside it. I thought they'd be easier to carry.
(TOM *puts the envelopes in his pocket, the large one with difficulty.*)

TOM

You were wrong.
(LILY *slams her book shut and tosses it upon the sofa.*)

LILY

—Another blonde heroine who won't take her milk, and Mama will throw up.
(*There is a silence, which* ALICE *finally breaks.*)

ALICE

—Did I tell you?—I saw the most amusing boat this afternoon: all white, with sienna sails, and a thin white prow——
(*Another silence.*)

TOM

—Gondolas are built in a rather curious way. You know how they seem to pivot—well——
(*But he relapses into silence.*)

HOPE

The air's so heavy—give me a glass of water, someone.

(TOM *gives her his glass of champagne.* HOPE *takes a swallow, and chokes.*)

HOPE

That isn't water.

TOM

The water in France isn't safe. It's full of Frenchmen.

PAT

—And sometimes an American, who swims out too far.

(LILY *turns on him, angrily.*)

LILY

Oh, damn you, Pat! Shut your trap, will you?

NORMAN

(*Quickly*). How long is the drive to Toulon?

TOM

Fifty minutes, Mr. Rose.

HOPE

(*Reflectively*).—Bags to be packed.

ANN

No, no—please—there's all the time in the world!

(*Another brief silence. Then* PAT *speaks.*)

PAT

It was funny motoring over here. We passed the old Hotel Beau-Site in Cannes. Lord, how it took me back. I had an English tutor there, named Briggs, when I was twelve. He fell in love with my mother.

ALICE

What did she do? Fire him?

PAT

Heavens, no.—Mother?

(NORMAN *starts a record on a portable gramophone which stands upon the wall—it is the "Naila" of Delibes.*)

LILY

Dear God, not that again. If you knew what that tune does to me.

(NORMAN *promptly turns it off and returns to his chair. Silence is again about to descend upon them, but* HOPE *will not have it.*)

HOPE

Seriously, Ann—how did you know we were at Antibes?

ANN

I told you: I had a hunch.

(TOM'S *elbow catches on the bulky envelope protruding from his coat pocket. Unnoticed by* PAT, *he takes it out, opens it and extracts four smaller envelopes from it.*)

HOPE

I know you said that. But seriously——

ANN

I have them, I tell you!—It's not my first one about Pat, is it Pat?—Do you remember my cable to London once, years ago?

PAT

What? Oh, yes—yes, sure.

ANN

I got a feeling that he was in some kind of trouble, so I cabled.—But what the trouble was, I never knew.

(TOM *is distributing the letters in his inside pockets and his wallet.*)

LILY

(*To* PAT). Don't tell me anything's ever gone against *you*, darling. I couldn't bear it.

ANN

—I asked you about it once before, didn't I?

PAT

Did you?

ANN

Yes. Don't you know what you said?

PAT

What?

(*Now,* TOM *has but one letter without a place for it. He reads the address upon it, starts slightly, frowns, and looks from it to* PAT, *and back again.*)

ANN

You said: "I'll tell you that the day before I die."

PAT

All right. That still goes.

NORMAN

It sounds ominous.

ANN

Doesn't it!
(TOM *taps the letter reflectively. Then:*)

TOM

(*Suddenly*). Pat—this—letter——
(PAT *turns swiftly, goes to him, and takes it from his hand.*)

PAT

Oh—oh, that—I'll tell you about that later.

TOM

I think you'd better.
(LILY *is watching* ANN.)

LILY

—I wish I was like Ann.—Ann, I do wish I was like you. I feel so inadequate near you.
(ANN *laughs and blows her a kiss.*)

ANN

Darling! You're famous—I'm nobody. I do nothing but read of your triumphs.

LILY

—The triumph of trash. You can have my public, if you'll give me your heart.

ANN

But you have it already!

LILY

I'd like to think that.

TOM

You may.

LILY

I want to play Cordelia in King Lear.

NORMAN

Cordelia?! You?

LILY

—And Booth turns a handspring in his grave. All right, but somehow that part fascinates me. Whenever I think of it I go absolutely cold. And still I know that if ever I have the guts to do Cordelia, my life will be a different thing.

PAT

Then why not try it? I'll back you, Lily.

LILY

(*In fright*). No! No! I wouldn't dare. (*Then she laughs.*)—No. I start my farewell tour any day now. I'm going to play the Styx instead.—That's a joke, the *river* Styx.

NORMAN

Everybody laugh.
(LILY *springs up.*)

LILY

Norman, there are times when I can't stand this damned Jewish superiority of yours, and this is one of them.

NORMAN

Really? I'm so sorry.

LILY

—The way you look down from your eminence of three thousand years—honestly, who do you think you are, some Disraeli?

NORMAN

He was later, wasn't he?

LILY

(*To the others*). You see?

NORMAN

Besides, I've always considered him enormously overrated.

LILY

I wouldn't mind so much if it made you happy. But you're one of the most wretched men I know.

TOM

Go on—bankers are always happy.

ALICE

Norman's more than a banker. He's a financial genius. My uncle says so.
(ANN *laughs.*)

ANN

There, Norman! Now are you happy?
(*A moment. Then:*)

NORMAN

No.—I'll tell you, Ann: here's how I see my life——

LILY

Tune in on Norman Rose Hour.

NORMAN

—There are several angles to it: When a man decides he wants to accumulate a fortune——

TOM

It's going to be a speech.

PAT

—I can't speak to Mr. Morgan just now. Tell him I'll call him back.

TOM

—Nine-thirty A. M. The great Norman Rose enters his office——
(*He goes to the table.*)

LILY

(*In three tones of voice*). Good morning, Mr. Rose. Good morning, Mr. Rose! Good morning, Mr. Rose!
(TOM *grunts, seats himself at the table and contemplates the bottles and glasses.*)

TOM

I see my desk is piled with work again.

LILY

You must learn to depute the smaller duties to underlings, Mr. Rose.

TOM

I have to think of my stock-holders. (LILY *knocks three times upon her book.* TOM *turns.*) Who's there?

LILY

It's me, Mr. Rose. Little Lily Malone. You know *me.*

TOM

(*Wearily*). Come in, come in!
(LILY *enters the great man's office.*)

LILY

—A gentleman to see you, sir.

TOM

I don't like gentlemen. It's ladies I like.—Come closer, Miss Malone.
(LILY *stiffens.*)

LILY

—A Mr. Patrick Farley, Morgan and Company. Sleighs and Violins Mended.

TOM

Show him in.

LILY

—Mr. Rose will see you now, Mr. Farley.
(PAT *comes in,* LILY *announces him.*) Mr. Farley, Mr. Rose.—I know you'll like each other.
(LILY *retires.* TOM *indicates a chair.* PAT *seats himself.*)

TOM

Well, Farley, what is it?

PAT

It's—just about everything, Doctor. I feel awful.

TOM

Your Chemistry is down. C-minus.

PAT

Yes, sir.

TOM

Your Physics is down. D.

PAT

Yes, sir.

TOM

Your English is down.

PAT

Yes, sir. I can keep everything down now, sir.

TOM

You were not so good at that last night, Farley.

PAT

I think you are forgetting your place, Rose. Please remember that my grandfather kept slaves, and your grandfather was one of them.

TOM

Yes, and a good one!

PAT

(*Sneering*).—Pride of race, eh?

TOM

If you like.

PAT

And if I don't?

TOM

Farley, I am a busy man.

PAT

—Just so. And that is why I want to ask you a question:—That shipment of ear-marked gold for Sweden——

TOM

My God.

PAT

Don't temporize, Mr. Rose. He is my God as well as yours.

TOM

But I must have a moment to myself, to think. (*Suddenly.*) I know what! I'll telephone about it!
(*He takes a long spoon from the table and holds the handle to his ear.*)

PAT

—That was the old Norman Rose speaking. That was the Norman Rose we once knew, and loved.
(TOM *speaks into the other end of the spoon.*)

TOM

Get me Equitable Trust. (*Then to* PAT.) What ever became of your Aunt Jessie Sprague?

PAT

None of that now? Don't try to get me off on sex.

TOM

(*To the telephone*). Hello?

PAT

Say this to him first: Say "what *is* ear-marked gold?"
(TOM *nods and waits a moment. Then.*)

TOM

Hello, is that you, Trust? Yes. This is Norman Rose speaking—the old Norman Rose. Listen now, Eq—about that gold for Sweden—Sweden, yes.—Look here, old man, maybe you can tell me: what *is* ear-marked gold? (PAT *nods approvingly. There is a silence.* TOM *holds his hand over the end of the spoon and turns to* PAT.)—He's bluffing. (*Another moment, then again to the spoon.*) Oh it *is,* is it? That's what it is, is it? Well, let me tell *you* something: you're not a big enough man to bluff Norman Rose. No sir!—Well, it's your *business* to know! (*To* PAT.)—Still bluffing. (*To the telephone.*) All right, all right—that's all right with me! But if you think you can—hello! Hello, are you there? Hello—hello—(*He puts down the spoon and turns to* PAT.) He's gone. He's hung up, the big bluffer.
(PAT *fixes him with his eye.*)

PAT

It's you who are bluffing, Rose. (*He points his finger at him.*) What *is* ear-marked gold?

TOM

(*Confused*). I—why, it's—I'm not sure, but I *think* it's——

PAT

We have no place here for men who are not sure.

TOM

Don't be hard on me, boy.

PAT

I'll give you two alternatives.

TOM

Make it three.

PAT

I'll give you three alternatives.

TOM

Four.

PAT

Four and a half.

TOM

Five. Five twenty-five!
(PAT's *fist descends upon the table.*)

PAT

Sold!—To the gentleman in the straw hat, for five twenty-five!

TOM

But who—who are you?
(PAT *rises, opens his coat, and points to his badge.*)

PAT

The Chairman of your Board of Directors.
(TOM *covers his face.* PAT *speaks quietly.*) Good afternoon, Mr. Rose. (TOM *rises, and makes one mute gesture of appeal.*) Good *afternoon,* Mr. Rose.
(TOM *hulks out of his office, a broken man.* PAT *seats himself at the table and pours a drink.*)

NORMAN

(*Laughing*). All right! I'll resign!

HOPE

Silly—they are so silly.

ANN

It was lovely! Do another——

HOPE

No, they mustn't. I'm always afraid they'll slip over the line and turn into the people they're pretending to be.

LILY

It would be grand just to let yourself go sometime. I wonder what would happen?

HOPE

I hate to think.

LILY

It couldn't be any worse than it is. (*She closes her eyes.*) Hopeless, hopeless——

NORMAN

What?

LILY

Hopeless.

PAT

(*Humming*). Rat-a-plan, rat-a-plan, rat-a-plan-plan-plan-plan.

NORMAN

(*To* LILY). But while there's life——

LILY

—There's the rent to pay.

PAT

—And what's the big premium on life, I'd like to know?

NORMAN

Well, it does look like all we've got.

PAT

There was a great big war, Pet, and we survived it. We're living on borrowed time.

TOM

Lost: one battalion.

PAT

We're not lost. Our schedule is different, that's all.—What I mean is, we'll have had the works at forty instead of eighty.

NORMAN

I've got a theory people expect too much from life.

ANN

But you can't! That's one thing that's not possible!

LILY

Then why is every one so disappointed in it?

ANN

Because all they concern themselves with are its probabilities. Think of the things that might happen, can happen, do happen! The possibilities!

LILY

There might be a ray of hope in that. Who, for instance, would ever have thought that the little backstage rat I was, would spend a week-end with the King of Spain?—Not that I enjoyed it.

ALICE

—Snob.

ANN

(*Laughing*). You might spend a week-end with yourself some time, Lily. You just might have a lovely time.

LILY

I'd bore myself stiff. I'd get to showing myself card-tricks.

TOM

A person's got to look for disillusionment all the way along. It's the price paid by every one who uses his head for anything but a hat-rack.

ANN

But Tom! What do you want with illusions in the first place?

LILY

Oh—just to make himself feel important. That's why he quit his business with such a great big gesture.

TOM

I quit publishing because it seemed ridiculous to devote my life to bringing out books about life.

LILY

Exactly—and how important the gesture made you feel. Sure. That's what we're all after—and that's all we're after.

ANN

You know, Lily, you're so completely debunked, there's very little of you left.

LILY

I tell you, to beat this game you've got to be born rich and healthy, and preferably a Farley—with Pat's private slant that nothing matters a damn any way.

PAT

Is that my slant?

LILY

Isn't it?

ANN

It wasn't when I knew him.

PAT

People change, they say.

ANN

It breaks my heart to have you change, Pat.
(PAT *glances at her, then looks away.* ALICE *stretches upon her cushion.*)

ALICE

Oh, you all think too much. Why don't you be like me?

LILY

Need you ask, dear?

ALICE

I know that when I die, I die. But in the meantime I hope to keep my days and nights fairly full.

LILY

Of what?

ALICE

I may not be as clever as you, Lily, but I'm a whole lot happier.
(*She yawns luxuriously.*)

LILY

I have a cat that is, too.

ALICE

I love cats. Cats have the right idea.

PAT

They also have kittens.
(NORMAN *clears his throat.*)

NORMAN

It all resolves itself into the fundamental problem of the location of Man in the Universe.

PAT

Really? Is that all?

TOM

Oh, Lord, how can anyone believe he matters any, when he knows that in a few years he'll be dead and done with?

ANN

You honestly think that *this* is all there is, then?

TOM

This what?

ANN

This life.

TOM

Why, of course. Don't you? (ANN *laughs.*)

ANN

Oh no, no, *no!* Of course not! Not possibly. (*They all look at her in astonishment. Even* ALICE *raises herself upon her elbows on the cushion.* LILY *murmurs.*)

LILY

—She's marvellous. She's really marvellous.

TOM

Chemistry is chemistry, Ann.

ANN

(*Still laughing*). Heavens, Tom, is that as far as you've got?

LILY

There's always the next step. Look: you see that nice little white scar there? (*She holds one hand out for her to see, wrist upward.* ANN *is serious in a moment.*)

ANN

Lily—what do you mean!

HOPE

Lily! You didn't!

LILY

—Didn't I, though.—At last a real use for old razor-blades.

HOPE

But when?

LILY

Oh—about a year ago. I forget, exactly.

HOPE

But my dear—*why?*

LILY

I just got sick of myself. (*She apologizes.*) —It wasn't very successful. I know too much. I made the tourniquet myself.

PAT

That's right, Actress, do your stuff. God's out front tonight.

LILY

—Will you tell the Kind Gentleman I enjoyed his little piece, but found no part in it for me?

TOM

Don't talk that way, Lily.

LILY

Why not?

TOM

It's blasphemy. I was born a Catholic, and I don't like it. (LILY *stares at him, finds him quite serious.*)

LILY

"Blasph—?" I haven't heard that word in years. Say another.

NORMAN

I thought you'd given up your religion?

TOM

So I have. But all the same, the only real dope on life I ever got was from an old priest at school. I'd like to see that old fellow again. He was a nice old fellow. Father Francis, his name was.

ANN

There's been a great space left in you, Tom. it will take some filling.

TOM

And with what?

LILY

They say cyanide is quite satisfactory.

HOPE

Don't, Lily——

LILY

Why? Don't tell me *you've* never thought of it.
(HOPE *is about to reply, but does not.*) Ha-ha! Caught you——

TOM

Darling—you haven't really——

HOPE

Well, haven't you?

TOM

I know, but——

HOPE

Is it anyone's special privilege? Am I not worthy?
(LILY *laughs, and turns to* ALICE.)

LILY

Alice?
(ALICE *sits up.*)

ALICE

Yes, dear?

LILY

No, there'd be no point in it for you—it would be too little change.—But what about you, Norman? Do you ever yearn out windows?
(NORMAN *smiles.*)

NORMAN

I can't say I've ever seriously contemplated it, no.

LILY

Then go on and contemplate it.
(*A brief pause. Then:*)

NORMAN

Well, I wouldn't do anything positive—but if I knew I could save my life by changing from this chair to that one, I doubt if I'd move.
(*Again* LILY *laughs.* ANN *is gazing at them in amazement.*)

LILY

This is grand! (*To* ANN.) I suppose we can count you out, though.

ANN

(*Briefly*). Yes. I'm out.

LILY

—And as for you, Patrick? How long since *your* last confession?

PAT

I'm sorry to disappoint you, but it's never crossed my mind.

LILY

And if I were you, I'd take precious good care it never did.

PAT

Thanks. You're kind. I'll remember.

LILY

—Because I don't think it would cross yours. I think it would stick there. (*She looks about her. Then, to* ANN.) Four out of six. Not a bad average, is it?

TOM

Pat, why was that letter addressed to me?
(PAT *smiles.*)

PAT

Suppose my foot should slip on an Alp?

TOM

Do you expect it to?

PAT

Not particularly, but there's always the hope.

TOM

You're not usually so foresighted.

PAT

But this time I am.

TOM

—I don't like it. May I read it now?

PAT

It would make me feel a little foolish. It's signed "oceans of love, Patrick."

ANN

What letter are you talking about?

PAT

One that he—

ALICE

(*Suddenly*). Oh, good Lord—

HOPE

What's the matter?

ALICE

Suddenly I had the most abominable chill.

LILY

On a night like this?

ALICE

What a fool I am, really.
(NORMAN *wraps a thin beach-blanket about her.*)

LILY

(*Sweetly*). Please dear, let *me* say that.

NORMAN

I wouldn't give two francs for any of our nervous systems.

HOPE

It's probably too much sun and too little sleep for a week.
(PAT *pours himself another brandy.*)

PAT

—And the grape—the grape and the grain.
(*And drains the glass. Again silence descends upon them.* HOPE *finally breaks it.*)

HOPE

Is it always so heavenly here, Ann?

ANN

—Except for some overcast nights in the Autumn with no moon, no stars. Then there's such blackness as you wouldn't believe.—Only the light from the lighthouse on the Ile de Port-Cros, crossing the terrace here—like the finger of God, Father says.
(*It has got darker, but the atmosphere possesses a luminous quality that imparts a strange definiteness of outline to the objects and the people upon the terrace. Again, silence. Then:*)

LILY

I'm sad.—I could cry.—I am crying.—Oh, behave yourself.
(*Suddenly* ANN *stands bolt upright, rigid.*)

HOPE

What is it?!

ANN

Wait a minute.

HOPE

Honestly, Ann, I do wish—

ANN

Wait! (*For a moment they wait, silent, tense. Then from the distance is heard one muffled report.*)—There. It's all right. Don't worry.

HOPE

But what on earth *was* it?

ANN

It's Father. He's at the bastide. Sometimes he fires a sunset-gun. I get to expect it.

ALICE

(*Awed*). He won't do it again tonight, will he?

ANN

I said a sunset-gun. It sets only once a day as a rule. (*There is a silence. She rises, abruptly.*) Well, why shouldn't he, if he likes? I think it's splendid of him! (*A moment. Then she laughs shortly.*) Sorry! (*Waits another moment, and continues.*)—I imagine he'd seem a trifle strange to you, but to me it's a pretty grand sort of strangeness. I believe he is a very wise man.

TOM

I don't doubt it.

ANN

I don't always understand him, but that's my fault. I understand better than I used to, and sometime I hope to understand all. So I just try to follow him wherever his mind leads. I've been beautiful places there with him.

TOM

(*After a pause*). I unearthed a marble tablet in the lower garden today. It was in Latin and said: "To Semptronius who, at age 12, danced here, and pleased."

ANN

But how charming that is!—Can't you see him?—Semptronius—
(TOM *rises. All at once he is as excited as a child.*)

TOM

I'd like to dance here too. (*To* PAT.) Will you play? And would anyone mind?

HOPE

—Now that's what I mean! Really, we're not acting at all sensibly, don't you realize it?
(TOM *looks at her, and returns to the wall.*)

TOM

—Ten years ago I wouldn't even have asked. It's a rotten feeling, knowing your youth's gone—knowing that all the brave things you once dreamed of doing, somehow just won't get done.

PAT

(*As a small boy would say it*). I wanna go out to the South Seas like Father Damien!

TOM

(*Soberly*). I did, at that.

ALICE

Who is Father Damien?

TOM

(*Reciting*). Father Damien was a noble priest who went to the South Seas to help the lepers and got it himself.

HOPE

Sometimes I don't know his voice from little Tommy's.
(*Suddenly* TOM *stands up upon the wall.*)

TOM

Look, Mummy! Look where *I* am!

HOPE

Get down, Tom, you'll fall.

TOM

Don't punish me, Mummy.—Reason with me.

HOPE

—Acting like that! I don't know where you think you are.
(TOM *descends from the wall.*)

TOM

—Under the piano. (*He moves away from them, toward the table.*)—Under the apple tree— (*He seats himself cross-legged beside the table, whistling a tune softly through his teeth and trying to wrench the top from a wooden champagne-stick. A moment, then he calls, as a small boy would.*) Hey, Pat! Pat! C'mon over!
(PAT *comes forward to him.*)

PAT

Hello, Tom.

TOM

Hello, yourself.

PAT

Where're the other fellows?

TOM

How should I know? I got better things to do than follow *them* all over everywheres.
(*He examines his stick with interest.* PAT *seats himself on the ground beside him.*)

HOPE

Don't, Tom.—Make them stop, Ann. They go too far with it.
(*But* ANN *is silent, watching them intently.*)

PAT

—Gosh, I feel good, don't you?

TOM

I feel all right.

PAT

—But don't you ever feel—gosh, I don't know—*good?*

TOM

You don't feel very good when you've got things the matter with you, like I have.

PAT

What have you got? (*No answer.*) Aw, come on, Tom—is it really bad?
(TOM's *head bends lower over his stick.*)

TOM

It's awful.

PAT

Aw gosh, I'm sorry—tell me, Tom—
(*A moment, then:*)

TOM

Will you promise never so long as you live— (PAT *nods eagerly.*)—I think I've got something, Pat.

PAT

What?

TOM

I think I got the leprosy.

PAT

(*Appalled*). You've—? Gosh, Tom, why do you think that?

TOM

I read a book last night about Father Damien in the South Seas and he got the leprosy and I think I've got it.

PAT

How—how do you suppose you ever—

TOM

I gave a old woman a dime the other day, and she went and kissed my hand, and I think it must of been her that gave it to me.

PAT

But didn't you wash or anything?

TOM

I couldn't till I got home. And it takes awful fast. Look at that—
(*He shows his wrist.*)

PAT

Where?
(*He almost touches* TOM's *wrist—but draws his hand back, fearfully.*)

TOM

Doesn't it look sort of—white to you?

PAT

It does, sort of.

TOM

—And scaly. That's the way it starts. My foot's the same way. I could tell for sure by putting it in hot water.

PAT

Hot water!

TOM

If you've got it, you don't feel anything, not even the water, even. Father Damien didn't. That's the way he knew.
(NORMAN *is drawn over to them. He too, has begun whistling softly. His tune is "Pony Boy."*)

PAT

Oh, he was prob'ly just a crazy ole priest. —H'lo Norman.
(TOM *scowls.* NORMAN *gestures "Hello," and goes on whistling, hands in pockets.*)

TOM

—A *what*, did you say?

PAT

Well, there *are* crazy priests. Anyways, I bet there have been, some time.

TOM

Never. Never one. God wouldn't let there be.

NORMAN

What about Theo-philus?

TOM

Who?

NORMAN

Theo-philus.

TOM

What did he do that was so crazy?

NORMAN

Just burnt the libary at Alexandria, that's all.

TOM

I never even heard of it.

PAT

I did. Alexander the Great built it, quite a long time ago, to please his vanity.

NORMAN

(*Reciting*).—And Theo-philus was a crazy Christian monk that burnt up the libary which was the greatest in the whole world and which history tells us contained over seventy thousand volumes.

TOM

Well, if he did, I bet he had some good reason. I bet they were impure books, or something.

NORMAN

He was crazy.

TOM

I bet he knew they were good and lashivious and he just burnt 'em to the honor and glory of God.

NORMAN

He was crazy.

PAT

(*Pointedly*). Of course you'd say so, anyway. I guess you'd say any Christian holy man of God was crazy.

NORMAN

I wouldn't either. (*A moment.*) *Why* would I?

PAT

I suppose you think we didn't notice you didn't eat that ham sandwich the other day and asked for a sardine.

NORMAN

I wanted a sardine. I like sardines better. I like their taste better.

PAT

Yes, you do!

TOM

(*To* PAT).—Any one says sardines taste better'n ham says so for some good alterior reason, you bet.

NORMAN

You know what *you* are, don't you?

TOM

What?

NORMAN

Cath'lic! Cath'lic!

TOM

(*Soberly*). I am a Catholic. Yes. I am proud to be a Catholic.

NORMAN

Yes—well, before *I'd* go to confession and things—

TOM

You know why?—You wouldn't get the chance. They wouldn't let you in. See, Mr. Jew?

PAT

You are a Jew, aren't you?
(NORMAN *raises his head proudly.*)

NORMAN

Of course I am. What about it?

TOM

You crucified our Lord, that's what about it.

NORMAN

Oh, no I didn't.

PAT

Who did, then?

NORMAN

—The Roman soldiers. See?

PAT

Oh, you think you know everything. All you do is sit around and read books, little Ikey.

NORMAN

I'm not an Ikey! Don't you call me that!

TOM

(*To* PAT)—You're just as bad as he is. A heretic's what *you* are—Protestant-dog-sit-on-a-log-and-eat-meat-on-*Friday!*

PAT

I'll eat anything I like any day I like—see? *And* ham.

TOM

It's all right now, only wait'll you die. Just wait'll then.

PAT

(*To* NORMAN). Pooh, "when I die." That's what the priest tells him—

TOM

Well, just let me tell *you:* when I grow up maybe *I'm* going to be a priest. See? Maybe I've got a vacation right this minute. See?

PAT

A what?

TOM

A vacation—a call.
(PAT *looks at him in wonder.*)

PAT

Gosh.

TOM

(*Closer to him*). Just think that over, Mr. Fresh.—And when you hear of me going out to the South Seas and places like Father Dami—
(*Awestruck, he remembers his malady. In fear he peers at his wrist again.*)

PAT

Is it any worse?

TOM

I—I think it's spread a little.

PAT

Listen—

TOM

What—

PAT

I know a fellow's got a doctor-book. Only he won't lend it. You got to look at it at his house. Shall we—?

TOM

All right. (*A moment. Then:*) Pat—

PAT

What?

TOM

What would you do if *you* had the—the you-know?

PAT

(*After thought*). I'd kill myself.

TOM

You couldn't. You'd go straight to hell. And the tortures of the you-know are as nothing to the tortures of hell.

PAT

Just the same I'd do it, though. I certainly wouldn't go around with the lepr— (TOM *claps his hand over his mouth.*) Let go!

TOM

—You promised! (*To* NORMAN.)—You get out. Get out, now!—If you know what's good for you—
(NORMAN *leaves them.* PAT *struggles.*)

PAT

Let go! I'm—I can't breathe. Let go—!
(*Still* TOM *holds him.* PAT *struggles harder. He begins to beat at him with his fists. Finally freeing himself, he goes at him more violently.* TOM *retaliates. They go up and down the terrace, advancing, retreating, clinching, separating, raining blows upon each other in dead earnest.* HOPE *suddenly realizes that they are no longer playing, and cries:*)

HOPE

Stop it! (*But they go on. She begins to strike at* PAT.) Stop! Stop it, do you hear me? (*She turns imploringly to* NORMAN.) Norman!
(NORMAN *goes to* TOM.)

NORMAN

Come on, now—that's enough! (*He holds his arms from behind.*) What's got into you two?
(HOPE *stands between* PAT *and* TOM, *protecting* TOM. *They are gasping for breath,*

glaring at each other. TOM *lurches forward once more.*)

HOPE

Stop, Tom!—How often must I tell you—(*Then she takes him in her arms.*) Oh, didn't I beg you not to!
(ANN *goes to* PAT.)

ANN

Pat—Pat, dear—
(PAT *stares at her blankly for a moment, then suddenly slumps down into a chair.*)

PAT

I'm—I don't know—
(NORMAN *releases* TOM, *who stares first at* HOPE, *then at* PAT, *amazement growing in his eyes.*)

ALICE

Well, of all the—

ANN

Wait!—Are you all right, Pat?

PAT

(*Weakly*). Sure.
(HOPE *covers her face.*)

HOPE

Oh, I'm scared—I'm so scared.

ANN

Of what, Hope—of seeing life burst the walls of the little room we try to keep it in?
(*Suddenly* TOM *turns upon her.*)

TOM

Well, Ann—if you know so much, what's the answer to the whole works?

ANN

If I could tell you—

HOPE

(*Gently*). Tom—listen—

TOM

(*Suddenly savage*). I say, what's the answer? I want to know! (*He averts his head, sharply.*) God help me, I've got to know!

ANN

—But I can't tell you!—I don't know how. —Oh, my dears—what is to become of you? How can I let you go to rove the world like ghosts this way? You're so pitiful, and I love you so!
(FELIX *comes in from the garden.*)

FELIX

(*To* ANN). Pardon, Mademoiselle—

ANN

Qui? Qu'est-ce-que c'est?

FELIX

C'est le père de Mademoiselle qui fait demander si elle a besoin de lui.

ANN

Ou est-il?

FELIX

À la bastide, Mademoiselle.
(*A moment.* ANN *looks about her, at the others. Then:*)

ANN

I'll go to him.
(*She turns and goes out, up the garden steps.* FELIX *turns to* PAT.)

FELIX

Pardon, Monsieur—il est neuf heures-et-demi, Monsieur.

PAT

Merci.
(FELIX *bows and goes out, into the house, taking the coffee-service with him. There is a long silence, then* LILY *collects herself and speaks.*)

LILY

What did he say to Ann?

ALICE

Her father sent to ask if she needed him. She's gone to him.

HOPE

Needed him!—For what, I wonder.
(*Another pause.* LILY *ventures hopefully:*)

LILY

It is not generally known that polo was invented by Chinese women.—An interesting fact, is it not? (*No one replies.*)—Nope.

NORMAN

(*Reflectively*).—I'd like to go all alone to Andorra.

ALICE

Where's that?

NORMAN

I don't know.

ALICE

Then what do you want to go for?

NORMAN

No Federal Reserve—no "giant mergers." —Time to think—Lord, time to think!

LILY

About what?

NORMAN

Lily, I'm sorrier for you than for any one I know.

LILY

I don't want your pity, Mr. Rose. I just want your money.

NORMAN

(*Pondering*). When I was working in that fur shop on Twenty-third Street, I was a free man. (*A moment. Then he rises abruptly.*) I think I'll go in and pack.
(*And goes out into the house.*)

TOM

Of course *I* think the trouble with Norman is, he's caught and he knows it. He'd like to retire now, but he can't. Too much depends on him.
(PAT *laughs shortly.*)

PAT

—All looking for the answer, when there isn't any answer. (*A moment.*)—Unless maybe it's "Off for Africa."

HOPE

—That will do, Pat. Don't even start it.

ALICE

I still don't see why men like you three can't enjoy life.

LILY

Promise me something, dear—

ALICE

What?

LILY

—When you die, leave your head to the Rockefeller Institute. It's a little gem.
(ALICE *rises and moves towards the house.*)

ALICE

Oh, you're always so bright—

LILY

I know. Isn't it the devil?

ALICE

If you weren't, *au fond*, such a common little piece—

LILY

—*N'est ce pas?* (*To the others.*)—She thinks in French.
(*At the door* ALICE *turns and contemplates them.*)

ALICE

Honestly, it's all so boring—
(*And goes out.*)

LILY

The trouble with that girl is complete lack of vitamins A to Z.

HOPE

Do you suppose Norman is really in love with her?

LILY

I don't know. Anyhow, there's a chink in that fine Semitic pride of his. It would never risk a refusal.

HOPE

But surely if she cared for him—

LILY

She doesn't—too much effort.
(*A pause.* TOM *rises.*)

TOM

Oh, Lord, if only I'd died at fifteen.

PAT

Maybe you did.

HOPE

It's been a ghastly week all around. No wonder we're depressed.
(TOM *looks at her.*)

TOM

Hope, sometimes I feel I don't know you at all. (*He mounts the steps to the house.*)—And we're supposed to be the lucky ones! We're the ones who've got the world by the top of the head.—I'll let you know when I'm packed, Hope.
(*And goes out.*)

HOPE

I'm coming now. (*To* PAT *and* LILY.)—He came abroad this time to study the origins of Ecclesiastical Precedence in Rome. He got as far as Antibes. He gets vaguer all the time. I'm so worried about him I can't see straight.

PAT

Of course *I* think Tom's trouble is having too much time on his hands.

HOPE

But it's his time to himself he always said he wanted! That would solve everything. And now that he's got it, *it's* not enough. I wish to heaven we were home with the children and he was still rushing madly for the 8:22. He cursed it, but it kept him going.

PAT

You're just travel-worn, that's all. Why not let him make his crusades for Truth by himself?

HOPE

—And get sent for the first day he's lonely? That's what's always happened.—Except once, just once, when he did go to Canada for a month. (*She rises.*) He accomplished two things toward his soul's salvation there—two great things.

PAT

What?

HOPE

—He grew a red beard and learned to whistle through his teeth. (*She moves toward the stairs.*)—Talk about children! He's the worst one I've got. Oh, if you *knew* how I want to stay home with my *real* babies!
(*And goes into the house.*)

LILY

—Which is the answer, of course, to Hope.

PAT

What is?

LILY

She's so peaceful, so normal. She's all home and babies.

PAT

That's not a bad thing to be.

LILY

It's a grand thing to be.—And so is it to be the fine, free, roving soul that Tom might. It's the combination that's wrong. Of course *I* think the real trouble with them both is—(*Suddenly she stops, and laughs.*) Do you realize what we've been doing?

PAT

What?

LILY

—When I go in, what will you say about me?—The trouble with Lily is what? What's wrong with Lily?

PAT

Is there anything?

LILY

Plenty. But Pat—

PAT

What?

LILY

I think we've been good for each other, don't you?

PAT

I suppose so.

LILY

You lie, you don't!
(PAT *looks at her mildly.*)

PAT

Don't be violent, Lily.
(LILY *groans.*)

LILY

—Now he's going to turn gent on me again. That's the catch with you: you were born a gent and you can't get over it.

PAT

I think I've done pretty well.

LILY

Oh, you do, do you? Well, listen to me—

PAT

Lily, I'm sunk.—And low, deep, full fathom five.
(*She looks at him curiously. There is a silence. Then she speaks in a different tone:*)

LILY

Have a drink.

PAT

No, thanks.

LILY

Pat, when I first knew you, your spine had turned to jelly—

PAT

Yes?

LILY

Yes. And your slant was all wrong. You'd been expecting too much of something—I don't know what—and hadn't got it. You were a mass of sobs.

PAT

That's a pretty picture.

LILY

It was you.—I'd knocked around enough, man and boy, to know what people really are. I taught you to expect nothing, didn't I?

PAT

Yes.
(*She raises her glass.*)

LILY

—And what a dandy little mother's-helper *this* is—
(*She drinks.*)

PAT

Yes.

LILY

—And that there's no de-lousing station big enough to pass the whole world through.

PAT

That's right.

LILY

Well—have a drink.
(*But he decides not to.*)

PAT

—I suppose they're good things to have learned.

LILY

I've changed your slant, haven't I?

PAT

Something has.

LILY

You've done a lot for me, too. How is it I don't fall in love with you, I wonder—

PAT

I don't know. Have you tried very hard?

LILY

Awfully hard.

PAT

I'm sorry. Maybe I'm just not your type.

LILY

Would you like to be?

PAT

I never gave it much thought.

LILY

Don't I attract you at all, Pat?

PAT

You might, if I thought about it.

LILY

Think about it. (*He does so. They look intently into each other's eyes.*) Have you thought?

PAT

Um.

LILY

What's the answer?

PAT

I'm attracted.

LILY

Much?

PAT

Quite a lot.

LILY

Would you mind kissing me, Pat?

PAT

On the contrary.

LILY

Then do, please. (*He kisses her. She clings to him briefly, then turns away.*) Oh, it's so awful—

PAT

Thanks! (*Then:*)—What is?

LILY

I don't feel anything. I don't feel anything at all.

PAT

No. I thought not.
(*She turns quickly.*)

LILY

You knew about me?

PAT

I imagined.

LILY

Don't get me wrong, Pat. I'm not one of the girls, either.

PAT

I never supposed you were.

LILY

I just—don't feel anything for any one.

PAT

Some people have all the luck.

LILY

Oh, no—don't say that! I want to, so much— (*A moment.*) It seems to me—dimly—way back somewhere, I loved someone terribly. I don't know who—my father, maybe.

PAT

There you go about your father again.

LILY

—All I know is, that since, there's been nothing.

PAT

Maybe that did the trick, Lily.

LILY

How?

PAT

Maybe that's all you get.

LILY

You're a wise guy, in a way.

PAT

You think?

LILY

(*Touching his forehead*).—The Farley brow, eight months gone with Minerva. Where do you get all your dope?

PAT

The ravens feed me.

LILY

Oh, hell—nothing happens any more.

PAT

Buck up, Lily. Something will before you know it.

LILY

A broken neck would be welcome.

PAT

Give things a chance. Don't try so hard for them.

LILY

All right, teacher.—Have another drink?

PAT

Later—when the night wears on a bit.

LILY

Yes—and won't it, though—
(ALICE *appears on the balcony.*)

ALICE

(*Lowly*). Listen, you two—
(LILY *puts on her humorless smile.*)

LILY

Yes, Angel? (*To* PAT.) Reach me my Winchester, will you?

ALICE

Honestly, I've got the queerest feeling.

LILY

I told you a week ago you swallow too fast.

ALICE

—I don't suppose we could decently leave *before* eleven—

PAT

No, I don't suppose we could.

ALICE

I was afraid we couldn't. (*She moves toward the doorway, but sways against the railing. She exclaims, weakly:*) Oh—come up here a minute, some one—will you? I feel awful.

LILY

Right away, dear.
(ALICE *goes out, into the house again.*)

PAT

You'd better go. She may be ill.
(LILY *is looking off into the garden.*)

LILY

Ann's coming back. One thing, Pat—

PAT

What?

LILY

(*As she moves to follow* ALICE). If I were you, I'd be careful tonight.

PAT

About what?

LILY

About Ann. You may not know it, but you're still the world to that girl.

PAT

You're talking tripe, Lily.

LILY

Just the same, I'd be careful. (PAT *turns abruptly and looks out over the wall.* FELIX *has come out upon the balcony, with three or four small candle-lamps, unlighted, which he arranges upon the balcony wall.* ANN *comes in from the garden.*) Ann—do you suppose your maid could give me a hand with my things?

ANN

But of course! She's in my room. Call her.
(LILY *mounts the steps.* FELIX *takes out his watch.*)

LILY

—And it isn't tripe, my Patrick.
(*From far in the distance beyond the wall a small pencil of light is cast. It performs an arc in space, sweeping across the terrace, flooding over the upper wall of the house and disappearing again in the garden above.*)

FELIX

Pardon, Monsieur— il manque dix-sept minutes de dix heure, Monsieur.

PAT

(*Without turning*). Bon.
(FELIX *goes into the house.*)

LILY

(*At the top of the steps*). What happens when you forget to wind him up?

(*She goes into the house by the other door.* ANN *stands silently watching* PAT *until the door has closed behind* LILY. *Then suddenly, swiftly, she goes to him, takes him by the shoulders and turns him about, facing her.*)

PAT

Oh, hello, Ann.
(*From the distance piano-music begins to be heard.*)

ANN

(*Lowly, intensely*). I won't have it, Pat. I just will not have it!

PAT

It?—What's that you won't have?

ANN

Something's burning you up. Tell me what it is!

PAT

I'm afraid you're imagining things. Where's the music from?

ANN

Réné Mayer has a house up the road. It's always full of musicians.—You've got to listen to me. I—

PAT

Have you heard Sandy Patch's new song? (*He moves toward the piano.*)—It's called "Drunk and Disorderly." It goes like this—

ANN

Don't Pat—we haven't time—

PAT

Then let's get the others down, shall we? —And enjoy what there is left.
(*He makes a move toward the house. Her hand upon his arm stops him.*)

ANN

Wait!
(*She looks away, to control herself, her hand still upon his arm.*)

PAT

I'm all right, my dear. Really I am.

ANN

We've known each other quite a few years, now—

PAT

We have, haven't we? I feel pretty spry, though, don't you?

ANN

We've always been able to talk.

PAT

They say I could talk when I was only—
(*Her hand tightens upon his arm.*)

ANN

—Which we've always done directly, and honestly.

PAT

Yes?

ANN

Shan't we now?

PAT

If you like. Why not?

ANN

When you leave tonight I shan't see you again for at least a year—maybe more—

PAT

Oh—before I forget—
(*From his pocket, in a fold of tissue-paper, he takes a very simple and fine ruby pendant, and gives it to her.*)

ANN

What is it?

PAT

It was Mother's. I'm sure she'd want you to have it. I know I do.

ANN

Beautiful—

PAT

I think so.

ANN

But Pat—it's priceless—

PAT

So was she. So is Ann.

ANN

Oh, thank you for it! Put it on for me— (*He catches it around her throat. She turns again, facing him, then stands for a moment with her forehead against his breast.*) Pat—my dear Pat—

PAT

Things don't go the way we'd like them to, Ann. (*A moment, then she leaves him.*)

ANN

—You've been dodging around corners, to get away from me.

PAT

I didn't know it.

ANN

I won't bite you, Pat.—What's been happening to you these past three years? I'm still a little interested.

PAT

It's been pretty much the same sort of life, thanks.

ANN

What are you doing with all that money?

PAT

Oh—spending some of it—giving away quite a lot of it. It's an awful pile to make a dent in.

ANN

You never found the job we used to talk so much about—
(PAT *smiles.*)

PAT

How well she knows me.

ANN

There are only two people in this world who are really important to me, you and Father.

PAT

I'm—thanks, Ann. That's good to know.

ANN

I've been able to help him a little—

PAT

I should think you had.

ANN

I'd give the eyes right out of my head, if I could help you. (*He lifts her hand to his lips, kisses it, and turns away.*) Oh, Pat, *Pat*—whatever has happened to you?

PAT

Myself.

ANN

—Don't you go telling yourself you're no good! You're the best there is.

PAT

You don't know.

ANN

Oh, yes I do!

PAT

Anyhow, let's not get solemn about—

ANN

—And what do you suppose it means to me to know that a person I love as I love you is breaking up into little pieces over something I've no share in?

PAT

But Ann—you don't love me any more.

ANN

I do, though. I've never got over it—never. I love you with all my heart. (*A silence. She smiles uncertainly.*)—I don't suppose by any chance you love me back—

PAT

(*With difficulty*). There's something in the way. Nothing can ever come of you and me now. There's something in the—
(*He turns away, with an exclamation.*)

ANN

Tell me.

PAT

I can't.

ANN

—You'll be shocked to hear I'm living with you in my mind. I've taught myself to dream about you nearly every night. That gives me—rights.

PAT

Ah, Ann—let it go—please let it go.

ANN

I can't. I simply can't.—You've always been a life-and-death person. You take things terribly hard. I'm sure it's not as hopeless as it seems. (*But he does not answer.*)—Do you remember the first time we met, on the Westbury Road?—me lost, with a sprained ankle, and you—

PAT

—When I forget anything about you and me—

ANN

I wish we could get back there. I wish we could start from the Westbury Road again.

PAT

—But we can't.

ANN

—Such a dear, serious boy you were. All the time you were in college you used to come to me with your little troubles—(*He laughs.*)

PAT

—Would I row on the Crew?—I didn't make the Dramatic Club.—What if they passed me up on Tap Day.—Poor Ann—

ANN

I was important to you then—

PAT

You still are.

ANN

Come to me now with your big trouble, Pat.

PAT

I'm just a flop, darling.

ANN

It's a little soon to decide that, don't you think?

PAT

I told you my schedule was different.

ANN

Pat, whatever happened, happened four years ago. You came back from a year in England, and you were changed. It was a girl, wasn't it? I saw her picture in your study. What was it—wouldn't she have you?
(PAT *smiles.*)

PAT

I forget. What did she look like?

ANN

Very young, quite English, very fair. A lovely face—pretty, oh, so pretty.

PAT

Funny—I've forgotten.

ANN

I haven't.—Then you went over again the next winter—for how long was it?

PAT

I don't know—three weeks—

ANN

That's when I had my hunch about you. It wasn't long after you'd sailed. I was walking up Madison Avenue and in a florist's window I saw a lot of hawthorn blossoms. (PAT *starts slightly.*)

PAT

Hawthorn—

ANN

Yes. They were lovely, and I was going in to get some when all at once I began to feel terribly queer. It was as if the bottom had dropped out of everything. I knew it had something to do with you, and I love you and I just went on home without them.

PAT

I don't get it at all.

ANN

Nor do I.—But the next morning I passed the same shop and saw that the hawthorn was gone. Somehow, that was terrible. I couldn't get warm again all day. I love you and I had to cable you.

PAT

I don't get it.

ANN

I've never known such a change in a person, as in you when you came back. Suddenly you were as hard as nails, and so bitter. I hated leaving you that way when I came here with Father. But I was sure you'd get through it somehow, back to yourself. Now I see that you haven't. I see that it's worse than it ever was, it's destroying you. Oh, Pat—it can't be just some fool of a girl who wouldn't have you.—What has done it?

PAT

Honestly, Ann—it's all so long ago.

ANN

But I've *got* to know. Tell me!
(PAT *shakes his head.*)

PAT

It's all too ridiculous. Really. I never even think of it any more.

ANN

Whether you do or not, it's got you still. Something awful's got you. Tell me—it will help to tell me. Ah, *please*—because I love you—

PAT

I would if I could. I want to. I simply can't.

ANN

I'll find out!

PAT

All right, Ann.

ANN

—But can't you *accept* it, somehow? Can't you take life whole—all of it—for what it is, and be glad of it? Why do you have to go at it with a tin box of paints, daubing it up pretty? You're grown-up, now.—Why, my dear! What have I said? What is there in that, to hurt you so?

PAT

Listen: you can have your marvelous life. I'm not taking any.

ANN

What are you talking about?!

PAT

—The lot of you—clutching, grabbing at some little satisfaction that lasts a day or two—a swell business.

ANN

You dare talk to me about my life like that!

PAT

Yours—theirs—anyone's—

ANN

Oh, you're horrible—
(PAT *looks at her intently.*)

PAT

So you're the last to go. You fail me too—

ANN

(*A cry*). —You?—And who are you, that you shouldn't be failed sometime?

PAT

I don't know, Ann. I've often wondered. (*Again he moves to the wall and stands looking out over it, the light from the lighthouse breaking over his head.* ANN *sinks into a corner of the sofa. From the distance, the piano-music begins to be heard more clearly. For a long time they are silent. Then* PAT *speaks. His voice is one of wonder, almost of fright.*)—They're right about this place—it *is* so, you know—it's really so—

ANN

What is?

PAT

—Like other places—like another place—

ANN

Where?

PAT

—A house my mother had in Florida, four years ago, when I came back from England—

ANN

That was the second time—

PAT

Yes. It was in March. I came straight down here from New York—I mean straight down there. Mother was in the patio all alone, having coffee—(*Still he looks out over the wall, without turning.*)—I had so much to tell her—I'll never foregt it—I thought if only I could talk to some one who—
(ANN *speaks, softly:*)

ANN

Hello, Son. It's good to have you back.

PAT

—Could talk to some one who might, just might, have some little faint idea of what I—

ANN

Hello, Son. It's good to have you back.
(*A moment. Then:*)

PAT

(*A murmur*). Hello, Mother. It's good to be back.
(*He comes forward to her, slowly.*)

ANN

I didn't expect you quite so soon.

PAT

I know.
(*He sinks down upon a cushion on the floor beside her. The eyes of both are straight ahead, not looking at each other.*)

ANN

You're looking tired.

PAT

It was a rotten trip. (*He goes on in a low voice, almost mechanically.*)—I think I'll stay a while this time.

ANN

I'm glad.

PAT

It seems like a pleasant place.

ANN

It's peaceful.

PAT

That's good.

ANN

Ah, Pat—what is it, dear? I've worried so about you.

PAT

Yes. I suppose.

ANN

I've wanted to ask, but—

PAT

I know. I just couldn't talk.

ANN

Are you so very much in love?

PAT

Yes.

ANN

Tell me about her. Who is she?

PAT

Oh, it's all over now.

ANN

Over?

PAT

Yes.

ANN

But are you sure?

PAT

I'm certain.
(*A moment. Then:*)

ANN

Who was she, then?

PAT

—Mary Carr—the niece of one of my dons at Cambridge. (*A moment. His voice hardens.*)—Cambridge—another of Father's fake ideas. Finish me off, eh? Turn me into the little gentleman. Every inch a Farley— God!

ANN

Hush, Pat—

PAT

—Be good at everything. Shine! Always shine! And if you can't, don't play.—I can still hear his voice.

ANN

—Mary Carr, I've seen her photograph. She's very lovely.

PAT

Yes.

ANN

—And young.

PAT

She was eighteen in November. (*A pause. Then suddenly.*) God, that is young. Father was right *there*, at least.

ANN

What happened when he went over to you last year—

PAT

I cabled I wanted to get married. He cabled me to wait, he was coming. I waited. He came. He talked me out of it. (*Bitterly.*)—She wasn't suitable.

ANN

But that wasn't *your* reason—

PAT

I tell you I let him talk me out of it!

ANN

You agreed to put it off, that's all.

PAT

Yes—that's what I told myself—and that's what I told Mary.—That's what the little swine I was, grunted at Mary—just put it off a while, that's all. But somehow the point missed Mary—somehow she didn't get me.—She just stopped talking in the middle of a word, and went into the house. And I took a train, and sailed with *him*. He was ill then—or said he was—we couldn't wait a day.

ANN

(*Hesitantly, after a pause*). You—I suppose you and she—you'd been a good deal to each other.

PAT

We'd been everything.

ANN

I see.

PAT

—But there wasn't to be a baby, if that's what you mean— (*Again the bitter voice returns.*) Wise boy, young Farley. *He* knows his way around!

ANN

But you wrote her. Surely you wrote her.

PAT

All the time, but I never had one little word from her. A dozen times I'd have gone over, but how could I with Father dying and then all that tangle settling the estate? (*He concludes, lowly.*)—It was a year and three months since I'd seen her, when I'd sailed. I didn't even wire—I was afraid she'd run away somewhere.

ANN

But she hadn't, had she?

PAT

No.

ANN

She was there—

PAT

She was there.
(*A moment. Then:*)

ANN

—And she just won't have you.
(*Her hand reaches to comfort him. He turns to her.*)

PAT

Mother, she just won't have me. (*Suddenly he stares at her.*) You're not—oh, damn you, Ann—
(*He rises, and leaves her. She follows him.*)

ANN

All right! But tell me. You've got to finish now! (*In another voice.*)—Surely it isn't hopeless. Surely you can—

PAT

But it is, you see.

ANN

I don't believe it. Where is she now?

PAT

Down in the ground.

ANN

Pat—she isn't—?

PAT

She is, though—as a doornail.

ANN

Oh, my poor boy—

PAT

My poor Mary.

ANN

But listen to me—listen—!

PAT

No. *You* do. (*He points his finger at her, and speaks.*) Three days before I came, she walked out under a tree where—she'd walked out under a hawthorn-tree at the end of a very sweet lane we knew, and stood there and shot herself.

ANN

Pat—Pat—
(*He moves away from her.*)

PAT

You wanted to know, didn't you?
(*She looks at him. Then:*)

ANN

—So I lose you to a dead girl.

PAT

I've lost myself to her.

ANN

You loved me first!

PAT

But she died— (*He goes to the piano and seats himself, running his fingers silently over the keys.*)—If only I could get back to her somehow. If I could just let her know I did come back.

ANN

How much of it is losing her—and how much the loss of yourself?

PAT

I don't understand that.

ANN

—You used to have a fair opinion of Pat Farley. That was essential to you—that *was* you.

PAT

All I know is that nothing's been any good to me since. I'm licked, Ann.

ANN

Well, what are you going to do about it? (*Unnoticed by them* STEPHEN FIELD *has appeared at the top of the garden-steps, where he stands, a figure in white, watching them. He is about fifty-eight, slight in build, gray-haired, with a face uncommonly strong, fine and sensitive, lined and worn as it is, gray, too, as it is.*)

PAT

What is there to?

ANN

(*Suddenly, sharply*). Pat!

PAT

(*Without turning*). What?

ANN

You said you'd tell me this the day before you died—
(*As she reaches the word, he strikes a chord and drowns it.*)

PAT

—But I changed my mind, didn't I?—And told you now! (*He turns toward the house, and calls:*) What'll I play? Call your tunes, gents—almost closing-time!

ANN

—And the letter to Tom—oh, my dear—what is it?

PAT

Don't be a fool.
(*A moment, then* STEPHEN *speaks:*)

STEPHEN

Pat—

PAT

(*Without turning*). What do you want?
(*He is completely unnerved now.*)

STEPHEN

I wouldn't do it, if I were you.

PAT

Do what?

STEPHEN

I really wouldn't. Things may change.
(*He speaks with a clear, incisive strength.*)

PAT

—Change? How? Who wants things changed? (*He turns, stares at him a moment, then rises.*) Oh, how do you do, Mr. Field. How are you?—Everything's fine with me. Everything is—

STEPHEN

—And yet I wouldn't do it. I would go from here to those high places—to that strange accident. I really wouldn't.
(PAT *laughs shortly.*)

PAT

Honestly!—If you think just because a fellow's planned a trip to climb an Alp or two—
(ANN *takes his shoulders in her hands, turns him about and gazes into his eyes.*)

ANN

Pat!

PAT

I don't know what he's talkng about. (*To* STEPHEN.) I don't know what you're talking about. You're beyond me. I can't follow all this—

ANN

Oh, my poor Sweet, why do you want to do it? (*She shakes his shoulders.*) *Why?*

PAT

Why not?—Maybe you can tell me that!—Why not?—I should have three years ago, but I was too yellow then. (*Still she stares. Another silence, then he pulls away from her, mumbling:*)—All right. Don't worry about me. It's all right. Small brain-storm, that's all.—Over now—

ANN

Promise it!
(*He gestures vaguely.*)

STEPHEN

It is not so easy. He is in love with death.
(PAT *turns to him and sings, beating time with his finger.*)

PAT

—Rat-a-plan, rat-a-plan, rat-a-plan-plan-plan-plan— (*He stops on the high note, holds out his arms, and cries:*) Yes!
(*And goes to the point of the wall, where he stands with his back to them.*)

ANN

Father—Pat's mine—I can't lose Pat!
(FELIX *comes out upon the balcony, watch in hand.* STEPHEN *descends the steps and comes upon the terrace.*)

STEPHEN

I know, dear. (*He is watching the house.*) —But let us take it quietly. Let us take it very quietly—

FELIX

(*To* PAT). Pardon, Monsieur— il est dix heure, juste.
(PAT *does not reply.* FELIX *goes out.*)

STEPHEN

—Here are your other friends.
(TOM *and* HOPE *enter.*)

TOM

(*To* HOPE, *on the balcony*). —No, no—what's the good of talking?

HOPE

Well maybe if you'd—
(*She sees* STEPHEN, *and stops.*)

ANN

This—these are Tom and Hope Ames.—My Father, Hope.

HOPE

How do you do, Mr. Field?

TOM

How do you do, Sir?
(STEPHEN *murmurs a greeting.* LILY *enters from the house.*)

LILY

—I gave Alice a bromide, and she's sleeping like a log. She's—
(*She sees* STEPHEN, *and stops.*)

STEPHEN

What a beautiful color you all are. You look like savages. People don't realize that the sun here in the Midi is—

TOM

Didn't I meet you once with Father Francis at St. Luke's?

STEPHEN

I'm afraid not.

TOM

Perhaps it's just that your voice reminds me of him. (LILY, *eyes wide, stands staring at* STEPHEN.)

STEPHEN

(*To* HOPE). What do you think of our little retreat here?

HOPE

It's lovely. The days have gone so quickly.

STEPHEN

—Quickly—so quickly. (*To* LILY.)—Why do you stare at me so?

LILY

Why I—I'm terribly sorry. I—

STEPHEN

But what is it?

LILY

It's just that you're so like my own father—

STEPHEN

Yes?

LILY

He was an actor in a touring-company. He died years ago in Cleveland. He wanted me to be a dancer. I used to dance for him, often. It was a great pleasure to him. I mean to say—

STEPHEN

(*Gently*). I am sure it was.
(NORMAN *comes in from the house.*)

LILY

(*In a burst*). —He was superb! He was so kind, so loving. He was the most beautiful man I've ever—! (*She stops suddenly, then continues:*)—But he deserted my mother, you know. He was simply foul to her.—Hell, I suppose he was just a ham actor—yes, and a drunkard, to boot. (*Again she stops.*)—What am I spilling all this for? What's biting me now?
(STEPHEN *turns inquiringly to* ANN.)

ANN

—Lily Malone, Father.

STEPHEN

Poor child. (*To* NORMAN.)—And this?

NORMAN

(*Advancing*). I'm Norman Rose, sir.
(*They shake hands.*)

STEPHEN

I understand that you must leave us soon.

NORMAN

I'm afraid we must, sir.—At eleven, to be exact.

STEPHEN

That is unfortunate. (*Again he smiles.*) Well—let us set the hour-glass on its side, and ask the Old Gentleman to put his sickle by, and sit down with us and rest a moment. (*He seats himself.*) Before you go I want you all to see my bed of white phlox in the lower garden. In the moonlight it is white as white was never. I have banked the petunias near it—

HOPE

(*Delightedly*). But *I* did that at home!
(STEPHEN *is watching the balcony.* ALICE *has appeared upon it.*)

STEPHEN

The odor at night is so sweet, so pungent—cinnamon and gunpowder.—And is this Alice?
(ALICE *comes down the stairway without touching the railing, eyes far away, walking as in a dream.* ANN *rises.*)

ANN

Yes—

LILY

Go back to bed, you foolish girl.
(ALICE *approaches them, unseeing.*)

ANN

—This is my father.—Alice Kendall, Father.

STEPHEN

How do you do, my dear?
(*But she does not regard him.*)

NORMAN

She's—!

ANN

Father, what is it?

STEPHEN

Sh! Be gentle with her—

HOPE

Oh, I don't like it!

ANN

I told you about that time she walked out into the hall, in Paris.
(ANN *goes to* ALICE.)

ANN

—There, dear, it's all right. Just be quiet—quiet—
(PAT *is watching her, fascinated.*)

PAT

Take her back. It's horrible—
(*Swiftly, directly* ALICE *walks to the angle of the wall.*)

HOPE

Norman—don't let her hurt herself!
(NORMAN *and* ANN *have followed her.*)

ANN

Alice—*Alice*—
(ALICE *turns to her. In a moment her eyes uncloud.*)

ALICE

—But hello, my dear. They didn't tell me you were coming down. Divine house, isn't it?
(*She speaks as if she were reading aloud.*)

ANN

Listen to me a moment, dear—

ALICE

They're right. There's nothing like May in England. Who's on the party, do you know?

ANN

Oh—lots of people. But Alice, listen—

ALICE

Any extra men?

ANN

I think so.
(PAT *goes to the wall and stands there with his back to them.*)

ALICE

I like this Norman person—

ANN

Yes, he's very nice. But—
(ALICE *laughs shrilly.*)

ALICE

I know!—But not too nice! (*Her voice lowers, confidentially.*) My dear, he burns me up. He looks so strong—so strong. I'll bet he'd give a girl a roll for her money, don't you? (*A moment. Then to herself, with real feeling:*)—Why can't he tell?—Why doesn't he know the way I ache for him?

PAT

Take her back, take her *back*—

ALICE

—Which one shall I wear?—I think the blue one, with the ruffle down the front—(*She unfastens a shoulder-clasp, and steps out of her dress.*)

HOPE

But she mustn't—!
(ANN *turns to* NORMAN *with a helpless gesture.*)

NORMAN

(ALICE *whispers:*) I'll speak to her.—Alice!

ALICE

Who's that?—Is that you, Norman?

NORMAN

Hello, Alice—

ALICE

It was naughty of you to bring me here, you know it was— (*She leans toward him.*) What did you tell the clerk at the desk?

NORMAN

Why, I just said that—

ALICE

Oh, I'm a pretty girl! (*She extends her arms.* NORMAN *takes one of her hands in his.*) Why does no one want me? What are they afraid of?

NORMAN

Maybe they do. (*He turns to the others, painfully.*) I love this girl. I've been crazy about her for years.

STEPHEN

Humble yourself before her beauty, sir.

ALICE

Come—there are people in the next room. I can hear them. They may come in—(*Suddenly she drags her hand from his and cries in terror:*)—Ann—Ann! (ANN *goes to her swiftly.*)—This man's been following me everywhere—

ANN

It's all right, darling, he won't hurt you. He's a nice man.
(ALICE *begins to whimper.*)

ALICE

Is he? (*She turns to* NORMAN *fearfully.*) Are you? (*He nods, speechless. She darts a glance at* ANN *and huddles herself in her arms.*)—But look at me—out on the street like this. Where's my little jacket? I want my little jacket—
(NORMAN *wraps a thin beach-blanket about her, and gives her her dress.*)

NORMAN

Here you are, dear.
(*He leads her gently to the steps. She looks up at him with a smile of childlike trust.*)

ALICE

You *are* a nice man—
(*They mount the steps. There is a silence until they have gone out, into the house.*)

LILY

She seemed to be so many places all at once.

STEPHEN

Sleep has freed her from time and space. One day sleep's sister will free her further. (*He hums a measure of a song, laughs softly, and concludes:*)—And near the white phlox I have a dappled pink variety which I developed by crossing a strain of crimson—

TOM

(*An appeal*). Mr. Field— What's the—? Mr. Field—!

STEPHEN

—Yes. It does bewilder one at first. I know. I too used to believe life had one aspect only. I was so sure that sleep and dreaming was—well, sleep and dreaming. And of course I knew that with death it was all over—

PAT

Well?

STEPHEN

Well, now I know I was mistaken.

PAT

How?

STEPHEN

I have found out a simple thing: that in existence there are three estates. There is this life of chairs and tables, of getting up and sitting down. There is the life one lives in one's imagining, in which one wishes, dreams, remembers. There is the life past death, which in itself contains the others. The three estates are one. We dwell now in this one, now in that—but in whichever we may be, breezes from the others still blow upon us.

PAT

I'm sorry, I don't follow you.

STEPHEN

There are no words for it. It is a sense, a knowing. It may come upon you in a field one day, or as you turn a corner, or one fine morning, as you stoop to lace your shoe (*A brief pause.*)—Or even as it came on me.

TOM

How was that, sir?

STEPHEN

Here on this terrace.

ANN

Father—

STEPHEN

I know, dear.

PAT

—So life does go on, does it?

STEPHEN

Oh, yes. Of course.

PAT

How, for instance?
(STEPHEN *smiles.*)

STEPHEN

—As it was in the beginning, is now, and ever shall be—

PAT

—World without end, eh?

STEPHEN

Without end.

PAT

Hah! That'd be a good joke.

LILY

Look out, Pat.
(NORMAN *comes out again upon the balcony and stands there, watching them.*)

STEPHEN

—Let us be bold and change the "world" to "universe."—A fine night, isn't it? (*His gesture includes the sky.*)—There is the space we one day shall inhabit, with all our memories and all our dreams. I ask you to admire this, gentlemen—

LILY

It's not always so fine, is it?

STEPHEN

But I ask you to admire that, too! (*To* PAT.) If one could but once see his life, whole, present and past together in one living instant, he would not wish to leave it before his time—oh, no!

PAT

I know my time.

STEPHEN

I thought I knew mine once. My mind was quite made up, that night. Nothing was to deter me.—But the light from the Ile de Port-Cros described its arc as it does now. (*He stands erect.*) It stopped me, held me. —How long I stood here, I don't know. But when I was aware again—

ANN

Father—

TOM

—What had happened to you? (HOPE *goes to him and tries to draw him away from the wall, murmuring "Tom—Tom!" but he does not answer and will not come.*) Say what had happened!
(*The terrace, in a brief space, has become flooded with moonlight. There is a silence. Then* STEPHEN *begins to speak again, this time more softly, gently, coaxingly.*)

STEPHEN

I had walked back in time. It is a very interesting excursion. You merely lift your foot, place it so, and there you are—or are you? One thinks one is going forward and one finds instead the remembered touch of water somewhere—the odor of geranium—sight of a blowing curtain—the faint sound of snow—the taste of apples. One finds the pattern of his life, traced with the dreadful clarity of dream. Then he knows that all that comes in remains—nothing is lost—all is important.

ANN

(*A small voice*). Father—

STEPHEN

Are you afrad?
(*A moment. Then:*)

ANN

No.

HOPE

(*In a whisper*). But I am, I am! Tom—Tom, listen—
(TOM *does not stir.* HOPE *leaves him.*)

STEPHEN

Here is the moon at last, you see?—Here is our day's reflection, hung in space. (*He hums another measure and again laughs softly.*) Space is an endless sea, and time the waves that swell within it, advancing and retreating. Now and again the waves are still and one may venture any way one wishes. (*A moment.*) They seem to be still now—quite still. So which way would you go—where would you travel?
(*A silence. Then* TOM *moves into the angle of the wall.*)

TOM

To what I was—
(*Another silence.* LILY *moves toward* STEPHEN.)

LILY

To him I love—

NORMAN

(*After a moment*). Wherever I should go—
(*He turns and goes into the house again.*)

HOPE

Nowhere. I'm happy as I am—or would be, if Tom were—
(*A silence. Then:*)

PAT

(*A murmur*). To Mary—Mary—

ANN

(*A cry*). No, no!—To the Westbury Road!
(PAT *hums softly.*)

PAT

—Rat-a-plan-plan-plan-plan.

STEPHEN

(*To* LILY). Listen: there is a turning. All things are turned to a roundness. Wherever there is an end, from it springs the beginning.

PAT

(*Barely audible*). —Ta-plan-plan-plan-plan.
(LILY *moves to the garden steps and out, following the movement of* STEPHEN'S *hand.* TOM *turns and gazes at* HOPE *with a* curious expression.

HOPE

What's the matter with you?

STEPHEN

Pat—Ann—it was not so long ago. Was it so long ago?
(ANN *shakes her head hopelessly, and moves toward the garden, mounts the steps and goes out. Slowly* PAT *crosses the terrace in the opposite direction, and enters the house.*)

HOPE

(*To* TOM). What are you staring at?
(TOM *smiles, but does not reply.* STEPHEN *turns to* TOM *and* HOPE.)

STEPHEN

And for us—shall we see my white phlox, first?

HOPE

Oh, Mr. Field—you mustn't let them go on like this! It's so frightening. (*She turns and sees* TOM *still staring at her.*) Tom's looking at me in the queerest way.—It's as if he didn't know me.

STEPHEN

Possibly you have changed.

HOPE

I—?

STEPHEN

—In his eyes. Perhaps you have one child too many.

HOPE

I don't know what you mean.

STEPHEN

It may be that he sees you not as a mother, but as a woman that he loves. I should not discourage that.
(TOM *goes to* HOPE *and gently turns her about, facing him. He looks at her with a curious smile.*)

HOPE

Tom, what's the matter with you, anyhow? (*His answer is to take her in his arms and kiss her. She frees herself.*) Honestly, I don't know what you're thinking of! What on earth has—(*He takes her face in his hands and kisses her again. She averts her head.*) I can't imagine what's come over you. I want to talk to Mr. Field. (*To* STEPHEN.) It seems to me that you're all—(TOM *comes to her again, takes both her hands in his and smiles into her eyes.*) I'm not fooling. I really mean it.

PAT

(*From the house*). Mary? *Mary!*

HOPE

(*To* STEPHEN). Who's he calling?—I tell you it isn't good for people to let themselves go that way—(TOM *draws her into his arms, and holds her there.*) It's a form of self-indulgence. — Stop, Tom! It's a — (*Again* TOM *kisses her.*) Tom, will you let me *go!*
(*He opens his arms suddenly and she is freed, almost falling. She recovers herself and turns once more, with dignity, to* STEPHEN.)

PAT

(*From the house*). Mary! Where are you?

HOPE

The things that are happening here to-night aren't natural, and what's not natural must be wrong.

STEPHEN

To me they are more natural than nature.

HOPE

Of course I don't pretend to follow *your* extraordinary—(*From behind her,* TOM *is taking the hair pins from her hair. She stamps her foot in exasperation.*) Honestly! This is *too* much! (*To* STEPHEN.) I hope you realize that goings on of this sort are not at all usual with us.

STEPHEN

I think that is a pity.
(*Tenderly, lovingly,* TOM *kisses the back of her neck.*)

HOPE

Tom—don't be an utter fool! (*To* STEPHEN.)—To me, life is a very simple thing.

STEPHEN

Is it?

HOPE

One has one's home, one's children and one's husband—

STEPHEN

Or has one home and children only?
(HOPE *looks at him, startled.* TOM *returns to the wall.*)

HOPE

You mean you think that to me, Tom's just another—?

STEPHEN

What do *you* think?
(HOPE *turns to* TOM.)

HOPE

Tom, darling—*surely* you must know that I—
(LILY'S *voice is heard from the garden, calling as a little girl would.*)

LILY

Good-bye, Pa! Good-bye!—Come right home after, won't you, Pa?

HOPE

(*To* STEPHEN). You see? That's Lily. Oh, I know she'll hurt herself! (*To* TOM.) Now

you stay right here, won't you? Please, Tom—like a good boy. (*She hurries off to the garden, calling.*) Lily! Wait, dear!
(*A moment, then* TOM *speaks from the depths of his wretchedness.*)

TOM

Oh, Father Francis—can't a fellow do anything without it's being sinful?
(STEPHEN *goes to a chair and seats himself.*)

STEPHEN

What have you to tell me?

TOM

—So much. I know it's after hours. I know you're tired, but—

STEPHEN

Come—
(TOM *comes, head down, hands clasped. He kneels beside* STEPHEN'S *chair and makes the Sign of the Cross.*)

TOM

—Bless me, Father, for I have sinned. It is about three months ago since my last confession. Since then, I accuse myself of the following sins: Father, I've cursed and sworn and taken the name of the Lord in vain. I've neglected my morning prayers and missed Mass once, and been distracted during Mass seven times—

STEPHEN

Yes—but what is really wrong?

TOM

I've been drunk, and had immodest thoughts, and eaten meat on an Ember-Day, and committed acts of impurity four times—

STEPHEN

But what is really wrong?
(TOM *chokes.*)

TOM

Oh, Father Francis—I don't believe any more! Nothing's got any meaning for me. I look around me, and nothing means anything at all—and I want it to! It must—it's got to—or I'll, or I'll—

STEPHEN

Your childhood faith is gone—

TOM

It wasn't true.

STEPHEN

Are you so sure?

TOM

Yes, and it meant so much to me. I even thought I ought to be a priest, but I lost my faith.

STEPHEN

Perhaps in order that you need not be one.

TOM

I know I've got no soul—nobody has.

STEPHEN

Look closer.

TOM

I have. It isn't there. There isn't any. There never was.

STEPHEN

At some time there is a soul born to every body—and like it, subject to many ills. But the soul's life is the only life there is, so the world is peopled with the living and with the dead. We know the living. Sometimes the dead deceive us.

TOM

You mean that maybe mine is—?

STEPHEN

No. The dead do not deceive me.—I mean that birth is painful. The infant suffers too.

TOM

It's awful—I can't stand it. Let me be damned!

STEPHEN

No.

TOM

But now I'm nothing—let me be *something!*

STEPHEN

Now you begin to be.

TOM

I keep wanting to do great things—too great for what I am—

STEPHEN

There are many men who would go to the ends of the earth for God—

TOM

I would! I keep starting to—

STEPHEN

—And cannot get through their own gardens.

TOM

Oh, don't! I'm such a weak soul—

STEPHEN

—Such a human being.

TOM

Something always stops me, always—

STEPHEN

Your own humanity.—But there are strong souls who never leave their gardens. Their strength is not in the doing, but in the wish to do. There is no strength anywhere, but in the wish. Once realized, it has spent itself, and must be born again.

TOM

But I don't know what I'm here at all for—

STEPHEN

To suffer and to rejoice. To gain, to lose. To love, and to be rejected. To be young and middle-aged and old. To know life as it happens, and then to say, "this is it."

TOM

Yes—but who *am* I? And what shall *I* be when it's over?

STEPHEN

You are the sum of all your possibilities, all your desires—each faint impression, each small experience—

TOM

—But when it's *over?!*

STEPHEN

You will be what your spirit wants and takes of them. Life is a wish. Wishing is never over.
(*A brief silence.* TOM *rises to his feet.*)

TOM

—Then everything about me *has* a meaning!—Everything I see and feel and think and do—dream, even!
(STEPHEN *closes his hand over* TOM'S.)

STEPHEN

Great heaven, yes!

TOM

I've got a feeling that I'm dreaming now.

STEPHEN

It may be.

PAT

(*From the house*). Mary!

TOM

—But Father Francis—are you ill?

STEPHEN

Why?

TOM

You look awfully white—and your hand—it was as cold as ice. I'm afraid I've been a strain for you. Good Lord, Father—you do look white. Here—take this— (*He goes to the table and pours a glass of brandy.* STEPHEN *goes to the fan-back chair in the shadow in the corner of the terrace.* TOM *turns with the glass.*) This will fix you. This—why, where are you, Father? (*He looks about him.*) Confound it, where's he gone to? He looked sick— (*He calls.*) Father Francis!
(STEPHEN *does not answer.* TOM *moves toward the house, with the brandy. As he reaches the steps,* NORMAN *darts out with a small, white fur-rug in his hands.*)

NORMAN

One minute, Mister!

TOM

What do you want? Have you seen Father Francis?

NORMAN

(*In a moderate Jewish accent*). How'd you like to buy a nice fur neck-piece?

TOM

Don't be a fool.

NORMAN

—Make a present to your lady-friend, eh? You can have it cheap—

TOM

No, thanks. Let me by—I'm in a hurry.

NORMAN

All right—I resign—I quit!—I'll get a job as runner in a bank. In five years I'll be rich—I'll be the biggest man in Wall Street! (*Again he offers the rug.*) Look—five dollars—it's worth fifty—
(TOM *tries to pass him.*)

TOM

Oh, for God's sake, Norman—Father Francis is ill—

NORMAN

I'll have money, power—that's what makes you happy—that's the life! (*Again, the rug.*) Look: It's a bargain. Buy it. An inside tip: the National City's taken half the issue at 91, and Pritchard, Ames is bidding for another hundred thousand at—

TOM

(*Suddenly*). I know—the bastide!

NORMAN

Don't you call me that, you leper!
(TOM *pulls away from him.*)

TOM

Get away, I'm not fooling. Let me by!
(*He crosses the terrace quickly, and goes up the garden steps and out.*)

NORMAN

But what a bargain! (*He shrugs.*) *I* should care. (*Then he turns and speaks to the empty chair in front of him.*) Look here, Mr. Sterner—I resign—I'm through!

STEPHEN

(*From the corner of the terrace, hidden in his chair.*) When I've given you such a fine opportunity, when I have even—?

NORMAN

Oh, I'll pay you back!—But I'm quitting, see? I've got better things to do than this. I'll educate myself. I'll—

STEPHEN

So ambitious, eh? Ah, you're all alike, you young people.—And next you marry a Gentile girl I suppose, and have her despise you—ruin you.

NORMAN

Oh, no!—Say, am I such a fool as that? Marry a *schiksa*—me? Whose uncle is a rabbi—? I guess not! But what I'll do is get an honest job—yes! "White fox"—this cat-fur! I'm sick of it—I'm through. I'll get up in the world. You watch me! Have educated people for my friends—

STEPHEN

May you be happy with them.

NORMAN

—Happy and strong and rich and honest! Watch me! (*He offers the despised rug to another unseen client, is refused, and shrugs again.*) No?—*I* should care!
(*And re-enters the house, whistling. For a moment* STEPHEN *is alone upon the terrace.* PAT'S *voice is heard from the house, in growing alarm.*)

PAT

—Aren't you here?—It's me—it's Pat, Mary!
(STEPHEN *passes his hand over his brow.*)

STEPHEN

My head—my head. (*A moment. Then.*) —But this is very strange. What is this mist that closes in around me? This is a winter mist, and it is summer. Wait a bit, you, I am not ready yet!
(*The distant music changes to "L'Enfant et les Sortilèges" from Ravel's ballet "Five o'Clock."* LILY, *her hair flying about her shoulders, runs down the steps from the garden. She is crossing in the direction of the house, when the music stops her. She listens intently for a moment, then with a swift motion slips the belt from her dress and drops it upon a chair. Her appearance has changed to that of a girl of thirteen.*

She begins to rise up and down upon her toes, in a formal movement of ballet-practice. Her breath becomes a little short. Frowning, she bends and feels her instep. STEPHEN *rises from his chair, and turns to her. She exclaims in joy.*)

LILY

Pa! Oh, Pa, you *did* come right home!
(*She runs and kisses him. He strokes her head.*)

STEPHEN

Well, well, well—and how has my little sprite endured her prison?
(*He speaks in the eloquent voice of an old-fashioned actor.*)

LILY

—Prison? Oh, I've been all right. I like it here. I think it's a nice hotel—nicer than the one in Harrisburg was, much nicer, warmer.—Pa, were you good to-night?

STEPHEN

I was splendid.
(*He seats himself in another chair, facing her.*)

LILY

How many curtain-calls were there?

STEPHEN

Alas, none. But I was magnificent.

LILY

I wish I'd gone. I wish you'd of let me. Could I maybe come to-morrow aft?

STEPHEN

Say "afternoon," child. Do not clip your words.

LILY

"Afternoon."—But could I?

STEPHEN

We shall see. (*With a gesture.*) Fix me my drink—(LILY *goes to the table and makes a brandy-and-soda.*)—And one for yourself.

LILY

I—I don't want any.

STEPHEN

And one for yourself, I said!—'Twill do you good.

LILY

Just a little one, then—it makes me feel so funny.
(STEPHEN's *manner begins to change.*)

STEPHEN

I like you funny.

LILY

Can I put sugar in it?

STEPHEN

Put anything you like in it. Put salt in it.

LILY

Oh—I wouldn't like that!
(*She brings him the glass, and a small one for herself. He seizes her glass and tastes it.*)

STEPHEN

Water!

LILY

(*In fright*). But Pa, I—

STEPHEN

—Your mother's daughter, eh? Lying, deceiving—

LILY

I'm not! I just didn't want—

STEPHEN

(*The actor*). Whose child are you, eh? Are you my child, at all?

LILY

Oh yes, yes! Pa—I *am* your child! Truly I am!

STEPHEN

Then obey me—without question, without equivocation. (*He drains his glass and gives it to her.*) Fill them both.

LILY

All right. I'll put some in—I'll put a lot in.
(*Again she goes to the table with the glasses, refills them and returns to him.*)

STEPHEN

Let me taste— (*He tastes her glass, and gives it back to her.*) That's better. You are your old man's daughter. Give me a kiss— (*She kisses his cheek. He takes a swallow from his glass and she does likewise.*)

LILY

—But you aren't an old man! You aren't old at all. And look, Pa: I don't ever lie to you. I love you too much to. I just can't tell you how much I— (*She strikes a posture, and declaims.*) "Then poor Cordelia!— And yet, not so; since I am sure, my love's more richer than my tongue . . . good, my Lord, you have begot me, bred me, loved me: I return those duties back as are right fit—obey you, love you, and most honor you."

STEPHEN

"Pray, do not mock me: I am a very foolish, fond old man. Fourscore and upward, and, to deal plainly, I fear I am not in my perfect mind. . . . Do not laugh at me: for, as I am a man, I think this lady to be my child, Cordelia."

LILY

"And so I am, I am!"

STEPHEN

—Not bad, not half bad. You get the feeling well enough, but you lack voice. You need filling out everywhere. You're thin all over. I don't like you thin.—What did you do while I was playing?

LILY

Well, you know how it snowed—

STEPHEN

Yes?
(*She is sipping from her glass.*)

LILY

Well, I got a whole shoe-box full off the window-sill and I was making a little girl out of it, only as fast as I made her she melted.

STEPHEN

What else?

LILY

Well, I did my toe-exercises.

STEPHEN

For how long?

LILY

A whole hour.—Well, almost a whole hour.

STEPHEN

You're lying to me.

LILY

Oh, no, Pa!

STEPHEN

Don't you ever lie to me.

LILY

Oh, no.

STEPHEN

If you do, I'll treat you the way I did your mother.

LILY

Pa! You wouldn't ever leave me!

STEPHEN

Just let me catch you lying once.

LILY

But I never, never!

STEPHEN

See that you don't.

LILY

I don't know what I'd do if ever you should leave me—

STEPHEN

—Pick up with some cheap tout, most likely, and go off with him.
(LILY *turns her innocent eyes upon him.*)

LILY

What?

STEPHEN

Never mind. (*She passes her hand vaguely over her eyes.*)—What ails you?

LILY

It's—beginning to feel, in my head.

STEPHEN

Drink it down.

LILY

I can't. My throat won't turn over any more. And—and things are going round—

STEPHEN

Then start the music and go around with them.
(*She giggles.*)

LILY

Oh, that's funny! That's so funny. You're such a funny man.

STEPHEN

Stop laughing.

LILY

I—I can't stop.

STEPHEN

Go start the music— (*Struggling hard to control her hysterics,* LILY *starts the gramophone. Again, it is the "Nailla" of Delibes. He follows the introductory bars with his hand, as if conducting an orchestra.*) Now then—
(*With difficulty, she empties her glass, and begins to dance, haltingly.*)

LILY

(*An appeal*). Oh, Pa—

STEPHEN

What?

LILY

I don't want to.

STEPHEN

Why not?

LILY

My foot hurts. I hurt my foot practising.

STEPHEN

If you'd done it right, you wouldn't have hurt it. Go on and dance.

LILY

I can't, truly I can't.

STEPHEN

Is a man to have no amusement when he comes home of nights after playing his heart out to silly fools who don't know art from turnips? Come on—get going.

LILY

(*Almost in tears*). Pa—this isn't like you. This isn't my you at all. My you tells me stories about queens and palaces and you hold me on your knee and rock me off to sleep and you tuck me in at night and say God love you, little daughter. That's what *you* do.

STEPHEN

Oh, I do, do I? And how often? In my tender moments twice a year.—Not like me, is it? I'll show you what's like me. Will you dance?

LILY

Oh, yes, yes. See? I'm dancing—
(*Again she begins to dance, this time more haltingly. He stands over her.*)

STEPHEN

Faster!—Wasn't Burbage amused when he came home? Wasn't Barrett and wasn't Booth? Is it too much to ask, eh?

LILY

Oh, no, Pa! See me, Pa?

STEPHEN

That's better.
(*She goes on, as well as she is able. At length.*)

LILY

(*Panting*).—My hurt foot—it won't go up any more—

STEPHEN

No? Try it.
(HOPE *appears at the top of the garden-steps, where she stands unseen by them, watching them in horror.*)

LILY

But I *am* trying!—Is it all right if I just—?
(*Again she tries to rise upon her toes, and cannot. She attempts a pitiful* pas seul, *fails*

in it, falls to the floor. Then, all at once she turns into a raging fury and screams.) God damn! Hell!
(*He laughs.*)

STEPHEN

Good!

LILY

Oh, I hate you. I hate you. I don't *love* you anymore!

STEPHEN

Splendid! Go on—more!
(*She rises to her feet and confronts him, trembling with rage.*)

LILY

You're a dirty drunk! You left my mother when she was sick. You can't act. You're just a super, that's all you are. You can't act any!
(*Laughing, he holds his arms out to her.*)

STEPHEN

Come here. Give us a kiss.

LILY

No. You smell of whisky and nasty grease-paint. You're dirty—I hate you! I won't stay with you any longer—I'll run away, that's what I'll do!

PAT

(*From the house*). Mary! I've come back. Where are you?
(STEPHEN'S *voice changes back to his own voice. Suddenly he seems very tired.*)

STEPHEN

—Then go quickly. Go very quickly. See—there is the door. It is open. Go in, and up the stairs, and to your room.
(*She gazes at him for a moment, then turns and walks directly to the steps and into the house. Again* STEPHEN *sinks into a chair, his hand over his eyes. There is a slight pause, then* HOPE *comes down from the garden.*)

HOPE

Oh, that was terrible! Why did you do it?

STEPHEN

I—? I did nothing. Tell me what happened—

HOPE

You know perfectly well what happened! —And she adored him. She— (*She turns and follows* LILY *into the house, calling.*) Lily!
(STEPHEN *is alone. He rises from his chair with effort, and moves toward the garden-steps. He stiffens suddenly, then exclaims in wonder.*)

STEPHEN

What's this? (*Another moment. Then, more sharply.*) Come now! What is it?! (*He slumps against the wall, and plucks at his left arm, which has gone limp, then tries to raise his right hand to his head, and cannot.*)—Cerebral hemorrhage, is that it? That's very interesting, I'm sure. The left side is quite numb—the lesion must be in the right lobe, in the Area of—God, when we crack we crack, don't we? (*A moment. Then summoning his remaining strength.*) —But I am not ready, yet! (*He makes his way to the fan-back chair in the corner of the terrace and slowly lets himself into it. He calls.*) Pat! Ann! (*Another moment.*) There—there's the pulse—it is quite hard, quite stringy—(*Again he calls.*) Ann!—But the breathing is regular, Doctor—difficult, but regular.—I say, not yet! I'll go, but in my proper time.—Curious there is no pain—only a sense of— (*He catches his breath.*)—No pain, did I say? (*And collects his strength for a final cry.*) Ann!
(*And sinks lower into his chair. From the distance piano-music begins to be heard again. It is a popular waltz, of ten years ago. A moment, then* ANN *comes down the steps from the garden. She is limping. As she crosses the terrace she murmurs to herself.*)

ANN

Poor dear—poor darling—what can I do for him? (*As she reaches the sofa her ankle gives way under her and she sinks down upon the floor, exclaiming.*) Ouch—*ouch*—oh, where *is* that road?
(PAT *comes in from the house, calling softly.*)

PAT

Mary! Where are you, Mary?

ANN

Ouch—ouch—
(PAT *hesitates a moment, then comes up to her.*)

PAT

Excuse me. Is there anything the—?
(ANN *starts in alarm.*)

ANN

—Oh!

PAT

I'm all right. I'm harmless.—But I was just wandering around here and I saw you from across the field and I thought something might be the matter, and—

ANN

—There is. Plenty.

PAT

What? Can I help?

ANN

Well, for one thing, I've probably broken my ankle. And for another, I'm lost. And for another—no, I'm not sure you can.

PAT

Does your ankle hurt?

ANN

Oh, no, it feels wonderful. They do, you know.—Ouch!

PAT

Maybe if I could get a car up into this field for you—

ANN

Have you got one that climbs fences?

PAT

What are you lost from?

ANN

The Westbury Road.
(*A breeze brings the music closer.*)

PAT

That's easy.

ANN

It hasn't been.

PAT

You're practically on it. It's just over there.

ANN

No!

PAT

Honest.

ANN

Then what's that music I've been hearing? Isn't it the Club?

PAT

No. It's from a party I'm at.

ANN

At?

PAT

Well, one I got away from.

ANN

Whose?

PAT

Mine. At my house.

ANN

I'm impressed. Why wasn't *I* asked?

PAT

You would have been.—Where do you live?

ANN

I'm staying down here with some people named Ames. But I got the wanders and had to walk.

PAT

So did I.—Tom and Hope Ames?

ANN

That's right.

PAT

They said they couldn't come.

ANN

Maybe they don't like parties. Or maybe they didn't want people to see me. In the Spring I get freckled.—Oh, this *damned* ankle!

PAT

Quit talking about your ankle. What's your name?

ANN

Ann Field. What's yours?

PAT

Don't laugh—

ANN

No.

PAT

Patrick— (*She laughs.*) You said you wouldn't.

ANN

But I've always wanted to know one!—What was it you said to Mike?

PAT

That's not very new, you know.—My last name's Farley.

ANN

—Not one of the great, enormous, important, rich ones!

PAT

Well—

ANN

—Please, forget everything I've said. You're beautiful. You'll get me home all right.

PAT

I'm—er—I came down for the Spring holidays, and I thought I'd swing a little party, and—

ANN

Why bless his heart, he's embarrassed! Lovely!

PAT

Oh, go to hell.

ANN

You're sweet. I think you're really sweet. (PAT *seats himself beside her.*)

PAT

Foolish to stay indoors a night like this. Foolish to sleep even.—You got awfully pretty hands.

ANN

Thanks. My eyes are nice, too. They don't cross, or anything.

PAT

Say—you come right back at a fellow, don't you?

ANN

Do I?

PAT

—Ever read a poem called "Pale hands I loved beside the Shal-i-mar?"

ANN

(*Suspiciously*). What about it?

PAT

I just wondered. Didn't you like it?

ANN

I thought it was awful.

PAT

Why?

ANN

I don't know. I just did.

PAT

You're a funny girl. Maybe you don't like poetry.

ANN

—Maybe I do! (*He laughs.*) I like the way you laugh.

PAT

I'll hire me a couple of expert ticklers. (*And then they both laugh.*)

ANN

You have awfully white teeth, haven't you?
(*Suddenly* PAT *frowns.*)

PAT

—What?

ANN

I said, you have—

PAT

(*Slowly*). I know—I'm trying to think: there was someone with white teeth that gleamed from the water—oh, never mind. (*Another moment. Then.*)—Funny, our meeting like this. I suppose that's the way good things happen.

ANN

Maybe.—I wish you'd brought a crutch, though, or a wheel-chair.
(*He eyes her reflectively.*)

PAT

How much do you weigh?

ANN

Something fairly serious—or I did. To-night I've walked a good deal of it off.

PAT

We've got to do something about moving you.

ANN

I hoped you'd get around to that.

PAT

That is, eventually. There's lots of time.—Say, are you moody?

ANN

Maybe.—Am I?

PAT

Because I am. That's why I got to walking to-night. I had something on my mind.

ANN

So had I.

PAT

Really? What?

ANN

My father.

PAT

Is he—is he sick?

ANN

I don't know.—What is it that worried you?

PAT

(*A moment*).—Well, you see, at Christmas I came down with the Copes—

ANN

Are they like the measles?
(PAT *laughs, and explains.*)

PAT

—Down *here,* with Johnny and Nora Cope. Well, one night we were coming home quite late from somewheres and we stopped in at the dog-wagon in the village to get—(*He stops suddenly and stares at her.*) Jeerusalem! I believe you're her!

ANN

"She," you should say.—Who?

PAT

(*Overcome with awe*). Good Lord Almighty—

ANN

I wonder if it's the same dog-wagon I know.

PAT

Of course!—But this is— Gosh! Do you know what this means to me?

ANN

I'm trying awfully hard to follow, but—

PAT

(*Still staring*). I had a Western, with a lot of onions, and we got up to go and there was a girl there sitting at the counter with a couple of other people and a great big glass of milk and she looked up as I went by, and—
(ANN *smiles.*)

ANN

I did, didn't I?

PAT

(*Excitedly*). Yes!—the milk had made a little white rim along your upper lip and—

ANN

(*Distressed*). Oh, dear—

PAT

It was beautiful.—And ever since, I've seen your face the whole time, in my mind, and I could never find you. It's been terrible.—And now—Oh, Lord!—Imagine!
(ANN *smiles.*)

ANN

Well—here I am.

PAT

It's just miraculous, that's all, it's miraculous. Gosh, I don't know what to say. You know this isn't like the usual—there's something terribly right about it.—Ever since that night I've been longing to—Jeez, I thought I'd go crazy if I couldn't find you—been longing to take your face in my hands like this, and—
(*He takes her face between his hands.*)

ANN

Wait. Let me look at you.
(*She looks.*)

PAT

I'm not much on looks—

ANN

Shhh! (*She looks a longer time.*) Why—it's the queerest thing. I think I—

PAT

—And to kiss that lovely mouth that had the white rim along the top of it—

ANN

But somehow—I don't think you'd better—yet—

PAT

No, I suppose not.—But I don't see why! (*A moment. Still they gaze at each other. Then.*) Look: do you ever get a feeling that you—oh, Lord—that you know all about it?

ANN

Sometimes.

PAT

I do now! I've never felt alive before! Everything's as clear as—(*Suddenly, directly.*) Look: I'll be at the Ameses for lunch to-morrow. Tell 'em I like steak.
(ANN *laughs.*)

ANN

I like *you!*

PAT

—As much as I like steak?

ANN

How much do you like steak?

PAT

I'm crazy for it. I dream about it. Well—?
(*Again* ANN *laughs, and rises.*)

ANN

Come on.
(*He catches her hand in his.*)

PAT

Ah, Ann—tell me, Ann!

ANN

No, no! This is ridiculous. It's—
(*She frees herself.*)

PAT

Oh, please! Tell me—do you like me?
(*A moment. Then.*)

ANN

Yes.

PAT

Much?

ANN

A lot. Terribly!
(*For* PAT *this is almost too much to bear.*)

PAT

Gosh, I'm glad.

ANN

I hope I'll be.—Come on—shall we?

PAT

Look: You've got to come up to the Spring Dance with me, and the ball games, and the boat races—I row Number Seven—and—oh, Ann—

ANN

What, Pat?

PAT

It's wonderful.

ANN

It is, it is.—Do come—come on—(*They go on another step or two, toward the garden-steps, where again her ankle gives way. He catches her in his arms. She recovers herself and, still in his arms, turns and looks at* him. *For a long moment their eyes hold them together. At length they kiss. For an instant* ANN *clings to him, then leaves him.*) Pat—Pat—we're crazy.

PAT

No!

ANN

(*Breathlessly*). Come on—. We must—(*She takes his hand. He turns.*)

PAT

First, let's look back at our meadow. (ANN *frowns half puzzled, half in alarm. Then.*)

ANN

(*Suddenly, sharply*). No! That's wrong! (*He had not said that. The spell is breaking.*)

PAT

What is? (*He takes a deep breath.*)—Um! Doesn't it smell good, though! What is it? Hawthorn?

ANN

No!

PAT

(*Slowly, from very far away*). But I—I guess they're right. I guess there's nothing like May in England—(*Suddenly he stops, releasing her hand. His face becomes troubled. He looks at the house, frowning.*) What's that house?

ANN

(*A sudden cry*). Don't think, Pat! Don't think at all! Come with me—

PAT

—But there's something I've got to do in this house.

ANN

No!

PAT

Yes. And I can't think what. And it's terribly important. I've waited too long. It's got to be done at once. It's getting late.—I know!—I've got to pack a bag. It's late. I've got to get that bag packed. I've got to pack a bag and catch a boat and go to England.
(ANN *is still at the garden-steps. His eyes have not left the house.*)

ANN

Stay with me, Pat! I'll lose you there!

PAT

I tell you she's waiting, and it's getting late. (*Again he moves toward the house.*)

ANN

Oh, why must I always lose you? (*She goes up the garden-steps and out.* PAT *advances further toward the house, but* STEPHEN *rises—*)

STEPHEN

Pat!
(PAT *halts, turns slowly, looks at him, then goes to him.*)

PAT

Why—why how do you do, Mr. Carr! I feel as if I'd been away for—I came across the fields and down the lane—the hawthorn's early, isn't it? I didn't wire, I thought I'd surprise her. How has she been?

STEPHEN

You cannot surprise her.

PAT

You mean she had a hunch that I was—? But where is she, then? I've been calling her all over everywhere. (STEPHEN *does not reply. Suddenly* PAT *becomes alarmed.*) Say, what is this—a joke? Because if it is —yes, and what about my letters? Why didn't she answer them? Did you and Father fix it so she wouldn't get them? I've been almost crazy. I've been—where is she? She's here—I know she's here—(*He calls.*) Ann! (*Then feeling something wrong, whispers.*)—Mary. (*Then, more confidently.*) It's Pat, Mary! (*He turns again to

STEPHEN.)—And you needn't think we're going to stay on with people who fixed it up to separate us, either. Not for one minute. I'm going to take her with me this very night, and—

STEPHEN

That is too soon.

PAT

It's not. Haven't we waited years already? We'll be wanting to get married right away. Tomorrow, most likely—or the next day—

STEPHEN

—Too soon.

PAT

Look here, Mr. Carr—(*Then correcting himself.*) Mr. Field.—I know you're a sick man. But Ann's got her whole life ahead of her. You can't take it from her. You've taken too much of it already. I don't hold with those old ideas. Ann and I are in love, and if you don't grant that that's the most important thing, it's time you did. I'm sorry to have to put it this way, but I've got to speak as I feel. I'll certainly never expect a child of mine to—to—

STEPHEN

—To what?

PAT

—To give her whole life up to me, and I don't think you should.

STEPHEN

I see.

PAT

You let her bring you here, away from all the—

STEPHEN

—She has needed me as much these last three years as I have needed her.

PAT

That may be. But—

STEPHEN

Wait! (*He looks at* PAT *intently, then speaks with a slow emphasis.*)—But now she does not need me any longer.

PAT

What are you looking like that for? What do you mean? (*Then suddenly, wildly.*) She's not! That's not true—you're lying. It's not possible—it can't be! She's here—I know she's here! (*Again he calls.*) Ann! Ann!

STEPHEN

She does not come.

PAT

Ann, dear! It's Pat, Ann!

STEPHEN

And still she does not come.

PAT

Oh, don't keep saying that! She's here—I can feel her all about me. (*He wheels about and looks around him.*) What kind of a deal is this, anyway? What am I doing—dreaming? (*Then one last despairing cry.*) Ann! (*And a long silence. Finally.*)—Because she thought I wasn't coming back—(*Another moment. Then, in anguish.*)—I can't believe—but how? *How* did she? She couldn't have hurt that sweet place at her temple, that lovely breast. What has death to do with her?

STEPHEN

—With anyone.

PAT

But I did come back! I wasn't the swine she thought me. I did come—she must know that. I'm sure she knows it!

STEPHEN

So then, you have your picture back—

PAT

My picture?

STEPHEN

The one you love so—your picture of yourself. Now your pet illusion is whole again, and all is well, eh?

PAT

I don't know what you're—

STEPHEN

You built your whole life upon an illusion—and it went—and still you want it back—from death, even!

PAT

I don't know what you're talking about.

STEPHEN

Your idea of your own perfection.

PAT

That's not true—

STEPHEN

No?—You came back, yes—but in your own time. A swine? Indeed you are!—But what brought you? How much of it was the self-contempt you felt for having left her?

PAT

None of it.

STEPHEN

—And how much your love of her, your want of her?

PAT

All!

STEPHEN

Which is it you can't live with, now? Which is it that spoils your picture?

PAT

Oh, be still about my picture! You're talking about a spoiled boy, stuffed with what he thought were fine ideals. Fakes, all of them! I've left that boy behind. I've got no picture anymore. I know I'm what I am—myself!

STEPHEN

Then can you face yourself—say good-bye to your last illusion, and come through alive?

PAT

Go—will you?

STEPHEN

If you cannot—what else is there for you? (*A moment. Then.*)

PAT

(*To himself*).—Off to Africa.

STEPHEN

Well—?
(PAT *moves toward the garden-steps.*)

PAT

Off to—! (*But half way up the steps, he stops. When he speaks, it is with a fine, saving scorn.*)—One big last shining gesture, eh? Watching myself go by. Another pretty picture: "He died for love." (*He raises his head.*) No!—That's for the weak ones. I stay.

STEPHEN

(*A murmur*). That's right, that's right.
(*He leaves him, and moves painfully toward his corner.*)

PAT

But I want her so. Ann—Ann—
(FELIX *comes in from house.*)

FELIX

Pardon, Monsieur—je regrette que j'avais laissé passer l'heure. Maintenant, il est onze heures moins douze. Je regrette beaucoup, Monsieur. C'est ma faute.
(PAT *does not reply.* FELIX *goes out. A moment, then* ANN'*s voice is heard softly, from the garden.*)

ANN

Pat?

PAT

(*A cry of joy*). Ann! (*In an instant he is up the garden-steps and out.*) I'll find you this time. Ann!
(STEPHEN *gropes for his chair in the corner and seats himself.*)

STEPHEN

—All right, you. Very well—I am ready. This ends, and that begins.—Oh, so you'd like to end it, would you? All of it, eh? (*He half rises, gasping for breath.*) Well, you can't!—I tell you—you cannot! (*Gasping.*) I tell you—!
(*There is a slight shuffling sound, as he slumps into death. A moment. Then* TOM *comes in from the garden with the brandy-glass, as* FELIX *enters from the house and crosses the terrace toward him, with three traveling-bags.*)

FELIX

Pardon, Monsieur—
(*He goes up the garden-steps and out.* HOPE *comes in from the house. She is dressed to leave. She sees* TOM *and goes to him quickly.*)

HOPE

Tom, Tom—

TOM

—I beg your pardon, but have you by any chance seen an old priest called Father—(*Then he recognizes her.*) Why—why, hello, Hope—

HOPE

—Who, did you say?

TOM

Why—I don't know—(*He frowns at the brandy-glass.*) I thought I—I had this for some one—who was it? I was taking it to him, to—Lord, *I* don't know—(*He looks at her closer.*)—How are the children?
(LILY *comes in from the house, also dressed for departure.*)

HOPE

—The children—that's good, that is!—Do you realize that that's just what you've been acting like?

TOM

(*To himself*).—Under the piano. Under the—
(ALICE *comes down the stairs from the balcony. She wears a coat and carries a small traveling-bag.*)

ALICE

Listen: could any one tell me what's got into the Rose man?

HOPE

Not Norman, too!

ALICE

—I opened my door into the hall, and there he was, stretched on the floor outside it, fast asleep on a fur-rug. (*She looks back over her shoulder.*)—And now he's—
(NORMAN *appears upon the balcony, the fur-rug still over his arm.*)

NORMAN

(*Heartily*). Well, everyone—how goes it?

TOM

What's that you've got?

NORMAN

How'd you like to—? (*He stops and frowns at the rug.*) Why, it's a—(*His accent leaves him.*) Damned if I know.
(*He drops it, and cleans his fastidious hands of it.*)

TOM

Was it a bargain?
(NORMAN *looks at him sharply.*)

NORMAN

—Am I right in believing that some pretty funny business went on here to-night?
(*All look troubled, eyeing one another furtively, trying to figure out how much the other remembers, how much one remembers oneself.*)

LILY

(*Finally*). Well, I don't know if you'd call it funny—but suddenly everything seems possible.—It's like beginning all over again.
(ALICE *stretches upon her cushion.*)

ALICE

I hope I didn't miss anything. I had a delicious nap.

LILY

—And did you dream?

ALICE

Dream?—I should say not. I was too dead.
(*Another silence. All stare in front of them. Finally* ALICE *speaks again, this time as if from a distance.*) Did I tell you?—Once when I was in England staying with the Potters, they had a—(*Then suddenly, with an air of discovery.*)—Why Norman! That was where I met you, wasn't it?

NORMAN

Yes.

ALICE

—Strange.
(*Again silence. Then.*)

TOM

At school the big idea used to be to sneak off in the afternoons and smoke real tobacco in real pipes.—Lord, how big that made us feel.

NORMAN

(*After another moment*).—I often wonder what happened to old Morris Sterner. He gave me my first real job.—Once he told me that—
(*But he relapses into silence, which* LILY *at length breaks.*)

LILY

It's fantastic, this terrace. It just hangs here. Some day it will float off into space, and anchor there, like an island in time.

HOPE

Don't!

ALICE

Don't what?

HOPE

Please, everyone make sense. It must be nearly time to leave.

TOM

Hope—(*She turns to him.*) Would you mind awfully if I don't sail with you?

HOPE

Why?

TOM

I want to go off somewhere by myself for a while. I think at last I've really got a line on something that may be the answer for me.

HOPE

(*Unconvinced*). Yes?

TOM

—In a way it's a kind of faith, in place of the old one—maybe it's the same. Anyhow, I want to work it out.

HOPE

Sweet Tom.
(PAT *and* ANN *are nearing the terrace from the garden.* PAT'S *voice is heard.*)

PAT

There's so much I'd have gone without—
(*They come in, her hand in his, and stand together upon the garden-steps.*)

TOM

(*To* HOPE).—I don't know how long it will take—but if I send for you——
(HOPE *smiles.*)

HOPE

Don't come——

TOM

Don't come.
(*Now everyone is talking in concert.*)

PAT

—Without so many good, quiet things——

TOM

I'm excited about this Hope.

HOPE

So am I, Tom—if you do it.

PAT

(*To* ANN). I want to sit with the wife I love, and read books, and look at maps——

LILY

You won't believe me when I tell you——

ALICE

What?

LILY

Next year I'm going to play Cordelia in King Lear.

PAT

—And fish trout-streams with my boys, and take my daughter walking——

HOPE

—What time is it, Norman? Oughtn't we be starting?

NORMAN

I'm not going to Paris.
(ALICE *glances at him in alarm.*)

HOPE

Really!—And who was it who simply had to be home by the tenth for a corporation meeting?

NORMAN

They can meet without me. They can whistle for me. I'll be in Andorra.

PAT

(*To* ANN).—And build a house and mend a fence, and be tired of a good day's work, and sleep——
(*Now they have come down the steps and joined the others.* ALICE *moves toward* NORMAN.)

ALICE

Norman——

NORMAN

What, Alice?

ALICE

I'll miss you.—Take me with you!
(NORMAN *starts forward.*)

NORMAN

You'd come!?

ALICE

Just ask me.

NORMAN

Alice——

ALICE

—Darling.
(*Then:*)

NORMAN

That's the way to see Andorra!
(ALICE *and* NORMAN *keep on gazing at each other as if they could never look their fill.*)

TOM

(*Suddenly*). Now I know how it happened! (*To* ANN.) Where's your father?
(LILY *rises quickly, and stares toward* STEPHEN'S *chair, which conceals him from their view.*)

ANN

He must have gone down to the bastide.—Why?

TOM

Hotel Universe!—*He'll* know.

ANN

What?

TOM

Don't you know the story?

ANN

Oh—you mean about Réné Mayer's house?

TOM

I mean about this house——

ANN

You must be mixed, Tom. This was built in nineteen-twelve by a man from Lyons.
(*A moment.* TOM *gazes at her. Then:*)

TOM

Are you sure?

ANN

Oh, yes. Father leased it from him.
(LILY *starts back from* STEPHEN'S *chair with a sudden cry.*)

LILY

Pa!

HOPE

Don't, Lily—please don't again——

LILY

Pat—Pat!
(*He goes to her.*)

PAT

What is it, Lily?

LILY

(*A moan*). I don't know, I don't know——

ANN

Lily—darling——

LILY

—I feel as if all that held me together had suddenly let go.
(*She begins to cry, softly.*)

ANN

Lily—darling—don't!

LILY

It's all right—I'll be all right——
(FELIX *re-enters from the garden and goes to* PAT.)

FELIX

Pardon, Monsieur—il est onze heure juste, Monsieur.
(HOPE *jumps up.*)

HOPE

Eleven! We've got to fly!
(*They all talk together.*)

ALICE

We'll probably be late at that.

NORMAN

Oh, no—not if we hurry.

TOM

You can make good time on these roads at night.

FELIX

(*To* ANN). Pardon, Mademoiselle, les valises sont dans les voitures.

ANN

—Your bags are all in.

TOM

Where's yours, Pat? Are you ready?

LILY

No! *You've* got to stay! Do you understand that?—You've got to stay!

PAT

Why yes, of course.—I'm not going.
(ANN *glances at him quickly.*)

ANN

Pat!

PAT

I'm staying, Ann.

TOM

Now there's a good idea!

HOPE

I had a hunch Pat was no mountain-climber!

NORMAN

That's the stuff, Pat.
(HOPE *goes to* ANN *and kisses her.* ALICE *slips her arm through* NORMAN'*s.*)

HOPE

Good-bye, Ann.

ANN

Good-bye, dear.

TOM

Good-bye, Pat. Take it easy for awhile.

PAT

Yes. Good-bye, Tom.

LILY

Hurry, *hurry!*
(TOM *kisses* ANN.)

TOM

Good-bye and thanks, Ann.—Say good-bye to your father for me.

HOPE

Yes.

NORMAN

Yes!
(TOM *frowns.*)

TOM

Say to him, that——

LILY

Hurry, hurry!

TOM

—Say good-bye to him.

NORMAN

Do you want to come with us, Tom?
(TOM *turns upon the garden-steps.*)

TOM

To Andorra? Why, it sounds like a good idea.

HOPE

No, no! Alone! You've got to go alone!

TOM

But Hope—you know what a friendly soul I am. You know how I need company.

HOPE

(*To the others*). What can you do with him?

(*They go out.* NORMAN *and* ALICE *mount the steps, calling over their shoulders.*)

NORMAN AND ALICE

Good-bye! Thanks! Good-bye!
(PAT, ANN *and* LILY *are left.*)

LILY

You two—you're for each other, aren't you?

PAT

I hope so.

ANN

Then we are.

LILY

(*To* ANN). Your father—remember what he said? It does go on. (ANN *looks at her.*) Wherever we may be—breezes from the other fields still blow upon us——

ANN

Why, yes. Why do you——?

LILY

I think that's good to know. God love him. God love you. Good-bye——
(*She mounts the steps, pauses for one brief instant to glance down at* STEPHEN, *then goes out into the garden.* PAT *and* ANN *are left alone.* ANN *touches his cheek.*)

ANN

Dear love.

PAT

I want to make love to you for years. Oh, it's a life, Ann!

ANN

I know, dear—don't I know! (*She murmurs.*)—Thank you, Father.

PAT

Yes—thanks! (*In the distance, far off in the garden, a cock crows hoarsely.* PAT *starts.*) What's that? What time is it?

ANN

Hush, darling, never mind.—It's just an old white rooster—one of Father's pets—his clock he calls him.

PAT

It must be dawn somewhere.

ANN

But of course, dear—always!

PAT

Wherever there is an end, he said——

ANN

—From it the beginning springs.
(*She stares straight in front of her, her apprehension growing in her eyes. Slowly, fearfully, her head turns in the direction of* STEPHEN. *Silence. Then again the cock exults.*)

CURTAIN

Robert Emmet Sherwood

REUNION IN VIENNA

To My Wife

ROBERT EMMET SHERWOOD

Robert Sherwood confesses that his literary career began in 1903, when, at the age of seven, he edited a magazine called *Children's Life.* From then until the time he won the Pulitzer Prize with *Idiot's Delight* in 1936, his career has been chiefly literary, with interludes for an elementary and college education at Harvard, service in the World War with the 42nd Battalion of the Canadian Black Watch, with journalistic ventures as dramatic critic of *Vanity Fair,* and motion-picture editor of *Life* and the *New York Herald.* His first play, *The Road to Rome,* was an immediate success. It was followed by *The Queen's Husband, Waterloo Bridge, This Is New York, Acropolis, Reunion in Vienna* and the 1936 Pulitzer Prize choice *Idiot's Delight.* Robert Sherwood is also the author of *The Virtuous Knight,* an historical novel dealing with the period of the Third Crusade.

"Wonder," says he, "is the basis of Worship: the reign of wonder is perennial, indestructible in Man; only at certain stages (as the present), it is, for some short season, a reign in *partibus infidelium.*" That progress of Science, which is to destroy Wonder, and in its stead substitute Mensuration and Numeration, finds small favor with Teufelsdröckh, much as he otherwsie venerates these two latter processes.

SARTOR RESARTUS.

CHARACTERS

KATHIE
ERNEST
ELENA
DOCTOR ANTON KRUG
OLD KRUG
ILSE
EMIL
FRAU LUCHER
COUNT VON STAINZ
COUNTESS VON STAINZ
POFFY
A PORTER
ANOTHER PORTER
STRUP
BREDZI
TWO WAITERS
TWO BUS-BOYS
A BELL-BOY
TORLINI
A POLICEMAN
CHEF
RUDOLF MAXIMILLIAN
GISELLA VON KRETT
GENERAL HOETZLER
SOPHIA
KOEPPKE
TALISZ
A VALET
JANSEI

SCENES

ACT I

The drawing-room in the house of Doctor Anton Krug, in Vienna. Late afternoon.

ACT II

The ante-room of the Imperial Suite, Hotel Lucher, in Vienna. Early evening.

ACT III

Same as Act I. Late evening.

(The curtain is lowered during Act III to indicate the passage of several hours.)

Time: August 18th, 1930.

REUNION IN VIENNA

ACT ONE

THE *scene is the living room in the home of* PROFESSOR DOCTOR ANTON KRUG *in Vienna. It is late in the afternoon of August 18th, 1930, a date which marks the one hundredth anniversary of the birth of the late Emperor Franz Joseph I.*

The room is ultra-modernistic in the style of its decorations and furnishings, but there is conveyed through the colors of the curtains and upholstery a suggestion of old-fashioned warmth.

At the right, down-stage, is a double door, leading to a hall and the staircase. In the up-stage right angle of the scene is a long window, looking out upon a sea of horse-chestnut trees. At the back of the room, in the center, a few steps lead up to a little landing; on this open the door leading to FRAU KRUG'S *boudoir and, to the left of it, the entrance to the hall which leads to the bedrooms.*

Up-stage left is the door leading to DR. KRUG'S *offices, and down-stage left, a fireplace.*

Before the fireplace is a seat. Slightly to the left of stage-center is a large couch, the back of which forms a bookcase. Towards the right is a thickly upholstered easy-chair, and two or three chairs that are not so easy. There is a window seat, and between it and the landing at the back is an American radio cabinet.

As the curtain rises, the stage is empty, but from the radio comes the sounds of a jazz tune.

After a moment, the door at the right opens and KATHIE *comes in. She is a stout, competent, middle-aged servant. Behind her comes* ERNEST, *a venerable, jovial laundryman, bearing a brimming hamper of clean linen.*

KATHIE

Put it down there. (*She indicates the couch, then goes up to the radio.*)

ERNEST

Yes, my dear. (*He puts the laundry basket by the sofa.*)

KATHIE

(*Muttering as she turns off the radio*). He always goes out and leaves it on when he knows it annoys the Herr Doctor. (*She goes up the steps and knocks on the door of* FRAU KRUG'S *room.*) Frau Krug.

ELENA

(*From off-stage*). Yes?

KATHIE

The laundry's here. (*She comes down and addresses* ERNEST *in a peremptory tone.*) She wants to count it herself—and heaven help you if there's anything missing.

ERNEST

Not so much as a doily, upon my word. (ELENA *comes out of her room, and walks quickly down to the couch. She is thirty-two years old, slim, serene, self-possessed and almost imperceptibly malicious. Unquestionably above reproach as the envied wife of the distinguished* DR. KRUG, ELENA *remains a lively subject for speculative discussion. There is no doubt that she is a lady of fashion—was born so, indeed—though she is now wearing a severely simple apron smock and appearing as a model of brisk, housewifely competence. She smiles amiably at* ERNEST.)

ELENA

Good afternoon, Ernest.

ERNEST

(*Bowing*). Frau Krug! Good afternoon. Warming up a bit, isn't it?

ELENA

Yes—it's lovely. . . . All right, Kathie. I have the list.
(KATHIE *starts taking the folded pairs of drawers from the basket, pair by pair, and putting them on the couch.* ELENA *holds a laundry book and pencil with which she confirms the numbers of items announced by* KATHIE.)

KATHIE

Seven pairs of drawers.

ELENA

Seven. That's right. . . . Here—let me see how they've been done.
(KATHIE *hands her a pair, which* ELENA *unfolds and inspects.*)

ERNEST

Beautifully laundered, Frau Krug, with creamy softness to caress your skin.

ELENA

Not my skin—my husband's.

ERNEST

(*Bowing*). Ten thousand pardons.

ELENA

How about the shirts?

KATHIE

(*Piling them up*). One—two—three—four—five—six—seven.
(DR. ANTON KRUG *has come in from the left. He is a tall, powerful, handsome man of forty-five, bespectacled, correctly dressed in an essentially Teutonic morning coat with striped trousers. His hands are those of a peasant rather than of a deft surgeon, and he is conscious of them. He speaks quietly, but in his deep voice is the resonance of assurance. He knows whereof he speaks.*)

ANTON

Elena . . . What are you doing? (*He comes close to* ELENA.)

ELENA

Now don't bother me, Anton. How many undershirts?

KATHIE

Two—four—six—seven.

ELENA

Seven. That's right. (*To* ANTON.) I'm counting the laundry.
(KATHIE *begins to count out socks.*)

KATHIE

One pair, two—three—four——(*She goes on.*)

ANTON

(*Smiling*). Forgive me, Elena—but will this great task keep you occupied for very long?

ELENA

No. Why?

ANTON

There are a couple of students of mine out there.

KATHIE

(*Mumbling*). Eleven pairs socks.

ANTON

Would you mind talking to them while they're waiting? I want them to have a good look at you.

ELENA

No, dear, by all means, send them in. Did you say eleven?

KATHIE

Yes, ma'am. Five woollen, six silk.

ELENA

That's right. I'd better not let them see me with all this wash.

ANTON

(*Smiling*). No, it might disillusion them. They imagine you as glamorous, regal.

ELENA

(*Interested*). Ah! *Do* they?

ANTON

Where they got such ideas, I don't know.

ELENA

Perhaps they're very young?
(KATHIE *is putting the laundry back into the basket.*)

ANTON

They are—young, and painfully earnest. They're badly in need of a few lessons in the cultivation of grace.

ELENA

(*Rising*). This apron isn't very glamorous, either.
(*Old* KRUG *ambles in from the right, carrying the evening paper. He is* ANTON's *father, a gentle old man, an ex-cobbler, who doesn't entirely like the way things have been going since Austria was made safe for democracy.*)

ANTON

No, I'm reasonably sure you can do better than that.

KRUG

Better than what?

ELENA

If you can keep them waiting a little while I *shall* do better. (*She goes up to the steps at the back.*)

ANTON

Thanks, Elena. I'll deposit them in here. (*He goes out at the left.*)

KRUG

Deposit who? What's happening?

ELENA

(*At the door to her room*). Bring the laundry in here. (*She goes out, leaving the door open.*)

ERNEST

Gladly, Frau Krug. (*He lifts the basket.* KATHIE *picks up the folded drawers and shirts from the couch and goes into the room.* ERNEST *is following her, but old* KRUG *intercepts him.*)

KRUG

Oh, Ernest!

ERNEST

(*Turning and bowing*). Herr Krug!

KRUG

(*Excitedly*). Have you heard any more about tonight?

ERNEST

(*Importantly*). I have! I was just over at Lucher's Hotel, and they're in a great state about it. They expect upwards of a hundred people!

KRUG

(*Impressed*). A hundred! The police aren't going to stop it, are they?

ERNEST

(*With assurance*). Noooo! Old Frau Lucher has bribed the authorities.
(KATHIE *appears in the bedroom door.*)

KATHIE

(*From the landing*). She told you to come in here!

ERNEST

Coming! (*He winks at* KRUG, *and goes out with his basket.* KRUG *goes over to the radio, twists the dials, then turns it on. A speech in Russian is coming through. He listens attentively.* ANTON *comes in from the left, followed by the students,* EMIL LOIBNER *and* ILSE HINRICH. EMIL *is dark, bespectacled, poorly, carelessly dressed.* ILSE *might be blondly beautiful if she cared to be. She is eager and ambitious, but a trifle bewildered.*)

ANTON

Right in here, please.

ILSE

I hope we're not disturbing Frau Krug.

ANTON

No, no! She's eager to meet you.

EMIL

She's very kind.

ANTON

(*To old* KRUG). Father! Turn that off!

KRUG

But it's that trial in Moscow.

ANTON

Yes, and you can't understand a word of it. Turn it off!

KRUG

(*With dejected resignation*). Oh, very well. (*He does so.*)

ANTON

This is my father. (ILSE *and* EMIL *bow and murmur: "Herr Krug—How do you do?"*) Two of my students—Ilse Hinrich and Emil Loibner. (KRUG *mumbles a churlish greeting and ambles up to the window seat, whereon he sits to read his paper.*) My wife will be here in a minute. I have one more patient to see before we can begin our work. A dreadful woman! She came all the way from—where is it?—Pennsylvania, to learn about the more elementary facts of life. She's married too. (*He laughs.*) What sort of husbands do you suppose they have in Pennsylvania that their wives must come all the way to Vienna to learn the facts? (EMIL *and* ISLE *laugh obediently at the Professor's little joke.*) Now when my wife comes in I want you both to be very charming—rather than scientific. Do you understand that?

EMIL

You don't need to tell us that, Herr Professor.

ANTON

Of course not. You're already a good psychiatrist. And you too, Ilse.

ILSE

Oh, I don't know anything yet.

ANTON

You stick at it for two or three years and you'll know everything—as Emil does. (*He slaps* EMIL'S *shoulder and goes out at the left. Ill at ease,* ILSE *sits down on the edge of the couch.* EMIL *takes up a defensive position before the fireplace.*)

ILSE

What shall we say to her?

EMIL

Well, I imagine we should flatter her. That's the right thing to do.

ILSE

I know—but about what?

EMIL

You ought to know. You're a woman.

KRUG

(*Unexpectedly*). Tell her you admire this room.

ILSE

Oh!
(*They are both startled, having forgotten* KRUG.)

KRUG

She likes to be praised about all this—decoration. (*With a none too approving sweep of the hand.*)

EMIL

Is it—is the decoration her work?

KRUG

Every bit of it. She stood over the carpenters and painters and told them what to do.

ILSE

It's tre*men*dously effective!

KRUG

Maybe. (*He rises and crosses toward* ILSE.) But as for me—it's—I don't know—I don't *like* it! It just isn't natural. . . . Do you know what she said when she was having it done? She said: "We won't have one thing in this house to look as if there ever was a past. We must believe we know nothing of what went on in the world before 1920. We are beginning new," she said. Crazy notions! (*He chuckles.*) But all the same, she's smart. She can tell you young people some things that are good for you to know. And what's more, she *will* tell you if you ask her the right . . .
(ERNEST *comes out of* ELENA'S *room, carrying his empty basket.*)

ERNEST

Well, the laundry added up perfectly.

KRUG

Good! I need a clean shirt. (*Together.*)

ILSE

(*In an undertone to* EMIL). I still don't know what to say to her. (*Together.*)

EMIL

Sh!

ERNEST

And if I hear any more about that certain affair I'll let you know.

KRUG

Oh, please do, Ernest, because if there is a rumpus, they won't let the papers print anything about it. Do you think there will be a rumpus?

ERNEST

(*Knowingly*). Unless I miss my guess, there'll be a good one. . . .

KRUG

Oh, I hope so.

ERNEST

Believe me, they're eager to have Frau Krug there.
(KATHIE *comes out of* ELENA'S *room.*)

KRUG

Oh, I can believe that.

KATHIE

Come on now—we're through with you. (*She crosses to the right.*)

ERNEST

Yes, my dear.

ILSE

(*To* EMIL). What was that about Frau Krug?
(EMIL *cautions her to silence.*)

KRUG

Good afternoon, Ernest.

ERNEST

Good afternoon, Herr Krug. (*He goes out at the right, followed by* KATHIE.)

KRUG

Herr Krug! (*He chuckles as he turns back to the students.*) He and I used to go to school together, and now he calls me "Herr" Krug. That's because I'm the father of my son. As if I deserved the credit. (*He comes close to* ILSE.) Do you want to know something?

ILSE

About Frau Krug?

KRUG

(*Paying no attention to her question*). I never saw what was in my boy. Neither did his mother. We wanted him to follow my trade, shoe-making. But he had big ideas. He had to be a surgeon *and* a revolutionist. Even when he was wearing short pants he was telling us that science was going to cure every one of everything. He was the wildest talker.

EMIL

Because he knew the truth.

KRUG

Well—he'd have been better off if he'd kept his mouth closed. They didn't like to be talked about the way he talked. They punished him. . . .

ILSE

Who were they?

EMIL

The Habsburgs!

ILSE

Oh!

KRUG

Yes—that's who it was. They were smart, too. Whenever things became too hot for 'em here at home they'd start another war, and send all the worst of the trouble makers into the front line. They did that with him. They put him to work patching up all the soldiers they'd broken there in Gorizia

—patching 'em up so that they could send 'em out to be broken again. But do you know what he said about it? He said it was murder they were doing—that the enemy were our comrades. Comrades! The Italians! And on top of all that, every soldier that was sent to him was marked unfit for further military service. He told 'em all to go home. But *they* soon put a stop to that. They took away his commission from him, and made him a laborer in their stone quarries; and that's why he could never be a surgeon again. They crushed his hands with their stones!

ILSE

How *hor*rible!

EMIL

(*Fervently*). That's one of the crimes that we must never forget!

KRUG

Oh, it didn't upset him. He said, "If I can't use my hands to chop people to pieces, I can still use *this*." (*He taps his head.*) And he did. And now they don't put him in prison for what he says. They *pay* him! Why—they sent for my boy all the way from America, and he went across the ocean to tell those Americans how to live. *They* didn't know. And when he came back he brought me a present—that wireless machine, there. Did you ever see as fine a one as that? (*He gazes lovingly at the radio.*) It's mine—but they won't let me play it.

(ELENA *comes in, now wearing a graceful tea-gown.*)

ILSE

Oh—that's too bad!

(EMIL *signals to* ILSE *to behold* FRAU KRUG.)

EMIL

(*Bowing*). Frau Krug!

ELENA

(*Shaking hands with* ILSE, *who rises*). How do you do?

ILSE

(*Timorously*). How do you do, Frau Krug?

ELENA

Father—aren't you going to introduce us?

KRUG

I don't know their names. They're students. (*He goes over to the right and sits down with his pipe and his newspaper.*)

ELENA

(*To* EMIL). I'm afraid I've kept you waiting.

EMIL

(*Stiffly*). Oh, no. We are the intruders. The Herr Professor's with a patient.

KRUG

It's a lady who came all the way from Pennsylvania with complaints.

EMIL

If I may say so, Frau Krug . . . I . . . well —I . . . (*There is an awkward pause.*)

ELENA

Why, my dear boy—of course you may say anything.

EMIL

Well, I . . . it was nothing. . . .

ELENA

Oh, come—it must have been something. You're embarrassed.

EMIL

(*With a sheepish laugh*). I'm afraid so.

KRUG

He was going to say that he doesn't believe *you* have any complaints, like that woman out there. . . .

EMIL

I was going to say nothing of the kind! It was something entirely different—a—a compliment——

ELENA

Oh—but that would have been the highest compliment of all!

ILSE

(*Nervously*). I think, Frau Krug—I think that Emil meant to say that we both admire the imaginativeness of this room.

ELENA

Oh! I should have liked that too. . . . Now—do sit down and tell me how you are getting on with your studies. (*They all sit.*)

ILSE

I'm afraid I don't know very much yet. You see I'm new. Emil is the Professor's favorite.

ELENA

Really! What does the Professor teach you?

ILSE

Everything!

ELENA

Oh?

ILSE

I mean, everything that's worth knowing.

ELENA

For example?

ILSE

(*Lamely*). Well—he makes us understand that if you'll only *think* right, you'll *live* right. I mean—if you can make what's in your subconscious come to the surface—then you'll know what it is—and you'll know what to do about it.

EMIL

(*Unable longer to curb his eloquence*). No, no! It's infinitely more than that. He's gone far beyond psychoanalysis. He teaches us the gospel of the better life—the life that is seen through the eyes of the biologist's microscope and in the changing colors of the chemist's test tube. He teaches us that the forward progress of man must be regulated by the statistician's inexorable curve, and not by the encyclicals of priests or the ukases of kings. He teaches us to banish from the world all false fear of God—to know Him, and recognize Him only as a measurable force in cosmic technology. He teaches us to look into ourselves—our bodies, our minds—and not to the vague hills of mysticism, for the knowledge that will set us free.

ELENA

Well—that *does* cover about everything, doesn't it? (*She treats* EMIL *to a sympathetic smile.*) And when you have absorbed all the knowledge there is, what will you do with it?

EMIL

I shall try to carry it to others—to share it with all mankind.

ELENA

I see. You're to be another Paul.

EMIL

Another Paul?

ELENA

Yes—Paul! The Apostle!

EMIL

Oh—yes.

ELENA

(*To* ILSE). And how about you?

ILSE

I suppose there'll be plenty of work for all of us.

EMIL

(*Rising*). You see, Madam—the world is very young.

ELENA

Very *young?*

EMIL

Why—hardly more than ten years ago we were living under conditions of mediæval-ism.

ELENA

Ten years!

EMIL

When I look at the decaying relics of the old order, the gaunt, empty palace of the Habsburgs, and the silly monuments they erected to their own glory—I bless the war and the revolution that delivered us from the tyranny of ignorance.

ELENA

And what do you say when you look at me?

ILSE

At *you,* Frau Krug? What possible connection has that . . .

ELENA

I'm one of the relics of the middle ages, of ten years ago.

(ANTON *comes in from the left.*)

EMIL

You are the wife of the most enlightened scientist in Austria.

ANTON

Emil! I overheard that last remark.

EMIL

Yes, sir.

ANTON

I'm afraid you must have misunderstood me. I wanted you to flatter her, not me. (*He goes to the bookcase at the back.*)

ELENA

They've been charming, both of them.

ANTON

(*Casually looking for a book*). I'm glad to hear it. . . . The one thing these students have difficulty in developing is the correct bedside manner. . . . Is that copy of *Sons and Lovers* here?

ELENA

I think it's there—somewhere.

ANTON

I want to give it to that Pennsylanvia woman. It might help her. . . . Ah—here it is.

ELENA

What's the trouble with her?

ANTON

The usual one—another frustration! For twenty years she's been measuring her poor husband in terms of her first love—the one that got away. . . .

ELENA

And what are you prescribing, besides that book?

ANTON

She must find her first lover, and have a good look at him as he is now. He's a manufacturer of dental supplies. I think she'll be cured. . . . (*He smiles at* ELENA *and goes out at the left.*)

ELENA

I hope he does help her. It must be awful to be always unsatisfied, and puzzled. . . .

EMIL

(*With complete conviction*). He'll cure her —if she has the capacity to understand.

ELENA

You worship him, don't you?

EMIL

All youth must worship him. He is leading us from the darkness—into the light.

ELENA

Do you hear that, father? Your son is a god.

KRUG

Yes—that's what they say.

ILSE

Frau Krug . . .

ELENA

Yes, dear.

ILSE

(*Hesitantly*). There's a question I'd like to ask. You see—the point is that we, Emil and I—we know only the present, the age of reason since the Revolution. You know something of the past.

EMIL

(*Reproving her quietly*). Ilse . . .

ELENA

That's quite all right. Why shouldn't I know the past? I'm old enough to be your mother. (*They both protest.*) Well, practically. . . . Now, come—what was the question that you want to ask?

KRUG

She wants you to tell her what you know of the Habsburgs.

EMIL

Frau Krug—I swear that we pay no attention to the scandalous gossip that evil, malicious bourgeois . . .

ELENA

(*Cutting in*). Oh, but you should. You want to be psychoanalysts, don't you?

ILSE

Well . . .

EMIL

Of course, we do!

ELENA

Then there's every reason for you to do research work.

EMIL

Research work is to be done in the laboratory—not in the drawing-room.

ELENA

My dear boy—when you have been fully inoculated with the germ of scientific culture you will realize that all the world is your laboratory—and all the men and women in it merely guinea-pigs. I'm one of them—and I'm here to be explored. As a matter of fact, I'm a peculiarly interesting specimen—ask my husband if I'm not. He'll tell you that most of his vast knowledge of human frailty comes from observation of me. (*To* ILSE.) Now, please! Just what did you want to know?

ILSE

It would be helpful to know how you see all the changes—whether you think we are advanced, for all our knowledge, or . . .

ELENA

Aren't you content to take my husband's word for it that the world has improved?

EMIL

I ask for no other assurance. I need none.

ELENA

(*To* EMIL). I know. But—(*To* ILSE.)—I gather that you're not so sure.

ILSE

(*Tremulous*). The trouble is—I'm not sure of my*self*.

ELENA

Oh?

ILSE

I—I had an experience.

ELENA

Ah! I see! (*She draws her chair closer to* ILSE. KRUG, *who has been listening, draws his a bit nearer.*) Tell me about it.

ILSE

(*Hesitantly*). It was very strange, and terribly disturbing. I've tried to account for my emotional reaction to it, but I can't do it. I was in Nice on my vacation, and I called a taxi. When I was in it, I happened to look in the little mirror, above the driver's seat, and I saw his eyes. He was staring at me, openly, insolently. They were the queerest eyes I've ever seen. I kept looking at them—although I didn't want to. I felt sure I'd seen him before. He was driving frightfully fast—on those narrow roads that run along the brinks of cliffs—crazily. That wasn't where I wanted to go at all, but I'd forgotten about that. I thought the cab would go over the edge any minute. Finally, I screamed out to him to stop—but I was so terrified that I forgot to say it in French. I spoke German. And with that he did stop, and stepped from his seat in the front and climbed into the inside of the taxi and sat down beside me. And he said, "I thought so! There was something about your eyelids that identified you as a Viennese. I am Viennese too. In fact, *I'm one of those who imparted to Vienna its now faded glory.*" Then he put his arms around me and gave me a long kiss.

KRUG

(*Softly*). Well—well——

ELENA

(*Slowly*). A taxi-driver.

ILSE

He kissed me so that I couldn't seem to utter a word of protest. I tried to tell myself that he was nothing more than an emotional extravert—but that didn't seem to help me. Then he said: "Permit me to introduce myself: I am the Archduke Rudolf Maximillian von Habsburg."

ELENA

(*Nodding*). Yes! (KRUG *laughs boisterously.* ELENA *rises.*) Father!
(KRUG *stifles his mirth.*)

EMIL

I don't believe it. It was probably some impostor.

ILSE

No. I asked them at the hotel when I got back. They told me he was well known in Nice.

KRUG

How long was it be*fore* you got back?

ILSE

Oh, he took me right back. . . . You see, he'd stopped his cab in the middle of the road, blocking traffic, and some policemen came along, so he had to remember he was a taxi-driver. . . . (*A little sadly.*)

KRUG

Oh, dear.

EMIL

(*To* ILSE, *in an undertone*). You've said about enough!

ELENA

What did he look like?

ILSE

He looked as if he'd stepped right out of one of those portraits in the old palace.

ELENA

Yes! I know. Those full, rich lips.

ILSE

(*In ardent agreement*). Yes! That's why I thought I'd seen him before. . . . And when I wanted to pay him the fare, he waved it away, and said, "Nonsense, my dear—on this ride, you have been my guest!"

KRUG

I should say you had. (*He laughs.*) Just like him! Isn't it, Elena? Just exactly like all of them.

EMIL

(*Vehemently*). If I had been there, I should have punched his nose.

ELENA

No—I don't think you would have

ILSE

Indeed, you wouldn't! It's all very well for you to talk—but if you'd seen him as I did, you wouldn't have been able to say a word except, "Yes, Your Imperial Highness!"

ELENA

(*To* ILSE). I gather that you considered the experience not entirely disagreeable.

ILSE

I can't decide what I think about it.

ELENA

Have you consulted Doctor Krug?

ILSE

I haven't had the courage to confess to him how weak I was.

KRUG

You don't have to consult him. . . . Elena—you know more about these things than Anton ever will, with all his experiments. Tell them about that time when the old Emperor caught you and Rudolf Maximillian, posing on the fountain at Schönbrunn, both naked as the day you were born.

ILSE

(*Gasping*). Oh—then you *knew* him!

KRUG

Knew him! (*He can't contain his merriment.*)

ILSE

Oh—then I've said something awful.

EMIL

Yes!

ELENA

No, my dear. It wasn't awful at all. I enjoyed every word of it.
(ANTON *has come in.*)

ELENA

Anton, you should have stayed away for another half hour. I was just about to give your students a lecture.

ANTON

On what subject?

ELENA

On the past.

ANTON

Whose?

ELENA

Mine.

ANTON

Then don't let me interrupt. Proceed with it, at once. It's very exciting.

ELENA

No, it isn't. It's very dull. But . . . (*To* ILSE.) . . . you were right about one thing—it is instructive. And you also (*To* EMIL.) were right, in all those eloquent speeches you made about the better life. Oh, Anton, you'd have been proud of him.

ANTON

(*Smiling*). Go on with your own lecture.

ELENA

(*To the students*). It is a better life—and I can say that with authority. I was one of the many evils of the old régime—I and that weird taxi-driver who entertained you in his cab.

ANTON

What *is* all this?

ELENA

She had an encounter with Rudolf.

ANTON

(*Startled*). Here in Vienna?

ELENA

No—in Nice.

ANTON

(*Relieved*). Oh!

ELENA

(*To* ILSE). You must tell him all about it. He'll analyze your emotional reactions, as he analyzed mine. I needed his treatment —(*She looks at* ANTON; *there is an exchange of understanding between them.*)—a great deal of it. He cured me—and I delivered myself, body and mind, to the new god. (*She puts her hand on* ANTON'*s shoulder.*) You need have no doubts as to the legitimacy of that god. You can believe in him, you can worship him, you can follow him to the last statistic!

EMIL

(*Fervently*). Your words are inspiring, Madam!

ELENA

I intended them to be.

ANTON

Well! All this is elevating our studies to an alarmingly high plane. (KATHIE *enters from the right, carrying a silver plate on which are several cards.*) However, if you neophytes will step into my office, we'll celebrate high mass.

KATHIE

Some callers, ma'am.

KRUG

(*Rising*). Who? Who *is* it?

ELENA

Just a minute, Kathie. Good-bye, Ilse, and don't worry about those emotions. They're not uncommon.

(*Together.*)

ILSE

I know—that's what worries me. (KRUG *has gone to* KATHIE *to have a look at the cards on the plate.*)

ELENA

Good-bye, Emil.

EMIL

You remember my name!

ELENA

Yes, that's one good result of my education under the Habsburgs.

KRUG

(*Excitedly*). Elena!

ELENA

(*Not stopping*). I was trained to remember. (*She beams upon* EMIL.)

KRUG

Elena! It's the Count and Countess Von Stainz.

ELENA

(*Startled*). Von Stainz? (*She leaves* EMIL *abruptly to look at the cards.*)

KRUG

And Frau Lucher, the old lady herself—and that Povoromo, that guide . . .

ELENA

(*To* KATHIE). They're *here?*

KATHIE

Yes, ma'am.

KRUG

Certainly they're here, and I know why.

KATHIE

They're downstairs in the hall—they beg to see you.

ANTON

(*To the students*). Will you wait in the office? I'll be with you in a minute.
(ILSE *and* EMIL *go out at the left.*)

KRUG

I can tell you *exactly* what they're after!

ANTON

What do they want?

KRUG

They want her to go to that party at Lucher's Hotel!

ANTON

Party! What party?

KRUG

They're having a big celebration! There's going to be a rumpus! (*He is in a high state of glee at this unexpected development, but no one is paying any attention to him.*)

ELENA

(*To* ANTON). It's the hundredth anniversary of the birth of that noble monarch, Franz Josef the First. Frau Lucher thought that it should be fittingly observed.

KRUG

Yes, and she's bribed the police!

ANTON

Well—what about it?

KRUG

They want Elena to go, that's what about it!

ANTON

Do you want to go, Elena?

ELENA

Anton!

ANTON

What?

ELENA

I don't want to see these people.

ANTON

Why not? They're friends of yours, aren't they?

ELENA

They were, a long time ago.

ANTON

Well, then—in that case—I can't see why . . . (*He sees* KATHIE.) Wait in the hall, Kathie.

KATHIE

Yes, Herr Doctor. (*She goes out at the right and shuts the door.*)

KRUG

Why do you want her to wait in the hall?

ANTON

If they're old friends of yours, I can't see any reason why you should refuse them. . . . Unless . . .

ELENA

Unless what?

ANTON

Unless there might be disagreeable associations.

ELENA

(*With surprising vehemence*). Of course there are disagreeable associations! The Count and Countess Von Stainz are dreadful people. They were two of the worst of the court toadies.

ANTON

But what about this Povoromo? He's a harmless and rather pathetic professional guide. There's nothing upsetting about . . .

KRUG

But don't you remember—he was one of the cronies of the Archduke. . . .

ANTON

And Frau Lucher—what's wrong with her?

ELENA

I hate her! I hate the sight of her hotel!

ANTON

Why? . . . Because it was the scene of so many of your youthful indiscretions with him!

KRUG

Are you talking about Rudolf Maximillian?

ANTON

That damned name again! (*He crosses to the door at the left.*) Now please, Elena—if you don't want to see them, then don't see them. But don't ask me what to do. I have those students on my hands. I'm very busy. (*He goes out.*)

KRUG

Did you hear what he said about that damned name? He can't seem to get over it.

(ELENA *crosses to the right.*)

ELENA

Kathie.

KATHIE

Yes, ma'am.

ELENA

Tell them to come up.

KATHIE

Yes, ma'am.

KRUG

(*Delighted*). That's the way, Elena! (*He sits down and makes himself entirely comfortable.*) It'll do you good to talk to 'em. I often think you don't see half enough of your old friends.

ELENA

Go to your room, Father.

KRUG

Why?

ELENA

Because I want you to.

KRUG

But I'd like to have a look at them.

ELENA

Go on! Please.

KRUG

(*Going*). Oh, dear! They never let me see anything interesting that goes on in this house. . . . (*He has shuffled out at the upper left.*)

(KATHIE *returns, holding open the door.*)

KATHIE

In here, please.

(FRAU LUCHER *comes in. She is a formidable old party, absurdly dressed in ancient clothes, but imposing. Her voice is gruff, her expression unchangeably hostile, her manner towards all arrogant and despotic. Behind her come the* COUNT *and* COUNTESS VON STAINZ *and* POFFY. *The* COUNT *is about fifty-five. On his gray countenance are the ravages of time, disappointment, and drink. His courtliness, however, is unimpaired. The* COUNTESS, *about fifty, is dowdy and excessively emotional.* POFFY *is a tragic but gallant ex-officer of the Imperial Army, who is now engaged in the great work of guiding American tourists about the Hofburg.*)

ELENA

Tatti! I'm *so* glad . . .

COUNTESS

Elena! My angel! My beautiful little angel! (*She rushes into an embrace.*)

ELENA

(*To the* COUNT, *over the* COUNTESS'S *shoulder*). Hello, Franz, how are you?

COUNT

Not very well, thank you.
(POFFY *and* LUCHER *have hung back, as though dubious of the quality of their reception.*)

ELENA

I'm so sorry. Hello, Poffy.

POFFY

(*Bowing*). Elena!

ELENA

Good afternoon, Frau Lucher.

LUCHER

Good afternoon, Frau Krug.

COUNTESS

But, my *darling!* Ten years have passed and you are not one day older. Look at her, Franz!

COUNT

I have been looking at her.

LUCHER

Would you mind if I sat down? (*She sits, heavily, on a chair at the left.*)

ELENA

No. Everybody sit down.

LUCHER

My feet hurt.

COUNTESS

I can't take my eyes off you, my little angel. You're lovely! I'm about to sob!

ELENA

Now don't be embarrassing, Tatti.

LUCHER

Let her sob if it'll make her any happier.

COUNT

Don't mind our gaping at you, Elena. It makes us think that maybe we haven't grown old, either.

ELENA

Where have you been?

COUNTESS

In a ghastly London suburb . . .

COUNT

Upper Tooting, if you must know.

COUNTESS

Breathing in English fog, eating English food . . .

COUNT

And drinking English beer.

LUCHER

That isn't beer!

COUNT

Which reminds me, Elena—my throat is parched.

COUNTESS

Franz!

COUNT

Would it be causing you too much trouble if I . . .

LUCHER

He's asking for a drink.
(ELENA *goes up to a table on which are a decanter and some glasses.*)

ELENA

I have some port here—would port do?

COUNT

Admirably!

COUNTESS

I told you you were not to touch a drop!

COUNT

We've had a long train journey and I simply must wash the cinders from my gullet.

COUNTESS

Elena, don't give it to him!

ELENA

Oh, a little port can't hurt him, Tatti. (*She hands him the glass.*)

COUNT

Of course not. Your health, my dear.

LUCHER

Do you mind if I smoke?

ELENA

No, have a cigarette.
(LUCHER *has opened her enormous black handbag and extracted therefrom a large silver cigar-case.*)

LUCHER

You needn't bother. (*She takes out a cigar, and bites off the end.*)

ELENA

Still smoking the same brand?

LUCHER

No, those Cubans no longer send the cream of the crop to Vienna.
(POFFY *steps forward to light the cigar.*)

COUNTESS

There is nothing the same here. After ten years of exile—to find this. Oh, Elena—if you only *knew* what we've been through. *I've* been a seamstress, my darling. A *seamstress!* Making sensible underwear for English frumps. We've gone without lunch for three months in order to save enough to be here. And I give you my word, when we arrived here this morning, and drove through the streets, we wept—we literally *wept*—to see that our beloved Vienna is undergoing its last, gruesome agonies.

ELENA

Those aren't death agonies that you see, Tatti. They're the throes of childbirth. A new life is being created.

COUNTESS

You may well say that. (*She looks about the room.*) The new life seems to have done well for you.

ELENA

Yes, it has! (*There is, perhaps, a suggestion of defiance in this.*)

COUNT

(*Tactfully*). And by the way—I hope we're to be presented to your husband.

ELENA

I'm afraid he's rather busy just now.

COUNTESS

What's he like, this doctor of yours?

ELENA

Well—he's brilliant, and charming, and kind . . .

POFFY

And famous! When I'm guiding American tourists past here, I point with pride—"Residence of the eminent Dr. Krug"—and they're thrilled.

ELENA

(*Smiling*). Especially the women.

POFFY

Ah, yes!

LUCHER

Isn't it about time to come to the main subject? That is—if you all feel that there have been enough polite preliminaries.

ELENA

There's no great hurry.

POFFY

By all means! Proceed, Lucher!

LUCHER

Well—the main subject is this, in so many words: they want you to change your mind about attending the party this evening. They begged me to come with them, and talk with you, on the supposition that I can terrorize any one into doing anything I ask. Strictly between ourselves, I don't think you'll be missing much if you don't come. By the looks of this gathering, it won't be very . . .

COUNTESS

If that's what you think, then why are you giving this party?

COUNT

Why have you invited us?

LUCHER

Even I have my sentimental moments, Countess. When I realized that this was the hundredth anniversary, I thought that we might have a revival of the old insanity, for one evening, at my expense. I thought there might be a bit of amusement. However, I've decided that I was over-optimistic . . . so now you know how I feel about all this, Frau Krug, and perhaps you'll be good enough to tell them how *you* feel, and get it over with.

COUNT

You really can't disappoint us, Elena. We've looked forward so to this, and to having you there, laughing, in the way you always laughed.

ELENA

But that's just it, Franz. I couldn't laugh. I'd probably weep.

COUNTESS

Splendid! We'll all weep together, and have a glorious time!

LUCHER

And when you've become sufficiently gloomy, you'll start throwing bottles through windows. I know!

ELENA

Who's to be here?

COUNT

Well—old General Hoetzler is expected . . .

ELENA

Is he?

COUNT

Do you know what he's doing now? He's a train announcer in the railway station at Erfurt.

ELENA

The poor old dear.

COUNTESS

And Talisz is coming. He's a bookkeeper, somewhere or other. And then the two Koeppkes—I forget what they do.

LUCHER

They run a lodging house in Zermatt—and I've *heard* . . .

ALL

Yes?

LUCHER

Well—never mind.

POFFY

And the beautiful Gisella Von Krett. She's here already.

ELENA

Gisella!

POFFY

She's a governess with a Sicilian family in Palermo.

ELENA

And who else? Is there any one else?

POFFY

Well—of course there were a good many who wanted to come but they were—lacking in funds.

COUNT

Oh, but more will turn up at the last minute to help us consume Lucher's champagne. It's sure to be the jolliest gathering.

LUCHER

Did I say that champagne would be served?

COUNT

I have never attended a party at the Hotel Lucher without champagne.

POFFY

You're thinking of the days when we paid—and well—for our drinks.

ELENA

Oh, I think Frau Lucher won't be stingy with her champagne. Will you?

COUNT

That's right, Elena. You were the only one who could ever order her about. You and Rudolf. (LUCHER *bursts out laughing.*) What in God's name are you roaring at?

LUCHER

I was just thinking of something. (*She is still emitting gusty, gaseous roars of laughter.*)

POFFY

(*To* ELENA). I gather it was something mildly amusing.

LUCHER

Oh, you remember it, Poffy—the night that Rudolf gave her the diamond necklace. You were there.

POFFY

I was indeed.

LUCHER

He came stalking into my café at two o'clock in the morning—cursing at me—cursing at Strup—presenting medals to the bus-boys. He said he had to have a magnum of 1812, a basket of pomegranates, and a diamond necklace for Fräulein Vervesz—*at once!*—or he'd break every bone in my old body. I had to rout Barnowsky the jeweler out of bed to get the diamonds.

COUNT

(*Laughing*). Served him right, the old bandit.

LUCHER

(*To* ELENA). And when I gave His Imperial Highness the necklace, he never said so much as a "Thank you." He merely snatched it, and then threw it into your lap.

ELENA

(*To* LUCHER). No, no! That wasn't what he did. He didn't give me the necklace until later, when we were upstairs. He first took hold of my hand and said, "Isn't it about time for a dance?" Then he waltzed me out of the room, and on the way out we bumped into you.
(ANTON *comes in.*)

LUCHER

But I burned his neck with my cigar. (*They all laugh—but their mirth congeals when they see* ANTON. *The* COUNT *and* POFFY *rise.*)

ELENA

Anton, are you finished with the students already?

ANTON

Yes, I dismissed them. I was anxious to meet your friends.

ELENA

(*Surprised*). Oh. . . . This is my husband.

ANTON

How do you do, Frau Lucher?

ELENA

The Count and Countess Von Stainz—Herr Povoromo. (*There are murmured salutations.*)

ANTON

Yes. I know Herr Povoromo.

COUNT

Herr Professor Doctor—permit me to felicitate you upon your wife. She is quite the most gracious, the most sympathetic and the loveliest of the ladies.

ANTON

(*Bowing*). I am inclined to agree with you.

COUNTESS

Herr Professor—we came to beg Elena, to plead with her, to be with us this evening.

COUNT

It isn't so much a matter of pleading—though we'll do that, too, heaven knows. But we do want to assure her what a delightful occasion . . .

LUCHER

(*Flatly*). The fact is that, without Frau Krug, the party will be a disaster.

ANTON

(*Amiably*). Well—in that case—I hope she'll go.

COUNTESS

There, Elena, that settles it! Your husband approves.

LUCHER

Perhaps the Herr Professor Doctor will also attend?

ANTON

Oh, that's very kind of you, but I really couldn't. I'm afraid I shouldn't quite belong.

ELENA

I've been afraid I shouldn't belong either. But now I'm beginning to think that it might be great fun.

COUNT

Good for you, Elena!

COUNTESS

And good for you, Herr Doctor! You are worthy of her!

COUNT

You're going to make this occasion a memorable one.

LUCHER

(*With an air of finality*). Well, now that that's settled, we can go.

POFFY

(*Stepping forward, hesitantly*). Just one minute, Elena.

ELENA

Yes, Poffy?

POFFY

Elena—I—think I know why you're changing your mind.

ELENA

Why?

POFFY

Because you realize this celebration will be nothing more than a gathering of broken-down old outcasts, like myself—with no one to give us animation, no one to give us the illusion of youth . . but . . . I'm afraid that it may not be quite what you expect.

LUCHER

What are you *talking* about?

POFFY

(*Deliberately*). I received a message this afternoon.

ELENA

Yes? (*As though she had expected this.*)

POFFY

I was instructed to say nothing about it to any one. But I think you should know about it before you go to that party; and you too should know, Herr Professor . . . If I might have a word with you in private . . .

COUNTESS

In private? What on earth . . .

POFFY

You'll forgive me . . .

COUNT

(*Stepping toward* POFFY). Rudolf?

ELENA

He's to be here?

LUCHER

No!

POFFY

He left Nice yesterday on his way to Vienna.

COUNTESS

Rudolf!

COUNT

(*Exultantly*). I can't believe it! It's too good to . . .

ANTON

Will they allow him to cross the border?

LUCHER

(*Emphatically*). No! They'll never let him in after all the things he's said and done. The officials are so stupid that the smaller fry can sneak past them, begging your pardon, Count and Countess, but they're not so stupid as to allow the most violent member of the Habsburg faction to get back into Austria.

POFFY

Regardless of all that, Elena—I thought you should know. I ask your pardon, Herr Professor, for having mentioned the subject.

ANTON

Not at all. There's nothing I can say. It's for Elena to decide.

ELENA

I'm not going.

COUNTESS

But, my little angel—what Lucher said is true. He couldn't possibly come into the country . . .

ELENA

I'm not going!

COUNT

You can't change your mind, Elena. We need you. You've always made things go. Have you forgotten those times when . . .

ELENA

Yes. I have forgotten. And my dear old friends, I advise you to forget, too.

COUNTESS

You're asking a great deal of people who have nothing but memories to live on.

ELENA

That's just it! You're trying to live on something that doesn't exist. That's why you're all so degraded and spent. That's why you have to drug yourselves with such infantile pretenses as this reunion. Wallowing in sentiment! Weeping into your beer!

COUNTESS

I never hope to hear a more heartless, brutal statement—and from you, Elena, of all people.

ELENA

I know it's brutal—and I feel miserable for having said it, if that's any consolation to you. But it's all true, every word of it. You know it is.

LUCHER

Of course it's true! I only wish you'd said it all to me before I'd let myself in for this nonsense.

COUNTESS

It would have been kinder to have told your servant to deny us admission. . . .

ELENA

Yes.

COUNTESS

To have slammed the door in our faces.

ELENA

You're right, Tatti.

COUNT

(*To* POFFY). Why didn't you have sense enough to obey orders and keep that information to yourself?

ELENA

(*Interrupting*). No, don't blame him. It was very good of you to warn me, Poffy. But the warning didn't make the slightest difference. You can see why—and so can you, Lucher. You've been in Vienna all through this. You know how changed everything is.

POFFY

I know, I know, my dear Elena. We've put you in a horribly unfair position.

COUNTESS

We're not doing that! It's not *our* fault that she's turned against her own kind.

POFFY

It's only proof of her good sense.

COUNT

Yes—and look at the results of her good sense! And then look at us, who wouldn't accept the inevitable.

COUNTESS

It's to our everlasting credit that we didn't. (*She goes over to the* COUNT, *and takes his arm.*)

LUCHER

(*Rising laboriously*). I'm not enjoying this discussion. . . . Come on. . . . I must arrange about the flowers for the party. I'm getting them second-hand from Gruen the undertaker. . . . Good-bye, Frau Krug. Stop in at the hotel some time for a cup of coffee. (*She goes out at the right.*)

COUNTESS

Good-bye, Elena. I doubt very much that we shall see you again. (*She goes out.*)

COUNT

(*With attempted courtesy*). You see—we start the homeward journey to England tomorrow.

ELENA

Good-bye, Franz.

COUNT

Herr Professor Doctor. (*He bows and goes.*)

POFFY

I'm sorry, Elena—very sorry. . . .

ELENA

Good-bye, Poffy. Come to see us again soon. Perhaps my husband can do . . .

POFFY

My duties as professional guide occupy much of my time—but perhaps I'll find a brief opportunity. Good-bye, Herr Doctor. Good-bye, Elena. (*He kisses her hand and goes. For a few moments,* ELENA *stares angrily at the door through which they have gone.*)

ANTON

You did not appear to best advantage in that encounter.

ELENA

(*Too heatedly*). What could I have said or done to make those imbeciles understand? They think I could sit there, and joke with them, and drink with them, as though nothing had happened.

ANTON

(*Gently*). You said that it might be great fun.

ELENA

Fun! Carousing with the Countess Von Stainz? And there'll be others at the party even worse than she is.

ANTON

When I came into this room, you were laughing with them. You were just about to accept their invitation.

ELENA

Why did you come in here at all, if you were so colossally busy? Why didn't you let me get rid of them by myself?

ANTON

I came to the conclusion that you should go to that party.

ELENA

What?

ANTON

There seems to me no reason why you shouldn't. . . .

ELENA

(*Facing him*). Are you going to carry on the attack?

ANTON

Attack against what?

ELENA

Against my peace of mind!

ANTON

I thought so.

ELENA

Oh! I suppose you consider that it will be good for me to go there and feel wretched and out of place, merely to assure myself that I'm right. Do I have to go there for that?

ANTON

Are you entirely sure that you are right?

ELENA

You can stand there and ask me that?

ANTON

If you take my advice, Elena, you'll go. You know, you may not be quite the calm, superior being that you fancy yourself.

ELENA

(*Interrupting*). Are you prescribing for me, as though I were . . .

ANTON

Yes, that's exactly what I'm doing. The tender spot has been uncovered. Now we can take measures to cure it. . . . Elena, as your family physician, as well as your husband, I order you to go to Lucher's tonight, and do the inane things you used to do, and that you still secretly think were gloriously romantic.

ELENA

Anton—I know you've been subjecting me to treatment ever since we were married. But you've at least been subtle about it. Now your methods are a little too obvious to be effective.

ANTON

I've revised my methods because I learned something myself when I saw you with your old friends. You deliver all this fine talk about the old days and the new—the woman who was reborn after the revolution. And now some pitiable spectres appear to you and you can't bear to face them.

ELENA

I can face anything, including your vast overpowering intellect.

ANTON

There are some things you can't face, my darling, because you can't see them. You're still in a state of emotional bondage. You're tied to those people by a cord that's strong even though it's invisible. You must cut that cord—and here's the chance to do it.

ELENA

When I require your professional services I shall make an appointment and come to your office.

ANTON

The appointment is now! (*They face each other through a moment of angry silence. Then* ELENA *goes to him.*)

ELENA

Oh, Anton—this is so silly.

ANTON

No, it isn't silly. (*They sit down together on the end of the couch.*)

ELENA

Two grown-up people, shouting at each other . . .

ANTON

Sometimes we have to shout. . . . Elena—there's never been a complete understanding between us. There's been a ghost in our house, an arrogant ghost, blocking the fulfillment of our life together. A thousand different times when I thought that at last we'd achieved the thing that we both want, he has stepped into the room, and laughed at me.
(ELENA *glances involuntarily towards the door at the right.*)

ELENA

The bearer of that damned name!

ANTON

Yes. . . . When I heard he might be there tonight it was something of a shock. . . . But then I thought of the advice I had given to other patients of mine. . . . You've seen what ten years have done to the Count and Countess Von Stainz. Well—see what the same years have done to him. . . . Go to that party, have a good look at him, and then come home and admit that I'm right.

ELENA

You're always right, Anton. That's your only fault.

ANTON

(*Laughing*). Yes—I've often worried about that. (*He kisses her hair.*) Now come, my dear, dress yourself up, and try to persuade your old friends that you're still one of them. Sing, dance, flirt—relax! Let yourself go completely! And see what happens.

ELENA

Let myself go. . . . Is that the prescription?

ANTON

Why not?
(*Old* KRUG *bustles in from the upper left.*)

KRUG

Well—I saw them! I had a good look at them from the window—and a more down-at-the-heel lot I never clapped eyes on. Oh, I laughed! I laughed when I thought of the old days when . . .

ANTON

You talk too much. (*He has risen and is going towards the door to his offices.*)

KRUG

Then maybe I can play the wireless?

ANTON

No. (*To* ELENA.) Put on that white dress. You know—the one you got in Paris. You look lovely in that. (*He goes out at the left.*)

KRUG

(*Mystified*). He wants you to dress up. What for? Does he want you to go to the party? (*He comes close to her.*)

ELENA

He's a little mixed up. He has me confused with that last patient of his—the one from Pennsylvania.

KRUG

I don't understand what you mean, Elena. Has anything gone wrong?

ELENA

No, father. Not yet. . . . Why don't you play the wireless?

KRUG

Now?

ELENA

Yes, dear—I want to hear it.

KRUG

Ah, Elena—*you're* my friend! (*He leans over her. She pats his cheek, tenderly. . . . He then turns, happily, goes up to the radio, and switches it on. It is playing "The Dollar Princess Waltz."*)

KRUG

Listen, Elena. It's the band at the Bristol. They always play the old tunes, for a half hour before supper—to give us old-timers an appetite. . . . It's beautiful, isn't it? (*He comes down, towards the right.*)

ELENA

No. (*Nevertheless, she is swaying ever so slightly in time to the music. Old* KRUG *watches her, fascinated. . . . At length she rises, crosses to the door at the left, and knocks.* KRUG *sits down at the right to await developments.*)

ELENA

(*Calling*). Anton!

KRUG

Oh, what do you want *him* for? He'll only make us turn it off.
(ANTON *appears in the doorway.*)

ANTON

What is it?

ELENA

Will you please look in the safe—in my jewel box? There's a necklace there—a diamond necklace.

ANTON

I'll get it. (*He goes out.*)
(*Swaying more perceptibly, exuberantly, to the rhythm of "The Dollar Princess," she crosses to the chair where old* KRUG *is sitting.*)

KRUG

You didn't mean what you said, about the music, did you, Elena? It really *is* beautiful, isn't it?

ELENA

Yes, father. Beautiful. (*She extends her arms. Gleefully, he jumps up. They waltz together.*)

CURTAIN

ACT TWO

THE *scene is a private room upstairs in the Hotel Lucher, a stuffy edifice built in the gaslit 'Eighties. Although redolent of stale plush, which is suggestive to the Anglo-Saxon mind of Victorianism and therefore of dreary propriety, this venerable tavern retains a winked intimation of Viennese caprice. Its somber salons can still sparkle with happy imaginings of frivolities which no longer are—and perhaps never were—but which eternally should be.*

At right, downstage, is a leather swinging door, leading to the pantries and kitchens. Upstage right and left are two more doors. In the center, at the back, double doors open upon a bedroom in which is an enormous, canopied bed. Downstage left, double doors open upon a larger room in which the banquet is to be held.

Above the door at the back, which is two or three steps up from the level of the stage, is hung an oval portrait of the late Emperor Franz Josef I. A PORTER, *on a step-ladder, is arranging laurel festoons about this portrait. Another* PORTER *is holding the ladder.*

At the left is a gilded couch with plum-colored brocade upholstery. By it is a small gilded, marble-topped tabouret. At the right is a round table, also marble-topped, behind which, as though enthroned, sits FRAU LUCHER, *administering orders to a respectful, palpitant group which includes* STRUP, *the aged head-waiter, and* BREDZI, *the band-leader, who is wearing a frogged green coat and is carrying his violin. He has given* LUCHER *the program of selections for the evening and is awaiting her verdict on it. . . . There are also present two lesser* WAITERS *and two quivering* BUS-BOYS. *A* BELL-BOY *is posted in the doorway at the left. . . . There are other chairs against the walls and perhaps a few potted palms. From the left, offstage, the small orchestra is playing a brisk march, as vigorously as its meager equipment and talents will allow.*

LUCHER

(*To* BREDZI). There is too much of the Mozart. . . .

BREDZI

No doubt, Frau Lucher.

LUCHER

No doubt whatever. They will want waltzes, appassionata, until they get drunk, and then they will want more waltzes. Sentimental ninnies! (*She hands the program back to* BREDZI.) They will want to weep on each others' shoulders. You understand?

BREDZI

Perfectly, ma'am.

LUCHER

Accompaniment for sobs—that's all that's expected of you. (*Her cigar has gone out. A* BUS-BOY *hastily strikes a match for her. She exhales a cloud of smoke, then turns to* STRUP.) Now, Strup, I'm ready for the wines.

(STRUP *hands her the wine card.*)

STRUP

(*Pridefully*). I have arranged everything.

LUCHER

Oh, have you! (*She scans the wine card with a practised eye.*) Champagne! Cliquot 1911! You are planning to serve that rabble Cliquot 1911?

STRUP

It's the best we have, madam.

LUCHER

And you're granting them the best!

STRUP

It is a matter of tradition.

LUCHER

So? You're putting tradition ahead of common sense, are you?

STRUP

(*Fearfully*). It isn't that, Frau Lucher, I only felt that . . .

LUCHER

(*Slapping the table*). The employees of this hotel will take their notions of tradition *and* of everything else from *me!* (*She includes all of them in the same decisive glare.*) You will serve Tizane with the roast—a half bottle for each of them. When they've guzzled that much, nothing but beer. Vienna beer, not Muenchner.

STRUP

Very good, ma'am.

LUCHER

A sage observation, Herr Strup. . . . Now, all of you, remember this: Courtesy, deference—treat them as if they were still lords of creation and as if you expected heavy tips for your services, which, I promise you, you won't get. All the old formalities, the old nonsense, from all of you—until they start breaking the furniture—then, *a firm hand!* If you can't manage them by yourselves, send for me.

STRUP

Yes, ma'am. We shall, ma'am.

LUCHER

You will serve the aperitifs in here. That is all.

STRUP

Yes, ma'am. To your posts, *march!* (*The* WAITERS *and* BUS-BOYS *hurry out.* LUCHER *turns her attention to the men at the ladder.*)

LUCHER

You! You have done enough fussing with the Emperor. Get that ladder out of here. (*Hastily, they fold up the ladder and depart. . . . A* BELL-BOY *appears in the large door at the right, ushering in* POFFY, *now wearing a once-resplendent uniform which reeks of moth-balls and naphtha.*)

BOY

Herr Povoromo!

STRUP

(*Bowing low*). Herr Baron.

POFFY

(*Mildly astonished*). What? Oh! I'm greatly obliged for the restoration of the title. (*He bows to* STRUP.)

LUCHER

Are they beginning to arrive?

POFFY

Yes—aperitifs are in order.

STRUP

Yes, Herr Baron.
(BREDZI *and* STRUP *go out at the left.* POFFY *advances jauntily towards* LUCHER.)

POFFY

I came to see you about the final arrangements.

LUCHER

The final arrangements are made.
(*The march music offstage stops.*)

POFFY

In particular reference to the wine. . .

LUCHER

(*Consulting her list*). With the soup, sherry—nine shillings. With the trout, Grinzinger—seven shillings. With the roast, Tizane—nine shillings.

POFFY

(*Shocked*). Tizane! Is that the best that this superior establishment can afford?

LUCHER

On this occasion, yes.

POFFY

There will be complaints.

LUCHER

You people are not paying for this affair. I am.

POFFY

We are aware of that condition. Nevertheless—I must insist—there will be complaints.

LUCHER

Did that message you received say what time he would arrive?

POFFY

I expected him on the afternoon train from Salzburg. But he was not on it.

LUCHER

(*With a look at her watch*). No. It is now half after eight.

POFFY

There will be another train.

LUCHER

Yes—and he won't be on that, either. It's just as I thought. They've stopped him at the border. . . . Are there any unexpected arrivals?

POFFY

No. Here's the complete list. Only eight names instead of the expected thirty.
(POFFY *takes the list from his pocket.*)

LUCHER

Let me see it.
(*He hands it to her. . . .* TORLINI, *the hotel's courier, enters from the upper left, accompanied by an officer of police.*)

TORLINI

Frau Lucher!

LUCHER

Yes?

TORLINI

The police, ma'am.
(LUCHER *is not in the least disturbed by this announcement. She is examining critically the list of guests.*)

LUCHER

(*To the* POLICEMAN). What do you want?

POLICEMAN

The Herr Inspector thought it might be as well for me to have a look around.

LUCHER

Go ahead and look. You'll observe nothing of the slightest interest.
(*The* POLICEMAN *nods and looks about the room, paying special attention to the portrait of Franz Josef.*)

POFFY

Surely, for only eight, you could afford Moët et Chandon, at the least.

LUCHER

No. There's not one on this list with a palate left to his name. The bottles of Tizane will be wrapped in napkins. No one will know the difference.

POFFY

(*Bowing*). As you say, my dear hostess.

LUCHER

Exactly as I say! (*She hands him back the list. The* POLICEMAN *is at the large door at the left.*)

POLICEMAN

(*Pointing off to the left*). Will the reception be held in there?

LUCHER

Yes. And it will be kept in there. (*The* POLICEMAN *steps out at the left.* LUCHER *speaks in an undertone to* POFFY.) If he had arrived it would have been different. I would have served the best. I'd even have done it if she had consented to come. But for the rest of you, Tizane is good enough.

POFFY

She was right, of course. She'd have had a poor time.

LUCHER

Yes. She was right. . . . But I'd like to have heard what the great psychologist said to her after we left.
(*The* POLICEMAN *has returned.*)

POLICEMAN

Who is to be present at this function?

POFFY

Here is the list. (*He hands the list to the* POLICEMAN, *then turns to* LUCHER.) And if he can find any cause for excitement in that group, then perhaps it may be a good party, after all.

POLICEMAN

Is this all?

LUCHER

That is all, and as I informed the inspector—there'll be no one of the slightest importance here tonight.
(*Having looked over the list, the* POLICEMAN *sticks it in the large note-book which he carries in a breast pocket.*)

POLICEMAN

If you don't mind, I think I'll have a look at these guests of yours and make certain that this list is correct.

LUCHER

You're calling me a liar?

POLICEMAN

No. I'm only being careful. (*He turns to the left and starts to go out.*)

POFFY

Perhaps you'd like me to present them to you formally. (*He and the* POLICEMAN *go out at the left.*)

LUCHER

Torlini, give that policeman a drink.

TORLINI

Yes, ma'am. (*He goes off at the left.* FRAU LUCHER *opens her hand-bag and takes therefrom a note-book and gold pencil. She is leaning over the little marble-topped table at the left, figuring out the cost of this affair. The aged* CHEF *rushes in from the right. He is in a state of terrific perturbation, as is a* WAITER, *who follows him.*)

CHEF

Frau Lucher!

LUCHER

(*Calmly*). Well—what is it?
(*Her back is towards the* CHEF *so that she does not see him bow low as the* ARCHDUKE RUDOLF MAXIMILLIAN *comes in from the right. . . .* RUDOLF *is tall, lean, deliberately ominous, consciously mad—an ageless prince who, despite the absurd inappropriateness of the Tyrolean costume that he now wears, brings back with him into the Hotel Lucher the semblance of imperial splendor which it had known when such outrageous beings as he were lords of Vienna. . . . He is followed by a* WAITER *and two* BUS-BOYS, *who carry his cape, haversack, blanket roll and sword holster. Even these* BUS-BOYS, *who were infants when the House of Habsburg fell—even they are awe-struck, trepidant in the presence of a magnificence which they have been rigorously taught to scorn. . . .* RUDOLF *crosses to* LUCHER *and administers a loving whack to her ample bottom.*)

RUDOLF

Good evening, venerable strumpet.
(LUCHER *turns, stares at him, mutters some blasphemous exclamation of dismay, curtsies involuntarily, then rushes to the doors at the left and shuts them.* RUDOLF *follows her.*)

RUDOLF

Still wearing the red flannel drawers? (*He lifts her skirts from behind.*) Thank God, there's something in Vienna that hasn't been changed.

LUCHER

(*Ferociously*). How did you come here?

RUDOLF

I came by various means of conveyance which I shall not describe in detail. My entrance to the hotel was made through the kitchens—and whatever appetite I may have had is now gone. You received no letter from me?

LUCHER

No.

RUDOLF

Good! I wrote none. (*He strolls towards the right, pauses, and sniffs.*) There's the same nauseating stench of fish in this hotel. By God—I believe it's the same *fish!*

LUCHER

Do *they* know?

RUDOLF

Who are they?

LUCHER

Poffy—Count von Stainz—Hoetzler . . .

RUDOLF

Is it necessary for me to advise *them* of my intentions? Is it?

LUCHER

They will be startled.

RUDOLF

As they should be! I will occupy the Imperial Suite . . .

LUCHER

The Imperial Suite no longer exists.

RUDOLF

Restore it!

LUCHER

(*To the* BUS-BOYS). Is that his luggage?

BUS-BOYS

(*Eagerly*). Yes, Frau Lucher. We were commanded to . . .

CHEF

Yes, Frau Lucher. His Imperial Highness ordered that we take it to. . . .

LUCHER

Put it in there. (*She indicates the door at the back. The* CHEF *motions to the two* BOYS *who hustle out as directed. The* WAITER *goes with them.*) Do you happen to know that the police are in the building?

RUDOLF

You! Were you addressing the chef?

LUCHER

(*Grudgingly*). Your Imperial Highness. . . . (*To the* CHEF.) You may go.
(*The* CHEF *starts to go out at the right.*)

RUDOLF

Wait! (*The* CHEF *stops, and bows.*) You recognized me, didn't you?

CHEF

(*Pleased*). Yes, Your Serene Highness. (*He bows again.*)

RUDOLF

You did *not* recognize me. I am traveling incognito.

CHEF

(*Bowing*). Yes, Your Serene Highness. (*He goes out at the right.*)

LUCHER

If your memory were better, you would remember that *this* was the Imperial Suite.

RUDOLF

(*Looking about the room*). By God, it is! (*He sees the portrait of Franz Josef, salutes it, then sits in the chair back of the table at the right and starts to take off his shoes. The* WAITER *comes out of the room at the back, followed by the* BUS-BOYS.) I want some brandy.

LUCHER

Brandy.

WAITER

(*Bowing*). At once, Your Serene Highness. (*He goes.* RUDOLF *is shaking some pebbles from one of his shoes into an ash-tray on the table.*)

RUDOLF

A cigarette.

LUCHER

Cigarette!
(*One of the* BUS-BOYS *places a cigarette between* RUDOLF'S *"full, rich lips." The other boy lights it.*)

BUS-BOYS

(*Bowing together*). Your Serene Highness. (*They scurry out at the right.* RUDOLF *exhales a huge cloud of smoke. Then he laughs.*)

RUDOLF

It's incredible! I believe that even the aged worms in your woodwork recognize me, and are thrilled by my return. I don't blame them—after all these years with nothing to do but sit back and watch themselves decay. How have you managed to keep this decrepit establishment going?

LUCHER

We have plenty of trade.
(*The* WAITER *comes in with a tray on which is a bottle of brandy and one enormous glass, which he puts on the table.*)

RUDOLF

Loud-mouthed American tourists, I suppose.

LUCHER

Yes! They flock here to ogle the scenes of your triumphs. (*She is pouring a drink of brandy.*)

RUDOLF

Disgusting!

LUCHER

(*To the* WAITER). Tell Torlini I want to see him.

WAITER

Yes, Frau Lucher. (*The* WAITER *goes out at the left.*)

RUDOLF

I find the whole aspect of this place depressing, and at the same time, rather gratifying. . . .

LUCHER

(*Interrupting him*). Now, I wasn't joking when I warned you about the police. . . .

RUDOLF

(*Through her speech*). Will you please not talk when I'm speaking? Sit down! (*Under protest,* LUCHER *has stopped talking and sits down across the table from him.*) Does this city realize that it's hopelessly defunct? It is like a corpse that twitches with the reflexes of life—a gruesome spectacle. I don't envy you, Lucher, having to abide here among the remains. . . . I didn't really mean that. I do envy you. (*He gulps some brandy.*) They drained the blood from Vienna when they removed us—and now observe the results! Serves the swine right. (*Another gulp.*)

LUCHER

Do you wish to change your clothes?

RUDOLF

Naturally, I don't intend to exhibit myself in this outlandish costume.

LUCHER

(*Rising*). Then you had better go in there, and *stay* in there, till I can get rid of the police.

RUDOLF

Sit down! (*Subduing several choice oaths, she again sits.*) Who is here, besides Poffy and that senile incompetent, General Hoetzler?

LUCHER

The Baroness von Krett, and Koeppke and his wife, and Talisz . . .

RUDOLF

And Elena Vervesz. She is here, too.

LUCHER

No.

RUDOLF

She is late.

LUCHER

She is not coming!

RUDOLF

What? She is not in Vienna?

LUCHER

Yes—but she has flatly refused to come!

RUDOLF

Oh! She didn't know I would be here. . . . Married, isn't she?

LUCHER

Yes. To a doctor—a very important doctor.

RUDOLF

I have a distinct feeling that he will be called out tonight, to some distant place—an emergency case. . . . Have you seen her lately?

LUCHER

I went to her house today.
(*The orchestra starts offstage, playing the opening bars of "The Blue Danube."*)

RUDOLF

How is she? Old?

LUCHER

No. (*Reminded by the music that the door is open, she rises and starts over towards the left.*)

RUDOLF

Does she bulge? (LUCHER *does not answer. He roars.*) Does she bulge? (LUCHER *turns to him.*) Here? (*He indicates breasts.*)

LUCHER

No! (*She shuts the doors at the left, so that the music can now be heard only faintly.*)

RUDOLF

Send for her.

LUCHER

She will not come.

RUDOLF

Tell her that her one true lover has condescended to be present.

LUCHER

I tell you, *she will not come!*

RUDOLF

(*Rising suddenly*). And I am telling you that she *will* come!

LUCHER

She has a different life now . . .

RUDOLF

(*Advancing*). If by any chance she should not be here when I am ready . . . (*He takes hold of her throat.*) But you know the consequences—don't you, old filthy? *You* know! (*He laughs, gives her a playful shake, and kisses her.*)

LUCHER

(*Through his kisses*). There is something else in Vienna that is not changed. You! You are the same maniac—like all your wretched family.

(RUDOLF *laughs, releases, her, and walks over to the table at the right.*)

RUDOLF

No—not a maniac. It is only that I am constantly intoxicated with my own charm. (*He starts to yodel. He picks up the bottle and glass, also his green Tyrolean hat.*) I want a valet. (*He puts on his hat and crosses to* LUCHER.) Tell Elena to take all the time she wants. I don't approve of women who jump into their clothes like fire-horses. She must make every possible effort to look alluring. (*He pinches her and strolls off yodelling into the bedroom at the back. He starts to remove his clothes.* LUCHER *nervously rushes up with unusual alacrity and closes the doors after him. Then she crosses to the doors at the left, opens them, and calls:*)

LUCHER

Strup! (*The music is playing loudly.*) *Strup!*

STRUP

(*From offstage*). Yes, Frau Lucher. (*He hurries in.*)

LUCHER

(*In measured tones*). You will take the Tizane off the ice. We will serve champagne —Cliquot 1911.

STRUP

What?

LUCHER

Did you hear!

STRUP

(*Astounded*). The Cliquot 1911.

(LUCHER *crosses slowly to the table at the right.*)

LUCHER

Yes, and there will be nine covers, instead of eight. Have them get that big chair that's in the office—that gold chair.

(TORLINI *has appeared in the doorway, followed by the* POLICEMAN, *whom* LUCHER *does not at first see.*)

STRUP

Yes, ma'am. Nine covers.

(*Hearing this, the* POLICEMAN *takes out his note-book and the list of guests which* POFFY *had given him.*)

LUCHER

Put the gold chair at the head of the table. And I want caviar served. . . .

TORLINI

You sent for me, Frau Lucher?

LUCHER

Yes, I did. (*She sees the* POLICEMAN.) But it's . . .

POLICEMAN

Nine covers? There are only eight here.

LUCHER

I neglected to count myself. I am to attend the party.

POLICEMAN

The gold chair will be for you?

LUCHER

Why not? It's my hotel, isn't it? Go on, Strup, do as you're told.

(STRUP *goes out at the left.* LUCHER *goes close to* TORLINI.)

LUCHER

I want to send a message—(*The* POLICEMAN *is evincing interest.* LUCHER *is frantically attempting to signal to* TORLINI *to get rid of the* POLICEMAN.)—to the florist's. The flowers they sent are all wilted. (*The* POLICEMAN *is watching too closely*—LUCHER *goes over to him, fire in her eye.*) And as for you—I'd be grateful if you'd go straight to the Herr Inspector and tell him that I consider this intrusion by the police an unpardonable outrage! Do you hear that?

POLICEMAN

Yes—Frau Lucher. I hear. But surely you'll agree that the police must be . . .

LUCHER

(*Shouting*). I'll agree to nothing! I've taken great pains to explain this whole affair to the authorities and they assured me that there would be no interference.

POLICEMAN

I only know that I have been ordered to look in here, and . . .

LUCHER

And you've obeyed your orders. (*She opens her hand-bag.*) You've seen everything and satisfied yourself that nothing harmful can come of this. It's all ridiculous stupidity, typical of the brainless asses who govern this city. (*She has fished some bills from her hand-bag.*) Here, my good man. (*She hands the money to him.*) Now run along to the inspector, and present to him my sincerest compliments. (*She pushes him towards the door.*)

POLICEMAN

I will, Frau Lucher! (*He pockets the money.*) And if he sends me back, it won't be my fault.

LUCHER

I know that. Go on. (*She pushes him out, then addresses* TORLINI, *rapidly, in a furious undertone.*) See that that policeman gets out of the hotel. Then telephone to Dr. Anton Krug's house, and tell Frau Krug that the worst has happened!

TORLINI

The worst?

LUCHER

She'll understand. Tell her to get into a car and drive out of Vienna just as fast as she can.

TORLINI

Yes, Frau Lucher. . . . But what about the florist?

LUCHER

(*At the top of her lungs*). Great God! Never mind the florist!

(*The door at the back opens, and* RUDOLF *appears wearing his shirt and nothing else.*)

RUDOLF

Where in hell is that valet?

LUCHER

Get back in that room!

TORLINI

(*Staring at* RUDOLF). It is impossible!

LUCHER

I told you to stay in . . .

RUDOLF

Is there such a thing as a valet in this brothel?

LUCHER

Yes, he's coming right up.

RUDOLF

Thank you, my sweet. (*He pinches her cheek.*)

TORLINI

(*Bowing low*). Your Imperial Highness.
(RUDOLF *reaches out and lifts* TORLINI'S *bowed head.*)

RUDOLF

I do not remember who you are—nevertheless, good evening. (*He bows to* TORLINI, *then turns and walks back with great dignity, albeit without trousers, into his room.* LUCHER *slams the door behind him.*)

LUCHER

Now do you know what I meant by the worst?

TORLINI

(*Trembling*). I do.

LUCHER

Tell her he's here. . . . When he finds out she isn't in this hotel, there'll be an uproar. He'll go after her. He'll break into her house, and have a fight with her husband. If she wants to avoid a nasty scene, she'll have to get herself out of the city, at once.
(*The* COUNT *has come in from the left. He is carrying a cocktail glass.* TORLINI *goes.*)

COUNT

Now let me tell you something, Frau Lucher: I just happened to take a look under the napkin in one of the ice buckets, and what did I see there? Tizane—that's what I saw! Tizane—sparkling dishwater!
(LUCHER *has been gathering up the papers from the table and stuffing them back into her hand-bag. She darts one look at the* COUNT.)

LUCHER

You're drunk already.

COUNT

Oh, now, that isn't worthy of you, Lucher. It hasn't been easy for us to come here, you know. If you had the heart to invite us here, I should think you'd have the decency to furnish us with wine that is at least potable.
(LUCHER, *however, has gone out at the right.* GISELLA VON KRETT *has come in from the left. She was once one of the haughtier beauties of the court. She is now a wasted, embittered governess, clinging grimly to the sense of snobbery which is all that she managed to salvage from the wreckage of the past. She is wearing an evening gown which was fashionable in* 1917.)

GISELLA

Well? Did you tell her we insisted on champagne?

COUNT

Yes, but she didn't seem to hear me.
(GISELLA *sits down at the left.*)

GISELLA

We should have known that this would happen. She dragged us here solely to humiliate us for the satisfaction of her own vulgarian sense of inferiority.

COUNT

Ah, well, my dear Gisella—Tizane isn't really so unbearable. I mean to say, after the first three glasses you hardly know what you're drinking. I shall consume the first three glasses rapidly.

HOETZLER

(*From offstage*). I hurled in the 19th army corps—or was it the 17th? (*He enters from the left with* SOPHIA KOEPPKE *on his arm.*) . . . And in another twelve hours we'd have smashed the Russian line. (*He sees the* COUNT.) Franz!

COUNT

General Hoetzler!
(*They bow formally and shake hands. . . . The old* GENERAL *is still fat but obviously shrunken; he hasn't flesh enough left to fill*

his skin. He wears a uniform coat, which is too large for him by many years, but moths have deprived him of the trousers that go with it and he is forced to wear a pair from his gray civilian suit. . . . In spite of which, he is wilfully hearty, and determined to make this a gay and carefree celebration. . . . SOPHIA *is a faded blonde, buxom and—unlike the others—too well fed, but still flagrantly girlish.*)

HOETZLER

This is splendid, old boy.

SOPHIA

(*Who has gone over to* GISELLA). My darling Gisella! How stunning you look!

GISELLA

(*Without emotion*). Good evening, Sophia.

HOETZLER

Gisella! Smart, distinguished, entrancing as ever!

SOPHIA

Now you must all be quiet, because dear General Hoetzler is telling me the most thrilling story about the campaign in 1915.

COUNT

Oh, yes, indeed—I remember it well. You had the Russians in a tight corner—eh, General? Now do sit down, Sophia.
(*She sits down at the right. . . . Offended at this abrupt dismissal of his favorite reminiscence, the* GENERAL *makes an attempt to continue.*)

HOETZLER

I was trying to explain to Sophia how curious it was that, at the very moment of complete triumph . . .
(*But the* COUNT *has his back turned.*)

COUNT

(*To* SOPHIA). I can't tell you what a delightful privilege it is to see a really stylish woman again.

SOPHIA

(*Giggling shrilly*). Oh, Franz—you're much too gallant.

COUNT

With provocation, my dear.

SOPHIA

But Koeppke and I do try to keep up appearances, even in the hopelessly middle-class atmosphere of Switzerland.

COUNT

As Tatti and I do, in Upper Tooting. But it's an endless struggle.

SOPHIA

Dreadful! People don't seem to understand the importance of those things any more. There are so many false standards.

COUNT

That's it! That's precisely it!
(*During all this,* HOETZLER *has sat down on the couch beside* GISELLA, *and is carrying on manfully with his narrative.*)

HOETZLER

I was just telling Sophia of the time early in 1915 when we had the Russians on the run. We were within *that* of breaking through the enemy's line; and they had no more than a corporal's guard in reserve. You can readily imagine the consequences. We'd have marched on to Petersburg, crushed the Russian Empire! But at the very moment when my plan of campaign had reached a climax . . . (*By this time the* COUNT *has said "That's precisely it!" and has been compelled, by the loudness of* HOETZLER'S *voice, to turn to listen.*) I received a telegram from Prince Max in Berlin telling me to withdraw! Now I ask you, I ask all of you, what was I to do?

COUNT

Withdraw.

HOETZLER

Exactly. And the baffling part of it all is that that telegram from Berlin has never been adequately explained. And I can tell you, my dear Gisella . . .

COUNTESS

(*From offstage*). They're all in here.
(*The* COUNTESS *and* TALISZ *come in, arm in arm. She is now wearing an evening dress,*

of her own manufacture, and there is an ostrich plume or so in her hair. . . . TALISZ *is very old, somewhat bemused and slightly deaf. He is wearing a frayed swallowtail coat, lustreless, black satin knee breeches, and black cotton stockings borrowed from his landlady. . . . There are general greetings, all very formal, very courtly.*)

COUNTESS

Gisella! Sophia! Well!

SOPHIA

Well!

GISELLA

(*Acidly*). The General is telling us about a telegram from Berlin.

HOETZLER

I was merely explaining that there was a certain faction in Prussia headed by Hindenburg that did not wish Austria to achieve . . .

TALISZ

(*To* SOPHIA). And where is Koeppke? I don't see him. Isn't he to be with us?
(*The* COUNTESS *takes his arm and indicates that he has interrupted the* GENERAL.)

HOETZLER

(*Giving* TALISZ *an angry look*). There can be no question of doubt that Hindenburg was jealous of the inevitable result of my coup. He knew my victory would destroy the Russian power and Austria would gain the credit for having won the war.

TALISZ

(*Who doesn't quite know what's happening*). Is His Imperial Highness here yet?

SOPHIA

No. Poffy's out now trying to find out if there's any word of him.

TALISZ

I beg your pardon?

COUNTESS

(*Distinctly, in his ear*). She said: "Poffy's out now trying to find out if there's any word of him."

TALISZ

Oh, yes, I knew that. I felt sure he'd come.

HOETZLER

Hindenburg, of course, was a Prussian of the Prussians—contemptuous of Austria, determined to . . .

TALISZ

What's the General saying?

COUNTESS

Something about the war.

TALISZ

Oh! Too bad. (*He moves away. . . . Nettled by the frequent interruptions,* HOETZLER *makes a supreme attempt to complete his story.*)

HOETZLER

I knew it at the time, but my obligations as a soldier to our allies compelled me to silence. Hindenburg blocked my plans and then deliberately stole them! Stole them—and used them himself in the Masurian Lakes region! That, my friends, is the true explanation of . . .
(POFFY *enters. The* COUNT, COUNTESS *and* SOPHIA *rush over to question him.*)

SOPHIA

Poffy, is there any news?

COUNT

What about Rudolf? Is he coming?

POFFY

No. The last train from Salzburg is in, but he wasn't on it.

COUNTESS

Oh! I can't bear to think they've caught him. (*She is apparently on the verge of tears, her favorite perch.*)

SOPHIA

He must come. He *must!*

POFFY

Of course with Rudolf there is always hope.

HOETZLER

Of course there is hope. Rudolf was always late. Do you remember the time, my dear Gisella, when the Emperor was holding a reception for King Edward VII?

GISELLA

No.

(STRUP *has come in, followed by two* WAITERS *with trays loaded with glasses of tepid vermouth.*)

STRUP

(*Speaking through* HOETZLER'S *lines*). Herr Baron, the aperitifs!

POFFY

By all means proceed with them.

STRUP

Thank you, Herr Baron.

(*The service of the aperitifs proceeds, under* STRUP'S *benign supervision, while* HOETZLER *continues with his reminiscence about the reception for King Edward VII.*)

HOETZLER

(*Taking* GISELLA'S *"No" as cue*). Matters of the utmost importance were at stake, and the Emperor had commanded all the members of the royal family to be most punctual. And of course they all were—with one exception. . . . (*The* WAITER *offers* HOETZLER *a drink, which he takes, and then continues:*) With one exception—Rudolf. He was a mere stripling then, but even so, he kept the King of England waiting for two hours while he . . .

(*The* VALET *has come in from the right and gone up to the bedroom door. He knocks.*)

RUDOLF

(*From within*). Come in.

HOETZLER

Who's in that room?

SOPHIA

(*Archly*). Now—now, General!

HOETZLER

But if there's anybody spying on us . . .

POFFY

He'll be bitterly disappointed. Now if you will all be good enough to rise. (*They all rise.* POFFY *turns and lifts his glass to the portrait of Franz Josef.*) To His Imperial Majesty!

(*They all drink and then give silent, facial testimony to the low quality of the vermouth. . . . The oppressive silence is broken by the entrance from the left of* KOEPPKE, *a brisk, obtrusive little man who, like his wife,* SOPHIA, *is too well nourished.*)

KOEPPKE

(*Breezily*). Well, here I am!

SOPHIA

You're late.

KOEPPKE

Yes, my love. (*He looks about.*) Is the party in full swing?

GISELLA

It is.

POFFY

Oh, come—let's go in to dinner.

GISELLA

I've lost my appetite. That loathsome vermouth . . .

POFFY

I know, my dear Gisella, you're accustomed to the best in Palermo. As for the rest of us, we have come here to conduct a celebration. It is going to be a difficult task, but I strongly urge that we all smother our justifiable grievances and pretend to be having a very devil of an uproarious carousal. Let us close our eyes to the fact that we all look a bit moth-eaten and concentrate on getting through this with a show of good grace.

(*The* COUNT *starts to sing: "Vilya, oh, Vilya, the witch of the wood."*)

GISELLA

We're not going to be very uproarious on Tizane.

HOETZLER

I beg of you, Gisella, be quiet.

SOPHIA

(*Referring to the* COUNT'S *song*). That's a cheerful selection!

GISELLA

(*To* POFFY). If you'd only taken the trouble to let us know what it would be like . . .

COUNTESS

It wasn't Poffy's fault.

KOEPPKE

Personally I'm in favor of abandoning the whole thing.
(*The* COUNTESS *has started to weep.* SOPHIA *is trying to calm her. The* COUNT *is slumped in a chair at the left, still singing "Vilya."* GISELLA *is seated at the right, regarding the* COUNTESS *with disgust.* HOETZLER *and* TALISZ *are behind her.* POFFY *has gone out at the left to beg the musicians for God's sake to play something lively.* KOEPPKE *is hovering over the couch, patronizing the* COUNTESS. *The following speeches are delivered in a jumble:*)

SOPHIA

I wish to heaven you'd all listen to Poffy. At least we can pre*tend* to be gay and—and jolly. . . . Now, please, Tatti, you won't help matters at all by crying your eyes out . . .

HOETZLER

Perhaps if Lucher would give us some really good beer it might take effect more quickly.

TALISZ

(*To* HOETZLER). What's everybody saying now?

KOEPPKE

(*To the* COUNTESS *and* SOPHIA). I'll tell you what. How about the three of us slipping down to the bar and having a few brandies? Just the three of us. Oh, don't worry—*I* can pay for them. I've over a hundred and fifty real marks in my pocket at this moment!

(ELENA *has entered on the cue from* TALISZ: *"What's everybody saying now?" She comes down from the upper right, so that* TALISZ *and* HOETZLER *see her first.*)

ELENA

Talisz! I did so hope you'd be here. And the dear General. How sweet it is to see you.

TALISZ

Elena! Elena! (*He kisses her hand.*)

HOETZLER

Elena, is it *you?*
(POFFY *has come back; he sees* ELENA, *and fairly whoops for joy.*)

POFFY

Elena!
(*The others are now aware of her presence. They cease their chattering, weeping and singing, and form a hilarious, welcoming group about her.*)

ELENA

Tatti! You should have *known.* I couldn't keep away. And Sophia! How charming you look! And Koeppke! I can't believe it! Hello, Franz—*you* knew I'd be here, didn't you!

COUNT

A good joke on us! A capital joke! Just like you, Elena. Bring some more drinks. Herr Ober! Herr Ober! (*The* COUNT *rushes out at the left.*)

HOETZLER

Where's that blackguard gone with the aperitifs?

ELENA

And here's Gisella. How are you, my darling? You're looking so chic, so exactly like yourself.

GISELLA

They told me you weren't coming.

COUNTESS

She wanted to surprise us—to make it all the better.

KOEPPKE

And that's what she's done.

ELENA

I changed my mind for no reason except a selfish one. I wanted to see all of you—and hear you laugh and joke.
(*A veritable orgy of ad-libbing is interrupted when the* COUNT *appears in the doorway at the left.*)

COUNT

(*Shouting*). Come in to dinner! They're serving *champagne!*

SOPHIA

What?

COUNT

Cliquot 1911! And caviar!
(*The* COUNT'S *announcement is greeted with cheers.* POFFY'S *request for lively music has been fulfilled by the orchestra offstage. There is a general movement towards the left.*)

HOETZLER

(*Offering* ELENA *his arm*). With your permission, I think I take the precedence.
(ELENA *takes the* GENERAL'S *arm and goes out at the left, followed by* KOEPPKE *and the* COUNTESS, POFFY *and* GISELLA, TALISZ *and* SOPHIA. *Just as* ELENA *reaches the door,* LUCHER *enters from the right and rushes across after them shouting:*)

LUCHER

Frau Krug! Frau Krug! Did you get my message?
(*Her voice is lost in the din of laughter, talk and music. . . .* ELENA *goes out.* LUCHER *is going after her, but she stops when cries for "Help!" are heard from the bedroom at the back. The bedroom door flies open and the* VALET *hurtles out, propelled by* RUDOLF, *who is now magnificent in his uniform. . . .* LUCHER *hastily shuts the doors at the left.*)

VALET

Frau Lucher! He threatened to strangle me!

RUDOLF

Do you mean to tell me that that stable-boy is dignified with the title of valet?

VALET

(*Terrified*). I was only trying to brush Your Highness's hair.

RUDOLF

He scratched my ear. (RUDOLF *slaps the* VALET, *who rushes out at the right.* RUDOLF *starts to fasten on his golden sash.*)

LUCHER

You're to stay in that room until I tell you it's safe to . . .

RUDOLF

Is she here?
(TORLINI *comes in from the upper left.*)

LUCHER

(*To* RUDOLF). I told you she wouldn't come!

TORLINI

They informed me that she had already left her house, on the way here. . . .

RUDOLF

(*Turning, to* LUCHER). Ah! Then she has arrived?

LUCHER

I've warned you that the police are on the watch . . .

RUDOLF

She's here, isn't she?

LUCHER

No! (*He tweaks her nose.*) Yes!

RUDOLF

Good! You have acted with unexpected competence. Bring her to me.

LUCHER

But they have just sat down to supper. You should join them.

RUDOLF

Bring her here! And champagne with her. I shall not be hungry for another forty-three minutes. (*He crosses to the right to examine himself in the mirror.*)

LUCHER

(*To* TORLINI). Request Frau Krug to come here for a moment. (TORLINI *goes out at the left.*)

RUDOLF

Frau Krug?

LUCHER

That is her name! (RUDOLF *turns again to the mirror, with an expression of disgust.*) You'd better be careful how you talk to her.

RUDOLF

You may now depart, Lucher.

LUCHER

She isn't the same one you used to make free with. Her husband is a very fine man —a big man, too, and . . .
(RUDOLF *steps up on a chair, the better to see the reflection of his sash in the mirror.*)

RUDOLF

I shall want some champagne—and also more cognac . . .

LUCHER

I tell you—you'd better not try any of your old tricks on her. She's different.
(*The doors at the left are open.* ELENA *appears, looking backward.*)

COUNTESS

(*From offstage*). But, my little angel, you're not going?

ELENA

No, no, Tatti, don't you worry, I'll be right back.

COUNT

Immediately——

ELENA

Yes, immediately. (*She turns and sees* RUDOLF *on the chair, his back to her.*)

RUDOLF

And one other thing: the towels in my bath room are soggy. Have them changed. . . . Get out, Lucher!
(LUCHER *darts one glance of commiseration at* ELENA, *folds her hands over her protuberant stomach, and goes out at the right.* ELENA *stares at* RUDOLF'S *back. He gazes at her image in the mirror. . . . After a few moments, he steps down from the chair, turns and confronts her. . . . The doors at the left have been closed, but the strains of a waltz are faintly audible. . . .* RUDOLF *starts towards her, pauses, then walks around her.* ELENA *does not move, but her eyes follow him. . . . He is behind her. He reaches out to touch her, but doesn't touch her. He walks around, in front of her, stares at her, then slaps her face. He seizes her in his arms and kisses her, fiercely. . . . A* WAITER *has come from the right with a bottle of cognac and glasses, followed by a* BUS-BOY *with an ice bucket containing a bottle of champagne. They deposit these at the right, gaping at* RUDOLF *and* ELENA *as they do so.*)

RUDOLF

How long has it been since you were kissed like that? Ten years? More than ten years! Think of it! (*The* WAITER *makes a slight clatter as he arranges the glasses on the table. . . .* RUDOLF, *still holding* ELENA *tightly, motions behind his back to the* WAITER *to get out. He does so, followed by the* BUS-BOY. RUDOLF *kisses* ELENA *more gently.*) Come—we'll have a drink! (*He steps aside, motions her to the table. She crosses slowly and sits down. He goes behind the table and fills each of the glasses with equal quantities of brandy and champagne.*)

ELENA

You know—I realize now how completely I had forgotten you.

RUDOLF

Yes—it's too bad. We're not equipped with the power to recall sensations. One of our Creator's more serious mistakes. . . . However—tonight we will both refresh our memories. (*He raises his glass, toasting her, then drains it. She raises her glass, slightly, then places it on the table, untouched.*) That's a very graceful tribute, Elena. I'm referring to the necklace. But—good God! That wedding ring! (*He laughs boisterously and seizes her hand for closer inspection of the ring.*)

ELENA

That's nothing to laugh at. (*She is trying

to pull her hand away, but he has a tight grip on her wrist.)

RUDOLF

Of all the bourgeois adornments! On you, it is a gross anachronism. Like a brassiere on the Venus de Milo. It offends me. We must remove it. (*He snatches the ring from her finger.*)

ELENA

Give it *back* to me!

RUDOLF

I told you it offends me.

ELENA

(*Struggling*). Are you going to give me back my ring?

RUDOLF

Yes, my darling—I'll give it back, cheerfully, in the morning. But in the meantime—well—surely, you can understand my point. That heavy gold band on your finger would strike a discordant note.

ELENA

I'm not planning to be in communication with you tomorrow morning. I want it now! (*She snatches for it.*)

RUDOLF

(*Pocketing the ring*). I must ask you to be careful, Elena. Refrain from irritating me. You will recall that the members of my family are subject to epileptic rages—sheer exuberance, you know—which invariably result in one form or another of physical violence. . . . I should not care to send you back to your husband with your lovely nose broken, and minus one or two conspicuous teeth. . . .

ELENA

(*Staring at him*). It can't be true!

RUDOLF

On the contrary, I can assure you that one more allusion to that detestable ring will prove that it *is* true. . . .

ELENA

I wasn't thinking about that. I was thinking of what ten years have failed to do to you.

RUDOLF

I chose to remain as I was.

ELENA

Ten years of exile, and humiliation, and poverty, haven't shaken in you the conviction that Franz Josef is still reigning in Schönbrunn.

RUDOLF

No—I admit that I have occasional qualms. There are moments when I suspect that the Habsburgs are not what they once were. But when I see you, my eternally beloved, and realize that you have had the pride to preserve your figure against the day of my return—then I know that there has been no revolution. (*He has sat down on the table, and is leaning over her, his face increasingly close to hers.*)

ELENA

Don't come near me.

RUDOLF

You don't wish to be kissed?

ELENA

I do not!

RUDOLF

Very well—if you feel that you need the inspiration of a little more champagne, you shall have it. . . . (*He goes to pour out another glass for her, but finds that she has had none. He empties her glass into the ice bucket, and refills it. He then hands it to her. She places it on the table. He pours out more for himself.*)

ELENA

(*Rising*). We must go in there and join the others.

RUDOLF

(*Pouring*). We must do nothing of the kind.

ELENA

I came here tonight to be with them . . .

RUDOLF

Whereas I came here to be with you. Those pitiful relics are of no interest whatever to me. . . . Come now—drink!

ELENA

I'm going in there.
(*He steps in front of her.*)

RUDOLF

No, you're not.

ELENA

Get out of my way. (*He laughs and gulps some more champagne, but does not budge. She softens her tone to one of persuasion.*) Oh, Rudolf—I'll tell them you're here. It's all that's needed to send the poor things into a complete state of delirium. Think of the excitement when they see you looking as young as ever, and as handsome, in your lovely uniform, with all the medals. Think how pleased *he'd* be (*pointing to the portrait*) if he knew that a Habsburg was again holding court in Vienna.

RUDOLF

(*With a glance at the portrait*). Very well—I'll show myself to them—for his sake. (*He kisses her lightly on the forehead, then crosses to the left and tries the door. It is locked. He turns to* ELENA, *delighted.*) Lucher's had us locked in—the tactful old bawd. (*He pounds on the door. It is opened. The guests at the banquet offstage are making a great deal of noise, indicative of well-bred hilarity. The voice of* STRUP *is heard to call out: "His Imperial Highness!"* RUDOLF *stands in the doorway. The shouts and murmurs stop as each of the guests sees him.* BREDZI'S *little orchestra strikes up the old national anthem.* RUDOLF *turns and glances at* ELENA. *She points to the portrait of the late Emperor, and he goes up and takes a position beneath it.* POFFY *comes in and bows low. The others follow him, the ladies going up to him to kiss his hand.* RUDOLF *greets each of them by name. He is impassive, regal, mildly disdainful—just as they want him to be. The* COUNTESS *begins to sob.*)

RUDOLF

That is enough—enough! (*He waves them out.*) I may join you later in the evening. (*They all back out. From offstage, the* COUNT *is heard to shout: "To His Imperial Highness."* ELENA *lifts her untouched glass of champagne and sips. There are sounds of shattered glasses from the left. The doors are closed, subduing the uproar of cheers.*)

RUDOLF

Why are they all so old? (*He gazes towards the left, despondently, then suddenly decides to give this depressing matter not another thought. He turns to* ELENA.) Well? Have I or have I not done my duty? (*He comes down to the table.*) Sit down, if you please. (*She sits down at the right of the table. He leans over and kisses her hair.*) Now! I suggest that we discuss briefly your husband, before we pass on to more mutually agreeable subjects. . . . Do you love him?

ELENA

Very much.

RUDOLF

I have no objection to that. . . . He's a doctor, isn't he?

ELENA

A psychoanalyst.

RUDOLF

Ah! A practitioner of Vienna's sole remaining industry. . . . I've been told he's quite brilliant. Written a book, hasn't he?

ELENA

Yes—eight volumes.

RUDOLF

I must meet him and let him study me. He could derive enough material for eight volumes more.

ELENA

He knows all about you already.

RUDOLF

Ah—you've told him!

ELENA

Yes. You'll find your type analyzed in one of his books under the heading, "Elephantiasis of the Ego."

RUDOLF

I doubt that I'd be interested. (*He sits down at the left of the table.*) Have you any children?

ELENA

No.

RUDOLF

I extend my condolences. (*He lifts his glass as in a toast. She bows slightly in acknowledgment.*) These purely intellectual husbands are not very productive, are they?

ELENA

It isn't his fault that there are no children. It's my fault. . . . Are there any more questions?

RUDOLF

Let me see . . . No—I think there aren't. We can dismiss the dreary topic of your domestic life—and press on to consideration of my own. But I suppose you know all about it.

ELENA

No, Rudolf. I have not followed your later career very closely.

RUDOLF

No?

ELENA

No. How have you supported yourself?

RUDOLF

In various ways. Now and then a good run at baccarat. One or two engagements in the cinema studios—did you see me in "The Shattered Idol?"

ELENA

No, I missed that, deliberately.

RUDOLF

You did well. As it turned out, I was virtually invisible. Then I conceived a great scheme for mulcting American tourists, but the authorities got wind of it, and took over the idea themselves. There have been other occupations.

ELENA

Some one told me you've been running a taxi.

RUDOLF

Merely an amusing whim. I've only driven people I know

ELENA

And if you don't know them when you start the drive, you do before it's finished.

RUDOLF

(*Laughing*). You've evidently been listening to gossip.

ELENA

Yes. I've heard how charming you are to your fares. You must have collected many delightful friends that way.

RUDOLF

(*Wistfully*). Friends? You can hardly call them that.

ELENA

No—I suppose not.

RUDOLF

As a matter of fact, Elena. Nice is a bore. I have been very lonely.

ELENA

I've been waiting for you to say that.

RUDOLF

You have no sympathy for me?

ELENA

No.

RUDOLF

Your heart wasn't always cold.

ELENA

You have never been lonely—never deserved one atom of sympathy, from any one.

RUDOLF

You don't understand me. No one has ever understood me. It's because I'm inscrutable.

ELENA

Perhaps. But I remain unimpressed by your appeal for pity.

RUDOLF

Pity! Have you the effrontery to suggest that I want you to pity me?

ELENA

Yes!

RUDOLF

I see. . . . Then I shall abandon that tack. (*He laughs.*) Elena—it has always seemed miraculous to me that any one could be as intelligent as you are and still alluring. And you *are* alluring!

ELENA

(*Bowing*). You're overwhelmingly kind.

RUDOLF

Oh—that wasn't intended as a tribute to you. It's a tribute to my own flawless taste.

ELENA

Ah! I see.

RUDOLF

I'm proud to think that it was I who first realized you, for the sight of you now assures me that, by God, I was right. . . . You're so beautiful, Elena. You delight me! You refresh me—and I am speaking nothing less than the truth when I tell you that refreshment is what I most urgently need.

ELENA

What tack are you off on now?

RUDOLF

None. I am driving straight to the point. . . . My room is in there.

ELENA

How convenient!

RUDOLF

Yes. It's a room that we have occupied before.

ELENA

I suppose we've occupied all of them.

RUDOLF

We have, indeed, my darling. We have made history in this hotel. Come—let us make some more.

ELENA

(*Pause*). Rudolf . . .

RUDOLF

Yes?

ELENA

I think it's time for me to announce that I'm not going to bed with you.

RUDOLF

(*After a while*). Very well. (*He stands up, as though accepting her rejection, and walks away. Drink in hand, he turns and looks at her.*) I can wait (*he sips the drink*) . . . a few minutes. (*He looks towards the left.*) Who's playing in there?

ELENA

Bredzi.

RUDOLF

(*Pleased*). Bredzi! (*He goes to the left and calls "Bredzi! Bredzi!" The doors are opened and* BREDZI *comes in, with his violin. He is in a fever of excitement, and knows precisely what is expected of him. Following him is* JANSEL, *an accordion player, similarly thrilled by this summons.*) A waltz! (*With appropriate flourishes, they start to play "Viennese Beauties."* RUDOLF *turns and crosses to the table where* ELENA *is sitting. The musicians follow him, playing as they go.* RUDOLF *bows before* ELENA. *Laughing, she rises and curtsies, and then they start to waltz around the room. The tempo is sprightly, exuberant. . . .* RUDOLF *manages to manœuvre* ELENA *to the bedroom door. He kicks it open and they waltz into the room and disappear. The musicians whisper to each other happily—for this is just as it should be. . . . However, after a moment,* ELENA *comes out alone, laughing.* RUDOLF *follows. She sits on the couch.*) You know—I'm being admirably patient with you.

ELENA

(*Still laughing*). Yes, Rudolf—I know.

RUDOLF

Because I understand you, too well. I can read your thoughts.

ELENA

No!

RUDOLF

I can see that as a result of your purely spiritual marriage you have developed a certain reluctance, which it is for me to overcome. Very well! I accept the challenge confidently! (*He has a drink of champagne, then turns to* BREDZI.) Play something more—more. . . . (BREDZI *understands, and obliges with a palpitantly passionate selection. For a moment,* RUDOLF *stands, silently regarding* ELENA.) Does that remind you of anything?

ELENA

Yes.

RUDOLF

What?

ELENA

Ischl!
(RUDOLF *crosses to the couch and lies down beside her. Knowing all the moves in this game,* BREDZI *goes close to* ELENA *and plays softly, persuasively.*)

RUDOLF

Ischl! Do you remember one night when it was too warm to stay indoors?

ELENA

Yes, we went out into the forest, and you took along an entire symphony orchestra to accompany us.

RUDOLF

I always adored music.

ELENA

And you had all the musicians blindfolded. The poor things. They couldn't play in harmony because they couldn't see.

RUDOLF

It was dreadful!

ELENA

And you cursed the leader horribly—and beat him with your cane.

RUDOLF

And when you tried to stop me, I knocked you down.

ELENA

Then you dismissed the orchestra—and we went on with our romance.

RUDOLF

Oh, God, what beautiful times! (ELENA *is now lying back on the couch, languorously.* RUDOLF *kisses the hollow of her throat. Then it occurs to him to kiss her ankle.* BREDZI *feels that it is time to shift the tune. . . . Raising up on his elbow,* RUDOLF *suddenly signals the musicians to be quiet.*) Do you imagine that I need any artificial stimulation from you. Get out! (*They hurry out at the left, closing the door after them.* RUDOLF *stands up.*) It's no use bantering this way and that about it, Elena. I know now if I didn't know before that I have never loved any woman as I love you. When I see you I know that I've never loved any one else at all. You were, you are and ever will be the one passion of my life. . . . Now! Glow with justifiable pride.

ELENA

I am glowing. . . . What other women have you known since then?

RUDOLF

Plenty. All kinds.

ELENA

All colors?

RUDOLF

All shades. There have been French women, English women, Americans. I've had a few tempting offers of marriage, but . . . Then there have been Russians, Moroccans, Siamese . . .

ELENA

Twins?

RUDOLF

No, unfortunately. But I can swear to you, Elena, that all of them were no more than incidents. Whatever enjoyment I've had from them—and I'll be generous and admit that there has been some enjoyment—has been vicarious. Every quivering one of them has been no more than a proxy for you. Ah, Elena—if you could know how

I've clung to you, how I've cherished you. Memory has been kind to me, my darling. It has kept you with me, through all the nights and days. (*He is again on the couch, at her side. She jumps to her feet, walks quickly away. There is a nervous irritability in her voice.*)

ELENA

It has been otherwise with me!

RUDOLF

What do you mean?

ELENA

Memory has been kinder to me. It has discreetly withdrawn . . .

RUDOLF

Behind the curtains of your imagination—but it is still there, alive and warm, aching to emerge.

ELENA

No, it is dead!

RUDOLF

I refuse to accept that, sight unseen.

ELENA

I have looked behind the curtains and seen it. It is decayed and loathsome.

RUDOLF

You're talking nonsense from your husband's books.

ELENA

I'm talking truth—bitter truth, for you, perhaps.

RUDOLF

I don't believe it.

ELENA

Because you will not face the one important fact.

RUDOLF

Which is what?

ELENA

I am happy with my husband. (*He laughs.*) I love him!

RUDOLF

You will notice that I am laughing.

ELENA

And you may notice that I am not going to bed with you.

RUDOLF

Elena! Will you tell me that never once while you've been enduring the physical intimacies of this great thinker, never once have you shut your eyes and assured yourself, "It's Rudolf Maximillian."

ELENA

Not in years have I thought of that.

RUDOLF

But there were times at first, weren't there? Many times?

ELENA

There may have been.

RUDOLF

I thought so—and they became less frequent as the years went by—not because you were learning to be happy with him, but because you were learning to be resigned. You see—I know something about your psychology, too. Now, come—we've had enough of debate. It's time for a little emotion. We'll see if we've forgotten what life tastes like.

ELENA

(*Indicating the door at the left*). I'm going back in there.

RUDOLF

You are not! (*He seizes her wrist and pulls her against him, then holds her tightly in his arms.*) You are now expected to shriek.

ELENA

I shall not shriek.

RUDOLF

Forgive me. I had forgotten that you are not the shrieking kind. That was always one of your most engaging qualities, Elena. You invariably knew when you were beaten. (*He kisses her several times, on her *eyes, ears, nose and throat. She offers no apparent resistance and no response.*) Ah, Elena, my only darling—it isn't easy for you to yield, is it? You keep on thinking of that wedding ring in my pocket. You're loyal to him, because you have the courage to be decent. You were always loyal, always brave. But with me, it isn't as it would be with any one else. Can't you see that? I loved you first. And you loved me. You weren't lying when you said you loved me. You never knew how to lie. And I'm only asking you to love me again, for a little while, reminiscently, not as a rival of your husband, but as the echo of a voice that enchanted you when you were innocent and impressionable and young. You can't tell me that those things have changed. I can see that they haven't. You have not grown old. The warmth is still in you. You can still make me adore you, and I can still make you love me! (*He sits down on the couch, still holding her tightly as she stands before him.*) Why not admit it, Elena? Why maintain that formidable rigidity, as though you were a pure-minded school girl in the clutches of an avid gorilla? Relax, my darling. Let yourself go. (*She has begun to laugh.*) Have I happened to say something witty? (ELENA *continues to laugh.*) There is something in the quality of that laughter which suggests that I'm wasting my time wooing you.

ELENA

You told me to let myself go!

RUDOLF

I did, but it was not intended as a pleasantry. (*He is seated on the couch. She is standing over him. Suddenly, she seizes his face and kisses him as ferociously as he had kissed her.*) Great God, Elena, I didn't expect . . .

ELENA

(*Passionately*). No, you didn't expect me to take your advice so quickly. (*She slaps his face.*) Did you? You thought I'd keep up the pretense of frigidity forever, didn't you? (*She kisses him again. As she does so, he pulls her down on to the couch. She rolls over him.*) Am I frozen now?

RUDOLF

No, there's been an unaccountable thaw. (*She kisses him again.*)

ELENA

Am I restraining myself now? Am I being subdued, repressed, coldly unresponsive? Am I? (*She slaps him again.*)

RUDOLF

No! But for God's sake, Elena—there is such a thing as going too far.

ELENA

No, there isn't. Let's open the doors.

RUDOLF

No.

ELENA

Yes! I want them to see that I haven't changed, that there are some things that can never change. (*She goes to the doors, flings them open, and shouts "Come on—come on!"* POFFY, GISELLA *and the rest come in, laughing, shouting.* BREDZI *and* JANSEI *are with them, playing "The Merry Widow" waltz.*)

RUDOLF

(*Through the happy din*). Look at her! Look at her! She has been hitting me—hitting me with all the old strength! Show them how you did it, my darling! (*She slaps him again. He kisses her gratefully. Then he picks her up in his arms and waltzes her into the bedroom. . . .* KOEPPKE *rushes after them and smirkingly closes the door. The others cheer lustily and wave their champagne glasses.*)

TALISZ

I give them both happiness!

SOPHIA

Happiness—and love!

POFFY

May the night last forever! (*He is standing on the sofa, singing, while* BREDZI *plays softly. The* COUNTESS *crosses to the* COUNT, *who kisses her.*)

COUNTESS

This is the most enchanting moment of my life.

(HOETZLER *bows to* GISELLA, *who curtsies, and they begin to waltz.* SOPHIA *goes to the couch.*)

SOPHIA

(*Transported*). It is the same Vienna—the same exquisite Vienna. . . .

COUNT

Just as it always was! Nothing has changed.

COUNTESS

I don't care if I die tomorrow. I really don't care at all.
(LUCHER *bustles in, terribly perturbed.*)

LUCHER

(*To* HOETZLER). Hush! Where has he gone? (*Waltzing with* GISELLA, *the* GENERAL *ignores* LUCHER, *who dashes to the left and shouts at* KOEPPKE.) Where is he?

KOEPPKE

We don't want to be disturbed now.

TALISZ

What is she saying?

LUCHER

(*Thundering*). Bredzi! Stop!
(*The music stops.* POFFY, *still standing on the couch and singing, turns to* LUCHER.)

POFFY

(*Sublimely unworried*). Is there anything the matter?

LUCHER

Herr Povoromo! Get down off that brocade! (POFFY *descends. They all laugh.*) The police are here! They've heard this racket and one of the bottles you threw hit somebody in the street.
(*Gleeful cheers hail this gratifying news.*)

HOEPPKE

(*Archly*). They'll hear no uproar from the arch-ducal chamber.

LUCHER

Where has he gone? And Frau Krug? What's he done with her?

SOPHIA

We haven't the faintest idea. (*They all laugh.*)

COUNT

Resume the music, Bredzi.
(*The general, mildly intoxicated laughter is interrupted by the sound of sharp knocking from within the bedroom.*)

HOETZLER

What is that?

RUDOLF

(*Offstage*). Elena! Elena!
(*More pounding is heard.* LUCHER *starts up to the door.* HOETZLER, SOPHIA, KOEPPKE *and* GISELLA *stop her.*)

LUCHER

Have you all gone crazy? The police will get him!

SOPHIA

Ssh!
(RUDOLPH *bursts out of the room, rushes to the right. Through the opened door, on the bed, is* ELENA's *white dress.*)

RUDOLF

Elena! Elena! (*He goes out at the right, then returns.*) Where is she? Why do you all stand there, frozen? Go after her. Find her. (HOETZLER, SOPHIA, *the* COUNT, TALISZ *and* KOEPPKE *go off, babbling "We'll find her. We'll bring her back," etc.*) I never should have trusted her to go into that bathroom alone.

COUNTESS

(*Frightened*). How did she get out? Did she jump out of the window?

RUDOLF

No. She went through another door. I wouldn't have trusted her if it hadn't been for the affectionate way she hit me. Elena! (*He is still pacing about frantically, from door to door.* SOPHIA *comes in again.*)

SOPHIA

She's left the hotel!

COUNTESS

She ought to be ashamed of herself.

LUCHER

She's gone home!

RUDOLF

Home? And where is that? Where does she live?

LUCHER

You've got to stay here.

RUDOLF

Why?

LUCHER

The police.

POFFY

They're in the hotel now.

RUDOLF

Get my cap.

LUCHER

I tell you she's gone back to her husband.

RUDOLF

That psychoanalyst? So much the better. Get my cap! (*He propels* LUCHER *towards the bedroom.*) Now which one of you verminous objects is going to tell me where she lives?

GISELLA

I don't know where she lives.

RUDOLF

(*To the* COUNTESS). Do you know?

COUNTESS

(*Timorously*). Poffy can tell you. Poffy knows.

RUDOLF

(*To* POFFY). You will escort me there.

POFFY

If you set foot out of this hotel you're insane.

RUDOLF

You're still threatening me with the police?

POFFY

They'll recognize you, Your Highness. . . .

SOPHIA

Oh, we *beg* of Your Highness . . .

RUDOLF

Any member of the Vienna police force who lays a hand on me will find himself at the bottom of the canal.

(LUCHER *has returned with the Tyrolean hat.*)

LUCHER

Here!

RUDOLF

No! My military cap!

LUCHER

That uniform is no longer worn in Vienna.

RUDOLF

I don't give ten thousand damns what's worn . . .

LUCHER

(*Screaming at him*). They'll shoot you. They'll jump at the chance to finish you.

RUDOLF

(*Calmly*). Very well. . . . Very well. (*He has put on the hat, and a cape which* POFFY *has brought for him.*)

LUCHER

She doesn't want you any more.

RUDOLF

Oh, yes, she does. She's leading me on. She wants the thrill of the chase. Well—she shall have it! (*He crosses to the right and picks up the brandy bottle from the table.*) And if the accommodations at her house are inadequate I'll bring her back here. So see to it that this party is still going on when I return, whether it's tomorrow—or the next day—or whenever. Come on, Poffy. (*He has gone out, followed by* POFFY.)

COUNTESS

(*Thrilled*). He'll do it! He'll do it!

GISELLA

Nothing will stop him!

SOPHIA

He'll bring her back, and the party will go on forever!

LUCHER

You fools! You fools! Don't you see what will happen? They'll catch him. They'll kill him. Tomorrow there'll be another Habsburg burning in hell.
(POFFY *comes in quickly.*)

POFFY

Frau Lucher!

LUCHER

(*Gasping*). Have they got him?

POFFY

No. . . . His Imperial Highness presents his compliments and wishes you to advance him a few schillings for his taxi-fare.
(LUCHER *is muttering a series of unprintable imprecations as she digs into her capacious handbag.*)

CURTAIN

ACT THREE

AGAIN *the living room in the* KRUG *home.*

The time is directly after the end of Act II.

There are spots of light about the room, but the surrounding shadows are deep. In one of the areas of shadow ANTON *is seated, listening to the radio, though not relaxed. He continually looks towards the window—towards the door. After a moment, he rises and crosses to the window, parts the curtains, and peers out.*

ELENA *comes in, breathless and agitated.* RUDOLF'S *cape is about her, clutched tightly, masking the absence of her white dress. . . . She hurries past* ANTON *and turns off the radio.*

ANTON

(*Turning from the window*). Well, how was it?

ELENA

Just about as I expected.

ANTON

Amusing?

ELENA

No.

ANTON

No excitement?

ELENA

None.

ANTON

You didn't stay there very long.

ELENA

Didn't I? (*She is going towards her room.*)

ANTON

(*Gently*). It was evidently a bit upsetting.

ELENA

It was nothing of the kind.

ANTON

I don't like to question you, Elena, but I'm rather afraid that . . .

ELENA

(*With uncharacteristic petulance*). You like nothing better than to question me. (*She is at the back. He is still by the window at the right.*)

ANTON

You know that's not so.

ELENA

Oh—not usually. But tonight . . . why did you ask me to go? Why?

ANTON

I thought you might have a good time.

ELENA

You were wrong. You know, Anton, your prescriptions are not infallible. . . . But—let's not talk about it now. I'm tired.
(*Old* KRUG *has come in from the upper left. He is in his bath-robe, night-shirt and slippers.*)

KRUG

Ah! So you're back. I *thought* I heard you come in. Well, how was the party? Did anything interesting happen? Tell us all about it.

ANTON

She's going to bed.

KRUG

Who all was there? Any famous people? (ELENA *has gone up to the door of her room.*) And what—where's your *dress?*

ELENA

Good night, father. Good night, Anton. (*She goes into her room.*)

KRUG

Hmm! Well, what do *you* make of it? (ANTON *crosses to the left, lights a cigarette, nervously.* KRUG *comes down slowly.*) Didn't you notice anything about the way she said good night? No kisses, nor sweet dreams, nor any affection. And that costume! She was wearing a dress when she left here, wasn't she? There's something the matter. Didn't you notice it?

ANTON

(*Sharply*). No!

KRUG

Well, if you didn't I *did!* And I don't set myself up as a great mind-reader, like you. . . . I could see that something happened there at Lucher's . . .

ANTON

She's tired, that's all.

KRUG

Yes—but *why* is she tired? That's what we ought to know. And what happened to her dress? That's what we ought to find out. You ought to ask a few questions about this . . .

(*The insistent ringing of the night bell is heard.*)

ANTON

There's nothing to find out.

KRUG

There's the night bell.

ANTON

I can hear it.

KRUG

What do you suppose it is?

ANTON

I haven't the faintest idea. (*From the right can be heard peremptory pounding on the front door and loud shouts.* ANTON *crosses to the right and goes out.*)

KRUG

But listen. . . . That sounds like trouble . . .

RUDOLF

(*Offstage*). You needn't announce me . . .

KATHIE

(*Shrieking, offstage*). Oh! Herr Professor! It's a madman.

KRUG

(*Excited*). You'd better get out your pistol, Anton. It's another one of your patients gone insane.

KATHIE

(*Offstage*). A maniac! His keeper is with him but he won't listen. . . . He forced his way in. I couldn't stop him.

POFFY

(*Offstage*). I'm sorry, Herr Professor. If there had been any conceivable way of avoiding this . . .

RUDOLF

A thousand pardons for the disturbance, but this dutiful handmaiden seemed to feel that I should be denied admittance. (*By now,* RUDOLF *has entered, followed by* POFFY, ANTON *and* KATHIE. RUDOLF *is still carry-*

ing the bottle of brandy, as a weapon. He addresses KRUG.) Are you the doctor?

KRUG

Yes! No!

RUDOLF

No?

KRUG

No! He is. (*He points to* ANTON. RUDOLF *turns and confronts the husband of* ELENA.) And I am his father . . .

RUDOLF

Ah! So you are the Herr Professor Doctor! I am frankly surprised. My imagination had adorned you with a gray beard, a long one. (*He bows.*) How do you do?

ANTON

Who are you?

RUDOLF

Eh? You are asking me who . . .?

KRUG

I can tell you who he is . . .

RUDOLF

He doesn't know who I am, Poffy. Come—step up! Present me.

POFFY

Professor Krug—this is the former Archduke Rudolf Maximillian.

RUDOLF

The former! One would think I had already joined my ancestors in their eternal empire.

KRUG

Oh! No!

RUDOLF

However, my dear doctor, you will readily observe that such is not the case. I am here, in your charming home, and I wish to see your wife.

ANTON

My wife has gone to bed.

RUDOLF

She will wish to be aroused.
(ANTON *regards* RUDOLF *for a moment, then crosses in front of him and addresses* KRUG.)

ANTON

Go to bed, father.

KRUG

Me?

ANTON

(*Motioning him off*). Yes! Do as you're told.
(*In a state of extreme disgruntlement, old* KRUG *turns and ambles slowly up towards the steps.* RUDOLF *removes his hat.*)

RUDOLF

(*To* POFFY). And you're no longer needed, Poffy. Go back to Lucher's and see that they carry on.

POFFY

You had better come with me.

RUDOLF

I may be detained a little longer than I had expected.

POFFY

I'll be at the hotel on call. (POFFY *goes out at the right.* KRUG *is now at the door of* ELENA'S *room.*)

KRUG

(*Calling through the door*). Elena, the Archduke Rudolf Maximillian von Habsburg is calling on us and they're sending me to bed. (KRUG *goes on out at the upper left. . . .* ANTON *confronts* RUDOLF, *who holds the brandy bottle at the alert. . . . After a moment,* ANTON *smiles and advances towards* RUDOLF.)

ANTON

I—I wish I could tell you how glad I am to see you.

RUDOLF

(*Startled*). You're *glad*—to see *me?*

ANTON

I should think you could imagine why. You've been something of a presence in my home, for a long time, ever since Elena and I were married. Not an entirely agreeable presence, I might add. (*He laughs.*) But one that we could never quite get rid of. At times, you've stalked about this house as if you owned it.

RUDOLF

(*Pleased*). I *have?*

ANTON

I naturally resented it, a little. But now that I have the chance to see you, and talk to you, I can feel much more friendly towards that presence.

RUDOLF

(*Bewildered*). Well! I've known husbands in my time—but you're the first one who ever granted me a kind word. . . . (*He steps forward. They bow and shake hands.*) I'm glad to see you, too, Herr Professor. Your vast reputation has not done you justice.

ANTON

A remarkably graceful compliment!

RUDOLF

Of course, I've known you through your books. Oh, yes! I've studied them, carefully.

ANTON

All eight volumes?

RUDOLF

You don't believe me, do you? Very well—cross-examine me!

ANTON

No, no. I don't like cross-examinations. I'm only too eager to take your word for it.

RUDOLF

It's very fortunate that you are. Otherwise I should have been proved a liar. (*He puts his hand affectionately on* ANTON's *shoulder. They both laugh. . . .* ELENA *comes in, now wearing a negligee.*) But I'm going to read them. I know now that they're good. (*He sees* ELENA.) Elena, we're friends!
(ELENA, *on the landing, looks from* RUDOLF *to* ANTON.)

ELENA

Are you?

ANTON

Of course we are. We see eye to eye on the most important subject.

RUDOLF

As a matter of fact, we're an incredibly happy combination. Your husband represents the sublimity of the intellectual, and I the quintessence of the emotional. You know—between us, just about there—(*he points to a spot on the carpet*)—there ought to be found the perfect man!
(ANTON *laughs.* ELENA *comes down, goes over to the left, beside* ANTON.)

ANTON

Please go on talking.

RUDOLF

Gladly! I have a great deal of interest to say. (*He sits down in a chair in the center.*)

ELENA

I hope you'll cut it short, Rudolf. Not that I'm unmindful of the great distinction conferred on our house by your presence here—but I'm sleepy. We're sleepy.

RUDOLF

I am still confident of my ability to keep you awake. But my words are not for you, my darling. They are for our mutual friend, your husband.

ANTON

I am anxious to hear them.

RUDOLF

I'm sure you are. And I'm equally sure that you'll be sympathetic. You're a brilliant psychologist—but more than that, you're a Viennese. You will know what I mean. . . . (ANTON *bows.*) But here—I seem to be the only one who's seated. Won't you please sit down?

ANTON

No—if you don't mind . . .
(ELENA *sits down on the edge of the couch.*)

RUDOLF

(*Settling back in the chair*). No, I don't mind. . . . Well—to begin at the beginning—always a suitable starting point: Herr Professor—I have been making advances to your wife. I am here now to continue them until the desired objective has been reached. Am I making myself clear?

ANTON

Perfectly clear.

ELENA

So far.

RUDOLF

Good! You are obviously a man of superior perception. You will not fail to see the validity of my claim. Fifteen years ago I became intimate with Elena. And when I say that I became intimate with her, I hope you will understand that I . . .

ANTON

I am familiar with the preface. You may skip it.

RUDOLF

No, no. I decline to do so. Indeed, I wish to dwell on it. She was then a maiden, exquisitely frail, standing hesitantly upon the threshold of infinite potentiality, if you will forgive my eloquence. Ah—she was lovely, Herr Professor. You would have adored her.

ANTON

I'm sure of it.

RUDOLF

As for myself, I was then, as now, a rank idealist—and when I first looked upon her, and felt the touch of her hand and saw the virginal invitation that was in her eyes, I vowed to myself, "This is the ultimate!" So I made her my mistress. For four beautiful years, I was devotedly . . .

ELENA

It was hardly more than two.

RUDOLF

Don't interrupt!

ELENA

Don't exaggerate!

RUDOLF

(*Rising enraged*). If I'm to be interrupted!

ELENA

Don't *exaggerate!*

RUDOLF

I do so only because of a desire to flatter you. (*He turns apologetically to* ANTON.) Permit me to continue: our idyllic romance was terminated by the revolution. Austria was compelled to give up most of her treasured provinces and possessions, including my family. (*He sits down again.*) We were at Lucher's together when the summons came. I promised her I'd return immediately—but I didn't return. I never even had a chance to say good-bye to her. (*He has said this almost to himself. He turns now to* ANTON.) We were denied the privilege of parting as most lovers do, with the customary romantic heroism—hypocritical self-sacrifice. We were wrenched apart. (*He indicates the arbitrary separation with a gesture of his clenched fists.*) Surely, Herr Doctor, *you* can see the significance of that wrench.

ANTON

I've seen a great deal of it.

RUDOLF

(*Resuming*). The pretense of adjustment had to be made. In my exile I concluded that I should never see my darling again and I made every effort to reconcile myself to that dismal realization. The effort was not completely successful. For ten years I have felt the lack of her. So I decided to return to Vienna, and have one more look at her, and let my youthful illusions be shattered once and for all.

ANTON

That was a highly intelligent decision—wasn't it, Elena?

ELENA

I'm not quite certain.

RUDOLF

Oh, it was, in theory. For I assumed that she would have become a commonplace, obese, bourgeois housewife.

ANTON

She has resisted the influences surrounding her.

RUDOLF

She has, indeed, and I've been grievously disappointed. I find that my acute want of her was no illusion. It remains a fact. (*He rises.*) A fact! (*He crosses and stands behind the couch.*) Which we all must face.

ELENA

Yes, Anton.

RUDOLF

Perhaps you don't believe that it is a fact. Elena didn't at first. I told her something this evening—something that I'd have confessed to no other woman. I told her that all the enjoyment I've had has been vicarious. I too, have been conscious of a presence. Elena has been in attendance at all the sordid little romances I have ever known. (*Turning to* ELENA.) Oh, my dear, you'd be horrified if you knew how many fantastic shapes you have assumed. (*To* ANTON.) That sounds a bit disgusting, doesn't it?

ANTON

Nothing is disgusting that is said with such artless sincerity.

RUDOLF

(*To* ELENA). He's charming—charming! (*To* ANTON.) I *knew* you were qualified to deal with this situation, Herr Doctor. You see, Elena told me: you've written a whole book about me.

ANTON

What?

ELENA

I told him nothing of the kind.

RUDOLF

You did. You distinctly said he'd analyzed me . . .

ELENA

(*Cutting in*). I did not. I said he'd written about that much, explaining your type. (*She indicates about two inches between her thumb and forefinger.*)

RUDOLF

(*To* ANTON). Evidently you can say volumes in a few words. Ah, Herr Doctor—it's enlightening to confront any one like you, who can view things impersonally, and with none of the usual moralistic indignation. You're a scientist—thank God—and I beg of you to consider me as your patient. Analyze me. Subject me to the treatment that you know I need.

ANTON

I'm afraid that's impossible, my friend.

ELENA

(*To* RUDOLF). That's absurd. It takes a long time to complete a treatment.

RUDOLF

So much the better. I don't mind remaining in Vienna indefinitely. But now is the time to begin, Herr Doctor. I want some professional advice.

ANTON

I can't give it.

RUDOLF

But I insist that you can.

ELENA

It's not his custom to give advice.

RUDOLF

Nonsense—he's a doctor—a distinguished one.

ELENA

By a process of suggestion, he compels the patient to advise himself.

RUDOLF

(*To* ANTON). Very well, then—suggest something.

ANTON

No. You have ideas of your own.

RUDOLF

A bewilderingly wide variety.

ANTON

I don't doubt it. But it is useless for me to try to consider this in the light of my own experience; because I have never confronted this problem in just this way before.

RUDOLF

Why, with Elena for a wife I should think that this sort of thing would be coming up all the time.

ANTON

I agree one would naturally think so. (ANTON *is beginning to betray evidences of impatience which might easily develop into violent wrath.*)

ELENA

But one would be wrong.

RUDOLF

Well, I'm glad.

ANTON

I'm only a psychiatrist. Your case requires the specialized services of a neuro-pathologist. There is a very good one in Munich.

RUDOLF

Munich? But that's a long way off—and the night is slipping through our fingers.

ANTON

That's the only advice I can give you, Herr von Habsburg. There's nothing I can do to help you.

RUDOLF

(*Appalled*). Herr von Habsburg! So that's my name? Herr von Habsburg! Oh—I'm not protesting. It *is* my name! It would have been patronizing to call me anything else. Forgive me for interrupting. . . . (*During the foregoing speech he has crossed to the left, close to* ANTON, *as though, for a moment, he had considered a demonstration of his resentment of the humiliating "Herr." . . . He now sits down, slumping, on a chair that is between* ANTON, *who is standing before the fireplace, and* ELENA, *on the couch. . . . It should be noted that through this dialogue* ELENA *is watching both of them with enthralled interest, alarmed expectancy and mounting excitement. . . . With apparent weariness,* RUDOLF *continues.*) You were saying something about a doctor in Munich.

ANTON

Yes. I'll give you a letter to him, and I urge that you go and consult him at once.

RUDOLF

(*With a flash of anger*). But I don't want to go to Munich! I want this problem to be settled now!

ANTON

I'm not a witch doctor. I can't straighten out a mass of glandular complications with a wave of the hand.

RUDOLF

(*Surprised but amused*). Oh, but I'm not complicated—even though I do like to represent myself as an enigma. (*To* ELENA.) You don't mind my talking about myself?

ELENA

Not at all. We're used to it.

RUDOLF

It's a fascinating subject. . . . You must realize, Herr Doctor, that for all my talk, I'm simply a man who lives on sensations. They're meat and drink and breath of life to me. At the moment, I'm desperately in need of nourishment—nourishment for my self-esteem. My ego is like the belly of a starving man—it's bloated but empty.

ANTON

And you imagine that *I* can furnish the necessary nourishment?

RUDOLF

If you can't—no one else can.

ANTON

If this could be dealt with in a rational manner, it would be simple. I'd tell you to look at her to your heart's content—fill your imagination with her. (RUDOLF *turns and stares at* ELENA *and continues to do so while* ANTON *snaps out the following.*) And then see for yourself that for you she has no substance; she's a dream that you've explained, and disposed of, and that you can never recapture. . . . But it isn't so simple as all that.

(*Slowly* RUDOLF *turns away from* ELENA, *rises, confronts* ANTON.)

RUDOLF

You're right, my friend. It isn't so simple. . . . I must do more than just look.
(ANTON *walks away, towards the right.*)

ELENA

Well, Anton—what have you to say to that?

ANTON

(*Irritably*). There's nothing for me to say. I don't want to have anything to say. (*There is a pregnant pause.*)

RUDOLF

I know—it's a damned awkward situation. And it wouldn't have arisen if it hadn't been for your decency. When I came in here I was ready to fight, and either be dragged out myself, or take Elena with me. But—you were so kind. You were so friendly. You showed me that this dispute should be settled by reason as opposed to force.

ANTON

I find that this dispute has become essentially unreasonable.

RUDOLF

It has not! My impulses are entirely natural.

ANTON

And so are my objections to your impulses.

RUDOLF

Oh! So you do object?

ANTON

Yes! I do! (*His attitude is now one of undisguised belligerence.*)

RUDOLF

You're not friendly with me any more. Why? Do you imagine that I want to take her away from you for good and all? I can reassure you on that point. I want her for one night only. That will give me enough to live on for another ten years—by which time I'll hardly be a serious menace to you or to any one. Now—surely—you can have no objection to that?

ANTON

You're forcing me into the hellishly uncomfortable position of a jealous husband.

RUDOLF

If you will permit me to say so, you assumed that position voluntarily when you married her.

ANTON

Yes, yes! I know that!

RUDOLF

You admitted the presence that is in your house, and now that the presence has materialized, are you afraid to face it?

ELENA

No! Anton! You won't let him say that.

RUDOLF

No! No! I don't believe it! You're a man of exalted intellect. You know that jealousy is merely a manifestation of fear, and you have banished fear as completely as you have banished the odious Habsburgs. Isn't that so?

ANTON

We've expelled the Habsburgs from Austria, but not all of us have expelled the Habsburgs from ourselves. . . . Now, I want you to leave.

RUDOLF

What?

ANTON

I'm asking you to go.

RUDOLF

Taking Elena with me?

ANTON

No.

RUDOLF

Even though she might want to go?

ANTON

Have you bothered to consult her as to that?
(ELENA *rises and crosses to the fire-place.*)

ELENA

Oh, leave me out of this. I'm only the guerdon in this conflict. You will have to dispose of me between yourselves.

ANTON

Get out!

RUDOLF

Oh—I'm disappointed in you, Herr Doctor. I thought you were one who had conquered all the baser emotions. But now I see that you *are* just a husband—no better than the rest of them.

ANTON

Unless you go of your own accord, I shall attempt to put you out—and I believe I shall succeed.

RUDOLF

I'm sure you can. But not without making a ridiculous spectacle of yourself.

ANTON

(*Taking off his glasses*). Then I shall not delay the process. (*He now starts to take off his coat. Observing this,* RUDOLF *starts to take off his coat, turning to* ELENA, *as he does so.*)

RUDOLF

There, Elena! I have exposed him before your eyes. This colossus of the intellect, this triumph of civilization, is behaving like a vindictive ape.

ANTON

Get out!

RUDOLF

(*Going up and putting his coat on the balcony rail*). I have to warn you that I'm not going to fight fair.

ANTON

You'd better not watch this, Elena.

ELENA

Nothing could induce me to leave now! (*She sits down on the bench before the fire-place.*) I've just realized that I've been waiting for this moment for years.

RUDOLF

That's right. Stay where you are. When I've had enough I'll call to you and you can drag him off me. (*He picks up a small, modernistic metal statue from the bookcase and brandishes it.*) Come on, Herr Professor. It's for you to begin the brawl. . . .

ELENA

Put that down!
(RUDOLF *examines the statue.*)

RUDOLF

Do you *like* that?

ELENA

Put it down!
(*Reluctantly he obeys.*)

RUDOLF

(*To* ANTON). I'm now unarmed. I'm a competent swordsman but I'm hopelessly inept with my fists. I'm forced to the indignity of treating with you. I'll make you an offer.

ANTON

Make it quickly.

RUDOLF

A very handsome one . . .

ANTON

Make it quickly!

RUDOLF

(*With convincing fervor*). Give her to me for this one night, and I shall give to you in return my one possession—namely, this carcass that I wear about my immortal soul, these priceless pounds of flesh. Tomorrow I shall go forth upon the Ringstrasse. I shall kick and insult policemen. My identity will become known. I shall be beaten to earth and shot, and I shall die gloriously in the gutter, my head pillowed on a pile of excrement. But before I take this suicidal action, I shall sign documents bequeathing my remains, unconditionally, to the eminent Professor Doctor . . . what's the name?

ELENA

Krug.

RUDOLF

Krug! All that is left of me will be yours. You will appreciate my value to science. You may lay me out on your operating table, you may probe, dissect me, discover just what it is about me that has made me what I am, the quality that dominated most of Europe for six hundred years. You will be able to say to your students: "Here, gentlemen—this revolting object that I hold before you is the heart of a Habsburg!" (*There is a prolonged pause.*) No? You reject my offer? You insist on being primitive? Very well, then! Come on, Herr Doctor— (*He steps back and achieves a pose.*) I'm waiting for that bull-like rush.

ANTON

You are succeeding in your object.

RUDOLF

I—succeeding?

ANTON

You are making a fool of me. I should have heeded your warning that you wouldn't fight fair. There are a thousand excellent reasons why I should hit you and I know all those reasons. But confronting you this way, in the presence of my wife, whom I wish above all others to impress, I can't do it. I could finish the fight, but I can't start it.

ELENA

No, Anton, you're wrong. You couldn't finish it. I am the only one who could do that. I should have known it there at Lucher's. (*The night bell rings.*) I shouldn't have tried to escape. That's the mistake I've always . . . (*The bell rings again.*) Who is that?

RUDOLF

Don't tell me that the doctor is being summoned to a patient! (*The bell rings again.*)

ELENA

Shall I go? (*She crosses to the right.*)

ANTON

No—Kathie is awake.
(*Old* KRUG *comes in.*)

KRUG

I heard the bell! I thought it might be something important.

RUDOLF

Let us hope it is not a matter of life and death.
(KATHIE *comes in at the right.*)

KATHIE

Herr Professor Doctor!
(POFFY *rushes in.*)

POFFY

Herr Professor Doctor, my deepest apologies for bursting in in this manner but . .

ANTON

What is it?

POFFY

It's the police.

KRUG

The police!

ANTON

What do they want?

POFFY

His Imperial Highness was seen tearing down the Kartnerstrasse in a taxi . . .
(*Old* KRUG *whistles.*)

ELENA

They want him! They've found out about him!

RUDOLF

By all means let them have me. It's an easy disposition of your problem, Herr Professor.

ELENA

No. You will have to hide. Go in there.

ANTON

What good will that do? The police will keep on till they find him.

RUDOLF

I shall not hide! I prefer to stand and face them.

ELENA

No, you won't. Go in there. . . . Kathie—tell the police that Dr. Krug will see them in a moment.

KATHIE

Yes, ma'am. (*She goes.*)

POFFY

(*To* RUDOLF). You must hide! The whole force is out searching for you.

RUDOLF

(*Going up*). This is the very depth of ignominy.

KRUG

In here, Your Imperial Highness.

ELENA

Here! (*She hands him his Tyrolean hat.*)

RUDOLF

I will not be arrested in this God-damned hat! (*He goes into the room at the back.*)

ELENA

Shut the door, father.

(KRUG *does so*—ELENA *motions him to his bedroom. He pouts but goes out, upper left.*)

ANTON

We'll have to see them.

POFFY

I beg of you, Herr Professor, go down and send them away.

ANTON

Do you think that will stop them from going on with their search?

POFFY

But, surely, they will listen to you. Your position . . .

ANTON

They know perfectly well that there was every likelihood of his coming here. I might get them out of this house, but I can't prevent them from keeping a close watch on it.

POFFY

But you have the greatest influence with the authorities. You can speak to them, persuade them . . .

ANTON

To do what? To allow him to remain here as my guest?

POFFY

No—to permit him to leave Austria, quietly. If you will only say a word to Herr Wreede, the prefect. He's out at Schönbrunn. . . . And I can swear to you that the Archduke will abide by any arrangement you choose to make.

ANTON

(*To* ELENA). So I'm to go to Schönbrunn and make all the arrangements.

ELENA

Oh, yes, Anton. You must do everything you can to help him. . . .

POFFY

You will be performing an act of the greatest generosity!

ELENA

Yes, Anton.

(ANTON *stares at* ELENA *for a moment, then turns to* POFFY.)

ANTON

Will you please wait for me downstairs?

POFFY

Yes, Herr Professor Doctor. (*He bows and goes. There is another pause.*)

ANTON

An act of great generosity! And let us hope of great wisdom.

ELENA

Have you any doubt of the wisdom, Anton?

ANTON

Yes, I have, but I must not admit it. (*He is making a gallant attempt to be ironic.*) You see, Elena—I am facing the test of my own relentless principles. You've heard what my students call me: "the messiah of a new faith." . . . Well—tonight I've heard the bitter injunction that is given to all messiahs: "Physician, heal thyself." It's not a comforting thought. . . . However—I must go out to Schönbrunn and see Wreede. I must make the necessary arrangements. I shan't be back before morning.

ELENA

Oh!

ANTON

Yes! (*He comes close to her.*) You saw the truth, Elena. You saw it, at last, when he goaded me into behaving like—like a vindictive ape. You are the only one who can settle it. If you can look at him, and laugh at him, and pity him, as you'd pity a deluded child; if you can see him for what he is, and not for what your memory tells you that he was—then you're free. He can never hurt you, whatever he does, or whatever you do.

ELENA

Very well, Anton.

ANTON

(*He stares at her for a moment*). Good-bye, Elena. . . . And tell him not to worry. . . . (*He turns and starts to go.*) Herr Wreede will be glad to do me a favor. His wife is one of my patients. (*He has gone out at the right. . . .* ELENA *stands still for a moment, then turns and calls, "Rudolf! Rudolf!"* RUDOLF *opens the door and peers out.* ELENA *crosses to the left.*)

ELENA

They've gone. You can come out.

(RUDOLF *emerges, still in his shirt sleeves, carrying his uniform coat. His tone during the subsequent scene is elaborately sardonic.*)

RUDOLF

Are you sure it's safe?

ELENA

Perfectly.

RUDOLF

Where is your husband?

ELENA

He has gone out.

RUDOLF

Where?

ELENA

To see the prefect of police.

RUDOLF

And what am I to do in the meanwhile—put on my coat and go?

ELENA

No. You can't. The police are down there.

RUDOLF

They were reluctant to take your husband's word?

ELENA

Yes—but you can rely on Anton. He has great influence with the officials. He'll see to it that you are allowed to leave Austria safely.

RUDOLF

(*Coming down*). So I'm to rely on him, am I?

ELENA

There's no one else who could do as much for you.

RUDOLF

The soul of magnanimity, isn't he!

ELENA

Yes.

RUDOLF

And trustful, too!

ELENA

Yes.

RUDOLF

And sublimely confident of your strength.

ELENA

Yes!

RUDOLF

And contemptuous of me. (*She says nothing. He throws his coat down on the couch, and glowers at the door through which* ANTON *departed.*) As effective a bit of foul play as I have ever witnessed! He's tricked me me into his debt—put me on my honor. He knows that I have that. It runs in the Habsburg blood—honor and epilepsy. We deserved to be thrown out—not because we were tyrants, but because we were all at heart rotten sentimentalists. The doctor has discovered the essential weakness.

ELENA

I told you his method of cure. He influences the patient to advise himself.

RUDOLF

Yes—and what he has made me advise myself is not very gratifying to my vanity or stimulating to my lecherous impulses. God damn him! He's devitalized me, emasculated me. (*He sits down on the end of the couch; his fury and much of his bumptiousness have gone out of him.*) While I was in there, hiding, waiting for him to protect me from the law, I looked at my coat, and the obsolete medals, and the worn-out lining, and a great truth dawned on me. It came to me in a revelation that I am no longer an Archduke, nephew of an Emperor; I am a taxi-driver, dressed up!

ELENA

And did your revelation also disclose to you what I am now?

RUDOLF

Yes! You're no longer a mistress—you're a wife—and consequently unprepossessing.

ELENA

Ah! You have realized that at last!

RUDOLF

I have.

ELENA

And you know that I can face you, and laugh at you, and pity you, as I'd pity a deluded child!

RUDOLF

Do we need to enlarge on it? If you mean to get satisfaction for all the indignities that I've lavished on you, you'll be up all night. . . . Go to bed and leave me alone. I'll promise to sit here and keep the faith.

ELENA

(*With sudden tenderness*). You'd better have some rest. You'll be travelling in the morning.

RUDOLF

Your solicitude is touching. But please don't have me on your mind.

ELENA

The police may come back.

RUDOLF

And you want me to know that it would grieve you sorely to have me receive my just deserts. I knew it!

ELENA

You'd better go in there and lie down and try to get some sleep.

RUDOLF

As you wish. (*He rises, crosses to the window, starts to look out upon the Viennese scene, but turns away.*) I shall rest peacefully, soothed by the knowledge that even I have influential friends in Austria. . . . Good night. . . . And when the benevolent doctor returns, please try to express to him some measure of my gratitude. Assure him that, thanks to his generosity, I shall leave Vienna, forever, and return to my taxi. (*He has gone up to the landing at the back.* ELENA *picks up his coat from the couch.*)

ELENA

You've forgotten your coat, Rudolf.

RUDOLF

Oh, thank you.

ELENA

(*Looking at the coat*). It needs mending. (*She goes up to the steps.*)

RUDOLF

Please don't bother. I'll never wear it again.

ELENA

You will, Rudolf. You'll always wear it, gallantly—even if the lining is a little torn. It's your coat. (*She hands him the coat.*)

RUDOLF

Yes! One of the meager possessions of Herr von Habsburg! (*He puts the coat on the balustrade.*) You're very sweet, Elena. I don't quite know why you should be, in view of the ridiculous trouble I've caused. But please remember that I'm grateful—and also sorry.
(*She takes his hand.*)

ELENA

No, Rudolf—you must never be sorry.

RUDOLF

Good night, my dear. (*He kisses her hand.*) Good-bye. (*He goes into the bedroom. . . . For some moments, she stands still. At length, she picks up his coat, looks at the worn lining and the tarnished medals, hanging limply. Then she turns, switches out the lights so that the stage is in darkness except for a faint glow from the hallway. She opens the door of her room. The light from within shines on her.*)

ELENA

Rudolf . . .

RUDOLF

(*From offstage*). Yes?
(*She goes into the room and closes the door behind her.*)

CURTAIN

The curtain is down a few seconds to indicate the passage of several hours. Its rise reveals morning, brilliantly sunny, warm and cheerful. KATHIE *is completing the arranging of the breakfast table which is at the left of the couch. It is set for three.*
Old KRUG *shuffles in from the left, carrying the morning paper.*

KRUG

(*Disgusted*). Just as I thought! Not a word in here about what happened last night. One of the most exciting things that's happened in this city in years, and then they hush it up. (*He sniffs and his expression changes.*) Mm! Kidneys!

KATHIE

You're not to touch them! They are for the Herr Professor Doctor.

KRUG

I thought as much. . . . Oh—well . . .
(KATHIE *starts to go,* KRUG *follows her, talking.*)

KRUG

Oh, Kathie! (*She pauses.*) What did you think of our guest, eh? Did you ever see any one like that before?

KATHIE

(*Scornfully*). No! (*She resumes her exit.*)

KRUG

I never did, either—I mean, close to. How did they get rid of him? What happened after I went to bed? (*He is following her out.*)

KATHIE

(*From offstage*). I haven't the faintest idea *what* happened!

KRUG

(*From offstage*). Well—I'd surely like to know. But it's a sure thing no one's going to tell me. Didn't you *hear* anything? (RUDOLF *comes out of the room at the back, and deposits his cape and his hat on the balustrade. . . .* KRUG, *still mumbling, returns.*) I've got to find out all these things for myself.

RUDOLF

Good morning. Good morning. Good morning! Whoever you are, I bid you good morning, and I can assure you I do so with the most profound sincerity. (KRUG *sees who it is, and is so startled he can only gape.* RUDOLF *goes to the window and looks out.*) It has been years since I have seen one like it. You know, it's an extraordinary thing about Vienna; in no other place on earth will you find a finer quality of mornings. They're ample, they're complete! They have character. Look at this one! It's a new day—and, don't forget, that's very different from saying "another day." You never hear people in Vienna say "another day has dawned," do you? For that's precisely like saying "another Chinaman has been born," an exact reproduction of all the countless millions and millions of Chinamen that have been born and lived and died. . . . It's an appalling thought, isn't it? (*He crosses towards the breakfast table, by which* KRUG, *utterly bewildered, is now standing.*) No, my dear friend—we Viennese are privileged beings. For us, each morning is an adventure, unprecedented and unforgettable. A new day! (*He inspects the array of breakfast.*) What have we here?

KRUG

(*Weakly*). I thought Your Imperial Highness had gone.

RUDOLF

What led you to that misconception? (*He is looking at the various dishes.*)

KRUG

After the police had left, I heard the front door close again.

RUDOLF

That was the excellent Herr Professor, going forth to clear the atmosphere. Ah! Kidneys. (*He takes the dish and sits down.*)

KRUG

Those are for my son!

RUDOLF

He likes kidneys, does he? (*He has begun to eat them.*)

KRUG

He does—and no one is allowed to touch . . .

RUDOLF

Please sit down. (KRUG *sits across the table.*) You know, the more I hear about that gifted scientist, the more I know him to be a gentleman of discernment and taste. He and I obviously appreciate the same delicacies.

KRUG

Where did you sleep last night?

RUDOLF

Now really, my friend—you're a man of the world, aren't you?

KRUG

(*Indignantly*). I am nothing of the kind.

RUDOLF

I envy you. It's a poor world. You do well to keep out of it. If you take my advice, you'll stay here, where you are, in this charming house, in this incomparable city, with a view of the horse-chestnuts; and leave investigation of the world to those who have no place else to go. (ELENA *comes in. She is radiant.*) Ah! Our lovely hostess!

KRUG

Look, Elena! Look at who is having breakfast with me!

ELENA

Good morning, father. Good morning, Rudolf. (*She waves towards the window.*) Gorgeous, isn't it?

RUDOLF

We've been discussing it, at some length.

KRUG

You should have heard him, Elena. I couldn't make out what he was talking about.

(ELENA *has come down to the table and taken possession of the coffee pot.*)

ELENA

Will you have coffee, Rudolf?

RUDOLF

Oh—I'll have everything: coffee, with whipped cream, rolls, honey, jam, jelly. . . . (*To* KRUG.) By the way, did you ever know why it was that our bakers started making rolls in the shape of crescents? (KRUG *shakes his head.*) It was intended as an expression of our contempt for the Turks. (*He is holding up a crescent roll while he talks.*)

KRUG

Was it really! (*He takes a bite of a roll, and munches it reflectively, as though appreciating for the first time its full flavor.*)

RUDOLF

Oh, I could tell you many similar facts of historical importance. For instance—about the Serbian pigs . . .

ELENA

(*Interrupting*). I've forgotten whether you take sugar.

RUDOLF

(*Gazing at her*). So have I.
(*Old* KRUG *laughs heartily.*)

ELENA

Father! What are you laughing at?

KRUG

He said he'd forgotten if he takes sugar.

RUDOLF

I don't blame you for laughing! I don't blame you a bit. It was a fatuous remark.

KRUG

What?

RUDOLF

A very silly remark. As a matter of fact, I take three lumps. (*They all laugh at that.*)

ELENA

(*To* KRUG). He's a fool, isn't he?

KRUG

I should say that he is! Why, do you know what he said about the morning? He said it was like a lot of Chinamen! (*He laughs uproariously. So do* ELENA *and* RUDOLF. . . . *The merriment is interrupted when* ANTON *comes in, accompanied by* POFFY.)

ANTON

Good morning.

ELENA

Anton! (*She rises and crosses to* ANTON.)

KRUG

(*Pointing to* RUDOLF). Look at *this,* Anton...

RUDOLF

Before any one else breaks the news, permit me to announce that I have devoured the kidneys.

ELENA

Kathie will cook some more. Sit down, Anton—and you too, Poffy.

ANTON

No, I've already had a huge breakfast at the Hotel Lucher. But I'm afraid this gentleman hasn't. He has been standing out in the street all night.

RUDOLF

Why in heaven's name have you been doing *that?*

POFFY

The police were still there, and I thought I might be needed.

RUDOLF

And you were ready to die for your Prince. Such gallantry must not pass unnoticed. (*He unpins a medal from his coat and tosses it to* POFFY, *who catches it.*)

KRUG

(*Wide-eyed*). Did you *see* that!

RUDOLF

You say you've been at Lucher's?

ANTON

Yes.

RUDOLF

Is the party still going on?

ANTON

Oh, Lord, yes. They all entertained me at breakfast.

ELENA

How are they now?

ANTON

They're getting a little sleepy.

RUDOLF

(*To old* KRUG). Then let's rush over and wake them up!
(KRUG *starts up, hopefully.*)

ANTON

I'm afraid we can't. I mean, you and I.

RUDOLF

Oh!

ANTON

We have to start immediately for Passau, where you will be allowed to cross the frontier. There's a government car downstairs.

RUDOLF

I see.

ANTON

I hate to drag you away.

RUDOLF

(*Rising*). But it's necessary. Of course it is. Do I have to wear that cape and that hat?

ELENA

Yes—help him, father.
(*Rising,* KRUG *throws his napkin down.*)

KRUG

Oh, *dear!* Now he has to *go!*

ELENA

But why do you have to go with him, Anton?

RUDOLF

I flatly refuse to hear of such a thing! I will not take you away from your duties, your home. Poffy will escort me.

POFFY

I should be delighted to.

ANTON

No. I have given my word that I myself will see you depart from Austria. The authorities wished me to explain that they will take extraordinary precautions to see that you do not return.

RUDOLF

I don't blame them. I don't blame them a bit. . . . Thank you. (*This to old* KRUG, *who has brought him his hat and cape.*)

ANTON

(*To* ELENA). I shan't be back much before evening. Will you tell Zenzi to cancel all my engagements for today?

ELENA

Yes, Anton. I'll tell her. And I'll send word to the university.

RUDOLF

A dutiful wife, Herr Professor. I commend her to you—and you to her. It is a remarkable union, and it will give me satisfaction to the end of my days to think that perhaps I, in my small way, have contributed something to it.

ELENA

It's time to go, Rudolf.

RUDOLF

I know it is. But before I depart, Herr Professor, let me say that I call your roof tree blessed! For beneath it, a Habsburg has been entertained—royally entertained—and has been granted, into the bargain, a superb demonstration of applied psychology. . . . Good-bye, Elena. (*He kisses her hand.*) No wistful tears, please. (*He crosses to* POFFY, *who bows and kisses* RUDOLF'*s hand.*) Good-bye, Poffy. If you sell that medal for a sou less than a thousand francs, I shall be insulted. (RUDOLF *slaps* POFFY *on the back and crosses to old* KRUG, *who is by the door at the right.*) Good-bye, my dear friend. Think of me in the mornings. (*He kisses old* KRUG *on both cheeks and goes out at the right.* POFFY *and* KRUG *go up to the window.*)

ANTON

(*To* ELENA). There'll be no trouble. . . .

ELENA

Anton—there's something I want to say . . .

ANTON

(*Hastily*). No, there isn't, Elena. You have nothing to say to me. I have only to look at you. (*He takes her hand.*) I must hurry.

ELENA

Yes, Anton—but I wanted to say—when you get to the frontier, ask him to give you back my wedding ring.

ANTON

I shall. And I left a package for you in the hall. Frau Lucher gave it to me. It's your white dress. (*He kisses* ELENA'S *hand and goes out.*)

KRUG

(*At the window*). A government car—with the shades drawn!
(ELENA *goes over to the table and sits down, wilfully indifferent to old* KRUG'S *excited reports of what is happening in the street below.*)

ELENA

Sit down, Poffy, and have some breakfast. You must be famished.

POFFY

(*Crossing to the table*). I rather imagine that I am. (POFFY *sits down.* ELENA *looks at the empty dish.*)

KRUG

They're just starting—and the policeman is *saluting* them!

ELENA

All the kidneys are gone. . . . Father! Ring the bell. I'll tell Kathie to cook some more.

KRUG

Enough for me, too? (*Pressing the bell button.*)

ELENA

Of course.

KRUG

Good! (*He is ambling over to the table.*)

ELENA

(*Pouring coffee*). Cream?

POFFY

No, thanks, Elena. I've got out of the habit of cream. (*She hands him the cup.*)

KRUG

You know, Elena—I've never, in all my life, had so much fun!

ELENA

Neither have I. (*She smiles at old* KRUG, *then sips her coffee.*)

CURTAIN

Maxwell Anderson

MARY OF SCOTLAND

MAXWELL ANDERSON

To the honor of having won the Pulitzer Prize for *Both Your Houses* in 1933, Maxwell Anderson can claim the added distinction of having been the first playwright to be awarded the Critic's Circle accolade for *Winterset* in 1936. Born in Atlantic, Pennsylvania, in 1888, Maxwell Anderson received his A.B. degree from the University of North Dakota and his master's degree from Leland Stanford. After a short career as a teacher, he turned to journalism and served successively on the staffs of the *Grand Forks* (North Dakota) *Herald, San Francisco Chronicle, San Francisco Bulletin, New Republic, New York Evening Globe* and *New York Morning World.* His work on the last-named newspaper brought friendship with Laurence Stallings, with whom he collaborated in the writing of the immensely successful *What Price Glory?* Since then Maxwell Anderson has won both critical and public acclaim with such plays as *Elizabeth the Queen* and *Mary of Scotland,* as well as the two dramatic works for which he won the highest honors our country can give.

CHARACTERS

FIRST GUARD, JAMIE
SECOND GUARD
THIRD GUARD
JOHN KNOX
JAMES HEPBURN, Earl of Bothwell
CHATELARD
MARY STUART
DUC DE CHATELHERAULT
MARY BEATON
MARY SETON
MARY LIVINGSTONE
MARY FLEMING
ELIZABETH TUDOR
LORD BURGHLEY
HENRY, LORD DARNLEY
LORD GORDON
DAVID RIZZIO
JAMES STUART, Earl of Moray
MAITLAND of Lethington
LORD HUNTLEY
LORD MORTON
LORD ERSKINE
LORD THROGMORTON
A PORTER
LORD RUTHVEN
LORD DOUGLAS
YOUNG RUTHVEN
FIRST SENTINEL
SECOND SENTINEL
A SERGEANT
A WARDEN
SOLDIERS AND OTHERS

MARY OF SCOTLAND

ACT ONE

SCENE I

SCENE: *A half-sheltered corner of the pier at Leith. It is a sleety, windy night, and the tall piles of the background and the planks underfoot shine black and icy with their coating of freezing rain. Long cables stretch away into the dark. The only light comes from the lantern of two iron-capped* GUARDS *who are playing cards morosely on the head of a fish-tub in the lee of a great coil of rope.*

FIRST GUARD

Na, na, put them away. I'm fair clabbered with the cold.

SECOND GUARD

Aye, you'd say that, wi' ma siller-piece laced in your brogues!

FIRST GUARD

Gie me the hand, then. But man, it's an unco bitter nicht for indoor pleasures.

SECOND GUARD

(*Throwing out cards*). It's a blastit wonner—

FIRST GUARD

Put out, put out!

SECOND GUARD

(*Laying down a coin*). Aye.

FIRST GUARD

And we'll just stop now, forbye to go on 'ud strain your two-year credit. (*He shows his hand.*)

SECOND GUARD

Dod, mon ye hae luck wi' the titties. Ye'll no refuse me ma revenge, Jamie?
(*A tall bearded* FIGURE *muffled in a cloak, has come in from the left.*)

FIRST GUARD

When ye can afford it. No earlier.

SECOND GUARD

Ye see yoursel', Jamie. I'm gouged out clean—

FIRST GUARD

And is that a reason I should risk my gains—?

THE OLD MAN

Aye, dicing, gaming, cards, drinking, dancing, whoring, and all the papistical uses of the flesh—they run before her like a foul air—

SECOND GUARD

It's the Master—wheest—put them awa'.

FIRST GUARD

An' what of it? I'm na member of his congregation.
(*A third* GUARD *runs in from the right.*)

THIRD GUARD

I was right, Jamie! 'Tis the queen's ship!

FIRST GUARD

The Queen's ship, you goik! How could it be the queen's ship? She's to come in a galley, and she's none due this month yet.

THIRD GUARD

My word on it, Tod, I rid out wi' the fishermen, and she's a galley wi' oars, and by God she carries the oriflamme!

SECOND GUARD

Would the queen's ship dock without notice to the lords, and no retinue at the pier?

THIRD GUARD

There it lies—yon wi' the lights!

FIRST GUARD

She's lights aplenty, afore God. Aweel, we've no orders aboot it.

THIRD GUARD

But we can do no less than give her what escort we can—

FIRST GUARD

We're set to guard the pier, and for nowt else.—And why are you so hot for a Romish sovereign to set foot on Scottish soil, do you mind if I ask?—For myself, I'm no member of the congregation, I'm a sojer doing what I'm set to, but it runs in my head we've had enough of the Guises and their Holy Father. Let them stick to their warm climates where they're welcome—and may they come to a hotter place before they set up another standard here!

THE OLD MAN

Ye may be na member of the congregation, friend, but you will be if you keep in that opinion. For her or against her it's to be in this land, and no half-way to stand on. The kirk of Christ or the hussy of Rome, drowned in wine, bestial with fornication, corrupt with all diseases of mind and blood—

SECOND GUARD

Is it the queen's galley, Master?

THE OLD MAN

Aye, is it.

SECOND GUARD

For there's been no herald of it, nor any one told—

THE OLD MAN

I have my ways of knowing. And, hearing of it, I came myself to see this white face they speak of, and these taking graces, and to tell her to that white face of hers and despite her enchantments that we want and will have none of her here. For whatever beauty she may possess, or whatever winning airs, they are given her of the devil to cozen us, they are born solely of the concupiscence of hell and set upon her like a sign. They say when she speaks she drips honey and she smells sweet with boughten perfumes, but I say the man who tastes of her or the people who trust in her will chew on dry ashes in the last day and find no remedy for that thirst! I say she comes with a milk-white body and a tongue of music, but beware her, for she will be to you a walking curse and a walking death!

THIRD GUARD

You will say this to the queen?

THE OLD MAN

I will say this to her whey face!
(BOTHWELL *enters from the right.*)

BOTHWELL

Leg it over to the inn, one of you lads, and fetch a chair—

FIRST GUARD

We're on guard here, my lord.

BOTHWELL

Damn your guard duty! The queen of Scotland's stepping out of a boat in velvet shoes—

THIRD GUARD

I doubt there's a chair nearer than Edinburgh town—

BOTHWELL

There's one at the Leith inn, as ye well know—

FIRST GUARD

We'd need the silver for that, in any case—

BOTHWELL

My mannie, if I was to lay a fist to the side of that iron pot of yours I doubt the dinge would come out in a hurry—. What the devil do ye mean bauchling over a dirty chair? Seize it, seize it in the queen's name!

THIRD GUARD

I'll fetch it, sir.
(*He starts out.*)

BOTHWELL

And do you go with him. I suspect ye of being a psalm-singer with that face.

(*The first* GUARD *goes with the third.*)
A verra braw evening to you, Master Knox.

THE OLD MAN

And to you, my lord.

BOTHWELL

It seems some here heard of her coming, though not perhaps those she'd have chosen. You're not here, by chance, to greet the daughter of Mary of Guise?

THE OLD MAN

If I have aught to say to her, it will be for her own ears.

BOTHWELL

No doubt, no doubt. And I have a little observe to make to you about that, too, sir. Whatever it is you have to say to her you won't say it.

THE OLD MAN

And why not? Are the Papists muzzling the ministers of God?

BOTHWELL

I'm no Papist, as ye're aware, Master Knox, and if I were I'm no such fool as to try to muzzle a minister, nevertheless, whatever it was you were going to say, you won't say it, that's my observe to you—

KNOX

I shall say what I have come to say.
(BOTHWELL *follows the Soldiers. A man's voice, speaking French in a light tenor, comes in from the right.*)

CHATELARD

(*Outside*). It is a badge of honor, I assure Your Majesty.

MARY

(*Outside*). Still, when next you toss your cloak in the mud, take note whether there are any watching to report it—

CHATELARD

(*Outside*). But if my queen and lady note it—ah, what other advertisement would a man desire?
(MARY *the Queen enters with* CHATELARD, CHATELHERAULT, *and the* FOUR MARYS-IN-WAITING.)

MARY

Tut, if it were not known, or suspected, that I was queen, I should have stepped in bog like a drover's daughter——

CHATELARD

Madame, that you are queen would be known if the world were stripped of subjects. The very trees and frozen mountains would bow down to you!

MARY

(*Laughing*). I can well imagine.
Body o' me, I could wish the clouds would stoop less to their queen in my native land.

CHATELHERAULT

One forgets how damn dismal this Scotland can be.

MARY

Dismal? Traitor, have you never plucked a gowan in spring—a fairy fresh gowan—?

CHATELHERAULT

Late—it comes late here—

MARY

Or gorged with bright thorn-apples in mid-August?

CHATELHERAULT

Is there an August in this heathenish climate? God, I can't remember it!

MARY

They are sweeter here than in France, as I recall, and all fruits are sweeter here, of those that grow—and the summer's sweeter—

CHATELHERAULT

They're short enough, God knows.

THE OLD MAN

And when they come they will bring excellent devices of masks and ornament to deceive the eye, and soft words and stenches to cumber the senses of mankind. Adulterers, jig-masters and the like will come in authority, and their counsel will be whoring and carousing, the flower and fruits of evil, of that great sin, that sin that

eats at the heart of the world, the church of abominations, the church of Rome.
(*He pauses.* MARY *stops to look back at him.*)

MARY

Chatelherault, I have been long away, and the speech of Scotland falls strangely on my ears, but is this talk usual among my people?

THE OLD MAN

Yet is there a place reserved for them, where the fire is unending and abates not, even as their desires abate not, where their tender flesh shall be torn from them with white-hot pincers, nor shall rank or station avail them, whether they be queens or kings or the lemans of queens and kings—!

MARY

(*Tremulous*). Surely this is some jest, sir. Surely this is not said in welcome to me.

THE OLD MAN

And what other welcome shall we give the whore of Babylon—the leprous and cankerous evangel of the Beast!
(BOTHWELL *returns from the right.*)

BOTHWELL

Your Majesty, they are preparing a room at the inn, and the chair will be here at once. If you would deign to take my cloak for your shoulders—
(*He lays his cloak around her.*)

MARY

Thank you. I wish to speak to this gentleman—

BOTHWELL

This is Master John Knox, of whom your Grace may have heard.

MARY

Nay, then I have heard of him, and I wish to speak to him. Master Knox, it is true that I am Mary Stuart, and your queen, and I have come back from France after many years away, to take up my rule in this country. It is true, too, that I am sad to leave the south and the sun, and I come here knowing that I shall meet with difficulties that would daunt many older and wiser than I am—for I am young and inexperienced and perhaps none too adept in statecraft. Yet this is my native place, Master Knox, and I loved it as a child and still love it—and whatever I may lack in experience, whatever I may have too much of youth, I shall try to make up for, if my people will help me, in tolerance and mercy, and a quick eye for wrongs and a quick hand to right them—

THE OLD MAN

Aye, they told me you spoke honey—

MARY

And cannot you also—you and your people and those you know—cannot you too be tolerant toward me a little space while I find my way? For it will be hard enough at the friendliest.

THE OLD MAN

Woman, I remember whose daughter and whose voice you are—

MARY

If I were your daughter, Master Knox, and this task before me, would you think it fitting to lay such hard terms on me, beast and whore and I know not what? For I am not a whore, I can say truly, but the daughter of a prince, softly nurtured and loving honor and truth. Neither is my body corrupt, nor my mind. Nay, I am near to tears that you should think so, and I was not far from tears before, finding myself unexpected on this coast, and no preparation to receive me. What you have said comes as very cold comfort now when I need greeting and reassurance.

BOTHWELL

Your Majesty, if the old goat has said anything that needs retracting—

MARY

He shall retract nothing in fear! I would have all men my friends in Scotland!

BOTHWELL

I'm afraid that's past praying for.

MARY

Look on me, sir—and judge my face and my words. In all fairness, am I the evangel of the Beast? Can we not be friends?

THE OLD MAN

I fear not, madame.

MARY

I strongly desire it. I have no wish for any enemy of mine except that he become my friend. You most of all, for I have met you first, and it is an augury.

THE OLD MAN

Your Majesty, I have said what I came to say.

MARY

But you no longer mean it! See—I give you my hand, Master Knox—it is a queen's hand, and fair—and I look at you out of honest eyes—and I mean well and fairly—you cannot refuse me! Do you still hesitate? It is clean.
(*She smiles. He bows stiffly over her hand.*)
And will you come to see me at Holyroodhouse, and give me counsel? For God knows I shall need counsel—and I shall listen, that I promise.

THE OLD MAN

Your Majesty, I should be untrue to myself and my calling if I refused counsel where it is asked.

MARY

You will come?

THE OLD MAN

I will come.

MARY

I will send for you, and soon.
(*Her words are a kindly dismissal.*)

THE OLD MAN

Good night, Your Majesty—

MARY

Good night, Master Knox.
(KNOX *goes to the left.*)
Now I wonder, will he hate me more or less?

BOTHWELL

More, probably. However, it's just as well to have him where you can watch him.

MARY

You're an outspoken man yourself, Captain.

BOTHWELL

I am.

MARY

You will forgive me, but so far I have not heard your name.

CHATELHERAULT

The Captain is James Hepburn, madame—the Earl of Bothwell.

MARY

Ah—you fought ably for my mother.

BOTHWELL

I have been of some slight service here and there.

MARY

You have indeed! Tell me, my lord of Bothwell, have I done well so far? Shall I not make this Scotland mine?

BOTHWELL

Madame, it is a cold, dour, sour, bastardly villainous country, and the folk on it are a cold, dour, sour, bastardly lot of close-shaving psalm-retching villains, and I can only hope no harm will come here to that bonny face of yours, and no misery to the spirit you bring.

MARY

Now here's a new kind of courtesy!

BOTHWELL

You'll hear far and wide I'm no courtier, madame—but I have eyes, and I can see that the new sovereign is a sonsie lass and a keen one, and I was for her from the first I saw her face—but from my heart I could wish her a better country to rule over—

MARY

Now, will no one speak well of this poor Scotland of mine—?

BOTHWELL

Your Majesty, shall I praise it for you—as high as it deserves—?

MARY

Say whatever good you can!

BOTHWELL

Then this is Scotland, my lady: To the north a few beggarly thousands of Highland Catholics who have not yet learned the trick of wearing britches, and to the south a few beggarly thousands of Lowland Protestants whose britches have no pockets to them—Their pleasures are drinking and fighting, both of which they do badly, and what they fight about is that half of them are willing to sell their souls for a florin, whereas the other half has no expectation of getting so much. What business they have is buying cheap and selling dear, but since none of them will sell cheap, and none will pay dear, the upshot is there's no business done——

MARY

Enough, enough!—solemnly and truly, sir—it may be they are not a happy race, but they have beliefs—and what they believe they believe from the heart! Even this Master Knox—

BOTHWELL

He? He believes whatever's to his own advantage, and prophesies whatever will line his nest if it comes to pass. He makes his living yelling nonsense into the lugs of these poor, benighted, superstitious savages—he's split the country wide open over your coming and leads the pack against you, brawling from his dung-hill! We'll have blood-shed over it yet—

MARY

Blood-shed?

BOTHWELL

And plenty.

MARY

No. If I thought that I should turn now and bid the mariners hoist sail and put back for France. I shall win, but I shall win in a woman's way, not by the sword.

BOTHWELL

Let us hope so.

MARY

Hope so! But I shall!

BOTHWELL

I am no courtier, madame. I say, let us hope so.

MARY BEATON

The chair has come, madame.

MARY

Yes, and in time. We're chilled to the heart here. Come.

(*She goes out with* BOTHWELL, *the others following. The first and third* GUARDS *return.*)

FIRST GUARD

Did the old man spit his venom?

SECOND GUARD

You'll not believe it. He kissed her hand.

THIRD GUARD

She's a witch, then.

SECOND GUARD

Aye, is she. The kind a man wouldna mind being bewitched by.

THIRD GUARD

No.

SECOND GUARD

I tell you she fair wenched him. The old man doddert a bit and then bent over like a popinjay.

FIRST GUARD

She's tha' kind then?

SECOND GUARD

She's tha' kind.

Curtain

SCENE II

SCENE: *A corner of Queen Elizabeth's study at Whitehall. It is morning, but the sun has not yet risen. She is up early to go over plans with* LORD BURGHLEY, *who sits opposite her at a small table on which an hour-glass stands like a paper-weight on their notes. She is a young woman, still beautiful, with a crafty face. Tall candles burn behind them in a sconce. Outside the circle of light the scene is indefinite.*

BURGHLEY

It still lacks something of dawn, Your Majesty.

ELIZABETH

We have one more hour before the palace will be stirring. You said, I believe, that you have made memoranda in regard to Mary Stuart?

BURGHLEY

I have set down the facts as we must face them, and alternative policies.

ELIZABETH

Read them, if you will. And turn the glass. It's run out.

BURGHLEY

(*Turning the glass and taking up a paper*). They are not in order, but the main points are covered. First, Mary Stuart has crossed from France to Scotland against your advice and without your safe conduct. This is in itself a slight to Your Majesty, and almost a challenge, though not one of which you can take public cognizance.

ELIZABETH

Yes.

BURGHLEY

Second, she has been crowned queen of Scotland, this also against your wish and in defiance of your policy. This may be construed as an open breach of friendship, or may be overlooked, as Your Majesty may desire—and as it may seem best.

ELIZABETH

Yes.

BURGHLEY

Third, she is a Catholic and related by blood to the most powerful Catholic house in France, which constitutes her a public danger to Protestant England. Fourth, she is next heir after Your Majesty to the throne of England, and is held by Catholic Europe to be the rightful queen of England at the present time, Your Majesty being regarded by all Catholics as a pretender, unjustly seated on your throne.

ELIZABETH

True. Proceed. You have more on that point. They believe me a bastard and say so. Very well, let us face that, too.

BURGHLEY

Fifth, then—you are held by the Catholic Europe to be the illegitimate daughter of Henry the Eighth, the divorce of Henry from Catherine of Arragon being unrecognized by the Church of Rome and his marriage to your mother, Anne Boleyn, deemed invalid. Sixth, these things being true, Your Majesty must not allow Mary Stuart to succeed as Queen of Scotland. For in so far as she is secure in Scotland you are insecure in England. Your Majesty will forgive my bad habit of setting down in writing what is so obvious, but it is only by looking hard at these premises that I am able to discover what must be done.

ELIZABETH

Out with it then. What must be done?

BURGHLEY

She must be defeated.

ELIZABETH

How?

BURGHLEY

Is there more than one way? We must pick our quarrel and send an army into Scotland.

ELIZABETH

Declare war?

BURGHLEY

Perhaps not openly—but we have excuse for it.

ELIZABETH

And reason?

BURGHLEY

She must be defeated.

ELIZABETH

Truly, but not so quick, not so quick with wars and troops and expenses. Have you no better counsel?

BURGHLEY

In all my reading I have found no case of a sovereign deposed without violence.

ELIZABETH

And in all those voluminous notes of yours you have set down no other method save warfare? The last resort, the most difficult, costly and hazardous of all?

BURGHLEY

It is the only sure method, and you cannot afford to fail.

ELIZABETH

My dear Burghley, in any project which affects England and our own person so nearly we have no intention of failing. But you have overlooked in your summary two considerations which simplify the problem. One is the internal dissension in Scotland, half Protestant, half Catholic, and divided in a mortal enmity—

BURGHLEY

Overlooked it! Madame, it is the main argument for an immediate declaration of war—Edinburgh would rally to your arms overnight! This is our opportunity to unite England and Scotland!

ELIZABETH

A war would unite Scotland against us—unite Scotland under Mary. No—it is necessary first to undermine her with her own subjects.

BURGHLEY

And how would that be accomplished?

ELIZABETH

This brings me to the second consideration which you overlook—the conduct and reputation of Mary herself.

BURGHLEY

Would that affect our policy?

ELIZABETH

It will make it. Merely to remind us, will you read over again the report of Mary's character in Randolph's latest budget of news?

BURGHLEY

This? "As for the person of Marie, our new Queen, I must say in truth that she is of high carriage, beautiful in a grave way—?"

ELIZABETH

So—go on.

BURGHLEY

"Beautiful, in a grave way, somewhat gamesome and given to lightness of manner among her lords as well as with other company, very quick-witted to answer back, and addicted to mirth and dancing, wherewith she hath made many converts to her cause among those most disaffected, though there be also those found to say her manners might more beseem the stews or places of low resort than so ancient a palace and line—"

ELIZABETH

You see, she is a Stuart.

BURGHLEY

"Moreover, she hath allowed herself to be seen much in the company of certain men, among them the Earl of Bothwell, and hath borne herself among these men, they being known of somewhat loose report, in such fashion as to give scandal to the stricter sort here, she not scanting to lend her eyes or hands or tongue to a kind of nimble and facile exchange of smiles and greetings which might better become the hostess of an ale-house, seeking to win custom. Natheless she is liked, and greatly liked by those on whom she hath smiled closely, they being won not as a wise sovereign wins subjects, but as a woman wins men."

ELIZABETH

Yes, a Stuart.

BURGHLEY

"Yet to be true again I must say also that she is of noble mind, greatly religious in her way, and the whispers against her name not justified by what she is in herself, but only by her manners, which she hath brought from France."

ELIZABETH

She has won our Randolph among others. He shall go north no more.

BURGHLEY

"And in addition she hath borne her power thus far with so discreet and tolerant a justness, impartial to north and south, to Catholic and Protestant alike, that if she persevere in this fashion she is like to reconcile the factions and establish herself firmly on the throne of Scotland. For vast numbers who thought to curse her now remain her fast friends."

ELIZABETH

Have you yet seen what we must do?

BURGHLEY

I find in this only a graver and more malicious danger.

ELIZABETH

And you would still make war?

BURGHLEY

Your Majesty, it will be war whether we like it or not—and there is imminent danger, danger to your throne and life. The more suddenly you act the less effort will be needed—

ELIZABETH

My lord, my lord, it is hard to thrust a queen from her throne, but suppose a queen were led to destroy herself, led carefully from one step to another in a long descent until at last she stood condemned among her own subjects, barren of royalty, stripped of force, and the people of Scotland were to deal with her for us?

BURGHLEY

She would crush a rebellion.

ELIZABETH

She would now, but wait. She is a Catholic, and for that half her people distrust her. She has a name for coquetry and easy smiling, and we shall build that up into a name for wantonness and loose behavior. She is seen to have French manners; we shall make it appear that these manners indicate a false heart and hollow faith.

BURGHLEY

Can this be done?

ELIZABETH

She is a woman, remember, and open to attack as a woman. We shall set tongues wagging about her. And since it may be true that she is of a keen and noble mind, let us take care of that too. Let us marry her to a weakling and a fool. A woman's mind and spirit are no better than those of the man she lies under in the night.

BURGHLEY

She will hardly marry to our convenience, madame.

ELIZABETH

Not if she were aware of it. But she is next heir to my throne; she will hope for children to sit on it, and she will therefore wish to marry a man acceptable as the father of kings. We can make use of that.

BURGHLEY

Only perhaps.

ELIZABETH

No, certainly. She is a woman and already jealous for the children she may bear. To my mind the man she marries must be of good appearance, in order that she may want him, but a fool, in order that he may ruin her, and a Catholic, in order to set half her people against her.

BURGHLEY

We know that she is seen much with Bothwell.

ELIZABETH

And he is a Protestant.

BURGHLEY

He is a Protestant. Now suddenly it occurs to me. If she were to marry a Protestant and turn Protestant herself, would she not make an acceptable ally?—

ELIZABETH

(*Rising*). I do not wish her for an ally! Have you not yet understood? I wish her a Catholic and an enemy, that I may see her blood run at my feet! Since Bothwell is a Protestant, the more reason for dangling some handsome youngster instantly in the north, as if by accident, nay, as if against my will, some youngster with courtly manners, lacking in brain, a Catholic, and of a blood-strain that would strengthen pretensions to the throne of England.

BURGHLEY

You have thought of some one?

ELIZABETH

I have thought of several. I shall even let it be rumored that I oppose such a marriage. I shall let it go abroad that I favor some one else.

BURGHLEY

Who is the man?

ELIZABETH

I have thought of Darnley.

BURGHLEY

But after herself Darnley is in fact heir to the English throne. An alliance with him would actually strengthen her claim to succeed to your place.

ELIZABETH

The better, the better. He is handsome, and of good bearing?

BURGHLEY

Yes.

ELIZABETH

And a fool?

BURGHLEY

A boasting, drunken boy.

ELIZABETH

And a Catholic.

BURGHLEY

As you know.

ELIZABETH

If I give out that I am determined against it, she will marry him, and he will drag her down, awaken her senses to become his slave, turn her people against her, make her a fool in council, curb this pretty strumpetry that gains her friends, haul her by the hair for jealousy, get her big with child, too, and spoil her beauty. I tell you a queen who marries is no queen, a woman who marries is a puppet—and she will marry—she must marry to staunch that Stuart blood.

BURGHLEY

This will take time.

ELIZABETH

It may take many years. I can wait.

BURGHLEY

And we shall need many devices.

ELIZABETH

You shall not find me lacking in devices, in the word to drop here, the rumor started there. We must have constant knowledge of her, and agents about her continually, so that her acts and sayings may be misconstrued and a net of half-lies woven about her, yes, till her people believe her a voluptuary, a scavenger of dirty loves, a bedder with grooms. Aye, till she herself think ill of herself and question her loves, lying awake in torment in the dark.—There is a man called Knox who can be used in this.

BURGHLEY

But that—to accomplish that—

ELIZABETH

We live in a world of shadows, my lord; we are not what we are, but what is said of us and what we read in others' eyes. More especially is this true of queens and kings. It will grow up about her in whispers that she is tainted in blood, given over to lechery and infamous pleasures. She will be known as double-tongued, a demon with an angel's face, insatiable in desire, an emissary of Rome, a prophetess of evil addicted to lascivious rites and poisonous revenges. And before all this her own mind will pause in doubt and terror of what she may be that these things should be said of her—she will lie awake in torment in the dark—and she will lie broken, nerveless there in the dark. Her own people will rise and take her sceptre from her.

BURGHLEY

(*Rising*). But Your Majesty—you—

ELIZABETH

However, I am not to appear in this. Always, and above all, I am to seem her friend.—You would say that I am in myself more nearly what will be said of her.

BURGHLEY

No, no—

ELIZABETH

Why, perhaps. But that is not what is said of me. Whatever I may be, it shall be said only that I am the queen of England, and that I rule well.

Curtain

SCENE III

SCENE: *A great hall in Mary Stuart's apartments at Holyroodhouse. The room is rectangular, with wide fireplaces glowing to the left and right. An entrance door opens to the right, and two doors at the left lead, one to Mary's study, and the other to her bedroom. The stone of the walls is largely covered with stamped leather hangings. A chair, slightly elevated, stands in the middle of the rear wall, the royal arms of Scotland draped above it. The floor is stone with a few Eastern rugs. There are two high, heavily draped windows at the rear, on either side of the queen's chair.*

MARY BEATON, MARY SETON, *and* MARY LIVINGSTONE *are concerning themselves with the hanging of the ensign behind the chair, and* LIVINGSTONE *has stepped upon a stool to reach a fold of it.* LORD DARNLEY *and* LORD GORDON *are warming themselves at one of the fires, having just come in.*

BEATON

(*To the men*). It's to hang there because she wants it there. Isn't that enough?

GORDON

I've heard my father say that the kings of Scotland were always plain folk, but queens are a fancy breed, and their ways are fancy.

DARNLEY

A thought higher with that fold, my dear —just a thought higher.

LIVINGSTONE

(*Turning*). And why?

DARNLEY

Dod, lady, it's a neat turn of ankle you show when you reach up. Reach a bit higher.

LIVINGSTONE

(*Back to her work*). Look your eyes full if it does you any good, my Lord Darnley.

DARNLEY

Man, man, but that's a pretty foot!

GORDON

Aye.

DARNLEY

Ye have heard it said, no doubt, what they say about a woman's foot?

GORDON

Aye.

SETON

What do they say?

DARNLEY

About a woman's foot? Only that it's, in a sort, a measure of her capacities.

BEATON

Oh, is it, indeed? I've heard the same in respect to a man's nose, and I can only say if it's true your nose is no great advertisement for you.

DARNLEY

The nose is a fallible signal, my lady, as I'll prove to you—you naming your own place and time.

BEATON

I to name the place?

DARNLEY

It is your privilege.

BEATON

Your own bed-chamber, then.

LIVINGSTONE

Beaton!

DARNLEY

Accepted! Accepted! My own bed-chamber! And the time?

BEATON

The night of your wedding, by God!

DARNLEY

My dear lady—

GORDON

She has you there, Darnley.

BEATON

Moreover, if there is one kind of man a woman dislikes more than another it's one so little experienced that he goes peeping at ankles for lack of better satisfaction.

DARNLEY

Stop there! I will furnish you with data—

BEATON

Unless indeed it be the kind of man whose experiences with women have been like nothing so much as those of a dog with lamp-posts—

LIVINGSTONE

Beaton!

(MARY FLEMING *enters from the queen's study.*)

BEATON

(*Clapping a hand to her mouth in mock chagrin*). Oh, what have I said, what have I said?

SETON

A great plenty!

DARNLEY

Mistress Fleming, is it true our sovereign is inaccessible this day?

FLEMING

Quite true, I fear.

DARNLEY

God help the man who tries to woo a queen.

FLEMING

And so he might if your Lordship prayed to him with any serious intent.

DARNLEY

Perhaps. And yet I doubt it might do more good if a man were to have studied in France.

FLEMING

Studied?

DARNLEY

The arts. The arts of Ovid. The arts of pleasing a maid.

BEATON

They are the same in France as elsewhere, no doubt.

DARNLEY

No doubt, says she, and a very pretty innocence.

GORDON

Aye, as though she'd never been there.

FLEMING

We're not denying that we've been in France.

DARNLEY

Then don't tell us that the art of Love is the same there as in England and Scotland, for the report runs different.

GORDON

It's a kennt thing that French love is none the same.

LIVINGSTONE

Will you tell us how?

GORDON

Eh, we're to tell you who've lived among them?

FLEMING

Aside from better manners the people of France are like the people of Scotland, both in love and war.

DARNLEY

It's not an easy matter to go into with my lady's bevy of beauty, nevertheless they say there are no virgins there above four years old.

LIVINGSTONE

Then they lie who say it, and you're fools to believe it.

DARNLEY

Nay, it may be a bit exaggerated, but I'd lay no more than a groat on any piece of French virginity. They have summat to tell in confession; they have had their three of a night; they have had their what-for, and come up all the fresher and more lisping for it.

BEATON

I must say I've never met nastier minds than hereabout, and that's something for John Knox to ponder on, too.

GORDON

Will ye come, man? Ye'll have no sight of the queen today, and these trollops have no time for plain Scotchmen.

DARNLEY

Aye.

FLEMING

Lord Darnley is to remain within call. It is her Majesty's pleasure.

DARNLEY

Ah, well that's something.

GORDON

It's dangling, to give it a plain name. (BOTHWELL *enters from the right.*)

LIVINGSTONE

Oh, my lord Bothwell.

BOTHWELL

By God, my name's remembered, and that's a triumph,
Tell the sweet queen Lord Bothwell would see her alone.

LIVINGSTONE

Sir, she is closeted with her secretary—
We are not free to speak with her.

BOTHWELL

Closeted? So?
I like not that word closeted. Who is there here
Who can speak with her and tell her?

FLEMING

My Lord, she has spaced
This day off into hours, so many to each,
And I fear your name is not scheduled.

BOTHWELL

Distrust your schedule,
Then, my prim, for I'll see her.

FLEMING

The ambassador

From England arrives today, for his audience,
And before that Her Majesty plans to hold
A conclave with the lords.

DARNLEY

We've been sloughed off
Much the same way, my lord.

BOTHWELL

Run along then, and practise
Wearing that tin sword you've got hung on you,
Before it trips you.

DARNLEY

Trips me?

BOTHWELL

Aye, run and play!
This one's been used. The nicks along the edge
Were made on tougher than you. Tell my lady queen
I wish to see her now.

FLEMING

I cannot myself.
I might speak to Master Rizzio.

BOTHWELL

Then do that. Is Scotland grown so formal
That a man's received like a money-lender?
(FLEMING *goes out.*)

LIVINGSTONE

No,
But these matters must be arranged.

BOTHWELL

(*To* DARNLEY). Are you still here?

DARNLEY

Still here.

BOTHWELL

I knew a pimp in Paris had much your look,
But the women he brought me were foul.

DARNLEY

But good enough,
I daresay.

BOTHWELL

You might have thought so.
(RIZZIO *enters,* FLEMING *following.*)

RIZZIO

Oh, my lord Bothwell,
There's such great pressure on our time today—
Matters that must be seen to; if you could come
Tomorrow—

BOTHWELL

Well, I cannot come tomorrow.
Tomorrow will not do. I am here today.
And will not be here tomorrow. Is that understood?
(RIZZIO *pauses.*)

DARNLEY

Let him run his suit into the ground.

GORDON

Aye, and himself.
(DARNLEY *and* GORDON *go out.*)

RIZZIO

My orders are strict, my lord. Her Majesty
Has great problems of state—

BOTHWELL

And they concern me
More than some others. Now, before Christ, I've argued
Enough with women and women-faced men! A room's a room
And a door's a door! Shall I enter without warning
Or will you announce me to her? Great pressure on
Our time! Our time, he says! My fine Italian—
(MARY STUART *enters. There is sudden quiet.*)

MARY

I will speak with my lord alone.
(*One by one, and silently,* RIZZIO *and the girls go out.*)
Do I find you angry?

BOTHWELL

At these pests and midges.

MARY

You saw me yesterday.

BOTHWELL

I have been standing since this early morning—
I and some hundred crows, out in the coppice
On the cliff's edge, waiting for the smoke to rise
From your breakfast chimney. And by the Lord these crows
Are a funny company. I've had four full hours
To study them.

MARY

You come to tell me this?

BOTHWELL

I come to tell you
I've never shown such patience for a woman,
Not in my life before.

MARY

Did you call it patience
On a time when I could not see you, to wreck an inn,
Leave mine host in the road with a broken head
And lie with his daughter?

BOTHWELL

That was not true. Or at least
I had her good will for it.

MARY

And another time
To besiege the governor's house with your border knaves
And rouse all Edinburgh? Are you a man
Or a storm at sea, not to be brought indoors?

BOTHWELL

When I would see my girl, why I must see her
Or I am a storm, and indoors, too.

MARY

Your girl? Give me leave,
Since I am a queen, with a kingdom to reign over,
To queen it once in a while.

BOTHWELL

I tell you truly
I've the manners of a rook, for we're all crows here,
And that's what's understood in this town, but I could
Be tame and split my tongue with courtly speeches
If I could be sure of you—if I could know from one day
To another what to make of your ways. You shut yourself up
With secretaries and ministers, harking for weeks
On end to their truffle—while I perch me on the rocks
And look my eyes out.

MARY

When I was but thirteen
A pretty lad fell in love with me; he'd come,
Oh, afternoons, late midnight, early dawn
Sopping with dew-fall; he'd stand there, waiting for a glance—
I've never had such tribute.

BOTHWELL

This is no boy.
This is a man comes beating your door in now.
It may be you're too young to know the difference,
But it's time you learned.

MARY

You've had your way, my lord;
We've spoken together, though I had no time to give,
And now, with your pardon—

BOTHWELL

You'll go about the business
Of marrying some one else. That's what this mangy
Meeting of councillors means, and that's what portends
From Elizabeth's ambassador! I warn you,
Make no decisions without me!

MARY

I cannot marry you.
I beg you, ask it not; speak not of it. Our day
Has come between us. Let me go now.

BOTHWELL

My lady,
I will speak softly. Have no fear of me
Or what I intend. But there have been days
I remember
When you had less care what hostages you
gave
The world. I think you showed more
royally then
Than now, for you loved then and spoke
your love, and I
Moved more than mortal for that while.
Oh, girl,
If we would be as the high gods, we must
live
From within outward! Let the heavens
rain fire
Or the earth mud. This is a muddy race
That breeds around us. Will you walk in
fear of mud-slingers,
Or walk proudly, and take my hand?

MARY

I am a queen.

BOTHWELL

They've made a slave of you,
This bastard half-brother of yours, this fox
of a Maitland,
This doddering Chatelherault! They
frighten you
With consequences. They're afraid of
men's tongues
And they've made you afraid. But what
they truly fear
Is that you'll win the country, be queen
here truly
And they'll be out of it. What they'd like
best of all
Is to wreck you, break you completely, rule
the country themselves,
And why they fear me is because I'm your
man alone,
And man enough to stop them.

MARY

Yes. You are man enough.
It's dangerous to be honest with you, my
Bothwell,
But honest I'll be. Since I've been woman
grown
There's been no man save you but I could
take
His hand steadily in mine, and look in his
eyes
Steadily, too, and feel in myself more
power
Than I felt in him. All but yourself. There
is aching
Fire between us, fire that could take deep
hold
And burn down all the marches of the west
And make us great or slay us. Yet it's not
to be trusted.
Our minds are not the same. If I gave my
hand
To you, I should be pledged to rule by
wrath
And violence, to take without denial,
And mount on others' ruin. That's your
way
And it's not mine.

BOTHWELL

You'll find no better way.
There's no other way for this nation of
churls and cravens.

MARY

I have been queen of France—a child-
queen and foolish—
But one thing I did learn, that to rule
gently
Is to rule wisely. The knives you turn on
your people
You must some time take in your breast.

BOTHWELL

You know not Scotland.
Here you strike first or die. Your brother
Moray
Seeks your death, Elizabeth of England
Seeks your death, and they work together.

MARY

Nay—
You mistrust too much—and even if this
were true
A sovereign lives always with death before
and after,
And many have tried to murder their way
to safety—
But there's no safety there. For each enemy
You kill, you make ten thousand, for each
one
You spare, you make one friend.

BOTHWELL

Friends? Friends? Oh, lass,
Thou'lt nurse these adders and they'll fang
thee—Thou'rt

Too tender and too just. My heart cries for thee—
Take my help, take my hands!

MARY

I would I could take both.
God knows how I wish it. But as I am queen
My heart shall not betray me, what I believe
And my faith. This is my faith, dear my lord, that all men
Love better good than evil, cling rather to truth
Than falseness, answer fair dealing with fair return;
And this too; those thrones will fall that are built on blood
And craft, that as you'd rule long, you must rule well.—
This has been true, and is true.

BOTHWELL

God help thee, child.

MARY

Be staunch to me. You have been staunchest of all.
Let me not lose your arm. No, nor your love—
You know how much you have of mine. I'm here
Alone, made queen in a set, hard, bitter time.
Aid me, and not hinder.

BOTHWELL

So it shall be.

MARY

And give me the help I'd have.

BOTHWELL

That I can't promise.
I'll help thee and defend thee. Lady dear,
Do you use guile on me?

MARY

No, sweet, I love thee,
And I could love thee well.
(*She goes to him. He kisses her hand and then her lips.*)
Go now, and leave me.
We've been seen too much together.

BOTHWELL

You must lay this hand
In no one's else. It's mine.

MARY

I have but lease on it,
Myself. It's not my own. But it would be yours
If it were mine to give.
(MARY LIVINGSTONE *comes to the right-hand door.*)

LIVINGSTONE

Your Majesty,
The Lords of the council are here.

MARY

Let them be admitted.
(LIVINGSTONE *goes out.*)

BOTHWELL

Has Your Majesty forgotten
That I am of the council, under your seal?

MARY

I could wish you were elsewhere. These are the men I least
Have wanted to find us alone. But stay, now you're here.
(*She goes pensively to her chair of state and seats herself.* LORD JAMES STUART, *Earl of Moray,* MAITLAND OF LETHINGTON, *the* DUC DE CHATELHERAULT, HUNTLEY, MORTON, *and* ERSKINE *are ushered in by* MARY LIVINGSTONE, *who withdraws. There is a brief silence.*)

MAITLAND

We have not interrupted Your Majesty?

MARY

No. The Earl of Bothwell is of the council.
I have asked him to take part.

MAITLAND

There was some agreement
That since the Earl's name might come up, it would be as well
If he were not here.

BOTHWELL

And then again, since my name
May be mentioned, and there's none so able as I

To defend it, it may be as well that I'm here.

MAITLAND

My lord,
There was small thought to attack you.

BOTHWELL

Less now, perhaps.

MARY

Lord Bothwell will remain.

MORAY

Sister, it may be that Bothwell will be offended
By something said.

MARY

You are courtier enough,
To couch it not to offend, my brother.

MAITLAND

Nay then,
What we have come to say must be softly said,
But meant no less strictly. The question of our queen's marriage,
Of which every one has spoken, let me add,
But which we have avoided here, must now come up
Whether or no we like it.

MARY

Be not so tender
With me, dear Maitland. I have been married. I am
A widow, and free to marry again.

HUNTLEY

That's the lass!
They say widows are always ready.

MARY

Do they say that?
Do they not say ready but—wary?

HUNTLEY

Aye, that too.

MARY

But the truth is I should prefer my own time for wedding.
I know of no prince or king whose hand is offered,
And whose hand I'd take.

MAITLAND

It's not to be treated lightly
I'm much afraid. The thrones of all the world
Are shaken with broils even as we stand here. The throne
On which you sit, our sovereign, is shaken, too,
Though Your Majesty has done more than I'd have dreamed
Could be done to still the factions. It's our belief
That a marriage, if the right one, would seat you more firmly,
Put an end to many questions.

MARY

There's more of this?

MAITLAND

That's all we wish—to see you safe on your throne
So that we may be safe in our houses. Until men know
What alliance we're to make, what hangs over us
In the way of foreign treaties, the clans will sleep
With dirks in their brogans, and a weather eye still open
For fire in the thatch. And yet to choose the man—
That's a point we can't agree on.

MARY

I'm with you there.
For you see, I'm hard to please.

MAITLAND

And more than that,
Of princes that offer, or have been suggested, each one
Commits us to some alliance of church or state
We'd find embarrassing. Philip of Spain, the Duke
Of Anjou—these are Catholic—

BOTHWELL

Has it crossed your mind
That there are lords in Scotland?

MAITLAND

And there, too—
If the choice were to fall on a Scottish earl, the houses

Passed over would take it ill—and it might well lead
To a breach in our peace—

BOTHWELL

Yes?

MAITLAND

Nay, even to civil war.

MARY

I cannot give myself out
As a virgin queen, yet our cousin Elizabeth's plan
Has virtues. Must I marry at all?

MORTON

Your Majesty,
We have not yet said what we came to say,
And it needs saying bluntly. The people of Scotland
Are given to morals almost as much as to drink.
I'll not say they're moral themselves, but they'll insist
On morals in high places. And they've got in their heads
That you're a light woman.
(MARY RISES.)
I don't know how it got there,
And I daresay it's not true—

MARY

Thank you. For your daresay.

MAITLAND

I could have wished to speak more delicately
Of this, but it's before us, and can't be denied.
Your Majesty, when you came to us from France
And I saw you first, I said to myself in my heart,
All will be well with Scotland. What I thought then
I can say now, for you are wiser even
Than I had supposed, and you have dealt more justly
Than any could have hoped, yet still it's true
Some spreading evil has gone out against you,
A crawling fog of whispers.

MARY

Who believes them?

MAITLAND

I'll not say they're believed. I'm not sure they are.
But there was the episode of the boy who was hidden
In your bed-chamber—

ERSKINE

Chatelard.

MAITLAND

Aye, he, and
That may have begun it. I believed at first it stemmed
From John Knox's preaching, for he holds all Catholics
To be the devil's own, but there's more than that—
A much more seeded, intentional crop of lyings
Planted here, till I've wondered if Chatelard
May not have been an agent, or one of many.

MARY

Planted by whom?

HUNTLEY

Why, by Elizabeth.
Who else?

MAITLAND

But that's not certain, either.
Chatelard came from France, and in all this scurril
I've traced no word to London.

MARY

It's what they say.
Not what they believe.

HUNTLEY

You've lent them some color for it,
Your Majesty. You've been no statue.

MARY

No,
Nor wish to be. My Lord of Lethington,
What you have said to me, how I was when you saw me,

How I seem to you now, I swear to you, you were not wrong.
I have not betrayed myself as woman or queen.

MAITLAND

I would swear that, too.

MARY

And since I know that is true,
I have thought very little of whispers. For there is judgment
Somehow in the air; what I am will be known, what's false
Will wash out in the rains.
(*She seats herself again.*)

MAITLAND

My sovereign, you are yet young.
I once believed that. But I have lived long enough
To see error grow up and prosper, and send its roots
A century deep. There's force enough in these winds
Of malice to blow us all down—

MARY

I'll try to be serious,
For I see you are. It's your thought, then, that a marriage
Would end the rumors?

MAITLAND

Aye.

MARY

But as to whom I'll marry—
Happily, that's not decided for me yet.

MORTON

By God,
If it was we'd see you to bed with him tonight.

MARY

Has the woman no voice in such matters?

MORTON

Not in such cases.

MARY

And what is my case, may I ask?

MORTON

Why, we've said nothing
About my Lord Bothwell. It's his name's coupled with yours;
His and young Rizzio's.

BOTHWELL

I've thought often, Morton,
One of us would die before the other. Now
I'm sure of it. And soon.

MORTON

I have you.

MARY

My lords,
Will you quarrel in council over your queen's virtue?
Let me defend my own honor, and let you
Defend your own. Do I understand that I
Am accused with Bothwell or Rizzio? Or both?

MAITLAND

You are accused of nothing.

MORTON

You are not accused,
Your Majesty. Moreover, you are queen
Of Scotland, and therefore no man here would dare
Accuse you—

MARY

Oh, speak out, man! Are you afraid?
When have I punished plain dealing?

MORTON

Why, then, you are queen,
And may set your own customs, but if my wife were seen
Abroad as you are, and half so free of contact
With young and old as you are, I'd not answer
For what was said about her!

MARY

I'm no man's wife.

MORTON

No. And the sense of this council
Is that it might be better if you were,
Better for your good name and better for Scotland.

MARY

I will answer these things: as for Rizzio,
He is my secretary; if I spend time
In private with him, that is the reason. If I
Had not liked him, he would not be my secretary.
As for Lord Bothwell, he has put more strength
Behind what I wished to do than any among you,
And at times when I had despaired. He is my good friend.
We were here alone before this conference
And we differed in opinion. To wipe that out
I went to him of myself and kissed his lips.
We had kissed but once before, may not kiss again,
But that's at my option, not yours.

HUNTLEY

Lassie, ye've been
Too honest for your own good.

MARY

Why, if so much weight
Is placed on a kiss in Scotland, come now, each one
And take your kiss—or if that's no recompense
Come to me then in private, and you shall have,
Each one, one kiss.

MORTON

And after that, there are kisses
Elsewhere—and when you've finished, whether you'll marry
Or not may not be the question, but whether we can find
A prince who'll have you.

MARY

(*Rising and taking a step down*).
And having heard that word—
My lords, when you wish to talk with me again
As civilized men, and not barbarians,
You shall have audience. This Scottish kirk of yours
Has misled you as to the meaning of kisses. I am
Unsullied and young, and have my own faith to plight
And more to think of than these maunderings
Over pantry gossip. I shall not marry till
I find it wise, nor until I have made quite sure
What effect it will have on my inheritance
Of the throne of England. You come here in high conclave
And spend three farthing's worth of wit to chaffer
Over a kiss in my audience-chamber! The question
Is not to save my name, I hope, nor my throne,
But how best to meet the destiny that has made me
Full heir to all this island.—Scotland is mine,
And England will come to me or to the child
I hope to have. It's this that makes my marriage
A matter of moment.—And this—with your good pardon—
Will be the last for today.
(*She goes into her study.*)

MORAY

Morton, I warned you
To leave all speech to Lethington.

MORTON

She sits on that throne
Only so long as we want her there, no longer.

BOTHWELL

If my lord of Morton
Would care to lose those black feathers from his crest
I await his pleasure.
(*He goes out.*)

MORAY

I'm for that, too. Settle it between you,
And may you both win. We'll all be the better for it.
(LIVINGSTONE *enters from the right.*)

LIVINGSTONE

Lord Throgmorton is here from England
With embassies for the queen.

MAITLAND

She's gone to her study.
She'll wish to admit him.

LIVINGSTONE

Yes.
(*She goes to the queen's study.* MORTON *goes out the other door.*)

MAITLAND

We get no further
Today, then.
(*He goes to the door.*)

HUNTLEY

No. Erskine, a word with you.
(ERSKINE *and* HUNTLEY *go out.* THROGMORTON *enters.*)

MAITLAND

Come in, Lord Throgmorton. You've been announced within.

THROGMORTON

Greetings, my lord, fair greetings.

MAITLAND

We can have speech later.

THROGMORTON

We shall.
(MAITLAND *goes out.* THROGMORTON *and* MORAY *are alone.*)
Greetings also to my Lord James Stuart,
In fine, the best of greetings.

MORAY

From Elizabeth?

THROGMORTON

I'm burdened with them—and more to you than any.

MORAY

May I know the drift?

THROGMORTON

This is hardly the place for that,
But this much for now: Elizabeth has determined
That you are to reign in Scotland, if not as king,
Then as regent again.

MORAY

Well, that's news.

THROGMORTON

She bids me to tell you
As if from herself, you are not to be disturbed
If her policy seems at variance with her mind.
It's a wide arc of intrigue, but she carries
These schemes in her head like a gambit, and she means
To play it to the end. Your sister Mary
Is not acceptable to her.

MORAY

But this scheme of hers?

THROGMORTON

Later, later. You're a silent man, I know.
No word.

MORAY

None.
(MARY *enters.*)

MARY

Lord Throgmorton?

THROGMORTON

Your Majesty.
(*He kneels. She comes to him and gives him her hand to kiss.*)
From one great queen to another, happiness.

MARY

A courtier in the grand style.

THROGMORTON

Nay, Majesty,
A plain man of business.

MARY

Let us to business, then.
(*She motions him to rise, and he does so.*)
My brother, did you wish further word with me?

MORAY

No, madame, only that I may see you tomorrow.

MARY

(*Goes to her chair*).
At your own time.

(MORAY *bows low and goes out.*)
You had more to say?

THROGMORTON

Much more. My poor brain's taxed with remembering.
But to begin, Queen Elizabeth sends her love
To her cousin of Scotland, wishes her well, and a reign
Both long and easy, and proffers to that end
Whatever friendship and amity between thrones
Your Majesty will accept.

MARY

Tell Elizabeth
She will not find me niggard of friendship or love.

THROGMORTON

I shall report Your Majesty so. Then, further,
I'm bid to say, what Elizabeth most desires
Is that all briars of discord that have grown
Between this city and England, be wed away,
And leave a path for peace.

MARY

I desire that, too.
Does she put a name to these briars?

THROGMORTON

Your Majesty, I am
Permitted to speak quite frankly?

MARY

I beg you to.

THROGMORTON

You are next heir to the throne of England, and you
Are a Catholic. This is a danger to you
As well as Elizabeth. Were you to turn Protestant
Elizabeth would at once recognize in you
Next heir to her succession.

MARY

I should think she might,
Since I am next heir.

THROGMORTON

Forgive me for speaking plainly.

MARY

Oh, forgive me!

THROGMORTON

If this seems difficult, I am bid to remind you
That Elizabeth was a Catholic, but became
A Protestant for political reasons.

MARY

That
I could never do. Nor do I see that one's faith
Should be touched by politics.

THROGMORTON

Why, not politics,
My gracious queen! God forbid me that I should bring
That word into such a context! We know, of course,
How one clings, shall we say for sentimental reasons,
To the rituals of his youth! Aye, and even a prince,
We admit, would rather say his pater nosters
The way he learned them when he was a child. And yet
Must we take these childish things so gravely now,
When war or peace hangs on them? There are Catholics
In England still. They still plot against our queen.
Were she struck down by one of them you'd take
Her throne and rule us. It follows that your faith
Is a challenge to her—yes, if your Grace will pardon
The word—a defiance.

MARY

You were bid to say this to me?

THROGMORTON

Madame, it was said so smoothly by my queen
There was no offense in it, but I have no gift
Of language. I must say things out.

MARY

Your manner
Is packed with the most magniloquent impudence
That's come my way. Do you or your queenly mistress
Deem me an inferior, to be given orders blithely,
With a high hand?

THROGMORTON

No, madame.

MARY

Say three words more
In this cavalier offensive style of yours
And you'll find yourself in the courtyard.

THROGMORTON

Madame, I—

MARY

Come down to earth, and speak without swaggering.

THROGMORTON

I've been in the wrong.

MARY

That's better.

THROGMORTON

It's true that I'd
Rehearsed my song and dance. Your wit is quicker
Than's been supposed in London.

MARY

Quick enough.
To perceive an insult, I hope.

THROGMORTON

Your Majesty,
There was none intended, but I might have spoken more wisely
Had I known your mettle. Elizabeth is concerned,
As I have said, with the differences that are certain
To arise over your religion. Further than that,
What arrangements may be made to avert a breach
In the present concord, if we may discuss these things
Frankly, and you will make frank replies, I have
No other mission.

MARY

Now you talk sense. And frankly.
I will not change my faith.

THROGMORTON

And, frankly again,
There was little hope that you would. There is some hope,
However, that when Your Majesty seeks a consort
You will not do so to bolster up your claim
To the English crown, which is strong enough already
To cause us uneasiness in London.

MARY

That
Had not occurred to me.

THROGMORTON

But surely your choice in marriage
Will imply your attitude?

MARY

I have no intention
Of plighting my troth at once, but if I had
I've received advice already on that point,
A mort of it—and I'm tender.

THROGMORTON

Say no more,
Madame, and I'll say no more.

MARY

Oh, out with it now,
Give the advice. I won't take it.

THROGMORTON

Why, it's only this:
If Your Majesty were to marry a Protestant lord
Of no royal pretensions, it would indicate
That you meant no danger to our Elizabeth.

MARY

She has chosen for me, I daresay? She has some lord
Of the sort in mind?

THROGMORTON

You embarrass me to go on.
She mentioned a name.

MARY

Yes?

THROGMORTON

Madame, the Earl of Leicester.

MARY

I hope her ears burn now. Leicester? Her cast-off!—
Her favorite—the one she's dangled? This is an affront—
She named Lord Leicester?

THROGMORTON

Nay, nay—only to show you
What it was she had in mind. The kind of match.

MARY

I would hope so.

THROGMORTON

For, you see, Your Majesty,
She had a fear of this—the young Lord Darnley
Has come north against her will. Why he's here we don't know.
Nor whether by invitation, nor what your plans
Might be concerning him.

MARY

I have none.

THROGMORTON

Then, if you will,
Forget what I've said. It was only that this Darnley
Combines to exactness what Elizabeth dreads
In case you marry. After you he's next to her throne,
And he's a Catholic. Should you marry Lord Darnley
And call up Catholic Europe to your back—
Well, we'd be ringed in steel.

MARY

I have offered your queen
My friendship and love. I meant that offer.

THROGMORTON

But even
If there were no quarrel, and you should marry Darnley
And have a son by him—he'd be heir to England—
And I think the plain fact is that Elizabeth
Would rather choose her own heir.

MARY

Now God forgive me!—
I am heir to the throne of England, and after me
Whatever children I have—unless by some chance
The virgin queen should bear sons! Is it part of her love
To cut me off from my right?

THROGMORTON

It must be remembered
That England is Protestant, and it might come hard
To accept a Romish sovereign. In brief, my queen
Has wished that you might choose Bothwell, or perhaps some other
Of Protestant persuasion!

MARY

And that's the message.
We're down to it at last. My lord Throgmorton,
I marry where I please—whether now or later,
And I abate not one jot of my good blood's lien
On the English throne. Nay, knowing now the gist
Of Elizabeth's polity toward that claim, I shall rather
Strengthen it if I can. The least worthy sovereign
Has a duty toward his blood, not to weaken it
Nor let it decline in place.

THROGMORTON

This will hardly please.

MARY

I could hardly expect it would. But I too am a power,

And it matters what pleases me. This was all?

THROGMORTON

This was all
I'm commissioned with.

MARY

I shall see to your safe-conduct.

THROGMORTON

I thank your Majesty.
(*He goes out.* MARY *is alone a moment, brooding.* RIZZIO *enters.*)

MARY

Oh, Rizzio, Rizzio,
They make a mock of me! It was as you predicted
To the utter syllable.

RIZZIO

A warning, then.

MARY

We'll expect no friendship from England.
She cuts me off, me and my line.

RIZZIO

May I say that this
Is only her wish, not accomplished?

MARY

Aye, and not to be.
I'd have stood her friend, Rizzio, meant to be her friend,
But now—this is not to be borne! Go and find Lord Darnley.

RIZZIO

Your Majesty—you have made a decision?

MARY

Yes.

RIZZIO

Now I thank you. Now, God helping us, we'll win.
She'll not stamp you out.

MARY

So I think. And now find him.

RIZZIO

Yes.
(MARY BEATON *comes to the outer door.*)

BEATON

Will your Majesty see a gentleman calling himself Lord Bothwell?
(BOTHWELL *comes to the door.*)

MARY

He's in again?

BEATON

There's no keeping him out.

BOTHWELL

(*Entering*). The doxy invited me in herself. She's a slut,
This Beaton of yours.
(RIZZIO *goes out the outer door.*)

MARY

Oh, I know.

BEATON

May I put in a word
For this gentleman, madame? Of all who come calling on you
He's the most ill-favored. It may be that he's honest,
I hope so, to go with that face. You're not afraid
To be left alone with him?

MARY

You may go, Beaton.

BEATON

Yes, Majesty.
(*She curtsies hurriedly, and goes out.*)

BOTHWELL

Now, what an inexperienced queen you are
To surround yourself with such taking bitches!

MARY

My lord,
I have heard from England.

BOTHWELL

Mary, my queen, what you heard

I could have guessed. She's your demon.
She bodes you ill.

MARY

I believe it now.

BOTHWELL

And moreover, between the two,
This cormorant brother of yours, and that English harpy
They'll have the heart out of you, and share it. Trust
Not one word they say to you, trust not even the anger
Their words rouse in you. They calculate effects.

MARY

Where is Lord Morton?

BOTHWELL

Lord Morton is not well.
(*He is very serious.*)
A sudden indisposition.

MARY

Bothwell, Bothwell—
You've fought with him!

BOTHWELL

A mere puncture. What men think
I cannot punish, nor what they say elsewhere but when
I hear them, by Christ, they'll learn manners.

MARY

I forbade it.

BOTHWELL

Forbade it! My dear, not God nor the holy angels
Forbid me when I'm angry.

MARY

I say I forbade it
It's I who's responsible for my kingdom—not you—
You were bound to keep the peace!

BOTHWELL

When my lady's slandered?
I'll teach them to hold their peace where you're concerned
Or find their sweet peace in heaven.

MARY

Would God I'd been born
Deep somewhere in the Highlands, and there met you—
A maid in your path, and you but a Highland bowman
Who needed me.

BOTHWELL

Why, if you love me, Marie,
You're my maid and I your soldier.

MARY

And it won't be.

BOTHWELL

Aye, it will be.

MARY

For, hear me, my lord of Bothwell.
I too have a will—a will as strong as your own,
And enemies of my own, and my long revenges
To carry through. I will have my way in my time
Though it burn my heart out and yours. The gods set us tasks,
My lord, what we must do.

BOTHWELL

Let me understand you.
The gods, supposing there are such, have thrown us together
Somewhat, of late.

MARY

Look, Bothwell. I am a sovereign,
And you obey no one. Were I married to you I'd be
Your woman to sleep with. You'd be king here in Edinburgh,
And I'd have no mind to your ruling.

BOTHWELL

They'll beat you alone.
Together we could cope them.

MARY

Love you I may—
Love you I have—but not now, and no more. It's for me
To rule, not you. I'll deliver up no land
To such a hot-head. If you'd been born to the blood

I'd say, aye, take it, the heavens had a meaning in this,
But the royal blood's in me.—It's to me they turn
To keep the peace, patch up old quarrels, bring home
Old exiles, make a truce to anarchy. Escape it I cannot.
Delegate it I cannot. The blame's my own
For whatever's done in my name.—I will have no master.
(BOTHWELL *is silent when she pauses.*)
Nay, I am jealous of this my Stuart blood.
Jealous of what it has meant in Scotland, jealous
Of what it may mean. They've attacked that blood, and I'm angry.
They'll meet more anger than they know.

BOTHWELL

And who
Has angered you? Not I?

MARY

Elizabeth.

BOTHWELL

I thought so.
She's afraid, if I'm half a prophet,
That you'll marry me.

MARY

Her fears run the other way.
She's afraid I'll marry a Catholic and threaten her throne!
She threatens disinheritance! Offers me Leicester!
Her leavings!

BOTHWELL

Yes, by God, that's a cold potato.

MARY

And means to choose another heir for her throne!
I may never sit on it, but the Stuart line
Shall not suffer by me!

BOTHWELL

Will you tell me what that means?

MARY

I mean if I have a son he'll govern England.

BOTHWELL

And so he might, if he were mine, too.

MARY

Nay, might—
But it must be!
She dares to threaten my heritage!

BOTHWELL

Does that mean Lord Darnley?
(*She is silent.*)
Aye, lady, will you stoop so low to choose
A weapon? This is not worthy of the girl
I've known. Am I to be ousted by a papejay
Who drinks in the morning and cannot carry his drink?
An end of mouldy string? You take too much
On yourself of the future. Think of us, and the hours
Close on us here we might have together. Leave something
To the gods in heaven! They look after lovers!

MARY

Oh, what's a little love, a trick of the eyes,
A liking, to be set beside the name
You'll have forever, or your son will have?

BOTHWELL

Well, it's been nibbling at you this long while,
And now it's got you, the blight of Charlemagne—
The itch to conquer.

MARY

I have an itch to conquer?

BOTHWELL

It goes deep, too, that itch. It eats out the brain.

MARY

Well, and my love for you, how worthy is that?
It's my body wants you. Something I've fought against
Comes out in me when you're near. You've not held it sacred.
You've taken others. I've known. And then come wooing.
It would happen again.

BOTHWELL

It's a man's way. I've loved you
None the less.

MARY

You don't offer enough, Lord Bothwell.
You're not true in it, and I'm not true to myself
In what I feel for you.

BOTHWELL

I'm no lute-player,
To languish and write sonnets when my lady
Says me nay. Faith, I've lived rough on the border,
And cut some throats. I don't forgive myself
Too easily, when I look back, but I tell you
If I give my pledge to you it's an honest pledge,
And I'll keep it. Yes, and when the tug begins
Around your throne, you'll be lost without me. Try
No threats toward England.—It will tax a hardy man
All his time to hold what you have.

MARY

We differ there, too.
What I have I'll defend for myself.

BOTHWELL

If you marry this Darnley
I take away my hand.

MARY

Before God, he believes
He's held me up so far, and I'd fall without him!

BOTHWELL

I believe it, and it's true! Darnley, sweet Christ!
No miracle could make him a king! He's a punk,
And he'll rule like a punk!

MARY

We shall see, Lord Bothwell.

BOTHWELL

Well, I'm sped. My suit's cold. But, dod, lady—Darnley—
He sticks in my craw—I can't go him. You'll find few that can.
Think twice about that. Let him not cross my way,
Or he'll lose his plumes like Morton!

MARY

Will you learn, Lord Bothwell,
That this is not your palace, but mine? Or must you
Be taught that lesson?

BOTHWELL

There's been a bond between us
We'll find it hard to forget.

MARY

You may. Not I.
I've set my face where I'm going.
(RIZZIO *enters.* DARNLEY *is seen behind him.*)

RIZZIO

Lord Darnley is here,
Your Majesty.

MARY

Let him enter.
(DARNLEY *enters from the doorway.*)

BOTHWELL

Lass, lass, God fend thee.
You've seen the last of me.

MARY

I've given no leave
For departure, Lord Bothwell!

BOTHWELL

I need no leave, nor leave-taking.
You see no more of me.
(*He goes out.* RIZZIO *bows and follows him.* MARY *crosses the room away from* DARNLEY *and looks for a moment in the fire. Then she turns to him.*)

MARY

I have sent for you.
Lord Darnley, to tell you your suit has prospered. You've asked
My hand in marriage, and I grant it.

DARNLEY

Your Majesty—
I hardly hoped—I haven't dared—this is fortune
To take one's breath!

(*He comes forward and falls to one knee.*)
I shall love you, keep you, defend you!

MARY

We shall face troubled times.

DARNLEY

We'll meet them bravely.
This is some dream—or a jest. It can't be.

MARY

Aye. I feel that.
And yet it's true.

DARNLEY

I'm to hold you in my arms!

MARY

Not yet. And yet, if you like, come, kiss me.

DARNLEY

They say
A kiss seals the bargain!
(*He rises, staggering slightly.*)

MARY

I've heard so.
(*He crosses to her.*)
You've drunk too much.

DARNLEY

Nay, only a morning cup. Oh, Lady, lady—
When you're kind the whole world's kind!

MARY

(*She faces him, then draws back a step in repulsion.*)
You're a boy, a child.

DARNLEY

Older than you, though.
It's a bargain, then?

MARY

Yes.
(*He puts out his arms to her. Her eyes hold him off.*)
Let the kissing go. Let it go till the bond's sealed.

DARNLEY

Aye, madame.
(*He drops his arms. They stand looking at each other.*)

Curtain

ACT TWO

SCENE I

SCENE: *The hall in the palace. Evening.* MARY *and the* FOUR MARY'S-IN-WAITING *are sitting near the fire, listening as* RIZZIO *sings to his lute.*

RIZZIO

My heart's in the north,
And my life's in the south,
False I've pledged with my hand,
False I've kissed with my mouth.

Oh, would we might lie
Where we lay by the firth,
With one cloak about us,
To keep us from earth,

With hand caught to hand
And the rain driving blind,
As the new years have driven
Old love out of mind.

MARY

What is the line, False I've pledged with my hand?

RIZZIO

False I've pledged with my hand,
False I've kissed with my mouth.

MARY

Where did you come by the song?

RIZZIO

It's one I made.

MARY

I thought so. Well, it's too true—and past time for crying.

BEATON

These poets make much of false pledges and false kisses—but they often turn out quite as well.

MARY

Nay, they turn out badly. If you should love, Beaton, give yourself where you love.

BEATON

There's one of these silly hackbuteers I could have a mind to but I gather he has his penny a day and no more.

MARY

Then if I were you I'd take him.

LIVINGSTONE

And live on a penny a day?

MARY

Or anything.

RIZZIO

My lady, I shall never forgive myself.

MARY

It was my own doing.

RIZZIO

My counsel weighed with you. I favored Darnley because he was of my faith. And he's our weakness, not our strength.

MARY

None could have known that.

RIZZIO

I should have known. Bothwell would have been better.

LIVINGSTONE

Bothwell!

RIZZIO

Aye, Bothwell. He'd have held them off. There's no trifling with him.

LIVINGSTONE

We do well enough without him.

RIZZIO

Well enough perhaps.

MARY

Let's have no talk of Bothwell.

LIVINGSTONE

He's better away. The country's been much quieter since he left it. Hasn't it, madame?

MARY

Much quieter.

FLEMING

You will have a child, your Majesty. You will have an heir, and then you will be happier.

MARY

With Darnley's child?

FLEMING

He will change, too. The man changes when there are children.

MARY

We must hope so.

SETON

His Majesty will return tomorrow?

MARY

He was to have returned three days since. But the hunting may have been delayed.

BEATON

The hunting! He does his hunting o' nights.

MARY

Nay, Beaton.

BEATON

Nor do I take much joy in hearing him called His Majesty.

SETON

But it's the correct address. Lord Darnley has been crowned.

BEATON

Is that a reason for giving him any deference among ourselves? He's a baby, and a spoilt one, and it would give me small pain if I never saw his foolish face again.

SETON

I think that's very treacherous talk!

MARY

It is, too.

BEATON

I'm true to my queen, and I'll be true to none else.
(*She goes to* MARY *and leans her head against her knee.*)

MARY

Not even your hackbuteer?

BEATON

Not even him.

RIZZIO

Your Majesty, I have a request which you have denied before, but which I must make again. It is necessary for me to leave Scotland.

MARY

David, David!

RIZZIO

I grow lonely for Italy.

MARY

And who will write my letters?

RIZZIO

There are many who could write letters.

MARY

Can you name one—both efficient and to be trusted?

RIZZIO

Maitland.

MARY

Would you trust him?

RIZZIO

I think I should go, Your Majesty.

MARY

We know why, David, and I won't have it. I won't have my friends driven from me.

RIZZIO

I think it's best.

MARY

Has His Majesty spoken to you?

RIZZIO

Only by the way.—I'm not wanted here—you know that.

MARY

The king is full of these whims and fancies, my dear Rizzio. If I gave way to one I should have to humor him in all. You and I know that I am quite innocent with you, and you with me.—And I can't spare you.

RIZZIO

God knows you are innocent, madame, and I too, unless it be a crime to love you. I do love you, I can't deny that.

MARY

Nor do I hold it a crime.

RIZZIO

Majesty, I tell you honestly it's torture to speak of going away—and yet—oh, I want no harm to come to you through me!

MARY

And none will. The king is jealous, of every one, my Rizzio, every one I see or have seen. It's just a brainsick notion. I know that he has acted and spoken foolishly in many such matters. But as for danger, there is none.

RIZZIO

I hope there is none.
(*There is a clatter of armor in the hall to the right.*)

MARY

Say no more of going.

RIZZIO

My queen, I am too easy to convince in this! Too much of me cries out to stay—and yet—say no more and let me go!

MARY

Why, very well.

RIZZIO

But not angrily—not in anger.

MARY

Not in anger.

RIZZIO

I thank Your Majesty.
(*A* PORTER *comes to the door at the right.*)

PORTER

Master Rizzio?

RIZZIO

Yes.

PORTER

Lord Maitland of Lethington and Master John Knox are here.

MARY

They are to come in.
(RIZZIO *makes a gesture to the* PORTER, *who goes out. The Queen rises.* RIZZIO *goes to the door and ushers in* MAITLAND *and* KNOX, *then goes out.* KNOX *stands at the door.*)

MAITLAND

Ah, Your Majesty—I was to bring Master Knox—

MARY

Yes, I remember.

MAITLAND

(*Looking about*). I gather that he wishes to speak with you in private.

MARY

I doubt that we shall find the subject makes it necessary. Master Knox, will you come closer to the fire?

KNOX

I am very well here, I thank Your Majesty.

MARY

You come—was it the word?—to make a protest?

KNOX

Would it be convenient that I speak with you alone?

MARY

When we last spoke alone, sir, there was some talk to the effect that I had used arts on you. I could wish to avoid a repetition of that.

KNOX

Why, then, I have but one thing to say and I shall make shift to say it quickly. You are a Catholic queen in a Protestant land, your Majesty—

MARY

Only in part Protestant.

KNOX

Protestant in great majority—

MARY

Yes.

KNOX

You have taken a Catholic husband and set him on the throne beside you, giving him what is called in the courts of this world the crown matrimonial. You have also set up an altar in this your palace, where the mass and other idolatrous rites are said for you. In these ways you encourage Lord Huntley and the Highland Catholics of the north in their heathenish practices, and in so doing bring grave dissension among your people. I come to warn you.

MARY

To warn me of what, Master Knox?

KNOX

That the forms and appurtenances of the Romish faith cannot be thrust upon us. That this will not be borne by the defenders of the Lord's word and church.

MARY

I ask no one to subscribe to my faith, sir. But it has been mine from a child, and I keep it.

KNOX

You seek to gain it a foothold here, and build it up about you. I wish no evil to you nor to this kingdom and I say the celebration of the mass must cease, for there are those among us to whom it is abhorrent. And though it cost civil war and the slaughter of brother by brother it will not be borne.

MARY

And are you among those who will not bear it?

KNOX

I am.

MARY

Do you find it written that all men must worship in one fashion?

KNOX

There is but one true faith and one true fashion of worship.

MARY

And would you enforce it with the sword?

KNOX

There is no tolerance for the idolator nor the adulterer. They are to be weeded out—and even now—before they come to the great pit and are given over to his unending fire—a fire not to be quenched nor remedied nor appeased.

MARY

I understand your attitude toward the idolator, Master Knox, but do you consider it apposite to bring adulterers also into this conversation?

KNOX

The idolator, the adulterer, the priests of Baal, they shall be uprooted, seed and seedling, and cast into the burning—

MARY

But Master Knox, Master Knox, let us have a meeting of minds! An idolator is not the same as an adulterer. Confine yourself to some meaning!

KNOX

They come among us in one person—the priests of the flesh and the worshippers of the flesh—

MARY

If you would but leave off prophesying for a moment and speak sense! Who is the idolator here?

KNOX

Have you not set up an altar?

MARY

A very little one, sir. Nothing to what I could wish. And does that make me an idolator?

KNOX

Will you deny it?

MARY

I do deny it. And now tell me who is the adulterer.

KNOX

Let them search in their hearts who came from France.

MARY

I have searched in mine, and find no adultery there. And shall not those who live in Scotland search in their hearts also?

MAITLAND

Your Majesty, I have brought Master Knox here only because I am convinced that he voices an attitude which must be seriously considered.

MARY

But I try to take him seriously and he speaks in parables. I ask him to define his words and he talks of a great fire. To him a priest is a priest of Baal, an idolator is the same as an adulterer, and those who come from France run especial danger of damnation. What can one say to such a man? Master Knox, I believe you mean well, but can you not see that I also mean well, and that there might be more than one opinion concerning the worship of Our Lord?

KNOX

There will be but one opinion held in that last day—when he comes with his armies, and driveth before him those who are not his children!

MARY

Look, what can one say to him? You ask him a question—and he threatens you with the Last Judgment! You see, Master Knox, you are not the judge who will sit over us in the Last Judgment! You are instead an elderly gentleman of provincial learning and fanatical beliefs, lately married to a niece of your own some forty years your junior, and one who conducts his conversations almost exclusively in quotations from the Old Testament. If you will talk sensibly with me I shall talk sensibly with you, but if you come here to frighten me I shall regard you as a most ridiculous antediluvian figure, and find you very funny. Which shall it be?

KNOX

Well I know you hold the Lord God as a jest and a mockery!

MARY

Do not confuse yourself with Lord God again! There's a difference!

KNOX

I am His spokesman.
(RIZZIO *comes to the door.*)

MARY

Indeed. Will you show me your commission?

KNOX

I call ruin to fall on this house, the shelter of the great beast—!

MARY

And there again! Maitland, can you, by any stretch of the imagination, look upon me as the great beast?

RIZZIO

Your Majesty, Lord Huntley is here.

MARY

Come in, Lord Huntley!
(HUNTLEY *enters.*)
Sir, I have just heard myself likened to the great beast of Revelations. Can you see any similarity there?

HUNTLEY

Why, lass, I'd say at the least it's an exaggeration.

MAITLAND

If Your Majesty wishes to give audience to Lord Huntley—
(*He starts to withdraw.*)

MARY

Nay, why should you go? And why should John Knox and Lord Huntley not meet face to face in one room? I am aware that Master Knox is a Protestant and that Huntley is a Catholic, but they dwell in the same kingdom, and it would be well if they understood each other.

KNOX

I am loath to say it, but I am of a mind that there can be no understanding between him and me, no, nor between myself and Your Majesty, lest I betray my Lord.

HUNTLEY

Madame, it's my opinion we understand each other dom well. Too dom well.

MARY

But since you must both live in this kingdom and one must be Catholic and one Protestant, surely it were wiser to be amiable over small matters, Maitland?

MAITLAND

Aye, it would be wiser.

KNOX

Not for what you have said to me or of my person, for that unto seventy times seven those who follow him forgive, but because the air of this house is offensive in his nostrils, I call ruin on it! Nor will I commune in it further, neither with those who make their beds here nor with those who come here for counsel! Yea, if there are any here who would avoid the wrath, let them turn now, for it is upon you and your servants!

MARY

Well—it would seem there's little to be done about that. You are dismissed if you wish to go.
(MAITLAND *and* KNOX *turn to leave.*)

MAITLAND

I offer my apologies, Your Majesty.

MARY

Oh, surely.

KNOX

Yea, those who breed and take their ease in the places of the anointed, turn, turn now, before the axe fall quickly and be followed by silence! For now it is not too late, but no man knows when he cometh, nor on the wings of what morning!

(MAITLAND *and* KNOX *go out.* RIZZIO *rejoins the group at the fire.*)

MARY

You are duly impressed by this talk, sir?

BEATON

Why, the solemn ass! He should have been booted!

HUNTLEY

My dear, you've been too easy with him, and if you continue to be easy we'll pay for it.

MARY

And in what way, sir?

HUNTLEY

You and I are alone here, Your Majesty, so far as Catholicism's concerned. My Highlanders are Catholic, it's true, and there's a plenty of them, and they're tough, but the rest are all against us, every noble and man of note. They're John Knox's men, and you heard yourself what he said.

BEATON

He with the persimmon-colored whiskers?

HUNTLEY

Aye, he. And he means it.

MARY

What does he mean?

HUNTLEY

Ruin to this house.

MARY

Is this a house to be blown down with windy talk?

HUNTLEY

My birdie—I canna call you Ye're Majesty and all that—

MARY

You need not.

HUNTLEY

Then, my bird, they draw their nets tight about us. I told you before, and it's coming.

MARY

And who draws the net?

HUNTLEY

(*Looking at the others*). Lady—

MARY

These five know my secret heart. They'll say nothing.

HUNTLEY

Lady, there's only one defence. Attack them first. And there's but one proper place for John Knox. He should be in Edinburgh Castle—and all those with him who are of his mind.

MARY

You'd imprison him?

HUNTLEY

He and some twenty others.

MARY

And then?

HUNTLEY

Then you can go to work. You're not safe here and I'm not safe here while a sect of Protestant lords divide your dominion with you. You rule by sufferance only.

MARY

They are here by my sufferance, Huntley.

HUNTLEY

You have heard of the sheep nursed the wolf-pups till they tore her to pieces.

MARY

But we're not sheep and wolves, my lord. There's room for all of us here, and for whatever faiths we may choose to have.

HUNTLEY

Never think it, my bird, never believe it! It's never yet happened that a state survived with two religions in it. Never. Elizabeth knows that. She's behind this Knox. He'd never dare be so bold if she weren't behind him.

MARY

But it's my thought that in Scotland, though it be the first time in the world, we shall all believe as we please and worship as we list. And Elizabeth may take it as she sees fit.

HUNTLEY

She uses it against you, my dear, and uses John Knox against you. Ladybird, I'm willing to beg it of you, take heed of me now or we're both done!

MARY

Rizzio?

RIZZIO

You know my mind. I'm with Lord Huntley in this.

MARY

But how can I bring myself to imprison men for no wrong they've done, on suspicion only, imprison them for their faith?

HUNTLEY

It's more than faith. It's works. You heard John Knox!

MARY

It cuts athwart every right instinct I have, my lord! Every fibre I have that's royal shrinks at such pennywise petty doings! And John Knox—a doddering imbecile, drooling prophecy!

HUNTLEY

He threatened you, lady.

MARY

No, no, I can't. Even if it were wisdom to do it, and it's not.
(*The right-hand door opens suddenly and* DARNLEY *stands in it.* MARY *turns toward him.*)
My lord!
(DARNLEY *walks slowly to the middle of the room and lays a hand on the table.*)

DARNLEY

I'm unexpected, perhaps? Too early? A thought
Too early? I'll retire. Come when I'm wanted.

MARY

No,
My lord, you've been long expected, and more than welcome.

DARNLEY

Why, a pretty wife, a huswife with her maids;
A pretty sight, and maybe a cavalier
Or two, for the maids' company. Dod, sit down, all!
Damn me if I'll intrude!

MARY

Will you speak to Lord Huntley?

DARNLEY

(*Focusing on* HUNTLEY).
Right. That's right. Lord Huntley, give me your hand.
I thank you for watching over the pretty wife here.
I've been away.

HUNTLEY

(*Turning*). Your Majesty, you've a wife
Such as I wish I'd had when I was young.

DARNLEY

Right—You have right. They all say that. I'd say it myself,
Only I know her better.
(*He turns to the door.*)
I know her too well.
And not well enough. She wouldn't care to hear it.
Not from me.

MARY

Darnley.

DARNLEY

She sleeps alone.
At least as far as I know.

HUNTLEY

I'll take my leave,
My lady.

MARY

Yes.

DARNLEY

Stay, stay, I'm going. I only
Tell you she sleeps alone as far as I know.
A pretty wife. These women—they get with child,
You never know how—and then they won't sleep with you.
(HUNTLEY *bows to* MARY, *turns deliberately, and goes out the door to the right, closing it.*)
What's the matter with him? He's an old married man.
He knows these things.

MARY

You're tired, my lord. Will you wish
Some service, something to eat and drink?

DARNLEY

She sends me
Off to bed, you note. You note it, Rizzio?
There's a service she could do me, but I doubt
She'll offer it. And I'm a king, by God, a king,
And you're a clark by office!

MARY

My lord, I hoped
You'd have some other word for me when you
Returned.

DARNLEY

My pink, if I gave you the word you've earned
The room would smell. I've been at the hunting. We had
Something to drink. Alban! Alban! Allons!

MARY

You call some one?

DARNLEY

Alban! God's right! St. Andrew! Alban!
I'm drunk, you see.

MARY

I think not.

DARNLEY

Yes, but I am.
Alban! Christ his sonties, am I left
Alone here! God and St. Andrew!

(*The right-hand door opens and* RUTHVEN *enters in full armor.*)

MARY

What is this?
(*To* RUTHVEN.)
You will retire, sir. Who are you?

DARNLEY

My good friend Ruthven.

MARY

Is this a place for armor? I will receive
Lord Ruthven another time.

DARNLEY

The callant's there,
Ruthven.

RUTHVEN

Aye.

MARY

I had heard that Lord Ruthven was ill,
And thought to go to him, not to see him here.

RUTHVEN

I am ill, and it's mortal, but I've sworn to be mortal
To another first.

MARY

This is my apartment, sir,
And I ask you to go.
(DOUGLAS *appears behind* RUTHVEN.)

MARY

I demand little courtesy,
But that little I must have. Are these your friends?
If so, take them elsewhere.

DARNLEY

Aye, I'm to have my friends
In my apartment—and you're to have yours here.
I say no—they're to mingle.—
(*He points to* RIZZIO.)
You see that grig
With the kinked hair there? He with the lady's hands
And feet? Where does he sleep nights? That's he, that's the one
We have in question!

MARY

My lord, when you've been drinking
I have little taste for your company, and to-night
Less, perhaps, than ever.

DARNLEY

He, he, I tell you!
That Italian spawn!
(RIZZIO, *trembling, steps back toward the queen's study.*)

MARY

(*Stepping in front of* RIZZIO).
Go into my study.
(LORD MORTON *enters.*)
Lord Morton,
Whatever you have in hand here, put no faith
In this king I've crowned and set beside me! His word
Is a paper shield.

DARNLEY

I'm king in this country, mistress—
And I know my rights.

MARY

Beaton, why were these men
Not stopped at my door?

DARNLEY

They came with me.

BEATON

(*Facing* MORTON).
Will you tell me
What you want with the queen?

MORTON

(*His dagger drawn*). Damme, do you want this bodkin
Through that bodice of yours?
(*She shrinks back.* RIZZIO, *having reached the study step by step, opens it and reveals a* GUARD, *a drawn claymore in his hand.*)

RIZZIO

Let me pass!

THE GUARD

Nay, lad.

FLEMING

Your Majesty,
They've broken into your rooms.
(MARY *turns and sees the guard.*)

MARY

Lord Darnley, was that
By your order?

RIZZIO

(*Hardly able to speak for fear*). Save me, my queen, save me!

MARY

Aye, Rizzio.
(*The five women retreat before the armed men, covering* RIZZIO *from them.*)

MORTON

Look to the women-folk, Darnley. We'll care for him.
(RIZZIO *turns suddenly and leaps behind the heavy drapes of the high window down-stage.* MORTON, DOUGLAS *and* RUTHVEN *follow him,* DOUGLAS *with his dagger raised.*)

MARY

Douglas, I'll remember this!
(*A fall is heard behind the curtains, but no cry.* MARY *runs toward the window, but is met by* RUTHVEN, *sheathing his dagger.*)
You've murdered him!
You pack of filthy cowards!

RUTHVEN

Yea, and done well.

MARY

Done well! Oh, fools and cowards!
(*She runs to the curtain and with* MARY BEATON *pulls it back from* RIZZIO, *then bends over him and draws back again in terror.*)
Oh, David, David,
It was I wouldn't let you go!

DARNLEY

(*Looking away*). You might cover that sight.

MARY

Is he dead, Beaton?

BEATON

Yes, madame.

MARY

Oh, you do well, you do well.
All of you!

(*She conquers her repulsion, and tries to loosen* RIZZIO'S *ruff.* FLEMING *comes to help her.*)
We'll help him if we can,
Fleming.

FLEMING

Yes.

MARY

You were too gentle for them,
David. They couldn't bear it—these boors and swine—
Your kerchief, Fleming! He bleeds so—

FLEMING

It's useless, madame.

MARY

(*Rising*). Yes.
(*To the lords.*) To take him unarmed, and poniard him—
One who had never hurt you!

RUTHVEN

(*Sinking to a chair*). Well, the work's done,
And my queen's wiped clear of him.

MARY

Wiped clear! You believed
I was guilty with him!

RUTHVEN

Were you not?

MARY

No!

RUTHVEN

I'd be sorry
If you were not. I struck him down for that.

MARY

I was not guilty. But will you tell me now
Who'll believe me innocent? You've branded me deep
With this murder, and you've killed a guiltless man!
Why do you sit in my presence?

RUTHVEN

Because I'm ill
And dying. I should be sorry if this thing
I've done were in error—for it's the last I'll do.

MARY

You'll stand in my presence! Whose order was it?

RUTHVEN

Why, ask His Majesty that—
And Morton there, and Moray.
(*He rises with difficulty.*)

MARY

Moray too?

RUTHVEN

Yea, your brother. For me—let me go home.

MARY

Go. Morton and Douglas, I give you three days
To leave this kingdom.

MORTON

And the king? I have the king's seal
For what I've done.

MARY

Is that true?

DARNLEY

Aye.

MARY

The worse for you.
The worse for you all.

DARNLEY

My lady, this long while past
You've denied me your chamber, and when I've seen you there's been
This Rizzio with you.

MARY

Never again while I live
Will you see me alone. I bear your child in me
Or you'd answer for this!

DARNLEY

There'll be no answering!
We know what we know about you!

MARY

I would I knew
In what strange dark chamber of your oafish brain

You found reasons for Rizzio's death. If I saw you seldom
Remember how often you drank yourself imbecile
Before you came to me. You've slain your last friend, sir.
It was Rizzio's counsel put you where you are
And kept you there. These are not your friends, these three,
Nor Moray. They wanted Rizzio out of the way,
And they wanted to drag you down, and drag me down,
And you play into their hands. I've never been
Unfaithful to you, but we're at an end, we two.
From this time forward if I touch your hand
May God blight me and my child!

DARNLEY

I wanted you!
You kept away from me, and it drove me mad!

MARY

You won't mend it now. Look, young Rizzio's dead,
You've blackened me, blackened yourself, thrown a black doubt
On the child who'll be your heir. The lords look on
And smile, knowing they've trapped you. You'll never climb
From the pit where you've fallen, and I may fall with you. Lord Moray
Weaves his web round us. You've helped him.

DARNLEY

God knows I wanted
Only my right.

MARY

You pitiful dolt! To think
Such a calf should rule, and at my choosing! God
May forgive you—not I. Nor forgive myself.—And Rizzio.—
Take yourselves out! You pollute the dead to stand there!
He wanted to go to Italy.

FLEMING

Yes.

MARY

Will you go?
(MORTON *beckons the guards, and they cross from the study to the outer door.*)

RUTHVEN

(*At the door*). You'll want some help, mayhap.

MARY

None of yours. I've noticed
It's men that kill, but women that wash the corpse
And weep for it. May none ever weep for you.

RUTHVEN

None will. I've been in the wrong.

MARY

I'm sorry, Lord Ruthven.
It's an ill thing to have on your heart when you die.

RUTHVEN

Aye, is it.
(*He goes out, and the men follow him.* DARNLEY *looks back as if he wished to speak to the queen, but goes silently.*)

MARY

And now we're alone. The lords have shown their hand.
Rizzio's gone—and Darnley, what there was to go.
We've been not long in Scotland, but time enough
To show I can lose it, have lost it in their minds
Already. We must lay the poor lad somewhere.
Could we lift him together?

SETON

Oh, madame, I'm afraid!

MARY

Of what?

SETON

I've never seen one dead before.
I've not known it was like this.

MARY

It's poor Rizzio.
No one to hurt us. And you and I will lie
Some time like this, and folk will be afraid
Because we lie so still. How strange it is
That he should frighten us who wished us well,
And would still if he lived. We must take him up
And lay him on my bed. I'll sleep with Beaton
Tonight.
(*She takes a step toward* RIZZIO.)

BEATON

Madame, the blood will stain your dress.

MARY

If that were all. This will bring more blood after.
Now I see it. Before I reign here clearly
There will be many men lie so for me
Slain in needless quarrel. Slain, and each one
With blood to spill but once, like his. And yet
One steps on into it—steps from life to life
Till there are thousands dead, and goes on still
Till the heart faints and sickens, and still goes on
And must go on.
(*An iron gate clangs outside.* BEATON *parts the curtains to look out.*)
I tell you, Fleming, my soul
Is aghast at this blood spilled for me, and yet
It hardens me, too. These are their manners, this
Is the way they go to work. I shall work on them,
And not too lightly. They think of me as a girl,
Afraid of them. They shall see.—And yet my mind
Believes nothing of what I say; I'm weak as grief,
Stripped and wept out before them. They press me close,
And I have no one to send.
(*There is a rattle of staves in the courtyard.*)

BEATON

(*Turning back*). It's the provost, madame,
I heard them call his name.

MARY

He's not to enter.
Let no one enter.
(BEATON *goes out right.*)
No one. In all this kingdom.
I can trust only five, and one's myself,
And we're women, all of us.—If they go scot-free
After this indignity I'm no queen. For Ruthven,
He'll pay his own score. He's dying. Morton and Douglas
Must die too.

FLEMING

They were under Lord Darnley's orders.

MARY

He was under theirs. It won't save them.

FLEMING

Your Majesty,
They've left the city by now. They should have been taken
While they were in your hands.

MARY

I know. It's true.
They've fled to raise troops. When next we find them they'll meet us
With culverins.
(BEATON *enters.*)
He's gone?

BEATON

Yes. But there's one
Below from France—says he has news.

MARY

From France?
Tomorrow, though. I wish I were still in France
And had never seen these stone walls.

LIVINGSTONE

And so do I.

MARY

What is his name?

BEATON

He gave me
This token for you, no name. It's a crow's feather.

MARY

(*Takes the feather, then pauses*). Tell my Lord Bothwell I have no wish to see him.
Now or later.

BEATON

Madame, you'll see him? I brought him
Along with me.

MARY

No. Not now. Not ever.
There's nothing to say between us now.

BEATON

He came
From France to see you.

MARY

Tell him.
(LORD BOTHWELL *is seen standing in the doorway.*)

BOTHWELL

Your Majesty,
You've had unwelcome company this hour,
If I've heard aright, and I care not to be another,
But I come to make an offer I made before—
To be your soldier.

MARY

I have no time to talk,
Lord Bothwell. Nor do I wish to see you. The time's
Gone by.

BOTHWELL

My queen, my queen, turn not away
Your friends. You've few enough, too few it seems
To prevent what's happened.

MARY

Go.

BOTHWELL

Does he still lie here?
I'll lay the poor boy away for you at least,
And then I'll go, since you wish it.
(*He crosses to* RIZZIO.)
Aye, they made sure,
Lad—and their dirks were sharp. Shall I place him within?

MARY

Yes.
(BOTHWELL *picks up* RIZZIO *and carries him into* MARY'S *chamber.*)
Must you betray me, too?

BEATON

I wished only—
If you'd but follow your heart!

MARY

We two must twain,
My Beaton. You take too much on you. Lord Bothwell,
May be your friend, not mine.

BEATON

Forgive me.

MARY

What warrant
Have you been given to vouch for my heart, or judge
Whether I should follow it?

BEATON

None.

MARY

Oh, God, this vice
Of women, crying and tears! To weep, weep now
When I need my anger! Say my farewells for me,
I've gone to my study.
(*She turns.* BOTHWELL *enters.*)

BOTHWELL

Good night, my queen.

MARY

Good night.
I'm not unkind. But I'm cut off from you.
You know that.

BOTHWELL

Yes. There's no need to hide your weeping.
He was over-young to die.

MARY

It's not for him.
No, it's for all I wanted my life to be,
And is not.

BOTHWELL

Majesty, you have a fortunate star.
It will come well yet.

MARY

If I have a star at all
It's an evil one. To violate my room,
Kill my servants before my eyes—How I must be hated!

BOTHWELL

They'll pay for that.

MARY

Perhaps.

BOTHWELL

I've taken an oath
They'll pay for it. Your Majesty, I wearied
Of France and exile, wearied of sun and wine,
And looked north over the water, longing for fog
And heather and my own country. Further, the news
Was none too happy from Scotland. They want your throne
And plan to have it. But I mean to live in this land
And mean you to be queen of it. The Earl of Bothwell
Is home, and spoiling for a fight. Before
Day dawns they'll hear from me.

MARY

My lord, I thank you—

BOTHWELL

Give me no thanks. I like a fight too well
To pretend it's a virtue. Moreover, if I'm to live here
I'd rather you were my liege than Moray. I'm none
So fond of your half-brother. This night's work
Should show you he's what I knew him, half-bred, half-faced
And double-tongued.

MARY

You have no army.

BOTHWELL

I have
My border men. Lord Huntley's joined with me
With his Highland kilties. If you'd call your clans
We could drive them to the wall.

MARY

It's a war then.

BOTHWELL

It's war,
Already. They've turned your Darnley against you. They'll use him
As long as they need his seal. Once they've got you out
They'll set Moray up as regent. They fear one chance:
That you and I should league together and balk them.
I've come back in time, not too soon.

MARY

I think you have.
My lord, I had no heart to face you. The fault
Was mine when we parted.

BOTHWELL

It's not too late. I've come
Only just in time, but in time.

MARY

It is too late—
For you and me. These faults we commit have lives
Of their own, and bind us to them.

BOTHWELL

(*Pointing toward her bedroom*). Yon was Darnley's work.
Are you still his?

MARY

Am I not?
(BEATON *gathers up the three others with a look and goes into the queen's study with them silently.*)
I'm to bear his child.
I cannot hate my child.

BOTHWELL

It's in the wind
This Darnley's not to live long.

MARY

I'd have no hand
In that—nor you!

BOTHWELL

It happens he's a pawn
In the game the lords are playing. They'll sacrifice him
When the time comes. It's no plot of mine.

MARY

But he lives
And I'm his wife, and my babe is his. I must drink
My cup down to the rinse. It was I that filled it,
And if there's grief at the bottom it's mine. I'll name you
My officer, but only if you can pledge
No harm will come through you to Darnley.

BOTHWELL

Lady,
I need you, and you need me, but I'll be damned
If Darnley's needed on this earth. I have
No project against him, but I'll give no pledge
To block me if I should have. There be men
Who wear their welcome out in this world early,
And Darnley's one of them.

MARY

You have never yet
Learned how to take an order.

BOTHWELL

And never will—
From man or woman living, sovereign or knave,
Judge or vicegerent. I have not been conquered
And will not be. But I offer you my fealty,
And it's worth the more for that.

MARY

You must make your own terms—
I'm but a beggar here.

BOTHWELL

Nay, nay, it's I
That sue, a beggar for what's impossible,
With this Darnley standing between us.
(*She pauses again.*)

MARY

You shall be
My Lord Admiral, and act for me. Yes, and to that
Let me add how my breath caught when I knew you here,
Hoping I know not what, things not to be,
Hopes I must strangle down. Oh, Bothwell, Bothwell!
I was wrong! I loved you all the time, and denied you!
Forgive me—even too late!

BOTHWELL

I tell you we
Shall be happy yet.

MARY

No, for I think I've been
At the top of what I'll have, and all the rest
Is going down. It's as if a queen should stand
High up, at the head of a stair—I see this now
As in a dream—and she in her dream should step
From level to level downward, all this while knowing
She should mount and not descend—till at last she walks
An outcast in the courtyard—bayed at by dogs
That were her hunters—walks there in harsh morning
And the dream's done.

BOTHWELL

(*Stepping toward her*). You're weary. You've borne too much.
They shall pay for this.

MARY

Come no nearer, my lord. It's not ours
To have. Go now.

BOTHWELL

Yes, your Majesty.
(*He turns.*) Yet
I tell you we shall be happy. And there will be nothing
Not ours to have.
(*He goes out.*)

Curtain

SCENE II

SCENE: ELIZABETH'S *study at Whitehall.* BURGHLEY *and* ELIZABETH *are seated across a table.* A THIRD FIGURE *approaches from the side.*

BURGHLEY

This will be Lord Throgmorton.

ELIZABETH

You're early, sir.

THROGMORTON

Madame, I rode all night.—I've news from the north.
Darnley's been murdered.

ELIZABETH

How?

THROGMORTON

Kirk o' Field was blown up.
The castle's in ruins.

ELIZABETH

Now that was a waste of powder—
And of castles too. But he's dead—

THROGMORTON

Yes, madame—they found him.
It was no accident. He'd been strangled.

ELIZABETH

So there's no more king in Scotland.
Who took this trouble?

THROGMORTON

Moray, and Morton, no doubt—perhaps Maitland—

ELIZABETH

Not Bothwell?—

THROGMORTON

No—though he must have known of it—

ELIZABETH

And the queen—
The queen weeps for her Darnley?

THROGMORTON

Madame—

ELIZABETH

Ah, yes—
She'll weep and wear black—it becomes her. A second time
She's a widow now. And she's borne a child. She begins
To wear a little, no doubt? She must ponder now
What costumes may become her?

THROGMORTON

Nay, truly, your Grace,
I'd say she charms as ever.

ELIZABETH

Would you say so?
But she weeps and puts on mourning?

THROGMORTON

No, madame, Bothwell
And the queen are friends again—or more than that.
They'd be married already, I think, only Moray's against it
And the earls behind him.

ELIZABETH

Now in my day and time
I have known fools and blockheads, but never, I swear,
In such numbers as among these Scotch earls. Moray's against it?
Against the queen's marriage with Bothwell?

BURGHLEY

Your Majesty—
If she were to marry Bothwell—we've opposed that, too,
And even prevented it.

ELIZABETH

Aye, times have changed,
And we change along with them. She loves this Bothwell?
It's a great love—a queen's love?

THROGMORTON

It is indeed.
A madness, almost.

ELIZABETH

Yes, yes—and it's well sometimes
To be mad with love, and let the world burn down
In your own white flame. One reads this in romances—
Such a love smokes with incense; oh, and it's grateful
In the nostrils of the gods! Now who would part them
For considerations of earth? Let them have this love
This little while—let them bed and board together—
Drink it deep, be happy—aye—

BURGHLEY

Madame, this Bothwell's
No man to play with, if they marry she'll crown him king—

ELIZABETH

You did well to ride fast, Throgmorton! Turn now
And ride as fast back again; you can sleep later
When we're old and the years are empty.—And tell my lord Moray
If he'd keep me a friend, let his sister marry Bothwell—
Tell him to favor it—hurry it.

BURGHLEY

And with Bothwell king
Do you think to conquer Mary?

ELIZABETH

Send next to John Knox,
But do this cleverly, giving Knox evidence
That Bothwell slew Darnley with the queen's connivance
And they bed together in blood. Have you wit enough
To see this well done?

THROGMORTON

I think so, Majesty.

ELIZABETH

See to it.
Who will deny that Bothwell murdered Darnley
When he lives with the queen, and enjoys the fruits? Or who
Will credit Bothwell's denial? Your brain, my Burghley!
Where do you wear it, or what has it hardened into
That you're so easily gulled?

BURGHLEY

But is it wise
To make a false accusation? This project hangs
By a thread. Make but one error and we shall lose
Whatever we've gained.

ELIZABETH

Go and do these things—
They are to marry—we sanction it—let none oppose it—
She refused him before when he could have saved her—
She'll take him now when it's fatal—Let her have this love
This little while—we grant her that—then raise
The winds against them—rouse the clans, cry vengeance
On their guilty sleep and love—I say within
This year at the very farthest, there's no more queen
Than king in Scotland!

Curtain

SCENE III

SCENE: *A hall in Dunbar Castle. A* SENTINEL *is at his post near the outer gate, another at the guard-room door. There is a step on the cobbles outside. The* FIRST SENTINEL *swings round to the gate.*

JAMIE

(*Outside*). Drop your point, man. Ye ken me.

FIRST SENTINEL

Eh, Jamie. What is it?

JAMIE

I'm late. It was tough getting through. The queen's taken prisoner. Her army's gone.

FIRST SENTINEL

Nay! And Bothwell?

JAMIE

Bothwell's free yet. Free and able to fight. We're to put the castle in posture of defence. Where's the sergeant?

FIRST SENTINEL

Call Graeme.

SECOND SENTINEL

Graeme!—I told you this was no lucky battle to be in.

FIRST SENTINEL

Says John Knox!
(GRAEME *enters.*)

JAMIE

I've orders for the guard. We're to man the walls and be ready on the gates.

GRAEME

It goes that way?
(BEATON *enters from the stair.*)

JAMIE

That way and worse.
(*They turn toward the gate.*)

BEATON

Jamie, what brings you?

JAMIE

Orders, lass.

BEATON

Quick, tell me!

JAMIE

It goes badly with us, lass.
(LORD HUNTLEY *enters.*)

BEATON

My lord—

HUNTLEY

There's to be a parley here. Make ready for it.

JAMIE

Watch that outer post.
(*The* SENTINELS *go out.*)

BEATON

A parley—the battle's over?

HUNTLEY

Aye, over and done. This is Moray's kingdom now.

BEATON

And the queen?

HUNTLEY

The queen's a prisoner, lass. My men have deserted, her own men turned against her.

BEATON

My lord, you'll forgive me, but how could that be?

HUNTLEY

This was John Knox's battle, lady. The auld limmer took a stance on a hill some half-mile to windward, and there he stood haranguing like the angel Gabriel, swearing Bothwell killed Darnley to have the queen. And the queen's men listened to him, the psalm-singing red-beards, and then turned and made her prisoner and delivered her up to Lord Moray.

GRAEME

Bothwell's returning.

JAMIE

Upstairs with you, lass.
(BEATON *goes up the lower stair.*)

GRAEME

Shall I set the guard?

HUNTLEY

Wait a moment.
(BOTHWELL *enters.*)

MARY

He rules by stealth—

ELIZABETH

But all this could be arranged,
Or so I'm told, if your son were to be crowned king,
And Moray made regent.

MARY

My son in Moray's hands—
Moray in power—

ELIZABETH

Is there any other way?
(*A pause.*)

MARY

Elizabeth—I have been here a long while
Already—it seems so. If it's your policy
To keep me—shut me up—. I can argue no more—
No—I beg now. There's one I love in the north,
You know that—and my life's there, my throne's there, my name
To be defended—and I must lie here darkened
From news and from the sun—lie here impaled
On a brain's agony—wondering even sometimes
If I were what they said me—a carrion-thing
In my desires—can you understand this?—I speak it
Too brokenly to be understood, but I beg you
As you are a woman and I am—and our brightness falls
Soon enough at best—let me go, let me have my life
Once more—and my dear health of mind again—
For I rot away here in my mind—in what
I think of myself—some death-tinge falls over one
In prisons—

ELIZABETH

It will grow worse, not better. I've known
Strong men shut up alone for years—it's not
Their hair turns white only; they sicken within
And scourge themselves. If you would think like a queen
This is no place for you. The brain taints here
Till all desires are alike. Be advised and sign
The abdication.

MARY

Stay now a moment. I begin to glimpse
Behind this basilisk mask of yours. It was this
You've wanted from the first.

ELIZABETH

This that I wanted?

MARY

It was you sent Lord Throgmorton long ago
When first I'd have married Bothwell. All this while
Some evil's touched my life at every turn.
To cripple what I'd do. And now—why now—
Looking on you—I see it incarnate before me—
It was your hand that touched me. Reaching out
In little ways—here a word, there an action—this
Was what you wanted. I thought perhaps a star—
Wildly I thought it—perhaps a star might ride
Astray—or a crone that burned an image down
In wax—filling the air with curses on me
And slander; the murder of Rizzio, Moray in that
And you behind Moray—the murder of Darnley, Throgmorton
Behind that too, you with them—and that winged scandal
You threw at us when we were married. Proof I have none
But I've felt it—would know it anywhere—in your eyes—
There—before me.

ELIZABETH

What may become a queen
Is to rule her kingdom. Had yo
yours I'd say
She has her ways, I mine. Li
And a merry world for t
But now

I must think this over—sadness has touched your brain.
I'm no witch to charm you, make no incantations;
You came here by your own road.

MARY

I see how I came.
Back, back, each step the wrong way, and each sign followed
As you'd have me go, till the skein picks up and we stand
Face to face here. It was you forced Bothwell from me—
You there, and always. Oh, I'm to blame in this, too!
I should have seen your hand!

ELIZABETH

It has not been my use
To speak much or spend my time—

MARY

How could I have been
Mistaken in you for an instant?

ELIZABETH

You were not mistaken.
I am all women I must be. One's a young girl,
Young and harrowed as you are—one who could weep
To see you here—and one's a bitterness
At what I have lost and can never have, and one's
The basilisk you saw. This last stands guard
And I obey it. Lady, you came to Scotland
A fixed and subtle enemy, more dangerous
To me than you've ever known. This could not be borne,
And I set myself to cull you out and down,
And down you are.

MARY

When was I your enemy?

ELIZABETH

Your life was a threat to mine, your throne to my throne,
Your policy a threat.

MARY

How? Why?

ELIZABETH

It was you
Or I. Do you know that? The one of us must win
And I must always win. Suppose one lad
With a knife in his hand, a Romish lad who planted
That knife between my shoulders—my kingdom was yours.
It was too easy. You might not have wished it.
But you'd take it if it came.

MARY

And you'd take my life
And love to avoid this threat?

ELIZABETH

Nay, keep your life.
And your love, too. The lords have brought a parchment
For you to sign. Sign it and live.

MARY

If I sign it
Do I live where I please? Go free?

ELIZABETH

Nay, I would you might,
But you'd go to Bothwell, and between you two
You might be too much for Moray. You'll live with me
In London. There are other loves, my dear.
You'll find amusement there in the court. I assure you
It's better than a cell.

MARY

And if I will not sign
This abdication?

ELIZABETH

You've tasted prison. Try
A diet of it.

MARY

And so I will.

ELIZABETH

I can wait.

MARY

And I can wait. I can better wait than you.
Bothwell will fight free again. Kirkaldy
Will fight beside him, and others will spring up

From these dragon's teeth you've sown.
Each week that passes
I'll be stronger, and Moray weaker.

ELIZABETH

And do you fancy
They'll rescue you from an English prison?
Why,
Let them try it.

MARY

Even that they may do. I wait for Bothwell—
And wait for him here.

ELIZABETH

Where you will wait, bear in mind,
Is for me to say. Give up Bothwell, give up your throne
If you'd have a life worth living.

MARY

I will not.

ELIZABETH

I can wait.

MARY

And will not because you play to lose. This trespass
Against God's right will be known. The nations will know it,
Mine and yours. They will see you as I see you
And pull you down.

ELIZABETH

Child, child, I've studied this gambit
Before I play it. I will send each year
This paper to you. Not signing, you will step
From one cell to another, step lower always,
Till you reach the last, forgotten, forgotten of men,
Forgotten among causes, a wraith that cries
To fallen gods in another generation
That's lost your name. Wait then for Bothwell's rescue.
It will never come.

MARY

I may never see him?

ELIZABETH

Never.
It would not be wise.

MARY

And suppose indeed you won
Within our life-time, still looking down from the heavens
And up from men around us, God's spies that watch
The fall of great and little, they will find you out—
I will wait for that, wait longer than a life,
Till men and the times unscroll you, study the tricks
You play, and laugh, as I shall laugh, being known
Your better, haunted by your demon, driven
To death or exile by you, unjustly. Why,
When all's done, it's my name I care for, my name and heart,
To keep them clean. Win now, take your triumph now,
For I'll win men's hearts in the end—though the sifting takes
This hundred years—or a thousand.

ELIZABETH

Child, child, are you gulled
By what men write in histories, this or that,
And never true? I am careful of my name.
As you are, for this day and longer. It's not what happens
That matters, no, not even what happens that's true,
But what men believe to have happened. They will believe
The worst of you, the best of me, and that
Will be true of you and me. I have seen to this.
What will be said about us in after-years
By men to come, I control that, being who I am.
It will be said of me that I governed well,
And wisely, but of you, cousin, that your life,
Shot through will ill-loves, battened on lechery, made you
An ensign of evil, that men tore down and trampled.
Shall I call for the lord's parchment?

MARY

This will be said—?
But who will say it? It's known as a lie!

ELIZABETH

You lived with Bothwell before Darnley died,
You and Bothwell murdered Darnley.

MARY

And that's a lie!

ELIZABETH

Your letters, my dear. Your letters to Bothwell prove it.
We have those letters.

MARY

Then they're forged and false!
For I never wrote them!

ELIZABETH

It may be they were forged.
But will that matter, Mary, if they're believed?
All history is forged.

MARY

You would do this?

ELIZABETH

It is already done.

MARY

And still I win.
A demon has no children, and you have none,
Will have none, can have none, perhaps. This crooked track
You've drawn me on, cover it, let it not be believed
That a woman was a fiend. Yes, cover it deep,
And heap my infamy over it, lest men peer
And catch sight of you as you were and are. In myself
I know you to be an eater of dust. Leave me here
And set me lower this year by year, as you promise,
Till the last is an oubliette, and my name inscribed
On the four winds. Still, STILL I win! I have been
A woman, and I have loved as a woman loves,
Lost as a woman loses. I have borne a son,
And he will rule Scotland—and England. You have no heir!
A devil has no children.

ELIZABETH

By God, you shall suffer
For this, but slowly.

MARY

And that I can do. A woman
Can do that. Come, turn the key. I have a hell
For you in mind, where you will burn and feel it,
Live where you live, and softly.

ELIZABETH

Once more I ask you,
And patiently. Give up your throne.

MARY

No, devil.
My pride is stronger than yours, and my heart beats blood
Such as yours has never known. And in this dungeon,
I win here, alone.

ELIZABETH

(*Turning*). Good night, then.

MARY

Aye, good night.
(ELIZABETH *goes to the door, which opens before her. She goes out slowly. As the door begins to close upon her* MARY *calls.*)
Beaton!

ELIZABETH

(*Turning*).
You will not see your maids again,
I think. It's said they bring you news from the north.

MARY

I thank you for all kindness.
(ELIZABETH *goes out.* MARY *stands for a moment in thought, then walks to the wall and lays her hand against the stone, pushing outward. The stone is cold, and she shudders. Going to the window she sits again in her old place and looks out into the darkness.*)

Curtain

S. N. Behrman

RAIN FROM HEAVEN

For

Elizabeth Bibesco

S. N. BEHRMAN

Like many of the dramatists who have had plays produced by the Theatre Guild, S. N. Behrman is an alumnus of Professor George Pierce Baker's 47 Workshop at Harvard University. Prior to his enrollment for this course, Behrman had studied under Professor G. Stanley Hall at Clark University in Worcester, Massachusetts, where he was born in 1893. When finally he came to New York, his ambition to become a playwright received scant encouragement. While searching for a job, he took a master's degree in English at Columbia University, and it was after waiting eleven years that he sold his first play, *The Second Man*. There was no such delay, however, for those that followed. *Serena Blandish, Meteor, Brief Moment, Biography, Rain from Heaven* and *End of Summer* were accepted and produced in rapid succession. In addition to these plays he has written many scenarios for Hollywood, where, from time to time, he goes to earn new laurels and such sums of money as he did not dare dream of during the lean eleven years of waiting to become a dramatist.

CHARACTERS

JOAN ELDRIDGE

MRS. DINGLE

RAND ELDRIDGE

HOBART ELDRIDGE

LADY LAEL WYNGATE *

HUGO WILLENS

SASCHA BARASHAEV

PHOEBE ELDRIDGE

CLENDON WYATT

NIKOLAI JURIN

SCENES

The action throughout takes place in the living room of Lady Wyngate's home, a short distance from London.

TIME

The present.

ACT I

A spring afternoon.

ACT II

SCENE I: Afternoon, four days later.

SCENE II: About 10:30 the same evening.

ACT III

The following day.

* This character was known as Lady Violet Wyngate in the Theatre Guild production of RAIN FROM HEAVEN. For the printed text, the author prefers to have her designated as Lady Lael Wyngate.

RAIN FROM HEAVEN

ACT ONE

SCENE: *The living room of an English country house not far from Brighton. It is not one of the "great houses" but rambling and informal and spaciously hospitable in a casual way. The garden seems almost to grow into the living room; the French windows at the back merely to beach its efflorescence. Cross the garden and you are in another living room; cross that and you are in another garden. The knack of combining an air of improvisation with solid comfort appears to be a special attribute of the British country house of this type.*

It is a sunny afternoon in spring.

MRS. DINGLE, *the ample housekeeper, and* JOAN ELDRIDGE, *an attractive young American girl, are awaiting the arrival by motor of two visitors. Each time they hear the sound of a car in the road which passes the house,* JOAN *leaps to the piano and strikes up "The Entrance of the Gladiators." At the rising of the curtain* JOAN *is discovered in one of these spasms of optimism.*

JOAN

(*As she runs to the piano*). There they are!

MRS. DINGLE

(*Lumbering to the window near the hall-door left, whence she may scan the road*). I believe it is, Miss Joan!
(JOAN *plays the music triumphantly. But the motor passes and dies down.*)

JOAN

(*In despair*). This is impossible.
(*She leaves the piano disconsolately*). I wish Lael hadn't left *me* to receive them. I'm getting more nervous every minute.

MRS. DINGLE

Nothing to be nervous about that I can see! Your own father . . . and your uncle . . . Tell me, Miss Joan, does your Uncle Rand look like a hero?

JOAN

That depends what your notion of a hero is. Besides, you've seen his picture in the papers, haven't you?

MRS. DINGLE

Don't know as I have.

JOAN

He's quite young, you know. And good-looking.

MRS. DINGLE

As good-looking as Lindbergh?

JOAN

(*Considering it*). Different style. Yes. Quite different.

MRS. DINGLE

Do they make a big fuss over him in America?

JOAN

Oh, no end.
(*Sound of motor car. Same business.* JOAN *rushes to the piano and plays.* MRS. DINGLE *stands at attention at French window. Same result. Motor car passes and dies down.* JOAN *rises from the piano.*)
I give up!

MRS. DINGLE

Perhaps they had an accident.

JOAN

I don't think so. It's just Father telling the driver to go slow. He's so damn cautious!

MRS. DINGLE

(*Shocked*). What a way to speak of your own father! In my day . . . !

JOAN

I know. In your day you suppressed your feelings! Such a bother, Lael not having a telephone! I'd like to ring up my young man in London to find out if he's all right. (MRS. DINGLE *starts to protest; she decides it's hopeless.*)

MRS. DINGLE

You mean Mr.—Mr.—?

JOAN

Barashaev.

MRS. DINGLE

I never will say that name.

JOAN

You will. With practice.

MRS. DINGLE

Is he your young man?

JOAN

I've been trying to persuade him ever since last winter in New York. Like him?

MRS. DINGLE

(*Thoughtfully*). He's a foreigner.

JOAN

Oh, Mrs. Dingle, how British!

MRS. DINGLE

He's worse than a foreigner. He's a Russian. But he can play the piano. I'll say that for him. He makes it talk.

JOAN

Sing, Mrs. Dingle. He makes it sing! (*Motor is heard approaching again. This time,* JOAN *doesn't stir.*)

MRS. DINGLE

(*Excited again*). Miss Joan, maybe . . .

JOAN

They don't fool me again!

MRS. DINGLE

But maybe . . .

JOAN

I don't care if it is! (*Motor stops with a squeak of brakes.*)

MRS. DINGLE

They've stopped! They've stopped! (MRS. DINGLE *rushes out.*)

JOAN

Really? (*She rushes to the piano and again strikes up the triumphant theme from "Heldenleben."*

RAND *enters, followed by his elder brother* HOBART ELDRIDGE. RAND ELDRIDGE *is a little over thirty, a Southern American and very attractive. The most attractive thing about him is a kind of shyness, a slightly uncomfortable awareness that he radiates an aura of fame which makes him conspicuous when really he would prefer to be unobserved.*

HOBART ELDRIDGE, *at least fifteen years older than* RAND, *has none of his younger brother's reticence. He understands completely the sources of his own power and is determined to insure their inexhaustibility. It is impossible for him to visualize a cosmos in which he and his kind are not the central suns.*)

(JOAN *rushes to her* UNCLE RAND). Hello! Hello!

RAND

(*With his arms around her*). Joan! How nice! How very nice!

JOAN

(*To her father*). Hello, Father.

HOBART

(*Annoyed that she is here*). I didn't know you knew Lady Wyngate, Joan!

JOAN

Oh, yes! We're great friends—met her in New York—She asked me down here to help entertain Uncle Rand!

RAND

Where *is* Lael?

JOAN

She had to run up to London. She left me to do the honors.

HOBART

Run up to London! Didn't she know? . . .

JOAN

It's a long story, Father. She said she'd explain to Uncle Rand.
(*She smiles bewitchingly at her uncle.*)

RAND

It's quite all right. I appreciate Lael's not treating me as a guest.

HOBART

(*Grimly*). If it's informality you're after, you'll get it all right here!

RAND

(*Looking round*). Sweet place!

JOAN

Wait till you see the garden!
(*To her father.*)
Shall I show him the garden?

MRS. DINGLE

Perhaps Captain Eldridge would like to go to his room?

RAND

No, thank you.

JOAN

This is Mrs. Dingle.
(MRS. DINGLE *bobs.*)

RAND

(*To* MRS. DINGLE). No, thank you, Mrs. Dingle. I'll just stretch here and talk to my brother for a bit. Seems we can't get talked out, doesn't it, Bart?
(*He takes his older brother affectionately by the shoulder.*)

JOAN

(*To* MRS. DINGLE). You might see that Rand's bags are put in his room.

MRS. DINGLE

Certainly, miss, I'll see to it.
(*She goes out.*)

RAND

(*To* JOAN, *affectionately*). Well, Joan, well! Well! It certainly was a great idea of Lael's to have you here.

JOAN

(*With real admiration*). You're looking wonderful. Very, very handsome.

RAND

You, on the other hand, are quite repulsive.

JOAN

Wherever did you get that beautiful tan? I thought it was freezing up there in the Antarctic.

RAND

It's not *up* there—it's *down* there. And coming back I passed through the tropics.

JOAN

(*Amazed*). Tropics!

RAND

(*Laughing, to* HOBART). Geographically, Joan seems a little vague.

HOBART

Vagueness is a charm she inherits from her mother.

RAND

(*To* JOAN). I'm a little hurt you didn't wait for me in New York.
(*Drily.*)
Seen the reception I had. Might have impressed you.

JOAN

I wish I had! How I should have loved to see you drive up Fifth Avenue. How was it? Were you thrilled?

RAND

Well, as you see, I survived that too.
(*They laugh.*)

HOBART

(*Breaking into this*). What's the inn like here, Joan?

JOAN

Very comfortable. Well, quite comfortable.

HOBART

You might ring up and reserve me some rooms. It's getting so late, I believe I'll stay the night.

RAND

Do, please.

JOAN

There's no telephone in this house. But I'll walk over . . .

HOBART

And while you're about it—would you mind telephoning your mother—she's at Wechsley, you know—ask her to pick me up at the White Hart because I shan't be able to get to Wechsley for her.

JOAN

Right!

HOBART

Thank you very much.

JOAN

(*As she runs out*). So long, Rand. Be seeing you.

RAND

Oh, Joan.

JOAN

(*Stopping*). Yes?

RAND

How is she? Lael? Is she all right?

JOAN

Oh, grand! Top of her form. Wait till you see . . .

RAND

(*Smiling*). I can't!

JOAN

(*To her father*). I'll get you the Royal Suite. The Royal Suite in the White Hart! (*She runs off through the house. There is a long pause.* RAND *takes a turn about the room. He is sorry* LAEL *hasn't been there to meet him, not for his own sake alone but because he knows the effect on his brother will be, from his point of view, unfortunate. Nor is he wrong.*)

HOBART

Well, this little incident illustrates a bit what I mean about your lady love.

RAND

(*Disingenuous*). This? What?

HOBART

(*Irritated at his evasion*). Well, her not being here! It's a bit thick, I must say.

RAND

I don't think so, Bart, really. She'll probably explain it perfectly. After all, she is a busy woman. She wirelessed me to come right down.

HOBART

I know! Come right down. Dying to see you! I won't be there, but come right down!

RAND

(*Remonstrating mildly*). Bart . . .

HOBART

It all comes under the head of being Bohemian, I suppose.

RAND

Come now! Lael's not Bohemian.

HOBART

Artistic, then. If you're artistic, you can be rude. I must say I'm not comfortable with artists. I get on much better with people who do things.

RAND

(*Shyly*). Bart . . . I . . .

HOBART

Yes, Rand.

RAND

You don't like Lael much, do you?

HOBART

Well, she's not my sort. Not your sort either, Rand—that's what I'd like to make you see.

RAND

Bart . . .

HOBART

She's all right in her place, I suppose, but . . .

RAND

Before you say any more, Bart, I want to tell you—I must tell you . . .

BART

Well?

RAND

I'm going to ask her to marry me. That's why I came to England.

HOBART

(*After a moment*). Rand . . .

RAND

Yes, Bart.

HOBART

You know I love you. You know how proud I am of you. You know how much your career and reputation mean to me.

RAND

And you know how grateful I am to you. I never speak of it, but don't think, Bart, I don't appreciate—deeply—all the money you've spent on my expeditions . . .

HOBART

Nonsense! What's that? What's money compared to what you've done for our name—the Eldridge name. I want that name kept high, Rand—at the highest . . .

RAND

(*Pleading for a clean bill*). There isn't anything against Lael, is there, Bart—nothing—serious?

HOBART

Well, it depends on what you call serious.

RAND

Well, is it anything to do with—anything to do with? . . .

HOBART

Nothing as far as I know—not in that way.

RAND

(*Completely relieved*). Thank God for that! That's all I care about.

HOBART

Her private life's all right, as far as I know, it's what you may call her—public life—that bother's me.

RAND

(*Ridicules idea*). Oh, if that's all!

HOBART

It's more important than you think, Rand. A little affair here and there I would forgive. . . .

RAND

(*Pained*). Please, Bart!

HOBART

Sorry. But the sort of thing Lady Wyngate goes in for . . .

RAND

(*Teasing him, completely relieved now and very happy—a sexual aspersion was the one thing he feared*). Well, now, big brother, what sort of thing *does* she go in for?

HOBART

Hardly know how to explain to you. Her reputation . . .

RAND

What *is* her reputation?

HOBART

Well, she's commonly considered—to put it mildly—eccentric.

RAND

How do you mean eccentric?

HOBART

For one thing her husband was little better than a fire-eater.

RAND

Did you know her husband?

HOBART

No, but I know plenty who did. I know the paper he edited—which her money supported and *still* supports.

RAND

She showed me a copy of it in New York. Seemed harmless—full of book reviews.

HOBART

It's communistic! That's what gets on *my* nerves—a woman of her class—whose fortune has been built up by a lot of hard-working manufacturers, supporting the *Clarion*—a Liberal weekly that's very dangerous—that wants to destroy the system that gives her her income. A woman of fine family whose father was knighted for war work, who might have her house full of the best people, surrounding herself with a lot of riff-raff.

RAND

I don't see any riff-raff.

HOBART

You will if you stay here—but I can't stop for that. What I have to convey to you is this: In the last year or so, while you've been away in the Antarctic, my mind has gradually crystallized to an important decision. I'm going to settle down permanently here in England—make my headquarters here.

RAND

Doesn't Phoebe want to live in America?

HOBART

It's got nothing to do with Phoebe! I've decided to give myself up, in a manner of speaking, to public service. I can see my way clear to becoming an influence, a power, not only here but, from here, in America as well. In fact—in fact . . .

RAND

(*Intrigued by the mystery*). You're wonderfully clever, Bart—you always were!

HOBART

I've formed a connection with one of the wealthiest men in England. You'd be startled, I think, if I told you who it was.

RAND

(*With perfect sincerity*). The Prime Minister!

HOBART

No, no! Lord—his name would be anathema in this house—Lord—
(*He whispers the name to* RAND.)

RAND

(*Registering the expected astonishment but still not having the faintest idea*). Really? Who is he?

HOBART

Well, I'm surprised. Don't you *ever* read the papers?

RAND

We don't get the papers in the Antarctic.

HOBART

Of course. Of course. Anyway, you'll soon learn about him. He admires you very much.

RAND

Admires me? Really?

HOBART

In fact—curious as it may sound—you are a factor in our schemes—an unconscious factor—but still a factor—none the less powerful because unseen—unspoken.

RAND

I? How? But how?

HOBART

Your name. Your magic name.

RAND

Really?

HOBART

Lord—
(*He can't bring himself to mention the sacred name. He looks around.*)

RAND

(*Interested*). You mean that Lord . . .

HOBART

(*Stopping him before he utters the name*). Yes! He's one of the most powerful newspaper proprietors in England—in the world. Before a week is out I shall be

definitely associated with him in a newspaper venture of great importance. I'm putting a good deal of money into it, but what he wants chiefly, I fancy, are my American connections. And I know you will be glad to hear that in my opinion *your* name, your unblemished and heroic reputation, finally turned the balance in my favor with Lord . . .
(*His voice hushes.*)
One of those imponderables that sometimes very subtly outweighs the greatest considerations. Yes, my instinct tells me you have been invaluable. You have aided me.

RAND

(*With complete sincerity*). Nothing you could say to me would make me happier.

HOBART

No man ever had a more loyal brother than you are. I know that.
(*A moment's silence.*)
Now you see, Rand—you understand what I am telling you is in the strictest confidence. . . .

RAND

Oh, absolutely . . .

HOBART

That includes Lady Wyngate—she's the last person I'd want to have know.

RAND

Of course, Bart. I never talk to Lael about things like that.

HOBART

Well, sometimes one thing leads to another.

RAND

(*With his half-shy smile*). I hope so!

HOBART

(*Clears his throat*). You see this venture I am going into with—the person I mentioned—is more that a newspaper venture. Much more important than that. The affairs of the world, as you probably know, are in a critical state.

RAND

You mean—the depression?

HOBART

Behind that—beyond that—beneath that.

RAND

(*Dimly*). I see!

HOBART

(*Grimly*). The line is becoming clearly marked. The issue is joined. At least we know which side we're on!

RAND

I think what you're going to do for the unemployed young men—get them interested in physical culture, give them jobs, give them something to live for—it's really wonderful, Bart—just like you—

HOBART

We've got to do something for them—or they'll drift into chaos, crime, anarchy—it's the New Crusade!
(*He is struck suddenly by an overwhelming idea*). My God, Rand!

RAND

(*Alarmed*). Bart? What's the matter?

HOBART

Nothing. Nothing. An idea! A terrific idea! The New Crusade—a motto—a picture slogan—for our masthead—don't you see?—The New Crusade—a Crusader in an airplane—don't you see—right on the masthead!

RAND

Masthead?

HOBART

(*His hands in front of his eyes to conserve the creative process*). You at the wheel!

RAND

(*Delicately*). Stick!

HOBART

You at the stick—in a Crusader's costume—driving a plane over a sea of chaos—communism—decadence—into the New Order—it's magnificent—I must telephone at once to Lord . . .

RAND

Won't it look as if you were trying to publicize me?

HOBART

Not a photograph of you—nothing realistic like that—an idealization—if I do say it myself, it's wonderful—how it bridges the centuries—the moral fervor of the . . .
(*Feels around for the century—can't remember it, compromises quickly.*)
Middle Ages—the science and heroism of the twentieth—it's superb!

RAND

Yes, I think it is, Bart. I think Lord . . .
(*He is about to say the sacred name.* HOBART *is terrified.*)

HOBART

(*Looks about room to see no one overhears them*). Sh!

RAND

Well, I think he's very lucky to have you for a partner!

HOBART

When I explain to you more clearly what it is we stand for—and when you've had a chance to observe Lady Wyngate in her own bailiwick, so to speak—you'll understand better why a marriage to her would be—well, to put it mildly—inexpedient.
(*Rises and starts to pace back and forth.*)

RAND

(*Rises*). But why? I don't see why. She's lovely. Everybody adores her.

HOBART

(*Facing* RAND). The right people don't adore her. After all—what do you know about her? You met her when she was on a flying trip to New York.

RAND

When I went down to Washington to get the—the medal from the Geographic Society.

HOBART

(*Turning away*). Well?

RAND

I met the British Ambassador.

HOBART

Well?

RAND

I asked him about her.

HOBART

Well?

RAND

His face lit up.

HOBART

(*Indulgently*). That, my boy, might mean many things.

RAND

He said he adored her.

HOBART

When he's in Washington, it's safe for him to adore her.

RAND

(*In despair*). But I don't understand—what is it—what is it that—?

HOBART

Shall I be blunt?

RAND

(*Dreading it*). Please—

HOBART

For a man in your position—with your reputation—to marry Lady Wyngate . . .

RAND

(*Very tense*). Well?

HOBART

(*Feeling for an analogy that* RAND *will understand*). Well—it would . . .
(*Hitting on it at last and pouncing on it happily.*)
Well—it would be like Lindbergh marrying a young Emma Goldman!
(*At this point, and before* RAND *can protest,* LAEL WYNGATE *comes in. She goes at once to* RAND, *embraces him, kisses him.*)

LAEL

Rand!

RAND

Lael, darling! *Can* you forgive me? You must think me most unbelievably rude. I left Joan here to receive you. Did she do well by you?
(HOBART *clears his throat.*)

RAND

This is my brother, Hobart Eldridge.

LAEL

Joan's father?

RAND

Yes.

LAEL

(*Shaking hands with him*). I'm so glad to see Mr. Eldridge.

HOBART

(*Formally*). How do you do?

LAEL

Such a morning! Do sit down! I went up to London to pick up a German refugee. I found him so alone and so charming that I've brought him back with me. You'll adore him.

HOBART

(*Sensing illustrative material*). German refugee?

LAEL

Yes.

RAND

(*Sensing it equally and to protect* LAEL). We didn't mind a bit waiting.

HOBART

What sort of refugee?

LAEL

Didn't I say? German!

HOBART

But what sort of German? Communist?

LAEL

I don't know. We didn't talk politics. He's a literary and music critic. A very prominent one. His name is Willens. Hugo Willens.

RAND

No! Willens! Not really!

LAEL

Do you know him?

RAND

I know him well. Where is he?

LAEL

He'll be down in a minute.

RAND

Well, imagine. Hugo Willens! Great chap. We used to go skiing together.

HOBART

Where was this?

RAND

Near Munich. When Phoebe was staying there.

LAEL

Phoebe?

RAND

Yes, Hobart's wife. Met him through Phoebe, as a matter of fact. Great friend of Phoebe's.

HOBART

Oh!

LAEL

Oh, then you know him too, Mr. Eldridge?

HOBART

No. I don't know all my wife's friends. Phoebe travels around quite a bit.

LAEL

Oh, I see. Well, won't it be nice for him to see you again? He hasn't the faintest idea, of course. And Mrs. Eldridge will have to come too. But, Rand, tell me! How splendid you look! How long were you gone this time?

RAND

Eight months!

LAEL

Were you? And did you have a triumphal on your return? Were they glad to see you?

RAND

They seemed to be.

LAEL

Seemed! Don't tell me. When Americans are glad, they're *glad!* How I adore them! And how is my dear, incomparable New York?

RAND

It's still there. Waiting to see you again.

LAEL

(*Makes an impulsive engagement*). I'll go back with you.

RAND

(*Eagerly*). Will you?

LAEL

(*To* HOBART). You must be very proud of him, Mr. Eldridge. You're staying for the week-end, aren't you?

HOBART

It's Tuesday. I'm afraid the week-end's over.

LAEL

I mean next week-end. Do stay. You live in England, don't you, Mr. Eldridge?

HOBART

I intend to.

LAEL

It's a great compliment to us. It's so reassuring for us that we attract Americans like you.

HOBART

(*Bows, and a little angrily*). Thank you.

LAEL

You know your brother is the most modest national hero I've ever met. That's why I adore him so. I'm so happy to see you again, Rand. What times we had in New York—what *good* times! Really, I believe I never had so much fun anywhere as I did in those two weeks.
(*To* HOBART *again.*)
In any case, Mr. Eldridge, whether you stay the week-end or not, you must stay for dinner.

RAND

I want you to meet Willens, Bart. How'd you corral him, Lael?

LAEL

Through Joan.

HOBART

Joan?

LAEL

When Joan's young man made his début in Berlin, Herr Willens gave him a great send-off. Yes, decidedly, it's one up for Joan.

RAND

(*To* HOBART). Has Joan a young man? *That's* why she wouldn't wait for me in New York! Well, Bart, are you prepared for that?

HOBART

Oh, Joan's young men come and go. It's not important.

LAEL

Well, anyway, you'll meet him in a minute. He's staying here. A young Russian-American, Sascha Barashaev. Plays the piano.

HOBART

Oh, then it's certainly not important.

LAEL

Between ourselves—all technique—magnificent—but not much feeling. Not what you'd expect, is it? Do you think Latins and Slavs actually have more feeling than we have? Do you, Mr. Eldridge? They're more expressive and that gives the impression of warmth, but actually I don't think they feel more intensely than we do, do you?

HOBART

Latins and Slavs are not my specialty, Lady Wyngate.

LAEL

Oh, well. It's that I get so tired of hearing about Anglo-Saxon coldness. We're such a sloppy, sentimental race. Only yesterday I ran into Lord Abercrombie at lunch . . .
(*As she mentions, so casually, the dread name,* RAND *is visibly struck.*)
What's the matter, Rand? Do you know him?

RAND

(*Gasping*). No! I don't.

LAEL

Very amusing, inflated, wrong-headed little man. Do you know him, Mr. Eldridge?

HOBART

(*With some fervor*). He's the hope of England.

LAEL

Has he told *you* that too? He believes it. He actually believes it. I hate messiahs. Fake ones, charlatan ones I enjoy. It's amusing to watch them do their stuff. I met Aimee McPherson in New York—you know, the woman who was lost in the desert—I found her in a cinema theatre. Now there's the kind of blonde messiah I like. But sincere ones, zealot ones I can't abide. When they tell you they're the hope of anything — and they're not faking—they're hopeless. But I'm not persuaded entirely about Lord Abercrombie. Are you, Mr. Eldridge? Perhaps he practices before a mirror. . . .

HOBART

In my opinion, Lady Wyngate, he is . . .

LAEL

I know! But on the side. Pretty good circulation-booster, isn't he? I haven't quite given him up. He may be—what do they call it in America—delicious word — a phony! Shall we bet on Lord Abercrombie, Mr. Eldridge?
(JOAN *comes in, followed by* MRS. DINGLE *with the tea things.*)

JOAN

Oh, Lael, I'm crazy about him—I'm just mad about him!

LAEL

That's not news. Ah, tea. Thank you, Mrs. Dingle.

JOAN

Not Sascha. The new one.

LAEL

Oh! Tea! Tea! Aren't you coming, Mr. Eldridge?

HOBART

Did you see about the room in the inn, Joan?

JOAN

Yes, Dad. I've reserved the Royal Suite for you. He's *so* charming. . . .

HOBART

Did you telephone to your mother?

JOAN

Yes. She's meeting you. He's so distinguished! So different! And he's been in a concentration camp.
(SASCHA *and* HUGO WILLENS *come in.*)

LAEL

Oh, here you are! Well, Herr Willens, I hear you're distinguished and different. How different are you, Herr Willens?

RAND

(*Stepping forward*). Hello, Hugo!

HUGO

(*Astonished*). No. Not really!
(*As they shake hands cordially, to* LAEL.)
Why didn't you tell me?

LAEL

I didn't know you and Rand were old friends.

RAND

This is my brother, Hobart Eldridge.

HUGO

(*Shaking hands with* HOBART). How do you do?

HOBART

How do you do?

RAND

Phoebe's husband.

HUGO

How do you do?
(HOBART *about to sit, looks at* HUGO *after the double greeting.*)

LAEL

And Mr. Eldridge, Mr. Barashaev.

SASCHA

How do you do?

HOBART

Oh, so you're Mr. Barashaev.

LAEL

And Captain Eldridge, Mr. Barashaev.

SASCHA

How do you do, Captain Eldridge. I've heard a lot about you.

RAND

Thank you.

LAEL

Come on, everybody! Tea! Please sit down!

RAND

Well, well, Hugo! What on earth's happened to you.

HUGO

That's a long story.

LAEL

Herr Willens has just emerged from a concentration camp.

RAND

Whatever for?

HUGO

(*Still rather quietly*). It was rather boring.

RAND

I mean—what did they put you in for?

HUGO

That's part of the long story.

LAEL

What was it like?

HUGO

No luxury. Plain. Simple.

LAEL

Showers or tubs?

HUGO

Barbed wire and truncheons.

LAEL

Both! How generous!
(*Pours* HUGO's *tea.*)

SASCHA

(*Gloomily*). That couldn't have been any joke.

RAND

Well, I can't conceive—Hugo, why?

LAEL

(*Holding* HUGO's *cup*). Before I give you tea . . .
(*A glance at* HOBART.)
We must know this—are you a Communist?

HUGO

I assure you, dear lady—I am a music critic.

LAEL

Thank heaven! Cream?

HUGO

(*Standing*). Please.
(LAEL *pours cream into cup and hands it to* HUGO, *who thanks her and sits down.*)

LAEL

(*As she pours the second cup*). Mr. Eldridge?

HOBART

Straight, please. I beg your pardon—plain.

LAEL

Rand? I know how you take yours.
(LAEL *hands* HOBART *his cup. She pours* RAND's *tea.* JOAN *rises and pours for* SASCHA

and herself. Gives SASCHA *his cup then sits down again.*)
You know, Herr Willens, Captain Eldridge has just discovered a new world—a bright, new, fresh, untainted world.

HUGO

Yes! I know!
(*Quietly—to* RAND.)
What a let-down it must be to return to this old one!

RAND

(*Quite buoyantly*). Oh, I don't know. I like it down there, but it's nice to be back too, Lael!

LAEL

(*Holds out* RAND's *cup for him. He rises and gets it and sits down again*). It seems to be easier to discover new worlds than to run them once you've found them.

HOBART

England has done pretty well.

LAEL

Has she? It's generous of you to say so, but some of us don't feel in the least complacent about it.

HOBART

There's plenty of strength in England. In America, too. It's not unified. It's not coordinated. Power not in the right hands, that's all.

LAEL

So Lord Abercrombie was telling me just the other day—his very phrase—"Power isn't in the right hands." He means to put it there.

HOBART

(*To* HUGO). Tell me Herr—Herr . . .

LAEL

Willens.

HOBART

Herr Willens. You say you're a music critic.

HUGO

I was.

HOBART

You're not a political writer then?

HUGO

Not at all.

HOBART

You don't mind I hope, if I—?

HUGO

Not at all.

HOBART

Then may I ask why you were put into a concentration camp?

HUGO

I wrote a pamphlet.

HOBART

(*In triumph*). Ah! Communist!

HUGO

Not at all! It was satiric.

HOBART

Making fun of the government!

LAEL

If he did make fun of the government, Mr. Eldridge, does that justify, in your opinion, his being put in a concentration camp?

HOBART

It's a government trying to make headway against tremendous odds. They're justified in putting down opposition. The Communists about whom we're so sentimental nowadays . . .

LAEL

Are we?

HOBART

They did it with bullets. They weren't sentimental. We might learn from them.

HUGO

As a matter of fact, Mr. Eldridge, my pamphlet had nothing to do with politics. It was pure fantasy.

LAEL

Really?

RAND

What was it about?

HUGO

I called it "The Last Jew."

LAEL

Where have I . . . ?

HUGO

They did me the honor to burn it—(*Deprecatingly.*) with other important works.

LAEL

Hugo Willens! Of course! I remember reading the title in the—fire list. "The Last Jew"—Hugo Willens. I remember thinking: Now who is Will—? I beg your pardon.

HUGO

Well, now, you know. I thought it amusing, really. As a writer of music I had, as a matter of course, innumerable Jewish friends. I was touched personally by their sudden misfortunes. Also, as a lover of music, I was devasted by what the Aryan standardization was doing to my world. I resented this gratuitous disturbance of my professional routine—so I sat down and wrote this pamphlet.

LAEL

What was it about?

HUGO

Well—

LAEL

Oh, do tell us, we want to know.

RAND

Yes, do.

HUGO

With the extermination of the Jews, the millennium has been promised the people. And with the efficiency of a well-organized machine the purpose is all but accomplished. They are all dead—but one—the last Jew. He is about to commit suicide when an excited deputation from the All-Highest comes to see him. There has been a meeting in the sanctum of the Minister of Propaganda. This expert and clever man has seen that the surviving Jew is the most valuable man in the Kingdom. He points out to the Council their dilemma. Let this man die and their policy is bankrupt. They are left naked, without an issue, without a programme, without a scapegoat. The Jews gone and still no millennium. They are in a panic—till finally a committee is dispatched—and the last Jew is given a handsome subsidy to propagate—

LAEL

(*Claps her hands in delight, jumps up*). Where is it? I must get my hands on it. I want to publish it in my magazine.

HOBART

(*Maliciously*). The Jew accepts the subsidy, I suppose!

HUGO

(*Calmly*). Not only does he accept it—he makes them double it. You see, Mr. Eldridge, he is not an idealist—he is a practical man. Idealism he leaves to his interlocutors.

LAEL

Why not? A subsidy to propagate for destruction. As an Imperialist Fascist, Mr. Eldridge, you must understand that perfectly. Where is your pamphlet, Herr Willens?

HUGO

It is destroyed. I have no copy.

LAEL

You must rewrite it—from memory.

HUGO

Why? Why should I be the Jewish apologist? I'm not a Jew. That is to say—

LAEL

Oh! Oh!

HUGO

I had a Jewish great-grandmother.

LAEL

But what an indiscretion! What an indulgence!

RAND

(*To* HUGO, *sympathetically*). Well, I never heard such nonsense! Do you mean to say they actually—

HUGO

Yes, and my father was a minister in the Protestant Church.

LAEL

(*Inexorable*). Still—that speck—that unfortunate—speck.

HUGO

Curiously enough, I was rather proud of that speck—when I thought of it—which wasn't often—it was not unpleasant to remember I had it. This odd and mysterious strain—did it give me sympathy and flavor, intellectual audacity, impudence and intensity? You see, Mr. Eldridge, it was rather like being left gold bonds in a vault —bonds which couldn't be touched but which, nevertheless, paid one an unseen and incalculable dividend. That's how I felt about—the speck. I was a Nordic with an interesting racial fillip. I was secretly vain about it—until it began!

LAEL

The chromosome-hunt!

HUGO

The chromosome-hunt! A curious experience—to find myself overnight a marked person, a special person. Curious discomfort. I kept saying to myself: What is it? What is it you feel? You are the same—in spite of these looks, these sudden stillnesses in conversation, this restraint—you are the same. But within forty-eight hours, it was not the same. Spiritually, I was in the ghetto.

HOBART

Imagination, of course!

HUGO

(*After a look at him—agreeing*). Of course — imagination — the only reality. The world in which one really lives and feels. And then the strangest thing happened. I cannot—still I cannot understand it. Atavism? The—*speck*—took possession of me. I became its creature. I moved under its ordering. I began to ask myself whether subconsciously I hadn't written the pamphlet to defend my antecedents.

LAEL

But—how absurd! Really, do you have to go to Freud to explain an act of simple humanity? You wrote the pamphlet because you are a generous human being. Don't you think—don't you really think—that the subconscious has been done to death and that it's high time someone rediscovered the conscious?

HUGO

(*Amused*). I admit that leaving the Fatherland has restored my balance a bit. I am quite over this aberration. I've returned to my Aryan inheritance.

LAEL

And very welcome you are.

RAND

(*Rises and puts down cup on tray. Warmly*). You bet you are! It's grand seeing you, old boy!

LAEL

Joan, will you like him even if he is an Aryan?

JOAN

I'll try. Sascha, come and play for me now, will you? I want to hear music.

LAEL

What's the matter with *this* piano?

JOAN

Sascha likes the tone of the upstairs one better.

LAEL

(*Realizing that they might want to be alone*). Oh.

JOAN

(*To* SASCHA). Come on.

SASCHA

(*Surly*). What if I don't feel like playing?

HUGO

Sascha, I'd love some Bach.

SASCHA

(*Capitulating at once*). Of course.

HUGO

(*Rising*). If Lady Wyngate will excuse us?

LAEL

Certainly.

JOAN

He'll play for you, Herr Willens. I'm jealous. (*She slips her arm through* SASCHA'S.)

LAEL

How did you get this hold on Sascha, Herr Willens?

HUGO

(*Quizzically*). By appreciating him—publicly.

SASCHA

(*Eagerly*). You know, I still carry that notice around with me. Whenever I get depressed, I read it.

LAEL

Where is it now?

SASCHA

(*Taking a German newspaper clipping from his breast pocket*). Right here!

LAEL

Really!

HUGO

Let me see it!
(HUGO *hands it to* LAEL.)

LAEL

May I see it?

JOAN

(*Wearily*). He's read it to me fifty times. (HUGO *and* LAEL *look at the yellowed clipping. In it he sees epitomized his vanished career, and another life. After a moment he gives the clipping back to* SASCHA.)

HUGO

Thank you.
(*A moment's pause. Then in a bantering tone.*)
I wanted to assure myself that I had actually once had an identity. I must have had. I told people to go to concerts and they went. I told them to stay away—they stayed away. Quite incredible, but it seems to be true!

SASCHA

My next appearance after that notice was sold out.

JOAN

Yes, but what about the Bach?

SASCHA

I'm out of practice.

JOAN

Are pianists ever in practice, Herr Willens?

HUGO

Not good ones.

LAEL

(*As they go out*). I'll join you presently. (*To* RAND *and* HOBART.)
Now then! Isn't he nice?

RAND

Oh, he's swell!

LAEL

Imagine your knowing him!

HOBART

(*Rises*). If you'll excuse me, I'll walk down to the post office. I have to send a telegram.

LAEL

I can give Robert the message and he can . . .

HOBART

Thank you. As a matter of fact, Phoebe—my wife . . .

LAEL

Where is she?

HOBART

She's picking me up at the White Hart. We were driving on to Boxwood.

LAEL

You'll bring her back to dine, of course. I'd love to meet her.

RAND

She'll probably want to see Hugo.

LAEL

Yes, of course.

RAND

Be sure you tell her he's here.

HOBART

I will.

RAND

She and Hugo were great pals.

LAEL

Oh, were they? Do make her come then. It will be so nice bringing them together again.

HOBART

I'll do my best. Thank you very much! I'm sure she'll be delighted. Besides, Mrs. Eldridge hasn't seen Rand yet. In his eagerness to come here he stopped for nothing—for nobody.
(*Piano is heard from upstairs—"Organ Fugue in G Minor."*)

LAEL

I'm very flattered.

HOBART

(*Heavily facetious*). The bridegroom runneth to his chambers.

LAEL

Now you're committing him and you don't want to be committed, do you, Rand? I'll expect you both for dinner. Tell Mrs. Eldridge she needn't fuss.

HOBART

(*Grimly*). She loves to fuss. Thank you very much. Good-bye.

LAEL

Good-bye.

HOBART

See you later, Rand.
(*He goes out. In the moment that follows* LAEL *and* RAND *turn and face each other.*)

LAEL

Well, Rand . . .

RAND

Awfully good of you to invite my entire . . .
(*They are in each other's arms. After a bit, from this close embrace emerges a whispered conversation.*)
Why did you run away from me?

LAEL

(*Muffled*). Had to.

RAND

It was hateful of you . . .

LAEL

It was. But I had to . . .

RAND

You won't again.

LAEL

I will again. I'll have to again.

RAND

Why? Why?

LAEL

If you give me a chance I'll tell you . . .

RAND

My dearest! I'll never let you go again—never let you go again!
(*They stand in silence a moment longer locked in each other's arms. Then they separate—still standing quite close, looking at each other.*)

LAEL

Tell me now—what was it like?

RAND

What?

LAEL

Your triumphal return. I saw pictures in the newsfilms. How I wish I could have been there! How I wish I could have fluttered telephone books at you! I'd have given anything—I adore parades.

RAND

Shall I tell you how it was? It was incomplete. It didn't mean much—because you weren't there. I'll never forgive you—for not being there.

LAEL

How very sweet of you! I've never had a nicer compliment.

RAND

It's true.

LAEL

What was it like? What were you thinking about? I'm enormously interested in fame. What is it like to be famous? To know—to be aware—that when you enter a room, its temperature alters? To be the Prince of Wales or Einstein—or yourself?

RAND

(*Embarrassed*). I never think of it.

LAEL

Not even when you're shaving?
(*They laugh.*)
Oh, come now, you must think of it when you're shaving. As a matter of fact I've never—and I've known very many famous people—I've never met anyone so genuinely modest, so unconscious of being haloed, as you.

RAND

(*Quite unaffectedly*). It bewilders me. I don't understand it. You know—I was thinking in New York—riding up Fifth Avenue—when they were making all that fuss—I was thinking—I remembered . . .

LAEL

That's just what I'd love to know—what does one think of on climactic occasions like that?

LAEL

I remembered—it'll sound foolish. . . .

LAEL

Please tell me!

RAND

When I was a kid—I hated school—I simply couldn't study. . . .

LAEL

Did you like mathematics?

RAND

I loathed it.

LAEL

Do you know, Rand, that to this day I can't add or subtract? And these days with the papers full of that awful rigamarole about inflated currencies and what not I'm very unhappy—when I read about frozen assets I really shiver—and the very idea of earmarking gold makes my nerves tingle, like gears grinding. But go on—tell me.

RAND

There was a hill—Mount Wachusett—it wasn't much more than that—I could see it out of the window of the little country schoolhouse, misty blue and very far away. One spring morning, when I should have been studying, I found myself looking at it—I had such a wish to climb it—to climb it, to discover it, for myself. I've never understood what came over me. But I just put down my book, left the schoolhouse and made for it.

LAEL

How old were you?

RAND

I was eight. It was farther away than I thought. When I got to it, it was nightfall. I spent the night in a barn. At sunrise I got up and climbed to the top. I'll never forget that instant—when I got to the summit and looked around at what seemed to me the whole world.

LAEL

How glorious! Like finding a Pole.

RAND

Much more thrilling because more definite. You wouldn't know you were at the Pole if your instruments didn't tell you so. When I got to the top of Mount Wachusett, I *knew!* But what I didn't know was that my poor mother, frantic with anxiety, was scouring the countryside for me.

LAEL

Did you catch it?

HUGO

Did I? That's what I remembered—that incident—riding up Fifth Avenue. And it seemed so funny—all this acclaim for doing what I'd been spanked for as a kid—the same thing exactly—for having fun—it was fun for me then—it is still— I don't know what they make all that fuss over—I honestly don't.

LAEL

(*Sincerely and tenderly*). I'm really frightfully flattered—that you should have left all that adulation and come to see me.

RAND

(*Hating to confess it*). And all the time I was remembering that I felt bitter against you—for not being there.

LAEL

I'm sorry.
(*A moment's pause.*)

RAND

(*To reassure her*). I kept your photograph in my cabin on the *Odyssey.*

LAEL

Did I give you a photograph?

RAND

I cut it out of the rotogravure section in a New York newspaper.

LAEL

Did I behold those awful vastnesses? Did I share those lonely vigils?

RAND

(*Laughing a bit*). We both did.

LAEL

Do you know, when I was a young girl, I met Admiral Scott?

RAND

(*Excited*). Did you really? What was he like?

LAEL

Well, rather like you. Very good-looking.

RAND

You'll give me a swelled head.

LAEL

I don't think so. Did you ever read Scott's "Diaries"?

RAND

Yes.

LAEL

Do you remember that passage about the death of Captain Oates?
(*Quoting from memory.*)
"We knew that poor Oates was walking to his death, but though we tried to dissuade him, we knew it was the act of a brave man and an English gentleman. We all hope to meet the end with a similar spirit and assuredly the end is not far."

RAND

Think of your knowing that—by heart. You're wonderful!

LAEL

(*Quietly*). Anyone can memorize a heroic bit of prose, Rand. To live that sort of thing—as you do—is much more difficult.
(*He is embarrassed. She laughs.*)
Sorry! You can't bear praise, can you? I won't do it again. Promise!
(*A pause. He is hung up. He wants to make love to her; he doesn't know how to bridge the gap. She shifts into a less delicate field. She hesitates, herself, to approach the explanation she must give him.*)
Your brother doesn't like me much, does he? I shock him, don't I? And, I must tell you, Rand, I don't mind a bit shocking him. I enjoy shocking him. What did he say to you about me? I wager he's frightened to death.

RAND

(*Very uncomfortable*). Well, you know Bart; he's a little strict.

LAEL

Oh, that's what it is. Strict!

RAND

He's the kindest brother a fellow ever had, only . . .

LAEL

Rand?

LAEL

(*Determined to be ruthless*). But don't you see— We're worlds apart.

RAND

Simply because you imagine we disagree theoretically—

LAEL

Your defence of me to your brother was touching but it only proves how little you know me. What did you say? I'm good-hearted and mean nothing by what I do. But I do, Rand—I try to mean a great deal. I'm a determined woman. Are you terrified?

RAND

No.

LAEL

How can I put you off? How can I finally put you off?

RAND

Do you want to?

LAEL

No!

RAND

There you are!

LAEL

(*Self-reproachful*). You bring out the worst in me, Rand—the most feminine. I haven't had this kind of conversation since before I married, when I lived in Heartbreak House.

RAND

Where?

LAEL

It's a fancy by Mr. Shaw. I'd like you to meet him. He'll probably put you in a play. Being a sedentary vegetarian he adores men who fly to unknown worlds and administer torrid continents. You and Lawrence . . .

RAND

Lawrence . . .

LAEL

Colonel, not D. H. . . . I refer to the exploit with Arabia—not with Lady Chatterly.

RAND

(*Laughs*). I don't mind. Usually I'm uncomfortable with brilliant people, but I'm not with you.

LAEL

You make *me* though!

RAND

(*Very sceptical*). Oh, yes! I'm sure I do!

LAEL

You do. Also you make me feel a little—horrid.

(RAND, *stung by this, suddenly takes her in his arms and kisses her passionately.*)

RAND

Do I! Do I! Do I!

LAEL

(*After recovery*). It is pleasanter off the pedestal, I admit. (*Sighs.*) Oh, dear!

RAND

What is it now?

LAEL

I have an awful foreboding that eventually I'll succumb to you but I feel I owe it to my conscience to put up an awful fight.

RAND

I want you—forever.

LAEL

No, you don't.

RAND

I'll never want anyone else but you.

LAEL

If you thoroughly knew me, you'd be bewildered by me—you might even be horrified by me.

RAND

(*His arms still around her*). You mean—darling, tell me—do you . . .

LAEL

What?

RAND

Do you have affairs with men?

LAEL

(*Between annoyance and laughter*). My dear!

RAND

Do you? I must know.

LAEL

(*Disengaging herself from him finally*). Well, if it's any comfort to you, I may tell you that though I'm intellectually sympathetic to any indulgence, emotionally, I'm fastidious and even puritanic.

RAND

(*Fervently*). Thank God!

LAEL

(*Bursts out laughing*). Oh, Rand!

RAND

(*Offended*). What's so funny?

LAEL

You make me feel that any progress is hopeless. How are we going to break down the indurated conservatism of men?

RAND

What's progress got to do with it?

LAEL

Imagine finding you—a great explorer, a hero—so—sex-ridden. It's disillusioning. I'm ashamed of you, Rand.

RAND

Sex-ridden? I love you!

LAEL

I mean your assumption that as long as I'm sexually monogamous, no other foible I might have could matter to you. I might be nourishing an idea to destroy the universe. I might be the incarnation of malice, a well, deep and poisonous; I might be anti-Christ, but so long as I didn't—well—you wouldn't mind, you wouldn't enquire. Your psyche, my dear Rand, is sex-ridden. It's obsessed. It's maggoty with possessive desire.

RAND

How can you say that when I want to marry you?

LAEL

How dare you marry me without knowing me! Much better if we—er—well—till you find me out!

RAND

I couldn't. You mean more to me than that.

LAEL

If I didn't know this rejection sprang from the purest chivalry, I should be humiliated.

RAND

Please don't be clever.
(HOBART *enters.*)

LAEL

(*Addressing them both*). Most men simply can't imagine any woman except in relation to themselves. Are you like that too, Mr. Eldridge? I imagine you are!

HOBART

(*Wary*). I wouldn't think of answering a question like that without preparation.

LAEL

I'm sure you are. An amusing instance of it happened during the one serious quarrel I ever had with my husband. It was during the Sacco-Vanzetti trial in America. I'd read everything there was to be found about it and felt passionately. I was coming up here one day in the train—I was living here alone then—for the moment Nick and I had separated. I had just read Vanzetti's farewell letter; I sat there thinking of this man being shunted in and out of the death-house, facing ignominious death and sitting down to write this patient, forgiving, beautiful letter and I began to cry. I just sat there—crying. A stranger was in the same carriage; I had forgotten his existence—a nice old Anglo-Indian colonel. He put his hand on my arm—"My dear young lady," he said, "Come! Come! A pretty young woman like you!" Life didn't seem long enough to explain to him that I was not crying about a lost lover but about Sacco and Vanzetti. "Think of all life has in store for you," he said. I was thinking about death but I couldn't help laughing. "Do you think so?" I asked. "That is right," he answered. "Keep a stiff upper lip!"

HOBART

Maybe your soldier friend wasn't far from right. Maybe your personal unhappiness was mixed up with those tears, Lady Wyngate.

LAEL

There you are!

HOBART

Maybe it was yourself you were crying for, after all.

LAEL

I see your resemblance to your brother, Rand. I'm sure you despise women, don't you, Mr. Eldridge?

HOBART

Well, I wouldn't exactly say that.

LAEL

Have you men been so successful in running the world that you can take the position of despising us?

HOBART

Surely you can't complain of Rand on that score? He's idolatrous.

LAEL

(*With a dazzling smile at* RAND). I certainly do. I complain of his idolatry more than of your contempt. He tells me, for example, that I don't mean anything at all. . . .

RAND

I didn't say that.

LAEL

You know better than that, don't you, Mr. Eldridge? You know that I mean a great deal.

HOBART

(*Showing* RAND *how fair he is*). I think that you do mean a great deal—but—you'll forgive me—I think that you're not nearly so certain of what it is that you mean. If you could visualize the ultimate implications of your conduct, I'm sure that you'd probably . . .

LAEL

What nonsense! But that would mean foreseeing to the end of time. It's difficult enough to visualize the immediate implications—and you talk about ultimate implications. What—you will forgive me—what conceit! Where is Mrs. Eldridge? Didn't you go to fetch Mrs. Eldridge?

HOBART

She hadn't arrived at White Hart. I left word for her to join me here. I hope you won't mind.

LAEL

Of course not! That's utterly delightful! You know, I can hardly wait to know you better because I am certain that the better we know each other the less we shall agree. I foresee enchanting vistas of antagonism. I love opposition. It solidifies my own position.

HOBART

What—you will forgive me—what conceit!

LAEL

(*Delighted—vamping* HOBART). I am beginning to see why you and Lord Abercrombie hit it off. He's a Puck.

HOBART

I beg your pardon!

LAEL

He's a Puck—and so are you—a malevolent Puck . . .
(JOAN *comes in.*)
Hello, Joan. What's Herr Willens doing?

JOAN

Arguing music with Sascha.

LAEL

That's one thing musicians can do. It appears music's more controversial than politics. Poor Herr Willens! What is he going to do? I have it! (*To* HOBART.) Why don't you let him review music for your new newspaper?

HOBART

We're not going in for that sort of thing.

LAEL

What are you going to fill it with?

HOBART

I'll send you advance sheets of the first issue.

LAEL

Please don't trouble. I can imagine. Racial solidarity and a higher tariff on wool. Rand, would you like to see the river view?

RAND

(*With alacrity*). I would indeed!

LAEL

We must find something though for that poor fellow Willens. To find yourself suddenly without a job and without a country . . . I'll take you on the most enchanting walk you ever . . . (*To* HOBART.) Won't you come too, Mr. Eldridge? Do you mind if I call you Hobart? Even if we do disagree to the death, there is no reason we can't be friends, is there? You will come, won't you, Hobart?

HOBART

No, thank you.

LAEL

I'm so sorry. Joan, will you be a dear and go tell Herr Willens that if he's bored with Sascha he might join us? We'll be walking the river path—slowly. Come on, Rand.

Curtain

ACT TWO

SCENE I

SCENE: *The same as* Act One.

Afternoon, four days later.

CLENDON WYATT'S *voice,* SASCHA *accompanying on the piano, is heard singing a spiritual.* NIKOLAI JURIN *sits by, listening. The curtain rises during the first lines of* WYATT'S *song.* WYATT *is an attractive young Southern American who won a Rhodes Scholarship for making a spectacular dash on the football field.* JURIN *is an aristocratic Russian, middle-aged, tired, very gentle.*

WYATT'S VOICE

Away up thar
My massa's settin'
Settin' on
His judgment chair
He looks down on
All creation
He sees sorrow
He knows care . . .
He sees sorrow
He knows care.

(*There is a moment's pause when he finishes singing.*)

JURIN

Thank you, Mr. Wyatt. I have always wanted to hear one of these songs. Sascha, please . . .

SASCHA

Yes?

JURIN

This spiritual which Mr. Wyatt has just

sung for us—did it make you think of anything, did it remind you of anything?

SASCHA

Musically, you mean?

JURIN

(*Eagerly*). Yes. Musically.

SASCHA

Not especially. Why?

JURIN

Ah, that's because you were never in Streilna before the Revolution, where Maria Nikolaevna used to sing the gypsy songs.
(*He closes his eyes and sings.*)

Utro Tumannoye
Utro Sedoye
Nivi Pechalnia
Snegom Pokritiya

Do you see what I mean about the resemblance?

WYATT

I see what you mean. . . .

SASCHA

(*Argumentative*). Not a bit alike! The Russian is sensuous, earthy . . .
(LAEL *comes in. Grouped around the piano, the others don't see her at once.*)

JURIN

(*Trying to persuade* SASCHA). But in the melancholy of both, there's . . .

WYATT

I know what it is they have in common—resignation!

JURIN

Yes! Resignation. Yes!

LAEL

(*Coming up to them*). What's this about resignation?
(*They all rise.*)
I don't approve of it. I think people ought to fight.

JURIN

(*Standing above his chair*). There comes a day, dear lady, when you cannot fight—then you need resignation.

LAEL

(*Briskly*). I don't admit that day!

JURIN

Had you been in Russia when the Bolsheviks came, you would have recognized such a day.

LAEL

Well, I'm prepared to admit that resignation may have its uses, a recuperative interval, a kind of hibernation of the soul—but you can't be resigned forever. That's Buddhism.

JURIN

No, pardon me, dear lady, but I do not agree with you. There comes a day when you wake up and you find yourself, though you are living and breathing, a part of the past.
(HUGO *enters.*).
You are historic. You realize that you have survived yourself. That's sad. That's strange. And for that day you need resignation.

LAEL

Oh, I understand it, but temperamentally I'm agin it.

JURIN

But really to understand it, you have to undergo persecution and contempt.

SASCHA

It's no joke the way things are going nowadays.

LAEL

It was never a joke at any time the way things were going. Was there ever a moment in history when you weren't surrounded by blood and tears?
(HOBART *enters. He is fingering a telegram and is very business-like.*)
It depended always on where you looked.
(*The last of this she has said looking at* HOBART.)
Oh, hello, Hobart.

HOBART

(*Aggressively*). I've got to go up to London. Where's Rand?

WYATT

On the tennis-court I believe. Shall I get him for you?

HOBART

If you please.
(*With a look at* LAEL, WYATT *goes out.*)

LAEL

I'll join you in a minute, Clen.

JURIN

What a nice boy that is. How does he, an American, happen to be at Oxford?

LAEL

He's a Rhodes Scholar. He says he's so grateful to Mr. Rhodes for letting him stay at Oxford that he's always wanting to write him a bread-and-butter letter.

JURIN

(*Puzzled*). But I thought Rhodes was dead?

LAEL

(*Laughs—in explanation to* JURIN). American humor, Jurin!
(JURIN *rises and kisses her hand.*)

SASCHA

I'll find Joan and we'll play doubles. Mrs. Eldridge doesn't want to play. What do you say, Jurin?

JURIN

I'll do my best. (*To* HUGO.) Perhaps you would like to play, Herr Willens?

HUGO

Thank you, no.

LAEL

(*To* SASCHA *and* JURIN). We'll be out in a second to watch you.
(SASCHA *and* JURIN *exit.*)
Now, then, Hobart, why must you go up to London? Why can't you relax? You're always so busy.

HOBART

I've just been down to the post-office . . .

LAEL

I could have a ticker-tape in your room?

HOBART

(*Smiling grimly*). A telephone would be some help. But this isn't the Stock Market. I've got to go up to London.
(RAND *comes in flushed from tennis.*)

LAEL

(*To* RAND). Your brother's going up to London. I'm hurt!

HOBART

Just for a few hours. And I've got to take Rand with me.

RAND

(*Appalled*). Oh, now, Bart . . .

HOBART

We'll be back in time for dinner. Right after, anyway. . . .

RAND

But I'm right in the middle of a set.

HOBART

An hour to London—half hour in Fleet Street—an hour back.

LAEL

(*Unable to resist it*). Shall I ask Lord Abercrombie here?

HOBART

(*Horrified*). Rand!

LAEL

Nonsense. Rand didn't tell me. I told him. *Shall* I ask him here?

HOBART

(*Recovered*). Don't think you could get him.

LAEL

(*Wickedly*). Shall I try?

HOBART

(*Fearful of her magic*). No, thank you. I'm afraid you might succeed and I'd rather see him in London—away from you. Probably, like everyone else, Lord Abercrombie can't resist you.

LAEL

Well, up to a point he can't resist me.

HOBART

(*Looking at his watch*). Please get ready, Rand. The longer you take . . .

RAND

(*Turning to obey*). Right! (*Stops.*) Why don't you drive up with us, Lael?

LAEL

Shall I, Hobart? Look how frightened he is. No, I can't leave my guests.

RAND

(*To* HOBART). Sure we will be back for dinner?

HOBART

If you hurry.

RAND

Be right down.
(RAND *exits.*)

LAEL

(*To* HUGO). Mr. Eldridge is organizing an Anglo-American Youth League.

HOBART

(*Surprised that she should speak of it to* HUGO). Hum?

LAEL

(*To* HOBART). Oh, it's everybody's secret. What are you going to ask the Anglo-American Youth to do for you?

HOBART

(*As if he had memorized it*). We are appealing to the generous spirit of the youth of both countries to mobilize against the subversive forces current in the world today.

LAEL

Are you appealing to it because it's generous or because it's uncritical?

HUGO

It's a myth about the generosity of youth. Youth is bloodthirsty and savage—it's only the exceptional youth that's generous—just as it's only the exceptional man.

LAEL

I don't agree with you, Hugo. I think the impulse of youth is to be generous.

HUGO

When it's well-fed and romping it may be occasionally, out of excess of energy—but normally it isn't. But then, normally, who is? No point in being quixotic, is there? Excuse me, Lady Wyngate, I think I'll watch the tennis.
(HUGO *saunters out.*)

LAEL

I hate Youth Movements. They all come to the same thing. Boy Scouts with bayonets. Do you want a private army, Hobart? Have you a little dictator hatching in your brain?

HOBART

(*Urbanely*). As a matter of fact, Lady Wyngate, it's commonly acknowledged that democracy is passé. At home, the historic system of "checks and balances"—(*He utters the phrase derisively.*)—has brought us where we are. And your Parliament is—what does Lord Abercrombie call it?

LAEL

Vestigial! He calls it vestigial!

HOBART

Exactly. Vestigial!

LAEL

I hate dictatorship because it implies omniscience, and I don't believe in omniscience. That's theology applied to politics, and I believe it's dangerous. I can believe in God only if He's invisible.

HOBART

(*Patronizingly*). Very good!

LAEL

Thank you!

HOBART

There's one thing about you—and people like you—that I *don't* understand . . .

LAEL

Oh, is there?

HOBART

. . . that I'd like to have explained to me.

LAEL

I have no secrets from you, Hobart.

HOBART

I can understand people who haven't anything being Communists. Naturally they want to take things away from the people who have. But why people like you, who have everything to lose by the destruction of our system, should be Communists, I never will understand. It baffles me. Frankly, it does.

LAEL

Well, in the first place, I'm not in the least bit a Communist. That's just an epithet that people like you apply to anyone like me who doesn't happen to share your prejudices. In the second place . . . Oh, dear . . .

HOBART

(*Patiently*). In the second place? . . .

LAEL

Dear, oh, dear, I find the prospect of arguing with you appals me.

HOBART

Why?

LAEL

Because the possibility of enlightening you —if you'll forgive me, Hobart, seems so—shall we say—remote?
(*He smiles benignly, patiently.*)
That benign smile!

HOBART

At least, I know where my interests lie.

LAEL

I'm sure you do.

HOBART

You don't. I'm fighting your battles.

LAEL

Thank you!

HOBART

You ought to pray for my success.

LAEL

I will, if you insist.

HOBART

It means the continuance of a world in which you can entertain Communists like Mr. Jurin and . . .

LAEL

Because he is a Russian—and my guest—you assume—you put two and two together—get a colossal sum—typical financier. As a matter of fact, Mr. Jurin is a victim of the Communists—as anti as possible.

HOBART

Humph!

LAEL

That irritates you, doesn't it?

HOBART

(*Still very bland*). Dear Lady Wyngate, inconsistency of any sort irritates me.

LAEL

Yes, I suppose it would.

HOBART

If I favor dictatorship as against democracy, it is because I've applied dictatorship in my business and in my private life, and have made it successful.

LAEL

(*Who is pondering, while he is talking, another problem*). Have you?

HOBART

I flatter myself I have. I am a very rich man, Lady Wyngate. I should never have become so through a system of divided powers. In the political realm also such a system is impractical. The state of the world today proves how impractical it is.

LAEL

(*On whom a light breaks*). Of course!

HOBART

(*Misunderstanding*). Don't tell me you agree with me. That would make me dubious of the soundness of my own premises.

LAEL

Lighter, Bart, lighter . . . I'm afraid these heavy broadsides are wasted on me. Do you know what's been worrying me while you've been making these pronunciamentos? Rand! What has Rand to do with all this? Why are you rushing him into town to meet Lord Abercrombie? Of course it's perfectly obvious—the whole scheme. Really, it is a trifle shabby.

HOBART

(*Olympian*). What is shabby, Lady Wyngate?

LAEL

(*Deliberately and firmly*). Exploiting your brother's name and reputation for a movement the real motive of which he doesn't understand and which he'd loathe if he did understand.

HOBART

And may I ask what makes you think he'd loathe it?

LAEL

(*Warmly*). Because he's generous-hearted and your movement isn't!

HOBART

In your opinion it isn't. As a matter of fact my brother does understand it and approves thoroughly.

LAEL

Will you risk my explaining it to him—from my point of view?

HOBART

That would hardly be fair.

LAEL

Why not?

HOBART

Because you are a lovely woman with whom he happens to be in love.
(*This gives her pause.*)

LAEL

(*Slowly, realizing* HOBART *is cleverer than he seems*). That's the most effective appeal you could have made. But perhaps I'll stop Rand joining you anyway. I must remember that people like you regard chivalry in others exactly as strategists in war regard weakness in defence. Shall I stop him? I can, you know.

HOBART

(*Steely now*). If I were you, Lady Wyngate, I really shouldn't try.

LAEL

Probably not. After all, why should I?

HOBART

That's wise.

LAEL

It's because I don't believe in your survival, no matter how many Youth Leagues you organize. But don't threaten me—even by implication. Because if you do—I *will* stop him. I'm perverse, you know, Hobart . . . (RAND *comes back. He has changed into a traveling suit.* HOBART *rises—looks at watch.*)

RAND

(*Transparently reluctant*). Well, here I am!

LAEL

(*Her customary chatter*). Of course, any hostess with a nature less adorably angelic than mine would simply poison you for taking away her most celebrated guest in the middle of the day like this. The trouble is you're so used to Rand you have no idea the glamor he sheds.

HOBART

(*Significantly*). I have some idea.

LAEL

I take it back. Of course you have!

RAND

I hate to go. (*He smiles at his brother.*) I wish, Hobart, you weren't so important!

HOBART

You two make me feel like the villain in the play separating the lovers. But it has to be done. Please, Rand . . .

RAND

(*Obedient but not apologetic*). I want to talk to Lael—for just a second.

HOBART

(*Looking at his watch*). I'll give you ten. (*Faces* LAEL.) Not so bad, am I? Any message to Lord Abercrombie?

LAEL

Give him my love—that's ambiguous enough.

HOBART

(*With a laugh*). I will! (*Holds up both his hands to* RAND.) Ten!
(*He goes out.* RAND *goes to her. Takes her in his arms. She is not very responsive.*)

RAND

What a bore! I have to go!
(*He sits on arm of* LAEL'*s chair.*)

LAEL

I think so!

RAND

I can't very well refuse Bart, can I?

LAEL

I suppose not.

RAND

He's done so much for me. It seems little enough to do in return.

LAEL

Does it?

RAND

After all—a few hours in London— I'll be back at the latest by . . .

LAEL

I wasn't referring to the time involved.

RAND

To what then?

LAEL

This illustrates what I mean when I . . . Oh, well, never mind.
(*She was about to tell him how it illustrates the essential incompatibility between them—his leaving her to go on a mission she detests—but she is inhibited by recalling* HOBART'*s accusation of unfairness.*)

RAND

But you must tell me. This illustrates—what?

LAEL

I can't tell you now—your brother's waiting for you—there isn't time.

RAND

There is. Tell me. Please, Lael, tell me.

LAEL

I promised your brother I wouldn't.

RAND

But . . .

LAEL

Oh, dear, life is very complicated!

RAND

You make it so.

LAEL

Do I?

RAND

I love you.

LAEL

You shouldn't.

RAND

I do though.

LAEL

Well, then—I shouldn't.

RAND

As long as you do! . . .

LAEL

You'd better go now, Rand, but when you come back . . .

RAND

Will you tell me then what all this mystery is?

LAEL

I will. I'll tell you then.

RAND

(*Smiling at her*). A showdown!

LAEL

That's it! A showdown!

RAND

That's what I've been waiting for. We've got to get clear. (*Takes her in his arms.*) Good-bye, darling.

LAEL

Good-bye.

RAND

(*Starts to leave, stops and faces her*). Come with me to the car, Lael, please.
(*He has returned to her.*)

LAEL

(*Crosses the room, stops at door and faces him*). All right. Rand—

RAND

Yes, Lael?

LAEL

Will you do me a favor?

RAND

Anything.

LAEL

After you've talked to Lord Abercrombie, tell him that before you make a final decision about anything you have promised to consult me.

RAND

Certainly I will.

LAEL

That'll cheer him up.
(*They exit through arch in alcove, laughing.*)
(HUGO *comes in through the French windows from the garden, crosses to the end table by sofa, picks up a cigarette and lights it. From the garden also* PHOEBE ELDRIDGE *comes in, blonde, exquisitely dressed, an adorable Kewpie.*)

PHOEBE

Are you afraid of me?

HUGO

Why, Phoebe?

PHOEBE

You seem to avoid me.

HUGO

Not at all.

PHOEBE

You've changed. You know that. You've got a lot of new lines in your face.

HUGO

Well, don't rub it in.

PHOEBE

At lunch I watched you. I thought: What is it about him that's changed?

HUGO

Age, my dear.

PHOEBE

No, not age. You don't somehow look older. Trouble, suffering. And I stopped hating you.

HUGO

(*Suddenly Mephistophelean, making passes with his fingers over his forehead*). Look, I erase the little lines.

PHOEBE

(*Piteously*). Do you want me to hate you?

HUGO

I don't want to be loved for a blemish. I am too vain!

PHOEBE

I didn't say that I loved you. I only said that I didn't hate you.

HUGO

In that dubious region between love and hate . . .

PHOEBE

What?

HUGO

Nothing. I succumbed to the cadence of that opening phrase. It seemed to be an opening phrase. Seemed to lead somewhere into some superb aphorism. But it doesn't. It doesn't lead anywhere. It gets ready to be magnificent and then dries up.

PHOEBE

There's one thing that I'd like to know—that I have a right to know.

HUGO

(*After a moment*). Well?

PHOEBE

About her?

HUGO

Her?

PHOEBE

The woman.

HUGO

What woman?

PHOEBE

The woman for whom you left me in Munich.

HUGO

Oh! That woman! What do you want to know?

PHOEBE

Are you still in love with her?

HUGO

You overestimate my fidelity.

PHOEBE

Are you trying to comfort me? It's nothing to me. I'm just curious.

HUGO

Well?

PHOEBE

Where is this mysterious woman now?

HUGO

I haven't the least idea.

PHOEBE

Haven't you? Are you sure you haven't?

HUGO

Quite.

PHOEBE

You must wonder why I'm so curious. . . . Really it's for the most trivial reason. You know how feminine I am.

HUGO

Yes, Phoebe, I do—I do. I assure you, Phoebe, that like the whole of my life—this woman—is part of the past.

PHOEBE

When you left me in Munich—that last time—where did you go to meet her?

HUGO

Where?

PHOEBE

Yes.

HUGO

Oh, er—Bayreuth, wasn't it?

PHOEBE

You know perfectly well it was Bayreuth. As a matter of fact, you heard "Tristan" with her—and you were going to take me. (*She bursts out suddenly at him.*) You don't see her any more, do you? You don't know where she is, do you?

HUGO

What are you? . . .

PHOEBE

This Wyngate woman . . .

HUGO

What!

PHOEBE

The moment I saw you together I knew it. I felt it. And then I found out. I was talking to her before luncheon. It wasn't difficult, clever as she's supposed to be.

HUGO

Phoebe, Phoebe! Of all your intuitions, this is the most brilliant.

PHOEBE

I found out where she was that summer—in Bayreuth—where you went to hear "Tristan" . . . "Tristan." You and your wonderful titled Englishwoman!

HUGO

Phoebe, does it occur to you that there must have been several hundred titled Englishwomen in Bayreuth that summer, that month, that day? You must believe me, Phoebe. This is a fantastic caprice of your imagination.

PHOEBE

Is it?

HUGO

I never saw Lady Wyngate until the other day—when Sascha brought her up to London to meet me.

PHOEBE

It's no use, Hugo.

HUGO

Very well, have it your own way. There's nothing to be done about it, is there?

PHOEBE

I can't help it, Hugo. I love you still. I've never stopped thinking of you. I can't do anything about it. I used to wonder who the other woman was. For three years I've wondered. I felt if I knew, it would be easier. Well, now I know—and it isn't.

HUGO

Phoebe! Phoebe, whatever you think about Lady Wyngate and me, it isn't true.

PHOEBE

Why did you come here then?

HUGO

I had to go somewhere. Phoebe, I assure you . . .

PHOEBE

Do you still love her?

HUGO

Oh, Phoebe!

PHOEBE

Is there anything between you now?

HUGO

Not a thing. You've got to believe me.

PHOEBE

Promise?

HUGO

Promise.

PHOEBE

Word of honor?

HUGO

(*Stands at attention and clicks his heels*). Word of honor.

PHOEBE

(*Leans back in chair, then speaks*). Still—I suppose I'd better leave here today.

HUGO

(*In panic—dreading a scene*). No, no! Don't do that! You mustn't do that! (*Going closer to her.*) Phoebe, I want you to stay.

PHOEBE

(*Coquettishly*). You don't—you don't in the least.

HUGO

I do. When I saw you here today, I felt . . .

PHOEBE

No, you didn't—you didn't feel anything.

HUGO

That's not true. Stay, Phoebe, and I'll show you how wrong you are.

PHOEBE

(*Rises—about to put her arm about his neck*). All right, Hugo. I'll give you a chance to explain.

(JURIN *enters from the French windows. He sees that he is interrupting and starts to leave.*)

HUGO

Phoebe . . .

(HUGO *sees* JURIN *and is delighted, grasping this as a means of escape from* PHOEBE.

He calls out to JURIN, *but remains standing at right of* PHOEBE.)
Oh, come in, Mr. Jurin, come in! I've been wanting to speak to you. It's most important that I speak to you!

JURIN

(*Crossing to left of* PHOEBE'S *chair*). Please?

HUGO

Are you fond of music, Mr. Jurin?

JURIN

Naturally.

HUGO

Ah! Then you can help me. You can help me no end!

JURIN

Can I?

HUGO

Yes. I want to do an article on Russian music.

JURIN

(*Interested*). Oh?

HUGO

Russian music since the Revolution. From Glazounov to Sostakhevitch. Did you by any chance know Glazounov, Mr. Jurin?

JURIN

No.
(*Sensing something is amiss, glances amusedly at* PHOEBE, *then continues.*)
I admire him greatly—but as a matter of fact . . .

HUGO

(*Interrupting him*). You see the point I want to make, Mr. Jurin, is that music is the only Russian art which has eluded political dictatorship—now Sostakhevitch . . .

JURIN

As a matter of fact, Herr Willens, Sostakhevitch . . .

PHOEBE

(*Unable to bear any more, rises and speaks to* JURIN—*rather coldly*). When you've both finished this fascinating subject . . .
(*To* HUGO—*warmly and sincerely.*)
I'll be waiting for you down by the river, Hugo.
(HUGO *and* JURIN *bow to her. She goes to the French windows and exits.* JURIN *and* HUGO *watch her go and then* HUGO *looks at* JURIN *and sinks into the chair.*)

JURIN

(*Quite aware of the situation—slightly teasing*). You see, Herr Willens—I left Russia in 1917. Sostakhevitch is a post-Revolutionary phenomenon. The first time I heard anything by Sostakhevitch was not in Russia but in the Bowl.

HUGO

(*Absent-mindedly*). The Bowl?

JURIN

Yes, the Bowl in Hollywood.

HUGO

Oh.

JURIN

But it is a very interesting topic, although I am very much afraid, Herr Willens, that you will have some difficulty in proving your point. These days it would seem nothing eludes political dictatorship. Not even music. To hear people talk you might think that music is a form of political pamphleteering. Hindemith is Bolshevik. Strauss is reactionary. Sostakhevitch is the orchestrator of the Five-Year Plan. Even dead composers are pulled out of their graves to hang in effigy.
(HUGO *is slumped in his chair.* JURIN *goes to him and glances off after* PHOEBE.)
However, my dear chap, if I can help you still further in any way, I shall be delighted.

HUGO

Thanks.

JURIN

You're welcome.
(LAEL *enters.*)

HUGO

(*Suddenly conscious of* JURIN). Mr. Jurin, have you been wandering over the face of the earth since 1917?

JURIN

Since 1917.

LAEL

(*Amused*). You ought to publish a refugee's hand-book, Jurin.

JURIN

A time-table?

LAEL

There ought to be a marvelous place set aside somewhere for all the refugees.

JURIN

But I thought it was *here,* Lady Wyngate!

LAEL

A little bigger, Jurin. My accommodations are so limited. A semi-tropical paradise set aside by the League of Nations. A government of refugees—by refugees—for refugees. What sort of a government would it be, I wonder.

JURIN

(*Humorously*). Probably a—dictatorship! (JURIN *exits through French windows into the garden.*)

LAEL

Great charm, that man! One of those rare souls whom suffering doesn't embitter but makes mellow somehow. Oh, dear—I'm very depressed, Hugo. I'm in a funk. I want building up.

HUGO

Then I'm afraid I'm the last person you want.

LAEL

If you let me talk I'll gradually build myself up. I'm irrepressible. Do you ever despise yourself, Hugo?

HUGO

Just now—before you came in here—I had occasion to despise myself.

LAEL

Did you? So did I! What a beautiful coincidence! Just now with Rand . . .

HUGO

(*Quickly*). Yes?

LAEL

I was strongly tempted to coquette him into doing something for me—like a film vampire shedding sex-appeal. Not nice!

HUGO

Well, we're even.

LAEL

How do you mean?

HUGO

Just now I overheard myself almost beginning to make insincere love to a woman for whom I feel nothing whatever—God knows why—but it was probably the only thing to do at the moment.

LAEL

(*After a moment—understanding*). Oh. Mrs. Eldridge?

HUGO

You know then?

LAEL

I found out today.

HUGO

Did you?

LAEL

Yes, just before luncheon.

HUGO

(*Realizing that* PHOEBE *hadn't put anything over on* LAEL). Oh.

LAEL

Nothing so thankless as to warm over an old love affair, is there?

HUGO

(*Rises*). Two weeks ago I was in a land suddenly hostile to me. I thought: If ever I get out of it—I'll live austerely. Now I am out and I find myself dawdling about and being agreeable where agreeableness is indicated. Really, human nature is too resilient!

LAEL

Isn't it lucky it is— How often—if it didn't bend, it would break!

HUGO

Better to break!

LAEL

That's too austere. That's Calvinist.

HUGO

(*Smiles*). Just now, while I was being agreeable to Phoebe, I kept saying to myself: "Why don't you tell her the plain truth—that you can't endure her?" I couldn't though. I kept on being agreeable.

LAEL

But of course you had to. The other would be too cruel.

HUGO

Would it? I wish I'd told her long ago in Munich—instead of what I did tell her then.

LAEL

What did you tell her then?

HUGO

I was so desperate to get rid of her and so determined to be ruthless that I told her there was another woman.

LAEL

Wasn't there?

HUGO

Not a soul. Pure improvisation. "Titled Englishwoman." I told her I was leaving her for a "Titled Englishwoman," a phrase from a tenpenny novel of "High Life." I heard it again today, the same phrase—she's treasured it: "Titled Englishwoman!"

LAEL

Did she demand to know who the "Titled Englishwoman" was?

HUGO

She did. Morbid curiosity.

LAEL

Not morbid at all. I'd have wanted to know too.

HUGO

(*Suddenly overcome by the grotesqueness of the situation, he bursts into laughter*). Really, it's too funny!

LAEL

I suppose you couldn't tell her there was nobody. No, that would be too pointed.

HUGO

Having improvised a rival, she tried to force me to produce one for her and since, for obvious reasons, I couldn't do that, she's done the job for me—conjured one out of the clear air! You!

LAEL

What?

HUGO

You! You are the "Titled Englishwoman." She is certain of it. Nothing I can say will dissuade her of it.

LAEL

But I . . .

HUGO

One of those sudden, irrational convictions jealous people get. The evidence is incontrovertible. A: You *are* a titled Englishwoman, aren't you? B: You *were* in Bayreuth during the Wagnerian cycle of the summer of '32, weren't you? C: So was I. A—B—C.

LAEL

(*Laughing*). Q. E. D.

HUGO

(*Ironically. Rises and bows to her*). I congratulate you!

LAEL

(*Enjoying it all*). But I think it's marvelous! (*All graciousness.*) And I may say —I congratulate *you!*

HUGO

(*Sits again on sofa beside* LAEL). I'm terribly sorry.

LAEL

But why? I don't mind, if you don't.

HUGO

It's too silly. It's so unfair to you.

LAEL

Nonsense! If I were to be upset by rumors about me—this is mild compared to some. I've given up years ago worrying about what people say. Do you know why? Because everybody else in the world is anonymous really except those few—it can never be more than a very few—who really matter to me. One, at most two absolute friends.

HUGO

(*Not too seriously*). There's no such thing as absolute friendship. Like everything else, friendship is relative—a thermometer of expediency.

LAEL

That's too cynical. Not bad as an epigram though. But you can't compress the truth about anything into a sentence. It's like pressing a drop of blood on a slide and saying: "This is the stuff that flows in your veins!" It isn't though. When it's in your veins it's something different.

HUGO

I'm glad you can believe in friendship. It must be a great comfort to you!

LAEL

Don't you? Don't you really?

HUGO

I did once.

LAEL

During the trouble at home—did no one stand by you?

HUGO

I was aware of one friend. He was an unknown playwright. I felt this man to be, though he was even then middle-aged, the freshest and the most living voice, since Ibsen, in Europe. In my first published book a large part was devoted to him. But the book brought me more success than it brought him—as a result of it I was invited to lecture in America. I took his plays with me, I translated them and lectured on them from New York to San Francisco. Now, you must understand that in all this, I was exalting myself; it was the most any critic can be, a disciple of greatness.

LAEL

(*Knowing he has begun to be afraid she will think him conceited*). I understand, Hugo.

HUGO

And I had the greatest reward such discipleship can have. As a result of my enthusiasm a curious phenomenon took place; the fame I created for him in America reverberated to Germany—and we began to accept him at home!

LAEL

You mean Lehrmann, I suppose?

HUGO

Yes, Lehrmann.

LAEL

He's your Grand Old Man, isn't he?

HUGO

Something like that. He's over sixty. I've hero-worshipped him for thirty years. I came to see him, sure that in his mellow greeting I would be in some sense—restored. Because I actually felt a wavering of sanity. I had sent him the manuscript of my pamphlet. I began to tell him how disturbed I was by the New Dispensation when I detected a new look in his eyes, a new manner. He had not smiled in greeting; he had not given me his hand. He refused point-blank to read my pamphlet; in a hard voice he advised me to tear it up. "This is a new day," he said to me. "There is no place in it for Oriental decadence!" Oriental! My family had lived in Germany for hundreds of years. I sat there staring at him. In his eyes, already glazed with mortality, I saw something impenetrable, incurably hostile, something that no appeal to the past could soften. That look did for me. I'd never had such a sense of helplessness. For in his youth this man had been the voice of the submerged—he had written the saga of the oppressed and the poor;

he had been a living instrument of justice. There he sat, impersonal, hard, fanatical. He let me go without asking me to come to see him again, as you let go a servant who has cheated you and to whom you refuse to give a reference. . . . Friendship!
(*A pause. He tries to gather himself together and speaks lightly.*)
After all—it's none of your affair, is it?

LAEL

(*Very quietly*). That's the unkindest thing, I think, that anyone's ever said to me.

HUGO

I'm sorry. But, really—I came here a complete stranger to you—you invite me to stay out of a fantastic goodness of heart. The least I can do in return is to be—jolly. As a matter of fact, I'm going away and that is partly why. It's too unfair to you.

LAEL

You mustn't go until you've had a chance to get a perspective on yourself. Besides, where would you go?

HUGO

I was going to borrow from Sascha passage-money to America. They've started something there they call the University in Exile. Maybe I could get into that. I've cabled the director.

LAEL

We'll see what can be done for you *here.*

HUGO

It won't be easy. To be at once an emigré and a critic—that is a double parasitism. Before I can be eloquent I need a masterpiece and before I can be witty I need something which fails to be a masterpiece.

LAEL

(*Amused*). Have you heard yet from America?

HUGO

Not yet.

LAEL

Well, I *do* wish you could feel welcome here, Hugo. Don't you like me?

HUGO

You've been very—gracious. It's that—! I feel—!
(*He doesn't finish. She gives him a quick look. She realizes that she has a problem on her hands that will not yield to simple tact merely.*)

LAEL

Hugo—

HUGO

Yes?

LAEL

Do you mind if I speak to you—frankly. That is to say, critically?

HUGO

(*Smiles quizzically*). Do you think I'm thin-skinned?

LAEL

I've avoided rather speaking to you about your—special experience. I've avoided it in a mistaken effort to keep your mind off it—but aren't you mistaking a mass antagonism for a personal one? Hugo, you don't want to develop a persecution mania.

HUGO

Is it a mania for the persecuted to believe in the reality of persecution?

LAEL

No. The truth is there's a pest over all the world just now, an epidemic of hatred and intolerance that may engulf us all. That is perfectly possible. People have suffered too much during the last twenty years—they can't stand any more, that's all. In one way or another they're letting off steam—the form it's taken against you is peculiarly detestable. Everyone here abhors it. The whole world revolts against it. That is what you must remember. This is a different climate, Hugo; you are like a man who continues to shiver when he's left the Arctic—and moved into the tropics. There are other worlds, you must remember, than the one you've left. . . .

HUGO

Are there?

LAEL

Oh, I know what you're saying to yourself: "It's easy enough for her to talk. She's at home, she's comfortable, she's secure." Am I though? There is no longer, in this curious moment of history, any security for anybody. What security should I have, as a liberal person, if the world goes Communist? Or Fascist? I think Hobart Eldridge and Lord Abercrombie might be—to say the least—unsympathetic to me. In any dictatorship, subtleties of opinion and temperament are swept away; you're either black or white.

HUGO

(*Quizzically*). But you're not a luxury commodity!

LAEL

I beg your pardon!

HUGO

Like the race of which I find myself suddenly as involuntary member!

LAEL

But, Hugo, these days *every* hereditary aristocracy is a luxury commodity!

HUGO

(*He takes her hand and kisses it*). You're very sweet—but I'm afraid the analogy is not quite complete. They, I suppose I ought to say we, are like passengers on a vessel that lets them stay on board—and even enter the first-class salons occasionally—as long as the weather is fair—but ho! for the sharks the minute there's a storm. Our science and our art are tolerated and even praised while the economic level is high. Once the golden stream is damned and constriction sets in we are the first to be squeezed. Of course the world has suffered, we among the rest, but, in its misery it singles us out to levy a secret and an ageless revenge.

LAEL

(*After a moment*). Where is your legendary patience, your legendary capacity for endurance, your legendary—resignation?

HUGO

(*Almost gleefully*). I haven't it! That's my special dilemma. I am neither patient, nor resigned, nor enduring. You forget I am only a Jew by fraction! I suffer the disabilities without the hereditary armors. The Aryan seven-eighths of me wars against the Semitic eighth—wars and retreats—and I'm afraid nothing can be done for me.

LAEL

That, Hugo, is a challenge to my resourcefulness! Promise me that you won't run away—if only because I like you and find you very sympathetic. (*Humorously*.) If you don't enjoy adapting yourself to Phoebe—adapt yourself to me.

HUGO

(*A slight pause, sincerely*). Shall I?

LAEL

(*After a second—candidly*). No. Don't.

HUGO

The idea tempts me.

LAEL

(*Resolutely*). It was automatically flirtatious. You deserve better than that of me—and so do I!

HUGO

(*Rather darting out at her*). You're in love with Rand!

LAEL

(*After a moment*). One's an awful mixture, Hugo.

HUGO

(*Accepting it instantly as a fact*). Don't you feel a sense of—incongruity?

LAEL

All the time. Yes. Keenly. It doesn't help though.
(*A moment's pause. She walks about the room impatiently. He watches her.*)
One gets so tired of one's own complexities. There's Rand, a symbol of simplicity, courage and directness. There, in a world of cruelty and chicanery, are honest purpose and generosity.

HUGO

So eloquent—and so unconvinced!

LAEL

(*Looks at him quickly, then away*). You're shrewd, Hugo. You're diabolically shrewd.

HUGO

(*Watching her*). Am I?

LAEL

Of course I'm unconvinced, but whether I'm convinced or not—there it is!

HUGO

(*Shrugging his shoulders*). Why attempt to rationalize the—elemental?

LAEL

(*As if to herself*). Isn't it extraordinary how one can go on being agreeable and alert—so-called normal—and all the time nourish an obsession that has a life of its own, independent and arrogant—a fugue that seeks stubbornly its own resolution—at no matter what cost—to oneself? (*Rises and faces him.*) Hugo . . .

HUGO

(*Rises*). Yes?

LAEL

(*Throwing away her pretences and appealing to him pitifully*). In you I feel—a special friend. Don't go. Please stay.

HUGO

(*Crosses to her*). All right. I'll stay. (*With great intensity.*) But not as a friend.

LAEL

(*Almost whispers*). Hugo . . .

HUGO

Not even as a special friend.

LAEL

On any terms.

HUGO

But because an obsession—may be destroyed.

LAEL

(*Realizes the implication of what he has said and looks at him in surprise*). Hugo!

HUGO

(*Terrific determination*). Yes! It may be destroyed!
(*His hand closes on her arm. They stand near together, close and warm spiritually also.* PHOEBE *comes in. She is eaten with jealousy, blind with rage, behaves almost like a person paralyzed with drugs. Speaks and walks as if in automatism.*)

PHOEBE

Do forgive me!

LAEL

Hello, Phoebe. Won't you . . .

PHOEBE

(*Without waiting to discover the invitation*). No, thank you very much.
(*She stands at door leading to staircase and addresses* HUGO.) Liar! Liar! Liar!
(*She disappears.*)

LAEL

Hugo! What does she mean? What did you tell her?

HUGO

(*Drily*). Well, she demanded to know whether there was anything between us, and I said there was not.

LAEL

(*Mischievously*). Well, you really shouldn't have lied to her, Hugo.

HUGO

That was twenty minutes ago—and I didn't know . . .
(*She is amused and provoked and still a little disturbed by* PHOEBE'S *plight. He stands looking at her, enchanted by her.*)

Quick Curtain

SCENE II

SCENE: *The same.*

Later that evening. Around 10:30.

JURIN *and* WYATT *are playing double patience and talking.*

WYATT

I wonder why the two Eldridges went so abruptly to London?

JURIN

I cannot suspect why.

WYATT

Didn't you feel a strain at dinner?

JURIN

Not especially. Mrs. Eldridge seemed a bit . . .

WYATT

Didn't she?
(*A moment's pause. They play in silence.*)

JURIN

The way Lady Wyngate rushed them all off to see the cinema in the village . . . They had no chance at all, did they? Whether they wanted to or not, to the cinema they went. You could tell she didn't mean to stand an evening of that by herself.

WYATT

The German didn't help much, did he?

JURIN

Not much.

WYATT

A burst of brilliance and then . . .

JURIN

A burst of brilliant silence! What do you think of him?

WYATT

I don't know. I can't tell. I think Lady Wyngate likes him. Do you like him?

JURIN

As a fellow refugee, I feel a sympathy for him. Poor fellow, he doesn't realize yet what being a refugee means.

WYATT

Maybe he does!

JURIN

He's new! I've had seventeen years of it.

WYATT

I can imagine—it's no fun.

JURIN

Half mendicant—half vagabond.

WYATT

Surely not for you—with your gift for languages.

JURIN

The English are really very kind. You'd be surprised how many of them are willing to begin to study Russian!
(WYATT *laughs.*)
They start with such enthusiasm, a mingling of philanthropy and really a romantic yearning to learn the language. But very soon, unhappily, they find that between the yearning to learn and learning is a gap which can only be bridged by a certain amount of hard work. This work is irksome and soon they begin to look on me, unconsciously perhaps, as a disagreeable taskmaster. They begin to miss lessons. They insist on paying for these missed lessons—at first I refuse to accept—now I accept for a while till it becomes only too apparent that the fees are only gifts. My pride intervenes. And I think: you have two children who must be fed—what right have you to pride? Pride is the last luxury one can train oneself to give up—like the traditional dress-suit of the impoverished swell. So it goes. Ah! The king I wanted.
(*He puts the king in place.*)

WYATT

Does Lady Wyngate miss many lessons?

JURIN

Oh, she misses them but with her it is different. When she misses a lesson it is because she really has something else to do. She works at it; she has made progress. But there is only one Lady Wyngate.

WYATT

Yes, isn't it lucky there is one!

JURIN

Oh, then why didn't you go along to the film?

JURIN

I have to cram for an exam.
(*He gets up.* HUGO *and* PHOEBE *come in,* PHOEBE *in evening dress.*)

JURIN

So soon back from the film?

HUGO

I left at the point where the first Lord Rothschild makes a loan to the Allied Powers out of sheer altruism!

PHOEBE

The stuffy place gave me a headache.

WYATT

Where is Lady Wyngate?

HUGO

Still there, I suppose. We couldn't find seats together—we got separated.

WYATT

Captain Eldridge came back just after you all left. Did he catch up to you?

HUGO

Yes, he did.
(*A moment's pause.*)

JURIN

(*Looks triumphantly at his cards*).
There—I've defeated myself—a brilliant victory—but a financial loss.

WYATT

How is that?

JURIN

I bet against myself—quietly.
(PHOEBE *goes to fireplace and sits by herself staring into it.* WYATT *gets up.*)

WYATT

Of course, Mr. Jurin, what you've been saying makes me timid about asking you to give me Russian lessons.

JURIN

My dear friend!

WYATT

(*To* HUGO). Mr. Jurin's been telling me what a hard time an emigré has even in a country as friendly as this is.

JURIN

Oh, please, I beg of you, do not repeat what I've been saying to Herr Willens!

HUGO

Why not?

JURIN

We don't want to discourage a novice!

HUGO

There is no novitiate in being a refugee. You are a veteran after you've left your country one day.

JURIN

(*Deprecatingly*). Well . . .

HUGO

To be a refugee is to belong to a lost cause. And people are bored by defeat.

JURIN

There have been refugees who have returned.

HUGO

Like Napoleon! When you still hope to return, you are not a refugee.

JURIN

(*Wistfully*). May not a lost cause be glamorous?

HUGO

(*Brutally*). In the amber of literature or history—yes. But not when it is contemporaneous. For a moment sympathetic people and generous people may be kind to the victim, but the average man has nothing but contempt for anyone who has been so footless as to put himself permanently in the wrong in the country of his origin. I saw it in people's faces the moment I crossed the frontier. A flicker of chivalry—merging almost instantly into a guarded boredom. No, it's a shabby martyrdom at best and if you will tell the truth, Mr. Jurin, you will have to admit that this is true.

JURIN

(*Sadly*). There are exceptions—that is to say, there is an exception—but in the main—yes—it is true.
(*A moment's pause.*)

WYATT

Mr. Jurin, if you don't mind I shall insist on studying Russian with you—not because you are a refugee—but because I want to learn the language.

JURIN

You will be unique among my pupils.

WYATT

Good night.
(*He goes out.*)
(JURIN *and* PHOEBE *and* HUGO *sit in silence.* JURIN *looks from one to the other, has some understanding of the situation and tries to stir up a little fire of conversation in these ashes.*)

JURIN

Evidently, Lady Wyngate likes the picture better than you did.

HUGO

I don't know. We weren't sitting together.

JURIN

It wouldn't matter if she didn't like it. She never can bear to leave anything in the middle. She always feels, she says, there may be something wonderful at the end.

PHOEBE

Oh, does she?

JURIN

Incorrigible optimist, isn't she?
(*A moment's pause.* JURIN *continues to* PHOEBE.)
Are they coming back after the film?

PHOEBE

I don't know. They said something about going to a Pier dance at Brighton. (*With perceptible irony.*) Lady Wyngate thought that would be fun!

JURIN

I won't wait up then. Will you say good night to her for me if she does come back?

PHOEBE

Yes, I will.

JURIN

Thank you, Mrs. Eldridge. (*To both of them.*) Good night.
(*He walks to French windows, stops.*)
I think I'll stroll through the garden. Really, the roses are overpowering at night. In the daytime I think they relax.
(*He goes out through the garden windows.* HUGO *and* PHOEBE *are left alone. He is so angry at her, he cannot bring himself to face her. He paces the room.*)

PHOEBE

(*At her most martyrish*). You're terrible! You act as if *I* had committed the grievance, as if *I* had hurt *you!*
(*A silence. He says nothing. He continues to pace.*)
You didn't say a word to me all the way here. Didn't you want me to leave the cinema with you? I couldn't sit there alone. How would it have looked afterwards—with Lady Wyngate and Rand? If you didn't want me to go, why didn't you say so?

HUGO

You've got it into your head that Lady Wyngate is the woman for whom I left you in Munich and nothing I can say will dissuade you of it. If you want to know the truth, there was nobody—nobody at all. I left you—not to meet Lady Wyngate nor anybody else—but for the blissful release of being away from you.

PHOEBE

You're very chivalrous, where she's concerned, aren't you? Anything to protect her!

HUGO

Well, whatever you may think, I want to be left alone now!

PHOEBE

I said I wanted to leave here this afternoon. Oh, no, you wouldn't have it! I mustn't go. Why? You'll be much more comfortable here without me, I should think. As for me, I'm quite reconciled, I assure you!

HUGO

(*Tensely*). Are you?

PHOEBE

You flatter yourself!

HUGO

You're behaving like a jealous schoolgirl. You're not a schoolgirl after all, Phoebe. You're the mother of a grown daughter.

PHOEBE

I know.

HUGO

You might behave with some dignity.

PHOEBE

Well, you needn't worry about it any longer.

HUGO

You say I needn't, but I do just the same. You act the martyr. You suffer. You whine.

PHOEBE

Hugo . .

HUGO

Um Gottes willen, I want to be left alone!

PHOEBE

Why didn't you tell me the truth then?

HUGO

Truth! Truth! What truth?

PHOEBE

This afternoon when I asked you if you still loved Lady Wyngate? You said you didn't. Why didn't you tell me the truth?

HUGO

Because I wanted to spare your feelings. Like all my other lies to you to spare your feelings!

PHOEBE

(*Gets very comfortable, then speaks*). Thank you, you needn't.

HUGO

Besides, you've always bullied me in your quiet way and I won't let you bully me any more. For that cowardly consideration I've always displayed to you—I apologize to you. I'll tell you the truth now—for all time. . . .

PHOEBE

Hugo . . .

HUGO

The truth is I can't endure you. Whether I love Lady Wyngate or anybody else can't possibly matter to you because I don't love you and never have. I detest your best qualities: your amiability, your patience, your clinging sweetness! You made me feel a cad and a sadist. You've done it for years and I'm sick to death of it. I repudiate it. I can't endure it. You drive me mad with boredom. You have almost from the beginning.

PHOEBE

That's a lie. I didn't before she came. You loved me before she came.

HUGO

You bored me before anybody came. The only reason our affair lasted as long as it did was because we were separated months at a time, because I hardly saw you for more than a few weeks each year. I beg of you, Phoebe, get interested in somebody else. Take up folk-dancing, or needlework, but for pity's sake, don't cling to me. Leave me alone.

PHOEBE

(*Not militantly*). All right, Hugo. You needn't worry. I will.

HUGO

You have a way of cringing before a blow when I speak harshly to you that's made a liar and a hypocrite of me for years. This conquest of me through meekness and patience and understanding has eroded me for years, and I'm not going to let it any longer. Do you understand that finally—not any longer!

PHOEBE

It's a pity your charming hostess won't make up her mind.

HUGO

I tell you she has nothing to do with it!

PHOEBE

(*Sweetly*). Whether she wants Rand or you. She sets her cap for him in New York and she got him over here. Why doesn't she make up her mind? Or maybe she's just using him. That's not very generous, I should say!

HUGO

(*In despair of her understanding—rises and faces her, then, as though explaining to a child*). Nothing would make any difference between you and me. How can I make it clear to you that if Lady Wyngate were blind or deaf or in a nunnery, it would make no difference to you and me? Nothing would make any difference between you and me!

PHOEBE

All right, Hugo.
(*He sits back in chair. She faces front. A pause.*)
No! No matter what you say to defend her—it was all right between us till she came. (*With quiet hatred.*) I owe this—to her! (JURIN *enters from the French windows.*)

JURIN

(*Seeing them*). Oh! Really, it is criminal to stay indoors on such a night. It is pure magic out there. Forgive me—one drink and I go.
(JURIN *comes to the secretaire and begins to mix himself a highball.* PHOEBE *and* HUGO *sit occupied with their own thoughts.* HOBART *enters. His face is set and grim. He has not had a happy or successful evening.* LORD ABERCROMBIE *has proved, at the critical moment, to be elusive.*)

HOBART

(*Taking in the frozen group*). Um! How very cozy!

JURIN

Oh, good evening, Mr. Eldridge.

HOBART

Good evening. I'll take a whiskey and soda, too, if you don't mind. I need it. Where's everybody?

PHOEBE

Rand is at the cinema with Lady Wyngate. So are Joan and Sascha.

HOBART

Should be back soon, shouldn't they?

PHOEBE

They said something about going to Brighton to a Pier dance hall.

HOBART

(*Incredulous*). What?

PHOEBE

(*Sarcastically*). Mingling with the people!

HOBART

Damn nonsense! I want to see Rand!

PHOEBE

You may have to wait up pretty late.

JURIN

Whiskey and soda, Hugo?

HUGO

(*Rises eagerly*). Yes, thanks.

JURIN

(*After a moment*). Why don't you all come out into the garden?

HOBART

Why? What's in the garden?

JURIN

(*Poetically*). The night.
(HUGO *understandingly pats* JURIN'*s arm and then goes to left of the sofa.* HOBART *looks at* JURIN *disgustedly and crosses to get another drink.* JURIN *then turns to* MRS. ELDRIDGE *and speaks to her from rear of the sofa.*)
Will you come, Mrs. Eldridge?

PHOEBE

No, thank you, Mr. Jurin.

HUGO

I'll go with you.

JURIN

(*Gallant*). I'd rather have Mrs. Eldridge, if *you* don't mind.

PHOEBE

I'm sorry.

JURIN

Then, thank you, Hugo.
(*Crosses to above the left end of the sofa, glances at* PHOEBE *and* HOBART *and indulging suddenly a personal sense of humor begins to declaim.*)
The moon shines bright: In such a night as this,
When the sweet wind did gently kiss the trees . . .
(HOBART *crosses to the right end of the sofa with his drink. He and* PHOEBE *exchange an incredulous glance and then he continues to the stool where he sits.*)
And they did make no noise, in such a night
Troilus methinks mounted the Trojan walls . . .
(JURIN *stops, glances at* HUGO, *then leans over and speaks to* PHOEBE.)
What comes next?
(PHOEBE *looks at him and then at* HOBART. JURIN *then turns to* HUGO.)
What comes after that?

HUGO

(*Smiling*). I only know the original . . .
In solcher Nacht
Erstieg wohl Troilus die Mauern Trojas
Und seufzte seine Seele zu den Zelten
Der Crichechn hin, so seine Cressida
Dies Nacht in Schlummer lag.
(JURIN *taking his arm affectionately.*)

JURIN

Still you must admit—"And Sigh'd his soul toward the Grecian tents, where Cressid lay that night" is not bad.

HUGO

Not bad—for a translation!

(*They both go out, carrying their highball glasses with them.* HOBART *has drained his highball and he goes to the tabouret to pour himself another.* PHOEBE *watches him.*)

PHOEBE

(*Dovelike to him suddenly*). What's the matter, Bart?

HOBART

(*Gruffly*). Why?

PHOEBE

Whenever you start drinking in that determined way, I know you're disappointed about something.

HOBART

Tired. Long day.

PHOEBE

(*After a moment*). Why didn't you and Rand come back together?

HOBART

I had to stay on to finish up with Lord Abercrombie.

PHOEBE

Did you finish up?

HOBART

Extraordinary interest you take in my affairs suddenly.

PHOEBE

If I know anything about them at all, it isn't because *you* confide in me.

HOBART

(*Mechanically*). What's the matter?
(*He knows there is something, but he's not interested much. He cannot possibly attribute gravity to* PHOEBE'S *preoccupations.*)

PHOEBE

Nothing. Why?

HOBART

(*After a moment, drinking*). Rand get back in time for dinner?

PHOEBE

No. Just after we all left for the cinema.

HOBART

Everything go off all right?

PHOEBE

Of course. Not that it would matter—Rand is so in love he's in complete oblivion as far as anything outside Lady Wyngate is concerned. He wouldn't notice anything anyway.

HOBART

What would there be to notice?

PHOEBE

Nothing. Nothing much.

HOBART

Well, what do you mean nothing much? What's on your mind? Speak up!

PHOEBE

Bart . . .

HOBART

Well?

PHOEBE

I think Rand ought to be warned . . .

HOBART

Warned?

PHOEBE

. . . about Lady Wyngate.

HOBART

How do you mean warned?

PHOEBE

(*With an air of dropping the whole thing*). Well, perhaps I'm crazy.
(*A pause.* HOBART *pours himself a third drink.* PHOEBE *walks about. He stands still, thinking, drinking his drink more slowly.*)
I think I'll take a turn in the garden.
(*She starts for garden doors, throwing a glance at him. He doesn't turn his head. She has to go through with it now and starts out, through the garden doors. At the last second, he calls her back.*)

HOBART

How do you mean warned? About what?

PHOEBE

It doesn't matter.

HOBART

(*Steely*). Come here.

PHOEBE

You're obviously in no mood to talk. (*A pause. He goes to her.*)

HOBART

What did you mean?

PHOEBE

I meant . . .

HOBART

Well?

PHOEBE

(*Her feelings get the better of her and she pours them out*).
I meant simply this: that Rand's precious idol is having an affair with that—immigrant—this Hugo Willens!
(*This makes considerable of an impression. So much so that, the moment she has uttered it,* PHOEBE *feels a bit frightened.*)

HOBART

(*After a pause*). What!

PHOEBE

Yes.

HOBART

Since coming to this house, you mean?

PHOEBE

Oh, no. It's been going on for years.

HOBART

How do you know?

PHOEBE

I know.

HOBART

How? This is important to me, Phoebe. More important than you realize. How do you know?

PHOEBE

(*More scared still and fighting for time—she realizes she hasn't worked her scheme out sufficiently in her mind*).
I can't tell you that.

HOBART

You've got to.

PHOEBE

I can't.

HOBART

You've got to. You will.

PHOEBE

Later perhaps—now I can't.

HOBART

Why not?

PHOEBE

It involves a friend.

HOBART

Who?

PHOEBE

That I can't tell you. You'd guess if I told you. I mean . . .
(*She has said it before she realizes it might be a clue. She is in a funk now about the whole thing. There is a pause.* HOBART *gathers himself together.*)

HOBART

(*At his cunningest*). Nonsense.

PHOEBE

What?

HOBART

You're crazy.

PHOEBE

What do you mean?

HOBART

It's absurd. Your notion is absurd. It's not possible. Willens? It's not possible. Somebody's been pulling your leg, my dear.

PHOEBE

(*Now she feels her quarry slipping from her and she is furious—determined not to let it go at all costs*). Have they?

HOBART

Of course they have!
(*He pours himself another drink.*)
Better go to bed, Phoebe. You're overwrought.
(*He turns away from her, his back to her as he drinks his highball. She feels the ground slipping from beneath her, her enemy escaping. A mania seizes her, a mania of cruelty and revenge—at any cost she must destroy* LAEL. *That is the first condition of her further being. Mixed in it is a desire to wound* HOBART *also, to destroy his complacency, to hurl a dart into that strong arrogant back.*)

PHOEBE

(*A new voice*). Am I?

HOBART

(*Without moving*). Of course you are.

PHOEBE

(*After a second*). Do you really want me to tell you—how I know?

HOBART

(*Knows he's got her, but his face revealing nothing—the poker face*). In the morning will do. I'm not interested much in female gossip.

PHOEBE

(*Her voice rising*). Aren't you?

HOBART

I advise you to go to bed, my dear.

PHOEBE

(*With an outburst of hysterical laughter*). You fool . . . You complacent fool! Can't you see that . . .
(*The sound of laughter and voices off stage*—RAND *and* LAEL.)

HOBART

(*Very annoyed at this interruption, still making the best of it*). You'd better . . .

PHOEBE

(*Hate in her voice*). She's back! I can't bear to . . .

HOBART

(*Close to her, quickly*). Go to your room. I'll join you there in a minute.
(*She crosses the room swiftly to opposite door and goes out. Left alone,* HOBART *decides rather quickly. He is pretty grim. He concludes there is no point in meeting* LAEL *now. Besides, it will delay the revelation he knows now he can get from his wife if he follows it up. He follows* PHOEBE *out. For a moment the stage is deserted—the voices and laughter of* RAND *and* LAEL *growing louder. They come in. They are in full evening dress. One gets a sense from* LAEL *that she has missed* HUGO *and is rather on the look-out for him.*)

LAEL

Where is everybody?

RAND

Do you miss them? I don't.
(*Following her.*)

LAEL

After all, I am a hostess.

RAND

Let's go to the Pier dance.

LAEL

(*Looking around toward the garden*). Shall we? Oh, Rand, remember that wonderful dance place in New York you took me to—all crystal and chromium and stratosphere!

RAND

I went there once afterwards without you; it was no good.

LAEL

Sometimes I get such a sudden homesickness for New York. I feel I want to be there on the instant—must walk those glittering streets, breathe that electric air.

RAND

Come back with me. I'll let you walk and breathe all you like.

LAEL

Don't spoil me.

RAND

(*Putting his arm around her shoulder*). Wouldn't I love to!

LAEL

(*In a dream of her own—rather drifts away from him*). Oh, Rand!

RAND

(*A slight pause—feels her mood*). Now, Lael, don't do that.

LAEL

What?

RAND

Drift away from me. Every once in a while you drift away from me.

LAEL

(*Coming back to the moment*). Little excursions. You take such big ones. Don't deny me the tiny ones.

RAND

Well, I don't like it.

LAEL

Tyrant!

RAND

I want to be with you on all the little excursions, do you hear? On all of them.

LAEL

Oh, you don't know what you're letting yourself in for. If you knew—in a day—in an hour—the thousand absurd and silly impulses I get. I wake up in the morning a sober woman with a sense of responsibility. An hour later I feel that I ought to be somewhere in Bali or Tahiti going native.

RAND

Well, why don't we?

LAEL

A graph of my impulses, Rand dear, would make you rather dizzy.
(*They both laugh.* LAEL *sits on arm of* RAND'*s chair.*)
I wonder—I wonder where Hugo is?

RAND

(*Immediately and sharply*). Why? Do you like him?

LAEL

(*His tone attracts her attention*). Yes, very much. Don't you?

RAND

(*Coldly*). I was brought up not to like his kind.

LAEL

(*Looking at him*). Oh!
(*Looking away from him.*)
One is brought up with so many prejudices.

RAND

(*After a pause—attempts to recapture the lost gaiety of a few moments before*). Let's go to the Pier dance, Lael.

LAEL

No, thank you, Rand.

RAND

Why not?

LAEL

I don't feel like it, really, Rand.

RAND

You said we'd drop in here to see where the others were and that if they weren't about you'd go on with me to Brighton.

LAEL

(*Rises*). I felt gay before. I don't any more.

RAND

(*Watches her*). Do I depress you?

LAEL

(*Sadly—facing him*). Rand.

RAND

I'm sorry.

LAEL

It's my fault. I'm sorry, Rand.

RAND

(*Irritated into demanding results*). Now, look here, Lael—you promised me a showdown and I mean to have it.

LAEL

(*Backing away a step*). Please, Rand, not now.

RAND

(*Following up*). Now! You're not going to put me off any longer. You're going to give me an answer. And it's going to be yes!

LAEL

Thank you for the choice.

RAND

Well, if it's no—I'm going to damn well know why. Lael, you're mixed up with a lot of funny notions about politics and theories and God knows what!

LAEL

Am I? Perhaps I am.

RAND

Do you think I'm going to let a lot of complicated *isms* stand between us? Well, I'm not. You've told me enough to let me see that once you let yourself go I can make you happy. All this "highbrow" atmosphere and these seedy people you have surrounded yourself with—it's all not you, Lael. I want to get you out of it—into some different environment where you can stop all this thinking. And where you can breathe deeply, and I'm going to do it.

LAEL

Oh, Rand, I'm so fond of you.

RAND

That's not enough.

LAEL

(*Finally*). It's all I can offer you.
(*A moment's pause.*) I'm sorry.

RAND

But you told me only the other day that some day you'd give in to me—and I believed you, Lael—I believed you.

LAEL

What I told you then was true. But since then . . .

RAND

What's happened since then?

LAEL

I can't bear to hurt you, Rand.

RAND

What's happened since then? I must know, I tell you. I've *got* to know.

(HUGO *and* JURIN *appear in the French windows; they are talking German to each other.* LAEL *rather rushes to them, grateful to have escaped the immediate necessity for inflicting on* RAND *the dreaded "show-down."*)

LAEL

My two lost children! Hugo, I'll never forgive you—never as long as I live!

HUGO

Won't you?

LAEL

For leaving that film—for missing the glory at the end of that film. Do you know what happened?

HUGO

Did Lord Rothschild go to heaven?

LAEL

He did and in color, my dear, in color! Suddenly and with divine unreasonableness, Lord Rothschild and everybody else became iridescent.

(*Everyone laughs.*)

He went to a big ball in the palace to be slapped on the back by the King. Good old Rothschild lends money to the Allies for patriotism and four per cent. You could see his pearl shirt-studs glisten with pride—you simply must come with me to see the end of that picture!

JURIN

I want to see it too.

LAEL

We'll all go.

(HOBART *enters. He has received* PHOEBE'S *information and stands there looking like Thor.*)

Now let's have some supper, shall we? Oh, there you are Hobart—just in time for supper. Mrs. Dingle's outdone herself.

(*She sees* HOBART *standing there like an angry and sullen god.*)

What's the matter, Hobart? You stand there looking like the Lord High Executioner. Did you give Lord Abercrombie my love? Did he send me his?

HOBART

He did!

LAEL

Well, that evens things up, doesn't it?

(*Crosses the others and goes to* HOBART.)

Let's go to supper—come on, everybody!

HOBART

I'm in no mood for supper, thank you!

LAEL

Oh, Hobart, do something for me, will you? Try to enjoy life. What can we do to cheer you up?

HOBART

Nothing, I'm afraid.

LAEL

(*Turns to others, appealing*). Jurin, Hugo, Rand—think of something.

(*To* HOBART.)

Lord Abercrombie is much more cheerful than you are, Hobart. I can always make him laugh.

HOBART

I'm sorry. My sense of humor is defective, I guess.

LAEL

Too bad. I wonder what we can do about it. Now let me see—I've known some very difficult cases but you—you—maybe you weren't a happy baby. Is that what it is? But anyway, do you mind if we have supper?

HOBART

No, thank you! I must speak to Rand alone.

RAND

What about?

LAEL

You're always taking him away from me.

HOBART

(*His tone is such that a chill falls over them*). Does that distress you, Lady Wyngate?

RAND

Bart!

LAEL

(*Quietly*). Of course it distresses me.
(*To* HUGO *and* JURIN.)
Shall we go?

RAND

I don't like your tone, Bart. I must tell you I don't like your tone to . . .

LAEL

Nonsense, Rand, Hobart and I understand each other. . . .

HOBART

No, we don't, Lady Wyngate—we don't in the least understand each other.

LAEL

Hobart, if you have a grievance against me I wish you'd tell me what it is.

HOBART

Shall I?

LAEL

Please do.

HOBART

Even you, Rand, will find out sooner or later; so you may as well know now. . . .
(*To* LADY WYNGATE.)
I hope at least, Lady Wyngate, that you're giving Rand value received.

RAND

What!

HOBART

You fool—you blind fool! The least she can do for you is to give up her present lover and take you on!

RAND

Hobart!

(HUGO *and* LAEL *exchange a sudden look of comprehension. It dawns on them both at once what has happened.*)

HOBART

(*Thundering at* RAND *and pointing accusingly at* LAEL *and* HUGO). Look at them! You have only to look at them!

RAND

Lael!

HOBART

Phoebe's just told me. And she ought to know because Lady Wyngate is her successor!

RAND

(*To* LAEL). So that's what you were going to tell me. That's why you kept putting me off! You were wondering where he was. Well, here he is!

HUGO

Captain Eldridge—

RAND

(*Turns on him*). You dirty Jew!

LAEL

(*Horrified*). Rand!

HUGO

It's all right, Lael. This makes me feel quite at home.

HOBART

You swine! Maybe those people over there are right.

LAEL

Hobart, please remember—Herr Willens is not only my lover he is also my guest.
(*Smiles at* HUGO.)
Hugo darling!

Curtain

ACT THREE

SCENE: *The same.*

Afternoon of the next day.

JOAN *and* SASCHA.

JOAN *is rather drawing* SASCHA *out; he is sulky and uncommunicative. He is at the piano with sheets of manuscript paper open before him making notes for an arrangement.*

JOAN

Something certainly happened last night, but I can't discover what it is. It's very tantalizing!
(SASCHA *doesn't answer. She looks at him. He has been especially taciturn lately. Also, there are other things which make her less than contented with him.*)
Have you seen Hugo?

SASCHA

Yes.

JOAN

Did *he* say anything?

SASCHA

What about?

JOAN

About—anything.

SASCHA

There was some sort of row!

JOAN

Was there?

SASCHA

Between him and Rand. I must say I blame Hugo for it.

JOAN

What was it about?

SASCHA

I can't tell you exactly. I wish Hugo would forget this race business.

JOAN

(*Studying him*). Why do you want him to forget it?

SASCHA

He'll bring a lot of trouble on himself. He has already.

JOAN

You manage to avoid trouble.

SASCHA

If everybody were as sensible about it as I am there'd be no problem.

JOAN

By sensible you mean—ashamed.

SASCHA

There's too much said about it. It's not important.

JOAN

I notice any time the question comes up you shy off.

SASCHA

Well, Hugo's too conscious about it. He's out of Germany now. Why doesn't he forget about it? It's the individual that's important.

JOAN

(*Slowly*). I understand better now, Sascha, your enthusiasm last night at the Pier dance for Lady Worrell.

SASCHA

Oh, that's it. Now it comes out.
(*As one above that sort of thing.*)
Jealous!

JOAN

Isn't she a bit elderly for you, Sascha?

SASCHA

I think she's marvelous. She's a marvelous woman.

JOAN

How could you tell?

SASCHA

Well, she's so—for one thing, she's so musical.

JOAN

Is she?

SASCHA

She invited me to play at Brierly.

JOAN

Did you tell her your fee?

SASCHA

Don't be vulgar!

JOAN

When is it going to be?

SASCHA

Thursday.

JOAN

Funny she didn't invite me.

SASCHA

I'll ask her if you like.

JOAN

No, thanks. I'm proud. As long as you're back on Friday for our jaunt to Cornwall.

SASCHA

Oh, Joan . . .

JOAN

Yes?

SASCHA

I'm staying the week-end at Brierly.

JOAN

(*Who knew it was coming, flaring up*). Are you? What about our date for Friday?

SASCHA

(*Rather miserably. He has dreaded it*). I thought I'd better pass it up. On account of . . . Frankly, Lady Worrell can do a lot for me.

JOAN

I dare say she can. You'll meet a lot of duchesses at Brierly. You'll like that!

SASCHA

What's wrong about liking duchesses? They're as good as other people, aren't they?

JOAN

Better. Their blood is so much bluer! (*A moment's pause.*)

SASCHA

(*Deciding it's expedient to concilate her, faces her*). I thought you were interested in my career. After all, I'm only doing it for you, you know—in a way. Once I get really established here in England I can turn my back on anybody I want to.

JOAN

Can you?

SASCHA

Except you. I can be independent. And then we—you and I—

JOAN

(*Turns away from him*). No, Sascha, this is the end.

SASCHA

(*Aggrieved*). Simply because I'm going to Lady Worrell's for the week-end! (*Realizes his mistake and controls himself —quietly.*) Now, Joan, please, I'll get her to ask you and we'll go together.

JOAN

I don't want to go. I'm through.

SASCHA

I'm not quite sure I understand.

JOAN

(*Turns on him—emotionally*). I think you do! Not that I'm not in love with you. I am and I'll have to take it, but I've always felt it. You're cold and calculating, and this about muffling your race is characteristic!

SASCHA

What do you want me to do? Shout it from the house-tops?

JOAN

It's characteristic! Instead of being proud and thrilled about it you are ashamed. That's contemptible, Sascha.

SASCHA

Oh, come now, Joan, don't take it so big. We'll talk it over when I get back on Monday.

JOAN

(*Very quietly*). Will we?

SASCHA

I'm going up to practise.

(SASCHA *walks up the stairs leaving her alone. She crosses to the piano seat and sits down. After a moment* HUGO *enters from the garden through the French windows.*)

HUGO

What's the matter, Joan?

JOAN

(*After a slight pause*). Well, the jig's up, Hugo. . . . Between Sascha and me. He prefers duchesses.

HUGO

Does it surprise you that he should?

JOAN

Yes. It surprises me.

HUGO

But why should it? Like so many insecure people, Sascha is a snob.

(LAEL *comes in. She takes them in. A moment's pause.*)

LAEL

Hello, Joan. You must have come back very late last night. How was the dance? Did you have a good time?

JOAN

Not very.

LAEL

I'm sorry. How was the Pier dance? Was it fun?

JOAN

It was very fashionable. It was overrun with duchesses. I wonder, really, where the lower classes go to dance.

(*She goes out.* LAEL *watches her. A moment's pause.*)

LAEL

What is it? Sascha?

HUGO

Yes.

LAEL

Sascha's stupid.

HUGO

Yes. He is stupid. He is also cunning and unscrupulous and greedy—and an exquisite artist, a superb artist!

LAEL

It's unfair that these attributes should go together. Poor Joan! What a pity she can't love the artist—and let the rest go!

HUGO

Pity the psyche isn't operable!

LAEL

(*Lightly*). According to you—it is! An obsession, you say, may be destroyed!

(*He looks at her. A pause. He lights a cigarette. His hand trembles slightly as he does so. She notices it.*)

Hugo! Your hand is trembling. Hugo . . .

HUGO

No sleep.

LAEL

I'm glad at least that you didn't sleep. I know I didn't.

(RAND *enters.*)

Oh, hello, Rand.

RAND

(*Stiffly—it's a great effort for him to do it*). Herr Willens . . .

HUGO

Yes, Captain Eldridge.

RAND

I want to apologize to you—for last night. For making a scene.

HUGO

Please don't. I understand it perfectly.

RAND

Whether you understand it or not—I beg you to accept my apology.

HUGO

Of course.
(*To* LAEL.)
You will excuse me.

LAEL

You needn't go, Hugo.

HUGO

I want to speak to Sascha.
(HUGO *exits through French windows.*)
(LAEL *looks at* RAND. RAND *is abject and broken. He has aged overnight. The fresh look in his face is gone.* RAND *looks at her, unable to speak.* LAEL *is stirred with pity for him.*)

LAEL

(*Involuntarily, moving towards him*). Rand!

RAND

(*In a dim voice*). I beg you—Lael—don't be nice to me!

LAEL

(*Devastated by him*). Rand!

RAND

(*In an ecstasy of self-reproach*). The Death of a Hero!

LAEL

What do you . . .

RAND

There was a picture of me once in the Sunday section of the newspaper in my home town. In color—very beautiful. Crossed flags over my head. Rosy cheeks. Perfect uniform. Clear-eyed look. Heroic expression. I joked about it when I saw it but now I realize—now that it is gone forever—that I took that picture seriously. I did. It was this picture of me which I've carried about in my mind all these years. It was my notion of myself. Decent fellow. Clean-cut. Well, he went to pieces last night—this wonderful effigy—smashed to bits like a lot of cheap crockery.

LAEL

After all, you thought you had some provocation. You mustn't . . .

RAND

(*Pacing about*). Don't tell me. I wanted to kill him. I wanted to tear him to bits. I wanted to lynch him.
(*Faces her suddenly.*)
All last night I was up—walking those roads—wishing I had him home. So I might lynch him. That's what I am!

LAEL

Poor Rand!

RAND

That's what I am!

LAEL

(*Rises and going to him*). In one way or another—that's what everybody is. Why do you suppose we're all staggering pitifully toward some incalculable abyss? Because, in one way or another, that's what everybody is. I'm sorry, Rand dear, that I had to take you out of the Happy Hunting Grounds into the Cave of Despair.

RAND

(*Sits in chair before her*). Well, you've done it all right.

LAEL

(*Gently*). Well, it's better than whistling away in the Never-Never Land.

RAND

What is there left?

LAEL

Instead of an effigy—a human being.

RAND

Pretty poor specimen.

LAEL

Not so bad, really. I like you!

RAND

(*Bitterly, without looking at her*). Do you?

LAEL

Now you can begin to live more—

RAND

After all these years!

LAEL

Why not? You're so young! And you'll find it's much more wholesome!

RAND

(*Jumps to his feet facing her*). Wholesome! Do you call this wholesome? Do you think that because I've apologized to him that I've forgiven him? Or you? Do you think my telling you cures me? I forced myself to apologize to him and while I was doing it I—and for me you're . . . in spite of anything I can say to myself—you're—you're —tainted! Now you know!

LAEL

(*Greatly troubled*). Poor Rand—what have I done to you?
(*He looks at her a moment, turns and walks out swiftly.* LAEL *starts to follow him, stops, realizing that her explanation will only increase his despair. She is overwhelmed herself with a kind of despair. The difficulty and the complexity of bringing human motives into some conformity with sanity and decency overwhelm her. Into the disturbed silence comes the sound of* SASCHA *upstairs playing the "Intermezzo in A Major" by Brahms. She lights a cigarette.* HUGO *comes in. He looks at her a moment standing there and comes to her impetuously. He is very tense. He has reached a decision and he must unburden himself to her.*)

HUGO

Lael—I must speak to you.

LAEL

Yes, Hugo . . .
(*Before he can go on* HOBART *enters. He sees them together; to him this is another "Love Scene." He is carrying a highball glass and crosses to the secretaire to mix himself another drink. He has been drinking steadily since last night. His eyes are bloodshot and he is quite drunk really but he holds his liquor wonderfully well, and, though he is quite shaky, you wouldn't know he was drunk first off unless you watched him closely.*)

HOBART

(*Seeing them*). Well, still at it, I see! And so am I . . .
(*Holds up his glass.*)
. . . at this! Just different ways of killing time, that's all. I'm not what you call a drinking man ordinarily . . .
(*Takes a drink.*)
. . . but lot to be said for it—makes you see things in—proportion!
(*To* HUGO.)
What is there about you fellows anyway that makes women go crazy about you?
(*To* LAEL.)
What is it, Lady Wyngate? Mystery? Romance? Passion? What is it?

LAEL

(*Starts to go*). Perhaps I'd better . . . Is Mrs. Eldridge? . . .

HOBART

Don't go. I'm not drunk—not very, anyway. I won't be objectionable—promise. Been all day without a soul to speak to. Phoebe has one of her headaches—she's had 'em for years. You can't go near her when she has a headache.
(*With a glare at* HUGO.)
I can't anyway.
(*He and* HUGO *look at each other.* HUGO *says nothing.* HOBART *goes on, laughing boisterously.*)
Maybe you think it's on account of Phoebe I'm drinking? Do you think *that* is the sorrow I'm trying to drown? That's good! That's very good! I've got more to worry about than that, my good fellow. You'll be glad to hear, Lady Wyngate, that my negotiations with Lord Abercrombie have broken down.

LAEL

Have they? I'm sorry.

HOBART

Why should you be sorry? Besides, you're not sorry! You're glad! He's a very clever man, isn't he, Lady Wyngate?

LAEL

Yes. He's clever!

HOBART

Knows a hell of a lot, doesn't he? That little smile of his—those little wrinkled eyes. Well, I thought I had him. Thought he realized how serious things were for us —the haves against the have-nots—the last fight. Thought he knew it, thought I'd convinced him of it. Thought it was all settled —feather in my cap—when all of sudden— last night—felt him slipping away from me—he began to joke—little jokes—flippant—then he told me . . .

LAEL

(*Curious*). What?

HOBART

That, "on mature consideration," he'd decided the idea of Anglo-American Youth League wouldn't go down. He'd be glad to advise me on any project I'd care to undertake, but he made it clear he couldn't be in on it. Press of business in London—demands of his papers—all that rot. He'd just decided—God knows what decided him— to let me down.
(*Fanatically.*)
I tell you he doesn't understand—none of them understand!

LAEL

Understand what?

HOBART

(*Same voice*). The danger—the danger they're heading for—we're all heading for —all last night I sat up facing it. . . .

LAEL

Facing it! Facing what?

HOBART

Losing everything I have, my fortune, my position, everything I've worked for. For money—for money—I've given up everything. My wife hates me, and my daughter —all of that—but my fortune and the power it gave me—were mine. Now they're threatened. They're in danger—terrible danger—and nobody'll do anything about it—nobody.
(*Turns on* HUGO *suddenly.*)
They're in danger from you! You think it's my wife I'm worried about? I've got a deeper grievance against you than that. You think it's because you killed Christ that we fear and hate you— No! It's because you gave birth to Lenin!

HUGO

(*Murmuring*). You over-estimate us!

LAEL

Really, Hobart, you mustn't drink any more. . . .

HOBART

(*In despair*). What is there left but to drink?

LAEL

Nonsense. Your fortune'll last you your lifetime. You needn't worry.

HOBART

What do you know about it—or the danger? Where it's a question of money in danger I'm as sensitive as a cat. I can tell you because I know. Better then Abercrombie with his cynical manner and his flippancy, better than anybody. We're doomed —all of us rich men. It's a question—as such things are reckoned—it's a question of minutes—and it'll overwhelm us all.

LAEL

Well, you'll be no worse off than the rest of us, will you?

HOBART

No worse off! No worse off! Where's the comparison? You don't care about money. You're sloppy about money. You don't love it as I do. You don't count on it as I do. It doesn't sustain you, it doesn't compensate you for everything else you've missed. And yet you say I'll be no worse off. You're as near-sighted as Abercrombie.

LAEL

He has as much to lose as you. His lightness should give you hope.

HOBART

(*Contemptuously*). Abercrombie! He's just a newspaper man—not a financier! When the Last Trumpet calls, it'll be just another headline to him!

LAEL

Well, you've had your innings—and a very good time too. If you have to give way— well, put a good face on it. Buck up. Be sporting.

HOBART

Can't—can't . . . Who's going to pay for everything—that's what I'd like to know? (*He again confronts* HUGO.) Who's going to pay? Will you Communists pay?

HUGO

If you capitalists lend us the money . . .

HOBART

(*A bit taken back*). Well, you shan't have it! And there's Rand . . . (*Very confidentially to* HUGO.) Do you know what his expeditions have cost? Do you know what I've spent in my lifetime for hospitals, scientific research, even art? Who's going to pay after we're gone? Who's going to pay?

LAEL

Bart, please . . .

HOBART

Poor Rand! Poor Rand! No more South Poles!

LAEL

Bart, please . . . (*Into the room from upstairs comes the sound of* SASCHA *playing the "Intermezzo in E Flat Minor" of Brahms.*)

HOBART

(*Turning to* LAEL *for sympathy this time*). Do you know, since the surtax, my income's shrunk to nothing? Do you know what I pay each year to the Government—State and Federal? (*He begins to weep. He becomes aware of the music and rushes to the foot of the stairs in the alcove, crying as he goes.*) There's another one! Listen to him up there! (*At the foot of the stairs.*) Who's going to pay for your God-damn concerts! (*Rushes to the secretaire and grabs a bottle of whiskey.*) You'll see! (*He starts out, crying like a baby, and through his blubbering says.*) You'll want us back! (*He goes out. There is an embarrassed pause. During the following scene between* LAEL *and* HUGO, *the Brahms goes on.*)

HUGO

To have in the world only one thing—and to face losing that—well, as Sascha might say, it's no joke!

LAEL

In the sixteenth century—when people went to the Tower to be executed—it's always struck me how casually they died. Something beyond gallantry. Just before they put their heads on the block—it's extraordinary how they prayed for king and country. We've lost that.

HUGO

They merely faced death. Mr. Eldridge faces extinction.

LAEL

That's true. Suspicion and fear . . .

HUGO

To be accused simultaneously of killing Christ and giving birth to Lenin—quite a feat, I must say! Just the same, Mr. Eldridge would do pretty well if he had the upper hand.

LAEL

(*Smiling*). Hobart's an American and doesn't really understand democracy.

HUGO

He's drowning in a reality he doesn't understand. He hates me because . . .

LAEL

He doesn't hate you. He's afraid of you. Suspicion and fear. They're suffocating the world.

HUGO

How're you going to get rid of them? Through some cosmic psycho-analysis?

LAEL

Through understanding.

HUGO

While you're understanding the enemy, he will destroy you.

LAEL

The eternal impasse.

HUGO

Unless—you destroy him first.

LAEL

(*A moment's pause*). You're inexorable, Hugo, ruthlessly analytical. You're always looking for the motive behind the motive.

HUGO

(*He looks at her a moment, then crosses to her, sitting beside her on the sofa*). Yesterday I fell in love.

LAEL

Hugo.

HUGO

All through dinner, sitting near you in the car going to the cinema, in the theatre—I was in love.

RAND

I know. I too.

HUGO

I thanked God for the miracle that filled me with longing for you. From my being alone, from my isolation, from the less than nothing I had to offer, from all these I gathered strength. When Mr. Eldridge turned on me, and Rand, too, I felt strong, omnipotent—but when you turned to me so magnanimously before them all, that did for me. I felt like a thief in the pillory to whom a sentimental bystander throws a rose.

LAEL

Your pride is devastating.

HUGO

Yes. And then I went up to my room. I sat at the window and looked over the garden, asleep in the moonlight. Enchantment. And suddenly the unreality of everything, of my presence here in this house overcame me. I thought: What can I hope for—what can I foresee—vistas of bliss in this pleasant country-house—with you. But what would it end in—a self-indulgent daydream. I thought: What am I doing here? What *am* I?

LAEL

What am *I*?

HUGO

It's your home. You belong here. But for me . . .

LAEL

But, Hugo, don't you see? I wanted my love to shield you from the odium of a graceless world.

HUGO

I hoped for love—without philanthropy.

LAEL

How untrue half truths are. I sat up last night too—thinking—about Rand and you—everything— For the first time in months it seemed to me I felt clear—I felt free. I had thought that never again would I be lost in an emotion that I could accept entirely without reservation. To love and not to be ashamed to love. This miracle I felt would never happen to me again—and now it has.

HUGO

(*Kisses her hand*). You are all there is left in the world for me to love. I'll never forget you. Your radiance, your goodness, your compassion.

LAEL

(*After a moment*). That has a valedictory sound, Hugo.

HUGO

Yes. I must leave you. I must go.

LAEL

Where?

HUGO

Back to Germany.

LAEL

(*Almost in terror*). Oh! But you can't go back, Hugo. They'll—stop you.

HUGO

I must risk it.

LAEL

Don't go, Hugo!

HUGO

I must. I must. Look at my career—a public taster of the arts—a dilettante in everything, except that I was paid. Behind this decorative curtain I was forced to discover that there is a harsh reality. Well, I must investigate this reality further. To stay here, to go to America would only be a continuation of my life before. Intellectual squirearchy! I was able to feed my vanity with the comfort of knowing that I made and unmade reputations. Lehrmann—I made Lehrmann—I created a world in which Lehrmann was king; and what sort of a world is it? Out of egotism and vanity I created worlds without testing the foundations on which they rested. A criminal architect who builds houses that topple on their hapless tenants. I see now that there is only one thing left: To destroy the inhuman—to discover humanity.

LAEL

You talk about humanity—discovering humanity—as if it were an abstraction—an essence like the elixir of life which you might find somewhere in a bottle and dispense. Hugo, listen, humanity is here, all around us. I tell you what I wish you'd do. Humor me. Let me take you for a holiday through our shires and let me show you our common folk. You'll find them kindly and gentle. In their faces you'll see how impossible, how far beyond them, are ferocity or brutality or mass-hate. Let me take you, Hugo, and you'll see—you'll be comforted.

HUGO

But I don't want to be comforted. I don't want to be soothed. What you say about England is true. I feel it in you who are the best of England. But what right have I to this immunity? A sybarite in a famine.

LAEL

You're an artist, Hugo. What have you to do with feuds and hatreds and rebellions? Can't you try to see it as I see it? You see, I believe in England. I believe in gradualness. I believe in muddling through. I believe—a poor foolish illusion, I suppose—I believe that in the main people are reasonable and corrigible and sweet—fragments of God.

HUGO

That isn't a belief. It's a mirage. A self-hypnosis. A wish-fulfillment.

LAEL

I allow for that. And is it your dream that the world, overnight, can be scrubbed clean of injustice and left glowing with humanity?

HUGO

It's that I must find certitude at last, and, having found it, if necessary, die for it.

LAEL

Or kill for it?

HUGO

Or kill for it.

LAEL

You are leaving to fight a mania as ravaging as a forest fire that burns down everything before it, leaving stumps and ashes where there had been strength and growth. I don't want it to consume you, Hugo, dearest Hugo. Don't go. You may be lost in it—and to me.

HUGO

Dearest Lael—I can't stay because of one thing—that I remember the past year. And what I remember . . .

LAEL

(*Understanding completely*). Wouldn't let you rest.

HUGO

No. I'm determined at last to view the world — including myself — completely without illusion. It's a matter of life and death. I see now that goodness is not enough, that kindness is not enough, that liberalism is not enough. I'm sick of evasions. They've done us in. Civilization, charity, progress, tolerance—all the catchwords. I'm sick of them. We'll have to redefine our terms.

LAEL

(*Seeing the inevitability of their separation*). The iron has entered into your soul, Hugo. You have crossed some frontier—into some region—where I cannot follow you.

HUGO

If I can ever return—it will be to you.

LAEL

(*Faces him*). You will find me here. There is a genius for wandering and a genius for remaining behind. There is the shooting star and the fixed. Perhaps when you come back—you will find that in our own way we have realized your dream.

HUGO

I know this—that while you live—one needn't despair.

LAEL

Then you need never despair. For nothing will destroy me.
(*With deep feeling, her valedictory.*)
I shall live forever and so will you. Our enemies will beat against us and find that we have a strength beyond their clamor, beyond their forces.
(HUGO *and* LAEL *look deeply into each other's eyes without moving. Then* HUGO *turns and goes out.* LAEL *watches him until he has left the room, starts instinctively to follow him, stops:* RAND *enters from the garden.*)

RAND

Lael!
(LAEL *stops but doesn't face him. She is looking away into some vision of her own.*)

RAND

Joan's just told me, Lael—that you never saw Willens until you met him in London. I can't tell you how I feel—how humiliated — If there was any way I could make you see how deeply ashamed I am—you'd—you'd . . .
(*There is the sound of a motor leaving the driveway.*)

LAEL

Hugo's gone.

RAND

I know now, Lael—whether he goes or stays—there's some awful fence in my mind and in my spirit, and you're on the other side, and no matter what I do I'll never be able to break through to you—never.

LAEL

We're all shut in behind our little fences, Rand—

The Curtain Falls

21